Vice-President Social Sciences: *Sean W. Wakely*
Developmental Editors: *Anne A. Reid, Sue Gleason*
Vice-President, Marketing: *Joyce Nilsen*
Editorial Assistants: *Jennifer Normandin, Erika Stuart*
Cover Administrator: *Linda Knowles*
Composition and Prepress Buyer: *Linda Cox*
Manufacturing Buyer: *Megan Cochran*
Editorial-Production Service: *Thomas E. Dorsaneo*
Text Design & Composition: *Seventeenth Street Studios*
Cover Designer: *Studio Nine*
Cover and chapter opening illustrations: *Lance Hidy, Lexington, VA*

A Viacom Company
160 Gould Street
Needham Heights, Massachusetts 02194

Library of Congress Cataloging-in-Publication Data

Berk, Laura E.
Child development / Laura E. Berk. — 4th ed.
p. cm.
Includes bibliographical references and index.
ISBN 0-205-19875-9
1. Child development. I. Title.
HQ767.9.B464 1997
305.23'1—dc20 96-7596
CIP

Printed in the United States of America
10 9 8 7 6 5 4 3 2 00 99 98 97

With gratitude, admiration, and love,
To Esther M. Lentschner
and in memory of my cousin
Walter S. Lentschner

Brief Contents

From Research to Practice

Cultural Influences

Social Issues

Detailed Contents

Part II Foundations of Development 40

Preface

My twenty-six years of teaching child development have brought me in contact with thousands of students having diverse college majors, future goals, interests, and needs. Some are affiliated with my own department, psychology, but many come from other child-related fields—education, family studies, sociology, anthropology, and biology, to name just a few. Each semester the aspirations of my students have proved to be as varied as their fields of study. Many look toward careers in applied work with children—teaching, caregiving, nursing, counseling, social work, school psychology, and program administration. Some plan to teach child development, and a few want to do research. Most hope someday to have children, whereas others are already parents who come with a desire to better understand and rear their own youngsters. And almost all my students arrive with a deep curiosity about how they themselves developed from tiny infants into the complex human beings they are today.

My goal in preparing this fourth edition of *Child Development* is to provide a textbook that meets the instructional goals of the course as well as the varied needs of students. I aimed for a text that is intellectually stimulating, that includes depth as well as breadth of coverage, and that portrays the complexities of child development in a way that captures student interest while helping them learn. To achieve these objectives, I have grounded this book in a carefully selected body of classic and current theory and research, emphasized how the research process helps solve real-world problems, highlighted commonalities and differences among ethnic groups and cultures, and paid special attention to policy issues that have a crucial bearing on the well-being of children in today's world. I have also used a clear, engaging writing style and provided a unique pedagogical program that assists students in mastering information, integrating the various aspects of development, and applying what they have learned.

TEXT PHILOSOPHY

The basic approach of this book has been shaped by my own professional and personal history as a teacher, researcher, and parent. It consists of five philosophical ingredients, which I regard as essential for students to emerge from a course with a thorough understanding of child development. I have woven each into every chapter:

■ **1. AN UNDERSTANDING OF THE DIVERSE ARRAY OF THEORIES IN THE FIELD AND THE STRENGTHS AND SHORTCOMINGS OF EACH.** The first chapter begins by emphasizing that only knowledge of multiple theories can do justice to the richness of child development. In each topical domain, I present a variety of theoretical perspectives, indicate how each highlights previously overlooked aspects of development, and discuss research that has been used to evaluate them. If one or two theories have emerged as specially prominent in a particular area, I indicate why, in terms of the theory's broad explanatory power. Discussion of contrasting theories also serves as the context for an evenhanded analysis of many controversial issues throughout the text.

■ **2. AN APPRECIATION OF BASIC RESEARCH STRATEGIES TO INVESTIGATE CHILD DEVELOPMENT.** To evaluate theories, students need a firm grounding in basic research design and methodology. I devote an entire chapter to a description and critique of research strategies. Throughout the book, numerous studies are discussed in sufficient detail for students to use what they have learned to critically assess the findings, conclusions, and implications of research.

■ 3. KNOWLEDGE OF BOTH THE SEQUENCE OF CHILD DEVELOPMENT AND THE PROCESSES THAT UNDERLIE IT. Students are provided a description of the organized sequence of development along with a discussion of processes of change. An understanding of process—how complex combinations of biological and environmental events produce development—has been the focus of most recent research. Accordingly, the text reflects this emphasis. But new information about the timetable of change has also emerged in recent years. In many ways, children are far more competent beings than they were believed to be in the past. Recent evidence on the timing and sequence of development, along with its implications for process, is presented in detail throughout the book.

■ 4. AN APPRECIATION OF THE IMPACT OF CONTEXT AND CULTURE ON CHILD DEVELOPMENT. A wealth of research indicates more powerfully than ever before that children live in rich contexts that affect all aspects of development. Throughout the text, consistent, even-handed attention is granted to both biological and social contexts for development. In addition, students travel to distant parts of the world as I review a growing body of cross-cultural evidence. The text narrative also discusses many findings on ethnically diverse children within the United States. Besides highlighting the role of immediate settings, such as family, neighborhood, and school, I underscore the impact of larger social structures—societal values, laws, and governmental programs—on children's well-being.

■ 5. A SENSE OF THE INTERDEPENDENCY OF ALL DOMAINS OF DEVELOPMENT—PHYSICAL, COGNITIVE, EMOTIONAL, AND SOCIAL. In every chapter, an integrated approach to child development is emphasized. I show how physical, cognitive, emotional, and social development are interwoven. Within the text narrative and in the Connections tables at the end of each chapter, students are referred to other sections of the book that deepen their understanding of relationships among various aspects of change.

■ 6. AN APPRECIATION OF THE INTERRELATEDNESS OF THEORY, RESEARCH, AND APPLICATIONS. Throughout this book, I stress that theories of child development and the research stimulated by them provide the foundation for sound, effective practices with children. The link between theory, research, and applications is reinforced by an organizational format in which theory and research are presented first, followed by implications for practice. In addition, a new focus in the field—harnessing child development knowledge to shape social policies that support children's needs—is reflected in every chapter. The text addresses the current condition of children in the United States and around the world and shows how theory and research have sparked successful interventions. Many important applied topics are considered—maternal nutrition and prenatal development, prevention of sudden infant death syndrome, brain growth spurts, teenage pregnancy and childbearing, the importance of make-believe play, early intervention for at-risk children, attention-deficit hyperactivity disorder, children's eyewitness testimony, bilingual education, maternal employment and day care, child maltreatment, and more.

TEXT ORGANIZATION

I have organized this text topically, in a manner best suited to a comprehensive, discussion of theory, research, and applications and an uninterrupted view of development within each domain. The book retains the same basic structure that received praise from users in its previous editions. It is divided into 5 parts and 15 chapters, each of which develops the six philosophical themes just described.

■ PART I. THEORY AND RESEARCH IN CHILD DEVELOPMENT. This section provides an overview of the history of the field, twentieth-century theories, and research strategies. **Chapter 1** stresses the importance of theories as organizing frameworks for understanding child development and traces changes in views of childhood from medieval to modern times. The study of child development is depicted as interdisciplinary endeavor that aims to both understand children and improve their life condition. **Chapter 2** is devoted to strategies for conducting scientifically sound research.

Commonly used research methods and both general and developmental research designs are explained and critiqued. The chapter concludes with a consideration of ethics in research on children.

■ PART II. FOUNDATIONS OF DEVELOPMENT. A trio of chapters introduces students to the foundations of development: **Chapter 3** combines a discussion of genetic mechanisms and prenatal and perinatal environmental influences into a single, integrated discussion of these earliest determinants of development. A concluding section takes up the various ways in which researchers conceive of the relationship between heredity and environment as a prelude to revisiting the nature–nurture controversy in later chapters. **Chapter 4** is devoted to an overview of the rapidly expanding literature on infant capacities. Research on newborn reflexes, states, and learning capacities is reviewed, followed by a consideration of early motor and perceptual development. The chapter closes with the question of whether infancy is a sensitive period in which certain experiences must occur to ensure healthy development. **Chapter 5** addresses physical growth, including development of the brain. The close connection between physical and psychological development is emphasized. A variety of hereditary and environmental influences on physical growth are considered.

■ PART III. COGNITIVE AND LANGUAGE DEVELOPMENT. Four chapters treat the diverse theories and wealth of research on cognitive and language development. **Chapter 6** is devoted to Piaget's cognitive-developmental theory and Vygotsky's sociocultural theory. Students are given a thorough grounding in Piagetian theory as a prerequisite to studying language, emotional, and social-cognitive development in later chapters. With its strong emphasis on the social context of cognition, Vygotsky's theory has recently risen to the forefront of the field, stands as a major competing approach to Piaget's, and therefore shares the title of Chapter 6. The chapter also introduces the nativist, modular view of the mind as yet another perspective that has recently become influential. **Chapter 7** offers an introduction to information processing. General and developmental models are reviewed along with research on each major facet of the information-processing system. The chapter also discusses recent applications of information processing to children's academic learning and concludes with an analysis of the strengths and weaknesses of the information-processing perspective. **Chapter 8**, on intelligence, provides an overview of the intelligence testing movement and addresses a wide variety of controversial issues and research findings, including ethnic and social class differences in IQ, heritability of intelligence, and cultural bias in the tests. The concluding section moves beyond IQ to a discussion of creativity. **Chapter 9** provides a comprehensive introduction to language development, including behaviorist, nativist, and interactionist theories. The main body of the chapter is organized around the four components of language: phonology, semantics, grammar, and pragmatics. The chapter also a addresses such questions as: Can nonhuman primates acquire language? Is there a sensitive period for language learning? How does bilingualism affect children's development?

■ PART IV. PERSONALITY AND SOCIAL DEVELOPMENT. Coverage of personality and social development is divided into four chapters: **Chapter 10,** on emotional development, provides an overview of theory and research on children's expression and understanding of emotion, the origins of temperament and its implications for cognitive and social development, and infant–caregiver attachment. The relationship of quality of caregiving, infant temperament, parents' internal working models, maternal employment and day care, and social and cultural contexts to the attachment bond are among the special issues considered. **Chapter 11** offers an overview of the development of social cognition. It is divided into three sections: children's understanding of self, other people, and relations among people. Among the topics included are young children's belief–desire reasoning; self-concept and self-esteem; achievement-related attributions; identity; perspective taking; friendship; and social problem solving. **Chapter 12** addresses moral development. The main body of the chapter is devoted to a review of sociobiological, psychoanalytic, social learning, and cognitive-developmental theories and related research. Child-rearing practices that foster moral internalization, cross-cultural research on moral reasoning, the controversial issue of whether males and females differ in moral understanding, and the development of self-control and aggression are among the special features of this chapter. **Chapter 13** focuses on sex-related differences and gender roles.

Biological and environmental influences on gender stereotyping and gender-role adoption, diverse theories and research on the development of gender-role identity, and sex-related differences in mental abilities and personality traits are discussed. The chapter also includes an applied section on developing non-gender-stereotyped children.

■ PART V. CONTEXTS FOR DEVELOPMENT. A final pair of chapters examines four highly influential contexts for development—family, peers, media, and schooling. **Chapter 14** considers the family from a social systems perspective. The bidirectional nature of parent–child interaction, the importance of links between the family and community for children's optimal development, and styles of child rearing are highlighted. The central portion of this chapter discusses the impact of family lifestyles and transitions in on children's development, including smaller families, one-child families, gay and lesbian families, adoptive families, and divorce, remarriage, maternal employment, and day care. The chapter concludes with a discussion of child maltreatment. In **Chapter 15**, the social systems perspective is extended to extrafamilial contexts for development. In the section on peer relations, research on the development of peer sociability, peer acceptance, peer groups, and peers as socialization agents is discussed. The middle portion of the chapter addresses the impact of television and computers on cognitive and social development. A concluding section on schooling considers such topics as educational philosophies, school transitions, teacher–pupil interaction, ability grouping, and cross-national research on academic achievement.

NEW COVERAGE IN THE FOURTH EDITION

In this edition, I continue to represent a burgeoning contemporary literature with theory and research from over 1,200 new citations. To make room for new coverage, I have condensed and reorganized some topics and eliminated others that are no longer as crucial in view of new evidence.

Since the last edition, findings on both biological and cultural contributions to development have greatly expanded. In addition, the field of child development continues to forge productive links between research and social policy—a theme that I have extended in this edition. Social policy is elevated to the forefront of the text through a special section in Chapter 1 that provides an overview of the current condition of children and the social policy process. A wide variety of social policy topics are integrated into succeeding chapters.

The following is a sampling of major content changes in this edition:

- Updated description of ecological systems theory, including the chronosystem (Chapter 1)
- Heightened attention to psychophysiological methods and related new findings on perceptual development, brain lateralization, brain growth spurts, information processing, attention-deficit hyperactivity disorder, individual differences in mental abilities, and temperament (Chapters 2, 4, 5, 7, 8, and 10)
- New discoveries in genetics, including genetic imprinting, mapping human chromosomes, gene splicing, and reproductive technologies (Chapter 3)
- Expanded discussion of the limitations of heritability estimates and concordance rates (Chapter 3)
- Updated findings on prevention of sudden infant death syndrome (Chapter 4)
- New section on dynamic systems theory of motor development, with special attention to microgenetic and cross-cultural research (Chapter 4)
- Expanded discussion of factors underlying development of visual capacities; new emphasis on affordances as guiding perceptual development (Chapter 4)
- Current evidence on adolescent sexual activity; new research on the development of sexual orientation (Chapter 5)
- Enhanced discussion of brain development, including synaptic pruning, lateralization, and brain growth spurts (Chapter 5)
- New section on physical reasoning in infancy (Chapter 6)

- Expanded discussion of alternatives to Piaget's account of domain-general, stagewise change, with special attention to the domain-specific, modular view of the mind (Chapter 6)
- New evidence on cultural and situational influences on mastery of Piagetian tasks, including the impact of schooling on logical operational abilities (Chapter 6)
- New section on Vygotsky's view of the importance of make-believe play: expanded coverage of the implications of Vygotsky's theory for education (Chapter 6)
- Updated research on information processing, including strategy development, planning, and children's awareness of mental activities; expanded treatment of reconstructive processing, including a new section on fuzzy trace theory (Chapter 7)
- New section on autobiographical memory, with updated research on infantile amnesia and development of personal narratives (Chapter 7)
- Inclusion of dynamic assessment as a mental testing alternative for ethnic minority children (Chapter 8)
- Extensively revised section on the development of creativity (Chapter 8)
- Updated research on individual and cultural differences in language development (Chapter 9)
- New hypotheses about children's strategies for acquiring word meanings, including syntactic bootstrapping and use of pragmatic cues (Chapter 9)
- Expanded discussion of cultural variations in emotional development, with coverage of self-conscious emotions, temperament, child problem behavior, and attachment (Chapter 10)
- New section on the relationship of parents' internal working models to children's attachment security (Chapter 10)
- New research on theory of mind, with special attention to children's belief–desire reasoning (Chapter 11)
- Updated presentation of Dodge's information-processing model of social problem solving (Chapter 11)
- Current findings on the influence of temperament on moral internalization (Chapter 12)
- Enhanced discussion of cultural variations in moral reasoning (Chapter 12)
- Expanded treatment of community and cultural influences on aggressive behavior and interventions for antisocial youths (Chapter 12)
- Updated evidence on sex-related differences in mental abilities and personality traits (Chapter 12)
- New research on ethnic variations in child rearing (Chapter 13)
- Enhanced coverage of family lifestyles and transitions, including new sections on adoptive families and gay and lesbian families (Chapter 14)
- New section on the impact of cultural values on peer sociability (Chapter 15)
- Updated evidence on the relationship of family ties to resistance to unfavorable peer pressure in adolescence (Chapter 15)
- Current evidence on the prevalence of television violence in the United States (Chapter 15)
- New research on the impact of teacher-directed versus child-centered classrooms on young children's intrinsic motivation and emotional well-being (Chapter 15)
- Recent cross-national comparisons of academic achievement (Chapter 15)
- Many new and revised boxes—addressing such topics as resilient children; policy-relevant research on day care; children's research risks; effects of vitamin–mineral supplements during pregnancy; educating children and adolescents about AIDS;

impact of low-level lead exposure on mental development; children's eyewitness testimony in court proceedings; implications of declaring English the official U.S. language for bilingual education; maternal depression and child development; building children's self-esteem; the impact of ethnic and political violence on children; regulating children's television; and the Reggio Emilia approach to early childhood education.

PEDAGOGICAL FEATURES

The pedagogical features of the text have been revised and expanded. A highly accessible writing style—one that is lucid and engaging without being simplistic—continues to be one of the text's strong points. I frequently converse with students, ask questions, and encourage them to relate what they read to their own lives. In doing so, I hope to make the study of child development involving and pleasurable.

■ CHAPTER INTRODUCTIONS AND END-OF-CHAPTER SUMMARIES. To provide students with a helpful preview of what they are about to read, I begin each chapter with an outline and overview of its content. Chapter introductions present lively examples of children's development and introduce controversial issues as a means of stimulating student interest. Comprehensive end-of-chapter summaries, organized according to the major divisions of each chapter and highlighting key terms, remind students of important points in the text discussion.

■ BRIEF REVIEWS. Interim summaries of text content appear at the end of most major sections in each chapter. They enhance retention by encouraging students to reflect on information they have just read before moving on to a new section.

■ BOXES. Three types of boxes accentuate the philosophical themes of this book. Among these, seventeen new boxes and twenty-three revised boxes appear. Cultural Influences boxes highlight the impact of context and culture on all aspects of development. From Research to Practice boxes integrate theory, research, and applications. Social Issues boxes discuss the condition of children in the United States and around the world and emphasize the need for sensitive social policies to ensure their well-being. Many Social Issues boxes have a "Point of View" theme, in that they encourage students to grapple with controversies and to express "Your Point of View . . ." through special activities.

■ MARGINAL GLOSSARY, END-OF-CHAPTER TERM LIST, AND END-OF-BOOK GLOSSARY. Mastery of the central vocabulary of the field is promoted through a marginal glossary, an end-of-chapter term list, and an end-of-book glossary. Important terms and concepts also appear in boldface type in the text narrative.

■ MILESTONES TABLES. Milestones Tables that provide students with an overview of the sequence and timing of achievements in each domain of development appear throughout the text. These tables are designed to help students keep track of major developments as they consider a wealth of theory and research. At the same time, each Milestones table reminds students that individual differences exist in the precise age at which milestones are attained, a point made throughout the text discussion.

■ CONNECTIONS TABLES. Each chapter concludes with a Connections table, which encourages students to continue exploring high-interest topics and integrate domains of development by turning to relevant information in other sections of the book. The Connections tables are designed to foster a coherent, unified picture of child development.

■ ADDITIONAL TABLES, ILLUSTRATIONS, AND PHOTOGRAPHS. Additional tables are liberally included to help students grasp essential points in the text discussion, extend information on a topic, and consider applications. The many full-color illustrations throughout the book depict important theories, methods, and research findings. Photos have been carefully selected to portray text content, illustrate the work of contemporary researchers, and represent the diversity of children around the world.

ACKNOWLEDGMENTS

The dedicated contributions of many individuals helped make this book a reality and contributed to refinements and improvements in each edition. An impressive cast of reviewers provided many helpful suggestions, constructive criticisms, and encouragement and enthusiasm for the organization and content of the book. I am grateful to each one of them:

Reviewers of the First Edition

Dana W. Birnbaum
University of Main at Orono
Kathryn N. Black
Purdue University
Cathryn L. Booth
University of Washington
Sam Boyd
University of Central Arkansas
Celia A. Brownell
University of Pittsburgh
Toni A. Campbell
San Jose State University
Beth Casey
Boston College
John Condry
Cornell University
James L. Dannemiller
University of Wisconsin, Madison
Darlene DeSantis
West Chester University
Kenneth Hill
Saint Mary's University, Halifax
Alice S. Honig
Synracuse University
Elizabeth J. Hrncir
University of Virginia
Mareile Koenig
George Washington University Hospital
Gary W. Ladd
Purdue University
Frank Laycock
Oberlin College
Robert S. Marvin
University of Virginia
Carolyn J. Mebert
University of New Hampshire
Gary B. Melton
University of Nebraska, Lincoln
Mary Evelyn Moore
Indiana University at Bloomington
Larry Nucci
University of Illinois at Chicago
Carol Pandey
Pierce College, Los Angeles
Thomas S. Parish
Kansas State University
B. Kay Pasley
Colorado State University
Ellen F. Potter
University of South Carolina at Columbia
Kathleen Preston
Humboldt State University
Maria E. Sera
The University of Iowa
Beth Shapiro
Emory University
Gregory J. Smith
Dickinson College
Harold Stevenson
The University of Michigan
Ross A. Thompson
University of Nebraska, Lincoln
Barbara A. Tinsley
University of Illinois at Urbana-Champaign
Kim F. Townley
University of Kentucky

Reviewers of the Second Edition

James L. Dannemiller
University of Wisconsin, Madison
Darlene DeSantis
West Chester University
Claire Etaugh
Bradley University
Katherine Green
Millersville University
Daniel Lapsley
University of Notre Dame
Mary D. Leinbach
University of Oregon
Gary Melton
University of Nebraska, Lincoln
Daniel Reschly
Iowa State University
Rosemary Rosser
The University of Arizona
Phil Schoggen
Cornell University
Harold Stevenson
The University of Michigan
Ross A. Thompson
University of Nebraska, Lincoln
Janet Valadez
Pan American University

Reviewers of the Third Edition

James L. Dannemiller
University of Wisconsin, Madison
Rebecca Eder
Bryn Mawr College
Bill Fabricius
Arizona State University
John Gibbs
Ohio State University
Peter Gordon
University of Pittsburgh
Beth Kurtz-Costes
University of North Carolina, Chapel Hill
Claire Kopp
University of California, Los Angeles
Mary Evelyn Moore
Illinois State University
Lois Muir
University of Wisconsin, La Crosse
Jane Rysberg
California State University, Chico
Rosemary Rosser
University of Arizona
Robert Siegler
Carnegie Mellon University
Ross A. Thompson
University of Nebraska, Lincoln

Reviewers of the Fourth Edition

Daniel Ashmead
Vanderbilt University
J. Paul Boudreau
University of Prince Edward Island
Rhoda Cummings
University of Nevada, Reno
James L. Dannemiller
University of Wisconsin, Madison
William Fabricius
Arizona State University
Beverly Fagot
University of Oregon
John C. Gibbs
Ohio State University
Tom McBride
Princeton University
Mary Evelyn Moore
Illinois State University
Bonnie K. Nastasi
State University of New York at Albany
Kimberly K. Powlishta
Northern Illinois University
Bud Protinsky
Virginia Polytechnic Institute and State University
Robert S. Siegler
Carnegie Mellon University
Robert J. Sternberg
Yale University
Amye R. Warren
University of Tennessee at Chattanooga

In addition, I thank the following individuals for responding to a survey that provided vital feedback for the new edition:

Leonard Abbeduto
University of Wisconsin, Madison
Radhi H. Al-Malink
University of Northern Iowa
Anne P. Copeland
Boston University
James L. Dannemiller
University of Wisconsin, Madison
Claire Etaugh
Bradley University
William Fabricius
Arizona State University
Larry Fenson
San Diego State University
Lee Fox
Kent State University, Stark Campus
Bridget A. Franks
University of Florida
Harry Freeman
University of Wisconsin, Madison
John C. Gibbs
Ohio State University
L. Greening
University of Alabama
Marie Hayes
University of Maine
Paula J. Hillmann
University of Wisconsin, Madison
Elana Joram
University of Northern Iowa
Janice H. Kennedy
Georgia Southern University
Wallace A. Kennedy
Florida State University
Claire Kopp
University of California, Los Angeles
Jupian Leung
University of Wisconsin, Oshkosh
Suzanne Lovett
Bowdoin College
Daniel O. Lynch
University of Wisconsin, Oshkosh
Margaret F. Lynch
San Francisco State University/ University of San Francisco
Teri Miller
Madison Area Technical College
Shitala P. Mishra
University of Arizona
R. H. Passman
University of Wisconsin, Milwaukee
Jane A. Rysberg
California State University, Chico
Nancy Segal
California State University, Fullerton
Ross A. Thompson
University of Nebraska, Lincoln
Eric Vernberg
University of Kansas
Nanci Weinberger
Bryant College

A wealth of new findings and clashing viewpoints created particular challenges for revision of the cognitive portions of the text. I extend a special thank you to Elyse Lehman of George Mason University for discussing with me the best direction for these chapters. Her keen observations helped me strike an effective balance between rapid changes in the field and student needs. Peter Ornstein, University of North Carolina, Chapel Hill, generously took time to comment on sections addressing information-processing theories, assisting me in shaping the opening part of Chapter 7. Andrew Meltzoff of the University of Washington has continually kept me abreast of new findings in his research program. As a result, I have been able to represent fascinating discoveries in infant cognition in up-to-the-minute fashion.

I am also indebted to colleagues and friends at Illinois State University and in the surrounding community for much encouragement and interest in this project. Walter Friedhoff, past chair of the Department of Psychology, provided a model of outstanding teaching that has energized my writing for students. Richard Payne, Department of

Political Science, is a kind and devoted friend with whom I have shared many profitable discussions about the writing process, the condition of children throughout the world, and other topics that have significantly influenced my vision of the text. Steven Landau, Neil Mulligan, and Mark Swerdlik, colleagues in the Department of Psychology, each provided consultation in their areas of expertise. My friendships with Laurie Bergner and Ruth Ann Friedberg have brought pleasurable walks on the Constitution Trail in Normal, Illinois, lively lunchtime conversations, and astute insights into the lives of children and families. Herman and Fran Brandau often asked how my work was progressing and provided invaluable advice and assistance.

Several students contributed significantly to this edition. Lisa Otte and Christy Mangione, my graduate assistants, secured permissions for use of copyrighted material and spent many long hours in the library gathering literature for the revision. Kimberly DeVico helped assemble the annotations for the Annotated Instructor's Edition.

The text supplement package benefited from the talent and diligence of several individuals. Rhoda Cummings, University of Nevada, Reno, and Kerry Krafft and Brenda Lohman, Illinois State University, are responsible for a greatly inhanced Instructor's Resource Manual. Carol Satterfield Tate, University of the South, prepared the Test Bank. I am pleased to have collaborated with Cynthia Elias, a graduate of Harvard University Law School and a doctoral candidate in school psychology at Illinois State University, on the Study Guide for this edition.

I have been fortunate to work with an outstanding publishing staff at Allyn and Bacon. *Child Development* has benefited greatly from the experience and dedication of several highly capable editors—John-Paul Lenney, Diane McOscar, and Susan Badger—with whom I am pleased to have continuing relationships. Sean Wakely, Vice President and Editor-in-Chief, edited this fourth edition with unusual sensitivity, forthrightness, and diplomatic problem solving. A short time after his arrival at Allyn and Bacon, he encouraged me to explore the possibilities of a new medium for teaching child development. The resulting observation video, coordinated with the text's content, has been among my most exciting endeavors in recent years. I look forward to working with Sean on future editions and on other projects in the years to come.

Sue Gleason, Senior Developmental Editor, assisted in planning the new Point of View boxes. Her prompt and patient responses to my concerns and queries are very much appreciated. Annie Reid handled the day-to-day development work on the text and its supplements. It is difficult to find words that do justice to her contributions. Annie worked closely with me as I revised each chapter, making sure that every line and paragraph would be clear, every thought and concept precisely expressed and well developed. Her keen visual sense enhanced the illustration and photo program for this edition. Annie also brought remarkable organizational skill and attention to detail to the coordination of text supplements, ensuring their high quality.

Tom Dorsaneo transformed the production of the book into a pleasant, efficient process that permitted me to complete filming for the observation video while the text was prepared for publication. His competence, courtesy, and interest as an involved grandfather of an energetic toddler have made working with him a great delight. I thank Elsa Peterson for obtaining the outstanding photos of culturally diverse children in this edition. Jennifer Normandin and Erika Stuart, Editorial Assistants, graciously arranged for manuscript reviews and attended to a wide variety of pressing, last-minute details.

A final word of gratitude goes to my family, whose love, patience, and understanding have enabled me to be wife, mother, teacher, researcher, and text author since I began this book in 1986. My sons, David and Peter, grew up with this text, passing from childhood to adolescence and then to young adulthood as successive editions were written. David, who received his Master's degree from Tulane University as the book went to press, has developed a special connection with its subject matter as he prepares for a career in teaching. Peter, a psychology major, business minor, and avid violinist, provided me with many an inspiring and restful respite from writing through his musical performances at Illinois Wesleyan University. My husband, Ken, willingly made room for this project in our family life and communicated his belief in its importance in a great many unspoken, caring ways.

—Laura E. Berk

About the Author

LAURA E. BERK is a distinguished professor of psychology at Illinois State University, where she has taught child development to undergraduate and graduate students for twenty-six years. She received her bachelor's degree in psychology from the University of California, Berkeley, and her masters and doctoral degrees in early childhood development and education from the University of Chicago. She has been a visiting scholar at Cornell University, UCLA, and Stanford University, and at the University of South Australia, where she was the recipient of the de Lissa fellowship in early childhood and family studies. She has published widely on the effects of school environments on children's development and, more recently, on the development of children's private speech. Her research has been funded by the U.S. Office of Education and the National Institute of Child Health and Human Development. It has appeared in many prominent journals, including *Child Development, Developmental Psychology, Merrill-Palmer Quarterly, Journal of Abnormal Child Psychology,* and *Development and Psychopathology.* Her empirical studies have also attracted the attention of the general public, leading to contributions to *Psychology Today* and *Scientific American.* Berk has served as research editor of *Young Children* and consulting editor of *Early Childhood Research Quarterly.* She is author of the chapter on the extracurriculum of schooling for the American Educational Research Association's *Handbook of Research on Curriculum.* Her books include *Private Speech: From Social Interaction to Self-Regulation; Scaffolding Children's Learning: Vygotsky and Early Childhood Education,* recently released by the National Association for the Education of Young Children; and the chronologically organized text *Infants, Children, and Adolescents,* published by Allyn and Bacon.

Child Development

1 History, Theory, and Applied Directions

Not long ago, I left my midwestern home to live for a year near the small city in northern California where I spent my childhood. One morning, I visited the neighborhood where I grew up—a place I had not been since I was 12 years old. I stood at the entrance to my old schoolyard. Buildings and grounds that looked large to me as a child now seemed strangely small from my grown-up vantage point. I peered through the window of my first-grade classroom. The desks were no longer arranged in rows but grouped in clusters around the room. A computer rested against the far wall, near the spot where I once sat. I walked my old route home from school, the distance shrunken by my larger stride. I stopped in front of my best friend Kathryn's house, where we once drew sidewalk pictures, crossed the street to play kick ball, produced plays for neighborhood audiences in the garage, and traded marbles and stamps in the backyard. In place of the small shop where I had purchased penny candy stood a neighborhood day care center, filled with the voices and vigorous activity of toddlers and preschoolers.

As I walked, I reflected on early experiences that contributed to who I am and what I am like today—weekends helping my father in his downtown clothing shop; the year during which my mother studied to become a high school teacher; moments of companionship and rivalry with my sister and brother; Sunday trips to museums and the seashore; and overnight visits to my grandmother's house, where I became someone extra special.

As I passed the homes of my childhood friends, I thought of what I knew about their present lives: my close friend Kathryn, star pupil and president of our sixth-grade class—today a successful corporate lawyer and mother of two children. Shy, withdrawn Phil, cruelly teased because of his cleft lip—now owner of a thriving chain of hardware stores and member of the city council. Julio, immigrant from Mexico who joined our class in third grade—today director of an elementary school bilingual education program and single parent of an adopted Mexican boy. And finally, my next-door neighbor Rick, who picked fights at recess, struggled with reading, repeated fourth grade, dropped out of high school, and (so I heard) moved from one job to another over the following 10 years.

As you begin this course in child development, perhaps you, too, have wondered about some of the same questions that crossed my mind during that nostalgic neighborhood walk:

- What determines the features human beings have in common and those that make each of us unique—in physical characteristics, capabilities, interests, and behaviors?
- Is the infant's and young child's perception of the world much the same as the adult's, or is it different in basic respects?
- Why do some of us, like Kathryn and Rick, retain the same styles of responding that characterized us as children, whereas others, like Phil, change in essential ways?
- How did Julio, transplanted to a foreign culture at 8 years of age, master its language and customs and succeed in its society, yet remain strongly identified with his ethnic community?
- In what ways are children's home, school, and neighborhood experiences the same today as they were in generations past, and in what ways are they different? How does cultural change—employed mothers, day care, divorce, smaller families, and new technologies—affect children's characteristics and skills?

These are central questions addressed by **child development**, a field devoted to understanding all aspects of human growth and change from conception through adolescence. Child development is part of a larger discipline known as **developmental psychology**, or (as it is referred to in its interdisciplinary sense) **human development**, which includes all changes we experience throughout the life span. Great diversity characterizes the interests and concerns of the thousands of investigators who study child development. But all have a single goal in common: to describe and identify those factors that influence the dramatic changes in young people during the first two decades of life.

Child Development as an Interdisciplinary, Scientific, and Applied Field

Look again at the questions just listed, and you will see that they are not just of scientific interest. Each is of *applied,* or practical importance, as well. In fact, scientific curiosity is just one factor that has led child development to become the exciting field of study it is today. Research about development has also been stimulated by social pressures to better the lives of children. For example, the beginning of public education in the early part of this century led to a demand for knowledge about what and how to teach children of different ages. The interest of pediatricians in improving children's health required an understanding of physical growth and nutrition. The social service profession's desire to treat children's anxieties and behavior problems required information about personality and social development. And parents have continually asked for advice about child-rearing practices and experiences that would promote the growth of their child.

Our large storehouse of information about child development is *interdisciplinary.* It has grown through the combined efforts of people from many fields of study. Because of the need for solutions to everyday problems concerning children, scientists from psychology, sociology, anthropology, and biology have joined forces in research with professionals from a variety of applied fields, including education, medicine, public health, and social service, to name just a few. Today, the field of child development is a melting pot of contributions. Its body of knowledge is not just scientifically important, but relevant and useful.

Basic Themes and Issues

Before scientific study of the child, questions about children were answered by turning to common sense, opinion, and belief. Systematic research on children did not begin until the late nineteenth and early twentieth centuries. Gradually it led to the construction of theories of child development, to which professionals and parents could turn for understanding and guidance. Although there are a great many definitions, for our purposes we can think of a **theory** as an orderly, integrated set of statements that describes, explains, and predicts behavior. For example, a good theory of infant–caregiver attachment would *describe* the behaviors that lead up to babies' strong desire to seek the affection and comfort of a familiar adult around 6 to 8 months of age. It would also *explain* why infants have such a strong desire. And it might also try to *predict* what might happen if babies do not develop this close emotional bond.

Theories are vital tools in child development (and any other scientific endeavor) for two reasons. First, they provide organizing frameworks for our observations of children. In other words, they *guide and give meaning* to what we see. To appreciate this idea, imagine a researcher who observes and measures, with no clear idea of what information is important to collect, at least for the moment, and what is unimportant. Such a person is likely to be overwhelmed by a multitude of trivial and disconnected facts because no "lens" is available to focus, integrate, and help make sense of the data (Thomas, 1992). Second, theories that are verified by research often serve as a sound basis for practical

Child development
A field of study devoted to understanding all aspects of human growth from conception through adolescence.

Developmental psychology
A branch of psychology devoted to understanding all changes that human beings experience throughout the life span.

Human development
An interdisciplinary field of study devoted to understanding all changes that human beings experience throughout the life span.

Theory
An orderly, integrated set of statements that describes, explains, and predicts behavior.

action. Once a theory helps us *understand* development, we are in a much better position to know *what to do* in our efforts to improve the welfare and treatment of children.

As we will see later, theories are influenced by the cultural values and belief systems of their times. But theories differ in one important way from mere opinion and belief: A theory's continued existence depends on *scientific verification* (Scarr, 1985). This means that the theory must be tested using a fair set of research procedures agreed on by the scientific community. (We will consider research strategies in Chapter 2.)

In the field of child development, there are many theories with very different ideas about what children are like and how they develop. The study of child development provides no ultimate truth, since investigators do not always agree on the meaning of what they see. In addition, children are complex beings; they grow physically, mentally, emotionally, and socially. As yet, no single theory has been able to explain all these aspects. Finally, the existence of many theories helps advance knowledge, since researchers are continually trying to support, contradict, and integrate these different points of view.

This chapter traces the emergence of the field of child development and provides an overview of major twentieth-century theories. (We will return to each modern theory in greater detail in later chapters of this book.) Although there are many theories, we can easily organize them, since almost all take a stand on three basic issues about child development: (1) How should we describe the developing child? (2) What is the course of development like? (3) What factors determine, or influence, development? To help you remember these controversial issues, they are briefly summarized in Table 1.1. Let's take a close look at each in the following sections.

VIEWS OF THE DEVELOPING CHILD

Recently, the mother of a 16-month-old boy named Angelo reported to me with amazement that her young son pushed a toy car across the living room floor while making a motorlike sound, "Brmmmm, brmmmm," for the first time. "We've never shown him how to do that!" exclaimed Angelo's mother. "Did he make that sound up himself," she inquired, "or did he copy it from some other child at day care?"

Angelo's mother has asked a puzzling question about the nature of children. It contrasts two basic perspectives: the organismic, or *active* position, with the mechanistic, or *passive* point of view.

Organismic theories assume that change is stimulated from *within the organism*—more specifically, that psychological structures exist inside the child that underlie and control development. Children are viewed as active, purposeful beings who make sense of their world and determine their own learning (Dixon & Lerner, 1992). For an organismic theorist, the surrounding environment supports development, as Angelo's mother did when she provided him with stimulating toys. But since children invent their own ways of understanding and responding to events around them, the environment does not bring about the child's growth. Instead, the "organism selects, modifies, or rejects environmental influences pressing upon it" (White, 1976, p. 100).

TABLE 1.1

Basic Issues in Child Development

Issue	Questions Raised About Development
View of the developing child: organismic versus mechanistic	Are children active beings with psychological structures that underlie and control development, or are they passive recipients of environmental inputs?
View of the course of development: continuous versus discontinuous	Is child development a matter of cumulative adding on of skills and behaviors, or does it involve qualitative, stagewise changes?
View of the determinants of development: nature versus nurture	Are genetic or environmental factors the most important determinants of development? If environment is crucial, to what extent do early experiences establish lifelong patterns of behavior? Can later experiences overcome early negative effects?

Organismic theory
A theory that assumes the existence of psychological structures inside the child that underlie and control development.

FIGURE 1.1

■ *Is development continuous or discontinuous? (a) Some theorists believe that development is a smooth, continuous process. Children gradually add more of the same types of skills. (b) Other theorists think that development takes place in abrupt, discontinuous stages. Children change rapidly as they step up to a new level of development and then change very little for a while. With each new step, the child interprets and responds to the world in a qualitatively different way.*

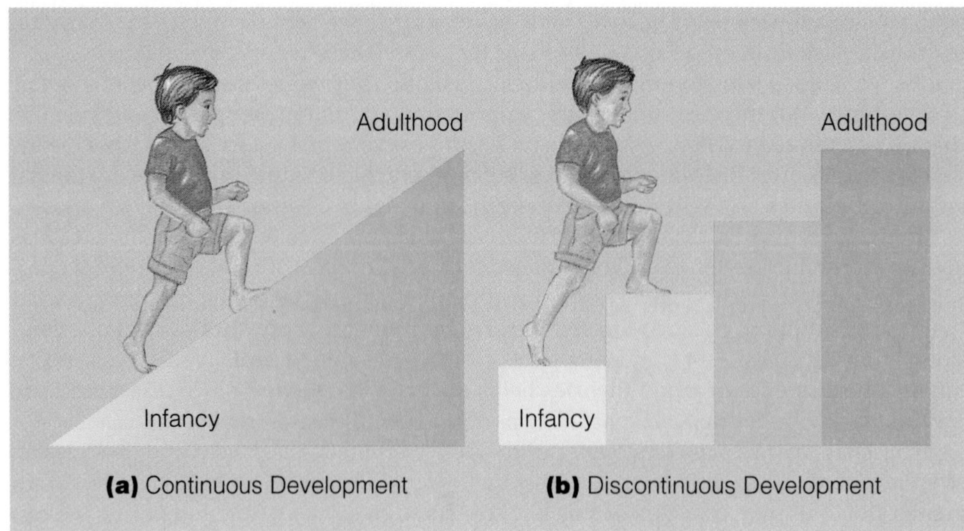

In contrast, **mechanistic theories** focus on relationships between environmental inputs and behavioral outputs. The approach is called *mechanistic* because children are likened to the workings of a machine. Change is stimulated by the environment, which shapes the behavior of the child, who is a passive reactor. For example, when Angelo's playmate says "Brmmmm," Angelo responds similarly. According to this view, new capacities result from external forces acting on the child. Development is treated as a straightforward, predictable consequence of events in the surrounding world (Miller, 1993; Smith, 1992).

VIEWS OF THE COURSE OF DEVELOPMENT

How can we best describe the differences in capacities and behavior among small infants, young children, adolescents, and adults? As Figure 1.1 illustrates, major theories recognize two possibilities.

On the one hand, babies and preschoolers may respond to the world in much the same way as adults. The difference between the immature and mature being may simply be one of *amount* or *complexity* of behavior. For example, little Angelo's thinking might be just as logical and well organized as our own. Perhaps (as his mother reports) he can sort objects into simple categories, recognize whether there are more of one kind than another, and remember where he left his favorite toy at day care the week before. Angelo's only limitation may be that he cannot perform these skills with as many pieces of information as we can. If this is true, then Angelo's development must be **continuous**—a process that consists of gradually adding on more of the same types of skills that were there to begin with.

On the other hand, Angelo may have unique ways of thinking, feeling, and behaving that must be understood on their own terms—ones quite different from our own. If so, then development is a **discontinuous** process in which new ways of understanding and responding to the world emerge at particular time periods. From this perspective, Angelo is not yet able to organize objects or remember experiences in the same way as adults. Instead, he will move through a series of developmental steps, each of which has unique features, until he reaches the highest level of human functioning.

Theories that accept the discontinuous perspective include a vital developmental concept: the concept of stage. **Stages** are *qualitative changes* in thinking, feeling, and behaving that characterize particular time periods of development. In stage theories, development is much like climbing a staircase, with each step corresponding to a more mature, reorganized way of functioning than the one that came before. The stage concept also assumes that children undergo periods of rapid transformation as they step up from one stage to the next, followed by plateaus during which they stand solidly within a stage. In other words, change is fairly sudden rather than gradual and ongoing. Finally, stages are always assumed to be universal across children and cultures; that is, stage theories assume that children everywhere follow the same sequence of development.

Mechanistic theory
A theory that regards the child as a passive reactor to environmental inputs.

Continuous development
A view that regards development as a cumulative process of adding on more of the same types of skills that were there to begin with.

Discontinuous development
A view in which new and different ways of interpreting and responding to the world emerge at particular time periods.

Stage
A qualitative change in thinking, feeling, and behaving that characterizes a particular time period of development.

Does development actually take place in a neat, orderly stepwise sequence that is identical for all human beings? For now, let's note that this is a very ambitious assumption that has not gone unchallenged. We will review some very influential stage theories later in this chapter.

VIEWS OF THE DETERMINANTS OF DEVELOPMENT

In addition to describing the course of child development, each theory takes a stand on a major question about its underlying causes: Are genetic or environmental factors most important? This is the age-old **nature–nurture controversy**. By *nature,* we mean inborn biological givens—the hereditary information we receive from our parents at the moment of conception that signals the body to grow and affects all our characteristics and skills. By *nurture,* we mean the complex forces of the physical and social world that children encounter in their homes, neighborhoods, schools, and communities.

Although all theories grant at least some role to both nature and nurture, they vary in the emphasis placed on each. For example, consider the following questions: Is the older child's ability to think in more complex ways largely the result of an inborn timetable of growth? Or is it primarily influenced by the way parents and teachers stimulate and encourage the child? Do children acquire language because they are genetically predisposed to do so or because parents intensively tutor them from an early age? And what accounts for the vast individual differences among children—in height, weight, physical coordination, intelligence, personality, and social skills? Is nature or nurture more responsible?

Notice how a theory's stance on the relative importance of nature versus nurture is related to its position on the two previously discussed issues. Look back at our discussion of organismic versus mechanistic views of the developing child. An organismic theorist would never assume that nurture is more powerful in development than nature. And a mechanistic theorist would always stress the importance of nurture.

Furthermore, the position a theory takes on nature versus nurture is linked to its explanation of individual differences. Some theorists emphasize *stability*—that children who are high or low in a characteristic (such as verbal ability, anxiety, or sociability) will remain so at later ages. These theorists typically stress the importance of *heredity.* If they regard environment as crucial, they generally point to *early experience* as establishing a lifelong pattern of behavior. Powerful negative events in the first few years, they argue, cannot be fully overcome by later, more positive ones (Bowlby, 1980; Sroufe, Egeland, & Kreutzer, 1990). Other theorists take a more optimistic view. They believe that *change* is possible and likely if new experiences support it (Chess & Thomas, 1984; Sampson & Laub, 1993; Werner & Smith, 1992).

Throughout this chapter and the remainder of this book, we will see that investigators disagree, often sharply, on the question of *stability versus change.* And the answers they provide are of great applied significance. If you believe that development is largely due to nature, then providing experiences aimed at inducing change would be of little value. If, on the other hand, you are convinced of the supreme importance of early experience, then you would intervene as soon as possible, offering children high-quality stimulation and support to ensure that they realize their potential. Finally, if you think that environment is profoundly influential throughout development, you would extend high-quality early experiences into later years. In addition, you would provide assistance any time children or adolescents run into difficulty, believing that they can recover from early negative events with the help of new opportunities and favorable life circumstances.

A BALANCED POINT OF VIEW

Up to now, we have discussed the basic issues of child development mostly in terms of extremes—solutions on one side or the other. As we trace the unfolding of the field in the rest of this chapter, you will see that the positions of many theories have softened. Modern ones, especially, recognize the merits of both sides. Some theorists take an intermediate stand between an organismic versus mechanistic perspective. They regard both the child and the surrounding environment as active and as collaborating to produce development. Similarly, some contemporary researchers believe that both continuous and discontinuous changes characterize development and alternate with one another.

Nature–nurture controversy Disagreement among theorists about whether genetic or environmental factors are the most important determinants of development and behavior.

Furthermore, investigators have moved away from asking which is more important—heredity or environment. Instead, they want to know precisely *how nature and nurture work together* to influence the child's traits and capacities.

Finally, as we will see in later parts of this book, the relative impact of early and later experiences varies substantially from one aspect of development to another and even (as the From Research to Practice box on the following page indicates) across individuals! Because of the intricate web of factors linked to human change and the challenges involved in isolating the effects of each, many theoretical points of view have amassed research support. Although debate continues, this circumstance has also sparked more balanced visions of child development.

■ *In this medieval painting, the young child is depicted as a miniature adult. His dress, expression, and activities resemble those of his elders. Through the fifteenth century, little emphasis was placed on childhood as a unique phase of the life cycle. (Giraudon/Art Resource)*

Historical Foundations

Modern theories of child development are the result of centuries of change in Western cultural values, philosophical thinking about children, and scientific progress. To understand the field as it exists today, we must return to its beginnings—to influences that long preceded scientific child study. We will see that many early ideas about children linger on as important forces in current theory and research.

MEDIEVAL TIMES

In medieval times (the sixth through the fifteenth centuries), little importance was placed on childhood as a separate phase of the life cycle. The idea accepted by many theories today, that children are unique and different from youths and adults, was much less common then. Instead, once children emerged from infancy, they were regarded as miniature, already formed adults, a view called **preformationism**. This attitude is reflected in the art, everyday entertainment, and language of the times. If you look carefully at medieval paintings, you will see that children are depicted in dress and expression as immature adults. Before the sixteenth century, toys and games were not designed to occupy and amuse children but were for all people. And consider age, so important an aspect of modern personal identity that children can recite how old they are almost as soon as they can talk. Age was unimportant in medieval custom and usage. People did not refer to it in everyday conversation, and it was not even recorded in family and civil records until the fifteenth and sixteenth centuries (Ariès, 1962).

Nevertheless, faint glimmerings of the idea that children are unique emerged during medieval times. The Church defended the innocence of children, spoke out against the common practice of infanticide, and encouraged parents to provide spiritual training. Medical works had sections acknowledging the fragility of infants and children and providing special instructions for their care. And some laws recognized that children needed protection from adults who might mistreat or take advantage of them. But even though in a practical sense there was some awareness of the smallness and vulnerability of children, as yet there were no theories about the uniqueness of childhood or separate developmental periods (Borstelmann, 1983; Sommerville, 1982).

THE REFORMATION

In the sixteenth century, a revised image of childhood sprang from the religious movement that gave birth to Protestantism—in particular, from the Puritan belief in original sin. According to Puritan doctrine, the child was a fragile creature of God who needed to be safeguarded but who also needed to be reformed. Born evil and stubborn, children had to be civilized toward a destiny of virtue and salvation (Ariès, 1962; Shahar, 1990).

Harsh, restrictive child-rearing practices were recommended as the most efficient means for taming the depraved child. Infants were tightly swaddled, and children were dressed in stiff, uncomfortable clothing that held them in adultlike postures. In schools, disobedient pupils were routinely beaten by their schoolmasters (Stone, 1977). Although these attitudes represented the prevailing child-rearing philosophy of the time, it is important to note that they probably were not typical of everyday practices in Puritan

Preformationism
Medieval view of the child as a miniature adult.

FROM RESEARCH TO PRACTICE

Resilient Children

John and his best friend Gary grew up in a run-down, crime-ridden inner-city neighborhood. By age 10, each had experienced years of family conflict followed by parental divorce. Reared for the rest of childhood and adolescence in mother-headed households, John and Gary rarely saw their fathers. Both achieved poorly in school, dropped out in their second year of high school, and spent their teenage years in and out of trouble with the police.

Although the first 18 years of John and Gary's lives were similar, their paths of development soon diverged. By age 30, John had fathered two children with women he never married, had spent time in prison, was unemployed, and drank alcohol heavily. In contrast, Gary had returned to finish high school, had studied auto mechanics at a community college, and became manager of a gas station and repair shop. Married with two children, Gary had saved his earnings and purchased a home in a pleasant, safe neighborhood. He was happy, healthy, and well adapted to life.

A wealth of evidence reveals that environmental risks—poverty, negative family interactions, parental divorce, job loss, mental illness, and drug abuse—predispose children to future problems. On the basis of these findings, we would have expected both John and Gary to develop serious health and psychological difficulties. Yet individuals with economically disadvantaged and stressful childhoods do not always repeat this pattern when they reach maturity (Garmezy, 1991; Rutter, 1987).

Research on *resiliency*—the ability to spring back from adversity—is receiving increasing attention because investigators want to find ways to protect young people from the damaging effects of stressful life events and conditions (Cicchetti & Garmezy, 1993). It was inspired by several long-term studies on the relationship of cumulative life stressors in childhood to competence and adjustment in adolescence and adulthood. In each, some children (like Gary) "beat the odds" and came through unscathed, whereas others (like John) showed many negative consequences (Garmezy, 1991, 1993; Rutter, 1985, 1987; Werner & Smith, 1992). What shields resilient children from adversity? Recent analyses of existing evidence have identified three broad factors:

- **PERSONAL CHARACTERISTICS OF CHILDREN.** A child's characteristics can reduce exposure to risk or lead to experiences that compensate for early stressful events. Temperament is particularly powerful. Children with calm, easy-going, sociable dispositions who are self-confident and willing to take initiative have a special capacity to adapt to change and elicit positive responses from others. Those who are emotionally reactive and irritable often strain the patience of people around them (Gribble et al., 1993; Milgram & Palti, 1993; Smith & Prior, 1995; Wyman et al., 1992). For example, both John and Gary moved several times during their childhoods. Each time, John became anxious and angry, picking arguments with his parents, siblings, and peers. In contrast, Gary reacted sadly to leaving his home but soon became excited about the prospect of making new friends and exploring new parts of the neighborhood. Intellectual ability is another protective factor. It increases the chances of rewarding experiences in school that may offset the impact of a stressful home life (Dubow & Luster, 1990).
- **A WARM PARENTAL RELATIONSHIP.** A close, supportive relationship with at least one parent who provides affection and assistance and introduces order and organization into the child's life fosters resilience. But note that this factor (as well as the next one) is not independent of children's personal characteristics! Children who are relaxed, socially responsive, and able to deal with change are easier to rear and more likely to enjoy positive relationships with parents and other people. Furthermore, some children may have developed more attractive dispositions as a result of parental warmth and attention (Luthar & Zigler, 1991; Smith & Prior, 1995).
- **SOCIAL SUPPORT OUTSIDE THE IMMEDIATE FAMILY.** Finally, a person outside the immediate family—perhaps a grandparent, teacher, or close friend—who forms a special relationship with the child can promote resilience. Gary may have succeeded in avoiding risks because of the support he received in adolescence from his maternal grandfather, who listened to Gary's concerns and helped him solve problems constructively. In addition, Gary's grandfather had a stable marriage and work life and handled stressors skillfully. Consequently, he served as a model of effective coping (Zimmerman & Arunkumar, 1994).

Research on resilience highlights the complex connections among determinants of development. Clearly, children are active in the resiliency process. Armed with positive characteristics (which may stem from innate endowment, favorable rearing environments, or both), they take action to reduce stressful situations. At the same time, an understanding adult can increase the young person's chances of developing effective coping skills.

Currently, researchers are examining the impact of various combinations of stressful and protective factors on development. So far, they know that when many risks pile up, it is increasingly difficult to overcome them (Capaldi & Patterson, 1991; Sameroff et al., 1993). Consequently, interventions need to reduce environmental risks as well as enhance relationships at home, in school, and in the community that inoculate children against the negative effects of risk. This means attending to both the person and the environment—building capacity as well as fixing problems.

families. Recent historical evidence suggests that love and affection for their children made many Puritan parents reluctant to use extremely repressive discipline (Moran & Vinovskis, 1986).

As the Puritans emigrated from England to the United States, they brought with them the belief that child rearing was one of their most important obligations. Although they continued to regard the child's soul as tainted by original sin, they tried to promote reason in their sons and daughters so they would be able to separate right from wrong and resist temptation. The Puritans were the first to develop special reading materials for children that instructed them in religious and moral ideals. As they trained their children in self-reliance and self-control, Puritan parents gradually adopted a moderate balance between discipline and indulgence, severity and permissiveness (Pollock, 1987).

PHILOSOPHIES OF THE ENLIGHTENMENT

The seventeenth-century Enlightenment brought new philosophies of reason and emphasized ideals of human dignity and respect. Conceptions of childhood appeared that were more humane than those of centuries past.

■ JOHN LOCKE. The writings of John Locke (1632–1704), a leading British philosopher, served as the forerunner of an important twentieth-century perspective that we will discuss shortly: behaviorism. Locke viewed the child as **tabula rasa**. Translated from Latin, this means "blank slate" or "white piece of paper." According to this idea, children were not basically evil. They were, to begin with, nothing at all, and their characters could be shaped by all kinds of experiences while growing up. Locke (1690/1892) described parents as rational tutors who could mold the child in any way they wished, through careful instruction, effective example, and rewards for good behavior. In addition, Locke was ahead of his time in recommending to parents child-rearing practices that were eventually supported by twentieth-century research. For example, he suggested that parents reward children not with money or sweets, but rather with praise and approval. Locke also opposed physical punishment: "The child repeatedly beaten in school cannot look upon books and teachers without experiencing fear and anger." Locke's philosophy led to a change from harshness toward children to kindness and compassion.

Look carefully at Locke's ideas, and you will see that he took a firm stand on each of the basic issues we discussed earlier in this chapter. As blank slates, children are viewed in passive, *mechanistic* terms. The course of growth is written on them by the environment. Locke also regarded development as *continuous*. Adultlike behaviors are gradually built up through the warm, consistent teachings of parents. Finally, Locke was a champion of *nurture*—of the power of the environment to determine whether children become good or bad, bright or dull, kind or selfish.

■ JEAN-JACQUES ROUSSEAU. In the eighteenth century, a new theory of childhood was introduced by the French philosopher of the Enlightenment, Jean-Jacques Rousseau (1712–1778). Children, Rousseau (1762/1955) thought, were not blank slates and empty containers to be filled by adult instruction. Instead, they were **noble savages**, naturally endowed with a sense of right and wrong and with an innate plan for orderly, healthy growth. Unlike Locke, Rousseau thought children's built-in moral sense and unique ways of thinking and feeling would only be harmed by adult training. His was a child-centered philosophy in which adults should be receptive to the children's needs at each of four stages of development: infancy, childhood, late childhood, and adolescence.

Rousseau's philosophy includes two vitally important concepts that are found in modern theories. The first is the concept of *stage,* which we discussed earlier in this chapter. The second is the concept of **maturation**, which refers to a genetically determined, naturally unfolding course of growth. If you accept the notion that children mature through a sequence of stages, then they cannot be preformed, miniature adults. Instead, they are unique and different from adults, and their development is determined by their own inner nature. Compared to Locke, Rousseau took a very different stand on basic developmental issues. He saw children as *organismic* (active shapers of their own destiny), development as a *discontinuous* stagewise process, and *nature* as having mapped out the path and timetable of growth.

Tabula rasa
Locke's view of the child as a blank slate whose character is shaped by experience.

Noble savage
Rousseau's view of the child as naturally endowed with an innate plan for orderly, healthy growth.

Maturation
A genetically determined, naturally unfolding course of growth.

DARWIN'S THEORY OF EVOLUTION

A century after Rousseau, another ancestor of modern child study—this time of its scientific foundations—emerged. In the mid-nineteenth century, Charles Darwin (1809–1882), a British naturalist, joined an expedition to distant parts of the world, where he made careful observations of fossils and animal and plant life. Darwin (1859/1936) noticed the infinite variation among species. He also saw that within a species, no two individuals are exactly alike. From these observations, he constructed his ground breaking theory of evolution.

The theory emphasized two related principles: *natural selection* and *survival of the fittest.* Darwin explained that certain species were selected by nature to survive in particular parts of the world because they had characteristics that fit with, or were adapted to, their surroundings. Other species died off because they were not well suited to their environments. Individuals within a species who best met the survival requirements of the environment lived long enough to reproduce and pass their more favorable characteristics to future generations.

Darwin's emphasis on the adaptive value of physical characteristics and behavior eventually found its way into important twentieth-century theories. For example, later in this chapter we will see that Darwin's ideas are central to ethology, an approach to development that emphasizes the evolutionary origins and adaptive value of human behavior. Jean Piaget, master theorist of children's thinking, was also influenced by Darwin. As will become clear shortly, Piaget believed that as children reason about the world in more mature, effective ways, they achieve a better adaptive fit with their surroundings (Dixon & Lerner, 1992).

During his explorations, Darwin discovered that the early prenatal growth of many species was strikingly similar. This suggested that all species, including human beings, were descended from a few common ancestors. Other scientists concluded from Darwin's observation that the development of the human child, from conception to maturity, followed the same general plan as the evolution of the human species. Although this belief eventually proved to be inaccurate, efforts to chart parallels between child growth and human evolution prompted researchers to make careful observations of all aspects of children's behavior. Out of these first attempts to document an idea about development, the science of child study was born.

EARLY SCIENTIFIC BEGINNINGS

Scientific child study evolved quickly during the early part of the twentieth century. As we will see in the following sections, rudimentary observations of single children were soon followed by improved methods and theoretical ideas. Each advance contributed to the firm foundation on which the field rests today.

■ THE BABY BIOGRAPHIES. Imagine yourself as a forerunner in the field of child development, confronted with studying children for the first time. How might you go about this challenging task? Scientists of the late nineteenth and early twentieth centuries did what most of us would probably do in their place. They selected a child of their own or of a close relative. Then, beginning in early infancy, they jotted down day-by-day descriptions and impressions of the youngster's behavior. Dozens of these baby biographies were published by the early twentieth century. In the following excerpt from one of them, the author reflects on the birth of her young niece, whose growth she followed during the first year of life:

> Its first act is a cry, not of wrath, . . . nor a shout of joy, . . . but a snuffling, and then a long, thin tearless á—á, with the timbre of a Scotch bagpipe, purely automatic, but of discomfort. With this monotonous and dismal cry, with its red, shriveled, parboiled skin . . . , it is not strange that, if the mother . . . has not come to love her child before birth, there is a brief interval occasionally dangerous to the child before the maternal instinct is fully aroused.
>
> It cannot be denied that this unflattering description is fair enough, and our baby was no handsomer than the rest of her kind. . . . Yet she did not lack admirers. I have never noticed that women (even those who are not mothers) mind a few little aesthetic defects, . . . with so many counterbalancing charms in the little warm, soft, living thing. (Shinn, 1900, pp. 20–21)

Can you tell from this passage why baby biographies have sometimes been upheld as examples of how *not* to study children? These first investigators tended to be emotionally invested in the infants they observed, and they seldom began with a clear idea of what they wanted to find out about the child. Not surprisingly, many of their records were eventually discarded as biased. But we must keep in mind that the baby biographers were like explorers first setting foot on alien soil. When a field is new, we cannot expect its theories and methods to be well formulated.

The baby biographies were clearly a step in the right direction. In fact, two theorists of the nineteenth century, Darwin (1877) and German biologist William Preyer (1882/1888), contributed to these early records of children's behavior. Preyer, especially, set high standards for making observations. He recorded what he saw immediately, as completely as possible, and at regular intervals. He also tried not to influence the child's behavior or to let his own interests and interpretations distort what he saw. And he checked the accuracy of his own notes against those of a second observer (Cairns, 1983). These are the same standards that modern researchers use when making observations of children. As a result of the biographers' pioneering efforts, in succeeding decades the child became a common subject of scientific research.

■ THE NORMATIVE PERIOD OF CHILD STUDY. G. Stanley Hall (1844–1924), one of the most influential American psychologists of the early twentieth century, is generally regarded as the founder of the child study movement (Dixon & Lerner, 1992). Inspired by Darwin's work, Hall and his well-known student Arnold Gesell (1880–1961) developed theories based on evolutionary ideas. These early leaders regarded child development as a genetically determined series of events that unfolds automatically, much like a blooming flower (Gesell, 1933; Hall, 1904).

Hall and Gesell are remembered less for their one-sided theories than for their intensive efforts to describe all aspects of child development. Aware of the limitations of baby biographies, Hall set out to collect a sound body of objective facts about children. This goal launched the **normative approach** to child study. In a normative investigation, measures of behavior are taken on large numbers of children. Then age-related averages are computed to represent the typical child's development. Using this approach, Hall constructed elaborate questionnaires asking children of different ages almost everything they could tell about themselves—interests, fears, imaginary playmates, dreams, friendships, favorite toys, and more (White, 1992).

In the same tradition, Gesell devoted a major part of his career to collecting detailed normative information on the behavior of infants and children. His schedules of infant development were particularly complete, and revised versions continue to be used today (see Figure 1.2). Gesell was also among the first to make knowledge about child development meaningful to parents. He provided them with descriptions of motor achievements, social behaviors, and personality characteristics (Gesell & Ilg, 1949). Gesell hoped to relieve parents' anxieties by informing them of what to expect at each age. If, as he believed, the timetable of development is the product of millions of years of evolution, then children are naturally knowledgeable about their needs. His child-rearing advice, in the tradition of Rousseau, recommended sensitivity and responsiveness to children's cues (Thelen & Adolph, 1992). Gesell's books were widely read. Along with Benjamin Spock's famous *Baby and Child Care,* they became a central part of a rapidly expanding literature for parents published over this century.

Although Hall and Gesell's work offered a large body of descriptive facts about children of different ages, it provided little information on *process*—the how and why of development. Yet the child's development had to be described before it could be understood, and the normative approach provided the foundation for more effective explanations of development that came later.

■ THE MENTAL TESTING MOVEMENT. While Hall and Gesell were developing their theories and methods in the United States, French psychologist Alfred Binet (1857–1911) was also taking a normative approach to child development, but for a different reason. In the early 1900s, Binet and his colleague Theodore Simon were asked to find a way to identify retarded children in the Paris school system who needed to be placed in special classes. The first successful intelligence test, which they constructed for this purpose, grew out of practical educational concerns.

Previous attempts to create a useful intelligence test had met with little success. But Binet's effort was unique in that he began with a well-developed theory. In contrast to earlier views, which reduced intelligence to simple elements of reaction time and sensitivity to physical stimuli, Binet captured the complexity of children's thinking (Siegler,

Normative approach
An approach in which age-related averages are computed to represent the typical child's development.

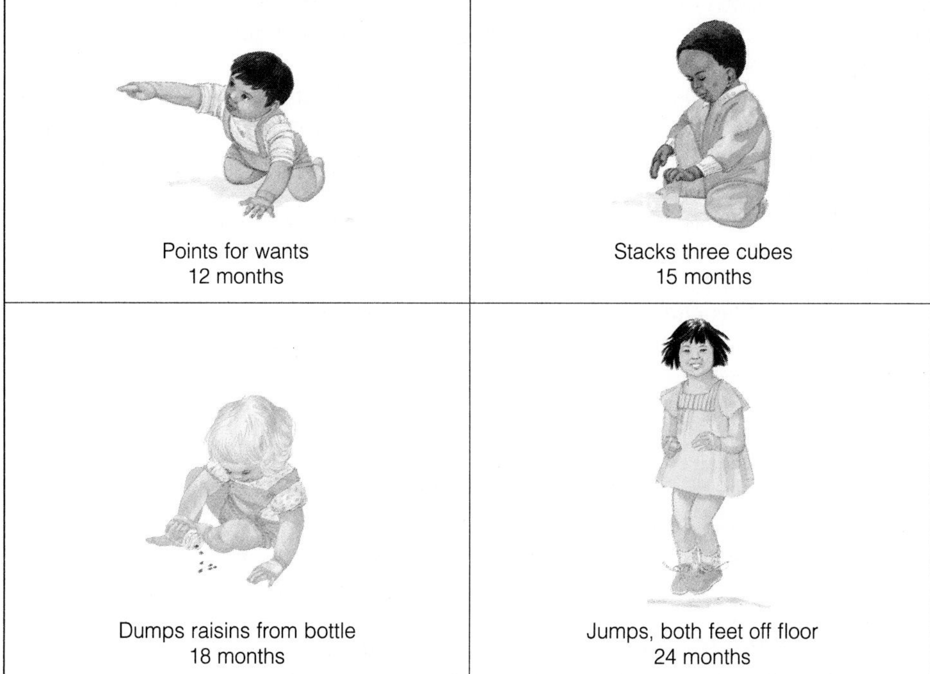

FIGURE 1.2

■ *Sample milestones from the most recent revision of Gesell's schedules of infant development, which include norms on hundreds of motor, mental, language, and social skills. Gesell's efforts to describe the course of development continue to be useful today. (Adapted from Knobloch, Stevens, & Malone, 1980.)*

1992). He defined intelligence as good judgment, planning, and critical reflection. Then he selected test questions that directly measured these abilities, creating a series of age-graded items that permitted him to compare the intellectual progress of different children.

In 1916, at Stanford University, Binet's test was translated into English and adapted for use with American children. It became known as the Stanford-Binet Intelligence Scale. Besides providing a score that could successfully predict school achievement, the Binet test sparked tremendous interest in individual differences in development. The mental testing movement was in motion. Comparisons of the intelligence test scores of children who vary in sex, ethnicity, birth order, family background, and other characteristics became a major focus of research. Intelligence tests also rose quickly to the forefront of the controversy over nature versus nurture that has continued throughout this century.

■ JAMES MARK BALDWIN: EARLY DEVELOPMENTAL THEORIST. A final important figure, overlooked in the history of child development for decades but now recognized as having had a major influence, is American psychologist James Mark Baldwin (1861–1934). A theorist rather than an observer of children, Baldwin's (1897) rich interpretations of development are experiencing a revival today. He believed that children's understanding of their physical and social worlds develops through a sequence of stages, beginning with the simplest behavior patterns of the newborn infant and concluding with the adult's capacity to think abstractly and reflectively (Cairns, 1992). Yet in describing the process of change, Baldwin differed from other leaders of his time in emphasizing diverse contributions to development.

Baldwin regarded neither the child nor the environment as in control of development. Instead, both nature and nurture were granted equal importance. Children, he argued, actively revise their ways of thinking about the world, but they also learn through habit, or simple copying of others' behaviors. As development proceeds, the child and his social surroundings influence each other, forming an inseparable, interwoven network. In other words, children are affected by those around them, but they too affect others' reactions toward them, in a reciprocal fashion.

Consider these ideas, and you will see why Baldwin (1895) argued that heredity and environment should not be viewed as distinct, opposing forces. Instead, he claimed, most human characteristics are "due to both causes working together" (p. 77). As we turn now to an overview of modern theories of child development, you will find Baldwin's ideas represented in several, especially the more recent ones.

BRIEF REVIEW

The modern field of child development has roots dating far back into the past. In medieval times, children were regarded as preformed, miniature adults. By the sixteenth century, childhood became a distinct phase of the life cycle. The Puritan belief in original sin fostered a harsh, authoritarian approach to child rearing. During the seventeenth century Enlightenment, Locke's "blank slate" and Rousseau's "inherently good" child promoted more humane treatment of children. Darwin's evolutionary ideas inspired maturational theories and the first attempts to study the child directly, in the form of baby biographies and Hall and Gesell's normative investigations. Out of the normative approach arose Binet's first successful intelligence test and a concern with individual differences among children. Baldwin's balanced view of the process of development survives in modern theories.

Mid-Twentieth-Century Theories

In the mid-twentieth century, the field of child development expanded into a legitimate discipline. Specialized societies were founded, and research journals were launched. As child development attracted increasing interest, a variety of mid-twentieth-century theories emerged, each of which continues to have followers today. In these theories, the European concern with the inner thoughts and feelings of the child contrasts sharply with the focus of American academic psychology on scientific precision and concrete, observable behavior.

THE PSYCHOANALYTIC PERSPECTIVE

By the 1930s and 1940s, many parents whose children suffered from serious emotional stress and behavior problems sought help from psychiatrists and social workers. The earlier normative movement had answered the question, What are children like? But to treat children's difficulties, child guidance professionals had to address the question, How and why did children become the way they are? They turned for help to the **psychoanalytic perspective** on personality development because of its emphasis on the unique developmental history of each child.

According to the psychoanalytic approach, children move through a series of stages in which they confront conflicts between biological drives and social expectations. The way these conflicts are resolved determines the individual's ability to learn, to get along with others, and to cope with anxiety. Although many individuals contributed to the psychoanalytic perspective, two have been especially influential: Sigmund Freud, founder of the psychoanalytic movement, and Erik Erikson.

■ FREUD'S PSYCHOSEXUAL THEORY. Freud (1856–1939), a Viennese physician, saw patients in his practice with a variety of nervous symptoms, such as hallucinations, fears, and paralyses, that appeared to have no physical basis. Seeking a cure for these troubled adults, Freud found that their symptoms could be relieved by having patients talk freely about painful events of their childhood. Using this "talking cure," he carefully examined the unconscious motivations of his patients. Startling the straitlaced Victorian society in which he lived, Freud concluded that infants and young children were sexual beings and that the way they were permitted to express their impulses lay at the heart of their adult behavior. Freud constructed his **psychosexual theory** of development on the basis of adult remembrances. He emphasized that how parents manage their child's sexual and aggressive drives in the first few years of life is crucial for healthy personality development.

Psychoanalytic perspective
An approach to personality development introduced by Sigmund Freud that assumes children move through a series of stages in which they confront conflicts between biological drives and social expectations. The way these conflicts are resolved determines psychological adjustment.

Psychosexual theory
Freud's theory, which emphasizes that how parents manage children's sexual and aggressive drives during the first few years is crucial for healthy personality development.

Id
In Freud's theory, the part of the personality that is the source of basic biological needs and desires.

Three Portions of the Personality. In Freud's theory, three parts of the personality—id, ego, and superego—become integrated during a sequence of five stages of development. The **id**, the largest portion of the mind, is inherited and present at birth. It is the source of basic biological needs and desires. The id seeks to satisfy its impulses head on, without delay. As a result, young babies cry vigorously when they are hungry or wet, or need to be held and cuddled.

TABLE 1.2

Freud's Psychosexual Stages

Psychosexual Stage	Period of Development	Description
Oral	Birth–1 year	The new ego directs the baby's sucking activities toward breast or bottle. If oral needs are not met appropriately, the individual may develop such habits as thumb sucking, fingernail biting, and pencil chewing in childhood and overeating and smoking in later life.
Anal	1–3 years	Young toddlers and preschoolers enjoy holding and releasing urine and feces. Toilet training becomes a major issue between parent and child. If parents insist that children be trained before they are ready or make too few demands, conflicts about anal control may appear in the form of extreme orderliness and cleanliness or messiness and disorder.
Phallic	3–6 years	Id impulses transfer to the genitals, and the child finds pleasure in genital stimulation. Freud's *Oedipus conflict* for boys and *Electra conflict* for girls take place. Young children feel a sexual desire for the opposite-sex parent. To avoid punishment, they give up this desire and, instead, adopt the same-sex parent's characteristics and values. As a result, the superego is formed. The relations between id, ego, and superego established at this time determine the individual's basic personality orientation.
Latency	6–11 years	Sexual instincts die down, and the superego develops further. The child acquires new social values from adults outside the family and from play with same-sex peers.
Genital	Adolescence	Puberty causes the sexual impulses of the phallic stage to reappear. If development has been successful during earlier stages, it leads to marriage, mature sexuality, and the birth and rearing of children.

The **ego**—the conscious, rational part of personality—emerges in early infancy to ensure that the id's desires are satisfied in accord with reality. Recalling times when parents helped the baby gratify the id, the ego redirects the impulses so they are discharged on appropriate objects at acceptable times and places. Aided by the ego, the hungry baby of a few months of age stops crying when he sees his mother unfasten her clothing for breast-feeding or warm a bottle. And the more competent preschooler goes into the kitchen and gets a snack on her own.

Between 3 and 6 years of age, the **superego**, or seat of conscience, appears. It contains the values of society and is often in conflict with the id's desires. The superego develops from interactions with parents, who eventually insist that children control their biological impulses. Once the superego is formed, the ego is faced with the increasingly complex task of reconciling the demands of the id, the external world, and conscience (Freud, 1923/1974). For example, when the ego is tempted to gratify an id impulse by hitting a playmate to get an attractive toy, the superego may warn that such behavior is wrong. The ego must decide which of the two forces (id or superego) will win this inner struggle or work out a reasonable compromise, such as asking for a turn with the toy. According to Freud, the relations established among the id, ego, and superego during the preschool years determine the individual's basic personality.

■ *Sigmund Freud founded the psychoanalytic movement. His psychosexual theory was the first approach to stress the importance of early experience for later development. (Lyrl Ahern)*

Psychosexual Development. Table 1.2 summarizes Freud's (1938/1973) stages of development. He believed that over the course of childhood, sexual impulses shift their focus from the oral to the anal to the genital regions of the body. In each stage, parents walk a fine line between permitting too much or too little gratification of their child's basic needs. Either extreme can cause the child's psychic energies to be *fixated,* or arrested, at a particular stage. Too much satisfaction makes the child unwilling to move on to a more mature level of behavior. Too little leads the child to continue seeking gratification of the frustrated drive. If parents strike an appropriate balance, then children grow into well-adjusted adults with the capacity for mature sexual behavior, investment in family life, and rearing of the next generation.

Freud's psychosexual theory highlighted the importance of family relationships for children's development. It was the first theory to stress the importance of early experience for later development. But Freud's perspective was eventually criticized for several reasons. First, the theory overemphasized the influence of sexual feelings in development. Second, because it was based on the problems of sexually repressed, well-to-do adults, some aspects of Freud's theory did not apply in cultures differing from nineteenth-century Victorian society. Finally, Freud's ideas were called into question because he did not study children directly.

Ego
In Freud's theory, the rational part of personality that reconciles the demands of the id, the external world, and the conscience.

Superego
In Freud's theory, the part of personality that is the seat of conscience and is often in conflict with the id's desires.

■ ERIKSON'S PSYCHOSOCIAL THEORY. Several of Freud's followers took what was useful from his theory and stretched and rearranged it in ways that improved on his vision. The most important of these neo-Freudians for the field of child development is Erik Erikson (1902–1994).

Although Erikson (1950) accepted Freud's basic psychosexual framework, he expanded the picture of development at each stage. In his **psychosocial theory**, Erikson emphasized that social experiences at each Freudian stage do not just lead to an embattled ego that mediates between id impulses and superego demands. The ego is also a positive force in development. At each stage, it acquires attitudes and skills that make the individual an active, contributing member of society. A basic psychosocial conflict, which is resolved along a continuum from positive to negative, determines healthy or maladaptive outcomes at each stage. As you can see in Table 1.3, Erikson's first five stages parallel Freud's stages. However, Erikson did not regard important developmental tasks as limited to early childhood. He believed that they occur throughout life. Note that Erikson added three adult stages to Freud's model and was one of the first to recognize the lifespan nature of development.

■ *Erik Erikson expanded Freud's theory, emphasizing the psychosocial outcomes of development. At each psychosexual stage, a major psychological conflict is resolved. If the outcome is positive, individuals acquire attitudes and skills that permit them to contribute constructively to society. (Lyrl Ahern)*

Finally, unlike Freud, Erikson pointed out that normal development must be understood in relation to each culture's unique life situation. For example, among the Yurok Indians (a tribe of fishermen and acorn gatherers on the northwest coast of the United States), babies are deprived of breast-feeding for the first 10 days after birth and are instead fed a thin soup from a small shell. At 6 months of age, infants are abruptly weaned, an event enforced, if necessary, by having the mother leave for a few days. These experiences, from our cultural vantage point, seem like cruel attempts to frustrate the child's oral needs. But Erikson explained that the Yurok live in a world in which salmon fill the river just once a year, a circumstance that requires the development of considerable self-restraint for survival. They can only be understood by making reference to the competencies valued and needed by the child's society as a whole.

■ CONTRIBUTIONS AND LIMITATIONS OF THE PSYCHOANALYTIC PERSPECTIVE. A special strength of the psychoanalytic perspective is its emphasis on the individual's unique life history as worthy of study and understanding (Emde, 1992). Consistent with this view, psychoanalytic theorists accept the *clinical method* (sometimes called the case study approach) as the most effective way to gather information about development. As we will see in Chapter 2, it combines data from a variety of sources—interviews with the child, family members, and others who know the child well; responses to psychological tests; and observations in the clinic setting and sometimes in everyday environments. The information is synthesized into a detailed picture of the personality functioning of a single child. Psychoanalytic theory has also inspired a wealth of research on many aspects of emotional and social development, including infant–caregiver attachment, aggression, sibling relationships, child-rearing practices, morality, gender roles, and adolescent identity.

Despite its extensive contributions, the psychoanalytic perspective is no longer in the mainstream of child development research. Psychoanalytic theorists may have become isolated from the rest of the field because they were so strongly committed to the clinical approach that they failed to consider other methods. In addition, many psychoanalytic ideas, such as Freud's Oedipus conflict and the psychosexual stages, were so vague and full of interpretation that they were difficult or impossible to test empirically (Miller, 1993).

Psychosocial theory
Erikson's theory, which emphasizes that the demands of society at each Freudian stage not only promote the development of a unique personality, but also ensure that individuals acquire attitudes and skills that help them become active, contributing members of their society.

Behaviorism
An approach that views directly observable events—stimuli and responses—as the appropriate focus of study and the development of behavior as taking place through classical and operant conditioning.

BEHAVIORISM AND SOCIAL LEARNING THEORY

At the same time that psychoanalytic theory gained in prominence, child study was also influenced by a very different perspective: **behaviorism**, a tradition consistent with Locke's image of tabula rasa. American behaviorism began with the work of psychologist John Watson (1878–1958) in the early part of the twentieth century. Watson wanted to create an objective science of psychology. Unlike psychoanalytic theorists, he believed in studying directly observable events—stimuli and responses—rather than the unseen workings of the mind (Horowitz, 1992).

■ TRADITIONAL BEHAVIORISM. Watson was inspired by studies of animal learning carried out by famous Russian physiologist Ivan Pavlov. Pavlov knew that dogs release

TABLE 1.3

Erikson's Psychosocial Stages

Psychosocial Stage	Period of Development	Description	Corresponding Psychosexual Stage
Basic trust versus mistrust	Birth–1 year	From warm, responsive care, infants gain a sense of trust, or confidence, that the world is good. Mistrust occurs when infants have to wait too long for comfort and are handled harshly.	Oral
Autonomy versus shame and doubt	1–3 years	Using new mental and motor skills, children want to choose and decide for themselves. Autonomy is fostered when parents permit reasonable free choice and do not force or shame the child.	Anal
Initiative versus guilt	3–6 years	Through make-believe play, children experiment with the kind of person they can become. Initiative—a sense of ambition and responsibility—develops when parents support their child's new sense of purpose and direction. The danger is that parents will demand too much self-control, which leads to overcontrol, or too much guilt.	Phallic
Industry versus inferiority	6–11 years	At school, children develop the capacity to work and cooperate with others. Inferiority develops when negative experiences at home, at school, or with peers lead to feelings of incompetence and inferiority.	Latency
Identity versus identity diffusion	Adolescence	The adolescent tries to answer the questions, Who am I, and what is my place in society? Self-chosen values and vocational goals lead to a lasting personal identity. The negative outcome is confusion about future adult roles.	Genital
Intimacy versus isolation	Young adulthood	Young people work on establishing intimate ties. Because of earlier disappointments, some individuals cannot form close relationships and remain isolated from others.	
Generativity versus stagnation	Middle adulthood	Generativity means giving to the next generation through child rearing, caring for other people, or productive work. The person who fails in these ways feels an absence of meaningful accomplishment.	
Ego integrity versus despair	Old age	In this final stage, individuals reflect on the kind of person they have been. Integrity results from feeling that life was worth living as it happened. Old people who are dissatisfied with their lives fear death.	

saliva as an innate reflex when they are given food. But he noticed that his dogs were salivating before they tasted any food—when they saw the trainer who usually fed them. The dogs, Pavlov reasoned, must have learned to associate a neutral stimulus (the trainer) with another stimulus (food) that produces a reflexive response (salivation). As a result of this association, the neutral stimulus could bring about the response by itself. Anxious to test this idea, Pavlov successfully taught dogs to salivate at the sound of a bell by pairing it with the presentation of food. He had discovered *classical conditioning.*

Watson wanted to find out if classical conditioning could be applied to children's behavior. In a historic experiment, he taught Albert, an 11-month-old infant, to fear a neutral stimulus—a soft white rat—by presenting it several times with a sharp, loud sound, which naturally scared the baby. Little Albert, who at first had reached out eagerly to touch the furry rat, cried and turned his head away when he caught sight of it (Watson & Raynor, 1920). In fact, Albert's fear was so intense that researchers eventually questioned the ethics of studies like this one (an issue we will take up in Chapter 2). On the basis of findings like these, Watson concluded that environment is the supreme force in child development. Adults could mold children's behavior in any way they wished, he thought, by carefully controlling stimulus–response associations.

After Watson, American behaviorism developed along several lines. The first was Clark Hull's *drive reduction theory.* According to this view, people continually act to satisfy physiological needs and reduce states of tension. As *primary drives* of hunger, thirst, and sex are met, a wide variety of stimuli associated with them become *secondary,* or *learned, drives.* For example, a Hullian theorist believes that infants prefer the closeness and attention of adults who have given them food and relieved their discomfort. To ensure adults' affection, children will acquire all sorts of responses that adults desire of them—politeness, honesty, patience, persistence, obedience, and more.

■ *B. F. Skinner rejected Hull's idea that primary drive reduction is the basis of all learning. He emphasized an alternative learning principle, operant conditioning, that has been widely applied in the field of child development. (Lyrl Ahern)*

Another form of behaviorism was B. F. Skinner's (1904–1990) *operant conditioning theory.* Skinner rejected Hull's idea that primary drive reduction is the only way to get children to learn. According to Skinner, a child's behavior can be increased by following it with a wide variety of *reinforcers* besides food and drink, such as praise, a friendly smile, or a new toy. It can also be decreased through *punishment,* such as withdrawal of privileges, parental disapproval, or being sent to be alone in one's room. As a result of Skinner's work, operant conditioning became a broadly applied learning principle in child psychology. We will consider these conditioning principles more fully when we explore the infant's learning capacities in Chapter 4.

■ SOCIAL LEARNING THEORY. Psychologists quickly became interested in whether behaviorism might offer a more direct and effective explanation of the development of children's social behavior than the less precise concepts of psychoanalytic theory. This concern sparked the emergence of **social learning theory**. Social learning theorists accepted the principles of conditioning and reinforcement that came before them. They also built on these principles, offering expanded views of how children and adults acquire new responses. By the 1950s, social learning theory had become a major force in child development research.

Several kinds of social learning theory emerged. The most influential was devised by Albert Bandura (1967, 1977), who demonstrated that *modeling,* otherwise known as *imitation* or *observational learning,* is the basis for a wide variety of children's behaviors. He recognized that children acquire many favorable and unfavorable responses simply by watching and listening to others around them. The baby who claps her hands after her mother does so, the child who angrily hits a playmate in the same way that he has been punished at home, and the teenager who wears the same clothes and hairstyle as her friends at school are all displaying observational learning.

Bandura's work continues to influence much research on children's social development. However, like changes in the field of child development as a whole, today his theory stresses the importance of *cognition,* or thinking. Bandura has shown that children's ability to listen, remember, and abstract general rules from complex sets of observed behavior affects their imitation and learning. In fact, the most recent revision of Bandura's (1986, 1989, 1992) theory places such strong emphasis on how children think about themselves and other people that he calls it a *social cognitive* rather than a social learning approach. According to this view, children gradually become more selective in what they imitate. From watching others engage in self-praise and self-blame and through feedback about the worth of their own actions, children develop *personal standards* for behavior and *a sense of self-efficacy*—beliefs about their own abilities and characteristics—that guide responses in particular situations (Grusec, 1992). For example, imagine a parent who often remarks, "I'm glad I kept working on that task, even though it was hard," who explains the value of persistence to her child, and who encourages it by saying, "I know you can do that homework very well!" As a result, the child starts to view himself as hard working and high achieving and, from the many people available in the environment, selects models with these characteristics to copy.

■ CONTRIBUTIONS AND LIMITATIONS OF BEHAVIORISM AND SOCIAL LEARNING THEORY. Like psychoanalytic theory, behaviorism and social learning theory have had a major impact on applied work with children. Yet the techniques used are decidedly different. **Applied behavior analysis** involves procedures that combine conditioning and modeling to eliminate children's undesirable behaviors and increase their socially acceptable responses. It has been used largely with children who have serious problems, such as persistent aggression and delayed language development (Patterson, 1982; Whitehurst et al., 1989). But it is also effective in dealing with more common difficulties of childhood. For example, in one study, preschoolers' anxious reactions during dental treatment were reduced by reinforcing them with small toys for answering questions about a story read to them while the dentist worked. Because the children could not listen to the story and kick and cry at the same time, their disruptive behaviors subsided (Stark et al., 1989).

Although the techniques of behaviorism are helpful in treating many problems, we must keep in mind that making something happen through modeling and reinforcement does not mean that these principles offer a complete account of development (Horowitz,

Social learning theory
An approach that emphasizes the role of modeling, or observational learning, in the development of behavior.

Applied behavior analysis
A set of practical procedures that combines reinforcement, modeling, and the manipulation of situational cues to change behavior.

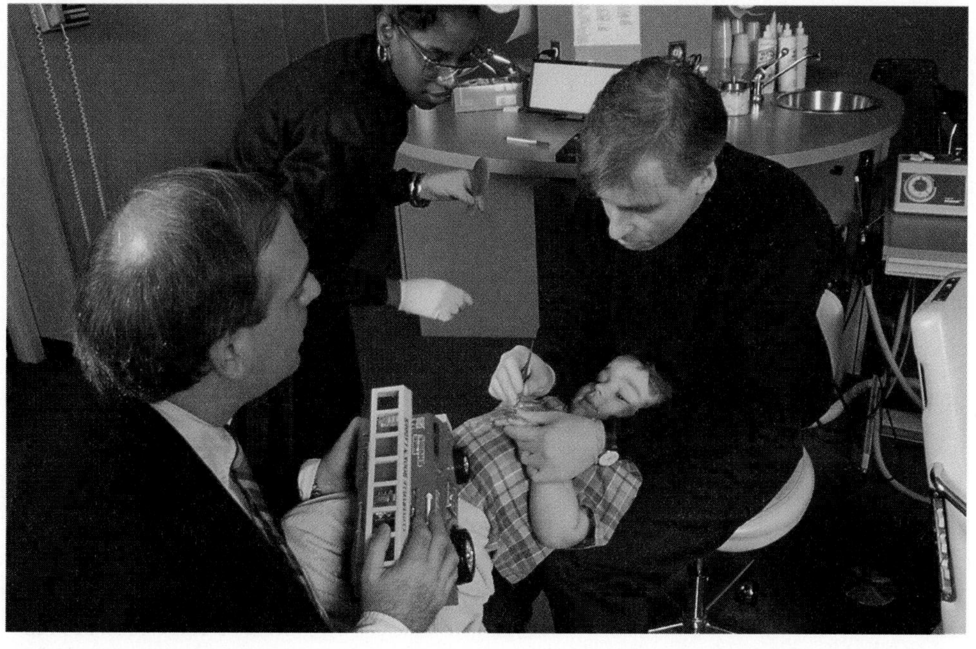

■ *Applied behavior analysis can be used to reduce a child's anxious reactions during dental treatment. This dentist engages in a counting game to relax his young patient before conducting an examination. While the dentist works on the boy's teeth, the boy's father will distract him with a toy fire engine. After the session is over, the father will reinforce the boy's cooperative behavior by permitting him to play with the toy. (Jacques Chenet/Woodfin Camp & Associates)*

1987). We will see in later sections that many theorists believe that behaviorism and social learning theory offer too narrow a view of important environmental influences. These extend beyond immediate reinforcements and modeled behaviors to the richness of children's physical and social worlds. Finally, we have seen that in emphasizing cognition, Bandura is unique among theorists whose work grew out of the behaviorist tradition in granting children an active role in their own learning. As we will see when we discuss Piaget's theory in the next section, behaviorism and social learning theory have been criticized for underestimating children's contributions to their own development.

PIAGET'S COGNITIVE-DEVELOPMENTAL THEORY

If there is one individual who has influenced the modern field of child development more than any other, it is the Swiss cognitive theorist Jean Piaget (1896–1980). Although American investigators had been aware of Piaget's work since 1930, they did not pay much attention to it until 1960. A major reason is that Piaget's ideas and methods of studying children were very much at odds with behaviorism, which dominated American psychology during the middle of the twentieth century (Beilin, 1992).

Recall that behaviorists did not study the child's mental life. In their view, thinking could be reduced to connections between stimuli and responses, and development was a continuous process, consisting of a gradual increase in the number and strength of these connections with age. In contrast, Piaget did not believe knowledge was imposed on a passive, reinforced child. According to his **cognitive-developmental theory**, children actively construct knowledge as they manipulate and explore their world, and their cognitive development takes place in stages.

■ PIAGET'S STAGES. Piaget's view of development was greatly influenced by his early training in biology. Central to his theory is the biological concept of *adaptation* (Piaget, 1971). Just as the structures of the body are adapted to fit with the environment, so the structures of the mind develop over the course of childhood to better fit with, or represent, the external world. In infancy and early childhood, children's understanding is very different from that of adults. For example, Piaget believed that young babies do not realize that something hidden from view—a favorite toy or even the mother—continues to exist. He also concluded that preschoolers' thinking is full of faulty logic and fantasy. For example, children younger than age 7 commonly say that the amount of milk or lemonade changes when it is poured into a differently shaped container. According to Piaget, children eventually revise these incorrect ideas in their ongoing efforts to achieve an *equilibrium,* or balance, between internal structures and information they encounter in their everyday worlds (Beilin, 1992; Kuhn, 1992).

Cognitive-developmental theory
An approach introduced by Piaget that views the child as actively building mental structures and cognitive development as taking place in stages.

TABLE 1.4

Piaget's Stages of Cognitive Development

Stage	Period of Development	Description
Sensorimotor	Birth–2 years	Infants "think" by acting on the world with their eyes, ears, and hands. As a result, they invent ways of solving sensorimotor problems, such as pulling a lever to hear the sound of a music box, finding hidden toys, and putting objects in and taking them out of containers.
Preoperational	2–7 years	Preschool children use symbols to represent their earlier sensorimotor discoveries. Language and make-believe play develop. However, thinking lacks the logical qualities of the two remaining stages.
Concrete operational	7–11 years	Children's reasoning becomes logical. School-age children understand that a certain amount of lemonade or play dough remains the same even after its appearance changes. They also organize objects into hierarchies of classes and subclasses. However, thinking falls short of adult intelligence. It is not yet abstract.
Formal operational	11 years on	The capacity for abstraction permits adolescents to reason with symbols that do not refer to objects in the real world, as in advanced mathematics. They can also think of all possible outcomes in a scientific problem, not just the most obvious ones.

■ *Through careful observations of and clinical interviews with children, Jean Piaget developed his comprehensive theory of cognitive development. His work has inspired more research on children than any other theory. (Yves de Braine/ Black Star)*

In Piaget's theory, children move through four broad stages of development, each of which is characterized by qualitatively distinct ways of thinking. Table 1.4 provides a brief description of Piaget's stages. In the *sensorimotor stage,* cognitive development begins with the baby's use of the senses and movements to explore the world. These action patterns evolve into the symbolic but illogical thinking of the preschooler in the *preoperational stage.* Then cognition is transformed into the more organized reasoning of the school-age child in the *concrete operational stage.* Finally, in the *formal operational stage,* thought becomes the complex, abstract reasoning system of the adolescent and adult.

■ PIAGET'S METHODS OF STUDY. Piaget devised special methods for investigating how children think. In the early part of his career, he carefully observed his three infant children and also presented them with everyday problems, such as an attractive object that could be grasped, mouthed, kicked, or searched for when hidden from view. From their reactions, Piaget derived his ideas about cognitive changes during the first 2 years of life.

In studying childhood and adolescent thought, Piaget took advantage of children's ability to describe their thinking. He adapted the clinical method of psychoanalysis, conducting open-ended clinical interviews in which a child's initial response to a task served as the basis for the next question Piaget would ask. We will look at an example of a Piagetian clinical interview, as well as the strengths and limitations of this technique, in Chapter 2.

■ CONTRIBUTIONS AND LIMITATIONS OF PIAGET'S THEORY. Piaget's cognitive-developmental perspective has stimulated more research on children than any other single theory. It also convinced many child development specialists that children are active learners whose minds are inhabited by rich structures of knowledge. Besides investigating children's understanding of the physical world, Piaget began some explorations into how children reason about the social world. As we will see in Chapters 11 and 12, Piaget's stages of cognitive development have sparked a wealth of research on children's conceptions of themselves, other people, and human relationships.

Practically speaking, Piaget's theory encouraged the development of educational philosophies and programs that emphasize discovery learning and direct contact with the environment. A Piagetian classroom contains richly equipped activity areas designed to stimulate children to revise their immature cognitive structures.

Despite Piaget's overwhelming contribution to child development and education, in recent years his theory has been challenged. Research indicates that Piaget underestimated the competencies of infants and preschoolers. We will see in Chapter 6 that when young children are given tasks scaled down in difficulty, their understanding appears closer to that of the older child and adult than Piaget believed. This discovery has led many researchers to conclude that the maturity of children's thinking may depend on their familiarity with the task and the kind of knowledge sampled. Finally, many studies show that children's performance on Piagetian problems can be improved with training. This finding raises questions about his assumption that discovery learning rather than adult teaching is the best way to foster development.

Today, the field of child development is divided over its loyalty to Piaget's ideas. Those who continue to find merit in Piaget's approach accept a modified view of his cognitive stages—one in which changes in children's thinking are not sudden and abrupt, but take place much more gradually than Piaget believed (Case, 1985, 1992a; Fischer & Pipp, 1984). Others have given up the idea of cognitive stages in favor of a continuous approach to development—information processing—that we will take up in the next section.

BRIEF REVIEW

Three perspectives dominated child development research in the middle of the twentieth century. Child guidance professionals turned to Freud's psychoanalytic approach, and Erikson's expansion of it, for help in understanding personality development and children's emotional difficulties. Behaviorism and social learning theory rely on conditioning and modeling to explain the appearance of new responses and to treat behavior problems. Piaget's stage theory of cognitive development revolutionized the field with its view of children as active beings who take responsibility for their own learning.

Recent Perspectives

New ways of understanding children are constantly emerging—questioning, building on, and enhancing the discoveries of earlier theories. Today, a burst of fresh approaches and research emphases, including information processing, ethology, ecological systems theory, and Vygotsky's sociocultural theory, is broadening our understanding of child development.

INFORMATION PROCESSING

During the 1970s, child development researchers became disenchanted with behaviorism as a complete account of children's learning and disappointed in their efforts to completely verify Piaget's ideas. They turned to the field of cognitive psychology for new ways to understand the development of children's thinking. Today, a leading perspective is **information processing**. It is a general approach that emerged with the design of complex computers that use mathematically specified steps to solve problems. These systems suggested to psychologists that the human mind might also be viewed as a symbol-manipulating system through which information flows (Klahr, 1992). From presentation to the senses at *input* and behavioral responses at *output*, information is actively coded, transformed, and organized.

Information processing is often thought of as a field of scripts, frames, and flowcharts. Diagrams are used to map the precise steps individuals use to solve problems and complete tasks, much like the plans devised by programmers to get computers to perform a series of "mental operations." Let's look at an example to clarify the usefulness

Information processing
An approach that views the human mind as a symbol-manipulating system through which information flows and that regards cognitive development as a continuous process.

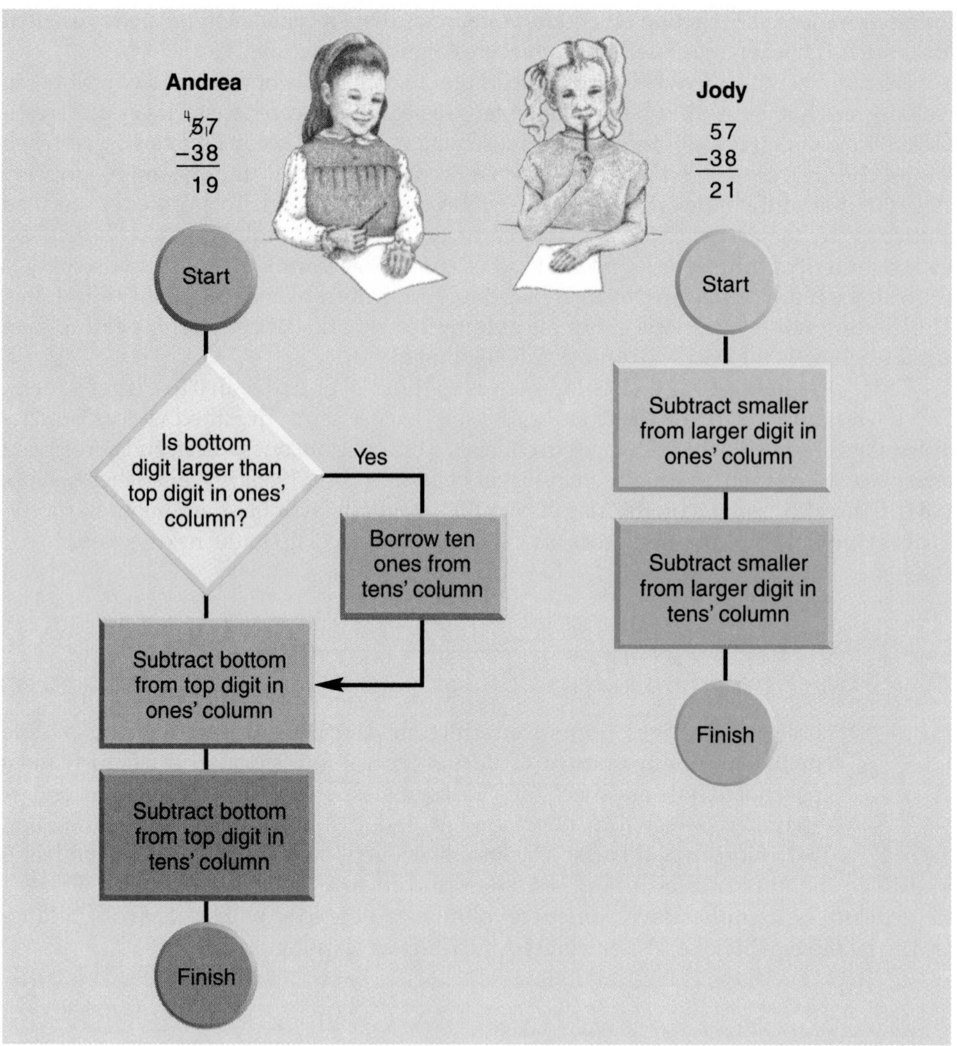

FIGURE 1.3

■ *Information-processing flowcharts showing the steps that two 8-year-olds used to solve a math problem. In this two-digit subtraction problem with a borrowing operation, Andrea's procedure is correct, whereas Jody's results in a wrong answer.*

of this approach. The left-hand side of Figure 1.3 shows the steps that Andrea, an academically successful 8-year-old, used to complete a two-digit subtraction problem. The right-hand side displays the faulty procedures of Jody, who arrived at the wrong answer. The flowchart approach ensures that models of child and adult thinking will be very clear. For example, by comparing the two procedures shown in Figure 1.3, we know exactly what is necessary for effective problem solving and where Jody went wrong in searching for a solution. As a result, we can pinpoint Jody's difficulties and design an intervention to improve her reasoning.

A wide variety of information-processing models exist. Some (like the one in Figure 1.3) are fairly narrow in that they track children's mastery of a single task. Others describe the human information-processing system as a whole (Atkinson & Shiffrin, 1968; Craik & Lockhart, 1972). These general models are used as guides for asking questions about broad age-related changes in children's thinking. For example, Does a child's ability to search the environment for information needed to solve a problem become more organized and planful with age? How much new information can preschoolers hold in memory compared to older children and adults? To what extent does children's current knowledge influence their ability to learn more? The information-processing approach is also being used to clarify the processing of social information—for example, how children come to view themselves and others in gender-linked terms (Martin & Halverson, 1987). If we can identify how rigid gender stereotypes arise in childhood, then we are in a good position to design interventions that promote more flexible conceptions of male and female role possibilities at an early age.

Like Piaget's theory, the information-processing approach regards children as active, sense-making beings who modify their own thinking in response to environmental demands (Klahr, 1992). But unlike Piaget, there are no stages of development. Rather, the thought processes studied—perception, attention, memory, planning strategies, categorization of information, and comprehension of written and spoken prose—are assumed to be similar at all ages but present to a lesser extent in children. Consequently, the view of development is one of continuous increase rather than abrupt, stagewise change.

A great strength of the information-processing approach is its commitment to careful, rigorous research methods to investigate cognition. Because it has provided precise accounts of how children of different ages engage in many aspects of thinking, its findings have important implications for education (Hall, 1989; Resnick, 1989; Siegler, 1983). But information processing has fallen short in some respects. Aspects of cognition that are not linear and logical, such as imagination and creativity, are all but ignored by this approach (Greeno, 1989). In addition, information-processing research has largely been conducted in artificial laboratory situations. Consequently, critics complain that it isolates children's thinking from important features of real-life learning situations. Recently, information-processing investigators have begun to address this concern by focusing on more realistic materials and tasks. Today, they can be found studying children's conversations, stories, memory for everyday events, and strategies for performing academic tasks (Miller, 1993).

Fortunately, a major advantage of having many theories is that they encourage one another to attend to previously neglected dimensions of children's lives. A unique feature of the final three perspectives we will discuss is the emphasis they place on *contexts for development.* The impact of context, or environment, can be examined at many levels. We will see that family, school, community, larger society, and culture all affect children's growth. In addition, human capacities have been shaped by a long evolutionary history in which our brains and bodies adapted to their surroundings. The next theory, ethology, emphasizes this biological side of development.

ETHOLOGY

Ethology is concerned with the adaptive, or survival, value of behavior and its evolutionary history (Hinde, 1989). It began to be applied to research on children in the 1960s but has become even more influential today. The origins of ethology can be traced to the work of Darwin. Its modern foundations were laid by two European zoologists, Konrad Lorenz and Niko Tinbergen (Dewsbury, 1992).

Watching the behaviors of diverse animal species in their natural habitats, Lorenz and Tinbergen observed behavior patterns that promote survival. The most well known of these is *imprinting,* the early following behavior of certain baby birds that ensures that the young will stay close to the mother and be fed and protected from danger. Imprinting takes place during an early, restricted time period of development. If the mother is not present during this time, but an object resembling her in important features is, young goslings may imprint on it instead (Lorenz, 1952).

Observations of imprinting led to a major concept that has been widely applied in child development: the *critical period.* It refers to a limited time span during which the child is biologically prepared to acquire certain adaptive behaviors but needs the support of an appropriately stimulating environment. Many researchers have conducted studies to find out whether complex cognitive and social behaviors must be acquired during

■ *Konrad Lorenz was one of the many founders of ethology and a keen observer of animal behavior. He developed the concept of imprinting. Here, young geese who were separated from their mother and placed in the company of Lorenz during an early, critical period show that they have imprinted on him. They follow him about as he swims through the water, a response that promotes survival. (Nina Leen/Life Magazine © Time Warner)*

Ethology
An approach concerned with the adaptive, or survival, value of behavior and its evolutionary history.

restricted time periods. For example, if children are deprived of adequate food or physical and social stimulation during their early years, will their intelligence be permanently impaired? If language is not mastered during early childhood, is the child's capacity to acquire it reduced?

As we address these and other similar questions in later chapters, we will discover that the term *sensitive period* offers a better account of human development than does the strict notion of a critical period (Bornstein, 1989). A **sensitive period** is a time that is optimal for certain capacities to emerge and in which the individual is especially responsive to environmental influences. However, its boundaries are less well defined than those of a critical period. It is possible for development to occur later, but it is harder to induce it at that time.

Inspired by observations of imprinting, British psychoanalyst John Bowlby (1969) applied ethological theory to the understanding of the human infant–caregiver relationship. He argued that attachment behaviors of babies, such as smiling, babbling, grasping, and crying, are built-in social signals that encourage the parent to approach, care for, and interact with the baby. By keeping the mother near, these behaviors help ensure that the infant will be fed, protected from danger, and provided with stimulation and affection necessary for healthy growth. The development of attachment in human infants is a lengthy process involving changes in psychological structures that lead the baby to form a deep affectional tie with the caregiver (Bretherton, 1992). As we will see in Chapter 10, it is far more complex than imprinting in baby birds. But for now, note how the ethological view of attachment, which emphasizes the role of innate infant signals, differs sharply from the behaviorist drive reduction explanation we mentioned earlier—that the baby's desire for closeness to the mother is a learned response based on feeding.

Observations by ethologists have shown that many aspects of children's social behavior, including emotional expressions, aggression, cooperation, and social play, resemble those of our primate ancestors. Although ethology emphasizes the genetic and biological roots of development, learning is also considered important because it lends flexibility and greater adaptiveness to behavior. Since ethologists believe that children's behavior can best be understood in terms of its adaptive value, they seek a full understanding of the environment, including physical, social, and cultural aspects. The interests of ethologists are broad. They want to understand the entire organism–environment system (Hinde, 1989; Miller, 1993). The next contextual perspective we will discuss, ecological systems theory, serves as an excellent complement to ethology, since it shows how various aspects of the environment, from immediate human relationships to larger societal forces, work together to affect children's development.

■ *Urie Bronfenbrenner is the originator of ecological systems theory. He views the child as developing within a complex system of relationships affected by multiple levels of the surrounding environment, from immediate settings to broad cultural values, laws, and customs. (Courtesy of Urie Bronfenbrenner, Cornell University)*

Sensitive period
A time span that is optimal for certain capacities to emerge and in which the individual is especially responsive to environmental influences.

Ecological systems theory
Bronfenbrenner's approach, which views the child as developing within a complex system of relationships affected by multiple levels of the environment, from immediate settings of family and school to broad cultural values and programs.

Microsystem
In ecological systems theory, the activities and interaction patterns in the child's immediate surroundings.

ECOLOGICAL SYSTEMS THEORY

Urie Bronfenbrenner, an American psychologist, is responsible for an approach to child development that has risen to the forefront of the field over the past decade. **Ecological systems theory** views the child as developing within a complex system of relationships affected by multiple levels of the surrounding environment. Since the child's biological dispositions join with environmental forces to mold development, Bronfenbrenner (1995) recently characterized his perspective as a *bioecological model.*

Before Bronfenbrenner's (1979, 1989, 1993) theory, most researchers viewed the environment fairly narrowly—as limited to events and conditions immediately surrounding the child. As Figure 1.4 shows, Bronfenbrenner expanded this view by envisioning the environment as a series of nested structures that includes but extends beyond home, school, and neighborhood settings in which children spend their everyday lives. Each layer of the environment is viewed as having a powerful impact on children's development.

■ THE MICROSYSTEM. The innermost level of the environment is the **microsystem,** which refers to activities and interaction patterns in the child's immediate surroundings. Until recently, researchers emphasized adults' effects on children when studying relationships in the microsystem. Bronfenbrenner emphasizes that to understand child development at this level, we must keep in mind that all relationships are *bidirectional and reciprocal.* In other words, adults affect children's responses, but children's biologically and socially determined characteristics—their physical attributes, personalities, and capacities—also influence the behavior of adults. For example, a friendly, attentive child is

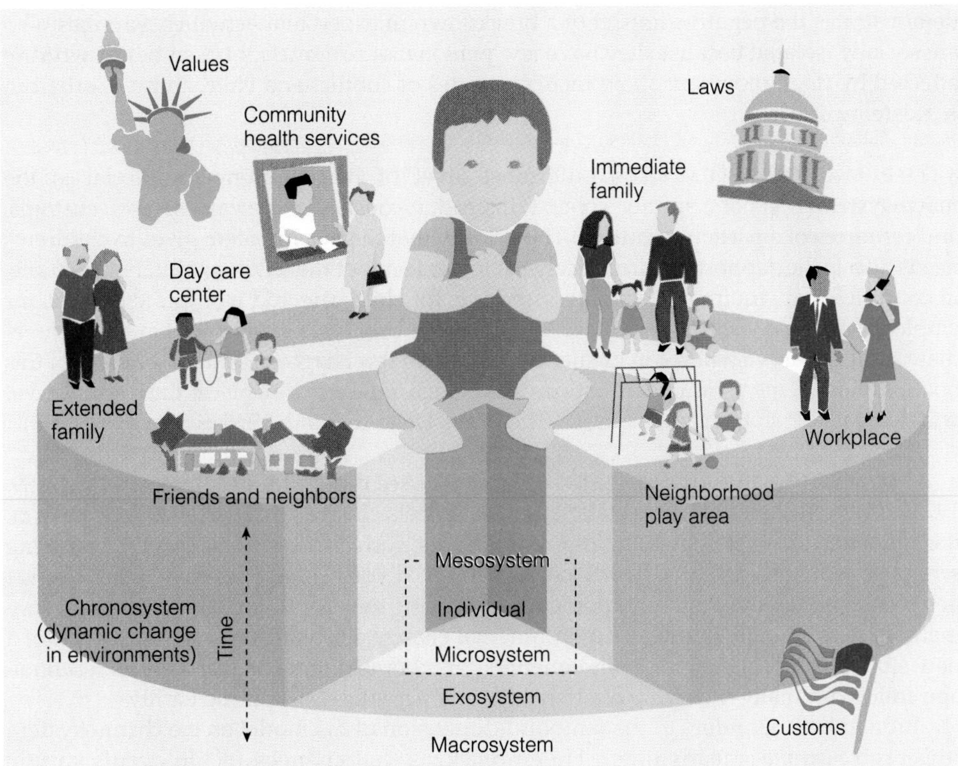

FIGURE 1.4

■ *Structure of the environment in ecological systems theory. The* microsystem *concerns relations between the child and the immediate environment; the* mesosystem, *connections among the child's immediate settings; the* exosystem, *social settings that affect but do not contain the child; and the* macrosystem, *the values, laws, and customs of the child's culture. The* chronosystem *is not a specific context. Instead, it refers to the dynamic, ever-changing nature of children's environments.*

likely to evoke positive and patient reactions from parents, whereas a distractible youngster is more likely to be responded to with restriction and punishment (Danforth, Barkley, & Stokes, 1990). As these reciprocal interactions become well established and occur often over time, they have an enduring impact on development (Bronfenbrenner, 1995).

But whether parent-child (or other two-person) relationships enhance or undermine development depends on environmental systems that surround and influence those relationships. Within the microsystem, interaction between any two individuals is influenced by the presence of *third parties.* If other individuals in the setting are supportive, the quality of relationships is enhanced. For example, when parents encourage one another in their child-rearing roles, each engages in more effective parenting (Gottfried, Gottfried, & Bathurst, 1988; Simons et al., 1992). In contrast, marital conflict is associated with inconsistent discipline and hostile reactions toward children (Hetherington & Clingempeel, 1992). Child development within the microsystem must be understood in terms of these complex, interacting forces.

■ THE MESOSYSTEM. For children to develop at their best, child-rearing supports must also exist in the larger environment. The second level of Bronfenbrenner's model is the **mesosystem**. It encompasses connections among microsystems, such as home, school, neighborhood, and day care center, that foster children's development. For example, a child's academic progress depends not just on activities that take place in classrooms. It is also promoted by parental involvement in school life and the extent to which academic learning is carried over into the home (Grolnick & Slowiaczek, 1994). Similarly, parent–child interaction is likely to be affected by the child's relationships with caregivers at day care, and vice versa. Parent–child and caregiver–child relationships are each likely to support development when there are links, in the form of visits and exchange of information, between home and day care setting.

■ THE EXOSYSTEM. The **exosystem** refers to social settings that do not contain children but nevertheless affect their experiences in immediate settings. These can be formal organizations, such as the parents' workplace or health and welfare services in the community. For example, flexible work schedules, paid maternity and paternity leave, and sick leave for parents whose children are ill are ways that work settings can help parents in their child-rearing roles and, indirectly, foster development. Exosystem supports can also be informal, such as parents' social networks—friends and extended family members who provide advice, companionship, and even financial assistance. Research

Mesosystem
In ecological systems theory, connections among children's immediate settings.

Exosystem
In ecological systems theory, settings that do not contain children but that affect their experiences in immediate settings. Examples are parents' workplace and health and welfare services in the community.

demonstrates the negative impact of a breakdown in exosystem activities. Families who are socially isolated because they have few personal or community-based ties or who are affected by unemployment show increased rates of conflict and child abuse (Garbarino & Kostelny, 1992).

■ THE MACROSYSTEM. The outermost level of Bronfenbrenner's model is the **macrosystem**. It is not a specific context. Instead, it consists of the values, laws, customs, and resources of a particular culture. The priority that the macrosystem gives to children's needs affects the support children receive at lower levels of the environment. For example, in countries that require high-quality standards for child care and workplace benefits for employed parents, children are more likely to have favorable experiences in their immediate settings. As we will see in greater detail later in this chapter and in other parts of this book, although most European nations have such programs in place, they are not yet widely available in the United States (Children's Defense Fund, 1996; Kamerman, 1993).

■ *According to Lev Semenovich Vygotsky, many cognitive processes and skills are socially transferred from more knowledgeable members of society to children. Vygotsky's sociocultural theory helps us understand the wide variation in cognitive competencies from culture to culture. Vygotsky is pictured here with his daughter. (Courtesy of James V. Wertsch, Washington University)*

■ A DYNAMIC, EVER-CHANGING SYSTEM. According to Bronfenbrenner (1989, 1993), the environment is not a static force that affects children in a uniform way. Instead, it is dynamic and ever-changing. Important events, such as the birth of a sibling, entering school, moving to a new neighborhood, or parents' divorce, modify existing relationships between children and their environments, producing new conditions that affect development. In addition, the timing of environmental change affects its impact. The arrival of a new sibling has very different consequences for a homebound toddler than for a school-age child with many satisfying relationships and activities beyond the family.

Bronfenbrenner refers to the temporal dimension of his model as the **chronosystem** (the prefix *chrono-* means time). He emphasizes that changes in life events can be imposed externally, as in the examples just given. Alternatively, they can arise from within the organism, since children select, modify, and create many of their own settings and experiences. How they do so depends on their physical, intellectual, and personality characteristics and the environmental opportunities available to them. Therefore, in ecological systems theory, development is neither controlled by environmental circumstances nor driven by inner dispositions. Instead, children are both products and producers of their environments, both of which form a network of interdependent effects. Notice how our discussion of resilient children on page 9 illustrates this idea. We will see many more examples in later chapters of this book.

■ INTERVENING IN THE ENVIRONMENT. Perhaps you can already tell that ecological systems theory is of tremendous applied significance, since it suggests that interventions at any level of the environment can enhance development. For example, at the level of the exosystem, providing socially isolated parents of abused children with access to parenting groups where they can discuss their problems and experience gratifying social relationships helps relieve distress and improve conditions for children. Bronfenbrenner (1989; Bronfenbrenner & Neville, 1994) believes that change at the level of the macrosystem is particularly important. Because the macrosystem affects all other environmental levels, revising established values and government programs in ways more favorable to child development has the most far-reaching impact on children's well-being.

Macrosystem
In ecological systems theory, the values, laws, and customs of a culture that influence experiences and interactions at lower levels of the environment.

Chronosystem
In ecological systems theory, temporal changes in children's environments, which produce new conditions that affect development. These changes can be imposed externally or arise from within the organism, since children select, modify, and create many of their own settings and experiences.

CROSS-CULTURAL RESEARCH AND VYGOTSKY'S SOCIOCULTURAL THEORY

Ecological systems theory, as well as Erikson's psychoanalytic theory, underscores the connection between culture and development. In line with this emphasis, child development research has recently seen a dramatic increase in cross-cultural studies. Investigations that make comparisons across cultures, and between ethnic and social-class groups within cultures, provide insight into whether developmental theories apply to all children or are limited to particular environmental conditions (Greenfield, 1994). As a result, cross-cultural research helps untangle the contributions of biological and environmental factors to the timing and order of appearance of children's behaviors.

In the past, cross-cultural studies focused on broad cultural differences in development—for example, whether children in one culture are more advanced in motor development or do better on intellectual tasks than children in another. However, this approach can lead us to conclude incorrectly that one culture is superior in enhancing development, whereas another is deficient. In addition, it does not help us understand the precise experiences that contribute to cultural differences in children's behavior.

Today, more research is examining the relationship of *culturally specific practices* to child development. The contributions of Russian psychologist Lev Semenovich Vygotsky (1896–1934) have played a major role in this trend. Vygotsky's (1934/1986) perspective is called **sociocultural theory**. It focuses on how *culture*—the values, beliefs, customs, and skills of a social group—is transmitted to the next generation. According to Vygotsky, *social interaction*—in particular, cooperative dialogues between children and more knowledgeable members of society—is necessary for children to acquire the ways of thinking and behaving that make up a community's culture (van der Veer & Valsiner, 1991). Vygotsky believed that as adults and more expert peers help children master culturally meaningful activities, the communication between them becomes part of children's thinking. As children internalize the essential features of these dialogues, they use the language within them to guide their own actions and acquire new skills (Wertsch & Tulviste, 1992). The young child instructing herself while working a puzzle or tying her shoes has started to produce the same kind of guiding comments that an adult previously used to help her master important tasks (Berk, 1994a).

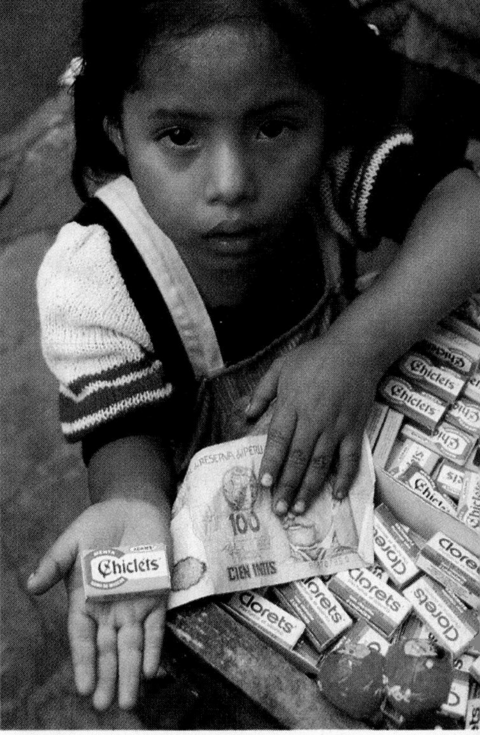

■ *This South American child candy seller is learning to solve arithmetic problems involving large currency values through everyday street vending activities. Her mathematical skills illustrate how culture and social experience influence cognitive development. (David Bartruff/Stock Boston)*

Perhaps you can tell from this brief description that Vygotsky's theory has been especially influential in the study of children's cognition. But Vygotsky's approach to cognitive development is different from Piaget's. Recall that Piaget did not regard direct teaching by adults as important for cognitive development. Instead, he emphasized children's active, independent efforts to make sense of their world. Vygotsky agreed with Piaget that children are active, constructive beings. But unlike Piaget, he viewed cognitive development as a *socially mediated process*—as dependent on the support that adults and more mature peers provide as children try new tasks. Finally, Vygotsky did not regard all children as moving through the same sequence of stages. Instead, as soon as children acquire language, their enhanced ability to communicate with others leads to continuous changes in thought and behavior that can vary greatly from culture to culture.

A major finding of cross-cultural research is that cultures select different tasks for children's learning. In line with Vygotsky's theory, social interaction surrounding these tasks leads to knowledge and skills essential for success in a particular culture (Rogoff & Chavajay, 1995). For example, among the Zinacanteco Indians of southern Mexico, girls become expert weavers of complex garments at an early age through the informal guidance of adult experts (Childs & Greenfield, 1982). In Brazil, child candy sellers with little or no schooling develop sophisticated mathematical abilities as the result of buying candy from wholesalers, pricing it in collaboration with adults and experienced peers, and bargaining with customers on city streets (Saxe, 1988). And as the research reported in the Cultural Influences box on page 28 indicates, adults begin to encourage culturally valued skills in children at a very early age.

Findings like these reveal that children in every culture develop unique strengths that are not present in others. The field of child development has again borrowed from another discipline—anthropology—to achieve this understanding. A cross-cultural perspective reminds us that the majority of child development specialists reside in the United States, and their research includes only a small minority of humankind. We cannot assume that the developmental sequences observed in our own children are "natural" or that the experiences fostering them are "ideal" without looking around the world.

BRIEF REVIEW

New child development theories are constantly emerging, questioning and building on earlier discoveries. Using computerlike models of mental activity, information processing has brought exactness and precision to the study of children's thinking. Ethology highlights the adaptive, or survival, value of children's behavior and its evolutionary history. Ecological systems theory stresses that adult–child interaction is a two-way street affected by a range of environmental influences, from immediate settings of home and school to broad cultural values and programs. Vygotsky's sociocultural theory takes a closer look at social relationships that foster development. Through cooperative dialogues with mature members of society, children acquire unique, culturally adaptive competencies.

Sociocultural theory
Vygotsky's sociocultural theory, in which children acquire the ways of thinking and behaving that make up a community's culture through cooperative dialogues with more knowledgeable members of that society.

CULTURAL INFLUENCES

!Kung Infancy: Acquiring Culture

Interaction between caregivers and infants takes different paths in different cultures. Through it, adults begin to transmit their society's values and skills to the next generation, channeling the course of future development.

Focusing on a culture very different from our own, researchers have studied how caregivers respond to infants' play with objects among the !Kung, a hunting and gathering society living in the desert regions of Botswana, Africa (Bakeman et al., 1990). Daily foraging missions take small numbers of adults several miles from the campground, but most obtain enough food to contribute to group survival by working only 3 out of every 7 days. A mobile way of life also prevents the !Kung from collecting many possessions that require extensive care and maintenance. Adults have many free hours to relax around the campfire, and they spend it in intense social contact with one another and with children (Draper & Cashdan, 1988).

In this culture of intimate social bonds and minimal property, objects are valued as things to be shared, not as personal possessions. This message is conveyed to !Kung children at a very early age. Between 6 and 12 months, grandmothers start to train babies in the importance of exchanging objects by guiding them in handing beads to relatives. The child's first words generally include *i* ("Here, take this") and *na* ("Give it to me").

In !Kung society, no toys are made for infants. Instead, natural objects, such as twigs, grass, stones, and nutshells, are always available, along with cooking implements. However, adults do not encourage babies to play with these objects. In fact, adults are unlikely to interact with infants while they are exploring objects independently. But when a baby offers an object to another person, adults become highly responsive, encouraging and vocalizing much more than at other times. Thus, the !Kung cultural emphasis on the interpersonal rather than physical aspects of existence is reflected in how adults interact with the very youngest members of their community.

When you next have a chance, observe the conditions under which parents respond to infants' involvement with objects in your own society. How is parental responsiveness linked to cultural values? How does it compare with findings on the !Kung?

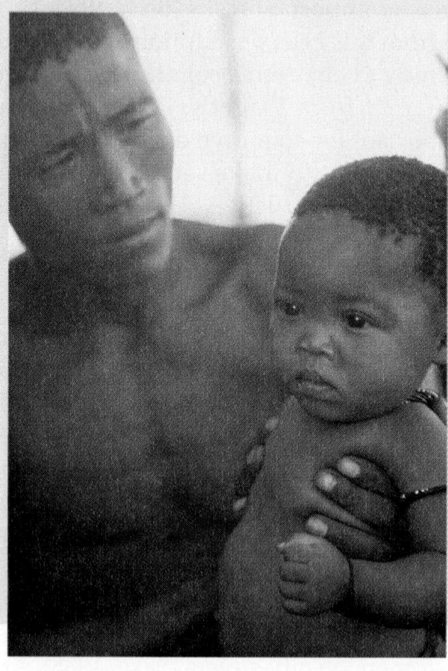

!Kung children grow up in a hunting-and-gathering society in which possessions are a burden rather than an asset. From an early age, children experience a rich, warm social contact with adults and are taught the importance of sharing. (Irven DeVore/Anthro-Photo)

Comparing Child Development Theories

In the preceding sections, we reviewed theoretical perspectives that are major forces in modern child development research. They differ in many respects.

First, they focus on different aspects of development. Some, such as psychoanalytic theory and ethology, emphasize children's social and emotional development. Others, such as Piaget's cognitive-developmental theory, information processing, and Vygotsky's sociocultural theory, stress important changes in children's thinking. The remaining approaches—behaviorism, social learning theory, and ecological systems theory—discuss factors assumed to affect all aspects of children's functioning.

Second, every theory contains a point of view about the nature of children and their development. As we conclude our review of theoretical perspectives, take a moment to identify the stand each theory takes on the three controversial issues presented at the beginning of this chapter. Then check your analysis of theories against Table 1.5. If you had difficulty classifying any of them, return to the relevant section of this chapter and reread the description of that theory.

Finally, we have seen that theories have strengths and weaknesses. This may remind you of an important point we made earlier in this chapter—that no single theory provides a complete account of development. Perhaps you found that you were attracted to some theories, but you had doubts about others. As you read more about child development research in later chapters of this book, you may find it useful to keep a notebook in

TABLE 1.5

Stance of Major Developmental Theories on Three Basic Issues in Child Development

Theory	The Developing Child: Organismic versus Mechanistic	The Course of Development: Continuous versus Discontinuous	The Determinants of Development: Nature versus Nurture Importance of Early Experiences
Psychoanalytic perspective	*Organismic:* Relations among structures of the mind (id, ego, and superego) determine personality.	*Discontinous:* Stages of psychosexual and psychosocial development are emphasized.	*Both nature and nurture:* Innate impulses are channeled and controlled through child-rearing experiences. *Early experiences* set the course of later development.
Behaviorism and social learning theory	*Mechanistic:* Development is the result of connections established between stimulus inputs and behavioral responses.	*Continuous:* Quantitative increase in learned behaviors occurs with age.	*Emphasis on nurture:* Learning principles of conditioning and modeling determine development. *Both early and later experiences* are important.
Piaget's cognitive-developmental theory	*Organismic:* Psychological structures determine the child's understanding of the world. The child actively constructs knowledge.	*Discontinuous:* Stages of cognitive development are emphasized.	*Both nature and nurture:* Children's innate drive to discover reality is emphasized. However, it must be† supported by a rich, stimulating environment. *Both early and later experiences* are important.
Information processing	*Both:* Active processing structures combine with a mechanistic, computerlike model of stimulus input and behavioral output to product development.	*Continuous:* A quantitative increase in perception, attention, memory, and problem-solving skills takes place with age.	*Both:* Maturation and learning opportunities affect information-processing skills. *Both early and later experiences* are important.
Ethology	*Organismic:* The infant is biologically prepared with social signals that actively promote survival. Over time, psychological structures develop that underlie infant–caregiver attachment and other adaptive behavior patterns.	*Both:* Adaptive behavior patterns increase in quantity over time. But sensitive periods—restricted time periods in which qualitatively distinct capacities and responses emerge fairly suddenly—are also emphasized.	*Both:* Biologically based, evolved behavior patterns are stressed, but an appropriately stimulating environment is necessary to elicit them. Also, learning can improve the adaptiveness of behavior. *Early experiences* set the course of later development.
Ecological systems theory	*Organismic:* Children's personality characteristics and ways of thinking actively contribute to their development.	*Not specified*	*Both:* Children's characteristics and the reactions of others affect each other in a bidirectional fashion. Layers of the environment influence child-rearing experiences. *Both early and later experiences* are important.
Vygotsky's sociocultural theory	*Organismic:* Children internalize essential features of social dialogues, forming psychological structures that they use to guide their own behavior.	*Continuous:* Interaction of the child with mature members of society leads to step-by-step changes in thought and behavior.	*Both:* Maturation and opportunities to interact with knowledgeable members of society affect the development of psychological structures and culturally adaptive skills. *Both early and later experiences* are important.

which you test your own theoretical likes and dislikes against the evidence. Do not be surprised if you revise your ideas many times, just as theorists have done throughout this century. By the end of the course, you will have built your own personal perspective on child development. It might turn out to be a blend of several theories, since each viewpoint we have discussed has contributed in important ways to what we know about children. And like researchers in the field of child development, you will be left with some unanswered questions. I hope they will motivate you to continue your quest to understand children in the years to come.

■ *In the United States, nearly 22 percent of children live in poverty, a circumstance that threatens all aspects of development. Poverty is especially high among ethnic minority children. (W. B. Spunbarg/PhotoEdit)*

New Applied Directions: Child Development and Social Policy

In recent years, the field of child development has become increasingly concerned with applying its vast knowledge base to the solution of pressing social problems faced by children and adolescents. In this final decade of the twentieth century, we know much more than ever before about family, school, and community contexts that foster the development of physically healthy, cognitively competent, and socially mature children. Although many American children fare well, the condition of a substantial minority is much less than satisfactory. Consider the following **childhood social indicators**, or periodic measures of children's health, living conditions, achievement, and psychological well-being that lend insight into their overall status:

- *Poverty.* Over the past 25 years, the poverty rate among American children has climbed from 14 to nearly 22 percent, a circumstance that threatens all aspects of development. Approximately 14.6 million young people under age 18 are affected. Nearly half of these are in desperate straits, with family incomes of less than half the *poverty line* (earnings judged by the federal government to be necessary for bare subsistence). Today, children are the poorest of any age sector of the American population. Poverty is as high as 54 percent among children in single-parent households, 40 percent among Hispanic children, and 47 percent among black children. Furthermore, economic disadvantage is far more likely to persist for most of childhood among Hispanics and African-Americans than Caucasian-Americans (Chase-Lansdale & Brooks-Gunn, 1994; Children's Defense Fund, 1996).
- *Homelessness.* Compounding the devastating effects of poverty, homelessness has risen in the United States over the past decade and a half. On any given night, approximately 735,000 people have no place to live (Wright, 1995). Homelessness has increased more among families with children than any other group. A recent survey of 30 cities revealed that nearly 40 percent of America's homeless population is made up of families, and 1 in every 4 homeless individuals is a child (U.S. Conference of Mayors, 1994).
- *Health insurance.* Approximately 14 percent of American children have no health insurance, making them the largest segment of the uninsured population. As employer-based health insurance became less available to families in the 1990s, the number of uninsured children increased. Among industrialized nations, only

Childhood social indicators
Periodic measures of children's health, living conditions, achievement, and psychological well-being that lend insight into their overall status in a community, state, or nation.

the United States and South Africa fail to guarantee every citizen basic health care services (Children's Defense Fund, 1996; Oberg, 1988).

- *Childhood immunization.* As many as 25 percent of American 2-year-olds are not fully immunized against preventable childhood diseases, leaving more than 1 million vulnerable to infectious illnesses, such as measles, tetanus, and polio (Children's Defense Fund, 1996).
- *Low birth weight and infant death.* Approximately 7 percent of American infants—about 250,000 babies—are born underweight annually. Low birth weight is a powerful predictor of serious health difficulties and early death. Nearly 8 out of every 1,000 American babies do not survive their first year, a figure that compares dismally to that of other industrialized nations (Guyer et al., 1995).
- *Teenage parenthood.* Each year, over 400,000 babies are born to American teenagers, who are neither psychologically nor economically prepared to raise a child (Chase-Lansdale & Brooks-Gunn, 1994; Jaskiewicz & McAnarney, 1994). The rates of adolescent pregnancy and childbearing in the United States are the highest in the industrialized world. Teenage parenthood is strongly linked to poverty and poses serious risks to the development of both adolescent and child.
- *Divorce.* Family breakdown is common in the lives of American children. One out of every 65 youngsters experiences parental divorce annually, a rate exceeding that of any other nation in the world (U.S. Bureau of the Census, 1995). In Chapter 14, we will see that marital dissolution is linked to temporary—and occasionally long-term—declines in family income and highly stressful living conditions.
- *Mental illness.* When environments undermine development during the early years, many children reach middle childhood and adolescence with serious mental health problems. Approximately 7.7 million American youngsters suffer from emotional and behavioral difficulties severe enough to warrant treatment. Chronic anxiety, antisocial behavior, eating disorders, depression, and suicide are among the problems we will discuss in later chapters. Yet only 20 to 30 percent of mentally ill children and adolescents have access to the treatment services they need (Children's Defense Fund, 1992, 1996).
- *Child abuse and neglect.* In 1994, 3.1 million reports of child abuse and neglect were made to juvenile authorities in the United States. The figure greatly underestimates the true number, since many cases go unreported (Children's Defense Fund, 1996).
- *Day care.* Sixty-five percent of American children under age 6 have mothers in the labor force. Yet unlike Western European nations, the United States has been slow to move toward a national system of day care to serve its single-parent and dual-earner families. According to recent surveys, much day care in the United States is substandard in quality. Low-income parents, who cannot afford the high cost of day care, often have no choice but to place their children in poor-quality settings (Shonkoff, 1995).
- *School achievement.* Many students are graduating from American high schools without the educational preparation they need to contribute fully to society. Although the majority master general information and basic skills, over 90 percent of 17-year-olds have difficulty with complex reasoning and problem solving in reading, writing, mathematics, and science (Mullis et al., 1994).
- *School dropout.* By age 18, 14 percent of American young people leave high school without a diploma. Those who do not return to finish their education are at risk for lifelong poverty. The dropout rate is especially high among low-income ethnic minority youths. In some inner-city areas, it approaches 50 percent (Children's Defense Fund, 1996).

The dire condition of so many American youngsters is particularly disturbing, since the United States has the largest gross national product[1] and the broadest knowledge

[1] Gross national product is the value of all goods and services produced by a nation during a specified time period. It serves as an overall measure of a nation's wealth.

TABLE 1.6

How Does the United States Compare to Other Nations on Indicators of Child Health and Well-Being?

Indicator	U.S. Rank	Some Countries the United States Trails
Childhood poverty	8th (among 8 industrialized nations studied)[a]	Australia, Canada, Germany, Great Britain, Norway, Sweden, Switzerland
Infant deaths in the first year of life	22nd (worldwide)	Hong Kong, Ireland, Singapore, Spain
Low birth weight newborns	28th (worldwide)	Bulgaria, Egypt, Greece, Iran, Jordan, Kuwait, Paraguay, Romania, Saudi Arabia
Percent of young children immunized against measles	21st (worldwide)	Chile, Czechoslovakia, Jordan, Poland
Number of school-age children per teacher	12th (worldwide)	Cuba, Lebanon, Libya
Expenditures on education as percentage of gross national product	14th (among 16 industrialized nations studied)	Canada, France, Great Britain, the Netherlands, Sweden
Teenage pregnancy rate	6th (among 6 industrialized nations studied)	Canada, England, France, the Netherlands, Sweden

[a]The U.S. childhood poverty rate of 22 percent is more than twice that of any of these nations. For example, the rate is 9 percent in Australia, 9.3 percent in Canada, 4.6 percent in France, and 1.6 percent in Sweden.

Sources: Children's Defense Fund, 1996; Danziger & Danziger, 1993; Grant, 1995; Sivard, 1993; Wegman, 1994.

base for intervening effectively in children's lives of any nation in the world. Yet, as Table 1.6 reveals, it does not rank among the top countries on any key measure of children's health and well-being. Let's consider why this is the case.

THE POLICY-MAKING PROCESS

Social policy is any planned set of actions directed at solving a social problem or attaining a social goal. The breadth of this definition indicates that social policies can take place at many levels. Policies can be proposed and implemented by small groups or large formal organizations; by private or public institutions such as schools, businesses, and social service agencies; and by governing bodies such as the U.S. Congress, state legislatures, the courts, and city councils.

When widespread social problems arise, nations attempt to solve them by developing a special type of social policy called **public policy**—laws and government programs designed to improve current conditions. Return for a moment to Bronfenbrenner's ecological systems theory on page 26, and notice how the concept of the macrosystem suggests that sound public policies are essential for protecting children's well-being. When governing bodies authorize programs to meet children's health, safety, and educational needs, they serve as broad societal plans for action. Events of the early 1980s provided a dramatic illustration of how critical government support of children and families truly is. When Aid to Families with Dependent Children (the nation's key welfare program) and food, housing, and medical benefits for the poor were cut in the face of rising inflation and unemployment, poverty, hunger, homelessness, and childhood disease climbed substantially (Children's Defense Fund, 1990; Hayes, 1989).

Why have attempts to help children been more difficult to realize in the United States than in other industrialized nations? To answer this question, we must have some understanding of the complex forces that combine to foster effective public policies. Among the most important are societal values, special interests, economic conditions, and child development research.

Social policy
Any planned set of actions directed at solving a social problem or attaining a social goal.

Public policy
Laws and government programs designed to improve current conditions.

CULTURAL VALUES. The *political culture* of a nation—dominant beliefs about the relationship that should exist between citizen and government—has a major impact on the policy-making process. When you next have a chance, ask several residents of your community the following question: "Who should be responsible for raising young children?" Many Americans respond in ways like these: "If parents decide to have a baby, then they should be ready to care for it." "Most people are not happy about others intruding into family matters."

These statements reflect a widespread opinion in the United States—that the care and rearing of children during the early years is the duty of parents, and only parents. This view has a long history, one in which independence, self-reliance, and the privacy of family life emerged as central American values (Goffin, 1988; Triandis, 1989). It is a major reason that the American public has been slow to accept the idea of government-supported health insurance and day care. These programs are broadly available in Europe, largely because European citizens are more approving of government intervention and control of family services.

■ SPECIAL INTERESTS. Of course, not all people hold the same political beliefs. In complex societies, distinct subcultures exist, based on such factors as geographic region, ethnicity, income, and age, that stand alongside a nation's dominant values. The diversity of American society has led *special interest groups* to play an especially strong role in policy making. In fact, policies generally arise out of conflicts and compromises among groups of people who have distinct beliefs and desires. In this clash of special interests from which new programs emerge, groups that are well organized, have skilled leadership, contribute to the economic welfare of a nation, and have a large membership are likely to fare much better than those that are poorly organized, a drain on economic reserves, and small in size.

In this effort to jockey for public influence, the needs of children can easily remain unrecognized. Instead of making immediate contributions to the welfare of a nation, children are a costly drain on economic resources that people with quite different interests want for their own pressing needs. In addition, children are not capable of organizing and speaking out to protect their own unique concerns, as adult citizens do. Because they must rely on the goodwill of others for becoming an important government priority, children are constantly in danger of becoming a "forgotten constituency" in the United States (Takanishi, DeLeon, & Pallak, 1983).

■ ECONOMIC CONDITIONS. Besides dominant values and the demands of special interests, the current state of a nation's economy affects what it does to improve the welfare of children and families. Scarce public resources are commonplace in less developed countries of the world, which depend on economic aid from richer nations like the United States to feed, educate, and provide health care for many citizens. But even in large industrialized nations, the government does not always have enough resources to solve pressing social problems. In times of economic difficulty, governments are less likely to initiate new social programs, and they may cut back or even eliminate those that exist. Over the past 15 years, the U.S. federal deficit quadrupled, reaching an astronomical $4.6 trillion in the mid-1990s (U.S. Office of Management and Budget, 1995). During this period, it is not surprising that federal support for the needs of children and families became difficult to secure and that funding of many child-related services declined (Garwood et al., 1989).

■ CHILD DEVELOPMENT RESEARCH. For a policy to be most effective in meeting children's needs, research should guide it at every step along the way—during design, implementation, and evaluation of the program. The recent trend toward greater involvement of child development researchers in the policy process was stimulated by events of the 1960s and 1970s, a time of greater economic prosperity and receptiveness to government-sponsored social services. Investigators quickly realized that they could have an impact on policy formation (Zigler & Finn-Stevenson, 1992).

For example, in 1965, research on the importance of early experience for children's intellectual development played a major role in the founding of Project Head Start, the nation's largest preschool intervention program for low-income families (Hunt, 1961). As we will see in Chapter 8, two decades of research on the long-term benefits of intervening with education and family social services in the first few years of life helped Head Start survive when its funding was threatened and contributed to the increase in support it has received in recent years (Zigler & Styfco, 1993). In another instance, findings on the

SOCIAL ISSUES ➤ POINT OF VIEW

Should Day Care Licensing Standards Be Upgraded in the United States?

In the United States, regulation of day care is the province of the states, not the federal government. As a result, licensing standards for day care facilities vary widely across the nation; some states have considerably more stringent requirements than do others. For example, in North Carolina, caregivers are not required to have any child-related educational preparation, and the adult–child ratio in settings for infants can be as low as 1 to 6. In contrast, caregivers in California must have earned at least 12 college-level credits in early childhood education, and the adult–infant ratio must be at least 1 to 4.

Will upgrading licensing standards actually enhance the quality of care American children receive? Two large-scale studies have addressed this question. Each carefully examined the daily lives of children and their caregivers in several hundred day care centers drawn from states that vary widely in the stringency of their regulations (Helburn, 1995; Phillips, Howes, & Whitebook, 1992). Besides checking to see if centers met or exceeded state requirements for features that can easily be regulated (caregiver education; adult–child ratios; and group size, or number of children in a single space), researchers carefully rated each setting on quality indicators that are difficult or impossible to control legally, such as the appropriateness of children's activities, the richness of their play environments, and the stimulation and sensitivity of caregiver–child interactions. Stability of caregivers (low staff turnover) was also examined. As we will see in Chapters 10 and 14, all of these nonregulable characteristics are consistently linked to children's cognitive, emotional, and social development (Hayes, Palmer, & Zaslow, 1990; Whitebook, Howes, & Phillips, 1990).

Results revealed that day care centers in states with more stringent regulations offered children higher-quality experiences in terms of both regulated and nonregulable characteristics. And when centers exceeded minimum state standards by meeting definitions of quality established by the early childhood education profession, children's learning opportunities, the warmth and support they received from adults, and the stability of caregivers were especially high. However, an overall look at centers participating in the two studies confirmed earlier reports that the quality of day care available to most American families is mediocre to poor. In one of the investigations, researchers judged that only 1 in 7

■ *The generous adult–child ratio in this day care center grants preschoolers the stimulation and sensitive interaction they need to develop at their best. Current licensing standards in the United States do not ensure that all children receive such high-quality care. Day care available to most American families is mediocre to poor. (Will Faller)*

severe impact of malnutrition on early brain development stimulated passage by Congress of the Special Supplemental Food Program for Women, Infants, and Children. Since the early 1970s, it has supplied food packages to many poverty-stricken pregnant women and young children (see Chapter 3).

Policy-relevant research, investigators soon realized, has the added benefit of expanding our knowledge base of child development. As researchers started to examine the impact of children's services, they became more aware of the power of settings remote from children's daily lives to affect their well-being. As a result, researchers broadened their focus of study to include development within a wider social context (Bronfenbrenner, 1979, 1989). Throughout this book, we will encounter a wealth of findings on the impact of larger social systems, such as school, workplace, community, mass media, and government. Researchers also began to address the impact of rapid societal change on children—poverty, homelessness, divorce, family violence, teenage parenthood, and day care. All these efforts have, in turn, helped to forge new policy directions.

Still, as we mentioned earlier, a large gap exists between what we know about children and the application of that knowledge. For several reasons, scientific research does not invariably affect policy making. First, the impact of research depends on its interactions with other components of the policy process. In the case of both Head Start and the Special Supplemental Food Program, if public sentiments had not been so receptive to helping poor children at the time these policies were proposed, compelling findings on the importance of early education and nutrition might have been less influential (Hayes,

centers provided a level of care sufficient to promote healthy psychological development (Helburn, 1995). Similar conclusions have been reached about children's experiences in family and relative day care (Galinsky et al., 1994).

Research clearly indicates that upgrading state regulations or imposing federal standards would enhance the quality of American day care. Still, many experts warn against taking these steps without considering how the *supply* of day care would be affected. High-quality day care is costly; the best centers are often nonprofit settings that receive more public funding and donated support. Consequently, they can hire better educated caregivers, pay them higher wages, and grant them more benefits—conditions that return to affect children's experiences. Tightening standards without providing additional funding may drive poorer-quality centers out of the market. This would leave many employed parents with no viable options, since day care (especially for infants) is already in short supply. In this respect, enhancing regulation is sometimes portrayed as restricting family choice and therefore in conflict with an important American ideal (Phillips, Howes, & Whitebook, 1992).

Day care in the United States is embedded in a complex, macrosystem context in which individualistic values, variable regulations, and limited economic resources constrain the quality of children's experiences (Bronfenbrenner, 1989). Recognizing this complexity, the researchers made the following recommendations to policy makers and the general public:

- The United States must implement higher standards for day care that go beyond protecting children's health and safety to ensuring their developmental needs. To do so, it must create a better balance of state and federal responsibility that reduces the unevenness of care to which children are exposed.
- Federal, state, and local governments as well as community organizations and businesses must increase their investment in day care to help families pay for high-quality services.
- Both the public and the private sector must launch consumer education efforts to help parents recognize signs of high-quality care. (For a preview of those signs, look ahead to pages 417 and 569.) At present, many parents overestimate the quality of their children's day care experiences. Over 90 percent rate programs in which their children are enrolled as very good, whereas trained observers rate most of the same programs as poor or mediocre (Helburn, 1995). Inability to identify good care implies that many parents do not demand it, thereby leaving day care providers with little incentive to improve quality.

Pressures to enhance the quality of American day care must come from multiple sources. These range from actions of legislative bodies to parental assertiveness in demanding better care and monitoring their children's daily experiences.

YOUR POINT OF VIEW . . .

- Contact a day care center in your community, and ask about state requirements for caregiver education, adult-child ratios, and group size for children of different ages. How stringent are day care standards in your state?
- Although substantial variation exists within each type of setting, several studies report that for-profit day care centers tend to offer children lower-quality care than do nonprofit centers. Why might this be so?

1982). Second, research that sheds light on policy often takes many years to conduct. Large numbers of studies that yield consensus on an issue are generally needed to arrive at an appropriate solution. Consequently, besides focusing on current concerns, researchers must anticipate future policy issues and work on them in advance. Third, child development researchers have had to learn how to communicate effectively with policymakers and the general public. Today, they are doing a better job than ever before of disseminating their findings in easily understandable ways, through television documentaries, newspaper stories, and magazine articles as well as direct reports to government officials (Huston, 1994). As a result, they are helping create a sense of immediacy about children's condition that is necessary to spur a society into action. For an example of policy-relevant research aimed at improving the quality of American day care, refer to the Social Issues box above.

CONTEMPORARY PROGRESS IN MEETING THE NEEDS OF AMERICAN CHILDREN

The design of public policies aimed at fostering children's development can be justified on two important grounds. The first is humanitarian—children's basic rights as human beings (Huston, 1991). In 1989, the United Nations' General Assembly drew up the *International Convention on the Rights of the Child*, a treaty written in the form of a legal agreement among nations. It commits each participating country to work toward guaranteeing children a standard of living and health care adequate for physical and psychological development, education that develops their capacities and talents as fully as possible, and protection from abuse and neglect. With the President's submission of the treaty to the Senate in 1995, the United States moved a step closer to the 180 nations that have ratified the treaty—a level of endorsement that reflects worldwide consensus on children's rights (Limber & Flekkøy, 1995). Second, child-oriented policies can be justified on the basis that children are the parents, workers, and citizens of tomorrow. Investing in them can yield valuable returns to a nation's quality of life. In contrast, failure to invest in children can result in "economic inefficiency, loss of productivity, shortages in needed skills, high health care costs, growing prison costs, and a nation that will be less safe, less caring, and less free." (Hernandez, 1994, p. 20).

To be sure, a wide variety of government-sponsored programs aimed at helping children and families do exist in the United States, and we will see many examples in later chapters. Nevertheless, analyses of these programs reveal that the majority have been enacted piecemeal, over a long period of time, with little attention to their interrelatedness. In addition, they are largely crisis oriented, aimed at handling the most severe family difficulties rather than preventing problems before they happen. Furthermore, funding for these efforts has waxed and waned and been seriously threatened at various times. In most cases, only a minority of needy individuals are being helped (Takanishi, DeLeon, & Pallak, 1983; Zigler & Finn-Stevenson, 1992).

Nevertheless, there are hopeful signs on the horizon. New policy initiatives are under way that promise to improve the status of American children. For example, a 1990 bill granted low-income parents increased tax relief to offset the cost of day care and offered modest funding to the states to enhance the quality and availability of day care services. A bill signed into law in 1992 provided funds to upgrade treatment programs for children with serious mental health problems. A 1993 bill granted workers 12 weeks of unpaid employment leave to deal with family emergencies, such as the birth or illness of a child. Furthermore, public health insurance coverage for children and pregnant women from low-income families has recently expanded. And beginning in 1994, all medically uninsured American children were guaranteed free vaccinations (Children's Defense Fund, 1996).

Additional policies are being initiated by a few businesses, such as on-site or nearby day care services, and by some state legislatures, such as enforcement of child support payments in divorce cases. Child-related professional organizations are also taking a strong leadership role. In the absence of federal guidelines for high-quality day care, the National Association for the Education of Young Children (NAEYC, an 86,000-member organization of early childhood educators) established a voluntary accreditation system for preschool and day care centers. It grants special professional recognition to programs that meet its rigorous standards of quality (National Association for the Education of Young Children, 1991). Efforts like these are serving as inspiring models for the nation as a whole.

■ *In 1973, Marion Wright Edelman founded the Children's Defense Fund, a private, non-profit organization that provides a strong, effective voice for American children, who cannot vote, lobby, or speak for themselves. Edelman continues to serve as president of the Children's Defense Fund today. (Westenberger/Liaiso, USA)*

Finally, child development specialists are joining with concerned citizens to become advocates for children's causes. Over the past two decades, several influential interest groups with children's well-being as their central purpose have emerged in the United States. One of the most vigorous is the Children's Defense Fund, a private nonprofit organization founded by Marion Wright Edelman in 1973. It engages in research, public education, legal action, drafting of legislation, congressional testimony, and community organizing. Each year, it publishes *The State of America's Children*, which provides a comprehensive analysis of the current condition of children, government-sponsored programs serving them, and proposals for improving child and family programs.[2]

By forging more effective partnerships with government and the general public, the field of child development is playing a significant role in spurring the policy process forward. As these efforts continue, there is every reason to expect increased attention to the needs of children and families in the years to come.

[2] To obtain a copy of *The State of America's Children*, contact The Children's Defense Fund, 122 C Street, N.W., Washington DC 20001. Telephone (800) 424-9602.

SUMMARY

CHILD DEVELOPMENT AS AN INTERDISCIPLINARY, SCIENTIFIC, AND APPLIED FIELD

- **Child development** is the study of human growth and change from conception through adolescence. It is part of a larger discipline known as **developmental psychology** or **human development**, which includes all changes that take place throughout the life span. Research on child development has been stimulated by both scientific curiosity and social pressures to better the lives of children.

BASIC THEMES AND ISSUES

- **Theories** provide organizing frameworks for our observations of the child and a sound basis for practical action. Major theories can be organized according to the stand they take on three controversial issues: (1) Is the child an **organismic** or **mechanistic** being? (2) Is development a **continuous** process, or does it follow a series of **discontinuous** stages? (3) Is development primarily determined by **nature** or **nurture**? Some theories, especially the more recent ones, take an intermediate stand on these issues.

HISTORICAL FOUNDATIONS

- Modern theories of child development have roots extending far back into the past. In medieval times, children were regarded as miniature adults, a view called **preformationism**. By the sixteenth century, childhood became a distinct phase of the life cycle. However, the Puritan conception of original sin led to a harsh philosophy of child rearing.
- The Enlightenment brought new ideas favoring more humane treatment of children. Locke's **tabula rasa** provided the basis for twentieth-century behaviorism, and Rousseau's **noble savage** foreshadowed the concepts of **stage** and **maturation**. A century later, Darwin's theory of evolution stimulated scientific child study.
- Efforts to observe children directly began in the late nineteenth and early twentieth centuries with baby biographies. Soon after, Hall and Gesell introduced the **normative approach**, which produced a large body of descriptive facts about children. Binet initiated the mental testing movement, an outgrowth of normative child study, which led to the first successful intelligence test. Baldwin's theory was ahead of its time in taking a balanced view on issues of organismic versus mechanistic child and nature versus nurture.

MID-TWENTIETH-CENTURY THEORIES

- In the 1930s and 1940s, child guidance professionals turned to the **psychoanalytic perspective** for help in understanding children with emotional problems. In Freud's **psychosexual theory**, children move through five stages, during which three portions of the personality—**id**, **ego**, and **superego**—become integrated. Erikson's **psychosocial theory** builds on Freud's theory by emphasizing the development of culturally relevant attitudes and skills and the lifespan nature of development.
- Academic psychology also influenced child study. From **behaviorism** and **social learning theory** came the principles of conditioning and modeling and practical procedures of **applied behavior analysis** with children.
- In contrast to behaviorism, Piaget's **cognitive-developmental theory** emphasizes an active child with a mind inhabited by rich structures of knowledge. According to Piaget, children move through four broad stages, beginning with baby's sensorimotor action patterns and ending with the elaborate, abstract reasoning system of the adolescent and adult. Piaget's theory has stimulated a wealth of research on children's thinking and encouraged educational programs that emphasize discovery learning.

RECENT PERSPECTIVES

- The field of child development continues to seek new directions. **Information processing** views the mind as a complex, symbol-manipulating system, operating much like a computer. This approach helps researchers achieve a clear understanding of what children of different ages do when faced with tasks or problems. Information processing has led to the design of instructional procedures that help children overcome cognitive limitations and approach tasks in more advanced ways.

- Three modern theories place special emphasis on contexts for development. **Ethology** stresses the adaptive, or survival, value of behavior and its origins in evolutionary history. In **ecological systems theory**, nested layers of the environment, which range from the child's immediate setting to broad cultural values and programs, undergo changes over time and are major influences on children's development. Vygotsky's **sociocultural theory** focuses on how culture is transmitted to the next generation. Through cooperative dialogues with mature members of society, children acquire culturally relevant knowledge and skills.

NEW APPLIED DIRECTIONS: CHILD DEVELOPMENT AND SOCIAL POLICY

- In recent years, the field of child development has become increasingly concerned with applying its vast knowledge base to the solution of pressing social problems. **Childhood social indicators** reveal that many children in the United States are growing up under conditions that threaten their well-being.
- A special type of **social policy** called **public policy**—laws and government programs designed to improve current conditions—is essential for protecting children's development. Dominant political values, competing claims of special interest groups, the state of a nation's economy, and child development research combine to influence the policy-making process. Policy-relevant research not only helps forge new policy directions, but also expands our understanding of child development.
- Although many government-sponsored child and family policies are in effect in the United States, they are largely crisis oriented and do not reach all individuals in need. A variety of new policies are under way, initiated by the federal government, state legislatures, businesses, and professional organizations. In addition, child development researchers are joining with concerned citizens to become advocates for children's causes. These efforts offer hope of improving the well-being of children and families in the years to come.

IMPORTANT TERMS AND CONCEPTS

child development (p. 4)
developmental psychology (p. 4)
human development (p. 4)
theory (p. 4)
organismic theories (p. 5)
mechanistic theories (p. 6)
continuous development (p. 6)
discontinuous development (p. 6)
stage (p. 6)
nature–nurture controversy (p. 7)
preformationism (p. 8)
tabula rasa (p. 10)
noble savage (p. 10)
maturation (p. 10)
normative approach (p. 12)
psychoanalytic perspective (p. 14)
psychosexual theory (p. 15)
id (p. 14)
ego (p. 15)
superego (p. 15)
psychosocial theory (p. 16)
behaviorism (p. 16)
social learning theory (p. 18)
applied behavior analysis (p. 18)
cognitive-developmental theory (p. 19)
information processing (p. 21)
ethology (p. 23)
sensitive period (p. 24)
ecological systems theory (p. 24)
microsystem (p. 24)
mesosystem (p. 25)
exosystem (p. 25)
macrosystem (p. 26)
chronosystem (p. 26)
sociocultural theory (p. 27)
childhood social indicators (p. 30)
social policy (p. 32)
public policy (p. 32)

CONNECTIONS for Chapter 1

If you are interested in . . .	turn to . . .	to learn about . . .
The nature-nurture controversy	Chapter 3, pp. 113–118	How researchers study the influence of heredity and environment on complex traits
	Chapter 4, pp. 141–146	Genetic and environmental influences on motor development
	Chapter 8, pp. 318–327	Genetic and environmental influences on intelligence
	Chapter 10, pp. 400–401	Genetic and environmental influences on temperament
	Chapter 13, pp. 524–533	Genetic and environmental influences on sex-related differences in mental abilities and personality traits

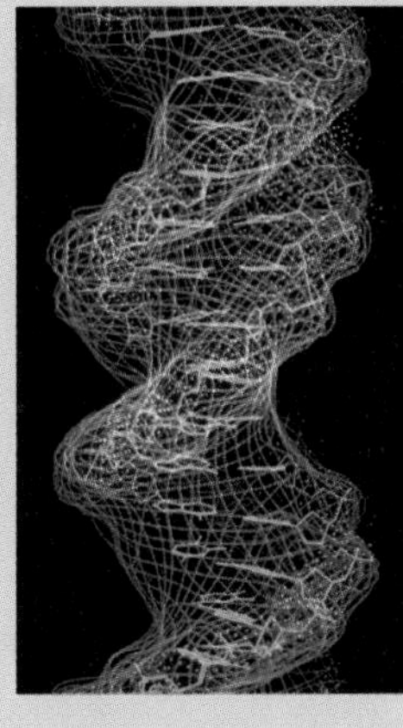

If you are interested in . . .	turn to . . .	to learn about . . .
Theories and their influence on child development research	Chapter 6, pp. 247–250	Vygotsky's sociocultural theory and the origins of higher cognitive processes
	Chapter 7, pp. 286–293	Applications of information processing to academic learning
	Chapter 10, pp. 406–408	Ethological theory and infant-caregiver attachment
	Chapter 11, pp. 438–440	Erikson's psychosocial theory and adolescent identity development
	Chapter 12, pp. 469–472	Piaget's cognitive-developmental theory and moral development
	Chapter 14, pp. 541–543	Ecological systems theory and family influences on development

If you are interested in . . .	turn to . . .	to learn about . . .
Child development and social policy	Chapter 3, pp. 100–101	Vitamin-mineral supplements and prenatal development
	Chapter 5, pp. 185–191	Teenage sexual activity, pregnancy, and childbearing
	Chapter 8, pp. 328–331	Early intervention and intellectual development
	Chapter 9, p. 376	Impact of declaring English the official U.S. language on bilingual education
	Chapter 15, p. 605	Regulating television to protect children's development

2 Research Strategies

One afternoon, my colleague Ron crossed the street between his academic department and our laboratory school, the expression on his face reflecting a deep sense of apprehension. After weeks of planning, Ron had looked forward to launching his study on the development of children's peer relations. Thinking back to his own elementary school years, he recalled the anguish experienced by several of his classmates, who were repeatedly ridiculed, taunted, and shunned by their peers. Ron wanted to find ways to help rejected children, many of whom go on to lead unhappy and troubled lives. In view of the importance of his research, Ron was puzzled by the request he had received to appear before the school's research committee.

Ron was joined at the committee meeting by teachers and administrators charged with evaluating research proposals on the basis of their ethical integrity. A third-grade teacher spoke up:

"Ron, I see the value of your work, but frankly, I'm very concerned about your asking my pupils whom they like most and whom they like least. I've got a couple of kids who are soundly disliked and real troublemakers, and I'm doing my best to keep the lid on the situation. If you come in and start sensitizing my class to whom they like and dislike, the children are going to share these opinions. Unfortunately, I think your study is likely to promote conflict and negative interaction in my classroom!"

Imagine the jolt Ron must have felt to hear someone suggest that the research he had been so carefully planning might have to be abandoned. Anyone who has undertaken the time-consuming process of preparing for such a study could commiserate with Ron's dismay. This chapter takes a close look at the research process—the many challenges investigators face as they plan and implement studies of children. Ron had already traveled a long and arduous path before he arrived at the door of the laboratory school, prepared to collect his data. First, he spent many weeks developing a researchable idea, based on theory and prior knowledge about children's peer relations. Next, he had to decide on an appropriate research strategy, which involves two main tasks. First, he had to choose from a wide variety of *research methods,* the specific activities of participants, such as taking tests, answering questionnaires, responding to interviews, or being observed. Second, he had to select a *research design,* an overall plan for his study that would permit the best possible test of his research idea. Finally, Ron scrutinized his procedures for any possible harm they might cause to the participants involved.

Still, as Ron approached a committee charged with protecting the welfare of young research participants, he faced an ethical dilemma. Research, whether on animals or humans, must meet certain standards that protect participants from stressful treatment. Because of children's immaturity and vulnerability, extra precautions must be taken to ensure that their rights are not violated in the course of a research study. In the final section of this chapter, we will see how Ron resolved the committee's earnest challenge to the ethical integrity of his research.

From Theory to Hypothesis

In Chapter 1, we saw how theories structure the research process by identifying important research concerns and, occasionally, preferred methods for collecting data. We also discussed how theories guide the application of findings to real-life circumstances and practices with children. In fact, research usually begins with a prediction about behavior drawn directly from a theory, or what we call a **hypothesis**. Think back to the various child development theories

Hypothesis
A prediction about behavior drawn from a theory.

presented in Chapter 1. Many hypotheses can be drawn from any one of them that, once tested, would reflect on the accuracy of the theory.

Sometimes research pits a hypothesis taken from one theory against a hypothesis taken from another. For example, a theorist emphasizing the role of maturation in development would predict that adult encouragement will have little effect on the age at which children utter their first words, learn to count, or tie their shoes. A sociocultural theorist, in contrast, would speculate that these skills can be promoted through adult teaching.

At other times, research tests predictions drawn from a single theory. For example, ecological systems theory suggests that providing isolated, divorced mothers with social supports will lead them to be more patient with their children. An ethologist might hypothesize that an infant's cry will stimulate strong physiological arousal in adults who hear it, motivating them to soothe and protect a suffering baby.

Occasionally, little or no theory exists on a topic of interest. In these instances, rather than making a specific prediction, the investigator may start with a *research question,* such as: Are children reaching puberty earlier and growing taller than they did a generation ago? What consequences does parental job loss have for children's psychological adjustment? Once formulated, hypotheses and research questions offer investigators vital guidance as they settle on research methods and a research design.

At this point, you may be wondering, Why learn about research strategies? Why not leave these matters to research specialists and concentrate on what is already known about the child and how this knowledge can be applied? There are two reasons. First, each of us must be wise and critical consumers of knowledge, not naive sponges who soak up facts about children. Knowing the strengths and weaknesses of various research strategies becomes important in separating dependable information from misleading results. Second, individuals who work directly with children are sometimes in a position to test hypotheses or research questions, either on their own or with an experienced investigator. At other times, they may have to provide information on how well their goals for children are being realized to justify continued financial support for their programs and activities. Under these circumstances, an understanding of the research process becomes essential practical knowledge.

Common Methods Used to Study Children

How does a researcher choose a basic approach to gathering information about children? Common methods in the field of child development include systematic observation, self-reports, psychophysiological measures, clinical or case studies of a single child, and ethnographies of the life circumstances of a particular group of children. As you read about these methods, you may find it helpful to refer to Table 2.1, which summarizes the strengths and limitations of each.

SYSTEMATIC OBSERVATION

To find out how children actually behave, a researcher may choose *systematic observation.* Observations of the behavior of children, and of the adults who are important in their lives, can be made in different ways. One approach is to go into the field, or the natural environment, and record the behavior of interest, a method called **naturalistic observation**.

A study of preschoolers' responses to their peers' distress provides a good example of this technique (Farver & Branstetter, 1994). Observing 3- and 4-year-olds in day care centers, the researchers recorded each instance of crying and the reactions of nearby children—whether they ignored, watched curiously, commented on the child's unhappiness, chastized or teased, or provided physical or emotional support in the form of sharing, helping, or expressing sympathy. Caregiver behaviors, such as explaining why a child was crying, mediating conflict, or offering comfort, were also noted to see if adult sensitivity was related to children's caring responses. A strong relationship emerged. The great strength of naturalistic observation in studies like this one is that investigators can see directly the everyday behaviors they hope to explain (Miller, 1997).

Naturalistic observation
A method in which the researcher goes into the natural environment to observe the behavior of interest.

TABLE 2.1

Strengths and Limitations of Common Research Methods

Method	Description	Strenths	Limitations
Systematic Observation			
Naturalistic observation	Observation of behavior in natural contexts	Observations reflect participants' everyday lives.	Conditions under which participants are observed cannot be controlled.
Structured observation	Observation of behavior in a laboratory	Conditions of observation are the same for all children.	Observations may not be typical of the way participants behave in everyday life.
Self-Reports			
Clinical interview	Flexible interviewing procedure in which the investigator obtains a complete account of the participant's thoughts	Comes as close as possible to the way participants think in everyday life; great breadth and depth of information can be obtained in a short time.	Pariticipants may not report information accurately; flexible procedure makes comparing individuals' responses difficult.
Structured interview, questionnaires, and tests	Self-report instruments in which each participant is asked the same questions in the same way	Standardized method of asking questions permits comparisons of participants' responses and efficient data collection and scoring.	Does not yield the same depth of information as a clinical interview; responses still subject to inaccurate reporting.
Psychophysiological Methods	Methods that measure the relationship between physiological processes and behavior	Reveals which central nervous system structures contribute to development and individual differences in certain competencies. Helps identify the perceptions, thoughts, and emotions of infants and young children, who cannot report them clearly.	Cannot reveal with certainty how an individual processes stimuli. Many factors besides those of interest to the researcher can influence a physiological response.
Clinical Method (Case Study)	A full picture of a single individual's psychological functioning, obtained by combining interviews, observations, test scores, and sometimes psychophysiological assessments	Provides rich, descriptive insights into processes of development.	May be biased by researcher's theoretical preferences; findings cannot be applied to individuals other than the participant.
Ethnography	Understanding a culture or distinct social group through participant observation; by making extensive field notes, the researcher tries to capture the culture's unique values and social processes	Provides a more complete and accurate description than can be derived from a single observational visit, interview, or questionnaire.	May be biased by researcher's values and theoretical preferences; findings cannot be applied to individuals and settings other than the ones studied.

Naturalistic observation also has a major limitation: Not all children have the same opportunity to display a particular behavior in everyday life. In the study just mentioned, some children might have witnessed child crying more often than others or been exposed to more cues for positive social responses from caregivers. For this reason, they might have displayed more compassion. Researchers commonly deal with this difficulty by making **structured observations** in a laboratory. In this approach, the investigator sets up a situation that evokes the behavior of interest so every participant has equal opportunity to display it. In one study, structured observations of children's comforting behavior were made by playing a tape recording simulating a baby crying in the next room. Using an intercom, children could either talk to the baby or flip a button so they did not have to listen. Children's facial reactions, the length of time they talked, and the extent to which they spoke in a comforting manner were recorded (Eisenberg et al., 1993).

Structured observation permits greater control over the research situation than does naturalistic observation. In addition, the method is especially useful for studying behaviors that investigators rarely have an opportunity to see in everyday life. For example, in a recent study, researchers wanted to find out how the presence of distracting toys

Structured observation
A method in which the researcher sets up a situation that evokes the behavior of interest and observes it in a laboratory.

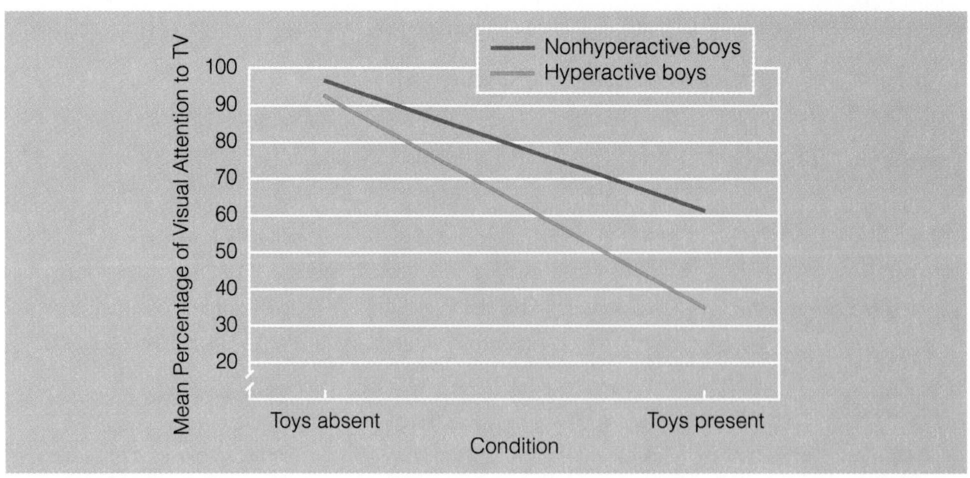

FIGURE 2.1

■ *Results of a study that used structured observations. The researchers wanted to know how the presence of distracting toys influenced hyperactive and nonhyperactive boys' attention to and learning from educational television. When toys were absent, attention to TV in the laboratory by both groups of boys was high. When toys were present, hyperactive boys spent only half as much time attending to TV as did their nonhyperactive counterparts. However, other findings revealed that both hyperactive and nonhyperactive boys remembered just as much information from the programs, suggesting that TV may be an especially effective medium for helping inattentive, overactive children learn. (From S. Landau, E. P. Lorch, & R. Milich, 1992, Visual attention to and comprehension of television in attention-deficit hyperactivity disordered and normal boys,* Child Development, *63, p. 933. © The Society for Research in Child Development, Inc. Reprinted by permission.)*

influences children's attention to and learning from educational television. They were particularly interested in hyperactive boys, who have great difficulty sitting still and paying attention. Television viewing, under these conditions, is hard to measure in children's homes. So the researchers furnished a laboratory like a living room, where they could control both TV programming and the presence of distracters. As expected, when toys were available, hyperactive 6- to 12-year-olds found them irresistible; they spent only half as much time watching the TV as did their nonhyperactive counterparts (see Figure 2.1). Yet surprisingly, recall of televised information in the presence of toys was similar for hyperactive and nonhyperactive boys. The inattentive, overactive participants appeared to learn effectively from TV, even when their attention was frequently diverted. These findings suggest that television may be an especially effective medium of instruction for hyperactive children, who typically do poorly in school (Landau, Lorch, & Milich, 1992). Of course, the great disadvantage of structured observations in studies like this one is that children may not behave in the laboratory as they do in their natural environments.

■ PROCEDURES FOR COLLECTING SYSTEMATIC OBSERVATIONS. The procedures used to collect systematic observations vary, depending on the research problem posed. Some investigators choose the **specimen record**, a description of the entire stream of behavior—everything said and done over a certain time period. In one of my own studies, I wanted to find out how sensitive, responsive, and verbally stimulating caregivers were when they interacted with children in day care centers (Berk, 1985). In this case, everything each caregiver said and did—even the amount of time she spent away from the children, taking coffee breaks and talking on the phone—was important.

In other studies, information on only one or a few kinds of behavior is needed, so it is not necessary to capture the entire behavior stream. In these instances, researchers may select more efficient observation procedures. One common approach is **event sampling**, in which the observer records all instances of a particular behavior of interest during a specified time period, ignoring other behaviors. In the study of preschoolers' responses to their peers' distress reported earlier, the researchers used event sampling by recording each instance in which a child cried at day care.

A second efficient means of observing is **time sampling**. In this procedure, the researcher records whether or not certain behaviors occur during a sample of short time

Specimen record
An observational procedure in which the researcher records a description of the participant's entire stream of behavior for a specified time period.

Event sampling
An observational procedure in which the researcher records all instances of a particular behavior during a specified time period.

Time sampling
An observational procedure in which the researcher records whether or not certain behaviors occur during a sample of short time intervals.

intervals. First, a checklist of the behaviors of interest is prepared. Then the observation period is divided into a series of brief time segments. For example, a half-hour observation period might be divided into 120 fifteen-second intervals. The observer collects data by alternately watching the child for an interval and then checking off behaviors during the next interval, repeating this process until the entire observation period is complete.

■ LIMITATIONS OF SYSTEMATIC OBSERVATION. A major problem in collecting systematic observations is the influence of the observer on the behavior being studied. The presence of a watchful, unfamiliar individual may cause children and adults to react in unnatural ways. For children below age 7 or 8, observer influence is generally limited to the first session or two that the unknown adult is present in the setting. Young children cannot stop "being themselves" for very long, and they quickly get used to the observer's presence. Older children and adults often engage in more positive, socially desirable behavior. In these instances, researchers can take their responses as an indication of the best behavior they can display under the circumstances.

There are ways that researchers can minimize **observer influence**. Adaptation periods, in which observers visit the research setting so participants have a chance to get used to their presence, are helpful. Another approach is to ask individuals who are part of the child's natural environment to do the observing. For example, in several studies, parents have been trained to record their children's behavior. Besides reducing the impact of an unfamiliar observer, this method permits information to be gathered on behaviors that would require observers to remain in the natural setting for a very long time to see them. In one such study, researchers wanted to know what kinds of TV programs children watch with their parents and which ones they watch alone. To find out, they asked parents to keep detailed diaries of the viewing behaviors of all family members for several 1-week periods (St. Peters et al., 1991).

In addition to observer influence, **observer bias** is a serious danger in observational research. When observers are aware of the purposes of a study, they may see and record what is expected rather than participants' actual behaviors. To guard against this problem, in most research it is wise to have people who have no knowledge of the investigator's hypotheses, or who at least have little personal investment in them, collect the observations.

Finally, although systematic observation provides invaluable information on how children and adults actually behave, it generally tells us little about the thinking and reasoning that underlie their behavior. For this kind of information, researchers must turn to another type of method—self-report techniques.

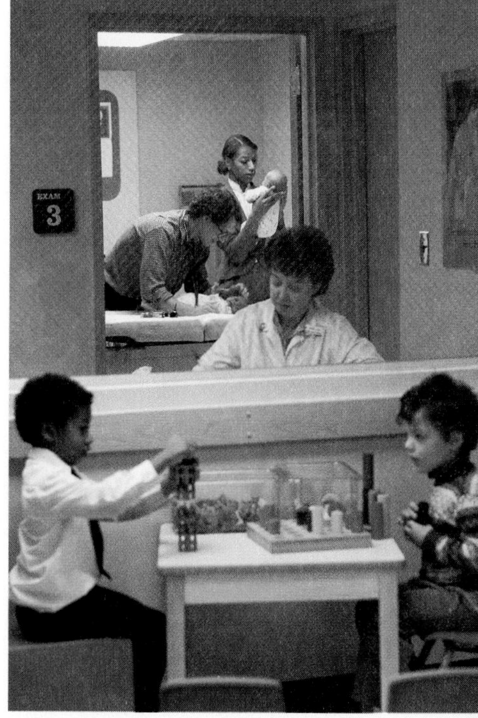

■ *By making structured observations in a laboratory, researchers can ensure that all paticipants have the same opportunity to display the behavior of interest. But participants may not respond in the laboratory as they do in everyday life.* (Dick Luria/FPG)

SELF-REPORTS: INTERVIEWS AND QUESTIONNAIRES

Self-reports are instruments that ask research participants to provide information on their perceptions, thoughts, abilities, feelings, attitudes, beliefs, and past experiences. They range from relatively unstructured clinical interviews, the method used by Piaget to study children's thinking, to highly structured interviews, questionnaires, and tests.

■ CLINICAL INTERVIEWS. Let's look at an example of a **clinical interview** in which Piaget questioned a 5-year-old child about his understanding of dreams:

> Where does the dream come from?—*I think you sleep so well that you dream.*—Does it come from us or from outside?—*From outside.*—What do we dream with?—*I don't know.*—With the hands? . . . With nothing?—*Yes, with nothing.*—When you are in bed and you dream, where is the dream?—*In my bed, under the blanket. I don't really know. If it was in my stomach, the bones would be in the way and I shouldn't see it.*—Is the dream there when you sleep?—*Yes it is in the bed beside me* . . . —You see the dream when you are in the room, but if I were in the room, too, should I see it?—*No, grownups don't ever dream.*—Can two people ever have the same dream?—*No, never.*—When the dream is in the room, is it near you?—*Yes, there!* (pointing to 30 cm in front of his eyes). (Piaget, 1926/1930, pp. 97–98)

Notice how Piaget used a flexible, conversational style to encourage the child to expand his ideas. Prompts are given to obtain a fuller picture of the child's reasoning.

Observer influence
The tendency of participants to react to the presence of an observer and behave in unnatural ways.

Observer bias
The tendency of observers who are aware of the purposes of a study to see and record what is expected rather than participants' actual behaviors.

Using the clinical interview, this researcher asks a mother to describe her child's development. The method permits large amounts of information to be gathered in a relatively short period of time. However, a major drawback of this method is that participants do not always report information accurately. (Tony Freeman/ Photo Edit)

The clinical interview has two major strengths. First, it permits people to display their thoughts in terms that are as close as possible to the way they think in everyday life. Second, it can provide a large amount of information in a fairly brief period of time. For example, in an hour-long session, a wide range of child-rearing information can be obtained from a parent—much more than could be captured by observing parent–child interaction for the same amount of time.

LIMITATIONS OF CLINICAL INTERVIEWS. A major limitation of the clinical interview has to do with the accuracy with which people report their own thoughts, feelings, and behaviors. Some participants, wanting to please the interviewer, may make up answers that do not represent their actual thinking. And because the clinical interview depends on verbal ability and expressiveness, it may not accurately assess individuals who have difficulty putting their thoughts into words. Skillful interviewers minimize these problems by wording questions carefully. They also watch for cues indicating that the participant may not have clearly understood a question or may need extra time to feel comfortable in the situation.

Interviews on certain topics are particularly vulnerable to distortion. In a few instances, researchers have been able to compare parents' and children's descriptions of events with information gathered years earlier, at the same time the events occurred. Reports of psychological states and family processes obtained on the two occasions show little or no agreement (Henry et al., 1994). Mothers, especially, are likely to speak about the past in glowing terms. They report faster development, fewer childhood problems, and child-rearing practices more in line with current expert advice than with records of their past behavior (Yarrow, Campbell, & Burton, 1970). Also, most parents find it difficult to recall specific instances of early events, although they can report general tendencies—for example, their disciplinary style as "strict" or "permissive." But strictness to one parent may register as permissiveness to another. Parents often have different definitions of these terms, making their recollections of child rearing virtually useless as predictors of children's development (Maccoby & Martin, 1983). Interviews that focus on current rather than past information and specific characteristics rather than global judgments show a better match with actual behavior. Even so, parents are far from perfect in describing their own practices and their children's personalities, preferences, and cognitive abilities (Kochanska, Kuczynski, & Radke-Yarrow, 1989; Miller & Davis, 1992).

Finally, we mentioned in Chapter 1 that the clinical interview has been criticized because of its flexibility. When questions are phrased differently for each participant, responses may be due to the manner of interviewing rather than real differences in the way people think about a certain topic. A second self-report method, the structured interview, reduces this problem.

Clinical interview
A method in which the researcher uses flexible, open-ended questions to probe for the participant's point of view.

Structured interview
A method in which the researcher asks each participant the same questions in the same way.

STRUCTURED INTERVIEWS, TESTS, AND QUESTIONNAIRES. In a **structured interview**, each individual is asked the same set of questions in the same way. As a result, this approach eliminates the possibility that an interviewer might press and prompt some participants more than others, thereby distorting the results. In addition, compared to clinical interviews, structured interviews are much more efficient. Answers are briefer, and researchers can obtain written responses from an entire class of children or group of parents at the same time. Also, when structured interviews use multiple choice, yes/no, and true/false formats, as is done on many tests and questionnaires, the answers can be tabulated by machine. However, keep in mind that these procedures do not yield the same depth of information as a clinical interview. And they can still be affected by the problem of inaccurate reporting.

PSYCHOPHYSIOLOGICAL METHODS

Researchers' desire to uncover the biological bases of children's perceptual, cognitive, and emotional responses has led to the use of **psychophysiological methods,** which measure the relationship between physiological processes and behavior. Investigators who rely on these methods want to find out which central nervous system structures contribute to development and individual differences in certain competencies. Another reason for psychophysiological methods is that they help identify the perceptions, thoughts, and emotions of infants and young children, who cannot report their psychological experiences clearly (Bornstein, 1992).

■ PSYCHOPHYSIOLOGICAL PROCEDURES. A wide variety of physiological responses have been recorded. Among the most common are measures of autonomic nervous system activity,[1] such as heart rate, blood pressure, respiration, pupil dilation, and electrical conductance of the skin. For example, heart rate is quite sensitive to psychological state. It can be used to infer whether an infant is staring blankly at a stimulus (heart rate is stable) or attending to and processing information (heart rate slows during concentration) (Izard et al., 1991; Porges, 1991). Heart rate variations are also linked to particular emotional expressions, such as interest, anger, and sadness (Fox & Fitzgerald, 1990). And as Chapter 10 will reveal, distinct patterns of autonomic activity are related to individual differences in temperament, such as shyness and sociability (Kagan, 1992).

Autonomic indicators of cognitive and emotional reactions have been enriched by measures of brain functioning. In an *electroencephalogram (EEG),* researchers tape electrodes to the scalp to record the electrical activity of the brain. EEG waves are related to different states of arousal (sleep–wakefulness), permitting precise determination of how these states vary with age. Investigators can also study *event-related potentials (ERPs),* or EEG waves that accompany particular events. For example, a unique wave pattern appears when infants over 4 months of age are re-exposed to a stimulus they saw only briefly before. It seems to reflect babies' efforts to search their memories for partially learned information (Nelson, 1993).

Finally, *functional brain-imaging techniques*, which yield three-dimensional pictures of brain activity, provide the most precise information currently available on which regions of the brain are specialized for certain functions, such as language or emotion. *Functional magnetic resonance imaging (fMRI)* is the most promising of these methods for research on children, since it does not depend on X-ray photography, which requires injection of radioactive substances. Instead, fMRI is completely noninvasive. Changes in blood flow within brain tissue in response to specific stimuli are detected magnetically, producing exceptionally clear computerized images of activated areas. Currently, fMRI is being used to study age-related changes in brain organization and the brain functioning of children with serious learning and emotional problems (Mattson, Jernigan, & Riley, 1994; Schifter et al., 1994; Schultz et al., 1994).

■ LIMITATIONS OF PSYCHOPHYSIOLOGICAL METHODS. Despite their virtues, psychophysiological methods have limitations. First, interpreting physiological responses involves a high degree of inference. Even though a stimulus produces a consistent pattern of autonomic or brain activity, investigators cannot be certain that an infant or child has consciously processed it in a particular way. Second, many factors besides those of

Psychophysiological methods
Methods that measure the relation between physiological processes and behavior. Among the most common are measures of autonomic nervous system activity (such as heart rate and respiration) and measures of brain functioning (such as the electroencephalogram [EEG], event-related potentials [ERPs], and functional magnetic resonance imaging [fMRI]).

[1] The autonomic nervous system regulates involuntary actions of the body. It is divided into two parts: the *sympathetic nervous system*, which mobilizes energy to deal with threatening situations (as when your heart rate rises in response to a fear-arousing event); and the *parasympathetic nervous sustem*, which acts to conserve energy (as when your heart rate slows as you focus on an interesting stimulus).

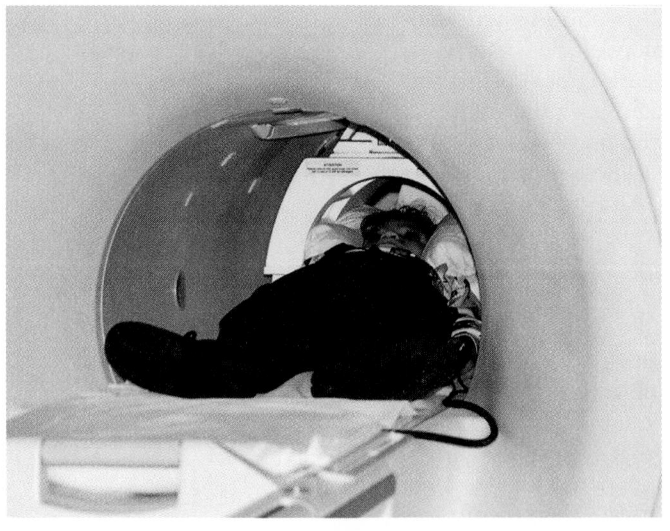

(a)

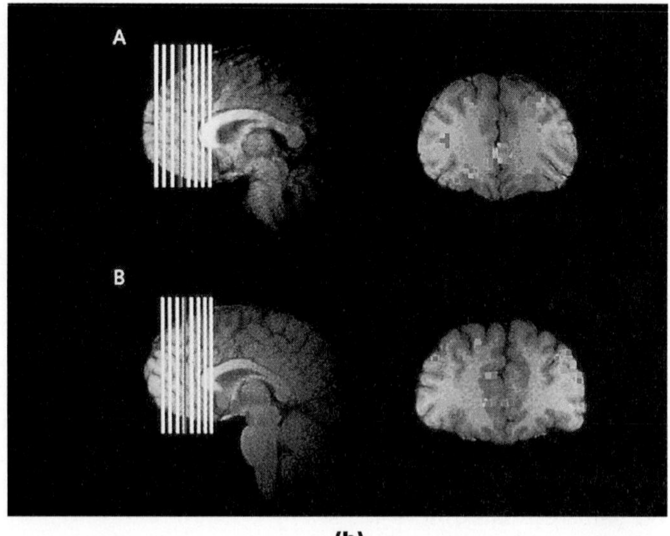

(b)

■ *In functional magnetic resonance imaging (fMRI), the child looks up at a stimulus, and changes in blood flow within brain tissue are detected magnetically (a). The result is a computerized image of activated areas (b), permitting study of age-related changes in brain organization and the brain functioning of children with serious learning and emotional problems. (B.J. Casey/UPMC)*

interest can influence a physiological response. A researcher who takes a change in heart rate, respiration, or brain activity as an indicator of information processing must make sure that it was not due to the child's fearful reaction to the laboratory equipment or (particularly with infants) to hunger, boredom, or fatigue (Tyc et al., 1995). Without efforts to minimize extraneous influences like these, detection of correspondences between physiological and psychological reactions is difficult or impossible.

THE CLINICAL OR CASE STUDY METHOD

In Chapter 1, we discussed the **clinical method** (sometimes called the *case study* approach) as an outgrowth of the psychoanalytic perspective, which stresses the importance of understanding the individual. Recall that the clinical method brings together a wide range of information on a single child, including interviews, observations, and test scores. Today, psychophysiological measures are sometimes included as well (Haynes, 1991). The aim is to obtain as complete a picture as possible of that child's psychological functioning and the experiences that led up to it.

Although clinical studies are usually carried out on children with developmental problems, they sometimes focus on well-adjusted youngsters. In one investigation, the researchers wanted to find out what contributes to the accomplishments of children with extraordinary intellectual talents. Among the six prodigies studied intensively was Adam, a boy who read, wrote, and composed musical pieces before he was out of diapers. Adam's parents provided a home exceedingly rich in stimulation, and raised him with affection, firmness, and humor. They searched for schools in which he could develop his talents while forming rewarding social relationships. By age 4, Adam was deeply involved in mastering human symbol systems—BASIC for the computer, French, German, Russian, Sanskrit, Greek, ancient hieroglyphs, music, and mathematics. Would Adam have realized his abilities without the chance combination of his special gift with nurturing, committed parents? Probably not, the investigators concluded (Feldman & Goldsmith, 1991). Adam's case illustrates the unique strengths of the clinical method. It yields case narratives that are rich in descriptive detail and that offer valuable insights into factors that affect development.

Clinical method
A method in which the researcher attempts to understand the unique individual child by combining interview data, observations, test scores, and sometimes psychophysiological assessments.

The clinical method, like all others, has drawbacks. Information is often collected unsystematically and subjectively, permitting too much leeway for researchers' theoretical preferences to bias their observations and interpretations. In addition, investigators cannot assume that the findings of clinical research apply to anyone other than the particular child studied. For these reasons, the insights drawn from clinical investigations need to be tested further with other research strategies before they can be accepted as accurate and generalizable.

ETHNOGRAPHY

Because of a growing interest in the impact of culture, child development researchers have begun to rely increasingly on a method borrowed from the field of anthropology—**ethnography**. Like the clinical method, ethnographic research is largely a descriptive, qualitative technique. But instead of aiming to understand a single individual, it is directed toward understanding a culture or a distinct social group (Winthrop, 1991).

The ethnographic method achieves its goals through *participant observation.* Typically, the researcher lives with the cultural community for a period of months or years, participating in all aspects of its daily life. Extensive field notes, which consist of a mix of observations, self-reports from members of the culture, and interpretations by the investigator, are gathered. Later, these notes are put together into a description of the community that tries to capture its unique values and social processes.

The ethnographic approach assumes that by entering into close and long-term contact with a social group, researchers can understand the beliefs and behavior of its members more accurately, in a way not possible with a single observational visit, interview, or questionnaire. Ethnographies of children from diverse cultures currently exist, and many more are being compiled. In some, investigators focus on many aspects of children's experience, as one team of researchers did in describing what it is like to grow up in a small American town (Peshkin, 1978). In other instances, the research is limited to one or a few settings, such as home or school life (Chang, 1992; LeVine et al., 1994). Because the ethnographic method is committed to trying to understand others' perspectives, it often overturns widely held stereotypes, as the Cultural Influences box on page 50 reveals.

Ethnographers strive to minimize their influence on the culture being studied by becoming part of it. Nevertheless, at times their presence does alter the situation. In addition, as with clinical research, investigators' cultural values and theoretical commitments sometimes lead them to observe selectively or misinterpret what they see. Finally, the findings of ethnographic studies cannot be assumed to generalize beyond the people and settings in which the research was originally conducted (Hammersley, 1992).

BRIEF REVIEW

Researchers use naturalistic observation to gather information on children's everyday behaviors. When it is necessary to control the conditions of observation, researchers often make structured observations in a laboratory. The flexible, conversational style of the clinical interview provides a wealth of information on the reasoning behind behavior. However, participants may not report their thoughts accurately, and comparing their responses is difficult. The structured interview is a more efficient method that questions each person in the same way, but it does not yield the same depth of information as a clinical interview. Psychophysiological methods are used to uncover the biological bases of children's behavior. However, they require a high degree of inference about the meaning of physiological responses. Clinical studies of individual children provide rich insights into processes of development, but the information obtained is often unsystematic and subjective. In ethnographic research, an investigator tries to understand a culture or distinct social group through participant observation. Like clinical studies, ethnographies can be affected by researchers' theoretical biases, and the findings may not generalize beyond the people studied.

Ethnography
A method in which the researcher attempts to understand the unique values and social processes of a culture or a distinct social group by living with its members and taking field notes for an extended period of time.

CULTURAL INFLUENCES

School Matters in Mexican-American Homes: An Ethnographic Study

For many years, the poor school achievement of low-income minority children was attributed to "cultural deficits"—home environments that place little value on education. Recent ethnographic research on Mexican-American families challenges this assumption. Concha Delgado-Gaitan (1992) spent many months getting to know the residents of a Mexican-American community in a small California city. There she collected extensive field notes on six families in which parents had recently immigrated to the United States. Each had a second-grade child. While in the homes, Delgado-Gaitan carefully examined children's experiences related to education.

Although the parents had little schooling themselves, they regarded education as a great privilege and supported their children's learning in many ways. Their homes were cramped, one-bedroom apartments, occasionally shared with relatives. Still, parents did their best to create a stable environment that encouraged children to think positively about school. They offered material rewards for good grades (such as a new book or dinner at a favorite restaurant), set regular bedtime hours, and where possible provided a special place for doing schoolwork. And they frequently spoke to their children about their own educational limitations and the importance of taking advantage of the opportunity to study.

■ *This Mexican-American mother tries to support her children's academic development by helping with homework and providing a quiet place for study. Ethnographic research reveals that how well she will succeed depends on access to information and resources from the school. (Comstock)*

During the week, most parent–child conversations revolved around homework. All parents tried to help with assignments and foster behaviors valued in school. But how well they succeeded depended on social networks through which they could obtain information about educational matters. Some parents relied on relatives who had more experience in dealing with the school system. Others sought out individuals at church or work as advisers.

When social support was available, perplexing school problems were quickly resolved. For example, one parent, Mrs. Matias, received repeated reports from her son Jorge's teacher about his unruly behavior. Finally, a note arrived threatening suspension if Jorge did not improve. Mrs. Matias consulted one of her co-workers, who suggested that she ask for permission to leave during the lunch hour to talk with Jorge's teacher. After a conference revealed that Jorge needed to stay away from certain boys who were provoking him, his fighting subsided.

Despite sincere efforts, lack of familiarity with school tasks hampered Mexican-American parents' ability to help their children. For example, Mrs. Serna insisted that her poorly achieving daughter Norma do her homework at regularly scheduled times, and she checked to make sure that Norma completed her assignments. But when she tried to assist Norma, Mrs. Serna frequently misinterpreted the instructions. And she did not understand the school environment well enough to contact teachers for information about how to support her child. As a result, Norma's progress remained below average.

Discontinuity between Mexican cultural values and the requirements of the school was often at the heart of children's academic difficulties. At home, respect for elders was emphasized. Mexican-American children learned not to express verbal opinions (especially contrary opinions) to adults, but instead to listen and follow directions. Yet in their classrooms, they were expected to demonstrate critical thinking by asking and responding to questions and formulating verbal arguments—behaviors in conflict with the teachings of their parents (Delgado-Gaitan, 1994).

Although the Mexican-American families had limited income and material resources, this did not detract from their desire to create conditions conducive to learning. As they became increasingly aware of cultural discontinuity between home and school, the parents formed a community organization whose major purpose was sharing knowledge about how to help their children succeed academically. Through regular meetings, they devised ways to make the home more compatible with the school while maintaining their cultural identity (Delgado-Gaitain, 1994). For example, parents began to accept their children's questions, particularly with respect to school matters, as necessary for academic progress. Gradually, the organization became a source of empowerment, opening lines of communication with school personnel so that parents had easier access to the resources they needed to strengthen their children's learning.

Delgado-Gaitan's ethnographic research shows that education of ethnic minority children can be promoted through informal social ties and community organizing. In this Mexican-American community, parents joined together as catalysts for cultural change, establishing vital links between home and school.

Reliability and Validity: Keys to Scientifically Sound Research

Once investigators choose their research methods, they must take special steps to make sure their procedures provide trustworthy information about the topic of interest. To be acceptable to the scientific community, observations, physiological measures, and self-reports must be both *reliable* and *valid*—two keys to scientifically sound research.

RELIABILITY

Suppose you go into a classroom and record the number of times a child behaves in a helpful and cooperative fashion toward others, but your research partner, in simultaneously observing the same child, comes up with a very different set of measurements. Or you ask a group of children some questions about their interests, but a week later when you question them again, their answers are very different. **Reliability** refers to the consistency, or repeatability, of measures of behavior. To be reliable, observations of peoples' actions cannot be unique to a single observer. Instead, observers must agree on what they see. And an interview, test, or questionnaire, when given again within a short period of time (before participants can reasonably be expected to change their opinions or develop more sophisticated responses) must yield similar results on both occasions.

Researchers determine the reliability of data in different ways. In observational research, observers are asked to record the same behavior sequences, and agreement between them is assessed. Reliability of self-report and psychophysiological data can be demonstrated by finding out how similar children's responses are when the same measures are given on another occasion. In the case of self-reports, children's scores can also be compared on different forms of the same test. If necessary, reliability can be estimated from a single testing session by comparing children's scores on different halves of the test.

VALIDITY

For research methods to have high **validity**, they must accurately measure characteristics that the researcher set out to measure. Think, for a moment, about this idea, and you will quickly see that reliability is absolutely essential for valid research. Methods that are implemented carelessly, unevenly, and inconsistently cannot possibly represent what an investigator originally intended to study.

But reliability by itself is not sufficient to ensure that a method will reflect the investigator's goals. Researchers must go further to guarantee validity, and they generally do so in several ways. They may carefully examine the content of observations and self-reports to make sure the behaviors of interest are included. For example, a test intended to measure fifth-grade children's knowledge of mathematics would not be valid if it contained addition problems but no subtraction, multiplication, or division problems (Miller, 1997). Another approach to validity is to see how effective a method is in predicting behavior in other situations that we would reasonably expect it to predict. If scores on a math test are valid, they should be related to how well children do on their math assignments in school or even to how quickly and accurately they can make change in a game of Monopoly.

As we turn now to research designs, you will discover that the concept of validity can also be applied more broadly, to the overall accuracy of research findings and conclusions. If, during any phase of carrying out a study—selecting participants, choosing research settings and tasks, and implementing procedures—the researcher permits factors unrelated to the hypothesis to influence behavior, then the validity of the results is in doubt, and they cannot be considered a fair test of the investigator's theory. As you read the following sections, keep a list of the many possible threats to the validity of research that can occur in the course of designing and conducting an investigation.

Reliability
The consistency, or repeatability, of measures of behavior.

Validity
The extent to which measures in a research study accurately reflect what the investigator intended to measure.

General Research Designs

In deciding which research design to use, investigators choose a way of setting up a study that permits them to test their hypotheses with the greatest certainty possible. Two main types of designs are used in all research on human behavior: correlational and experimental.

CORRELATIONAL DESIGN

In a **correlational design**, researchers gather information on already existing groups of individuals, generally in natural life circumstances, and no effort is made to alter their experiences in any way. Suppose we want to answer such questions as: Do structure and organization in the home make a difference in children's school performance? Does attending a day care center promote children's friendliness with peers? Do mothers' styles of interacting with their children have any bearing on the children's intelligence? In these and many other instances, the conditions of interest are very difficult to arrange and control.

The correlational design offers a way of looking at relationships between participants' experiences or characteristics and their behavior or development. But correlational studies have one major limitation: We cannot infer cause and effect. For example, if we find in a correlational study that maternal interaction does relate to children's intelligence, we would not know whether mothers' behavior actually causes intellectual differences among children. In fact, the opposite is certainly possible. The behaviors of highly intelligent children may be so attractive that they cause mothers to interact more favorably. Or a third variable that we did not even think about studying, such as the amount of noise and distraction in the home, may be causing both maternal interaction and children's intelligence to change together in the same direction.

In correlational studies, and in other types of research designs, investigators often examine relationships among variables by using a **correlation coefficient**, which is a number that describes how two measures, or variables, are associated with one another. Although other statistical approaches to examining relationships are also available, we will encounter the correlation coefficient in discussing research findings throughout this book. So let's look at what it is and how it is interpreted. A correlation coefficient can range in value from +1.00 to –1.00. The *magnitude, or size, of the number* shows the *strength of the relationship.* A zero correlation indicates no relationship; but the closer the value is to +1.00 or –1.00, the stronger the relationship that exists. For instance, a correlation of –.52 is a stronger relationship than –.25, but correlations of +.50 and –.50 are equally strong. The *sign of the number* (+ or –) refers to the *direction of the relationship.* A positive sign (+) means that as one variable increases, the other also increases. A negative sign (–) indicates that as one variable increases, the other decreases.

■ *Is warm, attentive parenting related to children's development? A correlational design can be used to answer this question, but it does not permit researchers to determine the precise cause of their findings. (Myrleen Ferguson Cate/PhotoEdit)*

Correlational design
A research design in which the investigator gathers information without altering participants' experiences and examines relationships between variables. Does not permit inferences about cause and effect.

Correlation coefficient
A number, ranging from +1.00 to -1.00, that describes the strength and direction of the relationship between two variables.

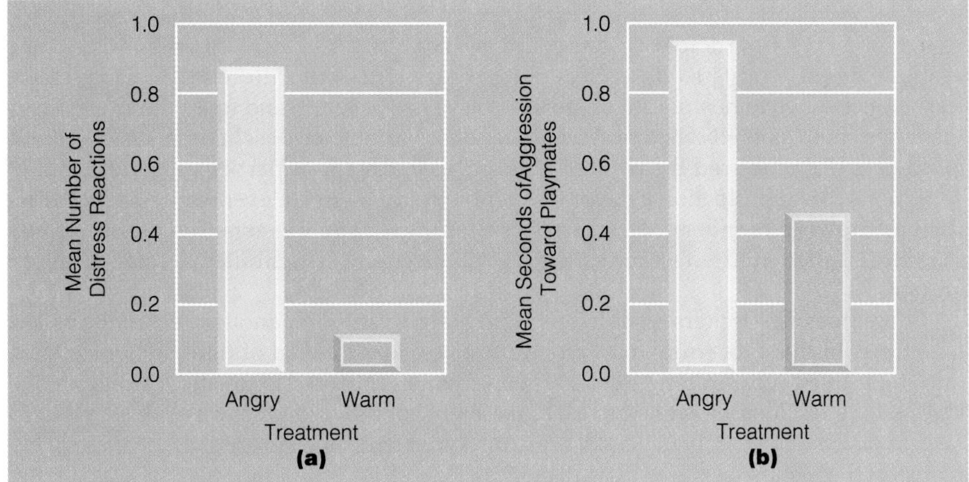

FIGURE 2.2

How does the quality of adult interaction affect 2-year-olds' emotional reactions? A laboratory experiment showed that exposure to angry adult interaction increased children's emotional distress (a) and aggressive behavior (b) toward playmates. (Adapted from Cummings, Iannotti, & Zahn-Waxler, 1985.)

Let's take some examples to illustrate how a correlation coefficient works. In one study, a researcher found that a measure of maternal language stimulation at 13 months was positively correlated with the size of children's vocabularies at 20 months, at +.50 (Tamis-LeMonda & Bornstein, 1994). This is a moderately high correlation, which indicates that the more mothers spoke to their infants, the more advanced their children were in spoken language during the second year of life. In another study, a researcher reported that the extent to which mothers ignored their 10-month-olds' bids for attention was negatively correlated with children's willingness to comply with parental demands 1 year later—at −.46 for boys and −.36 for girls (Martin, 1981). These moderate correlations reveal that the more mothers ignored their babies, the less cooperative their children were during the second year of life.

Both of these investigations found a relationship between maternal behavior in the first year and children's behavior in the second year. Although the researchers suspected that maternal behavior affected children's responses, in neither study could they really be sure about cause and effect. However, if we find a relationship in a correlational study, this suggests that it would be worthwhile to track down its cause with a more powerful experimental strategy, if possible.

EXPERIMENTAL DESIGN

Unlike correlational studies, an **experimental design** permits us to make inferences about cause and effect. In an experiment, the events and behaviors of interest are divided into two types: independent and dependent variables. The **independent variable** is the one anticipated by the investigator, on the basis of a hypothesis or research question, to cause changes in another variable. The **dependent variable** is the one the investigator expects to be influenced by the independent variable. Inferences about cause-and-effect relationships are possible because the researcher directly controls or manipulates changes in the independent variable. This is done by exposing participants to two or more treatment conditions and comparing their performance on measures of the dependent variable.

In one **laboratory experiment**, researchers wanted to know if the quality of interaction between adults (independent variable) affects young children's emotional reactions while playing with a familiar peer (dependent variable). Pairs of 2-year-olds were brought into a laboratory set up to look much like a family home. One group was exposed to a warm treatment in which two adults in the kitchen spoke in a friendly way while the children played in the living room. A second group received an angry treatment in which positive communication between the adults was interrupted by an argument in which they shouted, complained, and slammed the door. As Figure 2.2(a) reveals, children in the angry condition displayed much more distress (such as freezing in place, anxious facial expressions, and crying). And as Figure 2.2(b) shows, they also exhibited more aggression toward their playmates than did children in the warm treatment (Cummings, Iannotti, & Zahn-Waxler, 1985). The experiment revealed that exposure to even short episodes of intense adult anger can trigger negative emotions and antisocial behavior in very young children.

Experimental design
A research design in which the investigator randomly assigns participants to treatment conditions. Permits inferences about cause and effect.

Independent variable
The variable manipulated by the researcher in an experiment by randomly assigning participants to treatment conditions.

Dependent variable
The variable the researcher expects to be influenced by the independent variable in an experiment.

Laboratory experiment
An experiment conducted in the laboratory, which permits the maximum possible control over treatment conditions.

In experimental studies, investigators must take special precautions to control for characteristics of participants that could reduce the accuracy of their findings. For example, in the study just described, if a greater number of children who had already learned to behave in hostile and aggressive ways happened to end up in the angry treatment, we could not tell whether the independent variable or the children's background characteristics produced the results. **Random assignment** of participants to treatment conditions offers protection against this problem. By using an evenhanded procedure, such as drawing numbers out of a hat or flipping a coin, the experimenter increases the chances that children's characteristics will be equally distributed across treatment groups.

Sometimes researchers combine random assignment with another technique called **matching**. In this procedure, participants are measured ahead of time on the factor in question—in our example, aggression. Then equal numbers of high- and low-aggressive children are randomly assigned to each treatment condition. In this way, the experimental groups are deliberately matched, or made equivalent, on characteristics that are likely to distort the results.

MODIFIED EXPERIMENTAL DESIGNS

Most experiments are conducted in laboratories where researchers can achieve the maximum possible control over treatment conditions. But, as we have already indicated, findings obtained in laboratories may not always apply to everyday situations. The ideal solution to this problem is to do experiments in the field as a complement to laboratory investigations. In **field experiments**, researchers capitalize on rare opportunities to randomly assign people to treatment conditions in natural settings. In the experiment we just considered, we can conclude that the emotional climate established by adults affects children's behavior in the laboratory. But does it also do so in daily life?

Another study helps answer this question. This time, the research was carried out in a day care center. A caregiver deliberately interacted differently with two groups of preschoolers. In one condition (the *nurturant treatment*), she modeled many instances of warmth, helpfulness, and concern for others. In a second condition (the *control*, since it involved no treatment), she behaved as usual, with no special concern for others. Two weeks later, the researchers created several situations that called for helpfulness in a room adjoining the day care center. For example, a visiting mother asked each child to watch her baby for a few moments, but the baby's toys had fallen out of the playpen. The investigators recorded whether or not each child returned the toys to the baby. As Figure 2.3 shows, children exposed to the nurturant treatment behaved in a much more helpful way than those in the control condition (Yarrow, Scott, & Waxler, 1973).

FIGURE 2.3

■ *Does the emotional climate established by adults affect children's behavior in everyday life? In a field experiment conducted in a day care center, children exposed to a nurturant treatment in which a caregiver modeled helpfulness and concern for others were far more likely than children in the control condition to show helpfulness themselves. (Adapted from Yarrow, Scott, & Waxler, 1973.*

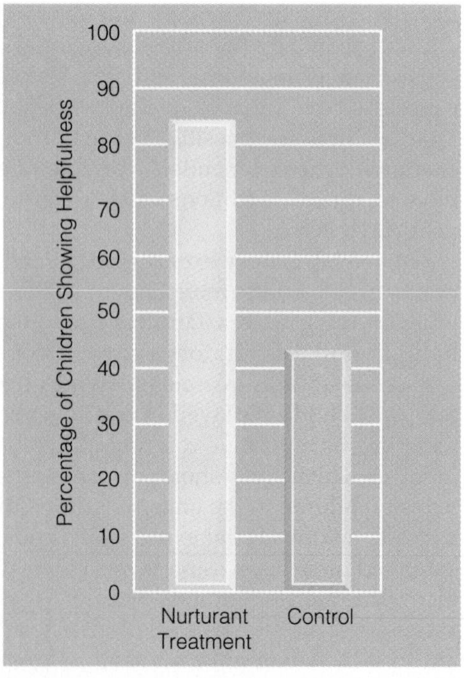

Random assignment
An evenhanded procedure for assigning participants to treatment groups, such as drawing numbers out of a hat or flipping a coin. Increases the chances that participants' characteristics will be equally distributed across treatment conditions in an experiment.

Matching
A procedure for assigning participants with similar characteristics in equal numbers to treatment conditions in an experiment. Ensures that groups will be equivalent on factors likely to distort the results.

Field experiment
A research design in which participants are randomly assigned to treatment conditions in natural settings.

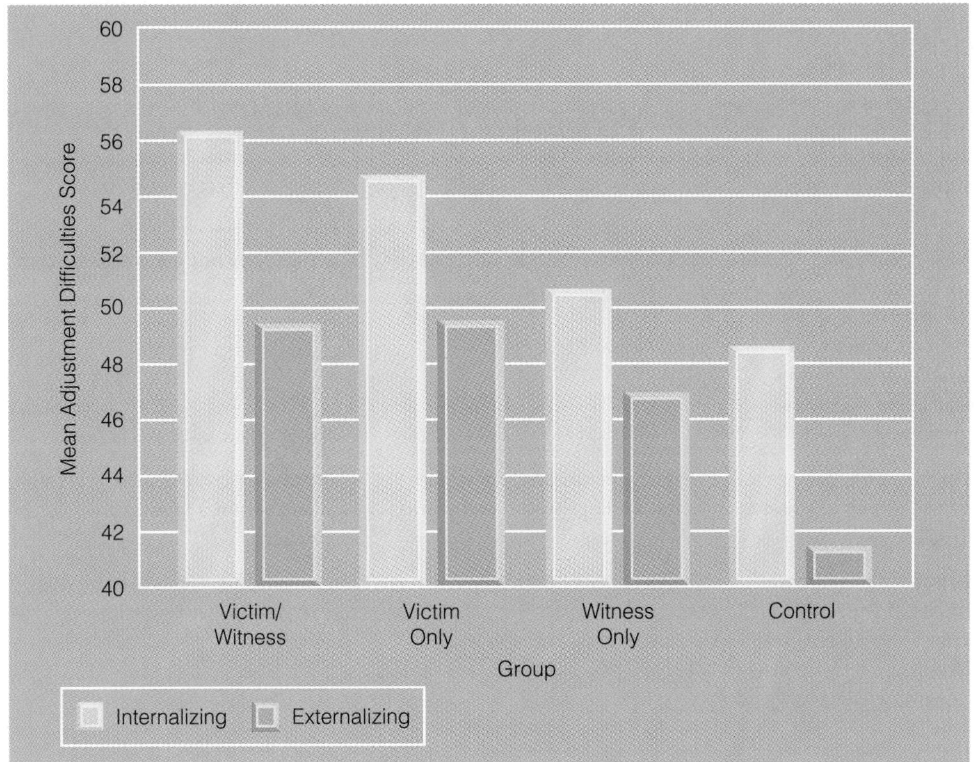

FIGURE 2.4

■ *Relationship of domestic violence to 8- to 12-year-olds' self-reports of two types of adjustment difficulties: internalizing problems (feeling sad, unwanted, and less healthy than peers) and externalizing problems (behaving in ways likely to get children in trouble with parents and teachers, such as aggressing or committing delinquent acts). Both victims and witnesses of violence reported more problems than did controls from nonviolent homes. However, children who experienced abuse reacted more strongly than did those who merely observed it. (Adapted from Sternberg et al., 1993.)*

In testing many hypotheses, researchers cannot randomly assign participants and manipulate conditions in the real world, as these investigators were able to do. Sometimes researchers can compromise by conducting **natural experiments**. Treatments that already exist, such as different family environments, schools, day care centers, and preschool programs, are compared. These studies differ from correlational research only in that groups of people are carefully chosen to ensure that their characteristics are as much alike as possible. In this way, investigators rule out as best they can alternative explanations for treatment effects.

In one such study, researchers wanted to know the extent to which witnessing spouse abuse (a husband physically hurting his wife) affects children's psychological adjustment. They conducted their investigation in Israel, where domestic violence is not as closely associated with other stressors (such as parental drug and alcohol abuse, divorce, and poverty) as it is in the United States. Consequently, they could control these factors more easily. As Figure 2.4 reveals, four groups of 8- to 12-year-olds were compared: children who were both victims and witnesses of abuse, victims only, witnesses only, and controls from nonviolent homes. Findings showed that experiencing abuse led children to report more unhappiness and troubled behavior than did observing abuse. Child witnesses, in turn, reported more adjustment difficulties than did controls matched with the other groups on a variety of background characteristics. In sum, exposure to either type of domestic violence appeared harmful, although children reacted more strongly as victims than witnesses (Sternberg et al., 1993). Despite careful efforts of investigators to equate existing groups, we must keep in mind that natural experiments cannot achieve the precision and rigor of true experimental research.

To help you compare the correlational and experimental designs we have discussed, Table 2.2 on page 56 summarizes their strengths and limitations. Now let's take a close look at designs for studying development.

Natural experiment
A research design in which the investigator studies already existing treatments in natural settings by carefully selecting groups of participants with similar characteristics.

TABLE 2.2

Strengths and Limitations of General Research Designs

Design	Description	Strengths	Limitations
Correlational design	The investigator obtains information on already existing groups, without altering participants' experiences.	Permits study of relationships between variables.	Does not permit inferences about cause-and-effect relationships.
Laboratory experiment	Under controlled laboratory conditions, the investigator manipulates an independent variable and looks at its effect on a dependent variable; requires random assignment of participants to treatment conditions.	Permits inferences about cause-and-effect relationships.	Findings may not generalize to the real world.
Field experiment	The investigator randomly assigns participants to treatment conditions in natural settings.	Permits generalization of experimental findings to the real world.	Control over treatment is generally weaker than in a laboratory experiment.
Natural experiment	The investigator compares already existing treatments in the real world, carefully selecting them to ensure that groups of participants are as much alike in characteristics as possible.	Permits study of naturally occurring variables not subject to experimenter manipulation.	Obtained differences may be due to variables other than the treatment.

Designs for Studying Development

Scientists interested in child development require information about the way research participants change over time. To answer questions about development, they must extend correlational and experimental approaches to include measurements at different ages. Longitudinal and cross-sectional designs are special *developmental* research strategies. In each, age comparisons form the basis of the research plan.

THE LONGITUDINAL DESIGN

In a **longitudinal design**, a group of participants is studied repeatedly at different ages, and changes are noted as they mature. The time span may be relatively short (a few months to several years) or very long (a decade or even a lifetime).

■ ADVANTAGES OF THE LONGITUDINAL DESIGN. The longitudinal approach has two major strengths. First, since it tracks the performance of each person over time, researchers can identify common patterns of development as well as individual differences in the paths children follow to maturity. Second, longitudinal studies permit investigators to examine relationships between early and later events and behaviors. Let's take an example to illustrate these ideas.

Recently, a group of researchers wondered whether children who display extreme personality styles—either angry and explosive or shy and withdrawn—retain the same dispositions when they become adults. In addition, they wanted to know what kinds of experiences promote stability or change in personality and what consequences explosiveness and shyness have for long-term adjustment. To answer these questions, the researchers delved into the archives of the Guidance Study, a well-known longitudinal investigation initiated in 1928 at the University of California, Berkeley, and continued over several decades (Caspi, Elder, & Bem, 1987, 1988).

Results revealed that the two styles were only moderately stable. Between ages 8 and 30, a good number of individuals remained the same, whereas others changed substantially. When stability did occur, it appeared to be due to a "snowballing effect," in which

Longitudinal design
A research design in which one group of participants is studied repeatedly at different ages.

children evoked responses from adults and peers that acted to maintain their dispositions. In other words, explosive youngsters were likely to be treated with anger and hostility (to which they reacted with even greater unruliness), whereas shy children were apt to be ignored.

Persistence of extreme personality styles affected many areas of adult adjustment, but these outcomes were different for males and females. For men, the results of early explosiveness were most apparent in their work lives, in the form of conflicts with supervisors, frequent job changes, and unemployment. Since few women in this sample of an earlier generation worked after marriage, their family lives were most affected. Explosive girls grew up to be hotheaded wives and mothers who were especially prone to divorce. Sex-related differences in the long-term consequences of shyness were even greater. Men who had been withdrawn in childhood were delayed in marrying, becoming fathers, and developing careers. Because a withdrawn, unassertive style was socially acceptable for females, women who had shy personalities showed no special adjustment problems.

■ PROBLEMS IN CONDUCTING LONGITUDINAL RESEARCH. Despite their strengths, longitudinal investigations confront researchers with a number of problems. There are practical difficulties, such as obtaining enough financial support and waiting the many years it takes for meaningful results in a long-term study. In addition, many factors can create serious difficulties for the validity of the findings.

Biased sampling is a common problem in longitudinal research. People who willingly participate in research that requires them to be continually observed and tested over many years are likely to have unique characteristics—at the very least, a special appreciation for the scientific value of research. As a result, we cannot easily generalize from them to the rest of the population. Furthermore, due to **selective attrition**, longitudinal samples generally become more biased as the investigation proceeds. Participants may move away or drop out for other reasons, and the ones who remain are likely to differ in important ways from the ones who do not continue.

The very experience of being repeatedly observed, interviewed, and tested can also threaten the validity of a longitudinal study. Children and adults may gradually be alerted to their own thoughts, feelings, and actions, think about them, and revise them in ways that have little to do with age-related change. In addition, with repeated testing, participants may become "test-wise." Their performance may improve as a result of **practice effects**—better test-taking skills and increased familiarity with the test, not because of factors commonly associated with development.

But the most widely discussed threat to the accuracy of longitudinal findings is cultural-historical change, or what are commonly called **cohort effects**. Longitudinal studies examine the development of *cohorts*—children born in the same time period who are influenced by a particular set of cultural and historical conditions. Results based on one cohort may not apply to children growing up at other times. For example, children's intelligence test performance may be affected by differences in the quality of public schooling from one decade to another or by generational changes in parental values regarding the importance of stimulating children's mental development. And a longitudinal study of adolescent social development would probably result in quite different findings if it were carried out in the 1990s, around the time of World War II, or during the Great Depression of the 1930s. (See the Cultural Influences box on page 58.)

Finally, changes occurring within the field of child development may create problems for longitudinal research covering an extended time period. Theories and methods are constantly changing, and those that first inspired a longitudinal study may become outdated (Nunnally, 1982). For this reason, as well as the others just mentioned, many recent longitudinal studies are short term, spanning only a few months or years in a child's life. In this way, researchers are spared some of the formidable obstacles that threaten longitudinal investigations lasting from childhood to maturity.

THE CROSS-SECTIONAL DESIGN

The length of time it takes for many behaviors to change, even in limited longitudinal studies, has led researchers to turn toward a more convenient strategy for studying development. In the **cross-sectional design**, groups of people differing in age are studied at the same point in time.

Biased sampling
Failure to select participants who are representative of the population of interest in a study.

Selective attrition
Selective loss of participants during an investigation, resulting in a biased sample.

Practice effects
Changes in participants' natural responses as a result of repeated testing.

Cohort effects
The effects of cultural-historical change on the accuracy of findings: Children born in one period of time are influenced by particular cultural and historical conditions.

Cross-sectional design
A research design in which groups of participants of different ages are studied at the same point in time.

SOCIAL ISSUES

Impact of Historical Times on Development: The Great Depression and World War II

Economic disaster, wars, and periods of rapid social change can profoundly affect people's lives. Yet their impact depends on when they strike during the life course. Glen Elder (1974) capitalized on the extent to which families experienced economic hardship during the Great Depression of the 1930s to study its influence on development. He delved into the vast archives of two major longitudinal studies: (1) the Oakland Growth Study, an investigation of individuals born in the early 1920s who were adolescents when the Depression took its toll; and (2) the Guidance Study, whose participants were born in the late 1920s and were young children when their families faced severe economic losses.

In both cohorts, relationships changed when economic deprivation struck. As unemployed fathers lost status, mothers were granted greater control over family affairs. This reversal of traditional gender roles often sparked conflict. Fathers sometimes became explosive and punitive toward their children. At other times, they withdrew from family interaction into passivity and depression. Mothers often became frantic with worry over the well-being of their husbands and children, and many entered the labor force to make ends meet (Elder, Liker, & Cross, 1984).

Although unusual burdens were placed on them as family lives changed, the Oakland Growth Study cohort—especially the boys—weathered economic hardship quite well. As adolescents, they were too old to be wholly dependent on their highly stressed parents, and their energies were often channeled into productive activities. Boys spent less time at home as they searched for part-time jobs, and many turned toward adults and peers outside the family for emotional support. Girls took over the responsibility of household chores and caring for younger siblings. Their greater involvement in family affairs led them to be exposed to more parental conflict and unhappiness. Consequently, adjustment of adolescent girls in economically deprived homes was somewhat less favorable than that of adolescent boys (Elder, Van Nguyen, & Caspi, 1985).

These changes in adolescents' lives had major consequences for their future aspirations. Girls' interests focused on home and family even more than was typical for that time period, and they were less likely to think about college and careers. Boys learned that economic resources could not be taken for granted, and they tended to make a very early commitment to an occupational choice.

The impact of the Depression continued to be apparent as adolescents entered adulthood. Girls from economically deprived homes remained committed to domestic life, and many married at an early age. Men had a strong desire for economic security, and they changed jobs less often than those from nondeprived backgrounds. The chance to become a parent was especially important to men whose lives had been disrupted by the Depression. Perhaps because they felt a rewarding career could not be guaranteed, these men viewed children as the most enduring benefit of their adult lives.

Unlike the Oakland Growth Study cohort, the Guidance Study participants were within the years of intense family dependency when the Depression struck. For young boys (who, as we will see in later chapters, are especially prone to adjustment problems in the face of family stress), the impact of economic strain was severe. They showed emotional difficulties and poor attitudes toward school and work that persisted through the teenage years (Elder & Caspi, 1988; Elder, Caspi, & Van Nguyen, 1986).

But as the Guidance Study sample became adolescents, another major historical event occurred: in 1939, the United States entered World War II. As a result, thousands of men left their communities for military bases, establishing conditions that favored dramatic life changes. Some heavy combat veterans came away with symptoms of emotional trauma that persisted for decades (Elder & Clipp, 1988). But for most young soldiers, war mobilization broke the hold of family hardship and vanishing opportunity. It broadened their range of knowledge and experience. It also granted time out from civilian responsibilities, giving many soldiers a chance to consider where their lives were and where they were going. And the GI Bill of Rights enabled them to expand their education and acquire new skills after the war. By middle adulthood, the Guidance Study war veterans had reversed the early negative impact of the Great Depression. They were more successful educationally and occupationally than their counterparts who had not entered the service (Elder & Hareven, 1993).

Clearly, cultural-historical change does not have a uniform impact on development. Outcomes can vary considerably, depending on the pattern of historical events and the age period in which they take place.

■ *The Great Depression of the 1930s left this farm family without a steady income. The adolescent girl (in the back row on the far right) may have been more negatively affected by economic hardship than her brother (second from left). And overall, younger children probably suffered more than older children. (Culver Pictures)*

A study in which children in grades 3, 6, 9, and 12 filled out a questionnaire asking about their sibling relationships provides a good illustration. Findings revealed that sibling interaction was characterized by greater equality and less power assertion with age. Also, feelings of sibling companionship declined during adolescence. The researchers thought these age-related changes were due to several factors. As later-born children become more competent and independent, they no longer need and are probably less willing to accept direction from older siblings. In addition, as adolescents move from psychological dependence on the family to greater involvement with peers, they may have less time and emotional need to invest in their siblings (Buhrmester & Furman, 1990). These intriguing ideas about the impact of development on sibling relationships, as we will see in Chapter 14, have been confirmed in subsequent research.

Notice how in cross-sectional studies, researchers do not have to worry about many difficulties that plague the longitudinal design. When participants are measured only once, investigators do not need to be concerned about selective attrition, practice effects, or changes in the field of child development that might make the findings obsolete by the time the study is complete.

■ PROBLEMS IN CONDUCTING CROSS-SECTIONAL RESEARCH. Although the cross-sectional design is a very efficient strategy for describing age-related trends, when researchers choose it they are shortchanged in the kind of information they can obtain about development. Evidence about change at the level at which it actually occurs—the individual—is not available. For example, in the cross-sectional study of sibling relationships just discussed, comparisons are limited to age group averages. We cannot tell if important individual differences exist in the development of sibling relationships. Indeed, recent longitudinal findings reveal that children vary considerably in the changing quality of their sibling relationships, some becoming more supportive and intimate and others becoming increasingly distant with age (Dunn, Slomkowski, & Beardsall, 1994).

Cross-sectional studies—especially those that cover a wide age span—have another problem. Like longitudinal research, their validity can be threatened by cohort effects. For example, comparisons of 5-year-old cohorts and 15-year-old cohorts—groups of children born and reared in different years—may not really represent age-related changes. Instead, they may reflect unique experiences associated with the different time periods in which the age groups were growing up.

IMPROVING DEVELOPMENTAL DESIGNS

In recent years, researchers have tackled the problems inherent in longitudinal and cross-sectional designs. They have devised ways of minimizing the weaknesses of each approach while continuing to take advantage of and even building on its strengths. Several modified developmental designs have resulted.

■ COMBINING LONGITUDINAL AND CROSS-SECTIONAL APPROACHES. To overcome some of the limitations of longitudinal and cross-sectional research, investigators sometimes combine the two approaches. One way of doing so is the **longitudinal-sequential design**, shown in Figure 2.5 on page 60. It is called a sequential design because it is composed of a sequence of samples, each of which is followed for a number of years (Schaie & Hertzog, 1982). In Figure 2.5, two groups are followed: one born in 1982, the other in 1985. Both are tracked longitudinally from 1988 to 1994. The first sample is followed from ages 3 to 9, the second from ages 6 to 12.

The design has three advantages. First, it permits researchers to find out whether cohort effects are operating by comparing children of the same age who were born in different years. In Figure 2.5, we can compare the behaviors of the two samples at ages 6 and 9. If they do not differ, we can rule out cohort effects. Second, it is possible to make both longitudinal and cross-sectional comparisons. If outcomes are similar in both, then we can be especially confident about our findings. Third, the design is efficient. In the example shown in Figure 2.5, the researcher can find out about change over a 9-year period by following each cohort for just 6 years. Although the longitudinal-sequential design is used only occasionally, it provides researchers with a convenient way to profit from the strengths of both longitudinal and cross-sectional approaches.

Longitudinal-sequential design
A research design with both longitudinal and cross-sectional components in which groups of participants born in different years are followed over time.

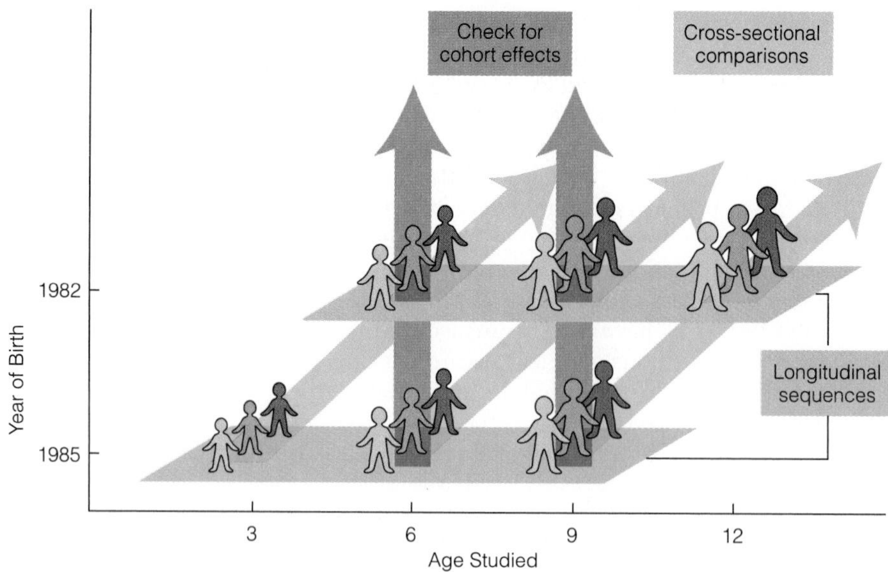

FIGURE 2.5

■ *Example of a longitudinal-sequential design. Two samples of children, one born in 1982 and the other in 1985, are observed longitudinally from 2 to 12 years of age. The design permits the researcher to check for cohort effects by comparing children of the same age who were born in different years. Also, both longitudinal and cross-sectional comparisons can be made.*

■ *What strategies does this child use to solve puzzles, and how does she become proficient at puzzle solving? Since a microgenetic design permits researchers to follow children's mastery of a challenging task, from the time change begins until it stabilizes, it is uniquely suited to answering these questions. (Alex Bartel/The Picture Cube, Inc.)*

■ EXAMINING MICROCOSMS OF DEVELOPMENT. Look back at the examples of developmental research we have discussed, and notice how in all instances observations of children are fairly widely spaced. When we observe at ages 4, 6, and 8, we can describe development, but we have little opportunity to capture the processes that produced the changes. A recent modification of the longitudinal approach, called the **microgenetic design**, is becoming more popular because it offers unique insights into how development takes place (Kuhn, 1995; Siegler & Crowley, 1991, 1992).

In microgenetic studies, researchers track change while it occurs, observing frequently from the time it begins until it stabilizes. Since it is not practical to use this approach over a long developmental period, investigators usually present children with a novel task or a task from their everyday environment and follow their mastery of it over a series of sessions. Within this "microcosm" of development, they see how change occurs.

In one microgenetic study, researchers watched how parents helped their fifth graders master challenging long-division problems. Children who progressed the fastest had parents who sensitively adjusted the help they offered to the child's moment-by-moment performance on the task. If the child failed in an attempt to solve a problem, the parent provided more direct guidance on the next try. If the child succeeded, the parent pulled back and gave less direct support, permitting the child to assume greater responsibility for the task (Pratt, Green, & MacVicar, 1992). In this investigation, the researchers focused on teaching techniques that support children's learning. In other microgenetic studies, they have examined the strategies children use to acquire various kinds of new knowledge, including reading, mathematical, and scientific concepts (Kuhn et al., 1995; Siegler & Munakata, 1993).

As these examples illustrate, the microgenetic design is especially useful for studying cognitive development. In Chapter 4, we will see that it has also been used to trace infants' mastery of motor skills. At the same time, microgenetic studies are very difficult to carry out. Researchers must pore over hours of videotaped records, analyzing each participant's behaviors. In addition, the time required for children to change is hard to

Microgenetic design
A research design in which change is tracked from the time it begins until it stabilizes, as participants master an everyday or novel task.

TABLE 2.3

Strengths and Limitations of Developmental Research Designs

Design	Description	Strengths	Limitations
Longitudinal design	The investigator studies the same groups of participants repeatedly at different ages.	Permits study of common patterns and individual differences in development and relationships between early and later events and behaviors.	Age-related changes may be distorted because of biased sampling, selective attrition, practice effects, and cohort effects.
Cross-sectional design	The investigator studies groups of participants differing in age at the same point in time.	More efficient than the longitudinal design.	Does not permit study of individual developmental trends. Age differences may be distorted because of cohort effects.
Longitudinal-sequential design	The investigator studies two or more groups of participants born in different years at the same point in time.	Permits both longitudinal and cross-sectional comparisons. Reveals existence of cohort effects.	May have the same problems as longitudinal and cross-sectional strategies, but the design itself helps identify difficulties.
Microgenetic design	The investigator tracks change from the time it begins until it stabilizes, as participants master an everyday or novel task.	Offers unique insights into the processes of development.	Requires intensive study of participants' moment-by-moment behaviors; the time required for participants to change is difficult to anticipate; practice effects may distort developmental trends.

anticipate. It depends on a careful match between the child's capabilities and the demands of the task (Siegler & Crowley, 1991). Finally, microgenetic studies are subject to practice effects. Repeated exposure to the task may distort developmental trends (Pressley, 1992). To find out whether this has occurred, researchers can compare microgenetic with cross-sectional observations. If new strategies that emerge microgenetically reflect change as it typically occurs, they should match the strategies displayed by more advanced participants in cross-sectional studies, who are observed only once (Kuhn, 1995). In sum, when researchers find ways to surmount the challenges of microgenetic research, they reap the benefits of witnessing development as it takes place.

■ COMBINING EXPERIMENTAL AND DEVELOPMENTAL DESIGNS. Perhaps you noticed that all the examples of longitudinal and cross-sectional research we have considered provide only correlational, and not causal, inferences about development. Yet ideally, causal information is desirable, both for testing theories and for coming up with ways to improve children's lives. If we find that children's experiences and behavior are related in a developmental design, in some instances we can explore the causal relationship between them by experimentally manipulating the experience in a later study. If, as a result, development is enhanced, we would have strong evidence for a causal association between experience and behavior. Today, research that combines an experimental strategy with either a longitudinal or cross-sectional approach appears with increasing frequency in the research literature. These designs are a vital force in helping investigators move beyond correlated variables to a causal account of developmental change. For a summary of the strengths and limitations of developmental research designs, refer to Table 2.3.

BRIEF REVIEW

A variety of research designs are commonly used to study children. In correlational research, information is gathered on existing groups of individuals. Investigators can examine relationships between variables, but they cannot infer cause and effect. Because the experimental design involves random assignment of participants to treatment groups, researchers can find out if an independent variable causes change in a dependent variable. Field and natural experiments permit generalization to everyday life, but they sacrifice rigorous experimental control.

Longitudinal and cross-sectional designs are uniquely suited for studying development. Longitudinal research provides information on common patterns as well as individual differences in development and the relationship between early and later events and behaviors. The cross-sectional approach is more efficient, but comparisons are limited to age group averages. The longitudinal-sequential design permits researchers to reap the benefits of both longitudinal and cross-sectional strategies. A special form of longitudinal research, the microgenetic design, offers unique insights into the processes of development. Experimental approaches can be combined with longitudinal or cross-sectional designs to examine causal influences on development.

Ethics in Research on Children

Research into human behavior creates ethical issues because, unfortunately, the quest for scientific knowledge can sometimes exploit people. When children take part in research, the ethical concerns are especially complex. Children are more vulnerable than adults to physical and psychological harm. In addition, immaturity makes it difficult or impossible for children to evaluate for themselves what participation in research will mean. For these reasons, special ethical guidelines for research on children have been developed by the federal government, by funding agencies, and by research-oriented associations such as the American Psychological Association (1992) and the Society for Research in Child Development (1993).

Table 2.4 presents a summary of children's basic research rights drawn from these guidelines. Once you have examined them, think back to the ethical controversy faced by my colleague Ron, described at the beginning of this chapter. Then take a close look at the following research situations, each of which poses an additional ethical dilemma. What precautions do you think should be taken to protect the rights of children in each instance? Is any one of these studies so threatening to children's well-being that it should not be carried out?

- To study children's willingness to separate from their caregivers, an investigator decides to ask mothers of 1- and 2-year-olds to leave their youngsters alone for a brief time period in an unfamiliar playroom. The researcher knows that under these circumstances, some children become very upset.
- In a study of moral development, a researcher wants to assess children's ability to resist temptation by videotaping their behavior without their knowledge. Seven-year-olds are promised an attractive prize for solving some very difficult puzzles. They are also told not to look at a classmate's correct solutions, which are deliberately placed at the back of the room. If the researcher has to tell children ahead of time that cheating is being studied or that their behavior is being closely monitored, she will destroy the purpose of her study.

Did you find it difficult to decide on the best course of action in these examples? Virtually every organization that has worked on developing ethical principles for research has concluded that the conflicts raised by studies like these cannot be resolved with simple right-or-wrong answers. The ultimate responsibility for the ethical integrity of research lies with the investigator. However, researchers are advised or, in the case of

TABLE 2.4

Children's Research Rights

Research Right	Description
Protection from harm	Children have the right to be protected from physical or psychological harm in research. If in doubt about the harmful effects of research, investigators should seek the opinion of others. When harm seems possible, investigators should find other means for obtaining the desired information or abandon the research.
Informed consent	All research participants, including children, have the right to have explained to them, in language appropriate to their level of understanding, all aspects of the research that may affect their willingness to participate. When children are participants, informed consent of parents as well as others who act on the child's behalf (such as school officials) should be obtained, preferably in writing. Children, and the adults responsible for them, have the right to discontinue participation in the research at any time.
Privacy	Children have the right to concealment of their identity on all information collected in the course of research. They also have this right with respect to written reports and any informal discussions about the research.
Knowledge of results	Children have the right to be informed of the results of research in language that is appropriate to their level of understanding.
Beneficial treatments	If experimental treatments believed to be beneficial are under investigation, children in control groups have the right to alternative beneficial treatments if they are available.

Sources: American Psychological Association, 1992; Society for Research in Child Development, 1993.

federally funded research, required to seek advice from others. Special committees, like the one that evaluated Ron's research, exist in colleges, universities, and other institutions for this purpose. These review boards evaluate research studies on the basis of a **risks-versus-benefits ratio**. This involves weighing the costs of the research to participants in terms of inconvenience and possible psychological or physical injury against the study's value for advancing knowledge and improving children's conditions of life.

Ron's procedures, the school's research committee claimed, might not offer children sufficient **protection from harm**. If there are any risks to the safety and welfare of participants that the research does not justify, then priority should always be given to the research participants. Vulnerability to harm, as the From Research to Practice box on page 64 reveals, varies with children's age and characteristics. Occasionally, further inquiry can help resolve perplexing ethical dilemmas about whether children might suffer. In Ron's case, he provided the research committee with findings showing that asking elementary school pupils to identify disliked peers does not lead them to interact less frequently or more negatively with those children (Bell-Dolan, Foster, & Sikora, 1989). At the same time, Ron agreed to take special precautions when requesting such information. He promised to ask all the children to keep their comments confidential. Also, he arranged to conduct the study at a time when classmates have limited opportunity to interact with one another—just before a school vacation. With these safeguards in place, the committee felt comfortable with Ron's research, and eventually they approved it.

The ethical principle of **informed consent** requires special interpretation when research participants are children. The competence of youngsters of different ages to make choices about their own participation must be taken into account. Parental consent is meant to protect the safety of children whose ability to make these decisions is not yet fully mature. Besides parental consent, agreement of other individuals who act on children's behalf, such as institutional officials when research is conducted in schools, day care centers, or hospitals, should be obtained. This is especially important when studies include special groups whose parents may not represent their best interests (refer again to the box on page 64).

Risks-versus-benefits ratio
A comparison of the costs of a research study to participants in terms of inconvenience and possible psychological or physical injury against its value for advancing knowledge and improving conditions of life. Used in assessing the ethics of research.

Protection from harm
The right of research participants to be protected from physical or psychological harm.

Informed consent
The right of research participants, including children, to have explained to them all aspects of a study that may affect their willingness to participate in language they can understand.

FROM RESEARCH TO PRACTICE

Children's Research Risks: Developmental and Individual Differences

Researchers interested in children's behavior face formidable challenges in defining their ethical responsibilities. Compared to adults, children are less capable of benefiting from research experiences. Furthermore, the risks they are likely to encounter are psychological rather than physical (as in medical research) and therefore difficult to anticipate and sometimes even detect (Thompson, 1992). Consider, for example, 7-year-old Henry, who did not want to answer a researcher's questions about how he feels about his younger brother, who has physical disabilities. Since Henry's parents told him they had granted permission for his participation, he did not feel free to say no to the researcher. Or take 11-year-old Isabelle, who tried to solve a problem unsuccessfully. Despite the researcher's assurances that the task was set up to be impossible, Isabelle returned to her classroom concerned about her own competence.

How can we make sure that children are subjected to the least research risk possible? One valuable resource is our expanding knowledge of age-related capacities and individual differences. A close look reveals that research risks vary with development in complex ways. Some risks decrease with age, others increase, and still others occur at many or all ages (Thompson, 1990b). And because of their personal characteristics and life circumstances, some children are more vulnerable to harm than others.

Research plans for younger children typically receive the most scrutiny, since their limited cognitive competencies restrict their ability to make reasoned decisions and resist violations of their rights. In addition, as Henry's predicament illustrates, young children's limited social power in the context of parental and school support for an investigation can make it difficult for them to refuse participation. In a study that examined 5- to 12-year-olds' understanding of research procedures, few children comprehended why they were asked to engage in the research activities. And although the majority understood that they could end their participation at any time, some believed there would be negative consequences for doing so (the experimentor might be upset) or that they could only stop on a temporary basis (for example, to go to the bathroom). The youngest children, especially, did not know how to go about terminating their involvement (Abramovitch et al., 1991). However, if the researcher explicitly says that she would not mind if the child stopped, children understand their right much better and are more likely to exercise it (Abramovitch et al., 1995).

Whereas young children have special difficulties understanding the research process, older children are more susceptible to procedures that threaten the way they think of themselves. In Chapter 11, we will see that compared to preschoolers, school-age children have a more coherent, differentiated understanding of their own strengths and weaknesses. As children become increasingly sensitive to the evaluations of others, giving false feedback or inducing failure (as happened to Isabelle) is more stressful. In adolescence, when views of the self are well established and questioning of authority is common, young people are probably better at sizing up and rejecting researchers' deceptive evaluations (Thompson, 1992).

At times, children's backgrounds, prior experiences, and other characteristics introduce special vulnerabilities. For example, parents of maltreated children are not always good advocates for the interests of their children. The consent of an additional adult invested in the child's welfare—perhaps a relative, teacher, or therapist—may be necessary to protect the child's rights. And because abuse is associated with deep psychological wounds, such children are at greater risk than their agemates when research procedures induce anxiety or threaten their self-image. In certain cases, such as adolescent substance abusers or delinquents, parents may be so eager to get their children into contact with professionals that they would agree to any research without much forethought (Fisher & Rosendahl, 1990). And even after a thorough explanation, their children may continue to believe that if they do not say yes, they will be punished by legal or school authorities. In these instances, researchers should take extra steps to assess each young person's understanding and motivation to make sure that the decision to participate is not influenced by real or imagined external pressures (Grisso, 1992).

Finding ways to reconcile the risks–benefits conflicts we have considered is vital, since research on children is of great value to society. In view of the complexity of children's research risks, convergent judgments of researchers, institutional review boards, child development experts, parents, and others responsible for children's welfare are likely to work best in safeguarding their interests. As each study is evaluated, participants' age and unique characteristics should be central to the discussion. Because of pressures they sometimes feel, children and adolescents need explanations of their right to dissent from participation. And their decision should be the final word in most investigations, even though this standard is not mandatory in current guidelines (Thompson, 1992).

For children 7 years and older, their own informed consent should be obtained in addition to parental consent (National Commission for the Protection of Human Subjects, 1977). Around age 7, changes in children's thinking permit them to better understand simple scientific principles and the needs of others. Researchers should respect and enhance these new capacities by providing school-age children with a full explanation of research activities in language they can understand (Ferguson, 1978; Thompson, 1992).

Debriefing
Providing a full account and justification of research activities to participants in a study in which deception was used.

Finally, young children rely on a basic faith in adults to feel secure in unfamiliar situations. For this reason, some types of research may be particularly disturbing to them. All ethical guidelines advise that special precautions be taken in the use of deception and concealment, as occurs when researchers observe children from behind one-way mirrors, give them false feedback about their performance, or do not tell them the truth regarding what the research is about. When these kinds of procedures are used with adults, **debriefing**, in which the experimenter provides a full account and justification of the activities, occurs after the research session is over. Debriefing should also take place with children, but it often does not work as well. Despite explanations, children may come away from the research situation with their belief in the honesty of adults undermined. Ethical standards permit deception in research with children if investigators satisfy institutional committees that such practices are necessary. Nevertheless, since deception may have serious emotional consequences for some youngsters, many child development specialists believe that its use is always unethical and that investigators should come up with other research strategies when children are involved (Cooke, 1982; Ferguson, 1978).

SUMMARY

FROM THEORY TO HYPOTHESIS

- Research usually begins with a **hypothesis**, or prediction about behavior drawn from a theory. In areas in which there is little or no existing theory, it starts with a research question. On the basis of the hypothesis or question, the investigator selects research methods (specific activities of participants) and a research design (overall plan for the study).

COMMON METHODS USED TO STUDY CHILDREN

- Common research methods in child development include systematic observation; self-reports; psychophysiological methods; the clinical, or case study, method; and ethnography. **Naturalistic observations** are gathered in children's everyday environments, whereas **structured observations** take place in laboratories, where investigators deliberately set up cues to elicit the behaviors of interest.
- Depending on the researcher's purpose, observations can preserve participants' entire behavior stream, as in the **specimen record**. Or they can be limited to one or a few behaviors of interest, as in **event sampling** and **time sampling**.
- Self-report methods can be flexible and open-ended, like the **clinical interview**, which yields a full picture of each participant's thoughts and feelings. Alternatively, **structured interviews**, questionnaires, and tests, which permit efficient administration and scoring, can be given.
- **Psychophysiological methods** assess the relation between physiological processes and behavior. Researchers use them to uncover the biological bases of children's perceptual, cognitive, and emotional responses.
- Investigators rely on the **clinical method** to obtain an in-depth understanding of a single child. In this approach, interviews, observations, test scores, and psychophysiological assessments are synthesized into a complete description of the participant's development and unique psychological functioning.
- A growing interest in the impact of culture has prompted child development researchers to borrow a method from the field of anthropology—**ethnography**. Like the clinical method, ethnographic research is descriptive and qualitative. But instead of focusing on a single individual, it uses participant observation to understand the unique values and social processes of a culture or distinct social group.

RELIABILITY AND VALIDITY: KEYS TO SCIENTIFICALLY SOUND RESEARCH

- To be acceptable to the scientific community, observations and self-reports must be both reliable and valid. **Reliability** refers to the consistency, or repeatability, of measures of behavior. A method has high **validity** if, after examining its content and relationships with other measures of behavior, the researcher finds that it reflects what it was intended to measure.
- The concept of validity can also be applied more broadly, to the overall accuracy of research findings and conclusions. In designing a study, investigators must take special precautions to make sure that factors unrelated to the hypothesis do not influence participants' behavior.

GENERAL RESEARCH DESIGNS

- Two main types of designs are used in all research on human behavior. The **correlational design** examines relationships between variables as they happen to occur, without any intervention. The **correlation coefficient** is often used to measure the association between variables. Correlational studies do not permit inferences about cause and effect. However, their use is justified when it is difficult or impossible to control the variables of interest.
- An **experimental design** permits inferences about cause and effect. Researchers manipulate an **independent variable** by exposing groups of participants to two or more treatment conditions. Then they determine what effect this has on a **dependent variable**. **Random assignment** and **matching** are techniques used to ensure that characteristics of participants do not reduce the accuracy of experimental findings.
- **Laboratory experiments** usually achieve high degrees of control, but their findings may not apply to everyday life. To overcome this problem, researchers sometimes conduct **field experiments**, in which they manipulate treatment conditions in the real world. When this is impossible, investigators may compromise and conduct **natural experiments**, in which already existing treatments, consisting of groups of people whose characteristics are as much alike as possible, are compared. This approach, however, is far less rigorous than a true experimental design.

DESIGNS FOR STUDYING DEVELOPMENT

- Longitudinal and cross-sectional designs are uniquely suited for studying development. In the **longitudinal design**, a group of participants is observed repeatedly at different ages. It permits study of common patterns as well as individual differences in development and the relationship between early and later events and behaviors.
- Researchers face a variety of problems in conducting longitudinal research, including **biased sampling**, **selective attrition**, and **practice effects**. But the most widely discussed threat to the accuracy of longitudinal findings is **cohort effects**—difficulties in generalizing to children growing up during different time periods.
- The **cross-sectional design**, in which groups of participants differing in age are studied at the same time, offers an efficient approach to studying development. However, it is limited to comparisons of age group averages. Like longitudinal research, cross-sectional studies can be threatened by cohort effects, especially when they cover a wide age span.
- New designs have been devised to overcome some of the limitations of longitudinal and cross-sectional research. By combining the two approaches, the **longitudinal-sequential design** benefits from the strengths of each and permits researchers to test for cohort effects. In the **microgenetic design**, researchers track change as it occurs. In doing so, they obtain unique insights into the processes of development. When experimental procedures are combined with developmental designs, researchers can examine causal influences on development.

ETHICS IN RESEARCH ON CHILDREN

- Research involving children raises special ethical concerns. Because of their immaturity, children are especially vulnerable. Ethical guidelines for research and special committees that weigh research in terms of a **risks-versus-benefits ratio** help ensure that children's rights are protected and that they are afforded **protection from harm**. In addition to parental consent, researchers should seek the **informed consent** of children age 7 and older for research participation. The use of deception in research with children is especially risky, since **debriefing** can undermine their basic faith in the trustworthiness of adults.

IMPORTANT TERMS AND CONCEPTS

hypothesis (p. 41)
naturalistic observation (p. 42)
structured observation (p. 43)
specimen record (p. 44)
event sampling (p. 44)
time sampling (p. 44)
observer influence (p. 45)
observer bias (p. 45)
clinical interview (p. 46)
structured interview (p. 46)
psychophysiological methods (p. 47)
clinical method (p. 48)
ethnography (p. 49)
reliability (p. 51)
validity (p. 51)
correlational design (p. 52)
correlation coefficient (p. 52)
experimental design (p. 53)
independent variable (p. 53)
dependent variable (p. 53)
laboratory experiment (p. 53)
random assignment (p. 54)
matching (p. 54)
field experiment (p. 54)
natural experiment (p. 55)
longitudinal design (p. 56)
biased sampling (p. 57)
selective attrition (p. 57)
practice effects (p. 57)
cohort effects (p. 57)
cross-sectional design (p. 57)
longitudinal-sequential design (p. 59)
microgenetic design (p. 60)
risks-versus-benefits ratio (p. 63)
protection from harm (p. 63)
informed consent (p. 63)
debriefing (p. 64)

CONNECTIONS for Chapter 2

If you are interested in . . .	turn to . . .	to learn about . . .
Common research methods used to study children	Chapter 4, pp. 134–140, 147	Methods for studying infant learning and perception
	Chapter 8, pp. 308–310	Intelligence testing of infants and children
	Chapter 9, p. 347	A clinical study of Genie, a child deprived of early language learning
	Chapter 10, pp. 398–399	Observational, parental report, and psycho-physiological measures of temperament
	Chapter 10, pp. 408–409	The Strange Situation: A laboratory observational procedure for studying infant–caregiver attachment security
	Chapter 12, p. 469 pp. 472–473	Clinical interviewing and questionnaire methods for studying moral reasoning
General and developmental research designs	Chapter 4, pp. 142–143	Microgenetic research on motor development
	Chapter 4, pp. 162–163	Longitudinal research on the importance of early experience for later development
	Chapter 8, pp. 328–329	Natural experiments on early intervention and intellectual development of at-risk children
	Chapter 14, pp. 543–545	Correlational research on child-rearing styles and children's cognitive and social competence
Ethics in research on children	Chapter 1, p. 17	Ethical implications of John Watson's classical conditioning of infant fear
	Chapter 3, pp. 82–83	Ethical implications of advances in fetal medicine
	Chapter 8, p. 317	Ethical implications of research on ethnic differences in intelligence
	Chapter 14, p. 571	Ethical implications of definitions of child maltreatment

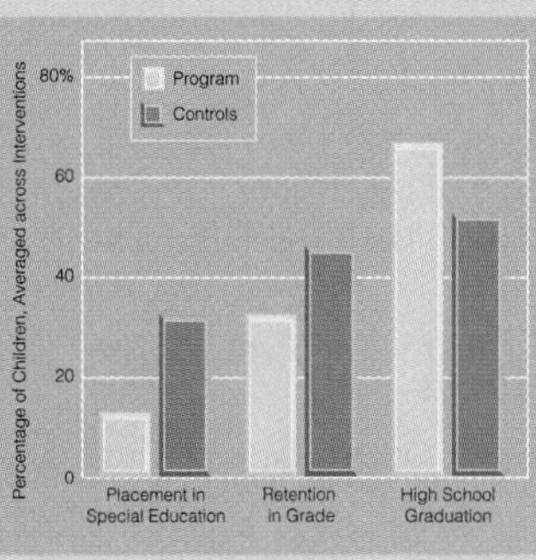

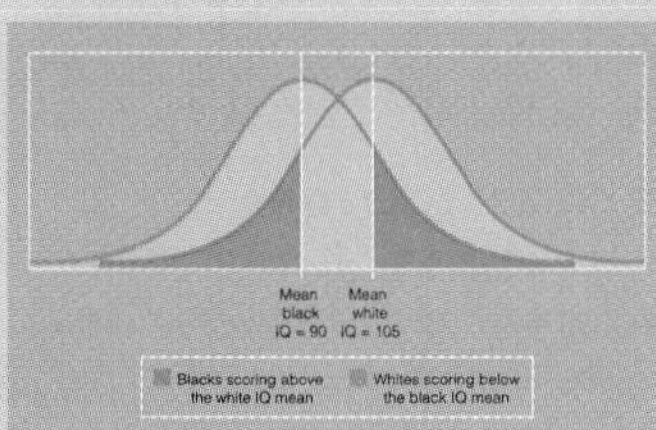

3 Biological Foundations, Prenatal Development, and Birth

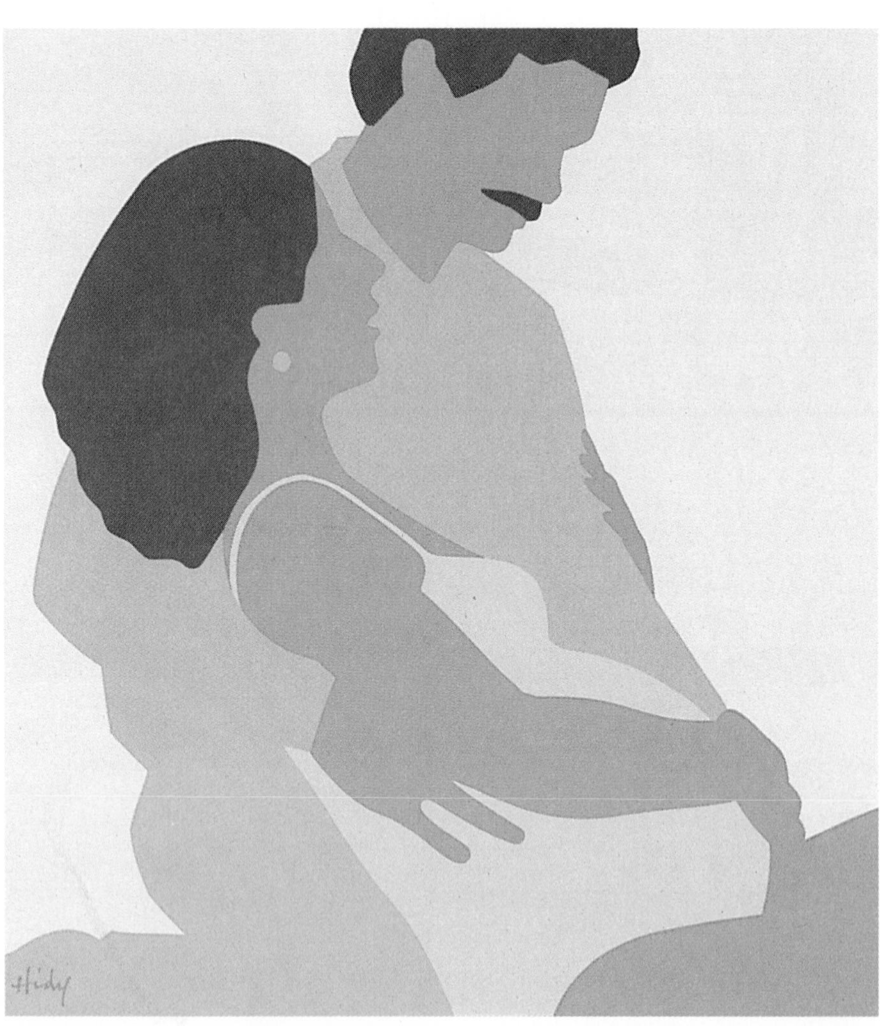

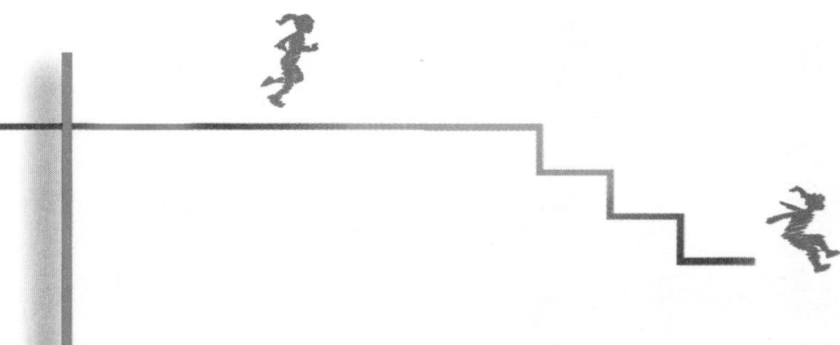

It's a girl," announces the doctor, who holds up the squalling little creature, while her new parents gaze with amazement at their miraculous creation.

"A girl! We've named her Sarah!" exclaims the proud father to eager relatives waiting by the telephone for word about their new family member.

As we join these parents in thinking about how this wondrous being came into existence and imagining her future, we are struck by many questions. How could this well-formed baby, equipped with everything necessary for life outside the womb, have developed from the union of two tiny cells? What ensures that Sarah will, in due time, roll over, reach for objects, walk, talk, make friends, imagine, and create—just like every other normal child born before her? Why is she a girl and not a boy, dark-haired rather than blond, calm and cuddly instead of wiry and energetic? What difference will it make that Sarah is given a name and place in one family, community, nation, and culture rather than another?

We begin our discussion of these questions by considering genetic foundations. Because nature has prepared us for survival, all human beings have features in common. Yet a brief period of time spent in the company of any child and his or her family reveals that each human being is unique. Take a moment to jot down the most obvious similarities in physical characteristics and behavior for several children and parents whom you know well. Did you find that one child shows combined features of both parents, another resembles just one parent, whereas still a third is not like either parent? These directly observable characteristics are called **phenotypes**. They depend in part on the individual's **genotype**—the complex blend of genetic information that determines our species and influences all our unique characteristics. But phenotypes, as our discussion will show, are also affected by a long history of environmental influences—ones that begin even before the moment of conception.

Next, we trace development during the most rapid phase of growth, the prenatal period, in which complex transactions between heredity and environment begin to shape the course of development. We consider environmental supports that are necessary for normal prenatal growth as well as damaging influences that threaten the child's health and survival. Then we turn to the drama of birth and to developmental risks for infants born underweight or prematurely, before the prenatal phase is complete.

Finally, we take a look ahead. This earliest period introduces us to the operation of the two basic determinants of development: heredity and environment. We will consider how researchers think about and study the relationship between nature and nurture as they continue to influence the individual's emerging characteristics from infancy through adolescence.

Genetic Foundations

Basic principles of genetics were unknown until the mid-nineteenth century, when Austrian monk and botanist Gregor Mendel began a series of experiments with pea plants in his monastery garden. Recording the number of times white- and pink-flowered plants had offspring with white or pink flowers, Mendel found that he could predict the characteristics of each new generation. Mendel inferred the presence of genes, factors controlling the physical traits he studied. Although peas and humans may seem completely unrelated, today we know that heredity operates in similar ways among all forms of life. Since Mendel's groundbreaking observations, our understanding of how genetic messages are coded and inherited has vastly expanded.

Phenotype
The individual's physical and behavioral characteristics, which are determined by both genetic and environmental factors.

Genotype
The genetic makeup of the individual.

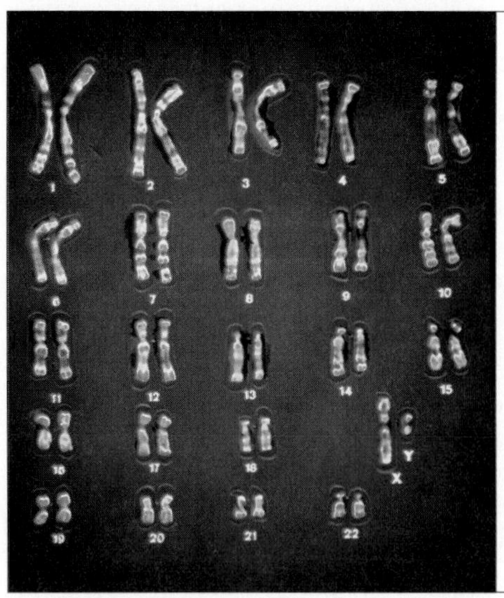

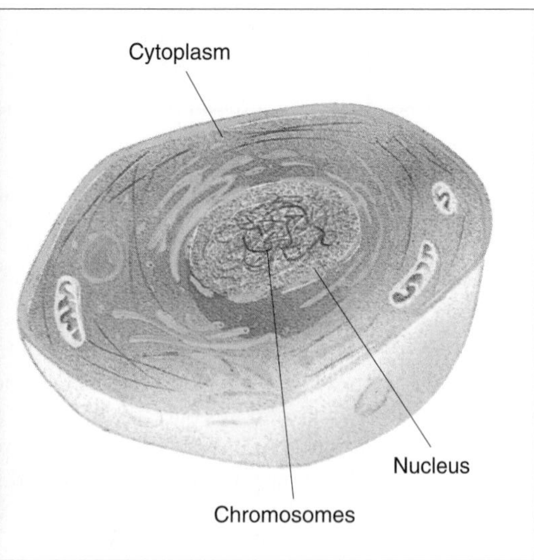

FIGURE 3.1

■ *A karyotype, or photograph, of human chromosomes. The 46 chromosomes shown here were isolated from a body cell, stained, greatly magnified, and arranged in pairs according to decreasing size of the upper arm of each chromosome. Note the twenty-third pair, XY. The cell donor is a male. In females, the twenty-third pair would be XX. (CNRI/Science Photo Library/Photo Researchers.)*

THE GENETIC CODE

Each of us is made up of trillions of independent units called cells. Inside every cell is a control center, or nucleus. When cells are chemically stained and viewed through a powerful microscope, rodlike structures called **chromosomes** are visible in the nucleus. Chromosomes store and transmit genetic information. Their number varies from species to species—48 for chimpanzees, 64 for horses, 40 for mice, and 46 for human beings. Chromosomes come in matching pairs (an exception is the XY pair in males, which we will discuss shortly). Each member of a pair corresponds to the other in size, shape, and genetic functions. One is inherited from the mother and one from the father. Therefore, in humans, we speak of 23 pairs of chromosomes residing in each human cell (see Figure 3.1).

Chromosomes are made up of a chemical substance called **deoxyribonucleic acid,** or **DNA**. As Figure 3.2 shows, DNA is a long, double-stranded molecule that looks like a twisted ladder. Notice that each rung of the ladder consists of a specific pair of chemical substances called bases, joined together between the two sides. Although the bases always pair up in the same way across the ladder rungs—A with T, and C with G—they can occur in any order along its sides. It is this sequence of bases that provides genetic instructions. A **gene** is a segment of DNA along the length of the chromosome. Genes can be of different lengths—perhaps 100 to several thousand ladder rungs long—and each differs from the next because of its special sequence of base pairs. Altogether, about 100,000 genes lie along the human chromosomes.

Genes accomplish their task by sending instructions for making a rich assortment of proteins to the cytoplasm, the area surrounding the nucleus of the cell. Proteins, which trigger chemical reactions throughout the body, are the biological foundation from which our characteristics and capacities are built.

A unique feature of DNA is that it can duplicate itself. This special ability makes it possible for the one-celled fertilized ovum to develop into a complex human being composed of a great many cells. The process of cell duplication is called **mitosis.** In mitosis, the DNA ladder splits down the middle, opening much like a zipper (refer again to Figure 3.2). Then, each base is free to pair up with a new mate from cytoplasm of the cell. Notice how this process creates two identical DNA ladders, each containing one new side and one old side of the previous ladder. At the level of chromosomes, during mitosis each chromosome copies itself. As a result, each new body cell contains the same number of chromosomes and the identical genetic information.

THE SEX CELLS

New individuals are created when two special cells called **gametes**, or sex cells—the sperm and ovum—combine. Gametes are unique in that they contain only 23 chromosomes, half as many as a regular body cell. They are formed through a process of cell division called **meiosis**, which halves the number of chromosomes normally present in body cells.

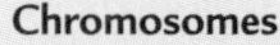

Chromosomes
Rodlike structures in the cell nucleus that store and transmit genetic information.

Deoxyribonucleic acid (DNA)
Long, double-stranded molecules that make up chromosomes.

Gene
A segment of a DNA molecule that contains instructions for production of various proteins that contribute to growth and functioning of the body.

Mitosis
The process of cell duplication, in which each new cell receives an exact copy of the original chromosomes.

Gametes
Human sperm and ova, which contain half as many chromosomes as a regular body cell.

Meiosis
The process of cell division through which gametes are formed and in which the number of chromosomes in each cell is halved.

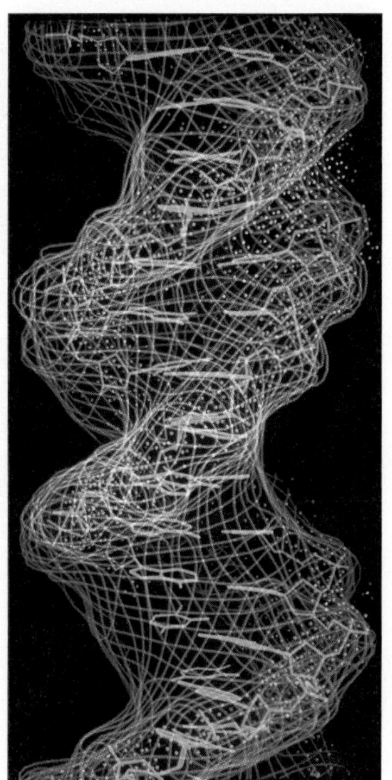

FIGURE 3.2

DNA's ladderlike structure. *The figure on the left shows that the pairings of bases across the rungs of the ladder are very specific: adenine (A) always appears with thymine (T), and cytosine (C) always appears with guanine (G). Here, the DNA ladder duplicates by splitting down the middle of its ladder rungs. Each free base picks up a new complementary partner from the area surrounding the cell nucleus.*
The photo on the right shows a computer-generated model of DNA. By simulating and color-coding DNA's structure, scientists can rotate the image and study it from different vantage points. (Jean-Claude Revy/Phototake)

Meiosis takes place according to the steps in Figure 3.3 on page 72. First, chromosomes pair up within the original cell, and each one copies itself. Then, a special event called **crossing over** occurs. Chromosomes next to each other break at one or more points along their length and exchange segments, so that genes from one are replaced by genes from another. This shuffling of genes creates new hereditary combinations. Next, the paired chromosomes separate into different cells, but chance determines which member of each pair will gather with others and end up in the same gamete. Finally, in the last phase of meiosis, each chromosome leaves its duplicate and becomes part of a sex cell containing 23 chromosomes instead of the usual 46.

In the male, four sperm are produced each time meiosis occurs. Also, the cells from which sperm arise are produced continuously throughout life. For this reason, a healthy man can father a child at any age after sexual maturity. In the female, gamete production is much more limited. Each cell division produces just one ovum. In addition, the female is born with all her ova already present in her ovaries, and she can bear children for only three to four decades. Still, there are plenty of female sex cells. About 1 million to 2 million are present at birth, 40,000 remain at adolescence, and approximately 350 to 450 will mature during a woman's childbearing years (Moore & Persaud, 1993).

Look again at the steps of meiosis in Figure 3.3, and notice how they ensure that a constant quantity of genetic material (46 chromosomes in each cell) is transmitted from one generation to the next. When sperm and ovum unite at fertilization, the cell that results, called a **zygote**, will again have 46 chromosomes. Can you also see how meiosis leads to variability among offspring? Crossing over and random sorting of each member

Crossing over
Exchange of genes between chromosomes next to each other during meiosis.

Zygote
The union of sperm and ovum at conception.

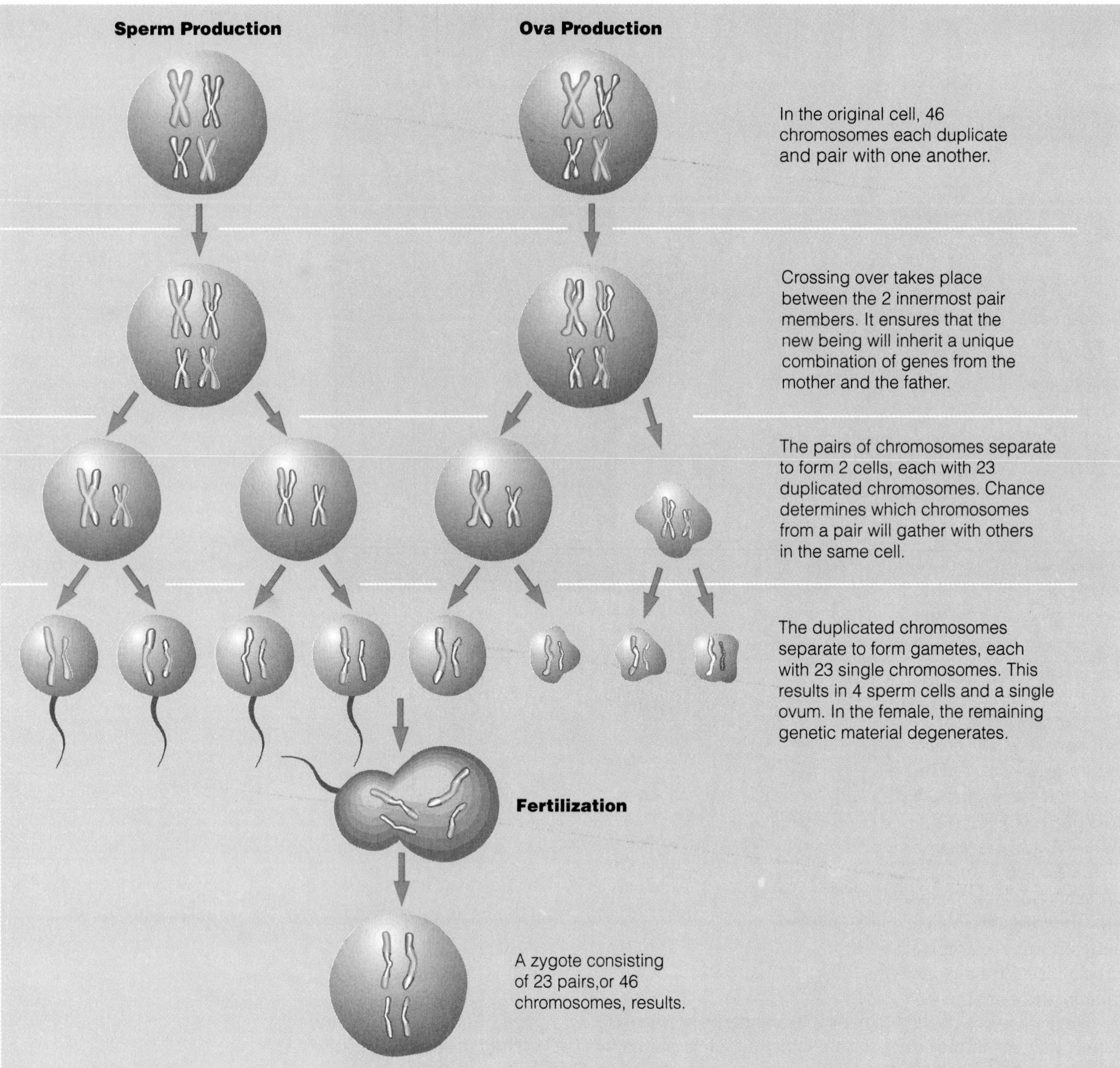

FIGURE 3.3

■ *The cell division process of meiosis leading to gamete formation. (Here, original cells are depicted with 2 rather than the full complement of 23 chromosome pairs.) Meiosis creates gametes with only half the usual number of chromosomes. When sperm and ovum unite at fertilization, the first cell of the new individual (the zygote) has the correct, full number of chromosomes.*

of a chromosome pair into separate sex cells means that no two gametes will ever be the same. Meiosis explains why siblings differ from each other even though they also have features in common, since their genotypes come from a common pool of parental genes. The genetic variability produced by meiosis is important in an evolutionary sense. It increases the chances that at least some members of a species will be able to cope with ever-changing environments and survive.

MULTIPLE OFFSPRING

Only under one circumstance do offspring *not* display the genetic variability we have just discussed. Sometimes a zygote that has started to duplicate separates into two clusters of cells that develop into two individuals. These are called **identical,** or **monozygotic, twins** because they have the same genetic makeup. The frequency of identical twins is about the same around the world—4 out of every 1,000 births. Animal research has uncovered a variety of environmental influences that prompt this type of twinning, including temperature changes, variation in oxygen levels, and late fertilization of the ovum.

Identical, or monozygotic, twins
Twins that result when a zygote, during the early stages of cell duplication, divides in two. They have the same genetic makeup.

TABLE 3.1

Maternal Factors Linked to Fraternal Twinning

Factor	Description
Ethnicity	About 8 per 1,000 births among whites, 12 to 16 per 1,000 among blacks, and 4 per 1,000 among Asians.
Family tendency to fraternal twinning	Women who are fraternal twins are more likely to give birth to fraternal twins; this tendency is not established for men.
Age	Rises with maternal age, peaking at 35 years, and then rapidly falls.
Nutrition	Occurs less often among women with poor diets; occurs more often among women who are tall and overweight or of normal weight as opposed to slight body build.
Fertility drugs and in vitro fertilization	Treatment of infertility with hormones and through in vitro fertilization (see page 84) increases the likelihood of multiple fraternal births, from twins to quintuplets.

Sources: Collins, 1994; Little & Thompson, 1988.

There is another way that twins can be created. **Fraternal**, or **dizygotic, twins**, the most common type of multiple birth, result when two ova are released at the same time. If both are fertilized, two offspring who are genetically no more alike than ordinary siblings develop. As Table 3.1 suggests, both hereditary and environmental factors seem to be involved in fraternal twinning.

BOY OR GIRL?

Using special microscopic techniques, the 23 pairs of chromosomes in each human cell can be distinguished from one another. Twenty-two of them are matching pairs, called **autosomes**. They are numbered by geneticists from longest (1) to shortest (22) (refer back to Figure 3.1). The twenty-third pair consists of **sex chromosomes**. In females, this pair is called XX; in males, it is called XY. The X is a relatively long chromosome, whereas the Y is short and carries very little genetic material. When gametes are formed in males, the X and Y chromosomes separate into different sperm cells. In females, all gametes carry an X chromosome. The sex of the new organism is determined by whether an X-bearing or a Y-bearing sperm fertilizes the ovum. In fact, scientists have isolated a gene on the Y chromosome that triggers male sexual development by switching on the production of male sex hormones. When that gene is absent, the fetus that develops is female (Page et al., 1987).

■ *These identical, or monozygotic, twins were created when a duplicating zygote separated into two clusters of cells, and two individuals with the same genetic makeup developed. Identical twins look alike, and, as we will see later in this chapter, tend to resemble each other in a variety of psychological characteristics. (Jeff Dunn/Stock Boston)*

Fraternal, or dizygotic, twins
Twins resulting from the release and fertilization of two ova. They are genetically no more alike than ordinary siblings.

Autosomes
The 22 matching chromosome pairs in each human cell.

Sex chromosomes
The twenty-third pair of chromosomes, which determines the sex of the child. In females, called XX; in males, called XY.

TABLE 3.2

Examples of Dominant and Recessive Characteristics

Dominant	Recessive
Dark hair	Blond hair
Normal hair	Pattern baldness
Curly hair	Straight hair
Nonred hair	Red hair
Facial dimples	No dimples
Normal hearing	Some forms of deafness
Normal vision	Nearsightedness
Farsightedness	Normal vision
Normal vision	Congenital eye cataracts
Normal color vision	Red–green color blindness
Normally pigmented skin	Albinism
Double-jointedness	Normal joints
Type A blood	Type O blood
Type B blood	Type O blood
Rh-positive blood	Rh-negative blood

Note: Many normal characteristics that were previously thought to be due to dominant–recessive inheritance, such as eye color, are now regarded as due to multiple genes. For the characteristics listed here, there still seems to be fairly common agreement that the simple dominant–recessive relationship holds.
Source: McKusick, 1995.

PATTERNS OF GENETIC INHERITANCE

Two or more forms of each gene occur at the same place on the chromosomes, one inherited from the mother and one from the father. Each different form of a gene is called an **allele**. If the alleles from both parents are alike, the child is said to be **homozygous** and will display the inherited trait. If the alleles are different, then the child is **heterozygous**, and relationships between the alleles determine the trait that will appear.

■ DOMINANT–RECESSIVE RELATIONSHIPS. In many heterozygous pairings, only one allele affects the child's characteristics. It is called *dominant;* the second allele, which has no effect, is called *recessive.* Hair color is an example of **dominant–recessive inheritance**. The allele for dark hair is dominant (we can represent it with a capital *D*), whereas the one for blond hair is recessive (symbolized by a lowercase *b*). Children who inherit either a homozygous pair of dominant alleles (*DD*) or a heterozygous pair (*Db*) will be dark-haired, even though their genetic makeup is different. Blond hair can result only from having two recessive alleles (*bb*). Still, heterozygous individuals with just one recessive allele (*Db*) can pass on that trait to their children. As a result, they are called **carriers** of the trait.

Some human characteristics and diseases that follow the rules of dominant–recessive inheritance are given in Table 3.2 and Table 3.3 on pages 76–77. As you can see, many defects and disorders are the product of recessive alleles. One of the most frequently occurring disorders is *phenylketonuria,* or *PKU.* PKU is an especially good example, since it shows that inheriting unfavorable genes does not always mean that the child's condition cannot be treated.

PKU affects the way the body breaks down proteins contained in many foods, such as cow's milk, bread, eggs, and fish. Infants born with two recessive alleles lack an enzyme that converts one of the basic amino acids that make up proteins (phenylalanine) into a by-product essential for body functioning (tyrosine). Without this enzyme, phenylalanine quickly builds to toxic levels that damage the central nervous system. Around 3 to 5 months, infants with untreated PKU start to lose interest in their surroundings. By 1 year, they are permanently retarded. All U.S. states require that each newborn be given a

Allele
Each of two or more forms of a gene located at the same place on the chromosomes.

Homozygous
Having two identical alleles at the same place on a pair of chromosomes.

Heterozygous
Having two different alleles at the same place on a pair of chromosomes.

Dominant–recessive inheritance
A pattern of inheritance in which, under heterozygous conditions, the influence of only one allele is apparent.

Carrier
A heterozygous individual who can pass a harmful gene to his or her offspring.

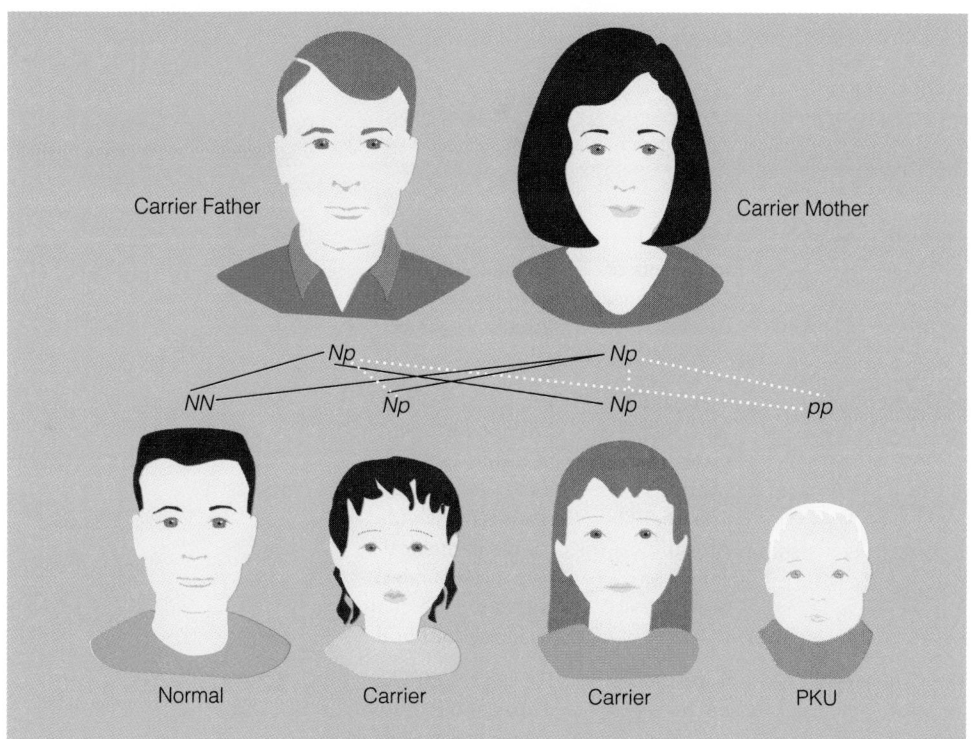

FIGURE 3.4

■ *Dominant–recessive mode of inheritance as illustrated by PKU. When both parents are heterozygous carriers of the recessive allele, we can predict that 25 percent of their offspring will be normal, 50 percent will be carriers, and 25 percent will inherit the disorder. Notice that the PKU-affected child, in contrast to his siblings, has light hair. The recessive gene for PKU is* pleiotropic *(affects more than one trait). It also leads to fair coloring.*

blood test for PKU. If the disease is found, doctors place the baby on a diet low in phenylalanine. Children who receive this treatment show delayed development of higher-order cognitive skills, such as planning and problem solving, in infancy and early childhood because even small amounts of phenylalanine interfere with brain functioning (Diamond et al., 1996; Welsh et al., 1990). But as long as dietary treatment begins early and continues, these deficits disappear by the school years, and children attain an average level of intelligence and have a normal life span (Mazzocco et al., 1994).

In dominant–recessive inheritance, if we know the genetic makeup of the parents, we can predict the percentage of children in a family who are likely to display a trait or be carriers of it. Figure 3.4 shows one example for PKU. Notice that for a child to inherit the condition, both parents must be carriers of a recessive allele (*p*). As the figure also illustrates, it is possible for a single gene to affect more than one trait—a genetic principle known as **pleiotropism**. Due to their inability to convert phenylalanine into tyrosine (which is responsible for pigmentation), children with PKU usually have light hair and blue eyes. Furthermore, children vary in the degree to which phenylalanine accumulates in their tissues and in the extent to which they respond to treatment. This is due to the action of **modifier genes,** which can enhance or dilute the effects of alleles controlling particular traits.

As Table 3.3 suggests, only rarely are serious diseases due to dominant alleles. Think about why this is the case. Children who inherit the dominant allele would always develop the disorder. They would seldom live long enough to reproduce, and the harmful allele would be eliminated from the family's heredity in a single generation. Some dominant disorders, however, do persist. One of them is *Huntington disease,* a condition in which the central nervous system degenerates. Why has this disease endured in some families? The reason is that its symptoms usually do not appear until age 35 or later, after the person has passed the dominant gene on to his or her children.

■ CODOMINANCE. In some heterozygous circumstances, the dominant–recessive relationship does not hold completely. Instead, we see **codominance**, a pattern of inheritance in which both alleles influence the person's characteristics.

The *sickle cell trait,* a heterozygous condition present in many black Africans, provides an example. *Sickle cell anemia* (see Table 3.3 on page 76) occurs in full form when a child inherits two recessive alleles. They cause the usually round red blood cells to become sickle shaped, a response that is especially great under low oxygen conditions. The sickled cells clog the blood vessels and block the flow of blood. Individuals who

Pleiotropism
The influence of a single gene on more than one characteristic.

Modifier genes
Genes that modify the effect of another gene on a characteristic by either enhancing or diluting its effects.

Codominance
A pattern of inheritance in which both alleles, in a heterozygous combination, are expressed.

TABLE 3.3

Examples of Dominant and Recessive Diseases

Disease	Description	Mode of Inheritance	Incidence	Treatment	Prenatal Diagnosis	Carrier Identification[a]
AUTOSOMAL DISEASES						
Cooley's anemia	Pale appearance, retarded physical growth, and lethargic behavior begin in infancy.	Recessive	1 in 500 births to parents of Mediterranean descent	Frequent blood transfusions; death from complications usually occurs by adolescence.	Yes	Yes
Cystic fibrosis	Lungs, liver, and pancreas secrete large amounts of thick mucus, leading to breathing and digestive difficulties.	Recessive	1 in 2,000 to 2,500 Caucasian births. 1 in 16,000 African-American births	Bronchial drainage, prompt treatment of respiratory infections, dietary management. Advances in medical care allow survival with good life quality into adulthood.	Yes	Yes
Phenylketonuria (PKU)	Inability to neutralize the harmful amino acid phenylalanine, contained in many proteins, causes severe central nervous system damage in the first year of life.	Recessive	1 in 8,000 births	Placing the child on a special diet results in average intelligence and normal life span. Subtle difficulties with planning and problem solving are often present.	Yes	Yes
Sickle cell anemia	Abnormal sickling of red blood cells causes oxygen deprivation, pain, swelling, and tissue damage. Anemia and susceptibility to infections, especially pneumonia, occur.	Recessive	1 in 500 African-American births	Blood transfusions, painkillers, prompt treatment of infections. No known cure; 50 percent die by age 20.	Yes	Yes
Tay-Sachs disease	Central nervous system degeneration, with onset at about 6 months, leads to poor muscle tone, blindness, deafness, and convulsions.	Recessive	1 in 3,600 births to Jews of European descent	None. Death by 3 to 4 years of age.	Yes	Yes
Huntington disease	Central nervous system degeneration leads to muscular coordination difficulties, mental deterioration, and personality changes. Symptoms usually do not appear until age 35 or later.	Dominant	1 in 18,000 to 25,000 American births	None. Death occurs 10 to 20 years after symptom onset.	Yes	Not applicable
Marfan syndrome	Tall, slender build; thin, elongated arms and legs. Heart defects and eye abnormalities, especially of the lens. Excessive lengthening of the body results in a variety of skeletal defects.	Dominant	1 in 20,000 births	Correction of heart and eye defects sometimes possible. Death from heart failure in young adulthood common.	Yes	Not applicable

TABLE 3.3 CONTINUED

Disease	Description	Mode of Inheritance	Incidence	Treatment	Prenatal Diagnosis	Carrier Identification[a]
X-LINKED DISEASES						
Duchenne muscular dystrophy	Degenerative muscle disease. Abnormal gait, loss of ability to walk between 7 and 13 years of age.	Recessive	1 in 3,000 to 5,000 male births	None. Death from respiratory infection or weakening of the heart muscle usually occurs in adolescence.	Yes	Yes
Hemophilia	Blood fails to clot normally. Can lead to severe internal bleeding and tissue damage.	Recessive	1 in 4,000 to 7,000 male births	Blood transfusions. Safety precautions to prevent injury.	Yes	Yes
Diabetes insipidus	A form of diabetes present at birth caused by insufficient production of the hormone vasopressin. Results in excessive thirst and urination. Dehydration can cause central nervous system damage.	Recessive	1 in 2,500 male births	Hormone replacement.	Yes	No

[a]Carrier status detectable in prospective parents through blood test or genetic analyses.
Sources: Behrman & Vaughan, 1987; Cohen, 1984; Fackelmann, 1992; Gilfillan et al., 1992; Martin, 1987; McKusick, 1995; Simpson & Harding, 1993.

have the disorder suffer severe attacks involving intense pain, swelling, and tissue damage. They generally die in the first 20 years of life; few live past age 40. Heterozygous individuals are protected from the disease under most circumstances. However, when they experience oxygen deprivation—for example, at high altitudes or after intense physical exercise—the single recessive allele asserts itself, and a temporary, mild form of the illness occurs (Sullivan, 1987).

The sickle cell allele is common among black Africans for a special reason. Carriers of it are more resistant to malaria than are individuals with two alleles for normal red blood cells. In Africa, where malaria occurs often, these carriers survived and reproduced more frequently than others, leading the gene to be maintained in the black population. In regions of the world where the risk of malaria is low, the gene is expected to become less common in future generations, until finally it is eliminated from the gene pool.

■ MUTATION. At this point, you may be wondering, How are harmful genes created in the first place? The answer is **mutation**, a sudden but permanent change in a segment of DNA. A mutation may affect only one or two genes, or it may involve many genes, as is the case for the chromosomal disorders we will discuss shortly. Some mutations occur spontaneously, simply by chance. Others are caused by a wide variety of hazardous environmental agents that enter our food supply or are present in the air we breathe.

For many years, ionizing radiation has been known to cause mutations. Women who receive repeated doses of radiation before conception are more likely to miscarry or give birth to children with hereditary defects (Zhang, Cai, & Lee, 1992). Genetic abnormalities are also higher when fathers are exposed to radiation in their occupations. In one instance, men who worked at a reprocessing plant for nuclear fuel in England fathered an unusually high number of children who developed cancer. Exposure to radiation at the plant is believed to have damaged chromosomes in male sex cells, causing cancer in the children years later (Gardner et al., 1990). Does this mean that routine chest and dental X-rays are dangerous to future generations? Research indicates that infrequent and mild exposure to radiation does not cause genetic damage. Instead, high doses over a long period of time appear to be required.

Although virtually all mutations that have been studied are harmful, we should keep in mind that some spontaneous ones (such as the sickle cell allele in malaria-ridden

Mutation
A sudden but permanent change in a segment of DNA.

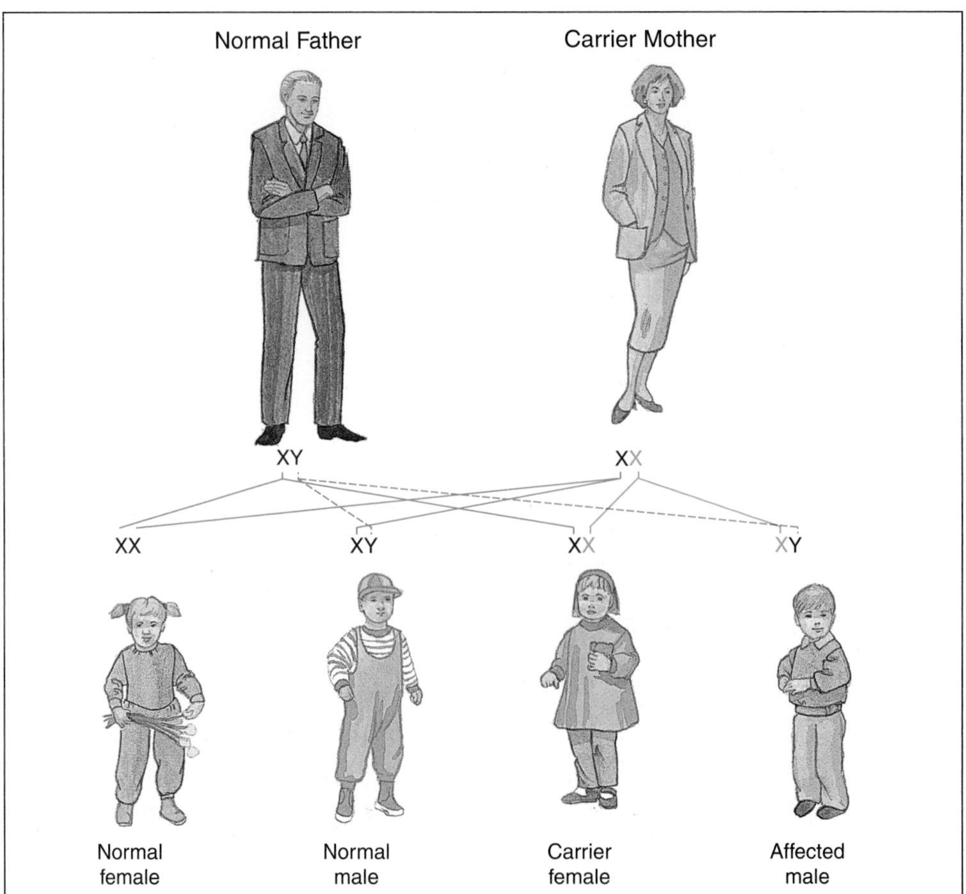

FIGURE 3.5

X-linked inheritance. In the example shown here, the allele on the father's X chromosome is normal. The mother has one normal and one abnormal allele on her X chromosomes. By looking at the possible combinations of the parents' alleles, we can predict that 50 percent of male children will have the disorder and 50 percent of female children will be carriers of it.

regions of the world) are desirable. By increasing genetic variability, they help individuals adapt to unexpected environmental challenges. However, scientists seldom go looking for mutations that underlie favorable traits, such as an exceptional talent or an especially sturdy immune system. Instead, they are far more concerned with identifying and eliminating unfavorable genes that threaten health and survival.

X-LINKED INHERITANCE. Males and females have an equal chance of inheriting recessive disorders carried on the autosomes, such as PKU and sickle cell anemia. But when a harmful allele is carried on the X chromosome, **X-linked inheritance** applies. Males are more likely to be affected because their sex chromosomes do not match. In females, any recessive allele on one X chromosome has a good chance of being suppressed by a dominant allele on the other X. But the Y chromosome is only about one-third as long and therefore lacks many corresponding alleles to override those on the X.

Red–green color blindness (a condition in which individuals cannot tell the difference between shades of red and green) is one example of an X-linked recessive trait. It affects males twice as often as females (Cohen, 1984). Return to Table 3.3 and review the diseases that are X-linked. A well-known example is *hemophilia,* a disorder in which the blood fails to clot normally. Figure 3.5 shows its greater likelihood of inheritance by male children whose mothers carry the abnormal allele.

Besides X-linked disorders, many sex-related differences reveal the male to be at a disadvantage. Rates of miscarriage and infant and childhood deaths are greater for males. Learning disabilities, behavior disorders, and mental retardation are also more common among boys (Richardson, Koller, & Katz, 1986). It is possible that these sex differences can be traced to the genetic code. The female, with two X chromosomes, benefits from a greater variety of genes. Nature, however, seems to have adjusted for the male's disadvantage. Because the Y-bearing sperm are lighter and swifter, they tend to reach the ovum more quickly. Consequently, about 106 boys are born for every 100 girls, and judging from miscarriage and abortion statistics, an even greater number of males are conceived (Shettles & Rorvik, 1984).

X-linked inheritance
A pattern of inheritance in which a recessive gene is carried on the X chromosome. Males are more likely to be affected.

■ GENETIC IMPRINTING. Over 1,000 human characteristics follow the rules of dominant–recessive and codominant inheritance (McKusick, 1995). In these cases, regardless of which parent contributes a gene to the new individual, the gene responds in the same way. Geneticists, however, have identified some exceptions governed by a newly discovered mode of inheritance. In **genetic imprinting**, alleles are *imprinted*, or chemically *marked*, in such a way that one pair member (either the mother's or the father's) is activated, regardless of its makeup. The imprint is often temporary; it may be erased in the next generation, and it may not occur in all individuals (Cassidy, 1995).

Imprinting helps us understand the confusion in inheritance of some disorders. For example, children are more likely to develop diabetes if their father, rather than their mother, suffers from it. And people with asthma or hay fever tend to have mothers, not fathers, with the illness. Scientists do not yet know what causes this parent-specific genetic transmission. At times, it reveals itself in heartbreaking ways. Imprinting is involved in several childhood cancers and in *Praeder-Willi syndrome,* a disorder with symptoms of mental retardation and severe obesity (Day, 1993).

In these examples, genetic imprinting affects traits carried on the autosomes. It can also operate on the sex chromosomes, as *fragile X syndrome* reveals. In this disorder, an abnormal repetition of a sequence of DNA bases occurs in a special spot on the X chromosome, damaging a particular gene (Ryynänen et al., 1995; Turk, 1995). Fragile X syndrome is a common inherited cause of mild to moderate mental retardation. It has also been linked to 2 to 3 percent of cases of infantile autism, a serious emotional disorder of early childhood involving bizarre, self-stimulating behavior and delayed or absent language and communication (Bailey et al., 1993). Recent research reveals that the defective gene at the fragile site is expressed only when it is passed from mother to child (Rose, 1995; Thapar et al., 1994).

■ *The flattened face and almond-shaped eyes of the younger child in this photo are typical physical features of Down syndrome. Although his intellectual development is impaired, this boy is doing well because he is growing up in a family in which his special needs are met and he is loved and accepted. (Frank Sitman/Stock Boston)*

■ POLYGENIC INHERITANCE. So far, we have discussed patterns of inheritance in which people either display a particular trait or do not. These cut-and-dried individual differences are much easier to trace to their genetic origins than are characteristics that vary continuously among people. Many traits of interest to child development specialists, such as height, weight, intelligence, and personality, are of this type. People are not just tall or short, bright or dull, outgoing or shy. Instead, they show gradations between these extremes. Continuous traits like these are due to **polygenic inheritance**, in which many genes determine the characteristic in question. Polygenic inheritance is complex, and much about it is still unknown. In the final section of this chapter, we will pay special attention to this form of genetic transmission by examining ways that researchers infer the influence of heredity on human attributes when knowledge of precise patterns of inheritance is unavailable.

Chromosomal Abnormalities

Besides inheriting harmful recessive alleles, abnormalities of the chromosomes are a major cause of serious developmental problems. Most chromosomal defects are the result of mistakes during meiosis when the ovum and sperm are formed. A chromosome pair does not separate properly, or part of a chromosome breaks off. Since these errors involve far more DNA than problems due to single genes, they usually produce disorders with many physical and mental symptoms.

DOWN SYNDROME

The most common chromosomal abnormality, occurring in 1 out of every 800 live births, is *Down syndrome.* In 95 percent of cases, it results from a failure of the twenty-first pair of chromosomes to separate during meiosis, so the new individual inherits three of these chromosomes rather than the normal two. For this reason, Down syndrome is sometimes called *trisomy 21*. In other less frequent forms, an extra broken piece of a twenty-first chromosome is present. Or an error occurs during the early stages of mitosis, causing some but not all body cells to have the defective chromosomal makeup (called a

Genetic imprinting
A pattern of inheritance in which alleles are imprinted, or chemically marked, in such a way that one pair member is activated, regardless of its makeup.

Polygenic inheritance
A pattern of inheritance involving many genes that applies to characteristics that vary continuously among people.

mosaic pattern). In these instances, since less genetic material is involved, symptoms of the disorder are less extreme (Epstein, 1993; Fishler & Koch, 1991).

Children with Down syndrome have distinct physical features—a short, stocky build, a flattened face, a protruding tongue, almond-shaped eyes, and an unusual crease running across the palm of the hand. In addition, infants with Down syndrome are often born with eye cataracts and heart and intestinal defects. Because of medical advances, fewer Down syndrome children die early than was the case in the past, but early death is still common. About 14 percent die by age 1, and 21 percent by age 10. The rest live until middle adulthood (Baird & Sadovnick, 1987).

The behavioral consequences of Down syndrome include mental retardation, speech difficulties, limited vocabulary, and slow motor development. These problems become more evident with age, since Down syndrome children show a gradual slowing in development from infancy onward when compared to normal children.

Down syndrome babies are more difficult to care for than are normal infants. Their facial deformities often lead to breathing and feeding difficulties. In addition, they smile less readily, show poor eye-to-eye contact, and explore objects less persistently. Therefore, caregivers need to be more assertive in getting these infants to become engaged in their surroundings (Loveland, 1987; MacTurk et al., 1985). When parents make this effort, their children show better developmental progress. Early intervention programs also foster the development of Down syndrome youngsters, although social, emotional, and motor skills improve more than intellectual performance (Gibson & Harris, 1988; Van Dyke et al., 1990). These findings indicate that even though Down syndrome is a genetic disorder, environmental factors affect how well these children fare in the long run.

As Table 3.4 shows, the incidence of Down syndrome rises dramatically with maternal age. Why is this so? Geneticists believe that the ova, present in the woman's body since her own prenatal period, weaken over time because of the aging process or increased exposure to harmful environmental agents. As a result, chromosomes do not separate properly during meiosis. A second possibility is that with age, mothers are less likely to miscarry defective conceptions (Antonarakis, 1992; Warburton, 1989). The mother's gamete, however, is not always the cause of a Down syndrome child. In about 20 percent of cases, the extra genetic material originates with the father. However, Down syndrome and other chromosomal abnormalities are not related to advanced paternal age. In these instances, the mutation occurs for other unknown reasons (Michelena et al., 1993; Phillips & Elias, 1993).

TABLE 3.4

Risk of Giving Birth to a Down Syndrome Child by Maternal Age

Maternal Age	Risk
20	1 in 1,900 births
25	1 in 1,200
30	1 in 900
33	1 in 600
36	1 in 280
39	1 in 130
42	1 in 65
45	1 in 30
48	1 in 15

Note: The risk of giving birth to a Down syndrome baby after age 35 has increased slightly over the past 20 years, due to improved medical interventions during pregnancy and consequent greater likelihood of a Down syndrome fetus surviving to be liveborn.
Sources: Adapted from Halliday et al., 1995; Hook, 1982.

ABNORMALITIES OF THE SEX CHROMOSOMES

Disorders of the autosomes other than Down syndrome usually disrupt development so severely that miscarriage occurs. When such babies are born, they rarely survive beyond early childhood. In contrast, abnormalities of the sex chromosomes usually lead to fewer problems. In fact, sex chromosome disorders are often not recognized until adolescence, when, in some of the deviations, puberty is delayed. The most common problems involve the presence of an extra chromosome (either X or Y) or the absence of one X chromosome in females (see Table 3.5).

A variety of myths about individuals with sex chromosome disorders exist. For example, many people think that males with *XYY syndrome* are more aggressive and antisocial than XY males. Yet by examining Table 3.5, you will see that this is not true. Also, it is widely believed that children with sex chromosome disorders suffer from mental retardation. Yet most do not. The intelligence of boys with XYY syndrome is similar to that of normal children (Netley, 1986; Stewart, 1982). And the intellectual problems of children with *triple X, Klinefelter, and Turner syndromes* are very specific. Verbal difficulties (for example, with reading and vocabulary) are common among girls with triple X syndrome and boys with Klinefelter syndrome, each of whom inherits an extra X chromosome (Netley, 1986). In contrast, Turner syndrome girls, who are missing an X, have trouble with spatial relationships. Their handwriting is poor, and they have difficulty telling right from left, following travel directions, and noticing changes in facial expressions (Money, 1993; Temple & Carney, 1995). These findings tell us that adding to or subtracting from the usual number of X chromosomes results in particular intellectual deficits. At present, geneticists do not know why this is the case.

TABLE 3.5

Sex Chromosomal Disorders

Disorder	Description	Incidence	Treatment
XYY syndrome	Inheritance of an extra Y chromosome. Typical characteristics are above-average height, large teeth, and sometimes severe acne. Intelligence, development of male sexual characteristics, and fertility are normal.	1 in 1,000 male births	No special treatment necessary.
Triple X syndrome (XXX)	Inheritance of an extra X chromosome. Impaired verbal intelligence. Affected girls are no different in appearance or sexual development from normal age-mates,except for a greater tendency toward tallness.	1 in 500 to 1,250 female births	Special education to treat verbal ability problems.
Klinefelter syndrome (XXY)	Inheritance of an extra X chromosome. Impaired verbal intelligence. Afflicted boys are unusually tall, have a body fat distribution resembling females, and show incomplete development of sex characteristics at puberty. They are usually sterile.	1 in 500 to 1,000 male births	Hormone therapy at puberty to stimulate development of sex characteristics. Special education to treat verbal ability problems.
Turner syndrome (XO)	All or part of the second X chromosome is missing. Impaired spatial intelligence. Ovaries usually do not develop prenatally. Incomplete development of sex characteristicsat puberty. Other features include short stature and webbed neck.	1 in 2,500 to 8,000 female births	Hormone therapy in childhood to stimulate physical growth and at puberty to promote development of sex characteristics. Special education to treat spatial ability problems.

Sources: Cohen, 1984; Money, 1993; Netley, 1986; Pennington et al., 1982; Ratcliffe, Pan, & McKie, 1992; Schaivi et al., 1984.

Reproductive Choices

In the past, many couples with genetic disorders in their families chose not to bear a child at all rather than risk having an abnormal baby. Today, genetic counseling and prenatal diagnosis permit people to make informed decisions about conceiving or carrying a pregnancy to term.

GENETIC COUNSELING

Genetic counseling helps couples assess their chances of giving birth to a baby with a hereditary disorder. Individuals likely to seek it are those who have had difficulties bearing children, such as repeated miscarriages, or who know that genetic problems exist in their families. When mental retardation, physical defects, or inherited diseases are present in the relatives of prospective parents, then genetic counseling is warranted (Fine, 1990).

The genetic counselor interviews the couple and prepares a *pedigree,* a picture of the family tree in which affected relatives are identified. The pedigree is used to estimate the likelihood that parents will have an abnormal child, using the same genetic principles we discussed earlier in this chapter. In the case of many disorders, blood tests or genetic analyses can reveal whether the parent is a carrier of the harmful gene. Turn back to pages 76–77, and you will see that carrier detection is possible for many of the diseases listed in Table 3.3. A carrier test has been developed for fragile X syndrome as well (Ryynänen et al., 1995).

Genetic counseling
Counseling that helps couples assess the likelihood of giving birth to a baby with a hereditary disorder.

TABLE 3.6

Prenatal Diagnostic Methods

Method	Description
Amniocentesis	The most widely used technique. A hollow needle is inserted through the abdominal wall to obtain a sample of fluid in the uterus. Cells are examined for genetic defects. Can be performed by 11 to 14 weeks after conception; 1 to 2 more weeks are required for test results. Small risk of miscarriage.
Chorionic villus sampling	A procedure that can be used if results are desired or needed very early in pregnancy. A thin tube is inserted into the uterus through the vagina or a hollow needle is inserted through the abdominal wall. A small plug of tissue is removed from the end of one or more chorionic villi, the hairlike projections on the membrane surrounding the developing organism. Cells are examined for genetic defects. Can be performed at 6 to 8 weeks after conception, and results are available within 24 hours. Entails a slightly greater risk of miscarriage than does amniocentesis. Also associated with a small risk of limb deformities, which increases the earlier the procedure is performed.
Ultrasound	High-frequency sound waves are beamed at the uterus; their reflection is translated into a picture on a videoscreen that reveals the size, shape, and placement of the fetus. By itself, permits assessment of fetal age, detection of multiple pregnancies, and identification of gross physical defects. Also used to guide amniocentesis, chorionic villi biopsy, and fetoscopy (see below). When used five or more times, may increase the chances of low birth weight.
Fetoscopy	A small tube with a light source at one end is inserted into the uterus to inspect the fetus for defects of the limbs and face. Also allows a sample of fetal blood to be obtained, permitting diagnosis of such disorders as hemophilia and sickle cell anemia as well as neural defects (see below). Usually performed between 15 to 18 weeks after conception, although can be done as early as 5 weeks. Entails some risk of miscarriage.
Maternal blood analysis	By the second month of pregnancy, some of the developing organism's cells enter the maternal bloodstream. An elevated level of alpha-fetoprotein may indicate kidney disease, abnormal closure of the esophagus, or neural tube defects, such as anencephaly (absence of most of the brain) and spina bifida (bulging of the spinal cord from the spinal column).

Sources: Benacerraf et al., 1988; Burton, 1992; Canick & Saller, 1993; Holmes, 1993; Newnham et al., 1993; Quintero, Puder, & Cotton, 1993; Shurtleff & Lemire, 1995.

When all of the relevant information is in, the genetic counselor helps people consider appropriate options. These include "taking a chance" and conceiving, adopting a child, or choosing from among a variety of reproductive technologies. The Social Issues box on pages 84–85 describes these medical interventions into conception along with the host of legal and ethical dilemmas that have arisen in their application.

PRENATAL DIAGNOSIS AND FETAL MEDICINE

If couples who might bear an abnormal child decide to conceive, several **prenatal diagnostic methods**—medical procedures that permit detection of problems before birth—are available (see Table 3.6). Women of advanced maternal age are prime candidates for *amniocentesis* or *chorionic villus sampling* (see Figure 3.6), since the overall rate of chromosomal problems rises sharply after age 35, from 1 in every 100 to as many as 1 in every 3 pregnancies at age 48 (Hook, 1988). Except for *ultrasound* and *maternal blood analysis,* prenatal diagnosis should not be used routinely, since each of the other methods described in Table 3.6 has some chance of injuring the developing organism.

Improvements in prenatal diagnosis have led to new advances in fetal medicine. Today, some medical problems are being treated before birth. For example, by inserting a needle into the uterus, drugs can be delivered to the fetus. Surgery has been performed to repair such problems as urinary tract obstructions and heart and neural defects. Nevertheless, these practices remain controversial. Although some babies are saved, the techniques frequently result in complications, premature birth, or miscarriage (Flake & Harrison, 1995). Yet when parents are told that their unborn child has a serious defect, they may be willing to try almost any option, even if there is only a slim chance of success. Currently, the medical profession is struggling with how to help parents make informed decisions about fetal surgery. One suggestion is that the advice of an independent counselor be provided—a doctor or nurse who understands the risks but is not involved in doing research on or performing the procedure.

Prenatal diagnostic methods
Methods that permit detection of developmental problems before birth.

Advances in *genetic engineering* also offer new hope for correcting hereditary defects. Genetic repair of the prenatal organism is one goal of today's genetic engineers. Researchers are mapping human chromosomes, finding the precise location of genes for

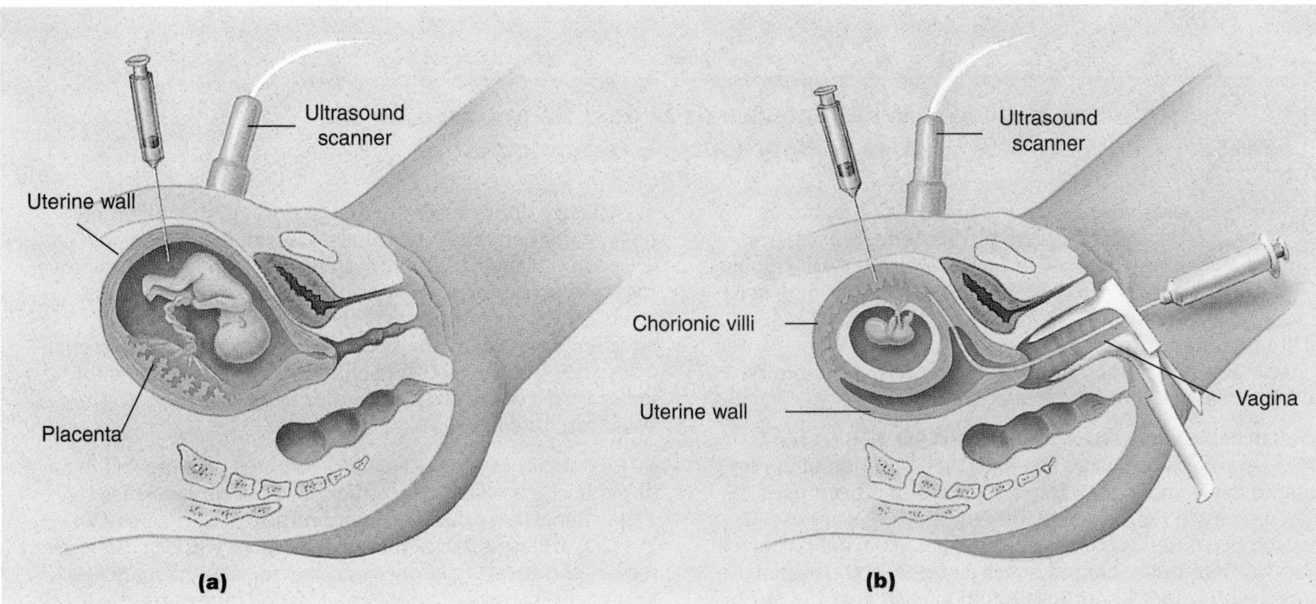

FIGURE 3.6

■ *Amniocentesis and chorionic villus sampling. Today, many defects and diseases can be detected before birth using these procedures. (a) In amniocentesis, a hollow needle is inserted through the abdominal wall into the uterus. Fluid is withdrawn and fetal cells are cultured, a process that takes 1 to 2 weeks. (b) Chorionic villus sampling can be performed much earlier in pregnancy, at 6 to 8 weeks after conception, and results are available within 24 hours. Two approaches to obtaining a sample of chorionic villi are shown: inserting a thin tube through the vagina into the uterus or a needle through the abdominal wall. In both amniocentesis and chorionic villus sampling, an ultrasound scanner is used for guidance. (From K. L. Moore & T. V. N. Persaud, 1993,* Before We Are Born, *4th ed., Philadelphia: Saunders, p. 89. Adapted by permission of the publisher and author.)*

specific traits and cloning (duplicating) these genes using chemical techniques in the laboratory. To date, DNA markers have been identified for over 5,000 human characteristics and hundreds of inherited diseases, including cystic fibrosis, Huntington disease, Marfan syndrome, Duchenne muscular dystrophy, some types of cancer, and the form of diabetes listed in Table 3.3 (Cox et al., 1994; Service, 1994). Scientists are using this information to identify abnormal conditions with greater accuracy before birth. They are also experimenting with *gene splicing*—replacing a harmful gene with a good one in the early zygote or in cells in the affected part of the body. At present, getting the healthy gene into target tissue and making sure it is passed on through cell duplication are major obstacles to the success of this technique (Begley, 1995; Marshall, 1995).

If prenatal diagnosis shows that the fetus has a condition that cannot be corrected, parents are faced with the difficult choice of whether or not to have an abortion. The decision to terminate a desired pregnancy is painful for all who have to make it. Parents must deal with the emotional shock of the news and decide what to do within a short period of time. If they choose abortion, they face the grief that comes with having lost a wanted child, worries about future pregnancies, and possible guilt about the abortion itself. Fortunately, 95 percent of fetuses examined through prenatal diagnosis are normal (Benacerraf et al., 1988). Because modern medicine makes such tests possible, many individuals whose age or family history would have caused them to avoid pregnancy entirely can now have healthy children.

BRIEF REVIEW

Each individual is made up of trillions of cells. Inside each cell nucleus are chromosomes composed of a molecule called DNA. Genes are segments of DNA that determine our species and unique characteristics. Gametes, or sex cells, are formed through a process of cell division called meiosis, which halves the usual number of chromosomes in human cells. Then, when sperm and ovum unite to form the zygote, each new being has the correct number of chromosomes.

SOCIAL ISSUES ➤ POINT OF VIEW

What Safeguards Should Be Imposed on the Use of Reproductive Technologies?

Some couples decide not to risk pregnancy because of a history of genetic disease. And many others—in fact, one-sixth of all couples who try to conceive—discover that they are sterile. Today, increasing numbers of individuals are turning to alternative methods of conception—technologies that, although fulfilling the wish of parenthood, have become the subject of heated debate.

DONOR INSEMINATION AND IN VITRO FERTILIZATION. For several decades, *donor insemination*—injection of sperm from an anonymous man into a woman—has been used to overcome male reproductive difficulties. In recent years, it has also permitted women without a heterosexual partner to bear children. In the United States alone, 30,000 children are conceived through donor insemination each year (Swanson, 1993).

In vitro fertilization is another reproductive technology that has become increasingly common. Since the first "test tube" baby was born in England in 1978, thousands of infants have been created this way. For in vitro fertilization, hormones are given to a woman, stimulating ripening of several ova. These are removed surgically and placed in a dish of nutrients, to which sperm are added. Once an ovum is fertilized and begins to duplicate into several cells, it is injected into the mother's uterus, where, hopefully, it will implant and develop.

In vitro fertilization is usually used to treat women whose fallopian tubes are permanently damaged, and it is successful for 20 percent of those who try it. These results have been encouraging enough that the technique has been expanded. By mixing and matching gametes, pregnancies can be brought about when either or both partners have a reproductive problem. In cases where couples might transmit harmful genes, single cells can be plucked from the duplicating zygote and screened for hereditary defects. Fertilized ova can even be frozen and stored in embryo banks for use at some future time, thereby guaranteeing healthy zygotes to older women (Edwards, 1991).

Children conceived through these methods may be genetically unrelated to one or both of their parents. Does lack of genetic ties, or secrecy surrounding these techniques (most parents do not tell their children), interfere with parent–child relationships? Apparently not. A recent study found that quality of parenting was superior (warmer and more emotionally involved) for 4- to 8-year-olds conceived through in vitro fertilization or donor insemination than for naturally conceived children. A strong desire for parenthood among couples who have experienced reproductive problems seems to enhance family functioning (Golombok et al., 1995).

Clearly donor insemination and in vitro fertilization have many benefits. Nevertheless, serious questions have arisen about their use. Many states have no legal guidelines for these procedures. As a result, donors are not always screened for genetic or sexually transmitted diseases. In addition, few American doctors keep records of donor characteristics. Yet the resulting children may someday want to know their genetic background or need to for medical reasons (Nachtigall, 1993).

SURROGATE MOTHERHOOD. A more controversial form of medically assisted conception is *surrogate motherhood.* Typically in this procedure, sperm from a man whose wife is infertile are used to inseminate a woman, who is paid a fee for her childbearing services. In return, the surrogate agrees to turn the baby over to the man (who is the natural father). The child is then adopted by his wife.

Although most of these arrangements proceed smoothly, those that end up in court highlight serious risks for all concerned. In one case, both parties rejected the handicapped infant that resulted from the pregnancy. In several others, the surrogate mother changed her mind and wanted to keep the baby. These children came into the world in midst of

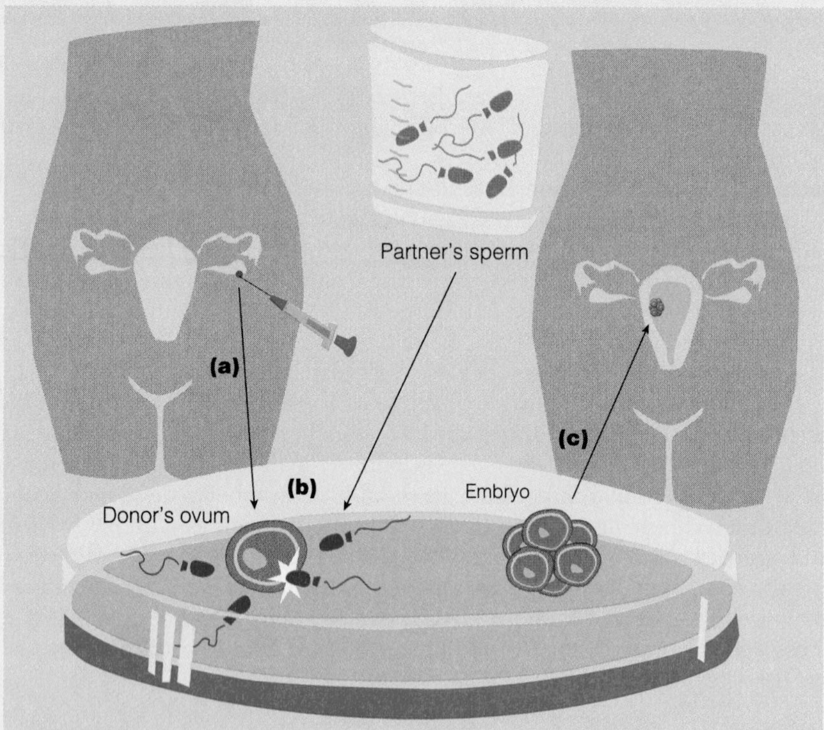

FIGURE 3.7

■ *In vitro fertilization procedure that can help postmenopausal women become pregnant. (a) A young female donor is given hormones to stimulate ovulation. Then a needle is inserted into her ovary, and several ova are extracted. (b) The donor's ova are fertilized in a dish of nutrients using sperm from the recipient's partner or from another male donor. (c) The prospective mother is given hormones to prepare her uterus to receive the fertilized ova, which are inserted.*

family conflict that threatened to last for years to come. Most surrogates already have children of their own, who may be deeply affected by the pregnancy. Knowledge that their mother would give away a baby for profit may cause these youngsters to worry about the security of their own family circumstances (McGinty & Zafran, 1988; Ryan, 1989).

NEW REPRODUCTIVE FRONTIERS. Reproductive technologies are evolving faster than societies can weigh the ethics of these procedures. Doctors have used donor ova from younger women in combination with in vitro fertilization to help postmenopausal women become pregnant (see Figure 3.7). Most recipients are in their forties, but in 1993, a 62-year-old woman gave birth in Italy (Beck, 1994). Even though candidates for postmenopausal assisted childbirth are selected on the basis of good health, serious questions arise about bringing children into the world whose parents may not live to see them reach adulthood.

Currently, experts are debating other reproductive options. At donor banks, customers can select ova or sperm on the basis of physical characteristics and even the IQ of potential donors. Some worry that this practice is a dangerous step toward selective breeding of the human species. Researchers have delivered baby mice using the transplanted ovaries of aborted fetuses (Hashimoto, Noguchi, & Nakatsuji, 1992). If the same procedure were eventually applied to human beings, it would create babies whose genetic mothers had never been born.

Finally, scientists have successfully cloned (made multiple copies of) fertilized ova in sheep and cattle, and they are working on effective ways of doing so in humans (Kolberg, 1993). By providing extra ova for injection, cloning might improve the success rate of in vitro fertilization. But it also opens the possibility of mass-producing genetically identical people.

Although new reproductive technologies permit many barren couples to rear healthy newborn babies, laws are needed to regulate them. In Great Britain and Sweden, individuals conceived with donated gametes have a right to information about their genetic origins. Pressures from those working in the field of assisted reproduction may soon lead to a similar policy in the United States (Daniels & Taylor, 1993).

In the case of surrogate motherhood, the ethical problems are so complex that 18 U.S. states have sharply restricted the practice, and many European governments have banned it (Belkin, 1992; Charo, 1994). Recently, England, France, and Italy took steps to prohibit in vitro fertilization for women past menopause (Beck, 1994). At present nothing is known about the psychological consequences of being a product of these procedures. Research on how such children grow up, including what they know and how they feel about their origins, is important for weighing the pros and cons of these techniques.

YOUR POINT OF VIEW . . .

- Locate newspaper and magazine articles on two highly publicized surrogate motherhood cases: Baby M of New Jersey (1987) and the Calvert case of California (1990). Do you think the problems that arose in each case justify limiting or banning the practice of surrogacy?

Identical twins have the same genetic makeup, whereas fraternal twins are genetically no more alike than ordinary siblings. Four patterns of inheritance—dominant–recessive, codominant, X-linked, and genetic imprinting—underlie many traits and disorders. Continuous characteristics, such as height and intelligence, result from the enormous complexities of polygenic inheritance, which involves many genes. Chromosomal abnormalities occur when meiosis is disrupted during gamete formation. Disorders of the autosomes are usually more severe than those of the sex chromosomes.

Genetic counseling helps people with a family history of reproductive problems or hereditary defects make informed decisions about bearing a child. Prenatal diagnostic methods permit early detection of fetal problems. Advances in fetal medicine and genetic engineering offer new hope for treating disorders before birth.

Prenatal Development

The sperm and ovum that will unite to form the new individual are uniquely suited for the task of reproduction. The ovum is a tiny sphere, measuring 1/175 of an inch in diameter, that is barely visible to the naked eye as a dot the size of a period at the end of this sentence. But in its microscopic world, it is a giant—the largest cell in the human body. The ovum's size makes it a perfect target for the much smaller sperm, which measure only 1/500 of an inch.

About once every 28 days, in the middle of a woman's menstrual cycle, an ovum bursts from one of her *ovaries,* two walnut-sized organs located deep inside her abdomen (see Figure 3.8 on page 86). Surrounded by thousands of nurse cells that will feed and protect it along its path, the ovum is drawn into one of two *fallopian tubes*—long, thin structures that lead to the hollow, soft-lined uterus. While the ovum is traveling, the spot on the ovary from which it was released, now called the *corpus luteum,* begins to secrete hormones that prepare the lining of the uterus to receive a fertilized ovum. If pregnancy

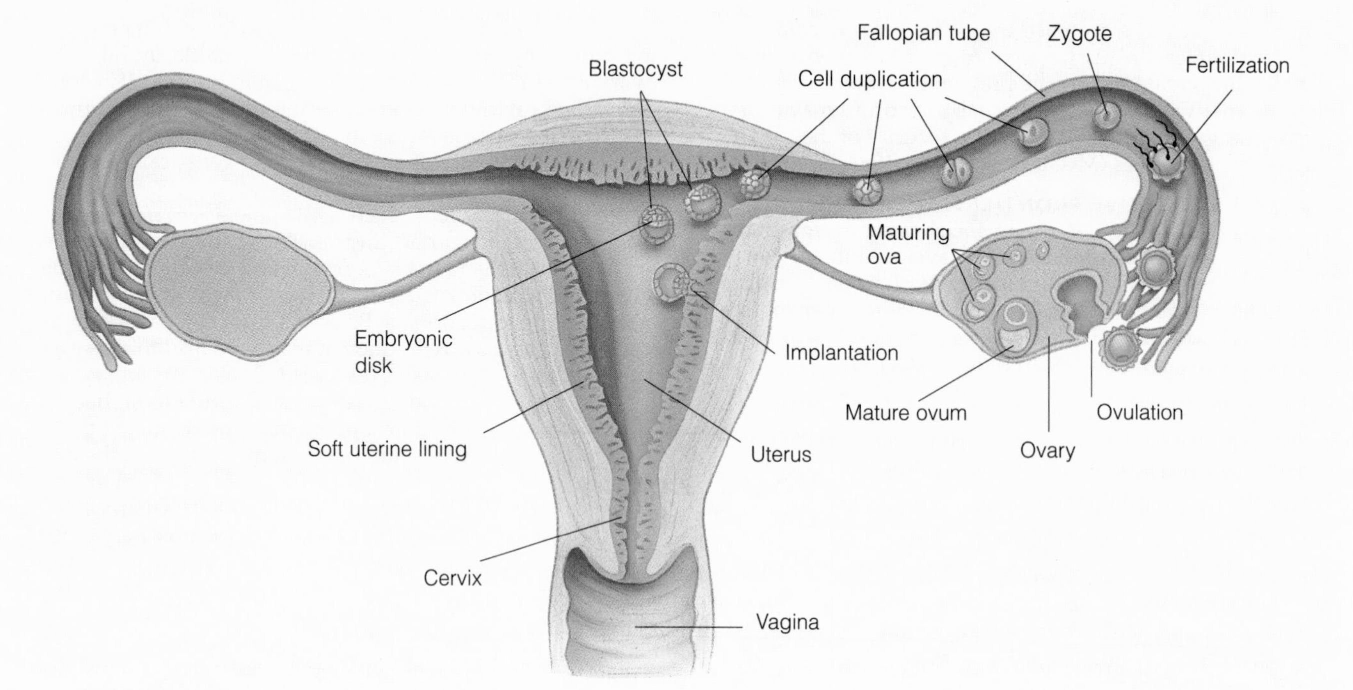

FIGURE 3.8

Journey of the ovum to the uterus. Once every 28 days, an ovum matures, is released from one of the woman's ovaries, and is drawn into the fallopian tube. After fertilization, it begins to duplicate, at first slowly and then more rapidly. By the fourth day, it forms a hollow, fluid-filled ball called a blastocyst. The inner cells, or the embryonic disk, will become the new organism; the outer cells will provide protective covering. At the end of the first week, the blastocyst begins to implant in the uterine lining. (From K. L. Moore & T. V. N. Persaud, 1993, Before We Are Born, *4th ed., Philadelphia: Saunders, p. 33. Reprinted by permission of the publisher and the author.)*

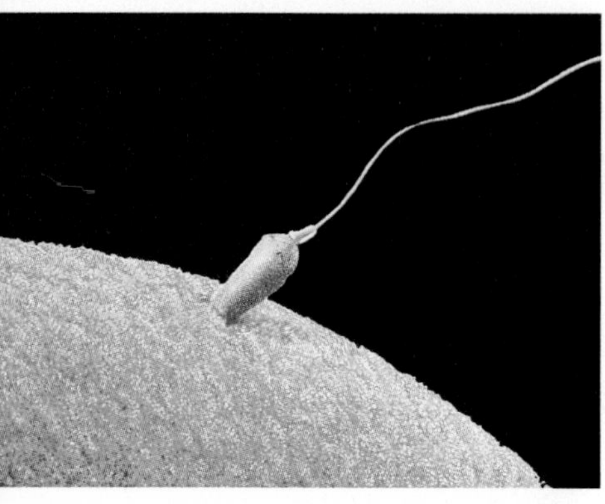

In this photograph of fertilization taken with the aid of a powerful microscope, a tiny sperm completes its journey and starts to penetrate the surface of an enormous-looking ovum, the largest cell in the human body. (Francis Leroy, Biocosmos/Science Photo Library/Photo Researchers)

Amnion
The inner membrane that forms a protective covering around the prenatal organism and encloses it in amniotic fluid, which helps keep temperature constant and provides a cushion against jolts caused by the mother's movement.

does not occur, the corpus luteum shrinks, and the lining of the uterus is discarded in 2 weeks with menstruation.

The male produces sperm in vast numbers—an average of 300 million a day. In the final process of maturation, each sperm develops a tail that permits it to swim long distances, upstream in the female reproductive tract and into the fallopian tube, where fertilization usually takes place. The journey is difficult, and many sperm die. Of the approximately 360 million sperm released during sexual intercourse, only 300 to 500 reach the ovum, if one happens to be present. Sperm live for up to 6 days and can lie in wait for the ovum, which survives for only 1 day after being released into the fallopian tube. However, most conceptions result from intercourse during a 3-day period—on the day of or the 2 days preceding ovulation (Wilcox, Weinberg, & Baird, 1995).

With fertilization, the story of prenatal development begins to unfold. The vast changes that take place during the 38 weeks of pregnancy are usually divided into three phases: (1) the period of the zygote, (2) the period of the embryo, and (3) the period of the fetus. As we look at what happens in each, you may find it useful to refer to the Milestones table on the following page.

THE PERIOD OF THE ZYGOTE

The period of the zygote lasts about 2 weeks, from fertilization until the tiny mass of cells drifts down and out of the fallopian tube and attaches itself to the wall of the uterus. The zygote's first cell duplication is long and drawn out; it is not complete until about 30 hours after conception. Gradually, new cells are added at a faster rate. By the fourth day, 60 to 70 cells exist that form a hollow, fluid-filled ball called a *blastocyst* (refer again to Figure 3.8). The cells on the inside, called the *embryonic disk,* will become the new organism; the outer ring will provide protective covering.

IMPLANTATION. Sometime between the seventh and ninth day, implantation occurs: the blastocyst burrows deep into the uterine lining. Surrounded by the woman's nour-

MILESTONES

Prenatal Development

Trimester	Period	Weeks	Length and Weight	Major Events
first	■ Zygote	■ 1		■ The one-celled zygote multiplies and forms a blastocyst.
		■ 2		■ The blastocyst burrows into the uterine lining. Structures that feed and protect the developing organism begin to form—amnion, chorion, yolk sac, placenta, and umbilical cord.
	■ Embryo	■ 3-4	■ 1/4 inch	■ A primitive brain and spinal cord appear. Heart and muscles, backbone, ribs, and digestive tract begin to develop.
		■ 5-8	■ 1 inch	■ Many external body structures (for example, face, arms, legs, toes, fingers) and internal organs form. The sense of touch begins to develop, and the embryo can move
	■ Fetus	■ 9-12	■ 3 inches; less than 1 ounce	■ Rapid increase in size begins. Nervous system, organs, and muscles become organized and connected, and new behavioral capacities (kicking, thumb sucking, mouth opening, and rehearsal of breathing) appear. External genitals are well formed, and the fetus's sex is evident.
second		■ 13-24	■ 12 inches; 1.8 pounds	■ The fetus continues to enlarge rapidly. In the middle of this period, fetal movements can be felt by the mother. Vernix and lanugo keep the fetus's from chapping in the amniotic fluid. All of the neurons that will ever be produced in the brain are present by 24 weeks. Eyes are sensitive to light, and the fetus reacts to sound.
third		■ 25-38	■ 20 inches; 7.5 pounds	■ The fetus has a chance of survival if born around this time. Size continues to increase. Lungs gradually mature. Rapid brain development causes sensory and behavioral capacities to expand. In the middle of this period, a layer of fat is added under the skin. Antibodies are transmitted from mother to fetus to protect against disease. Most fetuses rotate into an upside-down position in preparation for birth.

Sources: Moore & Persaud, 1993; Nilsson & Hamberger, 1990; Sadler, 1995.

ishing blood, now it starts to grow in earnest. At first, the protective outer layer multiplies fastest. A membrane, called the **amnion**, forms that encloses the developing organism in *amniotic fluid.* It helps keep the temperature of the prenatal world constant and provides a cushion against any jolts caused by the mother's movement. A *yolk sac* also appears. It produces blood cells until the developing liver, spleen, and bone marrow are mature enough to take over this function (Moore & Persaud, 1993).

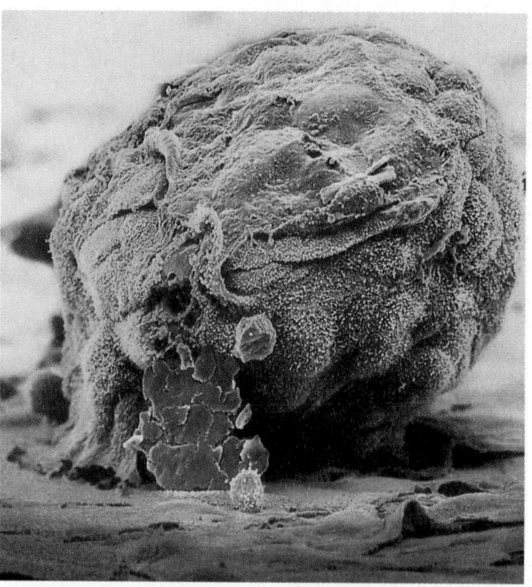

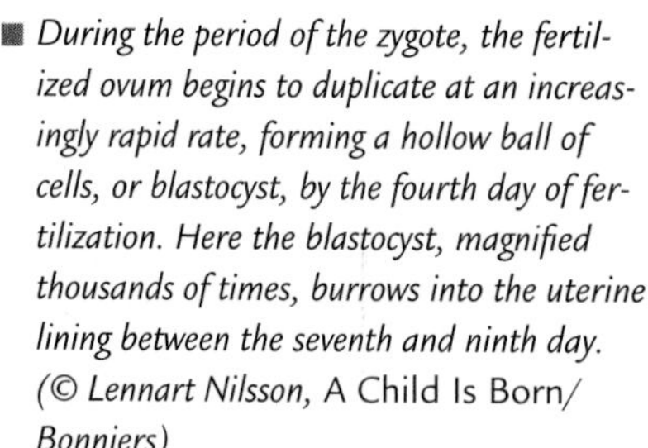

■ *During the period of the zygote, the fertilized ovum begins to duplicate at an increasingly rapid rate, forming a hollow ball of cells, or blastocyst, by the fourth day of fertilization. Here the blastocyst, magnified thousands of times, burrows into the uterine lining between the seventh and ninth day. (© Lennart Nilsson,* A Child Is Born/ *Bonniers)*

The events of these first 2 weeks are delicate and uncertain. As many as 30 percent of zygotes do not make it through this phase. In some, the sperm and ovum do not join properly. In others, for some unknown reason, cell duplication never begins. By preventing implantation in these cases, nature eliminates most prenatal abnormalities in the very earliest stages of development (Sadler, 1995).

■ THE PLACENTA AND UMBILICAL CORD. By the end of the second week, another protective membrane, called the **chorion**, surrounds the amnion. From the chorion, tiny hairlike *villi* begin to emerge.[1] As these villi burrow into the uterine wall and develop into blood vessels, a special organ called the **placenta** starts to develop. By bringing the embryo's and mother's blood close together, the placenta will permit food and oxygen to reach the organism and waste products to be carried away. A membrane forms that allows these substances to be exchanged but prevents the mother's and embryo's blood from mixing directly.

The placenta is connected to the developing organism by the **umbilical cord**. In the period of the zygote, it first appears as a primitive body stalk, but during the course of pregnancy, it grows to a length of 1 to 3 feet. The umbilical cord contains one large vein that delivers blood loaded with nutrients and two arteries that remove waste products. The force of blood flowing through the cord keeps it firm, much like a garden hose, so it seldom tangles while the embryo, like a space-walking astronaut, floats freely in its fluid-filled chamber (Moore & Persaud, 1993).

By the end of the period of the zygote, the developing organism has found food and shelter in the uterus. Already it is a very complex being. These dramatic beginnings take place before all but the most sensitive woman knows she is pregnant.

THE PERIOD OF THE EMBRYO

The period of the **embryo** lasts from implantation through the eighth week of pregnancy. During these brief 6 weeks, the most rapid prenatal changes take place as the groundwork for all body structures and internal organs is laid down. Because all parts of the body are forming, the embryo is especially vulnerable to interference in healthy development. But the fact that embryonic growth takes place over a fairly short time span helps limit opportunities for serious harm to occur.

■ LAST HALF OF THE FIRST MONTH. In the first week of this period, the embryonic disk forms three layers of cells: (1) the *ectoderm,* which will become the nervous system

Chorion
The outer membrane that forms a protective covering around the prenatal organism. It sends out tiny fingerlike villi, from which the placenta begins to emerge.

Placenta
The organ that separates the mother's bloodstream from the embryo or fetal bloodstream but permits exchange of nutrients and waste products.

Umbilical cord
The long cord connecting the prenatal organism to the placenta that delivers nutrients and removes waste products.

Embryo
The prenatal organism from 2 to 8 weeks after conception, during which time the foundations of all body structures and internal organs are laid down.

[1] Recall from Table 3.6 on page 82 that chorionic villus sampling is the prenatal diagnosis method that can be earliest, 6 to 8 weeks after conception. In this procedure, tissue from the ends of the villi is removed and examined for genetic abnormalities.

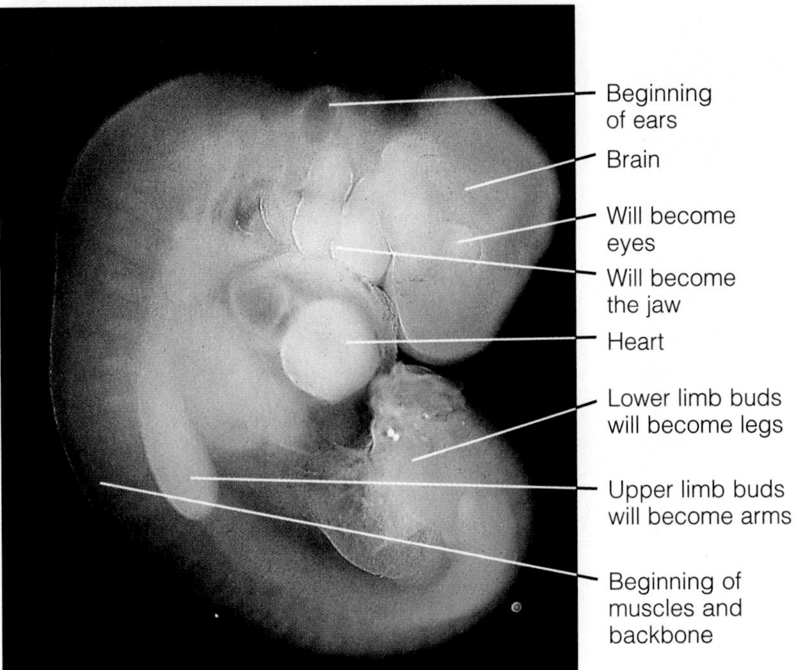

■ *This curled embryo is about 4 weeks old. In actual size, it is only 1/4-inch long, but many body structures have begun to form. The primitive tail will disappear by the end of the embryonic period. (© Lennart Nilsson, A Child Is Born/Bonniers)*

and skin; (2) the *mesoderm,* from which will develop the muscles, skeleton, circulatory system, and other internal organs; and (3) the *endoderm,* which will become the digestive system, lungs, urinary tract, and glands. These three layers give rise to all parts of the body.

At first, the nervous system develops fastest. The ectoderm folds over to form a *neural tube,* or primitive spinal cord. At 3 ½ weeks, the top swells to form a brain. Production of *neurons* (nerve cells that store and transmit information) begins deep inside the neural tube. Once formed, neurons travel along tiny threads to their permanent locations, where they will form the major parts of the brain (Casaer, 1993).

While the nervous system is developing, the heart begins to pump blood around the embryo's circulatory system, and muscles, backbone, ribs, and digestive tract start to appear. At the end of the first month, the curled embryo consists of millions of organized groups of cells with specific functions, although it is only one-fourth inch long.

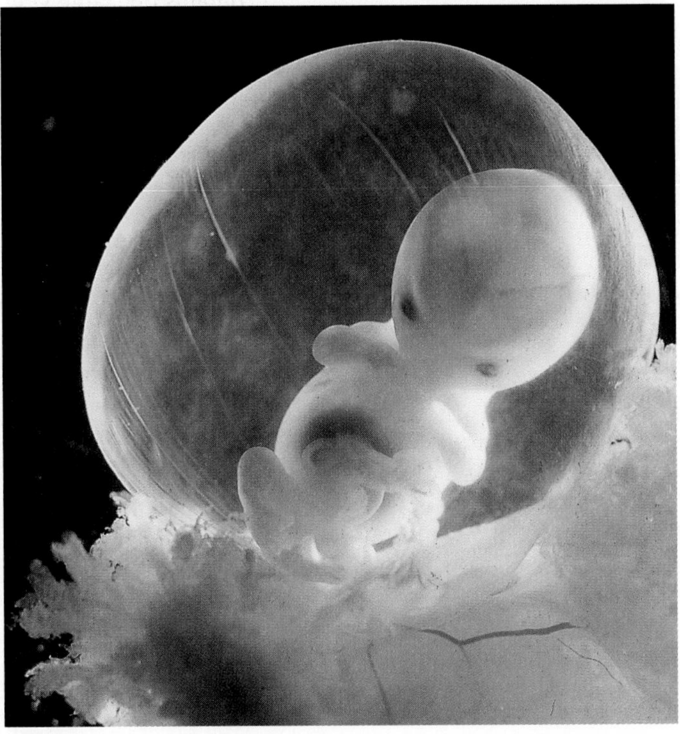

■ *By 7 weeks, the embryo's posture is more upright. Body structures—eyes, nose, arms, legs, and internal organs—are more distinct. An embryo of this age responds to touch. It can also move, although at less than an inch long and an ounce in weight, it is still too tiny to be felt by the mother. (© Lennart Nilsson,* A Child Is Born*/Bonniers)*

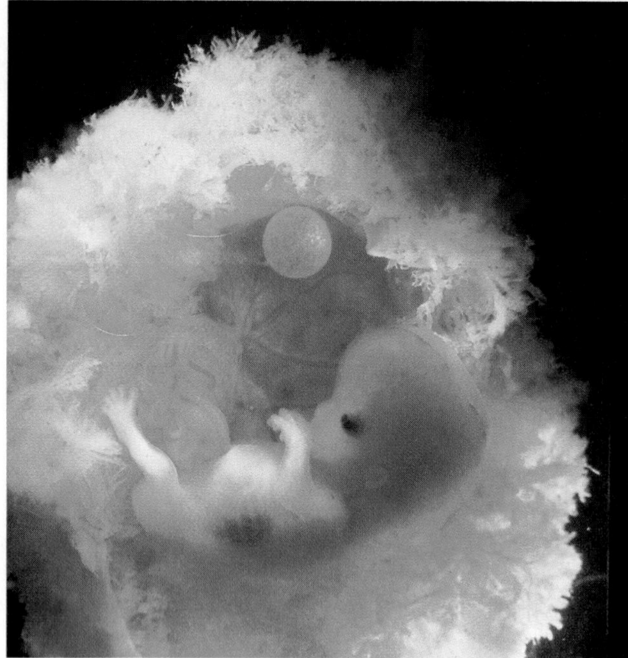

■ *During the period of the fetus, the organism increases rapidly in size, and body structures are completed. At 11 weeks, the brain and muscles are better connected. The fetus can kick, bend its arms, open and close its hands and mouth, and suck its thumb. Notice the yolk sac, which shrinks as pregnancy advances. The internal organs have taken over its function of producing blood cells. (© Lennart Nilsson,* A Child Is Born*/Bonniers)*

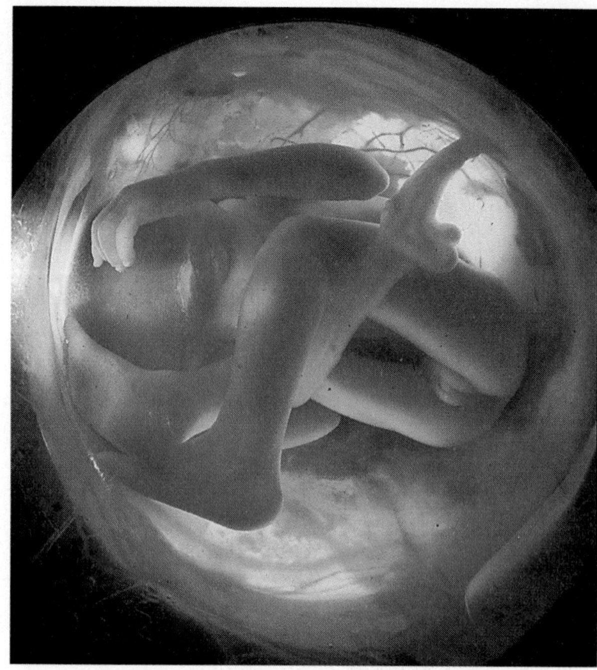

■ *At 22 weeks, this fetus is almost a foot long and slightly over a pound in weight. Its movements can be clearly felt by the mother and by other family members who place a hand on her abdomen. If born at this time, a baby has a slim chance of surviving. (© Lennart Nilsson,* A Child Is Born*/Bonniers)*

■ THE SECOND MONTH. In the second month, growth continues rapidly. The eyes, ears, nose, jaw, and neck form. Tiny buds become arms, legs, fingers, and toes. Internal organs are more distinct: the intestines grow, the heart develops separate chambers, and the liver and spleen take over production of blood cells so that the yolk sac is no longer needed. Changing body proportions cause the embryo's posture to become more upright. Now 1 inch long and one-seventh of an ounce in weight, the embryo can already sense its world. It responds to touch, particularly in the mouth area and on the soles of the feet. And it can move, although its tiny flutters are still too light to be felt by the mother (Nilsson & Hamberger, 1990).

THE PERIOD OF THE FETUS

Lasting from the ninth week until the end of pregnancy, the period of the **fetus** is the "growth and finishing" phase. During this longest prenatal period, the organism begins to increase rapidly in size. The rate of body growth is extraordinary, especially from the ninth to the twentieth week (Moore & Persaud, 1993).

■ THE THIRD MONTH. In the third month, the organs, muscles, and nervous system start to become organized and connected. The brain signals, and in response, the fetus kicks, bends its arms, forms a fist, curls its toes, opens its mouth, and even sucks its thumb. The tiny lungs begin to expand and contract in an early rehearsal of breathing movements. By the twelfth week, the external genitals are well formed, and the sex of the fetus can be detected with ultrasound. Other finishing touches appear, such as fingernails, toenails, tooth buds, and eyelids that open and close. The heartbeat is now stronger and can be heard through a stethoscope.

Prenatal development is often divided into *trimesters,* or three equal periods of time. At the end of the third month, the first trimester is complete. Two more must pass before the fetus is fully prepared to survive outside the womb.

Fetus
The prenatal organism from the beginning of the third month to the end of pregnancy, during which time completion of body structures and dramatic growth in size takes place.

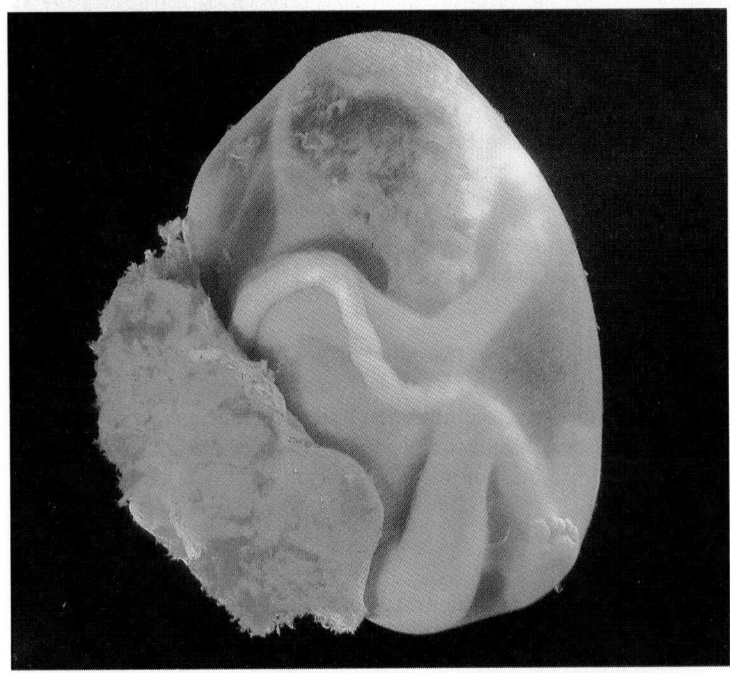

This 36-week-old fetus fills the uterus. To support its need for nourishment, the umbilical cord and placenta have grown very large. Notice the vernix (cheeselike substance), which protects the skin from chapping. The fetus has accumulated a layer of fat to assist with temperature regulation after birth. In another 2 weeks, it will be full term. (© Lennart Nilsson, A Child Is Born*/Bonniers)*

THE SECOND TRIMESTER. By the middle of the second trimester, between 17 and 20 weeks, the new being has grown large enough that its movements can be felt by the mother. If we could look inside the uterus at this time, we would find the fetus to be completely covered with a white, cheeselike substance called **vernix**. It protects the skin from chapping during the long months spent in the amniotic fluid. A white, downy hair covering called **lanugo** also appears over the entire body, helping the vernix stick to the skin.

At the end of the second trimester, many organs are quite well developed. And a major milestone is reached in brain development, in that all the neurons are now in place. No more will be produced in the individual's lifetime. However, *glial cells,* which support and feed the neurons, continue to increase at a rapid rate throughout the remaining months of pregnancy, as well as after birth (Nowakowski, 1987).

Brain growth means new behavioral capacities. The 20-week-old fetus can be stimulated as well as irritated by sounds. And if a doctor has reason to look inside the uterus with fetoscopy (see Table 3.6), fetuses try to shield their eyes from the light with their hands, indicating that the sense of sight has begun to emerge (Nilsson & Hamberger, 1990). Still, a fetus born at this time cannot survive. Its lungs are too immature, and the brain has not yet developed to the point at which it can control breathing movements and body temperature.

THE THIRD TRIMESTER. During the final trimester, a fetus born early has a chance for survival. The point at which the baby can first survive is called the **age of viability**. It occurs sometime between 22 and 26 weeks (Moore & Persaud, 1993). If born between the seventh and eighth month, breathing would still be a problem, and oxygen assistance would be necessary. Although the respiratory center of the brain is now mature, tiny air sacs in the lungs are not yet ready to inflate and exchange carbon dioxide for oxygen.

The brain continues to make great strides during the last 3 months. The *cerebral cortex,* the seat of human intelligence, enlarges. At the same time, the fetus responds more clearly to the external world. By 28 weeks, it blinks its eyes in reaction to nearby sounds (Birnholz & Benacerraf, 1983). And in the last weeks of pregnancy, the fetus learns to prefer the tone and rhythm of its mother's voice. In one clever study, mothers were asked to read aloud Dr. Seuss's lively book *The Cat in the Hat* to their unborn babies for the last 6 weeks of pregnancy. After birth, their infants were given a chance to suck on nipples that turned on recordings of the mother reading this book or different rhyming stories. The infants sucked hardest to hear *The Cat in the Hat,* the sounds they had come to know while still in the womb (DeCasper & Spence, 1986).

During the final 3 months, the fetus gains more than 5 pounds and grows 7 inches. In the eighth month, a layer of fat is added under the skin to assist with temperature

Vernix
A white, cheeselike substance covering the fetus and preventing the skin from chapping due to constant exposure to the amniotic fluid.

Lanugo
A white, downy hair that covers the entire body of the fetus, helping the vernix stick to the skin.

Age of viability
The age at which the fetus can first survive if born early. Occurs sometime between 22 and 26 weeks.

regulation. The fetus also receives antibodies from the mother's blood that protect against illnesses, since the newborn's own immune system will not work well until several months after birth.

In the last weeks, most fetuses assume an upside-down position, partly because of the shape of the uterus and because the head is heavier than the feet. Growth starts to slow, and birth is about to take place.

Prenatal Environmental Influences

Although the prenatal environment is far more constant than the world outside the womb, many factors can affect the embryo and fetus. In the following sections, we will see that there is much that parents—and society as a whole—can do to create a safe environment for development before birth.

TERATOGENS

The term **teratogen** refers to any environmental agent that causes damage during the prenatal period. It comes from the Greek word *teras,* meaning "malformation" or "monstrosity." This label was selected because scientists first learned about harmful prenatal influences from cases in which babies had been profoundly damaged.

Yet the harm done by teratogens is not always simple and straightforward. It depends on several factors. First, we will see as we discuss particular teratogens that amount and length of exposure make a difference. Larger doses over longer time periods usually have more negative effects. Second, the genetic makeup of the mother and baby plays an important role. Some individuals are better able to withstand harmful environments. Third, the presence of several negative factors at once, such as poor nutrition, lack of medical care, and additional teratogens, can worsen the impact of a single harmful agent. Fourth, the effects of teratogens vary with the age of the organism at time of exposure. We can best understand this idea if we think of prenatal development in terms of an important concept introduced in Chapter 1: the *sensitive period.* Recall that a sensitive period is a limited time span in which a part of the body or a behavior is biologically prepared to undergo rapid development. During that time, it is especially vulnerable to its surroundings. If the environment is harmful, then damage occurs that would not have otherwise happened, and recovery is difficult and sometimes impossible.

Figure 3.9 summarizes sensitive periods during prenatal development. Look carefully at it, and you will see that some parts of the body, such as the brain and eye, have long sensitive periods that extend throughout the prenatal phase. Other sensitive periods, such as those for the limbs and palate, are much shorter. Figure 3.9 also indicates that we can make some general statements about the timing of harmful influences. During the period of the zygote, before implantation, teratogens rarely have any impact. If they do, the tiny mass of cells is usually so completely damaged that it dies. The embryonic period is the time when serious defects are most likely to occur, since the foundations for all body parts are being laid down. During the fetal period, damage caused by teratogens is usually minor. However, some organs, such as the brain, eye, and genitals, can still be strongly affected.

The impact of teratogens is not limited to immediate physical damage. Although deformities of the body are easy to notice, important psychological consequences are harder to identify. Some may not show up until later in development. Others may occur as an indirect effect of physical damage. For example, a defect resulting from drugs the mother took during pregnancy can change reactions of others to the child as well as the child's ability to move about the environment. Over time, parent–child interaction, peer relations, and opportunities to explore may suffer. These experiences, in turn, can have far-reaching consequences for cognitive, emotional, and social development (Kopp & Kaler, 1989). Notice how an important idea about development discussed in Chapter 1 is at work here—that of *bidirectional* influences between child and environment. Now let's look at what scientists have discovered about a variety of teratogens.

Teratogen
Any environmental agent that causes damage during the prenatal period.

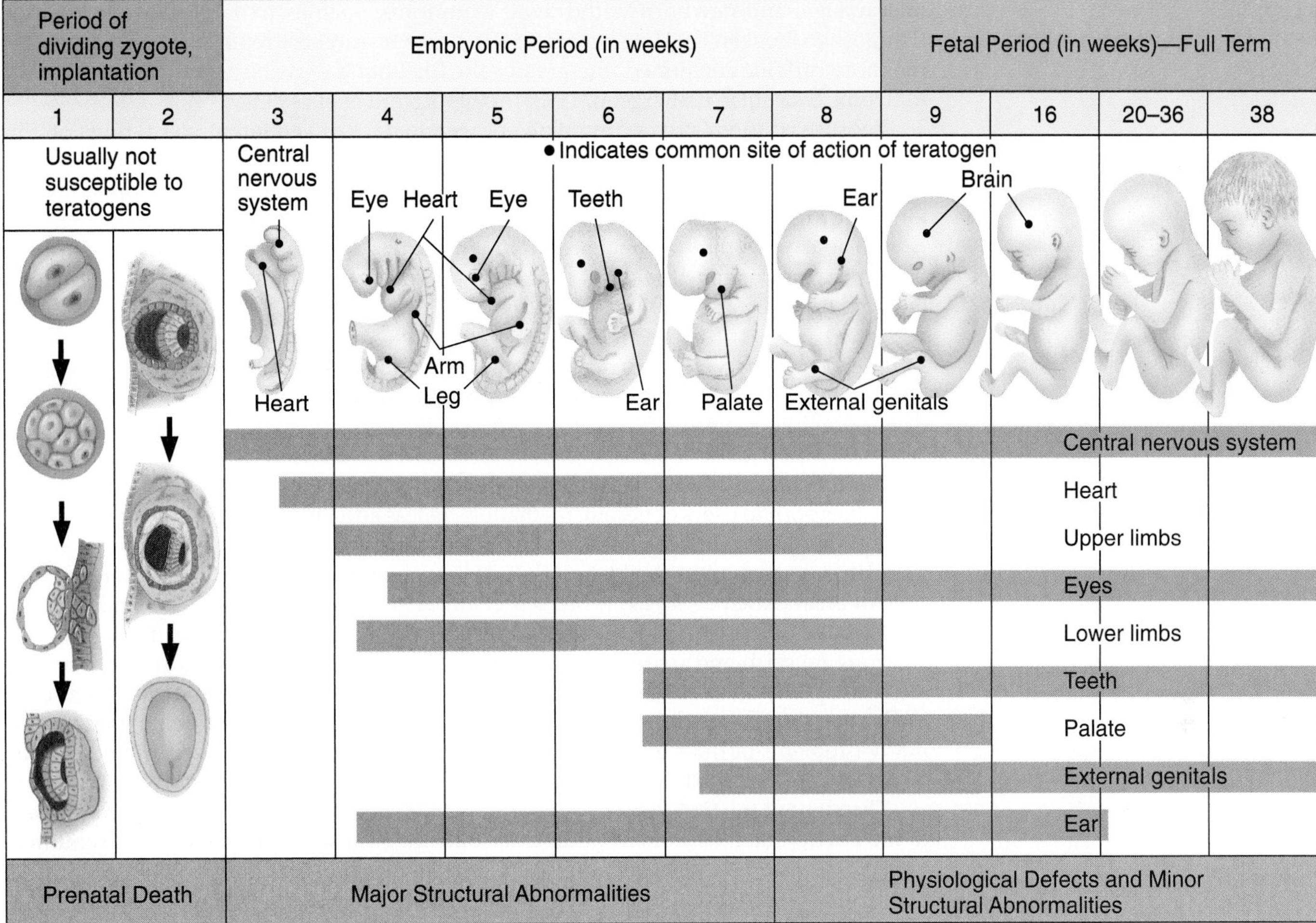

FIGURE 3.9

■ *Sensitive periods in prenatal development. Each organ or structure has a sensitive period during which its development may be disturbed. Gray horizontal lines indicate highly sensitive periods. Pink horizontal lines indicate periods that are somewhat less sensitive to teratogens, although damage can occur. (From K. L. Moore & T. V. N. Persaud, 1993,* Before We Are Born, *4th ed., Philadelphia: Saunders, p. 130. Reprinted by permission of the publisher and author.)*

■ PRESCRIPTION AND NONPRESCRIPTION DRUGS. Just about any drug a woman takes can enter the embryonic or fetal bloodstream. In the early 1960s, the world learned a tragic lesson about drugs and prenatal development. At that time, a sedative called thalidomide was widely available in Europe, Canada, and South America. Although the embryos of test animals were not harmed by it, in humans it had drastic effects. When taken by mothers between the fourth and sixth week after conception, thalidomide produced gross deformities of the embryo's developing arms and legs. About 7,000 infants around the world were affected (Moore & Persaud, 1993). As children exposed to thalidomide grew older, many scored below average in intelligence. Perhaps the drug damaged the central nervous system directly. Or the child-rearing conditions of these severely deformed youngsters may have impaired their intellectual development (Vorhees & Mollnow, 1987).

Despite the bitter lesson of thalidomide, many pregnant women continue to take over-the-counter drugs without consulting their doctors. Aspirin is one of the most common. Several studies suggest that regular use of aspirin is linked to low birth weight, infant death around the time of birth, poorer motor development, and lower intelligence test scores in early childhood (Barr et al., 1990; Streissguth et al., 1987). Other research, however, has failed to confirm these findings (see, for example, Hauth et al., 1995). Another frequently consumed drug is caffeine, contained in coffee, tea, cocoa, and cola. Heavy caffeine intake (over 3 cups of coffee per day) is associated with low birth weight, miscarriage, and newborn withdrawal symptoms, such as irritability and vomiting (Dlugosz & Bracken, 1992; Eskenazi, 1993). Some researchers report *dose-related* effects: the more caffeine consumed, the greater the likelihood of negative outcomes (Fortier, Marcoux, & Beaulac-Baillargeon, 1993; Infante-Rivard et al., 1993).

Because children's lives are involved, we must take even tentative findings on the harmful impact of medications seriously. At the same time, we cannot yet be sure that these drugs actually cause the problems mentioned. Often mothers take more than one kind of drug. If the prenatal organism is injured, it is hard to tell which drug might be responsible or if other factors correlated with drug taking are really at fault. Until we have more information, the safest course of action for pregnant women is to cut down on or avoid these drugs entirely.

■ ILLEGAL DRUGS. The use of highly addictive mood-altering drugs, such as cocaine and heroin, is widespread, especially in poverty-stricken inner-city areas, where these drugs provide a temporary escape from a daily life of hopelessness. The number of "cocaine babies" born in the United States has reached crisis levels in recent years. About 400,000 infants are affected annually (Waller, 1993).

Babies born to users of heroin, methadone (a less addictive drug used to wean people away from heroin), and cocaine are at risk for a wide variety of problems, including prematurity, low birth weight, physical defects, breathing difficulties, and death around the time of birth (Allen et al., 1991; Burkett et al., 1994; Handler et al., 1994; Kandall et al., 1993; Miller, Boudreaux, & Regan, 1995). In addition, these infants arrive drug addicted. They are feverish and irritable and have trouble sleeping. Their cries are abnormally shrill and piercing—a common symptom among stressed newborns that we will discuss in Chapter 4 (Doberczak, Kandall, & Friedmann, 1993; Fox, 1994). When mothers with many problems of their own must take care of these babies, who are difficult to calm down, cuddle, and feed, behavior problems are likely to persist.

Throughout the first year, heroin- and methadone-exposed infants are less attentive to the environment, and their motor development is slow. After infancy, some children get better, whereas others remain jittery and inattentive. The kind of parenting these youngsters receive may explain why there are long-term problems for some but not for others (Vorhees & Mollnow, 1987).

Unlike findings on heroin and methadone, evidence on cocaine suggests that many prenatally exposed babies have lasting difficulties. Cocaine is linked to a variety of physical defects, including eye, bone, genital, urinary tract, kidney, and heart deformities as well as brain hemorrhages and seizures (Fox, 1994; Holzman & Paneth, 1994; Moroney & Allen, 1994). Infants born to mothers who smoke crack (a cheap form of cocaine that delivers high doses quickly through the lungs) appear to be worst off in terms of low birth weight and damage to the central nervous system (Kaye et al., 1989). Fathers also seem to contribute to these effects. Research suggests that cocaine can attach itself to sperm, "hitchhike" its way into the zygote, and cause birth defects (Yazigi, Odem, & Polakoski, 1991). Still, it is difficult to isolate the precise damage caused by cocaine, since users often take several drugs and engage in other high-risk behaviors. For example, up to 85 percent of cocaine users smoke cigarettes. The joint impact of these substances may be responsible for the negative outcomes just described (Coles et al., 1992; Cotton, 1994).

Marijuana is another illegal drug that is used more widely than cocaine and heroin, but less is known about its prenatal effects. Studies examining its relationship to low birth weight and prematurity reveal mixed findings (Fried, 1993). After controlling for other factors, several researchers have linked prenatal marijuana exposure to newborn tremors, startles, disturbed sleep, an abnormally high-pitched cry, and reduced visual attention to the environment (Dahl et al., 1995; Fried & Makin, 1987; Lester & Dreher, 1989). These outcomes certainly put newborn babies at risk for future problems, even though long-term effects have not been established.

■ CIGARETTE SMOKING. Although smoking has declined in Western nations, an estimated one-fourth to one-third of adults are regular cigarette users. Among women under age 25, the rate of smoking is especially high—from 30 to 40 percent (Birenbaum-Carmeli, 1995; U.S. Bureau of the Census, 1995). The most well-known effect of smoking during pregnancy is low birth weight. But the likelihood of other serious consequences, such as prematurity, miscarriage, infant death, and cancer later in childhood, is also increased. The more cigarettes a mother smokes, the greater the chances that her baby will be affected. If a pregnant woman decides to stop smoking at any time, even during the last trimester, she can help her baby. She immediately reduces the likelihood that her infant will be born underweight and suffer from future problems (Ahlsten, Cnattingius, & Lindmark, 1993; Li, Windsor, & Perkins, 1993).

Even when a baby of a smoking mother appears to be born in good physical condition, slight behavioral abnormalities may threaten the child's development. Newborns of smoking mothers are less attentive to sounds and display more muscle tension (Fried & Makin, 1987). An unresponsive, restless baby may not evoke the kind of interaction from adults that promotes healthy psychological development. Some long-term studies report that prenatally exposed children have shorter attention spans and poorer mental test scores in early childhood, even after many other factors have been controlled (Fried & Watkinson, 1990; Kristjansson & Fried, 1989). But other researchers have not been able to confirm these findings, so long-term effects remain uncertain (Barr et al., 1990; Streissguth et al., 1989).

Exactly how can smoking harm the fetus? Nicotine, the addictive substance in tobacco, constricts the blood vessels and causes the placenta to grow abnormally. As a result, blood flow and transfer of nutrients is reduced, and the fetus gains weight poorly. Also, smoking raises the concentration of carbon monoxide in the bloodstreams of both mother and fetus. Carbon monoxide displaces oxygen from red blood cells. It damages the central nervous system and reduces birth weight in the fetuses of laboratory animals. Similar effects may occur in humans (Cotton, 1994; Fried, 1993).

Finally, from one-third to one-half of nonsmoking pregnant women are "passive smokers" because their husbands, relatives, and co-workers use cigarettes. Passive smoking is also related to low birth weight, infant death, and possible long-term impairments in attention and learning (Makin, Fried, & Watkinson, 1991; Fortier, Marcoux, & Brisson, 1994). Clearly, expectant mothers should do what they can to avoid smoke-filled environments, and family members, friends, and employers need to assist them in this effort.

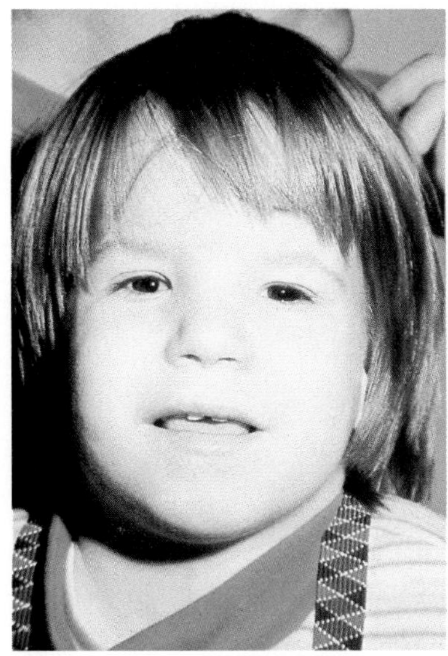

■ *The mother of this severely retarded boy drank heavily during pregnancy. His widely spaced eyes, thin upper lip, and short eyelid openings are typical of fetal alcohol syndrome. (Fetal Alcohol Syndrome Research Fund, University of Washington)*

■ ALCOHOL. In a moving story, Michael Dorris (1989), a Dartmouth University anthropology professor, described what it was like to rear his adopted son Adam, whose biological mother drank heavily throughout pregnancy and died of alcohol poisoning shortly after his birth. A Sioux Indian boy, Adam was 3 years old when he came into Dorris's life. He was short and underweight and had a vocabulary of only 20 words. Although he ate well, he grew slowly, remained painfully thin, and was prone to infection. When he was 7, testing revealed that Adam's intelligence was below average and that he had difficulty concentrating. At age 12, he could not add, subtract, or identify the town in which he lived. Now an adult, Adam has difficulty keeping a routine job and suffers from poor judgment. He might buy something and not wait for change, leave windows open on a bitterly cold night, or wander off in the middle of a task. His case and many others like it reveal that the damage done by alcohol to the embryo and fetus cannot be undone.

Fetal alcohol syndrome (FAS) is the scientific name for Adam's condition. Mental retardation, poor attention, and overactivity are typical of children with the disorder (Steinhausen, Willms, & Spohr, 1993). Distinct physical symptoms also accompany it. These include slow physical growth and a particular pattern of facial abnormalities: widely spaced eyes, short eyelid openings, a small, upturned nose, and a thin upper lip. The small heads of these children indicate that the brain has been prevented from reaching full development. Other defects—of the eyes, ears, nose, throat, heart, genitals, urinary tract, and immune system—may also be present. In all babies with FAS, the mother drank heavily through most or all of her pregnancy.

Sometimes children do not display all these abnormalities—only a few of them. In these cases, the child is said to suffer from **fetal alcohol effects (FAE)**. Usually mothers of these children drank alcohol in smaller quantities. The defects of FAE children vary with the timing and length of prenatal alcohol exposure.

How does alcohol produce its devastating consequences? Researchers believe it does so in two ways. First, alcohol quickly crosses the placental barrier, producing identical fetal and maternal blood concentrations within minutes. Besides disrupting the

Fetal alcohol syndrome (FAS) A set of defects that results when pregnant women consume large amounts of alcohol during most or all of pregnancy. Includes mental retardation, slow physical growth, and facial abnormalities.

Fetal alcohol effects (FAE) The condition of children who display some but not all of the defects of fetal alcohol syndrome. Usually their mothers drank alcohol in smaller quantities during pregnancy.

development of many body structures, alcohol interferes with cell duplication and migration in the neural tube (see page 89). When the brains of FAS babies who did not survive are examined, they show a reduced number of cells and major structural abnormalities (Moroney & Allen, 1994). Second, large quantities of oxygen are needed to metabolize alcohol. When pregnant women drink heavily, they draw oxygen away from the embryo or fetus that is vital for cell growth in the brain and other parts of the body (Vorhees & Mollnow, 1987).

Like heroin and cocaine, alcohol abuse is higher in poverty-stricken sectors of the population, especially among Native Americans. On the reservation where Adam was born, many children show symptoms of prenatal alcohol exposure. Unfortunately, when girls with FAS and FAE later become pregnant, the poor judgment caused by the syndrome often prevents them from understanding why they should avoid alcohol themselves. Thus, the tragedy is likely to be repeated in the next generation.

At this point, you may be wondering, How much alcohol is safe during pregnancy? Is it all right to have a drink or two, either daily or occasionally? One study found that as little as 2 ounces of alcohol a day, taken very early in pregnancy, was associated with FAS-like facial features (Astley et al., 1992). But recall that other factors—both genetic and environmental—can make some fetuses more vulnerable to teratogens. Therefore, a precise dividing line between safe and dangerous drinking levels cannot be established. Research shows that the more alcohol consumed during pregnancy, the poorer a child's motor coordination, intelligence, and achievement during childhood and adolescence (Barr et al., 1990; Jacobson et al., 1993; Streissguth et al., 1994). These dose-related effects indicate that it is best for pregnant women to avoid alcohol entirely.

■ HORMONES. Earlier in this chapter, we saw that the Y chromosome causes male sex hormones (called androgens) to be secreted prenatally, leading to formation of male reproductive organs. In the absence of male hormones, female structures develop. Hormones are released as part of a delicately balanced system. If their quantity or timing is off, then defects of the genitals and other organs can occur.

Between 1945 and 1970, a synthetic hormone called *diethylstilbestrol* (DES) was widely used in the United States to prevent miscarriages in women with a history of pregnancy problems. As the daughters of these mothers reached adolescence and young adulthood, they showed an unusually high rate of cancer of the vagina and malformations of the uterus. When they tried to have children, their pregnancies more often resulted in prematurity, low birth weight, and miscarriage than did those of non-DES-exposed women. Young men whose mothers took DES prenatally were also affected. They showed an increased risk of genital abnormalities and cancer of the testes (Linn et al., 1988; Stillman, 1982). Because of these findings, pregnant women are no longer treated with DES. But many children whose mothers took it are now of childbearing age, and they need to be carefully monitored by their doctors.

■ RADIATION. Earlier in this chapter, we saw that ionizing radiation can cause mutation, damaging the DNA in ova and sperm. When mothers are exposed to radiation during pregnancy, additional harm can come to the embryo or fetus. Defects due to radiation were tragically apparent in the children born to pregnant Japanese women who survived the atomic bombing of Hiroshima and Nagasaki near the end of World War II. Miscarriage, slow physical growth, an underdeveloped brain, and malformations of the skeleton and eyes were common (Michel, 1989). Even when an exposed child appears normal at birth, the possibility of later problems cannot be ruled out. For example, research suggests that even low-level radiation, as the result of industrial leakage or medical X-rays, can increase the risk of childhood cancer (Smith, 1992).

■ ENVIRONMENTAL POLLUTION. An astounding number of potentially dangerous chemicals are released into the environment in industrialized nations. In the United States, over 100,000 are in common use, and 1,000 new ones are introduced each year. Although many chemicals cause serious birth defects in laboratory animals, the impact on the human embryo and fetus is known for only a small number of them.

Among heavy metals, mercury and lead are established teratogens. In the 1950s, an industrial plant released waste containing high levels of mercury into a bay providing food and water for the town of Minimata, Japan. Many children born at the time were

TABLE 3.7

Effects of Some Infectious Diseases During Pregnancy

Disease	Miscarriage	Physical Malformations	Mental Retardation	Low Birth Weight and Prematurity
Viral				
Acquired immune deficiency syndrome (AIDS)	0	?	+	?
Chicken pox	0	+	+	+
Cytomegalovirus	+	+	+	+
Herpes simplex 2 (genital herpes)	+	+	+	+
Mumps	+	?	0	0
Rubella	+	+	+	+
Bacterial				
Syphilis	+	+	+	?
Tuberculosis	+	?	+	+
Parasitic				
Malaria	+	0	0	+
Toxoplasmosis	+	+	+	+

Note: + established finding, 0 = no present evidence, ? = possible effect that is not clearly established.
Sources: Adapted from *Clinical Genetics in Nursing Practice* (p. 232) by F. L. Cohen, 1984, Philadelphia: Lippincott. Reprinted by permission.
Additional sources: Chatkupt et al., 1989; Cohen, 1993a; Peckham & Logan, 1993; Samson, 1988; Sever, 1983; Vorhees, 1986; Qazi et al., 1988.

mentally retarded and showed other serious symptoms, including abnormal speech, difficulty in chewing and swallowing, and uncoordinated movements. Autopsies of those who died revealed widespread brain damage (Vorhees & Mollnow, 1987).

Pregnant women can absorb lead from car exhaust, paint flaking off the walls in old houses and apartment buildings, and other materials used in industrial occupations. High levels of lead exposure are consistently linked to prematurity, low birth weight, brain damage, and a wide variety of physical defects (Dye-White, 1986). Even a very low level of prenatal lead exposure seems to be dangerous. Affected babies show slightly poorer mental development during the first 2 years (Bellinger et al., 1987).

For many years, polychlorinated-biphenyls (PCBs) were used to insulate electrical equipment. In 1977, they were banned by the U.S. government after research showed that, like mercury, they found their way into waterways and entered the food supply. In one study, newborn babies of women who frequently ate PCB-contaminated fish were compared to newborns whose mothers ate little or no fish. The PCB-exposed babies had a variety of problems, including slightly reduced birth weight, smaller heads (suggesting brain damage), and less interest in their surroundings (Jacobson et al., 1984). When studied again at 7 months of age, infants whose mothers ate fish during pregnancy did more poorly on memory tests (Jacobson et al., 1985). A follow-up at 4 years of age showed persisting memory difficulties and lower verbal intelligence test scores (Jacobson, Jacobson, & Humphrey, 1990; Jacobson et al., 1992).

■ MATERNAL DISEASE. Five percent of women catch an infectious disease of some sort while pregnant. Most of these illnesses, such as the common cold and various strains of the flu, seem to have no impact on the embryo or fetus. However, as Table 3.7 indicates, a few diseases can cause extensive damage.

Rubella (3-day German measles) is a well-known teratogen. In the mid-1960s, a worldwide epidemic of rubella led to the birth of over 20,000 American babies with serious birth defects. Consistent with the sensitive period concept, the greatest damage occurs when rubella strikes during the embryonic period. Over 50 percent of infants whose mothers become ill during that time show heart defects; eye cataracts; deafness; genital, urinary, and intestinal abnormalities; and mental retardation. Infection during

FROM RESEARCH TO PRACTICE

Prenatal Transmission of AIDS

First-born child of Jean and Claire, Ginette was diagnosed with AIDS when she was 6 months old. She died from respiratory infections and a failure to grow normally at 11 months of age. Jean and Claire could not understand the social worker's explanation of why Ginette died. After all, neither parent felt sick. At the time, Claire was pregnant with a second baby. Several weeks after Ginette's death, Jeanine was born. When word spread that AIDS caused Ginette's death, Jean lost his job, and the family was evicted from their apartment. Over the next year, Claire gave birth to a son, Junior, and also became pregnant for a fourth time. During this pregnancy, both Claire and Jeanine began to show symptoms of AIDS. Claire gave birth prematurely, and she and the baby died soon after. Many months later, an uncle brought Jeanine and Junior to a hospital. Junior was tested for HIV infection. Unlike his sisters, he managed to escape it. Jean, heartsick over the death of his wife and two children, left the family and may have died of AIDS. He was never heard from again. (Paraphrased from Siebert et al., 1989, pp. 36–38)

AIDS is a relatively new viral disease that destroys the immune system. Affected individuals like Jean, Claire, and their children eventually die of a wide variety of illnesses that their bodies can no longer fight. Adults at greatest risk include male homosexuals and bisexuals, users of illegal drugs who share needles, and their heterosexual partners. Transfer of body fluids from one person to another is necessary for AIDS to spread.

The percentage of AIDS victims who are women has risen dramatically over the past decade—from 6 to 13 percent in the United States and to over 50 percent in Africa. More than 80 percent of infected women are of childbearing age (Grant, 1995; Provisional Committee on Pediatric AIDS, 1995). When they become pregnant, about 20 to 30 percent of the time they pass the deadly virus to the embryo or fetus. The likelihood of transmission is greatest when a woman already has AIDS symptoms, but (as Claire's case reveals) it can occur beforehand. Why only some offspring are affected is not well understood. It may depend on heredity, the timing of maternal infection, the condition of the placenta, and other factors. Besides prenatal infection, infants can contract HIV during the birth process, when exposure to maternal fluids increases. According to the U.S. Centers for Disease Control, nearly 4,000 childhood cases of AIDS have been diagnosed in the United States since 1981. Worldwide, about 1 million children are infected. The large majority (85 percent) are infants who received the virus before or during birth, often from a drug-abusing mother (Cohen, 1993a, 1993b).

AIDS symptoms generally take a long time to emerge in older children and adults—up to 5 years after HIV infection. In contrast, the disease proceeds rapidly in infants. Most infected babies are born with abnormalities of the immune system (Mayers et al., 1991). By 6 months of age, weight loss, fever, diarrhea, and repeated respiratory illnesses are common. The virus also causes brain damage. Infants with AIDS show a loss in brain weight over time, accompanied by seizures, delayed mental and motor development, and abnormal muscle tone and movements. Like Ginette, most survive for only 5 to 8 months after the appearance of these symptoms (Chamberlain, Nichols, & Chase, 1991; Chatkupt et al., 1989).

Prenatal AIDS babies are generally born to urban, poverty-stricken parents. Lack of money to pay for medical treatment, rejection by relatives and friends who do not understand the disease, and anxiety about the child's future cause tremendous stress in these families. Medical services for young children with AIDS and counseling for their parents are badly needed (Kurth, 1993).

Currently, scientists are searching for ways to interrupt prenatal HIV transmission. The antiviral drug AZT reduces it by 75 percent but can also cause birth defects (Chadwick & Yogev, 1995; Connor et al., 1995). Until a preventive method or cure is found, education of adolescents and adults about the disease, outreach programs that get at-risk women into drug treatment programs, and confidential HIV testing for all pregnant women (with their consent) are the only ways to stop continued spread of the virus to children.

the fetal period is less harmful, but low birth weight, hearing loss, and bone defects may still occur (Eberhart-Phillips, Frederick, & Baron, 1993; Samson, 1988). Since 1966, infants and young children have been routinely vaccinated against rubella, so the number of prenatal cases today is much less than it was a generation ago. Still, 10 to 20 percent of American women of childbearing age lack the rubella antibody, so new outbreaks of the disease are still possible (Lee et al., 1992).

The developing organism is also sensitive to the family of herpes viruses, for which there is no vaccine or treatment. Among these, cytomegalovirus (the most frequent prenatal infection, transmitted through respiratory or sexual contact) and herpes simplex 2 (which is sexually transmitted) are especially dangerous. In both, the virus invades the mother's genital tract. Babies can be infected either during pregnancy or at birth. The human immunodeficiency virus (HIV), which leads to acquired immune deficiency syndrome (AIDS), is affecting increasing numbers of babies. To find out about its prenatal transmission, refer to the From Research to Practice box above.

Also included in Table 3.7 are several bacterial and parasitic diseases. Among the most common is toxoplasmosis, caused by a parasite found in many animals. Pregnant women may become infected from eating raw or undercooked meat or from contact with the feces of infected cats. About 40 percent of women who have the disease transmit it to the developing organism. If it strikes during the first trimester, it is likely to cause eye and brain damage. Later infection is linked to mild visual and cognitive impairments (Peckham & Logan, 1993). Expectant mothers can avoid toxoplasmosis by making sure that the meat they eat is well cooked, having pet cats checked for the disease, and turning the care of litter boxes over to other family members.

OTHER MATERNAL FACTORS

Besides teratogens, maternal nutrition and emotional well-being affect the embryo and fetus. In addition, many prospective parents wonder about the impact of a woman's age on the course of pregnancy. We examine each of these influences in the following sections.

■ NUTRITION. Children grow more rapidly during the prenatal period than at any other phase of development. During this time, they depend totally on the mother for nutrients to support their growth. A healthy diet that results in a weight gain of 25 to 30 pounds helps ensure the health of mother and baby.

During World War II, a severe famine occurred in the Netherlands, giving scientists a rare opportunity to study the impact of nutrition on prenatal development. Findings revealed that the sensitive period concept operates with nutrition, just as it does with the teratogens discussed earlier in this chapter. Women affected by the famine during the first trimester were more likely to have miscarriages or to give birth to babies with physical defects. When women were past the first trimester, fetuses usually survived, but many were born underweight and had small heads (Stein et al., 1975).

We now know that prenatal malnutrition can cause serious damage to the central nervous system. Autopsies of malnourished babies who died at or shortly after birth reveal fewer brain cells and a brain weight as much as 36 percent below average. The poorer the mother's diet, the greater the loss in brain weight, especially if malnutrition occurred during the last trimester. During that time, the brain is growing rapidly in size, and a maternal diet high in all the basic nutrients is necessary for it to reach its full potential (Morgane et al., 1993). An inadequate diet during pregnancy can also distort the structure of other organs, including the pancreas, liver, and blood vessels, thereby increasing the risk of heart disease and diabetes in adulthood (Barker et al., 1993).

Prenatally malnourished babies enter the world with serious problems. They frequently catch respiratory illnesses, since poor nutrition suppresses development of the immune system (Chandra, 1991). In addition, these infants are irritable and unresponsive to stimulation around them. Like drug-addicted newborns, they have a high-pitched cry that is particularly distressing to their caregivers. The effects of poor nutrition quickly combine with an impoverished, stressful home life. With age, low intelligence test scores and serious learning problems become more apparent (Lozoff, 1989).

Many studies show that providing pregnant women with adequate food has a substantial impact on the health of their newborn babies. Yet the growth demands of the prenatal period require more than just increasing the quantity of a typical diet. As the Social Issues box on page 100 reveals, finding ways to optimize maternal nutrition through vitamin–mineral enrichment as early as possible—even before conception—is crucial.

When poor nutrition is allowed to continue throughout pregnancy, infants often require more than dietary enrichment. Their tired, restless behavior leads mothers to be less sensitive and stimulating, and in response, babies become even more passive and withdrawn. Successful interventions must break this cycle of apathetic mother–baby interaction. Some do so by teaching parents how to interact effectively with their infants, whereas others focus on stimulating infants to promote active engagement with their physical and social surroundings (Grantham-McGregor et al., 1994; Zeskind & Ramey, 1978, 1981).

Although prenatal malnutrition is highest in poverty-stricken regions of the world, it is not limited to developing countries. Each year, 80,000 to 120,000 American infants are born seriously undernourished. The federal government provides food packages to impoverished pregnant women through its Special Supplemental Food Program for Women, Infants, and Children. Unfortunately, because of funding shortages the program serves only 72 percent of those who are eligible (Children's Defense Fund, 1996).

SOCIAL ISSUES ➤ POINT OF VIEW

Should Vitamin–Mineral Supplements Be Recommended for All Women of Childbearing Age?

Many women of childbearing age do not consume major nutrients in sufficient quantity to meet recommended daily allowances. Levels are particularly low for women who are young or poverty stricken—groups least likely to take vitamin–mineral supplements on a regular basis to make up for their dietary inadequacies (Block & Abrams, 1993; Keen & Zidenberg-Cherr, 1994).

The impact of vitamin–mineral intake on pregnancy outcomes was strikingly revealed when iodine was added to commonly eaten foods, such as table salt. (Iodine is an essential component of thyroxine, a thyroid hormone necessary for central nervous system development and body growth.) As a result, iodine-induced cretinism, involving mental retardation, short stature, and bone deterioration, was virtually eradicated (Dunn, 1993).

Other vitamins and minerals also have established benefits. For example, enriching pregnant women's diets with calcium helps prevent maternal high blood pressure and premature births (Repke, 1992). Magnesium and zinc reduce the incidence of a wide variety of prenatal and birth complications (Facchinetti et al., 1992; Jameson, 1993; Spätling & Spätling, 1988). And a multivitamin supplement taken around the time of conception protects against cleft lip and palate (Tolarova, 1986).

Recently, the power of folic acid to prevent abnormalities of the neural tube, such as anencephaly and spina bifida

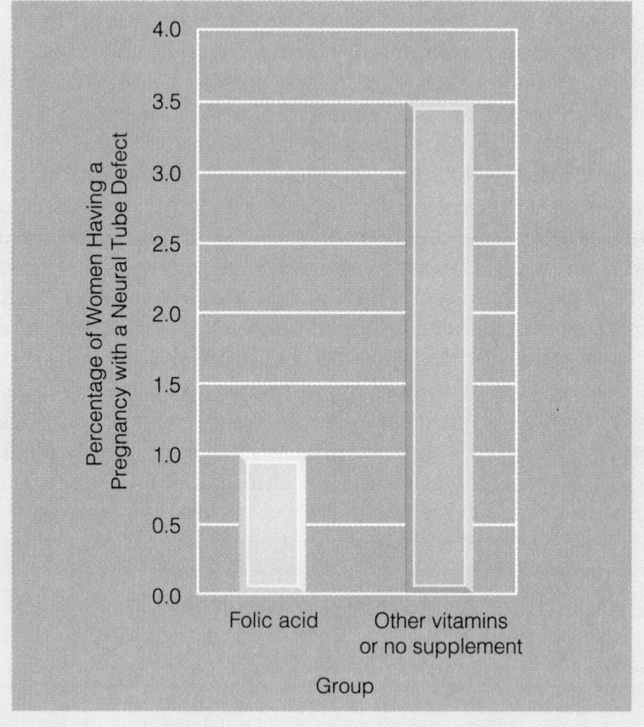

FIGURE 3.10

■ *Percentage of pregnancies with a neural tube defect in folic-acid-supplemented women versus other-vitamins or no-supplement controls. Folic acid taken around the time of conception dramatically reduced the incidence of neural tube defects. Note, however, that folic acid did not eliminate all neural tube defects. These abnormalities, like many others, have multiple origins in the embryo's genetic disposition and factors in the environment. (Adapted from MCR Vitamin Study Research Group, 1991.)*

■ PSYCHOLOGICAL STRESS. When women experience severe psychological stress during pregnancy, their babies are at risk for a wide variety of difficulties. Intense anxiety is associated with a higher rate of miscarriage, prematurity, low birth weight, and newborn respiratory illness. It is also related to certain physical defects, such as cleft lip and palate and pyloric stenosis (tightening of the infant's stomach outlet, which must be treated surgically) (Brandt & Nielsen, 1992; Norbeck & Tilden, 1983; Omer & Everly, 1988).

To understand how the developing organism is affected, think back to the way your own body felt the last time you were under considerable stress. When we experience fear and anxiety, stimulant hormones are released into our bloodstream. These cause us to be "poised for action." Large amounts of blood are sent to parts of the body involved in the defensive response—the brain, the heart, and muscles in the arms, legs, and trunk. Blood flow to other organs, including the uterus, is reduced. As a result, the fetus is deprived of a full supply of oxygen and nutrients. Stress hormones also cross the placenta, leading the fetus's heart rate and activity level to rise dramatically. In addition, stress weakens the immune system, making pregnant women more susceptible to infectious disease (Cohen & Williamson, 1991). Finally, women who experience long-term anxiety are more likely to smoke, drink, eat poorly, and engage in other behaviors that harm the embryo or fetus.

The risks of severe psychological stress are greatly reduced when mothers have husbands, other family members, and friends who offer social support. In a study of expec-

(see Table 3.6 on page 82), has captured the attention of medical and public health experts. This member of the vitamin B complex group can be found in green vegetables, fresh fruit, liver, and yeast. In a British study of nearly two thousand women in seven countries who had previously given birth to a baby with a neural tube defect, half were randomly selected to receive a folic acid supplement around the time of conception and half a mixture of other vitamins or no supplement. As Figure 3.10 reveals, the folic acid group showed a 72 percent reduction in rate of neural tube defects (MCR Vitamin Study Research Group, 1991). Large-scale studies carried out in Australia, Hungary, and the United States confirm these dramatic effects (Bower & Stanley, 1992; Czeizel & Dudas, 1992; Shaw et al., 1995).

Because the average American woman gets less than half the recommended amount of folic acid from her diet, the U.S. Food and Drug Administration recently proposed that it be added to flour, bread, and other grain products (Hopkins-Tanne, 1994). Yet even under these conditions, we cannot be sure that pregnant women will consume enough folic acid for a protective effect. Therefore, an intensive media campaign is under way to get all women of childbearing age to consume at least 0.4 mg but not more than 1 mg of folic acid per day through taking a regular vitamin–mineral supplement. Special emphasis is being placed on folic acid enrichment around the time of conception and during the early weeks of pregnancy, when the neural tube is forming.

However, recommending vitamin–mineral supplements for all potentially childbearing women is controversial. The greatest concern is that a national supplement program might lead some people to consume dangerously high levels of certain nutrients because they believe, incorrectly, that more is always better. For example, excessive daily intake of vitamins A and D (by taking even two or three multivitamin pills) can result in birth defects (Rosa, 1993; Rothman et al., 1995). Too much folic acid aggravates damage to the central nervous system in individuals with a severe form of anemia (Chanarin, 1994). Furthermore, if people conclude that taking a supplement means they need not worry about eating a well-balanced diet, a supplement program could reduce consumption of essential nutrients not provided in the supplement (Keen & Zidenberg-Cherr, 1994).

Experts agree that encouraging all women of childbearing age to take an appropriate vitamin–mineral supplement is vital for preventing birth defects. But without a public education campaign that emphasizes the dangers of excessive vitamin–mineral consumption and the importance of maintaining a high-quality diet, a national supplement program runs the risk of serious negative side effects.

Finally, a supplement policy should complement, not replace, economic programs designed to improve maternal diets during pregnancy. For women with low incomes who do not get enough food or an adequate variety of foods, multivitamin tablets are a necessary, but not sufficient, intervention.

YOUR POINT OF VIEW . . .

- Contact your local office of the March of Dimes Birth Defects Foundation or the national office at 1275 Mamaroneck Avenue, White Plains, NY 10605. Telephone (914) 428-7100. Ask for copies of brochures aimed at educating prospective mothers about the importance of dietary nutrients for preventing birth defects. To what extent does the literature describe both the benefits and risks of vitamin–mineral supplements?

tant women experiencing high life stress, those who reported having people on whom they could count for help had a complication rate of only 33 percent, compared to 91 percent for those who felt isolated (Nuckolls, Cassel, & Kaplan, 1972). Social support also reduces the incidence of low birth weight among newborns of highly stressed mothers (McLean et al., 1993). These results suggest that finding ways to provide supportive social ties can help prevent pregnancy problems.

■ MATERNAL AGE. First births to women in their 30s have increased greatly over the past quarter century in the United States and other Western nations (see Figure 3.11). Many more couples are putting off childbearing until their careers are well established and they know they can support a child. Earlier in this chapter, we indicated that women who delay having children face a greater risk of giving birth to babies with chromosomal defects. Are other pregnancy problems more common among older mothers?

For many years, scientists thought that aging and repeated use of the mother's reproductive organs increased the likelihood of a wide variety of complications. Recently, these ideas have been questioned. When women without serious health difficulties are considered, even those in their forties do not experience more prenatal problems than those in their twenties (Ales, Druzin, & Santini, 1990; Spellacy, Miller, & Winegar, 1986). And a large study of over 50,000 pregnancies showed no relationship between number of

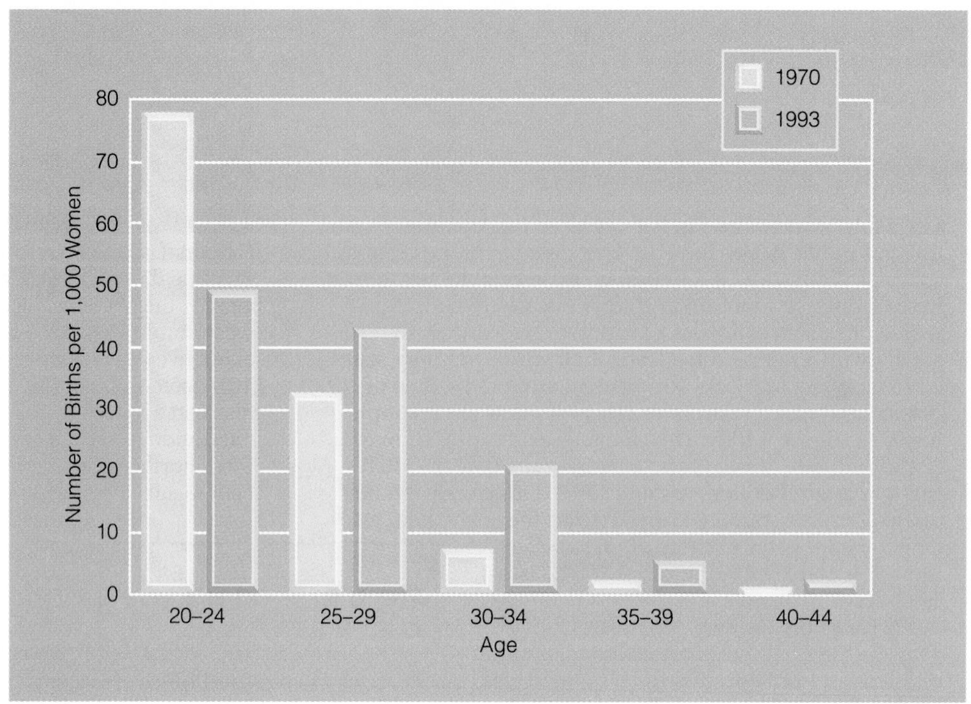

FIGURE 3.11

■ *First births to American women of different ages in 1970 and 1993. The birthrate decreased over this time period for women 20 to 24 years of age, whereas it increased for women 25 years and older. For women in their thirties, the birthrate more than doubled. (Adapted from Ventura, 1989; U.S. Department of Health and Human Services, 1995a.)*

previous births and pregnancy complications (Heinonen, Slone, & Shapiro, 1977). As long as an older woman is in good health, she can carry a baby successfully.

In the case of teenage mothers, does physical immaturity cause prenatal problems? Again, research shows that it does not. A teenager's body is large enough and strong enough to support pregnancy. In fact, as we will see in Chapter 5, young adolescent girls grow taller and heavier and their hips broaden (in preparation for childbearing) before their menstrual periods begin. Nature tries to ensure that once a girl can conceive, she is physically ready to carry and give birth to a baby. Infants of teenagers are born with a higher rate of problems for quite different reasons. Many teenagers do not have access to medical care or are afraid to seek it. In addition, most pregnant teenagers come from low-income backgrounds where stress, poor nutrition, and health problems are common (Ketterlinus, Henderson, & Lamb, 1990).

BRIEF REVIEW

The vast changes that take place during pregnancy are usually divided into three periods. In the period of the zygote, the tiny one-celled fertilized ovum begins to duplicate and implants itself in the uterine lining. In the period of the embryo, the foundations for all body tissues and organs are rapidly laid down. The longest prenatal phase, the period of the fetus, is devoted to growth in size and completion of body systems.

Teratogens—cigarettes, alcohol, certain drugs, radiation, environmental pollutants, and diseases—can seriously harm the embryo and fetus. The effects of teratogens depend on amount and length of exposure, the genetic makeup of mother and baby, and the presence of other harmful environmental agents. Teratogens operate according to the sensitive period concept. In general, greatest damage occurs during the embryonic phase, when body structures are formed. Poor maternal nutrition and severe psychological stress can also endanger the developing organism. As long as they are in good health, teenagers, women in their thirties and forties, and women who have given birth to several children have a high likelihood of problem-free pregnancies.

Childbirth

It is not surprising that childbirth is often referred to as labor. It is the hardest physical work a woman may ever do. A complex series of hormonal changes initiates the process, which naturally divides into three stages (see Figure 3.12):

1. *Dilation and effacement of the cervix.* This is the longest stage of labor, lasting, on the average, 12 to 14 hours in a first birth and 4 to 6 hours in later births. Contractions of the uterus gradually become more frequent and powerful, causing the cervix, or uterine opening, to widen and thin to nothing. As a result, a clear channel from the uterus into the vagina, or birth canal, is created.

Stage 1

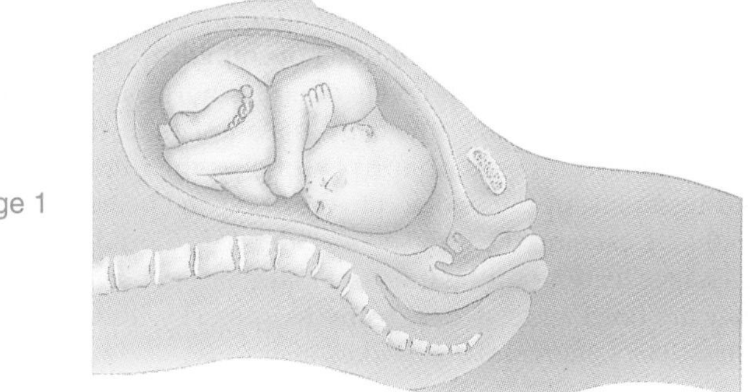

(a) Dilation and Effacement of the Cervix

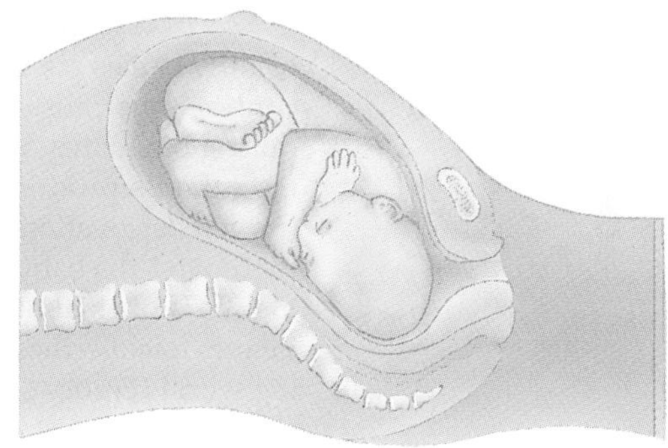

(b) Transition

Stage 2

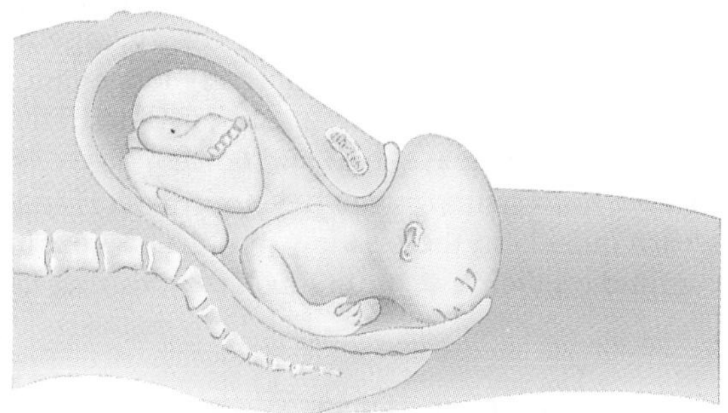

(c) Pushing

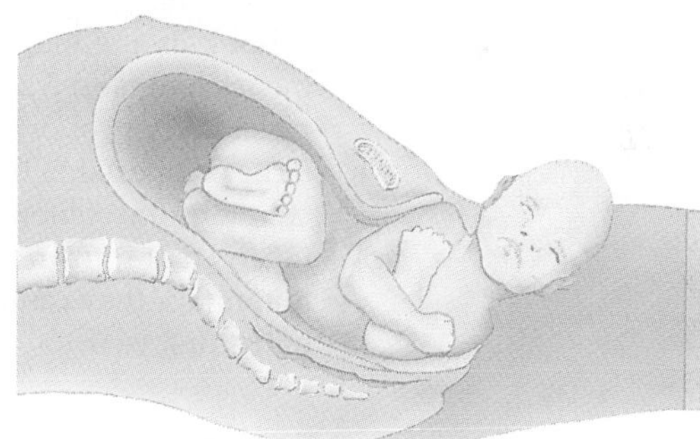

(d) Birth of the Baby

Stage 3

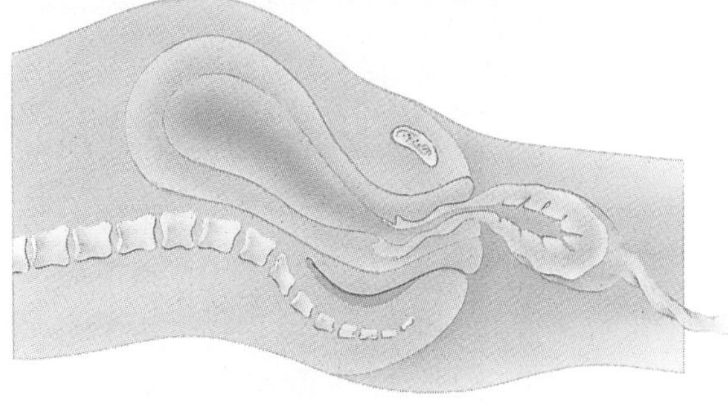

(e) Delivery of the Placenta

FIGURE 3.12

The three stages of labor. Stage 1: (a) Contractions of the uterus cause dilation and effacement of the cervix. (b) Transition is reached when the frequency and strength of the contractions are at their peak and the cervix opens completely. Stage 2: (c) The mother pushes with each contraction, forcing the baby down the birth canal, and the head appears. (d) Near the end of Stage 2, the shoulders emerge and are followed quickly by the rest of the baby's body. Stage 3: (e) With a few final pushes, the placenta is delivered.

2. *Delivery of the baby.* Once the cervix is fully open, the baby is ready to be born. This second stage is much shorter than the first, lasting about 50 minutes in a first birth and 20 minutes in later births. Strong contractions of the uterus continue, but they do not do the entire job. The most important factor is a natural urge that the mother feels to squeeze and push with her abdominal muscles. As she does so with each contraction, she forces the baby down and out.
3. *Birth of the placenta.* Labor comes to an end with a few final contractions and pushes. These cause the placenta to separate from the wall of the uterus and be delivered, a stage that usually lasts about 5 to 10 minutes.

THE BABY'S ADAPTATION TO LABOR AND DELIVERY

So far, we have described the events of childbirth from the outside looking in. Let's consider, for a moment, what the experience must be like for the baby. After being squeezed and pushed for many hours, the infant is forced to leave the warm, protective uterus for a cold, brightly lit external world. The strong contractions expose the head to a great deal of pressure, and they squeeze the placenta and umbilical cord repeatedly. Each time, the baby's supply of oxygen is reduced.

At first glance, these events may strike you as a dangerous ordeal. Fortunately, healthy babies are well equipped to withstand the trauma of childbirth. The force of the contractions causes the infant to produce high levels of stress hormones. Recall that during pregnancy, maternal stress can endanger the baby. In contrast, during childbirth, the infant's production of stress hormones is adaptive. It helps the infant withstand oxygen deprivation by sending a rich supply of blood to the brain and heart. In addition, it prepares the baby to breathe by causing the lungs to absorb excess liquid and expanding the bronchial tubes (passages leading to the lungs). Finally, stress hormones arouse infants into alertness so they are born wide awake, ready to interact with the surrounding world (Emory & Toomey, 1988; Lagercrantz & Slotkin, 1986).

THE NEWBORN BABY'S APPEARANCE

Parents are often surprised at the odd-looking newborn, who is a far cry from the storybook image many created in their minds before birth. The average newborn is 20 inches long and 7 ½ pounds in weight; boys tend to be slightly longer and heavier than girls. Body proportions contribute to the baby's strange appearance. The head is very large compared to the trunk and legs, which are short and bowed. As we will see in later chapters, the combination of a big head (with its well-developed brain) and a small body means that human infants learn quickly in the first few months of life. But unlike most mammals, they cannot get around on their own until much later, during the second half of the first year.

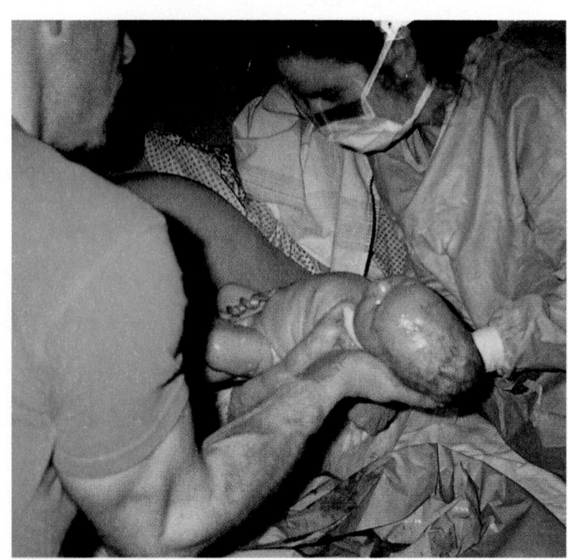

■ *This newborn baby is held by his mother's birthing coach (on the left) and midwife (on the right) just after delivery. The umbilical cord has not yet been cut. Notice how the infant's head is molded from being squeezed through the birth canal for many hours. It is also very large in relation to his body. As the infant takes his first few breaths, his body turns from blue to pink. He is wide awake and ready to get to know his new surroundings. (Courtesy of Dakoda Brandon Dorsaneo)*

TABLE 3.8

The Apgar Scale

Sign	Score		
	0	1	2
Heart rate	No heartbeat	Under 100 beats per minute	100 to 140 beats per minute
Respiratory effort	No breathing for 60 seconds	Irregular, shallow breathing	Strong breathing and crying
Reflex irritability (sneezing, coughing, and grimacing)	No response	Weak reflexive response	Strong reflexive response
Muscle tone	Completely limp	Weak movements of arms and legs	Strong movements of arms and legs
Color[a]	Blue body, arms, and legs	Body pink with blue arms and legs	Body, arms, and legs completely pink

[a]Color is the least reliable of the Apgar signs. Vernix, the white, cheesy substance that covers the skin, often interferes with the doctor's rating, and the skin tone of nonwhite babies makes it difficult to apply the "pink" criterion. However, newborns of all races can be rated for a pinkish glow that results from the flow of oxygen through body tissues, since skin color is generally lighter at birth than the baby's inherited pigmentation.

Source: Apgar, 1953.

Even though newborn babies may not match the idealized expectations of their parents, some features do make them attractive. Their round faces, chubby cheeks, large foreheads, and big eyes make adults feel like picking them up and cuddling them (Berman, 1980; Lorenz, 1943). These characteristics, as we will see in later chapters, are among the many ways in which nature helps get the parent–infant relationship off to a good start.

ASSESSING THE NEWBORN'S PHYSICAL CONDITION: THE APGAR SCALE

Infants who have difficulty making the transition to life outside the uterus require special assistance at once. To quickly assess the baby's physical condition, doctors and nurses use the **Apgar Scale**. As Table 3.8 shows, a rating from 0 to 2 on each of five characteristics is made at 1 and 5 minutes after birth. An Apgar score of 7 or better indicates that the infant is in good physical condition. If the score is between 4 and 6, the baby requires special help in establishing breathing and other vital signs. If the score is 3 or below, the infant is in serious danger, and emergency medical attention is needed. Two Apgar ratings are given, since some babies have trouble adjusting at first but are doing well after a few minutes (Apgar, 1953).

Approaches to Childbirth

Childbirth practices, like other aspects of family life, are molded by the society of which mother and baby are a part. In many village and tribal cultures, expectant mothers are well acquainted with the childbirth process. For example, the Jarara of South America and the Pukapukans of the Pacific Islands treat birth as a vital part of daily life. The Jarara mother gives birth in a passageway or shelter in full view of the entire community, including small children. The Pukapukan girl is so familiar with the events of labor and delivery that she can frequently be seen playing at it. Using a coconut to represent the baby, she stuffs it inside her dress, imitates the mother's pushing, and lets the nut fall at the proper moment. In most nonindustrialized cultures, women are assisted during the birth process, often by being held from behind. Among the Mayans of the Yucatán, the mother leans against the body and arms of a woman called the "head helper," who supports her weight and breathes with her during each contraction (Jordan, 1993; Mead & Newton, 1967).

In large Western nations, childbirth has changed dramatically over the centuries. Before the 1800s, birth usually took place at home and was a family-centered event. The

Apgar Scale
A rating used to assess the newborn baby's physical condition immediately after birth.

nineteenth-century industrial revolution brought greater crowding to cities along with new health problems. Childbirth moved from home to hospital, where the health of mothers and babies could be protected. Once doctors assumed responsibility for childbirth, women's knowledge about it declined, and relatives and friends were no longer welcome to participate (Lindell, 1988).

By the 1950s and 1960s, women started to question the medical procedures that came to be used routinely during labor and delivery. Many felt that frequent use of strong drugs and delivery instruments had robbed them of a precious experience and were often not necessary or safe for the baby. Gradually, a new natural childbirth movement arose in Europe and spread to the United States. Its purpose was to make hospital birth as comfortable and rewarding for mothers as possible. Today, most hospitals carry this theme further by offering birth centers that are family centered in approach and homelike in appearance. And a small but growing number of American women are rejecting institutional birth entirely and choosing to have their babies at home.

■ *Among the !Kung of Botswana, Africa, a mother gives birth in a sitting position, and she is surrounded by women who encourage and help her. (Shostak/Anthro-Photo)*

NATURAL, OR PREPARED, CHILDBIRTH

Natural, or **prepared, childbirth** tries to rid mothers of the idea that birth is a painful ordeal that requires extensive medical intervention. Although many natural childbirth programs exist, most draw on methods developed by Grantly Dick-Read (1959) in England and Ferdinand Lamaze (1958) in France. These physicians emphasized that cultural attitudes had taught women to fear the birth experience. An anxious, frightened woman in labor tenses muscles throughout her body, including those in the uterus. This turns the mild pain that sometimes accompanies strong contractions into a great deal of pain.

A typical natural childbirth program consists of three parts:

1. *Classes.* Expectant mothers and fathers attend a series of classes in which they learn about the anatomy and physiology of labor and delivery. Natural childbirth is based on the idea that knowledge about the birth process reduces a mother's fear.
2. *Relaxation and breathing techniques.* Expectant mothers are taught relaxation and breathing exercises aimed at counteracting any pain they might feel during uterine contractions. They also practice creating pleasant visual images in their minds instead of thinking about pain.
3. *Labor coach.* While the mother masters breathing and visualization techniques, the father (or another supportive companion) learns to be a "labor coach." The coach assists the mother by reminding her to relax and breathe, massaging her back, supporting her body during labor and delivery, and offering words of encouragement and affection.

Studies comparing mothers who experience natural childbirth with those who do not reveal many benefits. Mothers' attitudes toward labor and delivery are more positive, and they feel less pain. As a result, they require less medication—usually very little or none at all (Hetherington, 1990; Lindell, 1988). Research suggests that social support may be an important part of the success of natural childbirth techniques. In Guatemalan and American hospitals in which patients were routinely prevented from having friends and relatives with them during childbirth, some mothers were randomly assigned a companion who stayed with them throughout labor, talking to them, holding their hands, and rubbing their backs to promote relaxation. These mothers had fewer birth complications, and their labors were several hours shorter than those of women who did not have companionship. Observations of the Guatemalan mothers in the first hour after delivery showed that those receiving social support were more likely to respond to their babies by talking, smiling, and gently stroking (Kennell et al., 1991; Sosa et al., 1980).

Natural, or prepared, childbirth
An approach designed to reduce pain and medical intervention and to make childbirth a rewarding experience for parents.

HOME DELIVERY

Home birth has always been popular in certain industrialized nations, such as England, the Netherlands, and Sweden. The number of American women choosing to have their babies at home has increased since 1970, although it remains small, at about 1

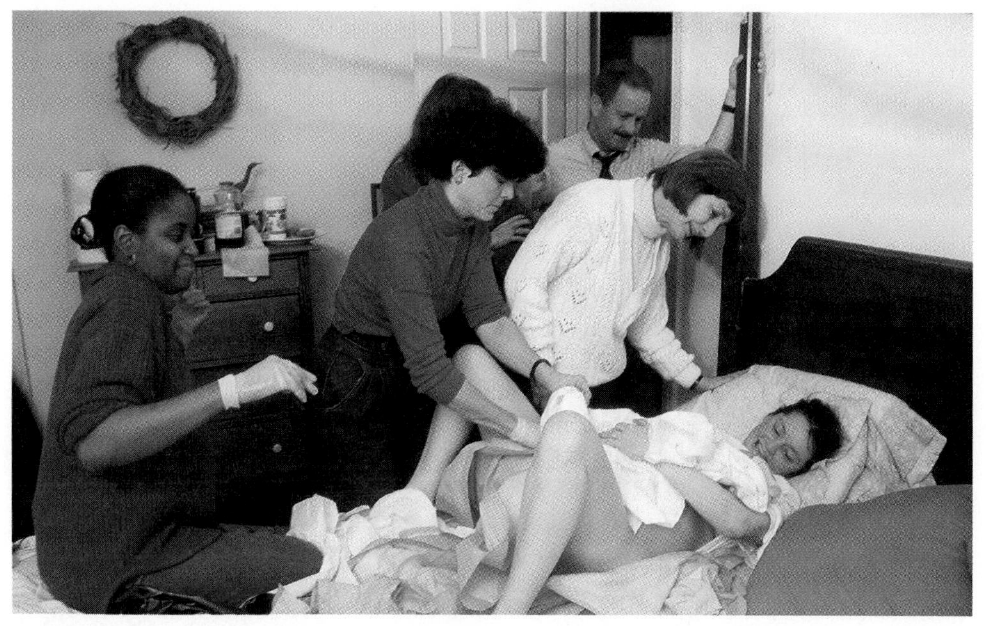

■ *Women who choose home birth want to share the joy of childbirth with family members, avoid unnecessary medical procedures, and exercise greater control over their own care and that of their babies. When assisted by a well-trained doctor or midwife, healthy women can give birth at home safely. (Franck Logue/Stock South)*

percent. These mothers want to recapture the time when birth was an important part of family life. In addition, most want to avoid unnecessary medical procedures and exercise greater control over their own care and that of their babies than hospitals typically permit (Bastian, 1993; O'Connor, 1993). Although some home births are attended by doctors, many more are handled by certified nurse-midwives who have degrees in nursing and additional training in childbirth management.

Is it just as safe to give birth at home as in a hospital? For healthy women who are assisted by a well-trained doctor or midwife, it seems so, since complications rarely occur. In fact, alternative birth settings, such as the home or *freestanding birth centers* (which operate independently of hospitals and offer less in the way of backup medical care), grant low-risk women the advantage of a less costly birth experience without any impact on birth outcomes (Albers & Katz, 1991). However, if attendants are not carefully trained and prepared to handle emergencies, the rate of infant death is high (Schramm, Barnes, & Bakewell, 1987). When mothers are at risk for any kind of complication, the appropriate place for labor and delivery is the hospital, where life-saving treatment is available should it be needed.

LABOR AND DELIVERY MEDICATION

Although natural childbirth techniques lessen or eliminate the need for pain-relieving drugs, some form of medication is still used in 80 to 95 percent of births in the United States. *Analgesics* are drugs that relieve pain. When given during labor, the dose is usually mild and intended to help a mother relax. *Anesthetics* are a stronger type of painkiller that blocks sensation. During childbirth, they are generally injected into the spinal column to numb the lower half of the body.

In complicated deliveries, pain-relieving drugs are essential because they permit life-saving medical interventions to be carried out. But when used routinely, they can cause problems. Anesthesia interferes with the mother's ability to feel contractions during the second stage of labor. As a result, she may not push effectively, increasing the likelihood that the baby may have to be pulled from the birth canal with *forceps* (a metal device placed around the infant's head) or a *vacuum extractor* (a plastic suction cup that fits over the top of the head). Both of these instruments involve some risk of injury to the baby (Hanigan et al., 1990; Johanson et al., 1993).

Labor and delivery medication rapidly crosses the placenta. When given in large doses, it produces a depressed state in the newborn baby that may last for days. The infant is sleepy and withdrawn, sucks poorly during feedings, and is likely to be irritable when awake (Brackbill, McManus, & Woodward, 1985; Brazelton, Nugent, & Lester, 1987).

Does the use of medication during childbirth have a lasting impact on the physical and mental development of the child? Some researchers claim so (Brackbill, McManus, &

Woodward, 1985), but their findings have been challenged, and contrary results exist (Broman, 1983). Anesthesia may be related to other risk factors that could account for long-term consequences in some studies, and more research is needed to sort out these effects. In the meantime, the negative impact of these drugs on the early infant–parent relationship supports the current trend to limit their use.

Birth Complications

In the preceding sections, we indicated that some babies—particularly those whose mothers are in poor health, do not receive good medical care, or have a history of pregnancy problems—are especially likely to experience birth complications. Insufficient oxygen, a pregnancy that ends too early, and a baby who is born underweight are serious difficulties that we have mentioned many times. Let's look more closely at the impact of each on development.

OXYGEN DEPRIVATION

A small number of infants are exposed to *anoxia*, or inadequate oxygen supply, during the birth process. Sometimes the problem results from a failure to start breathing immediately after delivery. Although newborns can survive periods without oxygen longer than adults, there is risk of brain damage if breathing is delayed for more than 3 minutes (Stechler & Halton, 1982). At other times, anoxia occurs during labor. Squeezing of the umbilical cord is a common cause, a condition that is especially likely when infants are in **breech position**—turned in such a way that the buttocks or feet would emerge first. Because of this danger, breech babies are often delivered by cesarean section, a surgical procedure in which the doctor makes an incision in the mother's abdomen and lifts the baby out of the uterus. Another cause of oxygen deprivation is *placenta previa*, or premature separation of the placenta, a life-threatening event that requires immediate delivery. Although the reasons for placenta previa are not well understood, teratogens that result in abnormal development of the placenta, such as cigarette smoking, are strongly related to it (Handler et al., 1994).

Incompatibility between mother and baby in a blood protein called the **Rh factor** can also lead to anoxia. When the mother is Rh negative (lacks the protein) and the father is Rh positive (has the protein), the baby may inherit the father's Rh-positive blood type. (Recall from Table 3.2 that Rh-positive blood is dominant and Rh-negative blood is recessive, so the chances are good that a baby will be Rh positive.) During the third trimester and at the time of birth, some maternal and fetal blood cells usually cross the placenta, generally in small enough amounts to be quite safe. But if even a little of the baby's Rh-positive blood passes into the mother's Rh-negative bloodstream, she begins to form antibodies to the foreign Rh protein. If these enter the baby's system, they destroy red blood cells, reducing the supply of oxygen. Mental retardation, damage to the heart muscle, and infant death can occur. Since it takes time for the mother to produce antibodies, first-born children are rarely affected. The danger increases with each additional pregnancy. Fortunately, the harmful effects of Rh incompatibility can be prevented in most cases. After the birth of each Rh-positive baby, Rh-negative mothers are routinely given a vaccine called RhoGam, which prevents the buildup of antibodies.

Children deprived of oxygen during labor and delivery remain behind their agemates in intellectual and motor progress throughout early childhood. But by the school years, most catch up in development (Corah et al., 1965; Graham et al., 1962). When problems do persist, the anoxia was usually extreme. Perhaps it was caused by prenatal damage to the baby's respiratory system, or it may have happened because the infant's lungs were not yet mature enough to breathe. For example, babies born more than 6 weeks early commonly have a disorder called *respiratory distress syndrome* (otherwise known as *hyaline membrane disease*). Their tiny lungs are so poorly developed that the air sacs collapse, causing serious breathing difficulties. Today, mechanical ventilators keep many such infants alive. In spite of these measures, some babies suffer permanent brain damage from lack of oxygen, and in other cases their delicate lungs are harmed by the

Breech position
A position of the baby in the uterus that would cause the buttocks or feet to be delivered first.

Rh factor
A protein that, when present in the fetus's blood but not in the mother's, can cause the mother to build up antibodies. If these return to the fetus's system, they destroy red blood cells, reducing the oxygen supply to organs and tissues.

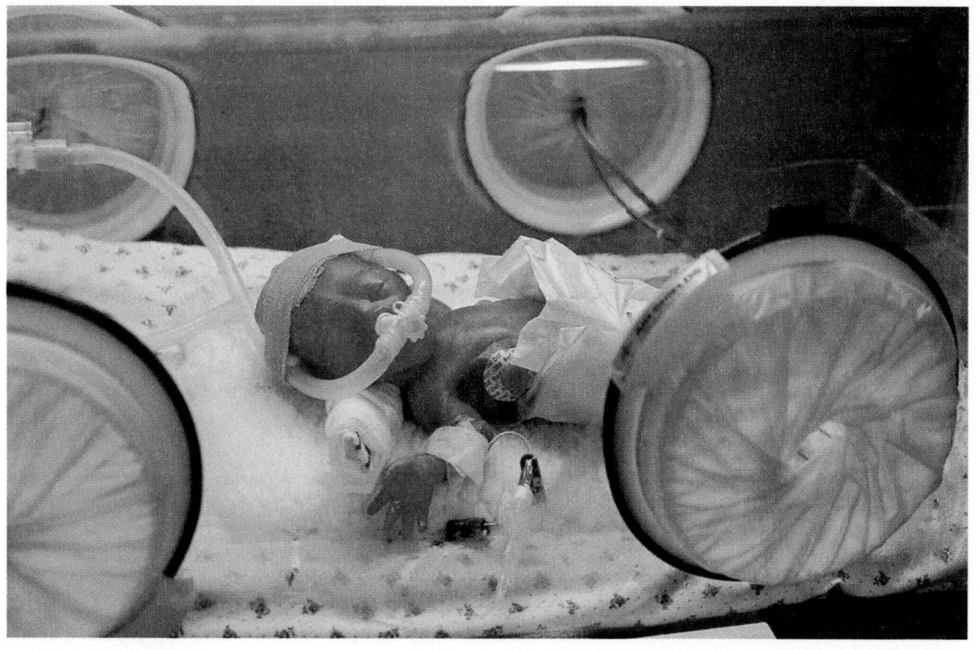

■ *This baby was born 13 weeks before her due date and weighs little more than 2 pounds. Since her lungs are too immature to function independently, she breathes with the aid of a respirator. Her survival and development are seriously at risk. (Simon Frazer/Princess Mary Hospital/Photo Researchers, Inc.)*

treatment itself (Vohr & Garcia-Coll, 1988). Respiratory distress syndrome is only one of many risks for babies born too soon, as we will see in the following section.

PRETERM AND LOW-BIRTH-WEIGHT INFANTS

Babies born 3 weeks or more before the end of a full 38-week pregnancy or who weigh less than 5 ½ pounds (2,500 grams) have, for many years, been referred to as "premature." A wealth of research indicates that premature babies are at risk for many problems. Birth weight is the best available predictor of infant survival and healthy development. Many newborns who weigh less than 3 ⅓ pounds (1,500 grams) experience difficulties that are not overcome, an effect that becomes stronger as birth weight decreases (Wilcox & Skjoerven, 1992). Frequent illness, inattention, overactivity, and deficits in motor coordination and school learning are some of the problems that extend into the childhood years (Hack et al., 1994; Liaw & Brooks-Gunn, 1993; McCormick, Gortmaker, & Sobol, 1990).

About 1 in 14 infants is born underweight in the United States. Although the problem can strike unexpectedly, it is highest among poverty-stricken pregnant women, especially ethnic minorities (Children's Defense Fund, 1996). These mothers, as we indicated earlier in this chapter, are more likely to be undernourished and to be exposed to other harmful environmental influences. In addition, they often do not receive the prenatal care necessary to protect their vulnerable babies.

Prematurity is also common when mothers are carrying twins. Twins are usually born about 3 weeks early, and because of restricted space inside the uterus, they gain less weight than singletons after the twentieth week of pregnancy.

■ PRETERM VERSUS SMALL FOR DATE. Although low-birth-weight infants face many obstacles to healthy development, individual differences exist in how well they do. Over half go on to lead normal lives—even some who weighed only a couple of pounds at birth (Vohr & Garcia-Coll, 1988). To better understand why some of these babies do better than others, researchers have divided them into two groups. The first is called **preterm**. These infants are born several weeks or more before their due date. Although small in size, their weight may still be appropriate for the amount of time they spent in the uterus. The second group is called **small for date**. These babies are below their expected weight when length of pregnancy is taken into account. Some small-for-date infants are actually full term. Others are preterm infants who are especially underweight.

Preterm
Infants born several weeks or more before their due date.

Small for date
Infants whose birth weight is below normal when length of pregnancy is taken into account.

Of the two types of babies, small-for-date infants usually have more serious problems. During the first year, they are more likely to die, catch infections, and show evidence of brain damage. By middle childhood, they have lower intelligence test scores, are less attentive, and achieve more poorly in school (Copper et al., 1993; Teberg, Walther, & Pena, 1988). Small-for-date infants probably experienced inadequate nutrition before birth. Perhaps their mothers did not eat properly, the placenta did not function normally, or the babies themselves had defects that prevented them from growing as they should.

■ CHARACTERISTICS OF PRETERM INFANTS: CONSEQUENCES FOR CAREGIVING. Imagine a scrawny, thin-skinned infant whose body is only a little larger than the size of your hand. You try to play with the baby by stroking and talking softly, but he is sleepy and unresponsive. When you feed him, he sucks poorly. He is usually irritable during the short, unpredictable periods in which he is awake.

Unfortunately, the appearance and behavior of preterm babies can lead parents to be less sensitive and responsive in caring for them. Compared to full-term infants, preterm babies—especially those who are very ill at birth—are less often held close, touched, and talked to gently. At times, mothers of these infants are overly intrusive, engaging in interfering pokes and verbal commands in an effort to obtain a higher level of response from a baby who is a passive, unrewarding social partner (Patteson & Barnard, 1990). Some parents may step up these intrusive acts when faced with continuing ungratifying infant behavior. This may explain why preterm babies as a group are at risk for child abuse. When these infants are born to isolated, poverty-stricken mothers who have difficulty managing their own lives, then the chances for unfavorable outcomes are increased. In contrast, parents with stable life circumstances and social supports can usually overcome the stresses of caring for a preterm infant. In these cases, even sick preterm babies have a good chance of catching up in development by middle childhood (Liaw & Brooks-Gunn, 1993).

These findings suggest that how well preterm infants develop has a great deal to do with the kind of relationship established between parent and child, to which both partners contribute. If a good relationship between mother and baby can help prevent the negative effects of early birth, then interventions directed at supporting this relationship should help these infants recover.

■ INTERVENTIONS FOR PRETERM INFANTS. In some intensive care nurseries, preterm infants can be seen rocking in suspended hammocks or lying on waterbeds—interventions designed to replace the gentle motion they would have received while being carried in the mother's uterus. Other forms of stimulation have also been used—for example, an attractive mobile or a tape recording of a heartbeat, soft music, or the mother's voice. Many studies show that these experiences have important short-term benefits. They promote faster weight gain, more predictable sleep patterns, and greater alertness during the weeks after birth (Cornell & Gottfried, 1976; Schaefer, Hatcher, & Bargelow, 1980).

Touch is an especially important form of stimulation for preterm newborns. In studies of baby animals, touching the skin releases certain brain chemicals that support physical growth. These effects are believed to occur in humans as well (Schanberg & Field, 1987). In one study, preterm infants who were gently massaged several times each day in the hospital gained weight faster and, at the end of the first year, were advanced in mental and motor development over preterm infants not given this stimulation (Field et al., 1986). In developing countries where hospitalization is not always possible, skin-to-skin "kangaroo baby care," in which the preterm infant is tucked between the mother's breasts and peers over the top of her clothing, is being encouraged. The technique is used often in Europe as a supplement to hospital intensive care. It fosters oxygenation of the baby's body, temperature regulation, improved feeding, and infant survival (Anderson, 1991; Hamelin & Ramachandran, 1993).

When effective stimulation helps preterm infants develop, parents are likely to feel good about their infant's growth and interact with the baby more effectively. Interventions that support the parenting side of this relationship generally teach parents about the infant's characteristics and promote caregiving skills. For parents with the economic and personal resources to care for a low-birth-weight infant, just a few sessions of coaching in recognizing and responding to the baby's needs is helpful. Infants of mothers randomly selected to receive this training in the months after hospital discharge, compared to infants of mothers who were not, gained steadily in mental test performance over the childhood years until their scores equaled those of full-term youngsters (Achenbach et al., 1990).

When preterm infants live in stressed, low-income households, long-term, intensive intervention is required to reduce developmental problems. In a recent study, preterm babies born into poverty received a comprehensive intervention that combined medical follow-up, weekly parent training sessions, and enrollment in cognitively stimulating day care from 1 to 3 years of age. As Figure 3.13 shows, compared to controls receiving only medical follow-up, nearly four times as many intervention children were within normal range at age 3 in intelligence, psychological adjustment, and physical growth. However, by age 5, differences between the two groups had declined. To sustain developmental gains in these very vulnerable children, it appears that high-quality intervention is needed well beyond age 3—even into the school years (Bradley et al., 1994; Brooks-Gunn et al., 1994).

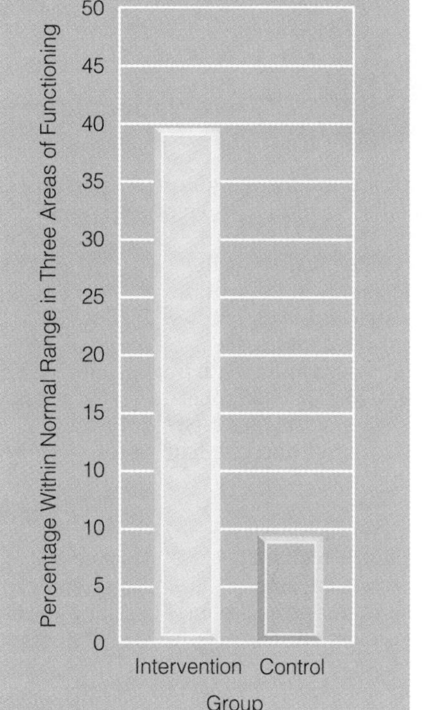

FIGURE 3.13

■ *Percentage of preterm infants assigned to an intensive intervention or a control group who were developing normally at age 3. Children who experienced the intervention, consisting of medical follow-up, parent training, and cognitively stimulating day care, were nearly four times more likely than medical-follow-up-only controls to be within normal range in intelligence, psychological adjustment, and physical growth. Without continued intervention, however, these gains are not sustained. (Adapted from Bradley et al., 1994.)*

Finally, the high rate of low birth weight and infant death in the United States—one of the worst in the industrialized world—could be greatly reduced by improving the health and social conditions described in the Cultural Influences box on page 112. Fortunately, today we can save many preterm infants. But an even better course of action would be to prevent this serious threat to infant survival and development before it happens.

UNDERSTANDING BIRTH COMPLICATIONS

In the preceding sections, we discussed a variety of birth complications that threaten children's well-being. Now let's try to put the evidence together. Are there any general principles that might help us understand how infants who survive a traumatic birth are likely to develop? A landmark longitudinal study carried out in Hawaii provides answers to this question.

In 1955, Emmy Werner and Ruth Smith began to track the development of nearly 700 infants on the island of Kauai who experienced either mild, moderate, or severe birth complications. Each was matched, on the basis of social class and ethnicity, with a healthy newborn. Findings revealed that the likelihood of long-term difficulties increased if birth trauma was severe. But among mildly to moderately stressed children, the best predictor of how well they did in later years was the quality of their home environments. Children growing up in stable families did almost as well on measures of intelligence and psychological adjustment as those with no birth problems. Those exposed to poverty, family disorganization, and mentally ill parents often developed serious learning difficulties, behavior problems, and emotional disturbance during childhood and adolescence (Werner & Smith, 1982).

The Kauai study tells us that as long as birth injuries are not overwhelming, a supportive home environment can restore children's growth. But the most intriguing cases in this study were the handful of exceptions to this rule. A few children with fairly serious birth complications and troubled family environments grew into competent adults who fared as well as controls in career attainment and psychological adjustment. Werner and Smith found that these resilient children relied on factors outside the family and within themselves to overcome stress. Some had especially attractive personalities that caused them to receive positive responses from relatives, neighbors, and peers. In other instances, a grandparent, aunt, uncle, or baby-sitter established a warm relationship with the child and provided the needed emotional support (Werner, 1989, 1993; Werner & Smith, 1992).

CULTURAL INFLUENCES

A Cross-National Perspective on Infant Mortality

Infant mortality is an index used around the world to assess the overall health of a nation's children. It refers to the number of deaths in the first year of life per 1,000 live births. Although the United States has the most up-to-date health care technology in the world, it has made less progress than many other countries in reducing infant deaths. Over the past three decades, it slipped down in the international rankings, from seventh in the 1950s to twenty-second in the 1990s. Members of poverty-stricken ethnic minorities, African-American babies especially, are at greatest risk. Black infants are two-and-one-half times more likely as white infants to die in the first year of life (Guyer et al., 1995).

Neonatal mortality, the rate of death within the first month of life, accounts for 67 percent of the high infant death rate in the United States. Two factors are largely responsible for neonatal mortality. The first is serious physical defects, many of which cannot be prevented. The percentage of babies born with physical defects is about the same in all ethnic and income groups. The second leading cause of neonatal mortality is low birth weight, which is largely preventable. Black babies are more than four times more likely to die because they are born early and underweight than are white infants. On an international scale, the number of underweight babies born in the United States is alarmingly high. It is greater than that of 28 other countries (Wegman, 1994).

Experts agree that widespread poverty and weak health care programs for mothers and young children are largely responsible for these trends. High-quality prenatal care beginning early in pregnancy is consistently related to birth weight and infant survival (Malloy, Kao, & Lee, 1992). Yet 5 percent of pregnant women in the United States wait until the end of pregnancy to seek prenatal care, or never get any at all (Children's Defense Fund, 1996).

Financial problems are a major barrier to early prenatal care. Most women who delay going to the doctor do not receive health insurance as a fringe benefit of their jobs. Others have no insurance because they are unemployed. Although the very poorest of these mothers are eligible for government-sponsored health services, many women who have low incomes and need benefits do not qualify. Unfortunately, expectant women who wait to see a doctor usually lead highly stressful lives and engage in harmful behaviors, such as smoking and drug abuse (Melnikow & Alemagno, 1993). These women, who have no medical attention for most or all of their pregnancies, are among those who need it most!

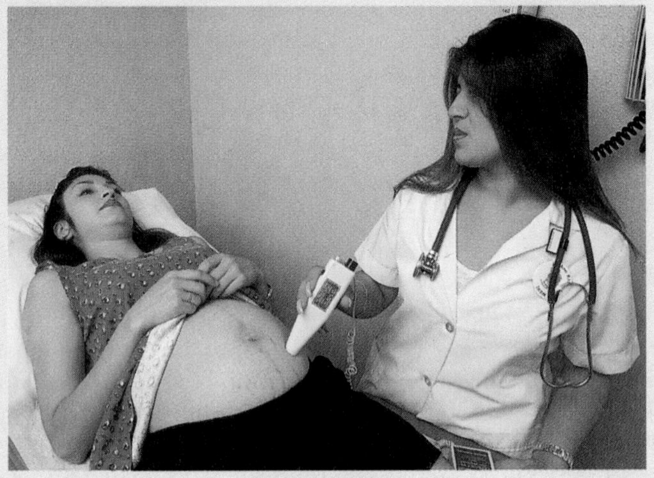

■ *During a routine check-up, a nurse uses an ultrasound scanner to check the growth of the fetus. Early prenatal care is vital to ensure the health of mothers and newborn babies. Yet many low-income women in the United States do not have access to affordable health care. (Michael Newman/PhotoEdit)*

The Kauai study reveals that as long as the overall balance of life events tips toward the favorable side, children with serious birth problems can develop successfully. When negative factors outweigh positive ones, even the sturdiest of newborn babies can become a lifelong casualty.

BRIEF REVIEW

The hard work of labor takes place in three stages: dilation and effacement of the cervix, birth of the baby, and delivery of the placenta. Stress hormones help the infant withstand the trauma of childbirth. The Apgar Scale provides a quick rating of the baby's physical condition immediately after birth. Natural, or prepared, childbirth improves mothers' attitudes toward labor and delivery and reduces the need for medication. Home births are safe for healthy women, provided attendants are well trained. Pain-relieving drugs can cross the placenta, producing a depressed state in the newborn baby. However, long-term effects of medication have not been established.

Birth complications can threaten children's development. Oxygen deprivation, when extreme, causes lasting brain damage. Preterm and low-birth-weight infants are at risk

Infant mortality
(see Cultural Influences box on page 112)
The number of deaths in the first year of life per 1,000 live births.

Except for the United States, each country listed in Figure 3.14 provides all its citizens with government-sponsored health care benefits. For example, all western European nations guarantee women a certain number of prenatal visits at very low or no cost. A health professional routinely visits the home after a baby is born to provide counseling about infant care and to arrange continuing medical services. Home assistance is especially extensive in the Netherlands. For a token fee, each mother is granted the services of a specially trained maternity helper, who assists with infant care, shopping, housekeeping, meal preparation, and the care of other children during the 10 days after delivery (Kamerman, 1993).

Paid employment leave for expectant and new parents is also available in Canada and Western Europe. It ranges from about 2 to 15 months, depending on the country. A few nations, such as Denmark, Finland, Norway, and Sweden, permit the father to take childbirth leave if he is the principal caregiver. The period of leave can usually be extended on an unpaid basis, and additional paid leave is granted in the event of maternal or child illness (Kamerman, 1993).

In countries with low infant mortality rates, expectant mothers need not wonder how or where they will get health and child care assistance, or who will pay for it. The clear link between high-quality maternal and infant health services and reduced infant mortality provides strong justification for implementing similar programs in the United States.

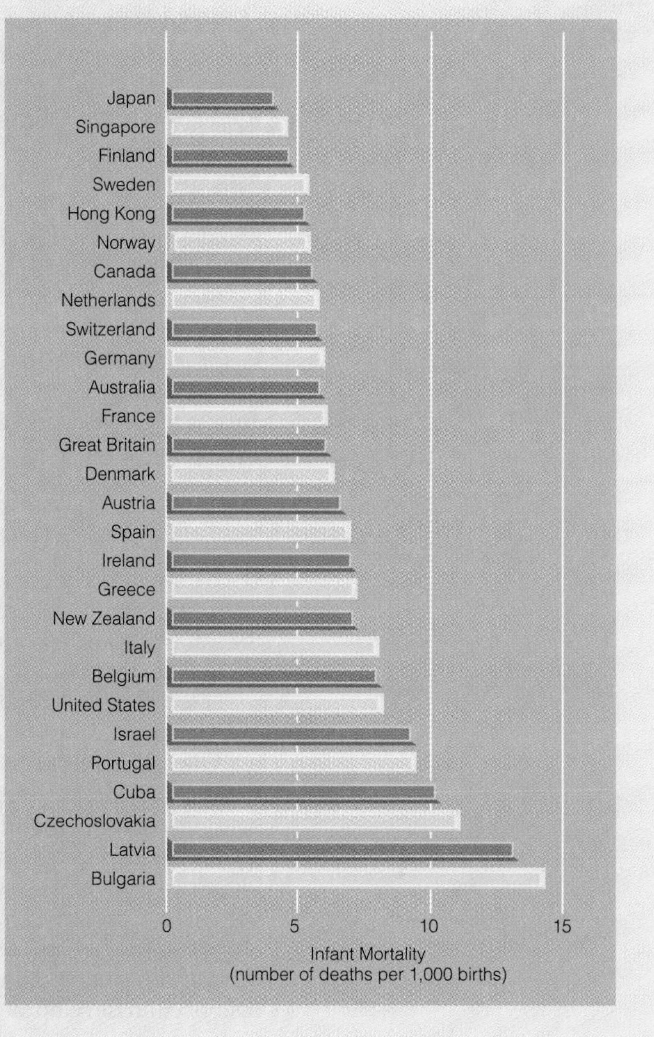

FIGURE 3.14

■ *Infant mortality in 28 nations. Despite its advanced health care technology, the United States ranks poorly. It is twenty-second in the world, with a death rate of 8.9 infants per 1,000 births. (Adapted from Wegman, 1994.)*

for many problems. Providing these babies with special stimulation and teaching parents how to care for and interact with them helps restore their growth. Preterm infants living in stressed, low-income households require long-term, intensive intervention to reduce developmental problems. As long as newborns with serious complications have access to favorable social environments, they have a good chance of catching up in development.

Heredity, Environment, and Behavior: A Look Ahead

Throughout this chapter, we have discussed a wide variety of genetic and early environmental influences, each of which has the power to alter the course of development. When we consider them together, it may seem surprising that any newborn babies arrive intact, but the vast majority do. Over 90 percent of pregnancies in the United States result in normal infants. Born healthy and vigorous, these developing members of the human species soon show wide variation in traits and abilities. Some are outgoing and sociable, whereas others are shy and reserved. By school age, one child loves to read, another is attracted to mathematics, while still a third excels at music or athletics. **Behavioral genetics** is a field devoted to discovering the origins of this great diversity in human characteristics. We have already seen that researchers are only beginning to understand the genetic and environmental events preceding birth that affect the child's potential. How, then, do they unravel the roots of the many characteristics emerging after birth that are the focus of the remaining chapters in this book?

All behavioral geneticists agree that both heredity and environment are involved in every aspect of development. There is no real controversy on this point because an environment is always needed for genetic information to be expressed (Plomin, 1994a). But for polygenic traits (due to many genes) like intelligence and personality, scientists are a long way from knowing the precise hereditary influences involved. They must study the impact of genes on these characteristics indirectly, and the nature–nurture controversy remains unresolved because researchers do not agree on how heredity and environment influence these complex traits.

Some believe it is useful and possible to answer the question of *how much* each factor contributes to differences among children. A second group regards the question of which factor is more important as neither useful nor answerable. These investigators believe heredity and environment do not make separate contributions to behavior. Instead, they are always related, and the real question we need to explore is *how* they work together. In the following sections, we consider each of these two positions.

THE QUESTION OF "HOW MUCH?"

Behavioral geneticists use two methods—heritability estimates and concordance rates—to infer the role of heredity in complex human characteristics. Let's look closely at the information these procedures yield, along with their limitations.

HERITABILITY. A **heritability estimate** measures the extent to which individual differences in complex traits are due to genetic factors. Researchers have obtained heritabilities for intelligence and a variety of personality characteristics. We will review their findings in detail in later chapters devoted to these topics and provide only a brief overview here. Heritability estimates are obtained from **kinship studies**, which compare the characteristics of family members. The most frequent type of kinship study compares identical twins, who share all their genes, with fraternal twins, who share only some. If people who are genetically more alike are also more similar in intelligence and personality, then the researcher assumes that heredity plays an important role.

Kinship studies of intelligence provide some of the most controversial findings in the field of child development. Some experts claim a strong role for heredity, whereas others believe genetic factors are barely involved. Currently, most researchers support a moderate role for heredity. When many twin studies are examined, correlations between the scores of identicals are consistently higher than those of fraternals. In a summary of over 30 such investigations, the correlation for intelligence was .86 for identical twins and .60 for fraternal twins (Bouchard & McGue, 1981). Heritability estimates take these correlations and compare them, arriving at a number ranging from 0 to 1.00. The value for intelligence is about .50, which indicates that half of the variation in intelligence can be explained by individual differences in genetic makeup (Plomin, 1994c). The fact that the intelligence of adopted children is more strongly related to the scores of their biological parents than

To study the role of heredity in complex human traits, researchers conduct kinship studies in which they compare the characteristics of family members. Sometimes the resemblance between parents and children—both physically and behaviorally—is striking. (Superstock)

Behavioral genetics
A field of study devoted to uncovering the hereditary and environmental origins of individual differences in human traits and abilities.

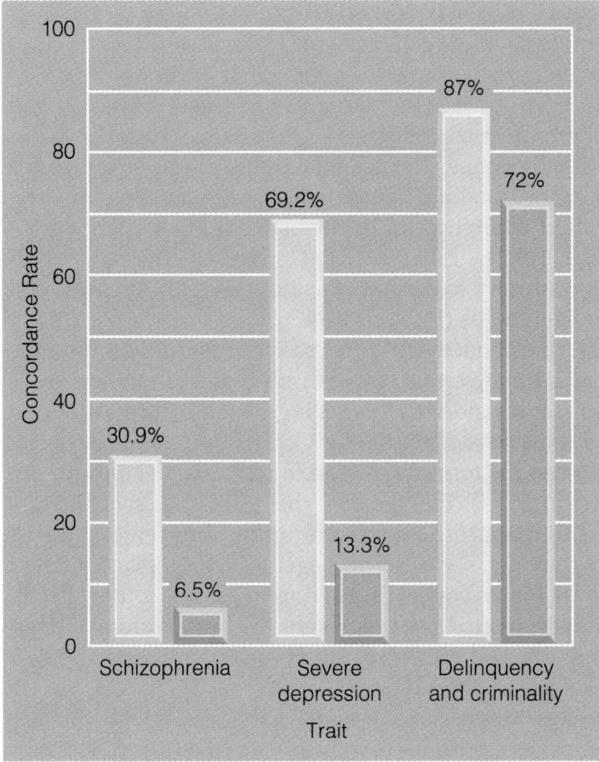

FIGURE 3.15

■ *Concordance rates for schizophrenia, severe depression, and delinquency and criminality, each based on over 100 twin pairs. By comparing identical and fraternal twins, we can see that heredity plays some role in schizophrenia and is even more influential in severe depression. The findings suggest that heredity contributes much less to delinquency and criminality. (From Gershon et al., 1977; Gottesman, Carey, & Hanson, 1983; Kendler & Robinette, 1983.)*

their adoptive parents offers further support for the role of heredity (Horn, 1983; Scarr & Weinberg, 1983).

Heritability research also reveals that genetic factors are important in personality. In fact, for personality traits that have been studied a great deal, such as sociability, emotional expressiveness, and activity level, heritability estimates are at about the same moderate level as that reported for intelligence (Braungart et al., 1992; Loehlin, 1992).

■ CONCORDANCE. A second measure that has been used to infer the contribution of heredity to complex characteristics is the **concordance rate**. It refers to the percentage of instances in which both twins show a trait when it is present in one twin. Researchers typically use concordance to study emotional and behavior disorders, which can be judged as either present or absent. A concordance rate ranges from 0 to 100 percent. A score of 0 indicates that if one twin has the trait, the other twin never has it. A score of 100 means that if one twin has the trait, the other one always has it. When a concordance rate is much higher for identical twins than for fraternal twins, then heredity is believed to play a major role. As Figure 3.15 reveals, twin studies of schizophrenia[2] and severe depression show this pattern of findings. Look carefully at the figure, and you will see that the evidence for heredity is less convincing for delinquency and criminality. In that case, the difference between the concordance rates for identical and fraternal twins is not great enough to support a strong genetic role (Plomin, 1994a). Once again, adoption studies lend support to these results. Biological relatives of schizophrenic and depressed adoptees are more likely to share the same disorder than are adoptive relatives (Loehlin, Willerman, & Horn, 1988).

Taken together, concordance and adoption research suggests that the tendency for schizophrenia and depression to run in families is partly due to genetic factors. However, we also know that environment is involved, since the concordance rate for identical twins would need to be 100 percent for heredity to be the only influence operating. Already we have seen that environmental stresses, such as poverty, family conflict, and a disorganized home life, are often associated with emotional and behavior disorders. We will encounter many more examples of this relationship in later chapters.

[2] Schizophrenia is a disorder involving serious difficulty distinguishing fantasy from reality, frequent delusions and hallucinations, and irrational and inappropriate behaviors.

Heritability estimate
A statistic that measures the extent to which individual differences in complex traits, such as intelligence and personality, are due to genetic factors.

Kinship studies
Studies comparing the characteristics of family members to determine the importance of heredity in complex human characteristics.

Concordance rate
The percentage of instances in which both twins show a trait when it is present in one twin.

■ LIMITATIONS OF HERITABILITY AND CONCORDANCE. Although heritability estimates and concordance rates provide evidence that genetic factors contribute to complex human characteristics, questions have been raised about their accuracy. First, we must keep in mind that each value refers only to the particular population studied and its unique range of genetic and environmental influences. If the range of either factor changes, then heritability estimates will change. To take an extreme example, imagine a country in which children's home, school, and neighborhood experiences are very similar. Under these conditions, individual differences in behavior would be largely due to heredity, and heritability estimates would be close to 1.00. Conversely, the more environments vary, the greater their opportunity to account for individual differences, and the lower heritability estimates are likely to be (Plomin, 1994c).

Second, the accuracy of heritability estimates and concordance rates depends on the extent to which the twin pairs on which they are computed reflect genetic and environmental variation in the population. Yet consider these findings: Identical twins reared together under highly similar conditions have more strongly correlated intelligence test scores than do those reared apart. When the former are used in research, the importance of heredity is overestimated (Hoffman, 1994). To overcome this difficulty, investigators try to find twins who have been reared apart in adoptive families. But few separated twin pairs are available, and when they are, social service agencies often place them in advantaged homes that are alike in many ways (Bronfenbrenner & Crouter, 1983). Because the environments of most twin pairs do not represent the broad range of environments found in the general population, it is often difficult to generalize heritability and concordance findings to the population as a whole.

Heritability estimates are controversial measures because they can easily be misapplied. For example, high heritabilities have been used to suggest that ethnic differences in intelligence, such as the poorer performance of black children compared to white children, have a genetic basis (Jensen, 1969, 1985). Yet this line of reasoning is widely regarded as incorrect. Heritabilities computed on mostly white twin samples do not tell us what is responsible for test score differences between ethnic groups. We have already seen that large economic and cultural differences are involved. In Chapter 8, we will discuss research indicating that when black children are adopted into economically advantaged homes at an early age, their scores are well above average and substantially higher than those of children growing up in impoverished families.

Perhaps the most serious criticism of heritability estimates and concordance rates has to do with their usefulness. Although they are interesting statistics that tell us heredity is undoubtedly involved in complex traits like intelligence and personality, they give us no precise information on how these traits develop or how children might respond when exposed to family, school, and peer experiences aimed at helping them develop as far as possible (Bronfenbrenner & Ceci, 1994; Wachs, 1994). Investigators who conduct heritability research respond that their studies are a first step. As more evidence accumulates to show that heredity underlies important human characteristics, then scientists can begin to ask better questions—about the specific genes involved, the way they affect development, and how their impact is modified by environmental factors (Plomin, Owen, & McGuffin, 1994).

THE QUESTION OF "HOW?"

According to a second perspective, heredity and environment cannot be divided into separate influences. Instead, behavior is the result of a dynamic interplay between these two forces. How do heredity and environment work together to affect development? Several important concepts shed light on this question.

■ REACTION RANGE. The first of these ideas is **range of reaction** (Gottesman, 1963). It emphasizes that each person responds to the environment in a unique way because of his or her genetic makeup. Let's explore this idea in Figure 3.16. Reaction range can apply to any characteristic; here it is illustrated for intelligence. Notice that when environments vary from extremely unstimulating to highly enriched, Ben's intelligence increases dramatically, Linda's only slightly, and Ron's hardly at all.

Range of reaction
Each person's unique, genetically determined response to a range of environmental conditions.

Reaction range highlights two important points about the relationship between heredity and environment. First, it shows that because each of us has a unique genetic

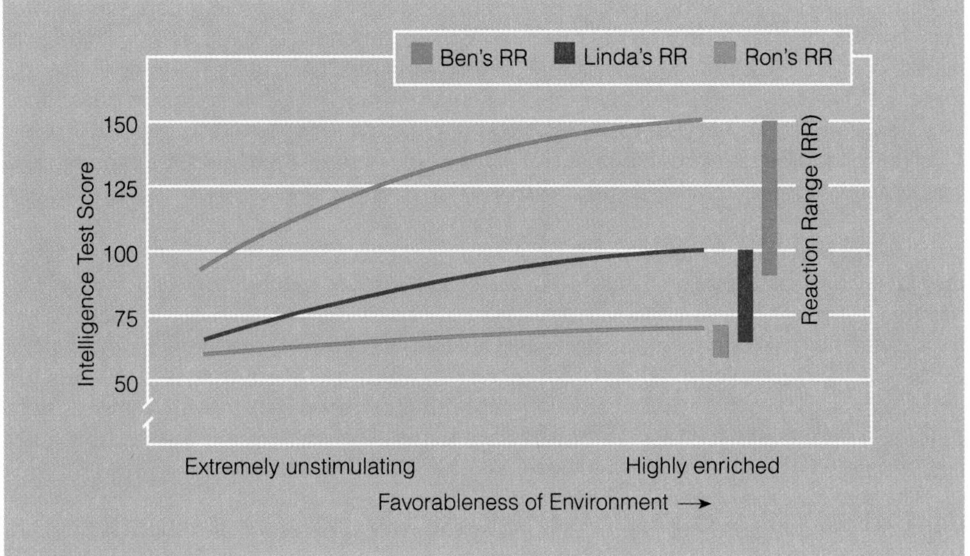

FIGURE 3.16

■ *Intellectual ranges of reaction (RR) for three children in environments that vary from unstimulating to highly enriched. (From I. I. Gottesman, 1963, "Genetic Aspects of Intelligent Behavior," in N. R. Ellis, ed.,* Handbook of Mental Deficiency, *New York: McGraw-Hill, p. 255. Adapted by permission.)*

makeup, we respond quite differently to the same environment. Again, look carefully at Figure 3.16, and notice how a poor environment results in a lower intelligence test score for Ron than Ben. Also, an advantaged environment raises Ben's score far above what is possible for Ron. Second, sometimes different genetic–environmental combinations can make two children look the same! For example, if Ben is reared in an unstimulating environment, his score will be about 100–average for children in general. Linda can also obtain this score, but to do so she must grow up in a very advantaged home. In other words, the concept of range of reaction tells us that children differ in their range of possible responses to the environment. And unique blends of heredity and environment lead to both similarities and differences in behavior.

■ CANALIZATION. The concept of **canalization** provides another way of understanding how heredity and environment combine. Canalization is the tendency of heredity to restrict the development of some characteristics to just one or a few outcomes. A behavior that is strongly canalized follows a genetically set growth plan, and only strong environmental forces can change it (Waddington, 1957). For example, infant perceptual and motor development seems to be strongly canalized, since all normal human babies eventually roll over, reach for objects, sit up, crawl, and walk. It takes extreme conditions to modify these behaviors or cause them not to appear. In contrast, intelligence and personality are less strongly canalized, since they vary much more with changes in the environment. When we look at the kinds of behaviors that are constrained by heredity, we can see that canalization is highly adaptive. Through it, nature ensures that children will develop certain species-typical skills under a wide range of rearing conditions, thereby promoting survival.

Recently, scientists have expanded the notion of canalization to include environmental influences. We now know that environments can also limit development (Gottlieb, 1991). For example, when children experience harmful environments early in life, there may be little that later experiences can do to change characteristics (such as intelligence) that were quite flexible to begin with. We have already seen that this is the case for babies who were prenatally exposed to high levels of alcohol, radiation, or anoxia. And later in this book, we will find that it is also true for children who spend many years living in extremely deprived homes and institutions (Turkheimer & Gottesman, 1991).

Using the concept of canalization, we learn that genes restrict the development of some characteristics more than others. And over time, even very flexible behaviors can become fixed and canalized, depending on the environments to which children were exposed.

Canalization
The tendency of heredity to restrict the development of some characteristics to just one or a few outcomes.

■ GENETIC-ENVIRONMENTAL CORRELATION. Nature and nurture work together in still another way. Several investigators point out that a major problem in trying to separate heredity and environment is that they are often correlated (Plomin, 1994b; Scarr &

McCartney, 1983). According to the concept of **genetic–environmental correlation**, our genes influence the environments to which we are exposed. In support of this idea, a recent study showed that the greater the genetic similarity between pairs of adolescents, the more alike they were on many aspects of child rearing, including parental discipline, affection, conflict, and monitoring of the young person's activities (Plomin et al., 1994).

These findings indicate that heredity plays a role in molding children's experiences. The way this happens changes with development.

Passive and Evocative Correlation. At younger ages, two types of genetic–environmental correlation are common. The first is called *passive* correlation because the child has no control over it. Early on, parents provide environments that are influenced by their own heredity. For example, parents who are good athletes are likely to emphasize outdoor activities and enroll their children in swimming and gymnastics lessons. Besides getting exposed to an "athletic environment," the children may have inherited their parents' athletic ability. As a result, they are likely to become good athletes for both genetic and environmental reasons.

The second type of genetic–environmental correlation is *evocative.* Children evoke responses from others that are influenced by the child's heredity, and these responses strengthen the child's original style of responding. For example, an active, friendly baby is likely to receive more social stimulation from those around her than a passive, quiet infant. And a cooperative, attentive preschooler will probably receive more patient and sensitive interactions from parents than an inattentive, distractible child.

Active Correlation. At older ages, *active* genetic–environmental correlation becomes common. As children extend their experiences beyond the immediate family to school, neighborhood, and community and are given the freedom to make more of their own choices, they play an increasingly active role in seeking out environments that fit with their genetic tendencies. The well-coordinated, muscular child spends more time at after-school sports, the musically talented youngster joins the school orchestra and practices his violin, and the intellectually curious child is a familiar patron at her local library.

This tendency to actively choose environments that complement our heredity is called **niche-picking** (Scarr & McCartney, 1983). Infants and young children cannot do much niche-picking, since adults select environments for them. In contrast, older children and adolescents are much more in charge of their own environments. The niche-picking idea explains why pairs of identical twins reared apart during childhood and later reunited often find, to their great surprise, that they have similar hobbies, food preferences, friendship choices, and vocations (Bouchard et al., 1990; Plomin, 1994a). It also helps us understand some curious longitudinal findings indicating that identical twins become somewhat more similar and fraternal twins and adopted siblings less similar in intelligence and personality from infancy to adolescence (Scarr & Weinberg, 1983; Wilson, 1983). The influence of heredity and environment is not constant but changes over time. With age, genetic factors may become more important in influencing the environments we experience and choose for ourselves.

A major reason child development researchers are interested in the nature–nurture issue is that they want to find ways to improve environments in order to help children develop as far as possible. The concepts of range of reaction, canalization, and niche–picking remind us that development is best understood as a series of complex exchanges between nature and nurture. When a characteristic is strongly influenced by heredity, it can still be modified. However, children cannot be changed in any way we might desire. The success of any attempt to improve development depends on the characteristics we want to change, the genetic makeup of the child, and the type and timing of our intervention.

Genetic–environmental correlation
The idea that heredity influences the environments to which individuals are exposed.

Niche-picking
A type of genetic-environmental correlation in which individuals actively choose environments that complement their heredity.

SUMMARY

GENETIC FOUNDATIONS

- Each individual's **phenotype**, or directly observable characteristics, is a product of both **genotype** and environment. **Chromosomes**, rodlike structures within the cell nucleus, contain our hereditary endowment. Along their length are **genes**, segments of **DNA** that make us distinctly human and influence our development and characteristics.
- **Gametes**, or sex cells, are produced through the process of cell division known as **meiosis**. **Crossing over** and independent assortment of chromosomes ensure that each gamete receives a unique set of genes from each parent. Once sperm and ovum unite to form the **zygote**, it starts to develop into a complex human being through cell duplication, or mitosis.
- **Identical**, or **monozygotic, twins** develop when a zygote divides in two during the early stages of cell duplication. **Fraternal**, or **dizygotic, twins** result when two ova are released from the mother's ovaries and each is fertilized. If the fertilizing sperm carries an X chromosome, the child will be a girl; if it contains a Y chromosome, a boy will be born.
- **Dominant–recessive** and **codominant** relationships are patterns of inheritance that apply to traits controlled by a single gene. **Pleiotropism**, the ability of a single gene to affect more than one trait, and **modifier genes**, which alter the expression of other genes, affect many characteristics. When recessive disorders are **X-linked** (carried on the X chromosome), males are more likely to be affected. Unfavorable genes arise from **mutations**, which can occur spontaneously or be induced by hazardous environmental agents. **Genetic imprinting** is a newly discovered pattern of inheritance in which one parent's allele is activated, regardless of its makeup.
- Human traits that vary continuously, such as intelligence and personality, are **polygenic**, or influenced by many genes. Since the genetic principles involved are unknown, scientists must study the influence of heredity on these characteristics indirectly.

CHROMOSOMAL ABNORMALITIES

- The most common chromosomal abnormality is Down syndrome, which results in physical defects and mental retardation. Effective parenting and early intervention can improve the development of these children.
- Disorders of the **sex chromosomes** are generally milder than defects of the **autosomes**. Contrary to popular belief, males with XYY syndrome are not prone to aggression. Studies of children with triple X, Klinefelter, and Turner syndromes reveal that adding to or subtracting from the usual number of X chromosomes leads to specific intellectual problems.

REPRODUCTIVE CHOICES

- **Genetic counseling** helps couples at risk for giving birth to children with hereditary defects decide whether or not to conceive. **Prenatal diagnostic methods** make early detection of abnormalities possible. In some cases, treatment can be initiated before birth. Although donor insemination, in vitro fertilization, and surrogate motherhood permit many barren couples to become parents, these reproductive technologies raise serious legal and ethical concerns.

PRENATAL DEVELOPMENT

- Prenatal development is usually divided into three phases. The period of the zygote lasts about 2 weeks, from fertilization until the blastocyst becomes deeply implanted into the uterine lining. The period of the **embryo** extends from 2 to 8 weeks, during which the foundations for all body structures are laid down. The period of the **fetus**, lasting until the end of pregnancy, involves a dramatic increase in body size and completion of physical structures. **Age of viability** occurs at the beginning of the final trimester, sometime between 22 and 26 weeks.

PRENATAL ENVIRONMENTAL INFLUENCES

- **Teratogens** are environmental agents that cause damage during the prenatal period. Their effects conform to the sensitive period concept. The organism is especially vulnerable during the embryonic period when body structures are rapidly emerging. The impact of teratogens differs from one case to the next, due to amount and length of exposure, the genetic makeup of mother and fetus, and the presence or absence of other harmful agents.
- The effects of teratogens are not limited to immediate physical damage. Serious psychological consequences may appear later in development. Drugs, cigarette smoking, alcohol, hormones, radiation, environmental pollution, and certain infectious diseases are teratogens that can endanger the prenatal organism.
- Other maternal factors can either support or complicate prenatal development. When the mother's diet is inadequate, low birth weight and brain damage are major concerns. Severe emotional stress is associated with many pregnancy complications. Its impact can be reduced by providing mothers with social support.
- Maternal age and number of previous births were once thought to be major causes of prenatal problems. Aside from the risk of chromosomal abnormalities in older women, this is not the case. Instead, poor health and environmental risks associated with poverty are the strongest predictors of pregnancy complications.

CHILDBIRTH

- Childbirth takes place in three stages, beginning with contractions that open the cervix so that the baby can be pushed through the birth canal and ending with delivery of the placenta. During labor, infants produce high levels of stress hormones, which help them withstand oxygen deprivation and arouse them into alertness at birth.
- Newborn babies' large heads and small bodies are odd-looking, but their attractive facial features contribute to adults' desire to pick them up and cuddle them. The

Apgar Scale is used to assess the newborn baby's physical condition at birth.

APPROACHES TO CHILDBIRTH

- Childbirth practices vary widely across cultures. In Western nations, **natural**, or **prepared, childbirth** helps reduce stress and pain during labor and delivery. As long as mothers are healthy and assisted by a well-trained doctor or midwife, it is just as safe to give birth at home as in a hospital.
- Pain-relieving drugs are necessary in complicated births. When given in large doses, they increase the likelihood of an instrument delivery and produce a depressed state in the baby that affects the early infant–parent relationship.

BIRTH COMPLICATIONS

- Anoxia is a serious birth complication that can damage the brain and other organs. As long as anoxia is not extreme, most affected children catch up in development by the school years.
- Preterm and low-birth-weight babies are especially likely to be born to poverty-stricken, ethnic minority mothers. **Small-for-date** infants usually have longer-lasting difficulties than **preterm** babies. Some interventions for low-birth-weight infants provide special stimulation in the intensive-care nursery. Others teach parents how to care for and interact with these fragile babies. When preterm infants live in stressed, low-income households, long-term, intensive intervention is necessary to reduce developmental problems.
- The Kauai study shows that when infants experience birth trauma, a supportive home environment can help restore their growth. Even children with fairly serious birth complications can recover with the help of favorable life events.

HEREDITY, ENVIRONMENT, AND BEHAVIOR: A LOOK AHEAD

- **Behavioral genetics** is a field devoted to discovering the hereditary and environmental origins of complex characteristics, such as intelligence and personality. Some researchers believe it is useful and possible to determine "how much" each factor contributes to individual differences. These investigators compute **heritability estimates** and **concordance rates** from **kinship studies**.
- Other researchers believe the important question is "how" heredity and environment work together. The concepts of **range of reaction**, **canalization**, and **genetic–environmental correlation** remind us that development is best understood as a series of complex transactions between nature and nurture.

IMPORTANT TERMS AND CONCEPTS

phenotype (p. 69)
genotype (p. 69)
chromosomes (p. 70)
deoxyribonucleic acid (DNA) (p. 70)
gene (p. 70)
mitosis (p. 70)
gametes (p. 70)
meiosis (p. 70)
crossing over (p. 71)
zygote (p. 71)
identical, or monozygotic, twins (p. 72)
fraternal, or dizygotic, twins (p. 73)
autosomes (p. 73)
sex chromosomes (p. 73)
allele (p. 74)
homozygous (p. 74)
heterozygous (p. 74)
dominant–recessive inheritance (p. 74)
carrier (p. 74)
pleiotropism (p. 75)
modifier genes (p. 75)
codominance (p. 75)
mutation (p. 77)
X-linked inheritance (p. 78)
genetic imprinting (p. 79)
polygenic inheritance (p. 79)
genetic counseling (p. 81)
prenatal diagnostic methods (p. 82)
amnion (p. 86)
chorion (p. 88)
placenta (p. 88)
umbilical cord (p. 88)
embryo (p. 88)
fetus (p. 90)
vernix (p. 91)
lanugo (p. 91)
age of viability (p. 91)
teratogen (p. 92)
fetal alcohol syndrome (FAS) (p. 95)
fetal alcohol effects (FAE) (p. 95)
Apgar Scale (p. 105)
natural, or prepared, childbirth (p. 106)
breech position (p. 108)
Rh factor (p. 108)
preterm (p. 109)
small for date (p. 109)
infant mortality (p. 112)
behavior genetics (p. 114)
heritability estimate (p. 115)
kinship studies (p. 115)
concordance rate (p. 115)
range of reaction (p. 116)
canalization (p. 117)
genetic–environmental correlation (p. 118)
niche-picking (p. 118)

for Chapter 3

If you are interested in . . .	turn to . . .	to learn about . . .
■ Prenatal risk factors and development 	■ Chapter 4, p. 132–134 ■ Chapter 4, p. 137 ■ Chapter 5, pp. 188–191 ■ Chapter 10, p. 412 ■ Chapter 13, p. 510–511	■ Neonatal behavioral assessment ■ Sudden infant death syndrome ■ Teenage pregnancy and childbearing ■ At-risk newborns and infant–caregiver attachment ■ Congenital adrenal hyperplasia
■ Nutrition, disease, and development 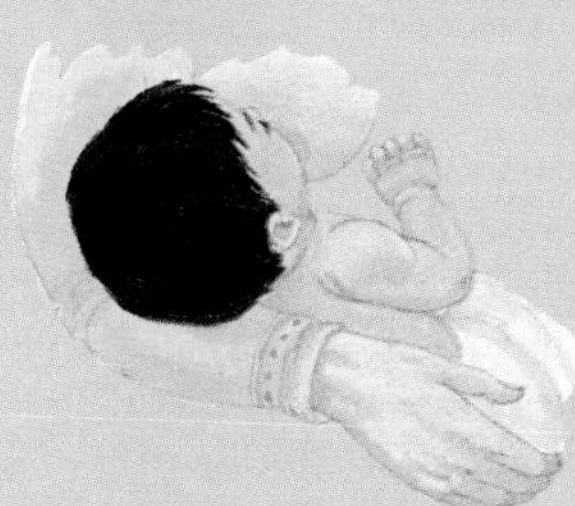	■ Chapter 5, p. 189 ■ Chapter 5, pp. 191–192 ■ Chapter 5, pp. 199 ■ Chapter 5, pp. 199–201 ■ Chapter 5, pp. 203–204 ■ Chapter 5, pp. 204–205	■ Educating children and adolescents about AIDS ■ Anorexia nervosa and bulimia in adolescence ■ Low-level led exposure and mental development ■ Age-related nutritional needs ■ Obesity ■ Malnutrition and infectious disease in childhood
■ Heritability 	■ Chapter 7, p. 270 ■ Chapter 8, pp. 319–321 ■ Chapter 10, p. 400	■ Heritability of attention-deficit hyperactivity disorder ■ Heritability of intelligence ■ Heritability of temperament
■ Genetic–environmental correlation 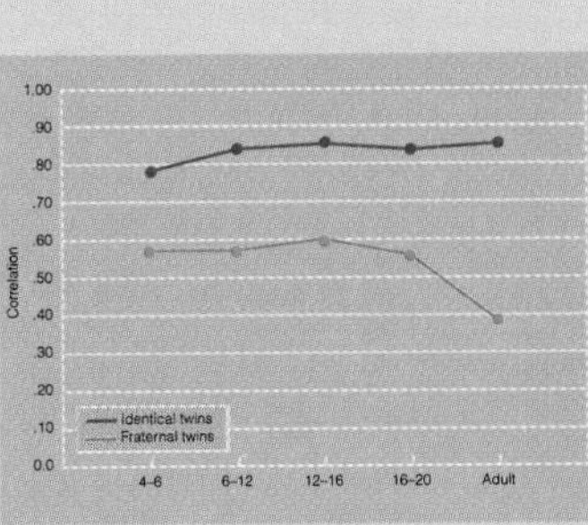 	■ Chapter 8, pp. 319–320 ■ Chapter 10, pp. 401–404 Chapter 14, pp. 545–546	■ Age-related change in IQ correlations of identical and fraternal twins ■ Temperament and child rearing

4 Infancy: Early Learning, Motor Skills, and Perceptual Capacities

THE ORGANIZED NEWBORN
Newborn Reflexes · Newborn States · Neonatal Behavioral Assessment · Learning Capacities

MOTOR DEVELOPMENT IN INFANCY
The Organization and Sequence of Motor Development · Motor Skills as Dynamic Systems · Dynamic Systems in Action: Microgenetic Research · Cultural Variations in Motor Development · Fine Motor Development: The Special Case of Voluntary Reaching

PERCEPTUAL DEVELOPMENT IN INFANCY
Touch · Taste and Smell · Hearing · Vision · Intermodal Perception · Understanding Perceptual Development

EARLY DEPRIVATION AND ENRICHMENT: IS INFANCY A SENSITIVE PERIOD OF DEVELOPMENT?

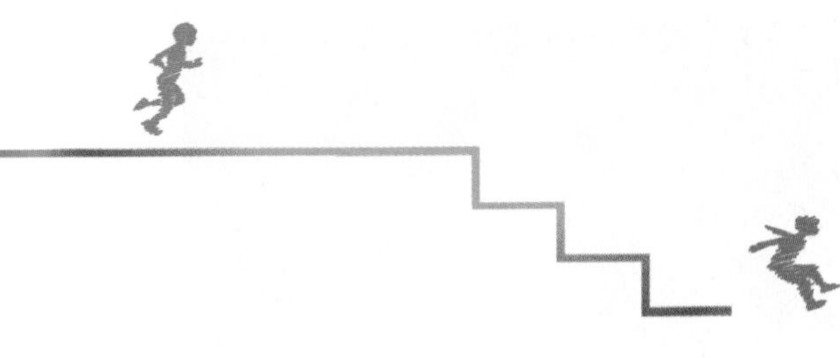

Infancy is the period of development that begins at birth and ends at about 18 months to 2 years of age with early language use. Although it comprises only 2 percent of the life span, it is one of the most remarkable and busiest times of development. The newborn baby, or *neonate,*[1] enters the world with surprisingly sophisticated perceptual and motor abilities, a set of skills for interacting with people, and a capacity to learn that is put to use immediately after birth. By the end of infancy, the small child is a self-assertive, purposeful being who walks on her own, has developed refined manual skills, and is prepared to acquire the most unique of human abilities—language.

Our view of the infant has changed drastically over this century. At one time, the newborn baby was considered a passive incompetent being whose world was, in the words of turn-of-the-century psychologist William James, "a blooming, buzzing confusion." Recently developed methods and equipment permitting researchers to test the young baby's capacities have shown this image to be wrong. Witness the following diary notes by a modern child development researcher about her own baby:

> At 3.5 weeks, you lift your head when I put you on your tummy, showing off your strength with shaky half-push-ups. In your crib, you stare at your mobile, your face serious and still, utterly absorbed. When you are bored, I carry you to a new place, sing to you. At the sound of my voice, your face perks up, and you turn toward me with rapt attention. When you are unhappy, I hold you close to my heart so you can feel its rhythmic sound. Your cry has become a language I can understand. Your tiny fingers grasp whatever comes near—the folds of my clothing, my fingers in your palm—and you hold on tightly. I marvel at your determination to master your world!

These observations clearly reflect the widely accepted view that infants, from the outset, are skilled, capable beings who display many complex human abilities.

Development during infancy proceeds at an astonishing pace. Excited relatives who visit just after the birth and return a few months later often remark that the baby does not seem like the same individual! Although researchers agree that infants are competent beings, fervent debates continue over questions like these: What capacities are present from the very beginning? Which must wait to mature with the passage of time? And which must be learned through constant interaction with the physical and social world?

In this chapter, we explore the infant's remarkable capabilities—early reflexive behaviors, learning mechanisms, motor skills, and perceptual capacities. Throughout our discussion, we will return to these controversial themes. We will also see how a burst of new findings adds to our practical understanding of experiences necessary to support the dramatic changes of the first 2 years.

The Organized Newborn

The newborn baby, as we saw in Chapter 3, is a homely looking creature. The head, misshapen from being squeezed through the narrow birth canal, is overly large compared to the potbellied trunk and bowlegged lower body. In addition, the baby's skin is usually wrinkled and "parboiled" in appearance. At first glance, many parents assume that this odd little being can do nothing but eat and sleep. Yet a few hours spent in the company of a neonate reveals that the tiny being is not a creature at all! Newborns display a

[1] The term *neonate* refers to infants from birth through the first month of life.

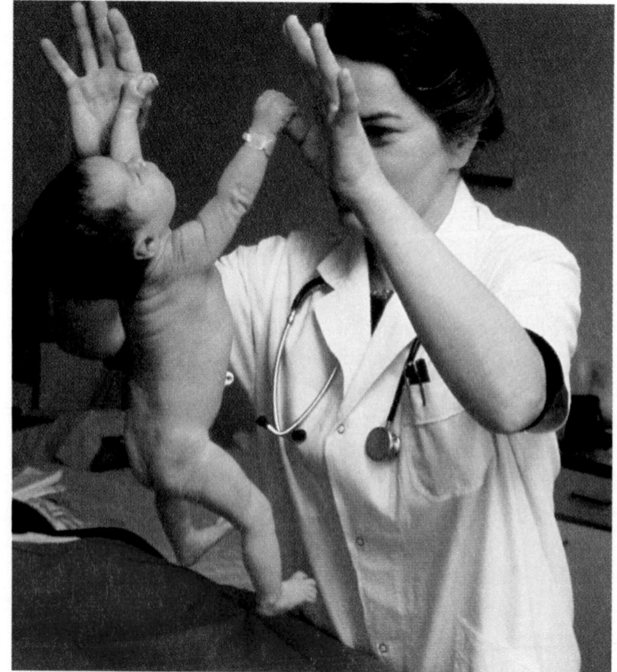

■ *The palmar grasp reflex is so strong during the first week after birth that many infants can use it to support their entire weight. (J. da Cunha/Petit Format/Photo Researchers, Inc.)*

wide variety of typically human capacities that are crucial for survival and that evoke the care and attention they receive from adults. In relating to the physical world and building their first social relationships, babies are active from the very start.

NEWBORN REFLEXES

A **reflex** is an inborn, automatic response to a particular form of stimulation. Reflexes are the neonate's most obvious organized patterns of behavior. Infants come into the world with dozens of them. A father, changing his newborn baby's diaper, accidentally bumps the side of the table. The infant reacts by flinging his arms wide and bringing them back toward his body. A mother softly strokes her infant's cheek, and the baby turns his head in her direction. Holding the infant upright with feet touching a flat surface, she watches the baby make little stepping movements. Table 4.1 lists the major newborn reflexes. See if you can identify the ones described here and in the diary excerpt at the beginning of this chapter. Then let's consider the meaning and purpose of these curious behaviors.

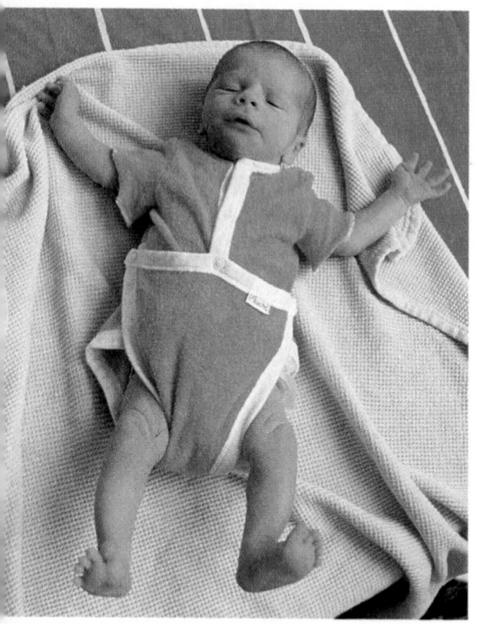

■ *In the Moro reflex, loss of support or a sudden loud sound causes this baby to arch his back, extend his arms outward, and then bring them in toward his body. (Elizabeth Crews)*

Reflex
An inborn, automatic response to a particular form of stimulation.

■ ADAPTIVE VALUE OF REFLEXES. Like breathing and swallowing, some newborn reflexes have survival value. The rooting reflex helps a breast-fed baby find the mother's nipple. Once the nipple is found, imagine what it would be like if we had to teach the infant the complex lip and tongue movements involved in sucking. If sucking were not automatic, our species would be unlikely to survive for a single generation! The swimming reflex helps a baby who is accidentally dropped into a body of water stay afloat, increasing the chances of retrieval by the caregiver.

Other reflexes protect infants from unwanted stimulation. For example, the eye blink reflex helps shield the baby from intense bright light, and the withdrawal reflex is a reaction to unpleasant tactile stimulation. At times, reflexive behavior can reduce infant distress. As any new mother who remembers to bring a pacifier on an outing with her young baby knows, sucking will reduce the mass, uncoordinated activity of a fussy neonate almost immediately.

A few reflexes probably helped babies survive during our evolutionary past but no longer serve any special purpose. For example, the Moro or "embracing" reflex is believed to have helped infants cling to their mothers during a time when babies were carried about all day. If the infant happened to lose support, the reflex caused the infant to embrace and, along with the powerful grasp reflex (so strong during the first week that it can support the baby's entire weight), regain its hold on the mother's body (Kessen, 1967; Prechtl, 1958).

TABLE 4.1

Some Newborn Reflexes

Reflex	Stimulation	Response	Age of Disappearance	Function
Rooting	Stroke cheek near corner of mouth.	Head turns toward source of stimulation.	3 weeks (becomes voluntary head turning at this time)	Helps infant find the nipple.
Sucking	Place finger in infant's mouth.	Infant sucks finger rhythmically.	Permanent	Permits feeding.
Swimming	Place infant face down in pool of water.	Baby paddles and kicks in swimming motion.	4–6 months	Helps infant survive if dropped into body of water.
Eye blink	Shine bright light at eyes or clap hand near head.	Infant quickly closes eyelids.	Permanent	Protects infant from strong stimulation.
Withdrawal	Prick sole of foot with pin.	Foot withdraws, with flexion of knee and hip.	Weakens after 10 days	Protects infant from unpleasant tactile stimulation.
Babinski	Stroke sole of foot from toe toward heel.	Toes fan out and curl as foot twists in.	8–12 months	Unknown.
Moro	Hold infant horizontally on back and let head drop slightly, or produce a sudden loud sound against surface supporting infant.	Infant makes an "embracing" motion by arching back, extending legs, throwing arms outward, and then bringing them in toward body.	6 months	In human evolutionary past, may have helped infant cling to mother.
Palmar grasp	Place finger in infant's hand and press against palm.	Spontaneous grasp of adult's finger.	3–4 months	Prepares infant for voluntary grasping.
Tonic neck	While baby lies on back, turn head to one side.	Infant assumes a "fencing position"; one arm is extended in front of eyes on side to which head is turned, other arm is flexed.	4 months	May prepare infant for voluntary reaching.
Body righting	Rotate shoulder or hips.	Rest of body turns in same direction.	12 months	Supports postural control.
Stepping	Hold infant under arms and permit bare feet to touch a flat surface.	Infant lifts one foot after another in stepping response.	2 months	Prepares infant for voluntary walking.

Source: Knobloch & Pasamanick, 1974; Prechtl & Beintema, 1965.

Finally, several reflexes help parents and babies establish gratifying interaction as soon as possible. An infant who searches for and successfully finds the nipple, sucks easily during feedings, and grasps when her hand is touched encourages parents to respond lovingly and increases their sense of competence as caregivers.

■ REFLEXES AND THE DEVELOPMENT OF MOTOR SKILLS. Most newborn reflexes disappear during the first 6 months, due to a gradual increase in voluntary control over behavior as the brain matures (Touwen, 1984). Currently, researchers disagree about the role reflexes play in the development of voluntary action. Do infant reflexes simply wane before voluntary behavior appears? Or are reflexes an integral and essential prelude to organizing the voluntary skills that come after them?

The fact that babies adapt their reflex actions to changes in stimulation immediately after birth suggests that many reflexes form the basis for complex purposeful behaviors. For example, different finger movements appear in the palmar grasp reflex, depending on how the palm of the hand is stimulated (Touwen, 1978).

A few reflexes appear to be related to voluntary behavior in subtle ways. For example, the tonic neck reflex may prepare the infant for voluntary reaching. When babies lie on their backs in this "fencing position," they naturally gaze at the hand in front of their eyes. The reflex may encourage them to combine vision with arm movements and, eventually, reach for objects (Knobloch & Pasamanick, 1974).

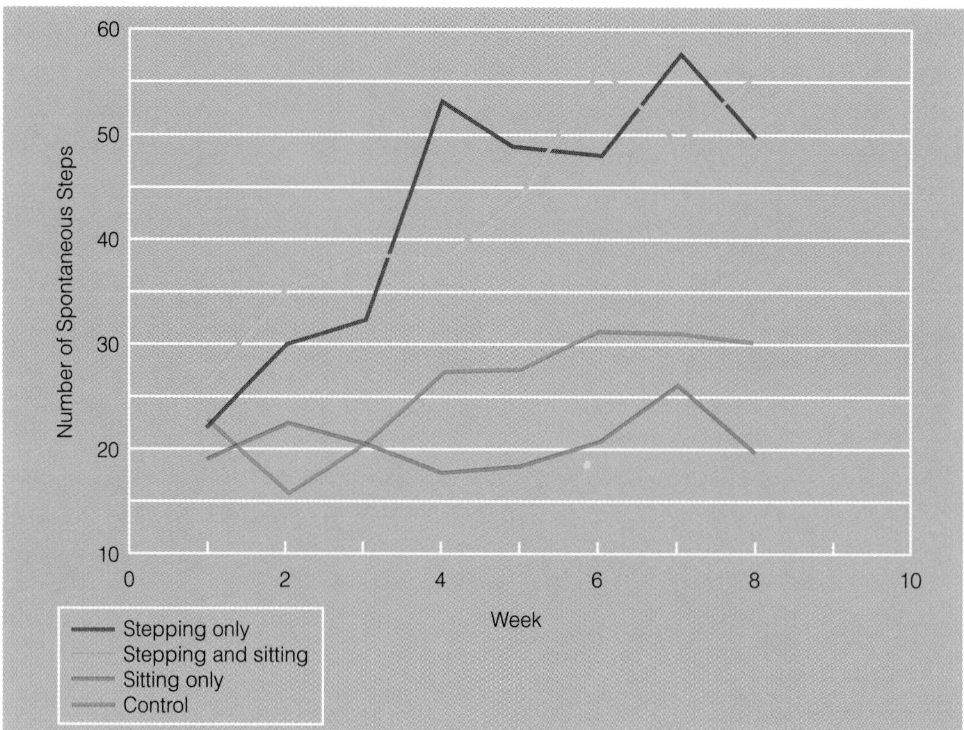

FIGURE 4.1

■ *Mean number of spontaneous stepping movements for infants given four types of motor practice during the first 2 months. Babies given daily stimulation of the stepping reflex showed a steady increase in spontaneous stepping movements over time, whereas groups receiving only sitting exercises or no motor practice displayed few spontaneous steps. How does stimulation of the stepping reflex promote the development of walking? Researchers disagree on answers to this question. (From Zelazo et al., 1993.)*

Certain reflexes drop out in early infancy, but the motor functions involved seem to be renewed later in development. Examples are the palmar grasp, swimming, and stepping responses. In a recent study, some babies were given daily stimulation of the stepping reflex during the first 2 months, whereas others received either sitting exercises or no motor practice. As Figure 4.1 reveals, infants in the stepping groups displayed more spontaneous stepping movements than did those in the nonstepping groups (Zelazo et al., 1993). In addition, infants with early stepping practice walk on their own several weeks earlier than do infants not given such practice (Zelazo, Zelazo, & Kolb, 1972).

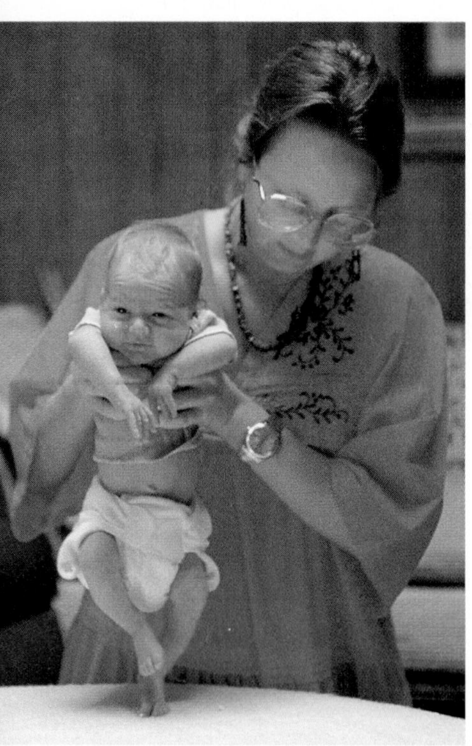

■ *When held upright under the arms, newborn babies show reflexive stepping movements. (Innervisions)*

Exactly how does early reflexive stimulation contribute to motor control? There are different answers to this question. Philip Zelazo (1983) believes that exercising the stepping reflex promotes development of areas of the cortex that govern voluntary walking. But research by Esther Thelen (1983) provides another explanation. She showed that babies who gained the most weight during the first month of life had the weakest stepping reflex. Also, when the lower part of the infant's body was dipped in water (which lightens the load on the baby's muscles), the reflex reappeared (Thelen, Fisher, & Ridley-Johnson, 1984). According to Thelen, the stepping reflex drops out because early infant weight gain is not matched by an increase in muscle strength, which permits babies to lift their increasingly heavy legs. But the infant permitted to exercise the stepping reflex builds leg strength early, in the same way that exercise causes an athlete to gain muscle power. Stronger leg muscles, in turn, enable infants to retain the reflex and to stand and walk at an earlier age. Regardless of which position is correct, the work of both Zelazo and Thelen reveals that even though reflexive stepping subsides in many infants, the mechanism responsible for it is used by the brain at a later age.

Do these findings suggest that parents should deliberately exercise newborn stepping and other responses? There is no special reason to do so, since reflexive practice does not produce a child who is a better walker! In the case of the swimming reflex, it is risky to try to build on it. Although young babies placed in a swimming pool will paddle and kick, they open their mouths and swallow large amounts of water. Consuming too much water lowers the concentration of salt in the baby's blood, which can cause swelling of the brain and seizures. Despite the presence of this remarkable reflex, swimming lessons are best postponed until at least 3 years of age (Micheli, 1985).

■ THE IMPORTANCE OF ASSESSING NEWBORN REFLEXES. Pediatricians test infant reflexes carefully, especially if a newborn has experienced birth trauma, since reflexes provide one way of assessing the health of the baby's nervous system. In brain-damaged infants, reflexes may be weak or absent, or in some cases exaggerated and

TABLE 4.2

Infant States of Arousal

State	Description	Daily Duration In Newborns
Regular sleep	The infant is at full rest and shows little or no body activity. The eyelids are closed, no eye movements occur, the face is relaxed, and breathing is slow and regular.	8–9 hours
Irregular sleep	Gentle limb movements, occasional stirring, and facial grimacing occur. Although the eyelids are closed, occasional rapid eye movements can be seen beneath them. Breathing is irregular.	8–9 hours
Drowsiness	The infant is either falling asleep or waking up. Body is less active than in irregular sleep but more active than in regular sleep. Eyes open and close; when open, they have a glazed look. Breathing is even but somewhat faster than in regular sleep.	Varies
Quiet alertness	Infant's body is relatively inactive. The eyes are open and attentive. Breathing is even.	2–3 hours
Waking activity	The infant shows frequent bursts of uncoordinated motor activity. Breathing is very irregular. The face may be relaxed or tense and wrinkled.	2–3 hours
Crying	Waking activity sometimes evolves into crying, which is accompanied by diffuse, vigorous motor activity.	1–2 hours

Source: Wolff, 1966.

overly rigid. Brain damage may also be indicated when reflexes persist past the point in development when they should normally disappear. However, individual differences in reflexive responses exist that are not cause for concern. Assessment of newborn reflexes must be combined with other observations of the baby to accurately distinguish normal from abnormal central nervous system functioning (Touwen, 1984).

NEWBORN STATES

Throughout the day and night, newborn infants move in and out of six different **states of arousal**, or degrees of sleep and wakefulness, which are described in Table 4.2. During the first month, these states alternate frequently. Quiet alertness is the most fleeting. It usually moves toward fussing and crying relatively quickly. Much to the relief of their fatigued parents, newborns spend the greatest amount of time asleep, taking round-the-clock naps that, on the average, add up to about 16 to 18 hours a day.

Between birth and 2 years, the organization of sleep and wakefulness changes substantially. The decline in total sleep time is not great; the average 2-year-old still needs 12 to 13 hours. Instead, short periods of sleep and wakefulness are gradually put together. Although from birth babies tend to sleep more at night than during the day, this pattern increases steadily with age (Whitney & Thoman, 1994). By 4 months, the typical American baby's nightly sleep period resembles that of the parents, in that it is 8 hours long. And over time, infants remain awake for longer daytime periods and need fewer naps—by the second year, only one or two (Berg & Berg, 1987).

These changes in arousal patterns are largely due to brain maturation, but they are affected by the social environment as well. In the United States, night waking is regarded as inconvenient. Parents try hard to get their infants to sleep through the night by offering an evening feeding and putting them down in a separate, quiet room. In doing so, they probably push babies to the limits of their neurological capacities. As the Cultural Influences box on page 128 shows, the practice of isolating infants to promote sleep is rare elsewhere in the world. In non-Western societies, babies typically remain in constant contact with their mothers throughout the day and night, sleeping and waking to nurse at will. For these infants, the average nightly sleep period remains constant, at about 3 hours, from 1 to 8 months of age. Only at the end of the first year do they move in the direction of an adultlike sleep–waking schedule (McKenna et al., 1994; Super & Harkness, 1982).

Although arousal states become more patterned and regular for all infants, striking individual differences in daily rhythms exist that affect parents' attitudes toward and interactions with the baby (Thoman & Whitney, 1990). A few infants sleep for long periods at an early age, increasing the rest their parents get and the energy they have for

States of arousal
Different degrees of sleep and wakefulness.

CULTURAL INFLUENCES

Cultural Variations in Infant Sleeping Arrangements

While awaiting the birth of a new baby, American middle-class parents typically furnish a special room as the infant's sleeping quarters. Initially, young babies may be placed in a bassinet or cradle in the parents' bedroom for reasons of convenience, but most are moved by 3 to 6 months of age. Many adults in the United States regard this nighttime separation of baby from parent as perfectly natural. Throughout this century, child-rearing advice from experts has strongly encouraged it. For example, Benjamin Spock, in each edition of *Baby and Child Care* from 1945 to the present, states with authority, "I think it is a sensible rule not to take a child into the parents' bed for any reason" (Spock & Rothenberg, 1992, p. 213).

Yet parent–infant "cosleeping" is common around the globe, even in industrialized societies, as a recent comparison of five culturally diverse groups of 6- to 48-month-olds revealed (see Figure 14.2). Japanese children usually lie next to their mothers throughout infancy and early childhood and continue to sleep with a parent or other family member until adolescence (Takahashi, 1990). Cosleeping is also frequent in some American subcultures. African-American children are more likely than Caucasian-American children to fall asleep with parents and to remain with them for part or all of the night (Lozoff et al., 1995). Appalachian children of eastern Kentucky typically sleep with their parents for the first 2 years of life (Abbott, 1992). Among the Maya of rural Guatemala, mother–infant cosleeping is interrupted only by the birth of a new baby, at which time the older child is moved beside the father or to another bed in the same room (Morelli et al., 1992).

Available household space plays a minor role in infant sleeping arrangements. Dominant child-rearing beliefs are much more important. In one study, researchers interviewed middle-class American and Guatemalan Mayan mothers about their sleeping practices. American mothers frequently mentioned the importance of early independence training, preventing bad habits, and ensuring their own privacy. In contrast, Mayan mothers explained that cosleeping helps build a close parent–child bond, which is necessary for children to learn the ways of people around them. When told that American infants sleep by themselves, Mayan mothers reacted with shock and disbelief, stating that it would be painful for them to leave their babies alone at night (Morelli et al., 1992).

Infant sleeping practices affect other aspects of family life. Sleep problems are not an issue for Mayan parents. Babies doze off in the midst of ongoing social activities, are carried to bed, and nurse on demand without waking the mother. In the United States, getting young children ready for bed often requires an elaborate ritual that consumes a good part of the evening. Many American infants and preschoolers insist on taking security objects to bed with them—a blanket or teddy bear that recaptures the soft, tactile comfort of physical closeness to the mother. In societies in which caregivers are continuously available to babies, children seldom develop these object attachments (Wolf & Lozoff, 1989). Perhaps bedtime struggles, so common in American middle-class homes but rare elsewhere in the world, are related to the stress young children feel when they are required to fall asleep without assistance (Kawasaki et al., 1994).

Infant sleeping arrangements, like other parenting practices, are meant to foster culturally valued characteristics in the young. American middle-class parents view babies as dependent beings who must be urged toward independence, and so they usually insist that they sleep alone. In contrast, Japanese, Mayan, and Appalachian parents regard young infants as separate beings who need to establish an interdependent relationship with the community to survive.

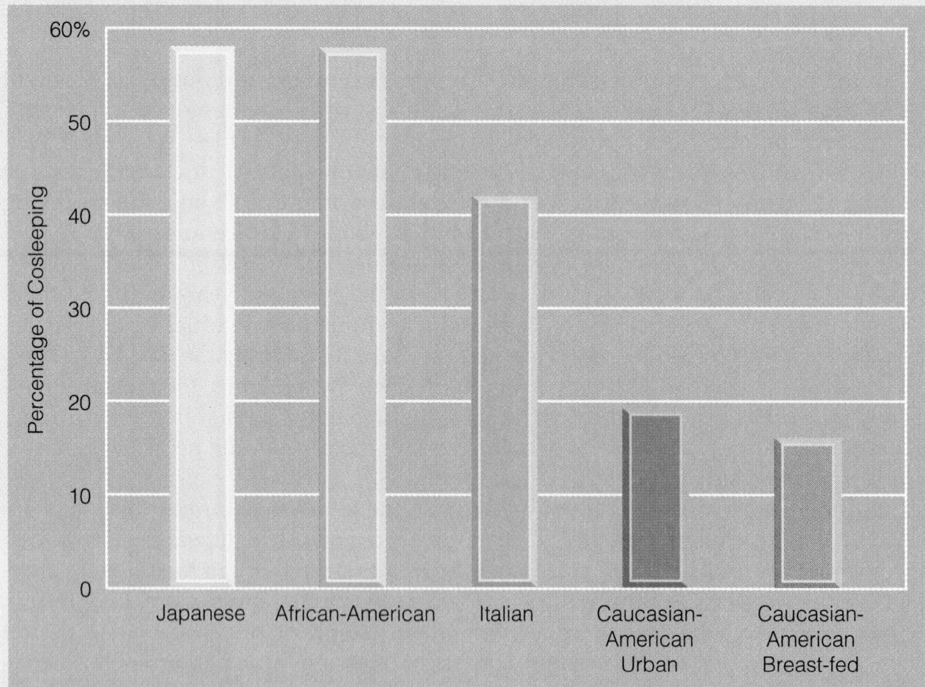

FIGURE 4.2

■ *Percentage of cosleeping in five groups of 6- to 48-month-old children. Cosleeping was much higher in Japanese, African-American, and Italian families than in Caucasian-American urban families. Even among Caucasian-American mothers who breast-fed their babies for 6 months or more, cosleeping was rare. Sleep practices seem to reflect the varying emphases of these cultures on independence versus interpersonal relatedness. (Lozoff et al., 1995.)*

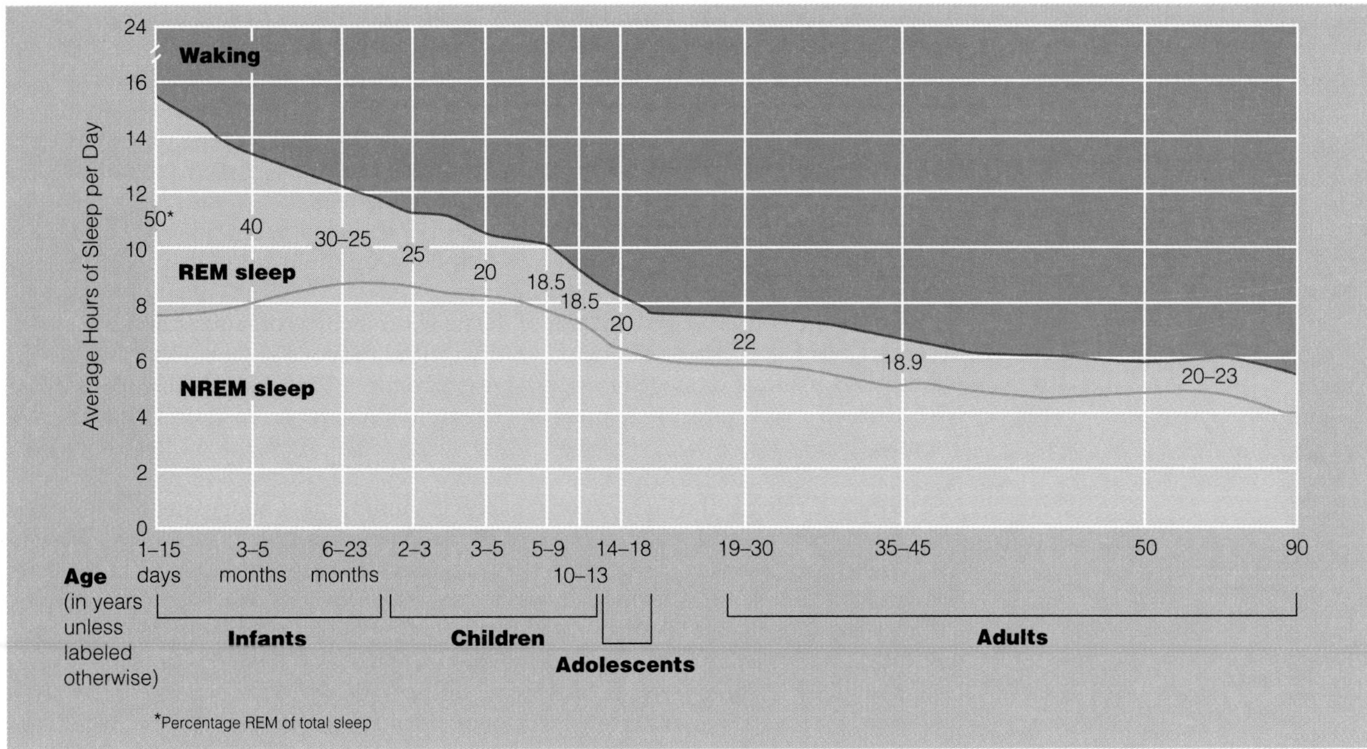

FIGURE 4.3

■ *Changes in REM sleep, NREM sleep, and the waking state from birth through adulthood. REM sleep declines steadily over the first few years of life. Between 3 and 5 years, it consumes about the same percentage of sleep time as it does in adulthood. In contrast, NREM sleep changes very little over infancy and childhood. It gradually declines in adolescence and adulthood as total sleep time drops off. (Adapted from H. P. Roffwarg, J. N. Muzio, & W. C. Dement, 1966, "Ontogenetic Development of the Human Sleep–Dream Cycle,"* Science, *152, p. 608. Copyright © 1966 by the AAAS. Revised from original publication by the authors in 1969 on the basis of additional data. Reprinted by permission.)*

sensitive, responsive care. Babies who cry a great deal require that parents try harder to soothe them. If these efforts are not successful, parents' positive feelings for the infant and sense of competence may suffer. Babies who spend more time in the alert state are likely to receive more social stimulation. And since this state provides opportunities to explore the environment, infants who favor it may have a slight advantage in cognitive development (Moss et al., 1988).

Of the states listed in Table 4.2, the two extremes—sleep and crying—have been of greatest interest to researchers. Each tells us something about normal and abnormal early development.

■ SLEEP. A mother and father I know watched one day while their newborn baby slept and wondered why his eyelids and body twitched and his rate of breathing varied, speeding up at some points and slowing down at others. "Is this how babies are supposed to sleep?" they asked, somewhat worried. "Indeed it is," I responded.

Sleep is made up of at least two states. Irregular, or **rapid-eye-movement (REM) sleep**, is the one these new parents happened to observe. The expression "sleeping like a baby" was probably not meant to describe this state! During REM sleep, the brain and parts of the body are highly active. Electrical brain wave activity, measured with an EEG, is remarkably similar to that of the waking state. The eyes dart beneath the lids; heart rate, blood pressure, and breathing are uneven; and slight body movements occur. In contrast, during regular, or **non-rapid-eye-movement (NREM) sleep**, the body is quiet, and heart rate, breathing, and brain-wave activity are slow and regular (Dittrichova et al., 1982).

Like children and adults, newborns alternate between REM and NREM sleep. However, as Figure 4.3 shows, they spend far more time in the REM state than they ever will again throughout their lives. REM sleep accounts for 50 percent of the newborn baby's sleep time. It declines steadily to 20 percent between 3 and 5 years of age, which is about the same percentage it consumes in adulthood.

Rapid-eye-movement (REM) sleep
An "irregular" sleep state in which brain wave activity is similar to that of the waking state; eyes dart beneath the lids; heart rate, blood pressure, and breathing are uneven; and slight body movements occur.

Non-rapid-eye-movement (NREM) sleep
A "regular" sleep state in which the body is quiet and heart rate, breathing, and brain wave activity are slow and regular.

Why do young infants spend so much time in REM sleep? **Autostimulation theory** provides the most widely accepted explanation (Roffwarg, Muzio, & Dement, 1966). In older children and adults, the REM state is associated with dreaming. Babies probably do not dream, at least not in the same way we do. Young infants are believed to have a special need for the stimulation of REM sleep because they spend little time in an alert state, when they can get input from the environment. REM sleep seems to be a way in which the brain stimulates itself. Sleep researchers believe this stimulation is vital for growth of the central nervous system. In support of this idea, when newborn babies are encouraged to spend more time awake, their REM sleep declines but their NREM sleep remains unchanged (Boismier, 1977).

Because the normal sleep behavior of the newborn baby is organized and patterned, observations of sleep states can help identify central nervous system abnormalities. In infants who are brain damaged or who have experienced birth trauma, disturbed REM-NREM sleep cycles are often present (Theorell, Prechtl, & Vos, 1974; Whitney & Thoman, 1993).

■ CRYING. Crying is the first way that babies communicate, letting parents know they need food, comfort, and stimulation. During the weeks after birth, all infants seem to have some fussy periods during which they are difficult to console. But most of the time, the nature of the cry helps guide parents toward its cause. The baby's cry is a complex auditory stimulus that varies in intensity, from a whimper to a message of all-out distress (Gustafson & Harris, 1990). As early as the first few weeks of life, individual infants can be identified by the unique vocal "signature" of their cries. The ability to recognize their own baby's cry helps parents locate their infant from a distance and is especially advantageous once babies move on their own (Gustafson, Green, & Cleland, 1994).

Events that cause young infants to cry usually have to do with physical needs. Hunger is the most common cause, but babies may also cry in response to temperature change when undressed, a sudden loud noise, or a painful stimulus. An infant's state often makes a difference in whether the baby will cry in response to a sight or sound. Infants who, when quietly alert, regard a colorful object or the sound of a toy horn with interest and pleasure may react to the same events with a burst of tears when in a state of mild discomfort and diffuse activity (Tennes et al., 1972).

■ ADULT RESPONSIVENESS TO INFANT CRIES. The next time you hear an infant cry, take a moment to observe your own mental and physical reaction. A crying baby stimulates strong feelings of arousal and discomfort in just about anyone—men and women and parents and nonparents alike (Boukydis & Burgess, 1982; Murray, 1985). The powerful effect of the cry is probably innately programmed in all human beings to make sure that babies receive the care and protection they need to survive.

Although parents are not always correct in interpreting the meaning of the baby's cry, experience quickly improves their accuracy (Green, Jones, & Gustafson, 1987). The intensity of the cry along with events that led up to it help parents tell what is wrong. If the baby has not eaten for several hours, she is likely to be hungry. If a period of wakefulness and stimulation preceded the cry, the infant may be tired. A wet diaper, indigestion, or just a desire to be held and cuddled may be the cause. A sharp, piercing cry usually means the baby is in pain. When caregivers hear this sound, they rush to the infant, anxious and worried. Very intense cries are rated as more unpleasant and produce greater physiological arousal in adults, as measured by heart rate and skin conductance (Crowe & Zeskind, 1992). These are adaptive reactions that help ensure an infant in danger will quickly get help.

■ SOOTHING A CRYING INFANT. Even when parents are fairly certain about the cause of the cry, the baby may not always calm down. Fortunately, as Table 4.3 indicates, there are many ways to soothe a crying newborn when feeding and diaper changing do not work. The technique that Western parents usually try first is lifting the baby to the shoulder. It is also the one that works the best. Being held upright against the parent's gently moving body not only encourages infants to stop crying, but also causes them to become quietly alert and attentive to the environment (Reisman, 1987).

Other common soothing methods are offering the baby a pacifier, talking gently or singing, and swaddling (wrapping the baby's body snugly in a blanket). Among the Quechua, who live in the cold, high-altitude desert regions of Peru, young babies are

Autostimulation theory
The theory that REM sleep provides stimulation necessary for central nervous system development in young infants.

TABLE 4.3

Ways of Soothing a Crying Newborn

Method	Explanation
Lift the baby to the shoulder and rock or walk.	This provides a combination of physical contact, upright posture, and motion. It is the most effective soothing technique.
Swaddle the baby.	Restricting movement while increasing warmth often soothes a young infant.
Offer a pacifier.	Sucking helps babies control their own level of arousal.
Talk softly or play rhythmic sounds.	Continuous, monotonous, rhythmic sounds, such as a clock ticking, a fan whirring, or peaceful music, are more effective than intermittent sounds.
Take the baby for a short car ride or walk in a baby carriage; swing the baby in a cradle.	Gentle, rhythmic motion of any kind helps lull the baby to sleep.
Massage the baby's body.	Stroke the baby's torso and limbs with continuous, gentle motions. This technique is used in some non-Western cultures to relax the baby's muscles.
Combine several of the methods listed above.	Stimulating several of the baby's senses at once is often more effective than stimulating only one.
If these methods do not work, permit the baby to cry for a short period of time.	Occasionally, a baby responds well to just being put down and will, after a few minutes, fall asleep.

Sources: Campos, 1989; Heinl, 1983; Lester, 1985; Reisman, 1987.

dressed in several layers of clothing and blankets. Then a cloth belt is tightly wound around the body, over which are placed additional blankets that cover the head and face and serve as a carrying cloth. The result—a nearly sealed, warm pouch placed on the mother's back that moves rhythmically as she walks—reduces crying and promotes sleep, thereby conserving energy for early growth in the harsh Peruvian highlands (Tronick, Thomas & Daltabuit, 1994).

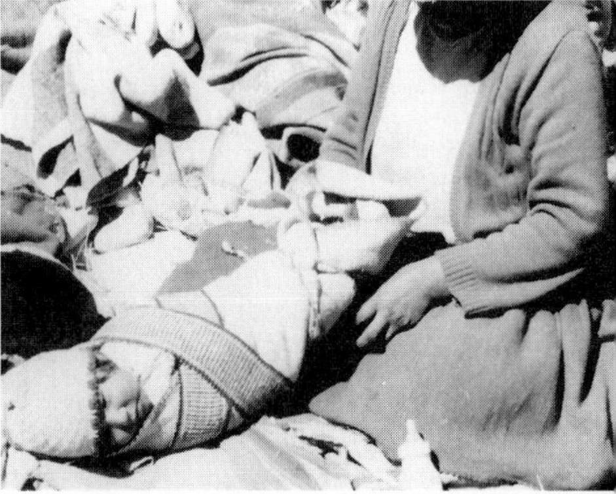

■ *This Quecha mother dresses her infant in several layers of clothing and blankets and winds a cloth belt tightly around the body, over which will be placed additional blankets. The resulting sealed, warm pouch placed on the mother's back reduces crying and promotes sleep, conserving energy for early growth in the harsh Peruvian highlands. (Dr. Edward Tronick)*

How quickly and how often should parents respond to their infant's cries? Will reacting promptly and consistently strengthen crying behavior and produce a miniature tyrant? Or will it give infants a sense of confidence that their needs will be met and, over time, reduce fussing and complaining? Available answers to this question are controversial and conflicting. In a well-known study, Sylvia Bell and Mary Ainsworth (1972) found that mothers who delayed or failed to respond to their young baby's cries had infants who cried more at the end of the first year. In addition, these babies developed fewer alternative ways of expressing their desires, such as gestures and vocalizations. The researchers used *ethological theory* to interpret their findings. According to this view, parental responsiveness is adaptive in that it ensures the infant's basic needs will be met and provides protection from danger. At the same time, it brings the baby into close contact with the caregiver, who can respond sensitively to a wide range of infant behaviors and, in the process, encourage the infant to communicate through means other than crying.

Other investigators, however, have challenged Bell and Ainsworth's conclusions. Jacob Gewirtz and Elizabeth Boyd (1977a, 1977b) criticized their methods and, instead, adopted a *behaviorist position.* From this perspective, consistently responding to a crying infant reinforces the crying response and results in a whiny, demanding child. A study carried out in Israel provides support for this position. Infants of Bedouin (nomadic) tribespeople, who believe that babies should never be left to fuss and cry, were compared to home-reared babies as well as infants raised together in children's houses on Israeli kibbutzim.[2] Bedouin babies (whose mothers rush to them at the first whimper) fussed

2. A *kibbutz* (plural: *kibbutzim*) is an Israeli cooperative agricultural settlement in which children are reared communally, freeing both parents for full participation in the economic life of the society.

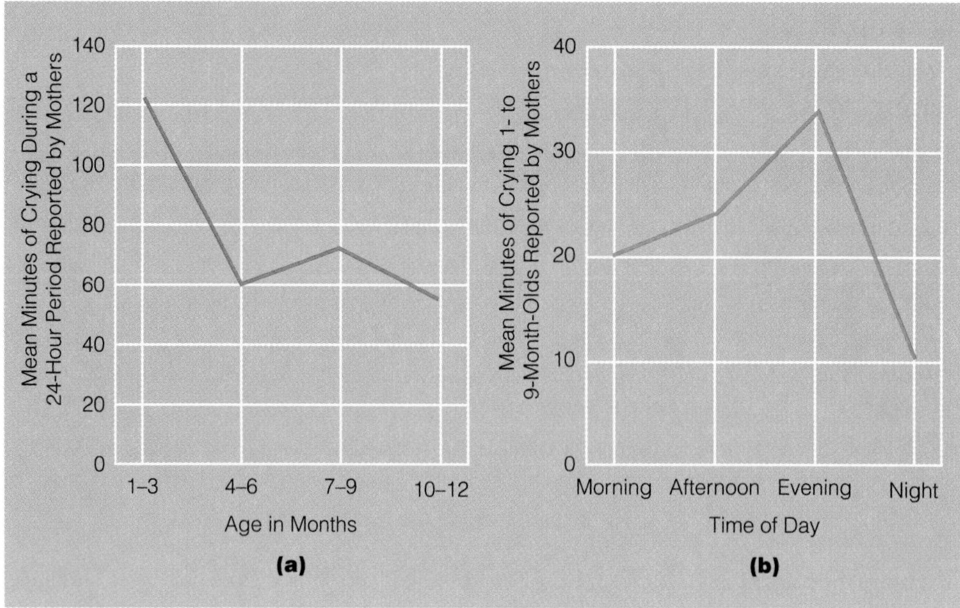

FIGURE 4.4

■ *Crying patterns during the first year of life. A sample of 400 mothers answered questions about how much time their infants spent crying. (a) Crying was greatest during the first 3 months but declined with age. The largest drop occurred after 3 months. (b) During the first 9 months, crying peaked in the evening. (Adapted from St James-Roberts & Halil, 1991.)*

and cried the most during the first year, followed by infants living in homes, where there is greater opportunity to respond promptly to a crying baby than on a kibbutz, where infants are cared for in groups (Landau, 1982).

These contrasting theories and findings reveal that there is no easy formula for how parents should respond to their infant's cries. The conditions that prompt infant crying are complex, and parents must make reasoned choices about what to do on the basis of culturally accepted practices, the suspected reason for the cry, its intensity, and the context in which it occurs—for example, in the privacy of the parents' own home or while having dinner at a restaurant. As Figure 4.4 shows, infant crying is greatest during the first 3 months of life, and through most of the first year it peaks in the evenings. Researchers believe that normal difficulties in readjusting the sleep–waking cycle as the central nervous system matures, not parental attention, are responsible for these trends, since they appear in many cultures (Barr et al., 1991; St James-Roberts, 1989). Fortunately, crying declines for most babies, and over time it occurs more often for psychological (demands for attention, expressions of frustration) than physical reasons. Both ethological and behaviorist investigators would probably agree that one way parents can lessen older babies' need to cry is to encourage more mature ways of expressing desires.

Like reflexes and sleep patterns, the infant's cry offers a clue to central nervous system distress. The cries of brain-damaged babies and those who have experienced prenatal and birth complications are often shrill and piercing (Huntington, Hans, & Zeskind, 1990; Lester, 1987). Most parents respond to a sick baby's call for help with extra care and attention. In some cases, however, the cry is so unpleasant and the infant so difficult to soothe that parents become frustrated, resentful, and angry. Research reveals that preterm and sick babies are more likely than healthy infants to be abused by their parents. Often these parents mention a high-pitched, grating cry as one factor that caused them to lose control and harm the baby (Boukydis, 1985; Frodi, 1985).

NEONATAL BEHAVIORAL ASSESSMENT

A variety of instruments permit doctors, nurses, and child development specialists to assess the overall behavioral status of the infant during the newborn period. The most widely used of these tests is T. Berry Brazelton's (1984) **Neonatal Behavioral Assessment Scale (NBAS)**. With it, the examiner can look at the baby's reflexes, state changes, responsiveness to physical and social stimuli, and other reactions. Table 4.4 lists some examples of NBAS items.

Neonatal Behavioral Assessment Scale (NBAS)
A test developed to assess the behavioral status of the infant during the newborn period.

Neonatal assessment is useful for several reasons. When scores are combined with information from a physical examination, they permit all but a very few cases of severe central nervous system impairment to be diagnosed in the first few weeks of life (Amiel-Tison, 1985). The NBAS and other similar instruments have also helped investigators

TABLE 4.4

Sample Items from Brazelton's Neonatal Behavioral Assessment Scale

Sample Item	Description
Reflexes	See Table 4.1 for examples.
Sensory and Motor Capacities	
Hearing	The examiner speaks softly into one of the infant's ears. The baby's ability to turn toward the sound is recorded.
Vision	A brightly colored ball is moved horizontally and then vertically before the baby's eyes. The baby's ability to track the ball is recorded.
Alertness	The overall alertness of the baby is rated.
Defensive movements	A small cloth is held lightly over the infant's eyes. The baby's effort to work free of the cloth is recorded.
State Changes	
Irritability	The number of times the infant fusses and the stimuli that lead to irritability are recorded.
Cuddliness	The infant's willingness to relax and mold to the examiner's body when held in an alert state is recorded.
Consolability	The effort the examiner must exert to bring the baby from an upset to a quiet state is recorded.
Autonomic Reactivity	
Tremulousness	Tremors of the infant's body are rated. If severe, tremulousness is an indication of central nervous system irritation.
Lability of skin color	Changes in skin color during the examination are noted. A normal newborn shows mild color changes after being undressed, disturbed, or upset, but the original color returns quickly. Difficult to score in nonwhite babies.

Source: Brazelton, 1984.

describe the effects of pregnancy and birth complications on infant behavior (Brazelton, Nugent, & Lester, 1987).

The NBAS has been given to many infants around the world. As a result, researchers have learned a great deal about individual and cultural differences in newborn behavior and how a baby's reactions can be maintained or changed by child-rearing practices. For example, NBAS scores of Asian and Native-American babies reveal that they are less irritable than Caucasian infants. Mothers in these cultures often encourage their babies' calm dispositions through swaddling, close physical contact, and nursing at the first signs of discomfort (Chisholm, 1989; Freedman & Freedman, 1969; Murett-Wagstaff & Moore, 1989). In contrast, the poor NBAS scores of undernourished infants born in Zambia, Africa, are quickly changed by the way their mothers care for them. The Zambian mother carries her baby about on her hip all day, providing a rich variety of sensory stimulation. By 1 week of age, a once unresponsive newborn has been transformed into an alert, contented baby (Brazelton, Koslowski, & Tronick, 1976).

Can you tell from these examples why a single NBAS score is not a good predictor of later development? Since newborn behavior and parenting styles combine to shape development, changes in NBAS scores over the first week or two of life (rather than a single score) provide the best estimate of the baby's ability to recover from the stress of birth. NBAS "recovery curves" predict intelligence with moderate success well into the preschool years (Brazelton, Nugent, & Lester, 1987).

The NBAS has also been used to help parents get to know their infants. In some hospitals, the examination is given in the presence of parents to teach them about their newborn baby's capacities and unique characteristics. These programs enhance early parent–infant interaction in many types of participants—mothers and fathers, adolescents and adults, low-income and middle-income parents, and full-term and preterm

■ *Similar to women in the Zambian culture, this Inuit mother of Northern Canada carries her baby about all day, providing close physical contact and a rich variety of stimulation. (Eastcott/ Momatiak/Woodfin Camp & Associates)*

newborns (Brazelton, Nugent, & Lester, 1987; Tedder, 1991). Although lasting effects on development have not been demonstrated, NBAS-based interventions are clearly useful in helping the parent–infant relationship get off to a good start.

LEARNING CAPACITIES

Learning refers to changes in behavior as the result of experience. Babies come into the world with built-in learning capacities that permit them to profit from experience immediately. Infants are capable of two basic forms of learning, which were introduced in Chapter 1: classical and operant conditioning. In addition, they learn through a natural preference they have for novel stimulation. Finally, one early learning mechanism is likely to surprise you: Newborn babies have a remarkable ability to imitate the facial expressions and gestures of adults.

■ CLASSICAL CONDITIONING. Earlier in this chapter, we discussed a variety of newborn reflexes. These make **classical conditioning** possible in the young infant. In this form of learning, a new stimulus is paired with a stimulus that leads to a reflexive response. Once the baby's nervous system makes the connection between the two stimuli, then the new stimulus by itself produces the behavior.

Recall from Chapter 1 that Russian physiologist Ivan Pavlov first demonstrated classical conditioning in his famous research with dogs (see pages 16–17). Classical conditioning is of great value to human infants, as well as other animals, because it helps them recognize which events usually occur together in the everyday world. As a result, they can anticipate what is about to happen next, and the environment becomes more orderly and predictable (Rovee-Collier, 1987). Let's take a closer look at the steps of classical conditioning.

Imagine a mother who gently strokes her infant's forehead each time she settles down to nurse the baby. Soon the mother notices that every time the baby's forehead is stroked, he makes active sucking movements. The infant has been classically conditioned. Here is how it happened (see Figure 4.5):

Classical conditioning
A form of learning that involves associating a neutral stimulus with a stimulus that leads to a reflexive response.

Unconditioned stimulus (UCS)
In classical conditioning, a stimulus that leads to a reflexive response.

Unconditioned response (UCR)
In classical conditioning, a reflexive response that is produced by an unconditioned stimulus (UCS).

1. Before learning takes place, an **unconditioned stimulus (UCS)** must consistently produce a reflexive, or **unconditioned, response (UCR)**. In our example, the stimulus of sweet breast milk (UCS) resulted in sucking (UCR).

2. To produce learning, a neutral stimulus that does not lead to the reflex is presented at about the same time as the UCS. Ideally, the neutral stimulus should occur just before the UCS. The mother stroked the baby's forehead as each nursing period began. Therefore, the stroking (neutral stimulus) was paired with the taste of milk (UCS).

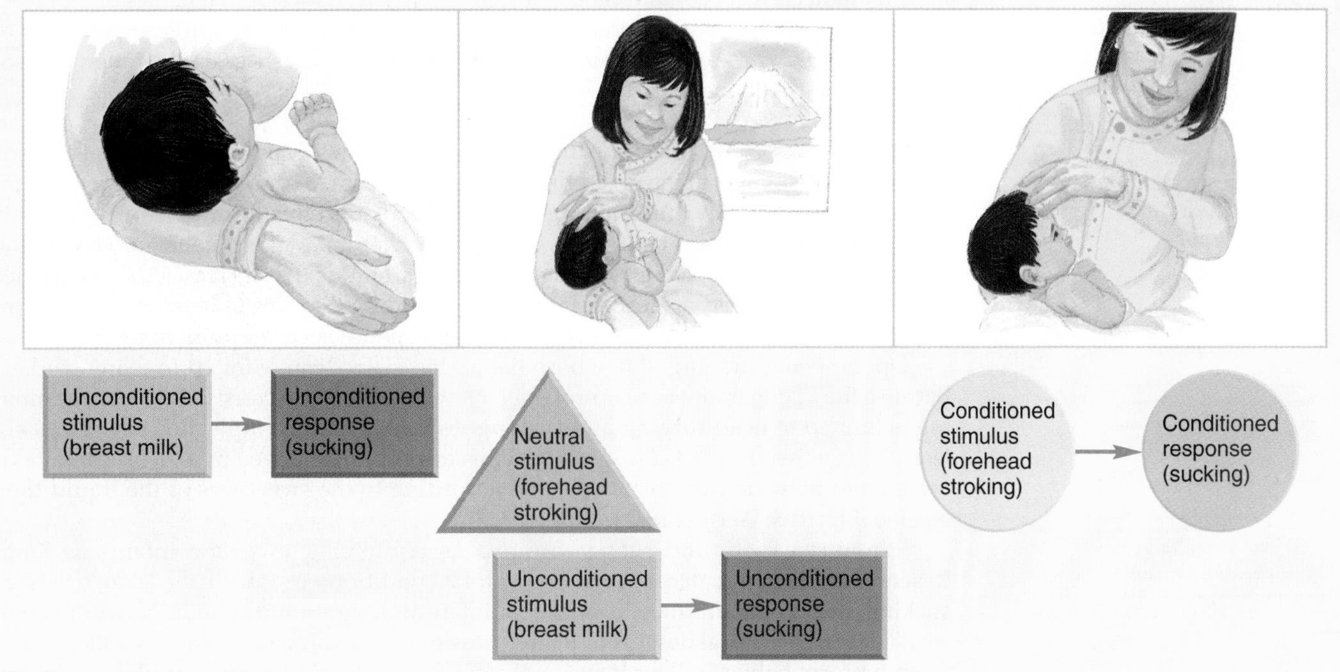

FIGURE 4.5

■ *The steps of classical conditioning. The example here shows how a mother classically conditioned her baby to make sucking movements by stroking his forehead at the beginning of feedings.*

3. If learning has occurred, the neutral stimulus by itself produces the reflexive response. The neutral stimulus is then called a **conditioned stimulus (CS)**, and the response it elicits is called a **conditioned response (CR)**. We know that the baby has been classically conditioned because stroking his forehead outside of the feeding situation (CS) results in sucking (CR).

If the CS is presented alone enough times without being paired with the UCS, the CR will no longer occur. In other words, if the mother strokes the infant's forehead again and again without feeding him, the baby will gradually stop sucking in response to stroking. This is referred to as **extinction**. In a classical conditioning experiment, the occurrence of responses to the CS during the extinction phase shows that learning has taken place.

Although young babies can be classically conditioned, they will not respond to just any pairing of stimuli. To be easily learned, the association between a UCS and a CS must have survival value. Not surprisingly, most CRs of newborns occur in the feeding situation. They are adaptive because they increase the efficiency of food-getting behavior (Blass, Ganchrow, & Steiner, 1984). In fact, babies are so sensitive to stimulus cues surrounding feeding that even the passage of time between meals can serve as an effective CS. Most newborns are fed about every 3 to 4 hours. As the end of this time period approaches (CS), mouthing, sucking, and salivation (CR) increase in frequency and intensity (Rovee-Collier, 1987).

Some responses are very difficult to classically condition in young infants. Fear is one of them. Until the last half of the first year, infants do not have the motor skills to escape unpleasant events. Because they depend on their parents for this kind of protection, they do not have a biological need to form these associations. But between 8 and 12 months, the conditioning of fear is easily accomplished, as seen in the famous example of little Albert, conditioned by John Watson to withdraw and cry at the sight of a furry white rat. Return to Chapter 1, page 17, to review this well-known experiment. Then test your knowledge of classical conditioning by identifying the UCS, UCR, CS, and CR in Watson's study. In Chapter 10, we will discuss the development of fear, as well as other emotional reactions, in detail.

Finally, an infant's state often affects classical conditioning. For example, when a baby is highly aroused and crying, the sight of the mother or the sound of her footsteps (CS) predicts relief from discomfort. Under these conditions, infants quickly learn to stop crying and to mouth and suck (CR) in preparation for feeding. However, when the infant is quietly alert, the mother's approach does not have this meaning, and the same response rarely appears (Gekoski, Rovee-Collier, & Carulli-Rabinowitz, 1983). When we

Conditioned stimulus (CS)
In classical conditioning, a neutral stimulus that through pairing with an unconditioned stimulus (UCS) leads to a new response (CR).

Conditioned response (CR)
In classical conditioning, an originally reflexive response that is produced by a conditioned stimulus (CS).

Extinction
In classical conditioning, decline of the CR, as a result of presenting the CS enough times without the UCS.

look at infant classical conditioning research as a whole, it is clear that babies do not react indiscriminately to environmental events. At the very least, the adaptive significance of what is to be learned and the state of the baby are major influences on the range of associations infants will make.

■ OPERANT CONDITIONING. In classical conditioning, babies build up expectations about stimulus events in the environment, but their behavior does not influence the stimuli that occur. **Operant conditioning** is quite different. In this form of learning, infants act (or operate) on the environment, and stimuli that follow their behavior change the probability that the behavior will occur again. A stimulus that increases the occurrence of a response is called a **reinforcer**. Removing a desirable stimulus or introducing an unpleasant one to decrease the occurrence of a response is called **punishment**.

Operant conditioning of newborn babies has been demonstrated in many studies. Because the young infant can control only a few behaviors, successful operant conditioning is limited to head-turning and sucking responses. For example, newborns quickly learn to turn their heads to the side when this response is followed by a sugar water reinforcer, and they vary their sucking rate according to the sweetness of the liquid they receive (Lipsitt & Werner, 1981).

Stimulus variety and change are just as reinforcing to young infants as food. Researchers have created special laboratory conditions in which the baby's rate of sucking on a nipple produces a variety of interesting sights and sounds. Newborns will suck faster to see visual designs or to hear music and human voices (Rovee-Collier, 1987). Even preterm babies will seek and make contact with reinforcing stimulation. In one study, they increased their contact with a soft teddy bear placed in the isolette that "breathed" quietly at a rate reflecting the infant's respiration, whereas they decreased their contact with a nonbreathing bear (Thoman & Ingersoll, 1993). As these findings suggest, operant conditioning has become a powerful tool for finding out what stimuli babies can perceive and which ones they prefer.

As infants get older, operant conditioning expands to include a wider range of stimuli and responses. For example, Carolyn Rovee-Collier places special mobiles over the cribs of 2- to 6-month-olds. When the baby's foot is attached to the mobile with a long cord, it takes only a few minutes for the infant to start kicking vigorously (Rovee-Collier & Hayne, 1987; Shields & Rovee-Collier, 1992). As we will see shortly, this technique has yielded important information about infant memory. And in Chapter 6, we will discover that it has also been used to study babies' ability to categorize stimulus events.

Operant conditioning soon modifies parents' and babies' reactions to each other. As the infant gazes into the adult's eyes, the adult looks and smiles back, and then the infant looks and smiles again. The behavior of each partner reinforces the other, and as a result, both parent and baby continue their pleasurable interaction. As Chapter 10 will reveal, this kind of contingent responsiveness plays an important role in the development of infant–caregiver attachment.

Recall from Chapter 1 that classical and operant conditioning originated with behaviorism, an approach that views the child as a relatively passive responder to environmental stimuli. If you look carefully at the findings just described, you will see that young babies are not passive. Instead, they use any means they can to explore and control their surroundings. In fact, when infants' environments are so disorganized that their behavior does not lead to predictable outcomes, developmental problems, ranging from intellectual retardation to apathy and depression, can result (Cicchetti & Aber, 1986; Seligman, 1975). In addition, as the Social Issues box on the following page reveals, deficits in brain functioning may prevent some babies from actively learning certain lifesaving responses; and the absence of such responses may lead to sudden infant death syndrome, a major cause of infant mortality.

■ HABITUATION AND DISHABITUATION: WINDOW INTO EARLY MEMORY. Take a moment to walk through the rooms of the library, your home, or wherever you happen to be reading this book. What did you notice? Probably those things that are new and different caught your attention first, such as a recently purchased picture on the wall or a piece of furniture that has been moved. At birth, the human brain is set up to be attracted to novelty. **Habituation** refers to a gradual reduction in the strength of a response due to repetitive stimulation. Looking, heart rate, and respiration may all decline, indicating a

Operant conditioning
A form of learning in which a spontaneous behavior is followed by a stimulus that changes the probability that the behavior will occur again.

Reinforcer
In operant conditioning, a stimulus that increases the occurrence of a response.

Punishment
In operant conditioning, removing a desirable stimulus or presenting an unpleasant one to decrease the occurrence of a response.

Habituation
A gradual reduction in the strength of a response as the result of repetitive stimulation.

SOCIAL ISSUES

The Mysterious Tragedy of Sudden Infant Death Syndrome

Before they went to bed, Millie and Stuart looked in on 3-month-old Sasha. She was sleeping soundly, her breathing no longer as labored as it had been 2 days before when she caught her first cold. There had been reasons to worry about Sasha at birth. She was born 3 weeks early, and it took over a minute before she started breathing. "Sasha's muscle tone seems a little weak," Millie remembered the doctor saying. "She just needs to get busy and gain a little weight, and then she'll be well on her way."

Millie awoke with a start the next morning and looked at the clock. It was 7:30, and Sasha had missed her night waking and early morning feeding. Wondering if she was all right, Millie tiptoed into the room. Sasha lay still, curled up under her blanket. She had died silently during her sleep.

Sasha was a victim of **sudden infant death syndrome (SIDS)**, the unexpected death, usually during the night, of an infant under 1 year of age that remains unexplained after thorough investigation. In industrialized nations, SIDS is the leading cause of infant mortality between 1 week and 12 months of age. It accounts for over one-third of these deaths in the United States (Cadoff, 1995). Millie and Stuart's grief was especially hard to bear because no one could give them a definite answer about why Sasha died. They felt guilty and under attack by relatives, and their 5-year-old daughter Jill reacted with sorrow that lasted for months.

Although the precise cause of SIDS is not known, infants who die of it usually show physical problems from the very beginning. Early medical records of SIDS babies reveal higher rates of prematurity, low birth weight, and limp muscle tone (Buck et al., 1989; Malloy & Hoffman, 1995). Abnormal heart rate, cry patterns, and respiration as well as disturbances in sleep–waking activity are also associated with the disorder (Corwin et al., 1995; Froggatt et al., 1988). At the time of death, over half of SIDS babies have a mild respiratory infection. This seems to increase the chances of respiratory failure in an already vulnerable baby (Cotton, 1990).

One hypothesis about the cause of SIDS is that problems in brain functioning prevent these infants from learning how to respond when their survival is threatened—for example, when respiration is suddenly interrupted (Lipsitt, 1990). Between 2 and 4 months of age, when SIDS is most likely to occur, reflexes decline and are replaced by voluntary, learned responses. Respiratory and muscular weaknesses of SIDS babies may stop them from acquiring behaviors that replace defensive reflexes. As a result, when breathing difficulties occur during sleep, they do not wake up, shift the position of their bodies, or cry out for help. Instead, they simply give in to oxygen deprivation and death.

In an effort to reduce the occurrence of SIDS, researchers are studying environmental factors related to it. Although babies of poverty-stricken, ethnic minority mothers are at greater risk, these findings may be due to mistaking other causes of infant death for SIDS. When SIDS diagnoses are "certain" rather than "questionable," family background closely resembles that of the general population (Haas et al., 1993; Taylor & Sanderson, 1995). In contrast, maternal cigarette smoking, both during and after pregnancy, as well as smoking by other caregivers is strongly predictive of the disorder. Babies exposed to cigarette smoke are two to three times more likely to die of SIDS than are nonexposed infants (Klonoffcohen et al., 1995; Poets et al., 1995).

Other consistent findings are that SIDS babies are more likely to sleep on their stomachs than their backs, are often wrapped very warmly in clothing and blankets, and are three times more likely to die in the winter than summer (Haglund et al., 1995; Irgens et al., 1995). Why are these factors associated with SIDS? Scientists think that smoke and excessive body warmth (which can be encouraged by putting babies down on their stomachs) place a strain on the respiratory control system in the brain. In an at-risk baby, the respiratory center may stop functioning. In other cases, healthy babies sleeping face down in soft bedding during the cold winter months may simply die from continually breathing their own exhaled breath (Kemp & Thach, 1993).

Can simple procedures like quitting smoking, changing an infant's sleeping position, and removing a few bedclothes prevent SIDS? Research suggests so. For example, if women refrained from smoking while pregnant, an estimated 30 percent of SIDS might be prevented. Public education campaigns that discourage parents from putting babies down on their stomachs have led to dramatic reductions in SIDS in England, New Zealand, and Tazmania. Similar efforts are under way in the United States (Taylor, 1991; Wigfield et al., 1992; Willinger, 1995). When SIDS does occur, surviving family members require a great deal of help to overcome a sudden and unexpected infant death. Parent support groups exist in many communities. As Millie commented 6 months after Sasha's death, "It's the worst crisis we've ever been through. What's helped us most are the comforting words of others who've experienced the same tragedy."

loss of interest. Once this has occurred, a new stimulus—some kind of change in the environment—causes responsiveness to return to a high level. This recovery is called **dishabituation**. Habituation and dishabituation permit infants to focus their attention on those aspects of the environment they know least about. As a result, learning is more efficient.

The habituation–dishabituation sequence provides researchers with a marvelous window into early memory development. Later in this chapter, we will see that it is also used to study infant perceptual capacities. Let's look at an example that illustrates how researchers capitalize on these responses. In one study, habituation and dishabituation were used to find out whether 5- and 6-month-olds could discriminate two similar

Sudden infant death syndrome (SIDS)
The unexpected death, usually during the night, of an infant under 1 year of age that remains unexplained after thorough investigation.

Dishabituation
Increase in responsiveness after stimulation changes.

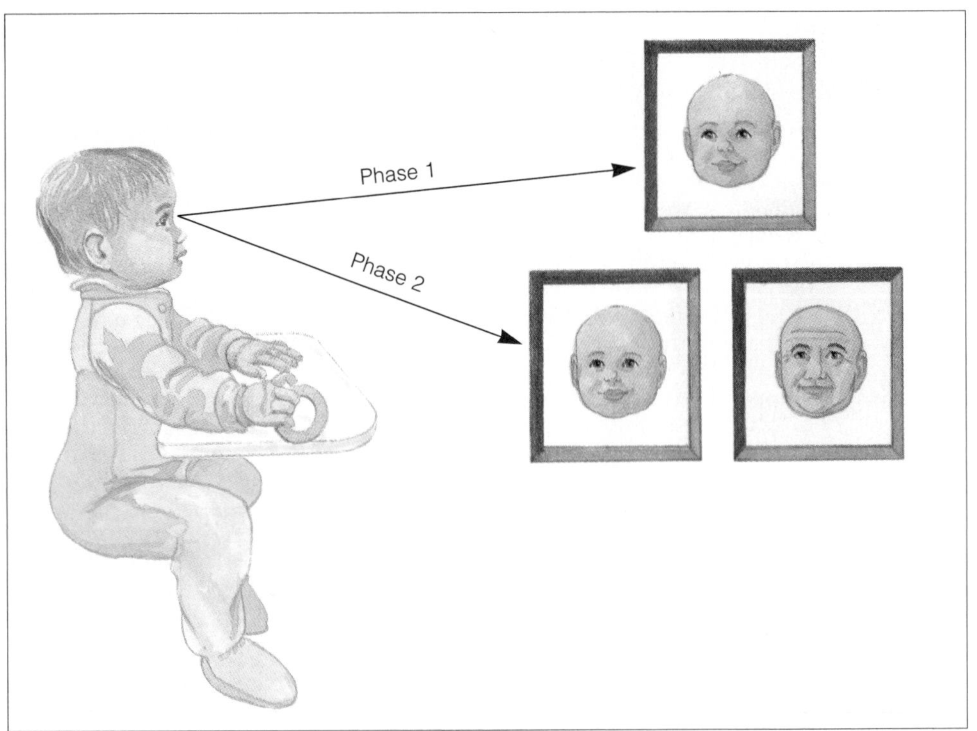

FIGURE 4.6

■ *Example of how the habituation–dishabituation sequence can be used to study infant perception and memory. In Phase 1, infants are shown (habituated to) a photo of a baby. In Phase 2, infants are again shown the baby photo, but this time it appears alongside a photo of a bald-headed man. Infants dishabituated to (spent more time looking at) the photo of the man, indicating that they remembered the baby and perceived the man's face as different from it. (Adapted from Fagan & Singer, 1979.)*

photos—one of a baby and the other of a bald man (see Figure 4.6). In Phase 1 (habituation), infants were shown the baby photo for a short time. Next, in Phase 2 (dishabituation), the baby photo was paired with a photo of a bald man. Because infants spent more time looking at the bald-headed man than the baby, the researchers concluded that infants both remembered the baby face and perceived the man as new and different from it (Fagan & Singer, 1979).

Habituation–dishabituation research reveals that neonates discriminate and remember a wide variety of distinct sights, sounds, and smells. Very young babies need long exposure times to stimuli to demonstrate the habituation–dishabituation response. With age, memory processing becomes more efficient. By the middle of the first year, infants require only 5 to 10 seconds of study time for immediate recognition. And gradually, they make finer distinctions among visual stimuli and remember them longer—at 3 months for about 24 hours; by the end of the first year for several days; and in the case of very familiar stimuli, such as a photo of the human face, even weeks (Fagan, 1973; Martin, 1975).

At this point, let's note that habituation–dishabituation research tells us how long babies retain a new stimulus in the laboratory, but it underestimates their ability to remember real-world events they can actively control. Recall Rovee-Collier's operant conditioning research, in which babies learned to make a mobile move by kicking. In a series of studies, she showed that 3-month-olds remember how to activate the mobile 1 week after training and, with a reminder (the experimenter briefly rotates the mobile for the baby), as long as 4 weeks (Fagen & Rovee-Collier, 1983). Rovee-Collier's findings also highlight a curious feature of infant memory. During the first 6 months, it is highly *context dependent.* That is, if babies are not tested in the same situation in which they were trained (on a very similar mobile in a crib with the identical patterned bumper), their retention is severely disrupted (Hayne & Rovee-Collier, 1995; Rovee-Collier & Shyi, 1992). According to Rovee-Collier, context-dependent memory is adaptive for infants. It protects early memories from being retrieved in inappropriate situations, where they can be easily modified or extinguished.

Although habituation and dishabituation to visual stimuli do not provide a full picture of early memory, at present they are the best available infant predictors of later cognitive development. Correlations between the speed of these responses and 3- to 11-year-old IQ consistently range from the .30s to the .60s (McCall & Carriger, 1993; Rose & Feldman, 1995). The habituation–dishabituation sequence seems to be an especially effective early index of intelligence because it assesses quickness of thinking, a character-

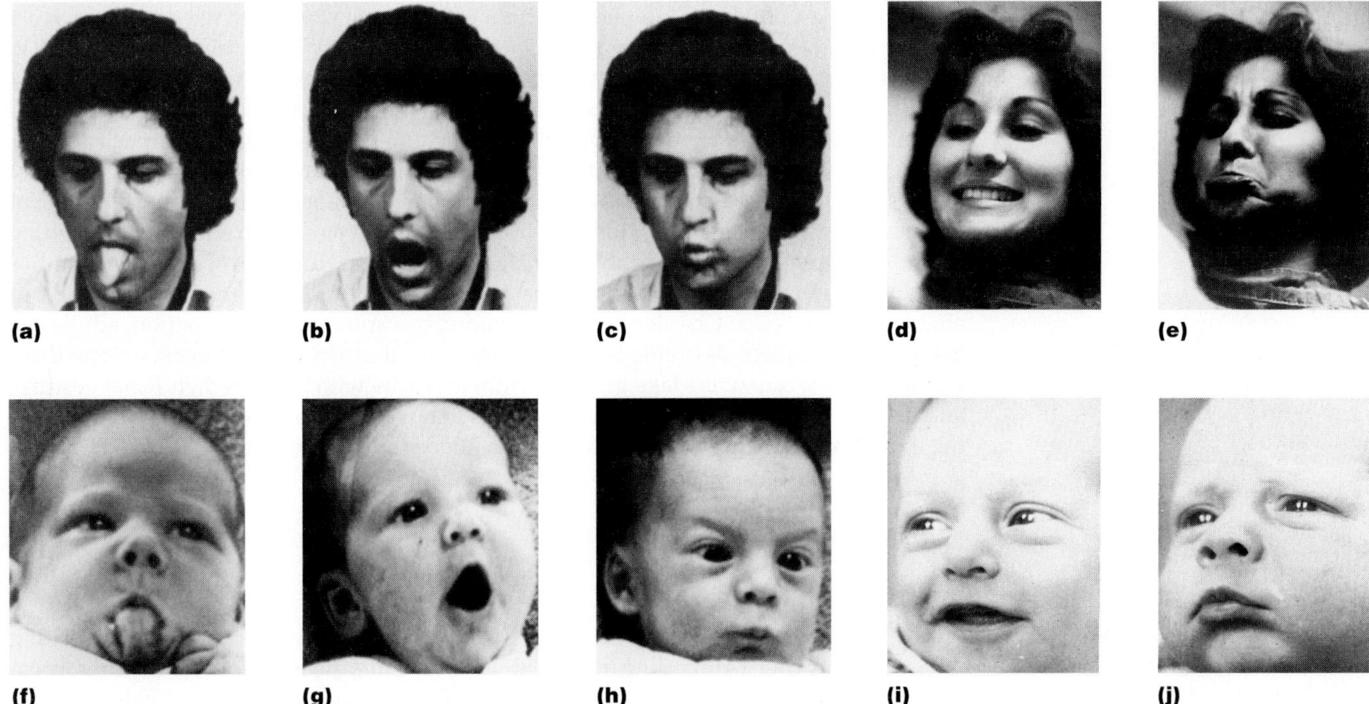

FIGURE 4.7

■ *Photographs from two of the first studies of newborn imitation. Those on the left show 2- to 3-week-old infants imitating tongue protrusion (a), mouth opening (b), and lip protrusion (c). Those on the right show 2-day-old infants imitating happy (d) and sad (e) adult facial expressions. (From A. N. Meltzoff & M. K. Moore, 1977, "Imitation of Facial and Manual Gestures by Human Neonates,"* Science, *198, p. 75; and T. M. Field et al., 1982, "Discrimination and Imitation of Facial Expressions by Neonates,"* Science, *218, p. 180. Copyright © 1977 and 1982, respectively, by the AAAS. Reprinted by permission.)*

istic of bright individuals (Colombo, 1995). It also taps basic cognitive processes—attention, memory, and response to novelty—that underlie intelligent behavior at all ages. In Chapter 8, we will describe an infant intelligence test made up entirely of habituation–dishabituation items.

So far, our discussion has considered only one type of memory—*recognition.* It is the simplest form of remembering because all babies have to do is indicate (by looking or kicking) whether a new stimulus is identical or similar to one previously experienced. *Recall* is a second, more challenging form of memory, since it involves remembering something that is not present. Can infants engage in recall? By the end of the first year, they can, since they find hidden objects and imitate the actions of others hours or days after they first observed the behavior. Recall undergoes much more extended and elaborate development than recognition. We will take it up in more detail in Chapter 7.

■ NEWBORN IMITATION. For many years, researchers believed that **imitation**—learning by copying the behavior of another person—was beyond the capacity of very young infants. They were not expected to imitate until several months after birth (Bayley, 1969; Piaget, 1945/1951). Then a growing number of studies began to report that newborns come into the world with the ability to imitate the behavior of their caregivers.

Figure 4.7 shows examples of responses obtained in two of the first studies of newborn imitation (Field et al., 1982; Meltzoff & Moore, 1977). As you can see, babies from 2 days to several weeks old imitated a wide variety of adult facial expressions. Since then, the neonate's capacity to imitate has been demonstrated in many ethnic groups and cultures (Meltzoff & Kuhl, 1994).

Explanations of the response are more controversial. Imitation is more difficult to induce in babies 2 to 3 months old than just after birth. Some investigators regard the capacity as little more than an automatic response to particular stimuli that recedes with age, much like a reflex. But Andrew Meltzoff (1990) points out that newborns model a wide variety of facial expressions, and they do so even after short delays—when the adult is no longer demonstrating the behavior. These observations suggest that the capacity is flexible and voluntary. Furthermore, imitation does not recede as reflexes do. Babies several months old often do not imitate an adult's behavior right away because they try to play social games of the sort they are used to in face-to-face interaction—smiling, cooing, and waving their arms. When an adult model displays a gesture repeatedly, older babies soon get down to business and imitate (Meltzoff & Moore, 1992).

Imitation
Learning by copying the behavior of another person. Also called modeling or observational learning.

According to Meltzoff, neonates imitate in much the same way we do—by actively matching body movements they "see" with ones they "feel" themselves make. Later in this chapter, we will encounter evidence that young infants are surprisingly adept at coordinating information across sensory systems. These findings provide additional support for Meltzoff's view of newborn imitation as a flexible, voluntary capacity.

As we will see in Chapter 6, infants' capacity to imitate changes greatly over the first 2 years. But however limited it is at birth, imitation provides the baby with a powerful means of learning. Using imitation, newborns begin to explore their social world, getting to know people by sharing behavioral states with them. In the process, babies notice equivalences between their own actions and those of others, and they start to find out about themselves (see Chapter 11). Furthermore, by capitalizing on imitation, adults can get infants to express desirable behaviors, and once they do, adults can encourage these further. Finally, caregivers take great pleasure in a baby who imitates their facial gestures and actions. Newborn imitation clearly seems to be one of those capacities that helps get the infant's relationship with parents off to a good start.

BRIEF REVIEW

The newborn baby is equipped with a wide variety of capacities for relating to the surrounding world. Reflexes are the neonate's most obvious organized patterns of behavior. Some, like sucking, have survival value, whereas others, like stepping, form the basis for motor skills that will develop later. Infants move in and out of six states of arousal that become more organized and predictable with age. Sleep is the dominant state; young infants spend far more time in REM sleep than they will at later ages. A crying baby stimulates strong feelings of discomfort in nearby adults. Fortunately, a crying infant can be soothed in many ways. Neonatal behavioral assessment permits doctors, nurses, and researchers to assess the remarkable capacities of newborn babies.

Infants are marvelously equipped to learn immediately after birth. Through classical conditioning, babies acquire stimulus associations that have survival value. Operant conditioning enables them to control events in the surrounding world. Habituation and dishabituation reveal that infants are naturally attracted to novel stimulation and that their recognition memory improves steadily with age. Finally, newborns' amazing ability to imitate the facial expressions and gestures of adults helps them get to know their social world.

Motor Development in Infancy

Virtually all parents eagerly await their infant's mastery of new motor skills. Baby books are filled with proud notations as soon as children hold up their heads, reach for objects, sit by themselves, crawl, and walk alone. Parents' enthusiasm for these achievements makes perfect sense. They are, indeed, milestones of development. With each new motor skill, babies master their bodies and the environment in a new way. For example, sitting alone grants infants an entirely different perspective on the world compared to when they spent much of the day lying on their backs and stomachs. Voluntary reaching permits babies to find out about objects by acting on them. And when infants can move on their own, their opportunities for exploration are multiplied.

Babies' motor achievements have a powerful effect on their social relationships. For example, once infants can crawl, parents start to restrict their activities by saying no and expressing mild anger and impatience—strategies that were unnecessary when the baby, placed on a blanket, would stay there! At the same time, parents' expressions of affection and game playing increase as their independently moving baby seeks them out for greetings, hugs, and entertainment (Campos, Kermoian, & Zumbahlen, 1992). Certain motor skills, such as pointing to and showing toys, permit infants to communicate more

MILESTONES

Gross and Fine Motor Development in the First Two Years

Motor Skill	Average Age Achieved	Age Range in Which 90 Percent of Infants Achieve the Skill
When held upright, head erect and steady	6 weeks	3 weeks–4 months
When prone, lifts self by arms	2 months	3 weeks–4 months
Rolls from side to back	2 months	3 weeks–5 months
Grasps cube	3 months, 3 weeks	2–7 months
Rolls from back to side	4 1/2 months	2–7 months
Sits alone	7 months	5–9 months
Crawls	7 months	5–11 months
Pulls to stand	8 months	5–12 months
Plays pat-a-cake	9 months, 3 weeks	7–15 months
Stands alone	11 months	9–16 months
Walks alone	11 months, 3 weeks	9–17 months
Builds tower of two cubes	13 months, 3 weeks	10–19 months
Scribbles vigorously	14 months	10–21 months
Walks up stairs with help	16 months	12–23 months
Jumps in place	23 months, 2 weeks	17–30 months

Note: These milestones represent overall age trends. Individual differences exist in the precise age at which each milestone is attained.
Source: Bayley, 1969.

effectively. Finally, babies' expressions of delight—laughing, smiling, and babbling—as they work on new motor competencies trigger pleasurable reactions in others, which encourage infants' efforts further (Mayes & Zigler, 1992). In this way, motor skills, emotional and social competencies, cognition, and language develop together and support one another.

THE ORGANIZATION AND SEQUENCE OF MOTOR DEVELOPMENT

Gross motor development refers to control over actions that help infants get around in the environment, such as crawling, standing, and walking. In contrast, *fine motor development* has to do with smaller movements, such as reaching and grasping. The Milestones table above shows the average ages at which a variety of gross and fine motor skills are achieved during infancy and toddlerhood.

Notice that the table also presents the age ranges during which the majority of infants accomplish each skill. These ranges indicate that although the sequence of motor development is fairly uniform across children, large individual differences exist in the rate at which motor development proceeds. Also, a baby who is a late reacher is not necessarily going to be a late crawler or walker. We would be concerned about a child's development only if many motor skills were seriously delayed.

Look at the table once more, and you will see that there is organization and direction to the infant's motor achievements. First, motor control of the head comes before control of the arms and trunk, and control of the arms and trunk is achieved before control of the legs. This head-to-tail sequence is called the **cephalocaudal trend**. Second, motor development proceeds from the center of the body outward, in that head, trunk, and arm control is mastered before coordination of the hands and fingers. This is the **proximodistal trend**. Physical growth follows these same trends during the prenatal period, infancy, and childhood (see Chapter 5). This physical–motor correspondence suggests a genetic contribution to the overall pattern of motor development.

However, we must be careful not to think of motor skills as isolated, unrelated accomplishments that follow a fixed, maturational timetable. Earlier in this century, researchers made this mistake. Today we know that each new motor skill is not only a product of change, but a contributor to future attainments (Thelen, 1995). Furthermore, many influences—both internal and external to the child—join together to support the vast transformations in motor competencies of the first 2 years.

MOTOR SKILLS AS DYNAMIC SYSTEMS

According to **dynamic systems theory**, motor development involves acquiring increasingly complex *systems of action.* When motor skills work as a system, separate abilities blend together, each cooperating with others to produce more effective ways of exploring and controlling the environment. For example, during infancy, control of the head and upper chest are combined into sitting with support. Kicking, rocking on all fours, and reaching are gradually put together into crawling. Then crawling, standing, and stepping are united into walking alone (Hofsten, 1989; Pick, 1989; Thelen, 1989).

Each new skill that develops is a joint product of central nervous system maturation, movement possibilities of the body, environmental supports for the skill, and the task the child has in mind. Change in any one of these elements leads to loss of stability in the system, and the child starts to explore and select new motor patterns. Which components disrupt stable organism–environment coordination to induce change may vary with age. In the early weeks of life, brain and body growth may be especially important as infants achieve postural control over the head, shoulders, and upper torso. Later, the tasks the baby wants to accomplish (getting a toy, crossing the room) and the environmental context (parental encouragement, objects in the infants' everyday setting) may play a greater role. Once new motor configurations are discovered, they must be refined to become accurate, smooth, and efficient. Consequently, for any particular skill, dynamic systems theory predicts a period in which behavior is highly variable and uncertain, followed by period in which it narrows to a stable pattern as the action is practiced and perfected.

Look carefully at dynamic systems theory, and you will see why motor development cannot be a genetically prewired process. Since it is motivated by exploration and the desire to master new tasks, it can only be mapped out by heredity at a very general level. Each skill—even ones that are universal, such as reaching, crawling, and walking—is learned by revising and combining earlier accomplishments to fit a new goal. Consequently, different pathways to the same outcome exist, and infants achieve motor milestones in unique ways.

Evidence for dynamic systems theory comes from two sources: (1) microgenetic studies of infants' acquiring new motor skills, in which behavior is followed from its initial stages until it is perfected, and (2) cross-cultural research, which highlights environmental contributions to the rate and form of motor progress. Let's look at examples of each.

DYNAMIC SYSTEMS IN ACTION: MICROGENETIC RESEARCH

Using the special mobile attached to the baby's foot with a long cord, described earlier in this chapter, Esther Thelen (1994) illustrated how infants learn motor skills by modifying what the body can already do to fit a new task. Typically, 3-month-olds kick with either one foot or two feet in alternation to make the mobile move. To see if infants could modify this preference, Thelen linked their legs together with a soft piece of elastic

Cephalocaudal trend
An organized pattern of physical growth and motor control that proceeds from head to tail.

Proximodistal trend
An organized pattern of physical growth and motor control that proceeds from the center of the body outward.

Dynamic systems theory
A theory that views new motor skills as reorganizations of previously mastered skills that lead to more effective ways of exploring and controlling the environment. Motor development is jointly influenced by central nervous system maturation, movement possibilities of the body, environmental supports for the skill, and the task the child has in mind.

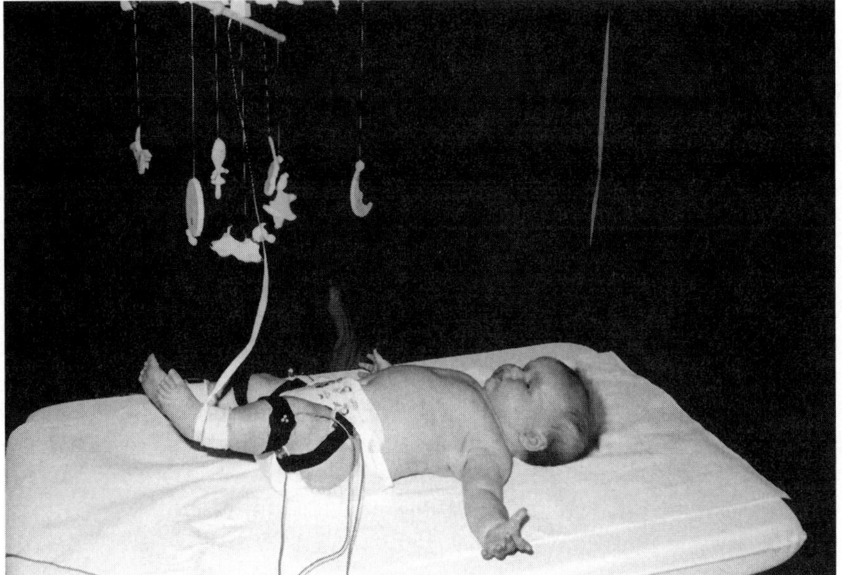

FIGURE 4.8

■ *Three-month-old infant in mobile experiment with legs linked together by an elastic ankle cuff. Consistent with dynamic systems theory, the baby revised previously learned motor acts into a more effective motor system. In response to the cuff, he replaced single- and alternate-leg kicking with simultaneous kicks. (Courtesy of Dr. Esther Thelen, Indiana University)*

attached to ankle cuffs (see Figure 4.8). This permitted single- or alternate-leg kicking, but it made kicking both legs in unison much more effective for activating the mobile. When the elastic was in place, infants gradually discovered the new motion. They began with a few tentative simultaneous kicks and, seeing the consequences, gradually replaced earlier movements with this new form. After the elastic was removed, infants quickly gave up the simultaneous pattern in favor of alternate or single-leg kicking. They readily experimented, revising their motor behavior appropriately to fit changing conditions of the task.

The way previously learned acts are reorganized into more effective motor systems is especially apparent in the area of fine motor skills. As we will see when we discuss the development of voluntary reaching, the various components—grasping, looking, and moving the arms—at first emerge independently. Then, as babies become increasingly aware of a world of objects to be explored, they combine these skills into successful reaching. Common to all infants is an effort to adapt current skills to get an object. As Thelen (1995) explains, the desire to accomplish a task motivates behavior. Then the new behavior enables the child to accomplish new tasks, and motor development changes again. In sum, infants are active in acquiring motor skills, and change occurs through their own problem-solving activity.

CULTURAL VARIATIONS IN MOTOR DEVELOPMENT

Cross-cultural research demonstrates how early movement opportunities and a stimulating environment contribute to motor development. Several decades ago, Wayne Dennis (1960) observed infants in Iranian orphanages who were deprived of the tantalizing surroundings that induce infants in most homes to acquire motor skills. The Iranian babies spent their days lying on their backs in cribs, without toys to play with. As a result, most did not move about on their own until after 2 years of age. When they finally did move, the constant experience of lying on their backs led them to scoot in a sitting position rather than crawl on their hands and knees the way infants raised in more normal situations do. This preference for scooting probably slowed the infants' motor development even further. Babies who scoot come up against furniture with their feet, not their hands. Consequently, they are far less likely to pull themselves to a standing position in preparation for walking. Indeed, only 15 percent of the Iranian orphans walked alone by 3 to 4 years of age.

Cultural variations in infant-rearing practices also affect motor development. Take a quick survey of several parents you know, asking these questions: Can babies profit from training? Should sitting, crawling, and walking be deliberately encouraged? Answers vary widely from culture to culture. Japanese mothers, for example, believe such efforts are unnecessary and unimportant (Caudill, 1973). Among the Zinacanteco Indians of southern Mexico, rapid motor progress is actively discouraged. Babies who walk before they know enough to keep away from cooking fires and weaving looms are viewed as dangerous to themselves and disruptive to others (Greenfield, 1992).

In contrast, among the Kipsigis of Kenya and the West Indians of Jamaica, babies hold their heads up, sit alone, and walk considerably earlier than North American infants. Kipsigi parents deliberately teach these motor skills. In the first few months, babies are seated in holes dug in the ground, and rolled blankets are used to keep them upright. Walking is promoted by frequently bouncing babies on their feet (Super, 1981). Unlike the Kipsigis, the West Indians of Jamaica do not train their infants in specific skills. Instead, beginning in the first few weeks of life, babies experience a highly stimulating, formal handling routine (see Figure 4.9). Asked why they use this routine, West Indian mothers refer to the traditions of their culture and the need to help babies grow up strong, healthy, and physically attractive (Hopkins & Westra, 1988).

Putting together the findings we have discussed so far, we must conclude that early motor skills, like other aspects of development, are due to complex transactions between nature and nurture. As dynamic systems theory suggests, heredity establishes the broad outlines of change, but experience contributes to the precise sequence of motor milestones and the rate at which they are reached.

FINE MOTOR DEVELOPMENT: THE SPECIAL CASE OF VOLUNTARY REACHING

Of all motor skills, voluntary reaching is believed to play the greatest role in infant cognitive development, since it opens up a whole new way of exploring the environment (Piaget, 1936/1952b). By grasping things, turning them over, and seeing what happens when they are released, infants learn a great deal about the sights, sounds, and feel of objects.

The development of reaching and grasping, shown in Figure 4.10 on page 146, provides an excellent example of how motor skills start out as gross, diffuse activity and move toward mastery of fine movements. When newborns are held in an upright posture, they direct their arms toward an object in front of them. These movements are called **prereaching** because they resemble poorly coordinated swipes or swings. Since newborn babies cannot control their arms and hands, they are rarely successful in contacting the object. Like newborn reflexes, prereaching eventually drops out, around 7 weeks of age.

At about 3 months, voluntary reaching appears and gradually improves in accuracy (Bushnell, 1985; Hofsten, 1984). Infants of this age reach just as effectively for a glowing object in the dark as for an object in the light. This indicates that early reaching does not require visual guidance of the arms and hands. Instead, it is controlled by *proprioception*, our sense of movement and location arising from stimuli within the body (Clifton et al., 1994). As a result, vision is freed from the basic act of reaching so it can focus on more complex adjustments. By 5 months, infants sensitively reduce their reaching behavior when an object is moved beyond their reach (Yonas & Hartman, 1993). At 9 months, they can redirect their reaching to obtain a moving object that changes direction (Ashmead et al., 1993).

Individual differences exist in how infants execute their first reaches. Babies with wild, flapping arm movements must damp them down to get their hands near the toy, whereas those with soft, quiet movements must use more muscle power to lift and extend their arms (Thelen et al., 1993). Each infant builds the act of reaching uniquely by exploring the match between current movements and those demanded by the task.

Once infants can reach, they start to modify the nature of their grasp. When the grasp reflex of the newborn period weakens, it is replaced by the **ulnar grasp**, a clumsy motion in which the fingers close against the palm. Around 4 to 5 months, when infants begin to master sitting, they no longer need their arms to maintain body balance. This frees both hands to become coordinated in exploring objects. Babies of this age can hold an object in one hand while the other scans it with the tips of the fingers, and they frequently transfer objects from hand to hand (Rochat, 1992; Rochat & Goubet, 1995). By the latter part of the first year, infants use the thumb and index finger opposably in a well-coordinated **pincer grasp** (Halverson, 1931). Then the ability to manipulate objects greatly expands. The 1-year-old can pick up raisins and blades of grass, turn knobs, and open and close small boxes.

By 8 to 11 months of age, reaching and grasping are so well practiced that they are executed smoothly and effortlessly. As a result, attention is released from coordinating

Prereaching
The poorly coordinated, primitive reaching movements of newborn babies.

Ulnar grasp
The clumsy grasp of the young infant, in which the fingers close against the palm.

Pincer grasp
The well-coordinated grasp emerging at the end of the first year, involving thumb and forefinger opposition.

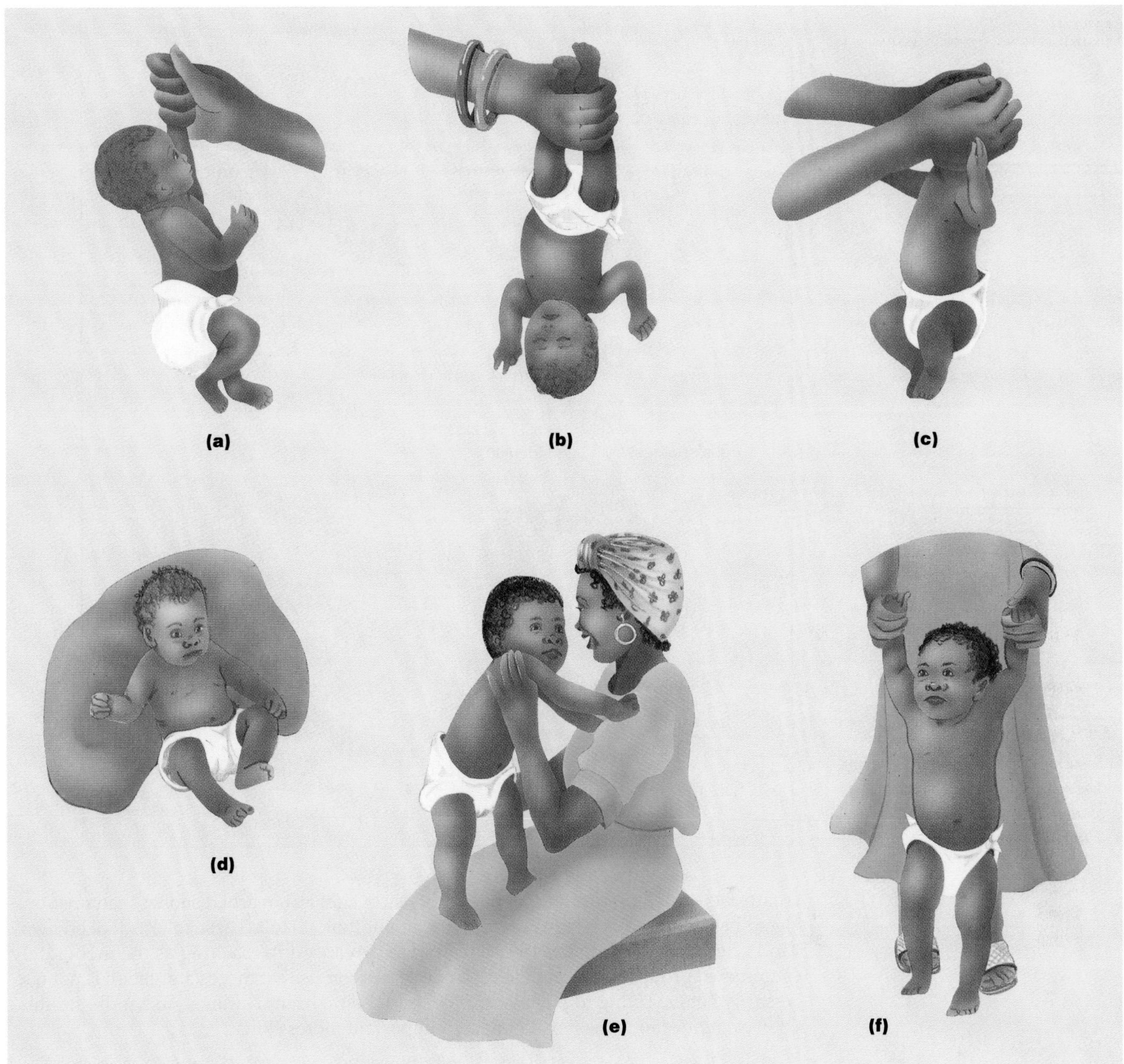

FIGURE 4.9

■ *West Indian mothers use a formal handling routine with their babies. Exercises practiced in the first few months include stretching each arm while suspending the baby (a); holding the infant upside-down by the ankles (b); grasping the baby's head on both sides, lifting upward, and stretching the neck (c); and propping the infant with cushions that are gradually removed as the baby begins to sit independently (d). Later in the first year, the baby is "walked" up the mother's body (e) and encouraged to take steps on the floor while supported (f). (Adapted from B. Hopkins & T. Westra, 1988, "Maternal Handling and Motor Development: An Intracultural Study,"* Genetic, Social and General Psychology Monographs, *14, pp. 385, 388, 389. Reprinted with permission of the Helen Dwight Reid Educational Foundation. Published by Heldref Publications, 1319 Eighteenth St., N.W., Washington, DC. 20036-1802. Copyright © 1988.)*

the motor skill itself to events that occur before and after obtaining the object. As we will see in Chapter 6, around this time infants can first solve simple problems involving reaching, such as searching for and finding a hidden toy.

Like other motor milestones, voluntary reaching is affected by early experience. In a well-known study, Burton White and Richard Held (1966) found that institutionalized babies provided with a moderate amount of visual stimulation (at first, simple designs; later, a mobile hung over their cribs) reached for objects 6 to 8 weeks earlier than infants given nothing to look at. A third group of babies provided with massive stimulation

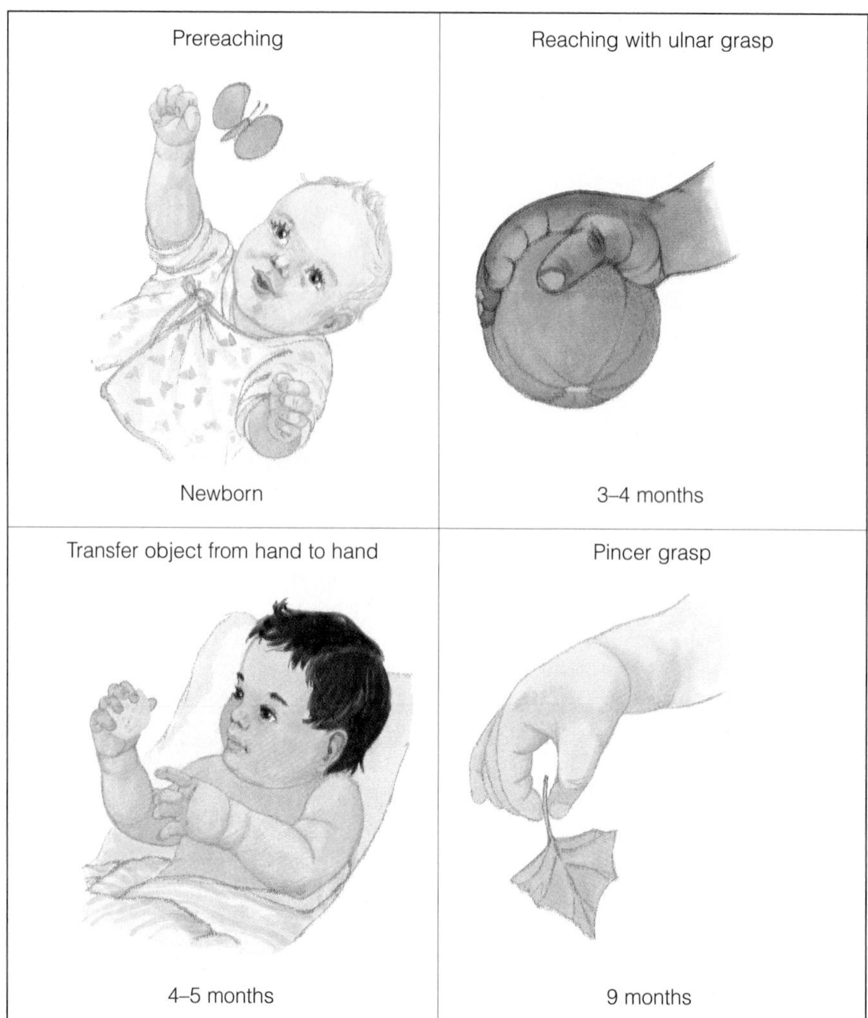

FIGURE 4.10

■ *Some milestones of voluntary reaching. The average age at which each skill is attained is given. (Ages from Bayley, 1969; Rochat & Goubet, 1995.)*

(patterned crib bumpers and mobiles at an early age) also reached sooner than unstimulated babies. But this heavy dose of enrichment took its toll. These infants looked away and cried a great deal, and they were not as advanced in reaching as the moderately stimulated group. White and Held's findings remind us that more stimulation is not necessarily better. Trying to push infants beyond their current readiness to handle stimulation can undermine the development of important motor skills.

BRIEF REVIEW

The overall sequence of early motor development follows the cephalocaudal and proximodistal trends. However, motor development is not programmed into the brain from the start. According to dynamic systems theory, it is energized by the baby's exploration and desire to master new tasks and jointly influenced by central nervous system maturation, movement possibilities of the body, and environmental supports for the skill. Microgenetic studies reveal how previously learned acts are reorganized into new motor attainments. Cross-cultural research underscores the contribution of movement opportunities, a stimulating environment, and infant-rearing practices to motor progress. Voluntary reaching plays a vital role in infant cognitive development. It begins with the uncoordinated prereaching of the newborn baby and gradually evolves into a refined pincer grasp by the end of the first year. Once reaching is well practiced, infants integrate it into increasingly elaborate motor skills.

Perceptual Development in Infancy

Think back to White and Held's study, described at the end of the previous section. It illustrates the close link between perception and action in discovering new skills. To reach for objects, maintain balance, or move across various surfaces, infants must continually coordinate their motor behavior with perceptual information (Lockman, 1990). Acting and perceiving are not separate aspects of experience. Instead, motor activity provides infants with a vital means for exploring and learning about the world, and improved perception brings about more effective motor activity. The union of perceptual and motor information is basic to our nervous systems, and each domain supports development of the other (Stein & Meredith, 1993).

What can young infants perceive with their senses, and how does perception change with age? Researchers have sought answers to these questions for two reasons. First, infant perception is relevant to the age-old nature–nurture controversy. Is an adultlike perceptual world given to the infant, or must it be acquired through experience? As we will see shortly, newborns have an impressive array of perceptual capacities. Nevertheless, since improvements occur as the result of both maturation and experience, an appropriate resolution to the nature–nurture debate seems, once again, to lie somewhere between the two extremes. Second, infant perception sheds light on other areas of development. For example, because touch, vision, and hearing permit us to interact with other human beings, they are a basic part of emotional and social development. Through hearing, language is learned. And perception provides the foundation for cognitive development, since knowledge about the world is first gathered through the senses.

Studying infant perception is especially challenging because babies cannot describe their experiences. Instead, researchers must find out about their perceptual world by observing the repertoire of behaviors infants do have. Fortunately, investigators can make use of a variety of infant responses that vary with stimulation, such as looking, sucking, head turning, facial expressions, and startle reactions. Psychophysiological measures, such as changes in respiration and heart rate, are also used. And as we noted earlier, researchers sometimes take advantage of operant conditioning and the habituation–dishabituation sequence to find out whether infants can make certain discriminations. We will see many examples of these methods as we explore the baby's sensitivity to touch, taste, smell, sound, and visual stimulation in the following sections.

TOUCH

Touch is a fundamental means of interaction between parents and young babies. Within the first few days of life, mothers can recognize their own newborn by stroking the infant's cheek or hand, and fathers can do the same by stroking the infant's hand (Kaitz et al., 1993a, 1993b). In our discussion of preterm infants in Chapter 3, we indicated that touch helps stimulate early physical growth. As we will see in Chapter 10, it is important for emotional development as well. Therefore it is not surprising that sensitivity to touch is well developed at birth. Return to the reflexes listed in Table 4.1 on page 125. They reveal that the newborn baby responds to touch, especially around the mouth and on the palms of the hands and soles of the feet. During the prenatal period, these areas, along with the genitals, are the first to become sensitive to touch, followed by other regions of the body (Humphrey, 1978).

Reactions to temperature change are also present at birth. When young infants are undressed, they often express discomfort by crying and becoming more active. Newborn babies are more sensitive to stimuli that are colder than body temperature than to those that are warmer (Humphrey, 1978).

At birth, infants are quite sensitive to pain. If male newborns are circumcised, the procedure is usually done without anesthesia because of the risk of giving pain-relieving drugs to a very young infant. Babies often respond with an intense, high-pitched, stressful cry (Hadjistavropoulos et al., 1994). In addition, heart rate and blood pressure rise, irritability increases, and the baby's sleep may be disturbed for hours afterward

(Anand, 1990). Recent research aimed at developing safe pain-relieving drugs for newborns promises to ease the stress of such procedures. One helpful approach is to offer a nipple that delivers a sugar solution, which quickly reduces crying and discomfort in young babies (Blass & Ciaramitaro, 1994). Doctors are becoming more aware that small infants, just like older children and adults, cannot be treated as if they are insensitive to pain.

■ *Touch is a major means through which babies investigate their world. These infants explore novel objects by running their lips and tongue over the surface. Then they remove the object to take a good look at it. In the next few months, this exploratory mouthing will give way to increasingly elaborate touching with the hands. (Tom McCarthy/PhotoEdit)*

Sensitivity to touch enhances infants' responsiveness to the environment. In one study, the soft caresses of an experimenter led babies to smile and become increasingly attentive to the adult's face (Stack & Muir, 1992). As soon as infants can grasp objects, touch becomes a major means through which they investigate their world. Watch babies at play, and you will see that they frequently mouth novel objects, running their lips and tongue over the surface, after which they remove the object to take a good look at it. Exploratory mouthing peaks in the middle of the first year and then declines in favor of increasingly elaborate touching with the hands, in which infants turn, poke, and feel the surface of things while knitting their brows and looking intently (Ruff et al., 1992). In Chapter 6, we will see that Piaget regarded this hands-on manipulation of objects, in which touch and vision combine, as essential for early cognitive development.

TASTE AND SMELL

All infants come into the world with the ability to communicate their taste preferences to caregivers. When given a sweet liquid instead of water, newborns use longer sucks with fewer pauses, indicating that they prefer sweetness and try to savor the taste of their favorite food (Crook & Lipsitt, 1976). Facial expressions reveal that infants can distinguish several basic tastes. Much like adults, newborns relax their facial muscles in response to sweetness, purse their lips when the taste is sour, and show a distinct archlike mouth opening when it is bitter (Rosenstein & Oster, 1988; Steiner, 1979). These built-in reactions are important for survival, since (as we will see in Chapter 5) the food that is ideally suited to support the infant's early growth is the sweet-tasting milk of the mother's breast. Salty taste develops differently from sweet, sour, or bitter. At birth, infants are either indifferent to or reject salt solutions in comparison to water. But by 4 months, they prefer the salty taste, a change that may prepare them to accept solid foods (Beauchamp et al., 1994).

Like taste, the newborn baby's responsiveness to the smell of certain foods is surprisingly similar to that of adults, suggesting that some odor preferences are innate. For example, the smell of bananas or chocolate causes a relaxed, pleasant facial expression, whereas the odor of rotten eggs makes the infant frown (Steiner, 1979). Newborns can also identify the location of an odor and, if it is unpleasant, defend themselves. When a whiff of ammonia is presented to one side of the baby's nostrils, infants less than 6 days old quickly turn their heads in the other direction (Reiser, Yonas, & Wikner, 1976).

In many mammals, the sense of smell plays an important role in eating and protecting the young from predators by helping mothers and babies identify each other. Although smell is less well developed in human beings than in other mammals, traces of its survival value are still present. Mothers can identify their own baby by smell shortly after birth, and the baby responds in kind. The ability to recognize the mother's smell within the first week of life occurs only in breast-fed newborns (Cernoch & Porter, 1985). However, bottle-fed babies prefer the smell of any lactating (milk-producing) woman to the smell of a nonlactating woman. And when given a choice between the smell of the lactating breast and their familiar formula, once again they choose the former (Makin & Porter, 1989; Porter et al., 1992). Neonates seem to have a built-in attraction to the odor of breast milk, which probably helps them locate an appropriate food source and, in the process, learn to identify their own mother.

At birth, babies seem to be quite adept at making taste and odor discriminations. Unfortunately, little is known about how these two senses develop as the result of further brain maturation and experience.

HEARING

Newborn infants can hear a wide variety of sounds, but they are more responsive to some than others. For example, they prefer complex sounds, such as noises and voices, to pure tones (Bench et al., 1976). In the first few days, infants can already tell the difference between a few sound patterns, such as a series of tones arranged in ascending and descending order and utterances with two as opposed to three syllables (Bijeljac-Babic, Bertoncini, & Mehler, 1993). Over the first year, they organize sounds into increasingly elaborate patterns. Between 4 to 6 months, babies even have a sense of musical phrasing. They prefer Mozart minuets with pauses between natural phrases to minuets with awkward breaks (Krumhansl & Jusczyk, 1990). And around 12 months, if two melodies differing only slightly are played, infants can tell that they are not the same (Morrongiello, 1986).

Responsiveness to sound provides support for the young baby's visual and tactile exploration of the environment. Infants as young as 3 days old turn their eyes and head in the general direction of a sound. By 4 months, they can reach fairly accurately toward a sounding object in the dark (Clifton et al., 1994). The ability to identify the precise location of a sound will improve greatly over the first 6 months (Ashmead et al., 1991; Hillier, Hewitt, & Morrongiello, 1992). By this time, infants start to make judgments about how far away a sound is. They are less likely to try to retrieve a sounding object in the dark if it is beyond their reach (Clifton, Perris, & Bullinger, 1991).

Neonates are particularly sensitive to sounds within the frequency range of the human voice, and they come into the world prepared to respond to the sounds of any human language. Tiny infants can make fine-grained distinctions among a wide variety of speech sounds—"ba" and "ga," "ma" and "na," and the short vowel sounds "a" and "i," to name just a few. In fact, there are only a few speech discriminations that young infants cannot detect, and their ability to perceive sounds not found in their language environment is more precise than an adult's (Jusczyk, 1995). As we will see in Chapter 9, by the middle of the first year, infants start to "screen out" sounds not used in their own language as they listen closely to the speech of those around them (Kuhl et al., 1992; Polka & Werker, 1994). These capacities reveal that the human baby is marvelously equipped for the awesome task of acquiring language.

Listen carefully to yourself the next time you talk to a young baby. You are likely to speak in a high-pitched, expressive voice and use a rising tone at the ends of phrases and sentences. Adults probably communicate this way because they notice that infants are more attentive when they do so. Indeed, newborns prefer human speech with these characteristics (Cooper & Aslin, 1990). They will also suck more on a nipple to hear a recording of their mother's voice than that of an unfamiliar woman, and to hear their mother's native tongue as opposed to a foreign language (Mehler et al., 1988; Spence & DeCasper, 1987). These preferences probably developed from hearing the muffled sounds of the mother's voice through the uterine wall before birth.

Infants' special responsiveness to their mother's speech probably encourages the mother to talk to the baby. As she does so, both readiness for language and the emotional bond between caregiver and child are strengthened. By 3 months of age, infants pick up information about the feelings of others through hearing. They can distinguish happy- from sad-sounding adult voices (Walker-Andrews & Grolnick, 1983). As we will see later, it will take somewhat more time before babies can discriminate these emotions visually.

Clearly, infants' acute sensitivity to sound supports the emergence of many competencies. Therefore, it is not surprising that even mild hearing impairments that go untreated in the early years can endanger development. To find out more about this topic, turn to the From Research to Practice box on page 150.

VISION

Humans depend on vision more than any other sense for active exploration of the environment. Yet vision is the least mature of the newborn baby's senses. Visual structures in both the eye and brain continue to develop after birth. For example, the muscles of the *lens,* the part of the eye that permits us to adjust our focus to varying distances of objects, are weak in the neonate. Also, cells in the *retina,* the membrane lining the inside of the eye that captures light and transforms it into messages that are sent to the brain, are not as mature or densely packed as they will be in several months (Banks & Bennett, 1988). Furthermore, the optic nerve and other pathways that relay these messages along with cells in the visual cortex that receive them will not be adultlike for several years (Hickey & Peduzzi, 1987).

FROM RESEARCH TO PRACTICE

Long-Term Impact of Early Hearing Loss on Development: The Case of Otitis Media

During his first year in day care, 18-month-old Alex caught five colds, had the flu on two occasions, and experienced repeated *otitis media* (middle ear infection). Alex is not unusual. By age 3, approximately 71 percent of children have had upper respiratory illnesses that lead to at least one bout of otitis media; 33 percent have had three or more bouts. Some episodes are acute, leading to severe ear pain, crying, irritability, and sleep disturbance. But as many as half are "silent"—accompanied by few or no symptoms. Parents either do not notice these or learn of them only on routine visits to the doctor. Antibiotics are effective in eliminating the bacteria responsible for otitis media, but they do not reduce fluid buildup in the middle ear, which causes mild to moderate hearing loss that can last for weeks or months after an episode (Feagans & Proctor, 1994).

The incidence of otitis media peaks between 6 months and 3 years of age, when children are first acquiring language and other important cognitive and social skills. Can repeated infections interfere with psychological development? Although some studies show no effects, others have produced worrisome findings. For example, in several large, well-designed investigations, otitis media in the first year of life predicted delayed language development between 1 and 7 years of age. Poorer academic performance in elementary school was also reported (Friel-Patti & Finitzo-Hieber, 1990; Menyuk, 1986; Teele et al., 1990).

How might otitis media disrupt language and academic progress? Difficulties in hearing speech sounds, particularly in noisy settings, may be responsible. Early and recurrent episodes of infection are consistently associated with impairments in speech perception and production (Feagans & Proctor, 1994; Gravel & Wallace, 1992). Furthermore, children who have had many bouts are less attentive to the speech of others and less persistent at tasks (Feagans et al., 1987; Roberts, Burchinal, & Campbell, 1994). Their distractibility may be due to repeated instances in which they could not make out what people around them were saying. When children have trouble paying attention, they may reduce the quality of others' interactions with them. In one study, mothers of preschoolers with many illness episodes were less effective in teaching their child a task (Chase et al., 1995).

Current evidence argues strongly in favor of early prevention of otitis media, especially since the illness is so widespread. Some children are at greater risk than others. The earlier the age of first infection, the more likely children are to have repeated bouts of illness. Crowded living conditions and exposure to cigarette smoke and other pollutants are also linked to the disease—factors that probably underlie its higher incidence among low-income children. In addition, enrollment of millions of infants and young children in day care creates opportunities for close contact, increasing the number of otitis media episodes by several fold (Froom & Culpepper, 1991).

How can negative developmental outcomes of early otitis media be prevented? Here are some ways:

- Frequent screening of infants and preschoolers for the disease followed by prompt medical intervention. (Plastic tubes that drain the inner ear are often used to treat chronic otitis media, although their effectiveness remains controversial.)
- Regular cleaning and design of day care settings to control infection. Because infants and young children often put toys in their mouths, these objects should be rinsed frequently with a disinfectant solution. Spatious, well-ventilated rooms and small group sizes also limit the spread of otitis media and other diseases.
- Verbally stimulating adult–child interaction. Developmental problems associated with otitis media are reduced or eliminated in high-quality day care centers where noise is kept to a minimum and caregivers engage in frequent, responsive communication with children, increasing their opportunities to hear spoken language (Feagans, Kipp, & Blood, 1994; Roberts, Burchinal, & Campbell, 1994).

Because of these factors, newborn babies cannot focus their eyes very well. In addition, their **visual acuity**, or fineness of discrimination, is limited. When you have your vision tested, the doctor estimates how finely you perceive stimuli in comparison to an adult with normal vision. Applying this same index to newborn babies, researchers have found that they see objects at a distance of 20 feet about as well as adults do at 600 feet (Courage & Adams, 1990; Held, 1993). Furthermore, unlike adults (who see nearby objects more clearly), newborn babies see *equally unclearly* across a wide range of distances. As a result, no visual cues are available to help them notice that a near or far object can be sharpened by refocusing the lens (Banks, 1980). Images such as a parent's face, even from close up, look much like the blur shown in Figure 4.11.

Newborn infants cannot yet see well, but they actively explore their environment with the limited visual abilities they do have. They scan the visual field for interesting sights and try to track moving objects, although their eye movements are slow and inaccurate (Aslin, 1993). The visual system matures rapidly over the first few months of life. By 3 months, infants can focus on objects just as well as adults can. Visual acuity improves steadily throughout infancy. By 6 months, it is about 20/100. At 2 years, it

Visual acuity
Fineness of visual discrimination.

(a) Newborn View **(b)** Adult View

FIGURE 4.11

The newborn baby's limited focusing ability and poor visual acuity lead the mother's face, even when viewed from close up, to look much like the fuzzy image in part (a) rather than the clear image in part (b).

reaches a near-adult level (Courage & Adams, 1990). Scanning and tracking also undergo rapid gains. By 1 month, babies can follow a slowly moving object with a smooth eye movement, a capacity that continues to improve during the first half-year (Aslin, 1987; Hainline, 1993).

Color perception is also refined in the early months. Newborns are sensitive to color, since they prefer to look at colored rather than gray stimuli, but they do not show a definite ability to distinguish particular hues (Adams, 1987). Pathways in the brain that process color information mature rapidly, since 2-month-olds can discriminate colors across the entire spectrum (Brown, 1990). By 4 to 5 months, they regard a particular color as the same, even under very different lighting conditions (Dannemiller, 1989). Once color sensitivity is well established, habituation–dishabituation research reveals that babies organize different hues into categories—red, blue, yellow, and green—just as adults do. Four-month-olds, for example, perceive two blues as more alike than a blue and a green (Bornstein, Kessen, & Weiskopf, 1976; Catherwood, Crassini, & Freiberg, 1989). This grouping of colors is probably an innate property of the visual system, since young infants could not have learned through language that a certain range of hues is called by the same name.

As babies see more clearly, explore the visual field more adeptly, and use color and brightness cues, they work on sorting out features of the environment and their arrangement in space. We can best understand how they do so by examining the development of three additional aspects of vision: depth, pattern, and object perception.

DEPTH PERCEPTION. Depth perception is the ability to judge the distance of objects from one another and from ourselves. It is important for understanding the layout of the environment and for guiding motor activity. To reach for objects, babies must have some idea about depth. Later, when infants learn to crawl, depth perception helps prevent them from bumping into furniture and falling down stairs.

Although we live in a three-dimensional world, the surface of the retina that captures visual images is two-dimensional. A variety of visual cues help us translate this two-dimensional representation into a three-dimensional view of reality. Research on depth perception focuses on two main questions: Do very young infants perceive depth? How does sensitivity to various cues for depth develop during the first year of life?

The earliest studies of depth perception used a well-known apparatus called the **visual cliff** (see Figure 4.12 on page 152). Devised by Eleanor Gibson and Richard Walk (1960), it consists of a glass-covered table with a platform at the center. On one side of the platform (the shallow side) is a checkerboard pattern just under the surface of the glass. On the other side (the deep side), the checkerboard is several feet beneath the glass. The researchers placed crawling infants on the platform and asked their mothers to entice them across both the deep and shallow sides by calling to them and holding out a toy. Although the babies readily crossed the shallow side, all but a few reacted with fear to

Visual cliff
An apparatus used to study depth perception in infants. Consists of a glass-covered table and a central platform, from which babies are encouraged to crawl. Patterns placed beneath the glass create the appearance of a shallow and deep side.

FIGURE 4.12

■ *The visual cliff. By refusing to cross the deep side and showing a preference for the shallow surface, this infant demonstrates the ability to perceive depth.* (*William Vandivert/Scientific American*)

the deep side. The researchers concluded that around the time infants crawl, most distinguish deep and shallow surfaces and avoid drop-offs that look dangerous (Walk & Gibson, 1961).

Gibson and Walk's research shows that crawling and avoidance of drop-offs are linked, but it does not tell us how they are related or when depth perception first appears. To better understand the development of depth perception, investigators have turned to babies' ability to detect particular depth cues, using methods that do not require that they crawl.

Kinetic Depth Cues. How do we know when an object is near rather than far away? Try these exercises to find out. Look toward the far wall while moving your head from side to side. Notice that objects close to your eye move past your field of vision more quickly than those far away. Next, pick up a small object (such as your cup) and move it toward and away from your face. Did its image grow larger as it approached and smaller as it receded?

Motion provides us with a great deal of information about depth, and **kinetic depth cues** are the first to which infants become sensitive. Babies 3 to 4 weeks of age blink their eyes defensively to a surface looming toward their face that looks as if it is going to hit them (Nánez, 1987; Nánez & Yonas, 1994). As they are carried about and as people and things turn and move before their eyes, infants pick up more information about depth. For example, complex habituation–dishabituation studies reveal that by 3 to 4 months, infants use motion to detect that objects are not flat shapes but are instead three-dimensional (Arterberry, Craton, & Yonas, 1993).

Binocular Depth Cues. Motion is not the only important depth cue. Because our eyes are separated, each receives a slightly different view of the visual field. In children and adults, the brain blends these two images but also registers the difference between them, providing us with **binocular** (meaning two eyes) **depth cues**. Researchers have used ingenious methods to find out if infants are sensitive to binocular cues. One approach is similar to a 3-D movie. The experimenter projects two overlapping images before the baby, who wears special goggles to ensure that each eye receives one of them. If babies use binocular cues, they see and visually track an organized form rather than random dots. Results reveal that binocular sensitivity emerges between 2 and 3 months and gradually improves over the first half-year (Birch, 1993). Infants quickly make use of binocular cues in their reaching, adjusting arm and hand movements to match the distance of objects from the eye.

Pictorial Depth Cues. We also use the same set of depth cues that artists rely on to make a painting look three-dimensional. These are called **pictorial depth cues**. Examples are receding lines that create the illusion of perspective (parallel railroad tracks appear to come closer and closer together until they vanish into the horizon), changes in texture

Kinetic depth cues
Depth cues created by movements of the body or of objects in the environment.

Binocular depth cues
Depth cues that rely on each eye receiving a slightly different view of the visual field; the brain blends the two images, creating three-dimensionality.

Pictorial depth cues
Depth cues artists use to make a painting look three-dimensional, such as receding lines, texture changes, and overlapping objects.

(a)

(b)

FIGURE 4.13

■ *Test of an infant's ability to perceive depth from pictorial cues. (a) A side view of an apparatus in which two toy ducks are placed on a background in which lines and texture create the illusion of depth. A baby reaching for the lower, or closer appearing, duck responds to pictorial cues. (b) This view shows how the experimental display looks to a baby who is sensitive to pictorial cues. (Adapted from Yonas et al., 1986.)*

(nearby textures are more detailed than ones far away), and overlapping objects (an object partially hidden by another object is perceived to be more distant).

Albert Yonas and his colleagues have explored infants' sensitivity to pictorial cues by covering one eye (so the baby cannot rely on binocular vision), presenting stimuli with certain cues, and watching what infants reach for. For example, Figure 4.13 shows two ducks placed on a vertical background in which lines and texture create the illusion of depth. If infants use pictorial cues, they should grasp the lower of the two toys. Experiments like this show that 7-month-olds respond to a variety of pictorial cues, but 5-month-olds do not (Arterberry, Yonas, & Bensen, 1989; Yonas et al., 1986). Pictorial depth perception is last to develop, emerging around the middle of the first year.

Explaining Sensitivity to Depth Cues. Why does perception of depth cues emerge in the order just described? According to researchers, kinetic sensitivity develops first (and may even be present at birth) because it provides the most dependable information about the location of objects and events (Kellman, 1993). Using motion-carried information, even neonates can protect themselves from harmful situations. For example, their capacity to avoid looming stimuli is adaptive, since their worlds are full of moving objects—blankets, objects, and their own hands—that might damage the delicate eye if allowed to contact it.

Proper alignment of the two eyes is essential for detection of binocular cues. Without early corrective surgery, infants with *strabismus* (a condition in which one eye does not focus with the other because of muscle weakness) show permanent deficits in binocular sensitivity, reduced visual acuity in the weak eye, and distorted perception of the spatial layout of the environment (Birch, 1993).

Motor development may also contribute to depth cue sensitivity. For example, control of the head during the early weeks of life may help babies notice kinetic cues. And around 5 to 6 months, the ability to turn, poke, and feel the surface of objects may promote perception of pictorial cues as infants use their hands to pick up information about the size, texture, and shape of objects (Bushnell & Boudreau, 1993). Indeed, as we will see next, research shows that one aspect of motor progress—the baby's ability to move about independently—plays a vital role in the refinement of depth perception.

■ INDEPENDENT MOVEMENT AND DEPTH PERCEPTION. A mother I know described her newly crawling baby daughter as a "fearless daredevil." "If I put April down in the middle of our bed, she crawls right over the edge," the mother exclaimed. "The same thing's happened by the stairs."

Will April become more wary of the side of the bed and the staircase as she becomes a more experienced crawler? Research suggests that she will. In one study, infants with more crawling experience (regardless of when they started to crawl) were far more likely to refuse to cross the deep side of the visual cliff (Bertenthal, Campos, & Barrett, 1984). Avoidance of heights, the investigators concluded, is "made possible by independent locomotion" (Bertenthal & Campos, 1987, p. 563).

Independent movement is related to other aspects of three-dimensional understanding as well. For example, crawling infants are better at remembering object locations and finding hidden objects than are their noncrawling agemates, and the more crawling experience they have, the better their performance on these tasks (Bai & Bertenthal, 1992; Campos & Bertenthal, 1989). Why does crawling make such a difference? Compare your own experience of the environment when you are driven from one place to another as opposed to when you walk or drive yourself. When you move on your own, you are much more aware of landmarks and routes of travel, and you take more careful note of what things look like from different points of view. The same is true for infants. In fact, researchers believe that crawling is so important in structuring babies' experience of the world that it may promote a new level of brain organization by strengthening certain neural connections in the cortex (Bertenthal & Campos, 1987; Fox, Calkins, & Bell, 1994).

■ *Crawling promotes three-dimensional understanding, such as wariness of dropoffs and memory for object locations. As this baby retrieves his pacifier, he takes note of how to get from place to place, where objects are in relation to himself and to other objects, and what they look like from different points of view. (Bob Daemmrich/Stock Boston)*

An estimated 80 to 90 percent of American parents place babies who are not yet crawling in "walkers" (Marcella & McDonald, 1990). These mechanical devices consist of a seat with a frame on casters in which babies can move around by pushing with their feet. Research suggests that walkers also help stimulate development in the ways just described (Bertenthal, Campos, & Barrett, 1984; Kermoian & Campos, 1988). However, walkers do not have any lasting effects, and they can be dangerous. Infants frequently tip over in them and careen down staircases, perhaps because the frame and seat provide a false sense of security. In the United States, walkers account for almost 28,000 infant injuries annually (Trinkoff & Parks, 1993). For safety's sake, it is best not to put babies in these devices. The reorganization of experience linked to independent movement eventually takes place for all normal infants.

■ PATTERN PERCEPTION. Are young babies sensitive to the pattern of things they see, and do they prefer some patterns to others? Early research revealed that even newborns prefer to look at patterned rather than plain stimuli—for example, a drawing of the human face or one with scrambled facial features to a black-and-white oval (Fantz, 1961). Since then, many studies have shown that as infants get older, they prefer more complex patterns. For example, when shown black-and-white checkerboards, 3-week-old infants look longest at ones with a few large squares, whereas 8- and 14-week-olds prefer those with many squares (Brennan, Ames, & Moore, 1966). Infant preferences for many other patterned stimuli have been tested—curved versus straight lines, connected versus disconnected elements, and whether the pattern is organized around a central focus (as in a bull's eye), to name just a few.

Contrast Sensitivity. For many years, investigators did not understand why babies of different ages find certain patterns more attractive than others. Then a general principle was discovered that accounts for early pattern preferences. It is called **contrast sensitivity** (Banks & Ginsburg, 1985; Banks & Salapatek, 1981). Contrast refers to the difference in the amount of light between adjacent regions in a pattern. If babies can detect the contrast in two or more patterns, they prefer the one with more contrast. To understand this idea, look at the two checkerboards in the top row of Figure 4.14. To the mature viewer, the one with many small squares has more contrasting elements. Now look at the bottom row, which shows how these checkerboards appear to infants in the first few weeks of life. Because of their poor vision, very young babies cannot resolve the small features in more complex patterns. To them, the large, bold checkerboard has more contrast, so they prefer to look at it. By 2 months of age, detection of fine-grained detail has improved considerably. As a result, infants become sensitive to the contrast in complex patterns and start to spend much more time looking at them (Dodwell, Humphrey, & Muir, 1987).

Contrast sensitivity
A general principle accounting for early pattern preferences, which states that if babies can detect a difference in contrast between two patterns, they will prefer the one with more contrast.

FIGURE 4.14

■ *The way two checkerboards differing in complexity look to infants in the first few weeks of life. Because of their poor vision, very young infants cannot resolve the fine detail in the more complex checkerboard. It appears blurred, like a gray field. The large, bold checkerboard appears to have more contrast, so babies prefer to look at it. (Adapted from M. S. Banks & P. Salapatek, 1983, "Infant Visual Perception," in M. M. Haith & J. J. Campos (Eds.),* Handbook of Child Psychology: Vol. 2. Infancy and Developmental Psychobiology *(4th ed.), New York: Wiley, p. 504. Copyright © 1983 by John Wiley & Sons. Reprinted by permission.)*

Combining Pattern Elements. In the early weeks of life, infants respond to the separate parts of a pattern. For example, when shown a triangle or a drawing of the human face, very young babies look at the outskirts of the stimulus and stare at single high-contrast features—one corner of the triangle or the hairline and chin of the face (see Figure 4.15 on page 156). At about 2 months, when scanning ability and contrast sensitivity have improved, infants inspect the entire border of a geometric shape. And they explore the internal features of complex stimuli like the human face, pausing briefly to look at each salient part (Bronson, 1991; Salapatek, 1975).

Once babies can take in all aspects of a pattern, at 2 to 3 months they start to combine pattern elements, integrating them into a unified whole. In fact, infants of 6 or 7 months are so good at detecting pattern organization that they even perceive subjective boundaries that are not really present. For example, look at Figure 4.16 on page 156. Seven-month-olds perceive a square in the center of this pattern, just as you do (Bertenthal, Campos, & Haith, 1980). Older infants carry this responsiveness to subjective form even further. As Figure 4.17 on page 157 shows, 9-month-olds can detect the organized, meaningful pattern in a series of moving lights that resemble a person walking, in that they look much longer at this display than they do at upside-down or disorganized versions (Bertenthal et al., 1985). Although 3- to 5-month-olds can tell the difference among these patterns, they do not show a preference for one with both an upright orientation and a humanlike movement pattern (Bertenthal et al., 1987).

By 12 months, infants can perceive a form on the basis of very little information, simply by watching a moving light trace the outline of a shape. In two studies, babies of this age preferred to look at a geometric shape that was different from the one they had just seen outlined by a blinking light. They extracted the shape by combining the light points into an orderly pattern, which they could distinguish from other shapes. Ten-month-olds were unable to make this discrimination (Rose, 1988; Skouteris, McKenzie, & Day, 1992).

Explaining Changes in Pattern Perception. Researchers believe that maturation of the visual system combined with exposure to a wide variety of stimuli underlie younger infants' increasing ability to detect more fine-grained pattern elements and integrated forms (Banks & Shannon, 1993; Proffitt & Bertenthal, 1990). As we saw earlier, visual acuity, scanning, and contrast sensitivity improve greatly during the first few months, supporting exploration of complex stimuli (Pipp & Haith, 1984). Also, studies of the

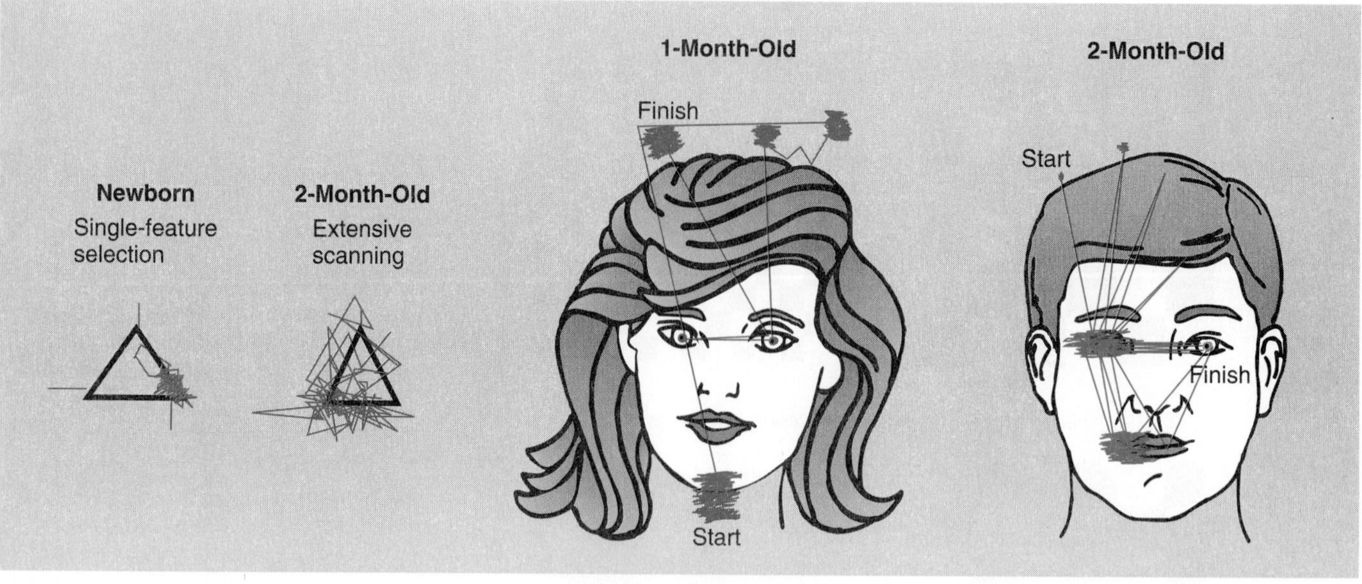

FIGURE 4.15

■ *Visual scanning of simple and complex patterns by young infants. When scanning a simple triangle, newborns focus only on a single feature, whereas 2-month-olds scan the entire border. When patterns are complex, such as a human face, 1-month-olds limit their scanning to single features on the outskirts of the stimulus, whereas 2-month-olds examine internal features. (From P. Salapatek, 1975, "Pattern Perception in Early Infancy," in L. B. Cohen & P. Salapatek (Eds.),* Infant Perception: From Sensation to Cognition, *New York: Academic Press, p. 201. Reprinted by permission.)*

visual cortex in animals, along with indirect research on humans, reveal that brain cells respond to specific pattern stimuli, such as vertical, horizontal, and curved lines. The sensitivity and organization of these receptors improve as babies search for regularities in their rich, patterned external world (Braddick, 1993).

Besides gains in basic sensory processes, infants' expanding knowledge of their surroundings affects perception of complex patterns, especially in the latter half of the first year. As we will see in Chapter 6, by 5 to 6 months of age, babies categorize their world, grouping together similar stimuli and extracting their common properties. Consider, for example, older infants' preference for a pattern of moving lights that corresponds to a person walking. From many occasions of observing people move, they build an image of the human gait as distinct from other stimuli. As evidence for this influence, when 5-month-olds are shown moving light displays of a person walking in different ways (forward, backward, and while marching), they extract the general pattern and show improved performance on the light display task (Pinto & Davis, 1991). In sum, over time, infants' knowledge of familiar actions, objects, and events increasingly governs pattern sensitivity (Bertenthal, 1993). As we turn now to perception of the human face, we will see additional examples of this idea.

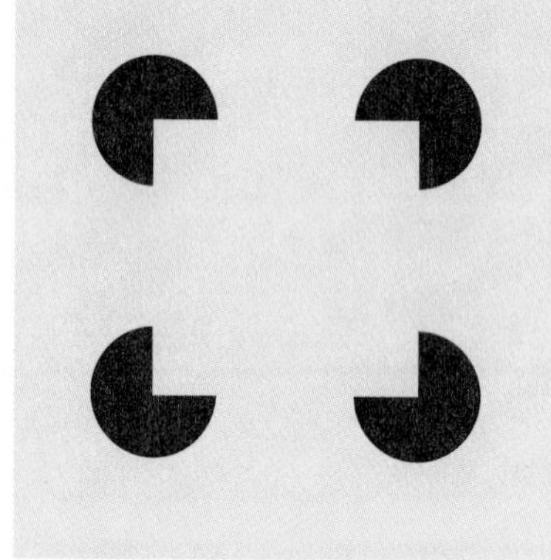

FIGURE 4.16

■ *Subjective boundaries in a visual pattern. Do you perceive a square in the middle of this figure? By 7 months of age, infants do, too. (Adapted from Bertenthal, Campos, & Haith, 1980.)*

■ PERCEPTION OF THE HUMAN FACE. Do newborn babies have an innate, primitive tendency to orient toward faces? Some researchers think so, since neonates will track a facelike pattern moving across their visual field farther than other stimuli (Morton & Johnson, 1991). But all agree that infants younger than 2 months cannot discriminate a static image of the human face from a pattern of equal complexity, such as one with scrambled facial features, largely because (as we noted earlier) 1-month-olds do not inspect the internal features of a stimulus.[3] At 2 to 3 months, when infants explore an entire stimulus, they do prefer a facial pattern over other similar configurations. For example, in one study, 3-month-olds, but not 6-week-olds, looked longer at a face than at the same pattern with its contrast reversed (that is, a negative of a face). They showed no similar preference when an abstract pattern was paired with its negative

[3] Perhaps you are wondering how neonates can display the remarkable imitative capacities described earlier in this chapter if they do not scan the internal features of a face. Recall that the facial expressions in newborn imitation research were not static poses but live demonstrations. Their dynamic quality probably caused infants to notice them.

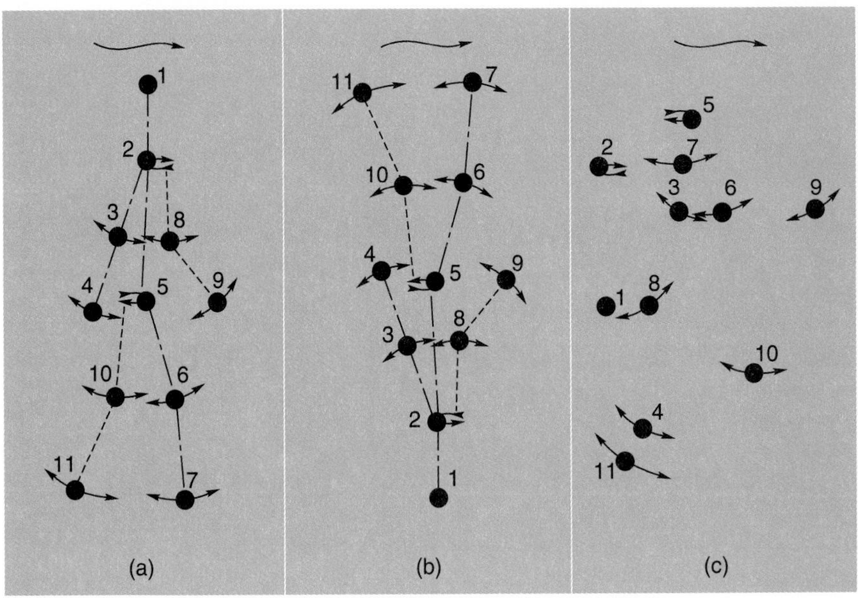

FIGURE 4.17

■ *Light displays used to test infants' preference for the motion of a human being walking. (a) Moving lights correspond to the head, shoulder, hip, elbows, wrists, knees, and ankles of a person walking. By 9 months of age, infants prefer this display to (b), an upside-down version, and to (c), a scrambled version. Three- to 5-month-olds can discriminate the three patterns, but they do not show a preference for (a). (From D. R. Proffitt & B. I. Bertenthal, 1990, "Converging Operations Revisited: Assessing What Infants Perceive Using Discrimination Measures,"* Perception and Psychophysics, *47, p. 5. Reprinted by permission of the Psychonomic Society.)*

(Dannemiller & Stephens, 1988). Infants' recognition of faces does not seem to be a built-in capacity. Instead, it follows the same developmental course as other aspects of visual perception.

The baby's tendency to search for structure in a patterned stimulus is quickly applied to face perception. By 3 months of age, infants make fine distinctions among the features of different faces. For example, they can tell the difference between the photos of two strangers, even when the faces are moderately similar (Barrera & Maurer, 1981a). Around this time, babies also recognize their mother's face in a photo, since they look longer at it than at the face of a stranger (Barrera & Maurer, 1981b). Between 7 and 10 months, infants start to react to emotional expressions as organized, meaningful wholes. They treat positive faces (happy and surprised) as different from negative ones (sad and fearful), even when these expressions are demonstrated in slightly varying ways by different models (Ludemann, 1991).

We must keep in mind that the evidence just reviewed is based only on photographed poses. Yet extensive face-to-face interaction between infants and their caregivers undoubtedly contributes greatly to the refinement of face perception. Therefore, the ability to extract meaning from a facial pattern may be more advanced in the context of live, animated faces infants encounter in everyday life (Caron, Caron, & MacLean, 1988). As we will see in Chapter 10, babies' developing sensitivity to the human face supports their earliest social relationships and helps regulate exploration of the environment in adaptive ways.

■ OBJECT PERCEPTION. Research on pattern perception involves only two-dimensional stimuli, but our environment is made up of stable, three-dimensional objects. Do infants perceive a world of independently existing objects, much like we do?

Size and Shape Constancy. As we move around the environment and look at objects, the images they cast on our retina are constantly changing in size and shape. To perceive objects as stable and unchanging, we must translate these varying retinal images into a single representation.

Size constancy—perception of an object's size as the same, despite changes in its retinal image size—is evident in the first week of life. To test for it, researchers habituated newborns to either a small or a large black-and-white cube at varying distances from the eye. In this way, they hoped to desensitize the infants to changes in the cube's retinal image size and direct their attention to its real size. Next, the large cube and the small cube were presented together, but at different distances so they cast the same size retinal image (see Figure 4.18 on page 158). All infants dishabituated to the novel-sized cube, indicating that despite equivalent retinal images, they distinguish objects on the basis of actual size (Slater, Mattock, and Brown, 1990).

Size constancy
Perception of an object's size as the same, despite changes in the size of its retinal image.

Shape constancy
Perception of an object's shape as the same, despite changes in the shape of its retinal image.

FIGURE 4.18

■ *Testing newborns for size constancy. (a) First, the infant was habituated to a small black-and-white cube at varying distances from the eye. (b) Next, the small cube and a new, large cube were presented together, but at different distances so they cast the same size retinal image. The baby dishabituated to (spent much more time looking at) the large cube, indicating that she distinguishes objects on the basis of actual size. (Adapted from Slater, Mattock, & Brown, 1990.)*

Perception of an object's shape as stable, despite changes in the shape projected on the retina, is called **shape constancy**. Habituation–dishabituation research reveals that it, too, is present within the first week of life, long before babies have an opportunity to actively rotate objects with their hands and view them from different angles (Slater & Morison, 1985). In sum, both shape and size constancy appear to be innate perceptual capacities that help infants organize their perceptual experiences immediately after birth.

Perception of Objects as Distinct, Bounded Wholes. Perceptual constancies provide only a partial picture of the extent to which infants perceive a world of independently existing objects. As adults, we distinguish a single object from its surroundings by looking for a regular shape and uniform texture and color. Observations by Piaget (1936/1952b) first suggested that young infants do not use these same cues. Piaget dangled a small, attractive object in front of his 6-month-old son Laurent, who eagerly grabbed it. But as soon as it was placed on top of a bigger object, such as a book or pillow, Laurent no longer reached for it. Instead, he reached for the larger, supporting object. Laurent's behavior indicates that he did not perceive the boundary between two objects created by their different sizes, shapes, and textures. Rather, he treated two objects close together as a single unit.

Recent research supports Piaget's informal observations and also reveals that it is the movement of objects relative to one another and to their background that gradually enables infants to construct a visual world of separate objects. In one series of studies, 3- to 5-month-olds were shown two objects. Sometimes the objects touched each other; at other times they were separated. Also, sometimes the objects were stationary; at other times they moved either independently or together. When objects touched and either stood still or moved in the same direction, infants reached for them as a whole. But when they were separated or moved in opposite directions, infants behaved as if the objects were distinct, and they reached for only one of them (Hofsten & Spelke, 1985; Spelke, Hofsten, & Kestenbaum, 1989).

These findings indicate that at first, motion and spatial arrangement determine infants' identification of objects, not shape, texture, and color (Kellman, 1993; Spelke, 1990). Indeed, young babies are fascinated by moving objects. They almost always prefer to look at a moving stimulus instead of an identical stationary one. As they do so, they pick up critical information about object characteristics. For example, as Figure 4.19 reveals, by 2 months of age, babies realize that a moving rod whose center is hidden behind a box is a complete rod rather than two rod pieces (Johnson & Aslin, 1995). When an object (such as a rod) moves across a background, its various features remain in the same relationship to one another and move together, helping the baby distinguish the object from other units in the visual field. During the second half-year, as infants become familiar with many types of objects, they start to rely on stationary cues to identify them as separate units (Spelke et al., 1993).

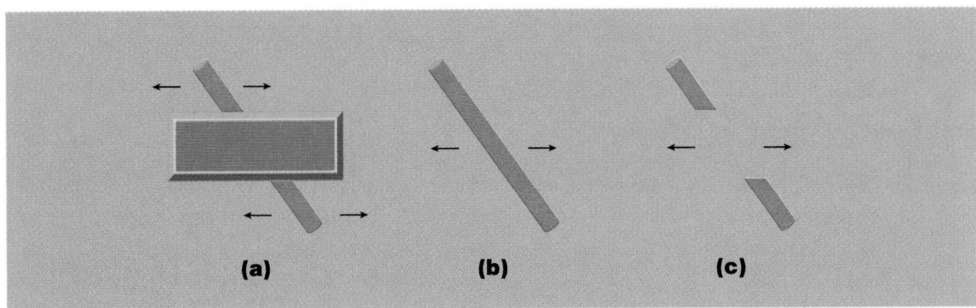

FIGURE 4.19

■ *Example of display used to test infants' ability to perceive object unity. (a) Infants are habituated to a rod moving back-and-forth behind a box. Next, they are shown (b) a complete rod or (c) a broken rod with a gap corresponding to the location of the box. Each of these stimuli is moved back and forth, in the same way as the habituation stimulus. Infants as young as 2 months typically dishabituate to (look longer at) the broken rod than the complete rod. This suggests that they perceive the rod behind the box in the first display as a single unit. (Adapted from Johnson & Aslin, 1995.)*

The Milestones table on page 160 provides an overview of the vast changes that take place in visual perception during the first year. Up to this point, we have considered the sensory systems one by one. Now let's turn to their coordination.

INTERMODAL PERCEPTION

When we take in information from the environment, we often use **intermodal perception**. That is, we combine stimulation from more than one modality, or sensory system. For example, we know that the shape of an object is the same whether we see it or touch it, that lip movements are closely coordinated with the sound of a voice, and that dropping a rigid object on a hard surface will cause a sharp, banging sound.

Are young infants, like adults, capable of intermodal perception, or do they have to learn how to put different types of sensory input together? Although researchers have debated this issue for years, recent evidence reveals that from the start, babies perceive the world in an intermodal fashion (Meltzoff, 1990; Spelke, 1987). Recall that newborns turn in the general direction of a sound, and they reach for objects in a primitive way. These behaviors suggest that infants expect sight, sound, and touch to go together.

By a few weeks after birth, infants show some impressive intermodal associations. In one study, 1-month-old babies were given a pacifier with either a smooth surface or a surface with nubs on it. After exploring it in their mouths, the infants were shown two pacifiers—one smooth and one nubbed. They preferred to look at the shape they had sucked, indicating that they could match touch and visual stimulation without spending months seeing and feeling objects (Meltzoff & Borton, 1979).

Other research reveals that by 4 months, vision and hearing are well coordinated. Lorraine Bahrick (1983) showed infants of this age two films side by side, one with two blocks banging and the other with two sponges being squashed together. At the same time, the sound track for only one of the films (either a sharp banging noise or a soft squashing sound) could be heard. Infants looked at the film that went with the sound track, indicating that they detected a common rhythm in what they saw and heard. In similar studies, 3- and 4-month-olds related the shape and tempo of an adult's moving lips to the corresponding sounds in speech (Pickens et al., 1994; Walton & Bower, 1993). And 7-month-olds united emotional expressions across modalities, matching a happy or angry sounding voice with the appropriate face of a speaking person (Soken & Pick, 1992; Walker-Andrews, 1986).

Of course, many intermodal matches, such as the way a train sounds or a teddy bear feels, must be based on experience. But what is so remarkable about intermodal perception is how quickly infants acquire these associations. Most of the time, they need just one exposure to a new situation (Spelke, 1987). In addition, when researchers try to teach intermodal relationships by pairing sights and sounds that do not naturally go together, babies will not learn them (Bahrick, 1988, 1992). Intermodal perception is yet another capacity that helps infants build an orderly, predictable perceptual world.

Intermodal perception
Perception that combines information from more than one sensory system.

MILESTONES

Visual Development in Infancy

Age	Visual Capacities
Birth–1 month	■ Displays size and shape constancy.
	■ Responds to kinetic depth cues.
2–3 months	■ Has adultlike focusing ability.
	■ Perceives colors across entire spectrum.
	■ Responds to binocular depth cues.
	■ Prefers patterns with fine details.
	■ Scans internal pattern features.
	■ Begins to perceive overall pattern structure.
	■ Prefers a facial pattern over patterns with scrambled facial features.
	■ Recognizes mother's face in a photo.
	■ Uses motion and spatial layout rather than stationary cues (shape, texture, and color) to identify objects as distinct from their surroundings.
4–5 months	■ Organizes colors into categories like those of adults.
	■ Shows gains in sensitivity to binocular depth cues.
6–8 months	■ Shows gains in visual acuity, from 20/600 at birth to 20/100 at 6 months.
	■ Tracks objects with smooth, efficient eye movements.
	■ Responds to pictorial depth cues.
	■ Detects subjective boundaries in patterns.
	■ Uses stationary cues rather than motion to identify objects as distinct from their surroundings.
9–12 months	■ Can extract information about a form in the absence of a full image (for example, from a moving light).
	■ Perceives patterns (including human walking movements and facial expressions of emotion) as organized, meaningful wholes.

Note: These milestones represent overall age trends. Individual differences exist in the precise age at which each milestone is attained.

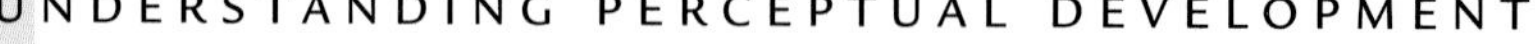

UNDERSTANDING PERCEPTUAL DEVELOPMENT

Differentiation theory
The view that perceptual development involves the detection of increasingly fine-grained, invariant features in the environment.

Invariant features
Features that remain stable in a constantly changing perceptual world.

Now that we have reviewed the development of infant perceptual capacities, how can we put together this diverse array of amazing achievements? Do any general principles account for perceptual development? Eleanor and James Gibson's **differentiation theory** provides widely accepted answers. According to the Gibsons, infants actively search for **invariant features** of the environment—those that remain stable—in a constantly changing perceptual world. For example, in pattern perception, at first babies are confronted with a confusing mass of stimulation. But very quickly, they search for features that stand out along the border of a stimulus. Then they explore its internal features, noticing stable relationships among those features. As a result, they distinguish patterns, such as crosses, squares, and faces. The development of intermodal perception also reflects this principle. Babies seem to seek out invariant relationships, such as a similar tempo in an object's motion and sound, that unite information across different modalities.

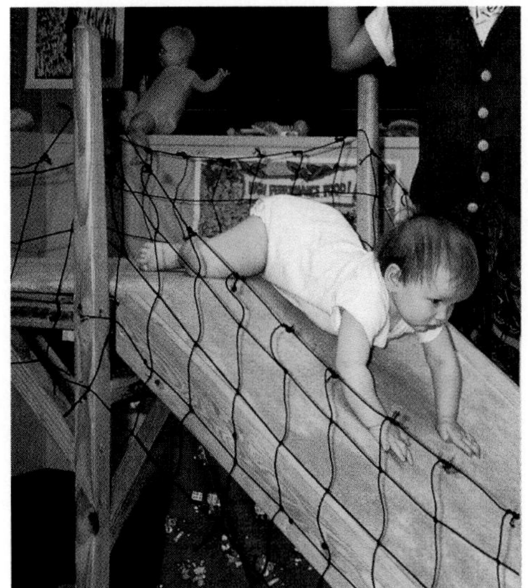

■ *Perception is guided by the discovery of* affordances. *The crawling infant on the left plunges headlong down a steeply sloping surface. He has not yet learned that it* affords *the possibility of falling. The newly walking toddler on the right approaches the slope more cautiously. Experience in trying to remain upright but frequently tumbling over has made him more aware of the consequences of his actions in this situation. He perceives the incline differently than he did at a younger age. (Courtesy of Karen Adolph, Emory University.)*

The Gibsons use the word *differentiation* (meaning analyze or break down) to describe their theory because over time, babies make finer and finer distinctions among stimuli. In addition to pattern perception, differentiation applies to depth and object perception. Recall how in each, sensitivity to motion precedes awareness of detailed stationary cues. So one way of understanding perceptual development is to think of it as a built-in tendency to search for order and stability in the surrounding world, a capacity that becomes increasingly fine-tuned with age (Gibson, 1970; Gibson, 1979).

Acting on the environment plays a major role in perceptual differentiation. According to the Gibsons, perception is guided by discovery of **affordances**—the action possibilities a situation offers an organism with certain motor capabilities (Gibson, 1988). As adults, we know when we can execute particular actions—when an object can be touched or a surface is appropriate for sitting or walking. Infants build these associations as they act on their world. For example, when they move from crawling to walking, they first realize that a steeply sloping surface *affords the possibility of falling* (they hesitate to go down it). Experience in trying to remain upright but frequently tumbling over on various surfaces seems to make new walkers more aware of the consequences of their actions in different situations. As a result, they differentiate surfaces in new ways and act more competently when confronted with them (Adolph, Eppler, & Gibson, 1993). Can you think of other links between motor milestones and perceptual development described in this chapter?

At this point, it is only fair to note that some researchers believe babies do not just make sense of their world by detecting invariant features and discovering affordances. Instead, they impose *meaning* on what they perceive, constructing categories of objects and events in the surrounding environment. We have seen the glimmerings of this cognitive point of view in this chapter. For example, older babies interpret a happy voice and face as a source of pleasure and affection and a pattern of blinking lights as a moving human being. We will save our discussion of infant cognition for later chapters, acknowledging for now that the cognitive perspective also has merit in understanding the achievements of infancy. In fact, many researchers combine these two positions, regarding infant development as proceeding from a perceptual to a cognitive emphasis over the first year of life (Mandler, 1992a; Salapatek & Cohen, 1987).

BRIEF REVIEW

Recent research has greatly expanded our understanding of infant perceptual development. Sensitivity to touch, taste, smell, and sound are well developed in the newborn baby. During the first year, infants organize sounds into more complex patterns and become sensitive to the sounds of their own language. Of all the senses, vision is least mature at birth. Visual acuity, scanning, tracking, and color perception improve during the early months. Depth perception develops as infants detect kinetic, binocular, and pictorial cues. Experience in

Affordances
The action possibilities a situation offers an organism with certain motor capabilities. Discovery of affordances is believed to guide perceptual development.

independent movement influences avoidance of heights as well as other aspects of three-dimensional understanding. Gradually, babies move from focusing on the parts of a pattern to perceiving it as an organized whole. Size and shape constancy are present at birth. At first, infants distinguish objects by attending to their motion and spatial arrangement; only later do they respond to stationary cues. Young babies have a remarkable ability to combine information across sensory modalities. The Gibsons's differentiation theory provides an overall account of perceptual development.

Early Deprivation and Enrichment: Is Infancy a Sensitive Period of Development?

Throughout this chapter, we have discussed how a variety of early experiences affect the development of perceptual and motor skills. In view of the findings already reported, it is not surprising that many investigations have found that stimulating physical surroundings and warm caregiving that is responsive to infants' self-initiated efforts promote active exploration of the environment and earlier achievement of developmental milestones (see, for example, Bendersky & Lewis, 1994; Bradley et al., 1989).

The powerful effect of early experience is dramatically apparent in the development of infants who lack the rich, varied stimulation of normal homes. Babies reared in severely deprived family situations or institutions show delays in early motor milestones, typically engage in stereotyped, immature play, and are overly fearful of new situations that present attractive opportunities for exploration (Collard, 1971). Although these children eventually catch up in motor functioning, their mental development remains substantially behind throughout childhood and adolescence (Dennis & Najarian, 1957; Fujinaga et al., 1990).

Although these findings indicate that early experience has a profound impact on development, they do not tell us for sure whether infancy is a sensitive period. That is, if babies do not experience appropriate stimulation of their senses in the first year or two of life, will there be lasting deficits from which they cannot fully recover? This question is highly controversial. Recall from Chapter 1 (see page 7) that some theorists argue that early experience leaves a lasting imprint on the child's competence. Others believe that experience operates much like a tape recording that can be made and erased. According to this view, the child's previous adaptations, and the events that led up to them, can be overcome by the quality of the current environment.

For ethical reasons, we cannot deliberately deprive some infants of normal rearing experiences and wait to observe the long-term consequences. However, several natural experiments in which children were victims of deprived early environments but were later exposed to stimulating, sensitive care provide the best available test of whether infancy is a sensitive period. A unique feature of these studies is that they allow us to examine the long-term effects of early deprivation without the contaminating influence of later deprivation. If the sensitive period hypothesis is correct, then the impact of deprivation during infancy should persist, even when children are moved into enriched settings.

In one study of this kind, Wayne Dennis (1973) followed the development of children who were placed in a Lebanese orphanage shortly after birth. Through most of the first year, they lay in their cribs and received practically no individual attention from caregivers. Extreme retardation in motor and language development resulted. Many did not sit up until 1 year of age or walk until well into the preschool years. Their IQs between 1 and 6 years were severely depressed, averaging only 53. In 1957, adoption was legalized in Lebanon, and children of a variety of ages left the orphanage for normal homes. By comparing those adopted early (before 2 years of age) with those adopted later, Dennis tested the sensitive period hypothesis. Findings showed that children adopted before age 2 overcame their earlier retardation, achieving an average IQ of 100 within 2 years. In contrast, those adopted later gained steadily in IQ during childhood but never fully recovered. After 6 to 8 years with their adoptive families, their IQs were only in the high 70s. Dennis concluded that environmental improvement by age 2 is necessary for complete recovery of deprived infants.

A more recent study suggests that less severe early deprivation can also have lasting consequences. Alan Sroufe, Byron Egeland, and Terri Kreutzer (1990) charted the experiences and competencies of a group of low-income children from infancy through middle childhood. Then they looked to see if early measures—attachment of infants to their mothers, exploration and problem solving at age 2, and quality of the home environment during the third year—added anything to later assessments in predicting cognitive, emotional, and social competence in childhood. Each of the early measures remained important. In addition, among children exposed to stresses during the preschool years, those with the greatest capacity for rebound in middle childhood had a history of positive adaptation during infancy (see Figure 4.20).

Unfortunately, most infants reared in underprivileged environments continue to be affected by disadvantaged conditions during their childhood years. Interventions that try to break this pattern by training caregivers to engage in warm, stimulating behaviors are highly effective and have lasting benefits (Andrews et al., 1982; Hunt et al., 1976). One of the most important outcomes of these programs is that passive, apathetic babies become active, alert beings with the capacity to evoke positive interactions from caregivers and initiate stimulating play for themselves.

Finally, it is important to keep in mind that besides impoverished environments, ones that overwhelm children with expectations beyond their current capacities also undermine development. In recent years, expensive early learning centers have sprung up around the United States in which infants are trained with letter and number flash cards and slightly older toddlers are given a full curriculum of reading, math, art, music, gym, and more. There is no evidence that these programs yield smarter, better "super babies." Instead, trying to prime infants with stimulation for which they are not ready can cause them to withdraw, threatening their spontaneous interest and pleasure in learning (Roe et al., 1991). In addition, when such programs promise but do not produce young geniuses, they are likely to lead to disappointed parents who view their children as failures at a very tender age (White, 1990). Thus, they rob infants of a psychologically healthy start on the road to maturity, and they deprive parents of relaxed, pleasurable participation in their children's early growth.

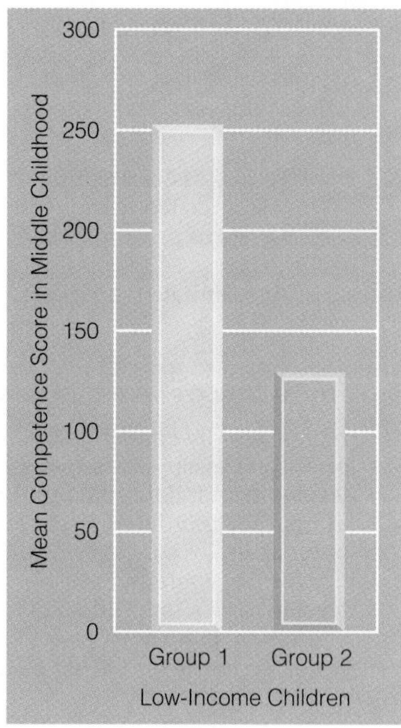

FIGURE 4.20

■ *Is infancy a sensitive period of development? In a recent study, two groups of low-income children were compared. Group 1 had a history of positive adaptation in infancy but then showed poor adaptation during the preschool years. Group 2 showed poor adaptation in both early and later periods. The first group displayed a much greater capacity for rebound in middle childhood, scoring more than twice as high on a measure of overall competence. (Adapted from Sroufe, Egeland, & Kreutzer, 1990.)*

SUMMARY

THE ORGANIZED NEWBORN

- Infants begin life with remarkable skills for relating to their physical and social worlds. **Reflexes** are the newborn baby's most obvious organized patterns of behavior. Some have survival value, whereas others provide the foundation for voluntary motor skills that will develop later.
- The neonate has a sleep–waking cycle that becomes more organized and patterned with age. Although newborns alternate frequently among various **states of arousal**, they spend most of their time asleep. Sleep consists of at least two states: **rapid-eye-movement (REM)** and **non-rapid-eye-movement (NREM) sleep**. REM sleep time is greater during the newborn period than at any later age. According to **autostimulation** theory, REM sleep provides young infants with stimulation essential for central nervous system development.
- A crying baby stimulates strong feelings of discomfort in nearby adults. The intensity of the cry and the events that led up to it help parents figure out what is wrong. Once feeding and diaper changing have been tried, lifting the baby to the shoulder is the most effective soothing technique. Ethological and behaviorist theories disagree on how promptly caregivers should respond to infant cries. A shrill, piercing cry is an indicator of central nervous system distress.
- The most widely used instrument for assessing the behavior of newborn infants is Brazelton's **Neonatal Behavioral Assessment Scale (NBAS)**. The NBAS has helped researchers understand individual and cultural differences in newborn behavior. Sometimes it is used to teach parents about their baby's capacities and unique characteristics.
- In **classical conditioning**, a neutral stimulus is paired with an **unconditioned stimulus (UCS)** that produces a reflexive, or **unconditioned, response (UCR)**. Once learning has occurred, the neutral stimulus, now called the **conditioned stimulus (CS)**, elicits the response, which is called the **conditioned response (CR)**. Young infants can be classically

conditioned when the pairing of a UCS with a CS has survival value. **Operant conditioning** of infants has been demonstrated in many studies. In addition to food, interesting sights and sounds serve as effective reinforcers, increasing the occurrence of a preceding behavior.

- **Habituation–dishabituation** research reveals that at birth, babies are attracted to novelty. Their ability to remember a wide variety of previously experienced stimuli improves over the first year. Newborn infants also have a remarkable capacity to **imitate** the facial expressions and gestures of adults.

MOTOR DEVELOPMENT IN INFANCY

- Infants' rapidly emerging motor skills support other aspects of development. Like physical development, motor development follows the **cephalocaudal** and **proximodistal trends**. According to **dynamic systems theory**, new motor skills are a matter of combining existing skills into increasingly complex systems of action. Each new skill develops as a joint product of central nervous system maturation, movement possibilities of the body, environmental supports for the skill, and the child's motivation to accomplish a task.
- Experience profoundly affects motor development, as shown by research on infants raised in deprived institutions. Stimulation of infant motor skills accounts for cross-cultural differences in motor development. During the first year, infants gradually perfect their reaching and grasping. The poorly coordinated **prereaching** of the newborn period eventually drops out. Once voluntary reaching appears, the clumsy **ulnar grasp** is gradually transformed into a refined **pincer grasp**.

PERCEPTUAL DEVELOPMENT IN INFANCY

- The study of infant perception sheds light on the nature–nurture controversy and helps us understand many aspects of psychological development. The senses of touch, taste, smell, and hearing are well developed at birth. Over the first year, babies organize sounds into more complex patterns. Newborns are especially responsive to high-pitched expressive voices, prefer the sound of their mother's voice, and can distinguish almost all sounds in human languages.
- Vision is the least mature of the newborn baby's senses. As the eye and visual centers in the brain mature during the first few months, focusing ability, **visual acuity**, scanning, tracking, and color perception improve rapidly.
- Depth perception helps infants understand the layout of the environment and guides motor activity. Responsiveness to **kinetic depth cues** appears by the end of the first month, followed by sensitivity to **binocular depth cues** between 3 and 6 months. Perception of **pictorial depth cues** emerges last, between 6 and 7 months of age. Experience in moving about independently enhances babies' three-dimensional understanding, including avoidance of edges and drop-offs, such as the deep side of the **visual cliff**.
- **Contrast sensitivity** accounts for infants' early pattern preferences. At first, babies look at the border of a stimulus and at single features. Around 2 months, they explore the internal features of a pattern, and soon they combine pattern elements into a unified whole. Over the first year, infants discriminate increasingly complex, meaningful patterns, including subjective forms based on moving lights. Perception of the human face follows the same sequence of development as sensitivity to other patterned stimuli. Between 7 and 10 months, babies react to emotional expressions as organized wholes.
- Infants gradually build a visual world made up of stable, three-dimensional objects. At birth, **size and shape constancy** help infants organize their perceptual experiences. The movement of objects relative to one another and their background enables infants to construct a visual world of independently existing objects.
- Infants have a remarkable, built-in capacity to engage in **intermodal perception**. Although many intermodal associations are learned, babies acquire them quickly, often after just one exposure to a new situation.
- **Differentiation theory** is the most widely accepted account of perceptual development. Over time, infants detect increasingly fine-grained, **invariant features** in a constantly changing perceptual world. Perception is guided by discovery of **affordances**—the action possibilities a situation offers the individual.

EARLY DEPRIVATION AND ENRICHMENT: IS INFANCY A SENSITIVE PERIOD OF DEVELOPMENT?

- Theorists disagree on whether infancy is a sensitive period in which warm caregiving and appropriate stimulation of the senses have a lasting impact on development. Research indicates that early experience combines with current conditions to affect the child's development. Recovery from a deprived early environment can occur if rearing conditions improve, but it may not be complete.

IMPORTANT TERMS AND CONCEPTS

reflex (p. 124)
states of arousal (p. 127)
rapid-eye-movement (REM) sleep (p. 129)
non-rapid-eye-movement (NREM) sleep (p. 129)
autostimulation theory (p. 130)
Neonatal Behavioral Assessment Scale (NBAS) (p. 132)
classical conditioning (p. 134)
unconditioned stimulus (UCS) (p. 134)
unconditioned response (UCR) (p. 134)
conditioned stimulus (CS) (p. 135)
conditioned response (CR) (p. 135)
extinction (p. 135)
operant conditioning (p. 136)
reinforcer (p. 136)
punishment (p. 136)
habituation (p. 136)
dishabituation (p. 137)
sudden infant death syndrome (SIDS) (p. 137)
imitation (p. 139)
cephalocaudal trend (p. 142)
proximodistal trend (p. 142)
dynamic systems theory (p. 142)
prereaching (p. 144)
ulnar grasp (p. 144)
pincer grasp (p. 144)
visual acuity (p. 150)
visual cliff (p. 151)
kinetic depth cues (p. 152)
binocular depth cues (p. 152)
pictorial depth cues (p. 152)
contrast sensitivity (p. 154)
size constancy (p. 157)
shape constancy (p. 157)
intermodal perception (p. 159)
differentiation theory (p. 160)
invariant features (p. 160)
affordances (p. 161)

CONNECTIONS for Chapter 4

If you are interested in . . .	turn to . . .	to learn about . . .
Assessment in infancy	Chapter 3, p. 105	Assessing the newborn's physical condition: The Apgar scale
	Chapter 8, p. 310	Infant intelligence tests
	Chapter 10, pp. 408–409	Assessing infant-caregiver attachment security
Early learning	Chapter 6, pp. 214–217	Piaget's sensorimotor stage
	Chapter 6, pp. 220–221	Early development of imitation and categorization
	Chapter 7, pp. 274–275	Recall in infancy
	Chapter 7, pp. 279–280	Infantile amnesia
	Chapter 9, pp. 349–352	Prelinguistic development
	Chapter 10, p. 390	Beginnings of emotional self-regulation
	Chapter 11, pp. 425–426	Emergence of self-recognition
	Chapter 12, pp. 486–487	Beginnings of self-control
	Chapter 15, p. 581	Beginnings of peer sociability
Sensitive periods of development	Chapter 1, pp. 23–24	Ethological theory, imprinting, and the sensitive period concept
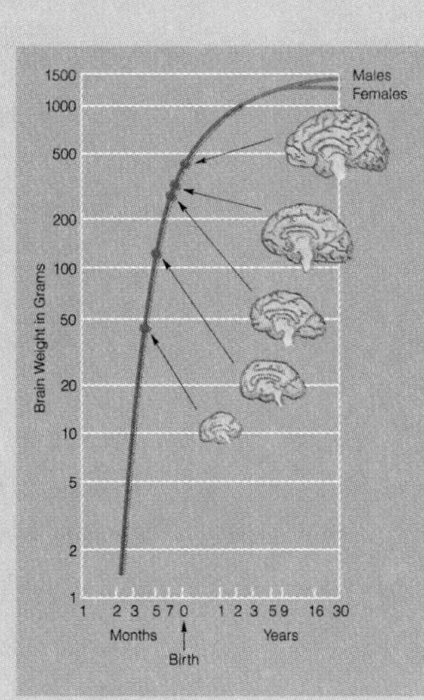	Chapter 3, pp. 92–93	Sensitive periods during prenatal development
	Chapter 5, pp. 196–197	Brain growth spurts and sensitive periods of development
	Chapter 9, p. 347	Sensitive period for language development
	Chapter 10, p. 410	Maternal deprivation in infancy

5 Physical Growth

As time passes during the first two decades of life, the human body changes continuously and dramatically, until it reaches the mature adult state. Think, for a moment, about the vast physical differences between a newborn baby and a full-grown young adult. From birth to maturity, the average individual's height multiplies more than threefold, and weight increases as much as fifteen- to twentyfold. The top-heavy, chubby infant, whose head represents a quarter of the body's total length, gradually becomes the better proportioned child and eventually the taller, broader, more muscular adolescent, whose head takes up only a seventh of the body's total length.

As we examine these changes closely, you will quickly see that the story of physical growth is not just a matter of becoming taller and larger. Instead, it involves a complex series of changes in body size, proportion, and composition. This chapter traces the course of human growth, along with biological and environmental factors that regulate and control it. We also consider how the brain develops and how it depends on precise interaction between the environment and maturing nerve cells.

Throughout our discussion, we will encounter many examples of the close link between physical and psychological development. But just how the child's transforming body is related to cognitive, emotional, and social changes has puzzled philosophers and scientists for centuries. And more than any other phase of growth, they have pondered this question with respect to **puberty**, the flood of biological events leading to an adult-sized body and sexual maturity at adolescence. When you next have a chance, ask several new parents what they expect their sons and daughters to be like as teenagers. You will probably get answers like these: "Rebellious and uncontrollable." "Full of rages and tempers." This view, widespread in contemporary American society, dates back to the writings of the eighteenth-century philosopher Jean-Jacques Rousseau, to whom you were introduced in Chapter 1. Rousseau believed that a natural outgrowth of the biological upheaval of puberty was heightened emotionality, conflict, and defiance of adults. Comparing adolescence to a violent storm, he cautioned parents:

> As the roaring of the waves precedes the tempest, so the murmur of rising passions . . . warns us of the approaching danger. A change of temper, frequent outbreaks of anger, a perpetual stirring of the mind, make the child ungovernable. . . . Keep your hand upon the helm or all is lost. (Rousseau, 1762/1955, pp. 172–173)

Although Rousseau's impressions were not based on scientific evidence, they were nevertheless picked up and extended by twentieth-century theorists. The most influential was G. Stanley Hall, whose view of development was grounded in Darwin's theory of evolution (see Chapter 1, page 12). Hall (1904) described adolescence as a cascade of instinctual passions, a phase of growth so turbulent that it resembled the period in which human beings evolved from savages into civilized beings.

Were Rousseau and Hall correct in this image of adolescence as a biologically determined, inevitable period of storm and stress? Or do social and cultural factors combine with biological change to shape psychological development? In the course of our discussion, we will see what modern research has to say about this issue.

Puberty
Biological changes during adolescence that lead to an adult-sized body and sexual maturity.

The Course of Physical Growth

Compared to other animals, primates (including humans) experience a prolonged period of physical growth. For example, among mice and rats, the time between birth and puberty is only a matter of weeks; it takes no more than 2 percent of the life span. In chimpanzees, who are closest to humans in the evolutionary hierarchy, growth is extended to about 7 years, or one-sixth of the life span. Physical immaturity is even more exaggerated in humans, who devote about one-fifth of their total years to growing.

Evolutionary reasons for this long period of physical growth are not hard to find. Because physical immaturity ensures that children remain dependent on adults, it provides added time for them to acquire the knowledge and skills necessary for life in a complex social world. In the words of anthropologist Weston LaBarre (1954), "Biologically, it takes more time to become human. Obviously, too, it is the human brain and human learning that gain particular advantages from this biological slow-down" (p. 153).

CHANGES IN BODY SIZE

To parents, the most obvious signs of physical growth are changes in the size of the child's body as a whole. During infancy, these changes are rapid—faster than they will be at any time after birth. By the end of the first year, the infant's height is 50 percent greater than it was at birth; and by 2 years, it is 75 percent greater. Weight shows similar dramatic gains. By 5 months, birth weight has doubled, at 1 year it has tripled, and at 2 years it has quadrupled. In fact, if children kept growing at the rate they do during the early months of life, by age 10 they would be 10 feet tall and weigh over 200 pounds! Fortunately, growth slows in early and middle childhood. Children add about 2 to 3 inches in height and 5 pounds in weight each year. Then, puberty brings a sharp acceleration in rate of growth. On the average, adolescents add nearly 10 inches in height and about 40 pounds in weight to reach a mature body size.

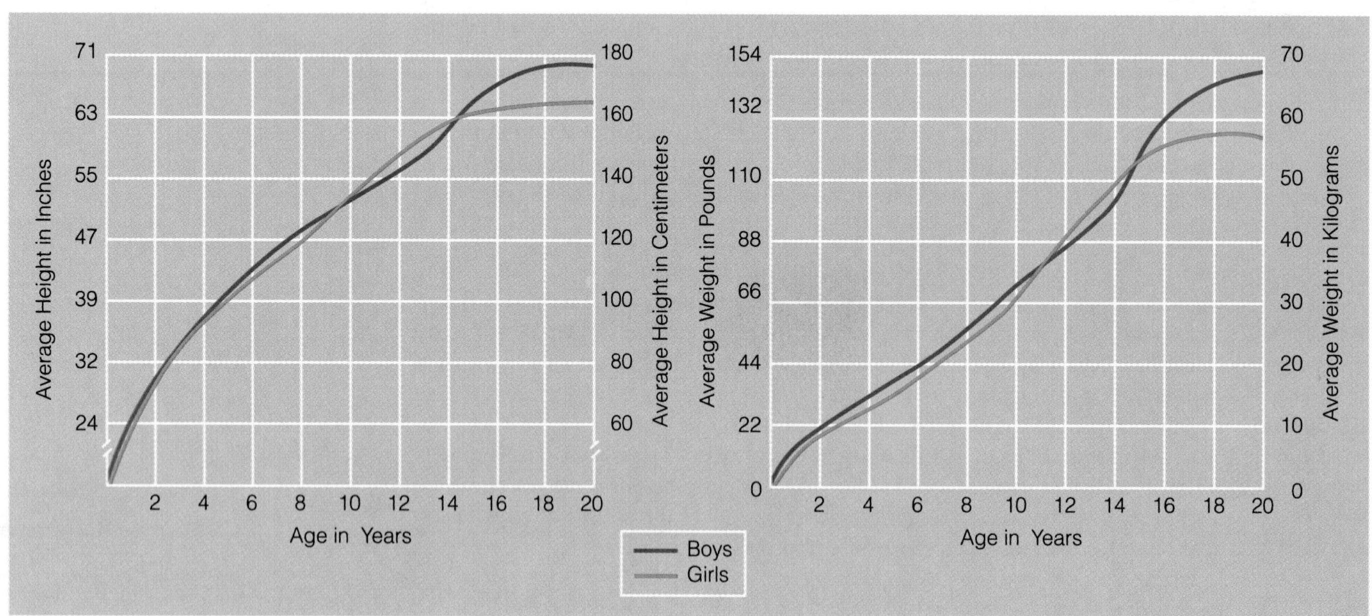

FIGURE 5.1

Height and weight distance curves for boys and girls, drawn from longitudinal measurements on approximately 175 individuals. (From R. M. Malina, 1975, Growth and Development: The First Twenty Years in Man, *p. 19. Minneapolis: Burgess Publishing Company. Copyright © 1975 by Burgess Publishing Company. Adapted by permission.)*

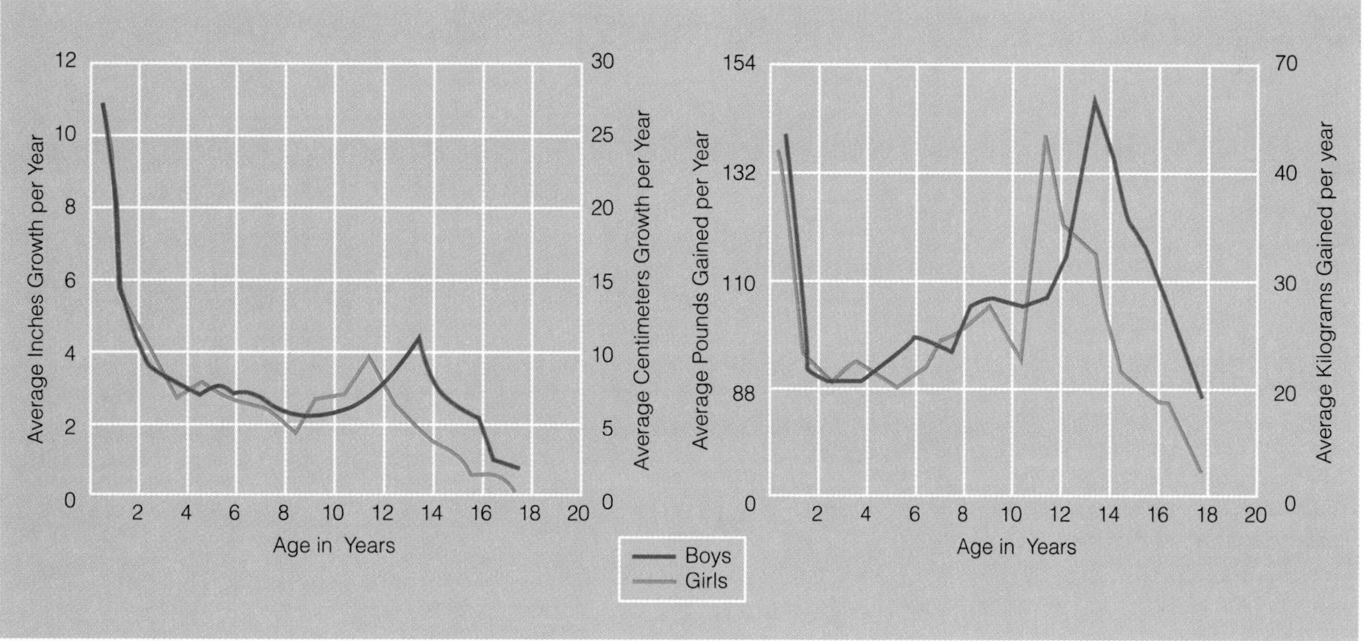

FIGURE 5.2

Height and weight velocity curves for boys and girls, drawn from longitudinal measurements on approximately 175 individuals. (From R. M. Malina, 1975, Growth and Development: The First Twenty Years in Man, *p. 20. Minneapolis: Burgess Publishing Company. Copyright © 1975 by Burgess Publishing Company. Adapted by permission.)*

Two types of growth curves are used to track these changes in height and weight. The first, shown in Figure 5.1, is a **distance curve**, which plots the average height and weight of a sample of children at each age. It is called a distance curve because it indicates typical yearly progress toward mature body size. The group averages are referred to as *growth norms* and serve as useful standards to which individual children can be compared. Other information about growth can also be obtained from these curves. Notice how during infancy and childhood the two sexes are similar, with the typical girl just slightly shorter and lighter than the typical boy. Around age 11, the girl becomes taller and heavier for a time because her pubertal growth spurt takes place 2 years earlier than the boy's. But this advantage is short-lived. At age 14, she is surpassed by the typical boy, whose growth spurt has started, whereas hers is almost finished. Growth in height is complete for most North American and European girls by age 16, for boys by age 17 ½ (Tanner, 1990).

A second type of growth curve is the **velocity curve**, depicted in Figure 5.2. It plots the average amount of growth at each yearly interval. As a result, it is much better than the distance curve in revealing the exact timing of growth spurts. Note the rapid but decelerating growth in infancy; a slower, constant rate of growth during childhood; and a sharp increase in growth in early adolescence followed by a swift decrease as the body approaches its adult size.

Since these overall growth trends are derived from group averages, they are deceiving in one respect. Researchers who have carefully tracked height changes of individual children report that rather than steady gains, little growth spurts occur. In one investigation, infants followed over the first 21 months of life went for periods of 7 to 63 days with no growth and then added as much as a half-inch in a 24-hour period. Almost always, parents described their babies as irritable, restless, and very hungry on the day before the spurt (Lampl, 1993; Lampl, Veldhuis, & Johnson, 1992). A study of Scottish children, who were followed between the ages of 3 and 10, revealed similar but more widely spaced spurts in height. Girls tended to forge ahead at ages 4 ½, 6 ½, 8 ½, and 10, boys slightly later, at 4 ½, 7, 9, and 10 ½. In between these spurts were lulls in which growth was slower (Butler, McKie, & Ratcliffe, 1990).

■ *The pubertal growth spurt takes place, on the average, 2 years earlier for girls than for boys. Although these adolescents are the same age, the girl is much taller and more mature looking. (Tony Freeman/ PhotoEdit)*

Distance curve
A growth curve that plots the average height and weight of a sample of children at each age. Shows typical yearly progress toward mature body size.

Velocity curve
A growth curve that plots the average amount of growth at each yearly interval for a sample of children. Clarifies the timing of growth spurts.

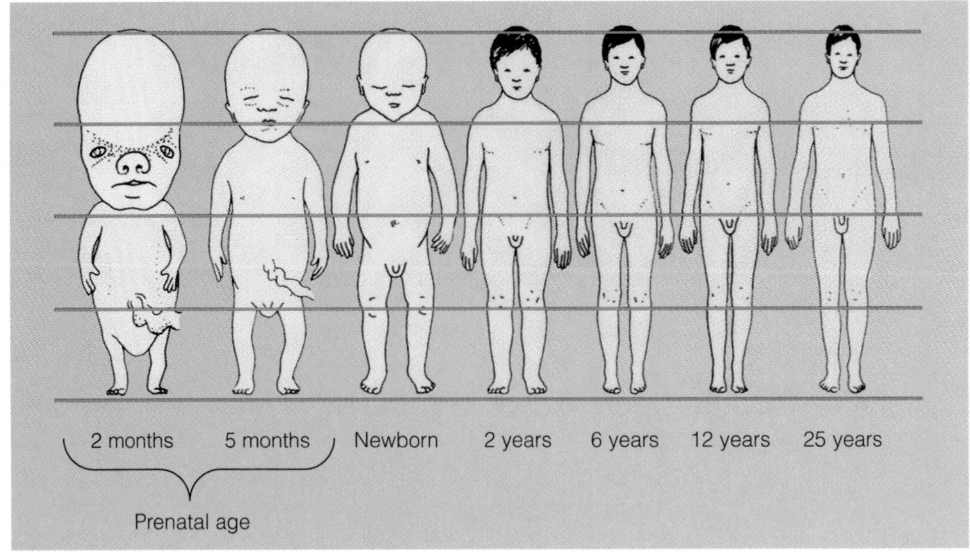

FIGURE 5.3

■ *Changes in body proportions from the early prenatal period to adulthood. This figure illustrates the cephalocaudal trend of physical growth. The head gradually becomes smaller, and the legs longer, in proportion to the rest of the body.*

CHANGES IN BODY PROPORTIONS

As the child's overall size increases, different parts of the body grow at different rates. Recall from Chapter 3 that during the prenatal period, the head develops first from the primitive embryonic disk, followed by the lower portion of the body. During infancy, the head and chest continue to have a growth advantage, but the trunk and legs gradually pick up speed. Do you recognize the familiar *cephalocaudal trend* we discussed in Chapter 4? You can see it depicted in Figure 5.3. Notice that the ratio of leg length to total height is less than 1:4 in the early prenatal period, increases to 1:3 at birth, and is 1:2 by adulthood. Physical growth during infancy and childhood also follows the *proximodistal trend.* It begins at the center of the body and moves outward, with the upper arms growing before the lower arms, which grow before the hands.

■ *Body proportions and muscle-fat makeup change dramatically between 1 and 5 years. The top-heavy, chubby infant gradually becomes the longer-legged, slender young child. (Bob Daemmrich/Stock Boston)*

Exceptions to these basic growth trends occur during puberty, when growth actually proceeds in the reverse direction. At first, the hands, legs, and feet accelerate, and then the torso, which accounts for most of the adolescent height gain (Wheeler, 1991). This pattern of development explains why young adolescents stop growing out of their shoes and pants before they stop growing out of their jackets. It also helps us understand why early adolescence is regarded as an awkward phase. Because growth is uneven, many young teenagers appear gawky and out of proportion—long legged with giant feet and hands.

Although body proportions of girls and boys are similar in infancy and childhood, major differences that are typical of young adults appear during adolescence. The most obvious are the broadening of the shoulders relative to the hips in boys and the broadening of the hips relative to the shoulders and waist in girls. These differences are caused by the action of sex hormones on skeletal growth. Of course, boys also end up much larger than girls, and their legs are longer in relation to the rest of the body. The major reason is that boys benefit from 2 extra years of preadolescent growth, when the legs are growing the fastest (Tanner, 1990).

CHANGES IN BODY COMPOSITION

Major changes in the body's muscle–fat makeup take place with age. Body fat (most of which lies just beneath the skin) begins to increase in the last few weeks of prenatal life and continues to do so after birth, reaching a peak at about 9 months of age. This very early rise in "baby fat" helps the small infant keep a constant body temperature. Then, beginning in the second year, children become more slender, a trend that continues into middle childhood. At birth, girls have slightly more body fat than boys, a difference that becomes greater over the course of childhood. Around age 8, girls start to add more fat than do boys on their arms, legs, and trunk, and they do so throughout puberty. In contrast, the arm and leg fat of adolescent boys decreases (Tanner & Whitehouse, 1975).

Muscle grows according to a different pattern than fat, accumulating very slowly throughout infancy and childhood. Then it rises dramatically at adolescence. Although

Skeletal age
An estimate of physical maturity based on development of the bones of the body.

Epiphyses
Growth centers in the bones where new cartilage cells are produced and gradually harden.

both sexes gain in muscle at puberty, the increase is much greater for boys, who develop larger skeletal muscles and hearts and a greater lung capacity. Also, the number of red blood cells, and therefore the ability to carry oxygen from the lungs to the muscles, increases in boys but not in girls (Katchadourian, 1977). The combined result of these changes is that boys gain far more muscle strength than do girls, a difference that contributes to boys' superior athletic performance during the teenage years. But size and strength cannot account for the childhood advantage of boys in a variety of gross motor skills. As the From Research to Practice box on page 172 reveals, beginning in the preschool years the social environment plays a prominent role.

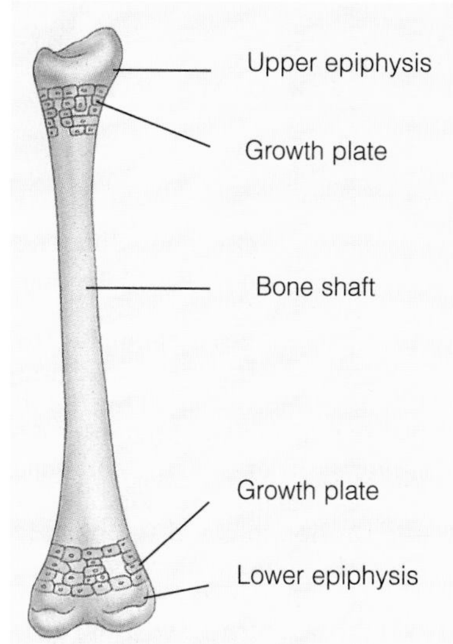

FIGURE 5.4

■ *Diagram of a long bone showing upper and lower epiphyses. Cartilage cells are produced at the growth plates and gradually harden into bone. (From J. M. Tanner, 1990,* Foetus into Man *(2nd ed.), Cambridge, MA: Harvard University Press, p. 32. Copyright © 1990 by J. M. Tanner. All rights reserved. Reprinted by permission of the publisher and author.)*

SKELETAL GROWTH

As we will see in a later section, children of the same age differ markedly in their rates of growth. As a result, researchers have devised methods for measuring progress toward physical maturity. These techniques are useful for studying the causes and consequences of individual differences in physical growth. They also provide rough estimates of children's chronological age in areas of the world where birth dates are not recorded.

■ SKELETAL AGE. The best way of estimating a child's physical maturity is to use **skeletal age**, a measure of development of the bones of the body. The embryonic skeleton is first formed out of soft, pliable tissue called *cartilage*. Then, beginning in the sixth week of pregnancy, cartilage cells harden into bone, a gradual process that continues throughout childhood and adolescence. Once bones have taken on their basic shape, special growth centers called **epiphyses** start to appear just before birth and increase throughout childhood. In the long bones of the body, epiphyses emerge at the two extreme ends of each bone (see Figure 5.4). As growth continues, the epiphyses get thinner and disappear. Once this occurs, no more growth of the bone is possible (Delecki, 1985). As Figure 5.5 shows, skeletal age can be estimated by X-raying the bones of the body and seeing how many epiphyses there are and the extent to which they are fused. These X-rays are compared to norms for bone maturity based on large representative samples of children (Malina & Bouchard, 1991).

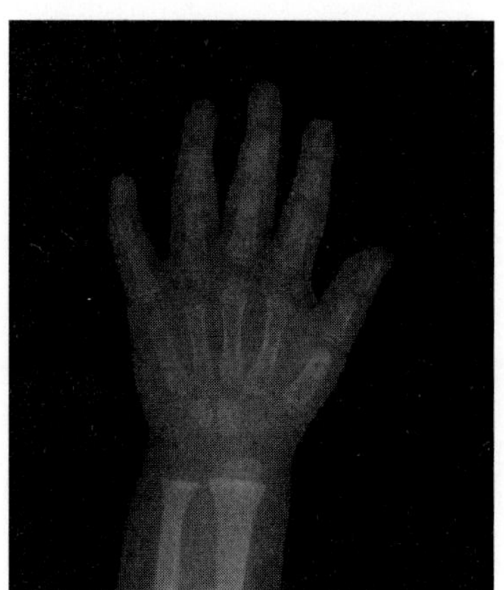

2½ years

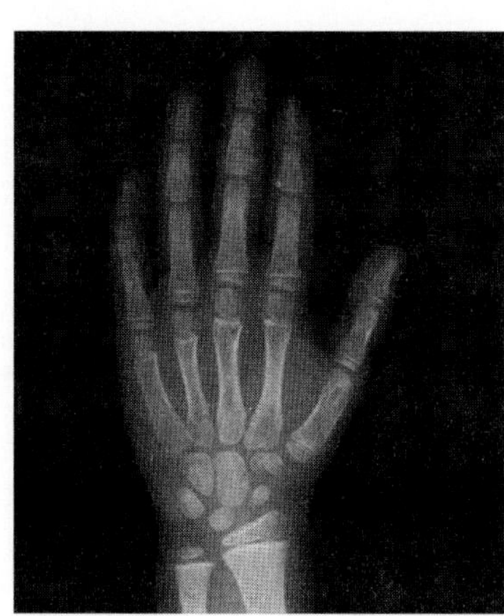

6½ years

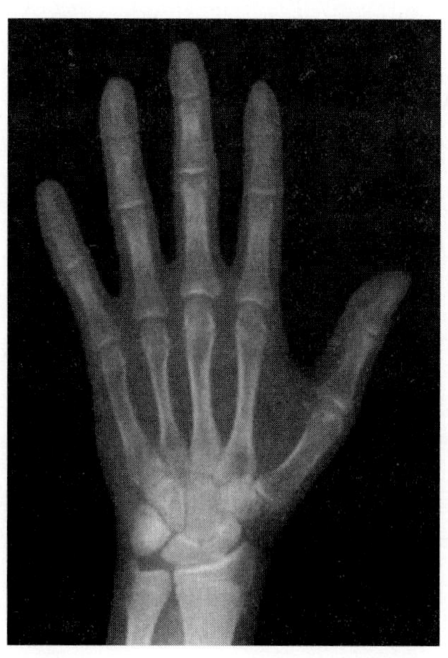

14½ years

FIGURE 5.5

■ *X-rays of a girl's hand, showing skeletal maturity at three ages. Notice how the wrist bones and epiphyses on the long bones of the fingers and forearms gradually close. (From J. M. Tanner, R. H. Whitehouse, N. Cameron, W. A. Marshall, M. J. R. Healey, & H. Goldstein, 1983,* Assessment of Skeletal Maturity and Prediction of Adult Height [TW2 Method], *2nd ed., Academic Press [London, Ltd.], p. 86. Reprinted by permission.)*

FROM RESEARCH TO PRACTICE

Sex-Related Differences in Motor Skills

Sex-related differences in motor development are present as early as the preschool years. Boys are slightly advanced over girls in abilities that emphasize force and power. By age 5, they can broad jump a little farther, run a little faster, and throw a ball much farther (about 5 feet beyond the distance covered by girls). Girls have an edge in fine motor skills of drawing and penmanship and in certain gross motor capacities that combine balance and foot movement, such as hopping and skipping. During middle childhood, these differences intensify. For example, a ball thrown by a 12-year-old boy travels, on the average, 43 feet farther than one thrown by a 12-year-old girl. Boys are also more adept at batting, kicking, dribbling, and catching (Cratty, 1986; Fischman, Moore, & Steele, 1992; Roberton, 1984).

Girls are ahead of boys in overall physical maturity, which may be partly responsible for their better balance and precision of movement. Boys' slightly greater muscle mass and (in the case of throwing) longer forearms probably contribute to their skill advantages. But sex-related differences in physical growth during childhood are not large enough to explain boys' superiority in so many gross motor capacities. Instead, adult encouragement and example are powerfully influential. From an early age, baseballs and footballs are purchased for boys; jump ropes, hula hoops, and games of jacks for girls. Although women's participation in athletics has increased since the 1970s, most public sports events continue to be dominated by males, a circumstance that provides few models of outstanding athletic accomplishment for girls (Coakley, 1990).

Parents also hold higher expectations for boys' athletic performance, and children absorb these social messages at an early age. In a study of over 800 elementary school pupils, kindergartners through third graders of both sexes viewed sports in a gender-stereotyped fashion—as much more important for boys. And boys more often stated that it was vital to their parents that they participate in athletics. These attitudes affected children's self-confidence and behavior. Girls saw themselves as having less talent at sports, and by sixth grade they devoted less time to athletics than did their male classmates (Eccles & Harold, 1991; Eccles, Jacobs, & Harold, 1990).

Not until puberty do sharp sex-related differences in physical size and muscle strength account for large differences in athletic ability. During adolescence, both sexes gain in gross motor performance, but girls' gains are slow and gradual, leveling off by age 14. In contrast, boys show a dramatic spurt in strength, speed, and endurance that continues through the end of the teenage years. Figure 5.6 illustrates this difference for running speed, broad jump, and throwing distance. Notice how the gender gap widens over time. By midadolescence, very few girls perform as well as the average boy, and practically no boys score as low as the average girl (Beunen et al., 1988).

The fact that the sexes are no longer evenly matched physically may heighten differential encouragement during the teenage years. Competence at sports is strongly related to peer admiration among adolescent boys, but it is not an important factor to girls. By high school, girls' sports participation falls far short of boys'. According to one recent esti-

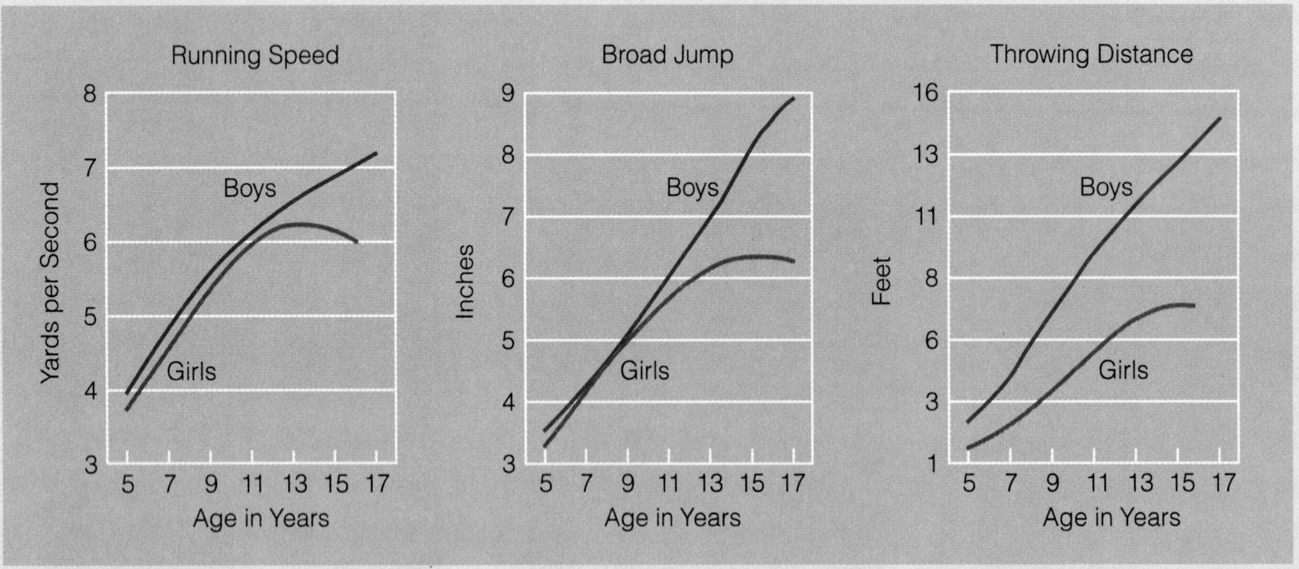

FIGURE 5.6

■ *Age changes in running speed, broad jump, and throwing distance for boys and girls. The gender gap in athletic performance widens during adolescence. (From A. Espenschade & H. Eckert, 1974, "Motor Development," in W. R. Warren & E. R. Buskirk, Eds.,* Science and Medicine of Exercise and Sport, *New York: Harper & Row, pp. 329–330. Adapted by permission of HarperCollins Publishers, Inc.)*

mate, about 64 percent of males but only 41 percent of females are active in high school athletics (Berk, 1992b).

Sports do not just improve motor performance. They influence cognitive and social development as well. Interschool and intramural athletics provide important lessons in competition, assertiveness, problem solving, and teamwork—experiences less available to girls. Clearly, special steps need to be taken to raise girls' confidence that they can do well at athletics. Educating parents about the minimal differences in school-age boys' and girls' physical capacities and sensitizing them to unfair biases against girls' athletic ability may prove helpful. In addition, greater emphasis on skill training, along with increased attention to the athletic achievements of girls, is likely to improve their participation and performance.

■ *These young softball players are likely to become far better at skills typically reserved for boys—batting, running, throwing, and catching—than their agemates who receive little encouragement for athletic participation. They are also learning important lessons in competition, assertiveness, problem solving, and teamwork. (Bob Daemmrich/Stock Boston)*

When the skeletal ages of infants and children are examined, African-American children tend to be slightly ahead of Caucasian-American children at all ages. In addition, girls are considerably ahead of boys. At birth, the difference between the sexes amounts to about 4 to 6 weeks, a gap that widens over infancy and childhood and is responsible for the fact that girls reach their full body size several years before boys. Girls are advanced in development of other organs as well. Their greater physical maturity may contribute to the fact that they are more resistant to harmful environmental influences. As we pointed out in Chapter 3, girls experience fewer developmental problems, and infant and childhood mortality for girls is also lower (Tanner, 1990).

■ GROWTH OF THE SKULL. Pediatricians are concerned with another aspect of skeletal development when they routinely measure children's head circumference during infancy. Skull growth is especially rapid during the first 2 years because of large increases in brain size. At birth, the bones of the skull are separated by six gaps, or "soft spots," called **fontanels** (see Figure 5.7 on page 174). The gaps permit the bones to overlap as the large head of the baby passes through the mother's narrow birth canal. You can easily feel the largest gap, the anterior fontanel, at the top of a baby's skull. It is slightly more than an inch across. It gradually shrinks and is filled in during the second year. The other fontanels are smaller and close more quickly. As the skull bones come in contact with one another, they form sutures, or seams. These permit the skull to expand easily as the brain grows. The sutures disappear completely after puberty, when skull growth is complete.

ASYNCHRONIES IN PHYSICAL GROWTH

From what you have learned so far, can you come up with a single overall description of physical growth? If you answered no to this question, you are correct. Figure 5.8 shows that physical growth is an *asynchronous* process. Different body systems have their own unique, carefully timed patterns of maturation. The **general growth curve** describes changes in overall body size (as measured by height and weight). It takes its name from the fact that outer dimensions of the body, as well as a variety of internal organs, follow

Fontanels
Six soft spots that separate the bones of the skull at birth.

General growth curve
Curve that represents overall changes in body size—rapid growth during infancy, slower gains in early and middle childhood, and rapid growth once more during adolescence.

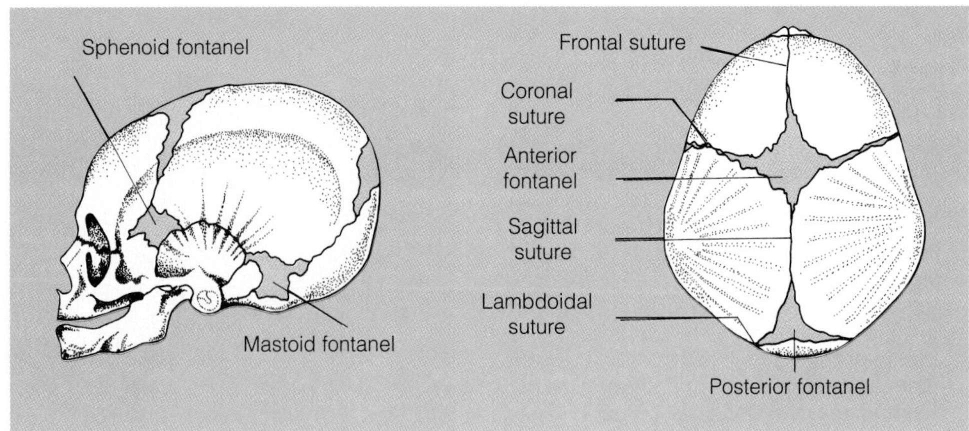

FIGURE 5.7

The skull at birth, showing the fontanels and sutures. (From P. M. Hill & P. Humphrey, 1982, Human Growth and Development Throughout Life, A Nursing Perspective, Albany, NY: Delmar Publishers, Inc., p. 42. Copyright 1982. Reprinted by permission.)

the same pattern—rapid growth during infancy, slower gains in early and middle childhood, and rapid growth again during adolescence.

Yet this trend has important exceptions. During the first few years, the brain grows faster than any other physical structure. The genitals show a slight rise from birth to age 4, followed by a period of little change throughout middle childhood, after which growth is especially rapid in adolescence. In contrast, lymph tissue (small clusters of glands found throughout the body) grows at an astounding pace throughout infancy and childhood, reaching a peak just before adolescence, at which point it declines. The lymph system plays a vital role in the body's ability to fight infection and also assists in the absorption of nutrients from foods (Malina & Bouchard, 1991). Rapid early growth of lymph tissue helps ensure children's health and survival.

INDIVIDUAL AND CULTURAL DIFFERENCES

Watch same-age children at play in any schoolyard, and you will see that they differ greatly in physical size. Most of this variation is within normal range. However, children at the far extremes—those who are either very large or very small for their age group—may have a serious growth problem, and they should be checked by a doctor (Tanner, 1990).

The diversity among children in physical growth is especially apparent when we travel to different nations. Measurements of 8-year-olds living in many parts of the world reveal a 9-inch gap between the smallest and largest youngsters. The shortest children tend to be found in South America, Asia, the Pacific Islands, and parts of Africa and include such ethnic groups as Colombian, Burmese, Thai, Vietnamese, Ethiopian, and Bantu. The tallest children reside in Australia, northern and central Europe, and the

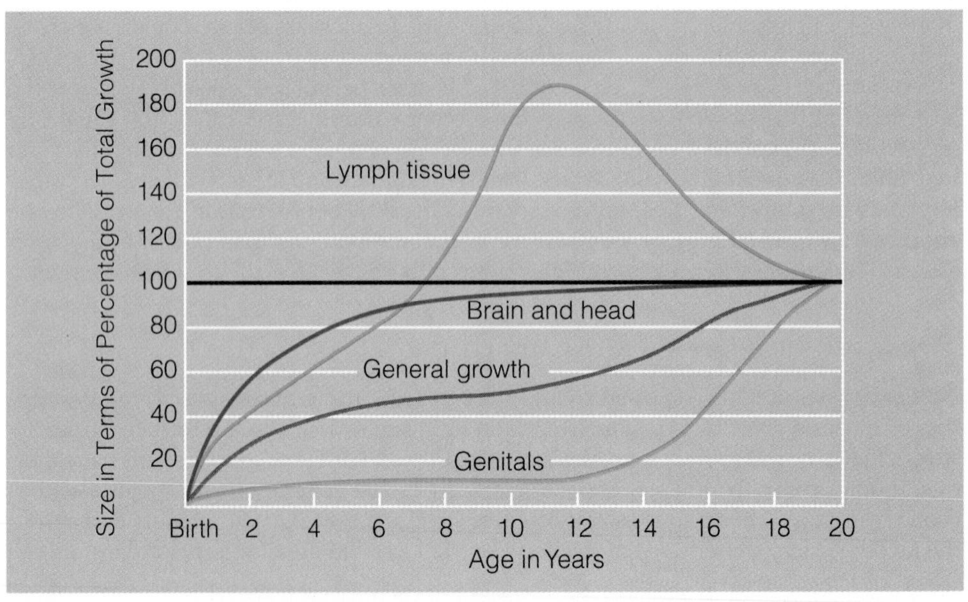

FIGURE 5.8

Growth of three different organ systems and tissues contrasted with the general growth curve. Growth is plotted in terms of percentage of change from birth to 20 years. Notice how the lymph tissue rises to twice its adult level by the end of childhood and then declines. (From J. M. Tanner, 1990, Foetus into Man *(2nd ed.), Cambridge, MA: Harvard University Press, p. 16. Copyright © 1990 by J. M. Tanner. All rights reserved. Reprinted by permission of the publisher and author.)*

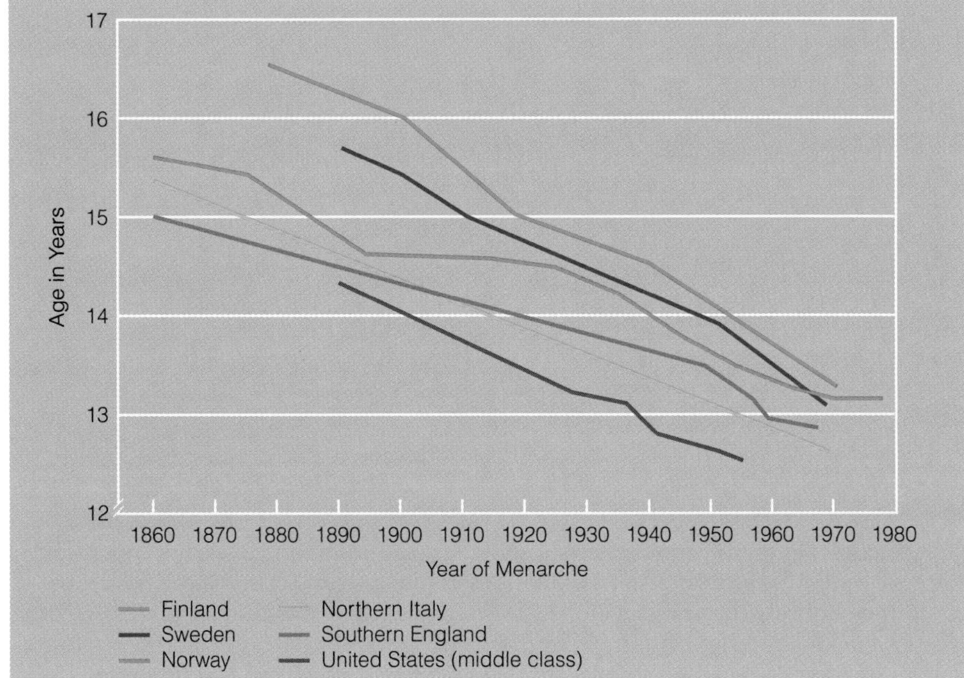

FIGURE 5.9

■ *Secular trend in age of first menstruation (menarche) from 1860 to 1970 in industrialized nations. Data for Norway, which extend to 1980, suggest that secular change has recently leveled off. (From J. M. Tanner, 1990,* Foetus into Man *(2nd ed.), Cambridge, MA: Harvard University Press, p. 160. Copyright © 1990 by J. M. Tanner. All rights reserved. Reprinted by permission of the publisher and author.)*

United States and consist of Czech, Dutch, Latvian, Norwegian, Swiss, and American black and white children (Meredith, 1978). Cultural differences in rate of growth are also common. For example, African-American and Asian children tend to mature faster than North American Caucasian children, who are slightly advanced over European children (Berkey et al., 1994; Eveleth & Tanner, 1990). These findings remind us that growth norms need to be interpreted cautiously, especially in countries like the United States, where many ethnic groups are represented.

What accounts for these vast differences in size and rate of growth? As we will see in greater detail at the end of this chapter, both heredity and environment are involved. Body size is sometimes the result of evolutionary adaptations to a particular climate. For example, long, lean physiques are typical in hot, tropical regions and short, stocky ones in cold, arctic areas. At the same time, children who grow tallest usually reside in developed countries, where food is plentiful and infectious diseases are largely controlled. In contrast, small children tend to live in less developed regions, where poverty, hunger, and disease are common (Tanner, 1990).

SECULAR TRENDS

Over the past century, **secular trends in physical growth**—changes in body size and rate of growth from one generation to the next—have taken place in industrialized nations. Most children today are taller and heavier than their parents and grandparents were as children. These trends have been found in nearly all European nations, in Japan, and among black and white children in the United States. The difference appears early in life and becomes greater over childhood and early adolescence. Then, as mature body size is reached, it declines. This pattern suggests that the larger size of modern children is mostly due to a faster rate of physical maturation. This speeding up of physical growth is especially apparent in age of first menstruation in girls. As Figure 5.9 shows, it declined steadily from 1860 to 1970, by about 3 to 4 months per decade.

Biologists believe improved nutrition and health are largely responsible for these secular gains. As evidence for these influences, orphaned babies from developing countries who are adopted by American parents often show faster physical growth and reach greater mature stature than do infants remaining in the land of origin. Furthermore, in many countries, secular trends are not as large for low-income children, who have poorer diets and are more likely to suffer from growth-stunting illnesses. And in regions of the world where poverty, famine, and disease are widespread, either no secular change or a secular decrease in body size has occurred (Barnes-Josiah & Augustin, 1995; Proos, 1993).

Secular trends in physical growth Changes in body size and rate of growth from one generation to the next.

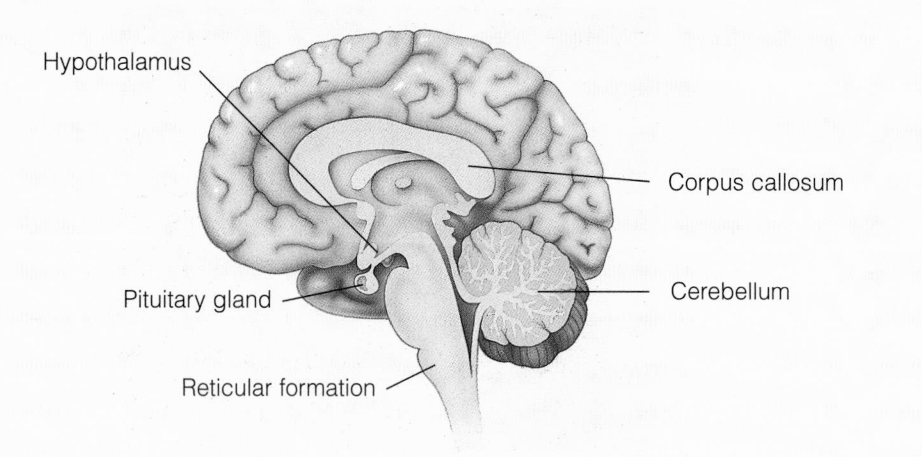

FIGURE 5.10

■ *Cross section of the human brain, showing the location of the hypothalamus and pituitary gland. Also shown are three additional structures—the cerebellum, the reticular formation, and the corpus callosum—that we will discuss in a later section.*

Of course, humans cannot keep growing larger and maturing earlier indefinitely, since we cannot exceed the genetic limitations of our species. Secular gains have slowed or stopped entirely in some developed countries, such as Canada, England, Sweden, Norway, Japan, and the United States (McAnarney et al., 1992; Roche, 1979). Consequently, modern children reared under good nutritional and social conditions are likely to resemble their parents in physical growth more than at any time during the previous 130 years.

HORMONAL INFLUENCES ON PHYSICAL GROWTH

The vast physical changes of childhood and adolescence are controlled by the endocrine glands of the body. These glands manufacture *hormones,* chemical substances secreted by specialized cells in one part of the body that pass to and influence cells in another. Because receptors in our cells respond to some hormones and not others, the action of each hormone is unique.

The most important hormones for human growth are released by the **pituitary gland**, which is located at the base of the brain near the **hypothalamus**, a structure that initiates and regulates pituitary secretions (see Figure 5.10). Once pituitary hormones enter the bloodstream, they act directly on body tissues to produce growth, or they stimulate the release of other hormones from endocrine glands located elsewhere in the body. The hypothalamus contains special receptors that detect hormone levels in the bloodstream. Through a highly sensitive feedback loop, it instructs the pituitary gland to increase or decrease the amount of each hormone. In this way, growth is carefully controlled. You may find it useful to refer to Figure 5.11 as we take up the major hormonal influences.

Growth hormone (GH) is the only pituitary secretion produced continuously throughout life. It affects the development of all body tissues, except the central nervous system and the genitals. GH acts directly on body tissues but also accomplishes its task with the help of an intermediary. It stimulates the liver and epiphyses of the skeleton to release another hormone called *somatomedin,* which triggers cell duplication in the bones. Although GH does not seem to affect prenatal growth, it is necessary for physical development from birth on. Children who lack it reach an average mature height of only 4 feet, 4 inches. When treated with injections of GH, such children grow faster than expected (a phenomenon called *catch-up growth,* discussed later in this chapter) and then continue to grow at a normal rate. Reaching their genetically expected height, however, depends on starting treatment early, before the epiphyses of the skeleton are very mature (Tanner, 1990).

Together, the hypothalamus and pituitary gland also prompt the thyroid gland (located in the neck) to release **thyroxine**, which is necessary for normal development of the nerve cells of the brain and for GH to have its full impact on body size. Infants born with a deficiency of thyroxine must receive it at once, or they will be mentally retarded. At later ages, children with too little thyroxine grow at a below-average rate. However, the central nervous system is no longer affected, since the most rapid period of brain

Pituitary gland
A gland located near the base of the brain that releases hormones affecting physical growth.

Hypothalamus
A structure located at the base of the brain that initiates and regulates pituitary secretions.

Growth hormone (GH)
A pituitary hormone that affects the development of all body tissues, except the central nervous system and the genitals.

Thyroxine
A hormone released by the thyroid gland that is necessary for central nervous system development and body growth.

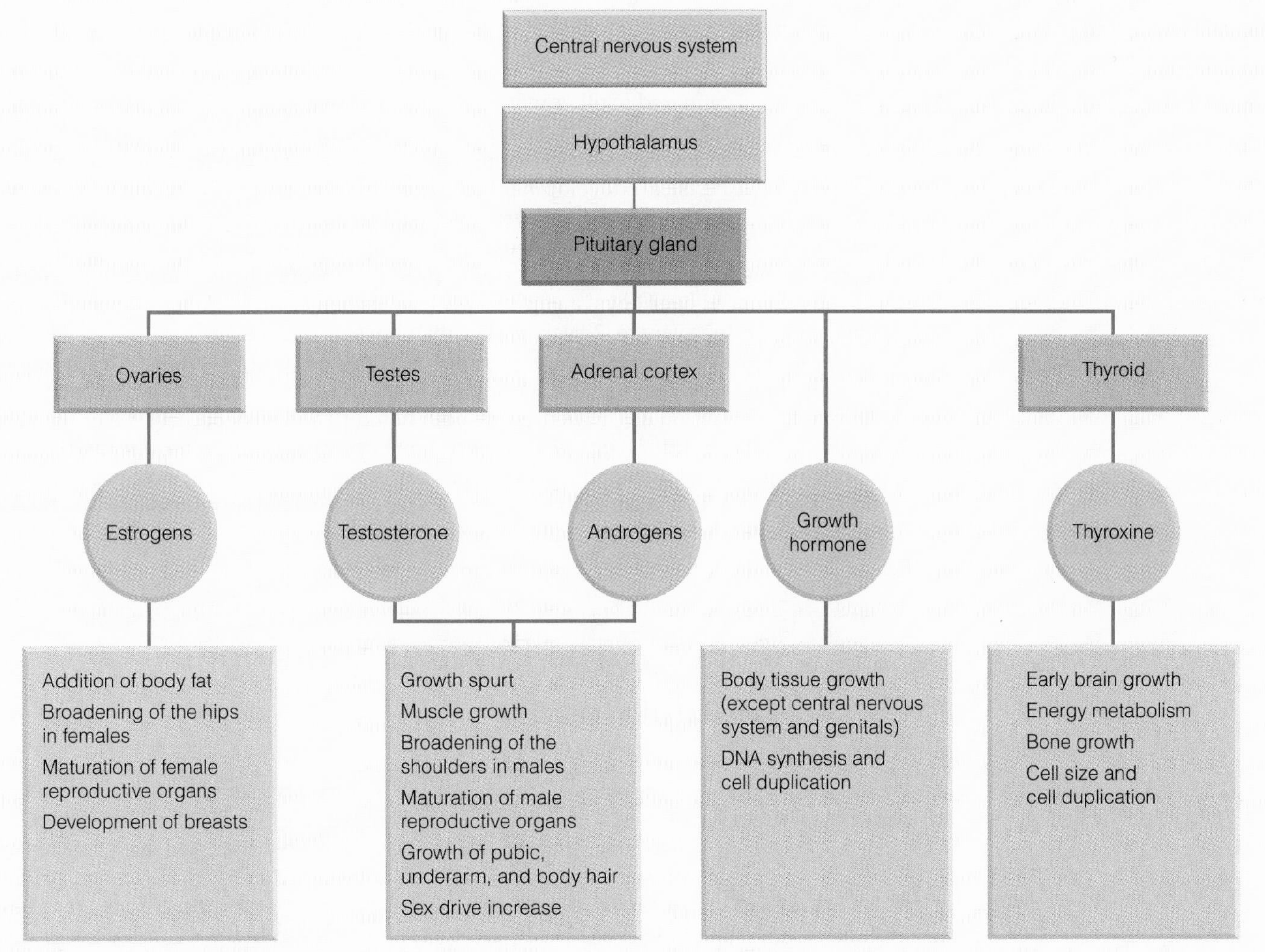

FIGURE 5.11

■ *Hormonal influences on postnatal growth.*

development is complete. With prompt treatment, such children catch up in body growth and eventually reach normal size (Tanner, 1990).

Sexual maturation is controlled by pituitary secretions that stimulate the release of sex hormones. Although **estrogens** are thought of as female hormones and **androgens** as male hormones, both types are present in each sex, but in different amounts. The boy's testes release large quantities of the androgen *testosterone,* which leads to muscle growth, body and facial hair, and other male sex characteristics. Testosterone also contributes to gains in body size. Estrogens released by the girl's ovaries cause the breasts, uterus, and vagina to mature and the body to take on feminine proportions. In addition, estrogens contribute to regulation of the menstrual cycle. Girls' changing bodies are also affected by the release of androgens from the adrenal glands, located on top of each kidney. *Adrenal androgens* influence the girl's growth spurt and stimulate the appearance of underarm and pubic hair. They have little impact on boys, whose physical characteristics are influenced mainly by androgen secretions from the testes.

What sets these complex hormonal processes in motion and eventually causes physical growth to draw to a close? At present, scientists are not sure. In females, a sharp rise in body weight and fat appears to play an important role in sexual maturation. Girls who begin serious athletic training at young ages or who eat very little (both of which reduce body fat) often show greatly delayed menstruation. In contrast, overweight girls typically start menstruating early (Post & Kemper, 1993; Rees, 1993). But body size and muscle–fat makeup are unrelated to other pubertal milestones, such as development of the breasts and reproductive organs (Tanner, 1990). The origins of these aspects of growth remain unknown.

Now let's take a closer look at the dramatic changes of puberty and the controversial issue, raised at the beginning of this chapter, of just how they contribute to psychological development.

Estrogens
Hormones produced chiefly by the ovaries that cause the breasts, uterus, and vagina to mature and the body to take on feminine proportions during puberty.

Androgens
Hormones produced chiefly by the testes, and in smaller quantities by the adrenal glands, that influence the pubertal growth spurt, the appearance of body hair, and male sex characteristics.

BRIEF REVIEW

Compared to other mammals, human beings experience a prolonged period of physical growth in which changes in body size take place rapidly in infancy, slowly during childhood, and rapidly again at adolescence. Physical development during infancy and childhood follows the cephalocaudal and proximodistal trends. Changes in body proportions and muscle–fat makeup that contribute to sex differences in athletic skill occur at adolescence. Skeletal age is the best indicator of progress toward physical maturity: At birth, girls are advanced over boys, a gap that widens with age. Girls' pubertal growth spurt takes place, on the average, 2 years earlier than boys'.

Physical growth is an asynchronous process. Different body systems follow unique, carefully timed patterns of maturation. Individual and cultural differences in body size and rate of maturation are influenced by both heredity and environment. Over the past century, secular trends in physical growth have occurred. Children in industrialized nations are growing larger and reaching maturity earlier than they did in previous generations. Body growth is controlled by a complex set of hormonal secretions released by the pituitary gland and regulated by the hypothalamus.

Puberty: The Physical Transition to Adulthood

During puberty, young people become physically mature and capable of producing offspring. Accompanying the rapid changes in body size and proportions we have already discussed are changes in physical features related to sexual functioning. Some, called **primary sexual characteristics**, involve the reproductive organs (ovaries, uterus, and vagina in females; penis, scrotum, and testes in males). Others, called **secondary sexual characteristics**, are visible on the outside of the body and serve as additional signs of sexual maturity (for example, breast development in females, appearance of underarm and pubic hair in both sexes). As you can see in the Milestones table on the following page, the age at which each of these characteristics appears and is completed varies greatly (Dubas & Petersen, 1993). Clearly, puberty is the period of greatest sexual differentiation since prenatal life.

SEXUAL MATURATION IN GIRLS

Menarche (from the Greek word *arche,* meaning "beginning") is the scientific name for first menstruation. Because most people view it as the major sign that puberty has arrived in girls, you may be surprised to learn that menarche actually occurs fairly late in the sequence of pubertal events. Female puberty usually begins with the budding of the breasts and the growth spurt. (For about 15 percent of girls, pubic hair is present before breast development.) Menarche typically happens around 12 ½ years for North American girls, 13 for Europeans. But the age range is wide, extending from 10 ½ to 15 ½ years. Following menarche, pubic hair and breast development are completed, and underarm hair appears. Most girls take about 3 to 4 years to complete this sequence. Some mature more rapidly, in as little as a year and a half. Others take longer, perhaps as much as 5 years (Tanner, 1990; Wheeler, 1991).

All girls experience menarche after the peak in the height spurt, once they have nearly reached their mature body size. This sequence has clear adaptive value. Nature delays menstruation until the girl's body is large enough for successful childbearing. As an extra measure of security, for 12 to 18 months following menarche, the menstrual cycle often takes place without an ovum being released from the ovaries. However, this temporary period of sterility does not apply to all girls, and it cannot be counted on for protection against pregnancy (Tanner, 1990).

Primary sexual characteristics
Physical features that involve the reproductive organs (ovaries, uterus, and vagina in females; penis, scrotum, and testes in males).

Secondary sexual characteristics
Features visible on the outside of the body that serve as signs of sexual maturity but do not involve the reproductive organs (for example, breast development in females, appearance of underarm and pubic hair in both sexes).

Menarche
First menstruation.

Pubertal Development in North American Boys and Girls

Girls	Average Age Attained	Age Range	Boys	Average Age Attained	Age Range
Breasts begin to "bud."	10	(8–13)	Testes begin to enlarge.	11.5	(9.5–13.5)
Height spurt begins.	10	(8–13)	Pubic hair appears.	12	(10–15)
Pubic hair appears.	10.5	(8–14)	Penis begins to enlarge.	12	(10.5–14.5)
Peak of strength spurt.	11.6	(9.5–14)	Height spurt begins.	12.5	(10.5–16)
Peak of height spurt.	11.7	(10–13.5)	Spermarche (first ejaculation) occurs.	13	(12–16)
Menarche (first menstruation) occurs.	12.5	(10.5–15.5)	Peak of height spurt.	14	(12.5–15.5)
Adult stature reached.	13	(10–16)	Facial hair begins to grow.	14	(12.5–15.5)
Breast growth completed.	14	(10–16)	Voice begins to deepen.	14	(12.5–15.5)
Pubic hair growth completed.	14.5	(14–15)	Penis growth completed.	14.5	(12.5–16)
			Peak of strength spurt.	15.3	(13–17)
			Adult stature reached.	15.5	(13.5–17.5)
			Pubic hair growth completed.	15.5	(14–17)

Note: These milestones represent overall age trends. Individual differences exist in the precise age at which each milestone is attained.
Sources: Malina & Bouchard, 1991; Tanner, 1990.

SEXUAL MATURATION IN BOYS

The first sign of puberty in boys is the enlargement of the testes (glands that manufacture sperm), accompanied by changes in the texture and color of the scrotum. Pubic hair emerges a short time later, about the same time the penis begins to enlarge in size (Wheeler, 1991).

Refer again to the Milestones table above, and you will see that the growth spurt occurs much later in the sequence of pubertal events for boys than girls. When it reaches its peak (at about age 14), enlargement of the testes and penis is nearly complete, and underarm hair appears soon after. Facial and body hair also emerges just after the peak in body growth, but it increases slowly, continuing to develop for several years after puberty. Another landmark of male physical maturity is the deepening of the voice as the larynx enlarges and the vocal cords lengthen. (Girls' voices also deepen slightly.) Voice change usually takes place at the peak of the male growth spurt and is often not complete until puberty is over. When it first occurs, many boys have difficulty with voice control. Occasionally, their newly acquired baritone breaks into a high-pitched sound (Katchadourian, 1977).

While the penis is growing, the prostate gland and seminal vesicles (which together produce semen, the fluid in which sperm are bathed) enlarge. Then, around age 13, **spermarche**, or first ejaculation, occurs (Jorgensen & Keiding, 1991). For a while, the semen contains few living sperm. So, like girls, many boys have an initial period of reduced fertility. Spermarche may be as psychologically significant for boys as menarche is for girls, an issue we will take up shortly.

The Psychological Impact of Pubertal Events

Think back to your late elementary school and junior high school days. Were you early, late, or about on time in physical maturation with respect to your peers? How did your feelings about yourself and your relationships with others change? Were your reactions similar to Rousseau and Hall's image of biologically determined storm and stress, described at the beginning of this chapter?

IS PUBERTY AN INEVITABLE PERIOD OF STORM AND STRESS?

Recent research on large numbers of teenagers suggests that Rousseau and Hall's conclusions are greatly exaggerated. A number of problems, such as eating disorders, depression, suicide (see Chapter 11), and lawbreaking (see Chapter 12), occur more often in adolescence than earlier. But the overall rate of severe psychological disturbance rises only slightly (by 2 percent) from childhood to adolescence, when it is the same as in the adult population—about 15 to 20 percent (Powers, Hauser, & Kilner, 1989). The serious difficulties some teenagers encounter should not be dismissed as unimportant. But emotional turbulence is not a routine feature of this phase of development.

The first researcher to point out the wide variability in adolescent adjustment and the contribution of social and cultural factors to it was anthropologist Margaret Mead (1901–1978). In 1926, she traveled to the Pacific islands of Samoa, returning a short time later with a startling conclusion: Samoan adolescence was free of all the characteristics that made it hazardous for young people and dreaded by adults in complex societies. Because of the culture's relaxed social relationships and openness toward sexuality, adolescence, Mead (1928) reported, "is perhaps the pleasantest time the Samoan girl (or boy) will ever know" (p. 308). Mead offered an alternative view—one in which the social environment was judged to be entirely responsible for the range of teenage experiences, from erratic and agitated to calm and stress free. Yet this conclusion is just as extreme as the biological perspective it tried to replace! Later researchers, who looked more closely at Samoan society, found that adolescence was not as smooth and untroubled as Mead made it out to be (Freeman, 1983).

Still, Mead's work had an enormous impact. Today we know that adolescence is neither biologically nor socially determined, but rather a product of the two. In line with Mead's observations, young people growing up in nonindustrialized societies generally experience a shorter and smoother transition to adulthood (Whiting, Burbank, & Ratner, 1986). But most of the time, adolescence is not absent. A study of 186 tribal and village cultures revealed that almost all had an intervening phase, however brief, between childhood and full assumption of adult roles (Schlegel & Barry, 1991).

In industrialized nations, successful participation in the economic life of society requires many years of education. Consequently, young people face extra years of dependence on parents and a long period in which they are expected to postpone sexual gratification while they master complex systems of knowledge essential to a productive worklife. As a result, adolescence is greatly extended, and teenagers confront a wider

Spermarche
First ejaculation of seminal fluid.

array of psychological challenges. A large body of research reveals that puberty is linked to important changes in self-image, mood, and interaction with parents and peers. In the following sections, we will see many examples of how biological and social forces combine to affect teenagers' adjustment.

REACTIONS TO PUBERTAL CHANGES

How do girls and boys react to the massive physical changes of puberty? Most research aimed at answering this question has focused on girls' feelings about menarche.

GIRLS' REACTIONS TO MENARCHE. Research of a generation or two indicated that menarche was often traumatic and disturbing. For example, one woman, who reached puberty in the 1950s, reported:

> I had no information whatsoever, no hint that anything was going to happen to me. . . . I thought I was on the point of death from internal hemorrhage. . . . What did my highly educated mother do? She read me a furious lecture about what a bad, evil, immoral thing I was to start menstruating at the age of eleven! So young and so vile! Even after thirty years, I can feel the shock of hearing her condemn me for "doing" something I had no idea occurred. (Weideger, 1976, cited in Brooks-Gunn & Reiter, 1990, p. 37)

Recent findings show that girls' reactions to menarche are rarely so unfavorable today. The most common response is "surprise," undoubtedly caused by the sudden onset of the event. Girls often report a mixture of positive and negative emotions—"excited and pleased" as well as "scared and upset." But there are wide individual differences. Some, like this girl, react with joy and elation:

> When I discovered it, I called my mother and she showed me what to do. Then she did something I'll never forget. She told me to come with her and we went to the living room to tell my father. She just looked at me and then at him and said, "Well, your little girl is a young lady now!" My dad gave me a hug and congratulated me and I felt grown-up and proud that I was really a lady at last. That was one of the most exciting days of my life. (Shipman, 1971, p. 331)

As these two accounts suggest, girls' feelings about menarche depend on prior knowledge and support from family members. Both are influenced by social and cultural attitudes toward puberty and sexuality.

For girls who have no advance information about sexuality, menarche can be shocking and disturbing. Fortunately, the number of girls with no preparation is much smaller today than it was several decades ago. In the 1950s, up to 50 percent were given no prior warning (Shainess, 1961). Today, no more than 10 to 15 percent are uninformed (Brooks-Gunn, 1988b). This shift is probably due to modern parents' greater willingness to discuss sexual matters with their children. Currently, almost all girls get some information from their mothers. And girls whose fathers are told about pubertal changes adjust especially well. Perhaps a father's involvement reflects a family atmosphere that is highly understanding and accepting of physical and sexual matters (Brooks-Gunn & Ruble, 1980, 1983).

BOYS' REACTIONS TO SPERMARCHE. Spermarche is the male pubertal event that is most similar to menarche, but we have much less information about its psychological impact. Available research indicates that like girls' reactions to menarche, boys' responses to spermarche are not intensely negative. Most report mixed feelings. Virtually all boys know about ejaculation ahead of time, but few get any information from parents. Usually they obtain it from reading material (Gaddis & Brooks-Gunn, 1985). In addition, although girls at first keep menarche secret from their peers, within 6 months almost all tell a friend they are menstruating. In contrast, far fewer boys ever tell anyone about spermarche (Brooks-Gunn et al., 1986; Downs & Fuller, 1991). Overall, boys seem to get much less social support for the physical changes of puberty than do girls. This suggests that boys might benefit, especially, from opportunities to ask questions and discuss feelings with a sympathetic male teacher at school.

■ *In this adolescent initiation ceremony, N'Jembe women of Gabon in west-central Africa celebrate the arrival of puberty in two young girls (located just behind the leader, wearing elaborate headdresses) with a special ritual. (Sylvain Grandadam/Photo Researchers, Inc.)*

■ THE FUNCTION OF ADOLESCENT INITIATION CEREMONIES. The experience of puberty is affected by the larger cultural context in which boys and girls live. Many tribal and village societies celebrate puberty with a rite of passage—a community-wide initiation ceremony that marks an important change in privilege and responsibility. Consequently, these young people know that pubertal changes are honored and valued in their culture (Ottenberg, 1994). In contrast, Western societies grant little formal recognition to movement from childhood to adolescence or from adolescence to adulthood. Certain religious ceremonies, such as confirmation and the Jewish bar or bat mitzvah, do resemble a rite of passage. But not all young people take part in these rituals, and they usually do not lead to any meaningful change in social status.

Instead, modern adolescents are confronted with many ages at which they are granted partial adult status—for example, an age for starting employment, for driving, for leaving high school, for voting, and for drinking. In some contexts (on the highway and at their place of work), they may be treated like adults. In others (at school and at home), they may still be regarded as children. The absence of a widely accepted marker of physical and social maturity makes the process of becoming an adult especially confusing. Perhaps modern adolescents would benefit from a socially and culturally appropriate substitute to serve the need that simpler societies meet with adolescent initiation rituals.

PUBERTAL CHANGE, EMOTION, AND SOCIAL BEHAVIOR

In the preceding sections, we considered adolescents' reactions to their sexually maturing bodies. Puberty can also affect the young person's emotional state and social behavior. A common belief is that pubertal change has something to do with adolescent moodiness and the desire for greater physical and emotional separation from parents.

■ ADOLESCENT MOODINESS. Recently, researchers have explored the role of sex hormones in adolescents' emotional reactions. Indeed, higher hormone levels are related to greater moodiness, in the form of anger and irritability for males and anger and depression for females, between 9 and 14 years of age (Brooks-Gunn & Warren, 1989; Nottelmann et al., 1990). But these links are not strong, and we cannot really be sure that a rise in pubertal hormones causes adolescent moodiness (Buchanan, Eccles, & Becker, 1992).

What else might contribute to the common observation that adolescents are moody creatures? In several studies, the mood fluctuations of children, adolescents, and adults were tracked over a week by having them carry electronic pagers. At random intervals, they were beeped and asked to write down what they were doing, whom they were with, and how they felt. As expected, adolescents reported somewhat lower moods than did school-age children and adults (Csikszentmihalyi & Larson, 1984; Larson & Lampman-Petraitis, 1989). But young people whose moods were especially negative were experiencing a greater number of negative life events, such as difficulties in getting along with parents, disciplinary actions at school, and breaking up with a boyfriend or girlfriend. Negative events increased steadily from childhood to adolescence, and teenagers also seemed to react to them with greater emotion than did children (Larson & Ham, 1993).

Furthermore, compared to the moods of adults, adolescents' feelings were less stable. They often varied from cheerful to sad and back again. But teenagers also moved from one situation to another more often, and their mood swings were strongly related to these changes. High points of their days were times spent with friends and in self-chosen leisure and hobby activities. Low points tended to occur in adult-structured settings—class, job, school halls, school library, and church (Csikszentmihalyi & Larson, 1984). Taken together, these findings suggest that situational factors may act in concert with hormonal influences to affect teenagers' moodiness—an explanation consistent with the balanced view of biological and social forces described earlier in this chapter.

■ PARENT–CHILD RELATIONSHIPS. Parents are quick to notice that as children enter adolescence, their bedroom doors start to close, they often resist spending time with the family, and they become more argumentative. Many studies report that puberty is related to a rise in parent–child conflict. Bickering and standoffs increase as adolescents move toward the peak of the growth spurt and, for girls, just after menarche occurs. During this time, both parents and teenagers report feeling less close to one another (Holmbeck & Hill, 1991; Paikoff & Brooks-Gunn, 1991).

Why should a youngster's more adultlike appearance and sexual maturity trigger these petty disputes between parent and child? Researchers believe the association may have some adaptive value. Among nonhuman primates, the young typically leave the family group around the time of puberty. The same is true in many nonindustrialized cultures (Caine, 1986; Schlegel & Barry, 1991). Departure of young people from the family discourages sexual relations among close blood relatives. But because children in industrialized societies usually remain economically dependent on parents long after they reach puberty, they cannot leave the family. Consequently, a modern substitute for physical departure seems to have emerged—increased psychological distancing between parents and children (Steinberg, 1987).

In later chapters, we will see that adolescents' new powers of reasoning may also contribute to a rise in family tensions. In addition, the need for families to redefine relationships as children become physically mature and demand to be treated in adultlike ways may produce a temporary period of conflict. The quarreling that does take place is generally mild. Only a small minority of families experience a serious break in parent–child relationships. In reality, parents and children display both conflict and affection toward one another throughout adolescence. This also makes sense from an evolutionary perspective. Although separation from parents is adaptive, both generations benefit from warm, protective family bonds that last for many years to come (Steinberg, 1990).

THE IMPORTANCE OF EARLY VERSUS LATE MATURATION

In addition to dramatic physical change, the timing of puberty has a major impact on psychological adjustment. As we will see in the following sections, having physical characteristics that help gain social acceptance can be very comforting to adolescent boys and girls.

■ EFFECTS OF MATURATIONAL TIMING. Findings of several longitudinal studies indicate that maturational timing acts in opposite directions for boys and girls. Early maturing boys appeared advantaged in many aspects of emotional and social functioning. Both adults and peers viewed them as relaxed, independent, self-confident, and physically attractive. Popular with agemates, they held many leadership positions in school and tended to be athletic stars. In contrast, late maturing boys were not well liked.

Peers and adults viewed them as anxious, overly talkative, and attention seeking in behavior (Clausen, 1975; Jones, 1965; Jones & Bayley, 1950).

Among girls, the impact of early versus late maturation was just the reverse. Early maturing girls had social difficulties. They were below average in popularity, appeared withdrawn and lacking in self-confidence, and held few positions of leadership. Instead, their late maturing counterparts were especially well off. They were regarded as physically attractive, lively, sociable, and leaders at school (Jones & Mussen, 1958).

■ EXPLAINING MATURATIONAL TIMING EFFECTS. Most research on maturational timing was completed in the 1950s and 1960s, but new studies reveal that the same trends persist today (Brooks-Gunn, 1988a; Dubas & Petersen, 1993). Two factors seem to account for them: (1) how closely the adolescent's body matches cultural ideals of physical attractiveness; and (2) how well young people "fit in" physically with their peers.

Flip through the pages of your favorite popular magazine, and look at the figures of men and women in the ads. You will see convincing evidence for our society's view of an attractive female as thin and long legged and a good-looking male as tall, broad shouldered, and muscular. The female image is a girlish shape that favors the late developer. The male image is consistent with that of the early maturing boy.

A consistent finding is that early maturing girls have a less positive **body image**—conception of and attitude toward their physical appearance—than do their on-time and late maturing agemates. Among boys, the opposite is true: Early maturation is linked to a positive body image, whereas late maturation predicts dissatisfaction with the physical self (Alsaker, 1995). Both boys and girls who have physical characteristics regarded by themselves and others as less attractive have a lower sense of self-esteem and are less well liked by peers (Langlois & Stephan, 1981; Lerner & Brackney, 1978). The adoption of society's "beauty is best" stereotype seems to be an important factor in the adjustment of early and late maturing boys and girls.

A second way of explaining differences in adjustment between early and late maturers is in terms of their physical status in relation to agemates. From this perspective, early maturing girls and late maturing boys have difficulty because they fall at the extremes in physical development. Support for this idea comes from evidence that adolescents feel most comfortable with peers who match their own level of biological maturity (Brooks-Gunn et al., 1986; Stattin & Magnusson, 1990).

Because few agemates of the same biological status are available, early maturing adolescents of both sexes seek out older companions—a tendency that can lead to some unfavorable consequences. Older peers often encourage early maturing youngsters into activities they find difficult to resist and are not yet ready to handle emotionally, including sexual activity, drug and alcohol use, and minor delinquent acts. Perhaps because of involvements like these, the academic performance of early maturers tends to suffer (Caspi et al., 1993; Stattin & Magnusson, 1990).

Interestingly, school contexts can modify these maturational timing effects. In one study, early maturing sixth-grade girls felt better about themselves when they attended kindergarten through sixth-grade (K–6) rather than kindergarten through eighth-grade (K–8) schools, where they could mix with older adolescents. In the K–6 settings, they were relieved of pressures to adopt behaviors for which they were not ready (Blyth, Simmons, & Zakin, 1985). Similarly, a New Zealand study found that delinquency among early maturing girls was greatly reduced in all-girl schools, which limit opportunities to associate with norm-violating peers (most of whom are boys) (Caspi et al., 1993).

■ LONG-TERM CONSEQUENCES. Longitudinal research reveals that several aspects of adolescent adjustment were still evident well into middle adulthood. At age 38, the social prestige of early maturing males could still be detected in greater social ease and responsible, self-controlled behavior. Similarly, late maturing males, who as adolescents often tried to compensate for their small size through clowning and other antics, remained more impulsive and assertive over the years (Livson & Peskin, 1980).

Beyond these few consistencies, long-term follow-ups show some striking turnabouts in overall well-being. Many early maturing boys and late maturing girls, who had been the focus of admiration in adolescence, became rigid, inflexible, conforming, and somewhat discontented adults. In contrast, late maturing boys and early maturing girls, who were stress-ridden as teenagers, often developed into adults who were independent,

Body image
Conception of and attitude toward one's physical appearance.

flexible, cognitively competent, and satisfied with the direction of their lives (Macfarlane, 1971). How can we explain these remarkable reversals? Perhaps the confidence-inducing adolescence of early maturing boys and late maturing girls does not promote the coping skills needed to solve life's later problems. In contrast, the painful experiences associated with off-time pubertal growth may, in time, contribute to sharpened awareness, clarified goals, and greater stability.

Finally, it is important to note that these long-term outcomes may not hold completely in all cultures. In a Swedish study, achievement difficulties of early maturing girls persisted into young adulthood. They were twice as likely to leave high school after completing the minimum years of compulsory education as their on-time and later maturing counterparts (Stattin & Magnusson, 1990). In countries with highly selective college entrance systems, perhaps it is harder for early maturers to recover from declines in school performance. Clearly, the effects of maturational timing involve a complex blend of biological, immediate social setting, and cultural factors.

ADOLESCENT SEXUALITY

Virtually all theorists agree that adolescence is an especially important time for the development of sexuality. With the arrival of puberty, hormonal changes—in particular, the production of androgens in young people of both sexes—lead to an increase in sex drive (Udry, 1990). In response, adolescents become very concerned about how to manage sexuality in social relationships, and new cognitive capacities affect their efforts to do so. Yet like the adjustment issues we have already discussed, adolescent sexuality is heavily influenced by the social context in which the young person is growing up.

■ *Adolescence is an especially important time for the development of sexuality. American teenagers receive contradictory and confusing messages from the social environment about the appropriateness of sex. Although the rate of premarital sex has risen among adolescents, most engage in low levels of sexuality and have only a single partner. (Richard Hutchings/PhotoEdit)*

■ **THE IMPORTANCE OF CULTURE.** Think, for a moment, about when you first learned about the "facts of life" and how you found out about them. In your family, was sex discussed openly or treated with secrecy? Cross-cultural research reveals that exposure to sex, education about it, and efforts to restrict the sexual curiosity of children and adolescents vary widely around the world. At one extreme are a number of Middle Eastern peoples, who are known to kill girls who dishonor their families by losing their virginity before marriage. At the other extreme are several Asian and Pacific Island groups with very permissive sexual attitudes and practices. For example, among the Trobriand Islanders of Melanesia, older companions provide children with explicit instruction in sexual practices. Bachelor houses are maintained, where adolescents are expected to engage in sexual experimentation with a variety of partners (Benedict, 1934b; Ford & Beach, 1951).

For all the publicity granted to the image of a sexually free modern adolescent, you may be surprised to learn that American society falls on the restrictive side of this cultural continuum. Typically, American parents give children little information about sex, discourage them from engaging in sex play, and rarely talk about sex in their presence. When young people become interested in sex, they seek information elsewhere, turning to friends, books, magazines, movies, and television. On prime-time television shows, which adolescents watch the most, premarital sex occurs two to three times each hour and is spontaneous and passionate. Characters are rarely shown taking steps to avoid pregnancy or sexually transmitted disease (Braverman & Strasburger, 1994; Strasburger, 1989).

Consider the messages delivered by these two sets of sources, and you will see that they are contradictory and confusing. On the one hand, adults emphasize that sex at a young age and outside of marriage is wrong. On the other hand, adolescents encounter much in the broader social environment that extols the excitement and romanticism of sex. These mixed messages leave many American teenagers bewildered, poorly informed about sexual facts, and with little sound advice on how to conduct their sex lives responsibly.

■ **ADOLESCENT SEXUAL ATTITUDES AND BEHAVIOR.** Although differences among subcultural groups exist, over the past 30 years the sexual attitudes of both adolescents and adults have become more liberal. Compared to a generation ago, more people believe that sexual intercourse before marriage is all right, as long as two people are emotionally committed to one another (Michael et al., 1994). Recently, a slight swing back in

TABLE 5.1

Teenage Sexual Activity Rates by Sex, Ethnic Group, and Grade

	Ethnic group			Grade				
Sex	**White**	**Black**	**Hispanic**	**9**	**10**	**11**	**12**	**Total**
Male	56.4	87.8	63.0	48.7	52.5	62.6	76.3	60.8
Female	47.0	60.0	45.0	31.9	42.9	52.7	66.6	48.0
Total	51.6	72.3	53.4	39.6	47.6	57.3	71.9	54.2

Note: Data reflect the percentage of high school students who report ever having had sexual intercourse.
Source: U.S. Centers for Disease Control, 1992.

the direction of conservative sexual beliefs has occurred. A growing number of young people say they are opposed to premarital sex, largely due to the risk of sexually transmitted disease (especially AIDS) (Roper Starch Worldwide, 1994).

Trends in sexual activity of adolescents are quite consistent with their beliefs. The rate of premarital sex among young people has risen over time. For example, among high school students, females claiming to have had sexual intercourse grew from 28 percent in 1971 to 48 percent in 1990 (Forrest & Singh, 1990; U.S. Centers for Disease Control, 1992). As Table 5.1 reveals, a substantial minority of boys and girls are sexually active quite early, by ninth grade. The table also indicates that males tend to have their first intercourse earlier than females, and sexual activity is especially high among black adolescents—particularly boys. Yet timing of first intercourse provides us with only a limited picture of adolescent sexual behavior. Most teenagers engage in relatively low levels of sexual activity. The typical 15- to 19-year-old sexually active male—white, black, or Hispanic—has relations with only one girl at a time and spends half the year with no partner at all (Sonenstein, Pleck, & Ku, 1991). When we look closely at adolescent sexual attitudes and behavior, we see that contrary to popular belief, a runaway sexual revolution does not characterize American young people. In fact, the rate of teenage sexual activity in the United States is about the same as in Western European nations (Alan Guttmacher Institute, 1994; Creatsas et al., 1995).

■ CHARACTERISTICS OF SEXUALLY ACTIVE ADOLESCENTS. Teenage sexual activity is linked to a wide range of personal, familial, peer, and educational variables, including early physical maturation, parental separation and divorce, large family size, sexually active friends and older siblings, poor school performance, and lower educational aspirations (Braverman & Strasburger, 1994; Ku, Sonenstein, & Pleck, 1993). Since many of these factors are associated with growing up in a low-income family, it is not surprising that early sexual activity is more common among young people from economically disadvantaged homes. In fact, the high rate of premarital intercourse among black teenagers can largely be accounted for by widespread poverty in the black population (Sullivan, 1993).

Unfortunately, one-third to one-half of sexually active American teenagers are at risk for unplanned pregnancy because they do not use contraception at all or use it only occasionally (Ambuel, 1995; Braverman & Strasburger, 1993). Why do so many teenagers fail to take precautions? In Chapter 6, we will see that compared to school-age children, adolescents can consider many more possibilities when faced with a problem. But at first, they fail to apply this reasoning to everyday situations. In several studies, teenagers were asked to explain why they did not use birth control. Here are some typical answers:

> You don't say, "Well, I'm going to his house, and he's probably going to try to get to bed with me, so I better make sure I'm prepared." I mean, you don't know it's coming, so how are you to be prepared?
>
> I wouldn't [use contraception] if I was going . . . to have sex casually, you know, like once a month or once every two months. I feel it's more for somebody who has a steady boyfriend. (Kisker, 1985, p. 84)

One reason for responses like these is that advances in perspective taking—the capacity to imagine what others may be thinking and feeling (see Chapters 6 and 11)—lead teenagers, for a time, to be extremely concerned about others' opinions of them.

Another reason for lack of planning before sex is that intense self-reflection leads many adolescents to believe they are unique and invulnerable to danger. Recent evidence indicates that teenagers and adults differ very little on questionnaires asking about consequences of engaging in risky behaviors; both report similar levels of vulnerability (Beyth-Marom et al., 1993; Quadrel, Fischhoff, & Davis, 1993). Still, in the midst of everyday social pressures, adolescents often seem to conclude that pregnancy happens to others, not to themselves (Jaskiewicz & McAnarney, 1994; Voydanoff & Donnelly, 1990).

Although adolescent cognition has much to do with teenagers' reluctance to use contraception, the social environment also contributes to it. Teenagers who talk openly with their parents about sex are not less sexually active, but they are more likely to use birth control (Brooks-Gunn, 1988b). Unfortunately, many adolescents say they are too scared or embarrassed to ask parents questions about sex or contraception. Although most get some sex education at school, teenagers' knowledge about sex and contraception is often incomplete or just plain wrong. Many do not know where to get birth control counseling and devices. When they do, they tend to be just as uncomfortable about going to a doctor or family planning clinic as they are about seeking advice from parents (Alan Guttmacher Institute, 1994; Winn, Roker, & Coleman, 1995).

■ SEXUAL ORIENTATION. Up to this point, our discussion has focused only on heterosexual behavior. About 3 to 6 percent of young people discover they are lesbian or gay, and an as yet unknown but significant number are bisexual (Michael et al., 1994; Patterson, 1995). Adolescence is an equally crucial time for the sexual development of these individuals, and societal attitudes, once again, loom large in how well they fare.

Although the extent to which homosexuality is due to genetic versus environmental forces remains highly controversial, new evidence indicates that heredity makes an important contribution. Identical twins of both sexes are much more likely than fraternal twins to share a homosexual orientation; the same is true for biological as opposed to adoptive relatives (Bailey & Pillard, 1991; Bailey et al., 1993). Furthermore, male homosexuality tends to be more common on the maternal than paternal side of families. This suggests that it might be X-linked (see Chapter 3). Indeed, a recent gene-mapping study found that among 40 pairs of homosexual brothers, 33 (85.5 percent) had an identical segment of DNA on the X chromosome. One or several genes in that region might predispose males to become homosexual (Hamer et al., 1993). How might heredity lead to homosexuality? According to some researchers, certain genes affect prenatal sex hormone levels, which modify brain structures in ways that induce homosexual feelings and behavior (Bailey et al., 1993; Blanchard et al., 1995; LeVay, 1993; Meyer-Bahlburg et al., 1995).

Yet these findings do not apply to all homosexuals, since some do not have the genetic markers just described. And many people prenatally exposed to very low or high levels of sex hormones are heterosexual. Family factors are also linked to homosexuality. Looking back on their childhoods, both male and female homosexuals tend to view their same-sex parent as cold, rejecting, or distant (Bell, Weinberg, & Hammersmith, 1981; McConaghy & Silove, 1992). This does not mean that parents cause their youngsters to become homosexual. Rather, for some children, an early genetic bias away from traditional gender-role behavior may lead them to feel alienated from same-sex parents and peers. A strong desire for affection from people of their own sex may join with biology to foster a homosexual orientation (Green, 1987). Once again, however, homosexuality does not always develop in this way, since some homosexuals are very comfortable with their gender role and have warm relationships with their parents. Homosexuality probably results from a variety of biological and environmental combinations that are not yet well understood (Horton, 1995).

A passing attraction to members of the same sex is common during adolescence. About 18 percent of boys and 6 percent of girls have participated in at least one homosexual act by age 19 (Braverman & Strasburger, 1993). In some tribal and village cultures, homosexual behavior among young males is encouraged, as a way of learning about sex and discharging the sex drive (Savin-Williams, 1990). But adolescents in industrialized nations who discover that they have a compelling interest in same-sex partners often experience intense inner conflict. They get little approval for their sexual orientation and feel a profound sense of isolation and loneliness. Family rejection and social stigma contribute to high rates of psychological distress and problem behaviors among homosexual teenagers, including depression, suicide, substance abuse, and high-risk sexual behavior (Baumrind, 1995; Hershberger & D'Augelli, 1995). Gay and lesbian adolescents have a special need for caring adults and peers who can help them establish a positive sexual identity and find social acceptance.

SEXUALLY TRANSMITTED DISEASE

Sexually active adolescents, both homosexual and heterosexual, face serious health risks. One out of six sexually active teenagers—2.5 million American young people—contract sexually transmitted diseases (STDs). If left untreated, sterility and life-threatening complications can result (Braverman & Strasburger, 1994). Teenagers in greatest danger of STD are the same ones who tend to engage in irresponsible sexual behavior—poverty-stricken young people who feel a sense of inferiority and hopelessness about their lives (Holmbeck, Waters, & Brookman, 1990).

By far the most serious STD is AIDS. Although not many adolescents have AIDS, over one-fifth of cases in the United States occur between ages 20 and 29. Nearly all of these originate in adolescence, since AIDS symptoms typically take 8 to 10 years to emerge in a person carrying the virus. Drug-abusing and homosexual teenagers account for most cases, but heterosexual spread is increasing, especially among females. It is at least twice as easy for a man to infect a woman with any STD, including AIDS, as it is for a woman to infect a man (U.S. Centers for Disease Control, 1995). To prevent this deadly disease, almost all parents favor AIDS education in the public schools, and most states now require it (see the From Research to Practice box on the following page).

TEENAGE PREGNANCY AND CHILDBEARING

Adolescent heterosexuals face another health concern: Unprotected sexual activity results in more than a million teenage pregnancies in the United States each year, 30,000 to young people under age 15. As Figure 5.12 shows, the adolescent pregnancy rate in the United States is twice that of England, Canada, and France, three times that of Sweden, and six times that of the Netherlands. The United States differs from these nations in three important ways: (1) effective sex education reaches fewer teenagers; (2) convenient, low-cost contraceptive services for adolescents are scarce; and (3) many more families live in poverty, which encourages young people to take risks without considering the future implications of their behavior (Jones et al., 1988).

Not all adolescents who conceive give birth to a baby. About 40 percent choose to have an abortion, and 13 percent of teenage pregnancies end in miscarriage (Chase-Lansdale & Brooks-Gunn, 1994; Jaskiewicz & McAnarney, 1994). Because the United States has one of the highest adolescent abortion rates of any developed country, the total number of teenage births is actually lower than it was 30 years ago. But teenage parenthood is a much greater problem today because modern adolescents are far less likely to marry before childbirth. In 1960, only 15 percent of teenage births were to unmarried females, whereas today, nearly 70 percent are (Children's Defense Fund, 1996). Increased social acceptance of a young single mother raising a child, along with the belief of many teenage girls that a baby might fill a void in their lives, has meant that only a small

FIGURE 5.12

■ *Teenage pregnancy rate in six industrialized nations. (Adapted from United Nations, 1991.)*

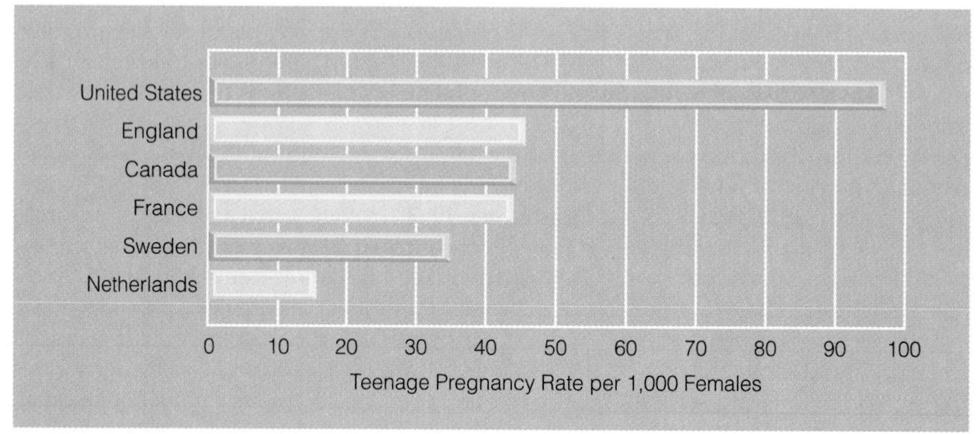

FROM RESEARCH TO PRACTICE

Educating Children and Adolescents About AIDS

Rates of HIV infection continue to grow among adolescents. In recent years, the largest annual increases have been among 13- to 19-year-olds (U.S. Centers for Disease Control, 1994).

Prenatal transmission is the major cause of childhood AIDS. Although few infected babies live until school age (see Chapter 3, page 98), many children have family members with the disease. These youngsters not only must face the repeated illnesses and eventual death of a parent or sibling, but are likely to be targets of prejudice in their schools and communities.

All fifty U.S. states mandate or strongly recommend AIDS education in school. Since an estimated 55 to 70 percent of adolescent HIV infections result from sexual contact, the vast majority of school programs focus on sex education for students old enough to be sexually active. But prevention through safe sex practices is not the only reason young people need AIDS education. Another consequence of spread of the disease is the greater probability of interacting with AIDS-infected people. Children and adolescents need help in responding appropriately to those who are, or may be, infected (Landau, Pryor, & Haefli, 1995).

What do children and adolescents know about AIDS, and how do they feel about people who have it? Interviews with preschool through high school students reveal that AIDS-related knowledge follows the same developmental sequence as knowledge of other illnesses. However, understanding of AIDS progresses more slowly, probably because children are less familiar with it than with other diseases and are influenced by social stigma against AIDS-infected people (Pryor & Reeder, 1993).

Because of their limited biological knowledge, preschoolers and kindergartners know practically nothing about AIDS. Understanding increases as children acquire more information about their bodies and are cognitively better able to make sense of it. By third to fifth grade, children have a fair amount of accurate information about the causes, consequences, and prevention of AIDS and other illnesses (Landau, Pryor, & Haefli, 1995; Schonfeld et al., 1993; Sigelman et al., 1993). At the same time, they harbor many misconceptions. Probe beneath 8- to 12-year-olds' correct answers—that people can get AIDS through sex, illegal drug use, or a transfusion of contaminated blood—and you will find that kernels of truth are often distorted by faulty generalizations from other diseases (such as colds and flu). Here are some examples:

> "If you get in bed with somebody who had AIDS, then you get AIDS, if like you kiss somebody with AIDS."
>
> "[You get it] if you get a blood transfusion and the needle is dirty and you get other germs, infections."
>
> "[You get it] when you donate blood to someone and they don't have very good blood."
>
> (Whalen et al., 1995, p. 434)

In one survey of fourth graders, 51 percent incorrectly believed that everyone is at risk for AIDS, and 59 percent said they "worry a lot" about getting it (Holcomb, 1990).

Misconceptions decline (but are not eliminated) by junior high and high school. Nevertheless, attitudes and feelings can create gaps between knowledge and behavior. Young children (who know less) voice more negative reactions to peers with AIDS. But even older youngsters who admit that they should not fear or avoid HIV-infected people say they would still feel uncomfortable around them:

> "I would be scared to even talk to them because they had AIDS, even though you can't get it that way."
>
> "I know it's not catchy, but I'd say I gotta go now."
>
> "I wouldn't be afraid of them really. I know you can't get it from, you know, by touching them or anything. But I would be more aware of what I'd do with them, though, for some reason like self-defense."
>
> (Whalen et al., 1995, p. 434)

AIDS education works best when it builds on current understandings. In the early grades, teachers should offer reassurance that young children usually do not get AIDS. Older children and adolescents can make use of more detailed explanations of HIV transmission and prevention (Walsh & Bibace, 1991). But school programs need to focus just as much on how AIDS is not spread (through sharing cups and utensils, coughing, sneezing, hugging, or holding hands) as how it is spread, so young people realize how it differs from other diseases. And since faulty beliefs can promote unnecessary anxiety and social rejection of AIDS victims, teachers must reach beyond simple knowledge and encourage students to examine their attitudes and feelings. Instruction that gives HIV "a human face," such as bringing infected people into the classroom, may help older children and adolescents respond constructively and compassionately (Pryor & Reeder, 1993).

number give their infants up for adoption. Each year, about 320,000 unmarried adolescent girls take on the responsibilities of parenthood before they are psychologically mature.

■ CORRELATES AND CONSEQUENCES OF TEENAGE PREGNANCY. Becoming a parent is challenging and stressful for any person, but it is especially difficult for adolescents. Teenage parents have not yet established a clear sense of direction for their own lives. As we have seen, adolescent sexual activity is linked to economic disadvantage. Teenage mothers are many times more likely to be poor than are women who postpone childbearing. The rate of out-of-wedlock births to members of low-income minorities, including African-American, Native-American, and Hispanic teenagers, is especially high. Many of these young people seem to turn to early parenthood as a way to move into adulthood when educational and career avenues are unavailable (Caldas, 1993; Murry, 1992).

Think about these characteristics of teenage parents, and you will quickly see why early childbirth imposes lasting hardships on two generations—adolescent and newborn baby. The lives of pregnant teenagers are often troubled in many ways, and after the baby is born, their circumstances worsen. Only 50 percent of girls who give birth before age 18 finish high school, compared to 96 percent of those who wait to become parents. Both teenage mothers and fathers are likely to be on welfare. If they are employed, their limited education restricts them to unsatisfying, low-paid jobs (Furstenberg, Brooks-Gunn, & Chase-Landsdale, 1989; Mott & Marsiglio, 1985).

In Chapter 3, we saw that poverty-stricken pregnant women are more likely to have inadequate diets and to expose their unborn babies to harmful environmental influences, such as illegal drugs. And many do not receive early prenatal care. These conditions are widespread among pregnant teenagers. As a result, adolescent mothers often experience prenatal and birth complications, and their infants are likely to be born underweight and premature (Scholl, Heidiger, & Belsky, 1996).

Children of teenagers are also at risk for poor parenting. Compared to adult mothers, adolescent mothers know less about child development, feel less positively about the parenting role, and interact less effectively with their infants (Sommer et al., 1993). As they get older, many children of adolescent mothers score low on intelligence tests, achieve poorly in school, and engage in disruptive social behavior. Too often, the cycle of adolescent pregnancy is repeated in the next generation. About one-third of girls who have a baby before age 19 were born to teenage mothers (Furstenberg, Levine, & Brooks-Gunn, 1990).

Still, how well adolescent parents and their children fare varies a great deal. Outcomes are more favorable when mothers return to school after giving birth and continue to live in their parents' homes, where child care can be shared with experienced adults. If the teenage mother finishes high school, avoids additional births, and finds a stable marriage partner, long-term disruptions in her own and her child's development are less severe. The small minority of young mothers who fail in all three of these ways face a life of continuing misfortune (Furstenberg, Brooks-Gunn, & Morgan, 1987).

■ **PREVENTION STRATEGIES.** Preventing teenage pregnancy and childbearing requires strategies addressing the many factors that underlie early sexual activity and lack of contraceptive use. Informing adolescents about sex and contraception is crucial. Too often, sex education courses are given late in high school (after sexual activity has begun), last no more than a few sessions, and are limited to a catalogue of facts about anatomy and reproduction. Sex education that goes beyond this bare minimum does not encourage early sex, as some opponents claim. It does improve awareness of sexual facts—knowledge that is necessary for responsible sexual behavior (Katchadourian, 1990).

Knowledge, however, is not sufficient to convince adolescents of the importance of postponing sexual activity and practicing contraception. To change teenagers' behavior, sex education must help them build a bridge between what they know and what they do in their everyday lives. Today, a new wave of more effective sex education programs has emerged in which creative discussion and role-playing techniques are being used to teach adolescents the decision-making and social skills they need to resist early and unprotected sex (Kirby, 1992; Kirby et al., 1994).

The most controversial aspect of adolescent pregnancy prevention is a growing movement to provide teenagers with easy access to contraceptives. In some large cities, school-based health clinics offering contraceptive services have been established (Seligmann, 1991). Many Americans argue that placing birth control pills or condoms in the hands of teenagers is equivalent to saying that early sex is okay. Yet in western Europe, where these clinics are common, teenage sexual activity is no higher than it is in the United States, but pregnancy, childbirth, and abortion rates are much lower (Hayes, 1987; Zabin & Hayward, 1993).

■ **INTERVENING WITH TEENAGE PARENTS.** The most difficult and costly way to deal with adolescent parenthood is to wait until after it has happened. Young single mothers need health care for themselves and their children, encouragement to stay in school, job training, instruction in parenting and life-management skills, and high-quality, affordable day care. School programs that provide these services reduce the incidence of low-birth-weight babies, increase mothers' educational success, and decrease their likelihood of rapid additional childbearing (Seitz & Apfel, 1993, 1994; Seitz, Apfel, & Rosenbaum, 1991). Interventions for fathers attempt to increase their financial and emotional commitment to the baby and strengthen the bond between teenage parents (Children's Defense Fund, 1996). But fathers are very difficult to reach because most either do not admit their paternity or abandon the young mother and baby after a short time. At present, the majority of adolescent parents of both sexes do not receive the help they need.

ANOREXIA NERVOSA AND BULIMIA

A group of adolescents with quite different characteristics than early childbearers also experience serious adjustment difficulties with the advent of puberty. As body fat rises, dieting and unhealthy eating behaviors increase, sometimes becoming extreme. **Anorexia nervosa** is a tragic eating disturbance in which young people starve themselves because of a compulsive fear of getting fat. About 1 in every 500 teenage girls in the United States is affected (Garner, 1993; Seligmann, 1994). Caucasian-Americans are at greater risk than African-Americans, who are more satisfied with their size and shape (Story et al., 1995). It is ironic that in industrialized nations, malnutrition severe enough to interfere with normal adolescent growth occurs most often in affluent homes, not in poverty-stricken families.

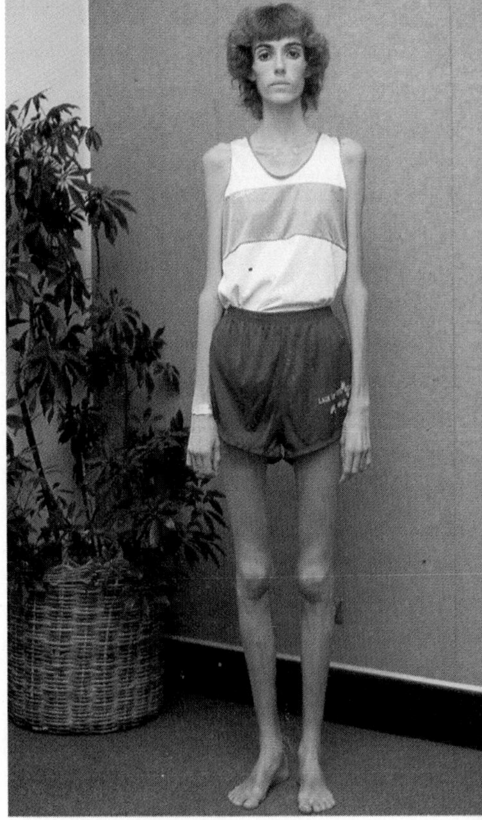

This anorexic girl's strict, self-imposed diet and obsession with strenuous physical exercise has led her to become painfully thin. Even so, her body image is so distorted that she probably regards herself as fat. (Wm. Thompson/The Picture Cube)

Anorexics have an extremely distorted body image. Even after they have become severely underweight, they conclude that they are fat. Most go on a self-imposed diet so strict that they struggle to avoid eating in response to hunger. To enhance weight loss, anorexics engage in strenuous physical exercise. If family members try to stop them, they seek other ways, such as pacing back and forth in their rooms or getting up in the middle of the night for an energetic workout.

The physical consequences of this attempt to reach "perfect" slimness are severe. Anorexics lose between 25 and 50 percent of their body weight and appear painfully thin. Because a normal menstrual cycle requires a body fat content of about 15 percent, either menarche does not occur or the girl's menstrual periods stop. Malnutrition causes additional physical symptoms—pale skin; brittle, discolored nails; fine dark hairs appearing all over the body; and extreme sensitivity to cold. If allowed to continue, anorexia nervosa can result in shrinking of the heart muscle and kidney failure. About 5 percent of those with the disorder die of it (Harris, 1991).

Anorexia is the combined result of forces within the individual, the family, and the larger culture. We have already seen that the societal image of "thin is beautiful" contributes to the poorer body image of early maturing girls, who are at greatest risk for anorexia (Graber et al., 1994). But though almost all adolescent girls go on diets at one time or another, anorexics persist in weight loss to an extreme. Many are perfectionists who have high standards for their own behavior and performance. Typically, these girls are excellent students who are responsible and well behaved—ideal daughters in many respects.

Yet researchers who have studied the interaction of parents with anorexic daughters have identified problems related to adolescent autonomy that may trigger the compulsive dieting. Often their mothers have high expectations for achievement and social acceptance, are overprotective and controlling, and have eating problems themselves (Pike & Rodin, 1991). Although the daughter tries to meet these demands, inside she is angry at not being recognized as an individual in her own right. Instead of rebelling openly, the anorexic girl expresses her feelings through dieting. Without saying so directly, she tells her parents, "I am a separate person from you, and I can do what I want with my own body!" At the same time, this youngster, who has been so used to having parents make decisions for her, responds to the challenges of adolescence with depression and lack of self-confidence. Starving herself is also a way of avoiding new expectations by returning to a much younger, preadolescent image (Halmi, 1987; Maloney & Kranz, 1991).

Because anorexic girls typically deny that any problem exists, treating the disorder is difficult. Hospitalization is often necessary to prevent life-threatening malnutrition. Family therapy, in which efforts are made to change parent–child interaction and expectations, is the most successful treatment. As a supplementary approach, applied behavior analysis, in which hospitalized anorexics are reinforced for gaining weight with praise, social contact, and opportunities for exercise, is helpful. Still, only 30 percent of anorexics

Anorexia nervosa
An eating disorder in which individuals (usually females) starve themselves because of a compulsive fear of getting fat.

fully recover. For many others, eating problems continue in less extreme form (Kreipe, Churchill, & Strauss, 1989).

One-third of anorexics develop **bulimia**, a less severe disorder in which young people (again, mainly girls) engage in binge eating followed by deliberate vomiting, other purging techniques such as heavy doses of laxatives, and strict dieting. However, bulimia is much more common than anorexia nervosa. About 1 to 3 percent of teenage girls have the disorder; only 5 percent have previously been anorexic (Fairburn & Beglin, 1990). Although bulimics share with anorexics a pathological fear of getting fat and a middle-class family background with high expectations, most have quite different personality characteristics. Typically, bulimics are not just impulsive eaters; they also lack self-control in other areas of their lives. Although they tend to be good students and liked by peers, many abuse alcohol and engage in petty shoplifting. Bulimics also differ from anorexics in that they are aware of their abnormal eating habits, feel extremely depressed and guilty about them, and are usually desperate to get help. As a result, bulimia is usually easier to treat through individual and family therapy, support groups, and nutrition education (Harris, 1991; Thakwray et al., 1993).

BRIEF REVIEW

Puberty is a time of dramatic physical change leading to an adult-sized body and sexual maturity. In contrast to early biologically oriented theories, modern researchers recognize that the psychological impact of pubertal events is a product of both biological and social forces. Typically, girls' emotional reactions to menarche and boys' reactions to spermarche are mixed, although prior knowledge and social support affect their responses. Adolescent moodiness is related to both sex hormone levels and changes in the social environment.

Puberty prompts increased conflict and psychological distancing between parents and children—reactions that appear to be modern substitutes for physical departure from the family in our evolutionary history. The standards and expectations of the culture and peer group lead early maturing boys and late maturing girls to be advantaged in emotional and social adjustment. In contrast, late maturing boys and early maturing girls experience more adjustment difficulties.

American adolescents receive mixed messages from adults and the larger culture about sexual activity. The percentage of sexually active teenagers has increased over time. Homosexual young people face special challenges in establishing a positive sexual identity.

Adolescent cognitive processes along with lack of social supports for responsible sexual behavior contribute to high rates of sexually transmitted disease, teenage pregnancy, abortion, and premarital childbirth in the United States. For many adolescent girls, the cultural ideal of thinness combines with family and psychological problems to produce the serious eating disturbances of anorexia nervosa and bulimia.

Bulimia
An eating disorder in which individuals (mainly females) go on eating binges followed by deliberate vomiting, other purging techniques such as heavy doses of laxatives, and strict dieting.

Neurons
Nerve cells that store and transmit information in the brain.

Synapses
The gap between neurons, across which chemical messages are sent.

Programmed cell death
Death of many neurons during the peak period of development in any brain area to make room for growth of neural fibers that form synaptic connections.

Development of the Brain

The human brain is the most elaborate and effective living structure on earth today. Despite its complexity, at birth the brain is nearer to its adult size than any other organ, and it continues to develop at an astounding pace during the first 2 years of life. To best understand brain growth, we need to look at it from two vantage points. The first is at the microscopic level of individual brain cells. The second is at the larger level of the cerebral cortex, the most complex brain structure and the one responsible for the highly developed intelligence of our species.

DEVELOPMENT OF NEURONS

The human brain has 100 billion to 200 billion **neurons**, or nerve cells that store and transmit information, many of which have thousands of direct connections with other neurons. Neurons differ from other body cells in that they are not tightly packed together. There are tiny gaps, or **synapses**, between them where fibers from different neurons come close together but do not touch. Neurons release chemicals that cross the synapse, thereby sending messages to one another.

The basic story of brain growth concerns how neurons form this intricate communication system. Each neuron passes through three developmental steps: (1) cell production, (2) cell migration, and (3) cell differentiation. In Chapter 3, we indicated that neurons are produced in the primitive neural tube of the embryo. From there, they migrate to form the major parts of the brain, traveling along threads produced by a special network of guiding cells. By the end of the second trimester of pregnancy, this process is complete; no more neurons will be generated in the individual's lifetime (Casaer, 1993; Nowakowski, 1987).

Once neurons are in place, they begin to differentiate, establishing their unique functions by extending their fibers to form synaptic connections with neighboring cells. Because developing neurons require space for these connective structures, a surprising aspect of brain growth is that many surrounding neurons die when synapses are formed. Consequently, the peak period of development in any brain area is also marked by the greatest rate of **programmed cell death** (Huttenlocher, 1994). Fortunately, during embryonic growth, the neural tube produces an excess of neurons—far more than the brain will ever need.

As neurons form connections, a new factor becomes important in their survival: stimulation. Neurons that are stimulated by input from the surrounding environment continue to establish new synapses, forming increasingly elaborate systems of communication that lead to more complex cortical functions. Neurons seldom stimulated soon lose their connective fibers, a process called **synaptic pruning**. Initially, stimulation leads to an overabundance of synapses, many of which serve identical functions, thereby helping to ensure that the child will acquire certain abilities. Pruning of synapses returns neurons not needed at the moment to an uncommitted state so they can support the development of future skills (Huttenlocher, 1994). Notice how, for this process to go forward, appropriate stimulation of the child's brain is vital during periods in which the formation of synapses is at its peak (Greenough et al., 1993).

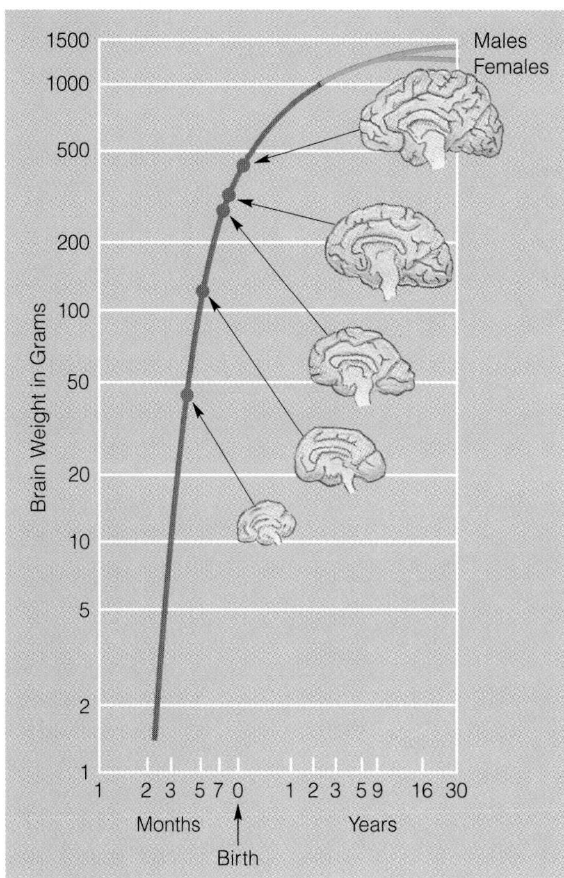

FIGURE 5.13

■ *Increase in weight of the human brain from the prenatal period to adulthood. The rise in brain weight is especially rapid between the fetal period and the child's second birthday (see red line), when glial cells are multiplying at a dramatic pace. As brain weight increases, the cortex becomes more convoluted, or folded. (From R. J. Lemire, J. D. Loeser, R. W. Leech, & E. C. Alvord, 1975,* Normal and Abnormal Development of the Human Nervous System, *New York: Harper & Row, p. 236. Adapted by permission.)*

At this point, you may be wondering, If no more neurons are produced after the prenatal period, what causes the dramatic increase in skull size we mentioned earlier in this chapter? Growth of neural fibers results in some increase in brain weight, but not as much as a second type of cell in the brain. About half the brain's volume is made up of **glial cells**, which do not carry messages. Instead, their most important function is **myelinization**, a process in which neural fibers are coated with an insulating fatty sheath (called *myelin*) that improves the efficiency of message transfer. Glial cells multiply at a dramatic pace from the fourth month of pregnancy through the second year, after which their rate of production continues at a slower pace (Casaer, 1993). Myelinization is responsible for the rapid gain in overall size of the brain (see Figure 5.13). By the time the child is 2 years old, the brain is already about 70 percent of its adult weight. At 6 years, it reaches 90 percent.

Synaptic pruning
Loss of connective fibers by seldom-stimulated neurons, thereby returning them to an uncommitted state so they can support the development of future skills.

Glial cells
Cells serving the function of myelinization.

Myelinization
A process in which neural fibers are coated with an insulating fatty sheath (called myelin) that improves the efficiency of message transfer.

Cerebral cortex
The largest structure of the human brain; accounts for the highly developed intelligence of the human species.

DEVELOPMENT OF THE CEREBRAL CORTEX

The **cerebral cortex** surrounds the rest of the brain, much like a half-shelled walnut. It is the largest structure of the human brain (accounting for 85 percent of brain weight) and the one responsible for the unique intelligence of our species. The cerebral cortex is also the last brain structure to stop growing. For this reason, it is believed to be much more sensitive to environmental influences than any other part of the brain.

As Figure 5.14 shows, different regions of the cerebral cortex have specific functions, such as receiving information from the senses, instructing the body to move, and think-

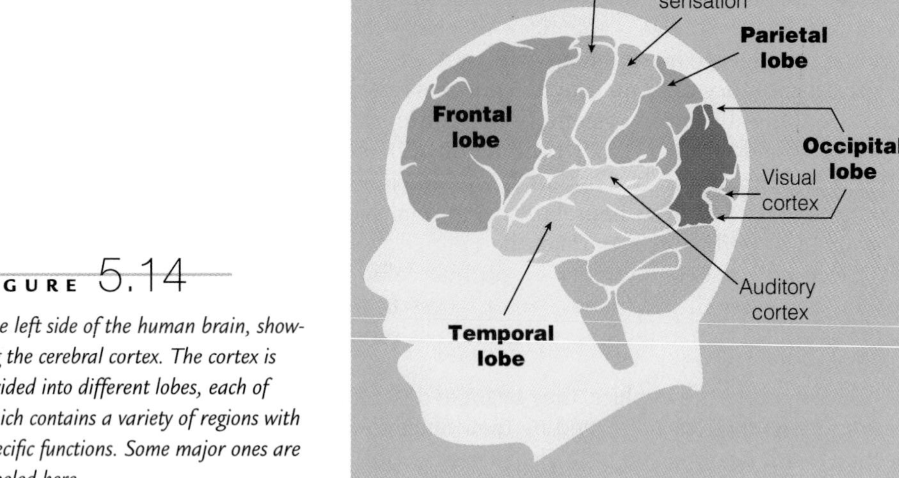

FIGURE 5.14

■ *The left side of the human brain, showing the cerebral cortex. The cortex is divided into different lobes, each of which contains a variety of regions with specific functions. Some major ones are labeled here.*

ing. To study the development of these regions, researchers examine age-related changes in brain activity, using such procedures as the EEG, ERP, or fMRI (see Chapter 2, page 47–48). In addition, they analyze the chemical makeup and myelinization of the brains of young children who have died. Their findings reveal that the order in which areas of the cortex develop corresponds to the sequence in which various capacities emerge during infancy and childhood. For example, among areas responsible for body movement, neurons that control the head, arms, and chest mature ahead of those that control the trunk and legs. Do you recognize a familiar developmental trend? The last portion of the cortex to develop neuronal connections and myelinate is the frontal lobe, which is responsible for thought and consciousness. From age 2 onward, this area functions more effectively, and it continues its growth for years, well into the second and third decades of life (Fischer & Rose, 1994, 1995).

■ LATERALIZATION OF THE CORTEX. Figure 5.14 shows only one hemisphere, or side, of the cortex. The brain has two hemispheres—left and right. Although they look alike, the hemispheres do not have precisely the same functions. Some tasks are done mostly by one and some by the other. For example, each hemisphere receives sensory information from and controls only one side of the body—the one opposite to it.[1] For most of us, the left hemisphere is responsible for verbal abilities (such as spoken and written language) and positive emotion (for example, joy), whereas the right hemisphere handles spatial abilities (judging distances, reading maps, and recognizing geometric shapes) and negative emotion (such as distress). This pattern may be reversed in left-handed people, but more often, the cortex of left-handers is less clearly specialized than that of right-handers.

Specialization of the two hemispheres is called **lateralization**. Few topics in child development have stimulated more interest than the question of when brain lateralization occurs. Researchers are interested in this issue because they want to know more about **brain plasticity**. A highly plastic cortex is still adaptable because many areas are not yet committed to specific functions. If a part of the brain is damaged, other parts can take over tasks that would have been handled by the damaged region. But once the hemispheres lateralize, damage to a particular region means that the abilities controlled by it will be lost forever.

Researchers used to think that lateralization of the cortex did not begin until after 2 years of age (Lenneberg, 1967). Today we know that hemispheric specialization is already under way at birth. For example, the majority of neonates favor the right side of the body in their reflexive responses (Grattan et al., 1992). And like adults, most infants show greater electrical activity in the left hemisphere while listening to speech sounds

Lateralization
Specialization of functions of the two hemispheres of the cortex.

Brain plasticity
The ability of other parts of the brain to take over functions of damaged regions.

[1] The eyes are an exception. Messages from the right halves of each retina go to the right hemisphere; messages from the left halves of each retina go to the left hemisphere. Thus, visual information from *both* eyes is received by *both* hemispheres.

and displaying positive emotion. In contrast, the right hemisphere reacts more strongly to nonspeech sounds as well as stimuli (such as a sour-tasting fluid) that cause infants to display negative emotion (Davidson, 1994; Fox & Davidson, 1986; Hahn, 1987).

Specialization of brain regions begins early in life, but it is not yet complete. Research on preterm babies with brain hemorrhages provides dramatic evidence for early plasticity. Although hemorrhaging led to brain damage, it turned out to be a poor predictor of mental and motor development at 2 years of age. As infants gained perceptual, cognitive, and motor experiences, other stimulated structures seemed to compensate for the injured areas (Sostek et al., 1987). Another illustration of how early experience can mold brain organization comes from studies of deaf adults who had been deprived of any spoken language since birth but, instead, learned to communicate visually and manually through signing. Electrical activity of brain regions revealed that compared to their hearing counterparts, these individuals depend more on the right hemisphere for language processing (Mills, Coffey-Corina, & Neville, 1994). Finally, research on children just beginning to acquire language reveals that 20-month-olds advanced in vocabulary development show greater left-hemispheric specialization for language than do their more slowly developing agemates. Apparently, the very process of acquiring spoken language promotes lateralization (Neville, 1991).

In sum, during the first few years, the brain is more plastic than at any later time in life, perhaps because many of its synapses have not yet been established. Although the cortex is programmed from the start for hemispheric specialization, the rate and success of this genetic program are greatly influenced by experience (Fox, Calkins, & Bell, 1994). A lateralized brain is certainly adaptive, since it permits a wider array of talents to be represented in the two hemispheres than if both sides served exactly the same functions.

■ LATERALIZATION AND HANDEDNESS. A growing literature on the development of handedness is also providing new insights into the joint contributions of nature and nurture to brain lateralization. A strong hand preference reflects the greater capacity of one side of the brain—often referred to as the individual's **dominant cerebral hemisphere**—to carry out skilled motor action. Other abilities located on the dominant side may be superior as well. In support of this idea, for right-handed people, who make up 90 percent of the population, language is housed with hand control in the left hemisphere. For the remaining 10 percent who are left-handed, language is often shared between the hemispheres rather than located in only one. This indicates that the brains of left-handers tend to be less strongly lateralized than those of right-handers (Hiscock & Kinsbourne, 1987). Consistent with this idea, many left-handed individuals are also ambidextrous. That is, although they prefer their left hand, they sometimes use their right hand skillfully as well (McManus et al., 1988).

Is handedness hereditary? Although researchers disagree on this issue, certain findings argue against a direct genetic explanation. Twins—whether identical or fraternal—are more likely than ordinary siblings to display opposite handedness, yet we would expect identical twins to be more alike if heredity played a powerful role. Furthermore, the hand preference of each twin is related to positioning in the uterus (twins usually lie in opposite orientations) (Perelle & Ehrman, 1994). According to one theory, cerebral dominance can be traced to prenatal events. The way most fetuses lie—turned toward the left—may promote greater postural control by the right side of the body (Previc, 1991).

Hand preference shows up early in development—by 5 or 6 months of age (McCormick & Maurer, 1988). However, it is not stable until 2 years, and some intriguing research suggests why. Handedness seems to undergo dips and recoveries that coincide with bursts in language competence. When language forges ahead at a quick pace, it seems to place extra demands on the left hemisphere, resulting in a temporary loss in motor dominance that returns as each new skill—at first babbling, then first words, and finally combining words—becomes well established (Ramsay, 1985; Ramsay & McCune, 1984). Then, in early and middle childhood, hand preference increases, indicating that specialization of brain regions strengthens during this time (McManus et al., 1988).

What about left-handed children, whose hand preference suggests an unusual organization of brain functions? Do these youngsters develop normally? Perhaps you have heard that left-handedness is more frequent among severely retarded and mentally ill people than it is in the general population. Although this is true, you also know that when two variables are correlated, this does not mean that one causes the other. Atypical lateralization is probably not responsible for the problems of these individuals. Instead,

Dominant cerebral hemisphere
The hemisphere of the brain responsible for skilled motor action. The left hemisphere is dominant in right-handed individuals. In left-handed individuals, the right hemisphere may be dominant, or motor and language skills may be shared between the hemispheres.

they may have suffered early brain damage to the left hemisphere, which caused their disabilities and, at the same time, led to a shift in handedness. In support of this idea, left-handedness shows a slight association with prenatal and birth difficulties that can result in brain damage, including prolonged labor, prematurity, Rh incompatibility, and breech delivery (Coren & Halpern, 1991; Williams, Buss, & Eskenazi, 1992).

Finally, in considering the evidence on handedness and development, keep in mind that only a small number of left-handers show developmental problems of any kind. In fact, the unusual lateralization of left-handed children may have certain advantages. Left- and mixed-handed youngsters are more likely than their right-handed agemates to develop outstanding verbal and mathematical talents. A genetic predisposition for more even distribution of cognitive functions across both hemispheres may be responsible for this trend (Benbow, 1986). Still, many left-handed children and adults may be bilateral and ambidextrous for environmental rather than genetic reasons, since they must learn to live in a right-hand biased world.

OTHER ADVANCES IN BRAIN DEVELOPMENT

Besides the cortex, other areas of the brain make strides during infancy and childhood. As we look at these changes, you will see that they have one feature in common. They all involve establishing links among different parts of the brain, increasing the coordinated functioning of the central nervous system. (To see where the structures we are about to discuss are located, turn back to Figure 5.10 on page 176.)

At the rear and base of the brain is the **cerebellum**, a structure that aids in balance and control of body movement. Fibers linking the cerebellum to the cerebral cortex begin to myelinate after birth, but they do not complete this process until about age 4 (Tanner, 1990). This change undoubtedly contributes to dramatic gains in motor control, so that by the end of the preschool years, children can play a game of hopscotch, pump a playground swing, and throw a ball with a well-organized set of movements.

The **reticular formation**, a structure in the brain stem that maintains alertness and consciousness, myelinates throughout early childhood, continuing its growth into adolescence. Neurons in the reticular formation send out fibers to other areas of the brain. Many go to the frontal lobe of the cortex (McGuinness & Pribram, 1980). Maturation of the reticular formation contributes to gains in sustained, controlled attention that we will discuss in Chapter 7.

A final brain structure that undergoes major changes during early childhood is the **corpus callosum**. It is a large bundle of fibers that connects the two hemispheres so that they can communicate with one another. Myelinization of the corpus callosum does not begin until the end of the first year of life. By 4 to 5 years, its development is fairly advanced (Witelson & Kigar, 1988). About this time, children become more proficient at tasks that require transfer of information between the cerebral hemispheres, such as comparing two textured stimuli when each is presented to a different hand (Galin et al., 1979). The corpus callosum continues to mature at a slower rate during middle childhood. More information on how it develops is likely to enhance our understanding of abilities that require collaboration among many parts of the brain, such as abstract thinking and creativity.

BRAIN GROWTH SPURTS AND SENSITIVE PERIODS OF DEVELOPMENT

Earlier we suggested that stimulation of the brain may be vital during periods in which it is growing most rapidly—when formation of synapses is at a peak. The existence of sensitive periods in postnatal development of the cortex has been amply demonstrated in studies of animals exposed to extreme forms of sensory deprivation. For example, there seems to be a time when rich and varied visual experiences must occur for the visual centers of the brain to develop normally. If a month-old kitten is deprived of light for as brief a time as 3 or 4 days, these areas of the brain start to degenerate. If the kitten is kept in the dark for as long as 2 months, the damage is permanent (Hubel & Wiesel, 1970). Severe stimulus deprivation also affects overall brain growth. When animals reared as pets are compared to animals reared in isolation, the brains of the pets are heavier and thicker (Greenough & Black, 1992; Greenough, Black, & Wallace, 1987).

Cerebellum
A brain structure that aids in balance and control of body movements.

Reticular formation
A brain structure that maintains alertness and consciousness.

Corpus callosum
The large bundle of fibers that connects the two hemispheres of the brain.

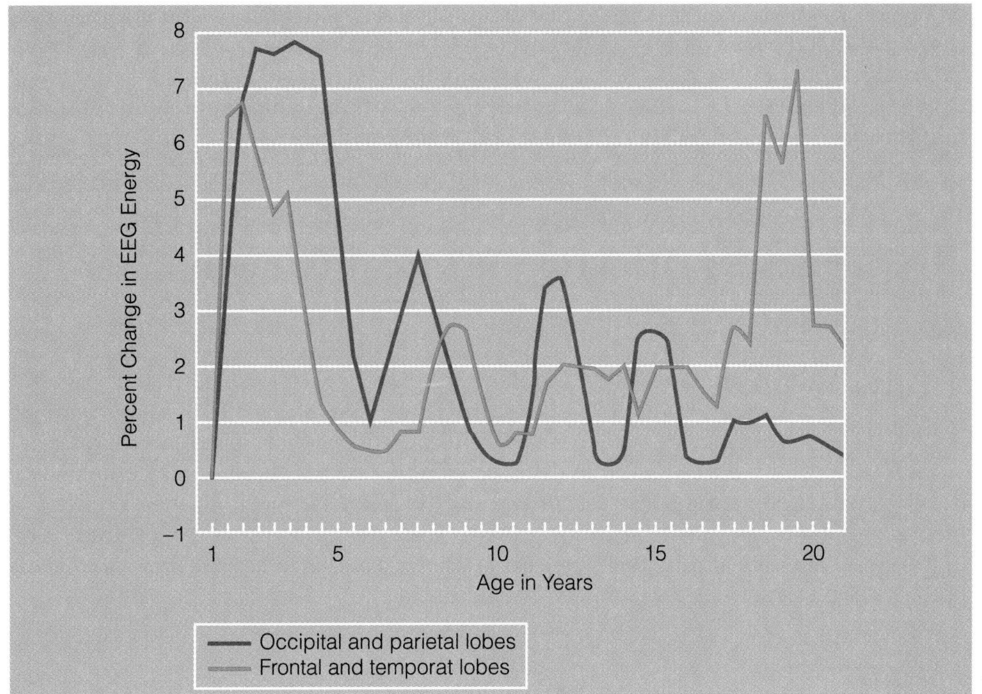

FIGURE 5.15

■ *Brain growth spurts, based on findings of a Swedish cross-sectional study in which EEGs were measured in individuals ranging from 1 to 21 years of age. EEG energy peaks indicate periods of rapid growth, troughs indicate periods of slow growth or no change. Spurts occurred around 1 1/2 to 2, 9, 12, 15, and 18 to 20 years of age in all lobes of the cortex (frontal, temporal, occipital, and parietal), suggesting that generalized growth took place at these times. The spurts coincide with peaks in children's intelligence test performance and major transformations in cognitive competence. (From K. W. Fischer & S. P. Rose, 1995,* Concurrent Cycles in the Dynamic Development of Brain and Behavior. *Newsletter of the Society for Research in Child Development, p. 16. Reprinted by permission of the authors.)*

Because we cannot ethically expose children to such experiments, researchers interested in identifying sensitive periods for human brain development must rely on less direct evidence. Several investigators have identified intermittent brain growth spurts from infancy into adolescence, based on gains in brain weight and skull size as well as changes in electrical activity of the cortex, as measured by the EEG (Epstein, 1980; Hudspeth & Pribram, 1992; Thatcher, 1991, 1994). These spurts coincide with peaks in children's intelligence test performance and major transformations in cognitive competence. For example, Figure 5.15 displays the findings of a Swedish study, in which EEGs were measured during a quiet, alert state in individuals ranging from 1 to 21 years of age. The first EEG energy spurt occurred around age 1½ to 2, a period in which representation and language flourish. The next three spurts, at ages 9, 12, and 15, probably reflect the emergence and refinement of abstract thinking. Another spurt, around age 18 to 20, may signal the capacity for mature, reflective thought (Fischer & Rose, 1995; Kitchener et al., 1993).

Researchers speculate that massive production of synapses in many cortical regions may underlie the earliest brain growth spurt. Development of more complex and efficient neural networks due to synaptic pruning, myelinization, and longer-distance connections between the frontal lobe and other cortical lobes may account for the later ones (Case, 1992b; Fischer & Rose, 1994; Thatcher, 1994). Exactly how brain development might be supported or disrupted by experience during each of these periods is still a question for future research. Once we have such information, it will have major implications for child-rearing and educational practices.

BRIEF REVIEW

The human brain grows faster early in development than any other organ of the body. Neurons develop in a three-step sequence—production, migration, and differentiation—that concludes with the formation of synapses and myelinization. Although the cerebral cortex has already begun to lateralize at birth, it retains considerable plasticity during the early years. Brain organization is a product of both a genetic program and experience. Hand preference is evident in infancy and strengthens over early childhood, a sign of increasing brain lateralization. Left-handedness is sometimes associated with developmental abnormalities; however, the majority of left-handed children show no problems of any kind. The cerebellum, the reticular formation, and the corpus callosum undergo considerable development during early childhood, contributing to connections between different parts of the brain. Research supports the existence of intermittent brain growth spurts from infancy through adolescence. Each may be a sensitive period during which appropriate stimulation is required for optimal development of human intelligence.

Factors Affecting Physical Growth

Physical growth, like other aspects of development, results from the continuous and complex interplay between heredity and environment. In the following sections, we take a closer look at this familiar theme. We will see that in addition to genetic makeup, nutrition, relative freedom from disease, and emotional well-being affect the body's development. And as the Social Issues box on the following page illustrates, environmental pollutants can threaten healthy growth. The extent to which low-level lead—one of the most common—undermines children's physical and mental well-being is currently the subject of intensive research and heated debate.

HEREDITY

Since identical twins are much more alike in body size than are fraternal twins, we know that heredity is an important factor in physical growth. However, this resemblance depends on when infant twins are measured. At birth, the differences in lengths and weights of identical twins are actually greater than those of fraternal twins. The reason is that identical twins share the same placenta, and one baby usually manages to get more nourishment. As long as negative environmental factors are not severe, the smaller baby recovers and swings back to her genetically determined path of growth within a few months. This tendency is called **catch-up growth**,[2] and it persists throughout childhood and adolescence.

Genes influence growth by controlling the body's production of and sensitivity to hormones. Sometimes mutations disrupt this process, leading to deviations in physical size. For example, return to Tables 3.2 and 3.3 on pages 74–77 to review the impact of hereditary defects on physical growth. Occasionally, a mutation becomes widespread in a population. Consider the Efe of Zaire, an African people who typically grow to an adult height of less than 5 feet. During early childhood, the growth of Efe children tapers off to a greater extent than that of other preschoolers because their bodies are less responsive to growth hormone (GH). By age 5, the average Efe child is shorter than over 97 percent of 5-year-olds in the United States (Bailey, 1990).

When environmental conditions are adequate, height and rate of physical maturity (as measured by skeletal age and timing of menarche) are strongly influenced by heredity. For example, identical twins generally reach menarche within a month or two of each other, whereas fraternal twins differ by about 12 months (Malina & Bouchard, 1991; Tanner, 1990). Body weight is also affected by hereditary makeup, since the weights of adopted children correlate more strongly with those of their biological than adoptive parents (Stunkard et al., 1986). Nevertheless, reaching genetic potential in any aspect of physical growth depends on appropriate environmental support, and good nutrition is essential.

NUTRITION

Table 5.2 on page 200 shows the many substances required for normal growth and daily functioning of the human body. Proteins, fats, and carbohydrates are the three basic components of the diet. Proteins are essential for growth, maintenance, and repair of body tissues; carbohydrates supply the primary fuel to meet the body's energy needs; and fats contribute to energy reserves and insulate the body against heat loss. We also need minerals, such as calcium for bone tissue and iron to support the oxygen-carrying power of red

Catch-up growth
Physical growth that returns to its genetically determined path after being delayed by environmental factors.

[2] Notice the resemblance of catch-up growth to the term canalization, which we discussed in Chapter 3, page 117. Body growth is a strongly canalized process.

SOCIAL ISSUES ➤ POINT OF VIEW

Should Children Be Treated for Low-Level Lead Exposure?

Four-year-old Desonia lives in an old, dilapidated tenement in a slum area of a large American city. Layers of paint applied over the years can be seen flaking off the inside walls and the back porch. The oldest paint chips are lead based. As an infant and young preschooler, Desonia picked them up and put them in her mouth. The slightly sweet taste of the leaded flakes encouraged her to nibble more. Soon Desonia became listless and irritable, and her appetite dropped off. When she complained of constant headaches, began to walk with an awkward gait, and experienced repeated convulsions (involuntary muscle contractions), her parents realized that she had more than a passing illness. At a nearby public health clinic, Desonia's blood was analyzed. She had severe lead poisoning, a condition that results in permanent brain damage and (if allowed to persist) early death (Friedman & Weinberger, 1990).

As more cases of severe lead poisoning were identified over this century, laws were passed restricting use of lead-based paint (the major source for children) and leaded gasoline, which releases lead into the air that can be absorbed through the skin and lungs. As a result, the average blood lead level of the American population declined in the late 1970s, and children like Desonia became increasingly rare (Berney, 1993).

Still, inner-city children growing up in deteriorated housing remain at high risk for lead exposure, since lead-based paint already in their homes is difficult to remove. And even when they reside in lead-free housing, children can absorb lead from residues in dust and soil—a danger that is especially great in industrial areas. The persistence of lead in the environment, along with accumulating evidence that it interferes with children's development at levels too low to produce obvious symptoms, sparked a broader question: Is lead contamination a "silent epidemic?" Do children exposed to even small quantities show impairments in intellectual functioning?

The impact of low-level lead is hard to determine, since its presence is related to other factors (such as poverty, poor nutrition, and stressful, unstimulating home environments) that might account for its association with poor mental development. To overcome this difficulty, investigators conducted longitudinal research in which lead exposure during the second year of life (the period in which blood levels peak) was used to predict later mental development. In each study, many variables that might alternatively explain the lead–IQ association were carefully controlled.

Seven investigations of this kind—three conducted in the United States, two in Australia, one in Costa Rica, and one in Yugoslavia—were completed during the past decade. Only two reported negative relationships between low lead levels and later IQ (Bellinger et al., 1991; McMichael, Baghurst, & Wigg, 1988). Yet the results of one suggested a pervasive impact—not just on mental test scores, but academic performance and educational attainment as well. Infants with more lead in their bodies were more likely to develop problems with reading, vocabulary, fine motor coordination, and sustained attention in middle childhood and to drop out of school in adolescence (Needleman et al., 1990). These associations occurred at very low blood concentrations—amounts found in 20 percent of all American children and 60 percent of African-American children in urban areas (Berney, 1993).

Alarmed by these findings, in 1991 the U.S. Public Health Service lowered the official "level of concern" for lead, mandating that children with minimal blood concentrations be followed up with efforts to reduce their exposure immediately. Although most experts agree with the need to control environmental lead contamination, the new policy has energized controversy. Supporters regard the more stringent standard as a necessary precaution. Critics point out that it is not based on sound evidence, since the majority of longitudinal investigations showed no effects of low-level lead exposure! They also worry that expensive, time-consuming monitoring of children for low blood lead will divert policymakers and health professionals from far more powerful causes of intellectual impairment, such as poverty and poor nutrition. In two longitudinal studies, iron deficiency anemia in infancy was strongly associated with lower mental test scores in early childhood, whereas low-level lead made little or no difference (Wasserman et al., 1992; Wolf, Jimenez, & Lozoff, 1994).

YOUR POINT OF VIEW . . .

- Return to pages 32–35 and review the factors that contribute to public policy formation. What might have prompted the U.S. Public Health Service to lower the "level of concern" for lead, despite inconsistent research findings? Do you agree with the new policy? Why or why not?
- Telephone a pediatrician's office or health clinic. Ask what kind of lead testing is routinely done as part of children's physical exams in your community. Find out what steps health professionals take when they find a child with a blood lead concentration at or above the U.S. Public Health Service's "level of concern?"

blood cells. Vitamins are critical as well, such as A for sight and D for skeletal growth. As extensive as it is, this list of essential nutrients is probably not exhaustive. Some substances are not included because they are not yet established as essential for humans.

■ AGE-RELATED NUTRITIONAL NEEDS. Nutrition is important at any time during development, but it is especially critical during infancy because of rapid brain and body growth. Pound for pound, a young baby's energy needs are twice as great as those of an adult. This is because 25 percent of the infant's total caloric intake is devoted to growth, and extra calories are needed to keep rapidly developing organs of the body functioning properly (Pipes, 1989).

TABLE 5.2

Essential Human Nutrients

Proteins			
Fats			
Carbohydrates			
Water			
Minerals	Calcium	Iron	Cobalt
	Phosphorus	Zinc	Chromium
	Potassium	Selenium	Fluorine
	Sulfur	Manganese	Silicon
	Sodium	Copper	Vanadium
	Chlorine	Iodine	Nickel
	Magnesium	Molybdenum	Tin
Vitamins	A	Riboflavin	
	D	Niacin	
	E	Pyroxidine	
	K	Pantothenic acid	
	Ascorbic acid	Folic acid	
	Thiamin	B_{12}	
Biotin			

■ *Breast-feeding is especially important in developing countries, where infants are at risk for malnutrition and early death due to widespread poverty. This baby of Rajasthan, India, is likely to grow normally during the first year because his mother decided to breast-feed. (Jane Schreirman/Photo Researchers)*

Babies do not just need enough food. They need the right kind of food. In early infancy, breast-feeding is especially suited to their needs, and bottled formulas try to imitate it. Table 5.3 summarizes the major nutritional and health advantages of breast milk. Because of these benefits, breast-fed babies in poverty-stricken regions of the world are much less likely to be malnourished and 6 to 14 times more likely to survive the first year of life. Too often, bottle-fed infants in developing countries are given low-grade nutrients, such as rice water or highly diluted cow's and goat's milk. When formula is available, it is generally contaminated due to poor sanitation. Also, because a mother is less likely to get pregnant while she is nursing, breast-feeding helps increase spacing among siblings, a major factor in reducing infant and childhood deaths in developing countries (Grant, 1995). (Note, however, that breast-feeding is not a reliable method of birth control.)

Partly as a result of the natural childbirth movement, over the past two decades, breast-feeding has become more common in industrialized nations, especially among well-educated, middle-class women. Today, over 60 percent of American mothers breast-feed their babies (National Center for Health Statistics, 1995). However, breast-feeding is not for everyone. Some mothers simply do not like it, or they are embarrassed by it. Occasionally, medical reasons prevent a mother from nursing. If she is taking certain drugs, they can be transmitted to the baby through the milk. If she has a serious viral or bacterial disease, such as AIDS or tuberculosis, she runs the risk of infecting her baby (Seltzer & Benjamin, 1990; Van de Perre et al., 1993). As we will see in Chapter 10, emotional well-being is affected by the warmth and sensitivity of caregiving, not by the type of milk offered. Breast- and bottle-fed youngsters show no differences in psychological development (Fergusson, Horwood, & Shannon, 1987).

By 6 months of age, infants require the nutritional diversity of solid foods, and around 1 year, their diets should include all the basic food groups. At about age 2, there is often a dramatic change in the quantity and variety of foods that children will eat. Many who as toddlers tried anything and everything become picky eaters. This decline in appetite is normal. It occurs because growth has slowed. And preschoolers' wariness of new foods may be adaptive. Young children are still learning which items are safe to eat and which are not. By sticking to familiar foods, they are less likely to swallow dangerous substances when adults are not around to protect them (Birch & Fisher, 1995; Rozin, 1990).

TABLE 5.3

Nutritional and Health Advantages of Breast-Feeding

Advantage	Description
Correct balance of fat and protein	Compared to the milk of other mammals, human milk is higher in fat and lower in protein. This balance, as well as the unique proteins and fats contained in human milk, is ideal for a rapidly myelinating nervous system.
Nutritional completeness	A mother who breast-feeds need not add other foods to her infant's diet until the baby is 6 months old. The milks of all mammals are low in iron, but the iron contained in breast milk is much more easily absorbed by the baby's system. Consequently, bottle-fed infants need iron-fortified formula.
Protection against disease	Through breast-feeding, antibodies are transferred from mother to child. As a result, breast-fed babies have far fewer respiratory and intestinal illnesses and allergic reactions than do bottle-fed infants.
Digestibility	Since breast-fed babies have a different kind of bacteria growing in their intestines than do bottle-fed infants, they rarely become constipated or have diarrhea.
Smoother transition to solid foods	Breast-fed infants accept new solid foods more easily than do bottle-fed infants, perhaps because of their greater experience with a variety of flavors, which pass from the maternal diet into the mother's milk and can be tasted by the baby.

Sources: Mennella & Beauchamp, 1991; Räihä & Axelsson, 1995; Shelov, 1993; Sullivan & Birch, 1994.

The wide variety of foods eaten in cultures around the world indicates that the social environment has a powerful impact on young children's food preferences. For example, Mexican preschoolers enthusiastically eat chili peppers, whereas American children quickly reject them. What accounts for this difference? Children tend to imitate the food choices of people they admire—peers as well as adults. In Mexico, children often see family members delighting in the taste of peppery foods (Birch, Zimmerman, & Hind, 1980). In addition, children's tastes are trained by the foods they encounter in their environment. Repeated exposure to a new food (without any direct pressure to eat it) increases children's acceptance (Sullivan & Birch, 1990, 1994).

Once puberty arrives, rapid body growth leads to a dramatic rise in food intake. This increase in nutritional requirements comes at a time when the eating habits of many young people are the poorest. Of all age groups, adolescents are the most likely to consume empty calories. As a result, about 75 percent of North American teenagers suffer from iron deficiency, the most common nutritional problem of adolescence. Most teenagers also do not get enough calcium, and they tend to be deficient in riboflavin (vitamin B_2) and magnesium, both of which support metabolism (Malina, 1990). Adolescents' poor diets do not have serious consequences if they are merely a temporary response to peer influences and a busy schedule, but they can be harmful if they extend a lifelong pattern of poor nutrition.

■ MALNUTRITION. In developing countries where food resources are limited, malnutrition is widespread. Recent evidence indicates that 40 to 60 percent of the world's children do not get enough to eat (Bread for the World Institute, 1994). Among the 4 to 7 percent who are severely affected, malnutrition leads to two dietary diseases: marasmus and kwashiorkor.

Marasmus is a wasted condition of the body that usually appears in the first year of life. It is caused by a diet that is low in all essential nutrients. The disease often occurs when a baby's mother is severely malnourished. As a result, she cannot produce enough breast milk, and bottle-feeding is also inadequate. Her starving baby becomes painfully thin and is in danger of dying.

Unlike marasmus, **kwashiorkor** is not the result of general starvation. Instead, it is due to an unbalanced diet, one that is very low in protein. Kwashiorkor usually strikes after weaning, between 1 and 3 years of age. It is common in areas of the world where children get just enough calories from starchy foods, but protein resources are scarce. The body responds by breaking down its own protein reserves. Soon the child's belly

Marasmus
A disease usually appearing in the first year of life that is caused by a diet low in all essential nutrients. Leads to a wasted condition of the body.

Kwashiorkor
A disease usually appearing between 1 and 3 years of age that is caused by a diet low in protein. Symptoms include an enlarged belly, swollen feet, hair loss, skin rash, and irritable, listless behavior.

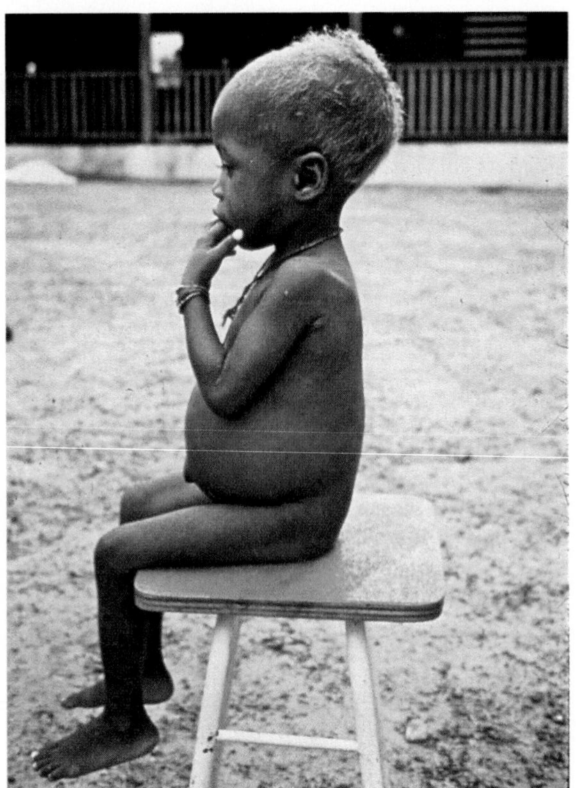

■ *The swollen abdomen and listless behavior of this child are classic symptoms of kwashiorkor, a nutritional illness that results from a diet very low in protein. (CNRI/Phototake)*

enlarges, the feet swell, the hair begins to fall out, and a rash appears on the skin. A once bright-eyed, curious youngster becomes irritable and listless.

Children who manage to survive these extreme forms of malnutrition grow to be smaller in all body dimensions (Galler, Ramsey, & Solimano, 1985a). In addition, their brains are seriously affected. One long-term study of marasmic children revealed that an improved diet led to some catch-up growth in height, but the children failed to catch up in head size (Stoch et al., 1982). The malnutrition probably interfered with myelinization, causing a permanent loss in brain weight. By the time these youngsters reach middle childhood, they score low on intelligence tests, show poor fine motor coordination, and have difficulty paying attention in school (Galler, Ramsey, & Solimano, 1985b; Galler et al., 1984, 1990).

Recall from our dicussion of prenatal malnutrition in Chapter 3 that the passivity and irritability of malnourished children make the impact of poor diet even worse. These behaviors appear even when protein-calorie deprivation is only mild to moderate (Ricciuti, 1993). They reduce the child's ability to pay attention, explore, and evoke sensitive caregiving from parents, whose lives are already disrupted by poverty and stressful living conditions (Wachs et al., 1992). For this reason, interventions for malnourished children must improve the family situation as well as the child's nutrition.

Even better are efforts at prevention—providing food and medical care before the effects of malnutrition run their course. Research in Guatemalan rural villages, where dietary deficiencies are common, underscores the importance of early nutritional intervention. Children receiving food supplements prenatally and during the first 2 years of life scored higher on a variety of mental tests in adolescence than did children given supplements only after their second birthday (Pollitt et al., 1993). Other longitudinal findings from Egypt, Kenya, and Mexico reveal that quality of food (protein, vitamin, and mineral content) is far more important than quantity of food in contributing to the favorable cognitive outcomes just described (Sigman, 1995).

Like prenatal malnutrition, malnutrition after birth is not confined to developing countries. Recent surveys indicate that over 12 percent of children in the United States go to bed hungry (Children's Defense Fund, 1996; Food Research and Action Center, 1991). Although few of these children have marasmus or kwashiorkor, their physical growth and ability to learn in school are still affected. Malnutrition is clearly a national and international crisis—one of the most serious problems confronting the human species today.

■ *Obesity is an emotionally painful and physically debilitating disorder. This boy has difficulty keeping up with his age-mates in a gunnysack race. Because of peer rejection, fat children often lead lonely lives. (Bob Daemmrich/Stock Boston)*

■ OBESITY. Approximately 27 percent of American children suffer from **obesity**, a greater than 20 percent increase over average body weight, based on the child's age, sex, and physical build. Overweight and obesity are growing problems in industrialized nations like the United States. Childhood obesity has climbed steadily since the 1960s, with over 80 percent of affected youngsters retaining their overweight status as adults (Dietz, Bandini, & Gortmaker, 1990; Muecke et al., 1992).

Obese children have serious emotional and social difficulties and are at risk for lifelong health problems. High blood pressure, high cholesterol levels, and respiratory abnormalities begin to appear in the early school years (Taitz, 1983; Unger, Kreeger, & Christoffel, 1990). These symptoms are powerful predictors of heart disease and early death.

Causes of Obesity. Childhood obesity is a complex physical disorder with many contributing factors. Not all children are equally at risk for becoming overweight. Fat children tend to have fat parents, and concordance for obesity is greater in identical than fraternal twins. These findings suggest that heredity has some effect. But similarity among family members is not strong enough to imply that genetics accounts for any more than a susceptibility to obesity (Bouchard, 1994; Dietz, Bandini, & Gortmaker, 1990). One indication that environment is powerfully important is the consistent relation between social class and overweight. Low-income youngsters in industrialized nations are not just at greater risk for malnutrition. They are also more likely to be obese (Stunkard & Sørenson, 1993). Among the factors responsible are lack of knowledge about healthy diet; a tendency to buy high-fat, low-cost foods; and family stress, which prompts overeating in some individuals.

Animal research indicates that overfeeding rats early in development causes their bodies to produce too many fat cells, which act to maintain the overweight condition (Knittle & Hirsch, 1968; Winick & Noble, 1966). Does this same biological factor operate in humans? Research reveals only a slight correlation between fatness in infancy and obesity at older ages. As yet, there is no evidence that a well-nourished human baby—even a very chubby one—can accumulate too many fat cells (Roche, 1981).

In instances in which fatness in infancy does extend into childhood, parental food choices and feeding practices seem to mediate the relationship. In a recent study, fatter preschoolers were more likely to prefer and eat larger quantities of high-fat foods,

Obesity
A greater than 20 percent increase over average body weight, based on the child's age, sex, and physical build.

perhaps because these foods were a prominent part of the diets offered by their parents, who also tended to be overweight (Fisher & Birch, 1995). Some parents anxiously overfeed their infants and young children, interpreting almost all their discomforts as a desire for food. Others are overly controlling, constantly monitoring what their children eat. In either case, they fail to help children learn to regulate their own energy intake appropriately. Finally, parents of obese children often use food as a reward. When food is used to reinforce other behaviors, children start to value the treat itself as well as other similar foods (Birch & Fisher, 1995). In families where these practices are common, high-calorie treats gradually come to symbolize warmth, comfort, and relief of tension.

Because of these feeding experiences, obese children soon develop maladaptive eating habits (Johnson & Birch, 1994). Research shows that they are more responsive to external stimuli associated with food—taste, sight, smell, and time of day—and less responsive to internal hunger cues than are normal-weight individuals. This difference is present in middle childhood and may develop even earlier (Ballard et al., 1980; Constanzo & Woody, 1979). Overweight individuals also eat faster and chew their food less thoroughly, a behavior pattern that appears in overweight children as early as 18 months of age (Drabman et al., 1979).

Fat children do not just eat more; they are less physically active than their normal-weight peers. This inactivity is both cause and consequence of their overweight condition. Recent evidence indicates that the rise in childhood obesity in the United States over the past 30 years is in part due to television viewing. Next to already existing obesity, time spent in front of the TV set is the best predictor of future obesity among school-age children (Gortmaker, Dietz, & Cheung, 1990). Television greatly reduces the time devoted to physical exercise. At the same time, TV ads encourage children to eat fattening, unhealthy snacks—soft drinks, sweets, and salty chips and popcorn (Carruth, Goldberg, & Skinner, 1991).

Psychological Consequences of Obesity. Unfortunately, physical attractiveness is a powerful predictor of social acceptance. Both children and adults rate obese youngsters as less likeable than children with a wide range of physical disabilities (Brenner & Hinsdale, 1978; Lerner & Schroeder, 1971). By middle childhood, obese children have a low sense of self-esteem, report feeling more depressed, and display more behavior problems than do their peers. A vicious cycle emerges in which unhappiness and overeating contribute to one another, and the child remains overweight (Banis et al., 1988).

These psychological consequences combine with continuing discrimination to result in reduced life chances. By young adulthood, overweight individuals have completed fewer years of schooling, have lower incomes, and marry less often than do individuals with other chronic health problems. These outcomes are particularly strong for females (Gortmaker et al., 1993).

Treating Obesity. Obesity is best treated in childhood, before the harmful behaviors that sustain it become well established. Yet childhood obesity is difficult to treat because it is a family disorder. A recent study comparing several treatment approaches found that the most effective intervention was family based and focused on changing behaviors. Both parent and child revised eating patterns, exercised daily, and reinforced each other with praise and points for progress, which they exchanged for special activities and times together (Epstein et al., 1987). A follow-up after 5 years showed that children maintained their weight loss more effectively than did adults. This finding underscores the importance of intervening with obese children at an early age (Epstein et al., 1990).

■ *To inform parents about the importance of immunizations, the U.S. Department of Health and Human Services distributes this poster free of charge. In the poster's next printing, chicken pox will be added to the list of preventable childhood diseases.*

INFECTIOUS DISEASES

Among well-nourished youngsters, ordinary childhood illnesses have no effect on physical growth. But when children are poorly fed, disease interacts with malnutrition in a vicious spiral, and the consequences can be severe.

In developing nations where a large proportion of the population lives in poverty, illnesses such as measles and chicken pox (which typically do not appear until after age 3 in industrialized nations) occur in infancy and take the form of severe illnesses. In these countries, many children do not receive a program of immunizations. In addition, poor diet depresses the body's immune system, making children far more susceptible to

■ *Widespread, government-sponsored immunization of infants and young children is a cost-effective means of supporting healthy growth by dramatically reducing the incidence of childhood diseases. Although this boy finds a routine inoculation painful, it will offer him lifelong protection. (Russell D. Curtis/Photo Researchers)*

disease (Eveleth & Tanner, 1990). Disease, in turn, is a major cause of malnutrition and, through it, affects physical growth. Illness reduces appetite, and it limits the body's ability to absorb foods that children do eat.

In industrialized nations, childhood diseases have declined dramatically during the past half-century, largely due to widespread immunization of infants and young children. Although the majority of preschoolers in the United States are immunized, a sizable minority do not receive full protection until 5 or 6 years of age, when it is required for school entry (Children's Defense Fund, 1996).

Figure 5.16 on page 206 compares immunization rates in the United States with those of a variety of Western nations. How is it that Canada and Western Europe manage to score so well, whereas the United States does poorly? In earlier chapters, we noted that because of lack of medical insurance, many families in the United States do not have access to the health care they need. Beginning in 1994, all medically uninsured American children were guaranteed free vaccinations through public health clinics.

Inability to pay for vaccines, however, is only one cause of low immunization rates. Misconceptions about safe medical practices also contribute. American parents often report that they delay bringing their child in for a vaccination because they fear that a mild illness might reduce its effectiveness or that the child might have an adverse physical reaction (Abbotts & Osborn, 1993; Shalala, 1993). In one case, a mother whose child reacted poorly to her first diphtheria–pertussis–tetanus (DPT) shot decided not to let her have any more of the vaccine. Two years later, the child caught pertussis (whooping cough) and infected her 1-month-old sister, who battled for her life (Friedman & Weiss, 1993). Public education programs directed at increasing parental knowledge about the importance of timely immunizations are badly needed.

EMOTIONAL WELL-BEING

We are not used to thinking of love and stimulation as necessary for healthy physical growth, but they are just as vital as food. Two serious growth disorders are the result of lack of affection and attention.

Nonorganic failure to thrive is usually present by 18 months of age. Infants who have it show all the signs of marasmus, described earlier in this chapter. However, no organic (or biological) cause for the baby's wasted appearance can be found. Enough food is offered, and the infant does not have a serious illness. The behavior of babies with failure to thrive provides a strong clue to its diagnosis. In addition to apathy and withdrawal, these infants keep their eyes on nearby adults, anxiously watching their every move. They rarely smile when the mother comes near or cuddle when picked up (Leonard, Rhymes, & Solnit, 1986; Oates, 1984).

Nonorganic failure to thrive
A growth disorder usually present by 18 months of age that is caused by lack of affection and stimulation.

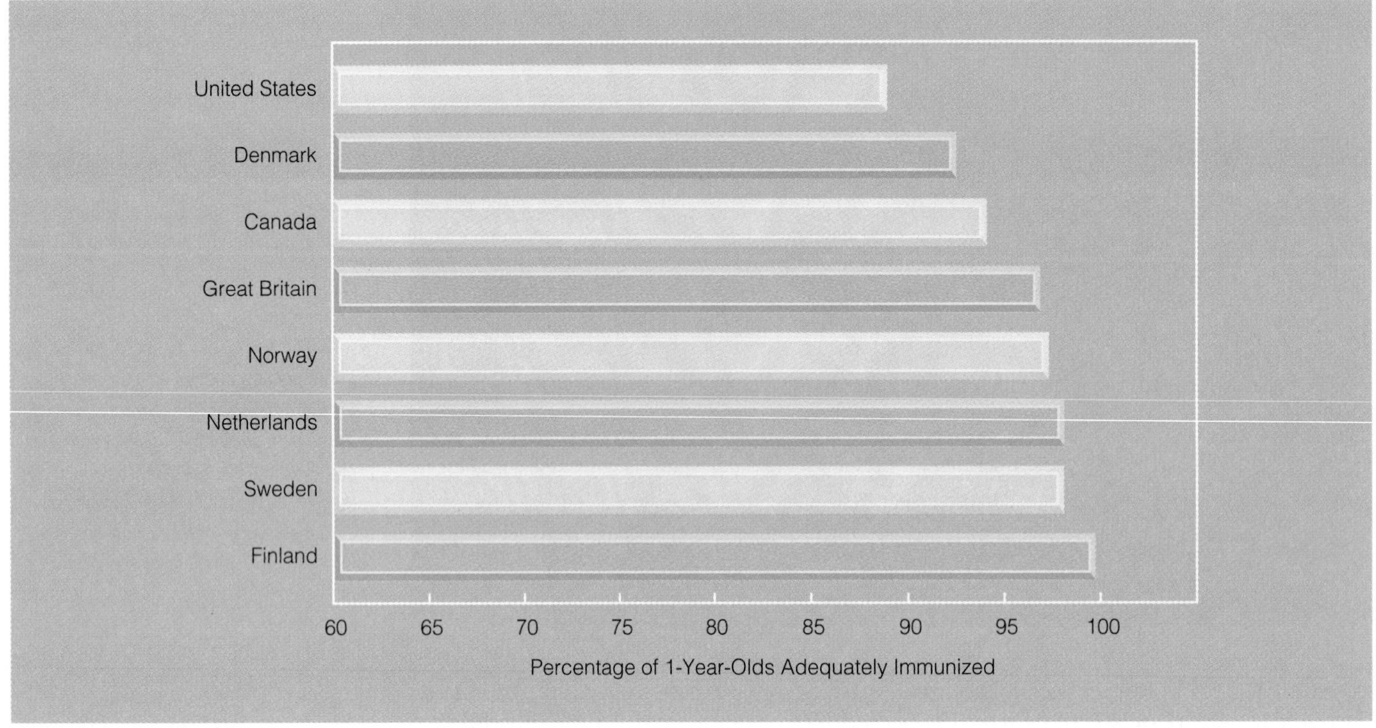

FIGURE 5.16

■ *Immunization rates for 1-year-olds in the United States, Canada, and Western European nations, based on the most recent cross-national data. Infants were immunized for diphtheria, pertussis whooping cough), tetanus, measles, and polio. (Adapted from Grant, 1995.)*

The family circumstances surrounding failure to thrive help explain these typical reactions. During feeding, diaper changing, and play sessions, mothers of these infants seem cold and distant, at other times impatient and hostile (Drotar et al., 1990). In response, babies try to protect themselves by keeping track of the threatening adult's whereabouts and, when she approaches, avoiding her gaze. Often an unhappy marriage or other family pressures contribute to these serious caregiving problems (Gorman, Leifer, & Grossman, 1993). Sometimes the baby displays abnormal feeding behaviors, such as poor sucking or vomiting—circumstances that stress the parent–child relationship further (Ramsay, Gisel, & Boutry, 1993). When treated early, through intensive family therapy or placement in a caring foster home, failure-to-thrive infants show quick catch-up growth. But if the problem is not corrected in infancy, some children remain small and display lasting cognitive and emotional difficulties (Drotar, 1992; Drotar & Sturm, 1988).

Deprivation dwarfism appears later than failure to thrive, usually between 2 and 15 years. Its most striking features are substantially below average stature, decreased GH secretion, and immature skeletal age. Children with the disorder do not look malnourished; their weight is usually appropriate for their height. Researchers believe that severe emotional deprivation affects communication between the hypothalamus and pituitary gland, resulting in stunted growth. When such children are removed from their emotionally inadequate environments, their GH levels quickly return to normal, and they grow rapidly. But if treatment is delayed until later in development, the dwarfism can be permanent (Oates, Peacock, & Forrest, 1985).

Caregiving problems associated with these growth disorders are often grounded in poverty and family disorganization, which place parents under severe stress. With their own emotional resources depleted, parents have little energy available to meet the psychological needs of their children. However, failure to thrive and deprivation dwarfism do not occur just among the poor. They sometimes appear in economically advantaged families when marital conflict or other pressures cause parents to behave insensitively and destructively toward their children (Gagan, 1984).

The study of growth disorders highlights important influences on physical growth that are not readily apparent when we observe the healthy, normally developing child. In the case of failure to thrive and deprivation dwarfism, we become consciously aware of the close connection between sensitive, loving care and how children grow.

Deprivation dwarfism
A growth disorder observed between 2 and 15 years of age. Characterized by substantially below-average stature, weight that is usually appropriate for height, immature skeletal age, and decreased GH secretion. Caused by emotional deprivation.

SUMMARY

THE COURSE OF PHYSICAL GROWTH

- Compared to other species, humans experience a prolonged period of physical growth. **Distance** and **velocity curves** show the overall pattern of change: Gains in height and weight are rapid during infancy, slow and steady during middle childhood, and rapid again during **puberty**.
- In childhood, physical growth follows cephalocaudal and proximodistal trends. During puberty, growth actually proceeds in the reverse direction, and sex-related differences in body proportions appear. Body fat is laid down quickly during the first 9 months, then rapidly again at adolescence for girls. In contrast, muscle development is slow and gradual until puberty, when it rises dramatically, especially for boys.
- **Skeletal age**, a measure based on the number of **epiphyses** and the extent to which they are fused, is the best way to estimate the child's overall physical maturity. Girls are advanced over boys, a gap that widens over infancy and childhood. At birth, infants have six **fontanels**, which permit skull bones to expand as the brain grows.
- Physical growth is an asynchronous process. The **general growth curve** refers to change in overall body size. Other systems of the body, such as the brain, the genitals, and the lymph tissue, have their own unique timetables of maturation.
- Large individual and group differences in body growth are the combined result of heredity and environment. **Secular trends in physical growth** have occurred in industrialized nations. Because of improved health and nutrition, many children are growing larger and reaching physical maturity earlier than their ancestors.
- Physical growth is controlled by hormones released by the **pituitary gland**, located at the base of the brain near the **hypothalamus**, which initiates and regulates pituitary secretions. **Growth hormone (GH)** affects the development of almost all body tissues. **Thyroxine**, released by the thyroid gland, influences brain growth and body size. Sexual maturation is controlled by the sex hormones—**estrogens** and **androgens**.

PUBERTY: THE PHYSICAL TRANSITION TO ADULTHOOD

- Accompanying rapid changes in body size and proportions at puberty are changes in **primary** and **secondary sexual characteristics**. **Menarche** (first menstruation) occurs relatively late in the girl's sequence of pubertal events, after the peak in the height spurt. In the following year, growth of the breasts and pubic hair are completed, and underarm hair appears. As the boy's body and sex organs enlarge and pubic and underarm hair emerges, **spermarche** (first ejaculation) and deepening of the voice take place, followed by growth of facial and body hair.

THE PSYCHOLOGICAL IMPACT OF PUBERTAL EVENTS

- Recent research shows that puberty is not a biologically determined, inevitable period of storm and stress. Instead, adolescent adjustment varies widely and is a product of both biological and social forces.
- Girls generally react to menarche with surprise and mixed emotions, but whether their feelings are more positive or negative depends on advance information and support from family members. Boys usually know ahead of time about spermarche, but they receive less social support for the physical changes of puberty than do girls.
- Besides hormone levels, situational changes are associated with adolescent moodiness. Puberty is accompanied by an increase in mild conflict and psychological distancing between parent and child.
- Timing of puberty influences psychological adjustment. Early maturing boys and late maturing girls, whose appearance closely matches cultural standards of physical attractiveness, have a more positive **body image**, feel more self-confident, and hold more positions of leadership. In contrast, early maturing girls and late maturing boys, who fit in least well physically with peers, experience emotional and social difficulties.
- The hormonal changes of puberty lead to an increase in sex drive, but social factors affect how teenagers manage their sexuality. Compared to most cultures, the United States is fairly restrictive in its attitude toward adolescent sex. Sexual attitudes of adolescents and adults have become more liberal in recent years, and the rate of teenage sexual activity has risen.
- One-third to one-half of sexually active American teenagers do not practice contraception regularly. Adolescent cognitive processes and a lack of social support for responsible sexual behavior underlie this trend.
- About 3 to 6 percent of young people discover they are lesbian or gay. Although heredity makes an important contribution, homosexuality probably results from a variety of biological and environmental combinations that are not yet well understood. Lesbian and gay teenagers face special problems in establishing a positive sexual identity.
- Sexually active teenagers are at risk for contracting sexually transmitted diseases (STDs). The most serious is AIDS. Drug-abusing and homosexual young people account for most cases, but heterosexual spread is increasing, especially for females.
- Adolescent pregnancy, abortion, and childbearing are higher in the United States than in many industrialized nations. Teenage parenthood is often associated with dropping out of school and poverty, circumstances that risk the well-being of both adolescent and newborn child. Improved sex education and contraceptive services for adolescents reduce teenage pregnancy and childbearing.

- Girls who reach puberty early, who are dissatisfied with their body images, and who grow up in economically advantaged homes are at risk for eating disorders. **Anorexia nervosa** tends to appear in girls who have perfectionist personalities and overprotective and controlling parents. The impulsive eating and purging of **bulimia** is associated with lack of self-control in other areas of life.

DEVELOPMENT OF THE BRAIN

- The human brain achieves its peak period of growth earlier than other organs. During infancy, **neurons** form **synapses** at a rapid rate. During the peak period of development in any brain area, **programmed cell death** makes room for growth of neural fibers that form synaptic connections. Stimulation determines which neurons will continue to establish new synapses and which will lose their connective fibers through **synaptic pruning**. **Glial cells**, which are responsible for **myelinization**, multiply dramatically through the second year and result in large gains in brain weight.
- **Lateralization** refers to specialization of the hemispheres of the cerebral cortex. Although some specialization exists at birth, in the first few years of life there is high **brain plasticity**. Both heredity and early experience contribute to brain organization.
- Hand preference reflects the individual's **dominant cerebral hemisphere**. It first appears in infancy and gradually increases, indicating that lateralization strengthens during early and middle childhood. Although left-handedness is more frequent among children with developmental problems, the great majority of left-handed children show no abnormalities of any kind.
- During infancy and early childhood, connections are established among different brain structures. Fibers linking the **cerebellum** to the cerebral cortex myelinate, enhancing children's balance and motor control. The **reticular formation**, responsible for alertness and consciousness, and the **corpus callosum**, which connects the two cerebral hemispheres, also develop rapidly.
- Changes in the electrical activity of the cortex, along with gains in brain weight and skull size, indicate that brain growth spurts occur intermittently from infancy into adolescence. These may be sensitive periods in which appropriate stimulation is necessary for full development of human intelligence.

FACTORS AFFECTING PHYSICAL GROWTH

- Twin and adoption studies reveal that heredity contributes to children's height, weight, and rate of physical maturation. Good nutrition is crucial for children to reach their full growth potential. Breast-feeding is especially suited to infants' growth needs. As growth slows in early childhood, appetite declines. It rises sharply during puberty.
- The importance of nutrition is tragically evident in the dietary diseases of **marasmus** and **kwashiorkor**, which affect large numbers of children in developing countries. In industrialized nations, **obesity** is a nutritional problem with severe health and psychological consequences.
- Infectious disease can combine with poor nutrition to undermine healthy physical development. **Nonorganic failure to thrive** and **deprivation dwarfism** illustrate the importance of affection and stimulation for normal human growth.

IMPORTANT TERMS AND CONCEPTS

puberty (p. 167)
distance curve (p. 169)
velocity curve (p. 169)
skeletal age (p. 170)
epiphyses (p. 170)
fontanels (p. 173)
general growth curve (p. 173)
secular trends in physical growth (p. 175)
pituitary gland (p. 176)
hypothalamus (p. 176)
growth hormone (GH) (p. 176)
thyroxine (p. 176)
estrogens (p. 177)
androgens (p. 177)
primary sexual characteristics (p. 178)
secondary sexual characteristics (p. 178)
menarche (p. 178)
spermarche (p. 180)
body image (p. 184)
anorexia nervosa (p. 191)
bulimia (p. 192)
neurons (p. 192)
synapses (p. 192)
programmed cell death (p. 192)
synaptic pruning (p. 193)
glial cells (p. 193)
myelinization (p. 193)
cerebral cortex (p. 193)
lateralization (p. 194)
brain plasticity (p. 194)
dominant cerebral hemisphere (p. 195)
cerebellum (p. 196)
reticular formation (p. 196)
corpus callosum (p. 196)
catch-up growth (p. 198)
marasmus (p. 201)
kwashiorkor (p. 201)
obesity (p. 204)
nonorganic failure to thrive (p. 205)
deprivation dwarfism (p. 206)

for Chapter 5

If you are interested in . . .	turn to . . .	to learn about . . .
■ Motor development	■ Chapter 4, pp. 125–126	■ Newborn reflexes and the development of motor skills
	■ Chapter 4, pp. 142–143	■ Dynamic systems theory and motor development
	■ Chapter 4, pp. 143–144	■ Cultural variations in motor development
	■ Chapter 4, pp. 147, 154, 161	■ Relationship between motor skills and infant perceptual development
	■ Chapter 6, pp. 216, 224	■ Relationship between motor skills and infant cognitive development
	■ Chapter 10, pp. 388–389	■ Relationship between motor skills and infant emotional development
■ Brain development	■ Chapter 3, pp. 89, 91	■ Brain development during the prenatal period
	■ Chapter 3, pp. 108–109	■ Birth complications and brain damage
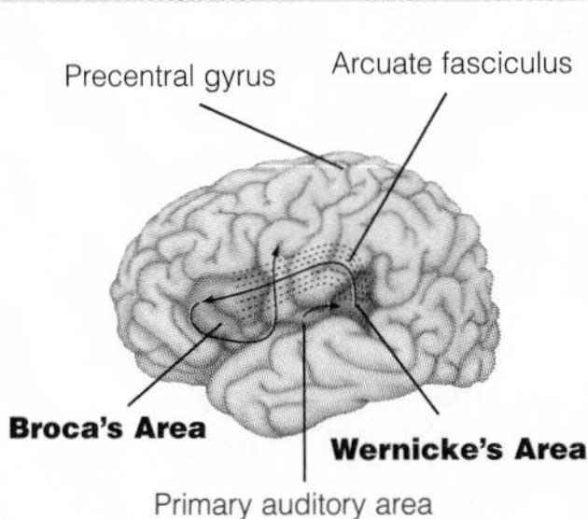	■ Chapter 4, pp. 126–127, 130, 132	■ Newborn reflexes, sleep, and crying and intactness of the central nervous system
	■ Chapter 7, p. 279	■ Brain maturation and infantile amnesia
	■ Chapter 9, pp. 346–347	■ Language areas in the brain
	■ Chapter 13, pp. 508–511, 528	■ Sex hormones and brain development
■ Adolescent adjustment	■ Chapter 6, p. 243	■ Formal operational egocentrism: The imaginary audience and personal fable
	■ Chapter 11, pp. 438–440	■ Adolescent identity development
	■ Chapter 11, p. 441	■ Adolescent suicide
	■ Chapter 12, p. 494	■ Juvenile delinquency
	■ Chapter 14, pp. 547–548	■ Adolescent autonomy
	■ Chapter 15, p. 596	■ Adolescent substance use and abuse
	■ Chapter 15, pp. 612–613	■ School transitions in adolescence

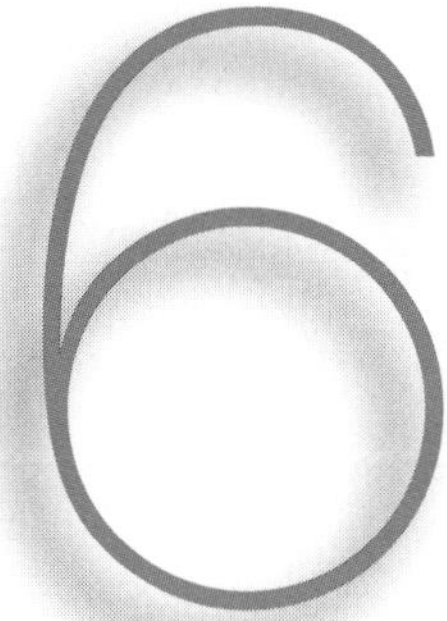

6 Cognitive Development: Piagetian and Vygotskian Perspectives

Cognition refers to the inner processes and products of the mind that lead to "knowing." It includes all mental activity—remembering, symbolizing, categorizing, problem solving, creating, fantasizing, and even dreaming. Indeed, we could easily expand this list, since mental processes make their way into virtually everything human beings do.

Among the great contributions of the Swiss theorist Jean Piaget was his view of human cognition as an integrated set of reasoning abilities that develop together and can be applied to any task. Piaget's *cognitive-developmental* stage theory stands as one of the three dominant twentieth-century positions on cognitive development (see Chapter 1). The other two are Lev Semenovich Vygotsky's *sociocultural theory,* which we consider alongside Piaget's perspective, and *information processing,* which we examine in Chapter 7.

The theories of Piaget and Vygotsky form a natural counterpoint. Both men were born in 1896, although they lived and worked in widely separated parts of the world—Piaget in Switzerland, Vygotsky in Russia. In their earliest investigations, each addressed the same puzzling issue—the role of language in cognitive development—in similarly titled volumes. Do children first master ideas and then translate them into words? Or does the capacity for language open new cognitive doors, enabling children to think in more advanced ways?

In *The Language and Thought of the Child,* Piaget (1923/1926) claimed that language was relatively unimportant in spurring the young child's thinking forward. Instead, he argued, major cognitive advances take place as children act directly on the physical world, discover the shortcomings of their current ways of thinking, and revise them to create a better fit with external reality.

A few years later, the bold young Vygotsky (1934/1986) challenged this conclusion. In *Thought and Language,* he claimed that human mental activity is the result of social, not independent, learning. According to Vygotsky, as children master challenging everyday tasks, they engage in cooperative dialogues with adults and more expert peers, who assist them in their efforts. During these interactions, cognitive processes that are adaptive in a particular culture are socially transferred to children. Since language is the primary means through which humans exchange social meanings, Vygotsky viewed it as crucial for cognitive change. Indeed, Vygotsky regarded the acquisition of language as the most significant achievement in children's development (Blanck, 1990).

On the basis of this brief description, do you find it difficult to decide between Piaget's and Vygotsky's perspectives? Before we can evaluate the work of these two giants of cognitive development, we must become thoroughly acquainted with each theory and the research it has stimulated.

As we do so, we will encounter additional controversies about the nature of the child's mind. Among the most widely debated are these:

- Is cognitive development a matter of **domain-general changes**—similar transformations across all types of knowledge, as Piaget claimed? Or does it involve a variety of **domain-specific changes**—the perfection of separate, specialized abilities, each adapted to handling certain types of information?
- Does a **constructivist approach** like Piaget's, in which children *discover virtually all knowledge about the world through their own activity,* provide an accurate account of cognitive development? Or is a **nativist approach** more effective—the idea that children *are born with substantial innate knowledge,* which guides their interpretations of reality and gets cognitive development off to a speedy, efficient start?

Domain-general changes
Similar transformations across all types of knowledge, resulting in the perfection of general reasoning abilities.

Domain-specific changes
Distinct transformations within each type of knowledge, resulting in the perfection of separate, specialized abilities.

Constructivist approach
An approach to cognitive development in which children discover virtually all knowledge about the world through their own activity. Consistent with Piaget's cognitive-developmental theory.

Nativist approach
An approach to cognitive development in which children are born with substantial innate knowledge, which guides their interpretations of reality and gets cognitive development off to a speedy, efficient start.

Piaget's Cognitive-Developmental Theory

Piaget conceived of human cognition as a network of mental structures created by an active organism constantly striving to make sense of experience. This view was revolutionary when it first reached the United States in the middle of the twentieth century. It represented a dramatic break with the then dominant perspective of behaviorism, which steered clear of any constructs of mind and regarded the child as passively shaped by external forces (Beilin, 1992). By the 1960s, American researchers embraced Piaget's ideas with enthusiasm. His vision of the child as an intrinsically motivated learner, the variety of tasks he devised to assess cognitive development, and the relevance of his theory for education made it especially attractive.

Piaget received his early training in biology and philosophy. As a young boy, he spent his afternoons at the Museum of Natural History in Neufchâtel, where he became interested in how the shell structures of mollusks, which populate the lakes of Switzerland, are uniquely adapted to the animals' habitat. During his teenage years, his godfather introduced him to epistemology, the branch of philosophy concerned with the foundations of knowledge. Shortly after completing his Ph.D. in zoology, Piaget began to construct a biological account of the origins of knowledge (Piaget, 1952a). As a result, his theory of cognitive development came to have a distinctly biological flavor.

■ *According to Piaget's theory, at first schemes are motor action patterns. As this 1-year-old takes apart, bangs, and drops these nesting cups, she discovers that her movements have predictable effects on objects and that objects influence one another in regular ways.* (Erika Stone)

KEY PIAGETIAN CONCEPTS

According to Piaget, just as the body has physical structures that enable it to adapt to the environment, so the mind builds psychological structures—organized ways of making sense of experience—that permit it to adapt to the external world. In the development of these structures, children are intensely active. They select and interpret experience in terms of their current structures, and they also modify those structures so that they take into account more subtle aspects of reality.

Piaget believed that children move through four stages of development—sensorimotor, preoperational, concrete operational, and formal operational—during which the exploratory behaviors of infants are transformed into the abstract, logical intelligence of adolescence and adulthood. To appreciate his view of how such vast change occurs, we must examine a set of important concepts. These convey Piaget's ideas about *what changes with development*, and *how cognitive change takes place.*

■ WHAT CHANGES WITH DEVELOPMENT? According to Piaget, specific psychological structures, or **schemes**, change with age. At first, schemes are motor action patterns. For example, watch a 6-month-old baby grasp and release objects, and you will see that the "dropping scheme" is fairly rigid; the infant simply lets go of a rattle or teething ring in her hand. But by 18 months, the "dropping scheme" has become much more deliberate and creative. Given an opportunity, a baby of this age is likely to toss all sorts of objects down the basement stairs, throwing some up in the air, bouncing others off walls, releasing some gently and others with all the force her little body can muster. Soon schemes will move from an action-based level to a mental level. When this happens, the child will show evidence of thinking before she acts. This change, as we will see later, marks the transition from sensorimotor to preoperational thought.

Piaget believed that children have a natural tendency to exercise their schemes repeatedly. For example, an infant who has just mastered voluntary reaching is likely to apply the new scheme to a wide variety of objects. And preschoolers often engage in tireless practice of representational schemes by demanding that the same story be read to them over and over again. As schemes are practiced, they come into contact with new information. Once children notice a gap between their current schemes and external reality, they try to reduce this discrepancy.

Scheme
In Piaget's theory, a specific structure, or organized way of making sense of experience, that changes with age.

■ HOW DOES COGNITIVE CHANGE TAKE PLACE? To explain how schemes change, Piaget identified two important intellectual *functions:* adaptation and organization. The basic properties of these functions remain the same throughout life, despite the wide variety of schemes they create.

Adaptation. **Adaptation** involves building schemes through direct interaction with the environment. It is made up of two complementary processes: assimilation and accommodation. During **assimilation,** we interpret the external world in terms of our current schemes. For example, the infant who puts a variety of objects in his mouth is assimilating them all into his sensorimotor sucking scheme. And the preschooler who sees her first camel at the zoo and calls out, "Horse!" has sifted through her collection of schemes until she finds one that resembles the strange-looking creature. In **accommodation**, we adjust old schemes or create new ones after noticing that our current thinking does not capture the environment completely. The baby who begins to suck differently on the edge of a blanket than on a nipple has started to modify the sucking scheme. And the preschooler who calls a camel a "lumpy horse" has noticed that certain characteristics of camels are not like horses and revised her "horse scheme" accordingly.

So far, we have referred to assimilation and accommodation as separate activities, but they always work together. That is, in every interchange with the environment, we interpret information using our existing structures, and we also refine them to achieve a better fit with experience. But the balance between assimilation and accommodation varies from one time period to another. When children are not changing very much, they assimilate more than they accommodate. Piaget called this a state of cognitive *equilibrium,* implying a steady, comfortable condition. During times of rapid cognitive change, however, children are in a state of *disequilibrium,* or cognitive discomfort. They realize that new information does not match their current schemes, so they shift away from assimilation toward accommodation. Once they have modified their schemes, they move back toward assimilation, exercising their newly changed structures until they are ready to be modified again.

Piaget used the term **equilibration** to sum up this back-and-forth movement between equilibrium and disequilibrium throughout development. Each time equilibration occurs, more effective schemes are produced. They take in a wider range of aspects of the environment, and there is less and less to throw them out of balance (Piaget, 1985). Consequently, the times of greatest accommodation are the earliest ones, and (as we will soon see) the sensorimotor stage is Piaget's most complex period of development.

Organization. Schemes also change through a second process called **organization**. It takes place internally, apart from direct contact with the environment. Once children form new structures, they start to rearrange them, linking them with other schemes so they are part of a strongly interconnected cognitive system. For example, eventually the baby will relate "grasping," "sucking," "dropping," and "throwing" to his developing understanding of "nearness" and "farness." And the preschooler will construct a separate "camel scheme," but it will be connected by similarities and differences to her understanding of horses and other animals. According to Piaget, schemes reach a true state of equilibrium when they become part of a broad network of structures that can be jointly applied to the surrounding world (Piaget, 1936/1952b).

Adaptation
In Piaget's theory, the process of building schemes through direct interaction with the environment. Made up of two complementary activities: assimilation and accommodation.

Assimilation
That part of adaptation in which the external world is interpreted in terms of current schemes.

Accommodation
That part of adaptation in which old schemes are adjusted and new ones created to produce a better fit with the environment.

Equilibration
In Piaget's theory, back-and-forth movement between cognitive equilibrium and disequilibrium throughout development, which leads to more effective schemes.

Organization
In Piaget's theory, the internal rearrangement and linking together of schemes so they form a strongly interconnected cognitive system.

THE PIAGETIAN NOTION OF STAGE

Each of Piaget's four stages groups together similar qualitative changes in many schemes that occur during the same time period of development (Tanner & Inhelder, 1956). As a result, his stage sequence has two important characteristics. First, it is *invariant,* which means that the stages always emerge in a fixed order; no stages can be skipped. Second, the stages are *universal;* they are assumed to describe the cognitive development of children everywhere (Piaget, Inhelder, & Szeminska, 1948/1960).

Although Piaget viewed the order of development as genetically determined, he emphasized that many factors—both hereditary and environmental—affect the speed with which individual children move through the stages (Piaget, 1926/1928). In the following sections, we will describe development as Piaget saw it, noting research that supports his observations. Then, for each stage, we will consider recent findings that seriously challenge his ideas. Before we begin, you may find it useful to return to Table 1.4 on page 20, which provides an overview of Piaget's sequence of development.

The Sensorimotor Stage (Birth to 2 Years)

The difference between the newborn baby and the 2-year-old child is so vast that the **sensorimotor stage** is divided into six substages. Piaget's observations of his own three children served as the basis for this description of development. Piaget watched carefully and also presented his son and two daughters with everyday problems (such as hidden objects) that helped reveal their understanding of the world. Nevertheless, the fact that Piaget's research on infant cognition was based on such a limited sample caused many investigators to question the validity of his sensorimotor stage. It is now widely agreed that Piaget underestimated the cognitive competence of young babies.

SENSORIMOTOR LEARNING MECHANISMS

According to Piaget, at birth infants know so little about the world that they cannot purposefully explore it. This presents a problem for young babies, since they need some way of adapting their first schemes. The **circular reaction** provides a special means of doing so. It involves stumbling onto a new experience caused by the baby's own motor activity. The reaction is "circular" because the infant tries to repeat the event again and again. As a result, a sensorimotor response that first occurred by chance becomes strengthened into a new scheme. For example, imagine a 2-month-old, who accidentally makes a smacking noise when finishing a feeding. The baby finds the sound intriguing, so she tries to repeat it until, after a few days, she becomes quite expert at smacking her lips.

During the first 2 years, the circular reaction changes in several ways. At first, it is centered around the infant's own body. Later, it turns outward, toward manipulation of objects. Finally, it becomes experimental and creative, aimed at producing novel effects in the environment. Piaget considered these revisions in the circular reaction so important that he named the sensorimotor substages after them.

Two additional capacities—*play* and *imitation*—first appear during the sensorimotor stage. They also serve as important mechanisms for solidifying old schemes and creating new ones. Piaget viewed play as the purest form of assimilation—practicing already acquired schemes just for the pleasure of doing so. (Later we will see that other theorists, including Vygotsky, regard this definition as too narrow.) In contrast, imitation emphasizes accommodation, since it involves copying behaviors that are not yet in the child's repertoire. According to Piaget, what infants and children play at and imitate provides excellent indicators of their advancing cognitive capacities.

THE SENSORIMOTOR SUBSTAGES

As we examine Piaget's six sensorimotor substages, you may find it helpful to refer to Table 6.1, which provides a summary of each.

■ SUBSTAGE 1: REFLEXIVE SCHEMES (BIRTH TO 1 MONTH). Piaget regarded newborn reflexes as the building blocks of sensorimotor intelligence. As we will see in Substage 2, sucking, grasping, and looking quickly change as they are applied to the environment. But at first, infants apply reflexive behaviors rather indiscriminately, to whatever stimulus comes in contact with their lips or the palms of their hands. In one amusing example, a mother reported to me that her 2-week-old daughter lay on the bed next to her father while he took a nap. Suddenly, he awoke with a start. The baby had latched on and begun to suck on his back!

According to Piaget, newborn babies are totally egocentric beings. *Egocentrism*—the inability to distinguish one's own cognitive perspective from the perspectives of others—reappears in several forms across his stages. **Sensorimotor egocentrism** involves a merging of the self with the surrounding world, an absence of the understanding that the self is an object in a world of objects. It declines over the sensorimotor period, as infants gradually discover that their own actions are separate from external reality (Piaget, 1936/1952b).

Sensorimotor stage
Piaget's first stage, during which infants "think" with their eyes, ears, hands, and other sensorimotor equipment. Spans the first 2 years of life.

Circular reaction
In Piaget's theory, a means of building schemes in which infants try to repeat a chance event caused by their own motor activity.

Sensorimotor egocentrism
A form of egocentrism present in infancy that involves a merging of the self with the surrounding world, an absence of the understanding that the self is an object in a world of objects.

TABLE 6.1

Summary of Cognitive Development During the Sensorimotor Stage

Sensorimotor Substage	Typical Adaptive Behaviors
1. Reflexive schemes (birth to 1 month)	Newborn reflexes (see Chapter 4, page 125)
2. Primary circular reactions (1–4 months)	Simple motor habits centered around the infant's own body; limited anticipation of events
3. Secondary circular reactions (4–8 months)	Actions aimed at repeating interesting effects in the surrounding world; imitation of familiar behaviors
4. Coordination of secondary circular reactions (8–12 months)	Intentional, or goal-directed action sequences; improved anticipation of events; imitation of behaviors slightly different from those the infant usually performs; ability to find a hidden object in the first location in which it is hidden (object permanence)
5. Tertiary circular reactions (12–18 months)	Exploration of the properties of objects by acting on them in novel ways; imitation of unfamiliar behaviors; ability to search in several locations for a hidden object (AB search)
6. Mental combinations (18 months–2 years)	Internal representation of objects and events; as indicated by sudden solutions to sensorimotor problems; ability to find an object that has been moved while out of sight (invisible displacement); deferred imitation; and make-believe play

■ **SUBSTAGE 2: PRIMARY CIRCULAR REACTIONS—THE FIRST LEARNED ADAPTATIONS (1 TO 4 MONTHS).** Infants start to gain voluntary control over their actions by repeating chance behaviors that lead to satisfying results. Consequently, they develop some simple motor habits, such as sucking their thumbs and opening and closing their hands. Babies in this substage also begin to vary their behavior in response to environmental demands. For example, they open their mouths differently to a nipple than a spoon. Young infants also show a limited ability to anticipate events. A hungry 3-month-old is likely to stop crying as soon as his mother enters the room and moves toward the crib—an event signaling that feeding time is near.

Piaget called the first circular reactions *primary,* and he regarded them as quite limited. Notice how, in the examples just given, infants' adaptations are oriented toward their own bodies and motivated by basic needs. According to Piaget, babies of this age are not yet very concerned with the effects of their actions on the external world. Therefore, the infant of a few months of age is still a very egocentric being.

In Substage 2, babies begin to exercise schemes playfully, smiling gleefully as they repeat a newly developed action. Piaget also believed that first efforts at imitation also appear, but they are limited to copying someone else's imitation of the baby's own actions. However, recall from Chapter 4 that neonates can imitate, so imitation seems to be one area in which Piaget misjudged the young baby's competence.

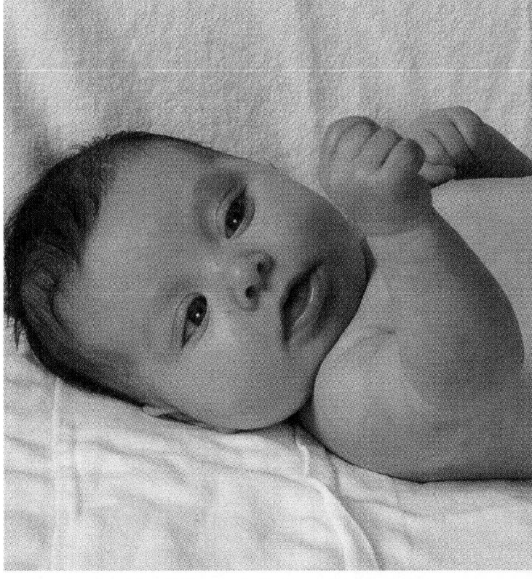

■ *During Piaget's Substage 2, infants' adaptations are oriented toward their own bodies. This young baby carefully watches the movements of her hands, a primary circular reaction that helps her gain voluntary control over her behavior. (Erika Stone)*

■ **SUBSTAGE 3: SECONDARY CIRCULAR REACTIONS—MAKING INTERESTING SIGHTS LAST (4 TO 8 MONTHS).** Between 4 and 8 months, infants sit up and become skilled at reaching for, grasping, and manipulating objects (see Chapter 4). These motor achievements play a major role in turning babies' attention outward toward the environment. Using the *secondary* circular reaction, they try to repeat interesting sights and sounds that are caused by their own actions. In the following illustration, notice how Piaget's 4-month-old son Laurent gradually builds the sensorimotor scheme of "hitting" over a 10-day period:

> At 4 months 7 days [Laurent] looks at a letter opener tangled in the strings of a doll hung in front of him. He tries to grasp (a scheme he already knows) the doll or the letter opener but each time, his attempts only result in his knocking the objects (so they swing out of his reach). . . . At 4 months 15 days, with another doll hung in front of him, Laurent tries to grasp it, then shakes himself to make it swing, knocks it accidentally, and then tries simply to hit it. . . . At 4 months 18 days, Laurent hits my hands without trying to grasp them, but he started by simply waving his arms around, and only afterwards went on to hit my hands. The next day, finally, Laurent immediately hits a doll hung in front of him. The [hitting] scheme is now completely differentiated [from grasping]. (Piaget, 1936/1952b, pp. 167–168)

Improved control over their own behavior permits infants of this substage to imitate the behaviors of others more effectively. However, babies under 8 months cannot adapt flexibly and quickly, copying behaviors that are very novel (Kaye & Marcus, 1981). Therefore, although 4- to 8-month-olds enjoy watching an adult demonstrate a game of pat-a-cake or peekaboo, they are not yet able to participate.

■ SUBSTAGE 4: COORDINATION OF SECONDARY CIRCULAR REACTIONS (8 TO 12 MONTHS). Now infants start to organize schemes. They combine secondary circular reactions into new, more complex action sequences. As a result, two landmark cognitive changes take place.

First, babies can engage in **intentional**, or **goal-directed, behavior**. Before this substage, actions that led to new schemes had a random, hit-or-miss quality to them—*accidentally* bringing the thumb to the mouth or *happening* to hit the doll hung over the crib. But by 8 months, infants have had enough practice with a variety of schemes that they coordinate them deliberately to solve sensorimotor problems. The clearest example is provided by Piaget's object-hiding tasks, in which he shows the baby an attractive toy and then hides it behind his hand or under a cover. Infants of this substage can find the object. In doing so, they coordinate two schemes: "pushing" aside the obstacle and "grasping" the toy. Piaget regarded these means–end action sequences as the first sign that babies appreciate **physical causality** (the causal action one object exerts on another through contact) and as the foundation for all later problem solving.

The fact that infants can retrieve hidden objects reveals that they have begun to attain a second cognitive milestone: **object permanence**, the understanding that objects continue to exist when out of sight. But awareness of object permanence is not yet complete. If an object is moved from one hiding place (A) to another (B), babies will search for it only in the first hiding place (A). Because 8- to 12-month-olds make this **AB search error**, Piaget concluded that they do not have a clear image of the object as persisting when hidden from view.

Substage 4 brings several additional advances. First, infants can anticipate events more effectively, and using their new capacity for intentional behavior, they sometimes try to change those experiences. For example, a baby of this age might crawl after his mother when she puts on her coat, whimpering and hanging on to keep her from leaving. Second, now babies imitate behaviors that are slightly different from those they usually perform. After watching someone else, they try to stir with a spoon, push a toy car, or drop raisins in a cup. Once again, they draw on their capacity for intentional behavior—purposefully modifying schemes to fit an observed action (Piaget, 1945/1951).

Finally, play extends to practicing the means in babies' new means–end action sequences. On one occasion, Piaget's son began by pushing an obstacle aside to obtain a toy but ended up ignoring the toy and instead pushing the obstacle (Piaget's hand or a piece of cardboard) again and again for fun (Piaget, 1945/1951).

■ SUBSTAGE 5: TERTIARY CIRCULAR REACTIONS—DISCOVERING NEW MEANS THROUGH ACTIVE EXPERIMENTATION (12 TO 18 MONTHS). At this substage, the circular reaction—now called *tertiary*—becomes experimental and creative. Toddlers do not just repeat behaviors that lead to familiar results. They repeat with variation, provoking new outcomes. Recall the example on page 212 of the child dropping objects down the basement steps, trying this, then that, and then another action in a deliberately exploratory approach. Because 12- to 18-month-olds deal with the world in this way, they are far better sensorimotor problem solvers than they were before. For example, they can figure out how to fit a shape through a hole in a container by turning and twisting it until it falls through, and they can use a stick to obtain a toy that is out of reach.

According to Piaget, this new capacity to experiment leads to a more advanced understanding of object permanence. Older infants look in not just one, but several locations to find a hidden toy. Thus, they no longer make the AB search error. Their more flexible action patterns also permit them to imitate many more behaviors, such as stacking blocks, scribbling on paper, and making funny faces. And once babies vary their actions with respect to objects, they clearly distinguish themselves from the surrounding world. As a result, sensorimotor egocentrism disappears.

Intentional, or goal-directed, behavior
A sequence of actions in which schemes are deliberately combined to solve a problem.

Physical causality
The causal action one object exerts on another through contact.

Object permanence
The understanding that objects continue to exist when they are out of sight.

AB search error
The error made by 8- to 12-month-olds after an object is moved from hiding place A to hiding place B. Infants in Piaget's Substage 4 search for it only in the first hiding place (A).

■ *As this 15-month-old masters the nuances of object permanence, she delights in hiding-and-finding games, such as peekaboo. Her flexible imitative abilities permit her to participate more actively in the game than she could at a younger age. (Tony Freeman/PhotoEdit)*

■ SUBSTAGE 6: MENTAL REPRESENTATION—INVENTING NEW MEANS THROUGH MENTAL COMBINATIONS (18 MONTHS TO 2 YEARS). Substage 5 is the last truly sensorimotor stage. Substage 6 brings with it the ability to make **mental representations** of reality—internal images of absent objects and past events. As a result, children can solve problems through symbolic means instead of trial-and-error behavior. One sign of this new capacity is that children arrive at solutions to sensorimotor problems suddenly, suggesting that they experiment with actions inside their heads. Faced with her doll carriage stuck against the wall, Piaget's daughter Lucienne paused for a moment, as if to "think," and then immediately went to the other side to push it in the reverse direction. Had she been in Substage 5, she would have bumped and pulled it in a random fashion until it was free to move again.

With the capacity to represent, toddlers arrive at a more advanced understanding of object permanence—that objects can move or be moved when out of sight. Try the following object-hiding task with an 18- to 24-month-old as well as a younger child: Put a small toy inside a box and the box under a cover. Then, while the box is out of sight, dump the toy out and show the toddler the empty box. The Substage 6 child finds the hidden toy in this **invisible displacement task** easily. Younger infants are baffled by this situation.

Representation also brings with it the capacity for **deferred imitation**—the ability to remember and copy the behavior of models who are not immediately present. A famous example is Piaget's daughter Jacqueline's imitation of another child's temper tantrum:

> Jacqueline had a visit from a little boy . . . who, in the course of the afternoon, got into a terrible temper. He screamed as he tried to get out of a playpen and pushed it backwards, stamping his feet. Jacqueline stood watching him in amazement. . . . The next day, she herself screamed in her playpen and tried to move it, stamping her foot lightly several times in succession. (Piaget, 1936/1952b, p. 63)

Finally, the emergence of representation leads to a major change in the nature of play. At the end of the sensorimotor period, children engage in **make-believe play**, in which they reenact familiar activities, such as pretending to eat, go to sleep, or drive a car. As the sensorimotor period draws to a close, mental symbols quickly become major instruments of thinking.

CHALLENGES TO PIAGET'S SENSORIMOTOR STAGE

Many researchers have tried to confirm Piaget's observations of sensorimotor development. Their findings show that infants display a wide array of cognitive capacities much sooner than Piaget believed. Earlier we noted the challenge posed by studies of newborn imitation, and you have already read about other conflicting evidence as well.

Mental representation
An internal image of an absent object or a past event.

Invisible displacement task
A type of object-hiding task in which the object is moved from one place to another while out of sight.

Deferred imitation
The ability to remember and copy the behavior of models who are not immediately present.

Make-believe play
A type of play in which children pretend, acting out everyday and imaginary activities.

Think back to the operant-conditioning research reviewed in Chapter 4 (page 136). Recall that newborns will suck vigorously on a nipple that produces a variety of interesting sights and sounds, a behavior that closely resembles Piaget's secondary circular reaction. It appears that infants try to explore and control the external world before 4 to 8 months. In fact, they do so as soon as they are born.

Piaget may have underestimated infant capacities because he did not have the sophisticated experimental techniques for studying early cognitive development that are available today. As we consider recent research on sensorimotor development, we will see that operant conditioning and the habituation–dishabituation response have been used ingeniously to find out what the young baby knows.

■ PHYSICAL REASONING. Piaget concluded that not until 8 to 12 months of age do infants appreciate important regularities of their physical world—that objects continue to exist when out of sight and act on one another in predictable ways. Yet as we will see in the following sections, even very young babies are quite knowledgeable about object characteristics.

Object Permanence. Before 8 months, do babies really believe that an object spirited out of sight no longer exists? It appears not. In a series of studies in which babies did not have to engage in active search, Renée Baillargeon (1987; Baillargeon & DeVos, 1991) found evidence for object permanence as early as 3½ months of age! In one study, infants were habituated to both a short and a tall smiley-faced carrot, each of which passed behind a screen on alternate trials (see Figure 6.1a). Then, using a screen with a large window in its upper half, the experimenter presented two test events, again on alternate trials. The first was a *possible event,* in which the short carrot (which was shorter than the window's lower edge) passed behind the screen and reappeared on the other side (Figure 6.1b). The second was an *impossible event,* in which the tall carrot passed behind the screen, did not appear in the window (although it was taller than the window's lower edge), and then emerged intact on the other side (Figure 6.1c). Young infants dishabituated to, or looked with much greater interest and surprise at, the impossible event, indicating that they are aware of the continued existence of objects that are hidden from view.

If 3½-month-olds grasp the idea of object permanence, then what explains Piaget's finding that much older infants (who are quite capable of voluntary reaching) do not try to search for hidden objects? One explanation is that just as Piaget's theory suggests, they cannot yet coordinate the separate means–end schemes—pushing aside the obstacle and

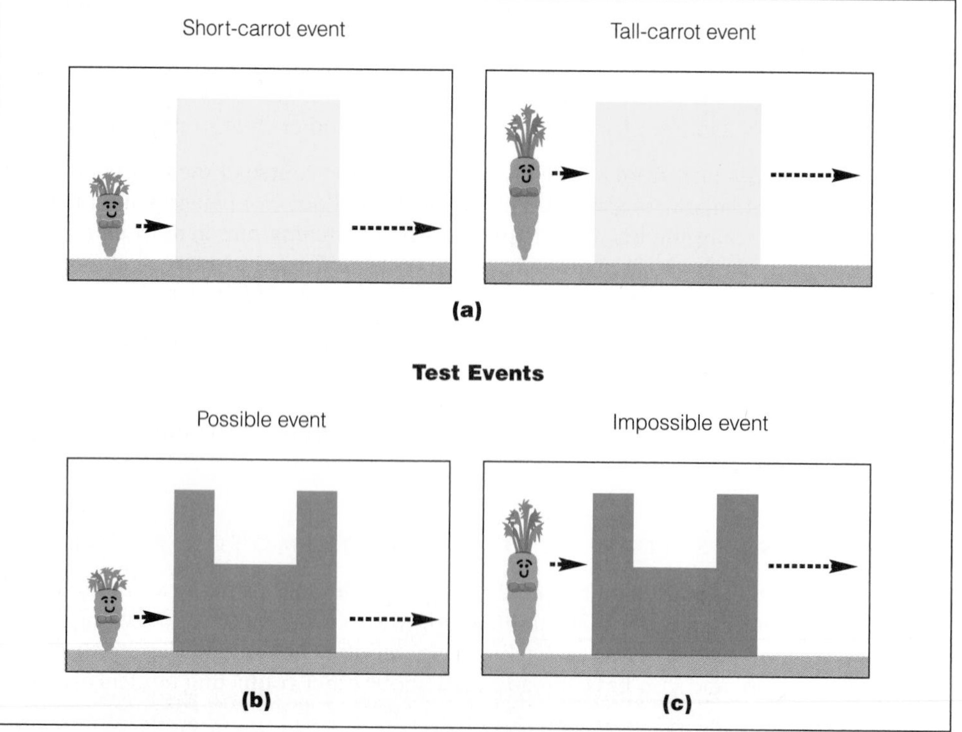

FIGURE 6.1

■ *Testing infants' understanding of object permanence using the habituation-dishabituation response. (a) First, infants were habituated to two events: a short carrot and a tall carrot moving behind a yellow screen, on alternative trials. Then two test events were presented, in which the color of the screen was changed to blue to help the infant notice that now it had a window. (b) In the possible event, the short carrot (which was shorter than the window's lower edge) moved behind the blue screen and reappeared on the other side. (c) In the impossible event, the tall carrot (which was taller than the window's lower edge) moved behind the screen, did not appear in the window, but then emerged intact on the other side. Infants as young as 3½ months dishabituated to the impossible event, suggesting that they understood object permanence. (Adapted from R. Baillargeon & J. DeVos, 1991, "Object Permanence in Young Infants: Further Evidence,"* Child Development, *62, p. 1230. © The Society for Research in Child Development, Inc. Reprinted by permission.)*

grasping the object—necessary to retrieve a hidden toy. In other words, what they *know* about object permanence is not yet evident in their searching behavior (Baillargeon et al., 1990).

Once 8- to 12-month-olds actively search for hidden objects, they make the AB search error. For some years, researchers thought babies had trouble remembering an object's new location after it was hidden in more than one place. But recent findings reveal that poor memory cannot fully account for infants' unsuccessful performance (Baillargeon, 1993). Another reason babies search at A (where they first found the object) instead of B (its most recent location) is that they have trouble inhibiting a previously rewarded response (Diamond, Cruttenden, & Neiderman, 1994). Once again, before 12 months, infants have difficulty translating what they know about an object moving from one place to another into a successful search strategy. This ability to integrate knowledge with action may depend on rapid maturation of the frontal lobe of the cortex at the end of the first year (Bell & Fox, 1992; Diamond, 1991; Nelson, 1995).

Other Aspects of Physical Reasoning. A wealth of research reveals that early in the first year, babies are aware of many object properties and the rules governing their behavior. For example, young infants are sensitive to principles of object substance. Elizabeth Spelke and her collaborators (1992) habituated 4-month-olds to a falling ball that landed on a supporting surface (see Figure 6.2a). Then babies watched either a *possible event,* in which the ball landed in a new location (Figure 6.2b), or an *impossible event,* in which the ball came to rest in the same location as in the habituation display but had to pass through a solid surface to do so (Figure 6.2c). Infants dishabituated to the impossible event, indicating that they do not expect one solid object to pass through another.

By the middle of the first year, infants know a great deal about physical limits on object motion. Habituation–dishabituation research reveals that 3-month-olds realize that an object much larger than an opening cannot pass through it (Spelke et al., 1992). Babies of this age are also sensitive to effects of gravity. They are surprised when a moving object stops in midair without support (Needham & Baillargeon, 1995; Sitskoorn & Smitsman, 1995). In the next few months, infants apply these understandings to a wider range of circumstances. For example, with respect to gravity, 7-month-olds (but not 5-month-olds) are aware that an object on a sloping surface will roll down, not up (Kim & Spelke, 1992). And as Figure 6.3 on page 220 shows, babies also realize that an object placed on top of another object will fall unless a large portion of its bottom surface contacts the lower object (Baillargeon, 1994a; Baillargeon, Needham, & DeVos, 1992).

A beginning grasp of physical causality also emerges quite early. When a moving object (such as a rolling ball) collides with a stationary object, infants as young as 2½ months expect the stationary object to be displaced. By 5½ to 6½ months, they figure out that *how far* the stationary object is displaced depends on the size of the moving object (Baillargeon, 1994b; Kotovsky & Baillargeon, 1995). Around 7 months, infants realize that an object hitting a second object will launch it on a continuous path of motion immediately (not after a delay). Soon infants extend their understanding of physical causality to more complex collision conditions. For example, after watching a blue ball disappear behind a screen and a red ball appear on the other side, 10-month-olds infer that the first object launched the second while out of their sight (Oakes, 1994; Oakes & Cohen, 1995).

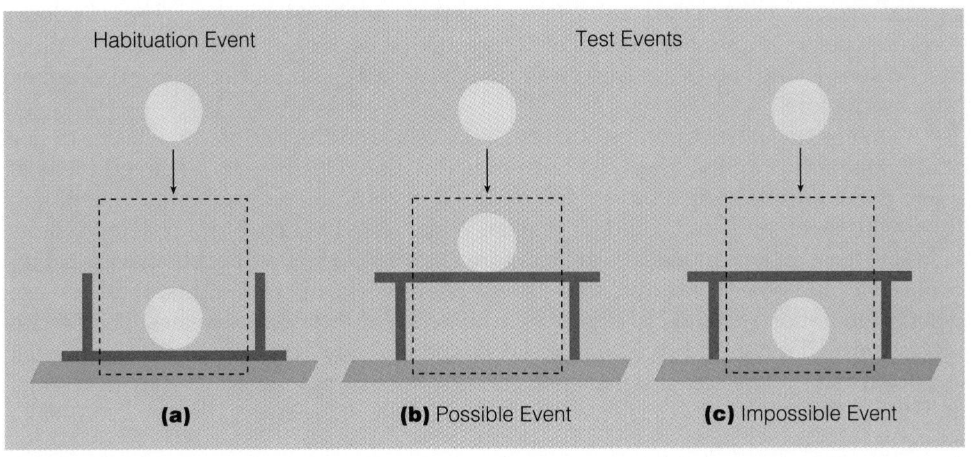

FIGURE 6.2

Testing infants' understanding of object solidity. (a) First, infants were habituated to a falling yellow ball that landed on a supporting red surface. Then two test events were presented. (b) In the possible event, the falling ball landed on a different, blue surface. (c) In the impossible event, the falling ball came to rest in the same location as in the habituation display but had to pass through a solid blue surface to do so. (To create the appearance of one object passing through another, the researchers introduced a screen behind which the ball fell in each condition.) Four-month-olds dishabituated to the impossible event, indicating that they are aware of object solidity. (From E. S. Spelke et al., 1992, "Origins of Knowledge," Psychological Review, *99, p. 611. Copyright © 1992 by the American Psychological Association. Reprinted by permission of the publisher and author.)*

FIGURE 6.3

■ *Testing infants' understanding of object support. First, infants were habituated to an event in which a hand pushed an attractive box part way across a long platform (not shown). Then two test events were presented in which the hand pushed the box across a shorter platform. (a) In the possible event, the box was pushed until its leading edge reached the end of the platform, so it remained fully supported. (b) In the impossible event, the box was pushed until only 15 percent of its bottom surface remained on the platform. Results indicated that 5½-month-olds looked equally at the two test events. In contrast, 6½-month-olds dishabituated to the impossible event, suggesting that they expect the object to fall unless a large portion of its bottom surface lies on the platform. (From R. Baillargeon, A. Needham, & J. DeVos, 1992, "The Development of Young Infants' Intuitions About Support,"* Early Development and Parenting, *1, 71. Reprinted by permission.)*

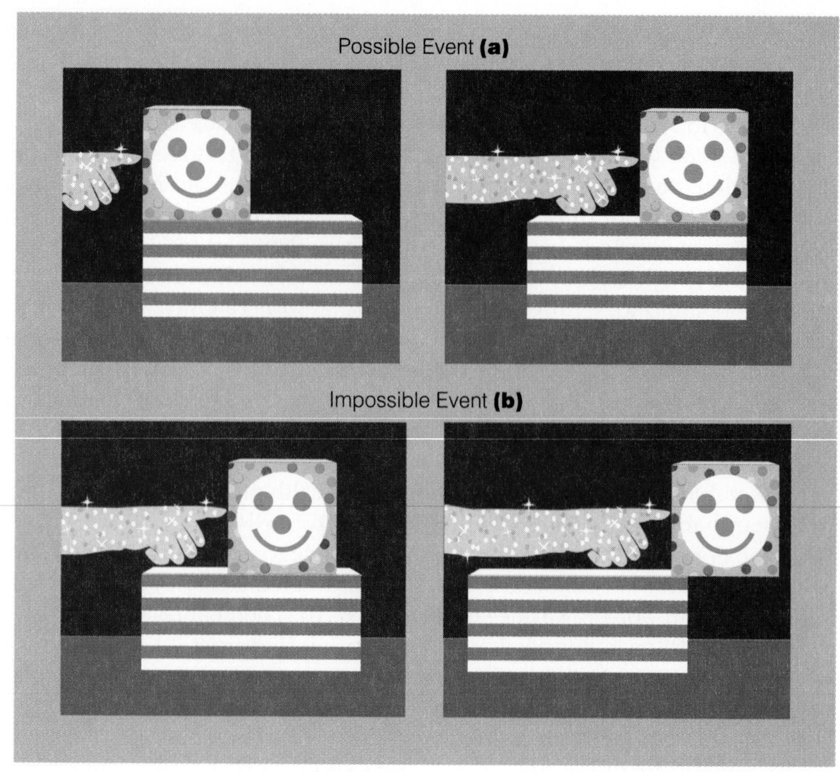

In sum, infants have a rich appreciation of the regularities of their physical world. Basic understandings—that objects continue to exist when masked by other objects, cannot move through the space occupied by other objects, fall without support, and move along continuous paths—are present within the first few months (long before infants can engage in Piagetian means–end action sequences) and are gradually refined over the first year.

■ MENTAL REPRESENTATION. In Piaget's theory, infants lead purely sensorimotor lives; they cannot represent experience until about 18 months of age. Yet new studies of deferred imitation and categorization reveal that the transition to mental representation takes place much earlier than Piaget predicted.

Deferred Imitation. Piaget studied imitation by noting when his own three children demonstrated it in their everyday behavior. Under these conditions, a great deal has to be known about the infant's daily life to be sure that deferred imitation has occurred. Also, some babies might be capable of deferred imitation but have very few opportunities to display it.

Recently, Andrew Meltzoff and Keith Moore (1994) brought 6-week-old babies into the laboratory and deliberately tried to induce deferred imitation of facial expressions. Infants who watched an adult open her mouth or stick out her tongue imitated the facial gesture when exposed to the passive face of the same adult 24 hours later. These findings show that deferred imitation, a form of representation, is present by the second month of life. Perhaps young babies use it as a way to identify and communicate with persons they have seen before.

As motor capacities improve, infants start to copy adults' actions on objects. In one study, Meltzoff (1988) showed 9-month-olds three novel toys—an L-shaped piece of wood that could be bent, a box with a button that could be pushed, and a plastic egg filled with metal nuts that could be shaken. When tested after a 24-hour delay, infants who saw these actions modeled were far more likely to reproduce them than were babies exposed to the objects but not shown how they work. By 14 months, toddlers use deferred imitation skillfully to enrich their range of sensorimotor schemes. They retain highly unusual modeled behaviors for several months, copy the actions of peers as well as adults, and imitate across a change in context—for example, enact a behavior learned at day care in the home (Hanna & Meltzoff, 1993; Meltzoff, 1994).

At the end of the second year, toddlers imitate not only an adult's behavior, but the actions he or she *tries* to produce, even if these are not fully realized (Meltzoff, 1995). This indicates that they have begun to infer others' intentions and goals. And once make-believe play is under way, 2-year-olds duplicate entire social roles, such as mommy, daddy, or baby.

■ BEGINNINGS OF CATEGORIZATION. Young babies' ability to categorize objects and events is also incompatible with a strictly sensorimotor approach to experience in which mental representation is absent. Recall the operant conditioning research in which infants kicked to make a mobile move that was attached to their foot by a long cord (see Chapter 4, page 134). By creatively varying the mobile stimuli, Carolyn Rovee-Collier and her colleagues have shown that the beginnings of categorization are present in the early months of life. In one series of studies, 3-month-olds kicked a mobile made of a uniform set of stimuli—small blocks, all with the letter L on them. After a delay, kicking returned to a high level only if the babies were given a mobile whose elements were labeled with the same form (the letter *L*). If the form was changed (from *L*'s to +'s), infants no longer kicked vigorously. While learning to make the mobile move, the babies had mentally grouped together its physical features, associating the kicking response with the category "*L*" and, at later testing, distinguishing it from the category "+" (Bhatt, Rovee-Collier, & Weiner, 1994; Hayne, Rovee-Collier, & Perris, 1987).

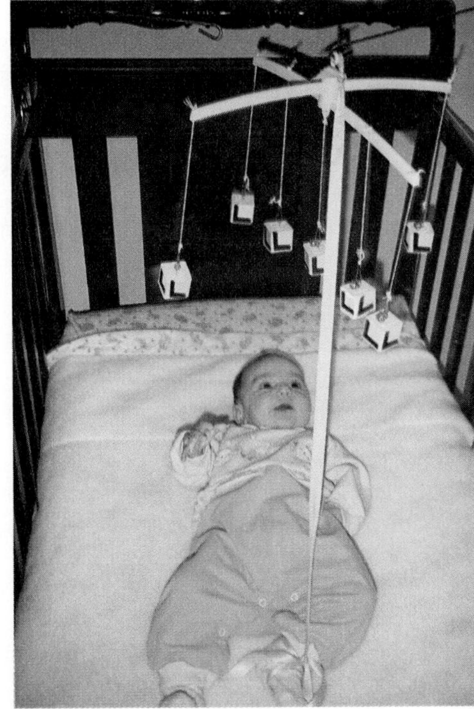

■ *This 3-month-old infant discovered that by kicking, she could shake a mobile made of small blocks with the letter L on them. After a delay, the baby continued to kick vigorously only if the mobile she saw was labeled with the same form (the letter L). She did not kick when given a mobile with a different form (a + sign). The infant's behavior shows that she groups similar stimuli into categories and can distinguish the category "L" from the category "+". (Courtesy of Carolyn Rovee-Collier, Rutgers University)*

Habituation–dishabituation research has also been used to study early categorization. For example, infants can be shown a series of pictures belonging to one category (such as hot dog, piece of bread, slice of salami). Then the experimenter observes whether they look longer at, or dishabituate to, a picture that is not a member of the category (chair) than one that is (apple). The findings of such studies reveal that 9- to 12-month-olds structure objects into an impressive array of meaningful categories—food items, birds, animals, vehicles, and more (Mandler & McDonough, 1993; Oakes, Madole, & Cohen, 1991; Ross, 1980; Younger, 1985, 1993). Besides organizing the physical world, infants of this age also categorize their social worlds. They sort people into males and females (Francis & McCroy, 1983; Poulin-Dubois et al., 1994), have begun to distinguish emotional expressions, and can separate the natural movements of people from other motions (see Chapter 4, page 157).

In the second year, children become active categorizers during their play. In one study, the emergence of object-sorting behavior was carefully observed (Gopnik & Meltzoff, 1987a). Twelve-month-olds merely touched objects that belong together, without grouping them. A little later, single-category grouping occurred. For example, when given four balls and four boxes, 16-month-olds put all the balls together but not the boxes. And finally, around 18 months, children could sort the objects exhaustively into two classes.

When we combine these capacities with other achievements of the first 2 years that we will discuss in later chapters—for example, that events taking place before 10 to 11 months can be recalled up to a year and a half later (see Chapter 7) and that around 1 year, infants start to communicate with symbolic gestures (see Chapter 9)—it seems clear that mental representation is not the culmination of sensorimotor development. Instead, sensorimotor and symbolic schemes appear to be developing concurrently over the course of infancy.

■ EVALUATION OF THE SENSORIMOTOR STAGE. The Milestones table on page 222 summarizes the remarkable cognitive attainments of infancy. To evaluate the accuracy of Piaget's sensorimotor stage, compare the entries in this table with the description of Piaget's sensorimotor substages on page 215. On the one hand, you will see that infants anticipate events, actively search for hidden objects, flexibly vary their sensorimotor schemes, and engage in make-believe play within Piaget's time frame. Yet on the other hand, many other capacities—including secondary circular reactions, understanding of object permanence and physical causality, deferred imitation, and categorization—emerge much earlier than Piaget expected.

Notice, also, that the cognitive attainments of infancy do not develop in the neat stepwise fashion predicted by Piaget's substages. For example, deferred imitation is present long before children pass invisible displacement tasks, probably because invisible displacement requires a more complex form of representation. To understand that an

MILESTONES

Some Cognitive Attainments of Infancy

Age	Typical Adaptive Behaviors	Physical Reasoning	Categorization	Imitation	Play
Birth–1month	■ Newborn reflexes; exploration of the surrounding world through circular reactions based on limited motor skills (head turning and sucking)	■ Size and shape constancy (see Chapter 4)	■ None 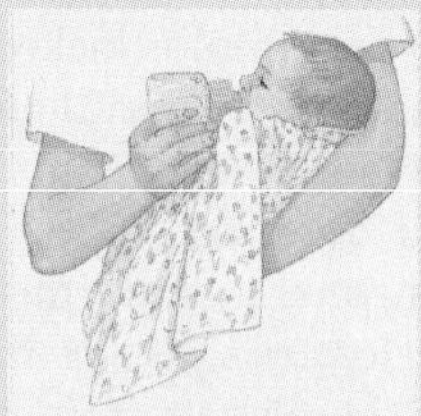	■ Imitation of adult facial expressions and gestures (see Chapter 4)	■ None
1–4 months	■ Circular reactions based on more advanced motor skills (kicking, reaching, and grasping); limited anticipation of events 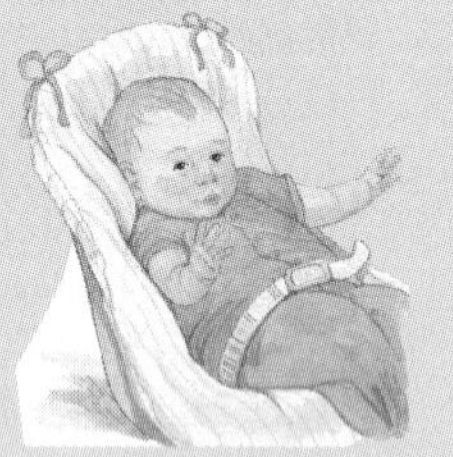	■ Awareness of object permanence ■ Awareness of object solidity and certain effects of gravity and object collision (physical causality) ■ Reliance on motion and spatial layout to identify objects as separate units (see Chapter 4)	■ Categorization of perceptually similar stimuli	■ Deferred imitation of adult facial expressions 	■ Beginnings of playful exercise of schemes
4–8 months	■ Circular reactions based on more advanced motor skills (for example, improved reaching and grasping; swiping, banging, throwing, and mouthing)	■ Ability to retrieve a partially hidden object ■ Improved understanding of the effects of gravity and object collision (physical causality) ■ Reliance on stationary cues (shape, texture, and color) to identify objects as separate units (see Chapter 4)	■ Same as above	■ Imitation of adults' actions on objects, but limited to behaviors the infant has practiced many times 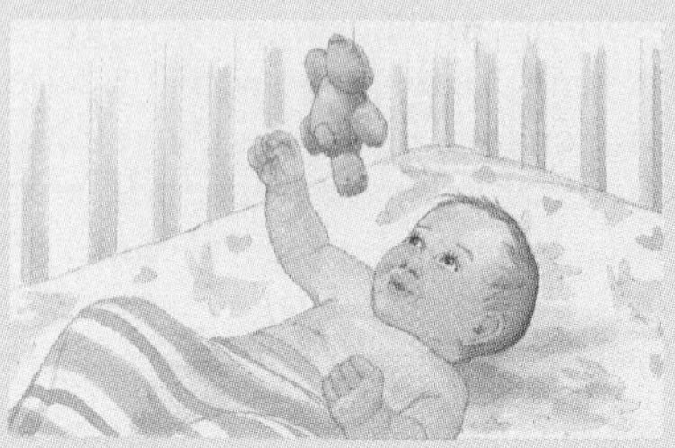	■ Same as above

MILESTONES

Some Cognitive Attainments of Infancy (continued)

Age	Typical Adaptive Behaviors	Physical Reasoning	Categorization	Imitation	Play
8–12 months	■ Intentional, or goal-directed, action sequences; improved anticipation of events	■ Ability to retrieve an object from the first location in which it is hidden 	■ Categorization of many objects by appearance and function ■ Categorization of many social stimuli (for example, emotional expressions, human versus nonhuman movement patterns)	■ Imitation of behaviors slightly different from ones the infant usually performs ■ Deferred imitation of adults' actions on objects over a short time interval (24 hours)	■ Playful exercise of means in means–end action sequences
12–18 months	■ Exploration of the properties of objects by acting on them in novel ways; trial-and-error solutions to sensorimotor problems	■ Ability to search in several locations for a hidden object (AB search)	■ Active object sorting: touching objects that go together followed by grouping objects into a single category	■ Imitation of adults' or peers' novel behaviors and action sequences ■ Deferred imitation of more behaviors over longer time intervals (up to 1 week) ■ Deferred imitation across a change in context (for example, from day care to home)	■ More varied and experimental sensorimotor play 
18 months–2 years	■ Sudden solutions to sensorimotor problems, suggesting experimentation with actions internally, through representation	■ Ability to find an object that has been moved while out of sight (invisible displacement)	■ Active object sorting: grouping objects into two categories 	■ Imitation of actions an adult tries to produce, even if these are not fully realized ■ Imitation of entire social roles in make-believe play	■ Beginnings of make-believe play

Note: These milestones represent overall age trends. Individual differences exist in the precise age at which each milestone is attained.

object can be moved while out of sight, infants must go beyond *recall of a past event* to *infer a novel unseen event* (Rast & Meltzoff, 1995). Yet Piaget assumed all representational capacities emerge in synchrony in Substage 6. These findings, and others like them, are among a rapidly accumulating body of evidence that questions Piaget's stagewise view of development.

Discrepancies between Piaget's observations and those of recent research also raise controversial questions about how early development takes place. Consistent with Piaget's constructivist ideas, motor activity facilitates the discovery of some forms of knowledge. For example, in Chapter 4, we indicated that babies who are experienced crawlers are better at finding hidden objects and perceiving depth on the visual cliff. But it is clear that infants comprehend a great deal about their world before they are capable of the motor behaviors Piaget assumed were responsible for these understandings. How can we account for babies' amazing cognitive accomplishments?

Some researchers believe that important schemes develop through perceptual means—by looking and listening—rather than solely through acting on the world. For example, Renée Baillargeon (1994b, 1995) argues that infants master physical phenomena by first making all-or-none distinctions, which they add to as they are exposed to relevant information. For example, 3-month-olds realize that an object will fall when released in midair and stop falling when it contacts a surface because they have seen adults drop toys in baskets and clothes in hampers many times. But not until the middle of the first year, when babies sit independently and can deposit objects on surfaces themselves, do they have a chance to see that an object will tumble over unless much of its bottom surface is supported. Similarly, Lisa Oakes and Leslie Cohen (1995) suggest that infants master physical causality as object perception improves and they have many opportunities to observe the regularities of physical events. And Jean Mandler (1992a, 1992b) proposes that babies form their first categories through a natural process of perceptual analysis in which they detect commonalities in the features and movements of objects and translate these into simplified images of experience.

Other investigators are convinced that infants' remarkable perceptual and reasoning abilities are based on innate knowledge. Development is a matter of these built-in, core understandings becoming better established and more elaborate as they come into contact with new information. For example, according to Elizabeth Spelke (1994), infants know from the start that objects move as connected wholes on continuous paths, do not change shape or pass through one another as they move, and cannot act on one another unless they come into contact. Later-emerging schemes are direct extensions of these innate structures, which channel infants' attention to relevant features of the environment and get their physical reasoning "off the ground" quickly. A growing number of researchers believe that innate, specialized knowledge guides development in other domains as well—for example, children's rapid mastery of number concepts (Chapter 7), language (Chapter 9), and understanding of people (Chapters 11 and 12) (Carey & Spelke, 1994; Chomsky, 1988; Gelman, 1990; Wellman & Gelman, 1992).

Think about the contemporary alternatives to Piaget's theory just described. Each grants newborns more built-in equipment for making sense of experience than did Piaget. But the first set of approaches, which emphasizes perceptual means, posits only a few procedures for analyzing stimulation as the starting point for development. Consequently, this view preserves Piaget's belief that rich, constructive interaction between the child and the environment is the primary force behind cognitive development. In contrast, the second perspective is a domain-specific, nativist view, which regards the mind as a collection of separate *modules*—genetically prewired, independent, special-purpose systems, each equipped with structures that trigger new understandings with exposure to stimulation (see Figure 6.4). According to this **modular view of the mind**, development is uneven because each module has its own neural basis in the brain and timetable of maturation (Fodor, 1983). Since so much is laid down in advance, the child is a far less active participant in the construction of knowledge than Piaget assumed.

Modular view of the mind
A domain-specific, nativist view that regards the mind as a collection of separate modules—genetically prewired, independent, special purpose systems, each of which is equipped with structures for making sense of a certain type of information.

This tension between a constructivist and nativist approach to cognitive development has been energized by disenchantment with Piaget's conception of a purely sensorimotor infant. We will be in a better position to reflect on this debate after we have discussed Piaget's childhood and adolescent stages and the research they have stimulated.

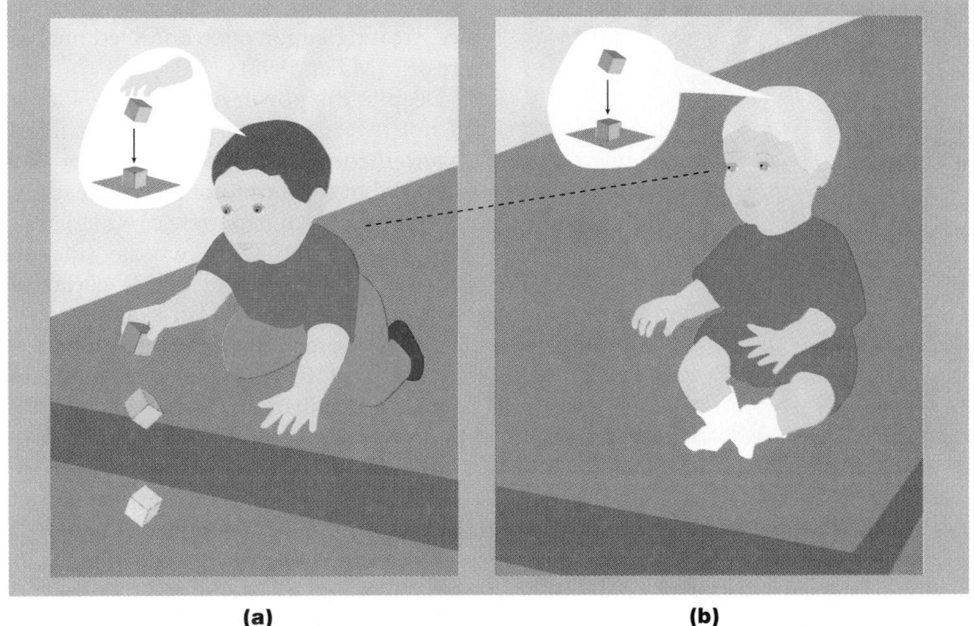

FIGURE 6.4

Constructivist, domain-general versus nativist, domain-specific (modular) view of the mind. (a) Do infants discover virtually all knowledge about their world through rich, constructive interaction with the enrvironment, as Piaget assumed? (b) Or do they begin life with a set of genetically prewired, independent, special-purpose mental systems called modules, each equipped with structures that trigger new understandings with exposure to stimulation?

BRIEF REVIEW

Piaget divides the vast changes of the sensorimotor stage into six substages. The circular reaction, a special means that infants use to adapt schemes, is first oriented toward the infants' own body, then turns outward to the surrounding world, and finally becomes experimental and creative. During the last three substages, infants make strides in intentional behavior and understanding object permanence. By the final substage, they represent reality through imitation and play. Recent evidence reveals that secondary circular reactions, understanding of object permanence and physical causality, deferred imitation, and categorization are present much earlier than Piaget assumed. These findings challenge his claim that infants construct all aspects of their world through motor activity and that early cognitive development is best characterized as a purely sensorimotor stage. Modern researchers regard infants as having more built-in equipment for making sense of experience than did Piaget, but they differ on whether newborns have only a few prewired procedures for constructing experience or substantial innate knowledge.

The Preoperational Stage (2 to 7 Years)

As children move from the sensorimotor to the **preoperational stage,** the most obvious change is an extraordinary increase in representational activity. Although infants have some ability to represent their world, between the ages of 2 and 7, this capacity blossoms.

LANGUAGE AND THOUGHT

As we will see in Chapter 9, around the end of the second and beginning of the third year, children make tremendous strides in language. Piaget acknowledged that language is our most flexible means of mental representation. By detaching thought from action, it permits cognition to be far more efficient than it was during the sensorimotor stage. When we think in words, we overcome the limits of immediate time and space. We can

Preoperational stage
Piaget's second stage, in which rapid development of representation takes place. However, thought is not yet logical. Spans the years from 2 to 7.

■ *During the preschool years, make-believe play blossoms. This child uses objects as active agents in a complex play scene.* *(M. Siluk/The Image Works)*

deal with the past, present, and future all at once, creating larger, interconnected images of reality (Miller, 1993).

Despite the power of language, Piaget did not regard it as responsible for more advanced forms of cognition. Instead, he believed that sensorimotor activity leads to internal images of experience, which children then label with words (Piaget, 1936/1952b). Some evidence is certainly consistent with this idea. For example, children's first words have a strong sensorimotor basis. They usually refer to objects that move or to familiar actions (see Chapter 9). Also, certain early words are linked to specific nonverbal cognitive achievements. Use of disappearance terms, like "All gone," occurs at about the same time as mastery of advanced object permanence problems. And success and failure expressions, such as "There!" and "Uh-oh," appear when children can solve sensorimotor problems suddenly, in Piaget's Substage 6. Finally, a sharp spurt in vocabulary between 18 months and 2 years coincides with the ability to sort objects into several categories (Gopnik & Meltzoff, 1987b). This "naming explosion" probably builds on infants' diverse preverbal categories, which become more elaborate by the end of the second year.

Still, Piaget's theory does not tell us exactly how sensorimotor schemes are transformed into images, and then into categories, to which words are eventually attached (Mandler, 1992b). And, as we have already suggested in the introduction to this chapter, Piaget may have misjudged the power of language to spur children's cognition forward. For example, we will see later that whereas language development is supported by early categories, learning names for things, in turn, enhances conceptual skills.

MAKE-BELIEVE PLAY

Make-believe play provides another excellent example of the development of representation during the preoperational stage. Like language, it increases dramatically during early childhood. Piaget believed that through pretending, children practice and strengthen newly acquired symbolic schemes. Drawing on Piaget's ideas, several investigators have traced changes in make-believe during early childhood.

■ CHANGES IN MAKE-BELIEVE. Compare an 18-month-old's pretending with that of a 2- to 3-year-old. You are likely to see examples of three important changes, each of which reflects the preschool child's growing symbolic mastery.

First, make-believe becomes increasingly detached from the real-life conditions associated with it. At first, toddlers use only realistic objects—for example, a toy telephone to talk into or a cup to drink from. Around age 2, they use less realistic toys, such as a block for a telephone receiver, more frequently. Soon after, children use body parts to stand for objects–for example, a finger for a toothbrush. Between 3 and 5 years, children become better at imagining objects and events without any support from the real world. This indicates that their representations are becoming more flexible, since a play symbol no longer has to resemble the object it denotes (Corrigan, 1987; O'Reilly, 1995).

Second, the way in which the "child as self" participates in play changes with age. When make-believe first appears, it is directed toward the self; that is, children pretend to feed or wash only themselves. A short time later, pretend actions are directed toward other objects, as when the child feeds a doll. And early in the third year, objects are used as active agents. The child becomes a detached participant who makes a doll feed itself or a parent doll feed a baby doll. This sequence reveals that make-believe gradually becomes less self-centered as children realize that agents and recipients of pretend actions can be independent of themselves (Corrigan, 1987; McCune, 1993).

Finally, over time, play includes increasingly complex scheme combinations. For example, the toddler can pretend to drink from a cup but does not yet combine pouring and drinking. Later, children coordinate pretend schemes, especially in **sociodramatic play**, the make-believe with others that is under way by age 2½ (Haight & Miller, 1993;

Sociodramatic play
The make-believe play with others that is under way by age 2½.

■ *These 4-year-olds coordinate several make-believe roles with the assistance of a very cooperative family pet. Their enjoyment of sociodramatic play contributes to cognitive, emotional, and social development. (Tom McCarthy/ Stock South)*

Howes & Matheson, 1992). By age 4 to 5, children build effectively on one another's play themes, create and coordinate several roles in an elaborate plot, and have a sophisticated understanding of story lines (Göncü, 1993).

These developments reflect a major change in representation. In complex sociodramatic play, children do not just represent their world. They display *awareness* that make-believe is a representational activity (Jarrold et al., 1994; Leslie, 1987). Listen closely to preschoolers as they jointly create an imaginary world. You will hear them assign roles and negotiate make-believe plans in ways like this: "*You pretend to be* the astronaut, *I'll act like* I'm operating the control tower!" "Wait, *I gotta set up* the spaceship." Communication about pretend reveals that around age 3½ to 4, children can reflect on and manipulate their own and others' fanciful representations. This indicates that they have begun to reason about peoples' thoughts, a topic we will return to in later chapters.

■ FUNCTIONS AND CONSEQUENCES OF MAKE-BELIEVE. Piaget clearly captured an important aspect of make-believe when he underscored the opportunities it affords for exercising symbolic schemes. He also noted its emotionally integrative function, a feature emphasized in psychoanalytic theory. An anxiety-provoking event, such as a visit to the doctor's office or discipline by a parent, is likely to be revisited in the young child's play, but with roles reversed so that the child is in command and compensates for the unpleasant experience (Erikson, 1950; Piaget, 1945/1951). In addition, Piaget commented that pretend allows children to become familiar with social role possibilities. In cultures around the world, young children act out family scenes and highly visible occupations—police officer, doctor, and nurse in Western nations; rabbit hunter and potter among the Hopi Indians; and hut builder and spear maker among the Baka of West Africa (Garvey, 1990). In this way, play provides young children with important insights into the link between self and wider society.

Nevertheless, today Piaget's view of make-believe as mere practice of symbolic schemes is regarded as too limited. Research indicates that play not only reflects, but contributes to children's cognitive and social skills (Nicolopoulou, 1993; Singer & Singer, 1990). Sociodramatic play has been studied most thoroughly. In contrast to social nonpretend activities (such as drawing or putting puzzles together), during social pretend, preschoolers' interactions last longer, show more involvement, draw larger numbers of children into the activity, and are more cooperative (Connolly, Doyle, & Reznick, 1988). When we consider these findings, it is not surprising that preschoolers who spend more time at sociodramatic play are advanced in general intellectual development, better understand the feelings of others, and are judged more socially competent by their teachers (Burns & Brainerd, 1979; Connolly & Doyle, 1984). Make-believe also seems to strengthen a wide variety of mental abilities, including memory, language, logical reasoning, imagination, and creativity (Dias & Harris, 1990; Ervin-Tripp, 1991; Newman, 1990; Pepler & Ross, 1981).

FROM RESEARCH TO PRACTICE

Where's Snoopy? Young Children's Understanding of Spatial Representations

For her second birthday, Marla's father built a beautiful doll house, replete with tiny furnishings like those in the family's home. Marla's 4-year-old brother Randy quickly took note of the relationship between the two dwellings and arranged the doll house furniture to match his real-world living room, kitchen, and bedroom. Although Marla used the doll house for make-believe, she remained unaware for many months that it symbolized her own house.

Spatial representations are powerful cognitive tools. When we understand that a photograph, model, or map corresponds to circumstances in everyday life, we can use it to acquire information about objects and places we have not experienced. When do children realize that spatial representation stands for a specific state of affairs in the real world?

To find out, Judy DeLoache and her collaborators had 2½- and 3-year-olds watch as a small toy (little Snoopy) was hidden in a scale model of a room. Then they were asked to find a larger toy (big Snoopy) hidden in the room that the model represented. Although children of both ages remembered where the original object was hidden equally well, 2½-year-olds could not apply this knowledge to the real-world situation. By age 3, most children could find the toy in the larger room (DeLoache, 1987).

These findings show that understanding of spatial representation improves rapidly over the third year of life. Although young children can represent their world, they are just beginning to represent relations between stimuli. Between ages 2½ and 3, children realize that the model is not just a toy room; it is a symbol of another room. At first, this understanding is fragile. For example, 3-year-olds' performance depends on a high degree of similarity between the model and the room, such as furniture in the same position and covered with the same fabric (DeLoache, Kolstad, & Anderson, 1991).

How do children become sensitive to spatial representation? Insight into one type of symbol–real world relation seems to help preschoolers understand others. Use of a photograph to show where Snoopy is hidden is grasped very early. Unlike a model, a photo's primary function is to stand for something. It is not an interesting object in its own right. Consequently, even 2-year-olds regard a photo as a real-world symbol. Furthermore, 2½-year-olds who receive the photo task first do better on the model task (DeLoache, 1991). And 3-year-olds who can pass the model task readily transfer their symbolic understanding to a new medium—use of a simple map to locate Snoopy (Marzolf & DeLoache, 1994).

These findings reveal that experience with symbols makes children more sensitive to the symbolic potential of new situations. As children notice the common structure between a variety of representations and the real world, they start to become consciously aware of the function of symbols. This awareness leads them to look for new correspondences. Granting young children opportunities to experiment with many symbolic forms—picture books, photographs, models, maps, drawings, and make-believe—enhances their understanding that one object or event can stand for another, thereby opening doors to new realms of knowledge.

These findings offer strong justification for play as a central part of preschool and day-care programs and the daily life of the preschool child. Later we will return to the origins and consequences of make-believe from an alternative perspective—Vygotsky's.

PICTORIAL REPRESENTATION

Children's drawings are another important mode of symbolic expression. Even the scrawls of toddlers, which seem to be little more than tangles of lines, are often "experiments in representation" (Winner, 1986, pp. 25–26). At first, children's artistic efforts take the form of gestures. For example, one 18-month-old took her crayon and hopped it around the page, explaining as she made a series of dots, "Rabbit goes hop-hop." Around age 2, children realize that pictures can depict pretend objects—a basic feature of artistic expression (Kavanaugh & Harris, 1994). Over the next year, scribbles start to become pictures. Often this happens after children make a gesture with the crayon, notice that they have drawn a recognizable shape, and label it. At the same time, children's understanding of representations of space, such as models and maps, improves rapidly (see the From Research to Practice box above), a change that might support the development of meaningful drawing.

A major milestone in children's artwork occurs when they begin to use lines to represent the boundaries of objects. This permits them to draw their first picture of a person by age 3 or 4. Look at the tadpole image on the left in Figure 6.5. It is a universal one in which the limits of the preschooler's fine motor skills reduce the figure to the simplest form that still looks like a human being (Gardner, 1980; Winner, 1986).

Unlike many adults, young children do not demand that a drawing be realistic. But as cognitive and fine motor skills improve, they learn to desire greater realism. As a

FIGURE 6.5

■ *Example of young children's drawings. The universal tadpolelike form that children use to draw their first picture of a person is shown on the left. The tadpole soon becomes an anchor for greater detail as arms, fingers, toes, and facial features sprout from the basic shape. By the end of the preschool years, children produce more complex, differentiated pictures like the one on the right, drawn by a 6-year-old child. (Tadpole drawings from H. Gardner, 1980,* Artful Scribbles: The Significance of Children's Drawings, *New York: Basic Books, p. 64. Reprinted by permission of Basic Books, a division of HarperCollins Publishers, Inc. Six-year-old's picture from E. Winner, August 1986, "Where Pelicans Kiss Seals,"* Psychology Today, *20[8], p. 35. Reprinted by permission of the author.)*

result, they create more complex drawings, like the one shown on the right in Figure 6.5, made by a 6-year-old child. Still, children of this age are not very particular about mirroring reality. Perceptual distortions help make their pictures look fanciful and inventive. Not until the elementary school years do children gradually represent depth in their drawings (Braine et al., 1993; Nicholls & Kennedy, 1992).

LIMITATIONS OF PREOPERATIONAL THOUGHT

Aside from the development of representation, Piaget described preschool children in terms of what they *cannot,* rather than *can,* understand (Beilin, 1992). The very name of the stage—*pre*operational—indicates that Piaget compared preschoolers to older, more capable concrete operational children. As a result, he discovered little of a positive nature about the young child's thinking. Later, when we take up recent research on preschoolers' thinking, we will see that Piaget underestimated the cognitive competencies of early childhood, just as he did with infancy. But first, let's consider the cognitive deficiencies of this period from Piaget's point of view.

For Piaget, **operations**—mental representations of actions that obey logical rules—are where cognitive development is headed. In the preoperational stage, children are not capable of operations. Instead, their thinking is rigid, limited to one aspect of a situation at a time, and strongly influenced by the way things appear at the moment. As a result, when judged by adult standards, preoperational reasoning often seems distorted and incorrect.

■ EGOCENTRISM AND ANIMISM. According to Piaget, the most serious deficiency of this stage, the one that underlies all others, is **preoperational egocentrism**. Now, with the emergence of new representational capacities, egocentrism appears in a different form. Preoperational children are egocentric with respect to their symbolic viewpoints. That is, they are unaware of perspectives other than their own, and they believe that everyone else perceives, thinks, and feels the same way they do (Piaget, 1950).

Operations
In Piaget's theory, mental representations of actions that obey logical rules.

Preoperational egocentrism
A form of egocentrism present during the preoperational stage involving the inability to distinguish the symbolic viewpoints of others from one's own.

FIGURE 6.6

Piaget's three-mountains problem. Each mountain is distinguished by its color and by its summit. One has a red cross, another small house, and the third a snow-capped peak. Piaget judged children at the preoperational stage to be egocentric because they cannot select a picture that shows the mountains from the doll's perspective. Instead, they simply choose the photo that shows their own vantage point.

Piaget's most convincing demonstration of egocentrism involves his *three-mountains problem* (see Figure 6.6). A child is permitted to walk around a display of three mountains of different heights arranged on a table. Then the child stands on one side, and a doll is placed at various locations around the display. The child must choose a photograph that shows what the display looks like from the doll's perspective. Below age 6 or 7, most children simply select the photo that shows the mountains from their own point of view (Piaget & Inhelder, 1948/1956).

Egocentrism, Piaget pointed out, is responsible for preoperational children's **animistic thinking**—the belief that inanimate objects have lifelike qualities, such as thoughts, wishes, feelings, and intentions, just like themselves (Piaget, 1926/1930). The 3-year-old who charmingly explains that the sun is angry at the clouds and has chased them away is demonstrating this kind of reasoning.

Piaget argued that egocentrism leads to the rigidity and illogical nature of preoperational thought. Young children's thinking proceeds so strongly from their own point of view that they do not accommodate, or revise their schemes, in response to feedback from the physical and social world. Egocentric thought is not reflective thought, which critically examines itself. But to fully appreciate these shortcomings of the preoperational stage, let's consider some additional tasks that Piaget presented to children.

Animistic thinking
The belief that inanimate objects have lifelike qualities, such as thoughts, wishes, feelings, and intentions.

Conservation
The understanding that certain physical characteristics of objects remain the same, even when their outward appearance changes.

Perception-bound
Being easily distracted by the concrete, perceptual appearance of objects.

Centration
The tendency to focus on one aspect of a situation to the neglect of other important features.

INABILITY TO CONSERVE. Piaget's most important tasks are the conservation problems. **Conservation** refers to the idea that certain physical characteristics of objects remain the same even when their outward appearance changes. A typical example is the conservation-of-liquid problem. The child is presented with two identical tall glasses of water and asked if they contain equal amounts. Once the child agrees, the water in one glass is poured into a short, wide container, changing the appearance of the water but not its amount. Then the child is asked whether the amount of water is still the same or whether it has changed. Preoperational children think the quantity of water is no longer the same. They explain their reasoning in ways like this: "There is less now because the water is way down here" (that is, its level is so low in the short, wide container) or "There is more water now because it is all spread out." In Figure 6.7, you will find other conservation tasks that you can try with children.

Preoperational children's inability to conserve highlights several related aspects of their thinking. First, their understanding is **perception-bound**. They are easily distracted by the concrete, perceptual appearance of objects (it *looks* like there is less water in the short, wide container, so there *must be* less water). Second, their thinking is *centered,* or characterized by **centration**. In other words, they focus on one aspect of a situation and neglect other important features. In the case of conservation of liquid, the child centers

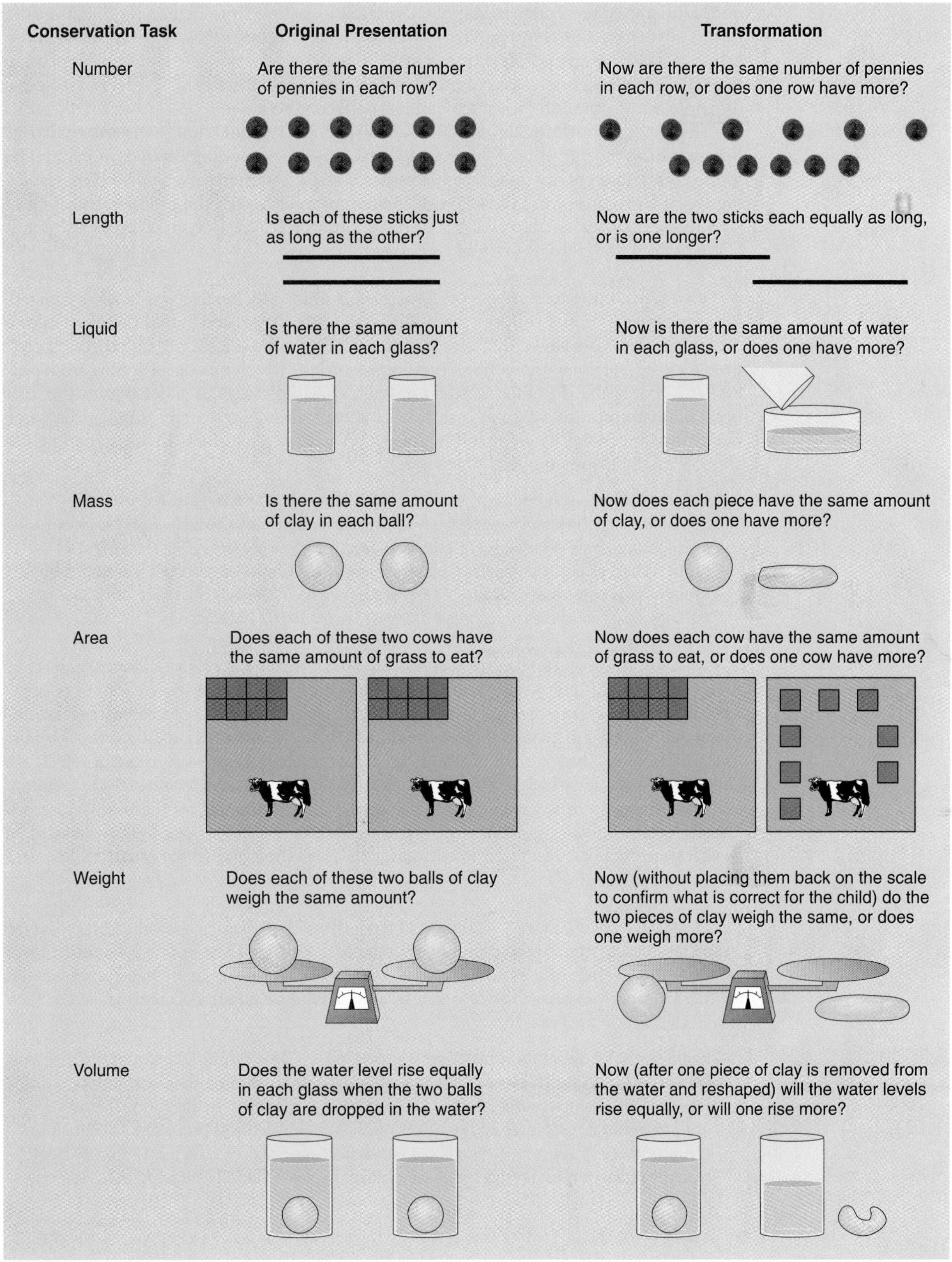

Conservation Task	Original Presentation	Transformation
Number	Are there the same number of pennies in each row?	Now are there the same number of pennies in each row, or does one row have more?
Length	Is each of these sticks just as long as the other?	Now are the two sticks each equally as long, or is one longer?
Liquid	Is there the same amount of water in each glass?	Now is there the same amount of water in each glass, or does one have more?
Mass	Is there the same amount of clay in each ball?	Now does each piece have the same amount of clay, or does one have more?
Area	Does each of these two cows have the same amount of grass to eat?	Now does each cow have the same amount of grass to eat, or does one cow have more?
Weight	Does each of these two balls of clay weigh the same amount?	Now (without placing them back on the scale to confirm what is correct for the child) do the two pieces of clay weigh the same, or does one weigh more?
Volume	Does the water level rise equally in each glass when the two balls of clay are dropped in the water?	Now (after one piece of clay is removed from the water and reshaped) will the water levels rise equally, or will one rise more?

FIGURE 6.7

■ *Some Piagetian conservation tasks. Children at the preoperational stage cannot yet conserve. These tasks are mastered gradually over the concrete operational period. Children in Western nations typically acquire conservation of number, length, liquid, and mass sometime between 6 and 7 years; area and weight between 8 and 10 years; and volume between 10 and 12 years.*

on the height of the water in the two containers, failing to realize that all changes in height are compensated by changes in width. Third, children of this stage focus on **states rather than transformations**. For example, in the conservation-of-liquid problem, they treat the initial and final states of the water as completely unrelated events, ignoring the dynamic transformation (pouring of water) between them.

The most important illogical feature of preoperational thought is *irreversibility*. **Reversibility**, the opposite of this concept, characterizes every logical operation. It refers to the ability to mentally go through a series of steps and then reverse direction, returning to the starting point. In the case of conservation of liquid, the preoperational child fails to see how the existence of the same amount of liquid is ensured by imagining it being poured back into its original container.

■ TRANSDUCTIVE REASONING. Reversible thinking is flexible and well organized. Because preoperational children are not capable of it, Piaget concluded that their causal reasoning often consists of disconnected facts and contradictions. He called young children's incorrect explanations **transductive reasoning**, which means reasoning from particular to particular. In other words, preschoolers simply link together two events that occur close in time and space in a cause-and-effect fashion. Sometimes this leads to some fantastic connections, as in the following interview Piaget conducted with a young child about why the clouds move:

> You have already seen the clouds moving along? What makes them move?—*When we move along, they move along too.*—Can you make them move?—*Everybody can, when they walk.*—When I walk and you are still, do they move?—*Yes.*—And at night, when everyone is asleep, do they move?—*Yes.*—But you tell me that they move when somebody walks.—*They always move. The cats, when they walk, and then the dogs, they make the clouds move along.* (Piaget, 1926/1929, p. 62)

■ LACK OF HIERARCHICAL CLASSIFICATION. During the preoperational stage, children also have difficulty with **hierarchical classification**. That is, they cannot yet organize objects into hierarchies of classes and subclasses on the basis of similarities and differences between the groups. Piaget illustrated this with his famous *class inclusion problem*. Children are shown a set of common objects, such as 16 flowers, most of which are yellow and a few of which are blue (see Figure 6.8). When asked whether there are more yellow flowers or more flowers, preoperational children respond confidently, "More yellow flowers!" They center on the overriding perceptual feature of yellow instead of thinking reversibly by moving from the whole class (flowers) to the parts (yellow and blue) and back again.

■ SUMMING UP PREOPERATIONAL THOUGHT. How can we combine the diverse characteristics of the preoperational stage into a unified description of what Piaget believed the young child's thought to be like? John Flavell suggests that Piaget viewed all these traits as expressions of a single, underlying orientation. Taken together, they reveal that preoperational thought

> bears the impress of its sensory-motor origins. . . . It is extremely concrete . . . concerned more with immobile, eye-catching configurations than with more subtle, less obvious components . . . it is unconcerned with proof or logical justification and, in general, unaware of the effect of its communication on others. In short, in more respects than not, it resembles sensory-motor action which has simply been transposed to a new (symbolic) arena of operation. (Flavell, 1963, p. 162)

CHALLENGES TO PIAGET'S PREOPERATIONAL STAGE

Over the past two decades, Piaget's account of a cognitively deficient preschool child has been seriously challenged. If researchers give his tasks in just the way he originally designed them, they indeed find that preschoolers perform poorly. But a close look at Piagetian problems reveals that many contain unfamiliar elements or too many pieces of information for young children to handle at once. As a result, preschoolers' responses often do not reflect their true abilities. Piaget also missed many naturally occurring instances of preschoolers' effective reasoning. Let's look at some examples to illustrate these points.

States rather than transformations
The tendency to treat the initial and final states in a problem as completely unrelated.

Reversibility
The ability to mentally go through a series of steps and then return to the starting point.

Transductive reasoning
Reasoning from one particular event to another particular event, instead of from general to particular or particular to general.

Hierarchical classification
The organization of objects into classes and subclasses on the basis of similarities and differences between the groups.

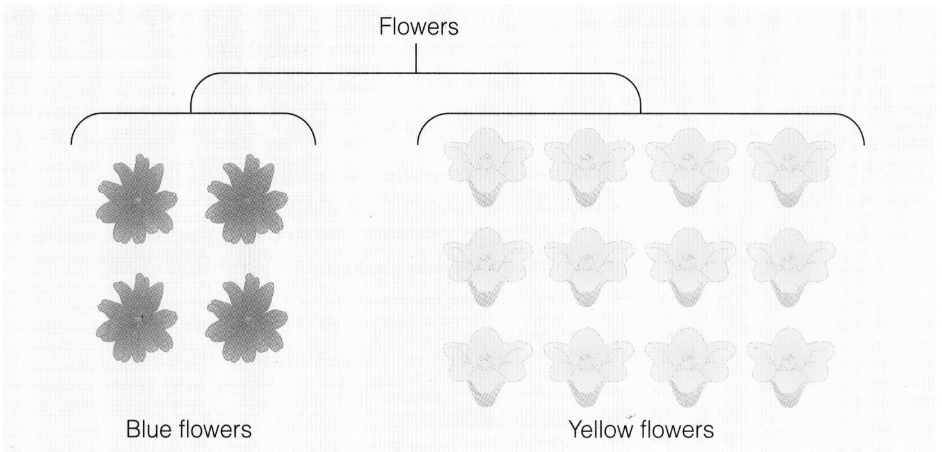

FIGURE 6.8

■ *A Piagetian class inclusion problem. Children are shown 16 flowers, 4 of which are blue and 12 of which are yellow. Asked whether there are more yellow flowers or more flowers, the preoperational child responds, "More yellow flowers," failing to realize that both yellow and blue flowers are included in the category "flowers."*

■ EGOCENTRIC, ANIMISTIC, AND MAGICAL THINKING. Are young children really so egocentric that they believe a person standing in a different location in a room sees the same thing they see? Although children's responses to Piaget's three-mountains task suggest that the answer is yes, more recent studies say no. When researchers include familiar objects in the display and use methods other than picture selection (which is difficult even for 10-year-olds), 4-year-olds show clear awareness of others' vantage points (Borke, 1975; Newcombe & Huttenlocher, 1992).

Nonegocentric responses also appear in young children's everyday interactions with people. For example, preschoolers adapt their speech to fit the needs of their listeners. Four-year-olds use shorter, simpler expressions when talking to 2-year-olds than to agemates or adults (Gelman & Shatz, 1978). Also, in describing objects, children do not use such words as "big" and "little" in a rigid, egocentric fashion. Instead, they adjust their descriptions, taking account of context. By age 3, children judge a 2-inch shoe as small when seen by itself (because it is much smaller than most shoes) but as big when asked about its appropriateness for a very tiny 5-inch doll (Ebeling & Gelman, 1994). These flexible communicative skills challenge Piaget's description of young children as strongly egocentric.

Recent studies also indicate that Piaget overestimated preschoolers' animistic beliefs because he asked children about objects with which they have little direct experience, such as the clouds, sun, and moon. Children as young as 3 rarely think that very familiar inanimate objects, like rocks and crayons, are alive. They do make errors when questioned about certain vehicles, such as trains and airplanes. But these objects appear to be self-moving, a characteristic of almost all living things. And they also have some lifelike features—for example, headlights that resemble eyes (Dolgin & Behrend, 1984; Massey & Gelman, 1988; Richards & Siegler, 1986). Children's responses result from incomplete knowledge about some objects, not from a rigid belief that inanimate objects are alive.

The same is true for other fantastic ideas of the preschool years. Most 3- and 4-year-olds believe in the supernatural powers of fairies, goblins, and other enchanted creatures that appear in storybooks, movies, and holiday legends. But they deny that magic can alter their everyday experiences—for example, turn a picture into a real object or living being (Subbotsky, 1994). Instead, they think magic accounts for events that violate their expectations and that they cannot otherwise explain. Between ages 4 and 8, as familiarity with physical events increases and scientific explanations are taught in school, magical beliefs decline. Children figure out who is really behind the activities of Santa Claus and the Tooth Fairy! They also realize that the antics of magicians are due to trickery, not special powers (Phelps & Woolley, 1994; Rosengren & Hickling, 1994).

■ ILLOGICAL CHARACTERISTICS OF THOUGHT. Many studies have reexamined the illogical characteristics that Piaget saw in the preoperational stage. Results show that when preschoolers are given tasks that are simplified and made relevant to their everyday lives, they do better than Piaget might have expected.

For example, when a conservation of number task is scaled down to include only three items instead of six or seven, 3-year-olds respond correctly (Gelman, 1972). And when preschoolers are asked carefully worded questions about what happens to substances (such as sugar) after they are dissolved in water, they display some surprisingly sophisticated understandings. Most 3- to 5-year-olds know that the substance is conserved—that it continues to exist, can be tasted, and makes the liquid heavier, even though it is invisible in the water. And the majority of 5-year-olds reconcile the apparent contradiction between invisibility and continued existence by indicating that particles too tiny to be seen are in the water (Au, Sidle, & Rollins, 1993; Rosen & Rozin, 1993).

Preschoolers' ability to notice and reason about transformations is also evident on other problems. In one study, children were shown "picture stories" of familiar experiences. In some, an object went from its basic state to a changed condition. For example, a cup became a wet cup. In others, it returned from its changed condition to its basic state. That is, a wet cup became a (dry) cup. Children were asked to pick an item from three choices (in this case, water, drying-up cloth, or feather) that caused the object to change. Most 3-year-olds had difficulty: they picked water for both transformations. But 4-year-olds did well. They selected the appropriate intermediate objects and reasoned effectively in either direction, from basic states to changed conditions and back again (Das Gupta & Bryant, 1989). This suggests that by age 4, preschoolers notice transformations, reverse their thinking, and understand causality in familiar contexts.

Indeed, a close look at 3- and 4-year-olds' conversations reveals that they use causal terms, such as "if–then" and "because," with the same degree of accuracy as adults do (McCabe & Peterson, 1988). Transductive reasoning occurs only when children grapple with unfamiliar topics. Consistent with this idea, recall that preschoolers are reluctant to resort to magical explanations unless they are faced with an extraordinary event. This supports the conclusion that they have a good understanding of causal principles that govern their everyday experiences. In sum, although young children cannot yet consider the complex interplay of forces that adolescents and adults can, they often analyze events accurately in terms of basic cause-and-effect relations.

■ CATEGORIZATION. Even though preschoolers have difficulty with Piagetian class inclusion tasks, their everyday knowledge is organized into nested categories at an early age. Earlier we saw that even young infants categorize, grouping together objects with similar physical features. By their first birthday, children have formed a variety of global categories consisting of objects that do not necessarily look alike but that are the same kind of thing. For example, 1- to 2½ -year-olds treat kitchen utensils, bathroom objects, animals, vehicles, plants, and furniture as distinct categories (Bauer & Mandler, 1989a; Mandler, Bauer, & McDonough, 1991; Mandler & McDonough, 1993). Consider these object groupings, and you will see that they provide yet another challenge to Piaget's assumption that young children's thinking is always perception bound (Keil, 1989). For example, the category of "kitchen utensils" includes objects that differ widely in appearance but that go together because of their common function and place of use.

Over the early preschool years, these global categories differentiate. Children form many *basic-level categories*—ones at an intermediate level of generality, such as "chairs," "tables," "dressers," and "beds." Language development may build on as well as facilitate these new categorical discriminations. A recent study revealed that 18-month-olds who use more object names in their everyday speech score higher on basic-level object-sorting tasks (Gopnik & Meltzoff, 1992). Perhaps the very act of naming helps young children recognize that all things can be classified. As a result, they detect more refined categories in the world of objects. In support of this idea, Korean children learn a language that emphasizes verbs rather than nouns, and object names are often omitted from sentences. They develop object-grouping skills later than do their English-speaking counterparts (Gopnik & Choi, 1990).

By the third year, preschoolers easily move back and forth between basic-level and *superordinate-level categories,* such as "furniture" (Blewitt, 1994). Soon after, they break down the basic-level categories into *subcategories,* such as "rocking chairs" and "desk chairs" (Mervis, 1987). Young children's category systems are not yet very complex, and concrete operational reasoning facilitates their development (Ricco, 1989). But the capacity to classify hierarchically is present in early childhood.

■ APPEARANCE VERSUS REALITY. So far, we have seen that young children show some remarkably advanced reasoning when presented with familiar situations and simplified problems. Yet in certain situations, preschoolers are easily tricked by the outward appearance of things.

John Flavell and his colleagues took a close look at the ability to distinguish appearance from reality. They presented children with objects that were disguised in various ways and asked what the items were, "really and truly." At age 3, children could separate the way an object appeared to feel from the way it truly felt. For example, they understood that even though an ice cube did not feel cold to their gloved finger, it "really and truly" was cold (Flavell, Green, & Flavell, 1989). In this task, the real and apparent object states were present at the same time, and children could easily compare them.

Preschoolers have more difficulty with problems involving sights and sounds, but not because they always confuse appearance and reality, as Piaget suggested. Instead, these tasks require them to recall the real image of an object in the face of a second, contradictory representation. When asked whether a white piece of paper placed behind a blue filter is "really and truly blue" or whether a can that sounds like a baby crying when turned over is "really and truly a baby," preschoolers often respond "Yes!" Not until 6 to 7 years do children do well on these problems (Flavell, 1993; Flavell, Green, & Flavell, 1987). Around this time, children also separate appearance from reality in the emotional domain. As we will see in Chapter 10, they begin to realize that an emotion a person expresses may not always be the one he or she truly feels (Friend & Davis, 1993).

How do children go about mastering distinctions between appearance and reality? Make-believe play may be important. Children can tell the difference between pretend play and real experiences long before they answer many appearance–reality problems correctly (Golomb & Galasso, 1995; Woolley & Wellman, 1990). During make-believe, we hear them say such things as "Let's use this block as a telephone" or "Pretend you're sad because the baby is sick." Experiencing the contrast between everyday and playful circumstances may help children refine their understanding of what is real and what is unreal in the surrounding world.

■ EVALUATION OF THE PREOPERATIONAL STAGE. How can we make sense of the contradictions between Piaget's conclusions and the findings of recent research? The evidence as a whole indicates that Piaget was partly wrong and partly right about young children's cognitive capacities. When given simplified tasks based on familiar experiences, preschoolers show the beginnings of logical operations long before the concrete operational stage. But their reasoning is not as well developed as that of school-age children, since they fail Piaget's three-mountains, conservation, and class inclusion tasks and have difficulty separating appearance from reality.

The fact that preschoolers have some logical understanding suggests that the attainment of operations takes place gradually. Over time, children rely on increasingly effective mental as opposed to perceptual approaches to solving problems. For example, recent research shows that children who cannot use counting to compare two sets of items do not conserve number (Sophian, 1995). Once preschoolers acquire this counting strategy, they apply it to conservation of number tasks with only a few items. As their counting improves, they extend the strategy to problems with more items. By age 6, they have formed a mental understanding that number remains the same after a transformation as long as nothing is added or taken away. Consequently, they no longer need to use counting to verify their answer (Siegler & Robinson, 1982). This sequence indicates that young children pass through several phases of understanding, although (as Piaget indicated) a full grasp of conservation is not attained until the early school years.

The fact that preschoolers can be trained to perform well on Piagetian problems, such as conservation and class inclusion, also supports the idea that operational thought is not absent at one point in time and present at another (Beilin, 1978; McCabe & Siegel, 1987). It makes sense that children who possess part of a capacity will benefit from training, unlike those with no understanding at all. In addition, a variety of training methods are effective, including language-based techniques, such as social interaction with more capable peers, adult instruction that points out contradictions in children's logic, and efforts to help children remember the component parts of a problem.

Still, the idea that logical operations develop gradually poses yet another challenge to Piaget's stage concept, which assumes sudden and abrupt change toward logical reasoning around 7 years of age. Although they still have a great deal of developing to do, new research shows that the minds of young children are considerably more coherent and organized than Piaget thought they were.

BRIEF REVIEW

During Piaget's preoperational stage, mental representation flourishes, as indicated by children's language, make-believe play, drawings and paintings, and grasp of spatial symbols. Aside from representation, Piaget's theory emphasizes the young child's cognitive limitations. Egocentrism underlies a variety of illogical features of preoperational thought, including animism, an inability to pass conservation tasks, transductive reasoning, and lack of hierarchical classification. Recent research reveals that when tasks are simplified and made relevant to children's everyday experiences, preschoolers show the beginnings of logical reasoning. These findings indicate that operational thought is not absent during early childhood, and they challenge Piaget's notion of stage.

The Concrete Operational Stage (7 to 11 Years)

Piaget viewed the **concrete operational stage,** which spans the years from 7 to 11, as a major turning point in cognitive development. When children attain it, their thought more closely resembles that of adults than that of the sensorimotor and preoperational child (Piaget & Inhelder, 1967/1969). According to Piaget, concrete operational reasoning is far more logical, flexible, and organized than cognition was during the preschool period. The Milestones table on the following page summarizes major cognitive changes from early to middle childhood, along with the attainments of adolescence that will follow.

OPERATIONAL THOUGHT

Concrete operations are evident in the school-age child's performance on a wide variety of Piagetian tasks. Let's look closely at these diverse cognitive accomplishments.

■ CONSERVATION. Piaget regarded *conservation* as the single most important achievement of the concrete operational stage, since it provides clear evidence of *operations.* In conservation of liquid, for example, children state that the amount of liquid has not changed, and they are likely to explain in ways like this: "The water's shorter but it's also wider. If you pour it back, you'll see that it's the same amount." Notice how in this response, the child coordinates several aspects of the task rather than centering on only one, as a preschooler would do. In other words, during middle childhood, children are capable of *decentration;* they recognize that a change in one aspect of the water (its height) is compensated for by a change in another aspect (its width). This explanation also illustrates *reversibility*—the capacity to imagine the water being returned to the original container as proof of conservation.

■ HIERARCHICAL CLASSIFICATION. By the end of middle childhood, operational thought permits children to categorize more effectively. Perhaps because they are more aware of classification hierarchies, they pass Piaget's *class inclusion problem* (Achenbach & Weisz, 1975; Hodges & French, 1988). You can see evidence for this in children's play activities. Collections of all kinds of objects become common during the school years. At age 10, one boy I know spent hours sorting and resorting his large box of baseball cards. At times he grouped them by league and team membership, at other times by playing position and batting average. He could separate the players into a variety of classes and subclasses and flexibly rearrange them. In contrast, most preschoolers insist that a set of objects can be sorted in only one way.

Concrete operational stage
Piaget's third stage, during which thought is logical, flexible, and organized in its application to concrete information. However, the capacity for abstract thinking is not yet present. Spans the years from 7 to 11.

MILESTONES

Some Cognitive Attainments of Childhood and Adolesence

Age	Cognitive Attainments
Early Childhood 2–4 years 	■ Shows a dramatic increase in representational activity, as reflected in the development of language, make-believe play, meaningful drawings, and understanding of spatial symbols (such as photographs, simple maps, and models) ■ Takes the perspective of others in simplified, familiar situations and in everyday communication ■ Distinguishes animate beings from inanimate objects; denies that magic can alter everyday experiences ■ Categorizes objects on the basis of common function and kind of thing, not just perceptual features ■ Classifies familiar objects hierarchically
4–7 years 	■ Replaces magical beliefs about fairies, goblins, and events that violate expectations with plausible explanations ■ Notices transformations, reverses thinking, and explains events causally in familiar contexts ■ Shows improved ability to distinguish appearance from reality
Middle Childhood 7–11 years 	■ Thinks in a more organized, logical fashion about concrete, tangible information, as indicated by the ability to pass Piagetian conservation, class inclusion, and seriation problems ■ Shows improved understanding of spatial concepts, as indicated by conservation of distance, ability to give clear directions, and well-organized cognitive maps ■ Displays sequential rather than complete mastery of logical reasoning in different content areas, according to the horizontal décalage
Adolescence 11–20 years	■ Reasons abstractly in situations that offer many opportunities for hypothetico-deductive reasoning and propositional thought ■ Displays the imaginary audience and personal fable, which are strongest in early adolescence and gradually decline

Note: These milestones represent overall age trends. Individual differences exist in the precise age at which each milestone is attained.

■ SERIATION. The ability to order items along a quantitative dimension, such as length or weight, is called **seriation**. To test for it, Piaget asked children to arrange sticks of different lengths from shortest to longest. Older preschoolers can form the series, but they do so haphazardly. They put the sticks in a row but make many errors and take a long time to correct them. In contrast, 6- to 7-year-olds are guided by an orderly plan. They create the series efficiently by beginning with the smallest stick, then moving to the next smallest, and so on, until the ordering is complete.

The concrete operational child's improved grasp of quantitative arrangements is also evident in a more challenging seriation problem—one that requires children to seriate mentally. This ability is called **transitive inference**. In a well-known transitive inference problem, Piaget showed children pairings of differently colored sticks. From observing that stick A is longer than stick B and stick B is longer than stick C, children must make the mental inference that A is longer than C. Not until age 9 or 10 do children perform well on this task (Chapman & Lindenberger, 1988; Piaget, 1967).

■ *An improved ability to categorize underlies children's interest in collecting objects during middle school. This boy enjoys sorting his shell collection into an elaborate structure of classes and subclasses. (Michael Newman/PhotoEdit)*

Piaget referred to the abilities we have considered so far—conservation, hierarchical classification, and seriation—as *logico-arithmetic operations.* He thought they were responsible for the school-age child's increased facility with quantitative tasks. As we will see in Chapter 7 when we consider the development of mathematical reasoning, preschoolers have some impressive numerical skills, including the ability to count small arrays and add and subtract small sets of items. But most mathematical knowledge is acquired after early childhood. Elementary school children do have a more quantitative, measurement-oriented approach to many tasks than do preschoolers.

■ SPATIAL OPERATIONS. In addition to logico-arithmetic operations, the concrete operational child also masters a variety of *spatial operations.* These deal with distance, directions, and spatial relationships among objects.

Distance. Piaget found that comprehension of distance improves during middle childhood, as a special conservation task reveals. To administer this problem, make two small trees out of modeling clay and place them apart on a table. Next, put a block or thick piece of cardboard between the trees. Then ask the child whether the trees are nearer together, farther apart, or still the same distance apart. Preschoolers say the distance has become smaller. They do not seem to realize that a filled space has the same value as an empty space (Piaget, Inhelder, & Szeminska, 1948/1960). By the early school years, children grasp this idea easily. Four-year-olds can conserve distance when questioned about a very familiar scene or when a path is marked between two objects, which helps them represent the distance. However, their understanding is not as solid and complete as that of the school-age child (Fabricius & Wellman, 1993; Miller & Baillargeon, 1990).

Directions. School-age children's more advanced understanding of space can also be seen in their ability to give directions. Stand facing a 5- or 6-year-old, and ask the child to name an object on your left and one on your right. Children of this age answer incorrectly; they apply their own frame of reference to that of others. Between 7 and 8 years, children start to perform *mental rotations,* in which they align the self's frame to match that of a person in a different orientation. As a result, they can identify left and right for positions they do not occupy (Roberts & Aman, 1993). Around this time, children begin to give clear, well-organized directions for how to get from one place to another. Aided by their capacity for operational thinking, they use a "mental walk" strategy in which they imagine another person's movements along a route (Gauvain & Rogoff, 1989a). Six-year-olds give more organized directions after they walk the route themselves or are specially prompted. Otherwise, they focus on the end point without describing exactly how to get there (Plumert et al., 1994).

Cognitive Maps. Children's drawings of familiar environments, such as their neighborhood or school, also undergo important changes from early to middle childhood (Piaget & Inhelder, 1948/1956). These mental representations of large-scale spaces are called **cognitive maps**. They require considerable perspective-taking skill, since the entire space cannot be seen at once. Instead, children must infer the overall layout by relating the separate parts to one another.

Seriation
The ability to arrange items along a quantitative dimension, such as length or weight.

Transitive inference
The ability to seriate—or arrange items along a quantitative dimension—mentally.

Cognitive maps
Mental representations of large-scale environments.

Preschoolers' maps display *landmarks,* but their placement is fragmented and disorganized. In the early school years, children start to arrange landmarks along an *organized route of travel,* such as the path they usually walk from home to school—an attainment that resembles their improved direction giving. However, they have not yet mastered the relationship of routes to one another. By the end of middle childhood, children form an *overall configuration of a large-scale space* in which landmarks and routes are interrelated (Newcombe, 1982; Siegel, 1981).

Once again, however, the ability to represent spatial layouts does not emerge suddenly. Children as young as 3 can use a simple map to navigate their way through a space they have never seen before (Uttal & Wellman, 1989). However, preschoolers cannot yet create an organized map of their own. "Map literacy" improves greatly during middle childhood (Liben & Downs, 1986; Spencer, Blades, & Morsley, 1989).

LIMITATIONS OF CONCRETE OPERATIONAL THOUGHT

Because of their improved ability to conserve, classify, seriate, and deal with spatial concepts, school-age children are far more capable problem solvers than they were during the preschool years. But concrete operational thinking suffers from one important limitation. Children think in an organized, logical fashion only when dealing with concrete information they can directly perceive. Their mental operations work poorly when applied to abstract ideas—ones not directly apparent in the real world.

Children's solutions to transitive inference problems provide a good illustration. When shown pairs of sticks of unequal length, 9-year-olds easily figure out that if stick A is longer than stick B and stick B is longer than stick C, then stick A is longer than stick C. But they have great difficulty with an entirely hypothetical version of this task, such as "Susan is taller than Sally and Sally is taller than Mary. Who is the tallest?" Not until age 11 or 12 can children solve this problem easily.

The fact that logical thought is at first tied to immediate situations helps account for a special feature of concrete operational reasoning. Perhaps you have already noticed that school-age children do not master all of Piaget's concrete operational tasks at once. Instead, they do so in a step-by-step fashion. For example, they usually grasp conservation problems in a certain order: first number; then length, mass, and liquid; and finally area and weight (Brainerd, 1978). Piaget used the term **horizontal décalage** (meaning development within a stage) to describe this gradual mastery of logical concepts. The horizontal décalage is another indication of the concrete operational child's difficulty with abstractions. School-age children do not come up with general logical principles and then apply them to all relevant situations. Instead, they seem to work out the logic of each problem they encounter separately.

CHALLENGES TO PIAGET'S CONCRETE OPERATIONAL STAGE

According to Piaget, brain maturation combined with experience in a rich and varied external world should lead children everywhere to reach the concrete operational stage. He did not believe that operational thinking depends on particular kinds of experiences. Yet recent evidence indicates that specific cultural practices have a great deal to do with children's mastery of Piagetian tasks (Rogoff, 1990).

A large body of evidence shows that conservation is often delayed in tribal and village societies. For example, among the Hausa of Nigeria, who live in small agricultural settlements and rarely send their children to school, even the most basic conservation tasks—number, length, and liquid—are not understood until age 11 or later (Fahrmeier, 1978). This suggests that for children to master conservation and other Piagetian concepts, they must take part in everyday activities that promote this way of thinking. Many children in Western nations, for example, have learned to think of fairness in terms of equal distribution—a value emphasized by their culture. They have many opportunities to divide materials, such as crayons and Halloween treats, equally among themselves and their friends. Because they often see the same quantity arranged in different ways, they grasp conservation early. But in cultures where these experiences are rare, conservation may not appear at the expected age (Light & Perrett-Clermont, 1989).

Horizontal décalage
Development within a Piagetian stage. Gradual mastery of logical concepts during the concrete operational stage is an example.

■ *In tribal and village societies, conservation is often delayed. This boy, who is growing up in Belize, Central America, gathers firewood for his family. His everyday activities may not promote the kind of reasoning required to pass Paigetian conservation tasks. Compared to his agemates in Western industrialized nations, he may have fewer opportunities to see the same quantity arranged in different ways. (Jeff Lawrence/Stock Boston)*

The very experience of going to school seems to promote mastery of Piagetian tasks. When children of the same age are tested, those who have been in school longer do better on transitive inference problems (Artman & Cahan, 1993). The many opportunities schooling affords for seriating objects, learning about order relations, and remembering the parts of a complex problem are probably responsible.

Yet certain nonschool, informal experiences can also foster operational thought! Their influence is simply not apparent outside the everyday situations in which that type of reasoning is useful. In one study, Brazilian 6- to 9-year-old street vendors (who seldom attend school) were given two class inclusion problems: (1) the traditional Piagetian task and (2) an informal version in which the researcher questioned the child during the course of customer–vendor interaction. As Figure 6.9 shows, street-vendor children were far more successful in the informal context, where the problem was meaningful to them and their interest and motivation were high. Middle-class Brazilian children showed the reverse trend: greater success on the Piagetian task than an informal version in which they were asked to role-play street vendors (an activity unfamiliar to them) (Ceci & Roazzi, 1994).

Besides specific experiences, the phrasing of questions and the objects to which they refer can have a profound effect on Piagetian task performance. In a recent study, researchers asked college students misleading questions about conservation of weight. Sometimes the question referred to the student's body ("When do you weigh more, when you are walking or running?") and sometimes it referred to an external object ("When did the modeling clay weigh more, when it was a ball or when it was in the shape of a sausage?"). Misleading questions led to many nonconserving responses, especially when they referred to the student's body. Interestingly, those students who were asked to explain their answers and who had heard of Piaget were less likely to be tricked by the misleading questions (Winer, Craig, & Weinbaum, 1992).

FIGURE 6.9

■ *Comparison of Brazilian street vendors with Brazilian middle-class children on the traditional Piagetian class inclusion task and an informal, street-vending version. For the informal task, the researcher asked the child for the price of two different kinds of chewing gum (mint and strawberry). After setting aside four units of mint and two units of strawberry, the investigator continued, "For you to get more money, is it better to sell me the mint chewing gum or [all] the chewing gum? Why?" Street vendors performed better on the informal version, whereas middle-class children did better on the Piagetian task. (Adapted from Ceci & Roazzi, 1994.)*

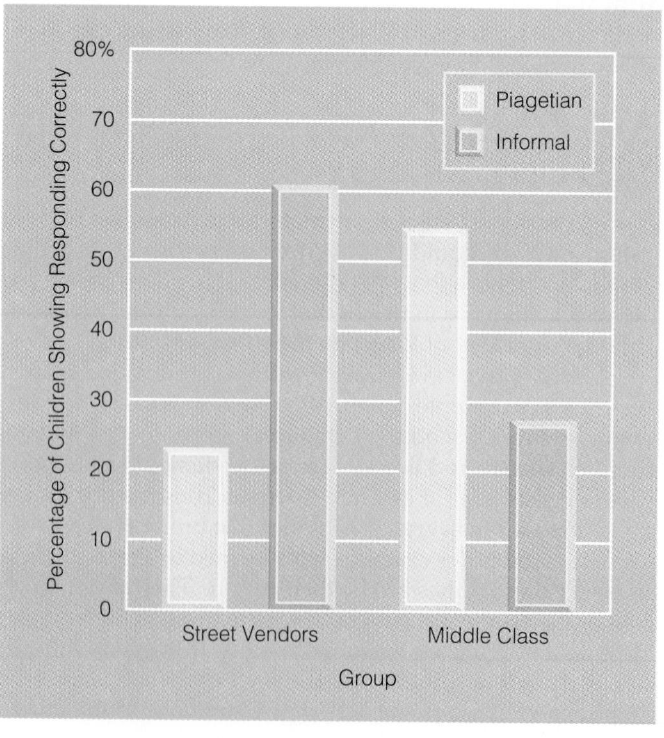

These findings reveal that concrete operations are not always used, even by adults! Instead, people seem to have at least two modes of thinking that are evoked in different situations: one that is person-centered and intuitive, and one that is object-centered and logically consistent. This is troublesome for Piaget's theory, since it indicates that concrete operational reasoning may not be a form of logic that emerges universally during middle childhood and, once present, overrides less mature ways of thinking. Instead, it may be a product of direct training, context, and cultural conditions (Gellatly, 1987; Light & Perrett-Clermont, 1989; Robert, 1989).

BRIEF REVIEW

During the concrete operational stage, thought is more logical, flexible, and organized than it was during the preschool years. The ability to conserve indicates that children can decenter and reverse their thinking. School-age children also have an improved grasp of classification, seriation, and spatial concepts. However, they cannot yet think abstractly. Recent research indicates that concrete operational reasoning is often delayed in non-Western societies, and it is strongly subject to situational conditions. These findings indicate that it may not be a natural form of thinking that emerges spontaneously and universally in middle childhood, as Piaget believed.

The Formal Operational Stage (11 Years and Older)

According to Piaget, the capacity for abstract thinking begins around age 11. At the **formal operational stage,** the adolescent reasons much like a scientist searching for solutions in the laboratory. Concrete operational children can only "operate on reality," but formal operational adolescents can "operate on operations." In other words, concrete things and events are no longer required as objects of thought (Inhelder & Piaget, 1955/1958). Instead, adolescents can come up with new, more general logical rules through internal reflection.

During the formal operational stage, adolescents display hypothetico-deductive reasoning. These high school students think of all possible hypotheses that could occur during a biology experiment. Then they test their predictions systematically to see which ones apply in the real world. (Bachmann/The Image Works)

HYPOTHETICO-DEDUCTIVE REASONING

At adolescence, young people first become capable of **hypothetico-deductive reasoning**. When faced with a problem, they start with a *general theory* of all possible factors that might affect an outcome and *deduce* from it specific *hypotheses* (or predictions) about what might happen. Then they test these hypotheses in an orderly fashion to see which ones work in the real world. Notice how this form of problem solving begins with possibility and proceeds to reality. In contrast, concrete operational children start with reality—with the most obvious predictions about a situation. When these are not confirmed, they cannot think of alternatives and fail to solve the problem.

Adolescents' performance on Piaget's famous pendulum problem illustrates this new hypothetico-deductive approach. Suppose we present several school-age children and adolescents with strings of different lengths, objects of different weights to attach to the strings, and a bar from which to hang the strings. Then we ask each of them to figure out what influences the speed with which a pendulum swings through its arc.

Formal operational adolescents come up with four hypotheses: (1) the length of the string, (2) the weight of the object hung on it, (3) how high the object is raised before it is released, and (4) how forcefully the object is pushed. Then, by varying one factor at a time while holding all others constant, they try out each of these possibilities. Eventually they discover that only string length makes a difference.

formal operational stage
Piaget's final stage, in which adolescents develop the capacity for abstract, scientific thinking, begins around age 11.

Hypothetico-deductive reasoning
A formal operational problem-solving strategy in which adolescents begin with a general theory of all possible factors that could affect an outcome in a problem and deduce specific hypotheses, which they test in an orderly fashion.

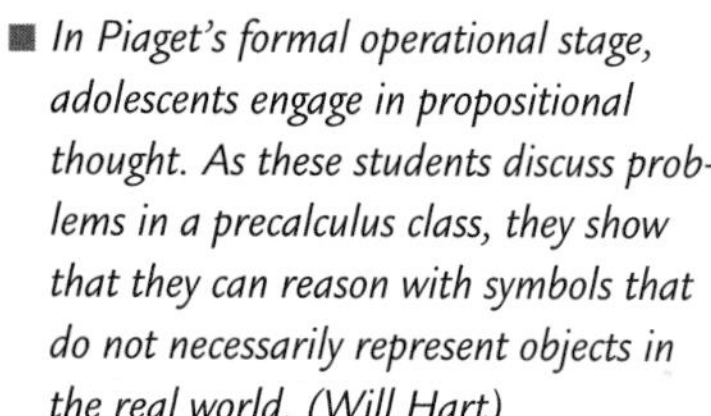

■ *In Piaget's formal operational stage, adolescents engage in propositional thought. As these students discuss problems in a precalculus class, they show that they can reason with symbols that do not necessarily represent objects in the real world. (Will Hart)*

In contrast, concrete operational children's experimentation is unsystematic. They cannot separate the effects of each variable. For example, they may test for the effect of string length without holding weight constant by comparing a short, light pendulum with a long, heavy one. Also, they fail to notice variables that are not immediately suggested by the concrete materials of the task—the height from which the pendulum is released and the forcefulness with which it is pushed.

PROPOSITIONAL THOUGHT

A second important characteristic of the formal operational stage is **propositional thought**. Adolescents can evaluate the logic of propositions (verbal statements) without referring to real-world circumstances. In contrast, concrete operational children can evaluate the logic of statements only by considering them against concrete evidence in the real world.

In one study of propositional reasoning, an experimenter showed children and adolescents a pile of poker chips and indicated that some statements would be made about them. The subject was asked to tell whether each statement was true, false, or uncertain. In one condition, the experimenter hid a chip in her hand and then asked the subject to evaluate the following propositions:

"Either the chip in my hand is green or it is not green."

"The chip in my hand is green and it is not green."

In another condition, the experimenter held either a red or a green chip in full view and made the same statements.

School-age children focused on the concrete properties of the poker chips rather than on the logic of the statements. As a result, they replied that they were uncertain to both statements when the chip was hidden from view. When it was visible, they judged both statements to be true if the chip was green and false if it was red. In contrast, adolescents analyzed the logic of the statements as propositions. They understood that the "either–or" statement is always true and the "and" statement is always false, regardless of the poker chip's color (Osherson & Markman, 1975).

Propositional thought
A type of formal operational reasoning in which adolescents evaluate the logic of verbal statements without making reference to real-world circumstances.

Although Piaget believed that language does not play a central role in children's cognitive development, he acknowledged that it is more important during adolescence. Abstract thought requires language-based systems of representation that do not stand for real things, such as those that exist in higher mathematics. Around age 14 or 15, high school students start to use these systems in algebra and geometry. Formal operational thought also involves verbal reasoning about abstract concepts. Adolescents demonstrate their capacity to think in this way when they ponder the relations among time, space, and matter in physics and wonder about justice and freedom in philosophy.

FORMAL OPERATIONAL EGOCENTRISM

Adolescents' capacity to think abstractly, combined with the physical changes they are undergoing, means that they start to think more about themselves. Piaget believed that the arrival of this stage is accompanied by **formal operational egocentrism**: the inability to distinguish the abstract perspectives of self and others (Inhelder & Piaget, 1955/1958). As teenagers imagine what others must be thinking, two distorted images of the relation between self and other appear.

The first is called the **imaginary audience**. Young teenagers regard themselves as always on stage. They are convinced that they are the focus of everyone else's attention and concern (Elkind & Bowen, 1979). As a result, they become extremely self-conscious, often going to great lengths to avoid embarrassment. The imaginary audience helps us understand the long hours adolescents spend in the bathroom inspecting every detail of their appearance as they envision the response of the rest of the world. It also accounts for their sensitivity to public criticism. To teenagers, who believe that everyone around them is monitoring their performance, a critical remark from a parent or teacher can be a mortifying event.

A second cognitive distortion is the **personal fable**. Because teenagers are so sure that others are observing and thinking about them, they develop an inflated opinion of their own importance. They start to feel that they are special and unique. Many adolescents view themselves as reaching great heights of glory as well as sinking to unusual depths of despair. As one teenager wrote in her diary, "My parents' lives are so ordinary, so stuck in a rut. Mine will be different. I'll realize my hopes and ambitions." The personal fable also contributes to adolescent risk taking. Teenagers who have sex without contraceptives or weave in and out of traffic at 80 miles an hour seem, at least for the moment, to be convinced of their uniqueness and invulnerability.

Consistent with Piaget's theory, the imaginary audience and personal fable are strongest during the transition to formal operations. They gradually decline over the adolescent years (Enright, Lapsley, & Shukla, 1979; Lapsley et al., 1988). Nevertheless, some experts believe that these distorted visions of the self may not represent a return to egocentrism. Instead, they may be an outgrowth of advances in perspective taking, which cause young teenagers to be very concerned with what others think (Lapsley et al., 1986). Adolescents may also cling to the idea that others are preoccupied with their appearance and behavior for emotional reasons. Doing so helps them maintain a hold on important relationships as they struggle to separate from parents and establish an independent sense of self (Lapsley, 1990).

RECENT RESEARCH ON FORMAL OPERATIONAL THOUGHT

Many researchers have conducted follow-up studies of formal operational thought, asking questions similar to those we discussed with respect to earlier stages: Is there evidence that abstract reasoning appears sooner than Piaget expected? Do all individuals reach formal operations during the teenage years?

ARE YOUNG CHILDREN CAPABLE OF ABSTRACT REASONING? School-age children show the glimmerings of abstract reasoning, but they are not as competent as adolescents and adults. For example, in simplified situations—ones involving no more than two possible causal variables—6-year-olds understand that hypotheses must be confirmed by appropriate evidence. They also realize that once supported, a hypothesis shapes predictions about what might happen in the future (Ruffman et al., 1993). But unlike adolescents, children cannot sort out evidence that bears on three or more variables at once. Clearly, adolescents reason much more effectively than do their younger counterparts. Consistent with this idea, training improves performance on hypothetico-deductive tasks like the pendulum problem for both children and adolescents. But the effects of training last longer and generalize more easily to new tasks with high school

Formal operational egocentrism
A form of egocentrism present during the formal operational stage involving an inability to distinguish the abstract perspectives of self and other.

Imaginary audience
Adolescents' belief that they are the focus of everyone else's attention and concern.

Personal fable
Adolescents' belief that they are special and unique. Leads them to conclude that others cannot possibly understand their thoughts and feelings. May promote a sense of invulnerability to danger.

or college students than with school-age children (Greenbowe et al., 1981; Kuhn, Ho, & Adams, 1979).

Similarly, children's capacity for propositional thought is quite limited. For example, they have great difficulty reasoning from premises that contradict reality or their own beliefs. Consider the following set of statements: "If dogs are bigger than elephants and elephants are bigger than mice, then dogs are bigger than mice." Children younger than 10 judge this reasoning to be false, since all the relations specified do not occur in real life (Moshman & Franks, 1986). As Piaget's theory indicates, around age 11 young people in Western nations are much better at analyzing the logic of propositions irrespective of their content. Propositional thought improves steadily over the adolescent years (Markovits & Vachon, 1989, 1990).

■ DO ALL INDIVIDUALS REACH THE FORMAL OPERATIONAL STAGE? Try giving one or two of Piaget's formal operational tasks to your friends, and see how well they do. You are likely to find that even well-educated adults have difficulty with abstract reasoning! About 40 to 60 percent of college students fail Piaget's formal operational problems (Keating, 1979).

Why is it that so many college students, and adults in general, are not fully formal operational? The reason is that people are most likely to think abstractly in situations in which they have had extensive experience. This is supported by evidence that taking college courses leads to improvements in formal reasoning related to course content. For example, math and science prompts gains in propositional thought, social science in methodological and statistical reasoning (Lehman & Nisbett, 1990). Consider these findings carefully, and you will see that formal operational thought, like the concrete stage that preceded it, appears to be a gradual development. And rather than emerging in all contexts at once, it is specific to situation and task.

Finally, in many tribal and village cultures, formal operational reasoning does not appear at all (Cole, 1990; Gellatly, 1987). Piaget acknowledged that because of lack of opportunity to solve hypothetical problems, abstract thought might not appear in some societies. Still, these findings raise questions similar to those discussed earlier. Is the highest stage really an outgrowth of children's independent efforts to make sense of their world? Or is it a culturally transmitted way of thinking that is specific to literate societies and taught in school? This issue, along with others, has prompted many investigators to doubt the overall validity of Piaget's theory.

Larger Questions About the Validity of Piaget's Theory

Piaget awakened psychologists and educators to a view of children as active knowledge seekers who undergo complex cognitive changes. Yet a wealth of research reveals that his theory has important shortcomings.

PROBLEMS OF CLARITY AND ACCURACY

Some of Piaget's ideas are not clearly spelled out. Think, for a moment, about Piaget's explanation of cognitive change—in particular, equilibration and its attendant processes of adaptation and organization. Just what the child does to equilibrate seems vague and imprecise. As an example of this problem, recall our description of organization, the notion that the structures of each stage form a coherent whole. Piaget is not very explicit about how the diverse achievements of each stage—for example, conservation, hierarchical classification, seriation, and spatial concepts during concrete operations—are bound together by a single, underlying form of thought.

Throughout this chapter, we have noted that several of Piaget's ideas are now regarded as either incorrect or only partially correct. For example, Piaget's belief that infants and young children must act on the environment to revise their cognitive structures is too narrow a notion of how learning takes place. As we will see when we turn to Vygotsky's sociocultural theory, cognitive development is not always self-generating. Left to their own devices, children may not always notice those aspects of a situation that are needed for an improved understanding. In addition, many efforts to verify Piaget's account of the timetable of development have not been successful. As Flavell (1992) states,

> The recent trend in the field has been to highlight the cognitive competencies of young children . . . , the cognitive shortcomings of adults, and the cognitive inconsistencies of both, effectively pushing from both ends of childhood towards the middle and blurring the differences between the two groups. (p. 1000)

ARE THERE STAGES OF COGNITIVE DEVELOPMENT?

This brings us to the most controversial question about Piaget's theory: Does cognitive development take place in stages? Throughout this chapter, we have seen that many changes proceed slowly and gradually. Few abilities are absent during one period and then suddenly present in another. Also, there seem to be few periods of cognitive equilibrium. Instead, children are constantly modifying structures and acquiring new skills. Today, virtually all experts agree that children's cognition is not as broadly stagelike as Piaget believed. At the same time, contemporary researchers disagree on how general or specific cognitive development actually is (Bjorklund, 1995; Flavell, 1992).

Some theorists regard development as domain-general, but they reject the existence of any stagewise change. They believe that thought processes are similar at all ages—just present to a greater or lesser extent—and that uneven performance across tasks can largely be accounted for by variations in children's knowledge and experience. These assumptions form the basis of a major competing approach to Piaget's theory—information processing, which we take up in Chapter 7.

Others think that the stage notion is still valid, but it must be modified. For example, in Chapter 7 we will consider the work of some neo-Piagetians, who combine Piaget's stage approach with information-processing ideas (Case, 1992a; Fischer & Farrar, 1987). They argue that Piaget's strict definition of stage needs to be transformed into a less tightly knit concept, one in which a related set of competencies develops over an extended time period, depending on both biological maturity and experience with different types of knowledge and tasks. These investigators point to findings indicating that as long as the complexity of tasks in different domains is carefully controlled, children and adolescents approach physical and social reasoning problems in similar, stage-consistent ways (Case et al., 1992; Marini & Case, 1989, 1994).

Still other theorists go further. They deny not only Piaget's stages, but his belief that the human mind is made up of general reasoning abilities that can be applied to any cognitive task. Recall the *modular view of the mind,* introduced earlier in this chapter, prompted by the remarkable competencies of young infants and the rapid development of many structures during the first few years. According to this nativist perspective, we begin life with well-defined, special-purpose knowledge systems, hardwired into the brain.

Is the modular view a satisfactory alternative to Piaget's domain-general account of the origins of knowledge? Critics claim that in emphasizing innate knowledge, the modular approach sidesteps vital questions about development. As infants search for hidden objects and children master conservation, they perform entirely new acts. How these arise from existing, built-in structures is not well specified (Thelen, 1992). In addition, the more predetermined we assume the child's mind to be, the less flexibility, creativity, and individual variability in thinking we would expect. Yet we have seen many examples of children's active and constructive efforts to make sense of experience as well as powerful situational and cultural influences on what they learn.

Furthermore, the modular approach implies that we should be able to localize domain-specific functions in the brain at an early age. Yet the evidence supports substantial brain plasticity in the early years and growth spurts across many areas of the cortex at once rather than in separate regions (see Chapter 5, pages 196–197). At present, neurological support for a separate brain/mind module is strongest for language, as we will see in Chapter 9.

How can we make sense of these clashing viewpoints? The future is likely to bring compromises among them. Clearly, there must be some innate, domain-specific predispositions, since the young baby is not knowledge free. However, according to Annette Karmiloff-Smith (1992), infants' initial mental equipment is unlikely to be as detailed as modular theorists assume. Instead, it is best viewed as a set of biases, each of which grants children an effective means for constructing and flexibly manipulating certain types of knowledge. As they do so, the brain and mind may take on greater domain-specific organization with age. At the same time, there is strong evidence for certain domain-general changes, such as the flourishing of representation in the second year and the move toward abstraction in adolescence—developments that profoundly affect performance across many types of tasks.

In sum, although Piaget's description of development is no longer fully accepted, researchers are a long way from consensus on how to modify or replace it. Yet they continue to draw inspiration from his portrait of rich, constructive interaction between the child and environment and his quest to understand how children acquire new capacities. As Flavell (1985) points out, "Perhaps what the field needs is another genius like Piaget to show us how, and to what extent, all those cognitive developmental strands within the growing child are really knotted together" (p. 297).

Piaget and Education

Piaget's theory has had a major impact on education, especially at the preschool and early elementary school levels. Three educational principles have served as the foundation for a variety of Piagetian-based curricula developed over the past 30 years:

1. *An emphasis on discovery learning.* In a Piagetian classroom, children are encouraged to discover for themselves through spontaneous interaction with the environment. Instead of presenting ready-made knowledge verbally, teachers provide a rich variety of activities designed to promote exploration and discovery and permit children to choose freely among them.

2. *Sensitivity to children's readiness to learn.* A Piagetian classroom does not try to speed up development. Instead, Piaget believed that appropriate learning experiences build on children's current level of thinking. Teachers watch and listen to their pupils, introducing experiences that permit them to practice new schemes and that are likely to challenge incorrect ways of viewing the world. But new skills are not imposed before children indicate they are interested or ready, since this leads to superficial memorization of adult formulas rather than true understanding (Johnson & Hooper, 1982).

3. *Acceptance of individual differences.* Piaget's theory assumes that all children go through the same sequence of development, but they do so at different rates. Therefore, teachers must make a special effort to arrange activities for individuals and small groups rather than for the total class (Ginsburg & Opper, 1988). In addition, teachers evaluate educational progress by comparing each child to his or her own previous development. They are less interested in how children measure up to normative standards or the average performance of same-age peers.

Educational applications of Piaget's theory, like his stages, have been criticized. Perhaps the greatest challenge has to do with his emphasis on action as children's major mode of learning to the neglect of other important avenues, such as verbal communication. Nevertheless, Piaget's influence on education has been powerful. He gave teachers new ways to observe, understand, and enhance young children's development and offered strong theoretical justification for child-oriented approaches to classroom teaching and learning.

In Piaget's formal operational stage, the capacity for abstraction appears, as indicated by hypothetico-deductive reasoning and propositional thought. New cognitive powers lead to formal operational egocentrism, in the form of the imaginary audience and personal fable. Adolescents and adults are most likely to display abstract thinking in areas in which they have had extensive experience. In village and tribal cultures, it does not appear at all. Major criticisms of Piaget's theory include the vagueness of his ideas about cognitive change, inaccuracies in his account of the timetable of development, and evidence that children's cognition is not as broadly stagelike and domain general as he assumed. Piaget's theory has had a powerful influence on education, promoting discovery learning, sensitivity to children's readiness to learn, and acceptance of individual differences.

Vygotsky's Sociocultural Theory

According to Piaget, the most important source of cognition is the child himself—a busy, self-motivated explorer who forms ideas and tests them against the world, without external pressure. Vygotsky also believed that children are active seekers of knowledge, but he did not view them as solitary agents. In his theory, the child and the social environment collaborate to mold cognition in culturally adaptive ways.

Early events in Vygotsky's life contributed to his vision of human cognition as inherently social and language-based. As a young boy in Russia, he was instructed at home by a private tutor, who conducted lessons using the Socratic dialogue—an interactive, question-and-answer approach that challenged current conceptions to promote heightened understanding. By the time Vygotsky entered the University of Moscow, his primary interest was a verbal field—literature. Upon graduation, he was first a teacher. Only later did he turn to psychology (Blanck, 1990; Kozulin, 1990).

Vygotsky died of tuberculosis when he was only 37 years old. Although he wrote prolifically, he had little more than a decade to formulate his ideas. Consequently, his theory is not as completely specified as that of Piaget. Nevertheless, the field of child development is currently experiencing a burst of interest in Vygotsky's sociocultural perspective. The major reason for his appeal lies in his rejection of an individualistic view of the developing child in favor of a socially formed mind (Wertsch & Tulviste, 1992; Rogoff & Chavajay, 1995).

According to Vygotsky, infants are endowed with basic perceptual, attentional, and memory capacities that they share with other animals. These undergo a natural course of development during the first 2 years through simple and direct contact with the environment. But once children become capable of mental representation, especially through language, their ability to participate in social dialogues while engaged in culturally important tasks is enhanced. Soon young children start to communicate with themselves in much the same way they converse with others. As a result, basic mental capacities are transformed into uniquely human, higher cognitive processes. Let's see how this happens, as we explore the Piagetian–Vygotskian controversy introduced at the beginning of this chapter in greater detail.

CHILDREN'S PRIVATE SPEECH

Watch preschoolers as they go about their daily activities, and you will see that they frequently talk out loud to themselves as they play and explore the environment. For example, as a 5-year-old worked a puzzle at preschool one day, I heard him say, "Where's the red piece? I need the red one. Now a blue one. No, it doesn't fit. Try it here." On another occasion, while sitting next to another child, he blurted out, "It broke," without explaining what or when.

■ *During the preschool years, children frequently talk to themselves as they play and explore the environment. Research supports Vygotsky's theory that children use private speech to guide their behavior when faced with challenging tasks. With age, private speech is transformed into silent, inner speech, or verbal thought. (Robert Brenner/PhotoEdit)*

Piaget (1923/1926) called these utterances *egocentric speech,* a term expressing his belief that they reflect the preoperational child's inability to imagine the perspectives of others. For this reason, Piaget said, young children's talk is often "talk for self" in which they run off thoughts in whatever form they happen to occur, regardless of whether they are understandable to a listener. Piaget believed that cognitive maturity and certain social experiences—namely, disagreements with peers—eventually bring an end to egocentric speech. Through arguments with agemates, children repeatedly see that others hold viewpoints different from their own. As a result, egocentric speech declines and is replaced by social speech, in which children adapt what they say to their listeners.

Vygotsky (1934/1986) voiced a powerful objection to Piaget's conclusion that young children's language is egocentric and nonsocial. He reasoned that children speak to themselves for self-guidance and self-direction. Because language helps children think about their own behavior and select courses of action, Vygotsky regarded it as the foundation for all higher cognitive processes, such as controlled, sustained attention; deliberate memorization and recall; categorization; planning; problem solving; and self-reflection. As children get older and find tasks easier, their self-directed speech declines and is internalized as silent, inner speech—the verbal dialogues we carry on with ourselves while thinking and acting in everyday situations.

Over the past two decades, researchers have carried out many studies to determine which of these two views is correct. Almost all the findings have sided with Vygotsky. As a result, children's speech-to-self is now referred to as **private speech** instead of egocentric speech. Research shows that children use more of it when tasks are difficult, after they make errors, or when they are confused about how to proceed (Berk, 1992a, 1994b). Also, just as Vygotsky predicted, with age private speech goes underground, changing from utterances spoken out loud into whispers and silent lip movements (Bivens & Berk, 1990). Furthermore, children who use private speech when faced with challenging tasks are more attentive and involved and show greater improvement in performance than their less talkative agemates (Behrend, Rosengren, & Perlmutter, 1992; Berk & Spuhl, 1995). Finally, children with learning problems engage in especially high rates of private speech over a long period of development. They seem to use self-directed verbalizations to help compensate for impairments in cognitive processing and attention, which make academic tasks more difficult for them (Berk & Landau, 1993; Diaz & Berk, 1995).

If private speech is a central force in cognitive development, where does it come from? Vygotsky's answer to this question highlights the social origins of cognition, his main difference of opinion with Piaget.

SOCIAL ORIGINS OF COGNITIVE DEVELOPMENT

Vygotsky (1930–1935/1978) believed that all higher cognitive processes develop out of social interaction. Through joint activities with more mature members of society, children come to master activities and think in ways that have meaning in their culture. A special concept, the **zone of proximal** (or potential) **development**, explains how this happens. It refers to a range of tasks that the child cannot yet handle alone but can accomplish with the help of adults and more skilled peers. As children engage in cooperative dialogues with more mature partners, they take the language of these dialogues, make it part of their private speech, and use this speech to organize their independent efforts in the same way.

Although Vygotsky was not very explicit about the features of these dialogues that promote transfer of cognitive processes to children, contemporary researchers believe that at least two characteristics are important. The first is **intersubjectivity**. It refers to the process whereby two participants who begin a task with different understandings arrive at a shared understanding (Newson & Newson, 1975). Intersubjectivity creates a common ground for communication as each partner adjusts to the perspective of the other. Adults try to promote it when they translate their own insights in ways that are

Private speech
Self-directed speech that children use to plan and guide their own behavior.

Zone of proximal development
In Vygotsky's theory, a range of tasks that the child cannot yet handle alone but can do with the help of more skilled partners.

Intersubjectivity
A process whereby two participants who begin a task with different understandings arrive at a shared understanding.

within the child's grasp. For example, an adult might point out the links between a new task and ones the child already knows. As the child stretches to understand the interpretation, she is drawn into a more mature approach to the situation (Rogoff, 1990).

A second feature of social experience that fosters children's development is **scaffolding** (Bruner, 1983; Wood, 1989). It refers to a changing quality of social support over the course of a teaching session. Adults who offer an effective scaffold for children's independent mastery adjust the assistance they provide to fit the child's current level of performance. When the child has little notion of how to proceed, the adult uses direct instruction, breaking the task down into manageable units and calling the child's attention to specific features. As the child's competence increases, effective scaffolders gradually and sensitively withdraw support in accord with the child's self-regulatory efforts and success cues.

Is there evidence to support these ideas on the social origins of cognitive development? Research shows that as early as the first few months, caregivers and babies engage in finely tuned emotional communication (see Chapter 10) and joint gazing at objects—forms of intersubjectivity that are related to advanced play, language, and problem-solving skills during the second year (Bornstein et al., 1992b; Frankel & Bates, 1990; Tamis-LeMonda & Bornstein, 1989). In early childhood, mothers who are effective scaffolders in teaching their children to solve a challenging puzzle have youngsters who use more private speech and who are more successful when asked to do a similar puzzle by themselves (Behrend, Rosengren, & Perlmutter, 1992; Berk & Spuhl, 1995).

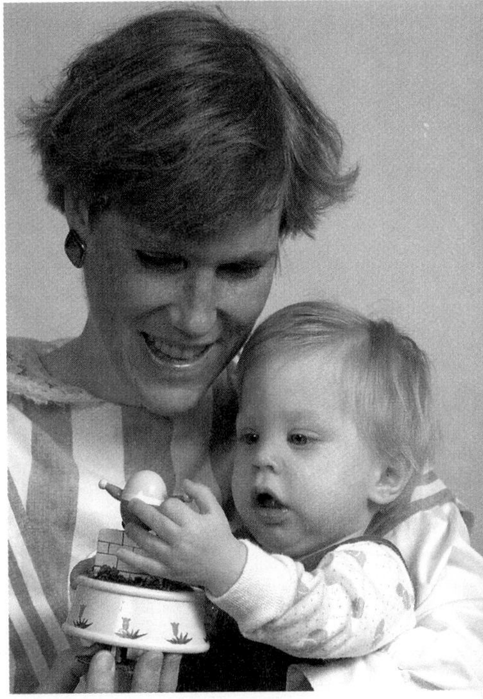

■ *This mother assists her young son in making a music box work. By presenting a task within the child's zone of proximal development and fine-tuning her support to fit his momentary needs, she promotes intersubjectivity and provides an effective scaffold for learning. (Erika Stone)*

VYGOTSKY'S VIEW OF MAKE-BELIEVE PLAY

In accord with his emphasis on social experience and language as vital forces in cognitive development, Vygotsky (1933/1978) granted make-believe play a prominent place in his theory. He regarded it as a unique, broadly influential zone of proximal development in which *children advance themselves* as they try out a wide variety of challenging skills:

> [Make-believe] play creates a zone of proximal development in the child. In play, the child always behaves beyond his average age, above his daily behavior; in play it is as though he were a head taller than himself. As in the focus of a magnifying glass, play contains all developmental tendencies in a condensed form and is itself a major source of development. (p. 102)

How does make-believe lead development forward? According to Vygotsky, it does so in two ways. First, as children create imaginary situations in play, they learn to act in accord with internal ideas, not just in response to external stimuli. The substitute objects that characterize make-believe are crucial in this process. When children use a stick to represent a horse or a folded blanket to represent a sleeping baby, they change an object's usual meaning. Gradually they begin to see that thinking (or the meaning of words) is separate from the actions and objects for which it stands and that ideas can be used to guide behavior.

A second feature of make-believe—its rule-based nature—also strengthens children's capacity to think before they act. Vygotsky pointed out that pretend play contains an interesting paradox. In play, children do what they most feel like doing, and to an outsider, their make-believe appears free and spontaneous. Nevertheless, it constantly demands that children act against their immediate impulses because they must follow social rules to execute the play scene. For example, a child pretending to go to sleep follows the rules of bedtime behavior. Another child imagining himself to be a father and a doll to be a child conforms to the rules of parental behavior. Make-believe, Vygotsky concluded, is not really "free"; instead, it requires self-restraint—willingly following social rules. As children enact rules in make-believe, they come to better understand social norms and expectations and strive to behave in ways to uphold them.

Vygotsky regarded the fantasy play of the preschool years as essential for further development of play—specifically, for movement toward game play in middle childhood. The games that captivate school-age children increasingly emphasize rules, thereby providing additional instruction in setting goals, regulating one's behavior in pursuit of those goals, and subordinating action to rules rather than impulse. Make-believe, in Vygotsky's theory, provides crucial preparation for cooperative and productive participation in social life.

Scaffolding
A changing quality of support over a teaching session in which adults adjust the assistance they provide to fit the child's current level of performance. Direct instruction is offered when a task is new; less help is provided as competence increases.

Was Vygotsky correct that make-believe serves as a zone of proximal development, supporting the emergence and refinement of a wide variety of competencies? Much evidence fits with Vygotsky's conclusion. Preschoolers' thinking about the pretend world seems to be more flexible and advanced than their thinking about the real world as they reason imaginatively about characters, events, and places (Lillard, 1993; Rubin, Fein, & Vandenberg, 1983). Turn back to page 225 to review findings that make-believe enhances a diverse array of cognitive and social skills.

Finally, Vygotsky took issue with the Piagetian view that make-believe arises spontaneously from symbolic tendencies within the child. Instead, Vygotsky argued that the elaborate pretending of the preschool years, like other higher cognitive processes, is the product of social collaboration (Berk, 1994a; Nicolopoulou, 1993). New evidence, reviewed in the Cultural Influences box on the following page, supports Vygotsky's view that children initially learn to pretend under the supportive guidance of experts.

Vygotsky and Education

Vygotsky's theory offers new visions of teaching and learning—ones that emphasize the importance of social context and collaboration. Today, educators are eager to use his ideas to enhance children's development.

Piagetian and Vygotskian classrooms clearly have features in common, such as opportunities for active participation and acceptance of individual differences. Yet Vygotsky differed from Piaget in that he believed education does not just refine structures that have already emerged. Instead, it plays a major role in development, leading it forward as children receive instruction from more expert partners on tasks within their zones of proximal development. Consequently, a Vygotskian classroom goes beyond self-initiated discovery; it promotes *assisted discovery.* Teachers guide children's learning with explanations, demonstrations, and verbal prompts, carefully tailoring their efforts to each child's zone of proximal development. Assisted discovery is also fostered by *peer collaboration.* Pupils who vary in ability work in groups, teaching and helping one another.

During the preschool years, Vygotsky's major educational message was to provide many challenging activities that promote teacher–child and child–child interaction. In addition, much time should be devoted to imaginative play—the ultimate means of fostering the self-discipline required for mastery of academic tasks after school entry (Berk & Winsler, 1995). Once formal schooling begins, Vygotsky placed special emphasis on literacy activities. Teachers in Vygotskian classrooms transform the environment into a highly literate setting in which many types of symbolic communication are integrated with one another (Bodrova & Leong, 1996; Moll & Whitmore, 1993). As children talk about reading and writing in literature, mathematics, science, social studies, and other academic contexts, they begin to reflect on their thought processes. As they do so, they develop the capacity to consciously manipulate and control the symbolic systems of their culture, and they shift to a higher level of cognitive activity (Vygotsky, 1934/1986).

The Social Issues box on page 252 summarizes a recent large-scale experiment in elementary education, grounded in sociocultural theory, that has been remarkably successful in helping low-income ethnic minority children learn. In the following sections, we examine two additional Vygotskian-based educational innovations, each of which incorporates assisted discovery and peer collaboration.

RECIPROCAL TEACHING

Reciprocal teaching is a method of instruction designed to improve reading comprehension in children who are at risk for academic difficulties or who are already experiencing difficulties (Palincsar & Brown, 1984). Recently, the approach has been adapted to other subject-matter areas, such as social studies and science lessons (Palincsar, 1992). A collaborative learning group is formed in which a teacher and two to four pupils take turns leading dialogues on the content of a text passage. Within the dialogues, group members flexibly apply four cognitive strategies: questioning, summarizing, clarifying, and predicting.

Reciprocal teaching
A method of teaching based on Vygotsky's theory in which a teacher and two to four pupils form a collaborative learning group. Dialogues occur that create a zone of proximal development in which reading comprehension improves.

CULTURAL INFLUENCES

Social Origins of Make-Believe Play

One of my husband Ken's shared activities with our two sons when they were young was to bake pineapple upside-down cake, a favorite treat. I remember well one Sunday afternoon when a cake was in the making. Little Peter, then 21 months old, stood on a chair at the kitchen sink, busy pouring water from one cup to another.

"He's in the way, Dad!" complained 4-year-old David, trying to pull Peter away from the sink.

"Maybe if we let him help, he'll give us some room," Ken suggested. As David stirred the batter, Ken poured some into a small bowl for Peter, moved his chair to the side of the sink, and handed him a spoon.

"Here's how you do it, Petey," instructed David, with an air of superiority. Peter watched as David stirred, then tried to copy his motion. When it was time to pour the batter, Ken helped Peter tip the small bowl so its contents flowed into the pan.

"Time to bake it," said Ken.

"Bake it, bake it," repeated Peter, as he watched Ken slip the pan into the oven.

Several hours later, we observed one of Peter's earliest instances of make-believe play. He got his pail from the sandbox and after filling it with a handful of sand, carried it into the kitchen and put it down on the floor in front of the oven. "Bake it, bake it," Peter called to Ken. Together, father and son lifted the pretend cake inside the oven.

Historically, the emergence of make-believe was studied in isolation from the social environment in which it usually occurs. Until recently, most researchers observed young children while playing alone. Probably for this reason, Piaget and his followers concluded that toddlers discover make-believe independently, as soon as they are capable of representational schemes. Vygotsky's theory has challenged this view. He believed that society provides children with opportunities to represent culturally meaningful activities in play. Make-believe, like other mental functions, is initially learned under the guidance of expert partners (Garvey, 1990; Smolucha, 1992). In the example just described, Peter's capacity to represent daily events was extended when Ken drew him into the baking task and helped him act it out in play.

New research supports the idea that early make-believe is the combined result of children's readiness to engage in it and social experiences that promote it. An observational study of middle-class American toddlers at play in their homes revealed that 75 to 80 percent of make-believe during the second year involved mother–child interaction. At 12 months, make-believe was fairly one-sided; almost all play episodes were initiated by caregivers. By the end of the second year, caregivers and children displayed mutual interest in getting make-believe started; half of pretend episodes were initiated by each. At all ages, caregivers elaborated on the child's contribution, resulting in joint activity in which both partners participated actively in an imaginative dialogue. Over time, the adult gradually released responsibility to the child for creating and guiding the fantasy theme (Haight & Miller, 1993).

What are the consequences of adult involvement in young children's pretending? In several studies, researchers compared toddlers' solitary play with their play while interacting with their mothers. In each case, caregiver support led early make-believe to move toward a more advanced level (Fiese, 1990; O'Reilly & Bornstein, 1993; Slade, 1987). For example, when adults took part, play themes were more varied, and maternal commentary was especially effective in extending the duration of make-believe. Also, toddlers were more likely to combine representational schemes into more complex sequences, as Peter did when he put the sand in the bucket ("making the batter"), carried it into the kitchen, and (with Ken's help) put it in the oven ("baking the cake").

In many cultures, adults do not spend much time playing with young children. Instead, older siblings take over this function. For example, in Indonesia and Mexico, where extended family households and sibling caregiving are common, make-believe is more frequent as well as complex with older siblings than with mothers. As early as 3 to 4 years of age, siblings join in the younger child's play activities and frequently make comments and suggestions for more elaborate pretending. In this way, they provide rich, challenging stimulation that serves as an important supplement to their mothers' less playful style of interaction. The fantasy play of toddlers in these cultures is just as well developed as that of their middle-class American counterparts (Farver, 1993; Farver & Wimbarti, 1995a; Gaskins, 1994).

Make-believe is a major means through which children extend their cognitive skills and learn about important activities in their culture. Vygotsky's theory, and the findings that support it, tell us that providing a stimulating environment is only part of what is necessary to promote early cognitive development. In addition, young children must be invited and encouraged by their elders to become active participants in the social world around them.

Once group members have read the passage, a dialogue leader (at first the teacher, later a pupil) begins by *asking questions* about its content. Pupils pose answers, raise additional questions, and in case of disagreement, reread the text. Next, the leader *summarizes* the passage, and discussion takes place to achieve consensus on the summary. Then a period occurs in which participants *clarify* ideas that are ambiguous or unfamiliar to any group members. Finally, the leader encourages pupils to *predict* upcoming content based on prior knowledge and clues in the passage (Palincsar & Klenk, 1992).

Over the past decade, hundreds of elementary and junior high school pupils have participated in reciprocal teaching. Such children show substantial gains in reading comprehension compared to controls exposed to alternative instructional strategies with the same reading materials (Lysynchuk, Pressley, & Vye, 1990; Palincsar, Brown, & Campione,

SOCIAL ISSUES

The Kamehameha Early Education Program (KEEP)

The Kamehameha Elementary Education Program (KEEP) is an educational experiment grounded in Vygotsky's sociocultural theory that is designed to foster high achievement as well as independence, positive social relationships, and excitement about learning. The zone of proximal development serves as the foundation for KEEP's theory of instruction. To motivate development, KEEP integrates a variety of strategies that have traditionally belonged to other theories into supportive teacher–pupil dialogues:

- Modeling, to introduce children to unfamiliar skills
- Instructing, to direct children toward the next specific act they need to learn in order to move through the zone of proximal development
- Verbal feedback (or reinforcement), to let children know how well they are progressing in relation to reasonable standards of performance
- Questioning, to encourage children to think about the task
- Explaining, to provide strategies and knowledge necessary for thinking in new ways

These techniques are applied in activity settings specially designed to enhance opportunities for teacher–child and child–child communication. In each setting, children work on a project that ensures that their learning will be active and directed toward a meaningful goal. For example, they might read a story and engage in lively discussion about its meaning or draw a map of the playground to promote understanding of geography. Sometimes activity settings include the whole class. More often, they involve small groups that foster cooperative learning and permit teachers to stay in touch with how well each child is doing. All children enter a focal activity setting, called "Center One," at least once each morning for 20 minutes. Here, scaffolding of challenging literacy skills takes place. Text content is carefully selected to relate to children's experiences, and instruction relies heavily on questioning, responding to, and building on children's ideas.

The precise organization of each KEEP classroom is adjusted to fit the unique learning styles of its pupils, creating culturally responsive environments (Tharp, 1994). For example, depending on pupil makeup, activity setting discourse might reflect the lively paced interactive style of native Hawaiians or the patient turn taking of the Navajo (Gallimore & Tharp, 1990).

An essential aspect of KEEP is that teaching and learning at each level of the school system is based on the zone of proximal development. Just as children require support in mastering activities in the classroom, teachers teach best when they are assisted by members of the educational system. Principals, supervisors, consultants, and other teachers help them improve their competence, transforming the school into a community of learners.

Thousands of low-income minority children have attended KEEP classrooms in the public schools of Hawaii, on a Navajo reservation in Arizona, and in Los Angeles. So far, research suggests that the approach is highly effective in helping children who typically achieve poorly learn. In KEEP schools, minority pupils performed at their expected grade level in reading achievement, much better than children of the same background enrolled in traditional schools (see Figure 6.10). Classroom observations also showed that KEEP pupils participated actively in class discussion, used elaborate language structures, frequently supported one another's learning, and were more attentive and involved than were non-KEEP controls (Tharp & Gallimore, 1988). As the KEEP model becomes more widely applied, perhaps it will prove successful with all types of children because of its comprehensive goals and effort to meet the learning needs of a wide range of pupils.

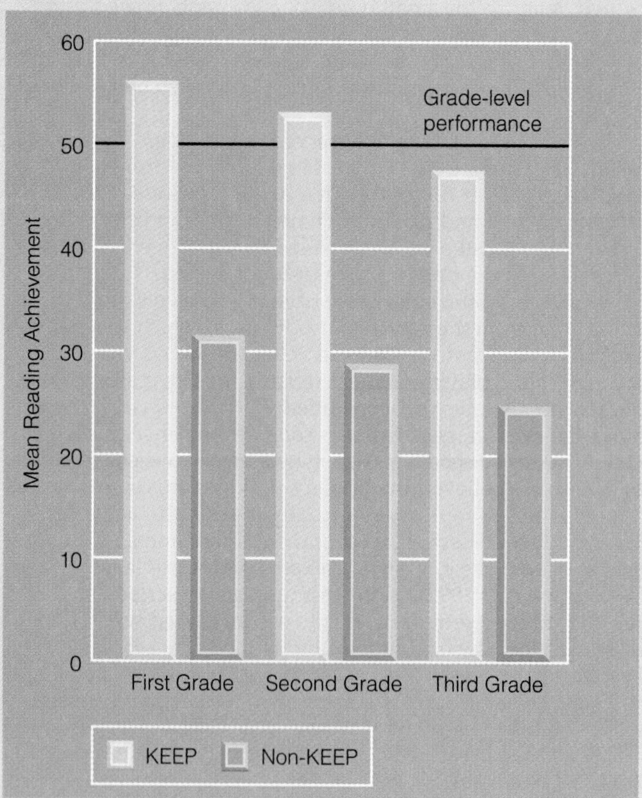

FIGURE 6.10

Reading achievement of KEEP-instructed and traditionally instructed first- through third-grade low-income minority pupils. The KEEP children performed at grade level; the non-KEEP pupils performed substantially below grade level. (Adapted from R. G. Tharp & R. Gallimore, 1988, Rousing Minds to Life: Teaching, Learning, and Schooling in Social Context, *New York: Cambridge University Press, p. 116. Adapted by permission.)*

■ *Consistent with Vygotsky's theory, the success of peer collaboration depends on cooperative learning. When peers work toward a common goal by resolving differences of opinion, sharing responsibility, and engaging in cooperative dialogues, cognitive development in enhanced. (Tony Freeman/PhotoEdit)*

1993). Notice how reciprocal teaching creates a zone of proximal development in which children, with the aid of teachers and peers, gradually assume more responsibility for the task. Reciprocal teaching also keeps reading activities whole rather than breaking them down into isolated skills removed from the complexities of real text passages (Engliert & Palincsar, 1991). In line with Vygotsky's theory, the method ensures that children learn within a culturally meaningful context that is applicable to their everyday lives.

COOPERATIVE LEARNING

Although reciprocal teaching uses peer collaboration, a teacher is present to guide it, helping to ensure its success. According to Vygotsky (1930–1935/1978), more knowledgeable peers can also lead children's learning forward, as long as they adjust the help they provide to fit the less mature child's zone of proximal development. Recall that Piaget, too, thought that peer interaction could contribute to cognitive change. In fact, he regarded discussion with agemates as more valuable than discussion with adults, since a child might superficially accept an adult's perspective without critically examining it, out of an unquestioning belief in the adult's authority. Piaget also asserted that clashing viewpoints—arguments jarring the young child into noticing a peer's point of view—were necessary for peer interaction to stimulate movement toward logical thought (Tudge & Winterhoff, 1993).

Today, peer collaboration is used in many classrooms, but evidence is mounting that it is successful only under certain conditions. A crucial factor is **cooperative learning**—structuring the peer group so that students work together toward a common goal. Conflict and disagreement do not seem to be as important in fostering development as the extent to which peers achieve intersubjectivity—by resolving differences of opinion, sharing responsibility, and engaging in cooperative dialogues (Forman & McPhail, 1993; Nastasi, Clements, & Battista, 1990; Tudge, 1992). And in line with Vygotsky's theory, children's planning and problem solving improve most when their peer partner is an "expert"—especially capable at the task (Azmitia, 1988; Radziszewska & Rogoff, 1988).

These findings indicate that teachers need to group together children of varied ages and abilities and provide guidelines for group interaction in order to reap the full benefits of peer collaboration. When these efforts are successful, pupils derive important benefits. Research conducted in Israel revealed that compared to teacher-directed instruction, cooperative learning in eighth-grade classrooms led to more harmonious and lively discussions, greater participation by low-income ethnic minority pupils, and higher academic achievement for both low-income and middle-income youngsters (Shachar & Sharan, 1994).

Cooperative learning
A learning environment structured into groups of peers who work together toward a common goal.

Evaluation of Vygotsky's Theory

Piaget and Vygotsky shared the belief that children arrive at knowledge through actively participating in the world around them. Yet in granting social experience a fundamental role in cognitive development, Vygotsky's theory is unique in helping us understand the wide variation in cognitive skills across cultures. Unlike Piaget, who emphasized universal cognitive change, Vygotsky's theory leads us to expect highly variable development, depending on the child's specific cultural experiences. For example, the reading, writing, and mathematical activities of children who go to school in literate societies generate cognitive capacities that differ from those in preliterate cultures. Yet the elaborate spatial skills of Australian aborigines, whose food-gathering missions require that they find their way through barren desert regions, or the proportional reasoning of Brazilian fishermen, promoted by their navigational experiences, are no less advanced (Carraher, Schliemann, & Carraher, 1988; Kearins, 1981). Instead, each is a unique form of thinking demanded by the particular settings that make up a culture's way of life (Rogoff & Chavajay, 1995; Tulviste, 1991).

Vygotsky's theory, like Piaget's, has not gone unchallenged. Although Vygotsky acknowledged the role of diverse symbol systems (such as pictures, maps, and algebraic expressions) in mediating the development of higher cognitive processes, he elevated language to highest importance. Yet verbal dialogue and finely tuned, scaffolded instruction is not the only means, or even the most important means, through which thought develops in some cultures.

In a recent study, Barbara Rogoff and her collaborators (1993) asked caregivers to help toddlers with challenging tasks (getting dressed and operating novel toys) in four communities—two middle-class urban areas, one in Turkey and one in the United States; a Mayan town in Guatemala; and a tribal village in India. In the middle-class communities, parents assumed much responsibility for children's motivation and involvement in the tasks. They often verbally instructed, conversed, and interacted playfully with the child. Their communication resembled the teaching that takes place in school, where their children will spend years preparing for adult life. In contrast, in the Mayan and Indian communities, adults expected toddlers to take greater responsibility for acquiring new skills through keen observation. As the child showed attentive interest, caregivers offered responsive assistance, often nonverbally. This style of interaction, which depended heavily on demonstration and gesture, appeared well suited to conditions in which young children learn by participating in daily activities of adult life.

■ *This young girl of the Urubamba Valley in Peru watches intently as her mother weaves an elaborately patterned cloth. Compared to children growing up in middleclass urban communities, she depends more on parental demonstration and gesture and less on finely tuned, scaffolded instrution to aquire culturally valued skills. (Inga Spence/The Picture Cube)*

In cultures everywhere, caregivers guide children's mastery of the practices of their community. Yet the type of assistance offered varies greatly, depending on the nature of adult–child involvement and the tasks essential for success in each society. So we are reminded once again that children learn in many ways, and as yet, no single theory provides a complete account of cognitive development.

Finally, recall that Vygotsky stated that the natural and cultural lines of development join, forming a single developmental pathway. But in focusing on the cultural line, he said little about the natural line—far less than did Piaget or information processing, to which we now turn. Consequently, we cannot tell from Vygotsky's theory exactly how elementary processes contribute to higher cognitive processes derived from social experience (Moll, 1994; Wertsch & Tulviste, 1992). It is intriguing to speculate about the broader theory that might exist today had these two giants of cognitive development had the chance to meet and weave together their extraordinary accomplishments.

SUMMARY

PIAGET'S COGNITIVE-DEVELOPMENTAL THEORY

- Influenced by his background in biology, Piaget viewed cognitive development as an adaptive process. By acting directly on the environment, children move through four stages in which internal structures achieve a better fit with external reality. According to Piaget, cognitive development is a matter of **domain-general** (rather than **domain-specific**) changes, and infants begin life with little in the way of built-in structures; they must **construct** virtually all knowledge about their world.
- In Piaget's theory, psychological structures, or **schemes**, change in two ways. The first is through adaptation, which is made up of two complementary processes: **assimilation** and **accommodation**. The second is through **organization**, the internal rearrangement of schemes so that they form a strongly interconnected cognitive system. **Equilibration** sums up the changing balance of assimilation and accommodation that gradually leads to more effective schemes. Piaget assumed that the stages are invariant and universal.

THE SENSORIMOTOR STAGE (BIRTH TO 2 YEARS)

- Piaget's **sensorimotor stage** is divided into six substages. Through the **circular reaction**, the newborn baby's reflexes are gradually transformed into the more flexible action patterns of the older infant, and **sensorimotor egocentrism** declines. During Substage 4, infants develop **intentional**, or **goal-directed, behavior** and begin to understand **physical causality** and **object permanence**. Substage 5 brings a more flexible, exploratory approach, and infants no longer make the **AB search error**. By Substage 6, they become capable of **mental representation**, as shown by sudden solutions to sensorimotor problems, **deferred imitation**, mastery of the **invisible displacement task**, and **make-believe play**.
- It is widely recognized that Piaget underestimated the capacities of young infants. Secondary circular reactions, physical reasoning (including object permanence and physical causality), and representation (in the form of deferred imitation and categorization), are present earlier than Piaget believed.
- Today, investigators believe newborns have more built-in equipment for making sense of their world than Piaget assumed. Some researchers speculate that infants begin life with a small set of innate perceptual procedures for interpreting experience. Others advocate a **nativist, modular view of the mind** that grants newborns substantial built-in, domain-specific knowledge.

THE PREOPERATIONAL STAGE (2 TO 7 YEARS)

- Rapid advances in **mental representation,** including language, make-believe play, meaningful drawings, and understanding of spatial symbols, mark the beginning of the **preoperational stage**. With age, make-believe becomes increasingly complex, evolving into **sociodramatic play** with others. Preschoolers' make-believe not only reflects, but contributes to cognitive development.
- Aside from representation, Piaget described the young child in terms of deficits rather than strengths. The most serious deficiency is **preoperational egocentrism**, an inability to distinguish the perspectives of others from one's own. It leads to a variety of illogical features of thought. According to Piaget, preschoolers engage in **animistic thinking**, and their cognitions are **perception bound**, centered, focused on **states rather than transformations**, and **irreversible**. In addition, preoperational children engage in **transductive reasoning** rather than truly causal reasoning. Because of these difficulties, they fail **conservation** and **hierarchical classification** (class inclusion) tasks.
- When young children are given simplified problems relevant to their everyday lives, their performance appears much more mature. This indicates that logical thought develops gradually over the preschool years, a finding that challenges Piaget's concept of stage.

THE CONCRETE OPERATIONAL STAGE (7 TO 11 YEARS)

- During the **concrete operational stage**, thought is far more logical and organized than it was during the preschool years. The ability to conserve indicates that children can decenter and reverse their thinking. In addition, they are better at hierarchical classification, **seriation**, and **transitive inference**. School-age youngsters have an improved understanding of distance and can give clear directions. **Cognitive maps** become more organized and accurate during middle childhood.
- Concrete operational thought is limited in that children can reason logically only about concrete, tangible information; they have difficulty with abstractions. Piaget used the term **horizontal décalage** to describe the school-age child's gradual mastery of logical concepts, such as conservation.
- Recent evidence indicates that specific cultural practices, the phrasing of questions, and the objects to which they refer can have a profound effect on Piagetian task performance. Concrete operations may not be a natural form of logic that emerges universally in middle childhood. Instead, it may be a product of direct training, context, and cultural conditions.

THE FORMAL OPERATIONAL STAGE (11 YEARS AND OLDER)

- In Piaget's **formal operational stage**, abstract thinking appears. Adolescents engage in **hypothetico-deductive reasoning**. When faced with a problem, they think of all possibilities, including ones that are not obvious, and test them against reality in an orderly fashion. **Propositional thought** also develops. Young people can evaluate the logic of verbal statements without considering them against real-world circumstances.
- Early in this stage, **formal operational egocentrism** appears. Adolescents have difficulty distinguishing the abstract perspectives of self and other. As a result, two distorted images of the relation between self and other appear: the **imaginary audience** and **personal fable**.

- Recent research reveals school-age children display the beginnings of abstract reasoning, but they are not as competent as adolescents and adults. In addition, many college students and adults are not fully formal operational, and formal thought does not appear at all in many village and tribal cultures. These findings indicate that Piaget's highest stage is reached gradually rather than abruptly and is affected by specific experiences.

LARGER QUESTIONS ABOUT THE VALIDITY OF PIAGET'S THEORY

- A wealth of research reveals that Piaget's theory has important shortcomings. Some ideas, such as his explanation of cognitive change, are not clearly spelled out. Others, such as the timetable of development, are not entirely accurate.
- Some researchers reject Piaget's stages but retain his view of cognitive development as an active, constructive process. Others argue that Piaget's strict stage definition needs to be modified into a less tightly knit concept. Still others deny both Piaget's stages and his conception of domain-general change in favor of a modular view of the mind. The future is likely to bring compromises among these clashing points of view.

PIAGET AND EDUCATION

- Piaget's theory has had a lasting impact on educational programs for young children. A Piagetian classroom promotes discovery learning, sensitivity to children's readiness to learn, and acceptance of individual differences.

VYGOTSKY'S SOCIOCULTURAL THEORY

- In contrast to Piaget, who viewed children as agents of their own development, Vygotsky constructed a theory in which the child and the social environment collaborate to mold cognition in culturally adaptive ways. Once children become capable of mental representation, especially through language, the natural line of mental development begins to be transformed by the social line.
- Whereas Piaget believed that language does not play a major role in cognitive development, Vygotsky regarded it as the foundation for all higher cognitive processes. As children engage in cooperative dialogues with more skilled partners while working on tasks within the **zone of proximal development**, they incorporate the language of these dialogues into their **private speech** and use it to organize their independent efforts in the same way. **Intersubjectivity** and **scaffolding** are features of social interaction that promote transfer of cognitive processes to children.
- According to Vygotsky, make-believe play is a unique, broadly influential zone of proximal development. As children create imaginary situations and follow the rules of the make-believe scene, they learn to act in accord with internal ideas rather than on impulse. In Vygotsky's theory, make-believe play, like other higher cognitive processes, is the product of social collaboration.

VYGOTSKY AND EDUCATION

- A Vygotskian classroom emphasizes assisted discovery in the form of verbal guidance from teachers and peer collaboration. Imaginative play in the preschool years and literacy activities during middle childhood foster important cognitive advances. Vygotskian educational innovations include **reciprocal teaching** and **cooperative learning**.

EVALUATION OF VYGOTSKY'S THEORY

- Vygotsky's theory helps us understand the wide variation in cognitive skills across cultures. However, verbal dialogues that scaffold children's efforts may not be the only means, or even the most important means, through which thought develops in some cultures. Piaget emphasized the natural line, Vygotsky the cultural line of development. A broader theory might exist today had these two contemporaries had the chance to meet and integrate their ideas.

IMPORTANT TERMS AND CONCEPTS

domain-general changes (p. 211)
domain-specific changes (p. 211)
constructivist approach (p. 211)
nativist approach (p. 211)
scheme (p. 212)
adaptation (p. 213)
assimilation (p. 213)
accommodation (p. 213)
equilibration (p. 213)
organization (p. 213)
sensorimotor stage (p. 214)
circular reaction (p. 214)
sensorimotor egocentrism (p. 214)
intentional, or goal-directed, behavior (p. 216)
physical causality (p. 216)
object permanence (p. 216)
AB search error (p. 216)
mental representation (p. 217)
invisible displacement task (p. 217)
deferred imitation (p. 217)
make-believe play (p. 217)
modular view of the mind (p. 224)
preoperational stage (p. 225)
sociodramatic play (p. 226)
operations (p. 229)
preoperational egocentrism (p. 229)
animistic thinking (p. 230)
conservation (p. 230)
perception-bound (p. 230)
centration (p. 230)
states rather than transformations (p. 232)
reversibility (p. 232)
transductive reasoning (p. 232)
hierarchical classification (p. 232)
concrete operational stage (p. 236)
seriation (p. 238)
transitive inference (p. 238)
cognitive maps (p. 238)
horizontal décalage (p. 239)
formal operational stage (p. 241)
hypothetico-deductive reasoning (p. 241)
propositional thought (p. 242)
formal operational egocentrism (p. 243)
imaginary audience (p. 243)
personal fable (p. 243)
private speech (p. 248)
zone of proximal development (p. 248)
intersubjectivity (p. 248)
scaffolding (p. 249)
reciprocal teaching (p. 250)
cooperative learning (p. 253)

CONNECTIONS for Chapter 6

If you are interested in . . .	turn to . . .	to learn about . . .
Play	Chapter 11, p. 428	Make-believe play and the child's theory of mind
	Chapter 13, pp. 509–510, 516	Sex-related differences in play
	Chapter 15, pp. 581–582	Social and cognitive maturity of play during the preschool years
	Chapter 15, pp. 584–585	Play materials and peer sociability
	Chapter 15, p. 586	Cultural values and play
	Chapter 15, pp. 603–604	Television and imaginative play
Influence of Piaget on child development research	Chapter 4, p. 158	Infant perception of objects as distinct, bounded wholes
	Chapter 7, pp. 264–266	Neo-Piagetian theories of cognitive development
	Chapter 7, pp. 275–277	Memory and reconstruction of information
	Chapter 8, p. 310	Piagetian-based intelligence tests
	Chapter 11, pp. 426–427	Emergence of self-recognition
	Chapter 11, pp. 428–429	Development of self-concept
	Chapter 11, pp. 444–448	Development of perspective taking
	Chapter 11, pp. 449–451	Understanding friendship
Jean Piaget	Chapter 12, pp. 469–472	Piaget's theory of moral development
	Chapter 13, p. 519	Emergence of gender-role identity
Vygotsky's sociocultural theory	Chapter 1, pp. 26–27	Cross-cultural research and Vygotsky's sociocultural theory
	Chapter 7, p. 285	Self-regulation of task performance
	Chapter 15, pp. 585–586	Mixed-age interaction and children's development
	Chapter 15, pp. 606–608	Computers and cognitive development
	Chapter 15, pp. 611–612	Vygotsky-inspired educational philosophies
Lev Vygotsky		

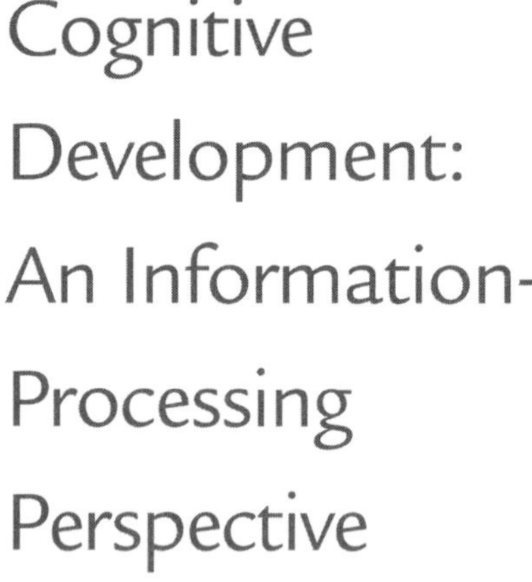

7 Cognitive Development: An Information-Processing Perspective

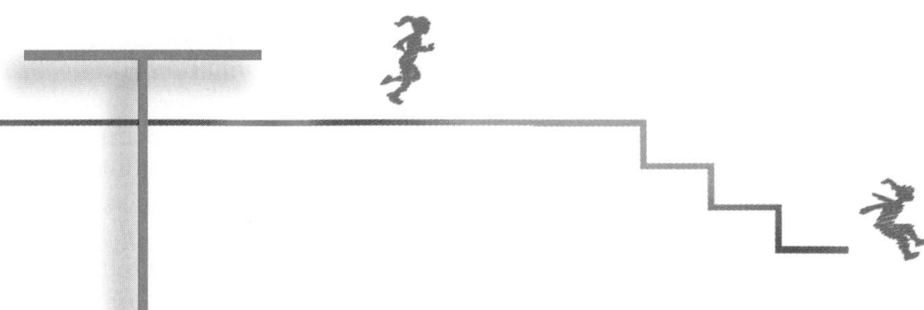

The information-processing view of cognition rose to the forefront of the field of child development partly as a reaction to the inadequacies of Piaget's theory. Unlike the Piagetian perspective, information processing does not offer a single, unified theory of children's thinking. Instead, it is an approach followed by researchers studying a wide variety of aspects of cognition. Their goal is to find out how children and adults operate on different kinds of information, coding, transforming, and organizing it as it makes its way through the cognitive system.

This chapter provides an overview of the information-processing perspective. First, we review general and developmental models of the human cognitive system that have served as major forces in research. Next, we turn to two basic operations that enter into all human thinking: attention and memory. We also consider how children's growing knowledge of the world and awareness of their own mental activities affect these basic operations.

As we examine each of these topics, we will return to a theme that surfaced many times in Chapter 6: the role of cultural context and task demands in cognitive performance. Consider the experience of one researcher, who interviewed Kpelle farmers of Liberia about how they would sort a set of 20 familiar objects as an aid to remembering them. Members of this preliterate society arranged the objects by function. For example, they placed a knife with an orange and a hoe with a potato rather than putting all the tools in one pile and the food items in another, as the researcher expected them to do (Glick, 1975). Puzzled that Kpelle adults would approach this task much like young children in Western nations, the researcher asked for an explanation. Many Kpelle replied that a wise person would do it that way. In exasperation, the researcher finally blurted out, "How would a fool do it?" Right away, he got the kinds of object groupings he had been looking for!

The Kpelle study suggests that societal definitions of skilled performance can mold information processing in certain directions. In this chapter, we pay special attention to how schooling, with its emphasis on literacy, mathematics, scientific reasoning, and retention of discrete pieces of information, channels cognition in culturally specific ways. Although information-processing theorists are especially interested in internal, self-generated changes that take place with age, they also want to find out how external influences—from teaching techniques to cultural values—affect the way children and adults approach various tasks. Our discussion concludes with an evaluation of the strengths and weaknesses of information processing as a framework for understanding cognitive development.

The Information-Processing Approach

Most information-processing theorists view the mind as a complex, symbol-manipulating system through which information flows, operating much like a digital computer. Information from the environment is encoded, or taken in by the system and retained in symbolic form. Then a variety of internal processes operate on it, recoding it, or revising its symbolic structure into a more effective representation, and then decoding it, or interpreting its meaning by comparing and combining it with other information in the system. When these cognitive operations are complete, output occurs in the form of a task solution.

Consider this brief description of information processing, and perhaps you can see why researchers have found the computer analogy of human mental functioning so attractive. It shares with Piaget's theory a view of the mind as an active processor of information. But beyond this, the computer model offers clarity and precision in a way that many Piagetian concepts do not. Using computerlike diagrams and flowcharts, investigators can map the exact series of steps children and adults execute when faced with a task or problem. Some do so in such detail that the same mental operations can be programmed into a computer. Then computer simulations are used to test predictions about how children and adults approach a variety of tasks.

Other information-processing investigators do not rely on computer simulations to test their ideas. Instead, they draw from a wealth of other methods, such as tracking eye movements, analyzing error patterns, and examining self-reports of mental processes. But all share a strong commitment to explicit models of cognitive functioning, each component of which must be thoroughly tested with research (Klahr, 1992; Kuhn, 1992).

General Models of Information Processing

How do information-processing researchers conceive of the human mental system? Two major models have influenced research on children's thinking.

ATKINSON AND SHIFFRIN'S STORE MODEL

The most widely known computerlike model of mental functioning is Atkinson and Shiffrin's (1968) **store model**. As Figure 7.1 shows, it is called a store model because information is assumed to be held, or stored, in three parts of the system for processing: the sensory register, short-term memory, and long-term memory. Atkinson and Shiffrin regard these stores as inborn and universal among all human beings. You can think of them as the *hardware* of the mental system. Each is limited in the speed with which it can process information. In addition, the sensory register and short-term memory are limited in capacity. They can hold onto only a certain amount of information for a brief period until it fades away entirely.

As information flows through each store, it can be operated on and transformed using **control processes**, or **mental strategies**—the *software* of the system. When we use strategies to manipulate input in various ways, we increase the efficiency of thinking as well as the chances that information will be retained for later use. According to Atkinson and Shiffrin, control processes are not innate; they are learned, and individuals differ in how well they use them. Let's take a brief look at each component of Atkinson and Shiffrin's model.

■ COMPONENTS OF THE STORE MODEL. First, information enters the **sensory register**. Here, sights and sounds are represented directly, but they cannot be held for long. For example, take a moment to look around, and then close your eyes. An image of what you saw persists briefly, but then it decays or disappears, unless you use control processes, or mental strategies, to preserve it. For example, you can attend to some details more carefully than others, thereby increasing the chances that the selected input will transfer to the next step of the information-processing system.

The second way station of the mind is **short-term memory**. This is the central processing unit, the conscious part of our mental system, where we actively operate on a limited amount of information. For example, if you are studying this book effectively, you are constantly applying mental strategies, manipulating input to ensure that it will be retained and available to solve problems. Perhaps you are attending to certain information that seems most important. Or you may be using a variety of memory strategies, such as taking notes, repeating information to yourself, or grouping pieces of information together, as the Kpelle farmers were asked to do in the study described at the beginning of this chapter.

Store model
Atkinson and Shiffrin's model of mental functioning, which views information as being held in three parts of the system for processing: the sensory register, short-term memory, and long-term memory.

Control processes, or mental strategies
Procedures that operate on and transform information, increasing the efficiency of thinking and the chances that information will be retained.

Sensory register
In Atkinson and Shiffrin's store model, the first part of the mental system, where sights and sounds are represented directly but held only briefly.

Short-term memory
In Atkinson and Shiffrin's store model, the central processing unit of the mental system, where information is consciously operated on using control processes, or mental strategies.

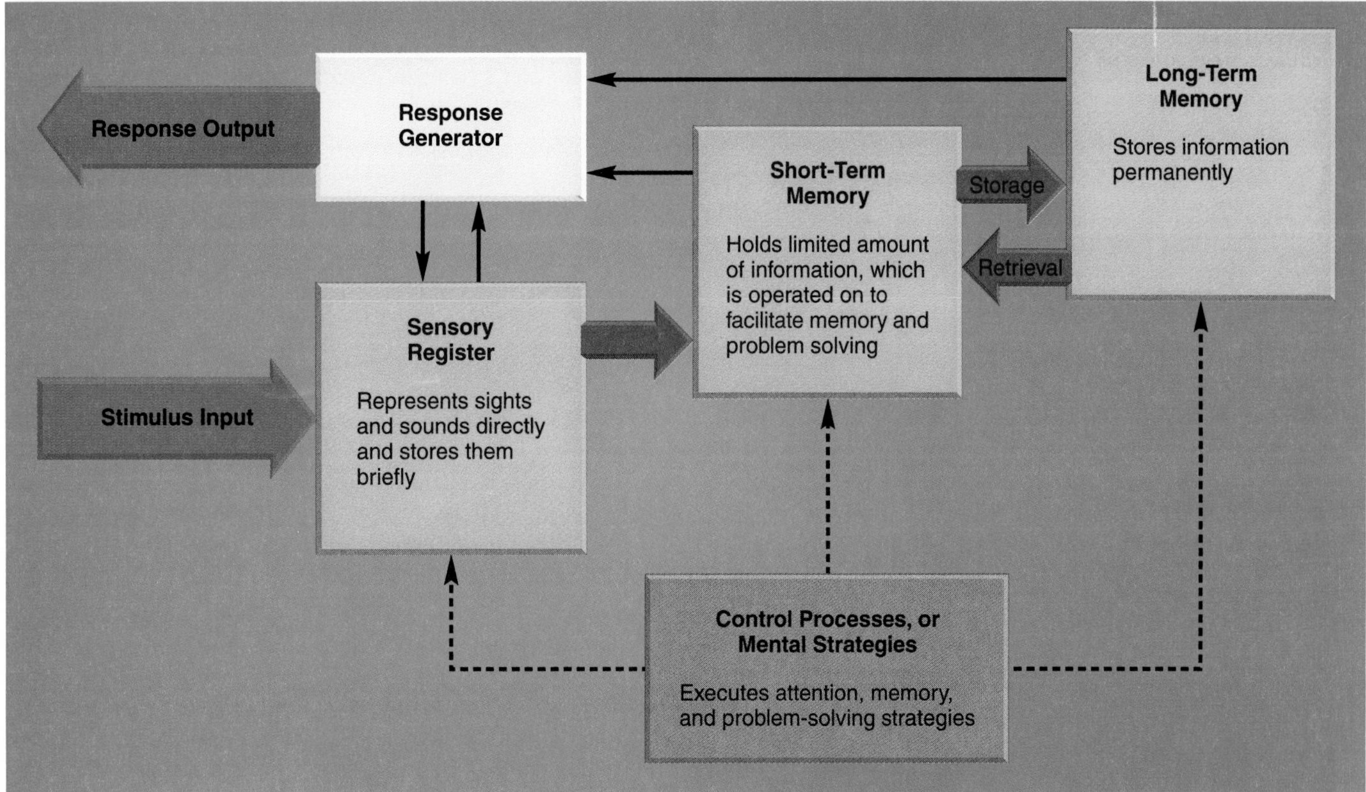

FIGURE 7.1

■ *Atkinson and Shiffrin's store model of the human information-processing system. Stimulus input flows through three parts of the mental system: the sensory register, short-term memory, and long-term memory. In each, control processes, or mental strategies, can be used to manipulate information, increasing the efficiency of thinking and the chances that information will be retained. (Adapted from R. M. Shiffrin & R. C. Atkinson, 1969, "Storage and retrieval processes in long-term memory,"* Psychological Review, *76, p. 180. Copyright © 1969 by the American Psychological Association. Adapted by permission of the publisher and author.)*

Think, for a moment, about why you apply strategies to retain information in short-term memory. The sensory register, although also limited, can take in a wide panorama of information. But when input reaches the short-term store, a bottleneck occurs. Once the limited number of slots in short-term memory is occupied, either new information cannot enter the system, or if it does, it will push out existing information. However, the capacity limit of short-term memory is not a matter of physical pieces of information, but of *meaningful chunks.* Therefore, by connecting separate pieces through strategy use, you can increase your memory capacity. And the longer information is retained in the system, the greater the chances that it will be transferred to the third, and largest, storage bin of the system.

Unlike the sensory register and working memory, the capacity of **long-term memory**, our permanent knowledge base, is limitless. In fact, so much input is stored in long-term memory that we sometimes have problems with *retrieval,* or getting information back from the system. To aid retrieval, we apply strategies in long-term memory just as we do in short-term memory. For example, consider how information in your long-term memory is arranged. According to Atkinson and Shiffrin (1968), it is categorized according to a master plan based on contents, much like a "library shelving system which is based upon the contents of books" (p. 181). When information is filed in this way, it can be retrieved quite easily by following the same network of associations that was used to store it in the first place.

■ RESEARCH TESTING THE STORE APPROACH. Much evidence is consistent with Atkinson and Shiffrin's store model. For example, the well-known **serial position effect** that occurs when you try to memorize a list of items supports the distinction between short- and long-term memory. Items in the middle are less likely to be remembered than those at the beginning or the end. Over time, however, items at the end decay from memory, whereas those at the beginning continue to be retained. Researchers believe this happens because items learned last are held only temporarily in short-term memory, whereas those learned first have had enough time to transfer to the long-term store.

In one study, researchers found this same effect as early as 7 months of age. Babies were shown three photos of women's faces. Then each infant was assigned to a condition in which the first, middle, or last photo was paired with a new photo. Memory for the

Long-term memory
In Atkinson and Shiffrin's store model, the part of the mental system that contains our permanent knowledge base.

Serial position effect
In memory tasks involving lists of items, the tendency to remember ones at the beginning and end better than those in the middle.

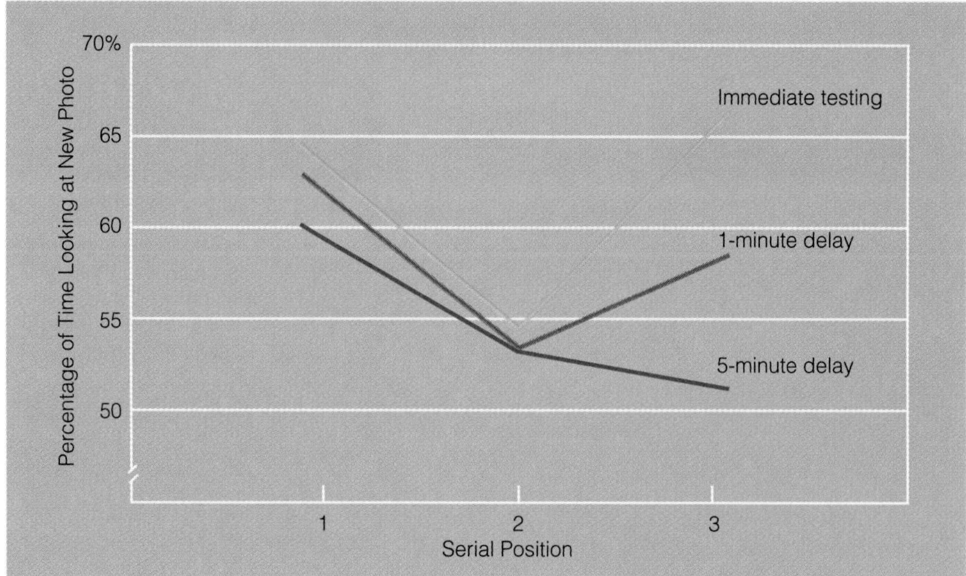

FIGURE 7.2

■ *Serial position findings in a study of 7-month-old infants. In the immediate testing condition, photos in the first and last serial positions were remembered best. After delays of 1 and 5 minutes, memory for the last photo declined and then disappeared. (Adapted from Cornell & Bergstrom, 1983.)*

original photo was determined by measuring the extent to which the babies dishabituated to, or spent more time looking at, the new photo. As Figure 7.2 shows, when babies were tested immediately, the first and last photos were remembered much more effectively than the middle photo. After a 1-minute delay, memory for the last photo declined, and at 5 minutes it disappeared (Cornell & Bergstrom, 1983). These findings are consistent with Atkinson and Shiffrin's assumption that separate short- and long-term memory stores are fundamental to the human information-processing system.

Other findings have raised questions about the store model. The capacity limits of the sensory register and short-term memory vary widely from study to study. For example, retention of visual information in the sensory register ranges from 250 milliseconds to 25 seconds. And the short-term store, once thought to be limited to 7 slots, actually varies from 2 to 20 (Baddeley, 1994; Siegler, 1983). Difficulties in identifying the precise size of these "hardware units" have led some researchers to doubt their existence and to turn toward a levels-of-processing view.

THE LEVELS-OF-PROCESSING MODEL

The **levels-of-processing model** abandons the idea of a series of containers with fixed limits on how much information can be grasped at once. Instead, it assumes that retention depends on the depth to which information is processed. For example, we could encode a written word superficially, according to its *perceptual features,* by noticing whether it is printed in capital or lowercase letters. At a slightly deeper level, we could encode the word by attending to its *phonemic features,* or how it sounds. In this instance, we might repeat the word aloud to ourselves, or rhyme it with another word, several times. At the deepest level of processing, we would encode the word according to its meaning, or *semantic features,* by relating it to other information already in our systems (Craik & Lockhart, 1972; Craik & Tulving, 1975). In the levels-of-processing model, information that is analyzed in a shallow way decays quickly and is soon forgotten. In contrast, information interpreted meaningfully and linked to existing knowledge is retained much longer.

According to the levels-of-processing view, the difficulty we experience in trying to handle many pieces of information at once is not due to a fixed-size memory container. Instead, it has to do with the extent to which we can distribute our attention across several activities at once. As a result, the limited-slot idea of short-term memory is replaced by the concept of **working memory**. It refers to the conscious pool of attentional resources from which our information-processing activities draw (Baddeley, 1992). The amount of attention a person must allocate to a task depends on how well learned, or automatic, the cognitive processes required by it happen to be. Unskilled individuals must devote more attention. As a result, resources are drawn away from other activities they might engage in at the same time. In contrast, automatic cognitive processes demand little or no attentional capacity, and individuals can engage in other tasks simultaneously.

Levels-of-processing model
A model of mental functioning in which retention of information depends on the depth to which it is analyzed. Attentional resources determine processing capacity.

Working memory
In the levels-of-processing model, the conscious pool of attentional resources from which our information-processing activities draw.

Let's use an example to illustrate this idea. Consider two children, one a novice and the other an expert bicycle rider. The attention of the novice is entirely consumed by efforts to steer, control the pedals, and maintain balance. Indeed, parents are best off insisting that this child practice in traffic-free areas, since little or no attentional resources remain for other cognitive activities, such as watching out for cars and pedestrians. In contrast, the practiced bicyclist rides easily around the neighborhood, delivering papers, chewing gum, and carrying on a conversation with a nearby rider at the same time.

RESEARCH ON THE STORE VERSUS LEVELS-OF-PROCESSING MODELS

When applied to development, the store and levels-of-processing models emphasize somewhat different features. The store approach suggests that both the hardware of the system (size of the information containers) and the software (control processes) change with age. That is, what develops may be both a bigger computer and a wider array of effective programs, or strategies. In contrast, the levels-of-processing model assumes that all changes have to do with software, or the functioning of the system. In other words, many cognitive processes become less capacity-consuming as the result of years of practice with strategies, which eventually leads to more efficient use of available space (Siegler, 1983).

Research we will review throughout this chapter indicates that without a doubt, control processes improve with age. Children gradually acquire a variety of strategies for conserving space within the limited-capacity systems they have, and they process information more deeply—an important cause of age-related memory gains (Ornstein, 1995).

Does the hardware of the system also expand? There is disagreement on this issue, but recent evidence on speed of processing suggests that overall capacity does increase. Robert Kail (1988, 1991, 1993) gave individuals between 7 and 22 years of age a variety of basic cognitive tasks in which they had to respond as quickly as possible. For example, in a visual search task, participants were shown a single digit and asked to signal if it was among a set of digits that appeared on a screen. In a mental rotation task, they were given pairs of letters in any of six different orientations and asked to decide whether the letters were identical or mirror images. And in a mental addition task, participants were presented with addition problems and answers, and they had to indicate whether or not the solution was correct.

As Figure 7.30 on page 264 reveals, Kail found that processing time decreased with age for all tasks. But even more important, the rate of change was the same across many activities—a fairly rapid decline that trailed off around 12 years of age. This pattern was also evident when participants performed perceptual–motor tasks, such as releasing a button or tapping as fast as possible—activities that do not rely heavily on mental strategies (Kail, 1991). Furthermore, after extensive practice on several tasks, the processing times of children and adults decreased proportionately, and the same age trends remained. This suggests that children and adults use the same steps to perform each of these tasks; older individuals simply perform the steps faster. Consequently, use of more effective strategies with age cannot account for the findings shown in Figure 7.3 (Hale, Fry, & Jessie, 1993).

The changes in processing speed just described have been reported for samples in Canada, Korea, and the United States (Kail & Park, 1992). Similarity in development across a diverse array of tasks in several cultures implies an age-related gain in basic information-processing resources, possibly due to myelinization or synaptic pruning of neural fibers in the brain (see Chapter 5) (Hale, Fry, & Jessie, 1993; Kail & Salthouse, 1994). As a result, older children and adults can hold more information in their cognitive systems at once, scan it more quickly, and generate faster responses in a wide range of situations. Kail reminds us, however, that neurological development is not the only factor that contributes to efficient information processing. On many tasks, older children, adolescents, and adults do use more adept strategies, which also quicken their performance (Kail & Park, 1994).

In sum, although the precise capacity limits of the cognitive system are hard to pin down, *both* its hardware and its software seem to change over the course of childhood. As we turn now to developmental models of information processing, we will see efforts to integrate these two aspects—the first emphasizing brain maturation, the second experience in transforming information—into an overall picture of how the cognitive system changes with age.

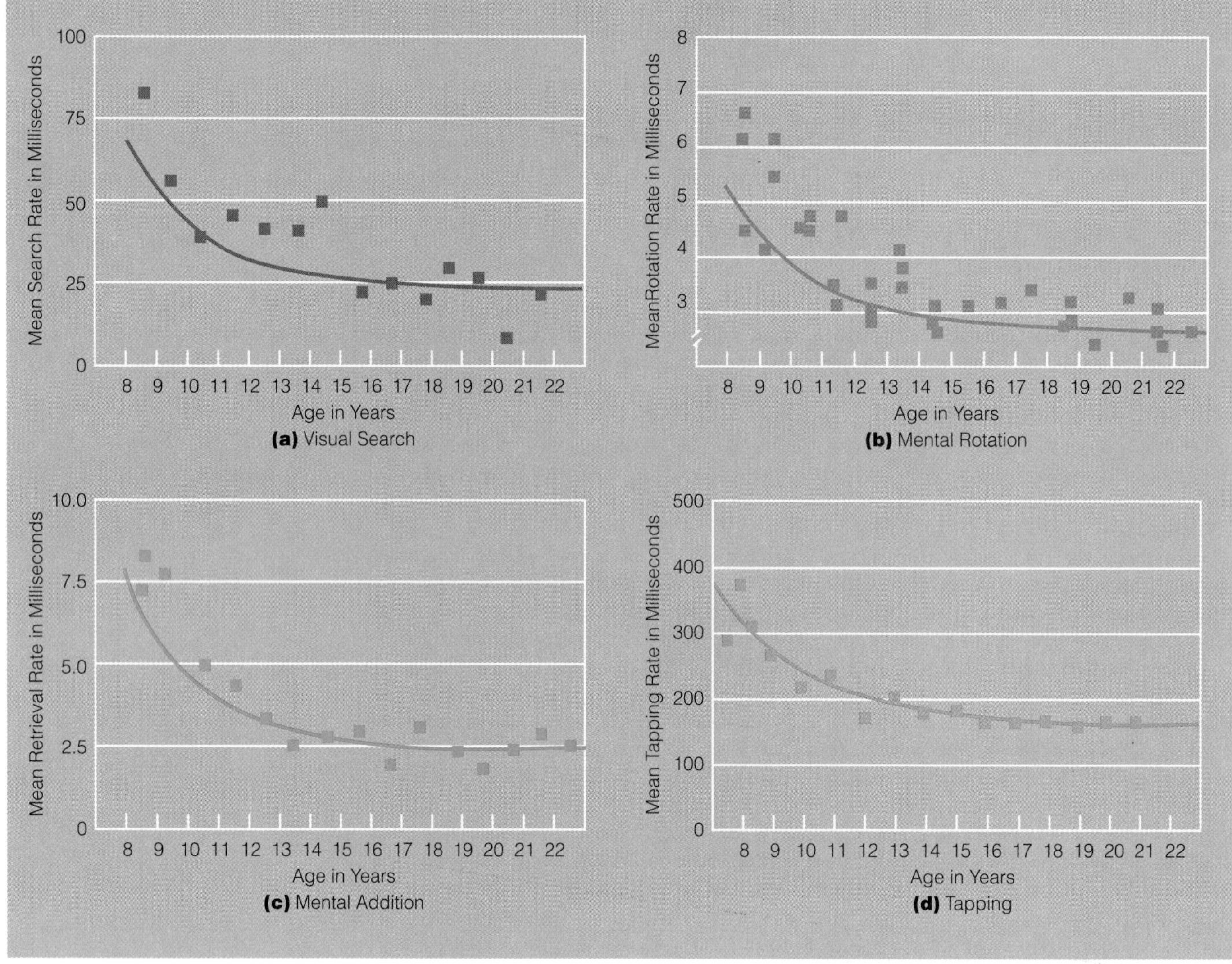

FIGURE 7.3

Decreases in processing time across a range of basic cognitive tasks over childhood and adolescence. That the rate of decline is so uniform across activities suggests that the overall capacity, or size, of the information-processing system is expanding. (Parts a–c from R. Kail, 1988, "Developmental functions for speeds of cognitive processes," Journal of Experimental Child Psychology, *45, p. 361. Copyright © 1988 by Academic Press. Reprinted by permission of the publisher and author. Part d from R. Kail, 1991, "Processing time declines exponentially during childhood and adolescence,"* Developmental Psychology, *27, p. 265. Copyright © 1991 by the American Psychological Association. Adapted by permission of the publisher and author.)*

Developmental Models of Information Processing

The store and levels-of-processing models are *general* approaches to information processing. Neither makes precise statements about how children's thinking changes with age. However, several *developmental* models have attracted widespread attention (Case, 1985, 1992a; Fischer & Pipp, 1984; Halford, 1993). To create an overall vision of development, each uses Piaget's theory as a starting point, reinterpreting it within an information-processing framework. Consequently, these theories are often termed *neo-Piagetian.* Let's take a brief look at two of them: Case's M-space and Fischer's skill theory.

CASE'S THEORY

Robbie Case (1985, 1992a) views cognitive development as a matter of increases in information-processing capacity that result from more efficient strategy use. Piagetian schemes, in Case's theory, constitute the child's mental strategies. With age, a computer-like construct called **mental space**, or **M-space**—a notion similar to working memory—expands (Pascual-Leone, 1970, 1987). Increases in M-space are due to three factors. The first is *brain maturation.* Myelinization improves the speed of neural processing and, thereby, the efficiency of thought. Second, *exercise of strategies* contributes. As schemes are repeatedly practiced, they become more automatic and require less attentional capacity, freeing up extra M-space for the child to work on combining old schemes and generating new ones. Once the schemes of a Piagetian stage become sufficiently automatized, enough M-space is available to consolidate them into an improved representational form. As a result, children acquire *central conceptual structures,* networks of concepts and relations that permit them to think about a wide range of situations in more advanced ways. These structures are a third way M-space expands, since they lead to more efficient approaches to interpreting experience and solving problems (Case & Griffin, 1990). When children acquire them, they move up to a new stage of development.

■ *This 9-year-old realizes that objects differing in size and shape can weigh the same amount, a principle he did not grasp at a younger age. According to Case's neo-Piagetian theory, brain maturation and exercise of previously mastered schemes enhance the efficiency of thought, freeing up space in working memory. As a result, children consolidate schemes into central conceptual structures—improved representations that permit them to think in more advanced ways. (Tony Freeman/ PhotoEdit)*

Case's theory also offers an information-processing account of horizontal décalage—that many Piagetian milestones, such as conservation, appear in specific situations at different times rather than being mastered all at once. Case assumes that different forms of the same logical insight vary in the processing demands they make of the child. Therefore, each successive Piagetian task requires more M-space for mastery.

Think back to the various Piagetian tasks we discussed in Chapter 6. A notable feature of them is that at each new stage of development, a greater number of features must be held in memory and combined to reach a correct solution. Children's ability to pass more advanced Piagetian tasks is correlated with their *digit span*—the number of discrete digits they can recall from a list, often used to assess the limits of working memory (Case, 1977, 1978). This finding is consistent with Case's suggestion that combining schemes in more complex problem solving is accompanied by an expansion of a central processing resource pool (M-space) with development.

FISCHER'S SKILL THEORY

Kurt Fischer's **skill theory** also reformulates Piaget's stages but places more emphasis on children's specific experiences than does Case. According to Fischer, a skill is a Piagetian scheme applied to a particular task or set of tasks. How broadly applicable a skill is depends on brain maturation and the range of environments to which the child has been exposed (Fischer & Bidell, 1991; Fischer & Farrar, 1987; Fischer & Pipp, 1984). To understand how these two factors work together, let's look at some concepts Fischer uses to describe skill development.

Each child has an optimal level of skill performance, or upper limit of processing capacity, that cannot be exceeded without further brain maturation. Fischer identifies three optimal skill levels that correspond to Piaget's stages: sensorimotor actions, representations, and abstractions. However, children (and adults) seldom function optimally, because using the most advanced skills possible depends on extensive support from the environment. Therefore, within each level, an extended period of skill learning takes place in which the child acquires new competencies on specific tasks, integrates them with others, and gradually transforms them into more general, higher-order skills.

For example, a 5-year-old who cannot yet conserve liquid may have some isolated skills, such as (1) after water is poured from a tall into a short glass, the height of the water level is reduced; and (2) after water is poured from a thin into a wide glass, the width of the water increases. But until the child has had enough experience transferring liquids from one container to another, she cannot combine these two separate skills into a conserving response. Once a more advanced skill is mastered in a particular situation, it can be transferred to other similar situations. In our example, conservation can then be applied to mass or weight. Eventually the child coordinates several task-specific skills into a new broadly applicable principle. When this happens, cognition moves to a higher level of functioning—in this case, from representation to abstraction.

Mental space, or M-space
In Case's theory, a construct similar to working memory. It expands with brain maturation, exercise of strategies, and formation of central conceptual structures, which permit the child to move up to a new Piagetian stage.

Skill theory
Fischer's theory, in which each Piagetian stage is viewed as an extended period of skill learning in which the child acquires new competencies on specific tasks, integrates them with others, and gradually transforms them into more general, higher-order skills. As a result, the child moves up to a new Piagetian stage.

EVALUATION OF CASE AND FISCHER'S THEORIES

In sum, the theories of Case and Fischer each build on Piaget's stage theory while attempting to deal with its problematic aspects. Both Case and Fischer view children's capacities as more heterogeneous than Piaget proposed and offer plausible information-processing accounts of development. A common thread is that each major advance in thinking coincides with a dramatic increase in working memory. Although more evidence is needed to support this idea, many researchers agree that surmounting memory limits is a crucial factor in cognitive development. These neo-Piagetian approaches are also unique in offering an integrated picture of how basic capacity, strategies, and learning interact to produce development (Bjorklund, 1995; Siegler, 1991).

Finally, Case and Fischer acknowledge greater domain-specificity in development than did Piaget, attributing it to variations in the complexity of tasks and children's experiences. At the same time, both theories, in the tradition of Piaget, are basically domain-general approaches, since each contends that there is level of performance extending across domains that a child cannot exceed. The question still remains: How domain-general is cognitive development? Some investigators, as we noted in Chapter 6, find it to be far more domain-specific than do these neo-Piagetians, arguing that the mind is modular in nature (see pages 224 and 245–246). This issue remains a major unresolved controversy in the field.

BRIEF REVIEW

Information-processing researchers are committed to explicit models of cognitive functioning that map the precise steps children and adults use when faced with a task or problem. Two general models of information processing have influenced research on children's cognition. Atkinson and Shiffrin's store model regards the limited capacity of our mental systems as due to fixed-size sensory and short-term memory stores. In contrast, the levels-of-processing view emphasizes allocation of attention as responsible for processing limitations. Two developmental models—Case's M-space and Fischer's skill theory—reinterpret Piaget's stages in information-processing terms. Each accounts for unevenness in development across tasks as well as broad cognitive changes.

Attentional Processing

Most information-processing research on how children encode sensory information focuses on infants—evidence discussed at length in Chapter 4. When individuals of different ages are shown arrays of visual stimuli and asked to report what they saw immediately, even 5-year-olds retain large quantities of information in the sensory register briefly—nearly as much as adults. Yet when questioned about what they saw a short time after removal of the stimulus display, young children perform considerably worse than older children, adolescents, and adults (Sheingold, 1973). This sharp decline in performance after a delay suggests that the capacity of the sensory register has little to do with younger children's less effective information processing. Instead, age differences in the ability to extract information from the sensory register and transfer it into short-term or working memory play a larger role.

Consequently, we begin our tour of the information-processing system with research on the development of attention. Attention is fundamental to human thinking, since it determines the sources of information that will be considered in any task or problem. Parents and teachers are quick to notice that young children spend only short times involved in tasks, have difficulty focusing on details, and are easily distracted. Attention improves greatly over the course of childhood, becoming more controlled, adaptable, and planful.

CONTROL

Watch young children at play, and you are likely to see that attention becomes more focused and sustained with age. In a recent study, infants and preschoolers were seated at a table with age-appropriate toys. Concentrated involvement rose steadily between 1 and 4 years. Infants' and older children's patterns of attention also differed. After playing for a short time, babies tended to habituate. Their loss of interest suggested that their attention was externally controlled by the physical properties of the toys. In contrast, preschoolers became increasingly attentive as the play session progressed. Their capacity to engage in complex play seemed to support focused engagement with objects (Ruff & Lawson, 1990). Nevertheless, even 5- and 6-year-olds do not remain attentive for very long. When observed during free play at preschool, the average time they spend in a single activity is about 7 minutes (Stodolsky, 1974).

As sustained attention improves, children become better at deliberately focusing on just those aspects of a situation that are relevant to their task goals, ignoring other sources of information. Researchers study this increasing selectivity of attention by introducing irrelevant stimuli into a task. Then they see how well children attend to its central elements (Lane & Pearson, 1982). In a typical experiment of this kind, school-age children and adults were asked to sort decks of cards as fast as possible on the basis of shapes appearing on each card—for example, circles in one pile and squares in another. Some decks contained no irrelevant information. Others included either one or two irrelevant stimuli, such as lines running across the shapes or stars appearing above or below them. Children's ability to ignore unnecessary information was determined by seeing how much longer it took them to sort decks with irrelevant stimuli. As Figure 7.4 indicates, the ability to keep attention on central features of the task improved sharply between 6 and 9 years of age (Strutt, Anderson, & Well, 1975).

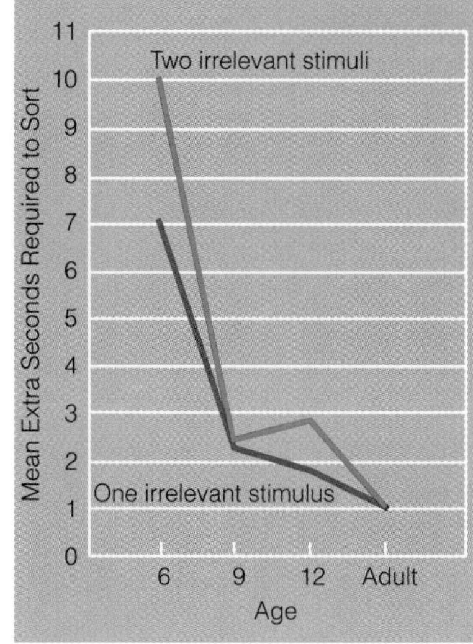

FIGURE 7.4

■ *Improvement in control of attention over the elementary school years. School-age children and adults were asked to sort decks of cards on the basis of shapes that appeared on each card. Six-year-olds took much longer to sort when the decks contained irrelevant stimuli (lines and stars) than when they did not. By age 9, sorting speed was only slightly affected by the presence of irrelevant information. (Adapted from G. F. Strutt, D. R. Anderson, & A. D. Well, 1975, "A developmental study of the effects of irrelevant information on speeded classification,"* Journal of Experimental Child Psychology, *20, p. 132. Copyright © 1975 by Academic Press. Adapted by permission of the publisher and author.)*

ADAPTABILITY

Children's attention gradually becomes more adaptable, flexibly adjusting to the momentary requirements of situations. For example, in judging whether pairs of stimuli are the same or different, sixth graders quickly shift their basis of judgment (from size to shape to color) when asked to do so. Second graders have trouble with this type of task (Pick & Frankel, 1974). Similarly, on tasks requiring a shift in attention from one part of the visual field to another (for example, pressing a button as fast as possible when a stimulus appears in the periphery of a computer screen), performance improves steadily over middle childhood and adolescence. Younger children do better when given a cue (such as an arrow) that directs their attention to the area in which the stimulus will appear (Pearson & Lane, 1990). But even with cueing, their performance is not as quick and accurate as that of older individuals.

Older children are also better at adapting their attention to changes in their own learning. When given lists of items to learn and allowed to select half for further study, first graders do not choose systematically. But by third grade, children show a strong tendency to select those they had previously missed (Masur, McIntyre, & Flavell, 1973). When learning more complex information, such as prose passages, the ability to allocate attention on the basis of previous performance continues to improve into the college years (Brown, Smiley, & Lawton, 1978).

How do children acquire and perfect attentional strategies that focus on relevant information and adapt to task requirements? Patricia Miller and her colleagues found that strategy development follows a predictable sequence. In a series of studies, they showed 3- to 9-year-olds a large box with rows of doors that could be opened. Half the doors had pictures of cages on them, signifying that behind each was a different animal. The other half had pictures of houses, indicating that they contained a variety of household objects. Children were asked to remember the precise location of all the objects in one group (DeMarie-Dreblow & Miller, 1988; Miller et al., 1986; Woody-Ramsey & Miller, 1988).

The youngest children did not use a selective attentional strategy; they simply opened all the doors, regardless of the pictures on them. In other words, they showed a **production deficiency**, a failure to use a strategy in situations in which it could be helpful. Slightly older children began to use the strategy, but they did not always apply

Production deficiency
The failure to use a mental strategy in situations where it could be helpful.

it; they still opened many irrelevant doors. These children displayed a **control deficiency**, an inability to execute a strategy effectively. When children began to apply the strategy more consistently, they suffered from a **utilization deficiency**, in that it did not improve their performance. Not until the mid-elementary school years could children use a selective attentional strategy and also benefit from it (Miller & Seier, 1994).

As we will see shortly, the three phases just described also characterize the development of memory strategies. Why, when young children first use a strategy, does it not work effectively? A likely reason is that applying a new strategy requires considerable mental effort, taking so much of children's attentional resources that they do not have enough to both execute the strategy and perform other parts of the task well (Miller et al., 1991; Miller, Woody-Ramsey, & Aloise, 1991). In support of this interpretation, reducing the demands of the task by having an adult perform the selective attention strategy for the child (by opening relevant doors) led to substantial gains in memory for object locations (DeMarie-Dreblow & Miller, 1988).

PLANFULNESS

With age, yet another change in children's attention is apparent: It becomes more planful. **Planning** involves thinking out a sequence of acts ahead of time and allocating attention accordingly to reach a goal (Scholnick, 1995). The seeds of effective planning are present in infancy. When researchers showed 2- and 3-month-olds a series of pictures that alternated in a predictable left–right sequence, they quickly learned to shift their focus to the location of the next stimulus before it appeared—a response not apparent when picture locations were random (Canfield & Haith, 1991). Even the attention of very young babies seems to be "future oriented," as indicated by their ability to anticipate routine events (Benson & Haith, 1995; Haith, Wentworth, & Canfield, 1993).

During the preschool years, children encounter circumstances that require planning on a larger scale. By age 4, they search for a lost object in a play yard systematically and exhaustively, looking only in locations between where they last saw the object and where they discovered it missing (Wellman, Somerville, & Haake, 1979).

Still, planful attentional strategies have a long way to go before they are very mature. When asked to compare detailed pictures like those in Figure 7.5, school-age children search much more thoroughly for similarities and differences (Vurpillot, 1968). And on complex tasks that require the coordination of many acts, they make decisions about what to do first and what to do next in a more orderly fashion. For example, when researchers gave 5- to 9-year-olds lists of items to obtain from a doll-sized grocery store, older children took more time to scan the store thoroughly before starting on a shopping trip. They also paused more often along the way to look for each item before moving to get it (see Figure 7.6). Consequently, they followed shorter routes through the aisles (Gauvain & Rogoff, 1989a; Szepkouski, Gauvain, & Carberry, 1994).

The development of planning illustrates how attention becomes coordinated with other cognitive processes we will take up later in this chapter. To solve problems involving multiple steps, children must postpone action in favor of mentally weighing alternatives, organizing task materials (such as items in a grocery list), and remembering the steps

FIGURE 7.5

■ *Pairs of houses children were asked to judge as the same or different. Preschoolers' eye movements showed that they did not examine all stimulus features systematically. As a result, they frequently judged different houses to be the same. In contrast, 6- to 9-year-olds used an exhaustive search strategy in which they compared the details of the houses window to window. (From E. Vurpillot, 1968, "The development of scanning strategies and their relation to visual differentiation,"* Journal of Experimental Child Psychology, 6, *p. 634. Copyright © 1968 by Academic Press. Reprinted by permission of the publisher and author.)*

Control deficiency
The inability to execute a mental strategy effectively.

Utilization deficiency
The failure to benefit from using a mental strategy.

Planning
Thinking out a sequence of acts ahead of time and allocating attention accordingly to reach a goal.

FIGURE 7.6

Play grocery store used to investigate children's planning. Five- to 9-year-olds were given "shopping lists," each consisting of five cards with a picture of a food item on it. Along the walls and on the shelves of the doll-sized store were pictures of food items that could be picked up by moving a figurine called the "shopper" down the aisles. Researchers recorded children's scanning of the store before starting on a shopping trip and along the way. The length of the route used to gather the items served as the measure of planning effectiveness. (Adapted from Szepkouski, Gauvain, & Carberry, 1994.)

of their plan so they can attend to each one in sequence. Along the way, they must monitor how well the plan is working and revise it if necessary. Clearly, planning places heavy demands on information-processing resources. Not surprisingly, even when young children do plan, they often forget to implement important steps. Practice in planning helps children understand its components and benefits and increases the likelihood that they will use this knowledge to guide future activities. As planning requires less effort, children narrow the gap between their intended plan and actual behavior (Scholnick, 1995; Friedman, Scholnick, & Cocking, 1987).

Finally, perhaps you noticed that each aspect of attention we have considered improves rapidly from early to middle childhood. Brain maturation and the demands of school tasks are probably jointly responsible. Controlled, adaptable, and planful attentional strategies are certainly essential for successful school performance. Unfortunately, some children have great difficulty paying attention during the school years. See the From Research to Practice box on page 270 for a discussion of the serious learning and behavior problems of children with attention-deficit hyperactivity disorder.

BRIEF REVIEW

Attention improves greatly from early to middle childhood. During the preschool years, children show gains in focused, sustained attention while playing. Over the school years, the ability to attend to relevant information and ignore irrelevant stimuli in a task improves. Older children are also better at adapting attention to momentary requirements of situations and deciding what to do first and what to do next in a planful, orderly fashion. Brain maturation and the demands of school tasks support rapid gains in attentional strategies.

FROM RESEARCH TO PRACTICE

Children with Attention-Deficit Hyperactivity Disorder

While the other fifth graders worked quietly at their desks, Calvin squirmed in his seat, dropped his pencil, looked out the window, fiddled with his shoelaces, and talked out. "Hey Joey," he yelled over the top of several desks, "wanna play ball after school?" Joey didn't answer. He and the other children weren't eager to play with Calvin. Out on the playground, Calvin was a poor listener and failed to follow the rules of the game. When up at bat, he had difficulty taking turns. In the outfield, he tossed his mitt up in the air and looked elsewhere when the ball came his way. Calvin's desk at school and his room at home were a chaotic mess. He often lost pencils, books, and other materials necessary for completing assignments. And very often, he had difficulty remembering his assignments and when they were due.

Calvin is one of 3 to 5 percent of school-age children with **attention-deficit hyperactivity disorder (ADHD)** (American Psychiatric Association, 1994). Although boys are diagnosed five to ten times more often than girls, recent evidence suggests that just as many girls may suffer from the disorder. Girls are less likely to be identified because their symptoms are usually not as flagrant (Hynd et al., 1991).

Children with ADHD have great difficulty staying on task for more than a few minutes. In addition, they often act impulsively, ignoring social rules and lashing out with hostility when frustrated. Many (but not all) are *hyperactive.* They charge through their days with excessive motor activity, leaving parents and teachers frazzled and other children annoyed. ADHD youngsters have few friends; they are soundly rejected by their classmates. According to one view that has amassed substantial research support, these diverse symptoms are unified by a common theme: an impaired ability to delay responding to stimuli (Barkley, 1994).

The intelligence of ADHD children is normal, and they show no signs of serious emotional disturbance. Instead, because they have trouble postponing action in favor of thought, they do poorly on laboratory tasks requiring sustained attention and find it hard to ignore irrelevant information (Douglas, 1983; Milich & Lorch, 1994). Their distractibility results in poor encoding of essential information, which may underlie their forgetfulness and difficulties with planning, reasoning, and problem solving in academic and social situations. Children with ADHD are behind their agemates in development of many information-processing capacities (Grodzinsky & Diamond, 1992). Although some outgrow these difficulties, most continue to have problems concentrating and finding friends into adolescence and adulthood (Claude & Firestone, 1995).

Heredity plays a major role in ADHD, since the disorder runs in families, and identical twins share it more often than do fraternal twins. Also, an adopted child who is inattentive and hyperactive is likely to have a biological parent (but not an adoptive parent) with similar symptoms (Faraone et al., 1995; Zametkin, 1995). Recent psychophysiological research, including EEG and fMRI studies, reveal structural differences between the brains of children with and without ADHD, particularly in the frontal lobe of the cortex and in other areas responsible for attention and inhibition of behavior (Riccio et al., 1993).

At the same time, ADHD is associated with a variety of environmental factors. These children are somewhat more likely to come from homes in which marriages are unhappy and family stress is high (Bernier & Siegel, 1994). But researchers agree that a stressful home life rarely causes ADHD. Instead, the behaviors of these children can contribute to family problems, which (in turn) are likely to intensify the child's preexisting difficulties. Furthermore, recall from earlier chapters that prenatal teratogens (including certain illegal drugs, alcohol, and cigarettes) are linked to inattention and hyperactivity. Dietary causes, such as food additives and sugar, have also been suggested, but there is little evidence that they play important roles (Hynd et al., 1991).

Calvin's doctor eventually prescribed stimulant medication, the most common treatment for ADHD. As long as dosage is carefully regulated, these drugs reduce activity level and improve attention, academic performance, and peer relations for 70 percent of children who take them (Barkley, DuPaul, & Costello, 1993; Rapport & Kelly, 1993). Researchers do not know precisely why stimulants are helpful. Some speculate that they change the chemical balance in brain regions that inhibit impulsiveness and hyperactivity, thereby decreasing the child's need to engage in off-task and self-stimulating behavior.

Although stimulant medication is relatively safe, its impact is only short term. Drugs cannot teach children ways of compensating for inattention and impulsivity (Whalen & Henker, 1991). Combining medication with interventions that model and reinforce appropriate academic and social behavior seems to be the most effective approach to treatment (Barkley, 1990, 1994). Teachers can also create conditions in classrooms that support these pupils' special learning needs. Short work periods followed by a chance to get up and move around help them concentrate. Finally, family intervention is particularly important. Inattentive, overactive children strain the patience of parents, who are likely to react punitively and inconsistently in return—a child-rearing style that strengthens inappropriate behavior. Breaking this cycle is as important for children with ADHD as it is for the defiant, aggressive youngsters we will discuss in Chapter 12. In fact, at least 35 percent of the time, these two sets of behavior problems occur together (Nottelmann & Jensen, 1995).

■ *While his classmates try to work, this boy constantly looks up from his assignment and fires paper airplanes across the room. Children with ADHD have great difficulty staying on task and often act impulsively, ignoring social rules. (David Young-Wolff/PhotoEdit)*

Short-Term or Working Memory

As attention improves with age, so do memory strategies, deliberate mental activities we use to increase the likelihood of holding information in short-term memory and transferring it to our long-term knowledge base. As we will see in the following sections, although memory strategies start to emerge during the preschool years, at first they are not very successful. Around the time children enter elementary school, these techniques take a giant leap forward.

STRATEGIES FOR STORING INFORMATION

Researchers have studied the development of three strategies that enhance memory for new information: rehearsal, organization, and elaboration.

■ REHEARSAL. The next time you look up a new phone number that you need to retain until you have a chance to dial it, take note of your own behavior. You will probably repeat the information to yourself, a memory strategy called **rehearsal**. Preschoolers show the beginnings of rehearsal. When asked to remember a set of familiar toys, they name, look at, and manipulate them more and play with them less than when not instructed to remember them. However, they do not name the toys consistently, and their rehearsal efforts have little effect on memory until about 6 years of age (Baker-Ward, Ornstein, & Holden, 1984). Furthermore, when young children are given less familiar materials, they rarely rehearse. In a well-known study, researchers presented 6- and 10-year-olds with pictures of objects to remember. Many more older than younger children audibly repeated the objects' names or moved their lips, and those who rehearsed recalled far more objects (Keeney, Canizzo, & Flavell, 1967).

Why are young children not very adept at rehearsal? Look closely at the findings we have reviewed so far, and you will see that both *production* and *control deficiencies* are involved. In addition, when children first use the strategy, they show a *utilization deficiency,* in that at first it has little or no impact on retention of information (Bjorklund & Coyle, 1995). Let's explore some additional evidence that supports these conclusions.

Studies in which nonrehearsing children have been taught to rehearse highlight an early production deficiency. Training improves recall on the task at hand. But when given an opportunity to rehearse later without prompting, most trained children abandon the strategy (Keeney, Canizzo, & Flavell, 1967). So although young children can be taught to rehearse, they fail to use the strategy in new situations or maintain it over time.

When children first rehearse spontaneously, control and utilization deficiencies are evident, since their efforts are neither efficient nor very successful. Eight-year-olds commonly repeat items one by one. For example, given a list beginning with "desk, man, yard, cat," most say "cat, cat, cat" after hearing the word "cat." In contrast, older children combine previously presented words with the newest item. After hearing "cat," they say "desk, man, yard, cat," an approach that greatly improves recall (Kunzinger, 1985; Ornstein, Naus, & Liberty, 1975). With age, children also become better at varying the strategy to fit the material to be learned. For example, 9- and 10-year-olds tend to rehearse repeatedly when given a random list of numbers (such as "5, 7, 3, 4, 6") but only once or not at all when given a serially ordered list ("4, 5, 6, 7, 8"), since they can rely on counting to retain it. In contrast, 5- and 6-year-olds often fail to take note of a list's features before deciding how to memorize (McGilly & Siegler, 1990).

The preschool child's minimal use of rehearsal and the young elementary school child's less effective execution of it reveal that the development of rehearsal skill is a gradual process. After much time and practice, the strategy becomes less of an effort and more automatic, and it can be used skillfully and adaptively in a wide range of situations.

■ ORGANIZATION. If in trying to remember a phone number, you group digits into meaningful chunks, you are using a second memory strategy, called **organization.** It causes recall to improve dramatically. Like rehearsal, the beginnings of organization can

Attention-deficit hyperactivity disorder
A childhood disorder involving inattention, impulsivity, and excessive motor activity. Often leads to academic failure and social problems.

Rehearsal
The memory strategy of repeating information.

Organization
The memory strategy of grouping information into meaningful chunks.

be seen in very young children. For example, when circumstances permit, they use spatial organization to aid their memories. In a study of 2- to 5-year-olds, an adult placed either an M&M or a wooden peg in each of 12 identical containers and handed them one by one to the child, who was asked to remember where the candy was hidden. By age 4, children put the candy containers in one place on the table and the peg containers in another, a strategy that almost always led to perfect recall (DeLoache & Todd, 1988). But preschoolers do not yet use *semantic organization*—grouping objects or words into meaningful categories—to aid recall. With intensive instruction they can be taught to do so, but training does not always improve their memory performance (Carr & Schneider, 1991; Lange & Pierce, 1992).

Once children semantically organize to retain information, the quality of their organizational strategies improves with age. Before age 9 or 10, children divide their lists into a greater number of categories and change their groupings from one trial to the next (Moely, 1977). Also, they tend to link items together by function. For example, consider the following items:

hat	carrot	head	rabbit
feet	monkey	banana	shoes

A 7- to 8-year-old is likely to say "hat–head," "feet–shoes," and "monkey–banana." In contrast, older children and adults group these items into clothing, body parts, animals, and food. The first approach is probably not a deliberate attempt to organize, since it appears to depend on involuntary associations between items. In other words, when asked to think of something that goes with "hat," we are more likely to say "head" than "shoes" because hat and head go together in everyday experience (Bjorklund & Jacobs, 1985).

These findings suggest that the first organizational efforts take place quite automatically, without much awareness on the part of the child. Indeed, unless items are highly familiar and strongly associated, children age 8 and younger do not group them at all (Best & Ornstein, 1986). When children first organize, their tendency to use many unstable, functional categories reduces the power of this memory strategy, and they retain little information.

As with rehearsal, organization requires substantial attentional resources on the part of younger children (Bjorklund & Harnishfeger, 1987). Experience with materials that form clear categories helps children organize more effectively, notice the strategy, and begin to apply it under less obvious task conditions. Still, utilization deficiencies remain. Only after considerable practice does organization lead to substantial gains in memory (Best, 1993; Bjorklund et al., 1994).

Once organization is well established, it becomes more flexible. For example, adolescents rely on semantic organization when recalling object names but switch to spatial organization when recalling object–location pairings. In contrast, children approach both recall tasks similarly (Plumert, 1994). Observing the effectiveness of organization in a variety of situations gradually leads to more discriminating strategy use.

■ ELABORATION. Sometimes information cannot be categorized easily. For example, suppose "fish" and "pipe" are among a list of words you need to learn. If to retain them, you imagine a fish smoking a pipe, you used a memory strategy called **elaboration**. It involves creating a relationship, or shared meaning, between two or more pieces of information that are not members of the same category.

Compared to other strategies, elaboration is a late-developing skill that rarely appears before age 11. Once individuals discover this memory technique, they find it so effective that it tends to replace other strategies (Schneider & Pressley, 1989). The very reason elaboration is so successful helps explain why it is late to emerge as a spontaneous strategy. It requires a great deal of mental effort to execute. To use elaboration, we must translate items into images and think of a relationship between them. Children's working memories must expand before they can carry out these activities simultaneously (Pressley et al., 1987).

Elaboration
The memory strategy of creating a relation between two or more items that are not members of the same category.

Perhaps for this reason, teaching children under age 11 to elaborate is not very successful. When they do try to use the strategy, they usually produce static images, such as "The dog had a car." In contrast, adolescents and adults generate active images that are more memorable, as in "The dog raced the car through town" (Reese, 1977). Increased knowledge of ways items can be combined in memory undoubtedly contributes to the older individual's more successful use of elaboration (Pressley, 1982).

CULTURAL AND SITUATIONAL INFLUENCES ON MEMORY STRATEGIES

In most of the laboratory studies we have reviewed so far, children were asked to learn discrete bits of information, and memorizing was the only goal of their activity. In everyday life, people rarely engage in retaining listlike material. Rather, they participate in a variety of daily activities that produce excellent memory as a natural by-product of the activity itself (Rogoff & Chavajay, 1995). In a study illustrating this idea, 4- and 5-year-olds were told either to play with a set of toys or to remember them. The play condition produced far better recall. Rather than just naming or touching objects, children instructed to play engaged in many spontaneous organizations that helped them recall. These included functional use of objects (pretending to eat a banana or putting a shoe on a doll) and narrating their activities, as in "I'm squeezing this lemon" or "Fly away in this helicopter, doggie" (Newman, 1990).

These findings help explain why the Kpelle farmers, described at the beginning of this chapter, viewed functional grouping as "the wise way" to organize familiar objects. Much like young children, people in non-Western cultures who have no formal schooling do not spontaneously use or benefit from instruction in memory strategies. They consistently do poorly when asked to learn material presented as isolated units, devoid of the structuring imposed by the way things appear and are used in their everyday lives (Rogoff & Mistry, 1985). Both young children and nonschooled people may seldom use the memorizing techniques we have discussed because they see little reason to remember information for its own sake.

In contrast, deliberate memorization is common in school, and academic tasks requiring list learning provide children with a great deal of motivation to use memory strategies. In fact, Western children may receive so much practice in acquiring discrete bits of information that they apply memory strategies inappropriately when trying to recall information embedded in meaningful contexts. For example, 9-year-old Guatemalan Mayan children do slightly better than American children when told to remember the placement of 40 familiar objects in a play scene (see Figure 7.7). Under these conditions, many American youngsters try to rehearse object names when it is more effective to keep track of spatial relations (Rogoff & Waddell, 1982). The skill shown by Mayan children in remembering contextually organized information contrasts sharply with their poor performance on list memory tasks (Kagan et al., 1979).

Looked at in this way, the development of memory strategies is not just a matter of a more competent information-processing system. It is also a product of task demands and cultural circumstances.

As these Guatemalan Mayan boys discuss the intricacies of effective kite-flying, they demonstrate a keen memory for information embedded in meaningful contexts. Yet when given a list-memory task of the kind American children often perform in school, they do poorly. (Ulrike Welsch/Photo Researchers)

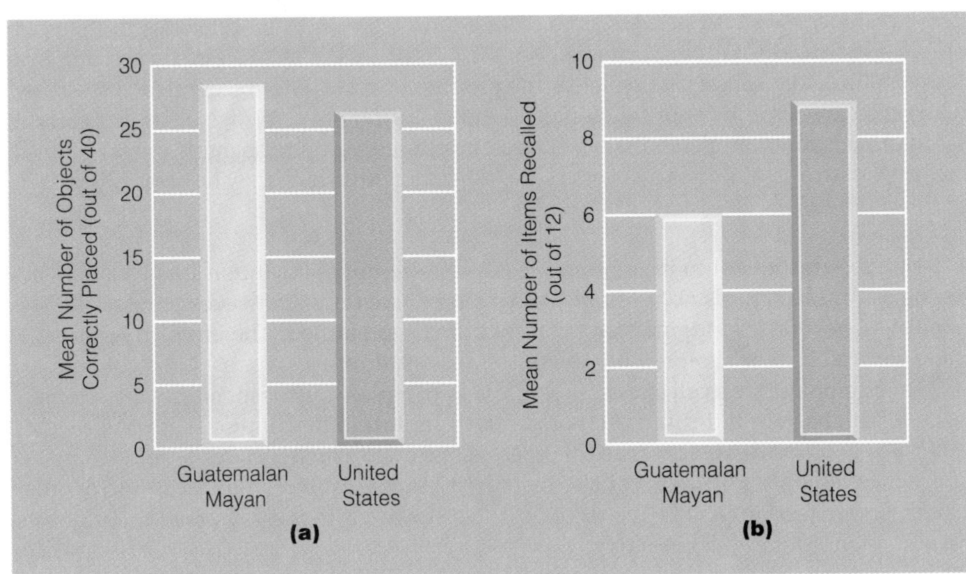

FIGURE 7.7

Comparison of 9-year-old Guatemalan Mayan and American children's memory for (a) placement of objects in a familiar play scene and (b) a word list. Mayan children did slightly better when asked to recall information in a meaningful context. American children were advantaged on a list-learning task. (Adapted from Kagan et al., 1979; Rogoff & Waddell, 1982.)

BRIEF REVIEW

Production, control, and utilization deficiencies characterize young children's use of memory strategies. Preschoolers seldom engage in deliberate efforts to improve their memory, nor do they show lasting gains from training. During the elementary school years, children use rehearsal and organization more effectively, and over time their efforts lead to better retention of information. Elaboration emerges later, after age 11. The need to learn isolated bits of information, a typical requirement of schooling in Western nations, influences the development of memory strategies.

Long-Term Memory

So far, we have discussed strategies for putting information into memory. Once it enters our long-term knowledge base, it must be *retrieved,* or recovered, to be used again. In the following sections, we consider how children retrieve information from long-term memory. Then we turn to their expanding long-term knowledge base and its impact on memory performance.

RETRIEVAL OF INFORMATION

Information can be retrieved from memory in three ways: through recognition, recall, and reconstruction. As we discuss the development of these approaches to remembering, we will also take up an intriguing, universal memory problem: our inability to recollect experiences that occurred during the first few years of our lives.

■ RECOGNITION. Noticing that a stimulus is identical or similar to one previously experienced is called **recognition**. It is the simplest form of retrieval, since the material to be remembered is fully present during testing to serve as its own retrieval cue. As the habituation research we discussed in Chapter 4 shows, even young infants are capable of recognition. The ability to recognize a larger number of stimuli over longer delays improves steadily from infancy through early childhood. By age 4, recognition memory is highly accurate. After viewing a series of 80 pictures, children of this age correctly discriminated 90 percent from pictures not in the original set (Brown & Campione, 1972).

Because recognition appears so early in life and preschoolers' performance approaches that of adults on many tasks, it is probably a fairly automatic process that does not depend on a deliberate search of long-term memory. Nevertheless, the ability of older individuals to apply strategies during storage, such as systematic scanning of visual stimuli and rehearsal, increases the number of items later recognized, especially when they are complex and unfamiliar (Mandler & Robinson, 1978; Nelson & Kosslyn, 1976). Also, growth in general knowledge undoubtedly supports gains in recognition memory. With age, children encounter fewer stimuli with which they have no experience (Perlmutter, 1984).

■ RECALL. In contrast to recognition, **recall** is more difficult, since it involves remembering a stimulus that is not present. Perhaps there are only a few cues to what it is, or none at all beyond the original context in which it was learned. Therefore, to recall, you must generate a mental representation of the absent stimulus.

The beginnings of recall appear before 1 year of age as long as memories are strongly cued. Think back to our discussion of deferred imitation in Chapter 6. Its presence in infancy is good evidence for recall. In other instances, researchers have asked parents to keep diary accounts of their babies' memories. Many examples of recall for people, places, and objects appear in the records. The following diary entry of a 7-month-old's memory of his father is an example:

> My husband called from work and I let him talk to Rob. (Rob) looked puzzled for a while and then he turned and looked at the door. Rob thought of the only time he

Recognition
A type of memory that involves noticing whether a stimulus is identical or similar to one previously experienced.

Recall
A type of memory that involves remembering a stimulus that is not present.

> hears his dad's voice when he knows Dad isn't home is when his Dad just got home. He heard his dad's voice and based on past experiences, he reasoned that his dad must be home, so he looked at the door. (Ashmead & Perlmutter, 1980, p. 4)

In other studies, children between 2 and 4 years recalled events many months and even years earlier, from a time before they had learned to talk (Bauer, 1996; Fivush, 1993). However, what is recalled about an event that happened long ago is only a portion of what can potentially be remembered. In one longitudinal study, sixth graders were asked to tell what happened when they went to an archaeological museum in kindergarten. They said much less about the experience than when they were asked the same question 6 weeks after the museum trip actually occurred. But in response to fairly specific external retrieval cues, including photos of the actual event, sixth graders remembered a great deal. And in some respects, their recall was more accurate. For example, they inferred that adults had hidden artifacts in a sandbox for them to find, whereas in kindergarten they simply recalled digging for relics (Hudson & Fivush, 1991).

When younger and older children are asked to recall information after an identical time lapse, older children's recall is considerably more accurate and complete. In fact, compared to recognition, recall shows much greater improvement with age (Perlmutter, 1984). One reason is that older individuals are much better at strategic processing. During the elementary school years, semantic organization of the knowledge base increases. Children develop more consistent and stable categories, which they arrange into more elaborate hierarchies. When stimuli are deeply processed at encoding so they are connected with other information in long-term memory, then a wide variety of internal retrieval cues can be used to recall them later.

■ RECONSTRUCTION. Read the following passage about George, a convict who has escaped from prison. Then close your book and try to write the story down or tell it to a friend:

> George was alone. He knew they would soon be here. They were not far behind him when he left the village, hungry and cold. He dared not stop for food or shelter for fear of falling into the hands of his pursuers. There were many of them; they were strong and he was weak. George could hear the noise as the uniformed band beat its way through the trees not far behind him. The sense of their presence was everywhere. His spine tingled with fear. Eagerly he awaited the darkness. In darkness he would find safety. (Brown et al., 1977, p. 1456)

Now compare your version with the original. Is it a faithful reproduction?

When people are given complex, meaningful material to remember, condensations, additions, and distortions appear that are not just the result of memory failure. Instead, they are due to a radical transformation of the information. This suggests that we do not always copy material into the system at storage and faithfully reproduce it at retrieval. Instead, much information we encounter in our daily lives, such as written and spoken language, is selected and interpreted in terms of our existing knowledge. And once the material is transformed, we often have difficulty distinguishing it from the original (Bartlett, 1932). Perhaps you noticed that this *constructivist approach* to information processing is quite consistent with Piaget's ideas. He believed that information cannot be imposed ready-made on the child. Instead, it is built by the mind through the functions of adaptation and organization.

Constructive processing can take place during any phase of information processing. It can occur during storage. In fact, the memory strategies of organization and elaboration are within the province of constructive memory, since both require us to generate relationships among stimuli. Yet earlier we saw that young children rarely use these strategies. Constructive processing can also involve **reconstruction** of information while it is in the system or being retrieved. Do children reconstruct stored information? The answer is clearly yes.

Children's reconstructive processing has been studied by asking them to recall prose material. Like adults, when children retell a story, they condense, integrate, and add information. For example, by age 6 or 7, children recall the important features of a story and forget the unimportant ones, combine information into more tightly knit units, and reorder the sequence of events to make it more logical (Bischofshausen, 1985; Christie & Schumacher, 1975; Mandler, 1984). And they often report information that fits with the meaning of a passage but that was not really presented. For example, after elementary

Reconstruction
A memory process in which complex, meaningful material is reinterpreted in terms of existing knowledge.

school pupils listened to the story of George, the escaped convict, the following statements appeared in their reconstructions:

> All the prison guards were chasing him.
>
> He climbed over the prison walls.
>
> He was running so the police would be so far away that their dogs would not catch his trail. (Brown et al., 1977, p. 1459)

In revising the information in meaningful ways, children provide themselves with a wealth of helpful retrieval cues that can be used during recall. By the early elementary school years, children's memory for prose material resembles that of adults in its emphasis on reconstruction of information.

Between ages 4 and 12, reconstruction goes further as the ability to draw inferences about actors and actions within a story improves. For example, preschoolers easily draw inferences when story statements concern the physical causes of events. When given the sentence "As Jennifer was walking to the store, she turned a somersault and lost her dollar," 4-year-olds infer how Jennifer lost her money. But not until the early to mid-elementary school years can children make inferences about psychological causes, as in the following sentence: "As Jennifer was walking to the store, she became very excited and lost her dollar." Young children have a much fuller understanding of physical than psychological causation, a difference that affects their ability to infer relationships (Thompson & Myers, 1985).

Since inference making is so important for comprehending and recalling complex information, are there ways to facilitate it? Think back to our discussion of reciprocal teaching in Chapter 6. Discussions aimed at clarifying and predicting future prose content require pupils to make inferences—one reason this method has been so successful.

■ ANOTHER VIEW OF RECONSTRUCTION: FUZZY-TRACE THEORY. So far, we have emphasized deliberate reconstruction of meaningful material by using the long-term knowledge base to interpret it. According to C. J. Brainerd and Valerie Reyna's (1990, 1993) **fuzzy-trace theory**, when we first encode information, we reconstruct it automatically, creating a vague, fuzzy version called a **gist**, which preserves essential content without details and is especially useful for reasoning. At the same time, we retain a verbatim version adapted for answering questions about specifics. For example, consider the following statement: "Farmer Brown owns many animals. He has 3 dogs, 5 sheep, 7 chickens, 9 horses, and 11 cows." Besides holding the precise numerical information in memory, you create a gist, such as "cows the most; dogs the least; horses, chickens, and sheep in the middle."

Fuzzy-trace theorists take issue with the assumption that all reconstructions are transformations of verbatim memory. Instead, they believe that both verbatim and gist memories are present from the outset and are stored separately so they can be used for different purposes. In support of this idea, shortly after being read a brief story, children can discriminate sentences they actually heard from ones they did not hear but that are consistent with the story's gist. Only over time, as the complete, verbatim memory decays more quickly than the efficiently represented gist, do children begin to say that statements consistent with but not in the story were ones they heard (Reyna & Kiernan, 1994). Fuzzy-trace theory also helps us understand why children (and adults) often reason effectively without recalling specifics. For example, when asked, "Which of Farmer Brown's animals are the most, cows or horses?" your gist memory yields the answer quickly and easily.

With age, children rely less on verbatim memory and more on fuzzy, reconstructed gists. In a recent study, researchers presented children with the description of Farmer Brown's barnyard and asked questions requiring only gist information (like the one just given) as well as questions requiring verbatim knowledge, such as "How many cows does Farmer Brown own, 11 or 3?" Preschoolers were better at answering verbatim- than gist-dependent questions, whereas the reverse was true for second graders (Brainerd & Gordon, 1994). Notice how relying on gist eases mental effort. Compared to a detailed statement, a fuzzy trace consumes less working memory, freeing attentional resources for the steps involved in thinking. Of course, for certain tasks, such as mental arithmetic, we need to have verbatim information. But in everyday life, the gist is often sufficient,

Fuzzy-trace theory
A theory that posits two encoding systems, one that automatically reconstructs information into a fuzzy version called a *gist* that is especially useful for reasoning and a second verbatim version that is adapted for answering questions about specifics.

Gist
A fuzzy representation of information that preserves essential content without details, is less likely to be forgotten than a verbatim representation, and requires less mental effort to use.

and if necessary, we can supplement it by referring to notes, lists, and other records (Reyna & Brainerd, 1992).

Fuzzy-trace theory adds to our understanding of reconstruction by pointing out that it can occur immediately, as soon as information is encoded, without distorting verbatim memories. The extent to which gist and verbatim representations undergo further reconstructive processing depends on the nature of the meaningful material, the type of task (telling an entire story versus answering a single question), and the passage of time. Fuzzy-trace research reveals that memory is vital for reasoning, but it is only loosely dependent on it. Getting bogged down in detail (as young children are prone to do) can interfere with effective cognitive processing. And since fuzzy traces are less likely than verbatim memories to be forgotten, gists may serve as enduring retrieval cues, contributing (along with strategy use) to improved recall with age (Brainerd & Reyna, 1995).

KNOWLEDGE AND MEMORY PERFORMANCE

At several points in our discussion, we suggested that children's expanding knowledge base may promote improved memory. Many researchers believe that cognitive development is largely a matter of acquiring domain-specific knowledge—knowledge of a specific content area that makes new, related information more meaningful so it is easier to store and retrieve (Bjorklund & Muir, 1988; Chi & Ceci, 1987).

If children's growing knowledge base accounts for better memory performance, then in areas in which children are more knowledgeable than adults, they should show better recall. To test this idea, Michelene Chi (1978) looked at how well third- through eighth-grade chess experts could remember complex chessboard arrangements. The children were compared to adults who knew how to play chess but were not especially knowledgeable. Just as expected, the children could reproduce the chessboard configurations considerably better than the adults could. These findings cannot be explained by the selection of very bright youngsters with exceptional memories. On a standard digit-span task in which the same subjects had to recall a list of numbers, the adults did better than the children. The children showed superior memory only in the domain of knowledge in which they were expert (see Figure 7.8).

In Chi's study of chess-playing children, better memory was largely attributed to a greater quantity of knowledge. Experts also have a more deeply and elaborately structured knowledge base that permits them to apply organizational strategies more adeptly and retrieve familiar items automatically. To illustrate this idea, Wolfgang Schneider and David Bjorklund (1992) classified elementary school children as experts or novices in knowledge of soccer. Then both groups were given lists of soccer and nonsoccer items to

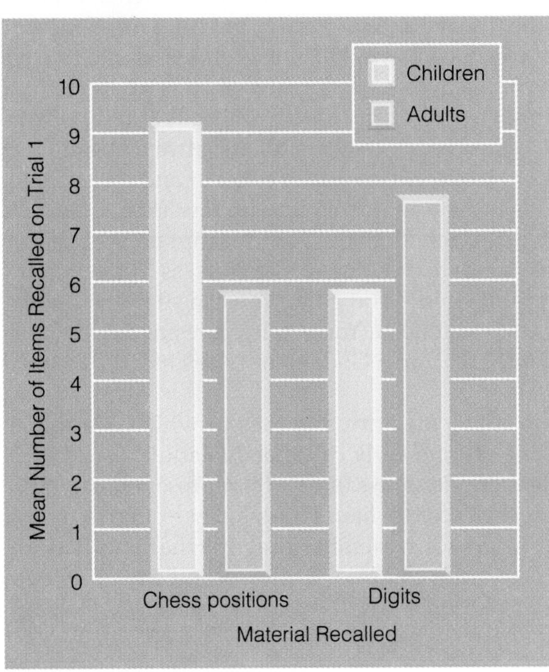

FIGURE 7.8

Performance of skilled child chess players and adults on two tasks: memory for complex chessboard arrangements and numerical digits. The child chess experts recalled more on the chess task, the adults on the digit task. These findings show that size of the knowledge base contributes to memory performance. (Adapted from Chi, 1978.)

learn. As in Chi's study, experts remembered far more items on the soccer list (but not on the nonsoccer list) than did nonexperts. In observing how fourth graders studied soccer items, the researchers found that both groups used organizational strategies. But experts were more likely to apply these strategies during retrieval (as indicated by clustering of items during recall). And within each category searched, experts remembered more items.

Although knowledge clearly plays a major role in memory development, it may have to be quite broad and well structured before it can facilitate memory performance. A brief series of lessons designed to increase knowledge in a particular area does not affect children's ability to recall information in that domain (DeMarie-Dreblow, 1991). Until children have enough knowledge and have time to connect it into stable, well-formed hierarchies, they may not be able to apply it to new memory problems.

Finally, we must keep in mind that knowledge is not the only factor involved in strategic memory processing. Children who are expert in a particular area, whether it be chess, math, social studies, or spelling, are usually highly motivated. Faced with new material, they say to themselves, "What can I do to clarify the meaning of this information so I can learn it more easily?" As a result, they not only acquire knowledge more quickly, but they actively use what they know to add more. Research reveals that academically successful and unsuccessful students differ in just this way. Poor students fail to approach memory tasks by asking how previously stored information can clarify new information. This, in turn, interferes with the development of a broad knowledge base (Bransford et al., 1981; Brown et al., 1983). Looked at in this way, knowledge acquisition and memory strategies are intimately related and support one another.

■ *Like adults, young children remember familiar experiences in terms of scripts. After brushing her teeth and getting ready for bed many times, this 3-year-old is unlikely to recall the details of a particular evening. But she will be able to describe what typically happens when you get ready for bed, and her account will become more elaborate with age. Scripts help us organize and interpret our everyday experiences. (David Young-Wolff/ PhotoEdit)*

SCRIPTS: BASIC BUILDING BLOCKS OF STRUCTURED KNOWLEDGE

Think back to research on children's ability to categorize in this chapter and in Chapter 6. It shows that a structured long-term knowledge base begins to form in infancy. How do children build a coherent network of knowledge, and in what ways does it change with age?

Our vast, intricately organized general knowledge system, which for purposes of clarity we now refer to as **semantic memory**, must grow out of the young child's **episodic memory**, or memory for many personally experienced events (Tulving, 1972). How semantic memory emerges from a foundation of specific, real-world experiences is considered by some researchers to be one of the most puzzling questions about memory development.

Like adults, preschoolers remember familiar experiences in terms of **scripts**, general representations of what occurs and when it occurs in a particular situation. For very young children, scripts begin as a structure of main acts. For example, when asked to tell what happens when you go to a restaurant, a 3-year-old might say, "You go in, get the food, eat, and then pay." Although children's first scripts contain only a few acts, as long as events in a situation take place in a logical order, they are almost always recalled in correct sequence (Fivush, Kuebli, & Clubb, 1992). This is true even for 1- and 2-year-olds, who cannot yet verbally describe events but who act them out with toys (Bauer & Dow, 1994; Bauer & Mandler, 1989b, 1992). With age, children can form a script on the basis of fewer repetitions of an event. Their scripts also become more elaborate, as in the following restaurant account given by a 5-year-old child: "You go in. You can sit in the booths or at a table. Then you tell the waitress what you want. You eat. If you want dessert, you can have some. Then you pay and go home" (Farrar & Goodman, 1992; Hudson, Fivush, & Kuebli, 1992).

Semantic memory
The vast, intricately organized knowledge system in long-term memory.

Episodic memory
Memory for personally experienced events.

Scripts
General representations of what occurs and when it occurs in a particular situation.

Scripts are a special form of reconstructive memory, and they provide yet another example of continuity in memory processing from early childhood to adulthood. When we experience repeated events, we fuse them into the same script representation. Then any specific instance of a scripted experience becomes hard to recall. For example, unless it was out of the ordinary, you probably cannot remember exactly what you had for dinner two days ago. The same is true for young children. By the second day of kindergarten, 5-year-olds have difficulty recalling specific events that occurred on the first day of class, although they can describe what happened in general terms (Fivush, 1984).

Once held in long-term memory, a script can be used to predict what will happen on similar occasions in the future. In this way, scripts serve as a basic means through which children (and adults) organize and interpret everyday experiences. For example, young children rely on scripts in make-believe play and when listening to and telling stories. They recall more events from stories that are based on familiar event sequences than on unfamiliar ones (Hudson & Nelson, 1983). Script structures also support children's earliest efforts at planning by helping them represent sequences of actions that lead to goals in familiar situations (Hudson, Shapiro, & Sosa, 1995).

According to Katherine Nelson, scripts may be the developmental link between early episodic memory and a semantically organized long-term memory store (Nelson & Gruendel, 1981, 1986). In one study, 3- and 4-year-olds remembered script-related items (such as peanut butter, bologna, cheese—foods often eaten at lunchtime) in clustered form and recalled them more easily than a typical categorical list (toast, cheese, ice cream—foods) (Lucariello & Nelson, 1985). It appears that relationships among items are first understood in terms of familiar events within an organized script framework. Once children develop an array of script sequences, objects that share the same function but occur in different scripts (eating toast for breakfast, peanut butter for lunch) may be joined together in a single, more typical semantic category (food).

AUTOBIOGRAPHICAL MEMORY

A special form of episodic memory is **autobiographical memory**, representations of one-time events that are long-lasting and particularly meaningful in terms of the life story each of us creates about ourselves. For example, perhaps you recall the day a sibling was born, the first time you took an airplane, a hospitalization, or a move to a new house. Memory for autobiographical events begins in early childhood. Practically none of us can retrieve experiences that happened to us before age 3—a phenomenon called **infantile amnesia**. Between ages 3 and 6, autobiographical memory becomes clearer and more detailed (Pillemer & White, 1989). Why do we experience infantile amnesia, and how do autobiographical events differentiate from other episodic memories and stand out for a lifetime?

THE MYSTERY OF INFANTILE AMNESIA. Some researchers speculate that brain maturation brings an end to the period of infantile amnesia. Perhaps growth of the frontal lobes of the cortex along with other structures is necessary before experiences can be stored in ways that permit them to be retrieved many years later (Boyer & Diamond, 1992).

Several psychological accounts of infantile amnesia are consistent with this explanation. For example, one hypothesis is that two levels of memory exist, one that operates unconsciously and automatically, another that is conscious and intentional. Infants' memories may be largely of the first kind, children's and adults' memories of the second; but the second system cannot access events stored by the first. In support of this idea, 9- and 10-year-olds shown pictures of their preschool classmates react physiologically in ways consistent with remembering, even when they do not consciously recall the child (Newcombe & Fox, 1994). Another conjecture is that adults often use verbal means for storing information, whereas infants' processing is nonverbal—an incompatibility that may prevent us from retrieving our earliest experiences (Neisser, 1967).

Yet the idea of vastly different approaches to remembering in very young and older individuals has been questioned. Turn back to our discussion of recall on pages 275–276, and you will see that 2- to 4-year-olds can describe their memories verbally and sometimes retain them for extensive periods. A growing number of researchers believe that rather than a radical change in the way experience is represented, two other developmental milestones lead to the offset of infantile amnesia.

First, for episodic memories to become autobiographical, the child must have a well-developed image of the self. In Chapter 11, we will see that the "psychological self" has only begun to emerge by age 3. In the first few years of life, it is not yet mature enough to serve as an anchor for one-time events, which become more difficult to retrieve over time if they do not take on personal meaning (Howe & Courage, 1993). Second, an autobiographical memory requires that children organize personally relevant events in narrative

Autobiographical memory
Long-lasting memory for one-time events that are particularly meaningful in terms of the life story each of us creates about ourselves.

Infantile amnesia
The inability of older children and adults to remember experiences that happened before age 3.

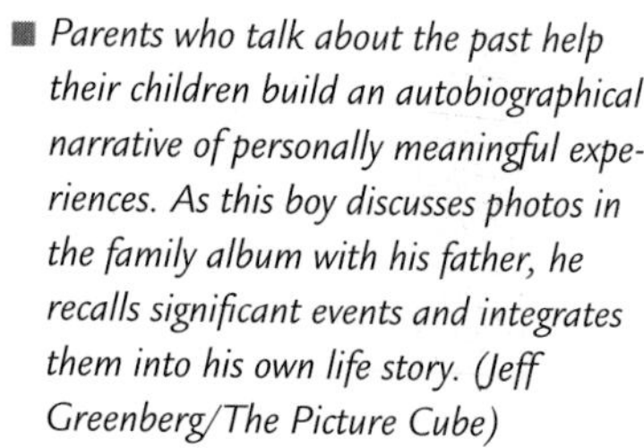

Parents who talk about the past help their children build an autobiographical narrative of personally meaningful experiences. As this boy discusses photos in the family album with his father, he recalls significant events and integrates them into his own life story. (Jeff Greenberg/The Picture Cube)

form so they become part of a life story. Recent evidence indicates that children learn to structure memories as narratives during the preschool years by talking about them with others (Nelson, 1993).

FORMING AN AUTOBIOGRAPHICAL NARRATIVE: TALKING ABOUT THE PAST. As early as 1½ to 2 years, children begin to talk about the past, guided by adults who expand on their fragmented recollections. Gradually, children adopt the narrative thinking generated in these dialogues, in the same way that Vygotsky indicated higher cognitive processes emerge out of social interaction with more expert partners (see Chapter 6). In one study, researchers observed mothers engaged in memory talk with their young preschoolers about a trip to a natural history museum. Those who elaborated on the child's experiences by explaining what happened when, where, and with whom (rather than simply identifying and categorizing museum artifacts) had children who recalled more about the trip a week later (Tessler, 1991).

Between 3 and 6 years of age, children's descriptions of special, one-time occurrences become better organized, detailed, and evaluative (and therefore imbued with personal meaning). Older children also add more background information, placing events in the larger context of their lives (Fivush, Haden, & Adam, 1995). Interestingly, girls are more advanced than boys in this sequence, a difference that fits with findings that parents talk about the past in more elaborate and evaluative ways with daughters than sons (Fivush & Reese, 1992). Perhaps because their early experiences were integrated into more coherent narratives, women report an earlier age of first memory and more vivid early memories than do men (Mullen, 1994).

Besides structuring memories in narrative form, talking about the past may serve the function of reinstating lost memories. In one study, researchers had 2-year-olds learn a sequence of novel actions involving a toy animal. Two weeks later, half the children were provided with an experience similar to the original: they reenacted the behaviors. At 3-month retesting, children whose memories had been reinstated showed no memory loss. They recalled as much as they had at two weeks and far more than children who had not reenacted the event (Fivush & Hamond, 1989). Verbal reinstatement is also highly effective in promoting 2- and 3-year-olds' long-term retention (Howe, Courage, & Bryant-Brown, 1995). As language develops and permits sharing and retaining of memories in socially and personally meaningful ways, autobiographical memory appears and expands in early childhood. As a result, children enter into the history of their family and community (Fivush, 1995).

The accuracy and completeness of children's autobiographical memories have recently taken on special applied significance. Increasingly, children are being called on to testify in court cases in which their recollections play a critical role in legal decisions affecting their own welfare. How reliable are children's memories under these conditions? See the Social Issues box on page 282 for a discussion of this topic.

BRIEF REVIEW

During infancy, retrieval changes from recognition of previously experienced stimuli to include recall in the presence of salient retrieval cues. Recall improves steadily in childhood and adolescence as the knowledge base becomes better organized and memory strategies are applied more effectively. Children, like adults, often recall complex, meaningful information in reconstructed form. Gains in reconstructive processing occur as the ability to draw inferences expands, a change that permits children to better understand and recall prose material. In addition, reconstruction often occurs at encoding, in the form of fuzzy traces called gists. With age, children rely less on verbatim memory and more on gist, which contributes to improved reasoning and recall with age.

Growth in size and structure of the knowledge base has a major impact on memory performance. Like adults, young children remember everyday experiences in terms of scripts—general representations that become more elaborate with age. Scripts may serve as the developmental link between episodic memory and our semantically organized, general knowledge system. As preschoolers' self-image and language skills develop, they form a personal narrative by talking about the past with adults, and autobiographical memory emerges.

Metacognition

Throughout this chapter, we have mentioned many ways in which cognitive processing becomes more reflective and deliberate with age. These trends suggest that another form of knowledge we have not yet considered may influence how well children remember and solve problems. The term **metacognition** refers to awareness and understanding of various aspects of thought.

During early and middle childhood, metacognition expands greatly. A wealth of research suggests that children construct a naive **theory of mind**, a coherent understanding of people as mental beings that they revise as they encounter and make sense of new evidence (Gopnik & Wellman, 1994). Most investigations into children's theory of mind have addressed their ability to be "mind readers"—to appreciate their own and other people's perceptions, thoughts, and feelings. We will take up this topic when we consider emotional and social understanding in Chapters 10 and 11. A second facet of metacognitive research concerns children's knowledge of mental activity, or *what it means to think.* To work most effectively, the information-processing system must be aware of itself. It must arrive at such realizations as "I'd better write that phone number down or I'll forget it" and "This paragraph is complicated; I'll have to read it again to grasp the author's point."

But for metacognitive knowledge to be helpful, children must apply it on a moment-by-moment basis. They must constantly monitor what they do, calling on what they know about thinking to overcome difficulties. In the following sections, we consider these higher-level, "executive" aspects of information processing.

METACOGNITIVE KNOWLEDGE

With age, children's knowledge of mental activities expands in three ways. They become increasingly conscious of cognitive capacities, strategies for processing information, and task variables that facilitate or impede performance.

■ KNOWLEDGE OF COGNITIVE CAPACITIES. Although Piaget suggested that young children have difficulty distinguishing between mental events and external reality, research reveals that they separate these realms at a remarkably early age. Such words as "think," "remember," and "pretend" are among the first verbs to appear in children's vocabularies. After age 2½, they use them appropriately to refer to internal states, as when they say, "It's not real, I was just pretending" or "I thought the socks were in the

Metacognition
Awareness and understanding of various aspects of thought.

Theory of mind
A coherent understanding of people as mental beings, that children revise as they encounter and make sense of new evidence. Includes children's knowledge of mental activity and their appreciation that people can have different perceptions, thoughts, and feelings about the same event.

SOCIAL ISSUES ➤ POINT OF VIEW

When Should Children Provide Eyewitness Testimony in Court Proceedings?

Renata, a physically abused and neglected 8-year-old, was taken from her parents and placed in foster care. There, she was seen engaging in sexually aggressive behavior toward other children, including grabbing their sex organs and using obscene language. Renata's foster mother suspected that sexual abuse had taken place in her natural home. She informed the child protective service worker, who met with Renata to gather information. But Renata seemed anxious and uncomfortable. She did not want to answer any questions.

Increasingly, children are being called on to testify in court cases involving child abuse and neglect, child custody, and other matters. Having to provide such information can be difficult and traumatic. Almost always, children must report on events that were highly stressful. In doing so, they may have to speak against a parent or other relative to whom they feel a strong sense of loyalty. In some family disputes, they may fear punishment for telling the truth. In addition, child witnesses are faced with a strange and unfamiliar situation—at the very least an interview in the judge's chambers, and at most an open courtroom with judge, jury, spectators, and the possibility of unsympathetic cross-examination. Not surprisingly, there is considerable debate about the accuracy of children's recall under these conditions.

In most states, it is rare for children under age 5 to be asked to testify, whereas those age 6 and older often are. Children between ages 10 and 14 are generally assumed competent to testify. These guidelines make good sense in terms of what we know about memory development. Compared to preschoolers, school-age children are better able to give detailed descriptions of past experiences and make accurate inferences about others' motives and intentions. Also, older children are more resistant to misleading questions of the sort asked by attorneys when they probe for more information or, in cross-examination, try to influence the content of the child's response (Ceci & Bruck, 1993b; Goodman & Tobey, 1994).

Nevertheless, when properly questioned, even 3-year-olds can recall recent events accurately—including ones that were highly stressful (Baker-Ward et al., 1993; Goodman et al., 1991). But court testimony often involves repeated interviews. When adults lead children by suggesting incorrect facts ("He touched you there, didn't he?"), they increase the likelihood of incorrect reporting—even among school-age children, whose descriptions are usually elaborate and dependable (Leichtman & Ceci, 1995; Ornstein et al., 1996). By the time children come to court, it is weeks, months, or even years after the occurrence of the target events. When a long delay is combined with suggestions about what happened, children can easily be misled into giving false information. Younger children are more likely to treat suggested memories as actually witnessed events (Ackil & Zaragoza, 1995; Ceci, Leichtman, & Bruck, 1994).

When children are interviewed in a frightening legal setting, their ability to report past events completely and accurately is reduced further (Saywitz & Nathanson, 1993). To ease the task of providing testimony, special interviewing methods have been devised for children. In Renata's case, a professional used puppets to ask questions and had Renata respond through them. In many child sexual abuse cases, anatomically correct dolls have been used to prompt children's recall. However, serious concerns have been raised about this method. Research indicates that it does not

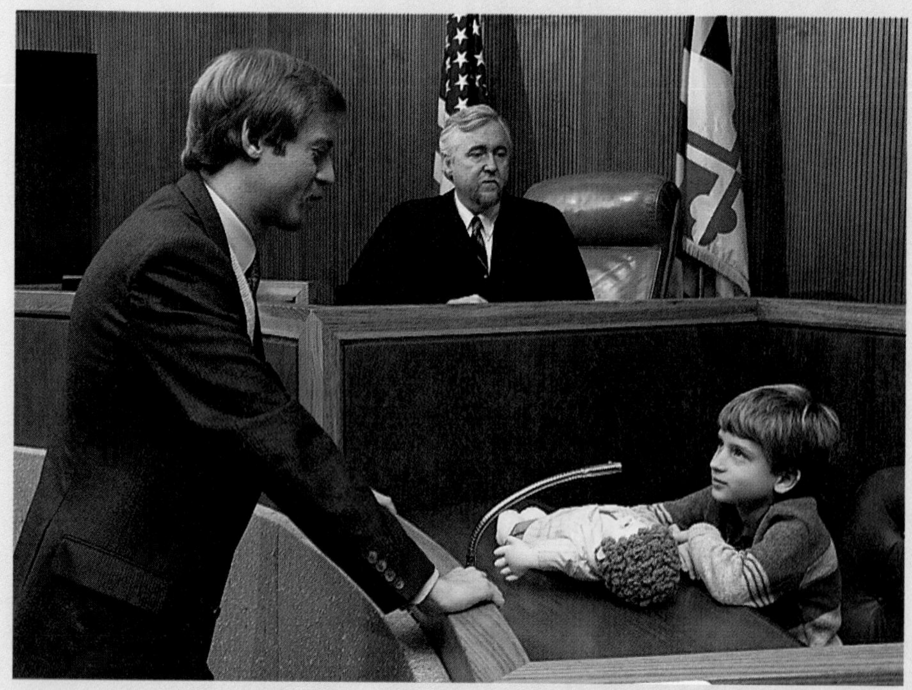

■ *Will this 6-year-old boy recount events accurately and completely on the witness stand? The answer to this question depends on many factors—his cognitive maturity, the way he is questioned, how long ago the events occurred, whether adults in his life have tried to influence his responses, how the doll is used to prompt his recall, and his understanding of the courtroom process. (Stacy Pick/ Stock Boston)*

improve the accuracy of young children's answers. And it can encourage them to report physical and sexual contact that, in fact, never happened (Bruck et al., 1995; Wolfner, Faust, & Dawes, 1993).

Child witnesses need to be prepared so that they understand the courtroom process and know what to expect. Below age 8, children have little grasp of the differing roles of judge, attorney, and police officer. Many regard the court negatively, as "a room you pass through on your way to jail" (Saywitz, 1987, p. 149). In some places, "court schools" exist in which children are taken through the setting and given an opportunity to role-play court activities. As part of this process, children can be encouraged to admit not knowing an answer rather than guessing or going along with what an adult expects of them. At the same time, legal professionals need to take steps to lessen the risk of suggestibility—by limiting the number of times children are interviewed, asking questions in nonleading ways, and being warm and patient (Ceci & Bruck, 1993).

If a child is likely to experience emotional trauma or later punishment (in a family dispute), then courtroom procedures can be adapted to protect them. For example, Renata eventually testified over closed-circuit TV so she would not have to face her abusive father. When it is not wise for a child to participate directly, expert witnesses can provide testimony that reports on the child's psychological condition and includes important elements of the child's story. But for such testimony to be worthwhile, witnesses need to be impartial and carefully trained in how to question children in ways that minimize false reporting (Ceci & Bruck, 1995).

YOUR POINT OF VIEW . . .

- Contact a local therapist, lawyer, or judge who has had experience interviewing children in court proceedings. Find out what procedures he or she uses to question children. How well do they match the recommendations of research on how to increase the chances of accurate reporting?
- Research shows that when faced with misleading questions, young children are more suggestible than older children. On the basis of what you know about the development of information processing, what factors might explain this finding?

drawer, 'cept they weren't" (Wellman, 1985, p. 176). By age 3, children distinguish thinking from other mental activities. They realize that it takes place inside their heads and that a person can think about something without seeing it, talking about it, or touching it (Flavell, Green, & Flavell, 1995; Woolley & Wellman, 1992).

But when questioned further, preschoolers' view of the workings of the mind appears limited. Without strong situational cues (a challenging task and a thoughtful expression), 3- and 4-year-olds deny that a person is thinking. They indicate that the minds of people waiting, talking, or engaged in such cognitive pursuits as looking at pictures, listening to stories, or reading books, are "empty of thoughts and ideas" (see Figure 7.9). This suggests that young children view mental activity as tied to a limited set of actions. They do not realize that people are constantly engaged in thought, even when there are no stimuli to perceive and no problems to solve (Flavell, Green, & Flavell, 1993, 1995).

Furthermore, preschoolers pay little attention to the process of acquiring knowledge. For example, 3-year-olds use the word "know" to refer to acting successfully (finding a hidden toy) and "forget" to refer to acting unsuccessfully (not finding the toy), even when a person had no prior relevant information (finds the toy because of a lucky guess) (Lyon & Flavell, 1994; Perner, 1991). Similarly, children under age 6 have difficulty recalling what they themselves (or others they observed) knew or were thinking just moments before. In one study, right after being taught a new fact, 4- and 5-year-olds claimed they had known it for a long time (Taylor, Esbensen, & Bennett, 1994). Children of this age also fail to realize that what they perceive influences what they know. They say that a puppet can tell a ball is blue by feeling it or a sponge is wet by looking at it (O'Neill, Astington, & Flavell, 1992). Finally, preschoolers think that all events must be directly observed to be known. They do not understand that *mental inferences* can be a source of knowledge (Sodian & Wimmer, 1987).

Even though their grasp of mental activities is incomplete, young children realize that the mind is a limited-capacity device, and both internal and external factors affect its functioning. Three- and 4-year-

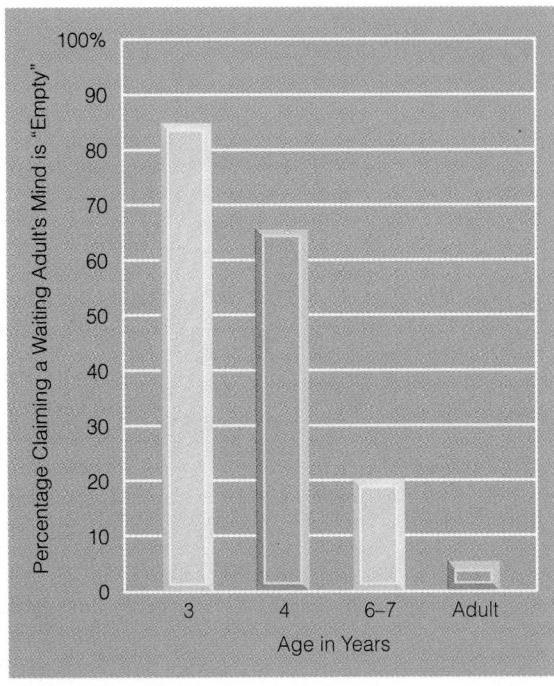

FIGURE 7.9

Age changes in children's ability to introspect about the mind's activities. As an adult sat waiting in a chair, an experimenter asked 3-, 4-, and 6- to 7-year-olds as well as young adults, "How about her mind right now? Is she having some thoughts and ideas, or is her mind empty of thoughts and ideas?" Many more preschoolers than school-age children claimed that the adult's mind was "empty." The ability to attribute an active mental life to another person when no obvious external cues suggest it improves sharply after the beginning of formal schooling. (Adapted from Flavell, Green, & Flavell, 1993.)

olds know that noise, lack of interest, and thinking about other things can interfere with attention to a task (Miller & Zalenski, 1982). And by age 5, most children understand that information briefly presented or that must be retained for a long time is more likely to be forgotten (Kreutzer, Leonard, & Flavell, 1975). Nevertheless, school-age youngsters have a more complete grasp of the impact of psychological factors on performance. For example, they recognize that doing well on a task depends on focusing attention—concentrating, wanting to do it, and not being tempted by anything else (Miller & Bigi, 1979). They also distinguish different types of cognitive processes—for example, memorizing as separate from inference-making (Schwanenflugel, Fabricius, & Alexander, 1994).

■ *School-age children show improved metacognitive knowledge. This child is aware that writing down a phone message is a very effective strategy for overcoming the limits of memory capacity.* (Will Faller)

How, then, should we describe the difference between the young child's understanding of cognitive capacities and that of the older child? Preschoolers know that we have an internal mental life, but they seem to view the mind as a passive container of information. Below age 4 or 5, they believe that physical experience determines mental experience. Consequently, they greatly underestimate the amount of mental activity that goes on in people and are poor at inferring what people know or are thinking about. In view of their limited awareness of how knowledge is acquired, it is not surprising that preschoolers rarely engage in planning or use memory strategies. In contrast, older children regard the mind as an active, constructive agent that selects and transforms information and affects how the world is perceived (Pillow, 1988a; Wellman, 1990). Look again at the findings we have discussed, and note how they illustrate this change.

What promotes this more reflective, process-oriented view of the mind? Researchers speculate that children may become aware of mental activities through quiet-time observation of their own thinking and exposure to talk about the mind in active terms, as when they hear people say, "I was thinking a lot" or "My mind wandered" (Wellman & Hickling, 1994). Formal schooling probably contributes as well. Instructing children to recall mental steps, think harder, and keep their minds on what they are doing calls attention to the workings of the mind. And as children engage in reading, writing, and arithmetic, they often use private speech, at first speaking aloud and later silently inside their heads. As they "hear themselves think," they may detect many aspects of mental life (Astington, 1995; Flavell, Green, & Flavell, 1995).

■ KNOWLEDGE OF STRATEGIES AND TASK VARIABLES. Consistent with their more active view of the mind, school-age children are far more conscious of strategies for processing information than are preschoolers. By third grade, they realize that in studying material for later recall, it is helpful to devote most effort to items you know least well. And they know quite a bit about effective memory strategies. Witness this 8-year-old's response to the question of what she would do to remember a phone number:

> Say the number is 663-8854. Then what I'd do is—say that my number is 663, so I won't have to remember that really. And then I would think now I've got to remember 88. Now I'm 8 years old, so I can remember, say, my age two times. Then I say how old my brother is, and how old he was last year. And that's how I'd usually remember that phone number. [Is that how you would most often remember a phone number?] Well, usually I write it down. (Kreutzer, Leonard, & Flavell, 1975, p. 11)

Older children also have a more complete understanding of task variables that affect performance. Kindergartners are aware of a few factors that make a memory task easy or hard—for example, the number of items, their familiarity, how much study time is available, and whether they must recognize or recall them (Speer & Flavell, 1979; Wellman, 1977). But by the mid-elementary school years, children know much more—for example, that a list of semantically related items is easier to remember than unrelated items and that recalling prose material word for word is more difficult than paraphrasing it (Kreutzer, Leonard, & Flavell, 1975).

Once children become conscious of the many factors that influence mental activity, they combine them into an integrated understanding. By the end of middle childhood, children take account of interactions among variables—how age and motivation of the learner, effective use of strategies, and nature and difficulty of the task work together to affect cognitive performance (Wellman, 1990). In this way, metacognition truly becomes a comprehensive theory.

SELF-REGULATION

Although knowledge of mental activity expands, many studies report that it is only weakly related to task performance (Byrd & Gholson, 1985; Pressley, 1995b). This suggests that school-age children have difficulty with the second aspect of metacognition mentioned earlier: putting what they know into action. They are not yet good at **self-regulation**, the process of continuously monitoring progress toward a goal, checking outcomes, and redirecting unsuccessful efforts.

One way self-regulation can be assessed is by looking at children's **comprehension monitoring**, or sensitivity to how well they understand a spoken or written message. In one study, fourth and sixth graders listened to short essays containing missing or inconsistent information, as in the following passage:

> Janet decided to play some records. She looked through all the songs and picked out her favorite. It was a song called "As Time Goes By." She said to herself, "I haven't played this one in a long time." She played it quietly so she would not disturb her family. She was out of practice so it sounded funny sometimes.* Janet sang along with the music. She knew some of the words and she hummed the rest. The last verse of the song was the part she liked the best. After that song was finished she played another one. [*Sentence is inconsistent with Janet playing records.] (Beal, 1990, p. 249)

Sixth graders detected more text problems than fourth graders, a finding confirmed by other research. In fact, school-age children even fail to notice gaps and contradictions in prose that they produce themselves—a major reason they rarely revise their writing (Fitzgerald, 1987). Their self-regulatory difficulties do not stem from an inability to adequately repair the text. Once problems are pointed out, they are quite good at correcting them (Beal, 1990).

Current evidence indicates that self-regulation of cognitive performance develops slowly over childhood and adolescence. This is not surprising, since monitoring learning outcomes is a cognitively demanding activity, requiring constant evaluation of effort and progress. By the time young people reach secondary school, self-regulation is a strong predictor of academic success. Students who do well know when they possess a skill and when they do not. If they run up against obstacles, such as poor study conditions, a confusing text passage, or an unclear class lecture, they take steps to organize the learning environment, review the material, or seek other sources of support. This active, purposeful approach contrasts sharply with the passive orientation of students who do poorly (Borkowski et al., 1990; Zimmerman, 1990).

Parents and teachers can foster children's self-regulatory skills by pointing out the special demands of tasks, encouraging the use of strategies, and emphasizing the value of self-correction. As adults ask children questions and help them monitor their own behavior in circumstances where they are likely to encounter difficulties, children internalize these procedures (Pressley, 1995a).

Think about these practical suggestions for fostering self-regulation. Do they resemble Vygotsky's theory of the social origins of higher cognitive processes? In fact, Vygotsky's theory has been a source of inspiration for metacognitive training. Many studies show that providing children with instructions to check and monitor their progress toward a goal has a substantial impact on their learning. In addition, training that goes beyond demonstrating a strategy to emphasizing why it is effective enhances children's use of it in new situations (Pressley & El-Dinary, 1993; Schunk & Zimmerman, 1994). When adults tell children why and not just what to do, they provide a rationale for future action. Then children learn not only how to get a particular task done, but what to do when faced with new problems.

In later chapters, we will return to the topic of self-regulation, since it also influences emotional and social development. And as we turn now to development within academic skill areas, notice how the importance of self-regulation is ever-present. But before we consider these domains of learning, you may find to helpful to review the Milestones table on page 287, which summarizes the diverse changes in general information processing that we have discussed.

Self-regulation
The process of continuously monitoring progress toward a goal, checking outcomes, and redirecting unsuccessful efforts.

Comprehension monitoring
Sensitivity to how well one understands a spoken or written message.

BRIEF REVIEW

Children's metacognitive knowledge changes from a passive to an active, constructive view of mental functioning as awareness of cognitive capacities, strategies, and task variables expands. Self-regulation develops slowly during childhood and adolescence; children do not always apply their metacognitive understanding. Teaching children self-regulatory skills can have broad effects on their learning.

Applications of Information Processing to Academic Learning

■ *Reading taxes all aspects of our information-processing systems. To become proficient, this young child will need to master many skills, from perceiving single letters and letter combinations to combing the meaning of various parts of a text passage into an understandable whole. (Sybil Shackman/Monkmeyer Press)*

Over the past decade, interest in the development of information processing has been extended to children's mastery of academic skills. A rapidly growing body of research focuses on learning in different subject-matter areas. Because paths to competence vary across knowledge domains, each area has been studied separately. Nevertheless, the research has features in common. First, investigators identify the cognitive capacities and strategies necessary for skilled performance, try to trace their development, and pinpoint the ways in which good and poor learners differ. Then, using this information, they design and test instructional procedures to improve children's learning. In the following sections, we discuss a sampling of these efforts in reading, mathematics, and scientific reasoning.

READING

As Table 7.1 shows, while reading we execute many skills simultaneously, taxing all aspects of our information-processing systems. We must perceive single letters and letter combinations, translate them into speech sounds, learn to recognize the visual appearance of many common words, hold chunks of text in working memory while interpreting their meaning, and combine the meanings of various parts of a text passage into an understandable whole. In fact, reading is such a demanding process that if one or more skills are poorly developed, they will compete for attentional resources in our limited memories, and reading performance will decline (Frederiksen & Warren, 1987; Perfetti, 1988).

TABLE 7.1

Cognitive Components of Skilled Reading

Lower-Level Skills	Higher-Level Skills
Perceptual encoding of single letters and letter combinations	Locating meanings of written words in long-term memory
Decoding single letters and letter combinations into speech sounds	Combining word meanings into clauses and sentences
Sight recognition of common words, to reduce time-consuming decoding	Using prose context to refine word, clause, and sentence meanings
Holding chunks of text in working memory for higher-level processing	Combining sentence meanings into higher-order relations
	Using previous knowledge to draw inferences about text meaning
	Engaging in comprehension monitoring to check processing accuracy

Sources: Frederiksen & Warren, 1987; Perfetti, 1988.

MILESTONES

Development of General Information Processing

Age	Basic Capacities	Strategies	Knowledge	Metacognition
2–5 years 	■ Organization of the mental system into sensory register, short-term memory, and long-term memory is adultlike. ■ Many basic capacities are present, including attention, recognition, recall, and reconstruction. ■ Overall capacity, or size, of the system increases.	■ Attention becomes more focused and sustained. ■ Beginnings of memory strategies are present, but they are seldom used spontaneously and have little impact on performance.	■ Knowledge expands. ■ Familiar events are remembered in terms of scripts, which become more elaborate with age. ■ Autobiographical memory emerges and becomes clearer and more detailed.	■ Knowledge of mental life emerges. ■ Differentiation of thinking from other mental activities occurs. ■ Awareness of a limited-capacity mental system is present, but preschoolers view it as a passive container of information.
6–10 years	■ Overall capacity, or size, of the system continues to increase.	■ Attention becomes more controlled, adaptable, and planful. ■ Memory strategies of rehearsal and semantic organization are executed spontaneously and more effectively. ■ Capacity to draw inferences in reconstructive processing expands. ■ Reliance on fuzzy, reconstructed gists for reasoning increases.	■ Knowledge continues to expand and become more intricately organized, which facilitates strategy use and retrieval. 	■ View of the mind as an active, constructive agent develops. ■ Knowledge of the impact of psychological factors on performance and different types of cognitive processes increases. ■ Knowledge of the impact of task variables on performance increases and is integrated with psychological factors. ■ Self-regulation improves slowly.
11 years–adulthood	■ Overall capacity, or size, of the system continues to increase, but at a slower pace than in childhood.	■ Memory strategy of elaboration appears and improves. 	■ Knowledge continues to expand and become better organized.	■ Metacognitive knowledge and self-regulation continue to improve.

Note: These milestones represent overall age trends. Individual differences exist in the precise age at which each milestone is attained.

How do children go about identifying written words when first learning to read? Using a microgenetic design to track children's mastery of new tasks (see Chapter 2), Robert Siegler (1986) devised and tested a **strategy-choice model**, which shows how strategies change over time. Children have multiple strategies available, and they choose adaptively among them. Automatic retrieval is the most efficient technique, and each time children encounter a new word, they may try it. But if a particular combination of letters is not strongly associated with any words they know, children resort to backup strategies, such as sounding out the word or asking for help. With practice, the appearance of each word becomes more strongly associated with its identity in long-term memory. When this happens, children gradually give up capacity-consuming backup strategies in favor of rapid retrieval. As we will see shortly, Siegler's model of strategy choice is broadly applicable. It describes how children make adaptive strategy choices that strike a balance between accuracy and speed on a diverse array of tasks.

■ *Parents who read to their young children provide vital preparation for the complex task of independent reading. (Tony Freeman/PhotoEdit)*

Currently, psychologists and educators are engaged in a "great debate" about how to teach beginning reading. On one side are those who take a **whole-language approach** to reading instruction. They argue that reading should be taught to young children in a way that parallels natural language learning. From the very beginning, children should be exposed to text in its complete form—stories, poems, letters, posters, and lists—so they can appreciate the communicative function of written language. According to these experts, as long as reading is kept whole and meaningful, children will be motivated to discover the specific skills they need as they gain experience with the printed word (Goodman, 1986; Watson, 1989). On the other side of the debate are those who advocate a **basic skills approach**. According to this view, children should be given simplified text materials. At first, they should be coached on *phonics*—the basic rules for translating written symbols into sounds. Only later, after they have mastered these skills, should they get complex reading material (Rayner & Pollatsek, 1989; Samuels, 1985).

Research does not show clear-cut superiority in reading attitudes or achievement for either of these approaches (McKenna et al., 1995; Stahl, McKenna, & Pagnucco, 1994). In fact, a third group of experts believes that children learn best when they receive a balanced mixture of both (Pressley, 1994; Stahl, 1992). Learning the basics—relations between letters and sounds—enables children to decipher words they have never seen before. As this process becomes more automatic, it releases children's attention to the higher-level activities involved in comprehending the text's meaning. But if practice in basic skills is overemphasized, children may lose sight of the goal of reading: understanding. Many teachers report cases of pupils who can read aloud fluently but who comprehend very little. These children might have been spared serious reading problems if they had received meaning-based instruction that included attention to basic skills.

Reading development begins long before formal schooling. It builds on a broad foundation of spoken language, experience with literacy materials, and understanding of the world. Parents who converse with their preschoolers, take them on outings, and expose them to print in everyday life have youngsters who arrive at school with both general and literacy-related knowledge that eases the task of early text processing (McGee & Richgels, 1996). Reading to young children is especially important. It is related to advances in language, understanding of the purpose and features of written symbols, and later success in school (Crain-Thoreson & Dale, 1992; Whitehurst et al., 1994).

Strategy-choice model
Siegler's model, which shows how strategies change over time as children master a diverse array of tasks. From multiple strategies available, children choose adaptively, striking a balance between accuracy and speed until answers are strongly associated with problems and can be retrieved automatically.

Whole-language approach
An approach to beginning reading instruction that parallels children's natural language learning and keeps reading materials whole and meaningful.

Basic skills approach
An approach to beginning reading instruction that emphasizes training in phonics—the basic rules for translating written symbols into sounds—and simplified reading materials.

Ordinality
A principle specifying order (more than and less than) relationships among quantities.

MATHEMATICS

Mathematical reasoning, like reading, builds on informal knowledge. Habituation–dishabituation research shows that newborn babies are sensitive to differences in the size of small sets (Antell & Keating, 1983). By 7 months, infants can recognize and match the same small quantity when it is presented in different sensory modalities. When shown two visual displays, they consistently look at the one with the same number of objects as a series of drumbeats. These findings indicate that young infants represent number in the same way, regardless of whether items are seen or heard (Starkey, Spelke, & Gelman, 1983). Around 16 months, infants display a beginning grasp of **ordinality**, or order relationships among quantities, such as three is more than two and two is more than one (Strauss & Curtis, 1984). These remarkable early understandings suggest the existence of an innate, numerical sensitivity that serves as the basis for more complex understandings (Gallistel & Gelman, 1992; Geary, 1995).

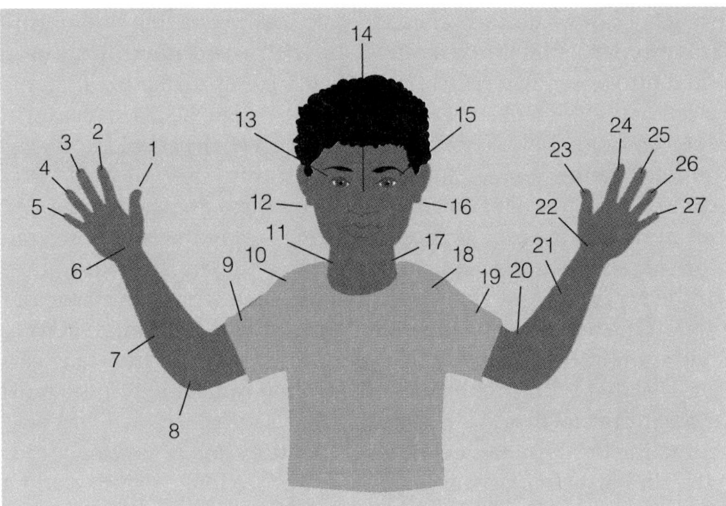

FIGURE 7.10

■ *Sequence of body parts used for counting by the Oksapmin of New Guinea. In the Oksapmin language, there are no terms for numbers aside from the body part names themselves (for example, "nose" represents "fourteen"). Children begin to use this system in the preschool years. When they enter school, they adapt body-part counting techniques to solve math problems, creating more complex computational procedures as the curriculum increases in difficulty. At their desks, Oksapmin children can often be seen pointing to body parts instead of counting on fingers. (From G. B. Saxe, 1985, "Effects of schooling on arithmetical understanding: Studies with Oksapmin children in Papua, New Guinea,"* Journal of Educational Psychology, *77, p. 505. (Copyright © 1985 by the American Psychological Association. Reprinted by permission of the publisher and author.)*

In the early preschool years, children start to attach verbal labels (such as *lots, little, big,* and *small*) to different amounts and sizes. And between ages 2 and 3, many begin to count. However, at first counting is little more than a memorized routine. Often numbers are recited in an unbroken string like this: "Onetwothreefourfivesix!" Or children repeat a few number words while vaguely pointing toward objects they have seen others count (Fuson, 1988).

Very soon, however, counting strategies become more precise. Most 3- to 4-year-olds have established an accurate one-to-one correspondence between a short sequence of number words and the items they represent (Gallistel & Gelman, 1992; Geary, 1994). Sometime between ages 4 and 5, they grasp the vital principle of **cardinality**. They understand that the last word in a counting sequence indicates the quantity of items in a set (Bermejo, 1996). They also know that if two groups of objects match up (for example, every jar has its own spoon or every doll its own cup), then each set contains the same number of items (Becker, 1989; Sophian, 1988).[1]

Mastery of cardinality quickly increases the efficiency of children's counting. By the late preschool years, children no longer need to start a counting sequence with the number "one." Instead, knowing that there are six items in one pile and some additional ones in another, they begin with the number "six" and count on to determine the total quantity. Eventually, they generalize this strategy and count down to find out how many items remain after some are taken away. Once these strategies are mastered, children start to manipulate numbers without requiring that countable objects be physically present (Fuson, 1988). At this point, counting on fingers often becomes an intermediate step on the way to automatic performance of basic arithmetic operations. By age 8 or 9, children naturally apply their additive understanding to multiplication, first approaching it as a kind of repeated addition (Geary, 1995).

■ *Counting on fingers is an early, spontaneous strategy that children use to learn basic math facts. As they repeatedly use this technique and others, answers become more strongly associated with problems, and children give up the strategy in favor of automatic retrieval. (Elizabeth Zuckerman/PhotoEdit)*

Cross-cultural evidence suggests that the basic arithmetic knowledge just described emerges universally around the world, although ways of representing number vary. For example, among the Oksapmin, an agricultural society of Papua, New Guinea, counting is mapped onto 27 body parts, which serve as number terms. To count as Oksapmins do, start with the thumb on one hand and move around the upper body, ending on the little finger of the opposite hand (see Figure 7.10). Using this system, Oksapmin children keep track of quantities, measure, and play number games. In elementary school classrooms, they can be seen pointing to body parts instead of counting on fingers, creating complex calculation procedures that tailor their already existing skills to new problems (Saxe, 1985).

Depending on the extent to which informal counting experiences are available in children's everyday lives, children may acquire early number understandings at different rates. In homes and preschools where adults provide many occasions and requests for quantification, children construct these basic concepts sooner (Geary, 1994). Then they are solidly available as supports for the wide variety of mathematical skills that are taught in school.

[1] As Piaget's conservation of number task reveals, at first preschoolers' understanding of cardinality is fragile. It is easily overcome by the appearance of a set of objects. However, the findings reported here indicate that young children understand much more about numbers than Piaget assumed.

Cardinality
A principle specifying that the last number in a counting sequence indicates the quantity of items in the set.

Once children reach school, how do they acquire basic math facts that will permit them to solve more advanced problems efficiently? As with word identification in reading, Siegler conducted microgenetic research in mathematics, applying his strategy-choice model (Siegler & Jenkins, 1989; Siegler & Shrager, 1984). Again, he discovered that children use diverse strategies adaptively. For example, when given the problem "5 + 3," children typically try to retrieve the answer automatically. If this does not work, they resort to backup procedures. They may count from one, put up three fingers on one hand and five on the other but recognize the total without counting, apply the count-on strategy described earlier, or sometimes guess. As children apply backup strategies, they receive feedback about the accuracy and speed with which each works on particular problems. This information influences their later choices. Gradually, children start to emphasize strategies that result in correct and quicker solutions. In the process, answers become more strongly associated with problems, and children move toward the most efficient technique—automatic retrieval.

Return for a moment to the description of children's identification of written words on page 288, and note the similarity in discovery of efficient procedures in both reading and math. Siegler (1989) reports similar findings for other domains as well, including time telling, spelling, and memory tasks. His research suggests a common approach to acquiring new knowledge in which diverse strategies are tried and the most successful ones survive, even though the specific strategies and information learned vary widely across domains. As Siegler comments, "[S]trategy choices are made through a general choice process that operates on task-specific representations" (p. 1). Notice how this conclusion supports the view that the mind has both general and domain-specific properties, which interact to produce cognitive change.

Arguments about how to teach mathematics resemble the positions discussed earlier in the area of reading. Extensive speeded practice to promote automatic retrieval is pitted against "number sense," or understanding. Further research is likely to show that some blend of these two approaches is most beneficial. In the case of basic number facts, compared to good students, poor students move too quickly toward trying to retrieve answers automatically. Their responses are often wrong because they have not used backup strategies accurately and long enough to build strong associations between problems and correct solutions (Siegler, 1989; Kerkman & Siegler, 1993). This suggests that teaching pupils how to apply backup strategies successfully and encouraging them to take time to do so is vital for promoting successful math fact retrieval.

A similar picture emerges when we look at pupils who experience difficulties with more complex skills, such as carrying in addition, borrowing in subtraction, and operating with decimals and fractions. Often these youngsters apply a method that is close to what they have been taught but that yields a wrong answer. Their mistakes indicate that they have tried to memorize a procedure but do not understand the basis for it. For example, look at the following subtraction errors:

$$\begin{array}{r} 4\,2\,7 \\ -\,1\,3\,8 \\ \hline 3\,1\,1 \end{array} \qquad \begin{array}{r} {}^{6}\not{7}\,0\,0\,{}^{1}2 \\ 5\,4\,4\,5 \\ \hline 1\,4\,4\,7 \end{array}$$

In the first problem, the child consistently subtracts a smaller from a larger digit, regardless of which is on top. In the second, columns with zeros are repeatedly skipped in a borrowing operation, and whenever there is a zero on top, the bottom digit is written as the answer. Researchers believe that an overemphasis on drill-oriented math that discourages children from using their naturally acquired counting strategies to grasp new skills underlies these difficulties (Fuson, 1990; Resnick, 1989).

Cross-cultural evidence suggests that American math instruction may have gone too far in emphasizing computational drill over numerical understanding. As we will see in greater detail in Chapter 15, children in Asian nations are ahead of American pupils in mathematical development at all levels of schooling. As the Cultural Influences box on the following page illustrates, they receive a variety of supports for acquiring mathematical knowledge that are not available to American children. The result is deeper processing—the formation of secure numerical concepts that provide a firm foundation for mastery of new skills.

CULTURAL INFLUENCES

Asian Children's Understanding of Multidigit Addition and Subtraction

Elementary school pupils in the United States find multidigit addition and subtraction problems requiring trades between columns to be very difficult. Many American children try to solve such problems by rote, without grasping crucial aspects of the procedure. They seem to have a confused, single-digit conception of multidigit numbers. For example, they tend to view the 3 in 5,386 as being just 3 rather than 300. As a result, when they carry to or borrow from this column, they are likely to compute the value incorrectly.

Chinese, Japanese, and Korean children, by contrast, are highly accurate at multidigit addition and subtraction. What accounts for their superior performance? To find out, Karen Fuson and Youngshim Kwon (1992) asked Korean second and third graders to solve a set of two- and three-digit problems, observed their methods, and asked questions about their knowledge. The performance of the children was excellent. For example, even though second graders had not yet received formal instruction on three-digit problems, their scores were nearly perfect in addition. In subtraction, they solved 78 percent of three-digit problems correctly.

Quantitative understanding of multidigit numbers was clearly responsible for the Korean pupils' exceptional competence. Almost all identified the tens' and hundreds' columns correctly as they described how to solve problems. And no Korean child viewed a "1" mark signaling trading to the tens column as "one," as American children typically do. Instead, they clearly identified it as "ten." Especially remarkable were third graders' clear explanations of how to perform complex multistep trading operations that stump their American agemates. Here are two examples:

> I borrowed one hundred. And I gave nine tens to the tens' column and the remainder, ten, to the ones' column.
>
> As four becomes three, the zero in the tens' column becomes nine and the zero in the ones' column becomes ten. (Fuson & Kwon, 1992, p. 502)

In fact, most Korean third graders no longer wrote extra marks when solving problems like this one. They could handle intricate trading procedures mentally.

Researchers point to several cultural and language-based factors that contribute to the sharp skill advantage of Asian over American pupils. First, use of the metric system in Asian countries, which presents one, ten, hundred, and thousand values in all areas of measurement, helps children think in ways consistent with place value. Second, English words for two-digit numbers (such as *twelve* and *thirteen*) are irregular and do not convey the idea of tens and ones. The structure of Asian-language number words ("ten two," "ten three") makes this composition obvious. Number words are also shorter and more quickly pronounced. This facilitates verbal counting strategies, since more digits can be held in working memory at once. It also increases the speed with which children can retrieve math facts from long-term memory (Geary et al., 1993; Jensen & Whang, 1994).

Asian instructional practices support rapid mastery of multidigit problems as well. For example, teachers use phrases that explicitly describe the trading operation. Instead of carrying, they say "raise up," and instead of borrowing, they say "bring down." Textbooks also do a much better job of helping children discriminate place values. Hundreds', tens', and ones' columns have separate color codes, and pictures depicting their relative sizes are often linked to addition and subtraction problems (Fuson, 1992). Finally, multidigit problems are introduced earlier in Asian schools. American pupils spend more time on problems requiring no trading, increasing the chances that they will apply single-digit concepts inappropriately to multidigit numbers.

In sum, what appears at first glance to be the same cognitive task is actually quite different for American than Asian pupils. These findings highlight several ways in which adults might ease children's mastery of numerical concepts in the United States.

■ *Cultural and language-based factors contribute to Asian children's skill at manipulating multidigit numbers. The abacus supports these Japanese pupils' understanding of place value. Ones, tens, hundreds, and thousands are each represented by a different column of beads, and calculations are performed by moving the beads to different positions. As children become skilled at using the abacus, they generate mental images that assist them is solving complex arithmetic problems. (Fuji Fotos/The Image Works)*

SCIENTIFIC REASONING

What does it mean to think scientifically? The heart of scientific reasoning is the coordination of theories with evidence. A scientist can clearly describe the theory that he or she favors, knows what evidence is needed to support it and what would refute it, and can explain how pitting evidence against available theories led to the acceptance of one theory as opposed to others.

Deanna Kuhn has conducted extensive research into the development of scientific reasoning. In one series of studies, third, sixth, and ninth graders; adults of mixed educational backgrounds; and professional scientists were all provided with evidence, sometimes consistent and sometimes conflicting with theories. This was followed by questions about the validity of each theory. For example, participants were asked to theorize about which of several features of sports balls, such as size, color, or surface texture, influences the quality of a player's serve. Then they were told about the theory of Mr. (or Ms.) S, who believed that size of the ball was important, and the theory of Mr. (or Ms.) C, who believed that color made a difference. Next, the interviewer presented evidence by placing balls with certain characteristics in two baskets labeled "good serve" and "bad serve."

Kuhn and her collaborators (1988) found that third and sixth graders, and older participants to a lesser degree, reason in ways that are very different from scientists. The youngest participants had the greatest difficulty coordinating theories with evidence. When evidence contradicted their preferred theory, they sometimes made slight but inadequate adjustments in the theory, without conscious awareness that they had done so. More often, children ignored conflicting evidence or misinterpreted it in ways consistent with their theory. Their willingness to distort evidence in this way is dramatically illustrated by Allen, a third grader, who judged that size was causal (with large balls producing good serves and small balls, bad serves). When shown incomplete evidence—a single, large light-colored ball in the "good serve" basket and no balls in the "bad serve" basket—Allen insisted that it proved Mr. S's theory (which was also his own) to be correct. Asked to explain, he stated flatly, "Because this ball is big . . . the color doesn't really matter" (Kuhn, 1989, p. 677).

These findings reveal that children have trouble discriminating theory from evidence in multiple variable situations. Instead of regarding pieces of evidence as separate from and bearing on a theory, they blend the two into a single representation of "the way things are." What are the cognitive skills that support scientific reasoning? According to Kuhn (1989, 1993), metacognition—thinking about thought—is most important. Individuals must represent the theory as an object of thought rather than a mirror image of reality. And they must also set aside their own preference for the theory and consider what the evidence says as their sole basis for judgment.

How does the development of skill in coordinating theory with evidence take place? Education clearly makes a difference. The performance of older individuals is strongly influenced by years of schooling, whether they grapple with traditional scientific tasks like those just described or engage in informal reasoning—for example, justify a theory about "what causes children to fail in school" (Kuhn, 1993). But even at advanced levels of education, scientific reasoning is rarely taught directly. Instead, in virtually all subject-matter areas, individuals receive practice in setting aside their own experiences and beliefs to infer conclusions that follow from information given. Research reveals that continuous opportunities to pit theory against evidence encourage children and adolescents to reflect on their current strategies, revise them, and think more scientifically (Kuhn et al., 1995; Schauble, 1996).

Perhaps you noticed that the capacity to coordinate theory with evidence shares features with Piaget's formal operational stage. Kuhn's work shows that scientific reasoning becomes more common during adolescence and develops similarly across different types of problems. It also depends on the metacognitive skills to which Piaget referred when he spoke of "operating on operations" (see Chapter 6, page 241). Nevertheless, recent findings indicate that scientific reasoning is not the result of an abrupt, stagewise change in general capacity. Instead, it develops gradually out of specific experiences that require individuals to match theories against evidence. Identifying contexts that promote scientific reasoning opens the door to instructional interventions that support its development. In all these ways, the new wave of research on scientific thinking skills reflects core tenets of the information-processing perspective.

BRIEF REVIEW

Recently, information-processing researchers have turned their attention to children's academic learning. Efficient reading requires simultaneous execution of many lower-level and higher-level skills. It builds on a firm foundation of language development and general and literacy-related knowledge acquired during the preschool years. Similarly, young children's spontaneously constructed number concepts and counting strategies serve as the basis for mathematics taught in school. Siegler's strategy-choice model explains how children use diverse strategies adaptively to master basic knowledge in academic domains. In both reading and math, instruction that provides balanced attention to basic skills and understanding seems most beneficial. Tasks that offer repeated practice in coordinating theory with evidence promote metacognitive skills necessary for scientific reasoning on diverse types of tasks.

Evaluation of the Information-Processing Approach

A major strength of the information-processing approach is its explicitness and precision in breaking down complex cognitive performance into its components. Information processing has provided a wealth of detailed evidence on how younger versus older and more skilled versus less skilled individuals perceive, attend to, memorize, and solve problems. Compared to Piaget's theory, it also offers a more precise account of cognitive change. Because information-processing researchers view thinking as a collection of separate skills rather than a single entity, they rely on many mechanisms to explain development. The most important ones are summarized in Table 7.2 on page 294. As you review them, think back to research discussed in this chapter that illustrates the role of each. Finally, information processing is beginning to clarify which aspects of cognitive development are domain-specific, which are general, and how they work together. In doing so, it is contributing to our understanding of academic learning and to instructional methods that enhance school performance.

Nevertheless, the information-processing perspective has several limitations that prevent it from serving as a complete account of cognitive development. The first, ironically, stems from its central strength: by analyzing cognition into its components, information processing has had difficulty putting them back together into a broad comprehensive theory. For this reason, many child development specialists resist abandoning Piaget's view in favor of it. In fact, efforts to build general theories of development within an information-processing framework, such as Case's and Fischer's theories, have succeeded only by retaining essential features of Piaget's stage sequence.

Furthermore, the computer metaphor, although bringing precision to research on the human mind, has drawbacks. Computer models of cognitive processing, though complex in their own right, do not reflect the richness of many real-life learning experiences. For example, they tell us little about aspects of cognition that are not linear and logical, such as imagination and creativity (Greeno, 1989). In addition, computers do not have desires, interests, and intentions. Although they interact with other machines through networks and modems, they cannot form friendships, take another's perspective, or adopt moral and social values. Perhaps because of the narrowness of the computer metaphor, information processing has not yet told us much about the links between cognition and other areas of development. Currently, researchers are intensely

TABLE 7.2

Mechanisms of Cognitive Change From the Information Processing Perspective

Mechanism	Description
Basic processing capacity	Size of the mental system increases as a result of brain maturation.
Processing efficiency	Speed of basic operations increases, consuming less capacity in working memory and freeing up resources for other mental activities.
Encoding of information	Encoding, in the form of attention, becomes more thorough and better adapted to task demands.
Strategy execution	Strategies become more effective, improving storage, representation, and retrieval of information.
Knowledge	Amount and structure of domain-specific knowledge increase, easing strategy use and retrieval.
Metacognition	Awareness and understanding of cognitive processes expand and self-regulation improves, leading strategies to be applied in a wider range of situations.

Source: Kuhn, 1992.

interested in whether information processing can enhance our understanding of how children think about their social world. We will see some examples of this emphasis in later chapters. But it is still true that extensions of Piaget's theory prevail when it comes to research on children's social and moral development.

Finally, information-processing research has been slow to respond to the growing interest in the biological basis of cognitive development. Critics argue that to fully understand cognitive change, theoretical revisions are needed that "take the brain as seriously as the mind" (Bjorklund, 1995, p. 127).

Despite its shortcomings, the information-processing approach holds great promise for the future. New breakthroughs in understanding the joint operation of mechanisms of cognitive development, neurological changes that underlie various mental activities, and instructional methods that support children's learning are likely to take place in the years to come.

SUMMARY

THE INFORMATION-PROCESSING APPROACH

- The information-processing approach views the mind as a complex, symbol-manipulating system that operates much like a computer. The computer analogy helps researchers analyze thought into separate components, each of which can be studied thoroughly to yield a detailed understanding of what children and adults do when faced with a task or problem.

GENERAL MODELS OF INFORMATION PROCESSING

- Atkinson and Shiffrin's **store model** assumes that information moves through three parts of the mental system, where **control processes**, or **mental strategies**, operate on it so that it can be retained and used efficiently. The **sensory register** and **short-term memory** are limited in capacity. **Long-term memory**, which contains our permanent knowledge base, is limitless. The **serial position effect** supports the distinction between short- and long-term memory.

- According to the **levels-of-processing model**, retention depends on the depth to which information is processed by the system. Instead of a short-term memory store, our limited cognitive capacity is due to **working memory**, a conscious pool of attentional resources from which our information-processing activities draw. As tasks become well learned, or automatic, they consume less attention, and resources are freed for other activities.

DEVELOPMENTAL MODELS OF INFORMATION PROCESSING

- Several developmental models that reinterpret Piaget's theory within an information-processing framework have attracted widespread attention. According to Case, development involves the expansion of **mental space**, or **M-space**, a computerlike construct similar to working memory. Brain maturation and automaticity of schemes due to practice release extra M-space for the child to combine old schemes and generate new ones. When schemes are consolidated into central conceptual structures, M-space increases further, and the child moves up to a new Piagetian stage.

- Fischer's **skill theory** emphasizes that each child has an optimal skill level that depends on brain maturation and corresponds to a Piagetian stage. Within each skill level, progress depends on the opportunities to practice schemes in a wide range of situations and integrate them into higher-order skills.

ATTENTIONAL PROCESSING

- With age, children sustain attention for longer periods of time and select stimuli on the basis of their relevance to task goals. Older children are also better at adapting attention to the momentary requirements of situations.
- Attentional (and memory) strategies develop in a three-phase sequence. At first, children show a **production deficiency**, a failure to use the strategy when it could be helpful. When they first acquire the strategy, they show a **control deficiency**, an inability to execute it effectively. Finally, when the strategy is perfected, a **utilization deficiency** is evident, in that initially it does not improve performance. Only after much time and practice do children benefit from strategy use.
- During middle childhood, children become better at **planning**. On tasks that require systematic visual search or the coordination of many acts, school-age children are more likely than preschoolers to decide ahead of time how to proceed and allocate their attention accordingly.

SHORT-TERM OR WORKING MEMORY

- Although the beginnings of memory strategies can be seen during the preschool years, young children seldom engage in **rehearsal** or **organization** when given unfamiliar materials. As use of these strategies improves, they gradually become more flexible; children vary them to fit the demands of the material to be learned. **Elaboration** is a late-developing memory skill that rarely appears before age 11.
- Like young children, people in non-Western cultures who have no formal schooling do not spontaneously use or benefit from instruction in memory strategies. Tasks requiring children to memorize unrelated pieces of information in school promote deliberate memory strategies in middle childhood.

LONG-TERM MEMORY

- **Recognition**, the simplest form of retrieval, is a fairly automatic process that is highly accurate by the preschool years. In contrast, **recall**, or remembering an absent stimulus, is more difficult and shows much greater improvement with age.
- Even young children engage in **reconstruction** when remembering complex, meaningful material. Over middle childhood, the ability to draw inferences from prose material expands. According to **fuzzy-trace theory**, information is reconstructed automatically at encoding into a vague, fuzzy version called a **gist** that is stored separately from the verbatim version. With age, children rely less on verbatim and more on gist memory, which contributes to improved reasoning and recall.
- Gains in the quantity and structure of domain-specific knowledge enhance memory performance by making new, related information easier to store and retrieve. However, children differ not only in what they know, but in how well they use their knowledge to acquire new information. Knowledge and memory strategies support one another.
- Like adults, young children remember familiar experiences in terms of **scripts**—general representations of what occurs and when it occurs in a particular situation. Scripts may be the developmental link in the transition from **episodic** to **semantic memory**.
- During the preschool years, **infantile amnesia** subsides as children's self-image and language skills develop and they begin to talk about the past with adults. Gradually, children adopt the narrative thinking generated in these dialogues, forming an **autobiographical memory**.

METACOGNITION

- **Metacognition** improves as children construct a naive **theory of mind**, a coherent understanding of people as mental beings. Children's awareness of cognitive capacities, strategies, and task variables changes from a passive to an active view of mental functioning in middle childhood. **Self-regulation**—using metacognitive knowledge to monitor performance—develops slowly over childhood and adolescence. Instruction that points out self-regulatory skills and explains why they are effective helps children generalize them to new situations.

APPLICATIONS OF INFORMATION PROCESSING TO ACADEMIC LEARNING

- Skilled reading involves executing many lower- and higher-level skills simultaneously, taxing all aspects of the information-processing system. Experts disagree on whether a **whole-language approach** or **basic skills approach** should be used to teach beginning reading. A balanced mixture of both is probably most effective. Reading builds on general and literacy-related knowledge acquired before formal schooling.
- Children develop counting strategies and construct basic mathematical concepts, including **ordinality** and **cardinality**, during the preschool years. Siegler's **strategy-choice model** explains how children use diverse strategies adaptively to learn basic math facts, identify written words in reading, and acquire knowledge in other domains. As with reading, instruction that combines practice in basic skills with conceptual understanding seems best in mathematics.
- Children (and to a lesser degree, adolescents and adults) have difficulty coordinating theories with evidence. Tasks that offer repeated practice in pitting theories against evidence promote the metacognitive skills necessary for scientific reasoning.

EVALUATION OF THE INFORMATION-PROCESSING APPROACH

- A major strength of the information-processing approach is its explicitness and precision in breaking down cognition into separate elements so each can be studied thoroughly. So far, information processing has not led to a comprehensive theory or told us much about the links between cognition and other areas of development. In addition, it has yet to integrate its findings with the burst of new research on the developing brain.

IMPORTANT TERMS AND CONCEPTS

store model (p. 260)
control processes, or mental strategies (p. 260)
sensory register (p. 260)
short-term memory (p. 260)
long-term memory (p. 261)
serial position effect (p. 261)
levels-of-processing model (p. 262)
working memory (p. 262)
mental space, or M-space (p. 265)
skill theory (p. 265)
production deficiency (p. 267)
control deficiency (p. 268)
utilization deficiency (p. 268)
planning (p. 268)
attention-deficit hyperactivity disorder (ADHD) (p. 271)
rehearsal (p. 271)
organization (p. 271)
elaboration (p. 272)
recognition (p. 274)
recall (p. 274)
reconstruction (p. 275)
fuzzy-trace theory (p. 276)
gist (p. 276)
semantic memory (p. 278)
episodic memory (p. 278)
scripts (p. 278)
autobiographical memory (p. 279)
infantile amnesia (p. 279)
metacognition (p. 281)
theory of mind (p. 281)
self-regulation (p. 285)
comprehension monitoring (p. 285)
strategy-choice model (p. 288)
whole-language approach (p. 288)
basic skills approach (p. 288)
ordinality (p. 288)
cardinality (p. 289)

CONNECTIONS for Chapter 7

If you are interested in . . .	turn to . . .	to learn about . . .
■ Information processing and other aspects of development	■ Chapter 9, pp. 360–361, 366–367	■ Ideas about how semantic and grammatical development take place
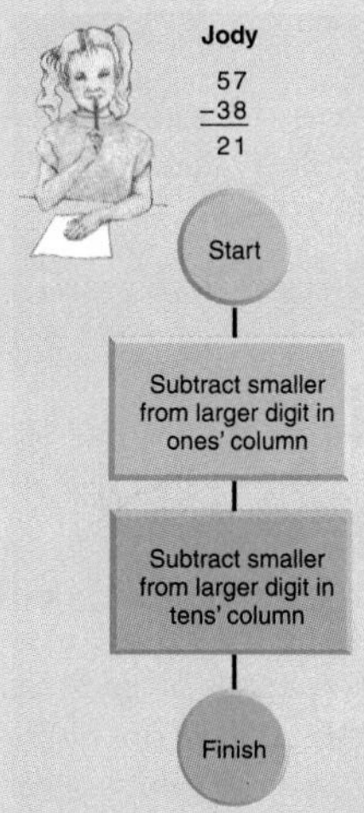	■ Chapter 11, pp. 426–428	■ Young children's theory of mind
	■ Chapter 11, pp. 433–438	■ Development of achievement-related attributions
	■ Chapter 11, pp. 453–455	■ An information-processing approach to social problem solving
	■ Chapter 12, p. 493	■ Social information processing of aggressive children
	■ Chapter 15, pp. 599–600	■ Development of television literacy
■ Self-regulation	■ Chapter 6, pp. 247–248	■ Private speech
 	■ Chapter 10, pp. 390–391	■ Emotional self-regulation
	■ Chapter 12, pp. 486–489	■ Self-control and moral self-regulation
■ Academic learning	■ Chapter 2, p. 50	■ School matters in Mexican-American families
	■ Chapter 6, pp. 250–253	■ Reciprocal teaching and reading comprehension
	■ Chapter 6, p. 253	■ Cooperative learning and academic performance
	■ Chapter 8, pp. 316–325 Chapter 15, pp. 616–617	■ Academic performance of low-income ethnic minority children
	■ Chapter 8, pp. 328–330	■ Early intervention and academic performance
	■ Chapter 9, pp. 374–376	■ Bilingual education and academic performance
	■ Chapter 14, pp. 543–545	■ Child-rearing styles and academic performance
	■ Chapter 15, pp. 603–604	■ Television and academic learning
	■ Chapter 15, pp. 610–611	■ Traditional versus open classrooms and academic performance
	■ Chapter 15, pp. 619–621	■ Cross-national research on academic achievement

8 Intelligence

Five-year-old Jermaine, an African-American child, sat in a small, unfamiliar testing room while Nora, an adult whom he had met only moments ago, prepared to give him an intelligence test. Eager to come when Nora had arrived at his kindergarten classroom, Jermaine became confused once the testing session began.

Starting with some word definitions, Nora asked, "Jermaine, how are wood and coal alike? How are they the same?"

Jermaine's eyebrows wrinkled in puzzlement. He shrugged his shoulders and said, "Well, they're both hard."

Nora continued, "And an apple and a peach?"

"They taste good," responded Jermaine, looking up at Nora's face for any sign that he was doing all right.

Nora looked back pleasantly but moved along in a businesslike way. "A ship and an automobile?"

Jermaine paused, unsure of what Nora meant. "They're hard," he finally replied, returning to his first response.

"Iron and silver?"

"They're hard," Jermaine repeated, still trying to figure out what these questions were all about. (Adapted from Miller-Jones, 1989, p. 362.)

The **psychometric approach** to cognitive development is the basis for the wide variety of intelligence tests available for assessing children's mental abilities. As Nora's testing of Jermaine illustrates, compared to Piagetian, Vygotskian, and information-processing views, the psychometric perspective is far more product oriented than process oriented. For the most part, it focuses on outcomes and results—how many and what kinds of questions children can answer correctly at different ages. How children arrive at solutions to problems is emphasized less. Researchers interested in intelligence testing ask such questions as, What factors, or dimensions, make up intelligence, and how do they change with age? How can cognitive development be measured so that scores are useful for predicting future academic achievement, career attainment, and other aspects of intellectual success? To what extent do children of the same age differ in intelligence, and what factors explain these differences?

As we examine these issues, we will quickly become immersed in the IQ nature–nurture debate, waged over the course of this century. We will look closely at genetic and environmental influences on intelligence as well as the controversy over whether intelligence tests yield biased estimates of the abilities of low-income ethnic minority children like Jermaine. As our discussion proceeds, we will see that the cognitive perspectives we have considered in previous chapters, as well as the work of many investigators examining contextual influences on development, have added much to our understanding of children's test performance.

Our discussion concludes by moving "beyond IQ" to the development of creativity and special talents. Although these are among the most highly valued human characteristics, they are not represented on current intelligence tests for children.

Psychometric approach
An approach to cognitive development that focuses on the construction of tests to assess mental abilities.

Definitions of Intelligence

Take a moment to jot down a list of behaviors you view as typical of people who are highly intelligent. Did you come up with just one or two characteristics or a great many? When Robert Sternberg asked nearly 500 laypeople and 24 experts to complete a similar exercise, he found that their responses were surprisingly similar. Both groups viewed intelligence as a complex construct made up of verbal ability, practical problem solving, and social competence (Sternberg, 1982; Sternberg & Detterman, 1986). These findings indicate that most people do not think of intelligence as a single ability. Instead, their definitions include a variety of attributes.

Now try another exercise. This time, list five traits you regard as characterizing intelligent 6-month-olds, 2-year-olds, 10-year-olds, and adults. The problem of defining children's intelligence is especially challenging, since behaviors that reflect intelligent behavior change with age. When students in an introductory psychology course were given this task, their descriptions differed greatly from one developmental period to the next. As Table 8.1 reveals, sensorimotor responsiveness became less important, whereas problem solving and reasoning became more important, in much the same way that Piaget suggested intelligence changes with age. Furthermore, after infancy, college students stressed the role of verbal and symbolic knowledge, an emphasis that fits with both Piagetian and information-processing views (Siegler & Richards, 1980).

The researchers also asked college students to estimate correlations among the mental abilities mentioned for each age. Students thought there would be some close connections, but they predicted considerable distinctiveness as well. As we will see in the following sections, scientific theories underlying the measurement of intelligence reveal this same tension between a single, overarching ability versus a collection of only loosely related skills.

ALFRED BINET: A HOLISTIC VIEW

The social and educational climate of the late nineteenth and early twentieth centuries led to the rise of the intelligence testing movement. Perhaps the most important influence was the beginning of universal public education in Europe and the United States. Once schools opened their doors to children of all social classes, not just society's privileged, educators called for methods that would help them identify pupils who could not profit from regular classroom instruction. The first successful intelligence test, completed by French psychologist Alfred Binet and his colleague Theodore Simon in 1905, responded to this need.

TABLE 8.1

Five Traits Most Frequently Mentioned by College Students as Characterizing Intelligence at Different Ages

6-Month-Olds	2-Year-Olds	10-Year-Olds	Adults
1. Recognition of people and objects	1. Verbal ability	1. Verbal ability	1. Reasoning
2. Motor coordination	2. Learning ability	2, 3, 4. Learning ability; problem solving; reasoning (all three tied)	2. Verbal ability
3. Alertness	3. Awareness of people and environment		3. Problem solving
4. Awareness of environment	4. Motor coordination		4. Learning ability
5. Verbalization	5. Curiosity	5. Creativity	5. Creativity

Source: R. S. Siegler & D. D. Richards. 1980, "College Students' Prototypes of Children's Intelligence." Paper presented at the annual meeting of the American Psychological Association, New York. Adapted by permission of the author.

Binet was asked by the French Ministry of Instruction to devise an objective method for identifying mentally retarded pupils who required assignment to special classes. The goal was to prevent unfair exclusion of disruptive pupils from regular education on the basis of their behavior rather than their intellectual ability. Other researchers had tried to assess intelligence using simple laboratory measures of sensory responsiveness and reaction time (Cattell, 1890; Galton, 1883). Binet believed that very different kinds of test items were needed—ones that did not dissect intelligence into elementary processes, but instead required individuals to apply complex functions involved in intelligent behavior, such as memory, good judgment, and abstraction. Consequently, Binet and Simon devised a test of "general mental ability" that included a variety of verbal and nonverbal reasoning tasks. Their test was also the first *developmental* approach to test construction. Items varied in difficulty, and each was classified according to the age at which a typical child could first pass it (Brody, 1992).

The Binet test was so successful in predicting school performance that it became the basis for new intelligence tests developed in other countries. In 1916, Lewis Terman at Stanford University adapted it for use with American schoolchildren. Since then, the American version has been known as the Stanford-Binet Intelligence Scale. The Stanford-Binet has been revised several times over this century. Later we will see that it no longer provides just a single, holistic measure of intelligence. Nevertheless, many of its items continue to resemble those on Binet's original scale.

THE FACTOR ANALYSTS: A MULTIFACETED VIEW

As intelligence tests became more widely used, psychologists and educators became increasingly aware that a single score might not adequately represent human mental functioning. As Figure 8.1 on page 302 shows, a wide variety of tasks typically appear on intelligence tests for children. Researchers seeking clearer definitions of intelligence had to confront the important issue of whether it really is a holistic trait or a collection of many different abilities.

To resolve this dilemma, a special technique was used to analyze the performances of individuals on intelligence tests. **Factor analysis** is a complicated statistical procedure in which scores on many separate items are combined into a few factors, which substitute for the separate scores. Then the researcher gives each factor a name, based on common characteristics of items that are closely correlated with the factor. For example, if vocabulary, verbal comprehension, and verbal analogies items all correlate highly with the same factor, it might be labeled "verbal ability." Using this method, many efforts were made to identify the mental abilities that contribute to successful performance on intelligence tests.

EARLY FACTOR ANALYSTS.

The first influential factor analyst was British psychologist Charles Spearman (1927), who found that all the test items he examined correlated to some degree with one another. Therefore, Spearman proposed the existence of a common underlying **general factor**, or what he termed "**g**." At the same time, he noticed that test items were not perfectly correlated. In other words, they varied in the extent to which they tapped "g." Consequently, he suggested that each item also measured a **specific factor**, called "**s**," that was unique to the task. Spearman's identification of "g" and "s" led his view of mental abilities to be called the *two-factor theory of intelligence.*

According to Spearman, "g" was central and supreme, and he was especially interested in its psychological characteristics. With further study, Spearman concluded that "g" represented some kind of abstract reasoning power. Test items that required individuals to form relationships and apply general principles seemed to be the strongest correlates of "g," and they were also the best predictors of intellectual performance outside the testing situation.

Louis Thurstone (1938), an American contemporary of Spearman, soon took issue with his emphasis on "g." Instead, Thurstone argued, separate, unrelated intellectual abilities exist. Thurstone gave over 50 intelligence tests to a large number of college students, and their scores produced seven clear factors. As a result, he concluded that intelligence consists of seven distinct **primary mental abilities**: verbal meaning, perceptual speed, reasoning, number, rote memory, word fluency, and spatial visualization.

Spearman's and Thurstone's findings represent two different ways of thinking about intelligence. Today, each is supported by research and accounts for part of the story.

Factor analysis
A complicated statistical procedure that combines scores from many separate test items into a few factors, which substitute for the separate scores. Used to identify mental abilities that contribute to performance on intelligence tests.

General factor, or "g"
In Spearman's theory of intelligence, a common factor representing abstract reasoning power that underlies a wide variety of test items.

Specific factor, or "s"
In Spearman's theory of intelligence, a mental ability factor that is unique to a particular task.

Primary mental abilities
In Thurstone's theory of intelligence, seven distinct mental abilities identified through factor analysis (verbal meaning, perceptual speed, reasoning, number, rote memory, word fluency, and spatial visualization).

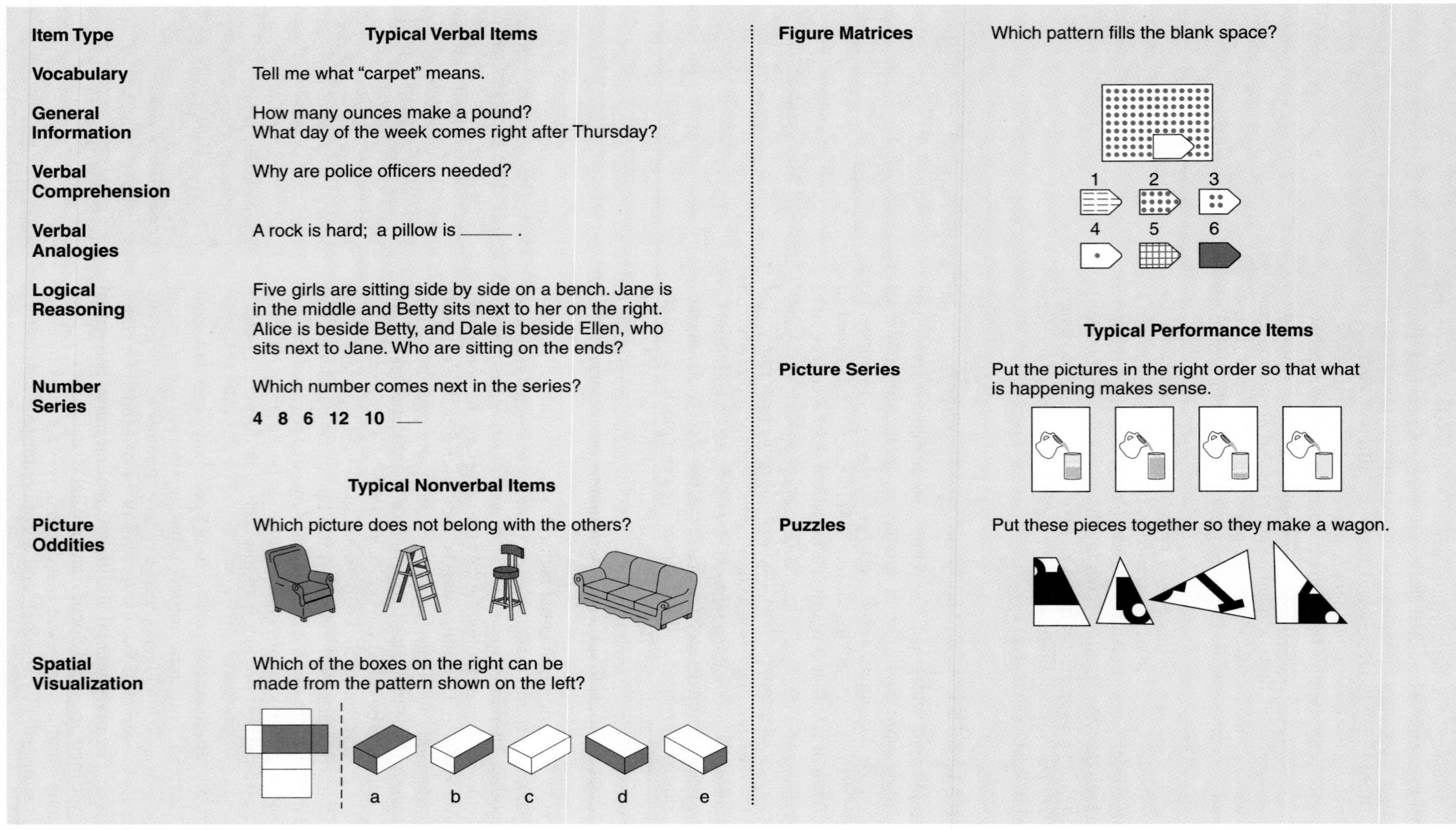

FIGURE 8.1

Items similar to those that appear on commonly used intelligence tests for children. In contrast to verbal items, nonverbal items do not require reading or direct use of language. Performance items are also nonverbal, but they require the child to draw or construct something rather than merely give a correct answer. (Logical reasoning, picture oddities, spatial visualization, and figure matrices items are adapted with the permission of The Free Press, a Division of Macmillan, Inc., from A. R. Jensen, 1980, Bias in Mental Testing, *New York: The Free Press, pp. 150, 154, 157.)*

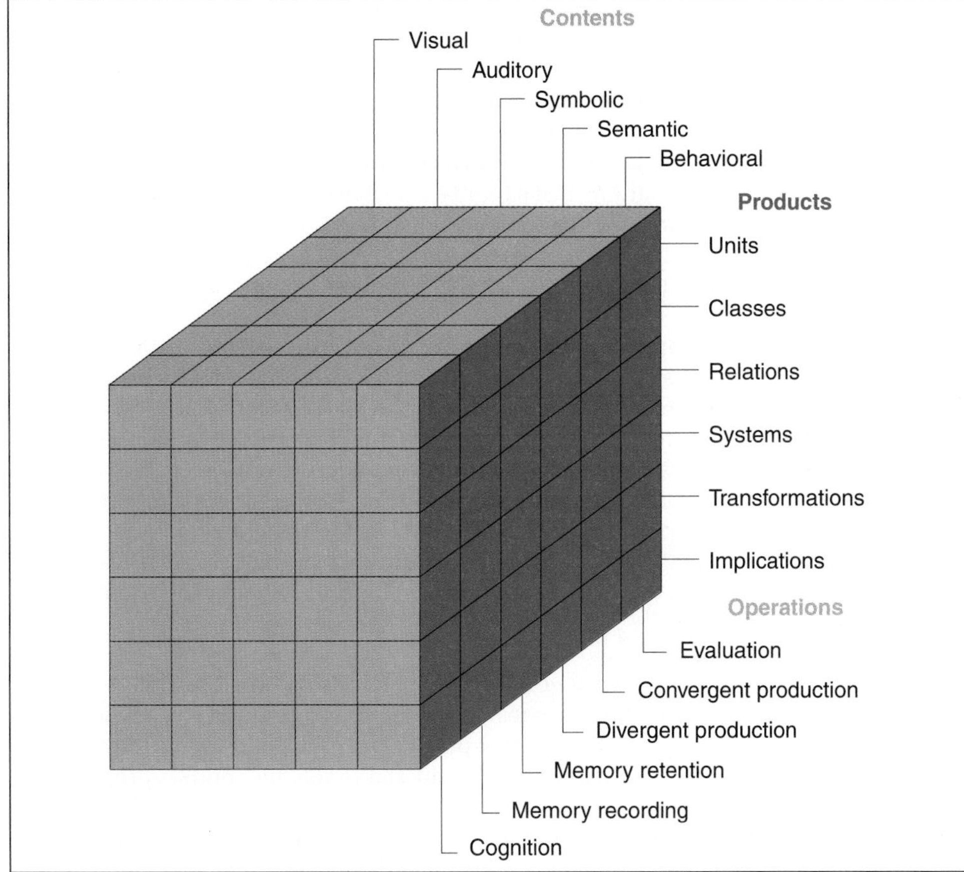

FIGURE 8.2

■ *Guilford's structure-of-intellect model. (From J. P. Guilford, 1988, "Some Changes in the Structure-of-Intellect Model,"* Educational and Psychological Measurement, *48, p. 3.)*

Later we will see that current theorists and test designers reconcile these two views by proposing *hierarchical models* of mental abilities. At the highest level is "g," assumed to be present to a greater or lesser degree in all specialized factors. These factors, in turn, are measured by subtests, or groups of related items. Subtest scores provide information about a child's strengths and weaknesses, and they can also be combined into an overall index of general intelligence (Brody, 1992).

■ MODERN FACTOR ANALYSTS. Several modern mental ability theorists have extended the efforts of the early factor analysts. Each offers a multifaceted perspective on intelligence with unique features.

Guilford's Structure-of-Intellect Model. J. P. Guilford (1967, 1985, 1988) rejected the existence of "g" and instead proposed a complex, three-dimensional **structure-of-intellect model** (see Figure 8.2). According to Guilford, every intellectual task can be classified according to (1) its content, (2) the mental operation involved, and (3) the product resulting from the operation. For example, think back to the similarities task Nora gave Jermaine, described at the beginning of this chapter. In Guilford's system, it would be classified as semantic (content), evaluation (operation), and relations (product). By combining the three dimensions in all possible ways, the structure-of-intellect model generates a total of 180 separate ability factors.

In addition to its large number of mental abilities, Guilford's model has other unusual features. Its "behavioral" content category acknowledges that a separate social intelligence exists, involving sensitivity to the mental states of others. Guilford also added tests of creative thinking to his factor analytic studies. He concluded that an essential operation for creativity is *divergent production*—the fluent generation of a wide variety of alternatives. In contrast, Guilford regarded *convergent production,* which involves arriving at a single correct answer, as noncreative.

Although Guilford's model has the largest number of mental abilities of any psychometric theory, other researchers have not obtained factor analytic support for it. Consequently, they question whether such an extensive list of factors accurately represents human intelligence. Recently, Guilford suggested that his 180 factors could be reduced to

Structure-of-intellect model
Guilford's 180-factor model of intelligence, which classifies each intellectual task according to three dimensions: content, mental operation, and product.

a smaller number of higher-order mental abilities. However, evidence for this hierarchical version of his theory is also limited (Brody, 1992).

R. B. Cattell's Crystallized versus Fluid Intelligence. Raymond B. Cattell's (1971, 1987) approach to defining intelligence differs sharply from Guilford's, as it accepts "g" and divides it into only two factors. **Crystallized intelligence** depends on culturally loaded, fact-oriented information. Tasks highly correlated with it include vocabulary, general information, and arithmetic problems. In contrast, **fluid intelligence** requires very little specific knowledge. It involves the ability to see complex relationships and solve problems, as in the number series, spatial visualization, and figure matrix items shown in Figure 8.1.

Among children who are similar in cultural and educational background, crystallized and fluid intelligence are highly correlated, and it is difficult to distinguish them. In these instances, the strong relationship is probably due to the fact that children who are high in fluid intelligence acquire specific information with greater ease. But when children who differ greatly in cultural and educational experiences are tested, the two abilities are easier to identify; children with the same fluid capacity may perform quite differently on tests that emphasize crystallized tasks. As these findings suggest, Cattell's theory has important implications for the issue of cultural bias in intelligence testing. We will see later that tests aimed at reducing culturally specific content usually emphasize fluid over crystallized items.

Carroll's Three-Stratum Theory of Intelligence. Recently, John Carroll (1993) used improved factor analytic techniques to reanalyze hundreds of studies of relationships among mental abilities carried out during the past 50 years. His findings yielded a **three-stratum theory of intelligence** that expands and elaborates the models proposed by Spearman, Thurstone, R. B. Cattell, and others. As Figure 8.3 shows, Carroll represents the structure of intelligence as a pyramid, with "g" at the top and eight broad abilities at the second stratum, arranged from left to right in terms of their decreasing strength of relationship with "g." Each broad ability is believed to be a basic, biological human characteristic that can influence a wide variety of behaviors. At the lowest stratum are narrow abilities—specific manifestations of second-stratum factors that result from experience with particular tasks.

Carroll's model is the most comprehensive classification of mental abilities to be confirmed by factor analytic research. As we will see in the next section, it provides a useful framework for investigators seeking to understand mental test performance in cognitive processing terms. The three-stratum theory highlights the multiplicity of intellectual factors sampled by current mental tests. Because there are so many, we can expect that a large proportion of the population can become quite good at one or several, and perhaps a great many (Carroll, 1993).

Crystallized intelligence
In Cattell's theory, a form of intelligence that depends on culturally loaded, fact-oriented information.

Fluid intelligence
In Cattell's theory, a form of intelligence that requires very little specific knowledge but involves the ability to see complex relationships and solve problems.

Three-stratum theory of intelligence
Carroll's theory, which represents the structure of intelligence as a pyramid, with "g" at the top; eight broad, biologically based abilities at the second stratum; and narrower manifestations of these abilities at the lowest stratum that result from experience with particular tasks. The most comprehensive classification of mental abilities to be confirmed by factor analytic research.

Componential analysis
A research procedure aimed at clarifying the cognitive processes responsible for intelligence test scores by correlating them with laboratory measures designed to assess the speed and effectiveness of information processing.

Recent Advances in Defining Intelligence

Although factor analysis has been the major approach to defining mental abilities, many researchers believe its usefulness will remain limited unless it is combined with other theoretical approaches to the study of human cognition. Factor analysts have been criticized for devoting too much attention to identifying factors and too little to clarifying the cognitive processes that underlie them. Once we discover exactly what separates individuals who can solve certain mental test items from those who cannot, we will know much more about why a particular child does well or poorly and what skills must be worked on to improve performance.

COMBINING PSYCHOMETRIC AND INFORMATION-PROCESSING APPROACHES

To overcome the limitations of factor analysis, some researchers have combined psychometric and information-processing approaches. These investigators conduct **componential analyses** of children's test scores by correlating them with laboratory measures

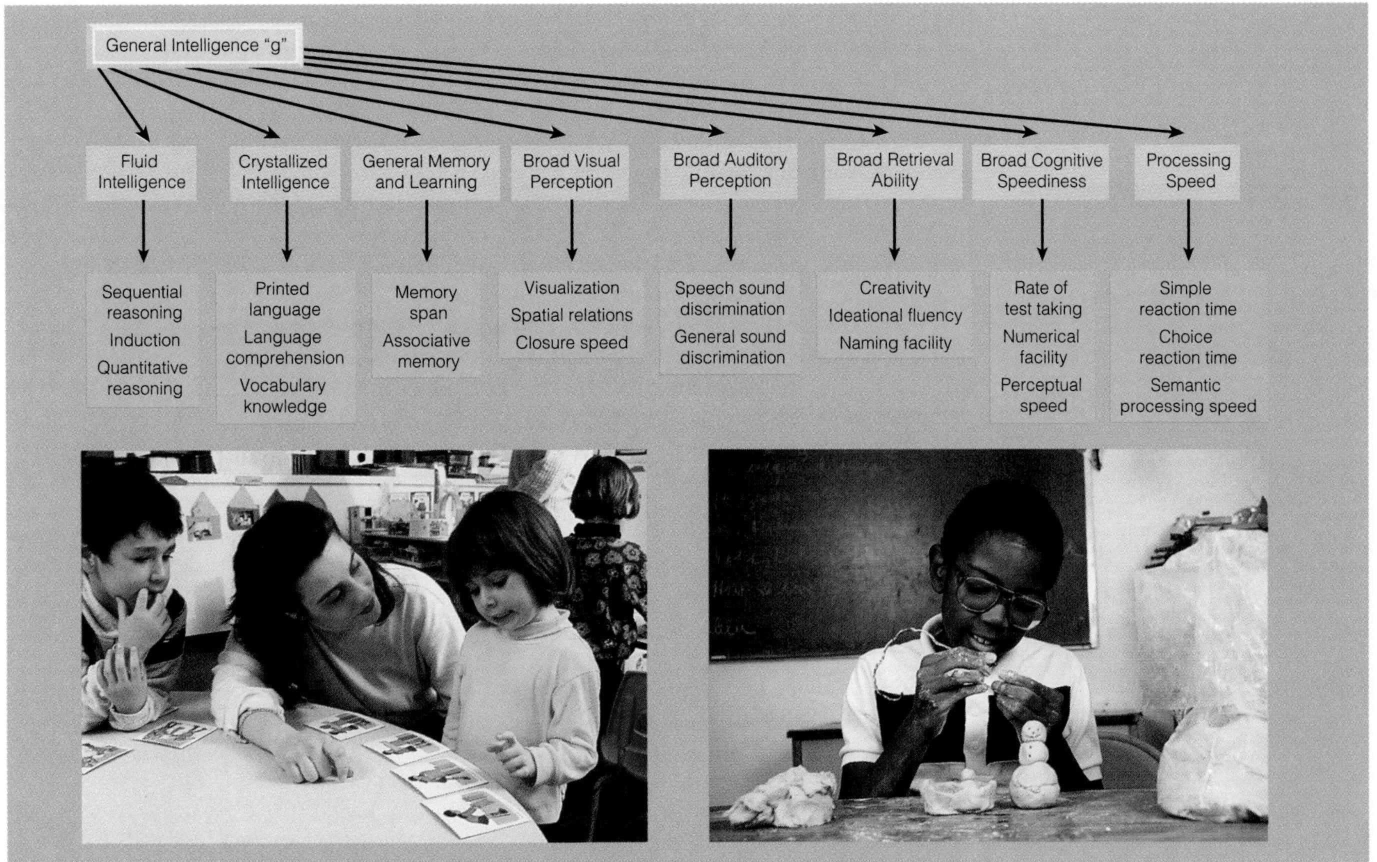

FIGURE 8.3

■ *Carroll's three-stratum theory of intelligence. Second-stratum abilities are arranged from left to right in terms of their decreasing strength of relationship with "g." The photos depict specific manifestations of second-stratum factors, listed at the lowest stratum. The child on the left completes a sequential reasoning task in which she arranges pictures to tell a story—a type of fluid intelligence. The child on the right uses art materials creatively to build a snowman, applying her broad retrieval ability. (Left, Will Faller; right, Myrleen Ferguson Cate) (From J. B. Carroll, 1993,* Human Cognitive Abilities: A Survey of Factor-Analytic Studies, *New York: Cambridge University Press, p. 626. Adapted by permission.)*

designed to assess the speed and effectiveness of information processing. In this way, they hope to provide process-oriented explanations of mental test performance (Sternberg, 1977).

Which information-processing components have turned out to be good predictors of intelligence? Many studies reveal that basic efficiency of thinking is correlated with the "g" factor. For example, speed of processing—measured in terms of reaction time to visual or auditory stimuli or through more complex tasks requiring scanning of information in working memory or retrieval from long-term memory—is moderately related to general intelligence and to gains in mental test performance over time (Deary, 1995; Kranzler & Jensen, 1989; Vernon, 1993).

These findings suggest that individuals whose nervous systems function more efficiently have an edge when it comes to intellectual skills. Because they can take in and manipulate information more quickly, they have more attentional resources available for using it to solve problems. In support of this interpretation, nerve conduction velocity and the rapidity and amplitude[1] of event-related potentials (ERPs, or EEG responses to specific stimulation) are modestly correlated with speed of processing and mental test scores (Vernon, 1993; Vernon & Mori, 1992). In addition, brain-imaging research reveals that the metabolic rate of the cortex when solving complex tasks is lower for more intelligent people, suggesting that they need to expend less mental effort (Haier et al., 1988, 1992).

Nevertheless, rapid responding is not the only processing correlate of mental test performance. Strategy use also makes a difference, and it explains some of the association

[1] The rapidity of ERPs is a measure of how quickly the brain responds to stimulation, and the amplitude reflects the amount of electrical activity that stimulation evokes. Both are associated with general intelligence.

between response speed and intelligence (Miller & Vernon, 1992). In one study, researchers used Siegler's strategy-choice model (see Chapter 7, page 288) to see if the way 4- to 6-year-olds apply strategies to simple addition problems is related to mental test scores. Adaptive strategy users—children who retrieved answers accurately, used backup techniques (such as counting) when they could not recall a math fact, and seldom guessed—did considerably better on a measure of general intelligence and on subtests of mathematical and spatial abilities than their less adaptive agemates (Geary & Burlingham-Dubree, 1989). As we saw in Chapter 7, children who apply strategies adaptively develop the capacity for fast, accurate retrieval in a skill area—an ability that seems to carry over to performance on intelligence test items.

■ *This boy solves a math problem with the help of a special set of small blocks. Children who apply strategies adaptively, using backup procedures when they cannot recall an answer rather than guessing, develop the capacity for fast, accurate retrieval and score higher on intelligence tests. (Stephen Marks)*

Componential research has also highlighted cognitive processes that appear unrelated to test performance but that children can rely on to compensate for tested mental ability. Recent evidence suggests that certain aspects of metacognition—awareness of problem-solving strategies and organizational and planning skills—are not good predictors of general intelligence (Casey et al., 1991; Kreitler & Kreitler, 1987). In one study, fourth and fifth graders who were average in mental ability but high in metacognitive knowledge about problem solving did far better on Piagetian formal operational tasks (such as the pendulum problem) than highly intelligent classmates who knew little about effective problem-solving techniques (Swanson, 1990).

As these findings illustrate, componential analyses are beginning to isolate specific cognitive skills on which training might be especially helpful to some children. Nevertheless, the componential approach has one major shortcoming. It attributes intelligence entirely to causes within the child. Yet throughout Chapter 7, we showed that cultural and situational factors profoundly affect children's cognitive skills. Recently, Robert Sternberg expanded the componential approach into a comprehensive theory that views intelligence as a product of both internal and external forces.

STERNBERG'S TRIARCHIC THEORY

Sternberg's (1985, 1988) **triarchic theory of intelligence** is made up of three interacting subtheories (see Figure 8.4). The first, the *componential subtheory,* spells out the information-processing skills that underlie intelligent behavior. You are already familiar with its main elements—metacognition, strategy application, and knowledge acquisition—from reading Chapter 7.

According to Sternberg, children's use of these components is not just a matter of internal capacity. It is also a function of the conditions under which intelligence is assessed. The *experiential subtheory* states that highly intelligent individuals, compared to

FIGURE 8.4

■ *Sternberg's triarchic theory of intelligence.*

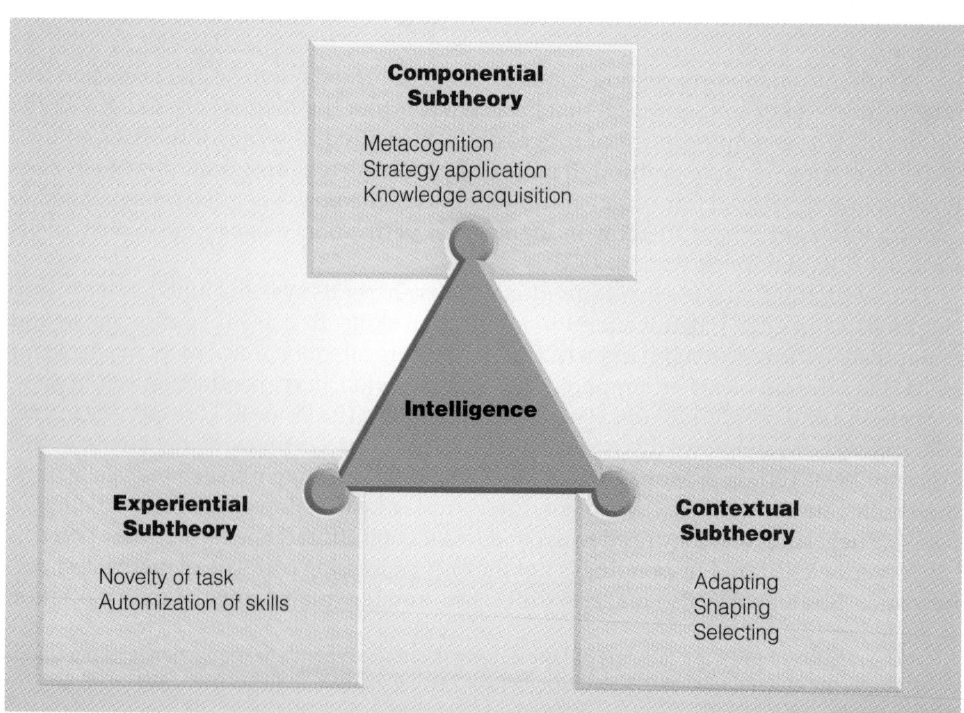

Triarchic theory of intelligence Sternberg's theory, which states that information processing skills, prior experience with tasks, and contextual (or cultural) factors interact to determine intelligent behavior.

less intelligent ones, process information more skillfully in novel situations. When given a relatively new task, the bright person learns rapidly, making strategies automatic so working memory is freed for more complex aspects of the situation.

Think, for a moment, about the implications of this idea for measuring children's intelligence. To accurately compare children in brightness—in ability to deal with novelty and learn efficiently—all children would need to be presented with equally unfamiliar test items. Otherwise, some children will appear more intelligent than others simply because of their past experiences, not because they are really more cognitively skilled. These children start with the unfair advantage of prior practice on the tasks.

This point brings us to the third part of Sternberg's model, his *contextual subtheory.* It proposes that intelligent people skillfully *adapt* their information-processing skills to fit with their personal desires and the demands of their everyday worlds. When they cannot adapt to a situation, they try to *shape,* or change, it to meet their needs. If they cannot shape it, they *select* new contexts that are consistent with their goals. The contextual subtheory emphasizes that intelligent behavior is never culture free. Because of their backgrounds, some children come to value behaviors required for success on intelligence tests, and they easily adapt to the tasks and testing conditions. Others with different life histories misinterpret the testing context or reject it entirely because it does not suit their needs. Yet such children may display very sophisticated abilities in daily life—for example, telling stories, engaging in elaborate artistic activities, accomplishing athletic feats, or interacting skillfully with other people (Sternberg, 1988).

Sternberg's theory emphasizes the complexity of human mental skills—in particular, their sensitivity to environmental contexts—and the limitations of current tests in assessing that complexity. Like Cattell's distinction between crystallized and fluid intelligence, Sternberg's ideas are relevant to the controversy surrounding cultural bias in intelligence testing, a topic we return to later in this chapter.

GARDNER'S THEORY OF MULTIPLE INTELLIGENCES

Howard Gardner's (1983, 1993) **theory of multiple intelligences** provides yet another view of how information-processing skills underlie intelligent behavior. But unlike the componential approach, it does not begin with existing mental tests and try to isolate the processing elements required to succeed on them. Instead, Gardner believes intelligence should be defined in terms of distinct sets of processing operations that permit individuals to solve problems, create products, and discover new knowledge in a diverse array of culturally valued activities. Accordingly, Gardner dismisses the idea of a single overarching mental ability, or "g," and proposes seven independent intelligences, which are described in Table 8.2.

Gardner acknowledges that if tests were available to assess all these abilities, factor analysis should yield low correlations among them. But he regards neurological support for their separateness as more persuasive. Research indicating that damage to a certain part of the adult brain influences only one ability (such as linguistic or spatial) while sparing others suggests that the affected ability is independent. The existence of prodigies, who show precocious development in only one area, such as language, music, or mathematics, also fits with Gardner's belief in distinct abilities.

Finally, Gardner argues that each intelligence has a unique biological potential, a distinct course of development, and different expert, or "end-state" performances. At the same time, he stresses that a lengthy process of education is required to transform any raw intellectual potential into a mature social role. This means that cultural values and learning opportunities have a great deal to do with the extent to which a child's strengths are realized and the ways they are expressed.

Does Gardner's theory remind you of the modular view of the mind we discussed in Chapter 6? Indeed, he is sympathetic to this position. Gardner's work has been especially helpful in efforts to understand and nurture children's special talents, a topic we will take up at the end of this chapter. At the same time, reservations have been raised about his theory. Neurological support for the independence of his intelligences is weak. Logico-mathematical ability, in particular, seems to be governed by many brain regions, not just one. Similarly, exceptionally gifted individuals exist whose abilities are broad rather than limited to a particular domain (Feldman & Goldsmith, 1991). Finally, current mental tests do tap several of Gardner's intelligences (linguistic, logico-mathematical, and spatial), and evidence for "g" suggests that they have common features.

Theory of multiple intelligences Gardner's theory, which identifies seven independent intelligences on the basis of distinct sets of processing operations applied in culturally meaningful activities (linguistic, logico-mathematical, musical, spatial, bodily/kinesthetic, interpersonal, intrapersonal).

TABLE 8.2

Gardner's Multiple Intelligences

Intelligence	Processing Operations	End-State Performance Possibilities
Linguistic	Sensitivity to the sounds, rhythms, and meanings of words and the different functions of language	Poet, journalist
Logico-mathematical	Sensitivity to, and capacity to detect, logical or numerical patterns; ability to handle long chains of logical reasoning	Mathematician, scientist
Musical	Ability to produce and appreciate pitch, rhythm (or melody), and aesthetic-sounding tones; understanding of the forms of musical expressiveness	Violinist, composer
Spatial	Ability to perceive the visual-spatial world accurately, to perform transformations on these perceptions, and to re-create aspects of visual experience in the absence of relevant stimuli	Sculptor, navigator
Bodily/kinesthetic	Ability to use the body skillfully for expressive as well as goal-directed purposes; ability to handle objects skillfully	Dancer, athlete
Interpersonal	Ability to detect and respond appropriately to the moods, temperaments, motivations, and intentions of others	Therapist, salesperson
Intrapersonal	Ability to discriminate complex inner feelings and to use them to guide one's own behavior; knowledge of one's own strengths, weaknesses, desires, and intelligences	Person with detailed, accurate self-knowledge

Sources: Gardner, 1983, 1993.

In sum, Gardner's list of abilities has yet to be firmly grounded in research. Nevertheless, his ideas have been powerful enough to reawaken the debate over a unitary versus multifaceted human intelligence. Still, without clear evidence in favor of one side or the other, most test designers (as we will see in the following sections) strike a balance between these two views.

BRIEF REVIEW

Binet and Simon's first successful intelligence test provided a single score designed to identify children who required assignment to special school classes. Factor analysts sought answers to the question of whether intelligence is a holistic trait or a collection of many different abilities. Their findings led to the identification of a general factor, or "g," as well as a wide variety of distinct mental abilities. Recently, researchers have combined the psychometric and information-processing approaches, conducting componential analyses aimed at uncovering the processing skills that predict mental test scores. Sternberg has expanded this approach into a triarchic theory that considers intelligence to be the combined result of processing skills, experience with tasks, and contextual (or cultural) influences. According to Gardner's theory of multiple intelligences, seven distinct domains of ability, each defined by unique processing operations, represent the diversity of human intelligence.

Representative Intelligence Tests for Children

A wide variety of tests are currently available to assess children's intelligence. Those that pupils take every two or three years in their classrooms are *group-administered tests.* They permit many children to be tested at once and require very little training of teachers who give them. Group tests are useful for instructional planning and identifying pupils who require more extensive evaluation with *individually administered tests.* Unlike group tests, individual tests demand considerable training and experience to give well. The examiner not only considers the child's answers but also carefully observes the child's behavior, noting such reactions as attentiveness to and interest in the tasks and wariness of the adult. These observations provide insights into whether the test score is accurate or underestimates the child's ability. Three individual tests are most often used to identify highly intelligent children and diagnose those with learning problems.

FIGURE 8.5

■ *"Unisex" child in the Stanford-Binet Intelligence Scale, designed to reduce gender bias in the test. (From R. L. Thorndike, E. P. Hagen, & J. M. Sattler, 1986,* The Stanford-Binet Intelligence Scale: Fourth Edition, Guide for Administering and Scoring, *Chicago: Riverside Publishing. Reprinted by permission.)*

THE STANFORD-BINET INTELLIGENCE SCALE

The **Stanford-Binet Intelligence Scale**, the modern descendant of Binet's first successful test, is appropriate for individuals between 2 years of age and adulthood. Its latest version measures both general intelligence and four intellectual factors: verbal reasoning, quantitative reasoning, abstract/visual (spatial) reasoning, and short-term memory (Thorndike, Hagen, & Sattler, 1986). Within these factors are 15 subtests that permit a detailed analysis of each child's mental abilities.

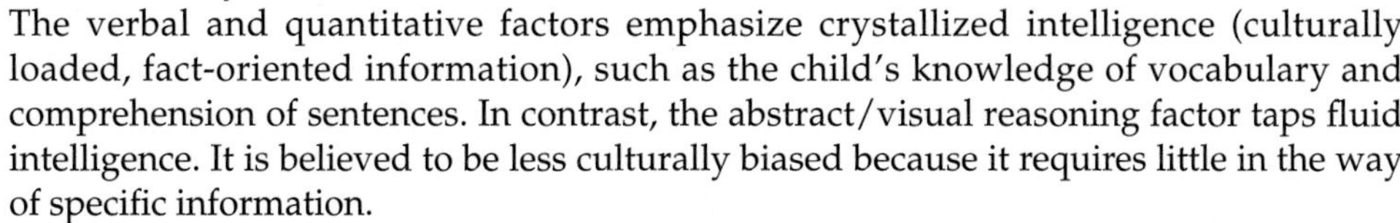

The verbal and quantitative factors emphasize crystallized intelligence (culturally loaded, fact-oriented information), such as the child's knowledge of vocabulary and comprehension of sentences. In contrast, the abstract/visual reasoning factor taps fluid intelligence. It is believed to be less culturally biased because it requires little in the way of specific information.

Like many current tests, the Stanford-Binet is designed to be sensitive to ethnic minority children and children with physical disabilities and to reduce gender bias. Pictures of children from different ethnic groups, a child in a wheelchair, and "unisex" figures that can be interpreted as male or female are included (see Figure 8.5).

THE WECHSLER INTELLIGENCE SCALE FOR CHILDREN

The **Wechsler Intelligence Scale for Children–III (WISC–III)** is the third edition of a widely used test for 6- through 16-year-olds. A downward extension of it, the *Wechsler Preschool and Primary Scale of Intelligence–Revised (WPPSI–R),* is appropriate for children 3 through 8 (Wechsler, 1989, 1991). The Wechsler tests offered both a measure of general intelligence and a variety of separate factor scores long before the Stanford-Binet. As a result, over the past two decades, psychologists and educators have come to prefer the WISC and the WPPSI for individual assessment of children.

Both the WISC–III and the WPPSI–R measure two broad intellectual factors: verbal and performance. Each contains 6 subtests, yielding 12 separate scores in all. Performance items (look back at Figure 8.1 on page 302 for examples) require the child to arrange materials rather than talk to the examiner. Consequently, these tests provided one of the first means through which non-English-speaking children and children with speech and language disorders could demonstrate their intellectual strengths.

The Wechsler tests were also the first to be standardized on children representing the total population of the United States, including ethnic minorities. Their broadly representative standardization samples have served as models for many other tests, including the recent version of the Stanford-Binet.

THE KAUFMAN ASSESSMENT BATTERY FOR CHILDREN

Although the Stanford-Binet and Wechsler scales are the most well-known intelligence tests, others based on alternative approaches do exist. The **Kaufman Assessment Battery for Children (K-ABC)** is one of the few tests to be grounded in an explicit cognitive theory (Luria, 1966). Published in 1983, the K-ABC measures the intelligence of children from ages 2½ through 12 on the basis of two broad cognitive processing skills. The

Stanford-Binet Intelligence Scale
An individually administered intelligence test that is the modern descendent of Alfred Binet's first successful test for children. Measures general intelligence and four factors: verbal reasoning, quantitative reasoning, abstract/visual (spatial) reasoning, and short-term memory.

Wechsler Intelligence Scale for Children–III (WISC–III)
An individually administered intelligence test that includes a measure of both general intelligence and a variety of verbal and performance scores.

Kaufman Assessment Battery for Children (K-ABC)
An individually administered intelligence test that measures two broad types of processing skills: simultaneous and sequential processing. One of the few tests to be grounded in an explicit cognitive theory.

first, *simultaneous processing,* demands that children integrate a variety of stimuli at the same time, as when they are asked to label an incomplete picture or recall the placement of objects on a page presented only briefly. The second, *sequential processing,* refers to problems that require children to think in a step-by-step fashion. Examples include repeating a series of digits or hand movements presented by the examiner.

The K-ABC makes a special effort to respond to the needs of culturally different children through its unusually flexible administration procedures. If a child fails one of the first three items on any subtest, the examiner is permitted to "teach the task." The tester can use alternative wording and gestures and may even communicate in a language other than English (Kaufman & Kaufman, 1983).

Like the most recent Stanford-Binet, the K-ABC is not without critics. Some point out that the test samples a narrow range of information-processing skills and that there is little research support for the simultaneous–sequential processing distinction (Conoley, 1990; Sternberg, 1984). Nevertheless, the K-ABC is responsive to a new trend to define intelligence in terms of cognitive processes, and it is likely to inspire new tests that draw on other theories.

INFANT INTELLIGENCE TESTS

Accurately measuring the intelligence of infants is an especially challenging task. Unlike children, babies cannot answer questions or follow directions. All we can do is present them with stimuli, coax them to respond, and observe their behavior. In addition, infants are not necessarily cooperative subjects. They are likely to become distracted, fatigued, or bored during testing. Some tests depend heavily on information supplied by parents to compensate for the uncertain behavior of these young test-takers.

Most infant measures consist largely of perceptual and motor responses. For example, the *Bayley Scales of Infant Development,* a commonly used infant test, was inspired by the early normative work of Arnold Gesell (see Chapter 1, page 12). It consists of two parts: (1) the Mental Scale, which includes such items as turning to a sound, looking for a fallen object, building a tower of cubes, and naming pictures; and (2) the Motor Scale, which assesses fine and gross motor skills, such as grasping, sitting, drinking from a cup, and jumping. Despite careful construction, infant tests emphasizing these types of items are poor predictors of intelligence during the childhood years, at least for samples of normal babies. The consistency of this finding has led researchers to conclude that infant perceptual and motor behaviors do not represent the same aspects of intelligence assessed in childhood.

In an effort to increase its predictive validity, the Bayley test has been extensively revised (The Psychological Corporation, 1993). Its new version includes items that emphasize infant memory, problem solving, categorization, and other complex cognitive skills—responses that, as we will see in a moment, are far more likely to correlate with later mental test scores. Nevertheless, traditional infant tests do show some predictability for very low-scoring babies (Colombo, 1993). As a result, they continue to be used for screening—helping to identify for further observation and intervention infants who have a high likelihood of experiencing future developmental problems.

Recall from Chapter 4 that dishabituation to visual stimuli is the best available infant correlate of childhood intelligence. Unlike typical infant test items, it seems to tap aspects of cognitive processing (speed of thinking and attention, memory, and response to novelty) that are important in the verbal, conceptual, and problem-solving skills assessed at later ages. Recently, a test made up entirely of habituation–dishabituation items, the *Fagan Test of Infant Intelligence,* was constructed. To take it, the infant sits on the mother's lap and views a series of pictures. After exposure to each one, looking time toward a novel picture that is paired with the familiar one is recorded. Scores on the Fagan test are moderately correlated with IQ during the preschool years. In addition, the Fagan test is highly effective in identifying babies who (without intervention) will soon show serious delays in mental development (Fagan & Detterman, 1992).

For many years, infant tests based on Piaget's theory have been available. For example, Užgiris and Hunt's (1975) *Infant Psychological Development Scale* contains eight subtests, each of which assesses an important sensorimotor milestone, such as imitation and object permanence. Like the habituation–dishabituation response, object permanence is a better predictor of preschool intelligence than traditional infant tests, perhaps because it, too, reflects a basic cognitive process—problem solving (Wachs, 1975).

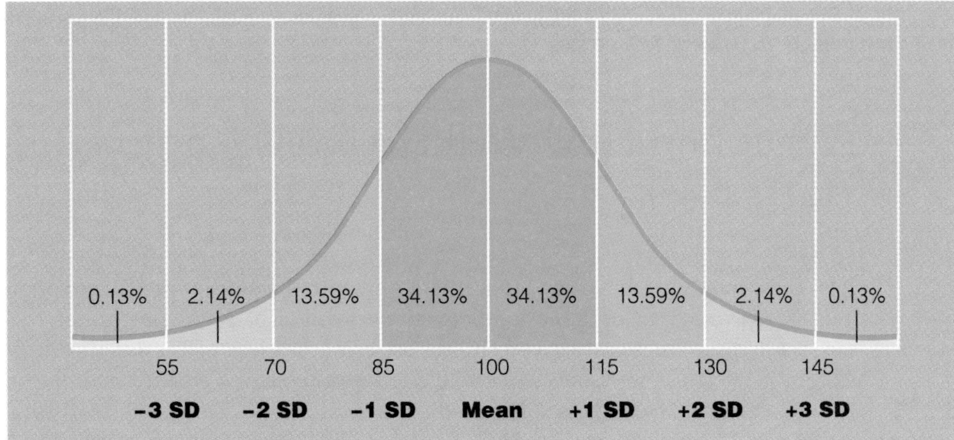

FIGURE 8.6

The normal curve, with the baseline scaled in both IQ and standard deviation (SD) units. Areas under the curve are given in percentages. By summing the percentages to the left of an individual's IQ, we can obtain a percentile rank, which refers to the proportion of people of the same age that individual scored better than on the test.

The Computation and Distribution of IQ Scores

Scores on intelligence tests, whether designed for infants, children, or adults, are usually arrived at in the same way—by computing an **intelligence quotient (IQ)**, which indicates the extent to which the raw score (number of items passed) deviates from the typical performance of same-age individuals. When a test is constructed, it is given to a large, representative sample of individuals. Performances at each age level form a *normal, or bell-shaped, curve* in which most people fall near the center and progressively fewer fall out toward the extremes. Two important features of the normal curve are its *mean,* or the average score, and its *standard deviation,* which provides a measure of the average variability, or "spread-outness," of the scores from the mean.

Most intelligence tests convert their raw scores so the mean is set at 100 and the standard deviation at 15. As Figure 8.6 shows, knowing the mean and standard deviation, we can determine the percentage of individuals at each age who fall above or below a certain score. Then, when we speak of a particular IQ, we know exactly what it means. For example, as Table 8.3 makes clear, a child with an IQ of 100 does better than 50 percent of same-age children. A child with an IQ of 85 does better than only 16 percent of her agemates, whereas a child with an IQ of 130 outperforms 98 percent of them. Look at Figure 8.6 once more, and notice how most scores cluster near the mean. The IQs of the great

TABLE 8.3

Meaning of Different IQ Scores

Score	Percentile Rank *Child does better than . . . percent of same-age children*
70	2
85	16
100 (average IQ)	50
115	84
130	98

Intelligence quotient (IQ)
A score that permits an individual's performance on an intelligence test to be compared to the typical performance of same-age individuals.

majority of the population (95.5 percent) fall between 70 and 130, with only a few people achieving very high or very low scores.

What and How Well Do Intelligence Tests Predict?

Already we have seen that infant perceptual and motor tasks are poor predictors of later intellectual performance. But what about the more frequently given childhood tests? Psychologists and educators who use test scores to make decisions about the educational placement of children assume that they are good indicators of future intelligence and scholastic performance. How well does IQ actually fare as a predictive measure?

STABILITY OF IQ SCORES

Stability refers to how effectively IQ predicts itself from one age to the next. Do children who obtain a particular IQ at 3 or 4 years perform about the same during elementary school and again when tested in high school? To answer this question, researchers rely on longitudinal studies in which the same children have been tested repeatedly over many ages.

■ **CORRELATIONAL STABILITY.** One way of examining the stability of IQ is to correlate scores obtained from repeated testings. This tells us whether children who score low or high in comparison to their agemates at one point in time continue to do so later. Examining these correlations, researchers have identified two generalizations about the stability of IQ:

1. *The older the child at time of first testing, the better the prediction of later IQ*. For example, in one longitudinal study, the correlation between scores at 2 and 5 years was only .32. It rose to .70 between ages 5 and 8, and .85 between 9 and 12 (Honzik, Macfarlane, & Allen, 1948). Preschool IQs do not predict school-age scores as well as later measures, but after age 6, there is good stability, with many correlations in the .70s and .80s. Relationships between two testings obtained in adolescence are as high as the .80s and .90s (Humphreys, 1989; Sontag, Baker, & Nelson, 1958).

2. The closer in time two testings are, the stronger the relationship between the scores. For example, a 4-year-old IQ correlates with a 5-year score at .72, but prediction drops by age 6 to .62. By age 18, it has declined to .42 (Honzik, Macfarlane, & Allen, 1948).

Taken together, these findings indicate that before 5 or 6 years, IQ is largely a measure of present ability, not a dependable, enduring measure. Why do preschool scores predict less well than later scores? One frequently cited reason is similar to the one we discussed with respect to infant tests: differences in the nature of test items. Concrete knowledge tends to be tested at younger ages, abstract problem solving later. Success on the first may require different skills than success on the second (Hayslip, 1994). Another explanation is that during early periods of rapid development, one child may spurt ahead of another and reach a plateau, whereas a second child, moving along slowly and steadily from behind, may catch up with and eventually overtake the first. Because children frequently change places with one another in a distribution during periods of rapid change, all measures of developmental progress, including height and weight, are less stable and predictable at these times. IQ seems to be no exception.

■ **STABILITY OF ABSOLUTE SCORES.** So far, we have looked at IQ stability in terms of how well children maintain their relative standing among agemates over time. We can also view stability in absolute terms by examining each child's profile of IQ scores on a series of repeated testings. Longitudinal research reveals that the majority of children

■ *A wealth of research indicates that IQ scores are effective predictors of scholastic performance. Researchers disagree, however, on the underlying basis of this relationship. (Dennis MacDonald/ The Picture Cube)*

experience substantial IQ fluctuations over childhood and adolescence—in most cases, 10 to 20 points, and sometimes much more (McCall, 1993).

Children who change the most tend to have orderly profiles in which scores either increase or decrease with age. A close look at their characteristics and life experiences highlights factors that may be responsible for these IQ variations. Gainers were more independent and competitive about doing well in school. In addition, their parents were more interested in their intellectual accomplishments, applied greater pressure to succeed, and used rational, democratic discipline. In contrast, decliners tended to have parents who made little effort to stimulate them and who showed extremes in child rearing, using either very severe or very lax discipline (Honzik, Macfarlane, & Allen, 1948; McCall, Appelbaum, & Hogarty, 1973; Sontag, Baker, & Nelson, 1958).

When ethnic minority children who live in poverty are selected for special study, many show IQ declines. Both genetic and environmental factors contribute to children's IQ profiles (Cardon et al., 1992). Yet environment seems to be the overriding factor in the decreasing scores of poverty-stricken youngsters. According to the **cumulative deficit hypothesis**, the effects of underprivileged rearing conditions worsen the longer children remain in them. As a result, early cognitive deficits lead to more deficits that become harder to overcome as children get older (Klineberg, 1963). This idea has served as the basis for many early intervention programs, which are intensive efforts to offset these declines.

What evidence exists to support the cumulative deficit? In a study of African-American children growing up under severely depressed conditions in the rural South, older siblings consistently obtained lower IQs than their younger brothers and sisters. But no such relation appeared for less disadvantaged African-American children living in California (Jensen, 1974). This finding is consistent with a cumulative deficit rather than a genetically determined IQ profile. To fit with a genetic explanation, both the southern and California-reared groups should have displayed age-related IQ declines.

In sum, many children show substantial changes in the absolute value of IQ that are the combined result of personal characteristics, child-rearing practices, and the quality of their living environments. Nevertheless, once IQ becomes reasonably stable in a correlational sense, it predicts a variety of outcomes, as we will see in the following sections.

IQ AS A PREDICTOR OF SCHOLASTIC PERFORMANCE

Thousands of studies reveal that intelligence tests have accomplished their goal of predicting academic achievement. Correlations range from .40 to .70 and are typically around .50 (Brody, 1992). Children with higher IQs also get better grades and stay in school longer. As early as age 7, IQ is moderately correlated with adult educational attainment (McCall, 1977).

Cumulative deficit hypothesis
A view that attributes the age-related decline in IQ among poverty-stricken ethnic minority children to the compounding effects of underprivileged rearing conditions.

Why is IQ an effective predictor of scholastic performance? Researchers differ in how they answer this question. Some believe IQ and achievement both depend on the same abstract reasoning processes that underlie Spearman's "g." A child well endowed with "g" is better able to acquire knowledge and skills taught in school. That IQ correlates best with achievement in the more abstract school subjects, such as English, mathematics, and science, is consistent with this interpretation (Jensen, 1980).

Other researchers argue that intelligence and achievement both sample from the same pool of culturally specific information. From this point of view, an intelligence test is partly an achievement test, and a child's past experiences affect performance on both measures. Support for this view comes from evidence that crystallized intelligence (which reflects acquired knowledge) does a much better job of predicting academic achievement than does its fluid counterpart (Kaufman, Kamphaus, & Kaufman, 1985).

As you can probably imagine, researchers who believe heredity plays a crucial role in individual differences in IQ prefer the first of these explanations. Those who favor the power of environment prefer the second. Since the IQ–achievement correlation is stronger among identical than fraternal twins, heredity does seem to be important (Thompson, Detterman, & Plomin, 1991). But children's experiences also contribute. For example, findings reviewed in the Cultural Influences box on the following page indicate that IQ not only predicts future achievement but is itself increased by years of schooling! Clearly, the relationship between intelligence and achievement is complex and determined by multiple factors.

Finally, although IQ predicts achievement better than any other tested measure, notice that the correlation is far from perfect. Other factors, such as motivation and personality characteristics that lead some children to try hard and want to do well in school, are just as important in accounting for individual differences in scholastic performance (Neisser et al., 1996).

IQ AS A PREDICTOR OF OCCUPATIONAL ATTAINMENT AND PERFORMANCE

Psychologists and educators would probably be less concerned with IQ scores if they were unrelated to long-term indicators of life success. But research indicates that childhood IQ predicts adult occupational attainment just about as well as it correlates with academic achievement. By second grade, pupils with the highest IQs are those who are most likely to enter prestigious professions, such as medicine, science, law, and engineering (McCall, 1977). Furthermore, IQ is modestly related to how successful a person is likely to be within an occupation. Employees who score higher on mental tests tend to receive higher job competence ratings from supervisors in a wide range of occupations (Hunter & Hunter, 1984).

Once again, however, we must keep in mind that the relationship between IQ and occupational attainment is far from perfect. Factors related to family background, such as parental encouragement, modeling of career success, and connections in the world of work, also predict occupational choice and attainment (Grotevant & Cooper, 1988). Furthermore, years of schooling is a stronger predictor of occupational success than is IQ (Featherman, 1980). And we have already seen that IQ and schooling appear to be mutually influential.

Personal variables also figure prominently in career achievement. In 1923, Lewis Terman initiated a longitudinal study of over 1,500 children with IQs above 135, who were followed well into mature adulthood. By middle age, more than 86 percent of the men in the sample had entered high-status professional and business occupations, a higher percentage than would have been expected for a random sample of individuals from similar home backgrounds (Terman & Oden, 1959).[2] But not all were professionally successful. Looking closely at those who fared best compared to those who fared worst, Terman found that their IQs were similar, averaging around 150. But the highly successful group appeared to have "a special drive to succeed, a need to achieve, that had been with them from grammar school onward" (Goleman, 1980, p. 31). They also experienced

[2] Born in the early part of this century during an era quite different from our own, nearly half the women in Terman's sample became housewives. However, of those who had professional careers, there were examples of outstanding accomplishments. Among them were scientists (one of whom contributed to the development of the polio vaccine), several novelists and journalists, and highly successful businesswomen (Terman & Oden, 1959).

CULTURAL INFLUENCES

Does Schooling Influence IQ?

It is widely accepted that intelligence affects achievement in school, but how important is schooling in the development of intelligence? Stephen Ceci (1990, 1991) reviewed hundreds of studies addressing this question. Taken together, they suggest that events taking place in classrooms have a profound effect on mental test performance.

Consider, first, the small but consistent drop in IQ that occurs over the summer months, especially among low-income children, whose summer activities least resemble school tasks. For advantaged children, whose vacation pursuits (such as academic-type camps) are often like those of school, the summer decline does not occur (Heyns, 1978).

Research dating back to the early part of this century reveals that irregular school attendance has an even greater impact on IQ. In one study, test scores of children growing up in "hollows" of the Blue Ridge Mountains were compared. All were descendants of Scottish-Irish and English immigrants, whose families had lived in the hollows for generations. One hollow was located at the foot of the mountains and had schools in session nine months of the year. In the other more isolated hollows, schooling was irregular. Children's IQs varied substantially with amount of schooling available. Those who received the most had a 10- to 30-point advantage (Sherman & Key, 1932).

■ *These Appalachian children check out books from a mobile library. Research in the early part of this century revealed that in the Blue Ridge Mountains, children whose schools were in session 9 months a year scored better on intelligence tests than did children living in isolated "hollows" where schooling was irregular. (Ken Fujihira/Monkmeyer)*

Delayed entry into school is similarly related to test scores. In the Netherlands during World War II, many schools were closed as a result of the Nazi occupation. The IQs of children who started school several years late dropped about 7 points (DeGroot, 1951). Similar findings come from a study of children of Indian settlers in South Africa, whose schooling was postponed up to 4 years because their villages did not have teachers. Compared to Indian children in nearby villages who attended school, they showed a loss of 5 IQ points per year (Ramphal, 1962).

Dropping out of school also has a detrimental effect on IQ. In a Swedish study, a large random sample of 13-year-old boys were given intelligence tests. At age 18, they were retested as part of the country's national military registration. The impact of dropping out was determined by comparing children who were similar in IQ, social class, and school grades at age 13. Each year of high school not completed amounted to a loss of 1.8 IQ points, up to a maximum of 8 points for all 4 years of high school (Härnqvist, 1968).

Although many factors contribute to individual differences in mental test performance, schooling clearly emerges as a major force. Ceci (1991) believes it influences IQ in at least three ways: (1) by teaching children factual knowledge relevant to test questions; (2) by promoting information-processing skills, such as memory strategies and categorization, that are tapped by test items; and (3) by encouraging attitudes and values that foster successful test taking, such as listening carefully to an adult's questions, answering under time pressure, and trying hard.

more intellectually stimulating home lives and a lower rate of family disruption due to parental divorce—factors that may have contributed to their achievement-oriented style.

Finally, once a person enters an occupation, abilities grouped under the label **practical intelligence** (because they are apparent in the real world but not in testing situations) predict on-the-job performance at least as well or better than IQ. Practical intelligence involves "knowing how" rather than "knowing that" (Sternberg et al., 1995). It can be seen in the assembly line worker who discovers the fewest moves needed to complete a product or the business manager who increases productivity by making her subordinates feel valued. Unlike IQ, no ethnic group differences in practical intelligence exist. And a growing body of evidence reveals that the two types of intelligence show little or no correlation with one another and make independent contributions to job success (Ceci & Liker, 1986; Scribner, 1986; Wagner & Sternberg, 1990).

In sum, occupational outcomes are a complex function of traditionally measured intelligence, education, motivation, family influences, special opportunity, and practical know-how. At present, no clear evidence indicates that IQ is more important than any of these other factors.

Practical intelligence
Abilities apparent in the real world, not in testing situations, that involve "knowing how" rather than "knowing that."

IQ AS A PREDICTOR OF PSYCHOLOGICAL ADJUSTMENT

Is IQ so influential that it predicts indicators of life success beyond school and the workplace, such as emotional and social adjustment? During middle childhood, children with higher IQs tend to be better liked by their agemates (Hartup, 1983). But the reasons for this association are not clear. A child's social competence is also related to child-rearing practices, health, physical appearance, and personality, all of which are correlated with IQ.

Another way of exploring the relationship between IQ and psychological adjustment is to look at the mental test performance of children who are clearly poorly adjusted, such as highly aggressive children who engage in norm-violating acts. Chronic delinquents do tend to have lower IQs, but the association is weak, and researchers believe that IQ probably does not play a causal role (Hirschi & Hindelang, 1977). Instead, the troubled family lives of these youngsters appear to increase the chances of slow mental development and poor school performance. Young people who fail repeatedly in school are likely to conclude that traditional routes to occupational success will be closed to them. Consequently, they may seek alternative sources of reward, turning to antisocial peer groups and criminal behavior (Patterson, DeBaryshe, & Ramsey, 1989).

Finally, many adjustment disorders, such as high anxiety, fearfulness, social withdrawal, and depression, are unrelated to mental test scores (Graham, 1979). When we look at the evidence as a whole, we must conclude that a high IQ offers little guarantee of happiness and life satisfaction. And its imperfect prediction of other indicators of success, such as scholastic performance and occupational attainment, provides strong justification for never relying on IQ alone to forecast a child's future or make important educational placement decisions.

BRIEF REVIEW

Intelligence tests for children typically measure overall intelligence as well as a variety of separate factors. The Stanford-Binet and Wechsler scales are the most commonly used individually administered tests. The Kaufman Assessment Battery for Children is among the first major tests to be grounded in an explicit cognitive theory. Traditional infant tests, which consist largely of perceptual and motor responses, predict childhood intelligence poorly. Because tests of recognition memory and object permanence tap basic cognitive processes, they are better predictors. Computation of IQ permits a direct comparison of a child's score with a representative sample of same-age children.

Research consistently shows that IQ is an effective predictor of scholastic performance and occupational attainment. It is also linked to some aspects of psychological adjustment. However, a wide variety of personal, familial, and experiential factors also contribute to these outcomes. Although a high IQ does offer certain advantages, IQ alone tells us little that is definite about a child's chances for future success.

Ethnic and Social-Class Differences in IQ

When we compare individuals in terms of academic achievement, years of education, and the status of their occupations, it quickly becomes clear that certain sectors of the population are advantaged over others. In searching for the roots of these disparities, researchers have compared the IQ scores of ethnic and social-class groups. Their findings are responsible for sparking the IQ nature–nurture debate. If group differences in IQ exist, then either there must be genetic differences between rich and poor and black and white children, or children from economically disadvantaged backgrounds must have fewer opportunities to acquire the skills needed for successful test performance.

■ *What are the origins of ethnic and social-class differences in intelligence? Research aimed at answering this question has been the subject of heated controversy. (Mary Kate Denny/PhotoEdit)*

In the 1970s, the IQ nature–nurture controversy escalated, after psychologist Arthur Jensen (1969) published a controversial article in the *Harvard Educational Review,* entitled "How Much Can We Boost IQ and Scholastic Achievement?" Jensen's answer to this question was "not much." He argued that heredity is largely responsible for individual, ethnic, and social-class differences in IQ, a position he continues to maintain (Jensen, 1980, 1985).

Jensen's work received widespread public attention. It was followed by an outpouring of responses and research studies. In addition, there were ethical challenges from scientists deeply concerned that his conclusions would be used inappropriately to fuel social prejudices. Recently, the controversy was rekindled in Richard Herrnstein and Charles Murray's *The Bell Curve* (1994). Like Jensen, these authors concluded that the contribution of heredity to individual and social-class differences in IQ is substantial. At the same time, they stated that the relative role of heredity and environment in the black–white IQ gap remains unresolved. Before we consider the evidence, let's look at group differences in IQ scores, since they are at the heart of the controversy.

DIFFERENCES IN GENERAL INTELLIGENCE

American black children score, on the average, 15 points below American white children on measures of general intelligence (Brody, 1992). A smaller social-class difference also exists. In one large-scale study, low-income children scored 9 points below middle-income children (Jensen & Figueroa, 1975). Since 47 percent of African-American children live in poverty compared to 23 percent of all children in the United States, a reasonable question is whether social class fully accounts for the black–white IQ difference. It accounts for some but not all of it. When black and white children are matched on family income, the black–white IQ gap is reduced by only a third (Jencks, 1972; Jensen & Reynolds, 1982).

No ethnic differences exist on infant measures of dishabituation to visual stimuli, which are good predictors of later IQ (Fagan & Singer, 1983). But before the third year of life, African-American children lag behind their white counterparts on other mental tests, a difference that persists into adulthood (Brody, 1992). Still, we must keep in mind that there is great variability in IQ *within* each ethnic and social-class group. For example, as Figure 8.7 shows, the IQ distributions of blacks and whites overlap greatly. About 16 percent of blacks score above the white mean, and the same percentage of whites score below the black mean. In fact, ethnicity and social class account for only about one-fourth of the total variation in IQ (Jensen, 1980). Nevertheless, these group differences are large enough and serious enough that they cannot be ignored.

DIFFERENCES IN SPECIFIC MENTAL ABILITIES

Are ethnic and social-class differences limited to certain kinds of mental abilities? Arthur Jensen believes so. In his **Level I–Level II theory**, Jensen distinguishes two kinds

Level I–Level II theory
Jensen's controversial theory, which states that ethnic and social-class differences in IQ are due to genetic differences in higher-order, abstract forms of intelligence (Level II) rather than basic memory skills (Level I).

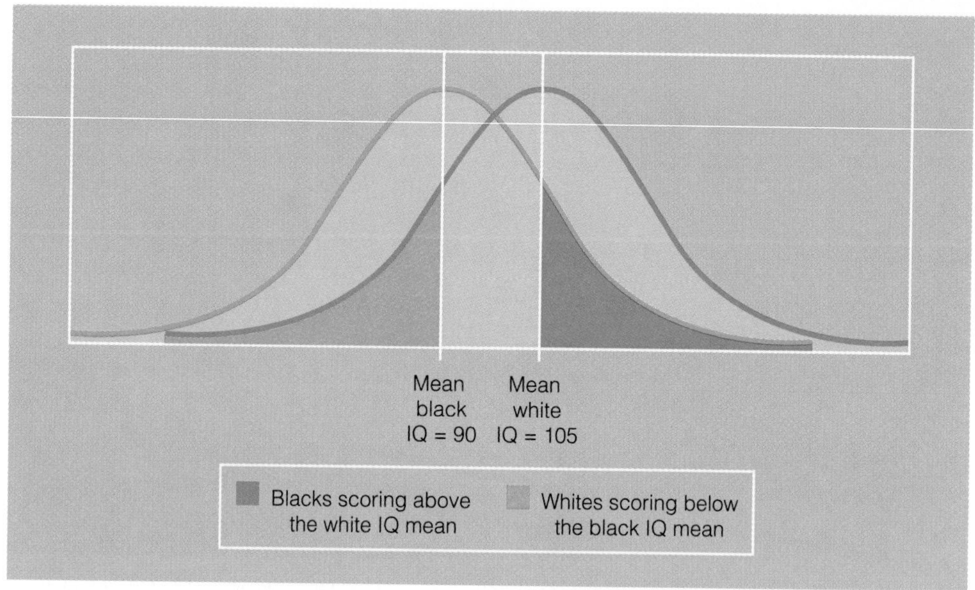

FIGURE 8.7

IQ score distributions for black and for white children. The means represent approximate values obtained in studies of children reared by their biological parents.

of intelligence. Level I refers to items emphasizing short-term and rote memory, such as digit span and recall of basic arithmetic facts. In contrast, Level II involves abstract reasoning and problem solving—items strongly correlated with Spearman's "g," such as vocabulary, verbal comprehension, spatial visualization, and figure matrices. (Turn back to Figure 8.1 on page 302 to review examples of these items.)

According to Jensen, black–white and (to a lesser extent) social-class differences in IQ are due to Level II abilities; the groups are about the same in Level I intelligence (Jensen, 1985, 1988). Furthermore, Jensen indicated that among Level II abilities, black children do worst on the least culturally loaded, fluid-type items (such as figure matrices) and best on crystallized tasks (such as vocabulary). Therefore, he argued, black–white IQ differences cannot be caused by cultural bias in the tests. Jensen's conclusion—that blacks are less well endowed than whites with higher-order, abstract forms of intelligence—intensified public outcries about the racist implications of his work.

Is there support for Jensen's Level I–Level II theory? In reviewing a large number of studies, one researcher judged that most were consistent with it (Vernon, 1981, 1987). But others have not been able to confirm the theory. For example, Nathan Brody (1987) found that test items strongly correlated with "g" did not always produce the largest black–white IQ differences. A second group of researchers reported that both Level I and Level II scores declined similarly with social class (Stankov, Horn, & Roy, 1980).

These findings suggest that "g" contributes to ethnic and social-class differences in IQ, but it is not the only basis for them. At present, the evidence on specific mental abilities is not clear enough to favor either a genetic or cultural-bias explanation. To explore the basis for individual and group differences in IQ, we must turn to a very different set of evidence.

Explaining Individual and Group Differences in IQ

Over the past two decades, researchers have conducted hundreds of studies aimed at uncovering the origins of ethnic, social-class, and individual differences in mental abilities. The research falls into three broad classes: (1) investigations addressing the importance of heredity; (2) those that look at whether IQ scores are biased measures of low-income and minority children's true abilities; and (3) those that examine the quality of children's home environments as a major influence on their mental test performance.

GENETIC INFLUENCES

Recall from Chapter 3 that behavioral geneticists examine the relative contributions of heredity and environment to complex human characteristics by conducting *kinship studies,* in which they compare individuals of differing degrees of genetic relationship to one another. Let's look closely at what they have discovered about genetic influences on IQ.

■ HERITABILITY OF INTELLIGENCE. In Chapter 3, we introduced the most common method for studying the role of heredity in IQ—the *heritability estimate.* To briefly review, first the IQs of pairs of family members who vary in the extent to which they share genes are correlated. Then, using a complicated statistical procedure, the correlations are compared to arrive at an index of heritability, ranging from 0 to 1, that indicates the proportion of variation among individuals due to genetic factors.

Let's begin our consideration of the importance of heredity by looking closely at the correlations on which heritability estimates are based. Thomas Bouchard and Matt McGue (1981) summarized worldwide findings on the IQs of kinship pairs. The correlations, listed in Table 8.4, clearly show that the greater the genetic similarity between family members, the more they resemble one another in IQ. In fact, two of the correlations reveal that heredity is, without question, partially responsible for individual differences in mental test performance. The correlation for identical twins reared apart (.72) is much higher than for fraternal twins reared together in the same household (.60).

When researchers look at how these kinship correlations change with age, they find additional support for the importance of heredity. As Figure 8.8 shows, correlations for identical twins increase modestly into adulthood, whereas those for fraternal twins drop sharply at adolescence. Do these trends remind you of the niche-picking idea we discussed in Chapter 3? Common rearing experiences support the similarity of fraternal twins during childhood. But as they get older and are released from the influence of their families, each fraternal twin follows a course of development, or finds a niche, that fits with his or her unique genetic makeup. As a result, their IQ scores diverge. In contrast, the genetic likeness of identical twins leads them to seek out similar niches in adolescence and adulthood. Consequently, their IQ resemblance is even greater than it was during childhood. Other studies agree that the contribution of heredity to intelligence strengthens with development (McGue et al., 1993).

TABLE 8.4

Worldwide Summary of IQ Correlations Between Kinship Pairs

Kinship Pair	Average Weighted Correlation	Total Number of Kinship Pairs Included	Number of Studies
Identical twins reared together	.86	4,672	34
Identical twins reared apart	.72	65	3
Fraternal twins reared together	.60	5,546	41
Siblings reared together	.47	26,473	69
Siblings reared apart	.24	203	2
Parent–biological child living together	.42	8,433	32
Parent–biological child living apart	.22[a]	814	4
Nonbiological siblings (adopted–natural pairings)	.29	345	5
Nonbiological siblings (adopted–adopted pairings)	.34	369	6
Parent–adopted child	.19	1,397	6

[a]This correlation is lower than the values obtained in three recent adoption studies, which reported correlations of .31, .37, and .43 (Horn, 1983; Phillips & Fulker, 1989; Scarr & Weinberg, 1983).

Source: T. J. Bouchard, Jr., & M. McGue, 1981, "Familial Studies of Intelligence: A Review," *Science,* 212, p. 1056.

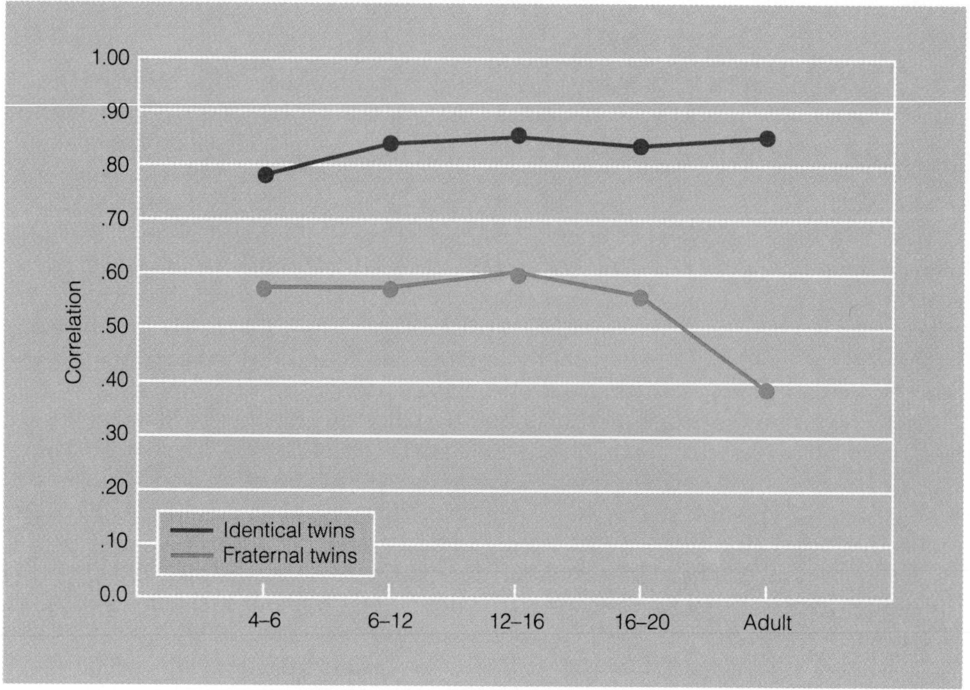

FIGURE 8.8

■ *Cross-sectional age-related changes in IQ correlations, derived from published studies including thousands of twin pairs. Correlations for identical twins increase modestly into adulthood, whereas those for fraternal twins drop sharply at adolescence. Similar trends appear when twins are followed longitudinally and IQ correlations are computed at successive ages. (From M. McGue, T. J. Bouchard, Jr., W. C. Iacono, & D. T. Lykken, 1993, "Behavioral Genetics of Cognitive Ability: A Life-Span Perspective," in R. Plomin & G. E. McClearn, Eds.,* Nature, Nurture, and Psychology, *p. 63. Washington, DC: American Psychological Association. Copyright © 1993 by the American Psychological Association. Adapted by permission.)*

Although kinship studies underscore the importance of heredity, a careful review of all the correlations in Table 8.4 reveals that environment is clearly involved. For example, the correlation for identical twins reared apart (.72) is considerably lower than for identical twins reared together (.86). Other comparisons that stress the role of environment include the stronger correlation for fraternal twins than ordinary siblings (due to twins' more similar rearing conditions); the stronger correlation for siblings reared together than apart; and the stronger correlation for parents and biological children living together than apart. Finally, parents and adopted children, as well as unrelated siblings, show low positive correlations, again providing support for the effects of common rearing conditions.

As we indicated in Chapter 3, heritability estimates are usually computed using correlations for identical and fraternal twins. The typical value in recent research is about .50, which means that half the variation in IQ is due to individual differences in heredity (Plomin, 1994c). This is a much more modest figure than the estimate of .80 arrived at by Jensen as part of his controversial 1969 article.

Furthermore, we noted in Chapter 3 that even this moderate value may be too high, since twins reared together often experience very similar overall environments. And even when they are reared apart, they are often placed in foster and adoptive homes that are advantaged and alike in many ways. When the range of environments to which twins are exposed is restricted, heritabilities underestimate the role of environment and overestimate the role of heredity. So although heritability research offers convincing evidence that genetic factors contribute to IQ, disagreement persists over how large the role of heredity really is (Ceci, 1990).

■ **DO HERITABILITY ESTIMATES EXPLAIN ETHNIC AND SOCIAL-CLASS DIFFERENCES IN IQ?** Despite the limitations of the heritability estimate, Jensen (1969, 1973) relied on it to support the argument that ethnic and social-class differences in IQ have a strong genetic basis. This line of reasoning is widely regarded as inappropriate. Although heritability estimates computed within black and white populations are similar, they provide no direct evidence about what is responsible for between-group differences in IQ (Brody, 1992; Plomin, 1990).

In a well-known example, Richard Lewontin (1976) showed that using within-group heritabilities to explain between-group differences is like comparing different seeds in different soil. Suppose we take a handful of corn seeds (which vary in genetic makeup) and plant them in the same pot with a rich supply of fertilizer designed to promote plant growth. Then we take another handful of seeds and grow them under quite different conditions, in a pot with half as much fertilizer. We find that although the plants in each group vary in height, the first group, on the average, grows taller than the second group. Within each group, individual differences in plant height are largely due to heredity, since growth environments of all plants were much the same. But the between-group difference is probably environmental, since the fertilizer given to the second group was far less plentiful.

To be sure of this conclusion, we could design a second study in which we expose the second group of seeds to a full supply of fertilizer and see if they reach an average height that equals that of the first group. If they do, then we would have more powerful evidence that environment is responsible for the previous group difference. In the next section, we will see that researchers have conducted natural experiments of this kind by studying the IQs of children adopted into homes very different from their family of origin.

■ ADOPTION RESEARCH. Adoption studies provide a wider range of information than the twin evidence on heritability we have considered so far. Correlations of children with their biological and adoptive family members can be examined for the relative contribution of heredity and environment. Even more important, researchers can gain insight into how malleable IQ is by looking at changes in the absolute value of test scores as the result of growing up in an advantaged family.

One of the earliest and best-known of these investigations was carried out nearly a half century ago by Marie Skodak and Harold Skeels (1949). They repeatedly tested the intelligence of 100 children who had been placed in adoptive homes before 6 months of age. Although the biological parents were largely low income, the adoptive parents were well above average in earnings and education. Children's scores remained above the population mean throughout middle childhood and into adolescence, suggesting that IQ is highly malleable! Nevertheless, children's IQs still showed substantial correlation with the scores of their biological mothers, providing support for the influence of heredity.

Skodak and Skeels's groundbreaking study suffered from an important limitation. Selective placement of adoptees took place. That is, children with the best-off biological parents tended to be placed with the most advantaged adoptive families. When this occurs, genetic and environmental influences on children's IQ scores cannot be separated completely.

But more recent adoption research, in which selective placement was judged to be minimal, agrees with Skodak and Skeels's findings. The Texas Adoption Project resulted from the discovery of a large private adoption agency that had routinely given IQ tests to unwed mothers staying in its residence until they gave birth. Children of two extreme groups of mothers—those with IQs below 95 and those with IQs above 120—were chosen for special study. As Figure 8.9 shows, when tested in middle childhood, both groups scored above average in IQ. But children of the low-IQ biological mothers did not do nearly as well as children of brighter mothers who were placed in similar adoptive families (Horn, 1983). And when correlations were examined, adopted children showed an increasing tendency to resemble their biological mothers as they grew older and a decreasing tendency to be similar to their adoptive parents (Loehlin, Horn, & Willerman, 1989). In sum, adoption research shows that both environment and heredity contribute significantly to IQ.

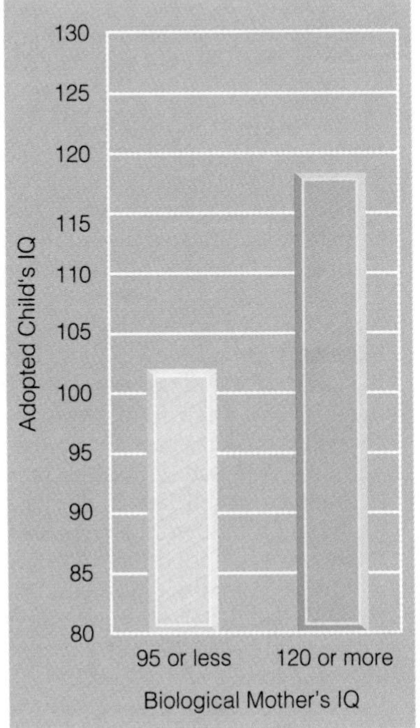

FIGURE 8.9

■ *IQs of adopted children as a function of biological mothers' IQ in the Texas Adoption Project. In this study, selective placement was not great enough to account for the large difference in performance between the two groups. (Adapted from Willerman, 1979.)*

The fact that adopted children have consistently been found to score above average in IQ suggests that the social-class difference in intelligence has a substantial environmental component. But concluding that it is entirely explained by environment is probably too extreme. Although children of low-IQ biological mothers adopted into middle-class families attain above-average IQs, they generally score somewhat lower than their adoptive parents' natural children, with whom they share equally privileged rearing conditions. This difference could be due to heredity, to environmental influences prior to adoption (such as prenatal conditions), or to both (Devlin et al., 1995). In addition, adoption studies repeatedly reveal stronger correlations between the IQ scores of biological than adoptive relatives (Horn, 1983; Plomin & DeFries, 1983; Scarr & Weinberg, 1983). On the basis of these findings, several researchers have concluded that the social class–IQ relationship is partly genetic (Bouchard & Segal, 1985; Scarr & Weinberg, 1978).

What about the black–white IQ gap? In this case, adoption research suggests it is environmental; it cannot be assigned to racially linked, inferior genes. See the Cultural Influences box on page 322 for a description of this important research.

CULTURAL INFLUENCES

Transracial Adoption: When Black Children Grow Up in White Homes

Two transracial adoption studies, both focusing on the development of black children growing up in white middle-class homes, provide evidence on the origins of IQ differences between black and white children. If Jensen's claim that black children are limited in potential is correct, then IQs of black adoptees should remain considerably below those of other children growing up in advantaged white families. If black children are as well equipped genetically as white children, then their IQs should rise when they are reared by white parents "in the culture of the tests and schools."

Sandra Scarr and Richard Weinberg (1976, 1983) gave IQ tests during childhood and adolescence to over one hundred transracially adopted black children. Two-thirds were placed during the first year of life, one-third after 12 months of age. The white adoptive parents had high-average to superior IQs, were well above average in occupational status and income, and had four to five more years of education than the children's biological parents. When tested in childhood, the adoptees attained an average IQ of 106, considerably above the general population mean. The scores of those who had been adopted within the first 12 months were even higher. They averaged 110, 20 points above the mean of children growing up in low-income black communities. Scarr and Weinberg concluded that heredity cannot account for black children's typically depressed intelligence test scores.

A decade later, the researchers restudied the sample and found that except for a decline in children's IQ scores (probably due to use of different tests at the two ages), the earlier findings persisted. Interracially adopted young people remained substantially above the IQ average for low-income African-Americans, and they scored slightly above the national norm in academic achievement. In sum, the adoptees continued to show the beneficial effects of their rearing environments as adolescents (Weinberg, Scarr, & Waldman, 1992; Waldman, Weinberg, & Scarr, 1994).

A second transracial study lends insight into cultural experiences that contributed to Scarr and Weinberg's findings. Elsie Moore (1986) compared the test-taking behavior and parent–child interaction of two groups of black adoptees: one growing up in white and the other growing up in black middle-class families. Tested between 7 and 10 years of age, the traditionally adopted children did well, attaining a mean IQ of 104. But scores of their transracially adopted counterparts were much higher, averaging 117.

Consistent with their superior scores, the transracially adopted group approached the test with attitudes and strategies conducive to success. They were more task-involved and persistent, and their responses were more elaborate. When they did not know an answer, they rarely attributed failure to their own inability. The transracially adopted group's greater test-taking confidence was, in turn, related to their mothers' special support of problem-solving behavior. When asked to teach their children a difficult task, the white mothers displayed more encouragement and enthusiasm for their children's efforts.

■ *When black children grow up "in the culture of the tests and schools," they perform substantially above the population mean in IQ. Transracial adoption research supports the view that rearing environment is responsible for the black–white IQ gap. (Tony Freeman/ PhotoEdit)*

These findings support the position that rearing environment accounts for the black–white IQ gap. However, the researchers were careful to point out that their findings are not an endorsement for widespread adoption of black children into white homes. Instead, they call for more research on ways in which ethnically different families promote a diverse array of cognitive skills.

CULTURAL BACKGROUND AND TEST BIAS

A controversial question raised about ethnic differences in IQ has to do with whether they are an artifact of test content and administration procedures. If a test samples culturally specific knowledge and skills that not all groups of children have had equal opportunity to learn, then is it a fair measure of the intelligence of all children?

This question has been the subject of heated debate. Some experts reject the idea that intelligence tests are biased, claiming that they were intended to represent important aspects of success in the common culture. According to this perspective, since current mental tests predict scholastic performance equally well for majority and minority children, they are fair measures for both groups (Jensen, 1980; Oakland & Parmelee, 1985). Others take a broader view of test bias. They believe that lack of prior exposure to test content, language customs, and motivational concerns lead IQ scores to underestimate the abilities of low-income minority children (Ceci, 1990; Ogbu, 1994; Sternberg, 1988). To evaluate this position, let's look at each of these factors.

■ PRIOR EXPOSURE TO TEST CONTENT. Many researchers argue that IQ scores are affected by specific information acquired as part of middle-class upbringing. Unfortunately, efforts to make tests fairer to minorities, either by basing them on more familiar content or by eliminating crystallized items and using only fluid tasks, have not raised the scores of these children very much (Kaplan, 1985). For example, Raven Progressive Matrices is one of the most commonly used tests of fluid intelligence. To see a typical item, look back at the figure matrix task in Figure 8.1. Yet low-income minority children continue to perform more poorly on the Raven test, and others like it, than their white middle-class agemates (Jensen, 1980).

Nevertheless, it is possible that high scores on fluid tests depend on subtle learning opportunities. In one study, children's performance on a spatial reasoning subscale of the WISC was related to the extent to which they had played a popular but expensive game that (like the test items) required them to arrange blocks to duplicate a design as quickly as possible (Dirks, 1982). Low-income minority children, who often grow up in more "people-oriented" than "object-oriented" homes, may lack experiences with games and objects that promote certain intellectual skills. In line with this possibility, when a large, ethnically diverse sample of parents were asked about characteristics important to their idea of an intelligent first grader, Anglo-Americans valued cognitive traits over noncognitive ones. In contrast, ethnic minorities (Cambodian, Filipino, Vietnamese, and Mexican immigrants) saw noncognitive attributes—motivation, self-management, and social skills—as equally or more important than cognitive skills. Mexican parents, especially, highly valued the social component of intelligence (Okagaki & Sternberg, 1993).

Finally, recall the evidence presented earlier in this chapter that the more time children spend in school, the higher their IQ scores. It also supports the conclusion that exposure to specific information resembling the content of intelligence tests affects performance on a wide range of mental ability tasks (Ceci, 1991).

■ LANGUAGE CUSTOMS. Ethnic minority families often foster unique language skills that do not match the expectations of most classrooms and testing situations. Shirley Brice Heath (1982, 1989), an anthropologist who spent many hours observing in low-income black homes in a southeastern American city, found that adults asked black children very different kinds of questions than is typical in white middle-class families. From an early age, white parents ask knowledge-training questions, such as "What color is it?" and "What's this story about?" that resemble the questioning style of tests and classrooms. In contrast, the black parents asked only "real" questions—ones that they themselves did not know the answer to. Often these were analogy questions ("What's that like?") or story-starter questions ("Didja hear Miss Sally this morning?") that called for elaborate responses about personal experiences and had no single right answer.

Heath and other researchers report that these experiences lead low-income black children to develop complex verbal skills at home, such as storytelling and exchanging quick-witted remarks. But their language differs from that of white middle-class children in emphasizing social and emotional topics rather than facts about the world (Blake, 1994). Not surprisingly, black children may be confused by the "objective" questions they encounter in classrooms and withdraw into silence.

Other minority youngsters also develop distinct language styles. For example, Navajo Indian children speak slowly and rhythmically, leaving much time between phrases and sentences. Teachers and testers often think these children have finished responding when they have only paused. In contrast, Native Hawaiian children prefer rapid-fire, overlapping speech. Non-Hawaiian adults may interpret this style as rude interruption, although in Hawaiian society it signals interest and involvement (Tharp, 1989, 1994).

When faced with the strangeness of the testing situation, the minority child may look to the examiner for cues about how to respond. Yet most intelligence tests permit tasks to be presented in only one way, and they allow no feedback. Consequently, minority children may simply give the first answer that comes to mind, not one that truly represents what they know. Turn back to the beginning of this chapter and review Jermaine's responses to Nora's questions. Jermaine appeared to repeat his first answer because he had trouble figuring out the task's meaning, not because he was unable to classify objects. Had Nora prompted him to look at the questions in a different way, his performance might have been better.

■ MOTIVATIONAL CONCERNS. When tested by an unfamiliar adult, children from poverty backgrounds often reply, "I don't know," to the simplest of questions, including "What's your name?" The response does not reflect lack of ability. Instead, it is due to wariness of the examiner and the testing situation. As a result, the fearful child behaves in ways aimed at minimizing interaction and terminating the unpleasant experience as quickly as possible (Zigler & Finn-Stevenson, 1992). Besides discomfort in the presence of strangers, many low-income minority children do not define testing conditions in achievement terms. They may be more concerned with attention and approval from the adult than answering as many questions correctly as possible (Zigler & Seitz, 1982).

Research indicates that IQs improve when testing conditions are modified so that the minority child has a chance to become familiar with the examiner, is praised frequently, and is given easier items after incorrect responses to minimize the emotional consequences of failure. In the most impressive of these studies, preschoolers from poverty-stricken backgrounds who experienced a short play period with the examiner or who were tested a second time showed gains of 10 points. In contrast, the scores of middle-class children increased by only 3 points (Zigler, Abelson, & Seitz, 1973).

Although these procedures ease adjustment of young children to the testing situation, many low-income minority children suffer from more deep-seated motivational difficulties. As they experience repeated academic failure, they are likely to develop a self-defeating style marked by withdrawal, disengagement, and reduced effort that severely affects their approach to tests and school tasks. Recent evidence indicates a growing discrepancy over the school years between high- and low-achieving children in their motivation to excel on standardized tests (Paris et al., 1991). As a result, IQs may become especially inaccurate indicators of these youngsters' learning potential at older ages.

REDUCING TEST BIAS

Although not all experts agree, today there is greater acknowledgment that IQ scores can underestimate the intelligence of culturally different children. A special concern exists about incorrectly labeling minority children as slow learners and assigning them to remedial classes, which are far less stimulating than regular school experiences. Because of this danger, precautions are advised when evaluating children for the purpose of educational placement. Besides test scores, assessments of children's adaptive behavior—their ability to cope with the demands of their everyday environments—should be obtained (Landesman & Ramey, 1989). The child who does poorly on an IQ test yet displays considerable practical intelligence by playing a complex game on the playground, figuring out how to rewire a broken TV, or caring for younger siblings responsibly is unlikely to be mentally deficient.

In addition, test designers are becoming more aware of the importance of using culturally relevant testing procedures. For example, Dalton Miller-Jones (1989) points out that minority children are often capable of the cognitive operations called for by test items. But because they are used to thinking in other ways in daily life, they may not access the required operation immediately. **Dynamic assessment**, an innovative approach to testing consistent with Vygotsky's concept of the zone of proximal development (see Chapter 6, page 248), narrows this gap between actual and potential performance. Instead of emphasizing previously acquired knowledge, dynamic assessment introduces purposeful teaching into the testing situation to find out what the child can attain with social support.

Dynamic assessment
An innovative approach to testing consistent with Vygotsky's concept of the zone of proximal development. Using a pretest–intervene–retest procedure, introduces purposeful teaching into the testing situation to find out what the child can attain with social support.

Several dynamic assessment models exist, each of which uses a pretest–intervene–retest procedure with traditional intelligence test items (Lidz, 1991). The best known of these is Reuben Feuerstein's (1979, 1980) *Learning Potential Assessment Device,* in which the adult tries to find the teaching style to which the child is most responsive and communicates principles and strategies that children can generalize to new situations.

Evidence on the effectiveness of dynamic assessment reveals that the IQs of ethnic minority children dramatically underestimate their ability to perform intellectual tasks after adult assistance. Instead, children's receptiveness to teaching and their capacity to transfer what they have learned to novel problems add substantially to the prediction of future performance (Brown & Ferrara, 1985; Rand & Kaniel, 1987; Tzuriel, 1989). An added benefit of dynamic assessment is that it helps identify forms of intervention likely to help children who are learning poorly in classrooms.

■ *Dynamic assessment introduces purposeful teaching into the testing situation to find out what the child can attain with social support. Many ethnic minority children perform more competently after adult assistance. And the approach helps identify the teaching style to which the child is most responsive. (Bob Daemmrich/Stock Boston)*

Dynamic assessment presents challenges much greater than those faced in traditional, static assessment. The approach is time consuming and requires extensive knowledge of cultural values and practices to work well with minority children. Until we have the resources to implement these procedures broadly, should we suspend the use of intelligence testing in schools? Most experts regard this solution as unacceptable, since important educational decisions would be based only on subjective impressions—a policy that could increase the discriminatory placement of minority children. Intelligence tests are useful as long as they are interpreted carefully by examiners who are sensitive to cultural influences on test performance. And despite their limitations, IQ scores continue to be valid measures of school learning potential for the majority of Western children.

HOME ENVIRONMENT AND IQ

Ethnic and social-class differences are not the only important IQ variations with environmental explanations. As we indicated earlier, children of the *same* ethnic and social-class background also vary in IQ. Many studies support the conclusion that home environmental factors contribute to these differences.

Researchers divide home influences into two broad types. The first, called **shared environmental influences**, are factors that pervade the general atmosphere of the home and, therefore, affect all children living in it to the same extent. The availability of stimulating toys and books and modeling by parents of intellectual activities are good examples. The second type, **nonshared environmental influences**, refers to factors that make siblings different from one another. Examples include unique treatment by parents, birth order and spacing, as well as certain events, such as moving to a new neighborhood, that affect one sibling more than another. Let's see what research says about each of these classes of environmental events.

■ SHARED ENVIRONMENTAL INFLUENCES. To assess the impact of home environment on intelligence, Bettye Caldwell and Robert Bradley developed the **Home Observation for Measurement of the Environment (HOME)**, a checklist for gathering information about the quality of children's home lives through observation and parental interview (Caldwell & Bradley, 1994). Separate infancy, preschool, and middle childhood versions exist. Table 8.5 shows the subscales measured by each.

Evidence on HOME confirms the findings of many years of research—that stimulation provided by parents is linked to mental development. All infant and preschool subscales are moderately correlated with IQ, although the most important ones change with age. In infancy, organization of the physical environment and variety in daily stimulation show strongest relationships with mental test scores. During the preschool years, warmth, stimulation of language and academic behavior, and provision of appropriate play materials are the best predictors (Bradley & Caldwell, 1976; Elardo, Bradley, & Caldwell, 1975, 1977). Furthermore, high HOME scores during infancy are associated with IQ gains between 1 and 3 years of age, whereas low HOME scores predict declines as large as 15 to 20 points (Bradley et al., 1989). The strength of the association between HOME

Shared environmental influences
Environmental influences that pervade the general atmosphere of the home and affect all children living in it to the same extent.

Nonshared environmental influences
Environmental influences that make children living in the same family different from one another.

Home Observation for Measurement of the Environment (HOME)
A checklist for gathering information about the quality of children's home lives through observation and parental interviews. Infancy, preschool, and middle childhood versions exist.

TABLE 8.5

Home Observation for Measurement of the Environment (HOME) Subscales

Infancy Version	Preschool Version	Middle Childhood Version
1. Emotional and verbal responsiveness of the parent	1. Pride, affection, and warmth	1. Emotional and verbal responsiveness of the parent
2. Acceptance of the child	2. Avoidance of physical punishment	2. Emotional climate of the parent–child relationship
3. Involvement with the child	3. Language stimulation	3. Encouragement of social maturity
4. Organization of the physical environment	4. Stimulation of academic behavior	4. Provision for active stimulation
5. Parental involvement with the child	5. Stimulation through toys, games, and reading material	5. Growth-fostering materials and experiences
6. Variety in daily stimulation	6. Modeling and encouragement of social maturity	6. Family participation in developmentally stimulating experiences
	7. Variety in daily stimulation	7. Physical environment: safe, clean, and conducive to development
	8. Physical environment: safe, clean, and conducive to development	8. Parental involvement in parenting

Sources: Bradley & Caldwell, 1979; Bradley et al., 1988; Elardo, Bradley, & Caldwell, 1975.

and IQ declines in middle childhood, perhaps because older children spend longer periods of time in other settings, such as school. Nevertheless, the relationship is still present (Luster & Dubow, 1992).[3]

When home environments within different social-class and ethnic groups are examined, the findings are much the same. A stimulating environment, encouragement of achievement, and affection are repeatedly linked to IQ, no matter what the child's background (Bradley & Caldwell, 1981, 1982; Bradley et al., 1989; Luster & Dubow, 1992). The extent to which parents talk to their young children seems to be particularly important. In a recent longitudinal study of children highly diverse in ethnic and social-class background, amount of verbal interaction in the home during the first 3 years was a powerful predictor of early language progress. Preschoolers' language competence, in turn, contributed substantially to their verbal intelligence and academic achievement in elementary school, after social class was controlled (Hart & Risley, 1995; Walker et al., 1994).

At the same time, we must be careful about interpreting these correlational findings, since they tell us nothing definite about causation. In all the studies reviewed so far, children were reared by their biological parents, with whom they share not just a common environment but also common heredity. It is possible that parents who are genetically more intelligent provide better experiences as well as give birth to genetically superior children. In addition, brighter children may evoke more stimulation from their parents. (Note that these hypotheses refer to genetic–environmental correlation; you may find it helpful to review this idea by returning to page 117 of Chapter 3.)

Indeed, there is support for a genetic contribution to the HOME–IQ association. When adopted children are studied, the correlation is not as strong as it is for biological children (Braungart, Fulker, & Plomin, 1992; Cherny, 1994). This suggests that genetic similarity between parent and child elevates the relationship. Using complicated statistical procedures, researchers estimate that as much as half the correlation between HOME and IQ is due to heredity (Coon et al., 1990). But so far, these findings are based only on white middle-class families. We do not yet know whether they generalize to children of all income and ethnic groups.

Furthermore, it is clear that heredity does not account for all of the association between home environment and mental test scores. In several studies, family living conditions continued to predict children's IQ beyond the effect of maternal intelligence—a finding that highlights the importance of environment (Luster & Dubow, 1992; Sameroff et al., 1993; Yeates et al., 1983). Also, one subscale of HOME—organization of the physical

Confluence model
A view that regards mental development as a function of family size, birth order, and spacing—factors that affect the quality of the environment each child experiences within the family.

[3] Because the middle childhood version of HOME is relatively new, we do not yet know which of its subscales predict IQ most effectively. In one study, two were especially strong predictors of academic achievement: provision for active stimulation (for example, encouraging hobbies, trips to the library, and organizational memberships) and family participation in stimulating experiences (visiting friends or relatives, attending musical or theater performances) (Bradley, Caldwell, & Rock, 1988).

environment—is unrelated to parental intelligence. Yet a measure of it in infancy predicts children's IQ well into middle childhood (Coon et al., 1990).

When the evidence is considered as a whole, we must conclude that the link between home environment and mental development is very complex. Caldwell and Bradley (1994) speculate that as children get older, the HOME–IQ relationship probably becomes increasingly bidirectional, with neither factor serving as the primary cause.

■ NONSHARED ENVIRONMENTAL FACTORS. Although children growing up in the same family are affected by common environments, in many ways their experiences are decidedly different. Parents may favor one child over another. Sibling relationships are experienced differently by each child. And children may be assigned special roles—for example, one expected to achieve, a second to get along well with others (Dunn & Plomin, 1990).

Very few studies have examined the effect of nonshared environmental influences on children's IQs. In fact, an explicit theory exists for only two nonshared variables: birth order and spacing. To explain their impact on intelligence, R. B. Zajonc and Gregory Markus proposed the **confluence model** (Zajonc, 1976; Zajonc & Markus, 1975; Zajonc, Markus, & Markus, 1979). It regards mental development as a function of the unique environment each child experiences within the family, which is affected by the contributions of other members. As each new child is born, environmental quality is diluted, since babies consume the attentions of mature family members but contribute little to intellectual stimulation in the home. However, as children get older and become more cognitively competent, they enrich the intellectual atmosphere of the family. Consequently, its overall quality rises.

Think about these ideas, and you will see that they lead to several predictions about the impact of family configurational factors on intelligence. First, IQs should be higher in smaller families with wider spacing among siblings, since children have more opportunity to profit from the stimulation of adults. Second, test scores should decline with birth order, except when wide spacing counteracts the negative impact of growing up with many siblings.

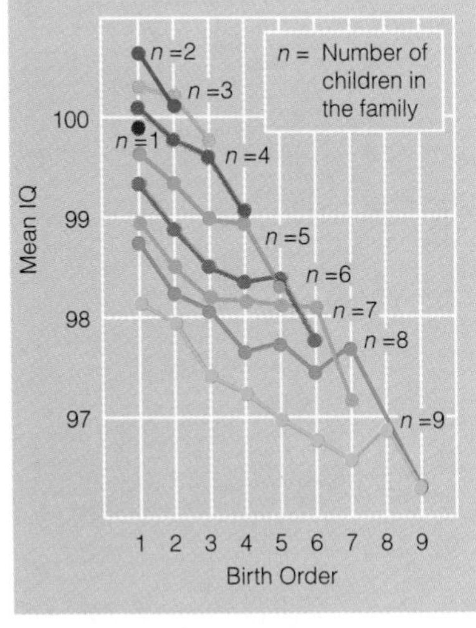

FIGURE 8.10

■ *IQ as a function of family size and birth order among 19-year-old males born in the Netherlands at the end of World War II. (From L. Belmont & F. A. Marolla, 1973, "Birth Order, Family Size, and Intelligence,"* Science, *182, p. 1097. Copyright © 1973 by the AAAS. Reprinted by permission.)*

Do the complex predictions of the confluence model fit with research evidence? A large study based on information drawn from military files on almost all males born in the Netherlands at the end of World War II yielded findings consistent with it. As Figure 8.10 reveals, IQ showed the predicted decrease with larger family size and later birth order (Belmont & Marolla, 1973). Nevertheless, other implications of the theory have not been confirmed. For example, children reared by a single parent do not always have lower IQs than children living with two parents. Nor does the presence of additional adults in the home, such as grandparents, aunts, and uncles, lead to a rise in IQ (Brackbill & Nichols, 1982). And although only children tend to do well intellectually, their IQs are about the same as those of firstborns with siblings—not higher, as the confluence model would lead us to expect (Falbo & Polit, 1986).

Overall, the confluence model has received only mixed support. Perhaps the greatest reservation about it is that family size and birth-order effects amount to no more than a few IQ points. Does this mean that nonshared environmental influences are unimportant? The evidence is not all in on this issue. Some potentially powerful nonshared factors are isolated, one-time events. A particularly inspiring English teacher, a summer at a special camp, or a period of intense rivalry with a sibling are examples. The most important nonshared influences may be of this kind. To understand their role in mental development, we need more intensive studies of children growing up in the same family than have been accomplished to date (Brody, 1992; McCall, 1993).

BRIEF REVIEW

The existence of ethnic and social-class differences in intelligence test performance has sparked the IQ nature–nurture debate. Heritability estimates indicate that genetic factors account for about half of the variation among individuals in mental test scores. However, heritabilities cannot explain ethnic and social-class differences in IQ. Adoption research reveals that IQ is highly malleable. At the same time, heredity remains important, since adopted children's scores are more strongly correlated with the IQs of their biological than adoptive relatives.

Researchers who view mental tests as biased point to test content, language customs, and motivational concerns that can lead IQs to underestimate the intelligence of low-income and ethnic minority children. Supplementing IQs with measures of adaptive behavior and adjusting testing procedures to take cultural differences into account are ways of reducing test bias. A stimulating home environment and parental warmth and encouragement of achievement consistently predict higher mental test scores. Factors considered by the confluence model, such as birth order and spacing, also predict IQ, but they are not very powerful.

Early Intervention and Intellectual Development

In the 1960s, during a decade in which the United States launched a "war on poverty," a wide variety of early intervention programs for economically disadvantaged preschoolers were initiated. They were based on the assumption that learning problems were best treated early, before the beginning of formal schooling, as well as the hope that early enrichment would offset the declines in IQ and achievement common among children from low-income and ethnic minority backgrounds.

Many intervention programs continue to exist today. The most widespread is **Project Head Start**, initiated by the federal government in 1965. A typical Head Start program provides children with a year or two of preschool education before they enter school, along with nutritional and medical services. In addition, parent involvement is a central part of the Head Start philosophy. Parents serve on policy councils and contribute to program planning. They also work directly with children in classrooms, attend special programs on parenting and child development, and receive services directed at their own social, emotional, and vocational needs. Currently, over 1,300 Head Start centers located around the country enroll about 720,000 children (Kassebaum, 1994; Zigler & Styfco, 1995).

IMPACT OF EARLY INTERVENTION

Over two decades of research on the long-term benefits of early intervention have played a major role in the survival of Head Start. The most important of these studies was coordinated by the Consortium for Longitudinal Studies, a group of investigators who combined data from seven university-based interventions. Results showed that children who attended programs scored higher in IQ and achievement than controls during the first 2 to 3 years of elementary school. After that time, differences in test scores declined.

Nevertheless, children who received intervention remained ahead on measures of real-life school adjustment into adolescence. As Figure 8.11 shows, they were less likely to be placed in special education classes or retained in grade, and a greater number graduated from high school. There were also lasting benefits in attitudes and motivation. Children who attended programs were more likely to give achievement-related reasons (such as school or job accomplishments) for being proud of themselves, and their mothers held higher vocational aspirations for them (Lazar & Darlington, 1982). A separate report on one program suggested benefits lasting into young adulthood. It was associated with a reduction in delinquency and teenage pregnancy and a greater likelihood of employment (Barnett, 1993; Berrueta-Clement et al., 1984).

Project Head Start
A federal program that provides low-income children with a year or two of preschool education before school entry and that encourages parent involvement in children's development.

EVALUATIONS OF HEAD START

Do these findings on outstanding university-based programs generalize to Head Start centers located in American communities? Although some studies report only minimal benefits, new evidence reveals that they are biased by one very important

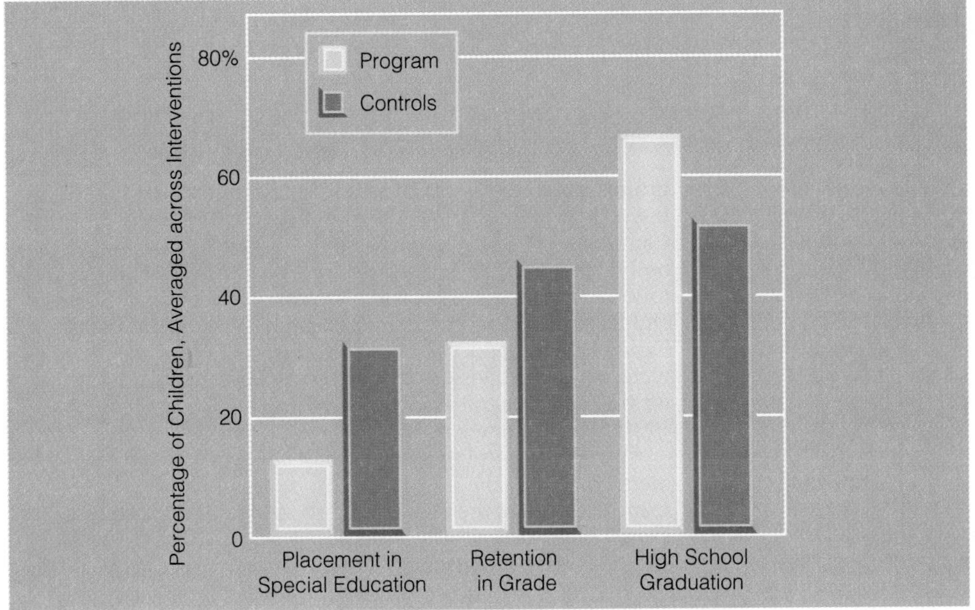

FIGURE 8.11

■ *Benefits of early intervention programs. Low-income children who received intervention fared better than controls on real-life indicators of school adjustment. (Adapted from Royce, Darlington, & Murray, 1983.)*

factor: Because not all poverty-stricken children can be served, Head Start typically enrolls the most economically disadvantaged preschoolers. Controls to whom they are compared often do not come from such extremely impoverished families (Schnur, Brooks-Gunn, & Shipman, 1992).

An investigation of Head Start programs in two large cities took this into account. It also looked carefully at the effectiveness of Head Start by comparing it to other preschool alternatives as well as to no preschool at all. Results showed that Head Start children, compared to "other preschool" and "no preschool" groups, had less educated mothers, came from more crowded households, and were more likely to be growing up in single-parent homes. Before entering the program, they scored well below the other groups on mental tests. Yet at the end of a year's intervention, Head Start children showed greater gains than both comparison groups (Lee, Brooks-Gunn, & Schnur, 1988). Furthermore, when African-American children, who comprised a majority of the sample, were followed up one to two years after Head Start, gains on several cognitive measures were sustained, although they were no longer as great as they had been immediately after the program (Lee et al., 1990).

A consistent finding of research on Head Start and other preschool interventions is that almost all children experience an eventual **washout effect**. In other words, improvements in IQ and achievement do not last for more than a few years (McKey et al., 1985). This is not surprising, since poverty-stricken children typically attend underfunded, poorer-quality schools, especially when they live in urban areas (Kozol, 1991; Wilson, 1987). Their elementary school experiences may cancel out earlier gains. To be most effective, interventions need to be supplemented with high-quality educational supports through the school years (Ramey & Ramey, 1990). More intensive programs that start earlier might also produce more enduring gains. Indeed, this is what is suggested by another intervention effort, the Carolina Abecedarian Project, which you can read about in the Social Issues box on page 330.

Despite declining test scores, graduates of high-quality Head Start centers (like those of university-based programs) show an improved ability to meet basic educational requirements during elementary and secondary school (Zigler & Styfco, 1994). Although researchers are not sure how these effects are achieved, one possibility is that they are largely the result of changes in the attitudes, behaviors, and life circumstances of parents, who create better rearing environments for their children. Consequently, new interventions are being conceived as two-generation models.

Washout effect
The loss of IQ and achievement gains resulting from early intervention within a few years after the program ends.

A TWO-GENERATION PROGRAM STRATEGY

A typical parent component of early intervention emphasizes teaching parenting skills and providing other supports that encourage parents to act as supplementary intervenors for their child. Researchers believe these efforts may not be enough (White,

SOCIAL ISSUES

The Carolina Abecedarian Project: A Model of Early Intervention

In the 1970s, an experiment was begun to find out if educational enrichment starting at a very early age could prevent the declines in mental development that affect children born into extreme poverty. The Carolina Abecedarian Project identified over a hundred infants at serious risk for school failure, based on parent education and income, a history of poor school achievement among older siblings, and other family problems. Shortly after birth, the babies were randomly assigned to either a treatment or a control group.

Between 3 weeks and 3 months of age, infants in the treatment group were enrolled in a full-time, year-round day care program, where they remained until they entered kindergarten. During the first three years, the children received stimulation aimed at promoting motor, cognitive, language, and social skills. After age 3, the goals of the program expanded to include prereading and math concepts. At all ages, special emphasis was placed on adult–child communication. Teachers were trained to engage in informative, helpful, and nondirective interaction with the children, who were talked to and read to daily. Both treatment and control children received nutrition and health services. The primary difference between them was the day care experience, designed to support the treatment group's mental development.

Intelligence test scores were gathered on the children regularly, and during infancy the performance of the two groups began to diverge. Treatment children scored higher than controls throughout the preschool years (Ramey & Campbell, 1984). Although the high-risk backgrounds of both groups led their IQs to decline over middle childhood, follow-up testing at ages 8 and 12 revealed that treatment children maintained their advantage in IQ over controls (see Figure 8.12). In addition, at age 12, treatment youngsters were achieving considerably better, especially in reading, writing, and general knowledge (Campbell & Ramey, 1991, 1994; Martin, Ramey, & Ramey, 1990).

When the Carolina Abecedarian children entered elementary school, the researchers conducted a second experiment to compare the impact of early and later intervention. From kindergarten through second grade, half the treatment and half the control group were provided with a special resource teacher. She introduced supplementary educational activities into the home addressing the child's specific learning needs. School-age intervention had little impact on IQ (refer again to Figure 8.12). And although it enhanced children's academic achievement, the effects were much weaker than the impact of very early intervention (Campbell & Ramey, 1994). The Carolina Abecedarian Project shows that providing children with continuous, high-quality enrichment from infancy through the preschool years is an effective way to reduce the devastating impact of poverty on children's mental development.

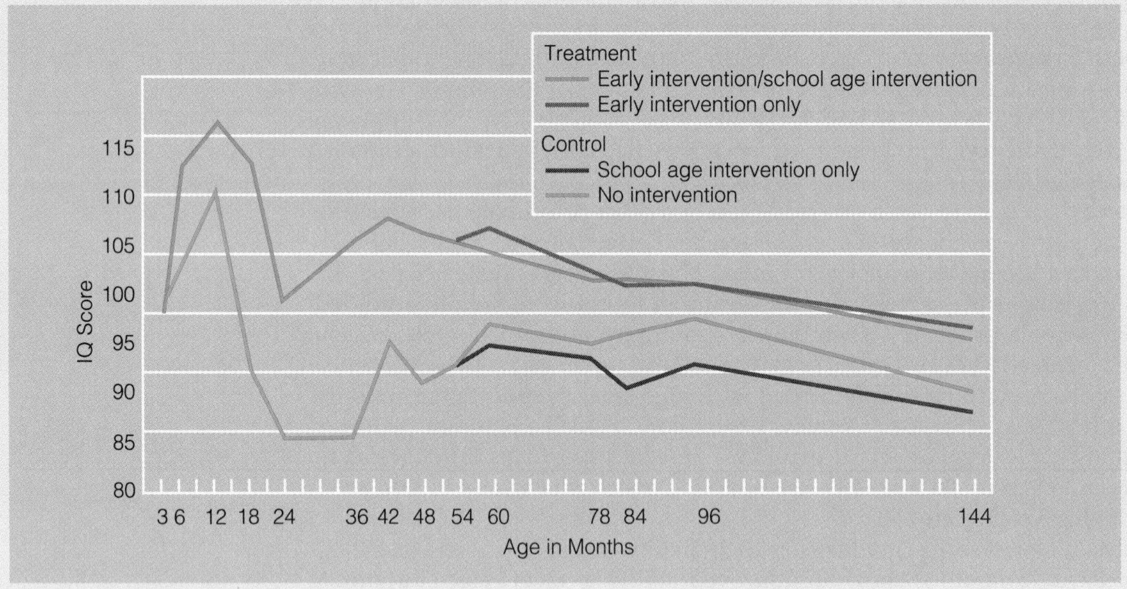

FIGURE 8.12

■ *IQ scores of treatment and control children from 6 months to 12 years in the Carolina Abecedarian Project. To compare the impact of early and later intervention, half the treatment and half the control group were provided with supplementary educational activities suited to their learning needs from kindergarten through second grade. School-based intervention had little impact on age-related changes in IQ; the effects of early intervention were far more powerful. (From F. A. Campbell & C. T. Ramey, 1994, "Effects of Early Intervention on Intellectual and Academic Achievement: A Follow-up Study of Children from Low-Income Families,"* Child Development, *65, p. 690. © The Society for Research in Child Development. Reprinted by permission.)*

Taylor, & Moss, 1992). By expanding intervention to include developmental goals for *both* parents and children, program benefits might be extended. A parent helped to move out of poverty with education, vocational training, and other social services is likely to show improved psychological well-being and greater interest in planning for the future. When combined with child-centered intervention, these gains may translate into lasting changes in parenting behavior and exceptionally strong, long-term benefits for children (Zigler & Styfco, 1994, 1995).

Currently, a variety of two-generation models are being tried—several in conjunction with Head Start (Smith, 1995). Although the approach is too new to have yielded much research, one pioneering effort, Project Redirection, is cause for optimism. In it, teenage mothers received a variety of services for themselves and their babies, including education, employment, family planning, life management, parent education, and child health care. A five-year follow-up revealed that participants obtained higher HOME scores, were less likely to be on welfare, and had higher family earnings than controls receiving less intensive intervention. In addition, program children were more likely to have enrolled in Head Start, and they had higher verbal IQs (Polit, Quint, & Riccio, 1988).

■ *Two-generation program strategies include developmental goals for both parents and children. Helping parents move out of poverty through education, vocational training, and other social services while providing high-quality preschool intervention may be the most effective route to long-term benefits for children. (Liane Enkelis/Stock Boston)*

THE FUTURE OF EARLY INTERVENTION

Although over one-fifth of American preschoolers are eligible for Head Start by virtue of their poverty level, at present the program serves only about one-third of these children. Yet Head Start and other interventions like it are highly cost effective. Program expenses are far less than the funds required to provide special education, treat delinquency, and support welfare dependency. Because of its demonstrated returns to society, a move is currently under way to expand Head Start to reach all eligible 3- and 4-year-olds (Collins, 1993; Hofferth, 1995).

Nevertheless, the distance in IQ and school achievement between Head Start graduates and their more economically advantaged peers remains considerable. As early intervention becomes more widespread, there is a need to find ways of increasing and sustaining the short-term cognitive gains that result from one- and two-year programs. The research we have considered indicates that more intensive, longer-lasting efforts that focus on the development of both parents and children offer hope of reaching these goals.

Beyond IQ: Development of Creativity

At the beginning of this chapter, we indicated that the concept of intelligence, to experts and laypeople alike, means much more than mental abilities that predict success in school. Today, educators recognize that gifted children—those who display exceptional intellectual strengths—have diverse characteristics. Some are high-IQ youngsters with scores above 130—the standard definition of giftedness based on intelligence test performance. High-IQ children, as we have seen, are particularly quick at academic work. They have keen memories and an exceptional capacity to analyze an existing problem and move toward a correct solution. Yet recognition that intelligence tests do not sample the entire range of human mental skills has prompted conceptions of giftedness to expand to include creativity (Feldhusen, 1986; Renzulli, 1986; Sternberg, 1986).

Creativity is the ability to produce work that is *original*—that others have not thought of before. Yet novelty is not enough for a product to be creative. It must also be *appropriate*—sensible or useful in some way. If a product is merely unusual but does not serve a social need, then it is not creative; it is, instead, an irrelevant response (Barron, 1988; Ochse, 1990; Sternberg & Lubart, 1991a). Besides the quality of the product, the process of arriving at it affects judgments of creativity. Rather than following established rules, a creative work pulls together previously disparate ideas. And it typically involves hard work and overcoming obstacles on the way to the final product (Amabile, 1983; Weisberg, 1993).

Creativity
The ability to produce work that is original (that others have not thought of before) and that is appropriate (sensible or useful in some way).

Creativity is of great value to individuals on the job and in daily life. In addition, it is vital for societal progress. Without it, there would be no new inventions, new scientific findings, new movements in art, and new social programs. Therefore, understanding its ingredients and nurturing them from childhood is of paramount concern. As we will see in the following sections, ideas about creativity have changed radically over the past decade.

THE PSYCHOMETRIC VIEW

Until recently, a purely cognitive perspective, inspired by Guilford's distinction between convergent and divergent production, dominated research on creativity. **Convergent thinking**, with its emphasis on arriving at a single correct answer to a problem, is the type of intelligence required for success on most mental tests. **Divergent thinking**, in contrast, refers to the generation of multiple and unusual possibilities when faced with a task or problem and is involved in creativity.

Recognizing that highly creative children (like high-IQ children) are often better at some types of tasks than others, researchers have devised verbal, figural, and "real-world-problem" tests of divergent thinking (Runco, 1992a, 1993; Torrance, 1988). A verbal measure might ask children to name as many uses for common objects (such as a newspaper) as they can. A figural measure might ask them to come up with as many drawings based on a circular motif as possible (see Figure 8.13). A "real-world problem" measure gives children an everyday dilemma (for example, how to use a broken, three-legged chair to sit at a table) and requires them to suggest solutions. Responses to each of these tests can be scored for the number of ideas generated, the flexibility of those ideas (number of different categories into which they fall), and their originality. For example, on a verbal test, saying that a newspaper can be used "as handgrips for a bicycle" would be more unusual than saying it can be used "to clean things."

Because tests of divergent thinking offer a convenient way of comparing people on a standard "creativity" scale, they are often referred to as the *psychometric approach to creativity* (Lubart, 1994). Yet critics of these measures point out that at best, they are imperfect predictors of creative accomplishment in everyday life because they tap only one of the complex, cognitive contributions to creativity. In addition, they say nothing about personality traits, motivational factors, and environmental circumstances that determine whether people with the necessary cognitive capacities will realize their creative potential (Amabile, 1983; Sternberg, 1989). Despite widespread agreement that tests of divergent thinking are incomplete measures of creativity, we will see that they do tap relevant skills, have been the major focus of research on children, and (as we will see shortly) have enhanced our understanding of the development of creativity.

A MULTIFACETED VIEW

Recent theories agree that many elements must converge for creativity to occur (Amabile, 1983; Csikszentmihalyi, 1988; Simonton, 1988; Weisberg, 1993). One influential multifaceted approach that represents this new view is Robert Sternberg and Todd Lubart's (1991a, 1995) **investment theory of creativity**. According to Sternberg and Lubart, people can invest in a variety of projects. Pursuing those that are novel (and therefore currently undervalued by others) will increase the chances of devising a creative, highly valued product. But whether a person invests in novelty—initiates an original project and brings it to fruition—depends on the availability of diverse intellectual, personality, motivational, and environmental resources, summarized in Table 8.6. Each must be present at a minimum level to catalyze creativity, although strength in one (such as perseverance) can compensate for weakness in another (an environment that is lukewarm toward novel ideas).

Sternberg and Lubart (1995) point out that contrary to popular belief, creativity is neither determined at birth nor the prized possession of an elite few. Instead, many people can develop it to varying degrees, and it is likely to reach greater heights when fostered from an early age. Let's look closely at the components of creativity and how we can strengthen them in children.

Convergent thinking
The generation of a single correct answer to a problem. Type of cognition emphasized on intelligence tests.

Divergent thinking
The generation of multiple and unusual possibilities when faced with a task or problem. Associated with creativity.

Investment theory of creativity
Sternberg and Lubart's theory, in which investment in novel projects depends on the availability of diverse intellectual, personality, motivational, and environmental resources, each of which must be present at some minimum level.

FIGURE 8.13

■ *Responses of an 8-year-old who scored high on a figural measure of divergent thinking. This child was asked to make as many pictures as she could from the circles on the page. Her responses are fluid and flexible—characteristics that increase the chances that some will be highly original. Tests of divergent thinking tap only one of the complex, cognitive contributions to creativity. (Test form copyright © 1980 by Scholastic Testing Service, Inc. Reprinted by permission of Scholastic Testing Service from E. P. Torrance, 1980, The Torrance Tests of Creative Thinking.)*

■ COGNITIVE RESOURCES. Creative work brings together a variety of high-level cognitive skills. Rather than just problem solving, it requires *problem finding*—detecting a gap in current knowledge, a need for a new product, or a deficiency with existing procedures. Once a problem is found, *the ability to define it*—to move it from a vague to a clearly specified state—becomes important. In both children and adults, the more effort devoted to defining the problem, the more original the final product (Getzels & Csikszentmihalyi, 1976; Runco & Okuda, 1988). In one study, elementary school pupils were asked to choose an object and write an essay about it. Children who explored more objects, investing heavily in problem discovery and definition, wrote more fluent and original essays (Moore, 1985).

Divergent thinking is an essential tool for generating novel solutions to problems. But the successful creator must also be able to set aside fruitless options in favor of the best responses. Therefore, rather than emphasizing only one mode of reasoning, creativity involves *alternating between divergent and convergent thinking* at opportune moments. And in narrowing the range of possibilities, creative individuals rely on *insight*

TABLE 8.6

Resources Necessary for Creativity

Cognitive	Personality	Motivational	Environmental
Problem finding Problem definition Divergent thinking Convergent thinking Insight processes Evaluation of competing ideas Knowledge	Innovative style of thinking Tolerance of ambiguity Perseverance Willingness to take intellectual risks Courage of one's convictions	Task focused rather than goal focused	Availability of stimulating activities Emphasis on intellectual curiosity Acceptance of child's individual characteristics Provision of systematic instruction relevant to child's talent Availability of time to reflect on ideas Encouragement of flexible and original use of knowledge Provision of challenging, extended assignments that promote tolerance of ambiguity, perseverance, and risk taking Emphasis on task-focused motivators

Sources: Sternberg & Lubart, 1991a, 1995.

processes—ones that combine and restructure elements in sudden but useful ways. For example, using analogies and metaphors to identify unique connections is common among people who have made outstanding creative contributions to literature, art, science, business, and other fields (Barron, 1988). Beginning in the preschool years, children are capable of this kind of thinking (see Chapter 9, page 359). Furthermore, *evaluating competing ideas* to select the most promising keeps creative problem solving moving efficiently toward a high-quality solution. School-age children's evaluative ability is related to their performance on divergent thinking tasks and can be enhanced by instructions to critically assess the originality of ideas (Runco, 1992b).

Finally, *knowledge* is necessary to make a creative contribution to any field, since without it, people cannot recognize or understand new ideas. Perhaps for this reason more than any other, individuals usually demonstrate creativity in only one or a few related domains. When researchers ask children and adults to describe their creative achievements or complete creativity tasks in several areas, cross-domain correlations among their performances are typically quite low, averaging about .20 (Baer, 1991; Lubart & Sternberg, 1995; Runco, 1987). Similarly, eminent creators rarely produce enduring work in more than one or two fields (Gray, 1966). Consequently, high creativity is usually manifested as a special talent.

Consider these multiple cognitive ingredients, and you will see why numerous studies report only a low positive correlation between IQ and creativity, typically around .20 to .30 (Baer, 1991; Torrance, 1988). Although some cognitive requirements for creativity overlap with factors on intelligence tests, others do not. Beyond a minimum level of general intelligence, the presence of other variables determines creative giftedness—which is quite distinct from the academic giftedness best predicted by IQ.

■ PERSONALITY RESOURCES. Personality characteristics facilitate the cognitive components of creativity, ensuring that they will be applied and reach fruition (Lubart, 1994; Sternberg & Lubart, 1995). The following traits are crucial:

1. *Innovative style of thinking.* Creative people not only have the capacity to see things in new ways, but like to do so. They prefer loosely structured activities

permitting innovative restructuring of problems to implementing already defined tasks. In a recent study of thinking styles in middle schools, teachers in the lower grades were more encouraging of the type of thinking linked to creativity, and pupils tended to match their teachers' preferred style (Sternberg & Grigorenko, 1993). These findings suggest that a creative thinking style is at least partially taught and that children adopt the styles of influential role models.

2. *Tolerance of ambiguity and perseverance.* Creative goals inevitably bring periods of uncertainty, when pieces of the problem do not fit together. During those times, we may feel pressure to give up or pursue the first available (but not the best) solution. Encouraging patience and persistence in the face of obstacles can help children develop a creative style.

3. *Willingness to take risks.* Creativity requires a willingness to "deviate from the crowd," to undertake challenge when outcomes are uncertain. Inducing a risk-oriented state of mind enhances divergent thinking scores (Glover, 1977). Yet children's willingness to take risks by choosing difficult over easy assignments declines as they progress through elementary school. As more emphasis is placed on getting good grades, children become less willing to take intellectual chances (Clifford, 1988).

4. *The courage of one's convictions.* Because their ideas are novel, creators may at times doubt them, especially when skeptical teachers or peers criticize them. Independence of judgment and high self-esteem are necessary for creative endeavors.

■ MOTIVATIONAL RESOURCES. Motivation for creativity must be *task focused* rather than *goal focused*. Task-focusing motivators, such as the desire to succeed at a high standard, energize work and keep attention on the problem itself. Goal-focusing motivators, often extrinsic rewards such as grades, divert attention from the task to other goals, thereby impairing performance. In one study, 7- to 11-year-old girls worked on collages, some competing for prizes and others expecting that the prizes would be raffled off. The products of those in the first group were substantially less creative (Amabile, 1982).

Extrinsic rewards, such as competitions and prizes, are not always detrimental to creativity. They communicate that it is socially valued and can encourage children to embark on innovative projects when they otherwise might not do so. But when rewards are overemphasized, children see only "the carrot at the end of the stick," and creativity suffers (Lubart, 1994).

■ ENVIRONMENTAL RESOURCES. Environments can provide physical and social conditions that help new ideas form and develop, or they can stifle them. This means that a child can appear creatively gifted in one context but quite ordinary in another.

Studies of the backgrounds of talented children and highly accomplished adults often reveal homes rich in reading materials and other stimulating activities and parents who emphasize intellectual curiosity and are highly accepting of their youngster's individual characteristics (Albert, 1994; Perleth & Heller, 1994). In addition, such parents recognize their child's creative potential and provide systematic instruction (in the form of out-of-school lessons), assistance with the child's learning, and (as the talent develops) apprenticeship under inspiring teachers (Bloom, 1985; Feldman & Goldsmith, 1991).

Classrooms in which children can take risks, challenge the instructor, and have time to reflect on ideas without being rushed to the next assignment are also facilitating. Elementary school teachers who are neither overly directive nor nondirective, but who balance structure with freedom of choice, have pupils who score higher in divergent thinking (Thomas & Berk, 1981). Unfortunately, creativity is discouraged in many classrooms. Knowledge acquisition is usually stressed over using it flexibly and originally, leading children's thinking to become *entrenched,* or limited to commonplace associations that produce correct answers. Assignments, which are usually short and well defined, do not promote the tolerance of ambiguity, perseverance, and risk taking necessary to sustain creative work. And goal-focusing motivators (grades and the desire to appear competent in front of teachers, parents, and peers) are widespread (Sternberg & Lubart, 1991b).

Although programs for the gifted exist in many schools, debate about their effectiveness typically focuses on factors irrelevant to creativity—whether to provide enrichment

■ *Gardner's theory of multiple intelligences has inspired programs that provide domain-specific enrichment to all pupils. An opportunity to write and perform their own play draws on the linguistic intelligence of these third graders. As specific intelligences are tapped outside of traditional academic assignments, the strengths of children previously thought to be unexceptional are revealed. (Elizabeth Crews/The Image Works)*

in regular classrooms, to offer pullout programs in which youngsters are gathered together for special instruction (the most common practice), or to provide accelerated learning opportunities in which very bright pupils are advanced to a higher grade. Children of all ages fare well academically and socially within each of these models (Moon & Feldhusen, 1994; Southern, Jones, & Stanley, 1994). Yet the extent to which they foster creativity depends on opportunities to acquire relevant skills.

Recently, Gardner's theory of multiple intelligences has served as the basis for several model programs that provide domain-specific enrichment to all pupils. A wide variety of meaningful activities, each designed to tap a specific intelligence or set of intelligences, serve as contexts for assessing strengths and weaknesses and, on that basis, teaching new knowledge and original thinking. For example, linguistic intelligence might be fostered and evaluated through storytelling or playwriting; spatial intelligence through drawing, sculpting, or taking apart and reassembling objects; and kinesthetic intelligence through dance or pantomime (Gardner, 1993).

Evidence is still needed on how effectively these programs nurture children's talents. But so far, they have succeeded in one way—by highlighting the strengths of some pupils who previously had been considered unexceptional or even at risk for school failure. Consequently, they may be especially useful in identifying talented minority children, who are underrepresented in school programs for the gifted (Frazier, 1994). How best to maximize the creative resources of the coming generation—the future poet and scientist as well as the everyday citizen—is a challenge for future research.

SUMMARY

DEFINITIONS OF INTELLIGENCE

- The **psychometric approach** to cognitive development is the basis for the wide variety of intelligence tests used to assess individual differences in children's mental abilities. In the early 1900s, Alfred Binet developed the first successful test, which provided a single, holistic measure of intelligence.
- **Factor analysis** soon emerged as a major means for determining whether intelligence is a single trait or a collection of many different abilities. The research of Spearman and Thurstone led to two schools of thought. The first regarded test items as having in common one **general factor,** or "**g.**" The second viewed intelligence as a set of distinct **primary mental abilities**.
- Modern factor analysts have extended the work of Spearman and Thurstone. Guilford's **structure-of-intellect model** defines a total of 180 separate abilities, several of which acknowledge the existence of social intelligence and creativity. Cattell's distinction between **crystallized** and **fluid intelligence** has influenced many attempts to create culture-fair tests. Carroll's **three-stratum theory of intelligence** is the most comprehensive classification of mental abilities to be confirmed by factor-analytic research.

RECENT ADVANCES IN DEFINING INTELLIGENCE

- To provide process-oriented explanations of mental test performance, some researchers conduct **componential analyses** of children's scores by correlating them with laboratory measures of information processing. So far, findings reveal that basic efficiency of thinking and adaptive strategy use are related to measures of general intelligence. Sternberg's **triarchic theory of intelligence** extends these efforts. It views intelligence as a complex interaction of information-processing skills, specific experiences, and contextual (or cultural) influences.
- According to Gardner's **theory of multiple intelligences,** mental abilities should be defined in terms of unique sets of processing operations applied in culturally meaningful activities. His list of seven distinct intelligences has been influential in efforts to understand and nurture children's special talents.

REPRESENTATIVE INTELLIGENCE TESTS FOR CHILDREN

- **The Stanford-Binet Intelligence Scale** and the **Wechsler Intelligence Scale for Children–III** are most often used to identify highly intelligent children and diagnose those with learning problems. The **Kaufman Assessment Battery for Children** is one of the few tests to be grounded in an explicit cognitive theory. Each of these tests provides an overall IQ as well as a profile of subtest scores.
- Traditional infant tests, which consist largely of perceptual and motor responses, predict childhood IQ poorly. The Fagan Test of Infant Intelligence, made up entirely of habituation–dishabituation items, taps basic aspects of cognitive processing and is the best available infant predictor of childhood IQ. Measures of object permanence also correlate better with preschool intelligence than do traditional infant tests.

THE COMPUTATION AND DISTRIBUTION OF IQ SCORES

- Scores on intelligence tests are arrived at by computing an **intelligence quotient (IQ)**. It compares a child's raw score to the performance of a large representative sample of same-age children.

WHAT AND HOW WELL DO INTELLIGENCE TESTS PREDICT?

- IQs obtained after age 6 show substantial correlational stability. Nevertheless, most children display considerable age-related change in the absolute value of their scores. Poverty-stricken ethnic minority children often experience declines due to a **cumulative deficit,** or the compounding effects of underprivileged rearing conditions.
- IQ is an effective predictor of scholastic performance, occupational attainment, and certain aspects of psychological adjustment. However, the underlying causes of these correlational findings are complex. Besides IQ, home background, personality, motivation, education, and **practical intelligence** contribute substantially to academic and life success.

ETHNIC AND SOCIAL-CLASS DIFFERENCES IN IQ

- Black and low-income children score lower on intelligence tests than do white and middle-income children, findings responsible for kindling the IQ nature–nurture debate. Jensen's **Level I–Level II theory** attributes the poorer scores of these children largely to a genetic deficiency in higher-order, abstract forms of ability. However, his theory has been challenged by subsequent research.

EXPLAINING INDIVIDUAL AND GROUP DIFFERENCES IN IQ

- Heritability estimates support a moderate role for heredity in accounting for individual differences in IQ. However, they cannot be used to explain ethnic and social-class differences in test scores.
- Adoption studies indicate that advantaged rearing conditions can raise the absolute value of children's IQs substantially. At the same time, adopted children's scores correlate more strongly with those of their biological than adoptive relatives, providing support for the influence of heredity. Research on black children reared in white middle-class homes reveals that the black–white IQ gap is environmentally determined.
- Experts disagree on whether intelligence tests yield biased measures of the mental abilities of low-income minority children. IQ predicts academic achievement equally well

for majority and minority children. However, lack of familiarity with test content, language customs, and motivational factors can lead test scores to underestimate minority children's intelligence. By introducing purposeful teaching into the testing situation, **dynamic assessment** narrows the gap between a child's actual and potential performance.

- Besides heredity, **shared** and **nonshared environmental influences** contribute to individual differences in intelligence. Research with the **Home Observation for Measurement of the Environment (HOME)** indicates that overall quality of the home environment consistently predicts IQ. Although the HOME–IQ relationship is partly mediated by heredity, a stimulating family environment does promote higher mental test scores. Factors considered by the **confluence model,** such as birth order and spacing, are also linked to IQ. However, these relationships are weak, and the confluence model has received only mixed support.

EARLY INTERVENTION AND INTELLECTUAL DEVELOPMENT

- Research on high-quality university-based early interventions as well as **Head Start** programs located in American communities shows that immediate IQ gains **wash out** with time. However, lasting benefits occur in school adjustment and ability to meet basic educational requirements.
- To induce larger and longer-lasting cognitive gains, early intervention needs to start earlier, last longer, and be more intensive. Two-generation program strategies are currently being tried to see if they lead to more powerful long-term outcomes.

BEYOND IQ: DEVELOPMENT OF CREATIVITY

- Recognition that intelligence tests do not sample the full range of human mental skills has led conceptions of giftedness to expand to include **creativity.** The psychometric approach to creativity, which emphasizes the distinction between **convergent** and **divergent thinking,** has given way to new, multifaceted approaches. According to Sternberg and Lubart's **investment theory of creativity,** a wide variety of intellectual, personality, motivational, and environmental resources must be present to initiate creative projects and bring them to fruition. Each can be fostered in children's homes and schools.

IMPORTANT TERMS AND CONCEPTS

psychometric approach (p. 299)
factor analysis (p. 301)
general factor, or "g" (p. 301)
specific factor, or "s" (p. 301)
primary mental abilities (p. 301)
structure-of-intellect model (p. 303)
crystallized intelligence (p. 304)
fluid intelligence (p. 304)
three-stratum theory of intelligence (p. 304)
componential analysis (p. 304)
triarchic theory of intelligence (p. 306)
theory of multiple intelligences (p. 307)
Stanford-Binet Intelligence Scale (p. 309)
Wechsler Intelligence Scale for Children–III (WISC–III) (p. 309)
Kaufman Assessment Battery for Children (K-ABC) (p. 309)
intelligence quotient (IQ) (p. 311)
cumulative deficit hypothesis (p. 313)
practical intelligence (p. 315)
Level I–Level II theory (p. 317)
dynamic assessment (p. 324)
shared environmental influences (p. 325)
nonshared environmental influences (p. 325)
Home Observation for Measurement of the Environment (HOME) (p. 325)
confluence model (p. 326)
Project Head Start (p. 328)
washout effect (p. 329)
creativity (p. 331)
convergent thinking (p. 332)
divergent thinking (p. 332)
investment theory of creativity (p. 332)

CONNECTIONS for Chapter 8

If you are interested in . . .	turn to . . .	to learn about . . .
Culture and intellectual skills	Chapter 1, p. 27	Cultural variation in cognitive skills
	Chapter 6, p. 239–240	Culture and concrete operational thought
	Chapter 6, p. 244	Culture and formal operational thought
	Chapter 7, p. 273	Culture and memory strategies
	Chapter 7, p. 291	Korean children's understanding of multidigit addition and subtraction
	Chapter 9, p. 345	Children invent language: The case of Hawaiian Creole English
	Chapter 9, pp. 374–375	Bilingualism in childhood and cognitive skills
	Chapter 12, pp. 479–480	Culture and moral reasoning
	Chapter 15, p. 621	Education in Japan, Taiwan, and the United States
Home environment and intellectual development	Chapter 3, pp. 110–111	Caregiving and development of preterm and low-birth-weight infants
	Chapter 6, p. 249	Parental scaffolding of cognitive skills
	Chapter 9, pp. 350, 360, 367, 368	Parent-child interaction and early language development
	Chapter 11, pp. 435, 436–437	Parental communication, achievement-related attributions, and cognitive performance
	Chapter 12, pp. 464, 478	Child-rearing practices
	Chapter 13, p. 512	Parent-child interaction and sex-related differences in mental abilities
	Chapter 14, pp. 543–545	Child-rearing styles and cognitive skills
	Chapter 14, pp. 549–550	Social class, poverty, and intellectual development
Early intervention	Chapter 3, p. 80	Intervention for children with Down syndrome
	Chapter 3, p. 99	Intervention for prenatally malnourished infants
	Chapter 3, pp. 110–111	Intervention for preterm infants
	Chapter 4, pp. 133–134	NBAS-based intervention
	Chapter 10, p. 417 Chapter 14, pp. 567–569	High-quality day care as effective early intervention

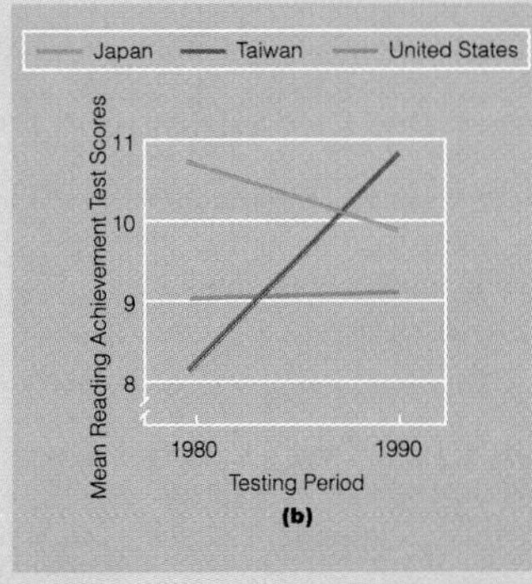

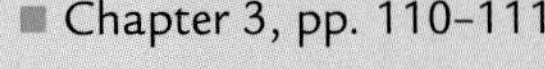

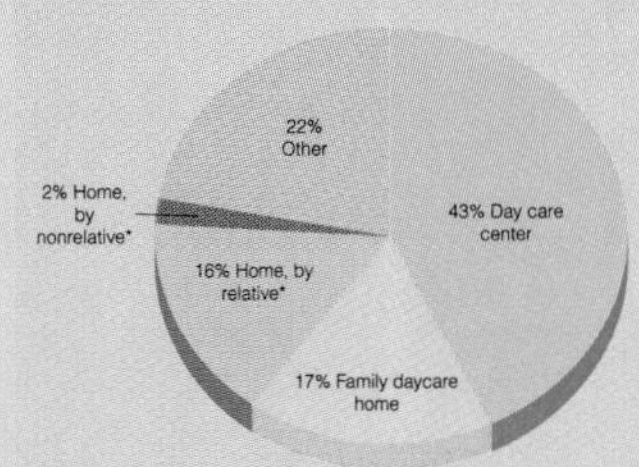

9 Language Development

"Bah-bah!" yells 1-year-old Mark while waving good-bye as his mother backs the car out of the driveway at grandmother's house. As she pulls onto the freeway and heads for home, Mark calls out insistently, "Bel! Bel!" He tugs at the seat belt, looking alternately at it and his mother beside him.

"The seat belt, Mark?" his mother responds. "Let's keep it on. Look!" she says. "Here's something," handing him a cracker.

"Caa-ca. Caa-ca," says Mark, who begins to eat contentedly.

"Can you shut the front door?" Susan's father shouts from upstairs to his 3-year-old daughter.

"There, I shutted it, Dad," calls Susan after closing the door. "No more wind's in here now."

Four-year-old Connie reaches for a piece of toast as she looks over the choices of jams and jellies at the breakfast table. "Mama, there's no more honey, is there?" she says.

"That's right, we ran out," her mother acknowledges. "We need to buy some more."

"There's a beehive at Uncle Joe's farm, so we could get some there," suggests Connie.

"We won't be seeing Uncle Joe until next summer," explains Connie's mother. "I'll get a jar at the store while you're at nursery school."

Language—the most awesome of universal human achievements—develops with extraordinary speed over the early childhood years. At age 1, Mark uses single words to name familiar objects and convey his desires. Three-year-old Susan already grasps some subtle conventions of human communication. Although her father's message is phrased as a question, she knows that he intends it to be a command and willingly complies by closing the door. In her report of the accomplished act, Susan combines words into meaningful sentences she has never heard before. Even her mistakes, such as "shutted," attest to her active, rule-oriented approach to language. Four-year-old Connie produces longer utterances and more sophisticated language structures. In making topic-relevant comments in a short exchange with her mother, Connie shows that she is a skilled conversational partner.

Children's amazing linguistic accomplishments raise some of the most puzzling questions about development. How are a vast vocabulary and an intricate grammatical system acquired in such a short time? Is language a separate capacity, or is it simply one aspect of our general cognitive ability? Without exposure to a rich verbal environment, will young children invent their own language? Do all children acquire language in the same way, or are there individual and cultural differences?

To explore these questions, we follow the common practice of dividing language into four components. By examining each separately, we can more fully appreciate the diverse skills children must master to become competent communicators. Our discussion of development opens with the fiery theoretical debate of the 1950s between behaviorist B. F. Skinner and linguist Noam Chomsky, which inspired the burst of research since that time. Then we turn to infant preparatory skills that set the stage for the child's first words during the second year of life. Next, for each component of language, we first describe what develops and then treat the more controversial question of how children acquire so much in so little time. We conclude with the challenges and benefits of bilingualism—mastering two languages—in childhood.

■ *To engage in effective verbal communication, children must combine four components of language that have to do with sound, meaning, overall structure, and everyday use. (Julie O'Neil/The Picture Cube)*

Components of Language

When children learn language, exactly what is it that they must learn? Language consists of several subsystems that have to do with sound, meaning, overall structure, and everyday use. Knowing language entails mastering each of these aspects and combining them into a flexible communicative system.

The first component, **phonology**, refers to the sounds of language. If you have ever visited a foreign country in which you did not know the language, you probably wondered how anyone could analyze the rapid flow of speech sounds into organized strings of words. Yet in English, you easily apply an intricate set of rules to comprehend and produce complicated sound patterns. How you acquired this ability is the story of phonological development.

Semantics involves vocabulary, or the way underlying concepts are expressed in words and word combinations. As we will see later, when young children first use a word, it often does not mean the same thing as it does to an adult. To build a versatile vocabulary, preschoolers must refine the meanings of thousands of words and connect them into elaborate networks of related terms. With age, children not only use many words correctly but become consciously aware of what they mean. As a result, they can define and experiment with words in imaginative ways.

Once mastery of vocabulary is underway, children begin to combine words and modify them in meaningful ways. Knowledge of **grammar** consists of two main parts: *syntax,* the rules by which words are arranged into sentences; and *morphology,* the use of grammatical markers that indicate number, tense, case, person, gender, active or passive voice, and other meanings (the "-s" and "-ed" endings are examples in English).

Finally, **pragmatics** refers to the communicative side of language. To interact effectively, children must learn to take turns, maintain topic relevance, and state their meaning clearly. In addition, they must figure out how gestures, tone of voice, and the context in which an utterance is spoken clarify meaning. Pragmatics also involves *sociolinguistic knowledge,* since society dictates how language should be spoken. To be successful communicators, children must acquire certain interaction rituals, such as verbal greetings and leave-takings. They must also adjust their speech to mark important social relationships, such as differences in age and status.

As we take up each of the four aspects of language, you will see that they are really interdependent. Acquisition of each one facilitates mastery of the others.

Phonology
The component of language concerned with understanding and producing speech sounds.

Semantics
The component of language concerned with understanding the meaning of words and word combinations.

Grammar
The component of language concerned with *syntax,* the rules by which words are arranged into sentences, and *morphology,* the use of grammatical markers that indicate number, tense, case, person, gender, and other meanings.

Pragmatics
The component of language concerned with how to engage in effective and appropriate communication with others.

Theories of Language Development

During the first half of this century, research on language development was primarily descriptive—aimed at establishing norms of development. The first studies identified milestones that applied to children around the globe: all babbled around 6 months, said their first words at about 1 year, combined words at the end of the second year, and were in command of a vast vocabulary and most grammatical constructions by 4 to 5 years of age. The regularity of these achievements suggested a process largely governed by maturation. Yet at the same time, language seemed to be learned, since without exposure to a spoken language, children who were born deaf or who were severely neglected did not acquire verbal communication. This apparent contradiction set the stage for a nature–nurture debate as intense as any that has been waged in the field of child development. By the end of the 1950s, two major figures had taken opposite sides in the controversy.

THE BEHAVIORIST PERSPECTIVE

In his book *Verbal Behavior,* published in 1957, B. F. Skinner concluded that language, just like any other behavior, is acquired through *operant conditioning*. As the baby makes sounds, parents reinforce those that are most like words with smiles, hugs, and speech in return. For example, at 12 months my older son David could often be heard babbling something like this: "book-a-book-a-dook-a-dook-a-book-a-nook-a-book-aaa." One day, I held up his picture book while he babbled away and said, "Book!" Very soon, David was saying "book-aaa" in the presence of books. *Imitation* has also been added to behaviorist accounts, to explain how children rapidly pick up complex utterances, such as whole phrases and sentences (Whitehurst & Vasta, 1975). And imitation can combine with reinforcement to promote language, as when a parent coaxes, "Say 'I want a cookie,'" and delivers praise and a treat after the child responds correctly.

As these examples indicate, reinforcement and imitation contribute to early language learning. At the same time, only a few researchers cling to the behaviorist perspective today (see, for example, Moerk, 1992). Think, for a moment, about the process of language development we have described. Adults must engage in intensive language tutoring—continuously modeling and reinforcing so that by age 6, children have an extensive vocabulary and produce an enormous number of complex sentences. This seems like a physically impossible task, even for the most conscientious parents. Furthermore, we have already seen that children create novel utterances that could not have been copied from or reinforced by others, such as Susan's use of "shutted" at the beginning of this chapter. This suggests that instead of learning specific sentences, young children develop a working knowledge of grammatical rules.

Nevertheless, the ideas of Skinner and other behaviorists should not be dismissed entirely. Throughout this chapter, we will see how adult responsiveness and example support children's language learning, even though they do not fully explain it. Behaviorist principles are also valuable to speech and language therapists in their efforts to help children with serious language delays and disabilities overcome their problems (Ratner, 1993).

THE NATIVIST PERSPECTIVE

Linguist Noam Chomsky's (1957) book *Syntactic Structures,* along with his critical review of Skinner's theory, first convinced the scientific community that children assume much responsibility for their own language learning. In contrast to behaviorism, Chomsky (1959) argued that internal mental structures are at the heart of our capacity to interpret and generate language. His alternative theory is a nativist account that regards language as a biologically based, uniquely human accomplishment.

Focusing on children's grammatical achievements, Chomsky reasoned that the rules for sentence organization are too complex to be directly taught to or discovered by cognitively immature young children. Instead, humans are born with a **language acquisition**

Language acquisition device (LAD) In Chomsky's theory, a biologically based, innate system for picking up language that permits children, as soon as they have acquired sufficient vocabulary, to combine words into grammatically consistent utterances and to understand the meaning of sentences they hear.

device (LAD), a biologically based, innate module[1] for picking up language that needs only to be triggered by verbal input from the environment. The LAD permits children, as soon as they have acquired sufficient vocabulary, to combine words into grammatically consistent, novel utterances and to understand the meaning of sentences they hear.

How can a single LAD account for children's mastery of diverse languages around the world? According to Chomsky (1976), within the LAD is a *universal grammar,* a built-in storehouse of rules that apply to all human languages. Young children use this knowledge to decipher grammatical categories and relationships in any language to which they are exposed. In proposing a universal grammar, Chomsky's theory emphasizes features the world's languages have in common. It assumes that wide variation in their structural properties can be reduced to the same underlying set of rules. Furthermore, since the LAD is specifically suited for language processing, sophisticated cognitive capacities are not required to master the structure of language. Instead, children do so spontaneously with only limited language exposure. Therefore, in sharp contrast to the behaviorist view, the nativist perspective regards deliberate training by parents as unnecessary for language development. Instead, the LAD ensures that language will be acquired early and swiftly, despite its inherent complexity (Pinker, 1994).

■ SUPPORT FOR THE NATIVIST PERSPECTIVE. Are children biologically primed to acquire language? Research reviewed in the Cultural Influences box on the following page, which suggests that children have a remarkable ability to invent new language systems, provides some of the most powerful support for this perspective. And three additional sets of evidence—efforts to teach nonhuman primates language systems, localization of language functions in the human brain, and investigations into whether a sensitive period exists for language development—are also consistent with Chomsky's view that humans are prepared for language in a specialized way. Let's look at each in turn.

Can Great Apes Acquire Language? Is the ability to master a grammatically complex language system a uniquely human attribute? To find out, many attempts have been made to teach language to chimpanzees, who are closest to humans in the evolutionary hierarchy. In some instances, researchers have created artificial languages for this purpose, such as plastic tokens that can be manipulated to represent sentences or computer consoles that generate strings of visual symbols (Premack, 1976; Rumbaugh, 1977). In other cases, chimps have been trained in American Sign Language, a gestural communication system used by the deaf that is as elaborate as any spoken language (Gardner & Gardner, 1969; Terrace et al., 1980).

Clearly, great apes have some capacity for symbolic communication. For example, in the wild, young chimpanzees and orangutans use intentional gestures, such as cupping

[1] Return to Chapter 6, pages 224 and 245 to review the modular view of the mind.

■ *Nim, a chimp taught American Sign Language, built a vocabulary of more than one hundred signs over several years of training. In addition, his two-sign combinations, such as "groom me," "hug Nim," and "Nim book," were similar to those of human toddlers. But for sign strings longer than two, Nim's productions showed little resemblance to human grammar. (Susan Kuklin/Photo Researchers)*

CULTURAL INFLUENCES

Children Invent Language: The Case of Hawaiian Creole English

Can instances be found in which children develop complex language systems with only minimal language input? If so, this evidence would serve as strong support for Chomsky's idea that humans are born with a biological program for language development.

In a series of studies, Susan Goldin-Meadow reported that deaf preschoolers who had not been taught sign language spontaneously produced a gestural communication system strikingly similar to hearing children's verbal language (Goldin-Meadow & Morford, 1985; Goldin-Meadow & Mylander, 1983). However, critics claim that the deaf children's competencies might have resulted from subtle gestural exchanges with their parents (Bohannon, 1993).

The study of *creoles* offers an alternative test of the nativist perspective. Creoles are languages that arise rapidly from *pidgins*, which are minimally developed "emergency" tongues that result when several language communities migrate to the same area and no dominant language exists to support interaction among them. In 1876, large numbers of immigrants from China, Japan, Korea, the Philippines, Puerto Rico, and Portugal came to Hawaii to work in the sugar industry. The multilingual population quickly outnumbered other residents—English speakers and native Hawaiians alike. Out of this melting pot, Hawaiian Pidgin English emerged, a communication system with a small vocabulary and narrow range of grammatical options that permitted new immigrants to "get by" in everyday life. Pidgin English, however, was so limited in its possibilities and applied so unsystematically that it may have offered young children too little language input from which to learn. Yet within 20 to 30 years, a new complex language, Hawaiian Creole English, which borrowed vocabulary from its pidgin and foreign-language predecessors, became widespread. How could this remarkable linguistic achievement have occurred?

Derek Bickerton (1981, 1990) concludes that the next generation of children must have invented the language, relying on innate mechanisms. Support for this conclusion is of two kinds. First, the structure of creole languages is similar around the world, suggesting that a common genetic program underlies them. Second, creole grammar resembles the linguistic structures children first use when acquiring any language and their incorrect hypotheses about complex grammatical forms. For example, expressions like "He no bite you" and "Where he put the toy?" are perfectly correct in Hawaiian Creole English. According to Bickerton,

> The child does not, initially, "learn language." As he develops, the genetic program for language which is his hominid inheritance unrolls exactly as does the genetic program that determines his increase in size (and) muscular control. . . . "Learning" consists of adapting this program, revising it, adjusting it to fit the realities of the cultural language he happens to encounter. Without such a program, the simplest of cultural languages would be quite unlearnable. (1981, pp. 296–297)

Bickerton believes that the child's biological language is always there, under the surface, ready to reemerge when cultural language is shattered. However, no one has yet been able to observe the language development of first-generation creole children directly. Some researchers claim that without such evidence, we cannot be entirely sure that adult input plays little role in the creation of creole (Tomasello, 1995).

■ *These children are descendants of immigrants who came from many parts of the world to work in the sugar industry in Hawaii in the 1870s. The multilingual population began to speak Hawaiian Pidgin English, a simplified communication system that permitted them to "get by" in everyday life. Yet the next generation spoke a new complex language, Hawaiian Creole English, believed to have been invented by children. The existence of creoles is among the most powerful evidence for Chomsky's idea that humans are born with a biological program for language development. (Bob Abraham/Pacific Stock)*

FIGURE 9.1

■ *Two structures in the left hemisphere of the cortex involved in language processing.* Broca's area *controls language production by creating a detailed program for articulation, which it sends to the face area of* precentral gyrus *(responsible for body movement and coordination.) Damage to Broca's area disrupts production but not comprehension of speech.* Wernicke's area *interprets language by receiving impulses from the* primary auditory area *(where sensations from the ears are sent). Damage to Wernicke's area results in speech laced with nonsense words and difficulty comprehending the speech of others. Wernicke's area communicates with Broca's area through a bundle of nerve fibers called the* arcuate fasciculus.

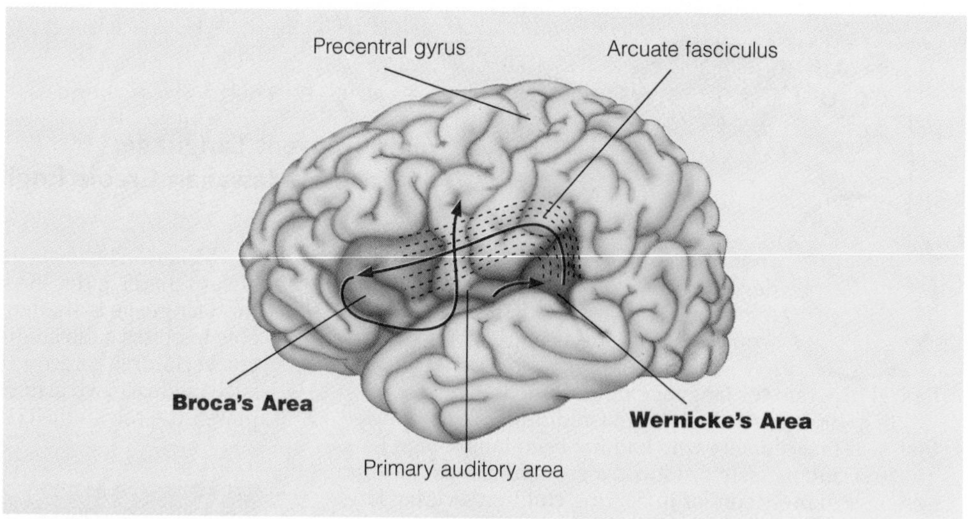

their hands to request food from their mothers, that precede spoken language in human children (Bard, 1992; Ghiglieri, 1988). Nevertheless, the ability of apes to acquire a humanlike language system appears to be limited. Many months and sometimes years of training and reinforcement are necessary to get them to master a basic vocabulary. And although their two-sign combinations resemble the two-word utterances of human toddlers, there is no convincing evidence that chimpanzees can master complex grammatical forms. Sign strings longer than two generally do not conform to a rule-based structure (Berko Gleason, 1993). For example, one chimp named Nim either repeated information or combined words nonsensically in his three- and four-word utterances. "Eat Nim eat" and "Play me Nim play" are typical examples (Terrace et al., 1980).

Still, these findings do not tell us for sure that humans are endowed with a specialized language capacity. Perhaps cognitive abilities or social and motivational factors account for the linguistic gap between chimpanzees and humans. Furthermore, not all species of apes have been studied as extensively as the common chimp, the subject of the research just described. Recently, Sue Savage-Rumbaugh and her collaborators (1990, 1993) investigated pygmy chimps, who are more socially skilled and adept at observational learning than are common chimps. The researchers also used a new instructional approach in which they encouraged these chimps to comprehend a wide range of expressions before requiring that they produce language—a form of learning resembling that of human children. Results revealed more rapid vocabulary development and better comprehension of novel sentences than ever before attained by nonhuman primates. Nevertheless, even pygmy chimps require several extra years of experience to attain the basic grammatical understandings of human 2- to 3-year-olds. And other evidence lends additional weight to the nativist argument.

Language Areas in the Brain. Humans have evolved specialized regions in the brain that support language skills. Recall from Chapter 5 that for most individuals, language is housed in the left hemisphere of the cortex. Within it are two language-specific structures (see Figure 9.1). **Broca's area**, located in the frontal lobe, controls language production. Damage to it results in a specific *aphasia,* or communication disorder, in which the person has good comprehension but speaks in a slow, labored, ungrammatical, and emotionally flat fashion. In contrast, **Wernicke's area**, located in the temporal lobe, is responsible for interpreting language. When it is damaged, speech is fluent and grammatical, but it contains many nonsense words. Comprehension of others' speech is also impaired.

Furthermore, psychophysiological research suggests that as children acquire language, the brain becomes increasingly specialized for language processing. When researchers recorded event-related potentials (ERPs) as 20-month-olds listened to words within their vocabularies, toddlers advanced in language development showed electrical activity concentrated in certain regions of the left hemisphere, whereas those less advanced displayed a more widely distributed response (Mills, Coffey-Corina, & Neville, 1993). This relationship between language competence and lateralization of language functions has also been found among language-impaired children and adults acquiring a second language (Neville et al., 1993; Weber-Fox & Neville, 1992). It is certainly consistent with the idea that a language module develops in a specific part of the brain.

Broca's area
A language structure located in the frontal lobe of the cerebral cortex that controls language production.

Wernicke's area
A language structure located in the temporal lobe of the cortex that is responsible for interpreting language.

Is There a Sensitive Period for Language Development? Recall from Chapter 5 that the brain, although already lateralized at birth, becomes increasingly specialized during childhood. Erik Lenneberg (1967) first proposed that children must acquire language during the age span of brain lateralization, which he believed to be complete by puberty. If this idea is correct, it would provide further support for the nativist position that language development has unique biological properties.

To test this sensitive period idea, researchers have tracked the recovery of severely abused children who experienced little human contact in childhood. The most recent thorough study is of Genie, a child isolated at 20 months in the back room of her parents' house and not discovered until she was 13½ years old.[2] Genie's early environment was linguistically and emotionally impoverished. No one was permitted to talk to her, and she was beaten when she made any noise. Over several years of training with dedicated caregivers, Genie's language developed, but not nearly to the same extent as that of normal children. Although she eventually acquired a large vocabulary and good comprehension of everyday conversation, her grammatical abilities (like those of the brain-damaged youngsters mentioned in the preceding section) were limited. Genie's case, along with findings on several other similar children, fits with Lenneberg's hypothesis that language learning is optimal during the period of brain lateralization (Curtiss, 1977, 1989).

What about acquiring a second language? Is this task harder during adolescence and adulthood, after a sensitive period for language development is passed? Once again, research says yes. In a study of Chinese and Korean adults who had immigrated to the United States at varying ages, those who began mastering English between 3 and 7 years scored as well as native speakers on a test of grammatical knowledge (see Figure 9.2). As age of arrival in the United States increased through adolescence, test scores gradually declined. Similar outcomes occur for deaf adults who learned American Sign Language at different ages (Johnson & Newport, 1989; Newport, 1991).

■ LIMITATIONS OF THE NATIVIST PERSPECTIVE. Chomsky's theory has had a major impact on current views of language development. It is now widely accepted that a uniquely human biological predisposition plays a powerful role in language learning. Still, Chomsky's account of development has been challenged on several grounds.

First, comparisons among languages reveal vastly different grammatical systems. Chomsky (1981) and others have attempted to specify an underlying universal grammar, but as yet a single set of rules that encompasses all languages has not been identified. Even simple grammatical distinctions, such as the use of *the* versus *a*, are made in quite different ways around the world. For example, several African languages rely on tone patterns to designate these articles. In Japanese and Chinese, they are inferred entirely from sentence context. In Finnish, *en* is attached to the front of a word to signify *the*, to the

[2] Medical records of Genie's early infancy suggest that she was an alert, responsive baby. Her motor development was normal, and she said her first words just before her confinement, after which all language disappeared. Therefore, mental retardation is an unlikely explanation for the course of her development.

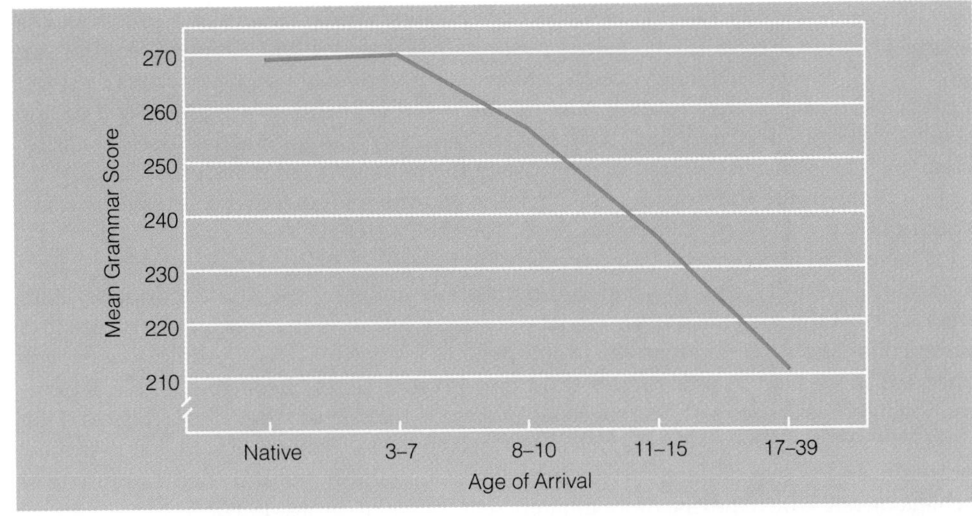

FIGURE 9.2

■ *Relationship between age of arrival of Chinese and Korean immigrants in the United States and performance on a test of English grammar. Individuals who began learning English in childhood attained the competence of native speakers. With increasing age through adolescence, scores declined. (From J. S. Johnson & E. L. Newport, 1989, "Critical Period Effects in Second Language Learning: The Influence of Maturational State on the Acquisition of English as a Second Language,"* Cognitive Psychology, *21, p. 79. Copyright © 1989 by Academic Press. Reprinted by permission.)*

back of a word to signify *a*. Critics of Chomsky's theory doubt the existence of a universal grammar that can account for such varied approaches to conveying the same grammatical forms (Maratsos, 1989; Tomasello, 1995).

Second, Chomsky's assumption that grammatical knowledge is innately determined does not fit with certain observations of language development. Although extraordinary strides are made during preschool years, children's acquisition of many sentence constructions is not immediate but steady and gradual. Complete mastery of some forms (such as the passive voice) is not achieved until well into middle childhood, and very subtle aspects of grammar continue to be refined into the adult years (Horgan, 1978; Menyuk, 1977). This suggests that more learning and discovery are involved in grammatical development than Chomsky assumed.

Third, although certain regions of the cortex are specialized for language, our knowledge of which parts deal with which language functions is very limited. Look back at the deficits resulting from damage to Broca's and Wernicke's areas, and you will see that several aspects of language—not just grammar—are involved in each. Other evidence reveals that additional parts of the cortex (for example, frontal lobe regions that permit us to relate concepts to one another) must support these specialized areas for effective language functioning (Bates, 1995; Blumstein, 1995). At present, the biological basis of Chomsky's LAD is far from clear.

Finally, dissatisfaction with Chomsky's theory has also arisen from its lack of comprehensiveness. For example, in focusing on language structure at the sentence level, it cannot explain how children weave statements together into connected discourse and develop strategies for sustaining meaningful conversations. Perhaps because Chomsky did not dwell on the pragmatic side of language, his theory grants little attention to quality of language input and social experience in supporting language development. Furthermore, we have already noted that the nativist perspective does not regard children's cognitive capacities as important. Yet in Chapter 6, we saw that attainment of cognitive milestones is involved in children's early vocabulary growth. And later in this chapter, we will encounter evidence that cognitive development has at least some effect on children's ability to detect grammatical structure as well.

THE INTERACTIONIST PERSPECTIVE

In recent years, new theories of language development have arisen, emphasizing interactions between inner predispositions and environmental inputs, replacing the dichotomy that grew out of the Skinner–Chomsky debate. Although several interactionist models exist, virtually all stress the social context of language learning. An active child, well endowed for acquiring language, observes and engages in social exchanges with others. Out of this experience, the child builds a communication system that relates the form and content of language to its social meaning. According to this view, native capacity, a strong desire to interact with others, and a rich linguistic and social environment combine to assist children in discovering the functions and regularities of language (Bohannon, 1993).

Although all interactionists regard the child as an active communicative being, debate continues over the precise nature of children's innate abilities. Some theorists accept a modified view of Chomsky's position, which states that although children are primed to make sense of language, they formulate and refine hypotheses about its structure based on input they receive (Slobin, 1985). Other theorists are impressed by the remarkable cognitive capacities of infants and preschoolers that we discussed in earlier chapters. They believe children make sense of their complex language environments by applying powerful analytic tools of a general cognitive kind rather than ones that are specifically tuned to language (Bates, 1995; Tomasello, 1995).

As we chart the course of language development, we will describe some of these new views, but we must keep in mind that none are completely verified yet. Indeed, even interactionist theories have not escaped the critical eye of modern researchers. Because interactionists assume that language competence grows out of communicative experience, we should not be able to find children who show large disparities between pragmatics and other aspects of language skill. Yet recall that Genie's development was quite uneven in this respect. And studies of severely retarded youngsters reveal that their semantic and conversational skills often lag considerably behind their grammatical achievements, which may be more innately determined (Curtiss, 1989).

Consequently, today there is increasing acknowledgment that biology, cognition, and social experience may operate in different balances with respect to each component of language. And to complicate matters further, the relative contributions of these factors may change with age (Owens, 1996). Research on children's language continues to face many theoretical puzzles. We still know much more about the course of language development than precisely how language acquisition takes place.

BRIEF REVIEW

In mastering language, children acquire four components—phonology, semantics, grammar, and pragmatics—that they combine into a flexible communication system. Three theories provide different accounts of how children develop language. According to Skinner and other behaviorists, language is learned through operant conditioning and imitation. However, these principles cannot account for the speed of early language development or children's novel, rule-based utterances. In contrast, Chomsky's nativist view regards children as biologically equipped with a language acquisition device (LAD) that supports rapid early mastery of the structure of language. Although much evidence supports a biological contribution to language development, Chomsky's theory fails to explain many aspects of language learning. Interactionist theories offer a compromise between these two views, stressing that innate abilities and social contexts combine to promote language development.

Prelinguistic Development: Getting Ready to Talk

From the very beginning, infants are prepared to acquire language. During the first year of life, inborn capabilities, cognitive and social milestones, and environmental supports pave the way for the onset of verbal communication.

RECEPTIVITY TO LANGUAGE

Recall from Chapter 4 that neonates are especially sensitive to the pitch range of the human voice and find speech to be more pleasing than other sounds. In addition, they have an astonishing ability to make fine-grained distinctions among the sounds of virtually any human language. Because this skill may help them crack the phonological code of their native tongue, let's look at it more closely.

As adults, we analyze the speech stream into **phonemes**, or sound categories—the smallest speech units we can perceive, such as the difference between the consonant sounds in "pa" and "ba." Phonemes are not the same across all languages. For example, "ra" and "la" are separate sounds to English speakers, but Japanese individuals hear them as the same. Similarly, an English speaker has trouble perceiving the difference between the two "p" sounds used in the Thai language. This tendency to perceive as identical a range of sounds that belong to the same phonemic class is called **categorical speech perception**. Like children and adults, 1-month-olds are capable of it. But unlike older individuals, they are sensitive to a much wider range of categories than exists in their own language environment (Jusczyk, 1995; Werker & Pegg, 1992).

Within the first few days after birth, babies distinguish and prefer the overall sound pattern of their native tongue to that of other languages (Mehler et al., 1988). As infants continue to listen actively to the talk of people around them, they learn to focus on meaningful sound variations. By 6 months of age, long before they are ready to talk, babies start to organize speech into the phonemic categories of their own language. That is, they stop responding to sound distinctions that are not useful in their language community (Kuhl et al., 1992).

Phoneme
The smallest speech unit that can be distinguished perceptually.

Categorical speech perception
The tendency to perceive a range of sounds that belong to the same phonemic class as identical.

This Nepalese mother speaks to her baby daughter in short, clearly pronounced sentences with high-pitched, exaggerated intonation. Adults in many countries use this form of language, called motherese, with infants and toddlers. It eases the task of early language learning. (David Austen/Stock Boston)

In the second half of the first year, babies focus on larger speech units that are crucial for making sense of what they hear. They start to respond to familiar words in spoken passages (Jusczyk & Aslin, 1995). And they can detect phrase units. In one study, researchers recorded two versions of a mother telling a story. In the first, she spoke naturally, with pauses occurring between clauses, like this: "Cinderella lived in a great big house [pause], but it was sort of dark [pause] because she had this mean stepmother." In the second version, the mother inserted pauses in unnatural places—in the middle of clauses: "Cinderella lived in a great big house, but it was [pause] sort of dark because she had [pause] this mean stepmother." Like adults, 7-month-olds clearly preferred speech with natural breaks (Hirsh-Pasek et al., 1987). By 9 months, infants extend this sensitivity to individual words. They listen much longer to a speech stream with stress patterns and phoneme sequences common in their own language, and they perceive it in wordlike segments (Jusczyk, Cutler, & Redanz, 1993; Jusczyk, Charles-Luce, & Luce, 1994; Morgan & Saffran, 1995).

At the same time, certain features of adult talk to young language learners assist babies in making sense of a complex speech stream. Adults in many countries speak to infants and toddlers in **motherese** (also called **child-directed speech**)—a form of language made up of short sentences with high-pitched, exaggerated intonation, clear pronunciation, and distinct pauses between speech segments (Fernald et al., 1989). Deaf mothers show a similar style of communication with their babies. They form signs at a slower tempo and exaggerate the movements associated with each (Masataka, 1992).

Why do adults use motherese? They do not seem to be deliberately trying to teach infants to talk, since many of the same speech qualities appear when they communicate with foreigners. Motherese probably arises from an unconscious desire to keep a young child's attention and ease the task of understanding, and it works effectively in these ways. From birth on, infants prefer to listen to motherese over other kinds of adult talk. When they hear it, they respond with visual focus, positive affect, and (at older ages) vocalizations that are similar in pitch and intonation (Cooper & Aslin, 1994; Fernald, 1993).

Furthermore, parents constantly fine-tune motherese, adjusting the length and content of their utterances to fit with children's needs. For example, in a recent study of "baby talk" in four cultures, Argentinean, French, Japanese, and American mothers tended to speak to 5-month-olds in affect-laden ways, emphasizing greetings, repeated sounds, and terms of endearment. At 13 months, when toddlers began to understand as well as respond, a greater percentage of maternal speech in each culture was information-laden—concerned with giving directions, asking questions, and describing what was happening at the moment (Bornstein et al., 1992). The more effectively parents modify speech complexity over the first year, the better their children's language comprehension at 18 months of age (Murray, Johnson, & Peters, 1990).

FIRST SPEECH SOUNDS

Around 2 months, babies begin to make vowel-like noises, called **cooing** because of their pleasant "oo" quality. Gradually, consonants are added, and around 6 months **babbling** appears, in which infants repeat consonant–vowel combinations in long strings, such as "babababababa" and "nanananana."

The timing of early babbling seems to be due to maturation, since babies everywhere (even those who are deaf) start babbling at about the same age and produce a similar range of early sounds (Stoel-Gammon & Otomo, 1986). However, for babbling to develop further, infants must be exposed to human speech. Around 7 months, babbling starts to include the sounds of mature spoken languages. However, if a baby is hearing impaired, these speechlike sounds emerge several months to years later and, in the case of deaf infants, are totally absent (Eilers & Oller, 1994; Oller & Eilers, 1988). But babbling is not restricted to the spoken modality. When deaf infants are exposed to sign language from birth, they babble manually in much the same way hearing infants do through speech (Petitto & Marentette, 1991).

Although language input is necessary for babbling to be sustained, maturation continues to affect its development through the second half of the first year. Adults cannot change a baby's babbled sounds through reinforcement and modeling, although they can, to some extent, influence the overall amount of babbling (Dodd, 1972). Also, the development of babbling follows a universal pattern. At first, infants produce a limited

Motherese, or child-directed speech
The form of language adopted by adults when speaking to infants and toddlers that is made up of short sentences with high-pitched, exaggerated intonation, clear pronunciation, and distinct pauses between speech segments.

Cooing
Pleasant vowel-like noises made by infants beginning around 2 months of age.

Babbling
Repetition of consonant–vowel combinations in long strings, beginning around 6 months of age.

number of sounds that expand to a much broader range by 12 months of age. Babbling continues for 4 or 5 months after infants say their first words (Locke, 1989).

Nevertheless, a careful look at babbling reveals that infants are applying the knowledge they have gained from many months of listening to their native tongue. By 1 year of age, intonation patterns of the babbling stream resemble those of the child's language community (Levitt & Wang, 1991). As a result, babbling often seems like conversational speech without intelligible words. In addition, as infants get ready to talk, they babble the consonant and vowel sounds of their own language with increasing frequency, some of which are transferred to their first words (Boysson-Bardies & Vihman, 1991; Levitt & Utmann, 1992). Finally, watch an older baby babble, and you are likely to see that certain patterns of sounds appear in particular contexts—for example, when manipulating objects, looking at books, and walking upright (Blake & Boysson-Bardies, 1992).

These features of babbling indicate that it paves the way for language in at least two ways. First, babbling permits speech sounds to be exercised in a preparatory way for early words. And second, links between babbled sounds and contexts suggest that these early vocalizations are meaningful from the baby's perspective. Through babbling, infants seem to experiment with the semantic function of language before they speak in more conventional ways.

BECOMING A COMMUNICATOR

At birth, infants are already prepared for some aspects of conversational behavior. For example, newborn babies can initiate interaction by making eye contact and terminate it by looking away. Around 4 months, they start to gaze in the same direction adults are looking, and adults follow the baby's line of vision as well. When this happens, parents often comment on what the infant sees. In this way, the environment is labeled for the baby. Researchers believe this kind of joint attention may be quite important for early language development. Infants who experience it often tend to talk earlier and show faster vocabulary development (Dunham & Dunham, 1992; Dunham, Dunham, & Curwin, 1993).

By 3 months, the beginnings of conversational turn-taking can be seen. The baby vocalizes, the caregiver vocalizes in return, waits for a response, and vocalizes again. In Western cultures, these vocal exchanges are common, but the adult is largely responsible for sustaining them (Schaffer, 1979). Several months later, turn-taking games, such as pat-a-cake and peekaboo, appear. At first, the parent starts the game and the infant is an amused observer. But by 12 months, infants become active participants, exchanging roles with the parent. As they do so, they practice the turn-taking pattern of human conversation, and they also hear words paired with the actions they perform (Ratner & Bruner, 1978).

At the end of the first year, as infants become capable of intentional behavior, they use two forms of preverbal gestures to influence the behavior of others. The first is the **protodeclarative**, in which the baby touches an object, holds it up, or points to it while looking at others to make sure they notice. In the second, the **protoimperative**, the infant gets another person to do something by pointing, reaching, and often making sounds at the same time (Bates, 1979; Fenson et al., 1994). Over time, some of these gestures become explicitly representational—much like those that appear in children's early make-believe play (see Chapter 6). For example, a 1- to 2-year-old might sniff to refer to flowers, lift her arms over her head to indicate big, and flap her arms to refer to a butterfly. In this way, gestural communication provides yet another context in which young children learn about the functions of language—that meanings can be symbolized and conveyed to others (Acredolo & Goodwyn, 1990).

Early in the second year, turn-taking and gestural communication come together, especially in situations in which children's messages do not communicate clearly. For example, witness the following efforts by a 14-month-old to get his mother to give him a sponge from the kitchen counter:

Jordan: (Vocalizes repeatedly until his mother turns around.)

Mother: (Turns around to look at him.)

Jordan: (Points to one of the objects on the counter.)

Protodeclarative
A preverbal gesture through which infants make an assertion about an object by touching it, holding it up, or pointing to it.

Protoimperative
A preverbal gesture in which infants point, reach, and make sounds to get another person to do something.

■ *These parents and their 1-year-old infant establish joint attention, and mother and baby use the protodeclarative, pointing to communicate. As adults label infants' preverbal gestures, they promote the transition to verbal language.*
(Fuji Fotos/The Image Works)

Mother:	Do you want this? (Holds up milk container.)
Jordan:	(Shakes his head "no.") (Vocalizes, continues to point.)
Mother:	Do you want this? (Holds up jelly jar.)
Jordan:	(Shakes his head "no.") (Continues to point.) (Two more offer–rejection pairs.)
Mother:	This? (Picks up sponge.)
Jordan:	(Leans back in highchair, puts arms down, tension leaves body.)
Mother:	(Hands Jordan sponge.) (Golinkoff, 1983, pp. 58–59)

Soon, words are uttered along with the gestures that made up the infant's preverbal communicative acts. Then the gestures diminish as children discover that words are more easily understood by others and as parents encourage their youngster's first meaningful verbalizations (Goldin-Meadow & Morford, 1985).

A final note: Throughout our discussion, we have stressed that progress toward spoken language is encouraged by caregivers who involve infants in dialoguelike exchanges. Yet how necessary are these early interactive experiences? In some societies, such as the Kaluli of Papua New Guinea and the people of Western Samoa, adults rarely treat infants as communicative partners and never play social games with them. Not until infants crawl and walk do sibling caregivers take charge, talk directly to babies, and respond to their vocalizations. Yet Kaluli and Samoan children acquire language within the normal time frame of development (Ochs, 1988; Schieffelin & Ochs, 1987). These findings suggest that adult molding of infant communication may not be essential. But when it occurs, it clearly supports the transition from the preverbal phase to the much longer, linguistic period of childhood.

BRIEF REVIEW

During infancy, biological predispositions, cognitive development, and a responsive social environment join together to prepare the child for language. Neonates have a built-in capacity to detect a wide variety of sound categories in human speech. By the second half of the first year, they become increasingly sensitive to the phonemes, words, and phrase structure of their native tongue. Cooing begins at about 2 months, babbling around 6 months. By 1 year, babbling reflects the intonation and sound patterns of the native language, and infants use preverbal gestures to influence the behavior of others. When adults use motherese, engage infants in turn-taking exchanges, and respond to babies' preverbal gestures, they support the transition to verbal communication.

Phonological Development

Think about the sounds you might hear if you listened in on a 1- or 2-year-old trying out her first handful of words. You probably imagined an assortment of interesting pronunciations, such as "nana" for banana, "oap" for soap, and "weddy" for ready, as well as some puzzling productions that the child uses like words but that do not resemble adult forms. For "translations" of these, you have to ask the child's parent. Phonological development is a complex process that depends on the child's ability to attend to the sound sequences of speech, produce sounds voluntarily, and combine them into understandable words and phrases. Between 1 and 4 years of age, children make considerable progress at this task.

Experts in phonology view children mastering the pronunciation of their language as young problem solvers. In trying to figure out how to talk like people around them, they adopt a variety of temporary strategies for producing sounds that bring adult words within their current range of physical and cognitive capabilities (Menn & Stoel-Gammon, 1993). Let's see how they do so.

THE EARLY PHASE

Children's first words are limited by the small number of sounds they can control. The easiest sound sequences start with consonants, end with vowels, and include repeated syllables, as in "mama," "dada," "bye-bye," and "nigh-nigh" (for "night-night"). In other instances, young speakers may use the same sound to represent a variety of words, a feature that makes their speech hard to understand. For example, one toddler substituted "bat" for as many as 12 different words, including "bad," "bark," "bent," and "bite" (Ingram, 1986).

These observations reveal that early phonological and semantic development are related. The words children choose to say are influenced partly by what they can pronounce (Hura & Echols, 1996; Vihman, 1993). Interestingly, languages cater to young children's phonological limitations. Throughout the world, sounds resembling "mama," "dadda," and "papa" refer to parents, so it is not surprising that these are among the first words children everywhere produce. Also, when speaking motherese, adults often use simplified words to talk about things of interest to toddlers. For example, rabbit becomes "bunny," stomach becomes "tummy," and train becomes "choo-choo." These word forms support the child's first attempts to talk.

APPEARANCE OF PHONOLOGICAL STRATEGIES

By the middle of the second year, children apply systematic strategies to words so they fit with their phonological capacities (Preisser, Hodson, & Paden, 1988). These strategies mark an intermediate phase of development in which pronunciation is partly right and partly wrong, but errors are fairly consistent. The rules children use are creative attempts to adapt sounds they can make to adult utterances (Vihman et al., 1994). Although children vary widely in the strategies they adopt, Table 9.1 on page 354 lists some typical ones.

Over the preschool years, children's pronunciation improves greatly. Maturation of the vocal tract and the child's active problem-solving efforts are largely responsible, since children's phonological errors are very resistant to adult correction. One father I know tried repeatedly to get his 2½-year-old daughter to pronounce the word "music," but each time she persisted with "ju-jic." Like other young children, she was well aware of the difference between her immature pronunciation and the correct version. When her father made one last effort, she replied, "Wait 'til I big. Then I say ju-jic, Daddy!"

LATER PHONOLOGICAL DEVELOPMENT

Although phonological development is largely complete by the time children go to school, a few accent patterns are not mastered until later childhood and adolescence. Pronunciations that signal subtle differences in meaning, as in the words "greenhouse" and "green house," develop gradually from first to sixth grade (Atkinson-King, 1973).

TABLE 9.1

Common Phonological Strategies Used by Young Children to Simplify Pronunciation of Adult Words

Strategy	Example
Repeating the first consonant–vowel in a multisyllable word	"TV" becomes "didi," "cookie" becomes "gege."
Deleting unstressed syllables in a multisyllable word	"Banana" becomes "nana," "giraffe" becomes "raffe."
Replacing fricatives (hissing sounds) with stop consonant sounds	"Sea" becomes "tea," "say" becomes "tay."
Replacing consonant sounds produced in the rear and palate area of the vocal tract with ones produced in the frontal area	"Shoe" becomes "zue," "goose" becomes "doose."
Replacing liquid sounds ("l" or "r") with glides ("j" or "w")	"Lap" becomes "jap," "ready" becomes "weddy."
Reducing consonant–vowel–consonant words to a consonant–vowel form by deleting the final consonant	"Bike" becomes "bai," "more" becomes "muh."
Replacing an ending consonant syllable with a vowel	"Apple" becomes "appo," "bottom" becomes "bada."
Reducing a consonant cluster to a single consonant	"Clown" becomes "cown," "play" becomes "pay."

Source: Ingram, 1986.

Changes in syllabic stress after certain abstract words take on endings—for example, "humid" to "humidity" and "method" to "methodical"—are not mastered until adolescence (Camarata & Leonard, 1986).

These late developments are probably affected by the semantic complexity of the words to which they apply. Even among young children, pronunciation is best for easily understood words. As we indicated in Chapter 7, the capacity of the human information-processing system is limited. Working on the sound and meaning of a new word simultaneously may overload the system, leading children to sacrifice sound temporarily until the word's meaning is better understood.

Semantic Development

aternal reports indicate that on the average, children say their first word around 12 months of age. By age 6, they have a vocabulary of about 10,000 words. To accomplish this extraordinary feat, children learn about 5 new words each day (Anglin, 1993).

The semantic achievements of early childhood are even more awesome if we consider that from infancy on, children's **comprehension**, the language they understand, develops ahead of **production**, or the language they use. For example, toddlers follow many simple directions, such as "Bring me your book" or "Don't touch the lamp," even though they cannot yet express all these words in their own speech. There is a 5-month lag between the time children comprehend 50 words (around 13 months) and the time they produce this many (around 18 months) (Menyuk, Liebergott, & Schultz, 1995).

Why is language comprehension ahead of production? Think back to the distinction we made in Chapter 7 between two types of memory: recognition and recall. Comprehension requires only that children recognize the meaning of a word, whereas production demands that they recall, or actively retrieve from their memories, the word as well as the concept for which it stands (Kuczaj, 1986). Language production is clearly a more difficult task. Failure to say a word does not mean that toddlers do not understand it. As we discuss semantic development, we need to keep both processes in mind. If we rely only on what children say, we will underestimate their language progress.

Comprehension
In language development, the words and word combinations that children understand.

Production
In language development, the words and word combinations that children use.

THE EARLY PHASE

Learning words is a matter of identifying which concept each label picks out in a particular language community. Ask several parents of toddlers to tell you which words appeared first in their children's vocabularies. You will quickly see that early language builds on the sensorimotor foundations Piaget described and on categories children construct during the first 2 years (see Chapter 6). First words refer to important people

TABLE 9.2

Types of Words Appearing in Toddlers' 50-Word Vocabularies

Word Type	Description	Typical Examples	Percentage of Total Word[a]
Object words	Words used to refer to the "thing world"	*Apple, ball, bird, boat, book, car, cookie, Dadda, doggie, kitty, milk, Mama, shoe, snow, truck*	65
Action words	Words that describe, demand, or accompany action or that express attention or demand attention	*Bye-bye, go, hi, look, more, out, up*	13
State words (modifers)	Words that refer to properties or qualities of things or events	*All gone, big, dirty, hot, mine, pretty, outside, red, uh-oh, wet*	9
Personal-social words	Words that express emotional states and social relationships	*No, ouch, please, want, yes, thank you*	8
Function words	Words that fill a solely grammatical function	*For, is, to, what, where*	4

[a]Average percentages are given, based on a sample of 18 American toddlers.
Source: Nelson, 1973.

("Mama," "Dadda"), objects that move or can be acted on ("ball," "car," "cat," "shoe"), familiar actions ("bye-bye," "more," "up"), or outcomes of familiar actions ("dirty," "hot," "wet"). As Table 9.2 reveals, in their first 50 words, toddlers rarely name things that just sit there, such as plate, table, towel, or vase (Nelson, 1973).

In Chapter 6, we noted that certain early words are linked to specific cognitive achievements. Recall that about the time children master advanced object permanence problems, they start to use disappearance terms, like "all gone." And when they solve sensorimotor problems suddenly (in Piaget's Substage 6), success and failure expressions, such as "there!" and "uh-oh!" appear in their vocabularies. As one pair of researchers concluded, "Children seem to be motivated to acquire words that are relevant to the particular cognitive problems they are working on at the moment" (Gopnik & Meltzoff, 1986, p. 1052).

At first, toddlers add to their vocabularies slowly, at a rate of 1 to 3 words a month. Over time, the number of words learned accelerates. As Figure 9.3 on page 356 shows, a spurt in vocabulary takes place between 18 and 24 months (Fenson et al., 1994; Reznick & Goldfield, 1992). Many children add 10 to 20 new words a week, a rise that (as we mentioned in Chapter 6) occurs at about the time their understanding of categories accelerates. As children become increasingly aware that objects belong in categories, they may simultaneously realize that all things can be named. Perhaps this new insight sparks greater interest in acquiring verbal labels. Expansion of working memory, improved phonological ability, and the capacity to represent more flexibly may also lead vocabulary to surge forward (McCune, 1995; Plunkett, 1993).

How do children manage to add new words to their vocabularies at such a phenomenal rate? Researchers have discovered that children can connect a new word with an underlying concept after only a brief encounter, a process called **fast-mapping** (Carey, 1978). In one study, an adult presented preschoolers with a novel nonsense word, "koob," in a game in which the object for which it stood (an oddly shaped plastic ring) was labeled only once. Children as young as 2 picked up the meaning of the word (Dollaghan, 1985).

Preschoolers can fast-map even new words they hear on television (Rice & Woodsmall, 1988). However, it would be wrong to conclude that TV exposure is sufficient for language development. Hearing children reared by deaf parents and exposed to spoken language only on television do not acquire normal speech (Bonvillian, Nelson, & Charrow, 1976). As research on individual differences (to which we now turn) reveals, a variety of factors interact in complex fashion to determine vocabulary growth—the cognitive foundations we have considered, rate of neurological maturation, personal styles of children, and the quantity and quality of adult–child communication.

■ INDIVIDUAL AND CULTURAL DIFFERENCES. Although the average age at which the first word is spoken is 12 months, the range is large, from 8 to 18 months. Individual differences in rate of language development have long been recognized. In Chapter 5, we

Fast-mapping
Connecting a new word with an underlying concept after only a brief encounter.

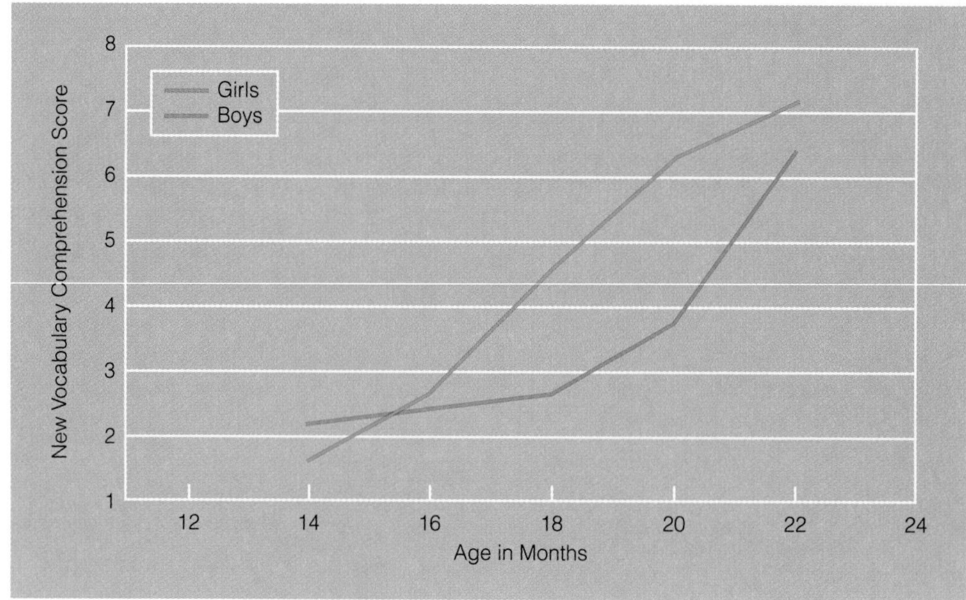

FIGURE 9.3

■ *Spurt in vocabulary between 18 and 24 months, averaged over 24 English-speaking children. Although the graph is based on a measure of language comprehension, a similar spurt appears when language production is assessed. Boys lag behind girls in size of their early vocabularies and in timing of the spurt. (From J. S. Reznick & B. A. Goldfield, 1992, "Rapid Change in Lexical Development in Comprehension and Production,"* Developmental Psychology, *28, p. 410. Copyright © 1992 by the American Psychological Association. Reprinted by permission.)*

noted that girls are consistently ahead of boys in physical maturity—a gap that extends to early language as well. Many studies show that girls are slightly advanced in vocabulary growth until about 2 years of age, after which time boys gradually catch up. (Look again at Figure 9.3 to see these trends.) Besides the child's sex, personality makes a difference. Toddlers who are very reserved and cautious often wait until they understand a great deal before trying to speak. When, finally, they do speak, their vocabularies increase rapidly (Nelson, 1973). Finally, sheer amount of parental speech is related to individual differences in vocabulary growth. The more words caregivers use when talking to toddlers, the greater the number that are integrated into the child's semantic repertoire. Furthermore, words parents say especially often tend to be acquired earliest by children (Hart, 1991; Huttenlocher et al., 1991).

Besides rate of development, striking individual differences in form of vocabulary growth exist. Following a sample of 18 children from 1 to 2½ years of age, Katherine Nelson (1973) noticed wide variation in the kinds of words they produced. The majority fit a **referential style** of language learning. Their early vocabularies consisted mainly of words that referred to objects. A smaller number of children used an **expressive style**. Compared to referential children, they used many more pronouns and social formulas, such as "Stop it," "Thank you," and "I want it," which were uttered as compressed phrases, much like single words (as in "Iwannit"). Nelson concluded that toddlers who use these styles have different early ideas about the functions of language. Referential children think words are for naming objects, whereas expressive children believe they are for talking about the feelings and needs of the self and other people. The vocabularies of referential-style children grow more quickly, since all languages contain many more object labels than social phrases (Bates, Bretherton, & Snyder, 1988).

What accounts for a toddler's choice of a particular language style? Once again, both biological and environmental factors seem to be involved. Rapidly developing, referential-style children often have an especially active interest in exploring objects and parents who eagerly respond with names of things to their first attempts to talk. And they freely imitate words outside their current repertoire that they hear others say—a strategy that supports swift early vocabulary growth, perhaps because it helps children encode new labels in memory (Masur, 1995). In contrast, expressive-style children spend more time watching other people, and their parents more often use verbal routines ("How are you?" "It's no trouble") designed to support social relationships (Goldfield, 1987).

Referential style
A style of early language learning in which toddlers use language mainly to label objects.

Expressive style
A style of early language learning in which toddlers use language mainly to talk about the feelings and needs of themselves and other people.

The two language styles are also linked to culture. For example, in Western societies, many mothers stress object labels to children, but Vietnamese toddlers learn an honorific pronoun system conveying respect for their elders first (Nelson, 1981). And compared to American mothers, Japanese mothers more often engage young children in social routines, probably because their culture stresses the importance of membership in the social group (Fernald & Morikawa, 1993). African mothers of Mali, Mauritania, and Senegal respond verbally to their infant's glances and vocalizations to other people, not to the

■ *In Western societies, many mothers stress object labels to young language learners. In contrast, these African mothers of Botswana respond verbally to their toddlers' glances and vocalizations to other people, not to exploration of objects. (DeVore/Anthro-Photo File)*

baby's exploration of objects (Jamin, 1994). When we consider these findings as a whole, early vocabulary development appears to support the interactionist's emphasis on the combined impact of children's inner predispositions and linguistic and social worlds.

■ TYPES OF WORDS. Look back at Table 9.2 on page 355, and you will see that three types of words—object, action, and state—are the most common in young children's vocabularies. Careful study of each provides researchers with important information about the course of semantic development.

Object and Action Words. Although children differ in the first words they choose to learn, virtually all early language learners have far more object than action words in their beginning vocabularies (Au, Dapretto, & Song, 1994; Menyuk, Liebergott, & Schultz, 1995). If actions are an especially important means through which infants find out about their world, then why this early emphasis on naming objects?

The major reason seems to be that concepts referred to by nouns are especially salient to young children because they are perceptually distinct, bounded wholes. As a result, when children start to talk, all they need to do is match objects with their appropriate labels. In contrast, verbs are cognitively more complex in that they require an understanding of the relationship between objects and actions (Gentner & Rattermann, 1991). Nevertheless, characteristics of the linguistic environment have some effect on toddlers' relative use of object and action words. For example, the structure of English emphasizes nouns more than do some non-Western languages. In Japanese and Korean, nouns are often omitted entirely from adult sentences, and verbs are stressed. In line with this difference, Japanese and Korean toddlers acquire action words earlier than their English-speaking counterparts do (Choi, 1991; Gopnik & Choi, 1995).

When English-speaking children first refer to actions, they often use a variety of words to represent them. For example, a toddler might use a noun, such as "door," or a preposition, such as "out," to convey the idea that she wants to open something. As their vocabularies expand at the end of the second and the beginning of the third year, children use many more words to refer to actions that for adults are verbs (Bates et al., 1994).

State Words. Between 2 and 2½ years, children's state (or modifier) words expand to include labels for attributes of objects, such as size and color ("big," "red") as well as possession ("my toy," "Mommy purse"). Words referring to the functions of objects appear soon after (for example, "dump truck," "pickup truck") (Nelson, 1976).

When state words are related in meaning, general distinctions (which are cognitively easier) appear first. For example, among words referring to the size of objects, children

■ *Cognitive development influences young children's mastery of state (or modifier) words. This 2-year-old is likely to say "big tower" before "tall tower" and "on" before "under." (Kopstein/Monkmeyer Press)*

acquire "big–small" first, followed by "tall–short," "high–low," and "long–short," and finally "wide–narrow" and "deep–shallow." The same is true for temporal terms, which modify actions. Between ages 3 and 5, children first master "now" versus "then" and "before" versus "after," followed by "today" versus "yesterday" and "tomorrow" (Clark, 1983; Stevenson & Pollitt, 1987).

State words referring to the location and movement of objects provide additional examples of how cognition influences vocabulary development. Below age 2, children can easily imitate an adult's action in putting an object "in" or "on" another object, but they have trouble imitating the placement of one object "under" another. These terms appear in children's vocabularies in just this order, with all three achieved around 2½ years of age (Clark, 1973). With respect to motion words, those that describe an object's source ("out," "off") and path of movement ("up," "down") appear before ones that refer to the place an object comes to rest ("here," "there"). The reason is that describing the end point of an object's motion demands that children grasp the relationship between all three concepts—where an object started, how it moved, and where it ended (Stockman & Vaughn-Cooke, 1992).

State terms serve a vital communicative function. Because they refer to the qualities of objects and actions, children can use them to express many more concepts than they could previously. As preschoolers master more of these words, their language becomes increasingly flexible.

■ UNDEREXTENSIONS AND OVEREXTENSIONS. When young children first learn new words, they often do not use them in just the way we do. Sometimes they apply the word too narrowly, an error called **underextension**. For example, at 16 months, my younger son used the word "bear" only to refer to a special teddy bear to which he had become attached. A more common error between 1 and 2½ years of age is **overextension**—applying the word to a wider collection of objects and events than is appropriate. For example, a toddler might use the word "car" to refer to a great many objects, including buses, trains, trucks, and fire engines.

Overextensions are yet another illustration of very young children's sensitivity to categorical relations. Children do not overextend words randomly. Instead, they apply them to a class of similar referents—for example, using "dog" to refer to a variety of furry, four-legged animals, or "open" to mean opening a door, peeling fruit, and undoing shoe laces (Behrend, 1988). Furthermore, children overextend many more words in production than they do in comprehension. That is, a 2-year-old may refer to trucks, trains, and bikes as "cars" but point to these objects correctly when given their names in a comprehension task (Naigles & Gelman, 1995). This suggests that children sometimes overextend deliberately because they have difficulty recalling or have not acquired a suitable word. In addition, when a word is hard to pronounce, toddlers are likely to substitute a related one they can say (Elsen, 1994). As vocabulary and phonology expand, overextensions gradually disappear.

■ WORD COINAGES AND METAPHORS. To fill in for words they have not yet learned, young children apply their vocabulary in other creative ways. As early as age 2, they coin new words based on ones they already know. At first, children operate on whole words, as in the technique of compounding. For example, a child might say "break-machine" for a machine that breaks things and "plant-man" for a gardener. Later they convert verbs into nouns and nouns into verbs, as in one child's use of "needle it" for mending something. Soon after, children discover more specialized word coinage techniques, such as adding "-er" to identify the doer of a particular action—for example, "crayoner" for a child using crayons instead of paints. Children give up coined words as soon as they acquire conventional labels for their intended meanings (Clark, 1995). Still, their ability to invent these expressions is evidence for a remarkable, rule-governed approach to language at an early age.

Underextension
An early vocabulary error in which a word is applied too narrowly, to a smaller number of objects or events than is appropriate.

Overextension
An early vocabulary error in which a word is applied too broadly, to a wider collection of objects and events than is appropriate.

Preschoolers also extend language meanings through metaphor. Some very clever ones appear in their everyday language. For example, one 3-year-old used the expression "fire engine in my tummy" to describe a recent stomachache (Winner, 1988). Not surprisingly, the metaphors young preschoolers use and understand are based largely on concrete, sensory comparisons, such as "clouds are pillows" and "leaves are dancers." Once their vocabulary and knowledge of the world expand, they start to appreciate ones based on nonsensory comparisons as well, such as "Friends are like magnets" (Karadsheh, 1991; Keil, 1986). Metaphors permit children to communicate in especially vivid and memorable ways. And sometimes they are the only means we have to convey what we want to say.

LATER SEMANTIC DEVELOPMENT

Because the average 6-year-old's vocabulary is already quite large, parents and teachers are less aware of gains in middle childhood and adolescence. Between the start of elementary school and young adulthood, vocabulary more than doubles, eventually exceeding 30,000 words. In addition, as we saw in Chapter 7, the knowledge base that underlies school-age children's vocabulary becomes better organized and hierarchically arranged. This permits them to use words more precisely and think about them differently than they did at younger ages.

If you look carefully at children's word definitions, you will see examples of this change. Five- and 6-year-olds give very concrete descriptions that refer to functions or appearance—for example, knife: "when you're cutting carrots"; bicycle: "it's got wheels, a chain, and handlebars." By the end of elementary school, their definitions emphasize more general, socially shared information. Synonyms and explanations of categorical relationships appear—for example, knife: "Something you could cut with. A saw is like a knife. It could also be a weapon" (Litowitz, 1977; Wehren, De Lisi, & Arnold, 1981). This advance reflects the older child's ability to deal with word meanings on an entirely verbal plane. Fifth and sixth graders no longer need to be shown what a word refers to in order to understand it. They can add new words to their vocabulary simply by being given a definition (Dickinson, 1984).

School-age children's more reflective, analytical approach to language permits them to appreciate the multiple meanings of words. For example, they recognize that many words, such as "sharp" or "cool," have psychological as well as physical meanings: "What a cool shirt!" or "That movie was really neat!" This grasp of double meanings permits 8- to 10-year-olds to comprehend subtle, mental metaphors, such as "sharp as a tack," "spilling the beans," and "left high and dry" (Wellman & Hickling, 1994; Winner, 1988). It also leads to a change in children's humor. In middle childhood, riddles and puns requiring children to go back and forth between different meanings of the same key word are common:

> "Hey, did you take a bath?" "No! Why, is one missing?"
>
> "Order! Order in the court!" "Ham and cheese on rye, your honor?"
>
> "Why did the old man tiptoe past the medicine cabinet?" "Because he didn't want to wake up the sleeping pills."

Preschoolers may laugh at these statements because they are nonsensical. But they cannot tell a good riddle or pun, nor do they understand why these jokes are funny (McGhee, 1979).

Finally, adolescents' capacity for abstract reasoning permits them to grasp words rarely used at younger ages, such as "counterintuitive," "incredible," and "philosophy." In addition, teenagers can understand subtle nonliteral word meanings. As a result, they become masters of irony and sarcasm (Winner, 1988). "Don't have a major brain explosion," one 16-year-old commented to his sister when she complained about having to write an essay for school. And on another occasion, when his mother fixed a dish for dinner that he disliked, he quipped, "Oh boy, my favorite!" Young children sometimes realize that a sarcastic remark is insincere if it is said in a very exaggerated, mocking tone of voice. But adolescents and adults need only notice the discrepancy between the statement and its context to grasp the intended meaning (Capelli, Nakagawa, & Madden, 1990).

IDEAS ABOUT HOW SEMANTIC DEVELOPMENT TAKES PLACE

Research shows that adult feedback facilitates semantic development. When adults go beyond correcting and provide an explanation ("That's not a car. It's a truck. See, it has a place to put things in"), toddlers are more likely to move toward conventional word meanings (Chapman, Leonard, & Mervis, 1986). Still, there is no way that adults can tell children exactly what concept each new word picks out. For example, if an adult points to a dog and calls it a "doggie," it is not clear whether the word refers to four-legged animals, the dog's shaggy ears, the shape of its wagging tail, or its barking sound. Therefore, the child's cognitive processing must play a major role in vocabulary development.

■ THE INFLUENCE OF MEMORY. A special part of working memory, a **phonological store** that permits us to retain speech-based information, supports young children's fast-mapping. The more rapidly 4-year-olds can repeat back nonsense words to an experimenter (a measure of phonological memory skill), the greater their vocabulary growth over the following year. This suggests that a child with good phonological memory produces traces of new words that are clear and persistent enough to increase their chances of being transferred to long-term memory and linked with relevant concepts.

But phonological memory does not provide a full account of word learning. After age 5, its ability to predict vocabulary growth breaks down. By then, the causal relationship reverses: Children's semantic knowledge influences how quickly they form phonological traces and acquire new words (Gathercole et al., 1992). And even at younger ages (as we will see next), there is good evidence that children rely heavily on words they already know to figure out the meanings of new ones.

■ STRATEGIES FOR WORD LEARNING. Recently, Eve Clark (1990, 1993, 1995) proposed an explanation of semantic development called **lexical contrast theory**. It assumes that two principles govern vocabulary growth. The first is *conventionality*, children's natural desire to acquire words and word meanings of their language community. The second is *contrast*, which explains how new word meanings are added. According to Clark, children assume that the meaning of each word they hear is unique. Therefore, when they hear a new label, they immediately try to figure out its meaning by contrasting it with words currently in their vocabulary.

Many researchers have criticized Clark for not being specific about the hypotheses young children use to determine new word meanings (Gathercole, 1987; Golinkoff et al., 1992). Ellen Markman (1989, 1992) makes a stronger claim about children's early word learning. She believes that in the early phases of vocabulary growth, children adopt a **principle of mutual exclusivity**. That is, they assume that words mark entirely separate (nonoverlapping) categories. The principle of mutual exclusivity works well as long as available referents are perceptually very distinct. For example, when 2-year-olds are told the names of two very different novel objects (a clip and a horn), they assign each label correctly, to the whole object and not a part of it. And they almost never call the horn a "clip" or the clip a "horn" on later occasions (Waxman & Senghas, 1992).

But mutual exclusivity cannot account for what young children do when adults call a single object by more than one name. Under these conditions, they look for cues in adult speech or behavior to determine whether the new word refers either to a higher- or lower-order category or to particular attributes, such as a part of the object, its shape, its color, or a proper name (Hall, 1996; Tomasello & Barton, 1994; Waxman & Hatch, 1992). When no such cues are available, children as young as 2 demonstrate remarkable flexibility in their word learning strategies. They abandon the mutual exclusivity principle and treat the new word as a second name for the object (Mervis, Golinkoff, & Bertrand, 1994).

Although these findings tell us something about how children master object labels, they say little about principles used for other types of words. Children seem to draw on other components of language for help in these instances. According to one proposal, children deduce many word meanings by observing how words are used syntactically, in the structure of sentences—a hypothesis called **syntactic bootstrapping** (Gleitman, 1990). Consider the sentence, "Please *give* me the doll." Notice how *give* is followed by an indirect object *(me)* and then a direct object *(doll)*—a strong cue that it is a verb of transfer, since transfer involves both an object transferred and a person to whom it is transferred.

Phonological store
A special part of working memory that permits us to retain speech-based information. Supports early vocabulary development.

Lexical contrast theory
A theory that attributes semantic development to two principles: conventionality, children's natural desire to acquire the words and word meanings of their language community; and contrast, children's discovery of meanings by contrasting new words with ones currently in their vocabulary.

Principle of mutual exclusivity
The assumption by children in the early stages of vocabulary growth that words mark entirely separate (nonoverlapping) categories.

Syntactic bootstrapping
Observing how words are used syntactically, in the structure of sentences, to deduce their meanings.

Analyses of mothers' speech to 2-year-olds reveal that different categories of verbs (for example, *give, take* versus *drop, move)* consistently appear in different syntactic contexts, supporting the idea of syntactic bootstrapping (Naigles & Hoff-Ginsberg, 1995).

Finally, children also rely on pragmatic cues to identify nonobject words. In one study, an adult performed an action on an object and then used a new label while looking back and forth between the child and the object, as if to invite the child to play. Two-year-olds capitalized on this social information to conclude that the label referred to the action, not the object (Tomasello & Akhtar, 1995).

In sum, children seem to draw on many sources of information to guide early word learning, all of which are not yet clearly specified. We still have much to discover about the processes responsible for the phenomenal pace of semantic development.

BRIEF REVIEW

Semantic development takes place with extraordinary speed as young children fast-map thousands of words into their vocabularies. Although individual differences exist, object words are emphasized first. Action and state words increase later. Errors of underextension and overextension gradually decline as preschoolers enlarge and refine their vocabularies. During middle childhood, understanding of word meanings becomes more flexible and precise. Adolescents acquire many abstract words and grasp subtle nonliteral word meanings. Adult feedback assists with word learning, but the child's cognitive processing plays a major role. Lexical contrast theory is a recent controversial account of how semantic development takes place. Research indicates that children use a wide variety of strategies to infer word meanings.

Grammatical Development

Grammar requires that children use more than one word in a single utterance. In studying grammatical development, researchers have puzzled over the following questions: Does the very young child use a consistent grammar, and if so, is it like that of the adult? Is grammatical learning special, or does it depend on more general cognitive processes? And what is the role of adult teaching—in particular, corrective feedback for errors—in acquiring grammar? Perhaps you already noticed that these questions have been prompted by Chomsky's theory. If a nativist account is plausible, then grammar should appear early, and the role of adult input should be minimal. We will consider evidence on these issues as we chart the course of grammatical development.

FIRST WORD COMBINATIONS

Sometime between 1½ and 2½ years, first sentences appear. Children combine two words, such as "Mommy shoe," "Go car," and "More cookie." Children's two-word utterances have been called **telegraphic speech**. Like a telegram, they focus on high-content words and leave out smaller, less important ones, such as "can," "the," and "to." In addition, word endings like "-s" and "-ed" are not yet present. However, keep in mind that telegraphic speech characterizes children learning languages that emphasize word order, like English and French. In languages where word order is flexible and small grammatical markers are stressed, children's first sentences include them from the start (de Villiers & de Villiers, 1992).

Even though the two-word utterance is limited in form, children the world over use it flexibly to express a wide variety of meanings (see Table 9.3 on page 362). In doing so, are children already applying a consistent grammar? At least to some extent they are, since children rarely engage in gross violations of the structure of their language. For example, English-speaking children usually say "Daddy eat" rather than "eat Daddy" and "my chair" rather than "chair my" (Bloom, 1990). This suggests that young children

Telegraphic speech
Children's two-word utterances that, like a telegram, leave out smaller and less important words.

TABLE 9.3

Common Meanings Expressed by Children's Two-Word Utterances

Meaning	Example
Agent–action	"Tommy hit"
Action–object	"Give cookie"
Agent–object	"Mommy truck" (meaning Mommy push the truck)
Action–location	"Put table" (meaning put *X* on the table)
Entity–location	"Daddy outside"
Possessor–possession	"My truck"
Attribution–entity	"Big ball"
Demonstrative–entity	"That doggie"
Notice–noticed object	"Hi mommy," "Hi truck"
Recurrence	"More milk"
Nonexistence–nonexistent or disappeared object	"No shirt," "No more milk"

Source: Brown, 1973.

have some sensitivity to word-order rules. Yet considerable controversy exists over the extent to which children at the two-word stage grasp the grammatical categories of their language. According to some investigators, a full adultlike grammar lies behind these two-word sentences, since children often use the same construction to express different underlying propositions. For example, a child might say "Mommy cookie" when he sees his mother eating a cookie and use the same phrase on another occasion to indicate that he wants his mother to give him a cookie. Perhaps the more elaborate structure is present in the child's mind, but an inability to remember and produce a longer word string prevents him from displaying it (Bloom, 1970).

Other researchers disagree, arguing that two-word sentences are based on a very limited structure that differs from the grammar of adults (Maratsos & Chalkley, 1980). For example, Jonathan, a child studied by Martin Braine (1976), produced several actor–action combinations, such as "Mommy sit," "Daddy sleep," and "Daddy work." However, these utterances did not reflect a general understanding of subject–verb relations, since Jonathan used the structure only in specific situations—when a person was moving from one place to another (such as his father going to bed or leaving for work). Also, many creative combinations that children produce during the two-word period do not conform to adult grammatical restrictions. For example, Andrew, another child studied by Braine, said "more hot" and "more read." He clearly applied a rule—"more + X"—in generating these utterances. But the combinations he created are not acceptable in English grammar.

These findings suggest that in first combining words, children are preoccupied with figuring out the meanings of words and using their limited vocabularies in whatever way possible to get their thoughts across to others (Maratsos, 1983). Some of their expressions match adult rules, whereas others seem to reflect their own hypotheses about particular word combinations (Owens, 1996). However, as we will see in the next section, it does not take long for children to grasp the basic structure of their language.

FROM TWO-WORD UTTERANCES TO COMPLEX SPEECH

Between 2 and 3 years of age, three-word sentences appear. In English-speaking children, they conform to a relatively fixed word order: subject–verb–object. Although at one time this sequence was thought to be a universal grammatical structure and to represent a natural order of thoughts, we now know that it is not. Instead, young children adopt the word orders of the adult speech to which they are exposed (de Villiers & de Villiers, 1992). For example, for "It is broken," a German 2-year-old says, "Kaputt is der" (literally translated as "Broken is it"). Yet German children find their native tongue no more difficult to learn than do children born into English-speaking homes.

TABLE 9.4

Order of Acquisition of English Grammatical Morphemes

Morpheme	Example
1. Verb present progressive ending ("-ing")	"He singing."
2. Preposition "on"	"On horsie."
3. Preposition "in"	"In wagon."
4. Noun plural ("-s")	"Cats."
5. Verb irregular past tense	"He ran." "It broke."
6. Noun possessive	"Daddy's hat."
7. Verb uncontractible "be" form used with adjective, preposition, or noun phrase	"Are kitties sleepy?"
8. Articles "a" and "the"	"A cookie." "The bunny."
9. Verb regular past tense ending ("-ed")	"He kicked it."
10. Verb present tense, third person singular irregular ending	"He likes it."
11. Verb present tense, third person singular irregular ending	"She has [from *have*] a cookie." "He does [from *do*] a good job."
12. Auxiliary verb uncontractible "be" forms	"Are you eating?"
13. Verb contractible "be" forms used with adjective, preposition, or noun phrase	"He's inside." "They're sleepy."
14. Auxiliary verb contractible "be" forms	"He's coming." "Doggie's eating."

Source: Brown, 1973.

■ DEVELOPMENT OF GRAMMATICAL MORPHEMES. As children move beyond two-word utterances, they clearly appreciate the formal grammatical categories of their language. In a study of the verbalizations of young preschoolers, by 2½ years, words clearly obeyed the regularities of adult English usage. Children created sentences in which adjectives, articles, nouns, noun phrases, prepositions, and prepositional phrases appeared in the same structural form as adults generate them (Valian, 1986).

At about the same time, a grammatical explosion takes place. Children add **grammatical morphemes**[3]—small markers that change the meaning of sentences, as in "John*'s* dog" and "he *is* eating." A striking finding is that these morphemes are acquired in a regular order by English-speaking 2- and 3-year-olds (Brown, 1973; de Villiers & de Villiers, 1973). The sequence is shown in Table 9.4. Nevertheless, children do not use these morphemes consistently for months or even years after they first appear (de Villiers & de Villiers, 1992).

Why does this regular order of development occur? Since adults' use of grammatical morphemes is unrelated to children's learning, language input cannot be responsible (Pinker, 1981). Instead, two characteristics of the morphemes themselves play important roles. The first is *structural complexity.* For example, adding the endings "-ing" or "-s" is structurally less complex than using various forms of the verb "to be." In these, the child has to take account of different forms that express tense and make the verb agree with the subject (for example, "I am coming" versus "They are coming"). Second, grammatical morphemes differ in *semantic complexity,* or the number and difficulty of the meanings they express. For example, adding "-s" to a word requires only one semantic distinction—the difference between one and more than one. In contrast, using the various forms of "to be" involves many more, including an understanding of person, number, and time of occurrence (Brown, 1973).

Research on children acquiring different languages illustrates the impact of both factors. For example, children learning English, Italian, and Turkish acquire morphemes that denote location (in English, these would be prepositions, such as "in" and "on") sooner than children learning Serbo-Croatian, in which expressing location is structurally more complex (Johnston & Slobin, 1979). At the same time, semantic complexity

[3] A *morpheme* is the smallest meaningful unit of speech (in contrast to a *phoneme,* which is the smallest perceptible unit of speech sound).

Grammatical morphemes Small markers that change the meaning of sentences, as in "John*'s* dog" and "he *is* eating."

FIGURE 9.4

■ *Two examples from Berko's "wug test." (From J. Berko, 1958, "The Child's Learning of English Morphology,"* Word, *14, pp. 154–155. Reprinted by permission.)*

is clearly involved, since across languages, there is considerable similarity in the order in which children acquire grammatical morphemes with the same meaning (Slobin, 1982).

■ OVERREGULARIZATION. Look again at Table 9.4, and you will see that some morphemes with irregular forms are acquired before those with regular forms. For example, children use past tense irregular verbs, such as "ran" and "broke," before they acquire the regular "-ed" ending. But once children grasp a regular morphological rule, they extend it to words that are exceptions, a type of error called **overregularization**. "My toy car breaked," "I runned faster than you," and "We each have two foots" are expressions that begin to appear between 2 and 3 years of age. Overregularization occurs only occasionally—in about 5 to 8 percent of instances in which children use irregular forms, a rate that remains constant into middle childhood. Therefore, it does not reflect a grammatical defect that must be unlearned. Instead, it shows that children apply grammatical rules creatively, since they do not hear mature speakers overregularize (Marcus et al., 1992; Marcus, 1995).

Additional evidence for the creative use of morphological rules comes from a classic study by Jean Berko (1958). She showed children pictures of unusual objects and actions that were given labels, such as "wug" for a birdlike creature and "rick" for a swinging motion. The labels occurred in sentences that Berko asked children to complete. Preschoolers easily added correct grammatical morphemes to many novel verbs. For example, they completed the sentences in Figure 9.4 with the expressions "wugs" and "ricked."

At this point, you may be wondering: Why do children use some correct irregular forms before they start to overregularize? In all languages, irregular forms are assigned to important, frequently used words. Since young children hear them often, they probably learn these instances by rote memory. But when they grasp a morphological rule, they apply it broadly, making their language more orderly than it actually is. Sometimes children even impose the rule on well-learned exceptions—for example, when they say "ated" or "felled" (Bybee & Slobin, 1982). At other times, children's memory for an irregular morpheme may fail. Then they call on the rule to generate the form, and overregularization results (Marcus, 1995).

DEVELOPMENT OF COMPLEX GRAMMATICAL FORMS

Once children master the auxiliary verb "to be," the door is open to a variety of new expressions. In English, auxiliary verbs play important roles in many sentence structures that are variations on the basic subject– verb–object form. Negatives and questions are examples.

Overregularization
Application of regular grammatical rules to words that are exceptions.

■ *Like English-speaking children, these Tamil-speaking preschoolers of India will master yes/no questions before wh- questions, which are both semantically and structurally more difficult. (Fujihira/ Monkmeyer Press)*

■ NEGATIVES. Three types of negation exist, which appear in children's speech in the following order: (1) *nonexistence,* in which the child remarks on the absence of something, such as "no cookie" or "all gone crackers"; (2) *rejection,* in which the child expresses opposition to something, such as "no take bath"; and (3) *denial,* in which the child denies the truthfulness of something, such as "That not my kitty" (Bloom, 1970; Clancy, 1985).

As these examples illustrate, before age 3, children tend to use the rule "no + utterance" to express nonexistence and rejection, but they use an internal form of negation to express denial. Their early constructions probably result from listening to parental speech. When parents express nonexistence or rejection, they often put "no" at the beginning of the sentence, as in "No more cookies" or "No, you can't have another cracker." Around 3 to 3½ years, children add auxiliary verbs to their sentences and become sensitive to the way they combine with negatives. As a result, appropriate grammatical constructions of all three kinds appear, such as, "There aren't any more cookies" (nonexistence), "I don't want a bath" (rejection), and "That isn't my kitty" (denial) (Tager-Flusberg, 1993).

■ QUESTIONS. Like negatives, questions first appear during the early preschool years and show an orderly pattern of development. English-speaking children can use rising intonation to convert an utterance into a yes/no question, as in "Mommy baking cookies?" As a result, they produce them earlier than children learning languages in which the structure of yes/no questions is more complex (Bowerman, 1973).

Correct question form requires that children invert the subject and auxiliary verb. In the case of *wh-* questions—ones that begin with "what," "where," "which," "who," "when," "why," and "how"—the *wh-* word must also be placed at the beginning of the sentence. When first creating questions, English-speaking children cling to the subject–verb–object word order that is so basic to the English language. As a result, they do not make the inversion. A 2-year-old is likely to say, "What you doing?" and "Where Daddy going?" A little later, children include the auxiliary without inverting, as in "What you are doing?" Finally, they can apply all the rules for producing a question. In languages as different as English, Korean, and Tamil (spoken in India), correct question form appears first for yes/no questions and later for *wh-* questions, which are both semantically and structurally more difficult (Clancy, 1989; Vaidyanathan, 1988).

■ OTHER COMPLEX CONSTRUCTIONS. Between ages 3 and 6, children begin to use increasingly complex grammatical forms. First, conjunctions appear connecting whole sentences ("Mom picked me up, *and* we went to the park") and verb phrases ("I got up *and* ate breakfast") (Bloom et al., 1980). Later, children produce embedded sentences ("I think he will come"), tag questions ("Dad's going to be home soon, isn't he?"), indirect object–direct object structures ("He showed his friend the present"), and passive sentences ("The dog was patted by the girl"). As the preschool years draw to a close, children use most of the grammatical structures of their native language competently (Tager-Flusberg, 1993).

LATER GRAMMATICAL DEVELOPMENT

Although preschoolers have an impressive mastery of grammar, development is not yet complete. During the school years, children's grasp of some constructions improves. The passive voice is one example. At all ages, children produce more abbreviated passives ("It got broken" or "They got lost") than full passives ("The glass was broken by Mary"). However, full passives are rarely used by 3- to 6-year-olds. They increase steadily during middle childhood and early adolescence (Horgan, 1978).

Older children also apply their understanding of the passive voice to a wider range of nouns and verbs. Preschoolers comprehend the passive best when the subject of the sentence is an animate being and the verb is an action word ("The boy is kissed by the girl"). Over the school years, the passive form extends to inanimate subjects, such as *drum* or *hat*, and experiential verbs, such as *like* or *know* (Lempert, 1989; Pinker, Lebeaux, & Frost, 1987). What accounts for this developmental trend? Recall that action is salient to young children in mastering vocabulary, a bias that may also influence their early acquisition of grammatical rules. But learning is also affected by input from the environment. Preschoolers rarely hear adults use experiential passives in everyday life, yet when exposed to them in the laboratory, they willingly integrate them into their own speech (Gordon & Chafetz, 1990).

Another grammatical achievement of middle childhood is an advanced understanding of pronoun reference. Consider the two sentences "Mickey told Barney that he liked Wonderwoman" and "Mickey told Barney that Wonderwoman liked him." In the first, the pronoun "he" can refer to Mickey, but in the second, the pronoun "him" cannot. Children's difficulties with these complex rules have been interpreted in many ways. One study revealed that an improved ability to take the perspective of others facilitates mastery. When 5- to 8-year-olds used a puppet representing the speaker to demonstrate the meaning of each sentence (thereby getting the child to take the role of the speaker), performance improved substantially (Smyth, 1995).

Like vocabulary, later grammatical achievements are fostered by children's cognitive development and improved ability to analyze and reflect on language. Older children can deal with more complex relationships and are more attentive to subtle linguistic and situational cues. These capacities play major roles in helping them understand the most intricate grammatical forms.

IDEAS ABOUT HOW GRAMMATICAL DEVELOPMENT TAKES PLACE

In view of the complexity of what is learned, preschoolers' mastery of most of the grammar of their language is truly astounding. There are various conjectures about how this early learning takes place.

STRATEGIES FOR ACQUIRING GRAMMAR.

Evidence that grammatical development is an extended rather than sudden process has raised questions about Chomsky's strict nativist account. Some experts have concluded that grammar is largely a product of general cognitive development, or children's tendency to search the environment for consistencies and patterns of all sorts (Bates & MacWhinney, 1987; Maratsos, 1983; Nelson, 1989). Yet among these theorists, there is intense debate about how children acquire the structure of their language.

According to one view, young children rely on the semantic properties of words to figure out basic grammatical regularities—an approach called **semantic bootstrapping**. For example, children might begin by grouping together words with "object qualities" as nouns and words with "action qualities" as verbs and then merge these semantic categories with observations they make about how particular words are used in sentences

Semantic bootstrapping
Relying on the semantic properties of words to figure out basic grammatical regularities.

(Bates & MacWhinney, 1987; Pinker, 1984). Others take the view that children form grammatical categories through direct observations of the structure of language. That is, they notice which words appear in the same positions in sentences, take the same morphological endings, and are similarly combined with other words and, over time, group them into the same grammatical class (Braine, 1992; Maratsos & Chalkley, 1980). It is also possible that some complex combination of semantic and structural analysis leads children to acquire the grammar of their language (Maratsos, 1983).

Still other theorists, while also focusing on processing mechanisms, agree with the essence of Chomsky's position that they are specially tuned for language learning. For example, Dan Slobin (1985) proposes that children do not start with an innate knowledge of grammatical rules, as Chomsky believed. However, they do have a special **language-making capacity (LMC)**—a set of procedures for analyzing the language they hear that supports the discovery of grammatical regularities. Studying the development of children acquiring over 40 different languages, Slobin found common patterns suggesting that a basic set of strategies exists. Nevertheless, controversy continues over whether there is a universal, built-in language-processing device or whether children in different parts of the world develop unique strategies that are influenced by the specific language they hear (Bowerman, 1989; de Villiers & de Villiers, 1992).

■ ENVIRONMENTAL SUPPORT FOR GRAMMATICAL DEVELOPMENT. Besides investigating inherent capacities, researchers have been interested in finding out what aspects of linguistic input might ease the task of mastering grammar. Research consistently shows that although adults correct children's semantics, they rarely provide direct feedback about grammar (de Villiers & de Villiers, 1992). For example, an early study reported that when a child said, "There's an animal farmhouse," the parent quickly explained that the building was really a lighthouse. In contrast, the statement "her curling my hair" was met with an approving response because the parent was, in fact, curling the child's hair (Brown & Hanlon, 1970). These findings confirm that young children must figure out the intricacies of grammar largely on their own.

Nevertheless, adults could be offering subtle, indirect feedback about grammatical errors through two techniques, which they generally use in combination: **expansions** and **recasts**. For example, a parent hearing a child say, "I gotted new red shoes," might respond, "Yes, you got a pair of new red shoes," *expanding* the complexity of the child's statement as well as *recasting* its incorrect features into appropriate form. Parents and nonparents alike are far more likely to respond in these ways after children make errors. When sentences are well formed, adults tend to either continue the topic of conversation or repeat exactly what the child just said (Bohannon & Stanowicz, 1988; Penner, 1987). Furthermore, children often imitate adult recasts, but they rarely imitate adult repetitions of their correct speech (Bohannon & Symons, 1988). Notice how expansions and recasts highlight the difference between a missing grammatical structure in the child's utterance and an adult sentence containing it.

However, the impact of such feedback has been challenged. Critics argue that it is not provided to all children in all cultures. And even when it is given, it may not be offered frequently enough and across a broad enough range of mistakes to serve as an important source of grammatical development (Marcus, 1993; Valian, 1993, 1996). Furthermore, whereas some studies report that parents' reformulations have a corrective effect, others show no impact on children's use of grammatical forms (Farrar, 1990; Morgan, Bonama, & Travis, 1995). Rather than eliminating specific errors, perhaps expansions and recasts serve the broader purpose of modeling a variety of grammatical alternatives and encouraging children to experiment with them.

In sum, virtually all investigators agree that young children are amazing processors of linguistic structure. But the extent to which factors in the language environment help them correct errors and take the next grammatical step forward remains a hotly contested issue in child language research.

Language-making capacity (LMC)
According to Slobin's theory, a built-in set of cognitive procedures for analyzing language that supports the discovery of grammatical regularities.

Expansions
Adult responses that elaborate on a child's utterance, increasing its complexity.

Recasts
Adult responses that restructure a child's incorrect speech into appropriate form.

BRIEF REVIEW

Children are active, rule-oriented learners whose earliest word combinations begin to reflect the grammar of their native tongue. As children move beyond two-word utterances, they add grammatical morphemes in a regular order influenced by the semantic and structural complexity of the forms to be learned. By age 6, children have mastered most of the grammar of their native tongue. They continue to refine certain complex forms in middle childhood. Powerful processing strategies are largely responsible for young children's grammatical achievements, but researchers disagree on whether they are of a general cognitive kind or especially tuned to language. Adult feedback may support children's mastery of grammar, but its impact continues to be debated.

Pragmatic Development

Besides phonology, vocabulary, and grammar, children must learn to use language effectively in social contexts. For a conversation to go well, participants must take turns, stay on the same topic, state their messages clearly, and conform to cultural rules that govern how individuals are supposed to interact. During the preschool years, children make considerable headway in mastering the pragmatics of language.

ACQUIRING CONVERSATIONAL SKILLS

At the beginning of early childhood, children are already skilled conversationalists. In face-to-face interaction with peers, they take turns, make eye contact, respond appropriately to their partner's remarks, and maintain a topic over time (Garvey, 1974; Podrouzek & Furrow, 1988). Nevertheless, certain conversational strategies that help sustain interaction are added at later ages. One of these is the **turnabout**, in which the speaker not only comments on what has just been said but also adds a request to get the partner to respond again. Turnabouts increase over the preschool years. Very young children may not use them because they cannot yet generate many words in each turn (Goelman, 1986). Between ages 5 and 9, more advanced conversational strategies appear, such as **shading**, in which a change of topic is initiated gradually rather than abruptly by modifying the focus of discussion (Wanska & Bedrosian, 1985).

Effective conversation also depends on understanding the **illocutionary intent** of utterances—that is, what a speaker means to say, regardless of whether the form of the utterance is perfectly consistent with it. For example, the statement "Would you like to make cookies?" can be a request for information, an offer to provide an activity, or a directive to do something, depending on its context. By age 3, children comprehend a variety of utterances as requests for action even when they are not directly expressed that way, such as "I need a pencil" or "Why don't you tickle me?" (Garvey, 1974). During middle childhood, illocutionary knowledge develops further. For example, in the context of having forgotten to do his chore of taking the garbage out, an 8-year-old understands that his mother's statement "The garbage is beginning to smell" really means, "Take the garbage out!" Appreciating form–intention pairings like this one requires children to make subtle inferences between content and utterance that are beyond preschoolers' cognitive capacities (Ackerman, 1978).

Still, surprisingly advanced conversational abilities are present at a very early age, and they probably grow out of early interactive experiences with adults and siblings. In fact, conversational give-and-take with skilled speakers seems to be an especially important context for all aspects of early language development. Opportunities to interact with adults, either at home or in preschool, are consistently related to general measures of language progress (Hart & Risley, 1995; McCartney, 1984). See the From Research to Practice box on the following page for additional evidence on the role of adult and sibling conversations in young children's pragmatic development.

Turnabout
A conversational strategy in which the speaker not only comments on what has just been said but also adds a request to get the partner to respond again.

Shading
A conversational strategy in which a change of topic is initiated gradually by modifying the focus of discussion.

Illocutionary intent
What a speaker means to say, regardless of whether the form of the utterance is perfectly consistent with it.

FROM RESEARCH TO PRACTICE

Language Learning in Multichild Family Contexts

Most research on the role of social interaction in language development has focused on mother–child pairs. Later-born children, however, typically spend their first few years in the presence of siblings. Only on rare occasions do these youngsters have the attention of a parent all to themselves.

Consistent with the confluence model we discussed in Chapter 8 (see page 327), several studies report that the presence of another child reduces the quantity and quality of parent–child interaction. Mothers of more than one child address each with fewer utterances, use more commands, and provide fewer comments and questions—factors thought to account for the slower early vocabulary growth of twins and, to a lesser extent, later-born children (Jones & Adamson, 1987; Tomasello, Mannle, & Kruger, 1986).

But vocabulary is only one aspect of language development. Research suggests that participating in multichild family interaction may have certain positive consequences. Recently, Michelle Barton and Michael Tomasello (1991) brought 19- to 25-month-old toddlers, their mothers, and their 3- to 5-year-old siblings into a laboratory and asked them to play with some novel toys. Even the youngest toddlers closely monitored the actions of their mothers and siblings, frequently establishing joint attentional focus with them. When they did so, toddlers were especially likely to join in interaction, sparking elaborate verbal exchanges.

■ *Mother-toddler-sibling interaction seems to offer a unique context for enhancing the pragmatics of language. The toddler in this family may become especially skilled at joining in conversations and adapting her speech to the needs of her listeners. (Charles Gupton/Stock Boston)*

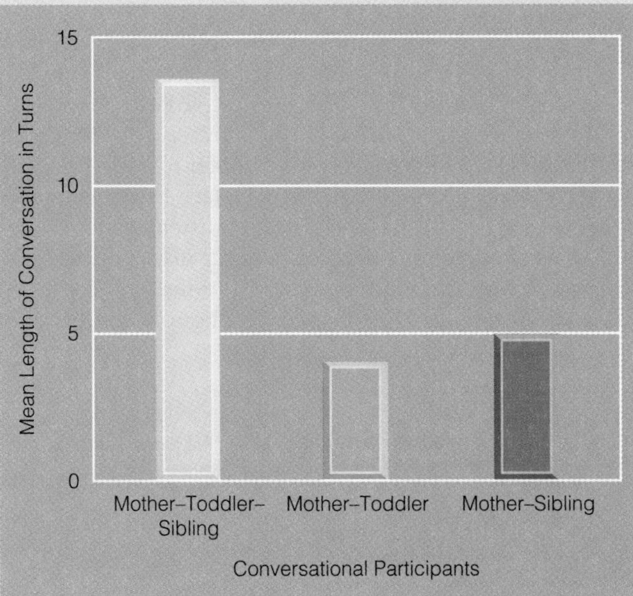

FIGURE 9.5

Average number of turns in mother-toddler-sibling conversations. When all three interacted together, conversations almost tripled in length, and each participant took more turns. (Adapted from Barton & Tomasello, 1991.)

As Figure 9.5 shows, mother–toddler–sibling conversations were almost three times longer than either mother–toddler or mother–sibling conversations. When all three interacted together, each participant took more turns.

Mother–toddler–sibling interaction seems to offer a unique context for acquiring the pragmatics of language. For example, successfully joining an ongoing conversation requires a toddler to understand the other speakers' topic and think of a way to add to it rather than just stating whatever comes to mind. Furthermore, as toddlers listen to the conversations of others, they are exposed to models that may be especially important for certain skills, such as use of personal pronouns ("I" versus "you"), which are more common in the first 50 to 100 words of younger than older siblings (Pine, 1995). Finally, communicating with siblings requires children to adapt their utterances to partners who may be far less willing than caregivers to give in to their wishes.

In sum, young children appear to profit in different ways from single and multichild language learning environments, and both are important for development. Although homes with older siblings may reduce adult sensitivity to individual children, they provide a rich variety of linguistic stimulation that helps children learn to use language for social purposes.

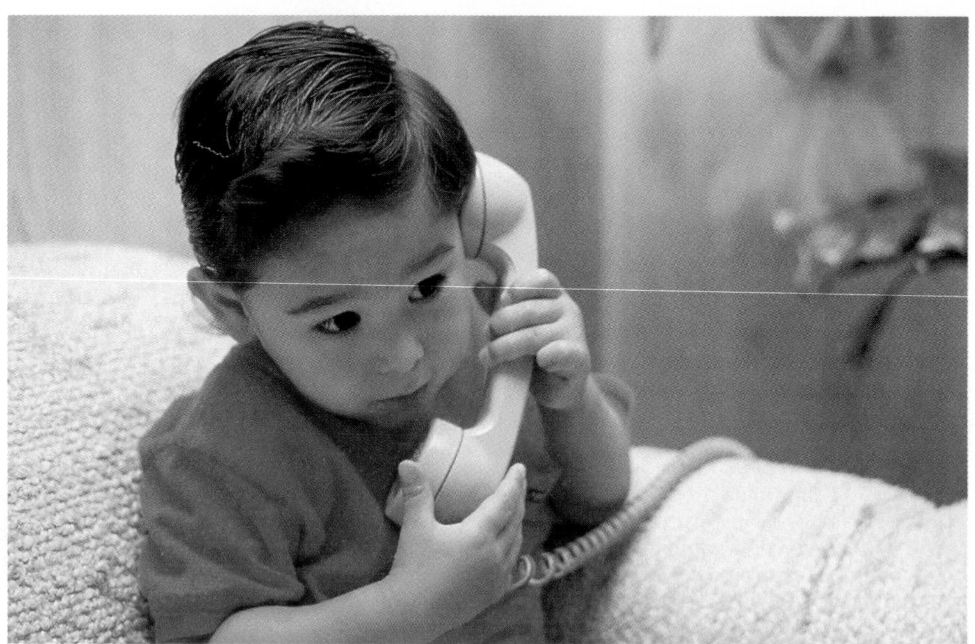

■ *Context affects young children's referential communication skills. When talking on the telephone, this 4-year-old is likely to have trouble communicating clearly because he lacks the supports available in face-to-face interaction, such as visual access to his partner's reaction and to objects that are topics of conversation. (Tony Freeman/PhotoEdit)*

LEARNING TO COMMUNICATE CLEARLY

Effective communication requires the ability to produce clear verbal messages as well as to recognize when messages we receive are unclear so we can ask for more information. These aspects of language are called **referential communication skills**.

Laboratory tasks designed to assess children's ability to communicate clearly typically present them with challenging situations in which they must describe one object among a group of very similar objects to a listener. For example, in one study, 3- to 10-year-olds were shown several eight-object arrays. In each, objects were similar in size, shape, and color. Children were asked to indicate which object they liked best as a birthday present for an imaginary friend. Most 3-year-olds gave ambiguous descriptions. When asked for clarification, they relied heavily on gestures, such as pointing. The ability to send clear messages improved steadily with age (Deutsch & Pechmann, 1982).

These findings may remind you of Piaget's notion of *egocentric speech*—that young children have difficulty taking the perspective of others (see Chapter 6). However, when preschoolers are given simpler communication tasks or engage in face-to-face interaction with familiar people, they adjust their speech to the needs of their listeners quite competently. This suggests that context has much to do with the clarity of young children's messages—a conclusion borne out by their telephone conversations. Have you tried talking on the phone with a 4-year-old lately? Here is an excerpt of one grandfather's attempt to do so:

Grandfather: "How old will you be?"
John: "Dis many." (Holding up four fingers.)
Grandfather: "Huh?"
John: "Dis many." (Again holding up four fingers.)
Grandfather: "How many is 'at?"
John: "Four. I'm gonna change ears, okay?"
Grandfather: "Okay."
John: "I'm back. I had ta change ears."
Grandfather: "Okay. Was one of your ears gettin' tired?"
John: "Yeah. This one is." (points to his left ear)
(Warren & Tate, 1992, pp. 259–260)

Referential communication skills
The ability to produce clear verbal messages and to recognize when the meaning of others' messages is unclear.

John used gestures that his grandfather could not see, and when his grandfather signaled that he could not understand ("Huh?"), John did not revise his message. Over time, children become more adept at communicating clearly in unfamiliar, highly demanding situations where they cannot see their listeners' reactions or rely on typical conversational aids, such as toys and objects to talk about (Lloyd, Boada, & Forns, 1992).

Children's ability to evaluate the adequacy of messages they receive also improves with age. Around age 3, preschoolers start to ask others to clarify ambiguous messages (Revelle, Karabenick, & Wellman, 1981). At first, children recognize when a message provides a poor description of a concrete object (Ackerman, 1993). Only later do they become good at telling when a message is inconsistent with something said earlier. Detection of this kind of difficulty requires the listener to retrieve previous discourse from memory and match it against currently spoken information. It depends on the comprehension monitoring skills we discussed in Chapter 7 and is a late developing achievement, improving gradually during middle childhood and adolescence (Sonnenschein, 1986a).

SOCIOLINGUISTIC UNDERSTANDING

Language adaptations to social expectations are called **speech registers**. As early as the preschool years, children are sensitive to them. In one study, 4- to 7-year-olds were asked to act out different roles with hand puppets. Even the youngest children showed that they understood the stereotypic features of different social positions. They used more commands when playing socially dominant and male roles, such as teacher, doctor, and father, and more politeness routines and indirect requests when playing less dominant and feminine roles, such as pupil, patient, and mother (Anderson, 1984).

Speech adjustments based on familiarity and age also appear during the preschool and early elementary school years. Children give fuller explanations to an unfamiliar listener than to someone with whom they share common experiences, such as a friend or family member (Sonnenschein, 1986b). They also simplify their speech when talking to a very young child (see Chapter 6, page 233). These abilities are refined in middle childhood. For example, when communicating with an unfamiliar listener or a 2-year-old, fourth graders include more redundant information than do first graders. Older children apply their more advanced referential communication skills to their speech register adjustments, taking extra steps to accommodate the needs of their listeners (Sonnenschein, 1988).

The importance of register adjustments is reflected in how often parents teach social routines as part of the child's first communicative acts. Infants are encouraged to wave "bye-bye" before they can grasp the meaning of the gesture. By age 2, when children fail to say "please," "thank you," or "hi" and "good-bye," parents usually model and demand an appropriate response (Becker, 1990). In some cultures, much greater emphasis is placed on tutoring young children in social routines than in language per se. For example, Kaluli mothers of New Guinea model socially appropriate statements, terminating their utterance with the word *ellema* (say it). If the child is too young to imitate, the mother may pitch her voice up and repeat the routine, as if the infant or toddler were speaking (Schieffelin & Ochs, 1987).

Parents everywhere seem to realize that a child can get by in the world without perfectly correct pronunciation, grammar, and a large vocabulary. But failing to use socially acceptable speech can lead to scorn and rejection, causing a child's message not to be received at all.

BRIEF REVIEW

During early and middle childhood, children acquire a variety of pragmatic devices that permit them to engage in more sustained and effective conversation with others. Over this same period, referential communication in unfamiliar, highly demanding situations improves. Sensitivity to speech registers is present during the preschool years. Parents the world over realize the importance of socially appropriate communication and tutor children in social routines from an early age.

Speech registers
Language adaptations to social expectations.

MILESTONES

Language Development

Age	Phonology	Semantics	Grammar	Pragmatics	Metalinguistic Awareness
Birth–1 year	■ Categorical speech perception is present. ■ Speech sounds become organized into phonemic categories of native language. ■ Sensitivity to stress patterns and phoneme sequences in words of native language develops. ■ Intonation and sound patterns of babbling begin to resemble those of native language.	■ Preference for words in own language develops. ■ Certain patterns of babbled sounds appear in particular contexts. ■ Preverbal gestures develop.	■ Sensitivity to natural phrase units develops.	■ Joint attention with caregiver is established. ■ Ability to engage in vocal exchanges with caregiver develops. ■ Participation in turn-taking games improves.	
1–2 years	■ Systematic strategies to simplify word pronunciation appear.	■ First words are produced; vocabulary builds to several hundred words. ■ Object words are emphasized first; action and state words follow soon after. ■ Word coinages appear.	■ Two-word utterances, in the form of telegraphic speech, appear. ■ A beginning appreciation of grammatical rules is present. ■ First grammatical morphemes are added.	■ Conversational turn-taking and topic maintenance are present.	
3–5 years	■ Pronunciation improves greatly.	■ Word coinage forms expand. ■ Metaphors based on concrete, sensory comparisons appear.	■ Sentences clearly reflect an appreciation of adult grammatical categories. ■ Grammatical morphemes continue to be added in a regular order. ■ Many complex grammatical structures are added.	■ Conversational strategies that help sustain interaction, such as the turnabout, appear. ■ Understanding of illocutionary intent is present. ■ Ability to adjust speech in accord with social expectations develops.	■ The beginnings of metalinguistic awareness emerge and support language and literacy development.

MILESTONES

Language Development (continued)

Age	Phonology	Semantics	Grammar	Pragmatics	Metalinguistic Awareness
6–10 years	■ Pronunciations signaling subtle differences in meaning are mastered. 	■ At school entry, vocabulary includes about 10,000 words. ■ Meanings of words are grasped on the basis of definitions. ■ Appreciation of multiple meanings of words leads to expanded understanding of metaphors and humor.	■ A few complex grammatical structures, such as the passive voice and pronoun reference, continue to be refined.	■ Advanced conversational strategies, such as shading, appear. ■ Understanding of illocutionary intent expands. ■ Referential communication in unfamiliar, highly demanding contexts improves.	■ Metalinguistic awareness develops rapidly and is enhanced by mastery of reading and spelling.
11 years–adulthood	■ Changes in syllabic stress after certain difficult words take on endings are mastered. 	■ Vocabulary builds to about 30,000 words. ■ Many abstract words are added to vocabulary. ■ Understanding of subtle nonliteral word meanings, as in irony and sarcasm, improves.	■ Refinement of complex grammatical structures continues.	■ Referential communication—especially, detection of unclear messages received—continues to improve.	■ Metalinguistic awareness continues to be refined. 

Note: These milestones represent overall age trends. Individual differences exist in the precise age at which each milestone is attained.

Development of Metalinguistic Awareness

In previous sections, we noted several times that older children's more reflective and analytical approach to language is involved in later linguistic achievements. The ability to think about language as a system is called **metalinguistic awareness**. Researchers have been especially interested in when it emerges and the role it plays in a variety of language-related accomplishments.

The beginnings of metalinguistic awareness are already present in early childhood. For example, by age 4, children are aware that word labels are arbitrary and not part of the objects to which they refer. When asked whether an object could be called by a different name in a new language, they respond "yes." Four-year-olds can also make some conscious syntactic judgments—for example, that a puppet who says, "Nose your touch" or "Dog the pat," is saying his sentences backward (Chaney, 1992). These early metalinguistic understandings are good predictors of vocabulary and grammatical development during the preschool years (Smith & Tager-Flusberg, 1982).

Nevertheless, young children view language primarily as a means of communication, and they seldom treat it as an object of thought. Full flowering of metalinguistic skills does not take place until middle childhood. For example, around age 8, children can identify phonemes (all the sounds in a word) (Tunmer & Nesdale, 1982). They can also judge the grammatical correctness of a sentence even if its meaning is false or senseless, whereas preschoolers cannot (Bialystok, 1986). School-age children's metalinguistic knowledge is also evident in their improved ability to define words and appreciate their multiple meanings in puns, riddles, and metaphors—skills that continue to be refined into adolescence (McGhee-Bidlack, 1991; Winner, 1988).

Metalinguistic awareness emerges as language use becomes more automatic, freeing children from the immediate linguistic context so they can attend to how messages are communicated. As early as the preschool years, *phonological awareness*—the ability to reflect on the sound structure of spoken language—predicts reading and spelling success. Four-year-olds who can categorize words on the basis of their beginning sounds and rhyming syllables make good use of this knowledge when they get to school and must map printed text onto oral language (Goswami & Bryant, 1990). Once reading and spelling are underway, they enhance more fine-grained aspects of phonological understanding, such as the ability (mentioned earlier) to divide words into phonemes (Morrison, Smith, & Dow-Ehrensberger, 1995). Training children in phonological awareness is a promising technique for encouraging early literacy development.

As we will see in the final section of this chapter, bilingual children are advanced in metalinguistic awareness (as well as other cognitive skills). But before we conclude with this topic, you may find it helpful to turn back to the Milestones table on pages 372–373, which provides an overview of the many aspects of language development we have discussed throughout this chapter.

Bilingualism: Learning Two Languages in Childhood

Most American children speak only one language, their native tongue of English. Yet throughout the United States and the world, many children grow up bilingual. They learn two languages, and sometimes more than two, during the childhood years. Current estimates indicate that 6 million American school-age children speak a language other than English at home, a figure expected to increase steadily into the twenty-first century (U.S. Bureau of the Census, 1995).

Children can become bilingual in two ways: (1) by acquiring both languages at the same time in early childhood, or (2) by learning a second language after mastering the first. Children of bilingual parents who teach both languages in the early years show no special problems with language development. For a time, they appear to develop more

Metalinguistic awareness
The ability to think about language as a system.

■ *Several million American school-age children speak a language other than English in their homes and neighborhoods. Research shows that bilingualism enhances many cognitive and linguistic skills. (Chet Seymour/The Picture Cube)*

slowly because they mix the two languages. But this is not an indication of linguistic confusion, since bilingual parents do not maintain strict language separation either. Instead, it reflects the young child's desire to use any means available to communicate (Baker, 1993). These bilingual youngsters acquire normal native ability in the language of their surrounding community and good to native ability in the second language, depending on their exposure to it. When children acquire a second language after they already speak a first language, it generally takes about a year to become as fluent in the second language as native-speaking agemates (Reich, 1986).

Until recently, a commonly held belief among Americans was that childhood bilingualism led to cognitive and linguistic deficits as well as a sense of personal rootlessness, since the bilingual child was thought to identify only weakly with mainstream American culture. This negative attitude has been fueled by ethnic prejudices, since bilingualism in the United States is strongly associated with low-income minority status. A large body of research now shows that bilingualism has a positive impact on development. Children who are fluent in two languages do better than others on tests of analytical reasoning, concept formation, and cognitive flexibility (Hakuta, Ferdman, & Diaz, 1987). And as we mentioned earlier, their metalinguistic skills are particularly well developed. They are more aware that words are arbitrary symbols, more conscious of language structure and detail, and better at noticing errors of grammar and meaning in spoken and written prose—capacities that enhance their reading achievement (Campbell & Sais, 1995; Ricciardelli, 1992).

The advantages of bilingualism provide strong justification for bilingual education programs in American schools. The Social Issues box on page 376 describes the current controversy over bilingual education in the United States. As you will see, bilingual children rarely receive support for their native language in classrooms. Yet bilingualism provides one of the best examples of how language, once learned, becomes an important tool of the mind and fosters cognitive development. In fact, the goals of schooling could reasonably be broadened to include helping all children become bilingual, thereby fostering the cognitive, language, and cultural enrichment of the entire nation (Hakuta, 1986; Ruiz, 1988).

SOCIAL ISSUES ➤ POINT OF VIEW

Should English Be Declared the Official U.S. Language? Impact on Bilingual Education

California, noted for its culturally diverse population, made national news in 1986 by passing a referendum declaring English as its official language. Over the next few years, 17 other states followed suit, each proclaiming their desire to protect a common language and culture in the United States. Supporters of these English-only laws believe they are vital for forging national unity and easing communication in education, business, and everyday life. They argue that immigrants who do not learn English are destined to become poverty-stricken, marginal members of society.

Opponents point out that when a country imposes a national language, ethnic minorities usually understand it as the majority's attempt to assert dominance. They react by striving all the harder to retain their linguistic heritage (Neier, 1994). Consequently, English-only laws are divisive. They defeat their purpose of integrating language minority people into the mainstream.

The battle over establishing English as the official language is fought most intensely on the front of education. English-only proponents believe that language minority children should be instructed from the start like all other American children—in English. According to this view, time spent communicating in the child's native tongue subtracts from English language achievement, which is crucial for success in the world of school and work.

On the other side are educators committed to truly *bilingual* education—developing the minority child's native language while fostering mastery of English. They believe that instruction in the native tongue lets minority children know that their heritage is respected (McGroarty, 1992). In addition, by avoiding abrupt submersion in an English-speaking environment, bilingual education prevents *semilingualism,* or inadequate proficiency in both languages. When minority children experience gradual loss of the first language as a result of being taught the second, they end up limited in both languages for a time, a circumstance that leads to serious academic difficulties. Semilingualism is one factor believed to contribute to the high rates of school failure and dropout among low-income Hispanic youngsters, who make up nearly 50 percent of the American language minority population (August & Garcia, 1988).

A wealth of research favors instruction in the child's native tongue with gradual introduction of English. In classrooms where both languages are integrated into the curriculum, minority children are more involved in learning, participate more actively in class discussions, and acquire the second language more easily. In addition, they readily transfer academic skills, such as reading and mathematics, from one language to another. They do not, as many people assume, learn in their native language at the expense of learning in English. To the contrary, when teachers speak only in a language their pupils can barely understand, children display frustration, withdrawal, and resentment toward the educational system (Cazden, 1984; Wong-Fillmore et al., 1985).

■ *When bilingual education programs provide instruction in both the child's native language and in English, children are more involved in learning and are advanced in language development. (Will Faller)*

The controversy over declaring English the official U.S. language highlights a curious paradox in American educational practice. Although minority children are encouraged to become English monolinguals, instruction in foreign languages is highly valued for middle-class, native English-speaking pupils (Hakuta & Garcia, 1989). Recently, a few schools have experimented with a new form of bilingual education designed to benefit both groups. In these programs, limited-English-proficient and fluent-English-speaking children are assigned in equal numbers to the same classroom, and instruction is directed at helping all achieve competence in English and a second language.

English-only supporters often point to Canada, which recognizes the linguistic rights of its French-speaking minority but where friction between English- and French-speaking groups is intense. Nevertheless, Canada continues to adhere to a policy in which both English and French are official languages, and most of its children become fluent in both—ideal conditions for building greater ethnic harmony (Piatt, 1993).

The United States has a centuries-old constitutional tradition of linguistic neutrality. English achieved its status as the majority language through societal forces acting on people's desire to secure education and employment and meet their social and commercial needs. Respect for the linguistic and cultural rights of minority groups is essential for achieving broad acceptance of a national language in the United States.

YOUR POINT OF VIEW . . .

■ Ask several people you know for their opinion on the value of bilingual education for ethnic minority children. Which side does each take on the controversy described here? For those who think children should be taught only in English, describe research findings on the benefits of bilingualism. Did any change their minds?

SUMMARY

COMPONENTS OF LANGUAGE

- Language consists of four subsystems: **phonology**, **semantics**, **grammar**, and **pragmatics**. In becoming competent speakers of their native tongue, children must master each component and combine them into a flexible communication system.

THEORIES OF LANGUAGE DEVELOPMENT

- Three theories provide different accounts of language development. According to the behaviorist perspective, language, like other behaviors, is learned through operant conditioning and imitation. Behaviorism has difficulty accounting for the speed of language progress and for children's novel, rule-based utterances. However, it has had a lasting impact on efforts to help children with serious language delays and disabilities.
- Chomsky's nativist perspective proposes that humans are born with a **language acquisition device (LAD)** that permits children, as soon as they have acquired sufficient vocabulary, to speak in a grammatically correct fashion and understand the language they hear. Consistent with nativist theory, evidence indicates that a complex language system is unique to humans, that language functions are housed in **Broca** and **Wernicke's areas**, and that a sensitive period for language development exists. However, vast diversity among the world languages and children's gradual acquisition of many constructions has raised questions about Chomsky's assumption of a universal grammar within the LAD ensuring built-in knowledge of grammatical rules.
- In recent years, interactionist theories have arisen, stressing that innate abilities and social contexts combine to promote language development. Today, there is increasing acknowledgment that biology, cognition, and social experience may operate in different balances with respect to each component of language. Grammar may be more innately determined than other aspects of linguistic skill.

PRELINGUISTIC DEVELOPMENT: GETTING READY TO TALK

- Infants are specially prepared for language learning. Newborn babies are capable of **categorical speech perception** and are sensitive to a much wider range of **phonemes** than are children and adults. By 6 months, infants focus more intently on the sound categories of their own language. In the second half of the first year, they start to detect phrase and word units. The special features of **motherese**, or **child-directed speech**, ease the young child's task of making sense of language.
- Infants begin **cooing** at about 2 months and **babbling** around 6 months. Over the first year, the range of babbled sounds expands. Then, as infants get ready to talk, the intonation and sound patterns of babbling start to resemble those of the child's language community. Also, certain patterns of babbles appear in particular contexts, suggesting that infants are experimenting with the semantic function of language.
- The beginnings of conversational behavior can be seen in the first few months as infants and caregivers establish joint attention, and the adult comments on what the baby sees. Turn-taking is present in early vocal exchanges, and by the end of the first year, babies become active participants in turn-taking games. Around this time, they start to use two preverbal gestures, the **protodeclarative** and **protoimperative**, to influence the behavior of others. Soon, words are uttered and gestures diminish as children make the transition to verbal communication.

PHONOLOGICAL DEVELOPMENT

- The first words children say are influenced partly by what they can pronounce. When learning to talk, children apply systematic phonological strategies to simplify adult pronunciations.
- Pronunciation improves greatly over the preschool years as the vocal tract matures and children engage in active problem solving. Certain accent patterns that signal subtle differences in meaning are not mastered until late childhood and adolescence.

SEMANTIC DEVELOPMENT

- Vocabulary increases at an extraordinary pace during early childhood, an accomplishment that is even more awesome when we consider that children's language **comprehension** develops ahead of **production**. To build an extensive vocabulary quickly, children engage in **fast-mapping**.
- Striking individual differences in rate and form of semantic development exist. Girls show faster early vocabulary growth than boys, and reserved, cautious toddlers may wait for a time before beginning to speak. Most toddlers use a **referential style** of language learning. A smaller number who use an **expressive style** have vocabularies that grow more slowly. Western mothers tend to foster the referential style by labeling objects; Asian and African mothers more often promote the expressive style by stressing social routines.
- Early vocabularies emphasize object words; action and state words appear soon after, an order influenced by cognitive development. When first learning new words, children make errors of **underextension** and **overextension**. Word coinages and metaphors permit children to expand the range of meanings they can express through language.
- In middle childhood, children can grasp word meanings from definitions, and comprehension of metaphor and humor expands. Adolescents' ability to reason abstractly leads to a wider vocabulary and appreciation of subtle meanings, as in irony and sarcasm.
- A special part of working memory, a **phonological store** that permits us to retain speech-based information, supports vocabulary growth in early childhood. According to **lexical contrast theory**, children figure out the meaning of new words by contrasting them with ones they already know. The **principle of mutual exclusivity** explains children's acquisition of some, but not all, early words. Children may deduce many word meanings through **syntactic bootstrapping**—observing how they are used in the structure of sentences.

GRAMMATICAL DEVELOPMENT

- Between 1½ and 2½ years, children combine two words to express a variety of meanings. These first sentences are called **telegraphic speech**, since they leave out smaller, less important words. Early word combinations do not always follow adult grammatical rules.
- As children move beyond two-word utterances, a grammatical explosion takes place. Their speech conforms to the formal grammatical categories of their language, and they add **grammatical morphemes** in a consistent order that is a product of both structural and semantic complexity. Once children acquire a regular morphological rule, they occasionally **overregularize**, or extend it to words that are exceptions. New expressions based on auxiliary verbs, such as negatives and questions, are soon mastered.
- Between ages 3 and 6, a variety of complex constructions are added. Still, certain forms, such as the passive voice and subtle pronoun reference, continue to be refined in middle childhood.
- Some experts believe grammar is a product of general cognitive development. According to one view, children engage in **semantic bootstrapping**, relying on common meanings of words to figure out grammatical regularities. Others agree with the essence of Chomsky's theory that children are specially tuned for language learning. One speculation is that children have a **language-making capacity (LMC)** that supports the discovery of grammatical regularities.
- Adults provide children with indirect feedback about grammatical errors, in the form of **expansions** and **recasts**. However, the impact of such feedback on grammatical development has been challenged.

PRAGMATIC DEVELOPMENT

- Young children are effective conversationalists. Strategies that help sustain interaction, such as the **turnabout** and **shading**, are added in early and middle childhood. During this time, children's understanding of **illocutionary intent** improves, and they also acquire more effective **referential communication skills**. Preschoolers are sensitive to **speech registers**. Parents tutor children in social routines at an early age, emphasizing the importance of adapting language to social expectations.

DEVELOPMENT OF METALINGUISTIC AWARENESS

- Although preschoolers show the beginnings of **metalinguistic awareness**, major advances do not take place until middle childhood. Phonological awareness predicts reading and spelling achievement, and literacy, in turn, enhances metalinguistic understanding.

BILINGUALISM: LEARNING TWO LANGUAGES IN CHILDHOOD

- Historically, Americans have held negative attitudes toward childhood bilingualism, a view that has been fueled by ethnic prejudices. A large body of research shows that children who are fluent in two languages are advanced in a variety of cognitive and metalinguistic skills.

IMPORTANT TERMS AND CONCEPTS

phonology (p. 342)
semantics (p. 342)
grammar (p. 342)
pragmatics (p. 342)
language acquisition device (LAD) (p. 343)
Broca's area (p. 346)
Wernicke's area (p. 346)
phoneme (p. 349)
categorical speech perception (p. 349)
motherese, or child-directed speech (p. 350)
cooing (p. 350)
babbling (p. 350)
protodeclarative (p. 351)
protoimperative (p. 351)
comprehension (p. 354)
production (p. 354)
fast-mapping (p. 355)
referential style (p. 356)
expressive style (p. 356)
underextension (p. 358)
overextension (p. 358)
phonological store (p. 360)
lexical contrast theory (p. 360)
principle of mutual exclusivity (p. 360)
syntactic bootstrapping (p. 360)
telegraphic speech (p. 361)
grammatical morphemes (p. 363)
overregularization (p. 364)
semantic bootstrapping (p. 366)
language-making capacity (LMC) (p. 367)
expansions (p. 367)
recasts (p. 367)
turnabout (p. 368)
shading (p. 368)
illocutionary intent (p. 368)
referential communication skills (p. 370)
speech registers (p. 371)
metalinguistic awareness (p. 372)

CONNECTIONS for Chapter 9

If you are interested in . . .	turn to . . .	to learn about . . .
Emergence of representation	Chapter 4, pp. 139–140	Newborn imitation
	Chapter 4, p. 155	Infant perception of pattern organization
	Chapter 6, pp. 220–221	Imitation and categorization in infancy
	Chapter 6, pp. 217, 226–228	Make-believe play
	Chapter 6, pp. 228–229	Pictorial representation
	Chapter 11, pp. 425–426	Self-recognition
Relationship between language and thought	Chapter 6, pp. 225–226	Piaget's view of the relationship between language and thought
	Chapter 6, p. 240	Phrasing of interview questions and conservation
	Chapter 6, pp. 242–243	Role of language in formal operational thought
	Chapter 6, p. 247	Vygotsky's view of the relationship between language and thought
	Chapter 7, p. 291	Language and Asian children's understanding of multidigit addition and subtraction
	Chapter 10, pp. 393–394	Language and emotional understanding
Culture and communication	Chapter 1, p. 28	!Kung infancy: Acquiring culture
	Chapter 8, pp. 323–324	Culture, language customs, and intelligence test performance
	Chapter 10, p. 391	Culture, parent–child communication, and emotional display rules
	Chapter 14, pp. 549–550	Impact of poverty on parent–child communication
	Chapter 15, p. 586	Culture and peer sociability

10 Emotional Development

On a spring day, 4-month-old Zach, cradled in the arms of his father, followed by 13-month-old Emily and 23-month-old Brenda, led by their mothers, arrived at the door of my classroom, which had been transformed into a playroom for the morning. My students and I spent the next hour watching closely for the wide variety of capacities that develop over the first 2 years. Especially captivating were the children's emotional reactions to people and things around them. As Zach's dad bounced him energetically on his knee and lifted him up in the air, Zach responded with a gleeful grin. A tickle followed by a lively kiss on the tummy produced an excited giggle. When I held a rattle in front of Zach, his brows knit, his face sobered, and he eyed it intently as he mobilized all his energies to reach for it.

Transferred to my arms and then to the laps of several students, Zach remained at ease with a variety of adults (although he reserved an unusually broad smile for his father). In contrast, Emily and Brenda were wary of this roomful of strangers. I held out a toy and coaxed Emily toward it. She pulled back and glanced at her mother, as if to check whether the new adult and tantalizing object were safe to explore. When her mother grinned and encouraged, Emily approached cautiously and accepted the toy. A greater capacity to understand the situation combined with her mother's explanations helped Brenda adjust quickly, and soon she was engrossed in play. During the hour, Brenda displayed a whole new range of emotional reactions, including embarrassment at seeing chocolate on her chin in a mirror and pride as I remarked on the tall tower she had built out of blocks.

In this chapter, we turn to the child's emotions, a topic that has captured the attention of researchers from virtually every major theoretical persuasion. Although the emotional side of development was overshadowed by cognition for several decades, new excitement surrounds the topic today. A large body of research indicates that emotions play a central role in all aspects of human experience.

Our discussion brings together several lines of evidence. We begin with major theories that provide contrasting views of the role of emotions in development and everyday life. Then we chart age-related changes in emotional expressiveness and understanding. As we do so, we will account for Zach, Emily, and Brenda's expanding range of emotional capacities. Next, our attention turns to temperament—individual differences in style of emotional responding. We will consider both biological and environmental contributions to these differences as well as their consequences for future development. Finally, we take up attachment to the caregiver, the child's first affectional tie that emerges during infancy. We will see how the feelings of security that grow out of this important bond provide a vital source of support for the child's exploration, sense of independence, and expanding social relationships.

Theories of Emotional Development

Three major viewpoints—behaviorism and social learning theory, cognitive-developmental discrepancy theory, and the more recent functionalist approach—have guided research on emotional development. Although the functionalist perspective has gained in popularity because of its broad explanatory power, each viewpoint has made lasting contributions to our understanding of children's emotions (Magai & McFadden, 1995).

BEHAVIORISM AND SOCIAL LEARNING THEORY

From the beginning of this century, behaviorists accorded emotional reactions an important role in children's development. According to John Watson, three innate emotions are present at birth: fear, induced by loud noises or loss of support; rage, prompted by restriction of body movements; and love, evoked by touching and caressing. As we indicated in Chapter 1, one of Watson's major findings was that emotional reactions to new stimuli, such as 11-month-old Albert's fearful reaction to a furry white rat, could be learned through classical conditioning. Watson concluded that all affective responses to objects and people were learned in this way (Watson & Raynor, 1920). In the 1960s, operant conditioning became an influential account of children's emotions as several researchers showed that infant smiling, vocalizing, and crying could be changed through caregivers' use of reinforcement and punishment (Etzel & Gewirtz, 1967; Rheingold, Gewirtz, & Ross, 1959).

Social learning theory emphasizes modeling of others' emotional reactions as another means through which children associate feelings with particular situations. In recent years, Albert Bandura (1989, 1992) expanded this view, adding a cognitive component to traditional social learning theory. According to Bandura, as children's representational ability improves, they can engage in emotional self-arousal by thinking about their own affectively charged past experiences or ones they have seen happen to others.

Although some emotional reactions are acquired through conditioning and modeling, behaviorist and social learning accounts are limited. They cannot explain why certain responses emerge spontaneously, without having been learned. For example, recall how Zach accepted unfamiliar adults, whereas Emily and Brenda were wary of them. As we will see later, fear of strangers typically appears during the second half of the first year, despite the fact that infants previously responded positively to unfamiliar people, who continue to smile at and offer toys to the baby. Throughout this chapter, we will see that children often react emotionally in ways that cannot be accounted for by basic learning mechanisms.

COGNITIVE-DEVELOPMENTAL DISCREPANCY THEORY

Instead of viewing emotions as central forces in development, cognitive-developmental theorists regard them as by-products of cognitive processing. The first to take this position was Donald Hebb (1949), whose **discrepancy theory** of emotional development explained how distress reactions came to be elicited by novel stimuli. According to Hebb, when children encounter a new stimulus, they compare it to a scheme, or internal representation, of a familiar object. The similarity between the novel stimulus and the child's scheme determines the emotional response. Little discrepancy produces very mild distress, but as the discrepancy increases, the child's distress reaction intensifies. When the discrepancy is very great, the stimulus can no longer be assimilated, and the distress reaction declines.

Later, other researchers modified Hebb's theory, suggesting that it could explain a wide variety of emotional reactions (Kagan, Kearsley, & Zelazo, 1978). For example, they argued that the positive emotions of interest and happiness are due to a moderate discrepancy between a current scheme and a new event. As the stimulus becomes more unusual, the child's reaction turns to anxiety and fear.

Discrepancy theory is especially effective in accounting for children's interest in and exploration of their physical world. Many studies show that infants look longer at visual stimuli that are moderately discrepant from ones they know well (McCall, Kennedy, & Appelbaum, 1977). Discrepancy theory also explains why young children often play happily with new toys but ignore familiar ones. It helps us understand why many parents and teachers find it useful to rotate toys in and out of children's play space to promote absorbed interest in objects.

Nevertheless, discrepancy theory does poorly when it comes to children's reactions to people. For example, it suggests that as soon as babies have a scheme for the familiar caregiver, they should begin to fear strangers (who deviate from this scheme). But babies have well-established memories of their mothers by 3 months of age (see Chapter 4), long before fear of strangers emerges during the second half of the first year. Furthermore, discrepancy theory cannot account for infants' reactions to different strangers—for

Discrepancy theory
A theory of emotional development in which a child's reaction to a novel stimulus is determined by the degree of similarity between the stimulus and a scheme of a familiar object, to which the stimulus is compared.

example, their wariness toward unfamiliar adults but friendliness toward children (Brooks & Lewis, 1976).

Finally, discrepancy theory does not tell us why children react to some very familiar experiences with interest and excitement rather than boredom. For example, the approach of the mother repeatedly elicits pleasure, even from older babies. And preschoolers frequently ask to have the same story read to them over and over, even after they have memorized it. Children clearly display great enthusiasm for certain thoroughly familiar events.

THE FUNCTIONALIST APPROACH

New theories, gathered together under the **functionalist approach**, emphasize that emotions are central, adaptive forces in all aspects of human activity—cognitive processing, social behavior, and even physical health (Barrett & Campos, 1987; Bretherton et al., 1986; Campos et al., 1983; Izard, 1991). To clarify this idea, let's examine the functions of emotions—the way they organize and regulate experience in each of these three areas.

EMOTIONS AS DETERMINANTS OF COGNITIVE PROCESSING. A large body of evidence indicates that emotions have a profound impact on cognitive processing. Emotional reactions can lead to learning that is crucial for survival. For example, the newly walking toddler does not need to receive a shock from an electric outlet or fall down a staircase to learn to avoid these dangerous situations. Instead, the caregiver's highly charged command is enough to get the child to acquire these self-protective behaviors (Campos et al., 1983).

To illustrate further, think about your own feelings on occasions in which you did poorly on a test or oral report even though you spent many hours preparing. Did anxiety affect your performance? Among children and adults, very high or low anxiety leads to poorer outcomes on cognitive tasks than does moderate anxiety, which can be facilitating (Sarason, 1980). Emotions also have powerful effects on memory. For example, children who were highly upset during an inoculation at the doctor's office remembered the event more clearly than did less stressed children (Goodman et al., 1991). At the same time, negative affect can impair children's encoding of information from the wider field (Bugental et al., 1992).

Unlike proponents of discrepancy theory, most functionalist theorists believe the relationship between emotion and cognition is bidirectional. Michael Lewis and his colleagues found evidence for this dynamic interplay as early as the first half-year of life. Two- to 8-month-olds were trained to pull a string attached to their wrists, which produced a slide of a smiling baby and a recording of a children's song. By tracking facial expressions, the researchers found that interest, happiness, and surprise increased as the infants learned the task—reactions that reflected pleasure at mastery of a new contingency. Next, a short nonreinforcement period followed in which pulling the string no longer activated the attractive stimuli. The babies' emotional reactions quickly changed—for most to anger but for a few to sadness. When the contingency was reinstated, babies who had reacted angrily to nonreinforcement showed renewed interest and enjoyment, pulling eagerly to produce the stimuli. In contrast, sad babies withdrew, displaying reduced involvement in the task (Lewis, Sullivan, & Ramsay, 1992). Emotions were intimately interwoven with cognitive processing, serving both as outcomes of mastery and as the foundation for infants' approach to the next learning phase.

EMOTIONS AS DETERMINANTS OF SOCIAL BEHAVIOR. Children's emotional signals, such as smiling, crying, and attentive interest, affect the behavior of other people in powerful ways. Similarly, emotional reactions of others regulate children's social behavior. For example, careful analyses of mother–infant face-to-face interaction reveal that by 3 months, a complex communication system is in place in which each partner responds in an appropriate and carefully timed fashion to the cues of the other (Tronick & Cohn, 1989). In several studies, this exchange of emotional signals was disrupted by having mothers assume either a still-faced, unreactive pose or a depressed emotional state. Infants tried facial expressions, vocalizations, and body movements to get their mothers to respond again. When these efforts failed, they reacted to their mother's sad, vacant gaze by turning away, frowning, and crying (Ellsworth, Muir, & Hains, 1993;

Functionalist approach
A theoretical perspective that regards emotions as central, adaptive forces in all aspects of human activity.

■ *Emotional signals are powerful determinants of social behavior. This child's unhappiness prompts her mother to respond with close body contact, soothing gestures, and comforting words. (Innervisions)*

Segal et al., 1995). To find out more about the powerful impact of maternal depression on children's emotional and social functioning, refer to the From Research to Practice box on the following page.

By the end of the first year, infants deliberately look to others for emotional cues to help them evaluate uncertain events, such as the approach of a stranger. Turn back to the beginning of this chapter and notice how Emily glanced at her mother to see if it was safe to interact with me. Yet another way that emotions regulate social interaction is through empathy, in which we respond in a caring way to the feelings of another person. We will consider the development of both of these emotional capacities in later sections.

■ EMOTIONS AS DETERMINANTS OF PHYSICAL HEALTH. In animal research, the link between emotions and physical health is well established. Studies of many species, from rats to monkeys, reveal that disrupting the mother–infant relationship (for example, by removing the baby from the mother either temporarily or permanently) depresses the animal's immune response—an effect that has long-term consequences for susceptibility to disease (Ackerman et al., 1988; Coe et al., 1992). Of course, for ethical reasons we cannot experiment with human children in these ways. But much naturalistic research indicates that emotions do influence children's physical well-being. For example, in Chapter 5 we discussed two childhood growth disorders—inorganic failure to thrive and deprivation dwarfism—that result from emotional deprivation. And other studies indicate that temporary or permanent separation from a loved one is associated with a variety of health difficulties from infancy into adulthood (Laudenslager & Reite, 1984).

■ OTHER FEATURES OF THE FUNCTIONALIST APPROACH. Besides the central role of emotions in cognitive, social, and physical experience, we will encounter some additional features of the functionalist approach throughout this chapter. First, emotions are viewed as important in the emergence of self-awareness. For example, the interest and excitement that babies display when acting on novel objects helps them develop a sense of self-efficacy—an awareness that they are capable of affecting events in their surrounding world (Alessandri, Sullivan, & Lewis, 1990). And once a beginning sense of self appears, the door is open to new emotional reactions. Recall Brenda's expressions of pride and embarrassment—two feeling states that have to do with evaluations of the self's goodness or badness (Barrett & Campos, 1987).

Second, the functionalist approach stresses that to adapt to their physical and social worlds, children must gradually gain voluntary control over their emotions, just as they do over motor, cognitive, and social behavior. At the same time, emotional expressions gradually become socialized, as children learn the circumstances in which it is acceptable to communicate feelings in their culture. As a result, by late childhood few emotions are expressed as openly and freely as they were in the early years of life (Thompson, 1990a). With these factors in mind, let's chart the course of emotional development.

FROM RESEARCH TO PRACTICE

Maternal Depression and Child Development

Approximately 8 to 10 percent of women experience chronic depression—mild to severe feelings of sadness and withdrawal that continue for months or years. Often the beginnings of this gloomy, distressed emotional state cannot be pinpointed; it has simply become a part of the person's daily life. In other instances, it emerges after childbirth but fails to subside as the new mother adjusts to hormonal changes in her body and gains confidence in caring for her baby. Stella experienced this latter form—called *postpartum depression*. Although genetic makeup increases the risk of depressive illness, Stella's case shows that social and cultural factors are also involved.

Stella's pregnancy went well until the last month, when her husband Kyle's lack of interest in the baby caused her to worry that having a child might be a mistake. Five days after Lucy was born, Stella's mood plunged. She was anxious and weepy, overwhelmed by Lucy's needs, and angry that she no longer had control over her own schedule. When Stella approached Kyle about her own fatigue and his unwillingness to help with the baby, he snapped that she overreacted to every move he made. Stella's friends, who did not have children, stopped by once to see Lucy and did not call again.

Children of depressed parents are two to five times more likely to develop behavior problems than are children of nondepressed parents (Cummings & Davies, 1994). Although heredity may be partly responsible (see Chapter 3, page 115), quality of parenting—in particular, less positive, responsive interaction—plays a major role. The more extreme the depression and the greater the number of stressors in a mother's life (such as marital discord, little or no social support, and poverty) the more the parent–child relationship is likely to be affected (Goodman et al., 1993). Stella, for example, rarely smiled and talked to Lucy, who responded to her mother's unhappy, detached demeanor with a sad, vacant gaze or, at times, with angry protest (Campbell, Cohn, & Meyers, 1995; Pickens & Field, 1993). Each time this happened, Stella felt inadequate as a mother, and her depression deepened. By 6 months of age, Lucy showed emotional symptoms common in babies of depressed mothers—a negative, irritable mood and attachment difficulties (Teti et al., 1995).

At older ages, parent–child relationship difficulties continue. Depressed parents use inconsistent discipline—sometimes lax, at other times too forceful—a pattern that reflects their disengaged as well as hostile behavior (Zahn-Waxler et al., 1990). As we will see in later chapters, children who experience these maladaptive parenting practices often show serious adjustment difficulties. To avoid their parent's insensitivity, they sometimes withdraw into depressive symptoms of their own. At other times, they mimic their parent's anger and become impulsive and antisocial (Conger, Patterson, & Ge, 1995). Furthermore, when teaching their child a task, depressed mothers are less sensitive to the child's level of understanding, less likely to use a variety of teaching strategies, and less likely to share decision making with the child than are other mothers (Goldsmith & Rogoff, 1995). Consequently, the impact of parental depression may extend beyond emotional and social functioning to cognition as well.

Over time, the parenting behaviors just described lead children to develop a negative worldview—one in which they perceive their parents and other people as a threat to their well-being. Children who constantly feel in danger and whose parents have not helped them learn how to manage their negative feelings are likely to become overly aroused in stressful situations, easily losing control when faced with cognitive or social challenges (Cummings & Cicchetti, 1990). Depressed parents are also more likely to have unhappy marriages. Repeated exposure to parental arguments sensitizes children to conflict, increasing their distress and aggression (Cummings & Zahn-Waxler, 1992). Impairments in regulating emotion (see page 391) compound these youngsters' cognitive and social difficulties.

Early treatment of maternal depression is vital, to prevent the disorder from interfering with the parent–child relationship and doing harm to children. Stella described her tearfulness, fatigue, and inability to comfort Lucy to her doctor. He referred her to a special program for depressed mothers and their babies, where a counselor worked with the family, helping Stella and Kyle with their marital problems and encouraging them to be more sensitive and patient with Lucy. In most cases of postpartum depression, treatment is successful (Steiner, 1990). When depressed mothers do not respond easily to treatment, a warm relationship with the father or another caregiver and efforts to reduce the many stressors that typically accompany depression can safeguard children's development.

BRIEF REVIEW

According to behaviorism and social learning theory, emotional reactions to new stimuli are learned through conditioning and modeling. In contrast, discrepancy theory regards emotions as by-products of cognitive processing. In comparison to these theories, the functionalist approach provides a more comprehensive account of emotional development. It regards emotions as vital adaptive forces in all aspects of human activity, as inseparably interwoven with cognition, and as becoming increasingly voluntary and socialized with age.

Development of the Expression of Discrete Emotions

Since infants cannot describe their feelings, researchers face a challenging task determining exactly which emotions they are experiencing. Although vocalizations and body movements provide some information, facial expressions seem to offer the most reliable cues. Cross-cultural evidence indicates that people around the world associate photographs of different facial gestures with emotions in the same way (Ekman & Friesen, 1972). These findings, which suggest that emotional expressions are built-in social signals, inspired researchers to carefully analyze infants' facial patterns to determine the range of emotions they display at different ages. A commonly used method for doing so, the MAX System, is illustrated in Figure 10.1.

Do infants come into the world with the ability to express a wide variety of emotions? Considerable controversy surrounds this question. Some researchers believe that all the **basic emotions**—those that can be directly inferred from facial expressions, such as happiness, interest, surprise, fear, anger, sadness, and disgust—are present in the first few weeks of life (Campos et al., 1983; Izard, 1991). Others regard the emotional life of the newborn baby as quite limited. For example, according to one view, separate emotions gradually emerge over the first year out of two global arousal states: the newborn's tendency to approach pleasant and withdraw from unpleasant stimulation (Fox, 1991; Sroufe, 1979).

Still, most researchers agree that signs of almost all the basic emotions are present in infancy (Izard et al., 1995; Malatesta-Magai, Izard, & Camras, 1991; Sroufe, 1979). Around 6 months, face, gaze, voice, and posture form distinct, coherent patterns that vary meaningfully with social events. For example, babies typically respond to their mother's playful interaction with a joyful face, positive vocalizations, and mouthing of body parts. In contrast, an unresponsive mother is likely to evoke a sad face and fussy vocalizations (sending the message "I'm overwhelmed") or an angry face, crying, and "pick-me-up" gestures (as if to say, "Change this unpleasant event!"). In sum, by the middle of the first year, emotional expressions are well organized and specific—and therefore able to tell us a great deal about the infant's internal state (Weinberg & Tronick, 1994).

Four emotions—happiness, anger, sadness, and fear—have received the most research attention. Let's see how they change with age.

HAPPINESS

Happiness—first in terms of blissful smiles and later through exuberant laughter—contributes to many aspects of development. Infants smile and laugh when they conquer

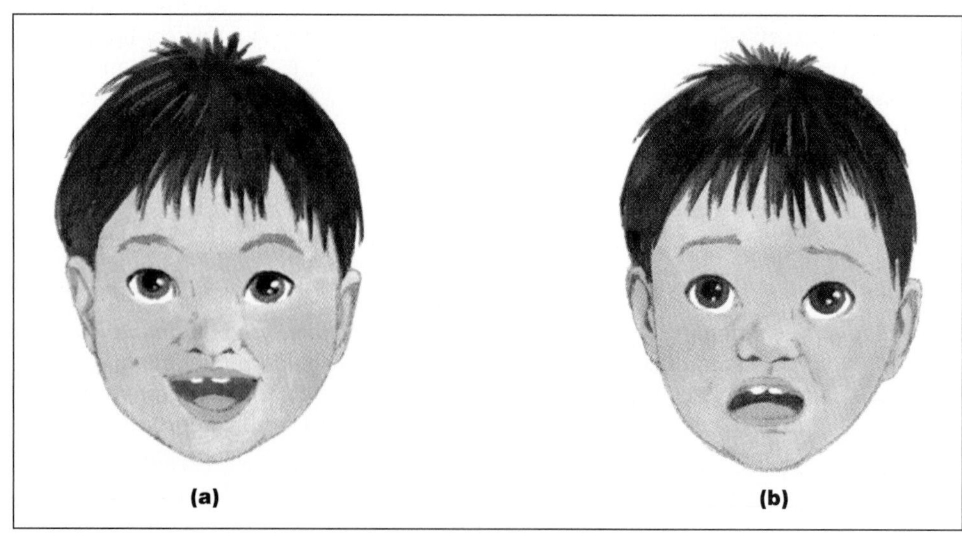

FIGURE 10.1

■ *Which emotions are these babies displaying? The MAX (Maximally Discriminative Facial Movement) System is a widely used method for classifying infants' emotional expressions. Facial muscle movements are carefully rated to determine their correspondence with basic feeling states. For example, cheeks raised and corners of the mouth pulled back and up signal happiness (a). Eyebrows raised, eyes widened, and mouth opened with corners pulled straight back denote fear (b). (From Izard, 1979.)*

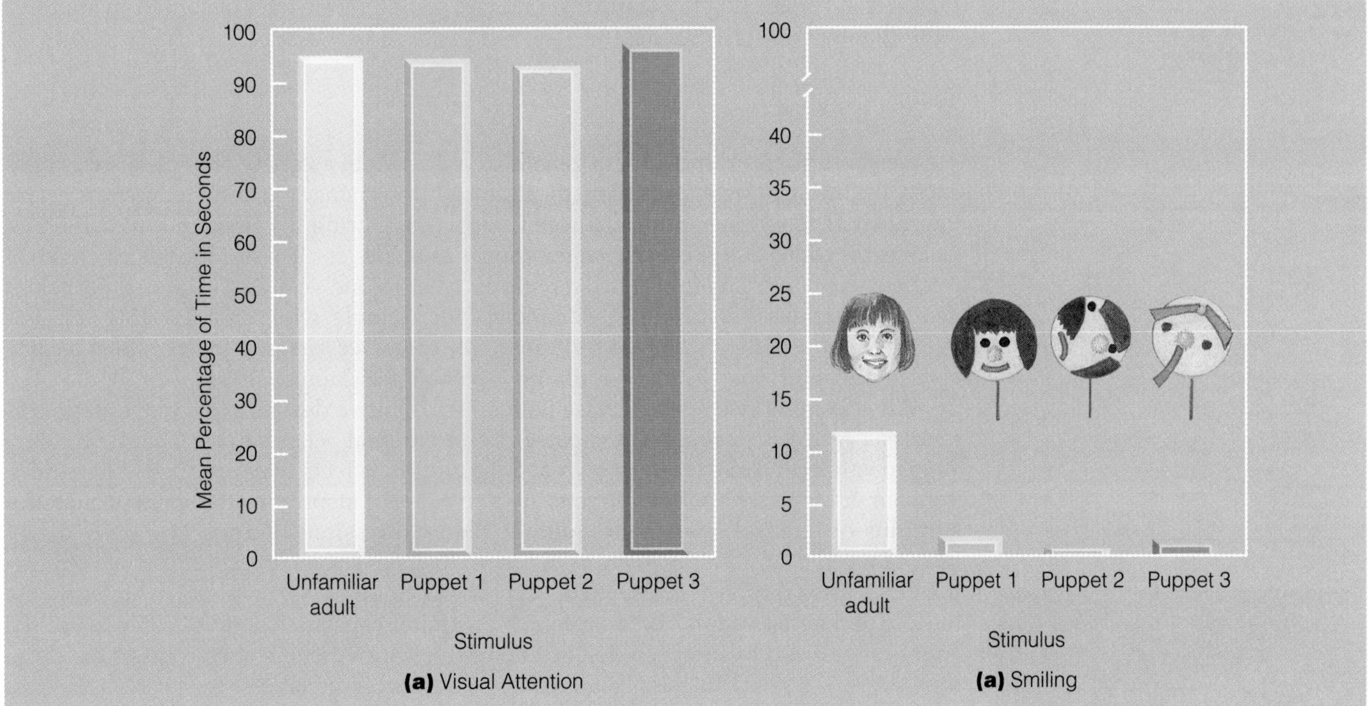

FIGURE 10.2

■ *Three-month-old infants' (a) visual attention to and (b) smiling at an unfamiliar adult and three hand puppets varying in resemblance to the human face, all of which responded contingently to the baby's behavior. Although the infants looked with just as much interest at the puppets as the adult, they spent much more time smiling at the human stimulus. (From C. P. Ellsworth, D. W., Muir, & S. M. J. Hains, 1993, "Social Competence and Person–Object Differentiation: An Analysis of the Still-Face Effect,"* Developmental Psychology, *29, p. 70. Copyright © 1993 by the American Psychological Association. Reprinted by permission.)*

new skills, expressing their delight in cognitive and motor mastery. The smile also encourages caregivers to be affectionate as well as stimulating, so the baby will smile even more. Happiness binds parent and baby into a warm, supportive relationship that fosters the infant's developing competence.

During the early weeks, newborn babies smile when full, during REM sleep, and in response to gentle touches and sounds, such as stroking of the skin, rocking, and the mother's soft, high-pitched voice. Already, the relation between smiling and tension release is present. EEG waves indicate that these early smiles are associated with spontaneous neural discharge in the limbic system, a set of brain structures involved in the regulation of emotional behavior (Sroufe & Waters, 1976).

By the end of the first month, infants start to smile at interesting sights, but these must be dynamic, eye-catching events, such as a bright object jumping suddenly across the baby's field of vision. Between 6 and 10 weeks, the human face evokes a broad grin called the **social smile,** which is soon accompanied by pleasurable cooing (Sroufe & Waters, 1976). Perhaps you can already tell that early changes in smiling parallel the development of infant perceptual capacities—in particular, babies' increasing sensitivity to visual patterns, including the human face—that we discussed in Chapter 4.

By 3 months, infants smile most often when interacting with people. In one study, babies were presented with four facial stimuli, each of which responded contingently to their behavior: an unfamiliar adult and three hand puppets that varied in resemblance to the human face (see Figure 10.2). Although infants looked with just as much interest at the moving, "talking" puppets as they did at the responsive adult, they rarely smiled at a puppet stimulus, even when it had humanlike features. In contrast, they directed frequent grins (as well as more vocalizations) toward the adult, indicating that they clearly identified human beings as having unique, social qualities (Ellsworth, Muir, & Hains, 1993).

Laughter, which appears around 3 to 4 months, reflects faster processing of information than does smiling. But like smiling, the first laughs occur in response to very active stimuli, such as the mother saying playfully, "I'm gonna get you!" and kissing the baby's tummy. As infants understand more about their world, they laugh at more subtle discrepancies from their usual experience, such as a soundless game of peekaboo or the caregiver approaching with a covered face (Sroufe & Wunsch, 1972).

By the middle of the first year, expressions of happiness become selective. Infants smile and laugh more when interacting with familiar people, a preference that supports and strengthens the parent–child bond. As preverbal gestures develop (see Chapter 9), the smile becomes a deliberate social signal. During the second year, toddlers break their

Basic emotions
Emotions that can be directly inferred from facial expressions, such as happiness, interest, surprise, fear, anger, sadness, and disgust.

Social smile
The smile evoked by the stimulus of the human face. First appears between 6 and 10 weeks.

play with an interesting toy to turn around and communicate their delight to an attentive adult (Jones & Raag, 1989).

ANGER AND SADNESS

Newborn babies respond with generalized distress to a variety of unpleasant experiences, including hunger, painful medical procedures, changes in body temperature, and too much or too little stimulation (see Chapter 4). During the first 2 months, fleeting facial expressions that seem like anger appear as babies cry. These gradually increase in frequency and intensity from 4 to 6 months into the second year. At the same time, babies display anger in a wider range of situations—for example, when an interesting object or event is removed, their arms are restrained, the caregiver leaves for a brief time, or they are put down for a nap (Camras et al., 1992; Stenberg & Campos, 1990).

Why do angry reactions increase with age? Cognitive development plays an important role. As infants acquire the capacity for intentional behavior (see Chapter 6), they start to value control over their own actions and the effects they produce (Alessandri, Sullivan, & Lewis, 1990). Older infants are also better at identifying the agent of a painful stimulus or blocked goal. Consequently, their expressions of anger are particularly intense when a familiar caregiver from whom they have come to expect warm, comforting behavior is responsible (Stenberg, Campos, & Emde, 1983). The rise in anger by the middle of the first year is also adaptive. New motor capacities permit babies to use the energy mobilized by anger to defend themselves or overcome obstacles. At the same time, anger is a powerful social signal that motivates caregivers to ease a baby's distress, and in the case of separation, may discourage them from leaving again soon.

■ *This 1-year-old uses her mother as a secure base from which to explore. As long as the familiar caregiver is nearby, newly mobile infants typically approach their surroundings with enthusiasm. (John Coletti/The Picture Cube)*

Expressions of sadness also occur in response to painful stimuli, removal of an object, and brief separations, but they are less frequent than anger (Alessandri, Sullivan, & Lewis, 1990; Izard, Hembree, & Huebner, 1987; Shiller, Izard, & Hembree, 1986). In contrast, sadness is common when caregiver–infant communication is seriously disrupted. The emotionally flat, disengaged caregiving of seriously depressed mothers dramatically illustrates young babies' capacity to express sadness (refer again to the From Research to Practice box on page 385). Extreme sadness can also be seen in infants separated from their mothers for long periods and who do not experience the care of a sensitive adult (Gaensbauer, 1980).

FEAR

Fear reactions are rare during early infancy, probably for adaptive reasons. Young babies do not yet have the motor skills to protect themselves from dangerous situations. Instead, they must rely on caregivers to do so (Izard & Malatesta, 1987). Like anger, fear rises during the second half of the first year. Older infants hesitate before playing with a new toy that they would have grasped immediately at an earlier age. And as we saw in Chapter 4, research with the visual cliff reveals that infants start to show fear of heights around this time, an attainment promoted by their newfound ability to move about independently. But the most frequent expression of fear is to unfamiliar adults, a reaction called **stranger anxiety.**

Stranger anxiety
The infant's expression of fear in response to unfamiliar adults. Appears in many babies after 7 months of age.

Secure base
The use of the familiar caregiver as a base from which the infant confidently explores the environment and to which the infant returns for emotional support.

Many infants and toddlers are quite wary of strangers, although the reaction does not always occur. It depends on several factors: the infant's temperament (some babies are more fearful), past experiences with strangers, and the context in which baby and stranger meet (Thompson & Limber, 1991). When an unfamiliar adult approaches and picks up the infant in a new situation, stranger anxiety is likely. But if the adult sits still while the baby moves around and a parent remains nearby, infants often show positive and curious behavior toward unfamiliar adults, although they rarely initiate physical contact (Horner, 1980). The stranger's style of interaction also makes a difference. Holding out an attractive toy, playing a familiar game, or approaching slowly rather than abruptly reduces the baby's fear (Ross & Goldman, 1977; Trause, 1977).

The impact of situational factors on stranger anxiety helps us understand the significance of greater fearfulness around 7 months of age. It holds in check the baby's compelling urge to venture away from the caregiver that comes with crawling and walking. Once wariness develops, babies start to use the familiar caregiver as a **secure base** from which to explore and a haven of safety when distress occurs. As part of this adaptive

■ *Children lean when to experience self-conscious emotions from adult instruction. Among the !Kung of Botswana, Africa, helping and sharing are encouraged at an early age. Perhaps this toddler already feels a sense of pride as she tries to assist her grandmother with food preparation. (Konner/Anthro-Photo)*

system, encounters with strangers lead to two conflicting tendencies in the baby: approach (indicated by interest and friendliness) and avoidance (indicated by fear). The infant's behavior is a matter of a balance between the two (Thompson & Limber, 1991).

Earlier we noted that infants are not wary of all unfamiliar people. They rarely respond with fear to small children, although why this is so is not entirely clear. According to one view, infants use themselves as a standard against which to evaluate strangers. A primitive awareness that other children are like the self leads babies to be less afraid (Lewis & Brooks, 1978). Another possibility is that the friendly, animated behavior of young children is so appealing to babies that it surmounts their fear.

Eventually, stranger anxiety declines as cognitive development permits toddlers to discriminate more effectively between threatening and nonthreatening people. This change is also adaptive, since adults other than caregivers will be important in children's development, and in later life many interactions will take place with unfamiliar people (Bornstein & Lamb, 1992). Fear also wanes as children acquire a wider array of strategies for coping with it, as we will see when we discuss emotional self-regulation shortly. In sum, early fear reactions are the combined result of several interacting factors—the adaptiveness of the fear response, the situational context, and infants' developing cognitive capacities.

SELF-CONSCIOUS EMOTIONS

Besides basic emotions, humans are capable of a second, higher-order set of feelings, including shame, embarrassment, guilt, envy, and pride. These are called **self-conscious emotions** because each involves injury to or enhancement of our sense of self. For example, when we are ashamed or embarrassed, we feel negatively about our behavior or accomplishments. In contrast, pride reflects delight in the self's achievements (Campos et al., 1983).

Self-conscious emotions first appear at the end of the second year, as the sense of self emerges. Between 18 and 24 months, children can be seen feeling ashamed and embarrassed as they lower their eyes, hang their heads, and hide their faces with their hands. Pride also emerges around this time, and envy and guilt are present by age 3 (Lewis et al., 1989; Sroufe, 1979).

Besides self-awareness, self-conscious emotions require an additional ingredient: adult instruction in when to feel proud, ashamed, or guilty. The situations in which adults encourage children to experience these feelings vary considerably from culture to culture. In most of the United States, children respond with pride to individual achievement, such as winning a game or getting good grades. Among the Zuni Indians, shame and embarrassment occur in response to purely individual success, whereas pride is evoked by generosity, helpfulness, and sharing (Benedict, 1934a). In Japan, violating cultural standards of concern for others' feelings and needs—those of a parent, teacher, or employer—is cause for intense shame (Lewis, 1992a).

Self-conscious emotions
Emotions that involve injury to or enhancement of the sense of self. Examples are shame, embarrassment, guilt, envy, and pride.

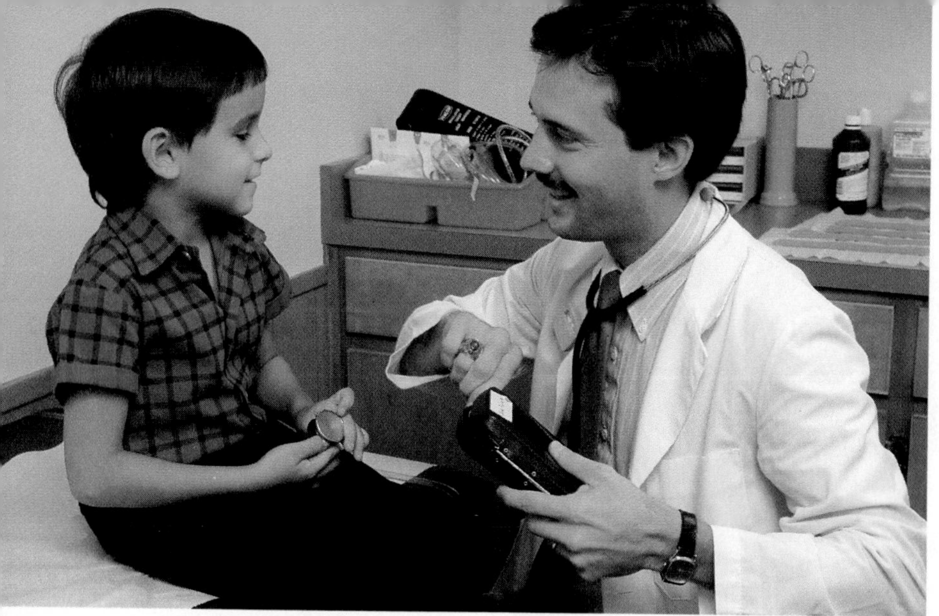

■ *Talking to children about potentially frightening experiences helps them develop effective strategies for emotional self-regulation. This doctor puts a young child at ease by explaining what will happen during a physical examination. (Bob Daemmrich/Stock Boston)*

At an early age, self-conscious emotions are clearly linked to self-evaluation. In one study, parents were asked to give their 3-year-olds easy and difficult problems to solve. Children showed much more pride when they succeeded on difficult than easy tasks and much more shame when they failed simple than hard tasks (Lewis, Alessandri, & Sullivan, 1992). In contrast, basic emotions of joy and sadness accompany success or failure, regardless of the challenge involved. They do not depend on judgments of self-worth.

Nevertheless, the conditions under which children experience self-conscious emotions do change with age. For example, when given stories designed to evoke pride (a child accomplishing a gymnastic feat) and shame (a child taking money that belongs to her parents) and asked how they would feel, preschoolers report the appropriate emotion only if an adult is present to observe the act. Older children report it in the absence of observation by others (Harter, Wright, & Bresnick, 1987). Furthermore, 6-year-olds are likely to experience guilt for any act that can be described as wrongdoing, even if it was accidental. In contrast, older children report guilt only for intentional misbehavior, such as ignoring responsibilities, cheating, or lying (Graham, Doubleday, & Guarino, 1984).

As these findings illustrate, self-conscious emotions play an important role in children's achievement-related and moral behavior. Once the sense of self is well established and includes clear standards for right action (see Chapters 11 and 12), the presence of others will no longer be necessary to evoke these emotions. In addition, they will be limited to situations in which children feel personally responsible for an outcome (Lewis, 1992b; Stipek, Recchia, & McClintic, 1992).

DEVELOPMENT OF EMOTIONAL SELF-REGULATION

Besides expressing a wider range of emotions, children acquire a variety of ways to manage their emotional experiences. **Emotional self-regulation** refers to the strategies we use to adjust our emotional state to a comfortable level of intensity so we can remain productively engaged in our surroundings. It involves attention focusing and shifting as well as the ability to inhibit behavior (Eisenberg et al., 1995; Thompson, 1994). If you drank a cup of coffee to wake yourself up this morning, reminded yourself that an anxiety-provoking event would be over soon, or decided not to see a horror movie because it might frighten you, you were engaging in emotional self-regulation.

In the early months of life, infants have only a limited capacity to regulate their emotional states. Although they can turn away from unpleasant stimulation and mouth and suck when their feelings get too intense, they are easily overwhelmed by internal and external stimuli. As a result, they depend on the soothing interventions of caregivers—lifting the distressed infant to the shoulder, rocking, and talking softly—for help in adjusting their emotional reactions.

Rapid development of the cortex increases the baby's tolerance for stimulation. Between 2 and 4 months, caregivers start to build on this capacity by initiating face-to-face play and attention to objects. In these rich interactional sequences in which emotional signals are exchanged, parents arouse pleasure in the baby while adjusting the pace of their own behavior so the infant does not become overwhelmed and distressed. As a result, the baby's tolerance for stimulation increases further (Field, 1994). By the end of the first year, crawling and walking enable infants to regulate feelings more effectively by approaching or retreating from various stimuli.

Gains in representation and language lead to new ways of regulating emotion. By describing their internal states, children can guide caregivers in ways that will help them feel better. After age 2, children frequently talk about their feelings and engage in active efforts to control them. For example, they might try to blunt emotional arousal by restricting sensory input (covering your eyes or ears), talking to themselves ("Mommy said she'll be back soon"), or changing their goals (deciding you don't want to play

Emotional self-regulation
Strategies for adjusting our emotional state to a comfortable level of intensity so we can remain productively engaged in our surroundings.

anyway after being excluded from a game). When adults prepare children for emotionally arousing experiences, such as the first day of school or a trip to the dentist's office, by suggesting ways to handle anxiety, they offer coping techniques that children can later apply to themselves (Thompson, 1990a).[1] As early as the preschool years, children who have trouble regulating their negative feelings freely vent their anger and frustration, respond with irritation to others' distress, and get along poorly with adults and peers (Eisenberg et al., 1994, 1995; Fabes et al., 1994).

From middle childhood to adolescence, children come up with many more ways to handle emotionally arousing situations. In several studies, 5- to 11-year-olds were told stories about positive and negative events, such as having to wait to receive an attractive prize or getting a bad grade on a test. Then they were asked what could be done to control their feelings. With age, children were less likely to mention complete avoidance, such as leaving the scene or going to sleep—a form of coping that is usually counterproductive. And although children of all ages were aware that they could distract themselves with alternative behaviors, such as reading or watching TV, older children more often mentioned cognitive strategies for overcoming emotion. Furthermore, when an event could not be changed, they came up with ways of reinterpreting it that helped them accept current conditions (Altshuler & Ruble, 1989; Band & Weisz, 1988). For example, in response to the story about receiving a bad grade, one child said, "Things could be worse. There'll be another test." The capacity to generate a diverse array of self-regulatory strategies and flexibly adjust them to situational demands permits adolescents to handle unanticipated daily stresses more effectively than they could at younger ages.

ACQUIRING EMOTIONAL DISPLAY RULES

In addition to regulating internal emotional states, children must acquire **emotional display rules** that specify when, where, and how it is appropriate to express emotions in their culture. As early as the first few months of life, American middle-class infants start to receive instruction in suppressing negative emotion. In several studies, mothers were carefully observed while playing with their 2- to 7-month-old babies. The mothers frequently imitated positive expressions of interest, happiness, and surprise, but they rarely imitated anger and sadness (Malatesta et al., 1986; Malatesta & Haviland, 1982).

At slightly older ages, parents provide children with direct instruction in emotional display rules. Peggy Miller and Linda Sperry (1987) studied the everyday interactions of three mother–toddler pairs in an urban working-class neighborhood. Consistent with the values of their community, the mothers encouraged children to express anger and aggression in self-defense—for example, when a playmate grabbed a toy or hit them—but not under other conditions. Children also learned how to behave emotionally by watching parents control their own expressions of feeling and by listening to them talk about reactions to daily experiences.

Although caregiver shaping of emotional behavior begins early, children only gradually become adept at modifying their own emotional displays. Not until age 3 can children pose an expression they do not feel. These emotional "masks" are largely limited to positive feelings of happiness and surprise. Children of all ages (and adults as well) find it harder to act angry, sad, or disgusted than pleased (Lewis, Sullivan, & Vasen, 1987). Over the school years, children become increasingly skilled at suppressing negative affect, although the extent to which they do so varies with the situation. For example, they are more likely to suppress anger in the presence of an adult authority figure than a peer, with whom angry interactions are more likely to have the desired impact (Underwood, Coie, & Herbsman, 1992).

Social pressures are undoubtedly responsible for these trends. To foster harmonious relationships, many cultures encourage children to communicate positive feelings and inhibit unpleasant emotional displays. Societies that stress collective over individual needs place particular emphasis on these rules. For example, compared to Americans, Japanese and Hindu Indian adults think that masking negative feelings toward family members, close friends, and higher-status individuals is more important, and they are also more emotionally controlled (Matsumoto, 1990; Roland, 1988).

Emotional display rules
Rules that specify when, where, and how it is culturally appropriate to express emotions.

[1] The central role of language in emotional self-regulation should remind you of Vygotsky's ideas on the social origins and self-guiding function of children's private speech, discussed in Chapter 6 (see pages 247–248).

Besides greater conformity to display rules, conscious awareness and understanding of them emerges in middle childhood. When given hypothetical stressful situations (for example, a child boasting about his skating ability to a friend but who later falls down), 10-year-olds can think of more display rules to handle them than can 6- and 8-year-olds. Also, older children justify display rules by referring to social norms ("It's impolite to show you feel that way"), whereas younger children justify them as a way to avoid scolding and ridicule. These findings suggest that at first, children obey display rules to avoid punishment and gain approval from others. Gradually, they see that each rule is followed by members of their culture, and they come to understand its value as a culturally accepted standard for expressive behavior (Saarni, 1989).

BRIEF REVIEW

The development of emotional expression is a gradual process that begins in infancy and continues into adolescence. Changes in happiness, anger, sadness, and fear reflect infants' developing cognitive capacities and serve social as well as survival functions. At the end of the second year, self-conscious emotions emerge. By middle childhood, these self-evaluative feelings occur in the absence of adult monitoring and are clearly to personal responsibility. Self-regulation of emotional experience begins in infancy and is supported by central nervous system maturation, cognitive and language development, and sensitive parenting. During the preschool years, children start to conform to the emotional display rules of their culture. In middle childhood, they become consciously aware of these rules.

Understanding and Responding to the Emotions of Others

Children's emotional expressiveness is intimately tied to their ability to recognize and interpret the feelings of others. Already we have seen that infants begin to detect emotional signals within the first few months, as they match the affective tone of the caregiver in face-to-face communication. Resonating in this way to another's feelings suggests that babies are beginning to discriminate emotional states. In Chapter 4, we indicated that by the middle of the first year, infants recognize some basic emotions on the basis of their separate features. Between 7 and 10 months, they react to facial expressions as organized patterns (see page 157). In addition, at 3 months, infants respond to variations in emotional messages conveyed through tone of voice. Around 7 months, they coordinate the vocal and facial emotional channels (see page 159).

Responding to emotional expressions as organized wholes rather than in component parts indicates that these signals have become meaningful to babies. Around 8 to 9 months, infants start to realize that an emotional expression not only has meaning, but is a meaningful reaction to a specific object or event (Bornstein & Lamb, 1992). Once these understandings are in place, infants actively seek emotional information from trusted caregivers and use it to guide their own behavior.

SOCIAL REFERENCING

Social referencing involves relying on another person's emotional reaction to appraise an uncertain situation. Besides the ability to interpret emotional signals, the tendency of older infants to evaluate objects and events in terms of their safety and security leads to the emergence of this new emotional capacity. Many studies show that a caregiver's emotional expression (happy, angry, or fearful) influences whether a 1-year-old will show wariness of strangers, play with an unfamiliar toy, or cross the deep side of the visual cliff (Rosen, Adamson, & Bakeman, 1992; Sorce et al., 1985; Walden & Ogan, 1988).

Social referencing
Relying on another person's emotional reaction to appraise an uncertain situation.

Mothers and fathers serve as equally effective sources of emotional information for babies. When parents are absent, infants and toddlers turn to other familiar adults, especially those who interact with them in an emotionally expressive way (Camras & Sachs, 1991). In fact, a caregiver's emotional cues during moments of uncertainty may be a major reason that she serves as a secure base for exploration. In an unfamiliar playroom, babies show a strong desire to remain within "eyeshot" of their mother. If she turns away, they will leave an attractive set of toys to relocate within her visual field so they can retain access to her facial and vocal cues (Carr, Dabbs, & Carr, 1975).

Although there is little research on social referencing beyond infancy, sensitivity to others' emotional evaluations undoubtedly becomes more finely tuned as cognitive and language development proceed and children consult a wider range of sources for emotional information (Feinman, 1982). Social referencing provides yet another example of how adults help children regulate their emotional experiences. And through it, children can see how mature members of their society react emotionally to many everyday events.

EMOTIONAL UNDERSTANDING IN CHILDHOOD

During the preschool years, children's emotional understanding expands rapidly, as their everyday talk about emotions reveals. Here are some excerpts from conversations in which 2-year-olds and 6-year-olds commented on emotionally charged experiences:

Two-year-old: (After father shouted at child, she became angry, shouting back.) "I'm mad at you, Daddy. I'm going away. Good-bye."

Two-year-old: (Commenting on another child who refused to take a nap and cried.) "Mom, Annie cry. Annie sad."

Six-year-old: (In response to mother's comment, "It's hard to hear the baby crying.") "Well, it's not as hard for me as it is for you." (When mother asked why) "Well, you like Johnny better than I do! I like him a little, and you like him a lot, so I think it's harder for you to hear him cry."

Six-year-old: (Trying to comfort a small boy in church whose mother had gone up to communion) "Aw, that's all right. She'll be right back. Don't be afraid. I'm here." (Bretherton et al., 1986, pp. 536, 540, 541)

As these examples show, early in the preschool years, children refer to causes, consequences, and behavioral signs of emotion, and over time their understanding becomes more accurate and complex. By age 4 to 5, children correctly judge the causes of many basic emotional reactions. When asked why a nearby playmate is happy, sad, or angry, they describe events similar to those identified by adults and that fit the emotion being expressed. However, they tend to emphasize external factors over internal states as explanations—a balance that changes with age (Fabes et al., 1991). For example, before age 7, children believe that people respond with anger when they have been wronged but can change the situation, whereas older children and adults associate anger with intent to do harm (Levine, 1995). Preschoolers are also good at predicting what a playmate expressing a certain emotion might do next. For example, they know that an angry child might hit someone or grab a toy and that a happy child is more likely to share (Russell, 1990). They are even aware that a lingering mood can affect a person's behavior for some time in the future (Bretherton et al., 1986).

An improved ability to consider multiple sources of information when explaining others' emotions develops during middle childhood. In one study, children were given conflicting cues about a person's feelings. One was situational, and the other was a facial expression. For example, they were shown a picture of a happy-faced child with a broken bicycle. When asked how the child in the picture felt, preschoolers tended to rely on the facial cue alone. By age 8 to 9, children showed no preference for one cue over the other (Gnepp, 1983). Around this time, they integrate both in accounting for another's feelings; that is, they might explain that a child with a broken bike is happy because her parent promised to fix it soon (Hoffner & Badzinski, 1989).

Similarly, older children also recognize that people can experience more than one emotion at a time—in other words, that they can have "mixed feelings" (Harter & Buddin, 1987; Wintre & Vallance, 1994). Preschoolers staunchly deny that two emotions can occur at once, in much the same way that they do not integrate two variables (height and width) in a Piagetian conservation-of-liquid task. For example, when asked about the feelings of a child who pushed a playmate off a swing to get a turn for himself, 4-year-olds report positive emotions—"happy" or "good" because he got what he wanted. By age 8, children spontaneously explain that in addition to feeling good, the naughty child also feels "sad," "bad," or "angry" because he did harm to another (Arsenio & Kramer, 1992).

Cognitive development clearly has much to do with these advanced emotional understandings, but social experience also contributes to them. Preschoolers growing up in families that frequently talk about feelings are better at judging the emotions of others when tested at later ages (Denham, Zoller, & Couchoud, 1994; Dunn et al., 1991). Discussions in which family members disagree over feeling states are particularly facilitating. These dialogues seem to help children step back from the experience of emotion, reflect on its causes and consequences, and establish joint meaning with a more mature person that leads to a higher-level appreciation. Furthermore, participation in make-believe play, particularly with siblings, is related to advanced emotional understanding. The intense nature of the sibling relationship, combined with frequent acting out of feelings, makes pretending a fertile context for early learning about emotions (Youngblade & Dunn, 1995).

Emotional knowledge is of great help to children in their efforts to get along with others. As early as 3 to 5 years, it is related to friendly, considerate behavior, willingness to make amends after harming another, and peer acceptance (Cassidy et al., 1992; Dunn, Brown, & Maguire, 1995; Garner, Jones, & Miner, 1994).

DEVELOPMENT OF EMPATHY

In **empathy,** understanding and expression of emotions are interwoven, since both awareness of the feelings of others and a sympathetic response to those feelings are required to experience empathy. Current theorists agree that empathy involves a complex interaction of cognition and affect. The ability to detect different emotions, the capacity to take another's perspective in order to comprehend that person's emotional state, and complementary feelings aroused within the self combine to produce a mature empathic response (Zahn-Waxler & Radke-Yarrow, 1990). Beginning in the preschool years, empathy is an important motivator of **prosocial,** or **altruistic, behavior**—actions that benefit another person without any expected reward for the self (Eisenberg & Miller, 1987).

Empathy has roots early in development. Newborn babies tend to cry in response to the cry of another baby, a reaction that may be the primitive beginnings of an empathic response (Hoffman, 1988). Like the self-conscious emotions we discussed earlier, true empathy requires children to understand that the self is distinct from other people. As self-awareness develops, 1-year-olds show empathy for the first time. They no longer cry and seek comfort for themselves in reaction to another person's distress. Instead, they try to relieve the other person's unhappiness, using methods that become more varied with age. For example, one 21-month-old reacted to his mother's simulated sadness by offering comforting words, giving her a hug, trying to distract her with a hand puppet, and asking the experimenter to help (Zahn-Waxler & Radke-Yarrow, 1990).

As language develops, children rely more on words to console others, a change that indicates a more reflective level of empathy. A 6-year-old said this to his mother after noticing she was distressed at not being able to find a motel after a long day's travel: "You're pretty upset, aren't you, Mom? You're pretty sad. Well, I think it's going to be all right. I think we'll find a nice place and it'll be all right" (Bretherton et al., 1986, p. 540).

Empathic responding increases over the elementary school years. Older children's understanding of a wider range of emotions and ability to take multiple cues into account in assessing another's feelings contribute to this change (Ricard & Kamberk-Kilicci, 1995). During late childhood and adolescence, advances in perspective taking permit an empathic response not just to people's immediate distress, but also to their general life condition. According to Martin Hoffman (1984), the ability to empathize with the poor, oppressed, and sick is the most mature form of empathic distress. It requires an advanced form of perspective taking in which the child understands that people lead continuous emotional lives beyond the current situation.

Besides cognitive development, child rearing has a profound impact on the development of empathy. Parents who are nurturant and encouraging and who show a sensitive,

Empathy
The ability to understand the feelings of others and respond with complementary emotions.

Prosocial, or altruistic, behavior
Actions that benefit another person without any expected reward for the self.

■ An increase in emphatic responding occurs over the elementary school years, due to the older child's improved ability to accurately detect the feelings of others and imagine the self in another's place. (Susan Johns/Photo Researchers)

empathic concern for their youngsters have children who are more likely to react in a concerned way to the distress of others (Radke-Yarrow & Zahn-Waxler, 1984). But empathy is fostered not just by modeling. Setting clear limits is also important. Parental intervention when children display inappropriate emotions and direct teaching about the importance of kindness predict high levels of empathic responding (Eisenberg et al., 1991; Zahn-Waxler & Radke-Yarrow, 1990).

In contrast, harsh, punitive parenting is related to disruptions in the development of empathy at an early age. In one study, severely physically abused toddlers were observed at a day care center to see how they reacted to other children's distress. Compared to their nonabused counterparts, they rarely showed signs of concern. Instead, they responded with fear, anger, and physical attacks (Klimes-Dougan & Kistner, 1990). By the second year of life, the reactions of abused children already resemble the behavior of their parents, since both respond with anger and aversion to others' distress.

These findings—as well as others discussed so far—suggest that there are important individual differences in children's emotional dispositions. As we take a closer look at these in the next section, we will discover that they are the combined result of biological and environmental influences. Even in the case of empathy, evidence from twin studies suggests a modest genetic contribution (Emde et al., 1992; Zahn-Waxler, Robinson, & Emde, 1992). But before we delve into the topic of individual differences, turn to the Milestones table on page 396 for an overview of the course of emotional development we have just considered.

BRIEF REVIEW

The ability to meaningfully interpret others' emotional expressions emerges at the end of the first year. Around this time, infants start to engage in social referencing, actively seeking emotional information from caregivers in uncertain situations. Over early and middle childhood, emotional understanding expands, a change that is influenced by cognitive development as well as family experiences that promote awareness of feelings. School-age children rely on multiple cues to evaluate the emotions of others, and they realize that people can experience more than one emotion at a time. Empathy increases from infancy into adolescence and is supported by genetic disposition, advances in perspective taking, sensitive child rearing, and parental intervention when children display hurtful emotions toward others.

MILESTONES

Emotional Development

Age	Emotional Expressiveness	Emotional Understanding
Birth–6 months	■ Signs of almost all basic emotions are present. ■ Social smile emerges. ■ Laughter appears. ■ Expressions of happiness are greater when interacting with familiar people. ■ Face, gaze, voice, and posture combine to form distinct, coherent emotional patterns that vary meaningfully with social events.	■ Matching adults' emotional expressions during face-to-face interaction occurs.
7–12 months	■ Anger and fear increase. ■ Use of caregiver as a secure base emerges. ■ Emotional self-regulation improves as crawling and walking permit approach and retreat from stimulation.	■ Ability to detect the meaning of others' emotional expressions emerges. ■ Social referencing develops.
1–2 years	■ Self-conscious emotions appear but depend on the presence of others.	■ Vocabulary of words for talking about feelings expands. ■ Empathic responding appears.
3–6 years	■ As representation and language improve, active behavioral and cognitive strategies for engaging in emotional self-regulation develop. ■ Ability to conform to display rules by posing a positive emotion one does not feel emerges.	■ Understanding of causes, consequences, and behavioral signs of emotion improves in accuracy and complexity. ■ As language develops, empathic responding becomes more reflective.
7–11 years	■ Self-conscious emotions become integrated with inner standards for right action. ■ Strategies for engaging in emotional self-regulation increase in variety, become more cognitive, and are adjusted to situational demands. ■ Conformity to and conscious awareness of emotional display rules improve.	■ Ability to consider multiple sources of information when explaining others' emotions appears. ■ Awareness that people can experience more than one emotion at a time emerges. ■ Empathic responding increases as emotional understanding improves.

Note: These milestones represent overall age trends. Individual differences exist in the precise age at which each milestone is attained.

Temperament and Development

When we describe one person as cheerful and upbeat, another as active and energetic, and still others as calm, cautious, or prone to angry outbursts, we are referring to **temperament**—stable individual differences in quality and intensity of emotional reaction (Goldsmith, 1987). Researchers have become increasingly interested in temperamental differences among infants and children, since the child's style of emotional responding is believed to form the cornerstone of the adult personality.

The New York Longitudinal Study, initiated in 1956 by Alexander Thomas and Stella Chess, is the most comprehensive and longest-lasting study of temperament to date. A total of 141 children were followed from the first few months of life over a period that now extends well into adulthood. Results showed that temperament is a major factor in increasing the chances that a child will experience psychological problems or, alternatively, be protected from the effects of a highly stressful home life. However, Thomas and Chess (1977) also found that temperament is not fixed and unchangeable. Environmental circumstances seemed to modify children's emotional styles considerably.

These findings stimulated a growing body of research on temperament, including its stability, its biological roots, and its interaction with child-rearing experiences. Let's begin to explore these issues by looking at some current models of temperament and methods for measuring it.

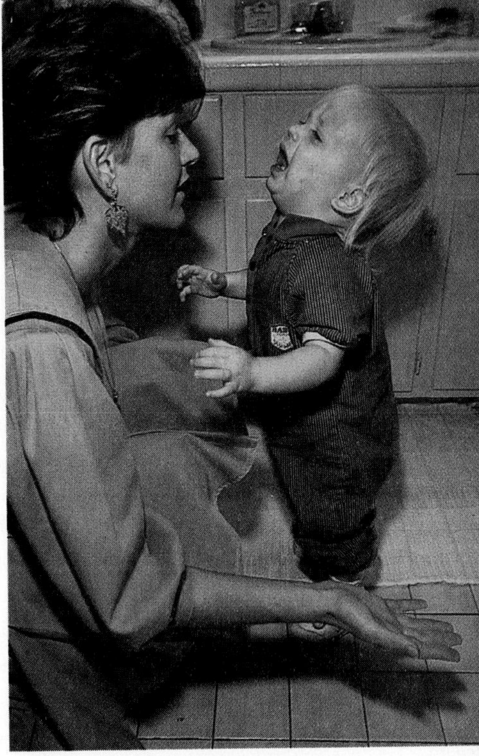

Difficult children have irregular daily routines, are slow to accept new experiences, and tend to react negatively and intensely. When parents are patient and provide opportunities for gradual, repeated exposure to new situations, difficultness often subsides. (Nubar Alexanian/Stock Boston)

MODELS OF TEMPERAMENT

Thomas and Chess's nine dimensions of temperament, listed in Table 10.1 on page 398, served as the first influential model, inspiring all others that followed. When detailed descriptions of infants' and children's behavior obtained from parental interviews were rated on these dimensions, certain characteristics clustered together, yielding three types of children that described the majority of their sample:

- The **easy child** (40 percent of the sample): This child quickly establishes regular routines in infancy, is generally cheerful, and adapts easily to new experiences.
- The **difficult child** (10 percent of the sample): This child has irregular daily routines, is slow to accept new experiences, and tends to react negatively and intensely.
- The **slow-to-warm-up child** (15 percent of the sample): This child is inactive, shows mild, low-key reactions to environmental stimuli, is negative in mood, and adjusts slowly to new experiences.

Note that 35 percent of the children did not fit any of these categories. Instead, they showed unique blends of temperamental characteristics.

Of the three temperamental types, the difficult pattern has sparked the most interest, since it places children at high risk for adjustment problems. In the New York Longitudinal Study, 70 percent of young preschoolers classified as difficult developed behavior problems by school age, whereas only 18 percent of the easy children did (Thomas, Chess, & Birch, 1968). Unlike difficult youngsters, slow-to-warm-up children do not present many problems in the early years. They encounter special challenges later, after they enter school and peer group settings in which they are expected to respond actively and quickly. Thomas and Chess found that by middle childhood, 50 percent of these children began to show adjustment difficulties (Chess & Thomas, 1984).

A second model of temperament, devised by Mary Rothbart (1981), is also shown in Table 10.1. Rothbart's system combines dimensions of Thomas and Chess that overlap (for example, "distractibility" and "attention span and persistence" are merged into "undisturbed persistence"). It also includes characteristics not represented by Thomas and Chess that place special emphasis on emotional self-regulation, such as soothability and distress to limitations. Other models of temperament, typically with fewer factors than Thomas and Chess's, also exist (Buss & Plomin, 1984; Sanson et al., 1994).

Temperament
Stable individual differences in quality and intensity of emotional reaction.

Easy child
A child whose temperament is such that he or she quickly establishes regular routines in infancy, is generally cheerful, and adapts easily to new experiences.

Difficult child
A child whose temperament is such that he or she is irregular in daily routines, is slow to accept new experiences, and tends to react negatively and intensely.

Slow-to-warm-up child
A child whose temperament is such that he or she is inactive, shows mild, low-key reactions to environmental stimuli, is negative in mood, and adjusts slowly to new experiences.

TABLE 10.1

Two Models of Temperment

Thomas and Chess		Rothbart	
Dimension	**Description**	**Dimension**	**Description**
Activity level	Proportion of active periods to inactive ones	*Activity level*	Level of gross motor activity
Rhythmicity	Regularity of functions, such as hunger, excretion, sleep, and wakefulness	*Smiling and laughter*	Frequency of expression of happiness and pleasure
Distractibility	Degree to which stimuli in the environment alter behavior	*Undisturbed persistence*	Duration of orienting and interest
Approach/withdrawal	Response to a new object or person, in terms of whether the child accepts the new experience or withdraws from it	*Fear*	Wariness and distress in response to intense or novel stimuli
Adaptability	Ease with which the child adapts to changes in the environment	*Soothability*	Reduction of fussing, crying, or distress when soothing techniques are used by the caregiver or child
Attention span and persistence	Amount of time devoted to an activity and the effect of distraction on the activity	*Distress to limitations*	Fussing, crying, and showing distress when desires are frustrated
Intensity of reaction	Intensity or energy level of response		
Threshold of responsiveness	Intensity of stimulation required to evoke a response		
Quality of mood	Amount of friendly, pleasant, joyful behavior as contrasted with unpleasant, unfriendly behavior		

Sources: A. Thomas, S. Chess, & H. G. Birch, 1970, "The Origins of Personality," *Scientific American, 223*(2), 106–107. Copyright © August 1970 by Scientific American, Inc. All rights reserved; M. K. Rothbart, 1981, "Measurement of Temperament in Infancy," *Child Development, 52,* p. 563. Copyright © The Society for Research in Child Development, Inc. Reprinted by permission.

Nevertheless, the dimensions given in Table 10.1 provide a fairly complete picture of the traits most often studied.

MEASURING TEMPERAMENT

Researchers measure temperament in diverse ways. Typically, they select from a variety of methods that assess children's behavior. But new techniques are focusing on physiological reactions in an effort to identify biological processes at the heart of temperamental styles.

ASSESSMENTS OF BEHAVIOR. Temperament is often assessed through interviews or questionnaires given to parents, although behavior ratings by pediatricians, teachers, and others familiar with the child as well as direct observations by researchers have also been used. Parental reports have been emphasized because of their convenience and parents' depth of knowledge about the child.

At the same time, information from parents has been criticized for being biased and subjective. For example, mothers with certain psychological characteristics—high anxiety, depression, and low self-esteem—tend to regard their babies as more difficult (Mebert, 1991; Vaughn et al., 1987). And parents' prebirth expectations for their infant's temperament have a substantial impact on their reports (Diener, Goldstein, & Mangelsdorf, 1995). Not surprisingly, parental ratings are only modestly related to observational measures of children's temperament (Seifer et al., 1994). Nevertheless, parent perceptions are useful for understanding the way parents view and respond to their child.

Most measures, whether parental report or observational, can assess temperament across only a narrow age range, because the way a child's emotional style is expressed changes with development. For example, a child high in fearfulness may reject his first spoonfuls of cereal at 3 months, cry in response to unfamiliar people at 8 months, avoid new children on the playground as a preschooler, and hide behind his mother when first entering kindergarten. Assessments of temperament also need to be made across different settings, since by definition, temperament is not a temporary response to a specific situation, but an enduring characteristic of the individual.

■ ASSESSMENTS OF PHYSIOLOGICAL REACTIONS. In recent years, researchers have begun to explore the biological substrate of temperament, searching for psychophysiological measures that underlie the same aspect of temperament at different ages. Besides providing insights into the origins of temperament, psychophysiological indices (like direct observations) are not hampered by the subjective elements of parental reports.

In one effort of this kind, Jerome Kagan followed several samples of infants over the first 2 years, focusing on two temperamental styles, which he labeled **inhibited** and **uninhibited.** At 4 months, inhibited children (who comprise about 10 to 15 percent of the Caucasian population) reacted with high rates of motor activity and crying to new sights and sounds, such as a moving mobile decorated with colorful toys. Observed again between 1 and 2 years, about half of these children were extremely shy and fearful when faced with unfamiliar rooms, toys, and people. In contrast, uninhibited 4-month-olds (about 20 to 25 percent of the Caucasian population) showed little motor activity and fussing in response to new stimuli. And when seen the following year in a laboratory session filled with novel experiences, only 10 percent responded with high fear; 60 percent showed none at all (Kagan, 1992; Kagan & Snidman, 1991).

Kagan believes individual differences in arousal of the limbic system contribute to these contrasting temperamental styles. In support of this hypothesis, as early as the first few weeks of life, the heart rates of many inhibited children speed up in response to unfamiliar or stressful events (Snidman et al., 1995). They also produce more cortisol (a hormone that regulates blood pressure and that is involved in resistance to stress) than do their uninhibited agemates (Gunnar & Nelson, 1994; Kagan & Snidman, 1991). Animal research suggests that these responses are mediated by a specific limbic structure called the amygdala, which governs avoidance reactions. Excitability of neurons in the amygdala may be an important determinant of behavioral inhibition in humans as well (Kagan, 1992).

Other researchers examining physiological correlates of temperament have focused on vagal tone, a measure of heart rate variability that taps responsiveness of the central nervous system to novel stimuli. High vagal tone predicts interest, friendliness, empathy and prosocial behavior, and adaptability to new situations, perhaps because it reflects the ability to regulate emotion effectively (Fox & Field, 1989; Porges, Doussard-Roosevelt, & Maiti, 1994; Zahn-Waxler et al., 1995).

Finally, yet another physiological mediator of approach–withdrawal to people and objects is the pattern of EEG waves in the frontal region of the cortex. Recall from Chapter 5 that the left cortical hemisphere is specialized to respond with positive emotion, the right hemisphere with negative emotion. Infants who are easily upset by maternal separation, preschoolers who display an inhibited temperamental style, and depressed adults and their babies show greater right than left frontal brain wave activity. Children with the opposite pattern—greater left than right activation—are less likely to respond negatively to novel and stressful events (Davidson & Fox, 1989; Field et al., 1995; Fox, Bell, & Jones, 1992).

Researchers do not yet know how or when these psychophysiological measures become interrelated—information that may shed new light on the role of various brain structures in the development of emotional reactivity. Nevertheless, individual differences in heart rate and EEG patterns are consistent enough that they are proving to be useful markers of temperamental styles, adding greater certainty to behavioral assessments.

STABILITY OF TEMPERAMENT

It would be difficult to claim that something like temperament really exists if children's emotional styles were not stable over time. Indeed, the findings of many studies provide support for the long-term stability of temperament. An infant or young child who scores low or high on attention span, activity level, irritability, sociability, or shyness is likely to respond in a similar way when assessed again a few years later and, occasionally, even into the adult years (Caspi & Silva, 1995; Kochanska & Radke-Yarrow, 1992; Riese, 1987; Ruff et al., 1990).

Inhibited child
A child who withdraws and displays negative emotion to novel stimuli.

Uninhibited child
A child who approaches and displays positive emotion to novel stimuli.

When the evidence as a whole is examined carefully, however, temperamental stability from one age period to the next is only modest. Although quite a few children remain the same, a good number have changed when assessed again as soon as a year or two later. Furthermore, some characteristics, such as the inhibited and uninhibited styles studied by Kagan, are stable over the long term only for children at the extremes—those who are very shy or very outgoing to begin with (Kerr et al., 1994; Robinson et al., 1992).

The fact that early in life, children show marked individual differences in temperament, some of which are related to physiological reactions, indicates that biological factors play an important role in children's emotional styles. At the same time, the changes that occur for many children suggest that temperament can be modified by experience. Finally, recall from Chapter 3 that it is possible for environmental influences to contribute to stability, since children's characteristics can shape the experiences to which they are exposed. With this idea in mind, let's take a close look at genetic and environmental contributions to temperament and personality.

GENETIC AND ENVIRONMENTAL INFLUENCES

The word *temperament* implies a genetic foundation for individual differences in emotional style. In recent years, many kinship studies have compared individuals of different degrees of genetic relationship to determine the extent to which temperament and personality are heritable. As with the heritability of intelligence, the most common approach has been to compare identical and fraternal twins.

■ HEREDITY. Identical twins are more similar than fraternal twins across a wide range of temperamental traits (activity level, sociability, shyness, distress to limitations, intensity of emotional reaction, attention span, and persistence) and personality measures (introversion, extroversion, anxiety, and impulsivity) (DiLalla, Kagan, & Reznick, 1994; Emde et al., 1992; Saudino & Eaton, 1991). Table 10.2 reveals that twin resemblance for temperament and personality is considerably lower than it is for intelligence. Nevertheless, when heritability estimates are computed by comparing the correlations of identical and fraternal twins, they are typically moderate, averaging around .50 (Emde et al., 1992; Robinson et al., 1992).

New evidence on shyness provides further support for genetic influences on temperament. Besides differing from their more sociable counterparts on the psychophysiological measures discussed earlier, shy children are more likely to have certain physical traits—blue eyes, thin faces, and hay fever—known to be affected by heredity (Arcus & Kagan, 1995). Researchers believe that the genes controlling these characteristics may also contribute to an inhibited temperamental style.

TABLE 10.2

Kinship Correlations for Temperament, Personality, and Intelligence

Kinship Pair	Temperment in Infancy	Personality in Childhood and Adulthood	Intelligence
Identical twins reared together	.36	.52	.86
Fraternal twins reared together	.18	.25	.60
Biological siblings reared together	.18	.20	.47
Nonbiological siblings (adopted-natural pairings)	-.03	.05	.34

Note: Correlations are averages across a variety of temperament and personality characteristics.
Sources: Braungart et al. (1992) and Emde et al. (1992) for temperament at 1 year of age; Nichols (1978) and Plomin, Chipuer, & Loehlin (1990) for personality in childhood and adulthood; and Bouchard & McGue (1981) for intelligence.

NONSHARED ENVIRONMENT. Recall from earlier chapters that adoption research can be useful in examining the relative contribution of heredity and environment to complex traits. The few such studies available for temperament and personality report very low correlations for both biological and nonbiological siblings, despite the fact that they are reared together in the same family (refer again to Table 10.2). How can this be explained when, once again, the resemblance between both types of siblings is considerably greater for intelligence?

In Chapter 8, we distinguished two broad classes of environmental factors: *shared environmental influences,* those that affect all children living in the same home to the same extent, and *nonshared environmental influences,* those that make siblings different from one another. The fact that siblings growing up in the same family show little or no resemblance in temperament and personality suggests that shared environmental factors, such as the overall climate of the home, do not make an important contribution. Instead, behavioral geneticists believe that nonshared environmental factors—those that bring out each child's uniqueness—are especially salient in personality development (Braungart et al., 1992; Emde et al., 1992; Plomin, 1994d).

Beginning at birth, Chinese infants are calmer, more easily soothed when upset, and better at quieting themselves than are Caucasian infants. These differences are probably hereditary, but cultural variations in child rearing support them. (Alan Oddie/PhotoEdit)

How might these nonshared influences operate? Although there is little research on this issue, behavioral geneticists believe that when it comes to children's personalities, parents may look for and emphasize differences. This is reflected in the comments many parents make after the birth of a second baby: "He's so much calmer," "She's a lot more active," or "He's more sociable." In one study, parents' descriptions of their children as temperamentally easy or difficult showed a sharp contrast effect. When one child was seen as easy, another was likely to be perceived as difficult (Schachter & Stone, 1985). Each child, in turn, evokes responses from caregivers that are consistent with parental beliefs and the child's actual temperamental style. Furthermore, as they get older, siblings often actively seek ways in which they can be different from one another. This is especially true when children are of the same sex or come from large families. Under these conditions, the child's need to stand out as special may be particularly great (Huston, 1983).

However, not everyone agrees that nonshared environmental influences are supreme in personality development. In Chapter 14, we will see that researchers who have assessed shared factors directly, such as family stress and child-rearing styles, report that they have a powerful impact on children's personalities. As Lois Hoffman (1991, 1994) points out, we must think of temperament and personality as resulting from many different inputs. For some qualities, child-specific experiences may be important. For others, the general family environment may be important. And perhaps for most, both nonshared and shared factors are involved.

CULTURAL VARIATIONS. Finally, consistent ethnic differences in infant temperament exist, implying a role for heredity. Compared to Caucasian infants, Chinese and Japanese babies are calmer, more easily soothed when upset, and better at quieting themselves (Kagan et al., 1994; Lewis, Ramsay, & Kawakami, 1993). Cultural variations in caregiving support these differences. When Japanese mothers are asked about their approach to child rearing, they respond that babies come into the world as independent beings who must learn to rely on their mothers through close physical contact. American mothers are likely to believe just the opposite—that they must wean the baby away from dependence into autonomy (Kojima, 1986). Consistent with these beliefs, Asian mothers interact gently, soothingly, and gesturally with their babies, whereas Caucasian mothers use a more active, stimulating verbal approach—behaviors that enhance early temperamental differences between their infants (Fogel, Toda, & Kawai, 1988).

Taken together, research on the nature–nurture issue in the realm of temperament and personality indicates that the importance of heredity cannot be ignored. At the same time, individual differences in personality can be understood only in terms of complex interdependencies between genetic and environmental factors.

TEMPERAMENT AS A PREDICTOR OF CHILDREN'S BEHAVIOR

In the first part of this chapter, we saw many examples of how emotions serve as powerful determinants of cognitive and social functioning. Since temperament represents an individual's typical style of emotional responding, it should be an effective predictor of those behaviors emotions are believed to organize (Campos et al., 1983). Many studies reveal that this is indeed the case.

■ TEMPERMENT AND COGNITIVE PERFORMANCE. Temperamental characteristics of interest and persistence are related to learning and cognitive performance almost as soon as they can be measured. For example, 2- to 3-month-olds rated high in persistence show faster operant conditioning than their less persistent counterparts (Dunst & Linderfelt, 1985). Persistence during the first year also correlates with infant mental test scores and preschool IQ (Matheny, 1989). During middle childhood, persistence, in the form of teacher-rated task orientation, continues to predict IQ as well as grades in school and teacher estimates of academic competence. In contrast, distractibility and high activity level are associated with poor school achievement (Martin, Olejnik, & Gaddis, 1994).

■ TEMPERMENT AND SOCIAL BEHAVIOR. Temperament also predicts important variations in social behavior. For example, highly active preschoolers are very sociable with peers, but they also become involved in more conflict than their less active agemates. Emotionally sensitive, excitable preschoolers tend to interact physically by hitting, touching, and grabbing objects from peers. Shy, inhibited children do more watching of classmates and engage in behaviors that discourage interaction, such as pushing other children away and speaking to them less often (Broberg, Lamb, & Hwang, 1990; Hinde, Stevenson-Hinde, & Tamplin, 1985). And as we will see in Chapter 12, temperament also influences conscience development. Inhibited youngsters' high anxiety leads them to be more prone to discomfort after wrongdoing and to feel a greater sense of responsibility to others.

In some cases, the social behavior seems to be a direct result of temperament, as is the case with shy children. In other instances, it is due to the way people respond to the child's emotional style. For example, active children are often targets of negative interaction, which leads to conflict. This is illustrated by research on sibling relationships; arguments between siblings increase when one member of a sibling pair is emotionally intense or highly active (Brody, Stoneman, & McCoy, 1994; Dunn, 1994). Early high activity level and emotional reactivity also predict aggression in adolescence, but the relationship seems to result from the tendency of many mothers to be permissive of antisocial behavior in children with these characteristics (Olweus, 1980). In sum, temperamental styles often stimulate consistent reactions from other people, which, in turn, mold the child's social development.

TEMPERAMENT AND CHILD REARING: THE GOODNESS-OF-FIT MODEL

We have already indicated that the temperaments of many children change with age. This suggests that environments do not always act to sustain a current temperamental style. If a child's disposition interferes with learning or getting along with others, then it is important for adults to gently but consistently counteract the child's maladaptive behavior.

Thomas and Chess (1977) proposed a **goodness-of-fit model** to describe how temperament and environmental pressures combine to affect the course of development. It states that when the child's style of responding and environmental demands are in harmony, or achieve a "good fit," then development is optimal. When dissonance, or a "poor fit" between temperament and environment exists, then the outcome is distorted development and maladjustment. To ensure goodness-of-fit, adults must create child-rearing environments that recognize each child's temperament while encouraging more adaptive functioning.

Goodness-of-fit model
Thomas and Chess's model, which states that an effective match, or "good fit," between child-rearing practices and a child's temperament leads to favorable development and psychological adjustment. When a "poor fit" exists, the outcome is distorted development and maladjustment.

The goodness-of-fit model helps explain why children with difficult temperaments are at high risk for later behavior problems. These children, at least in Western middle-class society, frequently experience parenting that fits poorly with their dispositions. As

CULTURAL INFLUENCES

Difficult Temperament and Infant Survival Among the Masai

In the midst of a study of infant development, a drought that swept the homeland of the Masai people of Kenya and Tanzania provided Marten deVries (1984) with a unique opportunity to examine the role of temperament in babies' capacity to cope with extreme stress. The Masai are a nomadic society who wander the plains of East Africa in small kinship groups, searching for suitable grazing land for their herds of cattle. In this society with an admired warrior class, assertive behavior is a cultural ideal, encouraged at an early age in the context of infant feeding. Although mothers are in constant contact with their babies from birth on, they offer the breast only when the infant fusses or cries. As a result, babies are responsible for signaling their need to be fed.

The drought devastated the Masai economy and social organization. Cattle died in large numbers, causing kinship networks to dissolve as families migrated to new areas in search of food for themselves and their dwindling herds. Soon, infants were deprived of supplementary cow's milk, and mothers were isolated from caregiving assistance typically provided by other women. As a result, infant malnutrition, illness, and mortality soared.

DeVries selected 10 easy and 10 difficult babies, identified on the basis of maternal report, and arranged to track their future development. But when he searched for the infants several months later, he could locate only 13 of their families, and he discovered that 7 of these babies (over 50 percent) had died. On the basis of Western research, deVries predicted that infants with easy temperaments would have an adaptive advantage, but he found just the opposite. All but one of the dead babies had been easy; the survivors were overwhelmingly difficult in temperamental style.

When first assessed, the easy and difficult groups had been similar on a wide range of factors, including maternal acceptance of the baby, plentifulness of breast milk, infant health, and family wealth. What, then, contributed to their different mortalities? According to deVries, the irritable behavior of difficult Masai infants prompted more frequent feeding, which led to greater weight gain and survival under conditions of marginal nutrition. In contrast, easy babies were not sufficiently demanding to induce enough feeding from their exhausted, undernourished mothers. As a result, the breast-milk supply diminished, and many died of starvation and disease. The unexpected mortality rates of Masai infants illustrate the interplay of temperament, child rearing, and cultural conditions in shaping developmental outcomes.

■ *When a drought swept the homeland of the Masai people of Kenya and Tanzania, many more difficult babies than easy babies survived. The irritable behavior of the difficult infants may have ensured that they were better fed. The adaptiveness of temperament varies with cultural circumstances. (Diane M. Love/Stock Boston)*

infants, they are far less likely to receive sensitive caregiving (van den Boom & Hoeksma, 1994). By the second year, parents of difficult children often resort to angry, punitive discipline. In response, the child reacts with defiance and disobedience. Then parents often behave inconsistently, rewarding the child's noncompliant behavior by giving into it, although they resisted at first (Lee & Bates, 1985). In these instances, the difficult child's temperament combined with harsh, inconsistent child rearing forms a poor fit that maintains and even increases the child's irritable, conflict-ridden style. In contrast, when parents are positive and involved with their babies and establish a happy, stable home life despite their child's negative, unpredictable behavior, infant difficultness declines with age (Belsky, Fish, & Isabella, 1991).

In the goodness-of-fit model, caregiving is not just responsive to the child's temperament. It also depends on cultural values and life conditions. For example, difficult children in working-class Puerto Rican families are treated with sensitivity and patience. They do not evoke severe child-rearing practices and are not at risk for adjustment problems (Gannon & Korn, 1983). Indeed, as the Cultural Influences box above reveals, under certain cultural circumstances, infant difficultness can even be adaptive and promote survival!

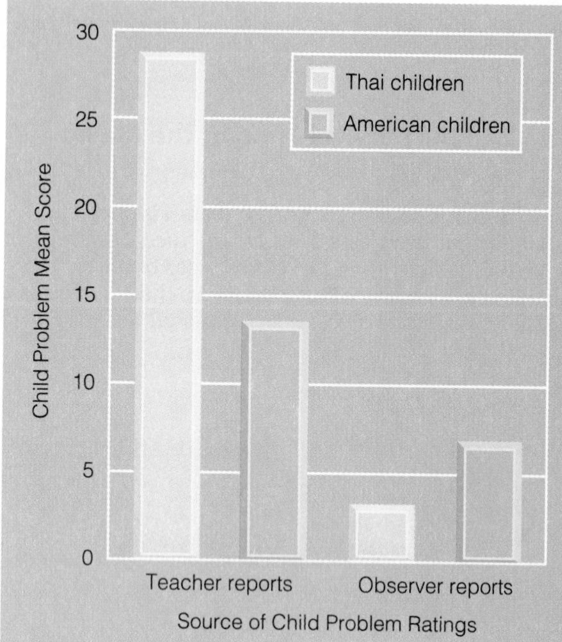

FIGURE 10.3

■ *Teacher and observer reports of Thai and American children's behavior problems. Notice that compared to observers, teachers in both countries reported more problem behavior overall, since they had much more exposure to the children. But in the eyes of teachers, Thai children were far more problem ridden than were American children. From the perspective of impartial observers, American children displayed substantially more problems. The high value placed on a polite, restrained temperamental style leads Thai teachers to identify a much lower level of difficult and off-task behavior as problematic than do American teachers. (From J. R. Weiss, W. Chaiyasit, B. Weiss, K. L., Eastman, & E. W. Jackson, 1995, "A Multimethod Study of Problem Behavior Among Thai and American Children in School: Teacher Reports versus Direct Observations,"* Child Development, *66, p. 410. © The Society for Research in Child Development, Inc. Reprinted by permission.) (Photo: Matthew Naythons/Stock Boston)*

Similarly, in Western nations, shy, withdrawn children are regarded as socially incompetent, yet in Chinese culture adults evaluate such children positively—as advanced in social maturity and understanding (Chen, Rubin, & Li, 1995). Expectations for polite, restrained child behavior are so strong in Thailand that Thai teachers rate pupils as having many more behavior problems than do American teachers. Yet as Figure 10.3 shows, in the eyes of impartial observers, Thai children are actually far better behaved in school than are their American counterparts! Thai teachers may be so used to respect and obedience that they regard children as disruptive, inattentive, and unmotivated who would be seen as quite normal in the United States (Weisz et al., 1995).

In cultures where particular temperamental styles are linked to adjustment problems, an effective match between rearing conditions and child temperament is best accomplished early, before unfavorable temperament–environment relationships have had a chance to produce maladjustment that is hard to undo. Both difficult and slow-to-warm-up children benefit from warm, accepting parenting that makes firm but reasonable demands for mastering new experiences (Chess & Thomas, 1984). In the case of reserved, inactive toddlers, research shows that highly stimulating maternal behavior (frequent questioning, instructing, and pointing out objects) fosters exploration of the environment. Yet these same parental behaviors inhibit exploration in very active toddlers. For these children, too much adult intervention dampens their natural curiosity (Gandour, 1989).

These findings provide yet another illustration of how effective parenting must harmonize with children's temperamental characteristics. We will encounter this theme again as we consider the development of attachment, to which the emotional communication of both caregiver and child contribute.

BRIEF REVIEW

Children's unique temperamental styles are apparent in early infancy. However, the stability of temperament is only modest. Heredity influences early temperament, but child-rearing experiences affect whether a child's emotional style is sustained or modified over time. Temperamental characteristics are good predictors of a variety of cognitive outcomes and social behaviors. A good fit between parenting practices and child temperament supports optimal development, helping children whose temperaments predispose them to adjustment problems achieve more adaptive functioning. The adaptiveness of different temperamental styles is powerfully affected by culture.

Development of Attachment

Attachment is the strong, affectional tie we feel for special people in our lives that leads us to feel pleasure and joy when we interact with them and to be comforted by their nearness during times of stress. By the second half of the first year, infants have become attached to familiar people who have responded to their need for physical care and stimulation. Watch babies of this age, and notice how parents are singled out for special attention. A whole range of responses is reserved just for them. For example, when the mother enters the room, the baby breaks into a broad, friendly smile. When she picks him up, he pats her face, explores her hair, and snuggles against her body. When he feels anxious or afraid, he crawls into her lap and clings closely.

EARLY THEORIES OF ATTACHMENT

Freud first suggested that the infant's emotional tie to the mother provides the foundation for all later relationships. We will see shortly that research on children deprived of an early caregiving relationship supports Freud's belief in the importance of the attachment bond. But attachment has also been the subject of intense theoretical debate for decades. Behaviorist and psychoanalytic theories were early views that competed to explain how attachment developed.

■ *Baby monkeys reared with "surrogate mothers" from birth preferred to cling to a soft terry cloth "mother" instead of a wire mesh "mother" that held a bottle. These findings reveal that the drive-reduction explanation of attachment, which assumes that the mother-infant relationship is based on feeding, is incorrect. (Martin Rogers/Stock Boston)*

■ BEHAVIORISM. Behaviorists believe that infants' attachment behaviors—seeking closeness to the mother, following her about, and crying and calling in her absence—are learned responses. The best-known behaviorist account is a **drive reduction model** that grants feeding a central role in the infant–caregiver relationship. As the baby's hunger *(primary drive)* is satisfied repeatedly by the mother, her presence becomes a *secondary* or *learned drive* because it is paired with tension relief. As a result, the baby learns to prefer all kinds of stimuli that accompany feeding, including the mother's soft caresses, warm smiles, and tender words of comfort (Sears, Maccoby, & Levin, 1957).

Although feeding is an important context in which mothers and babies build a close relationship, today we know that the attachment bond does not depend on satisfying an infant's hunger. In the 1950s, Harry Harlow's famous research on rhesus monkeys challenged the drive reduction explanation. Baby monkeys separated from their mothers at birth and reared with terrycloth and wire mesh surrogates spent their days clinging to the terrycloth substitute, even though the wire mesh "mother" held the bottle and infants had to climb on it to be fed (Harlow & Zimmerman, 1959). Contact comfort rather than feeding appeared to be central in the development of attachment.

Observations of human infants also revealed that they become attached to family members who seldom if ever feed them, including fathers, siblings, and grandparents (Schaffer & Emerson, 1964). And perhaps you have noticed that toddlers in Western cultures who sleep alone and experience frequent daytime separations from their parents sometimes develop a strong emotional tie to a soft, cuddly toy or blanket. These objects of attachment are effective sources of security that seem to substitute for special people when they are not available (Passman, 1987). Yet such objects have never played an active role in infant feeding!

A second behaviorist explanation of attachment is an **operant conditioning model** that emphasizes reciprocal responsiveness between caregiver and baby (Gewirtz, 1969). According to this view, babies look, smile, and seek closeness because their mothers respond contingently with smiles, pats, hugs, and vocalizations, thereby reinforcing the infant's social engagement. The greater the number of infant behaviors that have been consistently reinforced by and have therefore come under the stimulus control of another person, the stronger the attachment relationship is said to be. As we will see later, coordinated exchanges between parent and baby do influence the quality of the infant–caregiver relationship. But they cannot fully account for the formation of the attachment bond. One reason is that attachment behaviors emerge even under conditions of serious infant maltreatment. Harlow and his collaborators found that even though socially deprived mother monkeys (who had been raised in isolation) behaved violently toward their babies, the infants continued to seek physical contact (Seay, Alexander, & Harlow,

Attachment
The strong affectional tie that humans feel toward special people in their lives.

Drive reduction model of attachment
A behaviorist view that regards the mother's satisfaction of the baby's hunger (primary drive) as the basis for the infant's preference for her (secondary drive).

Operant conditioning model of attachment
A behaviorist view that regards the mother's contingent reinforcement of the baby's social behavior as the basis for the infant's preference for her.

■ *This infant becomes upset when her mother hands her to a caregiver and starts to leave for work. After 6 months of age, separation anxiety appears universally around the world. (Laura Dwight/ PhotoEdit)*

1964). Abused human children often make similar attempts to approach their nonreinforcing, punitive mothers.

A final problem with behaviorist accounts is that they cannot explain why the attachment relationship, once formed, tends to persist over long periods in which attachment figures are absent. Think about your own feelings of attachment for people whom you have not seen (and been reinforced by) in many months. Behaviorism would predict that your desire for closeness should *extinguish,* or disappear. Yet clearly it does not. Behaviorism has great difficulty explaining the remarkable endurance of human attachments over time and distance.

■ THE PSYCHOANALYTIC PERSPECTIVE. Psychoanalytic theorists, such as Freud and Erikson, emphasize that the central ingredient in attachment is the mother's caregiving during feeding, since the oral zone of the body is the locus of instinctual gratification during the first year of life. When the mother consistently satisfies the baby's pangs of hunger and her feeding practices are accompanied by sensitive, loving care, the baby builds a sense of trust that his needs will be met (Erikson, 1950). As a result, the infant feels confident about separating from her for brief periods of time to explore the environment. Eventually, the child forms a permanent, positive inner image of the mother that can be relied on for emotional support during brief absences.

Compared to behaviorism, the psychoanalytic approach provides a much richer view of the attachment bond, regarding it as critical for exploration of the environment, cognitive mastery, and emotional security. Psychoanalytic theories also recognize that deep affectional bonds, once formed, can endure over separations from loved individuals.

Despite its strengths, the psychoanalytic perspective has been criticized on two grounds. First, because it builds on Freud's oral stage, it (like the drive reduction model) overemphasizes the importance of feeding in the development of attachment. Second, although psychoanalytic theory has much to say about the mother's contribution to the attachment relationship, it grants far less importance to the infant's characteristics and behavior. As we will see in the following section, ethological theory is unique in emphasizing that babies are biologically prepared to contribute actively to ties established with their caregivers.

BOWLBY'S ETHOLOGICAL THEORY

Today, **ethological theory of attachment** is the most widely accepted view of the infant's emotional tie to the caregiver. Recall from Chapter 1 that according to ethology, many human behaviors have evolved over the history of our species because they promote survival. John Bowlby (1969), who first applied this idea to the infant–caregiver bond, was originally a psychoanalyst. As you will see shortly, his theory retains a number of psychoanalytic features. At the same time, Bowlby was inspired by Konrad Lorenz's studies of imprinting in baby geese (see Chapter 1). He believed that the human baby, like the young of other animal species, is endowed with a set of built-in behaviors that help keep the parent nearby, increasing the chances that the infant will be protected from danger. Contact with the parent also ensures that the baby will be fed, but Bowlby was careful to point out that feeding is not the basis for attachment. Instead, the attachment bond has strong biological roots. It can best be understood within an evolutionary framework in which survival of the species is of utmost importance.

According to Bowlby, the infant's relationship to the parent begins as a set of innate signals that call the adult to the baby's side. Over time, a true affectional bond develops, which is supported by new cognitive and emotional capacities as well as a history of sensitive, responsive care. The development of attachment takes place in four phases:

1. *The preattachment phase* (birth to 6 weeks). A variety of built-in signals—grasping, smiling, crying, and gazing into the adult's eyes—help bring newborn babies into close contact with other humans. Once an adult responds, infants encourage her to remain nearby, since they are comforted when picked up, stroked, and talked to softly. Babies of this age can recognize their own mother's smell and voice (see Chapter 4). However, they are not yet attached to her, since they do not mind being left with an unfamiliar adult.

Ethological theory of attachment
A theory formulated by Bowlby, which views the infant's emotional tie to the familiar caregiver as an evolved response that promotes survival.

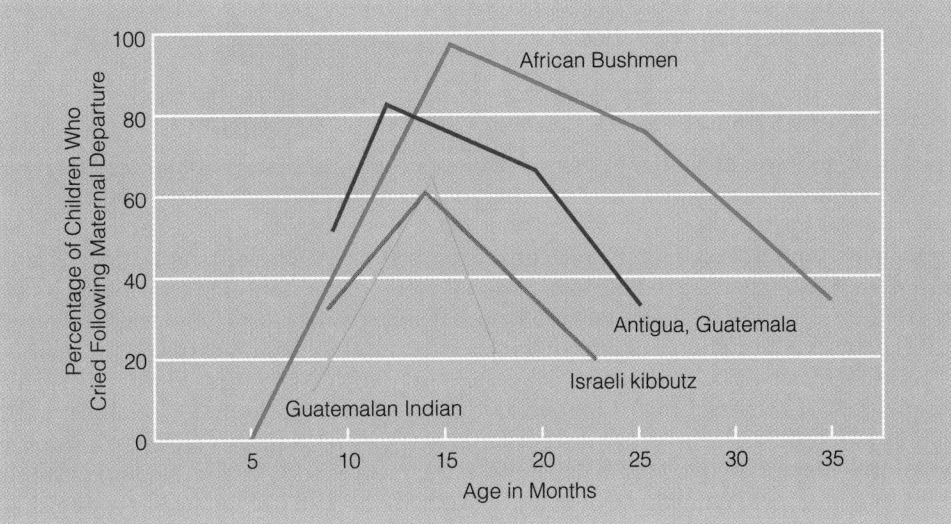

FIGURE 10.4

Development of separation anxiety. In cultures around the world, separation anxiety emerges in the second half of the first year, increasing until about 15 months and then declining. (From J. Kagan, R. B. Kearsley, & P. R. Zelazo, 1978, Infancy: Its Place in Human Development, Cambridge, MA: Harvard University Press, p. 107. Copyright © 1978 by the President and Fellows of Harvard College. All rights reserved. Reprinted by permission.)

2. *The "attachment-in-the-making" phase* (6 weeks to 6–8 months). During this phase, infants start to respond differently to a familiar caregiver than to a stranger. For example, the baby smiles, laughs, and babbles more freely when interacting with the mother and quiets more quickly when she picks him up. As infants engage in face-to-face interaction with the parent and experience relief from distress, they learn that their own actions affect the behavior of those around them. They begin to develop an expectation that the caregiver will respond when signaled. But babies still do not protest when separated from the parent, despite the fact that they can distinguish her from unfamiliar people.

3. *The phase of "clear-cut" attachment* (6–8 months to 18 months–2 years). Now attachment to the familiar caregiver is evident. Babies of this period show **separation anxiety,** in that they become very upset when the adult whom they have come to rely on leaves. Separation anxiety appears universally around the world after 6 months of age, increasing until about 15 months (see Figure 10.4). Its appearance suggests that infants have a clear understanding that the caregiver continues to exist when not in view. Consistent with this idea, babies who have not yet mastered Piagetian object permanence usually do not become anxious when separated from their mothers (Lester et al., 1974).

   Besides protesting the parent's departure, older infants and toddlers act more deliberately to maintain her presence. They approach, follow, and climb on her in preference to others. And they use her as a secure base from which to explore, venturing into the environment and then returning for emotional support, as we indicated earlier in this chapter.

4. *Formation of a reciprocal relationship* (18 months–2 years and on). By the end of the second year, rapid growth in representation and language permits toddlers to understand some of the factors that influence the parent's coming and going and to predict her return. As a result, separation protest declines. Now children start to negotiate with the caregiver, using requests and persuasion to alter her goals rather than crawling after and clinging to her. For example, one 2-year-old asked her mother to read a story before leaving her with a baby-sitter. The extra time with her mother, along with an explanation of where she was going ("to a movie with Daddy") and when she would be back ("right after you go to sleep") helped this child withstand her mother's absence.

According to Bowlby (1980), out of their experiences during these four phases, children construct an enduring affectional tie to the caregiver that permits them to use the attachment figure as a secure base across time and distance. Consequently, preschoolers no longer need to engage in behaviors that maintain the caregiver's nearness as insistently as they did before. This inner representation of the parent–child bond becomes a vital part of personality. It serves as an **internal working model,** or set of expectations about the availability of attachment figures, their likelihood of providing support during times of stress, and the self's interaction with those figures. This image becomes the

Separation anxiety
An infant's distressed reaction to the departure of the familiar caregiver.

Internal working model
A set of expectations derived from early caregiving experiences concerning the availability of attachment figures, their likelihood of providing support during times of stress, and the self's interaction with those figures that affect all future close relationships.

model, or guide, for all future close relationships—through childhood and adolescence and into adult life (Bretherton, 1992).

MEASURING THE SECURITY OF ATTACHMENT

Although virtually all family-reared babies become attached to a familiar caregiver by the second year, the quality of this relationship differs greatly from child to child. Some infants appear especially relaxed and secure in the presence of the caregiver; they know they can count on her for protection and support. Others seem more anxious and uncertain. Researchers have developed special methods for assessing attachment security so they can study the factors that influence it and its impact on later development.

The **Strange Situation** is the most widely used technique for measuring the quality of attachment between 1 and 2 years of age. In designing it, Mary Ainsworth and her colleagues (1978) reasoned that if the development of attachment has gone along well, infants and toddlers should use the parent as a secure base from which to explore an unfamiliar playroom. In addition, when the parent leaves for a brief period of time, the child should show separation anxiety, and an unfamiliar adult should be less comforting than the parent. As summarized in Table 10.3, the Strange Situation takes the baby through eight short episodes in which brief separations from and reunions with the parent occur.

Observing the responses of infants to these episodes, researchers have identified a secure attachment pattern and three patterns of insecurity (Ainsworth et al., 1978; Main & Solomon, 1990). They are as follows:

- **Secure attachment.** These infants use the parent as a secure base. When separated, they may or may not cry, but if they do, it is due to the parent's absence, since they show a strong preference for her over the stranger. When the parent returns, they actively seek contact, and their crying is reduced immediately. About 65 percent of American babies show this pattern.
- **Avoidant attachment.** These infants seem unresponsive to the parent when she is present. When she leaves, they are usually not distressed, and they react to the stranger in much the same way as the parent. During reunion, they avoid or are slow to greet the parent, and when picked up, they often fail to cling. About 20 percent of American babies show this pattern.
- **Resistant attachment.** Before separation, these infants seek closeness to the parent and often fail to explore. When she returns, they display angry, resistive

Strange Situation
A procedure involving short separations from and reunions with the parent that assesses the quality of the attachment bond.

Secure attachment
The quality of attachment characterizing infants who are distressed by parental separation and easily comforted by the parent when she returns.

Avoidant attachment
The quality of insecure attachment characterizing infants who are usually not distressed by parental separation and who avoid the parent when she returns.

Resistant attachment
The quality of insecure attachment characterizing infants who remain close to the parent before departure and display angry, resistive behavior when she returns.

TABLE 10.3
Episodes in the Strange Situation

Episode	Events	Attachment Behaviors Observed
1	Experimenter introduces parent and baby to playroom and then leaves.	
2	Parent is seated while baby plays with toys.	Parent as a secure base
3	Stranger enters, is seated, and talks to parent.	Reaction to unfamiliar adult
4	Parent leaves room. Stranger responds to baby and offers comfort if upset.	Separation anxiety
5	Parent returns, greets baby, and if necessary offers comfort. Stranger leaves room.	Reaction to reunion
6	Parent leaves room.	Separation anxiety
7	Stranger enters room and offers comfort.	Ability to be soothed by stranger
8	Parent returns, greets baby, if necessary offers comfort, and tries to reinterest baby in toys.	Reaction to reunion

Note: Episode 1 lasts about 30 seconds; the remaining episodes each last about 3 minutes. Separation episodes are cut short if the baby becomes very upset. Reunion episodes are extended if the baby needs more time to calm dowm and return to play.

behavior, sometimes hitting and pushing. In addition, many continue to cry after being picked up and cannot be comforted easily. This pattern is found in about 10 to 15 percent of American infants.

- **Disorganized/disoriented attachment.** This pattern seems to reflect the greatest insecurity. At reunion, these infants show a variety of confused, contradictory behaviors. For example, they might look away while being held by the parent or approach her with flat, depressed affect. Most of these babies communicate their disorientation with a dazed facial expression. A few cry out unexpectedly after having calmed down or display odd, frozen postures. About 5 to 10 percent of American infants show this pattern.

Infants' reactions in the Strange Situation closely resemble their use of the parent as a secure base and their response to separation in the home environment (Blanchard & Main, 1979). For this reason, the procedure is a powerful tool for assessing attachment security.

Recently, an alternative, more efficient method has become popular: the **Attachment Q-set**. An observer—the parent or an expert informant—sorts a set of 90 descriptors of attachment-related behaviors (such as "Child greets mother with a big smile when she enters the room" and "If mother moves very far, child follows along") into nine categories, ranging from highly descriptive to not at all descriptive of the child. The resulting profile indicates the degree to which the child displays secure-base behavior (Waters et al., 1995). Q-set assessments by expert informants correspond well with Strange Situation attachment classifications, those by mothers less so (van Dam & van IJzendoorn, 1988; Vaughn & Waters, 1990).

STABILITY OF ATTACHMENT AND CULTURAL VARIATIONS

For middle-class infants experiencing stable life conditions, quality of attachment to the caregiver is highly stable over the second year of life (Owen et al., 1984). In fact, evidence from two countries (Germany and the United States), summarized in Table 10.4, reveals that such children continue to respond to the parent in a similar fashion when reobserved in a laboratory reunion episode several years later, at age 6 (Main & Cassidy, 1988; Wartner et al., 1994). However, when families experience major life changes, such as a shift in employment or marital status, the quality of attachment often changes—sometimes positively and at other times negatively (Thompson, Lamb, & Estes, 1982). Mother–firstborn attachment is also likely to move in either direction after the birth of a sibling (Touris, Kromelow, & Harding, 1995). These are expected outcomes, since family transitions affect parent–child interaction, which, in turn, influences the attachment bond.

Nevertheless, cross-cultural evidence indicates that Strange Situation behavior may have to be interpreted differently in other cultures. For example, German infants show considerably more avoidant attachment than American babies do. However, German parents encourage their infants to be nonclingy and independent, so the baby's behavior may be an intended outcome of cultural beliefs and practices (Grossmann et al., 1985). An unusually high number of Japanese infants display a resistant response, but once again, the reaction may not represent true insecurity. Japanese mothers rarely leave their babies in the care of unfamiliar people, so the Strange Situation probably creates far greater stress for them than it does for infants who frequently experience maternal separations (Miyake, Chen, & Campos, 1985; Takahashi, 1990).

Despite these cultural variations, the secure pattern is still the most common attachment classification in all societies studied to date (van IJzendoorn & Kroonenberg, 1988). And when the Attachment Q-Set is used to assess conceptions of the ideal child, mothers in diverse cultures—China, Germany, Israel, Japan, Norway, and the United States—prefer that their young children express their feelings of attachment and use them as a secure base for exploration (Posada et al., 1995).

FACTORS THAT AFFECT ATTACHMENT SECURITY

A variety of factors might be expected to affect attachment security. First, simply having an opportunity to establish a close relationship with one or a few caregivers

Disorganized/disoriented attachment
The quality of insecure attachment characterizing infants who respond in a confused, contradictory fashion when reunited with the parent.

Attachment Q-set
An efficient method for assessing the quality of the attachment bond in which a parent or an expert informant sorts a set of 90 descriptors of attachment-related behaviors on the basis of how descriptive they are of the child. The resulting profile indicates the degree to which the child displays secure base behavior.

TABLE 10.4

Relationship of Attachment Classification in Infancy to Sixth-Year Attachment Behavior

Attachment Classification in Infancy	Sixth-Year Behavior When Reunited with Mother[a]
Secure	This child is relaxed throughout the reunion and either initiates pleasurable interaction or responds positively to the parent's initiations. Typically, the child seeks closeness or physical contact without seeming dependent.
Avoidant	This child keeps his or her distance from the parent, looking and speaking as little as possible by remaining occupied with toys or activities.
Resistant	This child shows exaggerated intimacy with the parent in movements, posture, and tone of voice. At the same time, the child displays avoidance (for example, by talking to the parent with back turned) as well as hostility and sometimes fear or sadness.
Disorganized/disoriented	This child tries to direct and control the parent's behavior, assuming a role that is more appropriate for a parent. In some cases, the child does so by humiliating or rejecting the parent, with such statements as "I told you, keep quiet!" or "Don't bother me!" In other cases, the child is overly solicitous or nervously cheerful at reunion, jumping, skipping, and clapping hands.

[a]Correspondences between attachment classification in infancy and sixth-year behavior when reunited with mother held for 84 percent of a sample of 32 American middle-class children and 82 percent of a sample of 39 German middle-class children.
Source: Main & Cassidy, 1988; Wartner et al., 1994.

should be crucial. Second, because it assures the infant that the caregiver will respond to his signals and needs, sensitive parenting should lead to greater attachment security. Third, since infants actively contribute to the attachment relationship, an infant's characteristics should make a difference in how well it proceeds. And finally, because children and parents are embedded in larger contexts, family circumstances should influence attachment quality. In the following sections, we examine each of these factors.

■ MATERNAL DEPRIVATION. The powerful impact of the baby's affectional tie to the caregiver is most evident when it is absent. In a series of landmark studies, René Spitz (1946) observed institutionalized babies who had been given up by their mothers between the third month and the end of the first year. The infants were placed on a large ward where they shared a nurse with at least seven other babies. In contrast to the happy, outgoing behavior they had shown before separation, they wept and withdrew from their surroundings, lost weight, and had difficulty sleeping. If a caregiver whom the baby could get to know did not replace the mother, the depression deepened rapidly.

According to Spitz, institutionalized infants experienced emotional difficulties because they were prevented from forming a bond with one or a few adults. A more recent study supports this conclusion. Researchers followed the development of infants reared in an institution that offered a good caregiver-child ratio and a rich selection of books and toys. However, staff turnover was so rapid that the average child had a total of 50 different caregivers by the age of 4½! Many of these children became "late adoptees" who were placed in homes after age 4. Most developed deep ties with their adoptive parents, indicating that a first attachment bond can develop as late as 4 to 6 years of age. But throughout childhood and adolescence, these youngsters were more likely to display emotional and social problems, including an excessive desire for adult attention, "over-friendliness" to unfamiliar adults and peers, and few friendships (Hodges & Tizard, 1989; Tizard & Hodges, 1978; Tizard & Rees, 1975). Although follow-ups into adulthood are necessary to be sure, these results leave open the possibility that fully normal development depends on establishing close bonds with caregivers during the first few years of life.

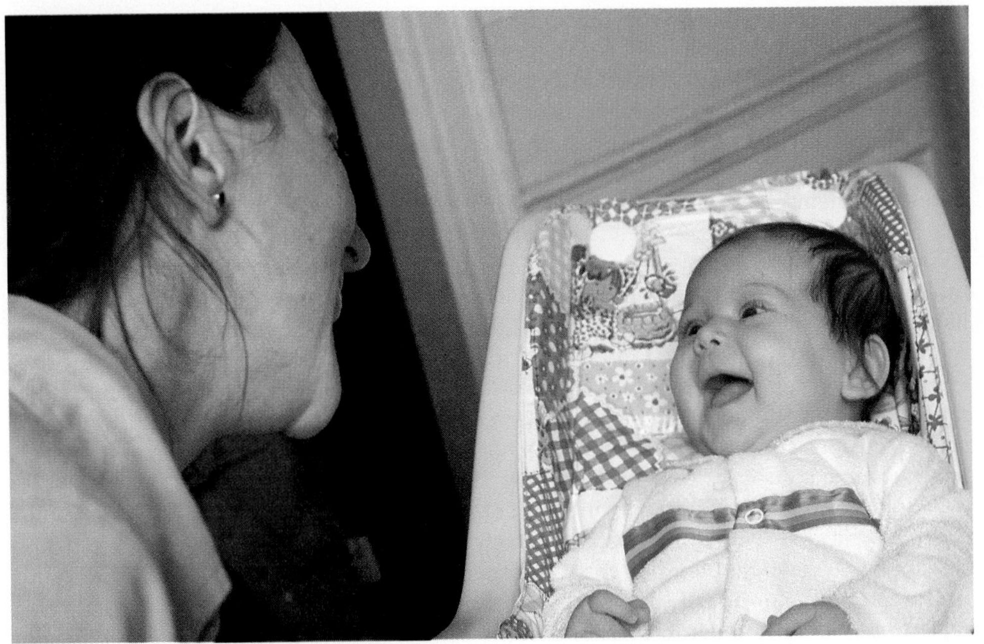

■ *This mother and baby engage in a sensitively tuned form of communication called interactional synchrony in which they match emotional states, especially the positive ones. Interactional synchrony may support the development of secure attachment, but it does not characterize mother-infant interaction in all cultures. (Julie O'Neil/The Picture Cube)*

■ QUALITY OF CAREGIVING. Even when infants experience the closeness of one or a few caregivers, parental behavior that is insensitive to their needs should lead to insecure attachment. To test this idea, researchers have related various aspects of maternal caregiving to the quality of the attachment bond. The findings of many studies reveal that securely attached infants have mothers who respond promptly to infant signals, express positive emotion, and handle their babies tenderly and carefully. In contrast, insecurely attached infants have mothers who dislike physical contact, handle them awkwardly, and behave insensitively when meeting the baby's needs (Ainsworth et al., 1978; Belsky, Rovine, & Taylor, 1984; Isabella, 1993).

Exactly what is it that mothers of securely attached babies do to support their infant's feelings of trust? In one study, mother–infant interaction was videotaped and carefully coded for each partner's behavior. Findings indicated that a special form of communication called **interactional synchrony** separated the experiences of secure from insecure babies (Isabella & Belsky, 1991). Interactional synchrony is best described as a sensitively tuned "emotional dance" in which the caregiver reacts to infant signals in a well-timed, appropriate fashion. In addition, both partners match emotional states, especially the positive ones (Stern, 1985).

But more research is needed to document the link between interactional synchrony and secure attachment. Other research reveals that only 30 percent of the time are exchanges between mothers and their babies perfectly "in sync" with one another. The remaining 70 percent of the time, interactive errors occur (Tronick, 1989). Perhaps warm, sensitive caregivers and their babies become especially skilled at repairing these errors and returning to a synchronous state. Nevertheless, finely tuned, coordinated interaction does not characterize mother–infant interaction everywhere. Among the Gusii of Kenya, mothers rarely cuddle, hug, and interact playfully with their babies, although they are very responsive to their infants' needs (LeVine et al., 1994). This suggests that secure attachment depends on attentive caregiving, but its association with moment-by-moment contingent interaction is probably culturally specific.

Compared to securely attached infants, avoidant babies tend to receive overstimulating, intrusive care. Their mothers might, for example, talk energetically to a baby who is looking away or falling asleep. By avoiding the mother, these infants appear to be escaping from overwhelming interaction. Resistant infants often experience inconsistent care. Their mothers are minimally involved in parenting and unresponsive to their signals. Yet when the baby begins to explore, these mothers interfere, shifting the infant's attention back to themselves. As a result, the baby shows exaggerated dependence as well as anger and frustration at the mother's lack of involvement (Cassidy & Berlin, 1994; Isabella & Belsky, 1991).

Interactional synchrony
A sensitively tuned "emotional dance," in which the caregiver responds to infant signals in a well-timed, appropriate fashion and both partners match emotional states, especially the positive ones.

When caregiving is extremely inadequate, it is a powerful predictor of disruptions in attachment. Child abuse and neglect (topics we will consider in Chapter 14) are associated with all three forms of attachment insecurity. Among maltreated infants, the most worrisome classification—disorganized/disoriented attachment—is especially high (Carlson et al., 1989). Infants of depressed mothers also show the uncertain behaviors of this pattern, mixing closeness, resistance, and avoidance while looking very sad and depressed themselves (Lyons-Ruth et al., 1990; Teti et al., 1995).

■ INFANT CHARACTERISTICS. Since attachment is the result of a relationship that builds between two partners, infant characteristics should affect how easily it is established. Indeed, there is good evidence that this is the case. In Chapter 3, we saw that prematurity, birth complications, and newborn illness make caregiving more taxing for parents. In poverty-stricken, stressed families, these infant conditions are linked to attachment insecurity (Wille, 1991). But when parents have the time and patience to care for a baby with special needs and the infant is not very sick, at-risk newborns fare quite well in attachment security (Pederson & Moran, 1995).

Infants also vary considerably in temperament, but the precise role that temperament plays in the development of secure attachment has been intensely debated. Some researchers believe that temperament is largely responsible for the way babies respond in the Strange Situation. They believe, for example, that babies who are irritable and fearful may simply react to brief separations with intense anxiety, regardless of the parent's sensitivity to the baby (Kagan, 1989). Consistent with this view, several studies report that proneness to distress in early infancy is moderately related to later insecure attachment (Seifer et al., 1996; Vaughn et al., 1992).

But other findings argue against the primacy of temperament in determining attachment pattern. First, quality of attachment to the mother and the father is often similar, a resemblance that could be due to parents' tendency to react similarly to their baby's temperamental characteristics (Fox, Kimmerly, & Schafer, 1991; Rosen & Rothbaum, 1993). Nevertheless, a substantial number of infants establish distinct attachment relationships with each parent and with their substitute caregivers (Goossens & van IJzendoorn, 1990). If infant temperament were the overriding determinant of attachment quality, we would expect attachment classification to be more constant across attachment figures than it is.

Second, the findings of several investigations suggest that when infant irritability is linked to attachment insecurity, caregiving mediates the relationship. For example, in one study, distress-prone infants who became insecurely attached were especially likely to have mothers with rigid, controlling personalities who probably had difficulty altering their immediate plans to comfort a baby who often fussed and cried (Mangelsdorf et al., 1990). And in another study, an intervention designed to promote sensitivity in mothers of irritable 6-month-olds led to gains in maternal responsiveness and in children's attachment security, exploration, cooperativeness, and sociability that were still evident at 3 ½ years of age. These findings support the view that caregiving is causally related to infant attachment (van den Boom, 1995).

Finally, additional evidence that caregiving can override the impact of infant characteristics comes from a study comparing the effects of maternal and child problem behaviors on the attachment bond. Combining data from over 34 studies including more than a thousand mother–infant pairs, the researchers found that maternal problems—such as mental illness, teenage parenthood, and child maltreatment—were associated with a sharp rise in attachment insecurity. In contrast, child problems—ranging from prematurity and developmental delays to serious physical disabilities and psychological disorders—had little impact on attachment quality (see Figure 10.5). Instead, the occurrence of security and insecurity resembled that of normal samples (van IJzendoorn et al., 1992).

A major reason that temperament and other child characteristics do not show strong relationships with attachment security may be that their influence depends on goodness-of-fit. From this perspective, many attributes of children can lead to secure attachment as long as the caregiver modifies her behavior to fit the needs of the baby (Seifer & Schiller, 1995; Sroufe, 1985). But when a mother's capacity to do so is limited—for example, by her own personality or by stressful living conditions—then infants with difficult temperaments and problem behaviors are at greater risk for attachment insecurity. In sum, the reason maternal sensitivity is an effective predictor of the quality of the attachment bond is that the very concept of sensitive caregiving implies a mother who adjusts her caregiving to suit the unique characteristics of her baby.

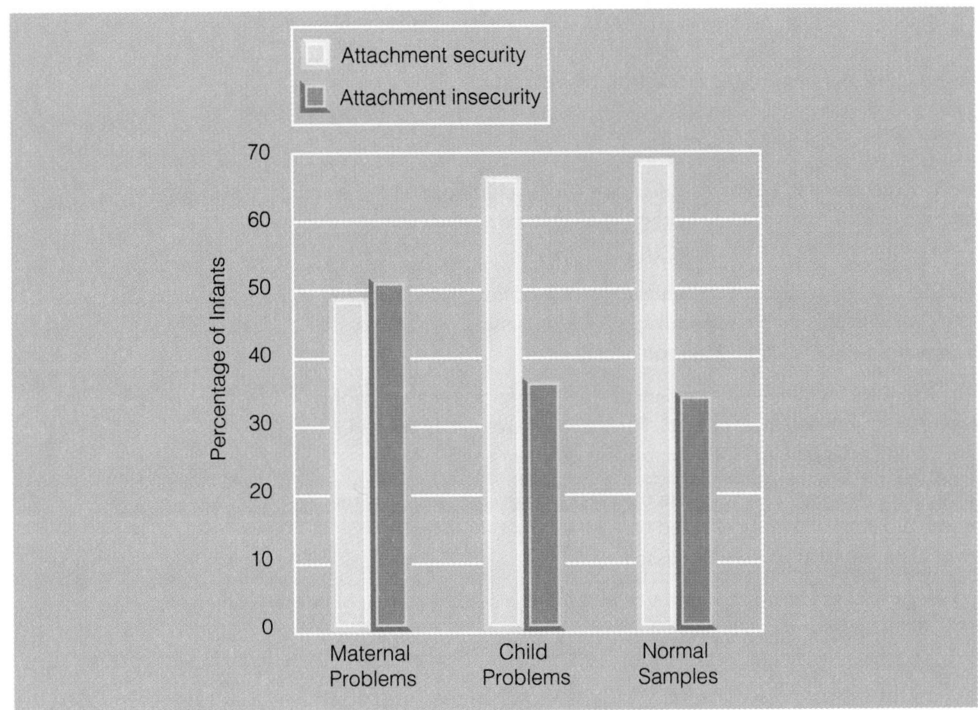

FIGURE 10.5

■ *Comparison of the effects of maternal and child problem behaviors on the attachment bond. Maternal problems were associated with a sharp rise in attachment insecurity. In contrast, child problems had little impact on the rate of attachment security and insecurity, which resembled that of normal samples. (Adapted from van IJzendoorn et al., 1992.)*

■ FAMILY CIRCUMSTANCES. We have already indicated, in this and previous chapters, that quality of caregiving can be fully understood only in terms of the larger social environment in which parent and child are embedded. In this respect, several factors influence parental contributions to attachment security. In families where there is stress and instability, insensitive parenting and insecure attachment are especially high. However, the availability of social supports, especially a good marital relationship and the spouse's assistance in caregiving, reduces stress and predicts greater attachment security (Howes & Markman, 1989; Pianta, Sroufe, & Egeland, 1989).

Unfortunately, not all parents have access to supportive family ties. In one study of poverty-stricken depressed and abusive mothers, home visitors provided an accepting, trustworthy relationship, offered help in making use of community resources, and modeled and reinforced more effective caregiving over a 9- to 18-month period. Compared to controls, home-visited babies scored 10 points higher in mental development and were twice as likely to be securely attached. The longer lasting the intervention, the more involved high-risk mothers were with their babies (Lyons-Ruth et al., 1990).

■ PARENTS' INTERNAL WORKING MODELS. Parents bring to the family context a long history of attachment experiences, out of which they construct internal working models that they apply to the bonds established with their babies. To assess parents' "state of mind" with respect to attachment, Carol George, Nancy Kaplan, and Mary Main (1985) devised the Adult Attachment Interview. It asks adults for childhood memories of attachment experiences along with an evaluation of those memories. How parents interpret their experiences, as opposed to the positive or negative nature of the events themselves, provides an overall impression of the adult's working model. Three types of attachment representations, summarized in Table 10.5, have been identified.

Quality of maternal working models is clearly related to attachment in infancy and early childhood—results replicated in studies carried out in Canada, Germany, Great Britain, the Netherlands, and the United States (Fonagy, Steele, & Steele, 1991; Das Eiden, Teti, & Corns, 1995; Main & Goldwyn, 1994; van IJzendoorn et al., 1991). Autonomous/secure mothers typically have secure infants, dismissing mothers have avoidant infants, preoccupied mothers have resistant infants, and unresolved mothers have disorganized infants. These correspondences hold for 60 percent of mother–infant pairs (Benoit & Parker, 1994; van IJzendoorn, 1995a). Furthermore, the relationship between maternal working model and child security seems to be mediated by caregiving behavior. Mothers who are autonomous/secure are warmer, more supportive of their children, and more likely to encourage learning and mastery. Their children, in turn, are more affectionate and comfortably interactive with them (Cohn et al., 1992).

TABLE 10.5

Relationship of Mothers' Internal Working Models to Infant Attachment Security

Type of Maternal Working Model	Description	Infant Attachment Classifications[a]
Autonomous/secure	These mothers show objectivity and balance in discussing their childhood experiences, whether they were positive or negative. They neither idealize their parents nor feel angry about the past. Their explanations are coherent and believable.	Secure
Dismissing	These mothers devalue the importance of their attachment relationships. They tend to idealize their parents without being able to recall specific experiences. What they do recall is discussed intellectually, with little emotion.	Avoidant
Overinvolved	These mothers talk about their childhood experiences with highly charged emotion, sometimes expressing anger toward their parents. They appear overwhelmed and confused about their early attachments and cannot discuss them coherently.	Resistant
Unresolved	These mothers show characteristics of any of the three other patterns. At the same time, they reason in a disorganized and confused way when loss of a loved one or experiences of physical or sexual abuse are discussed.	Disorganized/ disoriented

[a]Correspondences between type of maternal working model and infant attachment classification hold for 60 percent of mother–infant pairs.
Sources: Benoit & Parker, 1994; Main & Goldwyn, 1994.

Fathers' responses to the Adult Attachment Interview are less clearly related to attachment than are mothers' responses, perhaps because fathers typically spend less time with infants (van IJzendoorn & Bakermans-Kranenburg, 1996). Nevertheless, the quality of fathers' marital and parental relationships predicts their attitudes toward their babies. This suggests that working models also provide an important foundation for infant–father emotional ties (Cox et al., 1992).

These findings indicate, in line with both psychoanalytic and ethological theories, that parents' childhood experiences are transferred to the next generation by way of their internal working models of attachment relationships. This does not mean that adults with unhappy upbringings are destined to become insensitive parents. Instead, the way parents *view* their childhoods—their ability to integrate new information into their working models, to come to terms with negative events, and to look back on their own parents in an understanding, forgiving way—appears to be much more influential in how they rear their children than the actual history of care they received (van IJzendoorn, 1995b).

MULTIPLE ATTACHMENTS: THE FATHER'S SPECIAL ROLE

We have already indicated that babies develop attachments to a variety of familiar people—not just mothers, but fathers, siblings, grandparents, baby-sitters, and professional caregivers. Although Bowlby (1969) made room for multiple attachments in his theory, he believed that infants are predisposed to direct their attachment behaviors to a single attachment figure, especially when they are distressed. Observations of infants support this idea. When an anxious, unhappy 1-year-old is permitted to choose between the mother and father as a source of comfort and security, the infant usually chooses the mother (Lamb, 1976). This preference declines over the second year of life until, around 18 months, it is no longer present. And when babies are not distressed, they approach, touch, ask to be held, vocalize, and smile equally to both parents (Clarke-Stewart, 1978).

Fathers are salient figures in the lives of babies, beginning to build relationships with them shortly after birth. Observations of and interviews with fathers reveal that they respond to the arrival of their baby in much the same way as mothers. Most characterize the experience as "awesome," "indescribable," or "unforgettable" and display intense interest and involvement in their newborn child (Nichols, 1993). Regardless of their social class or whether they participated in childbirth classes, fathers touch, look at, talk to, and kiss their newborn babies just as much as mothers do (Parke & Tinsley, 1981).

Like mothers', fathers' sensitive caregiving predicts secure attachment—an effect that becomes stronger the more time they spend with their babies (Cox et al., 1992). Also, fathers of 1- to 5-year-olds enrolled in full-time day care because both parents are

■ *When playing with their babies, especially sons, fathers tend to engage in highly physical, bounding and lifting games. (Steve Starr/Stock Boston)*

employed report feeling just as much anxiety about separating from their child and just as much concern about the impact of these daily separations on the child's welfare as do mothers. Today, many fathers seem to "share anxieties that mothers have traditionally borne alone" (Deater-Deckard et al., 1994, p. 346).

As infancy progresses, mothers and fathers from a variety of cultures—Australia, Israel, India, Italy, Japan, and the United States—relate to babies in different ways. Mothers devote more time to physical care and expressing affection. In contrast, fathers spend more time in playful interaction (Lamb, 1987; Roopnarine et al., 1990). Also, when mothers and fathers play with babies, their behaviors tend to be different. Mothers more often provide toys, talk to infants, and initiate conventional games like pat-a-cake and peekaboo. In contrast, fathers tend to engage in more exciting, highly physical bouncing and lifting games, especially with their infant sons (Yogman, 1981). In view of these differences, it is not surprising that babies tend to look to their mothers when distressed and to their fathers for playful stimulation.

However, this picture of "mother as caregiver" and "father as playmate" has changed in some families as a result of the revised work status of women. Employed mothers tend to engage in more playful stimulation of their babies than do unemployed mothers, and their husbands are somewhat more involved in caregiving (Cox et al., 1992). When fathers are the primary caregivers, they usually retain their arousing play style in addition to looking after the baby's physical well-being (Lamb & Oppenheim, 1989). Such highly involved fathers are less gender stereotyped in their beliefs, have sympathetic, friendly personalities, and regard parenthood as an especially enriching experience (Lamb, 1987; Levy-Shiff & Israelashvili, 1988).

A warm marital bond supports both parents' involvement with babies, but cross-cultural evidence suggests that it is particularly important for fathers. Among the Aka hunters and gatherers of Central Africa, fathers devote more time to infant care than in any other known society. The relationship between Aka husband and wife is unusually cooperative and intimate. Throughout the day, they share hunting, food preparation, and social activities. The more they are together, the greater the Aka father's interaction with his baby (Hewlett, 1992b).

Research on fathers as attachment figures reminds us of the complex, multidimensional nature of the infant's social world. No evidence exists to support the commonly held assumption that women are biologically prepared to be more effective caregivers than are men.

ATTACHMENT AND LATER DEVELOPMENT

According to psychoanalytic and ethological theories, the inner feelings of affection and security that result from a healthy attachment relationship support all aspects of psychological development. Consistent with this view, research indicates that quality of attachment to the mother in infancy is related to cognitive and social development in early and middle childhood.

In one longitudinal study, securely attached infants showed more elaborate make-believe play and greater enthusiasm, flexibility, and persistence in problem solving by 2 years of age. At age 4, these children were rated by their preschool teachers as high in self-esteem, socially competent, cooperative, autonomous, popular, and empathic. In contrast, their avoidantly attached peers were viewed as isolated and disconnected, whereas those who were resistantly attached were regarded as disruptive and difficult. Studied again at age 11 while attending a summer camp, children who were secure as infants had more favorable relationships with peers, were more likely to form close friendships, and were judged as more socially skilled by their counselors (Elicker, Englund, & Sroufe, 1992; Matas, Arend, & Sroufe, 1978; Shulman, Elicker, & Sroufe, 1994).

Other studies report similar relationships between infant attachment security and childhood play, problem solving, and social competence (Frankel & Bates, 1990; Suess, Grossmann, & Sroufe, 1992). The consistency of these findings has been taken by some to mean that secure attachment in infancy causes increased cognitive and social competence during later years. Yet more evidence is needed before we can be certain of this conclusion. It is possible that differences in development are largely due to continuity of caregiving rather than the quality of early attachment per se (Lamb et al., 1985). In line with this view, parents who care for their infants in a sensitive, responsive fashion are more likely to provide effective support and guidance as their children move on to the challenges of school and peer relations (Booth, Rose-Krasnor, & Rubin, 1991).

Finally, earlier in this chapter we saw that infants deprived of a familiar caregiver showed long-term adjustment difficulties. But similar outcomes do not always occur for infants who do become attached but for whom the relationship is less than ideal. In some studies, insecurely attached infants developed into children with adjustment problems; in others, they did not (Fagot & Kavanaugh, 1990; Rothbaum et al., 1995). Clearly, more research is needed to determine how attachment security combines with other forces to affect children's internal working models and future development.

BRIEF REVIEW

Compared to behaviorist and psychoanalytic perspectives, ethological theory provides a more effective explanation of the development of attachment. According to this view, infants are biologically prepared to contribute to the attachment bond, which evolved to promote survival. In early infancy, babies' innate signals keep the parent nearby. By 6 to 8 months, separation anxiety and use of the caregiver as a secure base indicate that a true attachment has formed. Representation and language help older children tolerate brief separations from the parent.

Caregiving that is responsive to babies' needs supports the development of secure attachment; insensitive caregiving is linked to attachment insecurity. Infant illness and irritable and fearful temperamental styles make attachment security harder to achieve, but good parenting can override the impact of infant characteristics. Family conditions, including stress, instability, and parents' own attachment experiences as reflected in their internal working models, also contribute to attachment quality. Mothers more often relate to their babies through physical care and expressing affection, fathers through highly active play. Secure infant–mother attachment predicts cognitive and social competence at later ages, but continuity of caregiving may be largely responsible for this association.

Attachment and Social Change: Maternal Employment and Day Care

Over the past two decades, women have entered the labor force in record numbers. Today, over 60 percent of American mothers with a child under age 2 are employed (U.S. Bureau of the Census, 1995). In response to this trend, researchers and laypeople alike have raised questions about the impact of day care and daily separations of infant from parent on the attachment bond.

The Social Issues box on page 418 reviews the current controversy over whether day care threatens the emotional security of young children. As you will see, the weight of evidence suggests that quality of care and family conditions, rather than day care itself, may be the important factors. This conclusion is strengthened by the findings of research in Sweden, where day care is nationally regulated and liberally funded to ensure its high quality. Swedish children who entered day care before their first birthday received higher teacher ratings on cognitive, emotional, and social competence at ages 8 and 13 than did children who started day care later or experienced no day care at all (Andersson, 1989, 1992).

TABLE 10.6

Signs of High-Quality Infant and Toddler Day Care

Program Characteristic	Signs of Quality
Physical setting	Indoor environment is clean, in good repair, well lighted, and well ventilated. Fenced outdoor play space is available. Setting does not appear overcrowded when children are present.
Toys and equipment	Play materials are appropriate for infants and toddlers and stored on low shelves within easy reach. Cribs, highchairs, infant seats, and child-sized tables and chairs are available. Outdoor equipment includes small riding toys, swings, slide, and sandbox.
Caregiver–child ratio	In day care centers, caregiver–child ratio is no greater than 1 to 3 for infants and 1 to 6 for toddlers. Group size (number of children in one room) is no greater than 6 infants with 2 caregivers and 12 toddlers with 2 caregivers. In day care homes, caregiver is responsible for no more than 6 children; within this group, no more than 2 are infants and toddlers. Staffing is consistent, so infants and toddlers can form relationships with particular caregivers.
Daily activities	Daily schedule includes times for active play, quiet play, naps, snacks, and meals. It is flexible rather than rigid, to meet the needs of individual children. Atmosphere is warm and supportive, and children are never left unsupervised.
Interactions among adults and children	Caregivers respond promptly to infants' and toddlers' distress; hold, talk to, sing, and read to them; and interact with them in a contingent manner that respects the individual child's interests and tolerance for stimulation.
Caregiver qualifications	Caregiver has at least some training in child development, first aid, and safety.
Relationships with parents	Parents are welcome anytime. Caregivers talk frequently with parents about children's behavior and development.
Licensing and accreditation	Day care setting, whether a center or home, is licensed by the state. Accreditation by the National Academy of Early Childhood Programs or the National Family Day Care Association is evidence of an especially high-quality program.

SOCIAL ISSUES ➤ POINT OF VIEW

Is Infant Day Care a Threat to Attachment Security?

Recent research suggests that American infants placed in full-time day care before 12 months of age are more likely than home-reared babies to display insecure attachment—especially avoidance—in the Strange Situation. Does this mean that babies who experience daily separations from their employed mothers and early placement in day care are at risk for developmental problems? Some researchers think so (Belsky & Braungart, 1991; Sroufe, 1988), whereas others disagree (Clarke-Stewart, 1989; Scarr, Phillips, & McCartney, 1990). Yet a close look at the evidence reveals that we should be cautious about concluding that day care is harmful to infants.

First, in studies reporting a day care–attachment association, the rate of insecurity among day care infants is only slightly higher than that of home-reared infants (36 versus 29 percent), and it is similar to the overall figure reported for children in industrialized countries around the world (Lamb, Sternberg, & Prodromidis, 1992). In fact, most infants of employed mothers are securely attached! Furthermore, not all investigations report a difference in attachment quality between day care and home-reared infants (Roggman et al., 1994). This suggests that the early emotional development of day care children is within normal range.

Second, we have seen that family conditions affect attachment security. Many employed women find the pressures of handling two full-time jobs (work and motherhood) stressful. Some respond less sensitively to their babies because they are fatigued and harried, thereby risking the infant's security (Owen & Cox, 1988). Other employed mothers probably value and encourage their infant's independence. In these cases, avoidance in the Strange Situation may represent healthy autonomy rather than insecurity (Clarke-Stewart, 1989).

Third, poor-quality day care may contribute to a slightly higher rate of insecure attachment among infants of employed mothers. In one study, babies classified as insecurely attached to both mother and caregiver tended to be placed in day care environments with many children and few adults, where their bids for attention were frequently ignored (Howes et al., 1988).

Finally, when young children first enter day care, they must adjust to new routines and daily separations from the parent. Under these conditions, signs of distress are expected. But after a few months, infants and toddlers enrolled in high-quality programs become more comfortable. They smile, play actively, and begin to interact with agemates. These findings reveal that assessing attachment security during the period of adaptation to day care may not provide an accurate picture of its impact on early emotional adjustment (Fein, Gariboldi, & Boni, 1993). Indeed, having the opportunity to form a warm bond with a stable professional caregiver seems to be particularly helpful to infants whose relationship with one or both parents is insecure. When followed into the preschool and early school years, such children show higher self-esteem and more socially skilled behavior than their insecurely attached agemates who did not attend day care (Egeland & Hiester, 1995).

Taken together, research suggests that a small number of infants may be at risk for attachment insecurity due to inadequate day care and the joint pressures of full-time employment and parenthood experienced by their mothers. However, using this as evidence to justify a reduction in infant day care services is inappropriate. When family incomes are limited or mothers who want to work are forced to stay at home, children's emotional security is not promoted. Instead, it makes sense to increase the availability of high-quality day care and to educate parents about the vital role of sensitive caregiving in early emotional development.

YOUR POINT OF VIEW . . .

- Refer to the signs of high-quality day care in Table 10.6. Which ones are especially important for ensuring early emotional development? Visit a day care program serving infants and toddlers, and evaluate its quality on the basis of these standards. Do you think the program could play a protective role for young children whose attachment relationships with parents are insecure?

Recall from Chapter 1 that in contrast to most Western European countries, the quality of American day care is cause for deep concern (see pages 34–35). Children who enter poor-quality day care during the first year of life and remain there over the preschool years are rated by teachers as distractible, low in task involvement, and inconsiderate of others when they reach kindergarten (Howes, 1990).

Unfortunately, children most likely to receive inadequate day care come from low-income families. Their parents cannot afford to pay for the kind of services they need (Phillips et al., 1994). As a result, these children receive a double dose of vulnerability, both at home and in the day care environment. Table 10.6 lists signs of high-quality care that can be used in choosing a day care setting for an infant or toddler.

Of course, for parents to make this choice, there must be enough good day care available. Recognizing that American day care is in a state of crisis, in 1992 Congress allocated additional funds to upgrade its quality and assist parents—especially those with low incomes—in paying for it (Barnett, 1993). Although far from meeting the total need, the increase in resources has had a positive impact on the quality and accessibility of day care for low-income families (Children's Defense Fund, 1996). This is a hopeful sign, since good day care supports the development of all children, and it can serve as effective early intervention for children whose development is at risk, much like the programs we discussed in Chapter 8. We will return to maternal employment and day care in Chapter 14, when we consider their consequences for development during childhood and adolescence in greater detail.

SUMMARY

THEORIES OF EMOTIONAL DEVELOPMENT

- Three theoretical viewpoints have enhanced our understanding of emotional development. Although some emotional reactions are acquired through conditioning and modeling, behaviorism and social learning theory cannot explain why certain responses emerge spontaneously, without having been learned. Cognitive-developmental **discrepancy theory** is helpful in accounting for children's interest in and exploration of their physical world, but it has difficulty explaining their reactions to people. The **functionalist approach,** which emphasizes that emotions are central, adaptive forces in all aspects of human activity, including cognitive processing, social behavior, and physical health, has the broadest explanatory power.

DEVELOPMENT OF THE EXPRESSION OF DISCRETE EMOTIONS

- Signs of almost all the **basic emotions** are present in infancy. By the middle of the first year, emotional expressions are well organized and meaningfully related to social events. Consequently, they tell us a great deal about the infant's internal state.
- Happiness strengthens the parent–child bond and reflects as well as supports cognitive and physical mastery. The **social smile** appears between 6 and 10 weeks, laughter around 3 to 4 months.
- Anger and fear, especially in the form of **stranger anxiety**, increase in the second half of the first year as infants become better able to evaluate objects and events. These emotions have special adaptive value as infants' motor capacities improve. Once fear develops, infants start to use the familiar caregiver as a **secure base** from which to explore.
- At the end of the second year, self-awareness and socialization experiences provide the foundation for **self-conscious emotions**, such as shame, embarrassment, and pride. Self-conscious emotions become more internally governed with age.
- **Emotional self-regulation**—the ability to adjust emotional arousal to a comfortable level of intensity—emerges from the early infant–caregiver relationship. As motor, cognitive, and language development proceed, children gradually acquire a diverse array of self-regulatory strategies and flexibly adjust them to situational demands. During the preschool years, children start to conform to the **emotional display rules** of their culture. In middle childhood, they become consciously aware of these rules.

UNDERSTANDING AND RESPONDING TO THE EMOTIONS OF OTHERS

- As infants develop the capacity to meaningfully interpret emotional expressions, they actively seek emotional information from others. **Social referencing** appears at the end of the first year. Preschoolers have an impressive understanding of the causes, consequences, and behavioral signs of emotion. The capacity to consider multiple sources of information in interpreting others' feelings develops during middle childhood. Older children also realize that people can experience mixed emotions.
- The development of **empathy** involves a complex interaction of cognition and affect. As self-awareness emerges, 1-year-olds show empathy for the first time. Gains in language, emotional understanding, and perspective taking support an increase in empathic reactions over the childhood years. Parents who are nurturant and display empathic concern and who set clear limits on children's display of inappropriate emotions foster the development of empathy. Empathy is an important motivator of **prosocial**, or **altruistic, behavior**.

TEMPERAMENT AND DEVELOPMENT

- Children differ greatly in **temperament**, or style of emotional responding. Three temperamental patterns—the **easy child**, the **difficult child**, and the **slow-to-warm-up child**—were identified in the New York Longitudinal Study.
- Temperament is often assessed through parental self-reports, although behavior ratings by others familiar with the child and direct observations are also used. Researchers have begun to identify physiological reactions that are markers of temperament. For example, heart rate and electrical activity in the frontal region of the cerebral cortex distinguish **inhibited** from **uninhibited children**.
- Kinship studies reveal that temperament is moderately heritable. They also suggest that nonshared environmental influences are more important than shared influences in contributing to temperament, although not all researchers agree. Ethnic differences in temperament are due to the combined influence of heredity and cultural variations in child rearing.
- Temperament is consistently related to cognitive performance and social behavior throughout childhood. The **goodness-of-fit model** describes how temperament and environmental pressures combine to affect the course of development.

DEVELOPMENT OF ATTACHMENT

- The development of **attachment** has been the subject of intense theoretical debate. Although **drive reduction**, **operant conditioning**, and psychoanalytic explanations exist, the most widely accepted view is **ethological theory of attachment**. It regards babies as biologically prepared to contribute actively to ties established with their caregivers, which promote survival.
- In early infancy, a set of built-in behaviors encourages the parent to remain close to the baby. Around 6 to 8 months, **separation anxiety** and use of the parent as a secure base indicate that a true attachment bond has formed. As representation and language develop, preschoolers better understand the parent's goals, and separation anxiety declines. Out of early caregiving experiences, children construct an **internal working model** that serves as a guide for all future close relationships.
- The **Strange Situation** is the most widely used technique for measuring the quality of attachment between 1 and 2 years of age. A more efficient method, the **Attachment Q-set**, has also become popular. Four attachment classifications have been identified: **secure**, **avoidant**, **resistant**, and **disorganized/disoriented**. Cultural conditions must be considered in interpreting reactions in the Strange Situation.
- A variety of factors affect the development of attachment. Infants deprived of affectional ties with one or a few adults show lasting emotional and social problems. Sensitive, responsive caregiving promotes secure attachment; insensitive caregiving is linked to attachment insecurity. Even ill and temperamentally irritable infants are likely to become securely attached if parents adapt their caregiving to suit the baby's needs. Family conditions, including stress and instability, influence caregiving behavior and the attachment bond. Parents' internal working models show substantial correspondence with their children's attachment bonds in infancy and early childhood.
- Infants establish attachment relationships with a variety of familiar people. Fathers' affectional bonds with their babies are just as emotionally intense as mothers'. When interacting with infants, mothers devote more time to physical care and expressing affection, fathers to stimulating, playful interaction.
- Secure attachment during infancy predicts cognitive and social competence in early and middle childhood. However, continuity of caregiving may mediate this relationship.

ATTACHMENT AND SOCIAL CHANGE: MATERNAL EMPLOYMENT AND DAY CARE

- Today, the majority of American mothers with children under age 2 are employed. Infant day care is associated with a slight risk of attachment insecurity. Poor-quality day care and stressful conditions in some families with employed mothers may be responsible.

IMPORTANT TERMS AND CONCEPTS

discrepancy theory (p. 382)
functionalist approach (p. 383)
basic emotions (p. 387)
social smile (p. 387)
stranger anxiety (p. 388)
secure base (p. 388)
self-conscious emotions (p. 389)
emotional self-regulation (p. 390)
emotional display rules (p. 391)
social referencing (p. 392)
empathy (p. 394)
prosocial, or altruistic, behavior (p. 394)
temperament (p. 397)
easy child (p. 397)
difficult child (p. 397)
slow-to-warm-up child (p. 397)
inhibited child (p. 399)
uninhibited child (p. 399)
goodness-of-fit model (p. 402)
attachment (p. 405)
drive reduction model of attachment (p. 405)
operant conditioning model of attachment (p. 405)
ethological theory of attachment (p. 406)
separation anxiety (p. 407)
internal working model (p. 407)
Strange Situation (p. 408)
secure attachment (p. 408)
avoidant attachment (p. 408)
resistant attachment (p. 408)
disorganized/disoriented attachment (p. 409)
interactional synchrony (p. 411)
Attachment Q-set (p. 409)

CONNECTIONS for Chapter 10

If you are interested in . . .	turn to . . .	to learn about . . .
Emotions and Development	Chapter 3, p. 80	Emotional expressiveness of Down syndrome children
	Chapter 5, pp. 182–183	Pubertal change, emotion, and social behavior
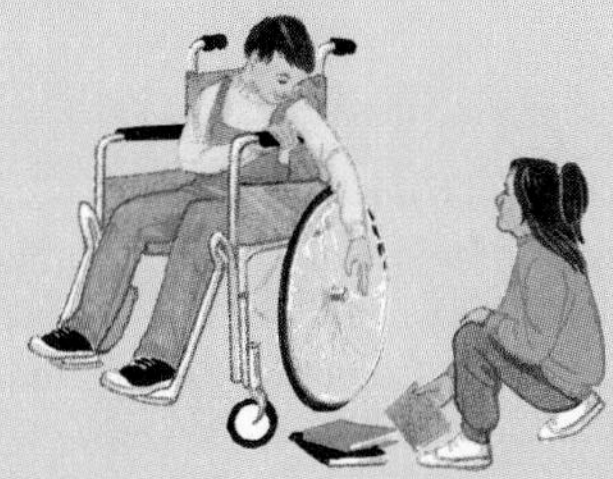	Chapter 11, pp. 436–438	Mastery-oriented versus learned helpless children and achievement motivation
	Chapter 12, p. 464	Inductive discipline, empathy, and conscience development
	Chapter 13, p. 530	Sex-related differences in emotional sensitivity
	Chapter 15, pp. 610–611	Teacher-directed versus child-centered classrooms and young children's emotional well-being
Temperament and Personality	Chapter 3, p. 115	Concordance for schizophrenia, depression, and delinquency and criminality
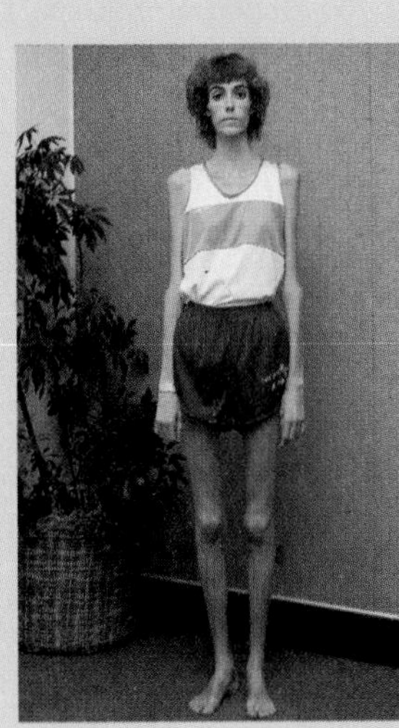	Chapter 5, pp. 191–192	Anorexia nervosa and bulimia
	Chapter 7, p. 270	Attention-deficit hyperactivity disorder
	Chapter 9, p. 356	Personality and language development
	Chapter 11, pp. 439–440	Adolescent identity status and personality
	Chapter 12, p. 465	Temperament and moral internalization
	Chapter 13, pp. 530–533	Sex-related differences in personality
	Chapter 14, pp. 543–545	Child-rearing styles and personality
	Chapter 14, p. 561	Temperament and adjustment to divorce
	Chapter 15, p. 596	Personality and substance abuse
Attachment	Chapter 11, p. 425	Attachment and self-development
	Chapter 11, pp. 449–453	Friendship
	Chapter 12, pp. 464–465	Attachment and moral development
	Chapter 14, pp. 554–556	Sibling relationships
	Chapter 15, p. 580	Peer-only rearing and attachment
	Chapter 15, p. 581	Attachment and peer sociability

11

Self and Social Understanding

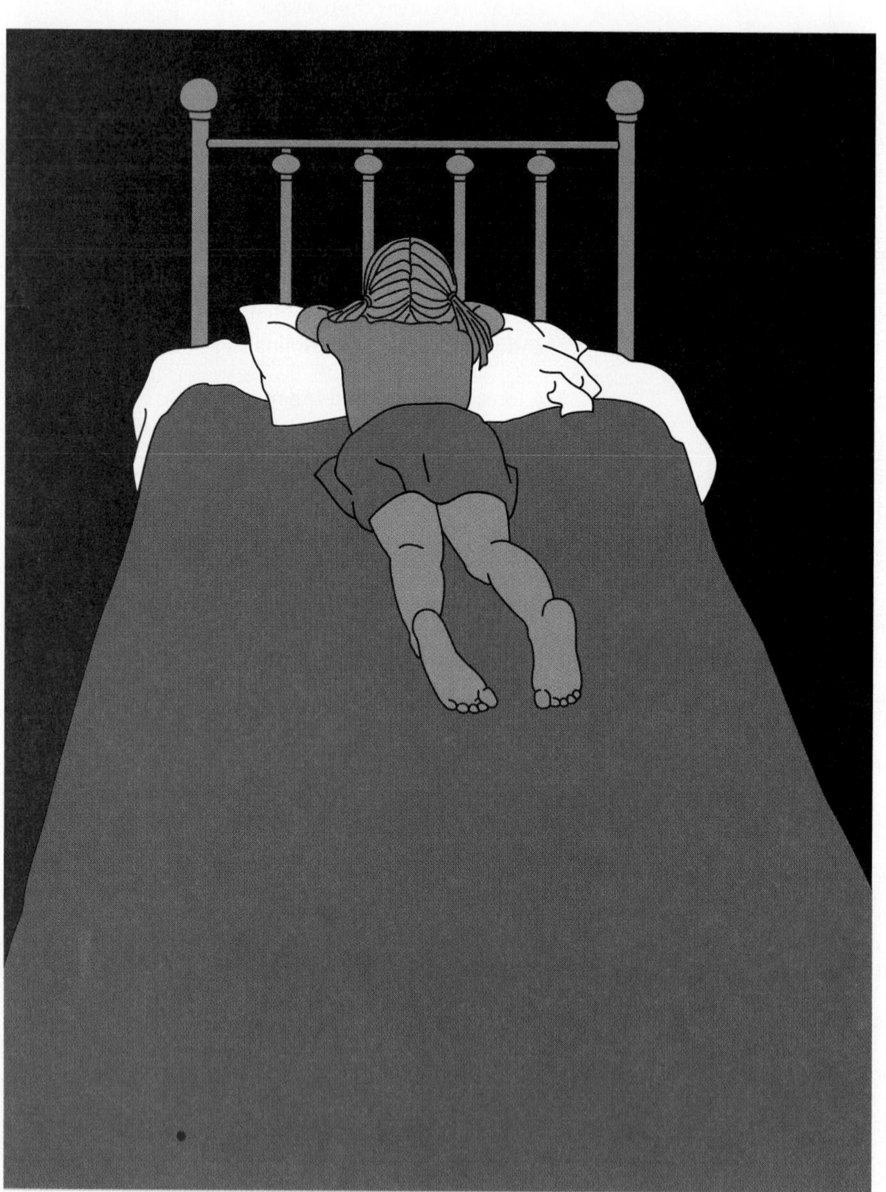

Grandpa, look at my new shirt!" exclaimed 4-year-old Ellen at her family's annual reunion. "See, it's got the three bears on it and their house and . . . ."

Ellen's voice trailed off as she realized all eyes were turned toward her 1-year-old cousin, who was about to take his first steps. As little David tottered forward, the grownups laughed and cheered. No one, not even Grandpa, who was usually so attentive and playful, took note of Ellen and her new shirt.

Ellen felt a twinge of jealousy and retreated to the bedroom, where she threw a blanket over her head. Arms outstretched, she peered through the blanket's loose weave and made her way back to the living room, where she saw Grandpa leading David about the room. "Here I come, the scary ghost," announced Ellen as she purposefully bumped into David, who toppled over and burst into tears.

Pulling off the blanket, Ellen quickly caught her mother's disapproving expression. "I couldn't see him, Mom! The blanket was over my face," Ellen sheepishly explained.

Ellen's mother insisted that she help David up and apologize at once. At the same time, she marveled at Ellen's skillful capacity for trickery.

This chapter addresses the development of **social cognition**, or how children come to understand their multifaceted social world. Like our discussion of cognitive development in Chapters 6 and 7, the changes to which we now turn are concerned with matters of thinking about and interpreting experience. But the experience of interest is no longer the child's physical surroundings. Instead, it is the inner characteristics of the self and other people.

Researchers interested in social cognition seek answers to questions like these: When do infants first discover that they are separate beings, distinct from other people and objects? How does children's understanding of their own and others' mental lives change with age? For example, what new realizations underlie Ellen's creative act of deception? When a 10-year-old calls another child "my best friend," what does he mean? In what ways are his ideas about friendship different from those of preschoolers, and how will they change during adolescence?

As we answer these and other questions, you will see that many of the trends we identified for nonsocial thinking also apply to children's understanding of their social world. Like nonsocial cognition, social cognition develops from *concrete* to *abstract*. Children first notice observable characteristics—the appearance and behavior of themselves and other people. Soon after, they become aware of internal processes—the existence of desires, beliefs, intentions, abilities, and attitudes. Social cognition also becomes *better organized* with age, as children gather together separate behaviors into an appreciation of their own and others' personalities and identities. In addition, children revise their ideas about the causes of people's behavior—from *simple, one-sided explanations* to *complex interacting relationships* that take into account both person and situational variables. Finally, social cognition moves toward a *metacognitive level of understanding*. As children get older, their thinking is no longer limited to social reality. They also think about their own and other people's social thoughts.

Although nonsocial and social cognition share many features, they differ in important respects. Consider, for a moment, how much easier it is to predict the motions of physical objects, such as a rolling ball, than the actions of people. Movements of things can be fully understood from the physical forces that act on them. In contrast, the behavior of people is not simply the result of others' actions toward them. It is also determined by inner states that cannot be observed directly.

In view of this complexity, we might expect social cognition to develop more slowly than nonsocial cognition. Yet surprisingly, it does not. We will see that children demonstrate some sophisticated understandings at early ages, even though others take a long

Social cognition
Thinking about the self, other people, and social relationships.

time to develop. Unique features of social experience probably help children make early sense of its complexity. First, the fact that people are animated beings and objects of deep emotional investment makes them especially interesting to think about. Second, social experience continually presents children with discrepancies between behaviors they expect and those that occur, which prompts them to revise their thoughts about social concerns. Finally, children and the people with whom they interact are all human beings, with the same basic nervous system and a shared background of experiences. This means that interpreting behavior from the self's point of view often helps us understand others' actions. When it does not, humans are equipped with a unique capacity—*perspective taking*—that permits them to imagine what another's thoughts and feelings might be. Perspective taking is so important for psychological development that we have already mentioned it many times in earlier parts of this book, and we will devote considerable attention to it in this chapter.

Our discussion is organized around three aspects of social-cognitive development: thinking about the self, thinking about other people, and thinking about relationships among people. Perhaps you have noticed that we have already considered some social-cognitive topics in previous chapters. Good examples are referential communication skills in Chapter 9 and emotional understanding in Chapter 10. Children's sense of morality is another important social-cognitive topic, but research on it is so extensive that it merits a chapter of its own. We will consider the development of moral reasoning in Chapter 12.

Thinking About the Self

Virtually all investigators agree that two distinct aspects of the self, first identified by philosopher William James (1890/1963) over a century ago, emerge and become more refined with age. The first is the "I," or the *existential self*—the part that initiates, organizes, and interprets experience. The "I" includes the following realizations: that the self is separate from the surrounding world, can act on and gain a sense of control over its environment, has a private, inner life not accessible to others, and maintains a continuous existence over time. The second facet of the self is the "me," a *reflective observer* that treats the self as an object of knowledge and evaluation by sizing up its diverse attributes. It consists of all qualities that make the self unique—material characteristics, such as physical appearance and possessions; mental characteristics, including desires, attitudes, beliefs, and thought processes; and social characteristics, such as personality traits, roles, and relationships with others.

Self-understanding begins with the dawning of self-awareness in the second year of life and gradually evolves into a rich, multifaceted view of the self's characteristics and

■ *This infant notices the correspondence between his own movements and the movements of the image in the mirror, a cue that helps him figure out that the grinning baby is really himself. (Paul Damien/Tony Stone Worldwide)*

capacities over childhood and adolescence. As we trace the blossoming of this increasingly elaborate and organized image of the self, we will see that the "I" and the "me" are intimately intertwined and influence each other.

EMERGENCE OF SELF-RECOGNITION

Self-recognition refers to perception of the self as a separate being, distinct from people and objects in the surrounding world. As early as the first few months of life, infants smile and return friendly behaviors to their reflection in a mirror. At what age do they realize that the charming baby gazing and grinning back is really the self?

To answer this question, researchers have conducted clever laboratory observations in which they expose infants and toddlers to images of themselves in mirrors, on videotapes, and in still photographs. In one study, 9- to 24-month-olds were placed in front of a mirror. Then, under the pretext of wiping the baby's face, each mother was asked to dab red dye on her infant's nose. Younger infants touched the mirror, as if the red mark had nothing to do with any aspect of themselves. But by 15 months, children began to rub their strange-looking little red noses, a response that rose steadily until age 2 (Lewis & Brooks-Gunn, 1979). In addition, some toddlers entertain themselves by acting silly or coy in front of the mirror—actions that also signify the beginnings of self-recognition (Bullock & Lutkenhaus, 1990).

At first, babies react to *contingency cues* when presented with their own moving image. A "live" video playback of their actions prompted 9- to 12-month-olds to play a kind of peek-a-boo game in which they moved their head, body, or hand in and out of the camera's view, a pattern of behavior that increased with age. By the middle of the second year, toddlers respond to *featural cues,* which have to do with their unique visual appearance. They behave differently when shown a film of another child rather than one of themselves—smiling, moving toward, and attending more closely to the unfamiliar toddler but imitating and trying contingent play with the self. Around age 2, recognition of the self is well established. Children look and smile more at a photo of themselves than one of another child. And almost all use their name or a personal pronoun ("I" or "me") to refer to themselves (Lewis & Brooks-Gunn, 1979).

■ *The struggle between these 2-year-olds over an attractive toy is a sign of developing selfhood. At first, children often assert their sense of self by becoming more possessive about objects. The ability to distinguish self from other also permits young children to learn how to resolve disputes and share. (Crews/The Image Works)*

■ THE IMPORTANCE OF A SENSE OF AGENCY. How do toddlers develop an awareness of the self's existence? As yet, little evidence is available to answer this question. Many theorists believe that the beginnings of self lie in infants' developing *sense of agency*—recognition that their own actions cause objects and people to react in predictable ways. In support of this idea, securely attached toddlers, whose parents have responded to their signals consistently and sensitively, are advanced in performance on agency tasks requiring them to engage in self- and mother-directed actions during make-believe play. They also show more complex featural knowledge of themselves and their parents (Pipp, Easterbrooks, & Brown, 1993; Pipp, Easterbrooks, & Harmon, 1992).

Once infants construct a sense of agency and explore their surroundings confidently, they notice different effects that may help them sort out self from other people and objects. For example, batting a mobile and seeing it swing in a pattern different from the infant's own actions informs the baby about the relation between self and physical world. Smiling and vocalizing at a caregiver who smiles and vocalizes back helps specify the relation between self and social world. And watching the movement of one's own hand provides still another kind of feedback—one under much more direct control than other people or objects. The contrast among these experiences may help infants build an image of self as separate from external reality (Lewis, 1991).

■ SELF-RECOGNITION AND EARLY EMOTIONAL AND SOCIAL DEVELOPMENT. Self-awareness quickly becomes a central part of children's emotional and social lives. At first, children's sense of self is so bound up with particular possessions and actions that they spend much time asserting their rights to objects. In one study, 2-year-olds' ability to distinguish between self and other was assessed. Then each child was observed interacting with a peer in a laboratory playroom. The stronger the children's self-definitions, the more possessive they were about objects, claiming them as "Mine!" This was despite the fact that the playroom contained duplicates of many toys (Levine, 1983). These findings suggest that rather than being a sign of selfishness, early struggles over objects are a sign of developing selfhood, an effort to clarify boundaries between self and other.

Self-recognition
Perception of the self as a separate being, distinct from people and objects in the surrounding world.

Besides prompting children's first disagreements, the ability to distinguish self from other supports the emergence of a wide variety of emotional and social skills. In Chapter 10, we saw that self-conscious emotions depend on self-awareness. Toddlers who pass the mirror self-recognition task are more likely to display empathy, prosocial behavior, and imitative play with adults and peers (Asendorpf, Warkentin, & Baudonnière, 1996; Bischof-Köhler, 1991). The ability to distinguish self from other also permits children to cooperate for the first time in playing games, solving simple problems, and resolving disputes over objects (Brownell & Carriger, 1990; Caplan et al., 1991).

Once children become self-aware, they use their representational and language capacities to relate themselves to other people, in much the same way that they group together physical objects (see Chapter 6). Between 18 and 30 months, children develop a **categorical self** as they classify themselves and others according to salient ways in which people differ, such as age ("baby," "boy," or "man"), sex ("boy" versus "girl" and "woman" versus "man"), physical characteristics ("big," "strong"), and even goodness and badness ("I good girl." "Tommy mean!"). They also start to refer to the self's competencies ("Did it!" "I can't") (Stipek, Gralinski, & Kopp, 1990). These are the first steps toward developing a psychological self—a major achievement of the childhood years.

YOUNG CHILDREN'S THEORY OF MIND

As children think more about themselves and others, they begin to form a naive *theory of mind*—a coherent understanding of their own and other's rich mental lives. Recall from Chapter 7 that after age 2½, children refer to mental states, such as "want," "think," and "pretend," frequently and appropriately in everyday language. Although they confuse certain mental terms (see page 283), young preschoolers are clearly aware of an *inner self* of private thoughts and imaginings.

What is the young child's view of the inner self like, and how does it change with age? Investigators are interested in answering this question because ideas about the mind are powerful tools in predicting and explaining our own and others' everyday behavior. Just as we cannot make sense of the physical world without a grasp of time, space, and the permanence of objects, so we cannot understand the social world without a theory of mind.

Research reveals that 2-year-olds have only a primitive grasp of the distinction between mental life and behavior. They think that people always behave in ways consistent with their desires and do not understand that a person's beliefs affect his actions (Wellman & Woolley, 1990). According to Henry Wellman (1990), from age 3 or 4 on, children's ideas about how the mind works are differentiated, organized, and accurate enough to qualify as a theory. Older preschoolers know that both *beliefs* and *desires* determine *actions,* and they understand the relationship among these three constructs. For example, turn back to the beginning of this chapter, and notice how 4-year-old Ellen deliberately tried to alter her mother's belief about the real motive behind her pretending—in hopes of warding off any desire on her mother's part to punish her. Wellman labels Ellen's more sophisticated view of the mind a **belief–desire theory**—a conception of mentality that closely resembles the everyday psychology of adults.

■ DEVELOPMENT OF BELIEF-DESIRE REASONING. To explore the emergence of belief–desire reasoning, researchers have presented children with stories about actors desiring or not desiring an outcome and believing or not believing it would happen. Then the outcome either happens or does not happen. Here is one example:

> Lisa wants it to be sunny today because she wants to play on her new swingset. But, Lisa thinks it's going to rain today. She thinks it's going to rain because she heard the weather man say it might rain. Look, it rains. (Wellman & Banerjee, 1991, p. 194)

Children are asked to indicate how Lisa would feel—happy or unhappy (a desire-related emotion) and surprised or unsurprised (a belief-related emotion). Both 3- and 4-year-olds easily give the appropriate desire-related feeling. They know that Lisa will be happy if she gets the weather she wants and unhappy if she does not (Hadwin & Perner, 1991; Wellman & Bartsch, 1988). And when the interviewing method is changed to clarify the meaning of emotional terms (preschoolers often confuse surprise with happiness),

Categorical self
Early classification of the self according to salient ways in which people differ, such as age, sex, and physical characteristics.

Belief–desire theory of mind
The theory of mind that emerges around age 4 in which both beliefs and desires determine behavior and that closely resembles the everyday psychology of adults.

FIGURE 11.1

■ *Game used to assess belief–desire reasoning. The child hides the driver of a toy truck underneath one of five cups in a sandbox so an adult, not in the room, cannot find it. The experimenter points out that the truck leaves telltale tracks in the sand as a sign of where it has been. Children who understand that people can hold false beliefs think of smoothing over the tracks to the driver's actual location, returning the truck to its starting place, and even laying false tracks to mislead the adult. (Adapted from Sodian et al., 1991.)*

even 3-year-olds display some awareness that surprise occurs in situations that violate prior beliefs, a response that becomes consistent around age 4 (Wellman & Banerjee, 1991).

A more dramatic illustration of belief–desire reasoning comes from games in which preschoolers are asked to mislead an adult. By age 4, children realize that people can hold *false beliefs* that combine with desire to determine behavior (Perner, 1991). In one study, 2 ½- to 4-year-olds were asked to hide the driver of a toy truck underneath one of five cups in a sandbox so that an adult, who happened to be out of the room, could not find it (see Figure 11.1). An experimenter alerted the child to the fact that the truck, after delivering the driver to the cup, left telltale tracks in the sand as a sign of where it had been. Most 2- and 3-year-olds needed explicit prompts to hide the evidence—smoothing over the tracks and returning the truck to its starting place. In contrast, 4-year-olds thought of doing these things on their own. They were also more likely to trick the adult by laying false tracks or giving incorrect information about where the driver was hidden (Sodian et al., 1991). Other research confirms that children's understanding of the role of false belief in guiding their own and others' actions strengthens over the preschool years, becoming more secure between ages 4 and 6 (Astington & Gopnik, 1991; Robinson & Mitchell, 1994; Wimmer & Hartl, 1991).

Preschoolers' mastery of false belief is a remarkable achievement. It signals a major advance in representation—the ability to view beliefs as *interpretations,* not just reflections, of reality. Does this remind you of the more active, reflective view of the mind that children develop as they move into middle childhood, discussed in Chapter 7? Perhaps belief–desire reasoning marks the beginnings of this overall change (Leekam, 1993). Interestingly, a grasp of false belief is associated with language ability equivalent to a child of age 4 or higher (Jenkins & Astington, 1996). This suggests that common representational capacities underlie gains in language and theory of mind at the end of the preschool years.

Children pass false belief tasks at about the same age among the Baka, a hunting and gathering people of Cameroon, West Africa, as in European and North American countries (Avis & Harris, 1991). The existence of a similar timetable of development in such different cultures strengthens the possibility that belief–desire reasoning is a universal feature of early childhood development.

■ WHERE DOES A THEORY OF MIND ORIGINATE? How do children manage to develop a theory of mind at such a young age? There are various speculations. Perhaps belief–desire reasoning originates in certain preverbal communicative acts, such as joint attention and social referencing, which require a beginning ability to represent another's mental state (Sigman & Kasari, 1995). Imitation may also contribute to an early grasp of

■ *Children with infantile autism are indifferent to other people, display poor knowledge of social rules, and show delayed or absent language development. Recent evidence suggests that they suffer from a specific impairment in reasoning about their own and others' mental states. (Andy Levin/Photo Researchers)*

mentality. Infants' primitive plan to copy an action, located inside the body, has much of the character of mental states. At the same time, imitation teaches infants that other people are like themselves. Perhaps this prompts them to conclude that others are also mental beings (Meltzoff & Gopnik, 1993). Make-believe play provides another foundation for thinking about the mind. As children observe themselves using one object to represent another, they notice that the mind can change what objects mean. These experiences may trigger an awareness of belief in determining behavior (Leslie, 1988).

Many researchers believe children are biologically prepared to develop a theory of mind, in much the same way they are primed to acquire language. The importance of an early grasp of mental states for normal development is tragically illustrated by children with infantile autism, who are indifferent to other people, display poor knowledge of social rules, and show delayed or absent language development. Recent evidence suggests that autistic individuals suffer from a specific impairment in mental reasoning and in the early capacities believed to underlie it. They fail tasks that require an understanding of others' cognitive states, and their vocabularies rarely contain such words as "believe," "think," "know," and "pretend." In addition, their ability to imitate and engage in make-believe play is limited. Yet other cognitive skills—especially those that involve the physical world—are intact (Baron-Cohen, 1991; Tager-Flusberg & Sullivan, 1994).

These findings support the assumption that the normal human brain is specially tuned to develop a belief–desire theory. At the same time, social experience clearly contributes. Preschoolers with siblings are advanced in performance on false belief tasks. And those with two siblings do better than those with only one (Jenkins & Astington, 1996). The presence of siblings may allow for more interactions in which the impact of beliefs on behavior is evident—through teasing, tricking another, and talking about internal states.

At older ages, children distinguish more clearly among different cognitive and emotional states (see Chapters 7 and 10) and between their own mental state and that of others, as we will see when we take up the development of perspective taking in a later section. Theorizing about the mind is a long developmental process, and we will add to our understanding of it throughout this chapter.

DEVELOPMENT OF SELF-CONCEPT

As children develop an appreciation of their inner mental world, they think more intently about themselves. During early childhood, they start to construct a **self-concept**, the sum total of attributes, abilities, attitudes, and values that an individual believes defines who he or she is. Studies in which children have been asked to describe themselves indicate that preschoolers' self-concepts are largely based on concrete characteristics, such as names, physical appearance, possessions, and typical behaviors. For example, in one investigation of 3- to 5-year-olds, the most frequently mentioned attributes were typical actions, such as "I go to school," "I can wash my hair by myself," and "I help Mommy" (Keller, Ford, & Meacham, 1978). These findings indicate, in agreement with Piaget and other theorists, that acting on the environment and finding out what one can do provide an especially important early basis for self-definition (Damon & Hart, 1988; Piaget, 1954).

But preschoolers' understanding of themselves is not limited to observable attributes. When questioned in a way that evokes descriptions of commonly experienced emotions and attitudes, children as young as 3½ demonstrate that they have begun to appreciate their unique psychological characteristics. For example, they describe themselves in ways like this: "I'm happy when I play with my friends" or "I don't like being with grown-ups" (Eder, 1989). And when read statements and asked to tell whether they are true of themselves (a much easier task than producing a self-description), 3½-year-olds often respond consistently. For example, a preschooler who says that she "doesn't push in front of other people in line" is also likely to indicate that she "feels like being quiet when angry" and "usually does what Mommy or the teacher says," as if she implicitly recognizes that she is high in self-control (Eder, 1990).

Over time, children organize these internal states and behaviors into dispositions that they are aware of and can verbalize to others. Between ages 8 and 11, a major shift

Self-concept
The sum total of attributes, abilities, attitudes, and values that an individual believes defines who he or she is.

takes place in children's self-descriptions, which begin to mention personality traits. Look at the following examples, and you will see evidence for this change.

> *A boy, age 7:* I am 7 and I have hazel brown hair and my hobby is stamp collecting. I am good at football and I am quite good at sums and my favourite game is football and I love school and I like reading books and my favourite car is an Austin. (Livesley & Bromley, 1973, p. 237)

> *A girl, age 11½:* My name is A. I'm a human being. I'm a girl. I'm a truthful person. I'm not pretty. I do so-so in my studies. I'm a very good cellist. I'm a very good pianist. I'm a little bit tall for my age. I like several boys. I like several girls. I'm old-fashioned. I play tennis. I am a very good swimmer. I try to be helpful. I'm always ready to be friends with anybody. Mostly I'm good, but I lose my temper. I'm not well-liked by some girls and boys. I don't know if I'm liked by boys or not. (Montemayor & Eisen, 1977, pp. 317–318)

> *A girl, almost age 13:* I have a fairly quick temper and it doesn't take much to rouse me. I can be a little bit sympathetic to the people I like, but to the poor people I dislike my temper can be shown quite easily. I'm not thoroughly honest, I can tell a white lie here and there when it's necessary, but I am trying my hardest to redeem myself, as after experience I've found it's not worth it. If I cannot get my way with various people I walk away and most likely never talk to that person again. I take an interest in other people and I like to hear about their problems as more than likely they can help me solve my own. My friends are used to me now and I don't really worry them. I worry a bit after I have just yelled somebody out and more than likely I am the first to apologize. (Livesley & Bromley, 1973, p. 239)

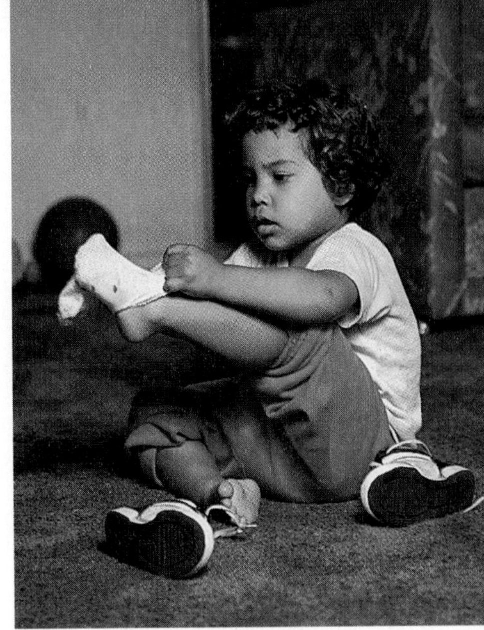

■ *Acting on the world is an especially important source of self-definition to preschoolers. When questioned about her self-concept, this child is likely to describe typicaly behaviors, such as "I can dress myself." She may also mention commonly experienced emotions and attitudes, indicating that she has a beginning appreciation of her unique psychological characteristics. (Mary Kate/Photo Edit)*

Notice that instead of specific behaviors, older children emphasize competencies, as in: "I am quite good at sums" or "I'm a very good cellist" (Damon & Hart, 1988). In addition, the number of psychological attributes increases with age. At first, children mention overall qualities—"smart," "honest," "friendly," "truthful," and "able to control my temper." When these general ideas about the self are firmly in place, adolescents start to qualify them: "I have a *fairly* quick temper," "I'm *not thoroughly* honest." This trend reflects an understanding that psychological qualities often change from one situation to the next (Barenboim, 1977). Finally, adolescents' self-descriptions place somewhat greater emphasis on social virtues, such as being considerate and cooperative, which reflects their greater concern with being liked and viewed positively by others (Rosenberg, 1979).

COGNITIVE, SOCIAL, AND CULTURAL INFLUENCES ON SELF-CONCEPT

What factors are responsible for these revisions in self-concept? Cognitive development certainly affects the changing *structure* of the self. School-age children, as we saw in Chapter 6, are better at coordinating several aspects of a situation and reasoning about their physical world. They also show an improved ability to relate separate observations in the social realm, combining typical experiences and behaviors into stable personality traits. In addition, by middle childhood, children have a clearer understanding of traits as causes of behavior and, for this reason, mention them more often (Paget & Kritt, 1986; Yuill, 1993).

The *content* of the developing self-concept, however, is largely derived from interaction with others. Early in this century, sociologists C. H. Cooley (1902) and George Herbert Mead (1934) described the self as a blend of what we imagine important people in our lives think of us. Mead called this reflected or social self the **generalized other**. He indicated that a well-organized, psychological self develops when children can comprehend the attitudes others take toward them. Mead's ideas indicate that *perspective-taking skills*—in particular, an improved ability to imagine what other people are thinking—are a crucial factor in the development of self-concept. Indeed, as we will see later in this chapter, perspective taking improves greatly over middle childhood and adolescence. Consequently, older children are better at reading the messages they receive from others and incorporating these into their self-definitions (Rosenberg, 1979). Consistent with the operation of the generalized other, both teacher and peer appraisals of fourth graders' competence are strong predictors of the adjustments they make in their self-concepts over the school year (Cole, 1991).

Generalized other
A blend of what we imagine important people in our lives think of us; determines the content of self-concept.

■ *During the school years, children's self-concepts expand to include feedback from a wider range of people as they spend more time in settings beyond the home. Girl scouting and its associated qualities of friendliness, helpfulness, and kindness are probably important aspects of the self-definitions of these two girls. (Joel Gordon)*

During middle childhood, children look to more people for information about themselves as they enter a wider range of settings in school and community. This is reflected in school-age children's frequent reference to social groups, such as scouting and athletic leagues, in their self-descriptions (Livesley & Bromley, 1973). Gradually, as children move into adolescence, their sources of self-definition become more selective. Although parents remain influential, between ages 8 and 15, peers become more important. And over time, self-concept becomes increasingly vested in the feedback children receive from their close friends (Rosenberg, 1979).

Finally, it is important to note that the changes we have described are based entirely on interviews with North American and Western European children. Cross-cultural research indicates that development of self-concept does not follow the same path in all societies. In cultures that value the collective over the individual, the self and social group are not differentiated so completely. Recall from earlier chapters that Asian parents stress harmonious interdependence with others, whereas Western parents emphasize the self's uniqueness and the importance of asserting the self. Consequently, in China and Japan, the self is defined in relation to the social group. In the United States, the self (once formed through social experience) usually becomes the "property" of a self-contained individual (Markus & Kitayama, 1991).

Yet even in Western nations, a strong theme of interdependence is reflected in the values of many subcultures. William Damon and Daniel Hart (1988) compared the self-descriptions of children in a Puerto Rican fishing village with those of children in an American town. Puerto Rican children more often characterized themselves as "polite," "nice," "respectful," and "obedient" and justified these social traits by noting the positive reactions they evoke from family members and friends. In contrast, American children more often mentioned individualistic traits, such as interests, preferences, and cognitive and social skills. In characterizing themselves, children from individualistic cultures seem to be more egoistic and competitive, those from collectivist cultures more concerned with the welfare of others—a finding that underscores the powerful impact of the social environment on the makeup of self-concept.

SELF-ESTEEM: THE EVALUATIVE SIDE OF SELF-CONCEPT

So far, we have focused on how the general structure and content of self-concept change with age. Another component of self-concept is **self-esteem**, the judgments we make about our own worth and the feelings associated with those judgments. According to Morris Rosenberg (1979), "a person with high self-esteem is fundamentally satisfied with the type of person he is, yet he may acknowledge his faults while hoping to overcome them" (p. 31). High self-esteem implies a realistic evaluation of the self's characteristics and competencies, coupled with an attitude of self-acceptance and self-respect.

Self-esteem
An aspect of self-concept that involves judgments about one's own worth and the feelings associated with those judgments.

Self-esteem ranks among the most important aspects of children's social-cognitive development. Children's evaluations of their own competencies affect their emotional experiences and future behavior in similar situations as well as their long-term psychological adjustment. Research reveals that as soon as a categorical self with features that can be judged positively and negatively is in place, children start to become self-evaluative beings. Around age 2, they call a parent's attention to an achievement, such as completing a puzzle, by pointing and saying something like "Look, Mom!" In addition, 2-year-olds are likely to smile when they succeed at a task set for them by an adult and look away or frown when they fail (Stipek, Recchia, & McClintic, 1992). Furthermore, recall from Chapter 10 that by age 3, self-conscious emotions of pride and shame are clearly linked to self-evaluation (see page 390). Self-esteem originates early in life, and (as we will see in the next section) its structure becomes increasingly elaborate over the childhood years.

ONE SELF-ESTEEM OR MANY? Take a moment to think about your own self-esteem. Besides a global appraisal of your worth as a person, you have a variety of separate self-judgments concerning how well you perform in different settings and activities. As early as the preschool years, children distinguish how they feel about various aspects of the self. In fact, children seem to develop an array of separate self-esteems first, only later integrating them into an overall impression (Harter, 1983, 1990).

Researchers have studied the multifaceted nature of self-esteem in the same way they have explored the question of whether there is one intelligence or many: by applying factor analysis[1] to children's ratings of themselves on many characteristics. For example, Susan Harter (1982, 1986) asked children to indicate the extent to which a variety of statements, such as "I am good at homework," "I'm usually the one chosen for games," and "Most kids like me," are true of themselves. Her findings reveal that before age 7, children distinguish how well others like them (social acceptance) from how "good" they are at doing things (competence). And when procedures are specially adapted for young children—for example, by questioning them individually and showing pictures of what each statement means—their sense of self-worth appears even more differentiated (Marsh, Craven, & Debus, 1991).

By 7 to 8 years, children have formed at least three separate self-esteems—academic, physical, and social—that become more refined with age. For example, academic self-worth divides into performance in different school subjects, social self-worth into peer and parental relationships (Marsh, 1990). Furthermore, school-age children combine their separate self-evaluations into a general appraisal of themselves—an overall sense of self-worth (Harter, 1990). Consequently, during middle childhood, self-esteem takes on the hierarchical structure shown in Figure 11.2 on page 432.

With the arrival of adolescence, several new dimensions of self-esteem are added—close friendship, romantic appeal, and job competence—that reflect salient concerns of this period. Furthermore, the hierarchical structure of self-esteem is reflected even more clearly in factor analytic studies, and it is similar for young people of different social classes and ethnic groups (Cauce, 1987; Harter, 1990; Marsh & Gouvernet, 1989).

CHANGES IN LEVEL OF SELF-ESTEEM. Once self-esteem is established, does it remain stable or does it fluctuate? Many studies show that self-esteem is very high during early childhood. Then it drops over the first few years of elementary school as children start to make **social comparisons**—that is, judge their abilities, behavior, appearance, and other characteristics in relation to those of others (Marsh et al., 1984; Stipek & MacIver, 1989). In one investigation, kindergartners through third graders rated their own and each of their classmates' "smartness" at school. Pupils in all grades could give estimates of classmates' abilities that were similar to those teachers gave. But the self-ratings of kindergartners and first graders were overly favorable and unrelated to teacher or peer judgments. Not until second grade did pupil self-ratings resemble the opinions of others (Stipek, 1981). In another study, second graders could make use of their own score along with the scores of several peers in judging their own task performance, but younger pupils could not (Ruble et al., 1980). Once children enter school, they receive frequent feedback about themselves in relation to their classmates. In addition, they become cognitively better able to make sense of such information. As a result, self-esteem adjusts to a more realistic level that matches the opinions of others as well as objective performance.

[1] If you need to review the meaning of factor analysis, return to Chapter 8, page 301.

Social comparisons
Judgments of abilities, behavior, appearance, and other characteristics in relation to those of others.

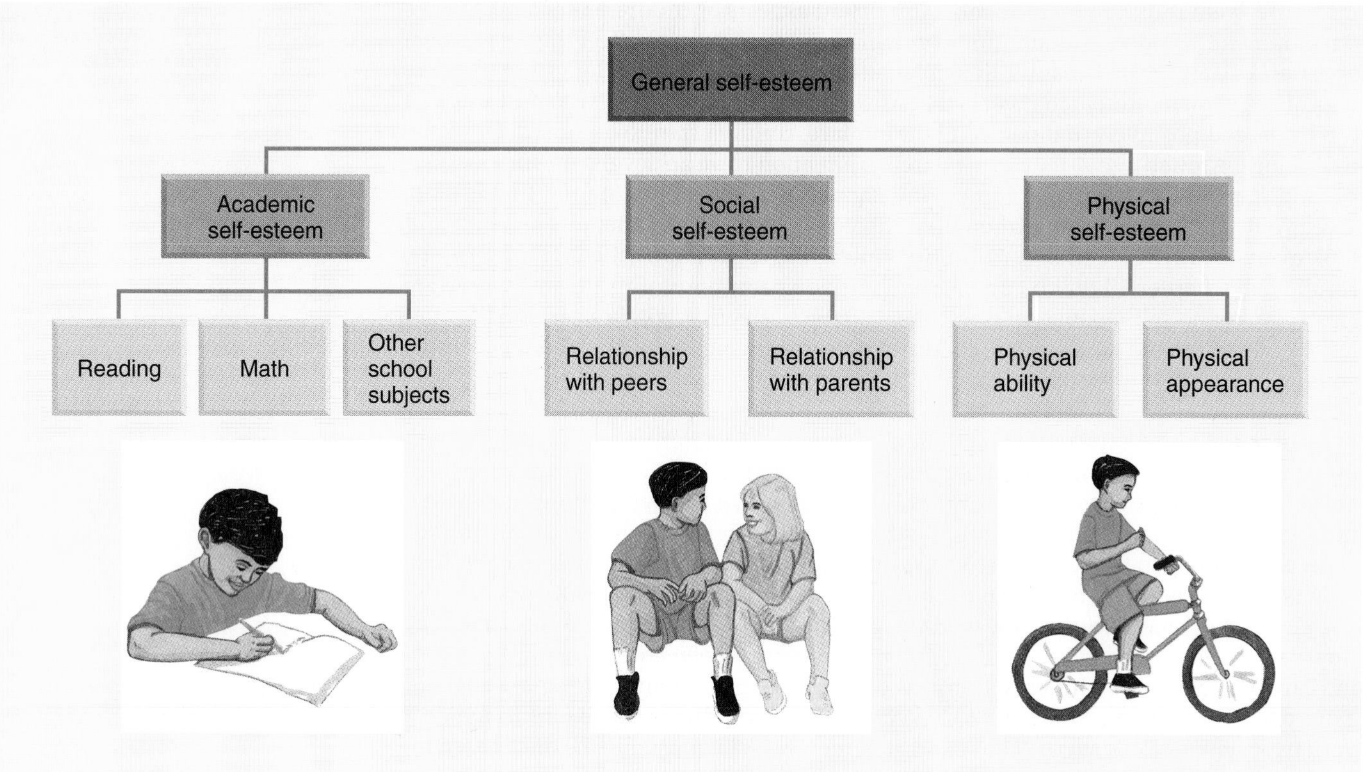

FIGURE 11.2

■ *Hierarchical structure of self-esteem in middle childhood. From their experiences in different settings, children form at least three separate self-esteems—academic, social, and physical. These differentiate into additional self-evaluations and combine to form an overall sense of self-worth.*

Typically, the drop in self-esteem is not great enough to be harmful. In fact, from fourth grade on, self-esteem rises for the majority of young people (Nottelmann, 1987). The only exceptions to this trend are a temporary decline in self-worth associated with the transition to junior high school and, occasionally, to high school. Entry into a new school, accompanied by new expectations by teachers and peers, may interfere with adolescents' ability to make realistic judgments about their behavior and performance for a period of time. In Chapter 15, we will take up these school transition effects in greater detail.

The increase in self-esteem just described is yet another reason that modern researchers question the widespread assumption discussed in Chapter 5—that adolescence is a time of emotional turmoil. To the contrary, the rise in self-worth suggests that for most young people, becoming an adolescent leads to feelings of pride and self-confidence (Powers, Hauser, & Kilner, 1989). This is true not just in the United States, but around the world. A study of self-esteem in 10 industrialized countries showed that the majority of teenagers had an optimistic outlook on life, a positive attitude toward school and work, and faith in their ability to cope with life's problems (Offer, 1988).

INFLUENCES ON SELF-ESTEEM

Up to this point, we have discussed general trends in the development of self-esteem. There are also wide individual differences that are strongly correlated with everyday behavior. For example, academic self-esteem predicts children's school achievement as well as their willingness to try hard at challenging tasks (Marsh, Smith, & Barnes, 1985). Children with high social self-esteem are consistently better liked by their peers (Harter, 1982). And as we saw in Chapter 5, boys come to believe they have more athletic talent than do girls, and they are also more advanced in a variety of physical skills.

Because self-esteem is so powerfully related to behavior, researchers have been intensely interested in uncovering factors that cause it to be high for some children and low for others. If ways can be found to improve children's sense of self-worth, then many aspects of child development might be enhanced as well.

■ CULTURE. Cultural forces have a profound impact on self-esteem. For example, in Chapter 5 we noted that during adolescence, early maturing girls and late maturing boys tend to feel poorly about themselves—outcomes influenced by cultural standards of physical beauty. Gender-stereotyped expectations for physical attractiveness and achievement have an especially detrimental effect on the self-esteem of girls. Beginning in adolescence, they score substantially lower than boys in overall sense of self-worth—partly because girls worry more about their appearance and partly because they feel more insecure about their abilities (Block & Robins, 1994).

Furthermore, the strong role of social comparison in self-esteem does not characterize children everywhere. Puerto Rican fishing village children, discussed earlier in this chapter, almost never make statements referring to social comparisons. Yet among American children, such statements are common, both in self-descriptions ("I'm better at kickball than any other kid in my class") and in everyday conversations ("Hey, how many math problems did you get right?") (Damon & Hart, 1988). An even greater emphasis on social comparison may underlie the finding that Japanese and Taiwanese children score lower in self-esteem than do American children, despite their higher academic achievement (Chiu, 1992–1993; Hawkins, 1994). In Asian classrooms, competition is tough and achievement pressure is high. Because so much stress is placed on school performance, Asian children may have fewer opportunities than American children to feel successful in other ways.

■ *Self-esteem rises during adolescence. Most young people have an optimistic outlook on life and are proud of their new competencies. (Joel Gordon)*

■ CHILD-REARING PRACTICES. Child-rearing practices are consistently related to self-esteem. Children and adolescents whose parents are warm and responsive and provide reasonable expectations for behavior feel especially good about themselves (Baumrind, 1971, 1991; Bishop & Ingersoll, 1989; Lord, Eccles, & McCarthy, 1994). If you think carefully about this finding, you will see that it makes perfect sense. Warm, positive parenting lets young people know they are accepted as competent and worthwhile. And firm but appropriate expectations, backed up with explanations, help them make sensible choices and evaluate their own behavior against reasonable standards. In contrast, highly coercive parenting communicates a sense of inadequacy to children. It suggests that their behavior needs to be controlled by adults because they are ineffective in managing it themselves. Finally, overly tolerant, indulgent parenting that promotes a feel-good attitude no matter how children behave creates a false sense of self-esteem, which is detrimental to development as well (see the Social Issues box on page 434).

Although parental acceptance and maturity demands are undoubtedly important ingredients of high self-esteem, we must keep in mind that these findings are correlational. We cannot really separate the extent to which child-rearing styles are causes of or reactions to children's characteristics and behavior. Research focusing on the precise content of adults' messages to children has been far more successful at isolating factors that affect children's sense of self-worth. Let's see how these communicative forces mold children's evaluations of themselves in achievement contexts.

DEVELOPMENT OF ACHIEVEMENT-RELATED ATTRIBUTIONS

Attributions are our common, everyday explanations for the causes of behavior—the answers we provide to the question "Why did I [or another person] do that?" We group the causes of our own and others' behavior into two broad categories: external, environmental causes and internal, psychological causes. Then we further divide the category of psychological causes into two types: ability and effort. In assigning a cause, we use certain rules. If a behavior occurs for many people but only in a single situation (the whole class gets *A*'s on Mrs. Apple's French test), we conclude that it is externally caused (the test was easy). In contrast, if an individual displays a behavior in many situations (Sally always gets *A*'s on French tests), we judge the behavior to be internally caused—by ability, effort, or both.

In Chapter 8, we showed that although intelligence predicts school achievement, the relationship is far from perfect. Differences among children in **achievement motivation**—the tendency to persist at challenging tasks—explain why some less intelligent pupils do better in school than their more intelligent classmates and why children who are equal in ability often respond differently in achievement situations. Today,

Attributions
Common, everyday explanations for the causes of behavior.

Achievement motivation
The tendency to persist at challenging tasks.

SOCIAL ISSUES ➤ POINT OF VIEW

How Should Parents Boost Children's Self-Esteem?

Jared, a bright adolescent growing up in a well-to-do American family, earned C's and D's in academic courses because he seldom turned in homework or studied for exams. His parents tried paying Jared for good grades, but to no avail. Next, they threatened to ground him on weekends. When Jared's report card again showed no improvement, his parents gave in to his pleas for weekend privileges, blaming his weak school performance on low self-esteem. "If only Jared liked himself better," his father reasoned, "he'd work harder in school and choose friends with more serious interests. We've *got* to find a way to make Jared feel better about himself!" Over the next 6 months, Jared's grades dropped further, and he and two of his friends were arrested for property destruction at a shopping mall.

A study of parents' and teachers' reports of American children's behavior, gathered in 1976 and again in 1989, showed declines for all ages and both sexes. Over the 13-year period, children were more likely to "do poorly on schoolwork," "hang around with peers who get into trouble," and "destroy things belonging to others." Fewer had found any activity that truly engaged them, including their education (Achenbach & Howell, 1993). Will parenting that boosts children's self-esteem help increasing numbers of young people like Jared, who lack character and direction? Or is Jared's parents' child-centeredness at the heart of his problems?

According to William Damon (1995), the child-centered philosophy was a major breakthrough when it was first introduced. It made parents and teachers aware that children have unique developmental needs and benefit from warmth and encouragement. Damon argues, however, that modern child-centeredness has been stretched to the point of indulgence. A common theme in popular child-rearing literature is that a child cannot develop meaningful goals and respect others without first coming to love himself. This idea is based on the assumption that self-esteem *precedes* healthy development. It must be built before anything else, through generous praise and unconditional acceptance.

But correlations between self-esteem and positive outcomes do not establish causality! Damon maintains that self-esteem is *the result* (not the cause) of accomplishment. From this perspective, it can be gained only indirectly—not through its own pursuit, but through socially useful commitment and responsibility. Yet instead of insisting on mastery of meaningful skills, too many American parents assure their children, regardless of circumstances, that they are "okay" in every way. Compliments, such as "You're great" or "You're terrific," that have no basis in real attainment disrupt children's potential for development. In Damon's view, sooner or later children see through them, come to mistrust the adults who repeat them, and begin to doubt themselves.

Is feeling good about oneself the producer of real accomplishment (as Jared's parents believe) or its product (as Damon contends)? Cross-cultural research sheds light on this controversy. As we will see in Chapter 15, the academic achievement of children in the United States falls behind that of children in Asian nations, such as Japan and Taiwan. Yet even though Japanese and Taiwanese high school students report higher parental expectations for school performance, they feel less stress and anxiety than do their American agemates and display very low rates of deviant behavior. Contrary to popular belief, Asian pupils do not attain their impressive levels of achievement at expense to their psychological well-being. Indeed, the highest Asian achievers report the fewest psychological symptoms. Strong parental support for achievement seems to contribute to Asian students' ability to meet rigorous academic standards while remaining well adjusted (Crystal et al., 1994).

According to Damon, parents serve children best when they guide them toward worthwhile activities and goals that result in genuine self-esteem. Parents serve children poorly when they promote in them a false sense of self-regard. Had Jared's parents helped him sustain effort in the face of difficulty and insisted that he meet his responsibilities years earlier, they might have prevented the current situation.

YOUR POINT OF VIEW . . .

- Ask several parents to describe what they expect of school-age children in terms of academic achievement and family responsibilities. How do their expectations compare to those of your own and your friends' parents when you were growing up? Could modern American children benefit from "greater expectations?"
- Check your bookstore or library for current titles offering child-rearing advice to parents. What do the authors recommend about promoting children's self-esteem? Do you agree with Damon's claim that the American "cult of self-esteem" is a threat to children's healthy development?

researchers regard achievement-related attributions as the main reason some children are competent learners who display initiative when faced with obstacles to success, whereas others give up easily when their task goals are not immediately achieved.

■ EMERGENCE OF ACHIEVEMENT-RELATED ATTRIBUTIONS. Infants start to engage in competence-increasing activities almost as soon as they enter the world. In earlier chapters, we showed that young babies express great pleasure at acquiring a new skill—satisfaction that reinforces their efforts and motivates similar behavior in the future. Because infants lack the cognitive capacities necessary for self-evaluation, they do not reflect on the implications of their achievements. Instead, they are naturally driven toward mastery of activities that support their development. Achievement motivation is believed to have roots in this early drive (White, 1959).

By the end of the second year, children turn to adults for evaluations of their accomplishments, and they react to approval and disapproval with expressions of pride and shame. In the process, they pick up information about the meaning of competence in their culture (Stipek, Recchia, & McClintic, 1992). And around age 3, they begin making attributions about their successes and failures. These attributions affect their expectancies of success, and expectancies, in turn, influence the extent to which children try hard in the future.

■ *Most preschoolers have a high sense of self-esteem, a quality that encourages them to persist at new tasks during a period in which many new skills must be mastered. (Miro Vintoniv/Stock Boston)*

Many studies show that preschoolers are "learning optimists" who rate their own ability as very high, often underestimate task difficulty, and hold positive expectancies of success. When asked to react to a situation in which one person does worse on a task than another, young children indicate that the lower-scoring person can still succeed if she keeps on trying (Nicholls, 1978). This does not mean that when working on a task, preschoolers never get frustrated or angry. Casual observation reveals that they do. But most young children recover easily from these experiences, and their attributions support a continuation of the initiative they displayed during infancy.

One reason that young children's attributions are often optimistic is that cognitively, they cannot yet separate effort and ability in explaining their successes and failures. Instead, they view all good things as going together: A person who tries hard is also a smart person who is going to succeed (Nicholls, 1978). Belief in their own capacities is also supported by the patience and encouragement of adults, who typically praise more than they criticize preschoolers in achievement situations. Most parents realize that young children are developing rapidly in a multitude of ways. They know that a child who has trouble riding a tricycle or cutting with scissors at age 3 is likely to be able to do so a short time later. Preschoolers, too, are aware that they are growing bigger and stronger, and most recognize that failure on one occasion often translates into success on another.

Nevertheless, by age 4, some children give up easily in the face of age-appropriate challenge, such as working a hard puzzle or building a tall block tower. These nonpersisters are likely to conclude that they are incapable at the task, to lower their evaluation of their work, and to report negative emotion after failure (Cain & Dweck, 1995; Smiley & Dweck, 1994). Furthermore, when nonpersisters are asked to act out an adult's reaction to such failures with dolls, they often respond with punitive statements like these: "He's punished cuz he can't do [the puzzle] and he didn't finish" and "Daddy's gonna be very mad and spank her." In contrast, persisters, who expect to succeed if they try harder or are given more time, more often portray adults as acknowledging and rewarding effort. They make an adult doll say things like this: "He worked hard but he just couldn't finish them. He wants to try them again later" (Burhans & Dweck, 1995, p. 1727).

Furthermore, although young children do not grasp the difference between ability and effort, they have formed general notions of their own goodness that, for some, are strongly affected by success and failure experiences. Nonpersisting 4- to 6-year-olds, who give up easily after criticism or failure, are likely to see themselves as bad and deserving of negative feedback. And they often report that their parents would berate them for making minor mistakes (Dweck, 1991; Heyman, Dweck, and Cain, 1992). These children have begun to develop the belief that their self-worth depends on the judgments of others, not on inner standards. Consequently, they show early signs of maladaptive achievement behaviors that, as we will see in the next section, become more common as performance evaluations increase.

■ Repeated negative evaluations about their ability can cause children to develop learned helplessness—low expectancies of success and debilitating anxiety when faced with challenging tasks. This learned-helpless boy is overwhelmed by a poor grade. He seems to have concluded that there is little he can do to improve his performance. (MacDonald Photography/Envision)

■ **MASTERY-ORIENTED VERSUS LEARNED-HELPLESS CHILDREN.** During middle childhood, children distinguish ability and effort, and they take more information into account in explaining their performance (Chapman & Skinner, 1989; Dweck & Leggett, 1988). Children who are high in achievement motivation develop **mastery-oriented attributions**. They believe their successes are due to ability—a characteristic they can improve through trying hard and can count on in the future when faced with new challenges. And when failure occurs, mastery-oriented children attribute it to factors about themselves or the environment that can be changed or controlled, such as insufficient effort or a very difficult task. So regardless of whether these children succeed or fail, they take an industrious, persistent, and enthusiastic approach to learning.

Unfortunately, other children, who develop **learned helplessness,** hold very discouraging explanations for their performance. They attribute their failures, not their successes, to ability. And on occasions in which they do succeed, they are likely to conclude that external factors, such as luck, are responsible. Furthermore, unlike their mastery-oriented counterparts, learned-helpless children have come to believe that ability is a fixed characteristic of the self that cannot be changed. They do not think competence can be improved by trying hard. So when a task is difficult, these children experience an anxious loss of control. They quickly give up, saying, "I can't do this," before they have really tried (Elliott & Dweck, 1988).

Over time, the ability of learned-helpless children ceases to predict their performance. Indeed, many are very bright pupils who have concluded that they are incompetent (Wagner & Phillips, 1992). Because they fail to make the connection between prior knowledge and what they can do, learned-helpless children do not develop the metacognitive and self-regulatory skills that are necessary for high achievement (see Chapter 7). Lack of effective learning strategies, reduced persistence, and a sense of being controlled by external forces sustain one another in a vicious cycle (Carr, Borkowski, & Maxwell, 1991; Heyman & Dweck, 1992).

Attributional styles affect the goals children pursue in learning situations. Mastery-oriented children focus on *learning goals*—increasing ability through effort and seeking information on how to do so. In contrast, the interests of learned-helpless children are much narrower. They focus on *performance goals*—obtaining positive and avoiding negative judgments of their fragile sense of ability. To protect themselves from painful feelings of failure, learned-helpless children soon begin to select less challenging tasks and, eventually, less challenging courses and even less demanding careers. As Figure 11.3 shows, learned helplessness prevents children from pursuing tasks they are capable of mastering and from realizing their potential.

■ **INFLUENCES ON ACHIEVEMENT-RELATED ATTRIBUTIONS.** What accounts for the very different attributions of mastery-oriented and learned-helpless children? The messages they receive from parents and teachers play a key role. Children who display a learned-helpless style tend to have parents who set unusually high standards yet believe their child is not very capable and has to work harder than others to succeed (Parsons, Adler, & Kaczala, 1982; Phillips, 1987).

Experimental research confirms the powerful impact of adult feedback on children's attributional styles. In one study, children were led to believe their ability to do a task was either high or low. Then they were given one of two types of task instructions: a message that emphasized a performance goal ("You'll be graded by experts on this task") or a message that highlighted a learning goal ("This task sharpens the mind and will help you with your studies"). Children who were told they had low ability and for whom a performance goal was emphasized responded to mistakes in a learned-helpless fashion—by giving up, displaying negative affect, and remarking on their lack of talent. In contrast, children encouraged to pursue a learning goal behaved in a mastery-oriented fashion, persisting in attempts to find solutions regardless of their perceived ability (Elliott & Dweck, 1988).

The achievement motivation of certain children is especially likely to be undermined by adult feedback. Girls more often than boys blame their ability for poor performance. Girls also tend to receive messages from teachers and parents that their ability is at fault when they do not do well (Phillips & Zimmerman, 1990). Low-income ethnic minority children are also vulnerable to learned helplessness. In several studies, African-American and Mexican-American children received less favorable teacher feedback than did other children (Aaron & Powell, 1982; Irvine, 1986; Losey, 1995). Also, when ethnic

Mastery-oriented attributions
Attributions that credit success to high ability and failure to insufficient effort. Leads to high self-esteem and a willingness to approach challenging tasks.

Learned helplessness
Attributions that credit success to luck and failure to low ability. Leads to low expectancies of success and anxious loss of control in the face of challenging tasks.

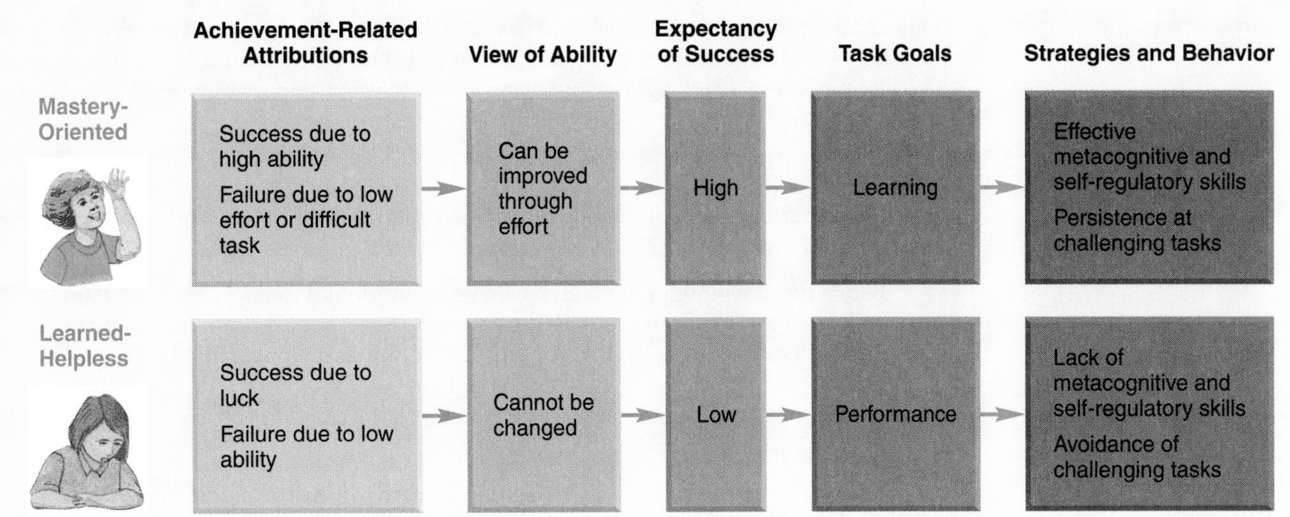

FIGURE 11.3

■ *Consequences of mastery-oriented and learned-helpless attributional styles.*

minority children observe that adults in their own family are not rewarded by society for their achievement efforts, they may give up themselves. Many African-American children may come to believe that even if they do try in school, social prejudice will prevent them from succeeding in the end (Ogbu, 1988).

Finally, cultural values affect the likelihood that children will develop learned helplessness. Compared to Americans, Chinese and Japanese parents and teachers believe that success in school depends much more on effort than innate ability—a message they transmit to children. Influenced by communist ideals of equality, Russian pupils regard one another as having about the same ability, and weight effort more heavily as well (Stetsenko et al., 1995). Similarly, Israeli children growing up on *kibbutzim* (cooperative agricultural settlements) are shielded from learned helplessness by classrooms that emphasize mastery and interpersonal harmony rather than ability and competition. When asked why children look at each other's work at school, kibbutz third graders more often give a mastery-oriented reason ("You need to be sure what you're supposed to do, so you might check"). In contrast, urban Israeli third graders are likely to make a social comparison assessing ability ("You'd want to see if someone else's picture is better than yours") (Butler & Ruzany, 1993).

■ ATTRIBUTION RETRAINING. Attribution research suggests that even adults who are, on the whole, warm and supportive may send subtle messages to children that undermine their competence. **Attribution retraining** is an effective approach to intervention that encourages learned-helpless children to believe that they can overcome failure if only they exert more effort. Most often, children are asked to work on tasks that are hard enough so that some failure experiences are bound to occur. Then they get repeated feedback that helps them revise their attributions, such as "You can do it if you try harder." Children are also taught to view their successes as due to both ability and effort rather than chance factors by giving them additional feedback after they succeed, such as "You're really good at this" or "You really tried hard on that one" (Schunk, 1983).

Another approach is to encourage these low-effort children to focus less on grades and more on mastering the task for its own sake. A large-scale study showed that classroom atmospheres that foster learning goals lead to positive changes in self-conceptions of ability and achievement motivation for failing pupils (Ames, 1990). At the same time, such children may need instruction in metacognitive and self-regulatory strategies to make up for learning lost in this area because of their debilitating attributional style (Borkowski et al., 1990).

To work well, attribution retraining is best begun early, before children's views of themselves become hard to change. An even better approach is for parents and teachers to prevent learned helplessness by carefully considering the feedback they give to children. Attribution research suggests that adults avoid statements that imply children's

Attribution retraining
An approach to intervention in which attributions of learned-helpless children are modified through feedback that encourages them to believe in themselves and persist in the face of task difficulty.

worth rests on external opinion ("I'm very disappointed in you!") and, instead, focus on effort and constructive strategies. Finally, extra measures need to be taken to support mastery-oriented attributions on the part of girls and ethnic minority children—by providing models of adult success and ensuring equality of opportunity in society at large.

CONSTRUCTING AN IDENTITY

During adolescence, thinking about the self extends further, as the following short essay written by a 17-year-old girl in response to the question "Who Am I?" indicates:

> I am a human being. I am a girl. I am an individual. I don't know who I am. I am a Pisces. I am a moody person. I am an indecisive person. I am a very curious person. I am not an individual. I am a loner. I am an American (God help me). I am a Democrat. I am a liberal person. I am a radical. I am a conservative. I am a pseudoliberal. I am an atheist. I am not a classifiable person (i.e., I don't want to be). (Montemayor & Eisen, 1977, p. 318)

This statement illustrates the quest for **identity**, first recognized by psychoanalyst Erik Erikson (1950, 1968) as the major personality achievement of adolescence and as a crucial step toward becoming a productive, happy adult. Constructing an identity involves defining who you are, what you value, and the directions you choose to pursue in life. This search for self is the driving force behind many new commitments—to a sexual orientation (see Chapter 5), to a vocation, and to ethical, political, religious, and cultural ideals.

Erikson regarded successful psychosocial outcomes in infancy and childhood as paving the way toward a positive identity formation. (Return to Chapter 1, page 17, to review Erikson's stages.) Although the seeds of identity are planted early, not until adolescence do young people become absorbed in this task. According to Erikson, in complex societies, teenagers experience an *identity crisis*—a temporary period of confusion and distress as they experiment with alternatives before settling on a set of values and goals. During this period, what adolescents once took for granted they question. Through a process of inner soul-searching, they sift through characteristics that defined the self in childhood and combine them with new commitments. Then they mold these into a solid inner core that provides a sense of sameness as they move through different roles in daily life.

Current theorists agree with Erikson that questioning of the self's values, plans, and priorities is necessary for a mature identity, but they no longer refer to this process as a *crisis* (Baumeister, 1990). The term suggests a sudden, intense upheaval of the self. For some young people, identity development is traumatic and disturbing, but for most it is not. *Exploration* better describes the typical adolescent's experience. Identity formation usually proceeds in a very gradual, uneventful way. The many daily choices teenagers make—"whom to date, whether or not to break up, having intercourse, taking drugs, going to college or working, which college, what major, studying or playing, being politically active"—and the reasons for them are gradually put together into an organized self-structure (Marcia, 1980, p. 161).

Erikson described the negative outcome of the adolescent period as *identity diffusion*. Some young people appear shallow and directionless, either because earlier conflicts have been resolved negatively or society restricts their choices to ones that do not match their abilities and desires. As a result, they are unprepared for the psychological challenges of adulthood. Is there research to support Erikson's ideas about identity development? In the following sections, we will see that adolescents go about the task of defining the self in ways that closely match Erikson's description.

■ PATHS TO IDENTITY. Using a clinical interviewing procedure, researchers have grouped adolescents into four categories, called identity statuses, which show the progress they have made toward forming a mature identity (Grotevant & Cooper, 1981). Table 11.1 summarizes these identity statuses: **identity achievement, moratorium, identity foreclosure,** and **identity diffusion.**

Adolescents often shift from one status to another until identity is attained. Both cross-sectional and longitudinal research reveals that young adolescents often start out as identity diffused and foreclosed and gradually move toward moratorium and identity achievement (Archer, 1982; Meilman, 1979). College triggers increased exploration as

Identity
A well-organized conception of the self made up of values, beliefs, and goals to which the individual is solidly committed.

Identity achievement
The identity status of individuals who have explored and committed themselves to self-chosen values and goals.

Moratorium
The identity status of individuals who are exploring alternatives in an effort to find values and goals to guide their life.

Identity foreclosure
The identity status of individuals who have accepted ready-made values and goals that authority figures have chosen for them.

Identity diffusion
The identity status of individuals who do not have firm commitments to values and goals and are not actively trying to reach them.

TABLE 11.1

The Four Identity Statuses

Identity Status	Description	Sample Response to Identity Interview
Identity achievement	Having already explored alternatives, identity achieved individuals are committed to a clearly formulated set of self-chosen values and goals. They feel a sense of psychological well-being, of sameness through time, and of knowing where they are going.	When asked how willing she would be to give up going into her chosen occupation if something better came along, the adolescent responds, "I might, but I doubt it. I've thought long and hard about law as a career. I'm pretty certain it's for me."
Moratorium	*Moratorium* means delay or holding pattern. These individuals have not yet made definite commitments. They are in the process of exploration—gathering information and trying out activites, with the desire to find values and goals to guide their life.	When asked if he had ever had doubts about his religious beliefs, the adolescent answers, "Yes, I guess I'm going through that right now. I just don't see how there can be a god and yet so much evil in the world."
Identity foreclosure	Identity-foreclosed individuals have committed themselves to values and goals without taking time to explore alternatives. Instead, they accept a ready-made identity that authority figures (usually parents but sometimes teachers, religious leaders, or romantic partners) have chosen for them.	When asked if she had ever reconsidered her religious beliefs, the adolescent states, "No, not really, our family is pretty much in agreement on these things."
Identity diffusion	Identity diffused individuals lack clear direction. They are not committed to values and goals, nor are they actively trying to reach them. They may have never explored alternatives, or they may have tried to do so but found the task too threatening and overwhelming.	When asked about his attitude toward nontraditional gender roles, the adolescent responds, "Oh, I don't know. It doesn't make much difference to me. I can take it or leave it."

young people are exposed to new career options and lifestyles. Most teenagers who go to work right after high school graduation settle on a self-definition earlier than do college-bound youths (Munro & Adams, 1977). But those who find it difficult to realize their occupational goals because of lack of training or vocational choices are at risk for identity diffusion (Archer, 1989b).

At one time, researchers thought that adolescent girls postponed the task of establishing an identity and, instead, focused their energies on Erikson's sixth stage, intimacy development. We now know that this is not the case. Girls do show more sophisticated reasoning in identity areas related to intimacy, such as sexuality and family–career priorities. In this respect, they are actually ahead of boys in identity development. Otherwise, the process and timing of identity formation are the same for boys and girls (Archer, 1989a; Streitmatter, 1993).

■ IDENTITY STATUS AND PERSONALITY CHARACTERISTICS. Identity achievement and moratorium are viewed as psychologically healthy routes to a mature self-definition, whereas foreclosure and diffusion are maladaptive. Studies of personality characteristics associated with the four identity statuses support this conclusion. Young people who are identity achieved or actively exploring have a higher sense of self-esteem, are more likely to engage in abstract and critical thinking, report greater similarity between their ideal self (what they hoped to become) and their real self, and are advanced in moral reasoning (Josselson, 1994; Marcia et al., 1993). Although they report spending more time thinking about themselves than do adolescents who lag behind in identity development, they are also more secure about revealing their true selves to others (O'Connor, 1995).

Adolescents who get stuck in foreclosure or diffusion have adjustment difficulties. Foreclosed individuals tend to be dogmatic, inflexible, and intolerant. Some use their commitments defensively, regarding any difference of opinion as a threat. Most are afraid of rejection by people on whom they depend for affection and self-esteem (Frank, Pirsch, & Wright, 1990; Kroger, 1995). A few foreclosed teenagers who are alienated from their families and society may join cults or other extremist groups, uncritically adopting a way of life that is different from their past.

Long-term diffused teenagers are the least mature in identity development. They typically entrust themselves to luck or fate, have an "I don't care" attitude, and tend to passively go along with whatever the "crowd" is doing at the moment. As a result, they are most likely to use and abuse drugs. At the heart of their apathy is often a sense of hopelessness about the future (Archer & Waterman, 1990). Many of these young people are at risk for serious depression and suicide—problems that rise sharply during adolescence (see the Social Issues box on the following page).

■ INFLUENCES ON IDENTITY DEVELOPMENT. Adolescent identity is the beginning of a lifelong process of refinement in personal commitments. In a fast-paced, changing world, individuals need to retain the capacity to engage in moratorium–achievement cycles throughout life (Archer, 1989b). A wide variety of factors influence identity development.

Cognitive development plays an important role. Although the attainment of formal operations is not related to identity status, the way adolescents grapple with competing beliefs and values makes a difference. Those who assume that absolute truth is always attainable tend to be foreclosed, whereas those who lack confidence in the prospect of ever knowing anything with certainty are more often identity diffused or in a state of moratorium. Adolescents who have come to appreciate that rational criteria can be used to choose among alternative visions are likely to have joined the ranks of the identity achieved (Boyes & Chandler, 1992).

Recall that infants who develop a healthy sense of agency have parents who provide both emotional support and freedom to explore. A similar link between parenting and identity exists at adolescence. When the family serves as a "secure base" from which teenagers can confidently move out into the wider world, identity development is enhanced. Adolescents who feel attached to their parents but who are also free to voice their own opinions tend to be identity achieved or in a state of moratorium (Grotevant & Cooper, 1985; Lapsley, Rice, & FitzGerald, 1990). Foreclosed teenagers usually have close bonds with parents, but they lack opportunities for healthy separation. And diffused young people report the lowest levels of warm, open communication at home (Papini, 1994).

Identity development also depends on schools and communities that provide young people with rich and varied opportunities for exploration. Erikson (1968) noted that it is "the inability to settle on an occupational identity which most disturbs young people" (p. 132). Classrooms that promote high-level thinking, extracurricular and community activities that enable teenagers to take on responsible roles, and vocational training programs that immerse young people in the real world of adult work foster identity achievement. A chance to talk with adults and older peers who have worked through identity questions can also help young people resolve doubts about identity-related matters (Waterman, 1989).

Finally, the larger cultural context and historical time period affect identity development. Among modern adolescents, exploration and commitment take place earlier in the identity domains of vocational choice and gender-role preference than in religious and political values. Yet a generation ago, when the Vietnam War divided Americans and disrupted the lives of thousands of young people, the political beliefs of American youths took shape sooner (Archer, 1989b; Waterman, 1985). Societal forces are also responsible for the special problems ethnic minority adolescents face in forming a secure personal identity, as the Cultural Influences box on page 443 describes.

BRIEF REVIEW

By the end of the second year, self-recognition is well established and underlies children's first struggles with peers over objects, prosocial acts, and formation of a categorical self. Early in the preschool years, children become aware of an inner self of private thoughts and imaginings. By age 4, they have formed a sophisticated theory of mind in which they understand the relationship of belief and desire to behavior. Self-concept evolves from an appreciation

SOCIAL ISSUES

Adolescent Suicide: Annihilation of the Self

The suicide rate increases over the life span. Although it is lowest in childhood and highest in old age, it jumps sharply from middle childhood into adolescence (see Figure 11.4). Among American 15- to 24-year-olds, suicide is the third leading cause of death, after motor vehicle injuries and homicides. It is a growing national problem, having tripled over the past 30 years, perhaps because modern teenagers face more stresses and have fewer supports than did those in decades past. Adolescent suicide has also risen throughout Europe, although not as much as it has in the United States (Diekstra, Kienhorst, & de Wilde, 1995; U.S. Department of Health and Human Services, 1995b).

Striking sex-related differences in suicidal behavior exist. Although girls show a higher rate of severe depression, the number of boys who kill themselves exceeds the number of girls by four or five to one. Yet these findings are not inconsistent. Girls make more unsuccessful suicide attempts and use methods with a greater likelihood of revival, such as a sleeping pill overdose. In contrast, boys tend to select more active techniques that lead to instant death, such as firearms or hanging. Gender-role expectations may account for these differences. There is less tolerance for feelings of helplessness and failed efforts in males than females (Garland & Zigler, 1993).

Suicidal adolescents often show signs of extreme despondency during the period before the suicidal act. Many verbalize the wish to die, lose interest in school and friends, neglect their personal appearance, and give away treasured possessions. These warning signs appear in two types of young people. In the first group are highly intelligent teenagers who are solitary, withdrawn, and unable to meet their own high standards or those of important people in their lives. A second, larger group shows antisocial tendencies. These young people express their unhappiness through bullying, fighting, stealing, and increased risk taking and drug use (Kandel, Raveis, & Davies, 1991; Lehnert, Overholser, & Spirito, 1995). Besides turning their anger and disappointment inward, they are hostile and destructive toward others.

Family turmoil, parental emotional problems, and marital breakup are common in the backgrounds of suicidal teenagers, who typically feel distant from parents and peers (Shagle & Barber, 1993). Their fragile self-esteem disintegrates in the face of stressful life events. Common circumstances just before a suicide include rejection by or conflict with a romantic partner or parent or the humiliation of having been caught engaging in irresponsible, antisocial acts.

Why is suicide rare in childhood but on the rise in adolescence? Teenagers' improved ability to plan ahead seems to be involved. Few successful suicides are sudden and impulsive. Instead, young people at risk usually take purposeful steps toward killing themselves. The cognitive changes of adolescence also contribute to the age-related increase in suicide. Belief in the personal fable (see Chapter 6) leads many depressed young people to conclude that no one could possibly understand the intense pain they feel. As a result, it deepens the isolation and despair of vulnerable teenagers.

Picking up on the signals that a troubled teenager sends is a crucial first step in preventing suicide. Parents and teachers need to be trained in warning signs. Unfortunately, because of the popular stereotype of adolescence as a period of storm and stress, some adults interpret these behaviors as "normal" and just a passing phase (Strober, McCracken, & Hanna, 1990). Schools can help by providing sympathetic counselors, peer support groups, and information about telephone hot lines that adolescents can call in an emergency.

Intervention with depressed and suicidal adolescents takes many forms—from antidepressant medication to individual, family, and group therapy. Sometimes hospitalization is necessary to ensure the teenager's safety and swift entry into treatment. Until the adolescent improves, parents are usually advised to remove weapons, knives, razors, scissors, and drugs from the home. On a broader scale, gun control legislation that limits adolescents' access to the most frequent and deadly suicide method would greatly reduce both the number of suicides and the high teenage homicide rate (Shaffer et al., 1988).

After a suicide, family and peer survivors need support to assist them in coping with grief, anger, and guilt for not having been able to help the victim. Teenage suicides often take place in clusters. When one occurs, it increases the likelihood of others among peers who knew the young person or heard about the death through the media. In view of this trend, an especially watchful eye needs to be kept on vulnerable adolescents after a suicide happens. Restraint by journalists in reporting teenage suicides on television or in newspapers can also aid in preventing them (Diekstra, Kienhorst, & de Wilde, 1995).

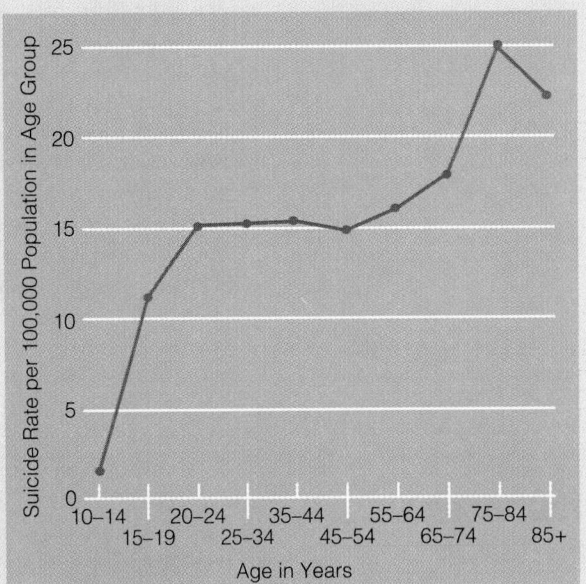

FIGURE 11.4

■ *Suicide rate over the life span. Although teenagers do not commit suicide as often as adults and the aged, suicide rises sharply from childhood to adolescence. (From U.S. Department of Health and Human Services, 1995).*

of typical emotions, attitudes, and observable characteristics to an emphasis on stable personality traits in middle childhood. At the same time, self-esteem differentiates, becomes hierarchically organized, and declines as school-age children begin to make social comparisons and evaluate their performance at different activities. From fourth grade on, self-esteem rises for the majority of young people. Adult communication affects children's attributions for success and failure in achievement contexts and willingness to persist at challenging tasks.

Four identity statuses describe the degree of progress adolescents have made toward forming a mature identity, or coherent set of values and life plans. Identity achievement and moratorium are adaptive statuses associated with positive personality characteristics. Teenagers in a long-term state of identity foreclosure or diffusion tend to have adjustment difficulties. Identity development is fostered by the realization that rational procedures can be used to choose among competing beliefs and values, by parents who provide emotional support and freedom to explore, by schools and communities that are rich in opportunities, and by societies that permit young people from all backgrounds to realize their personal goals.

Thinking About Other People

Children's understanding of other people—their descriptions of others' personalities and inferences about their behavior and mental states—has much in common with their developing understanding of themselves. In the following sections, we will see that this facet of social cognition also becomes increasingly differentiated and well organized with age.

PERSON PERCEPTION

Person perception concerns how we size up people with whom we are familiar in everyday life. To study it, researchers use methods similar to those that focus on children's self-concepts: asking them to describe people they know, such as "Can you tell me what kind of person ______ is?"

Like their self-descriptions, below age 8, children's descriptions of others focus on commonly experienced emotions and attitudes, concrete activities, and behaviors. Over time, children discover consistencies in the actions of people they know and begin to mention personality traits (Barenboim, 1977; Eder, 1989). At first, these references are closely tied to behavior and consist of implied dispositions, such as "He is always fighting with people" or "She steals and lies" (Peevers & Secord, 1973). Later, children mention traits directly, but they are vague and stereotyped—for example, "good," "nice," or "acts smart." Gradually, sharper descriptions appear, such as "honest," "trustworthy," "generous," "polite," and "selfish," and children become more convinced of the stability of such dispositions (Droege & Stipek, 1993; Livesley & Bromley, 1973).

About the time they begin comparing themselves to others, children start to make comparisons between people. These also change from concrete to abstract. At first, children cast comparisons in behavioral terms: "Billy runs a lot faster than Jason." Around age 10 to 12, after children have had sufficient experience inferring personality traits, they integrate these into social comparisons: "Paul's a lot more considerate than thickheaded Del" (Barenboim, 1981, p. 133).

During adolescence, as abstract thinking becomes better established, inferences about others' personalities are drawn together into organized character sketches (Livesley & Bromley, 1973; O'Mahoney, 1989). As a result, between ages 14 and 16, teenagers present much richer accounts of people they know that combine physical traits, typical behaviors, and inner dispositions. Adolescents also recognize that their own experiences with a person, and therefore their impressions, may differ from the opinions of other people (Barenboim, 1977).

Person perception
The way individuals size up people with whom they are familiar in everyday life.

CULTURAL INFLUENCES

Identity Development Among Ethnic Minority Adolescents

Most Caucasian-American adolescents are aware of their cultural ancestry, but it is usually not a matter of intense concern for them. Since the values of their home lives are consistent with mainstream American culture, ethnicity does not prompt intense identity exploration (Rotheram-Borus, 1993).

But for teenagers who are members of minority groups, ethnicity is a central part of the quest for identity, and it presents difficult, sometimes overwhelming challenges. Different skin colors, native languages, and neighborhoods set minority youths apart and increase the prejudices to which they are exposed. As they develop cognitively and become more sensitive to feedback from the social environment, they become painfully aware that they are targets of discrimination and inequality. This discovery complicates their efforts to develop a sense of cultural belonging and a set of personally meaningful life goals. One African-American journalist, looking back on his adolescence, remarked, "If you were black, you didn't quite measure up. . . . you didn't see any black people doing certain things, and you couldn't rationalize it. I mean, you don't think it out but you say, 'Well, it must mean that white people are better than we are. Smarter, brighter—whatever' " (Monroe, Goldman, & Smith, 1988, pp. 98–99).

Minority youths often feel caught between the standards of the larger society and the traditions of their culture of origin. Some respond by rejecting aspects of their ethnic background. In one study, Asian-American 15- to 17-year-olds were more likely than African-Americans and Hispanics to hold negative attitudes toward their subcultural group. Perhaps the absence of a social movement stressing ethnic pride of the kind available to African-American and Hispanic teenagers underlies this finding. Asian-American young people in this study had trouble naming well-known personalities who might serve as ethnic role models (Phinney, 1989). Some Asian parents are overly restrictive of their children out of fear that assimilation into the larger society will undermine cultural traditions, and their teenagers rebel. One Southeast Asian refugee described his daughter's behavior: "She complains about going to the Lao temple on the weekend and instead joined a youth group in a neighborhood Christian Church. She refused to wear traditional dress on the Lao New Year. The girl is setting a very bad example for her younger sisters and brothers" (Nidorf, 1985, pp. 422–423).

Other minority teenagers react to years of shattered self-esteem, school failure, and barriers to success in the American mainstream by defining themselves in contrast to majority values. A Mexican-American teenager who had given up on school commented, "Mexicans don't have a chance to go on to college and make something of themselves." Another, responding to the question of what it takes to be a successful adult, mentioned "being on the streets" and "knowing what's happening." He pointed to his uncle, leader of a local gang, as an example (Matute-Bianchi, 1986, pp. 250–251).

The challenges minority youths face in blending mainstream with ethnic group values are also apparent in the experiences of academically successful African-American adolescents. To avoid being labeled white by their peers, they frequently try to conceal their abilities and accomplishments (Clark, 1991). Because it is painful and confusing, minority high school students often dodge the task of forming an ethnic identity. Many are diffused or foreclosed on ethnic identity issues (Markstrom-Adams & Adams, 1995; Phinney, 1989).

How can society help minority adolescents resolve identity conflicts constructively? A variety of efforts are relevant, including reducing poverty, promoting effective parenting, and ensuring that schools respect minority youths' ethnic heritage and unique learning styles. Minority adolescents who are ethnic-identity-achieved—who have explored and adopted values from both their primary culture and the dominant culture—tend to be achieved in other areas of identity as well. They also have a higher sense of self-esteem, feel a greater sense of mastery over the environment, and show more positive family and peer relations (Phinney, 1989; Phinney & Alipuria, 1990). These findings support the notion that promoting the ethnic identity of minority youths enhances many aspects of emotional and social adjustment.

Finally, lack of concern by many white adolescents with their own ethnic origins (other than American) implies a view of the social world that is out of touch with the pluralistic nature of American society. The ethnic distinctions with which most of us are familiar (African-American, Asian-American, Caucasian, Hispanic, Native American) oversimplify the rich cultural diversity of the American populace (Spencer & Dornbusch, 1990). Interventions that increase the multicultural sensitivity of white teenagers lead to greater awareness of their own ethnic heritage. And majority adolescents who are secure in their own ethnic identity are less likely to hold negative stereotypes of their minority peers (Rosenthal, 1987; Rotheram-Borus, 1993).

■ *These Native-American adolescents dress in traditional costume in preparation for demonstrating a ceremonial dance to citizens of a small Wyoming town. When minority youths encounter respect for their cultural heritage in schools and communities, they are more likely to retain ethnic values and customs as an important part of their identities. (John Eastcott/Yva Momatiuk/The Image Works)*

UNDERSTANDING INTENTIONS

Besides getting to know others as personalities, children must learn how to interpret their behavior. Making behavior meaningful and deciding how to react to it often depend on distinguishing actions that are deliberate and intentional from those that are accidental. By age 2, preschoolers already have intentions on their minds. In everyday conversations, they say "gonna," "hafta," and "wanna" to announce actions they are about to perform. Think back to our discussion of children's theory of mind, and you will find further evidence for an early appreciation that intention, or desire, underlies action. Preschoolers often rely on this grasp of purposefulness to defend themselves. After being scolded for bumping into a playmate or spilling a glass of milk, they exclaim, "It was an accident!" or "I didn't do it on purpose!" (Shultz, 1980).

By 2½ to 3 years, this understanding extends to others. Preschoolers become sensitive to behavioral cues that help them tell if another person is acting intentionally. At first, they focus on the person's statements. If a person says he is going to do something and then does it, 3-year-olds judge the behavior as deliberate. If statements and actions do not match, then the behavior was not intended (Astington, 1991). By the end of the preschool years, children focus on a much wider range of information to judge intentionality. For example, 5-year-olds note whether a person is concentrating on what she is doing, whether her action leads to positive or negative outcomes (negative ones are usually not intended), and whether some external cause can account for the person's behavior (Smith, 1978).

Human intentional acts extend beyond the ones we have just considered. For example, we can deliberately refrain from acting but pretend that our lack of response was unintentional, by saying something like "I forgot all about it!" Between 5 and 9 years of age, children rely increasingly on a *verbal–nonverbal consistency rule* to evaluate the sincerity of others' stated intentions. For example, older children understand quite well that telling another person you like something when you look neutral or unhappy probably means you are not telling the truth (Rotenberg, Simourd, & Moore, 1989). The ability to detect more subtle efforts to conceal intentions depends on awareness of fine-grained features of a situation as well as sophisticated perspective-taking skills, a topic we examine in the next section.

Finally, children differ in how accurately they interpret others' intentions. Those who get along well with adults and peers make these judgments easily. In contrast, highly aggressive children show striking biases in inferring intentions; they often see hostility where it does not exist (Dodge & Price, 1994; Weiss et al., 1992). As we will see in Chapter 12, such children require special help in learning how to evaluate and respond appropriately to others' behavior.

DEVELOPMENT OF PERSPECTIVE TAKING

In this and previous chapters, we have emphasized that **perspective taking**—the capacity to imagine what other people may be thinking and feeling—is important for a wide variety of social-cognitive achievements, including referential communication skills (Chapter 9), understanding others' emotions (Chapter 10), self-concept and self-esteem, person perception, and inferring intentions. Recall that Piaget regarded egocentrism—preschoolers' inability to take the viewpoint of another—as the major feature responsible for the immaturity of their thought, in both the physical and social domains. But we have also seen much evidence that young children are not as egocentric as Piaget believed. Indeed, they show some capacity for perspective taking as soon as they separate self from others in the second year of life. Nevertheless, Piaget's ideas inspired a wealth of research on children's capacity to take another's perspective, which improves steadily over childhood and adolescence.

Perspective taking
The capacity to imagine what other people may be thinking and feeling.

■ SELMAN'S STAGES OF PERSPECTIVE TAKING. Robert Selman developed a five-stage model of major changes in perspective-taking skill. He asked preschool-age through adolescent youngsters to respond to social dilemmas in which the characters have differing information and opinions about an event. Here is one example:

> Holly is an 8-year-old girl who likes to climb trees. She is the best tree climber in the neighborhood. One day while climbing down from a tall tree she falls off the

bottom branch but does not hurt herself. Her father sees her fall. He is upset and asks her to promise not to climb trees anymore. Holly promises.

Later that day, Holly and her friends meet Sean. Sean's kitten is caught up in a tree and cannot get down. Something has to be done right away or the kitten may fall. Holly is the only one who climbs trees well enough to reach the kitten and get it down, but she remembers her promise to her father. (Selman & Byrne, 1974, p. 805)

After the dilemma is presented, children answer questions that highlight their ability to interpret the story from varying points of view, such as

Does Sean know why Holly cannot decide whether or not to climb the tree?

What will Holly's father think? Will he understand if she climbs the tree?

Does Holly think she will be punished for climbing the tree? Should she be punished for doing so?

Table 11.2 summarizes Selman's five stages of perspective taking. As you can see, children gradually include a wider range of information in their understanding of others' viewpoints. At first, they have only a limited idea of what other people might be thinking and feeling. Over time, they become more conscious of the fact that people can interpret the same event in different ways. Soon, children can "step in another person's shoes" and reflect on how that person might regard their own thoughts, feelings, and behavior. Finally, they can examine the relationship between two people's perspectives

TABLE 11.2

Selman's Stages of Perspective Taking

Stage	Approximate Age Range	Description	Typical Response to "Holly" Dilemma
Level 0: Undifferentiated perspective taking	3–6	Children recognize that self and other can have different thoughts and feelings, but they frequently confuse the two.	The child predicts that Holly will save the kitten because she does not want it to get hurt and believes that Holly's father will feel just as she does about her climbing the tree: "Happy—he likes kittens."
Level 1: Social-informational perspective taking	4–9	Children understand that different perspectives may result because people have access to different information.	When asked how Holly's father will react when he finds out that she climbed the tree, the child responds, "If he didn't know anything about the kitten, he would be angry. But if Holly shows him the kitten, he might change his mind."
Level 2: Self-reflective perspective taking	7–12	Children can "step into another person's shoes" and view their own thoughts, feelings, and behavior from the other person's perspective. They also recognize that others can do the same.	When asked whether Holly thinks she will be punished, the child says, "No. Holly knows that her father will understand why she climbed the tree." This response assumes that Holly's point of view is influenced by her father being able to "step in her shoes" and understand why she saved the kitten.
Level 3: Third-party perspective taking	10–15	Children can step outside a two-person situation and imagine how the self and other are viewed from the point of view of a third, impartial party.	When asked whether Holly should be punished, the child says, "No, because Holly thought it was important to save the kitten. But she also knows that her father told her not to climb the tree. So she'd only think she shouldn't be punished if she could get her father to understand why she had to climb the tree." This response steps outside the immediate situation to view both Holly's and her father's perspectives simultaneously.
Level 4: Societal perspective taking	14–adult	Individuals understand that third-party perspective taking can be influenced by one or more systems of larger societal values.	When asked if Holly should be punished, the individual responds, "No. The value of humane treatment of animals justifies Holly's action. Her father's appreciation of this value will lead him not to punish her."

Sources: Selman, 1976; Selman & Byrne, 1974.

TABLE 11.3

Percentage of Individuals from Four Years to Adulthood at Each of Selman's Perspective-Taking Levels

Level	Age 4	Age 6	Age 8	Age 10	Age 13	Age 16	Adult
0	80	10	0	0	0	0	0
1	20	90	40	20	7	0	0
2	0	0	50	60	50	21	0
3	0	0	10	20	36	58	0
4	—	—	—	—	7	21	100

Source: R. L. Selman & D. F. Byrne, 1974, "A Structural-Developmental Analysis of Levels of Role Taking in Middle Childhood," *Child Development, 45,* 803–806. Additional data from D. F. Byrne, 1973, "The Development of Role Taking in Adolescence," unpublished doctoral dissertation, Harvard University.

simultaneously, at first from the vantage point of a disinterested spectator and later by making reference to societal values.

■ RESEARCH CONFIRMING SELMAN'S DEVELOPMENTAL SEQUENCE. As Table 11.3 indicates, cross-sectional findings on Selman's dilemmas show that maturity of perspective taking rises steadily with age. Also, longitudinal research reveals gradual movement to the next higher stage over 2 to 5 years, with no individuals skipping stages and practically none moving back to a previous stage (Gurucharri & Selman, 1982; Selman, 1980). These findings provide strong support for Selman's assumption that his stages form an age-related, invariant sequence.

Cognitive Development and Perspective Taking. Selman's stages are also related to nonsocial-cognitive milestones—findings that offer additional support for his developmental progression. Individuals who fail Piaget's concrete operational tasks tend to be at Selman's Level 0; those who pass concrete but not formal operational tasks tend to be at Levels 1 and 2; and those who are increasingly formal operational tend to be at Levels 3 and 4 (Keating & Clark, 1980; Krebs & Gillmore, 1982). Furthermore, each set of Piagetian tasks tends to be mastered somewhat earlier than its related perspective-taking level (Walker, 1980). This suggests that Piagetian milestones are a necessary but not sufficient condition for attaining Selman's perspective-taking stages. Additional social-cognitive capacities are required, as we will see in the following section.

Perspective-Taking Games. Besides responses to social dilemmas, "games and the delights of deception" offer ideal opportunities to study perspective taking (Selman, 1980, p. 49). According to several researchers, preschoolers' limited perspective-taking skills are largely due to their passive view of the mind—their assumption that what a person knows is the result of simply observing rather than actively interpreting experience (Chandler, 1988; Pillow, 1988b). In agreement with this idea, 4-year-olds understand quite clearly that because of greater experience, children and adults know more than babies do. Nevertheless, when asked to play a special "privileged information game" that challenges their perspective-taking capacities, these same preschoolers run into difficulty.

In one study, an experimenter showed 4- to 6-year-olds pictures of objects and then covered them in such a way that either a nondescript part or an identifiable part of the object was left showing (see Figure 11.5). Next, children were asked whether two observers—a baby and a child—who had never seen the full pictures could recognize the objects from the incomplete versions. Four-year-olds often said that an observer could tell from a nondescript part what the object was. They made little allowance for another's difficulty in inferring the meaning of a tiny part without having seen the full picture. And although 4-year-olds were well aware that children are more knowledgeable than babies, they did not apply this understanding to the perspective-taking game. They thought a baby would be able to recognize pictures of nondescript and identifiable object parts just as easily as an older child, even when the objects (a horse or teeter-totter) were unfamiliar to infants. Not until age 6 did children realize that simply seeing a picture does not determine a person's view of it. Instead, what the observer brings to the situation in terms of prior experience and knowledge affects their ability to interpret it

Recursive thought
The self-embedded form of perspective taking that involves thinking about what another person is thinking.

FIGURE 11.5

■ *In viewing each of these pictures for the first time, can a baby or a child tell that the object depicted is a horse? In a recent study, 4-year-olds thought that both observers could recognize the horse, even from a nondescript part. Not until age 6 did they realize that prior experience (having seen the full picture) as well as greater knowledge (being older and familiar with horses) affects an individual's ability to interpret pictures. (Adapted from Taylor, Cartwright, & Bowden, 1991.)*

(Taylor, Cartwright, & Bowden, 1991). Around 6 to 8 years, children understand that besides knowledge, people's beliefs and expectations can also lead to quite different views of new information (Pillow, 1991).

Other gamelike tasks have focused on **recursive thought**, the self-embedded form of perspective taking that involves thinking about what another person is thinking. Selman's stages suggest that the capacity to think recursively (Levels 3 and 4) improves over the adolescent years, a trend that is supported by research. Patricia Miller, Frank Kessel, and John Flavell (1970) asked first through sixth graders to describe cartoon drawings showing one- and two-loop recursive thought (see Figure 11.6 on page 448). By sixth grade, only 50 percent of children had mastered one-loop recursions, and two-loop recursions were rare. Not until midadolescence do young people master the complexities of recursive understanding (Flavell et al., 1968).

Recursive thought is a feature of perspective taking that makes human interaction truly reciprocal. People often call on it to clear up misunderstandings, as when they say, "I thought you would think I was just kidding when I said that." Recursive thinking is also involved in our attempts to disguise our real thoughts and feelings, when we reason in ways like this: "He'll think I'm jealous if I tell him I don't like his new car, so I'll pretend I do" (Perner, 1988). Finally, the capacity to think recursively contributes to the intense self-focusing and concern with the imaginary audience typical of early adolescence (see Chapter 6). As Miller, Kessel, and Flavell (1970) point out, "Often to their pain, adolescents are much more gifted at this sort of wondering than first graders are" (p. 623).

■ PERSPECTIVE TAKING AND SOCIAL BEHAVIOR. Children's developing perspective-taking skills help them get along with other people. When we anticipate another person's point of view, social relationships become more predictable. Each individual can plan actions with some knowledge of what the other person is likely to do in return. In addition, when children recognize that other people may have thoughts and feelings different from their own, they can respond to the momentary needs of others more effectively. It is not surprising that perspective taking is related to a wide variety of social skills. Good perspective takers are more likely to display empathy and compassion, and they are better at thinking of effective ways to handle difficult social situations (Eisenberg et al., 1987; Marsh, Serafica, & Barenboim, 1981). For these reasons, they tend to be especially well liked by peers (LeMare & Rubin, 1987).

Although good perspective taking is a crucial ingredient of mature social behavior, we must keep in mind that it does not always result in prosocial acts. How children apply their ability to imagine another person's viewpoint depends on the situation. In a competitive task, skilled perspective takers are often as good at defending their own viewpoint as they are at cooperating with other people. Also, even when children appreciate another person's thoughts and feelings, additional factors, such as personality, influence whether they will act on their social awareness. For example, children who have learned to regulate their emotions effectively can avoid being overwhelmed by their own feelings

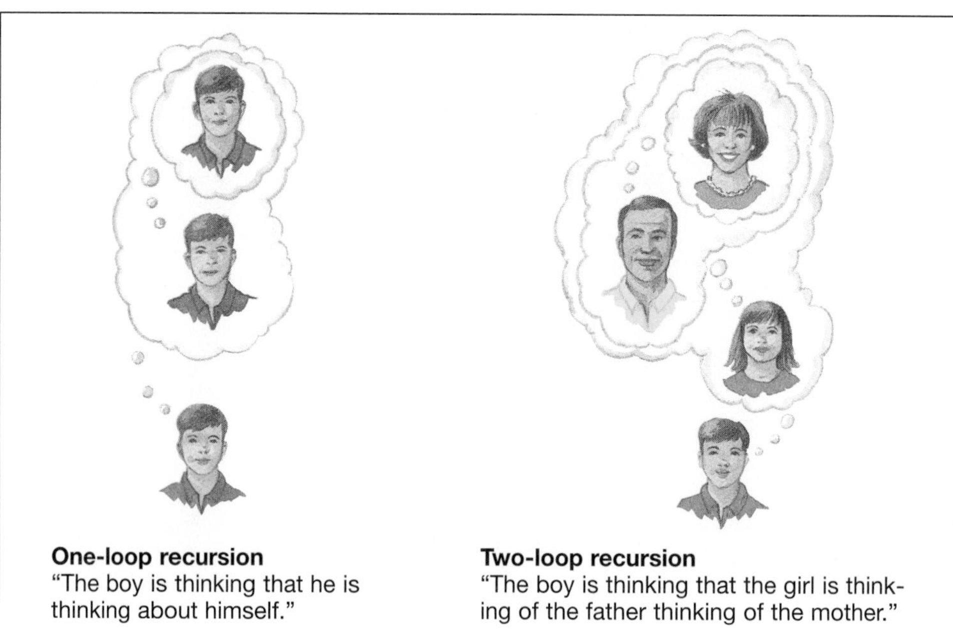

FIGURE 11.6

Cartoon drawings depicting recursive thought. Not until midadolescence do young people master the complexities of this self-embedded form of perspective taking. (From P. H. Miller, F. S. Kessel, & J. H. Flavell, 1970, "Thinking About People Thinking About People Thinking About . . . : A Study of Social Cognitive Development," Child Development, *41, p. 616. © The Society for Research in Child Development, Inc. Reprinted by permission.)*

and are therefore more likely to help others in distress and handle peer social conflicts constructively (Eisenberg & Fabes, 1995; Fabes, Eisenberg, & Eisenbud, 1993).

Finally, children and adolescents with very poor social skills—in particular, the angry, aggressive styles that we will take up in Chapter 12—have great difficulty imagining the thoughts and feelings of others. They often mistreat adults and peers without experiencing the guilt and remorse prompted by awareness of another's point of view. Interventions that provide coaching and practice in perspective taking are helpful in reducing antisocial behavior and increasing prosocial responding (Chalmers & Townsend, 1990; Chandler, 1973).

BRIEF REVIEW

Like self-concept, person perception shifts from a focus on concrete activities and behaviors to an emphasis on personality traits in middle childhood. During adolescence, inferences about others' psychological characteristics are drawn together into organized character sketches. The ability to infer intentions from others' behavior emerges during the preschool years and becomes refined in middle childhood. Perspective taking undergoes vast changes from early childhood into adolescence. It begins with limited awareness of others' thoughts and feelings and evolves into advanced recursive and societal perspective-taking capacities. The development of perspective taking builds on nonsocial cognitive milestones and children's awareness that the mind actively interprets experience. Perspective taking is related to a wide variety of social skills.

Thinking About Relations Among People

As children develop, they apply their insights into the inner psychological worlds of themselves and others to an understanding of relations among people. Most research on this aspect of social cognition has to do with reasoning about friendship and interpersonal conflict—topics we will explore in the following sections. Investigators have also begun to examine children's understanding of ethnicity and social class, since views formed in childhood may have long-term implications for fostering positive intergroup relations and a tolerant, peaceful society (see the Cultural Influences box on the following page).

CULTURAL INFLUENCES

Children's Understanding of Ethnicity and Social Class

How do children make sense of diversity and inequality in society? Already we have seen that at an early age, preschoolers sort people into categories. By age 3 to 4, most have formed basic concepts of race and ethnicity, in that they can apply labels of black and white to pictures, dolls, and people. Many indicators of social class, such as education and occupational prestige, are not accessible to young children. Nevertheless, they can distinguish rich from poor on the basis of salient physical characteristics, such as clothing, residence, and possessions (Ramsey, 1991).

Do race, ethnicity, and social class dominate young children's views? Not necessarily. For example, both black and white preschoolers categorize people according to sex more readily than race (McGraw, Durm, & Durnam, 1989). Nevertheless, children absorb prevailing attitudes about social groups by the early school years. By that time, they associate physical characteristics with social information, such as the status of different groups. Since race, ethnicity, and social class are closely linked, American children quickly connect power and privilege with white people and poverty and subordinate status with people of color (Ramsey, 1995).

Children are more likely to hold negative attitudes toward groups to which they themselves do not belong—a bias that also characterizes adults. Yet recall from our discussion of person perception that with age, children pay more attention to internal characteristics and make finer distinctions among people. The capacity to classify the social world in multiple ways permits school-age children to understand that people can be both "the same" and "different"—that those who look different need not think, feel, or act differently (Bigler & Liben, 1993). Consequently, verbalized prejudice declines with cognitive maturity in middle childhood.

Nevertheless, children vary in the extent to which they hold racial, ethnic, and social-class biases. Studies of adults reveal the existence of intolerant personalities—people who hold a broad array of negative stereotypes, against the elderly, homosexuals, women, and people of various ethnic and political groups. But traitlike prejudice is rare among children. A recent study showed that 5- to 12-year-olds' ethnic bias does not predict their gender bias or their dislike of overweight people (Powlishta et al., 1994). This suggests that specific learning experiences are very influential in the development of childhood prejudice. Children who come to believe that personality is fixed are more likely to make rigid, long-term social judgments than are those who see it as changeable (Erdley & Dweck, 1993). The broader social world is also a powerful force in children's views. For example, in the few societies in which skin color has no social implications (such as Sweden), children perceive it accurately, as a continuously varying property of people rather than in terms of white versus black (Hughes, 1975).

Children and adolescents with a tolerant outlook may still display prejudice in their behavior. As we will see later, racial, ethnic, and social-class segregation is common in children's friendships at all ages. Contact and collaboration among different groups in neighborhoods, schools, and communities are the best ways to overcome these biases—in both thought and action (Ramsey, 1995).

■ *In the few societies in which skin color has no social implications (such as Sweden), children perceive it accurately, as a continuously varying property of people rather than in terms of white versus black. (Peter Southwick/Stock Boston)*

UNDERSTANDING FRIENDSHIP

To an adult, friendship is not a one-sided relationship. You can like someone without being a friend to that person, since your liking may not be returned. Instead, friendship is a mutual relationship involving companionship, sharing, understanding of thoughts and feelings, and caring for and comforting one another in times of need. In addition, mature friendships endure over time and survive occasional conflicts.

Children's ideas about friendship do not start out this way. Researchers have interviewed children of different ages, asking them to name a best friend, explain why that person is a friend, and indicate what they expect of a close friend. In addition, children sometimes respond to dilemmas about friendship that tap motives for friendship formation, characteristics of friendship, ways in which good friends solve conflicts, and how and why friendships break up. From children's answers, several theories of the development of friendship understanding have emerged. All emphasize that friendship begins as a concrete relationship based on pleasurable activity and evolves into a more abstract relationship based on mutual consideration and psychological satisfaction (Damon,

1977; Selman, 1980; Youniss, 1980). William Damon has combined the work of other investigators into a three-stage sequence:

LEVEL 1: FRIENDSHIP AS A HANDY PLAYMATE[2] (ABOUT 4 TO 7 YEARS). Interviews with preschoolers show that they already understand something about the uniqueness of friendship. They know that a friend is someone "who likes you," with whom you spend a lot of time playing, and with whom you share toys. As yet, there is little sense of appreciating another person's personality traits, since (as we saw earlier) young children are only beginning to size up themselves and others in terms of unique psychological characteristics.

Because friendship is viewed concretely, in terms of play and exchange of material goods, young children regard it as easily begun—for example, by meeting in the neighborhood and saying, "Hi." However, friendship does not yet have a long-term, enduring quality. Level 1 children say that a friendship can dissolve when one partner refuses to share, hits, or is not available to play. The following answer of a 5-year-old boy to the question "What makes a good friend?" sums up the young child's view of friendship: "Boys play with boys, trucks play with trucks, dogs play with dogs." When the interviewer probed, "Why does that make them good friends?" the child answered, "Because they do the same things" (Selman, 1980, p. 136).

During middle childhood, concepts of friendship become more psychologically based. Although these boys enjoy playing baseball, they want to spend time together because they like each other's personal qualities. Mutual trust is a defining feature of their friendship. Each child counts on the other to provide support and assistance. (Richard Hutchings/PhotoEdit)

LEVEL 2: FRIENDSHIP AS MUTUAL TRUST AND ASSISTANCE (ABOUT 8 TO 10 YEARS). During middle childhood, children's concepts of friendship become more complex and psychologically based. Look closely at the responses of this 8-year-old to questions about what makes a best friend:

> Who's your best friend? *Shelly.* Why is Shelly your best friend? *Because she helps me when I'm sad, and she shares. . . .* What makes Shelly so special? *I've known her longer, I sit next to her and got to know her better. . . .* How come you like Shelly better than anyone else? *She's done the most for me. She never disagrees, she never eats in front of me, she never walks away when I'm crying, and she helps me on my homework. . . .* How do you get someone to like you? . . . *If you're nice to [your friends], they'll be nice to you.* (Damon, 1988, pp. 80–81)

As these statements show, friendship is no longer just a matter of engaging in the same activities. Instead, it is a mutually agreed-on relationship in which children like each other's personal qualities and respond to one another's needs and desires. Since friendship is a matter of both children wanting to be together, getting it started takes more time and effort than it did at earlier ages. Once a friendship is formed, trust becomes its defining feature. School-age children state that a good friendship is based on acts of kindness that signify each person can be counted on to support the other. Consequently, events that break up a friendship are quite different than they were during the preschool years. Older children regard violations of trust, such as not helping when others need help, breaking promises, and gossiping behind the other's back, as serious breaches of friendship. And once a rift occurs, it cannot be patched up as easily as it could at younger ages—by playing nicely after a conflict. Instead, apologies and explanations for violating friendship expectations are necessary (Damon, 1977; Selman, 1980).

LEVEL 3: FRIENDSHIP AS INTIMACY AND LOYALTY (11 TO 15 YEARS AND OLDER). By early adolescence, friendship takes on greater depth. When asked to comment on the meaning of friendship, teenagers stress two characteristics. The first, and most important, is intimacy. Adolescents seek psychological closeness and mutual understanding from their friends. Second, more than younger children, teenagers want their friends to be loyal—to stick up for them and not to leave them for somebody else (Berndt & Perry, 1990).

Because friendship has this depth dimension to it, adolescents regard it as a relationship formed over a long period of time by "getting to know someone." In addition, friends are viewed as important in relieving psychological distress, such as loneliness, sadness, and fear. And because true mutual understanding implies forgiveness, only an extreme falling out can lead Level 3 relationships to dissolve. Here is how one teenager described his best friendship:

[2] I have provided titles for each of the stages to help you remember them.

Well, you need someone you can tell anything to, all kinds of things that you don't want to spread around. That's why you're someone's friend. Is that why Jimmy is your friend? Because he can keep a secret? *Yes, and we like the same kinds of things. We speak the same language. My mother says we're two peas in a pod. . . .* Do you ever get mad at Jimmy? *Not really.* What if he did something that got you really mad? *He'd still be my best friend. I'd tell him what he did wrong and maybe he'd understand. I could be wrong too, it depends.* (Damon, 1977, p. 163)

■ RESEARCH ON CHILDREN'S DEVELOPING UNDERSTANDING OF FRIENDSHIP. Both cross-sectional and longitudinal research confirm the sequence of friendship understanding just described (Bigelow, 1977; Bigelow & LaGaipa, 1975; Keller & Wood, 1989). Also, virtually every study shows that even after a psychological appreciation of friendship emerges, early concepts, such as sharing common activities, are not abandoned. Instead, they are integrated into more mature concepts. Furthermore, friendship reasoning is related to advances in perspective taking (Selman, 1981). We would certainly expect this to be so, since a more advanced appreciation of friendship implies greater awareness of others' thoughts and feelings.

■ ARE CHILDREN'S CONCEPTS OF FRIENDSHIP RELATED TO FEATURES OF THEIR REAL FRIENDSHIPS? If social cognition plays a vital role in everyday behavior, then children's developing ideas about friendship should predict qualities of their real friendships. There is good evidence for this relationship in three areas: friendship stability, interaction, and resemblance.

Stability of Friendships. First, we would expect greater friendship stability as mutual trust and loyalty become more important in children's expectations of their friends. In one study, friendship choices of first, fourth, and eighth graders were gathered in the fall and spring of the school year. Friendships did become more stable from first to fourth grade, but no change occurred from fourth to eighth grade. The researchers discovered that eighth graders permitted a larger number of friendships to dissolve and were very selective about adding new friends (Berndt & Hoyle, 1985). Two factors seem to be responsible for this trend. First, friendships become more exclusive with age, especially for girls, because (as we will see shortly) they typically demand greater closeness in the relationship than do boys. Second, as children approach puberty, varying rates of development and new interests lead to a period of change in choice of friends (Berndt, 1988).

Although friendship stability does increase with age, children's friendships are remarkably stable at all ages. Even during the preschool years, two-thirds of children who identify one another as friends do so again 4 to 6 months later (Gershman & Hayes, 1983). However, lasting friendships at younger ages are more a function of the constancy of social environments, such as preschool and neighborhood, than of social cognition. At older ages, friendships endure for psychological reasons, although they often undergo temporary shifts in the strength of each partner's commitment (Cairns et al., 1995).

Interaction Among Friends. Second, a more mature understanding of friendship should lead older children to behave with more mutual responsiveness and sensitivity toward friends. Actually, interactions among friends have a unique quality at all ages. Preschoolers give twice as much reinforcement, in the form of greetings, praise, and compliance, to children whom they identify as friends, and they also receive more from them. Friends are also more emotionally expressive—talking, laughing, and looking at each other more often than nonfriends (Hartup, 1996). Apparently, spontaneity and intimacy characterize rewarding friendships very early, although children are not able to verbalize that these qualities are essential to a good friendship until much later.

Prosocial behavior toward friends does increase with age. When working on a task together, school-age friends help, share, refer to each other's comments, and spend more time focused on the task than first-grade friends do (Hartup, 1996; Newcomb & Bagwell, 1995). Cooperation, generosity, and mutual affirmation between friends continue to rise into adolescence—a trend that may reflect greater effort and skill at preserving the relationship as well as increased sensitivity to a friend's needs and desires (Windle, 1994). Children with close friends also behave in a more caring way toward others in general (McGuire & Weisz, 1982). Many prosocial behaviors may emerge first in the context of friendship and then transfer to other people.

■ *In integrated schools and neighborhoods, many children form close other-race friendships. (Carol Palmer/The Picture Cube)*

School-age friends do not just behave more prosocially. They also freely compete with each other to a greater extent than nonfriends. Since children regard friendship as based on equality, they seem especially concerned about losing a contest to a friend. Also, when children hold differing opinions, friends are more likely to voice them than are nonfriends (Azmitia & Montgomery, 1993). As early as middle childhood, friends seem to be secure enough in their approval of one another to risk being direct about their opinions. As a result, friendship probably provides an important context in which children learn to tolerate argument, disagreement, and criticism (Hartup et al., 1993).

Resemblance Among Friends. Finally, we would expect the value adolescents attach to feeling especially "in sync" with their friends to mean that friendship pairs will become increasingly similar in attitudes and values at older ages. Actually, the attributes on which friends are most alike throughout childhood and adolescence are race, ethnicity, sex,[3] and social class. But friends also resemble one another in personality (sociability versus shyness), peer popularity, and academic achievement (Hartup, 1996; Kupersmidt, DeRosier, & Patterson, 1995). And by adolescence, they tend to be alike in educational aspirations, political beliefs, and willingness to try drugs and engage in lawbreaking acts. Perhaps children choose companions like themselves to increase the supportiveness of friendship. Once they do so, friends influence each other. Adolescent friends become more alike in attitudes, values, school grades, and social behavior over time (Berndt & Keefe, 1995; Savin-Williams & Berndt, 1990).

Still, we must keep in mind that some aspects of friendship similarity are due to the way the social world is organized. Most children and adolescents live in neighborhoods that are fairly homogeneous in terms of ethnicity, income, and belief systems. In one study of friendships in an integrated junior high school, over 50 percent of seventh to ninth graders reported at least one close other-race school friend. But these friendships seldom extended to out-of-school contexts unless adolescents lived in integrated neighborhoods (DuBois & Hirsch, 1990).

■ SEX-RELATED DIFFERENCES IN FRIENDSHIPS. Ask several girls and boys age 8 or older to describe their close friendships, and you are likely to find a consistent difference. Emotional closeness and trust are more common in girls' talk about friends than in boys' (Buhrmester & Furman, 1987; Parker & Asher, 1993). This does not mean that boys rarely form close friendship ties. They often do, but the quality of their friendships is

[3] Although interaction between boys and girls increases during adolescence, stable friendships continue to be limited to members of the same sex. In one survey of nearly 2,000 high school students between 13 and 18 years of age, 91 percent reported that their best friend was of their own sex (Kandel, 1978).

more variable. In one survey of high school students, 45 percent of boys described their best friendships as highly intimate; 35 percent said they were guarded in communication. In contrast, 65 percent of girls reported very intimate best friendships, whereas only 5 percent had relationships that were distant and superficial (Youniss & Smollar, 1986). The intimacy of boys' friendships is related to their gender-role identity. Boys who identify strongly with the traditional masculine role are less likely to form close friendships than those who are more flexible in their gender-related preferences (Jones & Dembo, 1989).

■ DEVELOPMENTAL CONSEQUENCES OF FRIENDSHIPS. Although young people who are well adjusted to begin with are better able to form and sustain close peer ties, warm supportive friendships further their development. The reasons are several:

1. *Close friendships provide opportunities to develop a wide variety of social-cognitive skills.* Through open, honest communication, friends become sensitive to each other's strengths and weaknesses, needs and desires. They get to know themselves and their partners especially well, a process that supports the development of self-concept, perspective taking, identity, and intimate ties beyond the family.

2. *Close friendships provide support in dealing with the stresses of everyday life.* Because friendship enhances sensitivity to and concern for another, it increases the likelihood of empathy and prosocial behavior. Adolescents with supportive friendships report fewer daily hassles and more "uplifts" than do others (Kanner et al., 1987). As a result, anxiety and loneliness are reduced while self-esteem and sense of well-being are fostered.

3. *Close friendships can improve attitudes toward and involvement in school.* Young people with satisfying friendships tend to do well in school. The link between friendship and academic performance depends, of course, on the extent to which each friend values achievement. But overall, close friendship ties promote good school adjustment. When children and adolescents enjoy interacting with friends at school, perhaps they begin to view all aspects of school life more positively (Berndt & Keefe, 1995; Vandell & Hembree, 1994).

In sum, supportive, gratifying friendships provide invaluable contexts for forming new attachments and developing a deep understanding of another person. As a result, they may be as vital for long-term psychological well-being as early family relationships. Several decades ago, psychiatrist Harry Stack Sullivan (1953) wrote about the significance of childhood friendships:

> If you will look very closely at one of your children when he finally finds a chum—somewhere between eight-and-a-half and ten—you will discover something very different in the relationship—namely, that your child begins to develop a real sensitivity to what matters to another person. And this is not in the sense of "what should I do to get what I want," but instead "what should I do to contribute to the happiness or to support the prestige and feeling of worthwhileness of my chum." So far as I have been able to discover, nothing remotely like this appears before. . . . Thus the developmental epoch of preadolescence is marked by the coming of integrating tendencies which, when they are completely developed, we call love. (pp. 245–246)

Recent research on the development of friendship confirms Sullivan's vision.

UNDERSTANDING CONFLICT: SOCIAL PROBLEM SOLVING

Children, even when they are best friends, sometimes come into conflict with one another. Recall that Piaget (1923/1926) granted social conflict an important role in development. He believed that arguments and disagreements help children notice others' viewpoints, which leads to a decline in egocentrism. In Chapter 6, we noted that resolution of conflict, rather than conflict per se, encourages development. Indeed, even preschoolers seem to handle most of their quarrels constructively. Observations show that only rarely do conflicts lead to intensely hostile encounters. Instead, arguments, refusals, denials, and opposition are much more common. Furthermore, conflicts are not very frequent when compared to children's friendly, cooperative interactions (Hay, 1984). And when conflicts do occur, they are usually brief and settled by children themselves (O'Keefe & Benoit, 1982).

Despite their infrequency and brevity, peer conflicts are important. Watch children work out their disputes over play objects ("That's mine!" "I had it first!"), entry into and control over play activities ("I'm on your team, Jerry." "No, you're not!"), and disagreements over facts, ideas, and beliefs ("I'm taller than he is." "No, you aren't!"). You will see that they take these matters quite seriously. Recent research reveals that social conflicts offer children invaluable learning opportunities in **social problem solving**. In their efforts to resolve conflicts effectively—in ways that are both acceptable to others and beneficial to the self—children must bring together a variety of social-cognitive skills. These include encoding and interpreting social cues, clarifying a social goal, generating strategies for reaching the goal, evaluating the effectiveness of each strategy in preparation for choosing one, and enacting it.

■ *Conflicts are not very frequent when compared to children's friendly, cooperative interactions. When conflicts do occur, children must bring together a variety of social-cognitive skills to solve social problems effectively.(Ken Lax/ Photo Researchers*

Kenneth Dodge regards social problem solving as a special, interpersonal form of the more general problem-solving process. He organizes the steps of social problem solving into the circular model shown in Figure 11.7. Notice how this flowchart takes an *information-processing approach* to social cognition. It clarifies the exact series of steps a child might use in grappling with a social problem and arriving at a solution. Once these are known, then specific processing deficits can be identified, and treatment programs can be tailored to meet children's individual needs (Crick & Dodge, 1994; Dodge, 1985).

Researchers are especially interested in social problem solving because of its profound impact on social competence. Well-adjusted children who get along with peers interpret social cues accurately, formulate goals that enhance relationships (such as being helpful to peers), and have a repertoire of effective strategies that they apply adaptively. In contrast, maladjusted children who are disliked by peers, either because they are highly aggressive or because they are anxious and withdrawn, have great difficulty solving social problems. They attend selectively to certain social cues, such as hostile acts. Their social goals (getting even with or avoiding a peer) often damage relationships. And they also form biased expectations for how a situation is going to proceed that interfere with their ability to process social information correctly (Crick & Dodge, 1994; Vitaro & Pelletier, 1991). When social problem-solving skills improve, both children and adolescents show gains in academic, emotional, and social functioning (Dubow et al., 1991; Elias et al., 1986).

■ DEVELOPMENT OF SOCIAL PROBLEM SOLVING. George Spivack and Myrna Shure (1974, 1985) conducted pioneering research on social problem solving, stimulating the large body of research that exists today. Focusing on strategy generation, they asked young children to think of as many ways as they could to deal with hypothetical conflicts, such as wanting to play with a toy someone else has. Their findings, and the results of more recent studies, show that the ability to generate a variety of solutions to social conflicts increases over the preschool and early school years (Dubow & Tisak, 1989; Rubin & Krasnor, 1985).

The quality of children's strategies also improves with age. Younger children, as well as children with especially poor peer relations, describe strategies that impulsively meet their needs, such as grabbing, hitting, or ordering another child to obey. Older children and those with good peer relations assert their needs in ways that take into account the needs of others. They rely on friendly persuasion and compromise, sometimes suggesting that a conflict might be solved by creating new mutual goals. In doing so, they recognize that solutions to immediate problems have an important bearing on the future of the relationship (Downey & Walker, 1989; Yeates, Schultz, & Selman, 1991).

Other researchers have expanded the study of social problem solving in an effort to find out at what points, besides strategy generation, socially competent children differ from less competent children. Dodge and his collaborators (1986) assessed school-age children's skillfulness at five of the problem-solving steps in Figure 11.7. A videotape dramatized a problem involving entry into a play group. In the first scene, two children played a board game, and the researchers measured each participant's ability to *encode and interpret social cues* about the video characters' willingness to let the child join the game. Then children *generated strategies* for joining the game, and their responses were coded in the following ways:

Social problem solving
Resolving social conflicts in ways that are both acceptable to others and beneficial to the self.

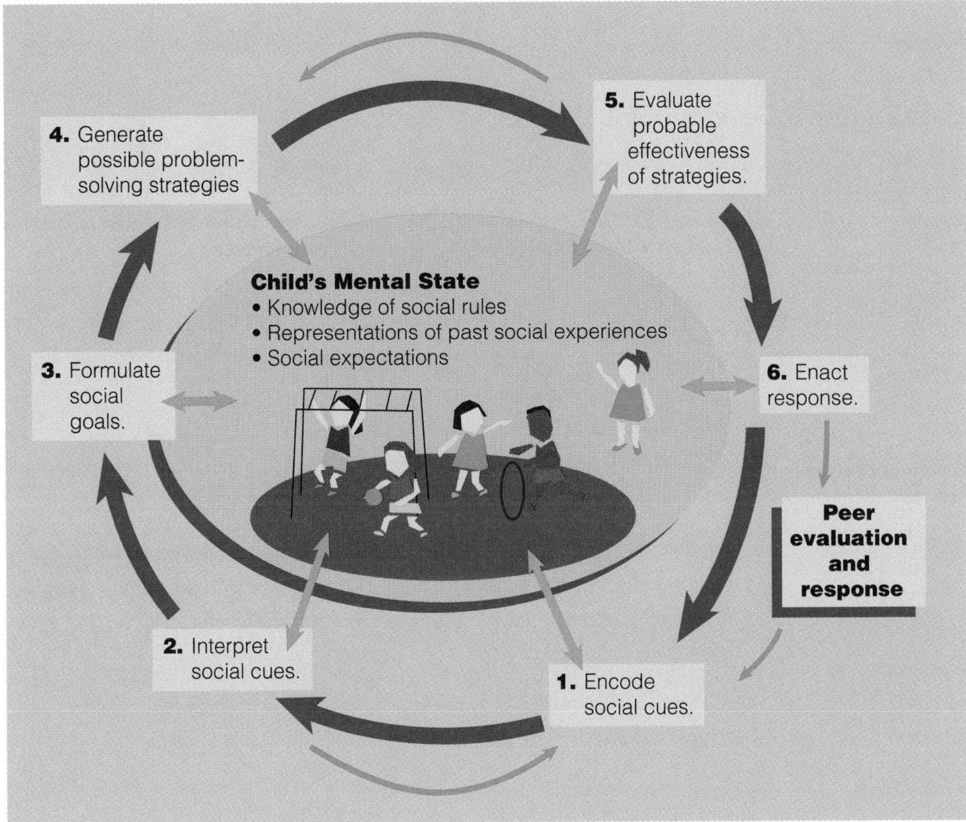

FIGURE 11.7

Dodge's information-processing model of the steps a child is likely to use when confronted with a social problem. The model is circular, since children often engage in several information-processing activities at once—for example, interpreting information as they encode it and continuing to consider the meaning of another's behavior while they generate and evaluate problem-solving strategies. The model also takes into account the impact of children's mental state on social information processing—in particular, their knowledge of social rules, their representations of past social experiences, and their expectations for future experiences. Peer evaluations and responses to enacted strategies, along with the way children think about those responses, are also important factors in social problem solving. (Adapted from N. R. Crick & K. A. Dodge, 1994, "A Review and Reformulation of Social Information-Processing Mechanisms in Children's Social Adjustment," Psychological Bulletin, *115*, 74–101. Copyright © 1994 by the American Psychological Association. Adapted by permission.)

- *Competent:* polite requests to play and other friendly comments
- *Aggressive:* threats, physical force, and barging in without asking
- *Self-centered:* statements about the self, such as "Hey, I know how to play that!"
- *Passive:* shy, hovering responses, such as waiting and "hanging around"
- *Appeals to authority:* for example, "The teacher said I could play"

Next, participants viewed five more scenes in which a child tried to enter the game using each of these strategies, and they engaged in *strategy evaluation* by indicating whether or not the technique would succeed. Finally, participants *enacted a response* by demonstrating a way of joining the game.

In a separate session, the investigators assessed children's actual social competence by having them gain entry into a real peer group activity in the laboratory. Results showed that all five social problem-solving skills were related to children's performance. Each social-cognitive measure also predicted how effectively children joined play activities while being observed on their school playground. In sum, children's processing of social information in a hypothetical situation is highly effective in explaining their behavior in similar everyday social contexts.

Over the early elementary school years, the various components of social problem solving become more strongly associated with socially competent behavior. As children move through the first few years of schooling, they confront increasingly complex social situations, which demand more sophisticated social information-processing skills. These, in turn, become increasingly important for getting along with others (Dodge & Price, 1994).

TRAINING SOCIAL PROBLEM SOLVING. Intervening with children who are poor social problem solvers can enhance development in several ways. Besides improving peer relations, effective social problem solving provides children with a sense of mastery and self-worth in the face of stressful life events. It reduces the risk of adjustment difficulties in children from low-income and troubled families (Downey & Walker, 1989; Goodman, Gravitt, & Kaslow, 1995).

MILESTONES

Social-Cognitive Development

Age	Thinking About the Self	Thinking About Other People	Thinking About Relations Among People
1–2 years	■ Self-recognition emerges and becomes well established. ■ By age 2, a categorical self develops. ■ Self-evaluative statements appear.	■ By age 2, ability to categorize people according to salient characteristics develops. ■ Beginnings of perspective taking emerge.	
3–5 years	■ A belief–desire theory of mind emerges. ■ Self-concept emphasizes observable characteristics and commonly experienced emotions and attitudes. ■ Self-esteem is typically high and consists of least two dimensions: social acceptance and competence. ■ Achievement-related attributions appear.	■ Person perception emphasizes observable characteristics and commonly experienced emotions and attitudes. ■ Inferring others' intentions from behavioral cues improves. ■ Perspective taking is limited; children assume that what people observe determines their perspective.	■ Friendship is viewed concretely, in terms of play and exchange of material goods. ■ Variety of social problem-solving strategies expands. 
6–10 years "Peter is nicer than you!"	■ Self-concept emphasizes personality traits. ■ Self-esteem becomes hierarchically organized: At least three dimensions (academic, physical, and social) are present, which are combined into an overall impression. ■ Self-esteem declines as children start to make social comparisons, then rises. ■ Achievement-related attributions differentiate into ability and effort.	■ Person perception emphasizes personality traits and social comparisons. ■ Understanding deceptive forms of intentional behavior improves. ■ Perspective taking expands; children understand that people can interpret the same event in different ways.	■ Friendship emphasizes mutual trust and assistance. ■ Quality of social problem-solving strategies improves. ■ Components of social problem solving become more strongly associated with socially competent behavior. ■ Prevailing attitudes about racial, ethnic, and social-class groups are acquired, although prejudice declines with cognitive maturity.
11 years–adulthood	■ New aspects of self-esteem are added (close friendship, romantic appeal, and job competence). ■ Self-esteem continues to rise. ■ Identity develops.	■ Person perception consists of organized character sketches. ■ Recursive and societal perspective taking develops.	■ Friendship emphasizes intimacy and loyalty. 

Note: These milestones represent overall age trends. Individual differences exist in the precise age at which each milestone is attained.

Spivack and Shure (1974) devised a well-known and widely applied social problem-solving training program. For several months, preschoolers and kindergartners participate in daily sessions in which puppets act out social problems and children discuss ways to resolve them. In addition, teachers intervene as conflicts arise in the classroom, pointing out consequences of children's behavior and suggesting alternative strategies. In several studies, trained pupils, in contrast to untrained controls, improved in both social reasoning and teacher-rated adjustment—gains still evident months after the program ended (Feis & Simons, 1985; Ridley & Vaughn, 1982). Older elementary school children benefit from similar interventions (Gettinger, Doll, & Salmon, 1994).

At present, researchers are not sure which ingredients of social problem-solving training are most effective. Some evidence suggests that practice in enacting responses needs to accompany social-cognitive training. When children have had many opportunities to engage in maladaptive behaviors, repeated rehearsal of new techniques may be necessary to overcome their habitual responses (Mize & Ladd, 1988). Also, current programs have not been tailored to fit the social-cognitive deficits of particular children. But it is in precisely these ways that the information-processing approach to social problem solving promises to make a unique contribution.

On a final note, social-cognitive training is not the only means for helping children with poor social competence. In Chapter 15, we will take up other approaches, including reinforcement, modeling, and direct teaching of social skills. The Milestones table on the previous page provides an overview of the changes in social cognition we have considered in this chapter.

SUMMARY

- The development of **social cognition** deals with how children's understanding of themselves, other people, and relationships between people changes with age.

THINKING ABOUT THE SELF

- Reactions of infants to images of themselves indicate that **self-recognition** is well established by the end of the second year. The emergence of representational and language capacities permits toddlers to construct a **categorical self** as they classify themselves and others on the basis of salient characteristics, such as age, sex, and physical characteristics. Self-awareness provides the foundation for early struggles over objects as well as cooperation and prosocial behavior.
- Around age 4, children's theory of mind becomes a **belief–desire theory** that closely resembles the everyday psychology of adults. Early emergence of a theory of mind may be supported by infants' sense of agency as well as make-believe play and imitation. Many researchers believe that the normal human brain is biologically prepared to develop a belief–desire theory. Social experience also contributes, since children with siblings are advanced in understanding of false belief.
- During the preschool years, children begin to construct a **self-concept**, or set of beliefs about their own characteristics. In middle childhood, self-concept changes from an appreciation of typical emotions, attitudes, and observable characteristics to an emphasis on personality traits, a transformation supported by cognitive development and perspective-taking skills. In describing themselves, children tend to be more egoistic and competitive in individualistic cultures, more concerned with the welfare of others in collectivist cultures.
- **Self-esteem**, the judgments we make about our own worth, differentiates, becomes hierarchically organized, and declines over the first few years of elementary school as children start to make **social comparisons**. Except for a temporary drop associated with school transition, self-esteem rises from fourth grade on. For most young people, becoming an adolescent leads to feelings of pride and self-confidence. Self-esteem is influenced by cultural forces. Child-rearing practices that are warm and responsive and that provide reasonable expectations for mature behavior are consistently related to high self-esteem.
- Research on achievement-related **attributions** has identified adult communication styles that affect children's self-esteem and **achievement motivation**. Children with **mastery-oriented attributions** credit their successes to high ability and failures to insufficient effort. They believe that ability can be improved through trying hard. In contrast, children with **learned helplessness** attribute their successes to luck and failures to low ability. They are convinced that ability is fixed and cannot be changed. Children who receive negative feedback about their ability and pressure to focus on performance goals are likely to develop learned helplessness. **Attribution retraining** has succeeded in improving the self-evaluations and task performance of learned-helpless children.
- Erikson first recognized **identity**—the construction of a solid self-definition consisting of self-chosen values and goals—as the major personality achievement of adolescence. In complex societies, a period of exploration is necessary to form a personally meaningful identity.
- **Identity achievement** and **moratorium** are psychologically healthy identity statuses. **Identity foreclosure** and **identity diffusion** are related to adjustment difficulties. Adolescents

who recognize that rational criteria can be used to choose among beliefs and values and who feel attached to parents but free to disagree are likely to be advanced in identity development. Schools and communities that provide young people with rich and varied options for exploration support the search for identity.

THINKING ABOUT OTHER PEOPLE

- Like self-concept, **person perception** places greater emphasis on personality traits and becomes more differentiated and organized with age. Over the preschool years, children become increasingly skilled at distinguishing intentional from unintentional acts. During middle childhood, they begin to detect deceptive forms of intentional behavior.
- **Perspective taking** improves greatly from childhood to adolescence, as Selman's five-stage sequence indicates. Mastery of Piagetian tasks and a view of the mind as an active interpreter of experience are related to advances in perspective taking. During adolescence, **recursive thought** is mastered.
- The ability to understand the viewpoints of others contributes to a wide variety of social skills. Young people who display extremes of antisocial behavior are often greatly delayed in the development of perspective taking. Interventions that train perspective-taking skills by having troubled adolescents role-play interpersonal problems result in improvements in social cognition and behavior.

THINKING ABOUT RELATIONS AMONG PEOPLE

- Children's understanding of friendship evolves from a concrete relationship based on sharing activities and material goods to more abstract conceptions based on mutual trust and intimacy. In line with this change, children's real friendships are characterized by greater stability, prosocial responding, and similarity in attitudes and values with age. Girls emphasize emotional closeness and trust in their friendships more than boys do. Close friendships foster a wide variety of social-cognitive skills, provide support in dealing with everyday stresses, and can improve attitudes toward and involvement in school.
- With age, children become better at resolving conflict through **social problem solving**. All components of the social problem-solving process—encoding and interpreting social cues, clarifying social goals, generating and evaluating strategies, and enacting responses—predict social competence. Training in social problem solving leads to gains in psychological adjustment for both preschool and school-age children.

IMPORTANT TERMS AND CONCEPTS

social cognition (p. 423)
self-recognition (p. 425)
categorical self (p. 426)
belief–desire theory of mind (p. 426)
self-concept (p. 428)
generalized other (p. 429)
self-esteem (p. 430)
social comparisons (p. 431)
attributions (p. 433)
achievement motivation (p. 433)
mastery-oriented attributions (p. 436)
learned helplessness (p. 436)
attribution retraining (p. 437)
identity (p. 438)
identity achievement (p. 438)
moratorium (p. 438)
identity foreclosure (p. 438)
identity diffusion (p. 438)
person perception (p. 442)
perspective taking (p. 444)
recursive thought (p. 446)
social problem solving (p. 454)

CONNECTIONS for Chapter 11

If you are interested in . . .	turn to . . .	to learn about . . .
Self-understanding	Chapter 5, pp. 181–182	Adolescent reactions to pubertal changes
	Chapter 5, pp. 187–188	Sexual identity of homosexual adolescents
	Chapter 6, pp. 214, 229–230, 243	Egocentrism in Piaget's theory
	Chapter 7, pp. 281–284	Metacognitive knowledge
	Chapter 10, pp. 393–394	Emotional understanding in childhood
	Chapter 13, pp. 518–519	Gender-role identity
Perspective taking	Chapter 6, p. 248	Peer interaction and perspective taking in Piaget's theory
	Chapter 6, pp. 238–239	Perspective taking and children's cognitive maps
	Chapter 6, pp. 248–249	Intersubjectivity, perspective taking, and transfer of cognitive skills to children
	Chapter 10, p. 394	Perspective taking and empathy
	Chapter 12, pp. 473, 476	Perspective taking and moral understanding
	Chapter 13, pp. 518–522	Perspective taking and gender-role identity in adolescence
	Chapter 15, pp. 582–583	Perspective taking and peer sociability in middle childhood
Aggression in childhood	Chapter 7, p. 270	Attention-deficit hyperactivity disorder and aggression
	Chapter 12, pp. 489–495	Development of aggression
	Chapter 12, p. 496	Impact of ethnic and political violence on children
	Chapter 15, p. 588	Peer rejection and aggression
	Chapter 15, p. 589	Bullies and their victims
	Chapter 15, p. 593	Dominance hierarchies and control of peer group aggression
	Chapter 15, p. 594	Peer reinforcement of aggressive behavior
	Chapter 15, pp. 600–601	Television and aggression

12 Moral Development

In cultures as diverse as the American middle class, Vietnamese immigrants to California, and the Fiji Islanders of the South Pacific, a profound change in reactions to certain events takes place during the latter half of the second year. Around 17 to 20 months, children start to show great concern with deviations from the way objects should be and people should act. Toddlers of this age point to destroyed property, such as holes in clothing, spots on furniture, or broken toys, with an expression of discomfort, often exclaiming, "Uh-oh!" At about this time, they react with distress to behaviors that are aggressive or that might otherwise endanger their own or another's welfare. And by age 2, language includes clear references to standards of conduct, such as "broken," "dirty," or "boo-boo," and evaluations of one's own and others' actions as "good" or "bad" (Kagan, 1987; Kochanska, Casey, & Fukumoto, 1995).

As these observations reveal, accompanying the emergence of new representational capacities and self-awareness in the second year is another crowning achievement: The child becomes a moral being. Throughout the world, adults take note of this budding capacity to distinguish right from wrong. In some cultures, special terms are used to describe it. The Utku Indians of Hudson Bay say the child develops *ihuma* (reason). The Fijians believe that *vakayalo* (sense) appears. In response, parents hold children more responsible for their behavior (Kagan, 1989).

What accounts for the early emergence of morality and children's expanding appreciation of standards of conduct with age? Philosophers have pondered this question for centuries, and modern investigators have addressed it with such intensity that today the research on moral development exceeds that on all other aspects of social development. Understanding morality and the related practical matter of how to encourage it in children are age-old concerns. People have long recognized that behaviors respecting the rights and needs of others are essential for the continued existence of human groups.

Think, for a moment, about factors that constrain you to act morally. You will quickly see that the determinants of morality exist on many levels. In all societies, morality is protected by an overarching social organization that specifies rules for good conduct. At the same time, morality has roots in each major aspect of our psychological makeup. First, as we indicated in Chapter 10, morality has an *emotional component,* since powerful feelings cause us to empathize with another's distress or feel guilty when we are the cause of it. Second, morality has an important *cognitive component.* As we showed in Chapter 11, humans think about their social experiences, and children's developing social understanding permits them to make more profound judgments about actions they believe to be right or wrong. Third, morality has a vital *behavioral component,* since experiencing morally relevant thoughts and feelings only increases the chances, but does not guarantee, that people will act in accord with them.

Traditionally, these three facets of morality have been studied separately: biological and psychoanalytic theories focused on emotions, cognitive-developmental theory on moral thought, and social learning theory on moral behavior. Today, a growing body of research reveals that all three facets are interrelated. Still, major theories continue to disagree on which is primary. We will see that the aspect a theory emphasizes has major implications for how it conceptualizes the basic age trend of moral development: the shift from superficial, or externally controlled, responses to behavior that is based on inner standards. Truly moral individuals do not just do the right thing for the sake of social conformity or when authority figures are around. Instead, they have developed principles of good conduct, which they follow in a wide variety of situations.

Our discussion of moral development takes a close look at the four theories just mentioned, highlighting the strengths and limitations of each based on current research. Then we consider self-control. The development of a personal resolve to keep the self from doing anything it feels like doing—from painting on the walls and playing with matches in the young preschooler to ignoring chores, insulting a playmate, or breaking a promise in the older child—is crucial for translating moral commitments into action. We conclude with a discussion of the "other side" of self-control—the development of aggression.

Morality as Rooted in Human Nature

During the 1970s, biological theories of human social behavior became prominent, spurred by a controversial new field called **sociobiology**. It suggested that many morally relevant prosocial behaviors, such as helping, sharing, and cooperating, were rooted in the genetic heritage of our species (Wilson, 1975). This view was supported by the work of ethologists, who observed animals aiding other members of their species, often at great risk to their own safety. For example, some small birds, including robins and thrushes, use a special call that warns others of an approaching predator, even though the sound might betray the caller's presence. Certain species of insects, such as ants, bees, and termites, show extremes of self-sacrifice. Large numbers will sting or bite an animal that threatens the hive, a response that often results in their own death. Among primates, chimpanzees often share meat after a cooperative hunt and practice adoption when a baby loses its mother (Goodall, 1990). On the basis of this evidence, sociobiologists reasoned that evolution must have made similar provisions for prosocial acts in human beings.

How might genes influence behaviors that protect the social group and, thereby, the survival of the species? Although sociobiologists admit that this process is not fully understood, many believe prewired emotional reactions are involved (Hoffman, 1981; Trivers, 1971). In Chapter 10, we noted that newborns show primitive signs of empathy, since they cry when they hear another baby cry. By the second year, empathic concern is present, and toddlers react with distress to behaviors that threaten not just their own well-being, but that of others. Perhaps these emotions underlie early sharing as well as other prosocial acts. Indeed, research reveals that 2-year-olds in a play group share more often when toys are scarce than when they are plentiful (Hay et al., 1991). Consistent with sociobiological theory, the tendency to sacrifice personal gain in favor of group welfare is present at an early age.

But like most other human behaviors, morality cannot be fully explained by its biological foundations. Recall from Chapter 10 that morally relevant emotions, such as empathy, require strong caregiving supports to develop. And their mature expression depends on

■ *According to sociobiologists, many morally relevant prosocial behaviors, such as helping, sharing, and cooperating, are rooted in the genetic heritage of our species. These chimpanzees retreat to a safe, secluded spot in a tree to share meat after a cooperative hunt. (Baron Hugo Van Lawick/National Geographic Society Image Collection)*

Sociobiology
A field that assumes many complex social behaviors, including morally relevant prosocial acts, are rooted in our genetic heritage and have evolved because of their survival value.

cognitive development as well. Finally, although emotion is one basis for moral action, it is not a complete account, since following our empathic feelings is not always moral. For example, most of us would question the behavior of a parent who decides not to take a sick child to the doctor out of empathy for the child's fear and anxiety.

Still, the biological perspective on morality is useful, since it reminds us of the adaptive significance of moral behavior. Because the capacity to serve the self's needs is present early, nature seems to have made sure that counteracting tendencies are also in place that limit disruptive acts and promote concern for the well-being of others.

■ *This 9-year-old girl reacts with guilt as her teacher uses inductive discipline, explaining the effects of her transgression on others. Induction supports conscience development by clarifying how the child should behave and fostering empathy. (Stephen Marks)*

Morality as the Adoption of Societal Norms

The two perspectives we are about to discuss, psychoanalytic and social learning theory, offer quite different perspectives on how children become moral beings. Yet both regard moral development as a matter of **internalization**: adopting preexisting, ready-made standards for right action as one's own. Each view focuses on how morality moves from society to individual—that is, how children acquire norms, or prescriptions for good conduct, widely held by members of their social group (Gibbs & Schnell, 1985).

PSYCHOANALYTIC THEORY

According to Sigmund Freud, morality emerges between ages 3 and 6 during the phallic stage, a time when sexual impulses transfer to the genital region of the body, and the well-known Oedipus conflict arises. The young boy wishes to have his mother all to himself and feels jealous of and hostile toward his father. A similar Electra conflict exists for girls, who want to possess their fathers and who envy their mothers. These feelings soon lead to intense anxiety, since children fear they will lose their parents' love and be punished for their unacceptable wishes. To master the anxiety, avoid punishment, and maintain the affection of parents, children form a **superego**, or conscience, through **identification** with the same-sex parent. This means that they take the parent's characteristics into their personality, thereby internalizing standards that reflect society's norms. Finally, children turn the hostility previously aimed at the same-sex parent toward themselves, which leads to painful feelings of guilt each time the superego is disobeyed (Freud, 1925/1961).

In sum, Freud believed that children obtain their morality directly from their parents and act in accord with moral prescriptions to avoid punitive feelings of guilt from a harsh, restrictive superego. He viewed moral development as largely complete by age 5 or 6, with some strengthening of the superego in middle childhood.

■ IS FREUD'S THEORY SUPPORTED BY RESEARCH? Today, most child development researchers disagree with Freud's account of conscience development on several grounds. First, Freud's view of guilt as a hostile impulse redirected toward the self is no longer widely accepted. As we will see, high levels of self-blame are not associated with moral internalization. Instead, recent evidence suggests that guilt arises when a person intentionally engages in an unacceptable act and feels personally responsible for the outcome. From this perspective, children cannot experience a mature form of guilt without several cognitive capacities. These include awareness of themselves as autonomous beings who make choices about actions and the ability to distinguish intentional from unintentional acts. In Chapters 10 and 11, we saw that these understandings emerge during the preschool years and are refined in middle childhood. Although this is the same period Freud assigned to conscience formation, the basis of the guilt response differs sharply from his theory.

Second, if you look carefully at the Oedipus and Electra conflicts, you will see that discipline promoting fear of punishment and loss of parental love should motivate young children to behave morally (Hoffman, 1988; Kochanska, 1993). Yet research shows that children whose parents frequently use threats, commands, or physical force tend to

Internalization
The process of moral development in which children adopt preexisting, ready-made standards for right action as their own.

Superego
In Freud's theory, the part of the personality that is the seat of conscience and is often in conflict with the id's desires.

Identification
In Freud's theory, the process leading to formation of the superego in which children take the same-sex parent's characteristics into their personality.

violate normative standards often and feel little guilt after harming others. In the case of love withdrawal—for example, when a parent refuses to speak to or actually states a dislike for the child—children often respond with high levels of self-blame after misbehaving. They might think to themselves, "I'm no good" or "Nobody loves me." Eventually, these children may protect themselves from overwhelming feelings of guilt by denying the emotion when they do something wrong. So they, too, develop a weak conscience (Zahn-Waxler et al., 1990).

In contrast to these techniques, a special type of discipline called **induction** does support conscience formation. It involves pointing out the effects of the child's misbehavior on others. At younger ages, referring to simple, direct outcomes works best, as in: "If you keep pushing him, he'll fall down and cry." Later, parents can explain why the child's action was inappropriate, perhaps by referring to the other person's intentions: "Don't yell at him. He was only trying to help." And with further cognitive advances, more subtle psychological explanations can be given: "He feels proud of his tower and you knocked it down" (Hoffman, 1983, p. 246). As long as the explanation matches the child's ability to understand and the child's attention is elicited by generally nurturant parents, induction is effective as early as 2 years of age. In one study, mothers who consistently used inductive reasoning had preschoolers who were more likely to make up for their misdeeds. They also showed more prosocial behavior, in that they spontaneously gave hugs, toys, and verbal sympathy to others in distress (Zahn-Waxler, Radke-Yarrow, & King, 1979).

Why is induction so effective? First, it tells children how to behave so they can call on this information in future situations. Second, by pointing out the impact of the child's actions on others, parents encourage children to empathize, which motivates use of the inductive information in prosocial behavior (Krevans & Gibbs, 1996). In contrast, discipline that relies too heavily on threats of punishment or love withdrawal produces such high levels of fear and anxiety that children cannot think clearly enough to figure out what they should do. These practices may stop unacceptable behavior temporarily, but in the long run they do not get children to internalize moral norms. However, mild warnings and disapproval may sometimes be necessary to get children to listen to the inductive message.

Although there is little support for Freudian mechanisms of conscience development, Freud was correct that guilt can be an important motivator of moral action. In one study, 4- to 11-year-olds were asked to complete ambiguous stories in which a child like themselves could have caused another person's distress. Children who made reference to empathy-related guilt reactions (expressions of personal responsibility, such as "She's sorry she pushed him down") were far more likely to help an adult in need in the laboratory (Chapman et al., 1987). Furthermore, 10- to 12-year-olds often end such stories by having the main character resolve to be less selfish and more considerate in the future. In older children, guilt may contribute to moral behavior by triggering a general motive to act morally that goes well beyond the immediate situation (Hoffman, 1980).

Despite the effectiveness of guilt in prompting moral action, Freud's theory is one-sided in viewing it as the only force that compels us to act morally. In addition, a wealth of research we will review later in this chapter indicates that contrary to what Freud believed, moral development is not an abrupt event that is virtually complete by the end of the preschool years. Instead, it is a far more gradual process, beginning in early childhood and extending into adulthood.

Finally, Freud's theory places a heavy burden on parents, who must ensure through their disciplinary practices that children develop an internalized conscience. The research we have reviewed indicates parental discipline is vitally important. Yet in earlier chapters we emphasized that parent–child interaction is a two-way street; children's characteristics can affect the success of certain parenting techniques. Turn to the From Research to Practice box on the following page for recent findings on the role of temperament in moral internalization.

Induction
A type of discipline in which the effects of the child's misbehavior on others are communicated to the child.

■ RECENT PSYCHOANALYTIC IDEAS. Recognizing the limitations of Freud's theory, recent psychoanalytic ideas underscore the importance of a positive parent–child relationship and much earlier development of morality. According to Robert Emde, sensitive emotional exchanges between caregiver and infant that support the attachment bond also serve as a vital foundation for acquiring moral standards. Toddlers who feel a secure sense of connection with the parent are more likely to be responsive to adult signals

FROM RESEARCH TO PRACTICE

Temperament and Moral Internalization in Young Children

When her mother reprimanded her sharply for pouring water on the floor as she played in her bath, 2-year-old Katherine burst into tears. An anxious, sensitive child, Katherine was so distressed that it took her mother 10 minutes to calm her down. Outside in the front yard the next day, Katherine's mother watched as her next-door neighbor patiently asked her 3-year-old son, who was about to pick the first tulips to blossom in the garden, not to touch the flowers. Alex, an active, adventurous child, paid no attention. As he pulled at another tulip, Alex's mother grabbed him, scolded him harshly, and carried him inside. Alex responded by kicking, hitting, and screaming, "Let me down, let me down!"

What explains Katherine and Alex's very different reactions to firm parental discipline? Grazyna Kochanska (1993) points out that children's temperaments affect the parenting procedures that best promote internalized patterns of concern and responsibility. In a recent study, she found that for temperamentally inhibited 2- and 3-year-olds, gentle maternal discipline—reasoning, polite requests, suggestions, and distractions—predicted conscience development, measured in terms of compliance to directives and obedience to a prohibition (not touching some attractive toys) while the mother stepped out of a laboratory room. In contrast, for relatively fearless, impulsive children, mild disciplinary tactics showed no relationship to moral internalization. Instead, a secure attachment bond with the mother predicted compliance and obedience (Kochanska, 1995).

According to Kochanska, inhibited children like Katherine, who are prone to anxiety, are easily overcome by intense psychological discipline. Mild, patient tactics are sufficient to motivate them to internalize parental messages. In fact, research indicates that inhibited toddlers exposed to gentle intervention continue to show a more firmly internalized conscience, in the form of self-reported guilt and willingness to make amends after a transgression, during the school years (Kochanska, 1991). But impulsive children, such as Alex, may not respond to gentle interventions with enough discomfort to promote internalization. Yet frequent use of power-assertive methods is not effective either, since these techniques spark anger and resentment, which interfere with the child's processing of parental messages.

Why is secure attachment predictive of conscience development in nonanxious children? Kochanska suggests that when children are so low in anxiety that typically effective disciplinary practices fail, a close bond with the caregiver provides an alternative foundation for conscience formation. It motivates children unlikely to experience negative emotion to internalize rules as a means of preserving a spirit of affection and cooperation with the parent.

To foster early moral development, parents must tailor their child-rearing strategies to their child's temperament. In Katherine's case, a soft-spoken correction would probably have been effective. For Alex, taking extra steps to build a warm, caring relationship during times when he behaves well is likely to promote moral internalization. Although Alex's parents need to use firmer and more frequent discipline than Katherine's do, emphasizing power assertion is counterproductive for both children. Do these findings remind you of the notion of goodness of fit, discussed in Chapter 10? Return to page 402 to review this idea.

about how to behave, which increase in the second year of life (Emde et al., 1991; Kochanska & Aksan, 1995).

Furthermore, current psychoanalytic theorists believe that the superego children build from parental teachings consists not just of prohibitions or "don'ts" (as Freud emphasized), but also of positive guidelines for behavior, or "do's." After formulating a punitive superego, Freud acknowledged that conscience includes a set of ideals based on love rather than threats of punishment, but he placed less emphasis on this aspect.[1] The positive side of conscience probably develops first, out of toddlers' participation in morally relevant activities with caregivers, such as helping to wipe up spilled milk or move a delicate object from one place to another. In these situations, parents offer generous praise, and the small child smiles broadly with pride—an early sign of internalization of parental moral standards.

A short time later, parents' warnings and disapproval of forbidden acts evoke shame along with "hurt feelings"—blends of sadness, anger, and pouting—that may be the forerunners of guilt. Soon, toddlers use their capacity for social referencing to check back with the parent, searching for emotional information that can serve as a guide for moral conduct. With a disapproving glance or shake of the head, parents respond with subtle but powerful messages about the moral meaning of the child's actions. Around age 3, guilt reactions are clearly evident (see Chapter 10) (Emde & Buchsbaum, 1990).

[1] Erik Erikson's psychosocial theory, which builds on Freud's stage sequence, accepts the restrictive side of the superego but also views it as a positive, constructive force in development. For example, Erikson described the outcome of the phallic stage as a sense of initiative, which provides the foundation for ambition and purpose in life (see Chapter 1, page 17). In addition, Erikson (1968) believed conscience development extended into the adult years. Recall from Chapter 11 that an important part of identity development involves the search for a set of moral values. These are selected during late adolescence as identity is achieved, and they are refined during adulthood.

Notice how recent psychoanalytic formulations retain continuity with Freud's theory in regarding emotion as the primary basis for early moral development. Although little attention is paid to young children's reasoning about moral norms, values, or decisions (the emphasis of cognitive-developmental theory), it is possible that early morally relevant feelings are the platform on which a mature understanding of moral principles is built (Hoffman, 1991).

SOCIAL LEARNING THEORY

Unlike psychoanalytic theory, the social learning perspective does not consider morality to be a special form of human activity that follows a unique course of development. Instead, moral behavior is acquired just like any other set of responses: through modeling and reinforcement.

THE IMPORTANCE OF MODELING. According to the traditional behaviorist view, *operant conditioning* is an important way in which children pick up new responses. From this perspective, children start to behave in ways consistent with adult moral standards because parents and teachers follow up "good behavior" with *positive reinforcement* in the form of approval, affection, and other rewards.

However, it is unlikely that very many moral responses are initially acquired through operant conditioning. For a behavior to be reinforced, it must first occur spontaneously and then be rewarded. Yet many prosocial acts, such as sharing, helping, or comforting an unhappy playmate, do not occur often enough at first for reinforcement to explain their rapid development in early childhood. Instead, social learning theorists believe children learn to behave morally largely through *modeling*—by observing and imitating adults who demonstrate appropriate behavior (Bandura, 1977; Grusec, 1988). Once children acquire a moral response, such as sharing or telling the truth, reinforcement in the form of praising the act ("That was a nice thing to do") and attributing good behavior to the character of the child ("You're a very kind and considerate boy") increases its frequency (Mills & Grusec, 1989).

Many studies show that models who behave helpfully or generously increase young children's prosocial responses. Models exert their most powerful effect on prosocial development during the preschool years. At the end of early childhood, children who have a history of consistent exposure to caring adults tend to behave prosocially regardless of whether a model is present. By that time, they have internalized prosocial rules from repeated experiences in which they have seen others help and give and have been encouraged to behave in a similar way themselves (Mussen & Eisenberg-Berg, 1977). In contrast, younger children are still formulating these norms and finding out the conditions under which to apply them. Consequently, they look to adult models for information about where, when, and what kinds of prosocial behaviors are appropriate (Peterson, 1982).

A model's characteristics have a major impact on children's willingness to imitate their behavior. First, preschoolers are more likely to copy the prosocial actions of an adult who is warm and responsive than one who is cold and distant (Yarrow, Scott, & Waxler, 1973). Warmth may make children more receptive to the model and therefore more attentive to the model's behavior. Also, warm, affectionate responding is an example of altruism, and part of what children may be imitating is this aspect of the model's behavior. Second, children tend to select competent, powerful models to imitate—the reason they are especially willing to copy the behavior of older peers and adults. Powerful individuals serve as effective models because children want to acquire their prestige and mastery for themselves (Bandura, 1977). A final characteristic that affects children's willingness to imitate is whether adults "practice what they preach." When models say one thing and do another—for example, announce that "it's important to help others" but rarely engage in helpful acts—children generally choose the most lenient standard of behavior that adults demonstrate (Mischel & Liebert, 1966).

So far, we have seen that children can pick up many positive behaviors through observing others. Can modeling also help children learn how to inhibit unfavorable acts? Research suggests that it can under certain conditions. Joan Grusec and her colleagues (1979) had a person first try to lure an adult model and then 5- to 8-year-olds away from a boring task to play with toys that the experimenter had forbidden them to touch. A model who verbalized that she was resisting temptation and clearly stated her reason for doing so ("I can't come play with the toys because I'm here to sort cards, and I always try to do what's right") was more effective in promoting children's self-restraint than a model who merely did not touch the toys. These findings indicate that to inspire resistance to temptation, models need to make their own efforts explicit by verbalizing them. The verbalization also provides children with a rationale for self-restraint that they can call on when similar situations arise in the future.

■ *One alternative to harsh punishment is time out, in which children are removed from the immediate setting until they are ready to act appropriately. Time out is useful when a child is out of control and other effective methods of discipline cannot be applied at the moment. Once this child calms down, induction can help her understand how to behave in the future. (Tom Pollak/Monkmeyer Press)*

■ EFFECTS OF PUNISHMENT. One social learning approach to moral development regards punishment as a prime motivator of moral action. According to this view, when children experience scolding, criticism, and spankings for misbehavior, painful anxiety is associated with the unacceptable behavior. Since anxiety is reexperienced each time the child starts to transgress again, it is best avoided by not engaging in the act (Aronfreed, 1968). Yet we have already seen in our discussion of Freud's theory that harsh, punitive discipline is less effective in promoting conscience formation than rational, inductive techniques. The use of sharp reprimands or physical force to restrain or move a child is justified when immediate obedience is necessary—for example, when a 3-year-old is about to run into the street. In fact, parents are most likely to use forceful methods under these conditions. When they are interested in fostering long-term goals, such as acting kindly toward others, they tend to rely on warmth and reasoning (Kuczynski, 1984).

Most parents realize that the usefulness of punishment is limited and that it should be applied sparingly, and the majority of social learning theorists agree. Indeed, a great deal of research shows that punishment promotes only momentary compliance, not lasting changes in children's behavior. Children who are frequently criticized, shouted at, or slapped are likely to display the unacceptable response again as soon as adults are out of sight and they can get away with it. In fact, children of highly punitive parents are known to be especially aggressive and defiant outside the home (Strassberg et al., 1994).

Harsh punishment also has undesirable side effects. First, it provides children with adult models of aggression. Second, children who are frequently punished soon learn to avoid the punishing adult. When children refrain from interacting with adults who are responsible for their upbringing, those adults have little opportunity to teach desirable behaviors that can replace unacceptable responses. Finally, since punishment "works" to stop children's misbehavior temporarily, it offers immediate relief to adults, and they are reinforced for using coercive discipline. For this reason, a punitive adult is likely to punish with greater frequency over time, a course of action that can spiral into serious abuse.

■ ALTERNATIVES TO HARSH PUNISHMENT. Alternatives to verbal and physical punishment can reduce the side effects of coercive tactics. One technique is called **time out**, in which children are removed from the immediate setting—for example, by sending them to their rooms—until they are ready to act appropriately. Time out is useful when a child is out of control and other effective methods of discipline cannot be applied at the moment (Betz, 1994). It usually requires only a few minutes to change children's behavior, and it also offers a "cooling off" period for parents, who may be highly angered by children's unacceptable acts. Another approach is withdrawal of privileges, such as loss of allowance or deprivation of a special experience like going to the movies or watching a favorite TV program. Removing privileges often generates some resentment in children, but it allows parents to avoid using harsh techniques that could easily intensify into violence (Parke, 1977).

Although its usefulness is limited, punishment can play a valuable role in moral development. Earlier we noted that mild warnings and disapproval are occasionally necessary if induction is to be effective. And recall William Damon's (1995) argument, discussed in Chapter 11, that parents must be willing to assert their authority to avoid the dangers of excessive child-centeredness (see page 434).

When parents do decide to use punishment, its effectiveness can be increased in several ways. The first involves consistency. Punishment that is unpredictable is related to especially high rates of disobedience in children. When parents permit children to act inappropriately on some occasions but not others, children are confused about how to behave, and the unacceptable act persists. Second, a warm parent–child relationship

Time out
A form of mild punishment in which children are removed from the immediate setting until they are ready to act appropriately.

increases the effectiveness of an occasional punishment (Parke & Walters, 1967). Children of involved, caring parents find the interruption in parental affection that accompanies punishment to be especially unpleasant. As a result, they want to regain the warmth and approval of parents as quickly as possible. Third, punishment works best when it is accompanied by a rationale. Explanations permit children to internalize the adult's reasoning, recall the misdeed in similar situations, and relate it to expectations for behavior (Walters & Andres, 1967).

Finally, parenting practices that do not wait for children to misbehave but that encourage and reward good conduct are the most effective forms of discipline. This means letting children know ahead of time how to act, serving as a good example, and praising children when they behave well (Zahn-Waxler & Robinson, 1995). When parents use a proactive approach with 1- to 3-year-olds that makes appropriate demands for competent behavior, children are more likely to comply and less likely to display behavior problems at age 5 (Kuczynski & Kochanska, 1995). Adults can also reduce opportunities for misbehavior. For example, at the supermarket, where exciting temptations abound, they can engage young children in conversations and encourage them to help with shopping rather than waiting for them to get into mischief before intervening (Holden, 1983; Holden & West, 1989). When adults help children acquire acceptable behaviors that they can use to replace forbidden acts, the need for punishment is greatly reduced.

LIMITATIONS OF "MORALITY AS THE ADOPTION OF SOCIETAL NORMS" PERSPECTIVE

Learning to conform to societal norms is, without question, an essential aspect of moral development. Without a shared moral code, people would disregard each other's rights whenever their desires conflicted. Furthermore, external sanctions are not enough to ensure morality. The emphasis psychoanalytic and social learning theories place on internalization is vital, since people must continuously govern their own behavior in countless everyday situations in which moral violations would remain unobserved and undetected by others (Bandura, 1991).

Nevertheless, a major criticism of theories that treat morality as entirely a matter of social conformity is that prevailing standards sometimes are at odds with important ethical principles and social goals. Under these conditions, deliberate violation of norms is not immoral. It is justifiable and courageous. Think, for a moment, about historical figures who rose to greatness because they refused to accept the validity of prevailing societal norms. Abraham Lincoln's opposition to slavery, Susan B. Anthony's leadership in the crusade for women's suffrage, and Martin Luther King's campaign to end racial prejudice are only a few examples. Few of us would place these leaders in the same moral class as Al Capone or Jack the Ripper. Yet all have in common the fact that their conduct was seriously at odds with widely accepted standards (Rest, 1983).

Cognitive-developmental theorists believe that neither identification with parents nor direct teaching, modeling, and reinforcement are the major means through which children become moral beings. Instead of simply internalizing existing rules and expectations, the cognitive-developmental perspective assumes that individuals develop morally through **construction**—actively attending to and interrelating multiple aspects of situations in which social conflicts arise and deriving new moral understandings. As James Rest (1983) explains, "Children do not just learn lists of prescriptions and prohibitions; they also come to understand the nature and function of social arrangements," including promises, bargains, divisions of labor, and fair principles and procedures for regulating human relationships (p. 616). In other words, children make moral judgments on the basis of concepts they construct about justice and fairness (Gibbs, 1991).

Construction
The process of moral development in which children actively attend to and interrealte multiple aspects of situations in which social conflicts arise and derive new moral understandings.

The cognitive-developmental position on morality is unique in its view of the child as a thinking moral being who wonders about right and wrong and searches for moral truth. We will see in the following sections that cognitive-developmental theorists differ in the methods they use to study moral understanding and in their timing of certain moral advances. But all agree that changes in children's reasoning are at the heart of moral development.

BRIEF REVIEW

According to sociobiology, morality is grounded in our genetic heritage through prewired emotional reactions. Although psychoanalytic and social learning theories offer different accounts of development, both emphasize internalization—children's adoption of preexisting standards for behavior as their own. Contrary to predictions from Freudian theory, power assertion and love withdrawal do not promote conscience formation. Instead, induction, against a backdrop of nurturance, is far more effective. Social learning theorists have shown that modeling combined with reinforcement in the form of praise is effective in encouraging prosocial acts. In contrast, harsh punishment promotes only temporary compliance, not lasting changes in children's behavior. A major criticism of theories that view morality as entirely a matter of internalization is that sometimes violation of normative prescriptions is ethically valid. The cognitive-developmental perspective regards construction—actively thinking about right and wrong in situations in which social conflicts arise and deriving new moral understandings—as central to moral development.

Morality as Social Understanding

According to the cognitive-developmental perspective, cognitive maturity and social experience lead to advances in moral understanding, from a superficial orientation to physical power and external consequences to a more profound appreciation of interpersonal relationships, societal institutions, and lawmaking systems. As their grasp of social cooperation expands, children's ideas about what ought to be done when the needs and desires of people conflict also change, toward increasingly just, fair, and balanced solutions to moral problems (Gibbs, 1995; Rest, 1983).

PIAGET'S THEORY OF MORAL DEVELOPMENT

Piaget's (1932/1965) early work on children's moral judgments was the original inspiration for the cognitive-developmental perspective and continues to stimulate new research. To study children's ideas about morality, Piaget relied on open-ended clinical interviews, questioning Swiss children between ages 5 and 13 about their understanding of rules in the game of marbles. In addition, he gave children stories in which characters' intentions to engage in right or wrong action and the consequences of their behavior were varied. In the best known of these stories, children were asked which of two boys—well-intentioned John, who breaks 15 cups while on his way to dinner, or ill-intentioned Henry, who breaks 1 cup while stealing some jam—is naughtier and why.

> *Story A:* A little boy who is called John is in his room. He is called to dinner. He goes into the dining room. But behind the door there was a chair, and on the chair there was a tray with fifteen cups on it. John couldn't have known that there was all this behind the door. He goes in, the door knocks against the tray, bang go the fifteen cups, and they all get broken!
>
> *Story B:* Once there was a little boy whose name was Henry. One day when his mother was out he tried to get some jam out of the cupboard. He climbed up on to a chair and stretched out his arm. But the jam was too high up and he couldn't reach it and have any. But while he was trying to get it he knocked over a cup. The cup fell down and broke. (Piaget, 1932/1965, p. 122)

From children's responses, Piaget identified two broad stages of moral understanding: heteronomous and autonomous morality.

HETERONOMOUS MORALITY, OR MORAL REALISM (ABOUT 5 TO 10 YEARS). During the early preschool years and before the beginning of this stage, children show little understanding of rules that govern social behavior. When they play rule-oriented games, they are unconcerned about winning, losing, or coordinating their actions with those of others. Around age 5, as children enter the period of **heteronomous morality**, they start to show great concern with and respect for rules.

The word *heteronomous* means under the authority of another. As the term suggests, children of this stage view rules as handed down by authorities (God, parents, and teachers), as having a permanent existence, as unchangeable, and as requiring strict obedience. For example, young children state that the rules of the game of marbles cannot be changed, explaining that "God didn't teach [the new rules]," "you couldn't play any other way," or "it would be cheating. . . . A fair rule is one that is in the game" (Piaget, 1932/1965, pp. 58, 59, 63).

According to Piaget, two factors limit children's moral understanding: (1) the power of adults to insist that children comply, which promotes unquestioning respect for rules and those who enforce them; and (2) cognitive immaturity, especially egocentrism. Because young children think all people view rules in the same way, their moral understanding is characterized by **realism**. That is, they regard rules as external features of reality rather than as cooperative principles that can be modified at will.

Together, adult power, egocentrism, and realism result in superficial moral understandings. In judging an act's wrongness, younger children focus on objective consequences rather than intent to do harm. For example, in the stories about John and Henry mentioned earlier, they regard John as naughtier because he broke more cups, despite his innocent intentions.

AUTONOMOUS MORALITY, OR THE MORALITY OF COOPERATION (ABOUT 10 YEARS AND OLDER). Cognitive development, gradual release from adult control, and peer interaction lead children to make the transition to **autonomous morality**. Piaget regarded arguments and disagreements between peers as especially facilitating (see Chapter 6). Through them, children become aware that people can have different perspectives about moral action and that intentions, not objective consequences, should serve as the basis for judging behavior.

Furthermore, as children participate as equals in activities with peers, they learn to settle conflicts in mutually beneficial ways. Gradually, they start to use a standard of fairness called **reciprocity**, in which they express the same concern for the welfare of others as they do for themselves. Most of us are familiar with reciprocity in the form of the Golden Rule: "Do unto others as you would have them do unto you." But Piaget found that the way to the Golden Rule must be paved with a "cruder" form of reciprocity: "You scratch my back and I'll scratch yours." It defines the beginning of the morality of cooperation.

According to Piaget, reciprocity helps children realize that rules are flexible, socially agreed-on principles that can be revised to suit the will of the majority. Children of the autonomous stage no longer regard unquestioning obedience to adults as a sound basis for moral action. They recognize that at times there may be good reason to break or change a rule.

Furthermore, reciprocity leads to a new perspective on punishment: it should be reciprocity based, or rationally related to the offense. In other words, it should fit the seriousness of the transgression and, whenever possible, be a logical consequence of it—for example, a cheater whom no one will play with, a liar whom no one will believe anymore, even when he tells the truth. Finally, punishment should be meted out in a fair, even-handed fashion to everyone responsible for an offense, guaranteeing equal justice for all.

Heteronomous morality
Piaget's first stage of moral development, in which children view rules as having a permanent existence, as unchangeable, and as requiring strict obedience.

Realism
A view of rules as external features of reality rather than cooperative principles. Characterizes Piaget's heteronomous stage.

Autonomous morality
Piaget's second stage of moral development, in which children view rules as flexible, socially agreed-on principles that can be revised to suit the will of the majority.

Reciprocity
A standard of fairness in which individuals express the same concern for the welfare of others as they do for themselves.

EVALUATION OF PIAGET'S THEORY

Follow-up research on Piaget's theory indicates that it describes the general direction of change in moral judgment fairly well. In many studies, some conducted in different cultures, the diverse characteristics that distinguish heteronomous from autonomous reasoning are related to age. Also, much evidence supports Piaget's conclusion that moral understanding is supported by cognitive maturity, gradual release from adult control, and peer interaction (Lickona, 1976). We will consider these findings in greater detail when we turn to extensions of Piaget's work by Lawrence Kohlberg and his followers. Nevertheless, several aspects of Piaget's theory have been questioned because they underestimate the moral capacities of young children.

INTENTIONS AND MORAL JUDGMENTS. Look again at the stories about John and Henry on page 469. Because bad intentions are paired with little damage and good intentions with a great deal of damage, Piaget's method yields a conservative picture of young children's ability to make moral judgments. In Chapter 11, we showed that 3- to 5-year-olds are often sensitive to cues about others' intentions. When questioned about moral issues in a way that makes a person's intent stand out as strongly as the harm they do, preschool and early school-age children are quite capable of judging ill-intentioned people as naughtier than well-intentioned ones (Nelson-Le Gall, 1985; Yuill & Perner, 1988). As further evidence, by age 4, children clearly recognize the difference between two morally relevant intentional behaviors: truthfulness and lying. They approve of telling the truth and disapprove of lying, even when a lie remains undetected (Bussey, 1992).

Nevertheless, an advanced understanding of the morality of intentions does await the emergence of autonomous morality. Research indicates that 5- and 6-year-olds interpret statements of intention in a rigid, heteronomous fashion. They believe that once you say you will do something, you are obligated to follow through, even if uncontrollable circumstances (such as an accident) make it difficult or impossible for you to do so. By age 9 or 10, children realize that not keeping your word is much worse in some situations than others—namely, when you are able to do so and permit another person to count on your actions (Mant & Perner, 1988). Appeals to intangible considerations, such as trust (as opposed to external, physical consequences) are also much more prevalent among these older children (Peterson, Peterson, & Seeto, 1983). In sum, Piaget was partly right and partly wrong about this aspect of moral reasoning.

REASONING ABOUT AUTHORITY. New evidence on young children's understanding of authority reveals that they do not regard adults with the unquestioning respect Piaget assumed. Later in this chapter, we will see that preschoolers judge certain acts, such as hitting and stealing, to be wrong regardless of the opinions of authorities. When asked to explain why they think these behaviors should be prohibited, even 3- and 4-year-olds express concerns about harming or otherwise violating the welfare of other people rather than obeying the dictates of adults (Nucci & Turiel, 1978; Smetana, 1981, 1985).

By age 4, children have formed differentiated notions about the legitimacy of authority figures that are refined further during the school years (Laupa, 1995). In one study, kindergartners through sixth graders were asked questions designed to assess their view of how broad a school principal's authority should be. Pupils of all ages did not conceive of an authority as having general powers that apply across all situations. Most rejected a principal's right to set rules and issue directives in settings other than his own school, a response that strengthened with age. However, when an act (fighting) could harm another person, children made an exception: They thought a principal should intervene and stop the behavior if it occurred in an out-of-school public context (a city park). But most did not extend this right to a private context (the child's home) (Laupa & Turiel, 1993).

Young children's notions of authority are not limited to unquestioning respect for adults, as Piaget assumed. These pupils recognize their principal's right to set rules and issue directives in his own school, but they are likely to reject his authority in most other situations. (Jeffrey Dunn/Stock Boston)

Furthermore, adult status is not required for preschool and school-age children to accept someone as an authority. Peers are also regarded as legitimate authorities when they hold certain positions (such as safety-patrol member) or are particularly knowledgeable in a skill area (Laupa, 1991, 1995). Although young children's concepts of authority tend to focus on power and status, several factors are coordinated at a much earlier age than Piaget anticipated—the attributes of the individual, the type of behavior to be controlled, and the context in which it occurs.

STAGEWISE PROGRESSION. An additional point about Piaget's theory is that the characteristics associated with each stage do not correlate very highly, as we would expect if each represented a general, unifying organization of moral judgment. As Thomas Lickona (1976) puts it, "The child's moral thought, as it unfolds in Piagetian interviews, is not all of a piece but more of a patchwork of diverse parts" (p. 240). But in fairness, Piaget (1932/1965) observed a mixture of heteronomous and autonomous reasoning in the responses of many children and recommended that the two moralities be viewed as fluid, overlapping phases rather than tightly knit stages.

Finally, moral development is currently regarded as a more extended process than Piaget believed. In fact, Kohlberg's theory, to which we now turn, identifies three stages beyond the first appearance of autonomous morality. Over the past two decades, Piaget's groundbreaking work has been supplanted by Kohlberg's more comprehensive six-stage sequence. Nevertheless, it is clear that Kohlberg's theory is a direct continuation of the research Piaget began—the search for universal stages of moral development and the study of how moral understanding is intimately tied to cognitive growth.

KOHLBERG'S EXTENSION OF PIAGET'S THEORY

Like Piaget, Kohlberg used a clinical interviewing procedure to study moral development, but he based his stage sequence on situations quite different from Piaget's stories. Whereas Piaget asked children to judge the naughtiness of a character who had already decided on a moral course of action, Kohlberg presented people with **moral dilemmas** and asked them to decide both what the main actor should do and why. Perhaps as a result, he obtained a clearer picture of the reasoning on which moral decisions are based. Today, Kohlberg's clinical interviewing procedure is widely used to assess moral understanding. More efficient, questionnaire approaches have also been devised.

THE CLINICAL INTERVIEW. Each of Kohlberg's dilemmas presents a genuine crisis that pits one moral value against another. The best known of these is the "Heinz dilemma," which asks individuals to choose between the value of obeying the law (not stealing) and the value of human life (saving a dying person):

> In Europe, a woman was near death from cancer. There was one drug the doctors thought might save her. A druggist in the same town had discovered it, but he was charging ten times what the drug cost him to make. The sick woman's husband, Heinz, went to everyone he knew to borrow the money, but he could only get together half of what it cost. The druggist refused to sell it cheaper or let Heinz pay later. So Heinz got desperate and broke into the man's store to steal the drug for his wife. Should Heinz have done that? Why or why not? (paraphrased from Colby et al., 1983, p. 77)

Kohlberg emphasized that it is the *structure* of the answer—the way an individual reasons about the dilemma—and not the *content* of the response (whether to steal or not to steal) that determines moral maturity. Individuals who believe Heinz should take the drug and those who think he should not can be found at each of Kohlberg's first four stages. To bring out the structure of moral understanding, the interview is lengthy and free-ranging. After a dilemma is presented, follow-up questions elicit views on such issues as obedience to laws and authority figures and understanding of higher moral values, such as respect for human life. In the Heinz dilemma, the interviewer would ask: "If Heinz does not love his wife, should he still steal the drug for her?" "Why or why not?" "Is it important for people to do everything they can to save another's life?" "Why?" "It is against the law for Heinz to steal. Does that make it morally wrong?" "Why or why not?"

Although structure is the primary consideration for determining an individual's moral progress, at the highest two stages content is also relevant. Morally mature individuals do not just agree on why certain actions are justified. They also agree on what people ought to do when faced with a moral dilemma. Given a choice between obeying the law and preserving individual rights, the most advanced moral thinkers support individual rights (in the Heinz dilemma, stealing the drug to save a life). As we look at development in Kohlberg's scheme, we will see that moral reasoning and content are at first independent, but eventually they are integrated into a coherent ethical system (Kohlberg, Levine, & Hewer, 1983). Does this remind you of adolescents' efforts to formulate a sound, well-organized set of personal values in identity development, discussed in Chapter 11? According to some theorists, the development of identity and moral understanding are part of the same process (Davidson & Youniss, 1991; Marcia, 1988).

THE SOCIOMORAL REFLECTION MEASURE–SHORT FORM. The most recently developed questionnaire instrument for assessing moral understanding is the **Sociomoral Reflection Measure–Short Form (SRM–SF)**. Like Kohlberg's clinical interview, the SRM–SF asks individuals to evaluate the importance of moral values and produce moral reasoning. Here are four of its eleven questions:

> Let's say a friend of yours needs help and may even die, and you're the only person who can save him or her. How important is it for a person (without losing his or her own life) to save the life of a friend?

Moral dilemma
A conflict situation presented to research participants, who are asked to decide both what the main actor should do and why. Used to assess the development of moral reasoning.

Sociomoral Reflection Measure–Short Form (SRM–SF)
A questionnaire for assessing moral understanding in which individuals rate the importance of moral values addressed by brief questions and explain their ratings. Does not require research participants to read and think about lengthy moral dilemmas.

What about saving the life of anyone? How important is it for a person (without losing his or her own life) to save the life of a stranger?

How important is it for people not to take things that belong to other people?

How important is it for people to obey the law? (Gibbs, Basinger, & Fuller, 1992, pp. 151–152)

After reading each question, participants rate the importance of the value it addresses (as "very important," "important," or "not important") and write a brief explanation of their rating. The explanations are coded for thinking that reflects an adaptation of Kohlberg's stages.

The SRM–SF is far less time consuming than clinical interviewing because it does not require people to read and think about lengthy moral dilemmas. Instead, they merely evaluate moral values and justify their evaluations. Nevertheless, scores on the SRM–SF correlate well with those obtained from clinical interviews (Basinger, Gibbs, & Fuller, 1995). Apparently, moral judgment can be measured without using dilemmas—a discovery that is likely to ease the task of conducting moral development research.

KOHLBERG'S STAGES OF MORAL UNDERSTANDING. Kohlberg organized his six stages into three general levels and made strong statements about the properties of this sequence. First, he regarded the stages as invariant and universal—a sequence of steps that people everywhere move through in a fixed order. Second, he viewed each new stage as building on reasoning of the preceding stage, resulting in a more logically consistent and morally adequate concept of justice. Finally, he saw each stage as an organized whole—a qualitatively distinct pattern of moral reasoning that a person applies across a wide range of situations (Colby & Kohlberg, 1987). Recall from Chapter 6 that these characteristics are the very ones Piaget used to describe his cognitive stages.

Furthermore, Kohlberg believed that moral understanding is promoted by the same factors that Piaget thought were important for cognitive development: disequilibrium, or actively grappling with moral issues and noticing weaknesses in one's current thinking; and gains in perspective taking, which permit individuals to resolve moral conflicts in more complex and effective ways. As we examine Kohlberg's developmental sequence and illustrate it with responses to the Heinz dilemma, look for changes in cognition and perspective taking that each stage assumes.

The Preconventional Level. At the **preconventional level**, morality is externally controlled. As in Piaget's heteronomous stage, children accept the rules of authority figures, and actions are judged by their consequences. Behaviors that result in punishment are viewed as bad, and those that lead to rewards are seen as good.

- *Stage 1: The punishment and obedience orientation.* Children at this stage find it difficult to consider two points of view in a moral dilemma. As a result, they ignore people's intentions and instead focus on fear of authority and avoidance of punishment as reasons for behaving morally.

Prostealing: "If you let your wife die, you will get in trouble. You'll be blamed for not spending the money to help her, and there'll be an investigation of you and the druggist for your wife's death." (Kohlberg, 1969, p. 381)

Antistealing: "You shouldn't steal the drug because you'll be caught and sent to jail if you do. If you do get away, [you'd be scared that] the police would catch up with you any minute." (Kohlberg, 1969, p. 381)

- *Stage 2: The instrumental purpose orientation.* Awareness that people can have different perspectives in a moral dilemma appears, but at first this understanding is very concrete. Individuals view right action as what satisfies their needs or otherwise results in a personal advantage, and they believe others also act out of self-interest. Reciprocity is understood as equal exchange of favors—"you do this for me and I'll do that for you."

Prostealing: "The druggist can do what he wants and Heinz can do what he wants to do. . . . But if Heinz decides to risk jail to save his wife, it's his life he's risking; he can do what he wants with it. And the same goes for the druggist; it's up to him to decide what he wants to do." (Rest, 1979, p. 26)

Preconventional level
Kohlberg's first level of moral development, in which moral understanding is based on rewards, punishment, and the power of authority figures.

Antistealing: "[Heinz] is running more risk than it's worth unless he's so crazy about her he can't live without her. Neither of them will enjoy life if she's an invalid." (Rest, 1979, p. 27)

The Conventional Level. At the **conventional level**, individuals continue to regard conformity to social rules as important, but not for reasons of self-interest. They believe that actively maintaining the current social system is important for ensuring positive human relationships and societal order.

- *Stage 3: The "good boy–good girl" orientation, or the morality of interpersonal cooperation.* The desire to obey rules because they promote social harmony first appears in the context of close personal ties. Stage 3 individuals want to maintain the affection and approval of friends and relatives by being a "good person"—trustworthy, loyal, respectful, helpful, and nice. The capacity to view a two-person relationship from the vantage point of an impartial, outside observer supports this new approach to morality. At this stage, the individual understands reciprocity in terms of the Golden Rule.

Prostealing: "No one will think you're bad if you steal the drug, but your family will think you're an inhuman husband if you don't. If you let your wife die, you'll never be able to look anyone in the face again." (Kohlberg, 1969, p. 381)

Antistealing: "It isn't just the druggist who will think you're a criminal, everyone else will too. After you steal it, you'll feel bad thinking how you brought dishonor on your family and yourself; you won't be able to face anyone again." (Kohlberg, 1969, p. 381)

- *Stage 4: The social-order-maintaining orientation.* At this stage, the individual takes into account a larger perspective—that of societal laws. Moral choices no longer depend on close ties to others. Instead, rules must be enforced in the same even-handed fashion for everyone, and each member of society has a personal duty to uphold them. The Stage 4 individual believes laws cannot be disobeyed under any circumstances because they are vital for ensuring societal order.

Prostealing: "He should steal it. Heinz has a duty to protect his wife's life; it's a vow he took in marriage. But it's wrong to steal, so he would have to take the drug with the idea of paying the druggist for it and accepting the penalty for breaking the law later."

Antistealing: "It's a natural thing for Heinz to want to save his wife but. . . . You have to follow the rules regardless of how you feel or regardless of the special circumstances. Even if his wife is dying, it's still his duty as a citizen to obey the law. No one else is allowed to steal, why should he be? If everyone starts breaking the law in a jam, there'd be no civilization, just crime and violence." (Rest, 1979, p. 30)

The Postconventional or Principled Level. Individuals at the **postconventional level** move beyond unquestioning support for the rules and laws of their own society. They define morality in terms of abstract principles and values that apply to all situations and societies.

- *Stage 5: The social-contract orientation.* At Stage 5, individuals regard laws and rules as flexible instruments for furthering human purposes. They can imagine alternatives to their social order, and they emphasize fair procedures for interpreting and changing the law when there is a good reason to do so. When laws are consistent with individual rights and the interests of the majority, each person follows them because of a social-contract orientation—free and willing participation in the system because it brings about more good for people than if it did not exist.

Prostealing: "Although there is a law against stealing, the law wasn't meant to violate a person's right to life. Taking the drug does violate the law, but Heinz is justified in stealing in this instance. If Heinz is prosecuted for stealing, the law needs to be reinterpreted to take into account situations in which it goes against people's natural right to keep on living."

Conventional level
Kohlberg's second level of moral development, in which moral understanding is based on conforming to social rules to ensure positive human relationships and societal order.

Postconventional level
Kohlberg's highest level of moral development, in which individuals define morality in terms of abstract principles and values that apply to all situations and societies.

- *Stage 6: The universal ethical principle orientation.* At this highest stage, right action is defined by self-chosen ethical principles of conscience that are valid for all humanity, regardless of law and social agreement. These values are abstract, not concrete moral rules like the Ten Commandments. Stage 6 individuals typically mention such principles as equal consideration of the claims of all human beings and respect for the worth and dignity of each person.

Prostealing: "If Heinz does not do everything he can to save his wife, then he is putting some value higher than the value of life. It doesn't make sense to put respect for property above respect for life itself. [People] could live together without private property at all. Respect for human life and personality is absolute and accordingly [people] have a mutual duty to save one another from dying." (Rest, 1979, p. 37)

RESEARCH ON KOHLBERG'S STAGES

Is there support for Kohlberg's developmental sequence? If his theory is correct, movement through the stages should be related to age, cognitive development, and gains in perspective taking. Also, moral development should conform to the strict stage properties that Kohlberg assumed.

AGE-RELATED CHANGE AND INVARIANT STAGES. A wealth of cross-sectional research reveals that progress through Kohlberg's stages is strongly related to age (Rest, 1986). But longitudinal studies provide the most convincing evidence for Kohlberg's developmental sequence. The most extensive of these is a 20-year continuation of Kohlberg's first study of adolescent boys in which 58 of the 84 original participants were reinterviewed at regular 3- to 4-year intervals. Like cross-sectional findings, the correlation between age and moral maturity was strong, at .78. In addition, the stages formed an invariant developmental sequence. Almost all the individuals moved through them in the predicted order, without skipping steps or returning to less mature reasoning once a stage had been attained (Colby et al., 1983). Other longitudinal findings also confirm the invariance of Kohlberg's stages (Rest, 1986; Walker, 1989; Walker & Taylor, 1991b).

A striking feature of age trends in moral reasoning is that development is very slow and gradual. Figure 12.1 shows the extent to which individuals used each stage of moral reasoning between ages 10 and 36 in the longitudinal study just described. Notice how Stages 1 and 2 decrease in early adolescence, whereas Stage 3 increases through midadolescence and then declines. Stage 4 rises over the teenage years until, by early adulthood, it is the typical response. Few people move beyond it to Stage 5. In fact, postconventional morality is so rare that there is no clear evidence that Kohlberg's Stage 6 actually follows Stage 5. The highest stage of moral development is still a matter of speculation.

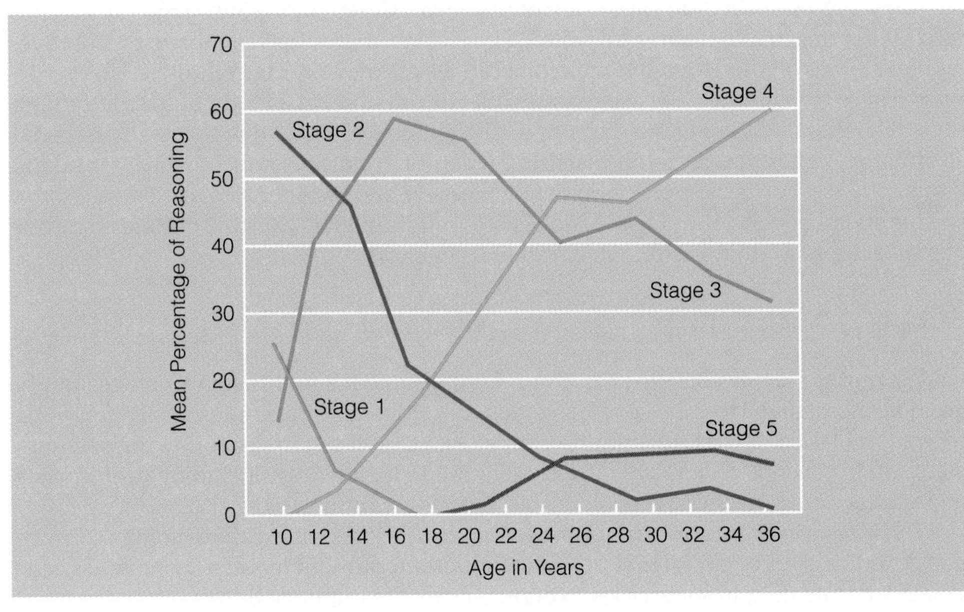

FIGURE 12.1

Mean percentage of moral reasoning at each stage by age in Kohlberg's 20-year longitudinal study of adolescent boys. (From A. Colby, L. Kohlberg, J. C. Gibbs, & M. Lieberman, 1983, "A Longitudinal Study of Moral Judgement," Monographs of the Society for Research in Child Development, *48 (1–2, Serial No. 200), p. 46. © The Society for Research in Child Development, Inc. Reprinted by permission.)*

ARE KOHLBERG'S STAGES ORGANIZED WHOLES? As you read the Heinz dilemma, you probably came up with your own solution to it. Now, try to think of a moral problem you recently faced in everyday life. How did you solve it? Did your reasoning fall at the same stage as your thinking about Heinz and his dying wife? If each of Kohlberg's stages forms an organized whole, then individuals should use the same level of moral reasoning across many tasks and situations.

When Kohlberg's interviewing procedure is used, most individuals do show fairly uniform reasoning from one moral dilemma to another (Walker, 1988). But Kohlberg's scoring procedure tends to minimize variability in people's responses. Alternative scoring approaches produce greater diversity in moral thought (Gibbs, Basinger, & Fuller, 1992; Rest, 1983).

Furthermore, when aspects of the dilemmas are changed, quality of thinking changes as well. When people generate real-life moral problems of their own, they tend to fall at a lower stage than on hypothetical dilemmas (Trevethan & Walker, 1989). Perhaps real-life problems elicit moral reasoning below a person's actual capacity because they bring out the many practical considerations involved in an actual moral conflict. Consistent with this idea, moral responses also become less mature when dilemmas highlight the possibility of punishment for the main actor—for example, stating that if Heinz decides to steal the drug, he will "be caught for sure and sent to prison" (Sobesky, 1983, p. 578). Emphasizing punishment increases concern with self-interest, a major preconventional basis of morality.

The influence of situational factors on moral judgment suggests that like Piaget's cognitive stages, Kohlberg's moral stages are best viewed in terms of a loose rather than strict concept of stage. Rather than developing in a neat, stepwise fashion, each individual seems to draw on a range of moral responses that vary with context. With age, this range shifts upward as less mature moral reasoning is gradually replaced by more advanced moral thought (Rest, 1979). Apparently, Piaget was right to think of less mature and more mature moralities as overlapping phases.

COGNITIVE PREREQUISITES FOR MORAL REASONING. Moral maturity, whether based on Piaget's or Kohlberg's theories, is positively correlated with IQ, performance on Piagetian cognitive tasks, and perspective-taking skill (Kurdek, 1980; Lickona, 1976; Rest, 1979). However, Kohlberg (1976) believed that moral development depends on cognition and perspective taking in a very specific way. He argued that each moral stage requires certain cognitive and perspective-taking capacities, but these are not enough to ensure moral advances. In addition, reorganization of thought unique to the moral domain is necessary. In other words, Kohlberg hypothesized that cognitive and perspective-taking, attainments are *necessary but not sufficient conditions* for each of the moral stages.

Recall from Chapter 11 that the "necessary but not sufficient" criterion also applies to the relation between Piaget's cognitive and Selman's perspective-taking stages, so Kohlberg's hypothesis is an expansion of this idea. Although no single study has examined all the stage relationships in Table 12.1, research shows that cognitive, perspective-taking, and moral development are related in ways consistent with Kohlberg's predictions (Krebs & Gillmore, 1982; Selman, 1976). For example, in a study of fourth through seventh graders, with only one exception all children at Stage 3 moral reasoning scored at either a higher stage or the matching stage of cognition and perspective taking (Walker, 1980). Furthermore, attempts to increase moral reasoning reveal that it cannot be stimulated beyond the stage for which an individual has the appropriate cognitive prerequisites (Arbuthnot et al., 1983; Walker & Richards, 1979).

ENVIRONMENTAL INFLUENCES ON MORAL REASONING

What other factors besides the attainment of Piaget's and Selman's stages might promote moral maturity? Earlier we mentioned Kohlberg's belief that actively grappling with moral issues is vital for moral change. As we will see in the following sections, many environmental factors are related to moral understanding, including peer interaction, child-rearing practices, schooling, and aspects of culture.

The weakness of this research is one we have mentioned many times before: Correlational studies cannot tell us for sure that an important cause of moral reasoning has been isolated. Fortunately, in some cases, experiments that manipulate the experience in question have been conducted, demonstrating its role in moral development. Furthermore, a

■ *Intense, animated discussions about moral issues in which peers confront, critique, and attempt to clarify one another's statements lead to gains in moral understanding. (Stephen Marks)*

growing body of evidence suggests that the way these experiences work is by inducing disequilibrium—presenting young people with cognitive challenges, which stimulate them to think about moral problems in more complex ways.

■ PEER INTERACTION. Research relating peer experiences to progress through Kohlberg's stages supports Piaget's belief that interaction with agemates can promote moral understanding. Maturity of moral reasoning is correlated with peer popularity, participation in social organizations, and service in leadership roles (Enright & Sutterfield, 1980; Harris, Mussen, & Rutherford, 1976). Studies conducted in Africa underline the importance of exposure to diverse peer value systems for stimulating moral thought. Kenyan and Nigerian students enrolled in ethnically and racially mixed high schools and colleges were advanced in moral development compared to those enrolled in homogeneous settings (Edwards, 1978; Maqsud, 1977).

Peer experiences have provided the framework for many interventions aimed at improving moral understanding. A major feature of most of them is peer discussion and

TABLE 12.1

Relations Among Kohlberg's Moral, Piaget's Cognitive, and Selman's Perspective-Taking Stages

Kohlberg's Moral Stage	Description	Piaget's Cognitive Stage	Selman's Perspective-Taking Stage
Punishment and obedience orientation	Fear of authority and avoidance of punishment are reasons for behaving morally.	Preoperational, early concrete operational	Social-informational
Instrumental purpose orientation	Satisfying personal needs determines moral choice.	Concrete operational	Self-reflective
"Good boy–good girl" orientation	Maintaining the affection and approval of friends and relatives motivates good behavior.	Early formal operational	Third-party
Social-order-maintaining orientation	A duty to uphold laws and rules for their own sake justifies moral conformity.	Formal operational	Societal
Social-contract orientation	Fair procedures for changing laws to protect individual rights and the needs of the majority are emphasized.		
Universal ethical principle orientation	Abstract universal principles that are valid for all humanity guide moral decision making.		

role-playing of moral problems. A study by Moshe Blatt and Lawrence Kohlberg (1975) yielded particularly impressive findings. After participating in either teacher- or student-led classroom discussions of moral dilemmas for one semester, many sixth and tenth graders moved partially or totally to the next moral stage, a change not found in pupils who did not receive the intervention. A year later, these differences were still evident. Other peer discussion interventions have also produced gains in moral reasoning, although in most instances the change is slight.

Which aspects of peer discussion stimulate moral development? In one study, college students who confronted, critiqued, and attempted to clarify one another's statements gained in moral maturity. In contrast, nongainers made assertions, told personal anecdotes, or expressed confusion about the task (Berkowitz & Gibbs, 1983). In another study, small friendship groups of university students participated in weekly interaction sessions. Some discussed hypothetical moral dilemmas, whereas others played games designed to stir up actual moral problems—for example, a game called "Ghetto" in which citizens confront a corrupt staff person who represents "the system." In the games, students engaged in more intense expressions of disagreement. During discussions, interactions tended to be emotionally controlled, intellectual responses to conflict. Games facilitated moral reasoning far more effectively than did discussions (Haan, Aerts, & Cooper, 1985).

Taken together, these findings indicate that cognitively probing, emotionally involved exchanges between peers are especially effective in stimulating moral understanding. Finally, because moral development is a gradual process, it usually takes many peer interaction sessions over weeks or months to produce moral change.

■ *Years of schooling is a powerful predictor of moral maturity. The social diversity of many college campuses, which introduces young people to issues that involve entire political and cultural groups, probably contributes to gains in moral reasoning. (Randy Matusow/Monkmeyer Press)*

■ CHILD-REARING PRACTICES. Child-rearing practices associated with mature moral reasoning reflect rational, democratic processes. Lawrence Walker and John Taylor (1991a) assessed level of moral reasoning and interaction styles of mothers and fathers as they discussed moral dilemmas with their first- through tenth-grade children. Parents who created a supportive atmosphere by listening sensitively, asking clarifying questions, presenting higher-level reasoning, and using praise and humor had children who gained most in moral understanding when interviewed 2 years later. In contrast, parents who lectured, used threats, or made sarcastic remarks had children who changed little or not at all. These effects were especially strong when families discussed a child-generated rather than hypothetical moral dilemma. Because the child's moral problem was directly relevant to parents' and children's lives, it probably provoked discussion that better resembled day-to-day family interaction.

Other research reveals that parents who use low levels of power assertion and high levels of warmth and inductive discipline and who encourage participation in family decision making have morally mature children (Boyes & Allen, 1993; Parikh, 1980). In sum, the kind of parent who facilitates moral understanding is verbal, rational, and affectionate and promotes a cooperative style of family life (Edwards, 1981).

■ SCHOOLING. Years of schooling completed is one of the most powerful predictors of moral development. In one study, adolescents graduating from high school were followed over a 10-year period. Some did not go to college (the "low" education group), others went for a short time (the "moderate" education group), and still others graduated from college (the "high" education group). College graduates continued to gain in moral maturity, those with some college leveled off after they left college, and those with no college education declined (Rest & Narvaez, 1991). Other research confirms that moral reasoning advances in late adolescence and young adulthood only as long as a person remains in school (Speicher, 1994).

Why does schooling make such a difference in moral maturity? There could be many reasons, including exposure to morally relevant subject matter and opportunities to interact with teachers and peers about moral concerns. Kohlberg (1984) suggested that higher education is an especially important arena for moral development because it introduces young people to social issues that extend beyond familiar, face-to-face relationships to entire political or cultural groups. Consistent with this idea, college students who report more academic perspective-taking opportunities (for example, classes that emphasize open discussion of opinions) and who indicate that they have become more aware of social diversity tend to be more advanced in moral reasoning (Mason & Gibbs, 1993a, 1993b).

SOCIAL ISSUES ➤ POINT OF VIEW

Should the Public Schools Teach Moral Values?

Debate over whether to teach moral values in the public schools is vigorous and polemical. Supporters point to moral demise in our culture, noting the rising rates of violence and apathetic, unmotivated children and adolescents. Opponents argue that too many areas of hot disagreement exist in our pluralistic society to devise one educational approach that would be suitable for all young people.

The history of moral education in the United States reflects similar polarization. Early in this century, the *character education approach* arose, committed to training students in a common set of virtues. A typical list includes honesty, kindness, fairness, responsibility, and moral courage. Critics claimed that beneath popular consensus on the worth of these values lies substantial disagreement on their meaning. For example, one person's honesty might be another's stubbornness or insensitivity.

In response, educators designed the *values clarification approach.* It stresses that people have different values and asks students to explore and rationally select their own, with the goal of encouraging tolerance for many value positions, none of which are better than any others. Values clarification has obvious strengths, including promoting awareness of value alternatives and open-mindedness. Yet it has dangers as well. Within this system, children and adolescents can justify immoral acts, such as cheating and stealing, by simply referring to their own self-chosen convictions.

Kohlberg's *cognitive-developmental approach* has been the dominant force in moral education for the past quarter-century (Sockett, 1992). His ideas changed over the course of his career, reflecting the tension between the two views of moral education just described. At first, Kohlberg rejected teaching moral character, or a ready-made "bag of virtues." Instead, he stressed improving moral reasoning through discussion of moral dilemmas. But Kohlberg came to question the ability of these interventions to change moral thinking and behavior in everyday life. Eventually he concluded that teaching moral values is necessary and compatible with his theory, as long as educators use a rational approach to rule making (Higgins, 1995; Power, Higgins, & Kohlberg, 1989).

Kohlberg enlarged his concept of moral education to include training in values, reasoning, and behavior through the **just community**, a small society within a school in which teachers and students practice a democratic way of life. A central feature of the program is the weekly community meeting, in which the entire group gathers to create and refine school policy. Once rules are made, teachers do not stand back; they help students build a commitment to them. For example, at one meeting in a just community school, the group agreed not to allow smoking during a field trip to a movie. Yet as soon as the lights dimmed, several students lit up. The teachers stopped the film and led a short discussion about the importance of upholding agreements. Morality is also fostered through the teaching of subject matter. Students identify moral dilemmas in literature and evaluate and justify courses of action. In social studies, they consider questions of human rights and good citizenship. And in science, they address such moral problems as environmental pollution and nuclear arms.

Do just community programs make a difference in the moral lives of students? When effectively implemented, they can be highly successful. As the moral atmosphere of the school takes shape, students usually express a strong commitment to it. Here is a typical comment of a just community participant: "[Our school] is a real community. People have rights and can bring up issues of concern . . . and people listen to what you have to say, and therefore make you feel like a real person" (Power, Higgins, & Kohlberg, 1989, p. 190). Research indicates that advances in moral maturity from one year to the next were much greater in just community settings than in traditional or other alternative high schools. And students who felt the strongest sense of community showed the greatest moral stage gains (Higgins, 1991). Themes of community and participatory democracy, appropriately adapted, are also found in moral education programs at the elementary school level (Lickona, 1991).

Integrating moral instruction into public education acknowledges that young people receive messages about what is right and wrong from all people in their lives—not just their family, but also their school and the larger society. The most effective approach to moral education may be one that neither indoctrinates students in adult-chosen values nor rejects the possibility of a common moral culture. According to Kohlberg, to understand and feel justice, children and adolescents have to be both justly treated and called on to act justly. This requires a school in which everyone has a voice and in which the worth of rules is judged by their fairness to all involved.

YOUR POINT OF VIEW . . .

- Ask several elementary and secondary school teachers whether and how they teach moral values in their classrooms. To what extent is morality granted an important place in the curriculum? Which of the educational approaches just described is emphasized? If morality is not directly taught, how is it likely to be conveyed in other ways?

The question of how best to foster moral development in schools has been the focus of much research and debate. To find out more about Kohlberg's approach to moral education, turn to the Social Issues box above.

Just community
Kohlberg's approach to moral education, in which a small society of teachers and students practice a democratic way of life.

CULTURE. Cross-cultural research reveals that individuals in technologically advanced, urban cultures move through Kohlberg's stages more rapidly and advance to a higher level than do individuals in nonindustrialized, village societies. Stages 4 and above are not reached by members of isolated peasant communities, whereas they are attained by high school- and college-educated adolescents and adults in developed

■ *Young people growing up on Israeli kibbutzim receive training in the governance of their society at an early age. As a result, they understand the role of societal laws and rules in resolving moral conflict and are advanced in moral reasoning. (Louis Goldman/Photo Researchers)*

nations (Snarey, 1995). (Recall, however, that Stages 5 and 6 are not commonly reached even by adults in industrialized countries.)

Why these cultural differences exist is a matter of considerable debate. One explanation addresses the role of societal institutions in advanced moral understanding. In traditional village cultures, moral cooperation is based on direct relations between people. Yet Stage 4 to 6 reasoning depends on understanding the role of laws and government institutions in resolving moral conflict (Kohlberg, 1969). In support of this view, in cultures where young people participate in the institutions of their society at early ages, moral reasoning is advanced. For example, on kibbutzim, small but technologically complex agricultural settlements in Israel, children receive training in the governance of their community beginning in middle childhood. By third grade, they mention more concerns about societal laws and rules when discussing moral conflicts than do Israeli city-reared or American children (Fuchs et al., 1986). During adolescence and adulthood, a greater percentage of kibbutz than American individuals reach Kohlberg's Stages 4 and 5 (Snarey, Reimer, & Kohlberg, 1985).

A second possible reason for cultural variation in moral understanding is that Kohlberg's dilemmas are not well suited to certain cultures. At times, people respond in ways not easily scorable in Kohlberg's scheme. Recall from Chapter 11 that self-concepts in collectivist cultures (including village societies) are more other-directed than in Western Europe and North America. This very difference seems to characterize moral reasoning as well (Miller, 1994). In village cultures, moral statements that portray the individual as vitally connected to the social group through a deep sense of community responsibility are common. For example, one New Guinea village leader placed the blame for the Heinz dilemma on the entire social group, stating, "If I were the judge, I would give him only light punishment because he asked everybody for help but nobody helped him" (Tietjen & Walker, 1985, p. 990).

Similarly, in some Eastern nations, well-educated adults expected to be at Stages 5 and 6 often think in ways that differ from typical postconventional reasoning. In a study conducted in India, the most morally mature individuals rarely appealed to personal ethical principles in discussing the Heinz dilemma. Instead, they resisted choosing a course of action, explaining that a moral solution should not be the burden of a single individual but of the entire society. As one woman explained:

> The problems that Heinz is up against are not individual problems that are affecting 1 or 2 Heinzes of the world. These are social problems. Forget Heinz in Europe, just come to India . . . . Heinz's story is being repeated all around us all the time with wives dying, with children dying, and there is no money to save them . . . . So Heinz in his individual capacity—yes, okay, steal the drug, but it's not going to make any difference on a large scale . . . . I don't think in the final analysis a solution can be worked out on an individual basis . . . . It will probably have to be tackled on a macro level. (Vasudev & Hummel, 1987, p. 110)

These findings raise the question of whether Kohlberg's highest stages represent a culturally specific rather than universal way of thinking—one limited to Western societies that emphasize individual rights and an appeal to an inner, private conscience.

ARE THERE SEX-RELATED DIFFERENCES IN MORAL REASONING?

The debate over the universality of Kohlberg's stages has also been extended to gender. Carol Gilligan (1982) is the most well-known figure among those who have argued that Kohlberg's theory does not adequately represent the morality of females. She believes that feminine morality emphasizes an "ethic of care," but Kohlberg's system devalues it. Return to the description of Kohlberg's stages on pages 473–475 and notice how Stage 3 is based on interpersonal obligations. In contrast, Stages 4 to 6 stress justice—an abstract, rational commitment to moral ideals that according to Gilligan, tends to be encouraged in males. In her view, a concern for others is a *different,* not less valid basis for moral judgment than a focus on impersonal rights.

Many studies have tested Gilligan's claim that Kohlberg's approach underestimates the moral maturity of females, and most do not support it. On hypothetical dilemmas as well as everyday moral problems, adolescent and adult females do not fall behind males in development. Also, themes of justice and caring appear in the responses of both sexes, and when girls do raise interpersonal concerns, they are not downscored in Kohlberg's system (Jadack et al., 1995; Kahn, 1992; Walker, 1995). These findings suggest that although Kohlberg emphasized justice rather than caring as the highest of moral ideals, his theory does include both sets of values.

Still, Gilligan's claim that research on moral development has been limited by too much attention to rights and justice (a "masculine" ideal) and too little attention to care and responsiveness (a "feminine" ideal) is a powerful one. Some evidence shows that although the morality of males and females taps both orientations, females do tend to stress care, or empathic perspective taking, whereas males either stress justice or use justice and care equally (Galotti, Kozberg, & Farmer, 1991; Garmon et al., 1996; Wark & Krebs, 1996). The difference in emphasis appears most often on real-life rather than hypothetical dilemmas. Consequently, it may be largely a function of men's and women's daily lives. In support of this idea, one study found that restricting moral problems to child-rearing concerns eliminated gender differences in reasoning between mothers and fathers. As the researchers noted, men "only needed to have their attention drawn to an important part of their lives to manifest the care concerns already abundantly present" (Clopton & Sorell, 1993, p. 99).

Although current evidence indicates that justice and caring are not gender-specific moralities, Gilligan's work has had the effect of broadening conceptions of the highly moral person. Mary Brabeck (1983) notes,

> When Gilligan and Kohlberg's theories are taken together, the moral person is seen as one whose moral choices reflect reasoned and deliberate judgments that ensure justice be accorded each person while maintaining a passionate concern for the well-being and care of each individual. Justice and care are then joined . . . and the need for autonomy and for interconnection are united in an enlarged and more adequate conception of morality. (p. 289)

MORAL REASONING AND BEHAVIOR

A central assumption of the cognitive-developmental perspective is that moral understanding should affect moral motivation. As young people grasp the underlying moral "logic" of human social cooperation, they are upset when this logic is violated. As a result, they gradually realize that behaving in line with the way one thinks is an important part of creating and maintaining a just social world (Gibbs, 1995; Narvaez & Rest, 1995). On the basis of this idea, Kohlberg predicted a very specific relationship between moral thought and behavior: The two should come closer together as individuals move toward the higher stages of moral understanding (Blasi, 1990).

Consistent with Kohlberg's prediction, advanced moral reasoning is related to many aspects of social behavior. Higher-stage adolescents more often engage in prosocial acts, such as helping, sharing, and defending victims of injustice (Gibbs et al., 1986). They are also more honest. For example, they are less likely to cheat on assignments and tests in school (Harris, Mussen, & Rutherford, 1976). Conversely, lower-stage adolescents are likely to be less honest and to engage in antisocial behavoir (Gregg, Gibbs, & Fuller, 1994).

Yet even though a clear connection between moral thought and action exists, it is important to keep in mind that it is only moderate. We have already seen that moral behavior is also influenced by noncognitive factors, including the emotions of empathy and guilt, individual differences in temperament, and a long history of experiences that affect moral choice and decision making. Researchers have yet to discover how all these complex facets of morality work together.

FURTHER QUESTIONS ABOUT KOHLBERG'S THEORY

Although there is much support for Kohlberg's theory, it continues to face some challenges. The most important of these concern Kohlberg's conception of moral maturity and the appropriateness of his stages for characterizing the moral reasoning of young children.

A key controversy has to do with Kohlberg's belief that moral maturity is not achieved until the postconventional level. Yet if people had to reach Stages 5 and 6 to be considered truly morally mature, few individuals anywhere would measure up! John Gibbs (1991) believes that "postconventional morality" should not be viewed as the standard against which other levels are judged immature. Instead, he regards such reasoning as a reflective, philosophical orientation beyond the realm of spontaneous, everyday moral thought. Gibbs finds maturity in the ethically ideal aspects of Stages 3 and 4, which are not necessarily "conventional" or based on social conformity, as Kohlberg assumed. Instead, Stages 3 and 4 require vital moral constructions—an understanding of mutual trust as the basis for obligations between people and of widely accepted moral standards as necessary for society.

Finally, Kohlberg's stages largely describe changes in moral reasoning during adolescence and adulthood. They tell us little about moral understanding in early and middle childhood. Indeed, Kohlberg's moral dilemmas are remote from the experiences of most young children and may not be clearly understood by them. When children are given moral problems related to their everyday lives, their responses indicate that Kohlberg's preconventional level, much like Piaget's heteronomous morality, underestimates their moral reasoning. We take a close look at this evidence in the following sections.

BRIEF REVIEW

According to Kohlberg's three-level, six-stage theory, morality changes from concrete, externally oriented reasoning to more abstract, principled justifications for moral choices. Each moral stage builds on cognitive and perspective-taking capacities. Research suggests a powerful role for environmental contexts in the development of moral understanding. Advanced moral reasoning is not attained unless supports exist on many levels, including family, peers, schooling, and wider society. Although Kohlberg's theory emphasizes a morality of justice rather than a morality of care, it does not underestimate the moral maturity of females. As individuals advance through Kohlberg's stages, moral reasoning becomes better related to behavior. Recent challenges to Kohlberg's theory question its definition of moral maturity and its view of the moral reasoning of young children.

Moral Reasoning of Young Children

Researchers using moral dilemmas specifically designed for children have addressed three facets of their moral understanding: (1) their ability to distinguish moral rules from social conventions; (2) their ideas about fair distribution of rewards; and (3) their prosocial reasoning—how they choose between self-interest and meeting the needs of others. Besides being relevant to children's real-life experiences, the moral problems used in these studies differ from Kohlberg's in that the role of laws and the possibility of punishment are deemphasized. When dilemmas are formulated in these ways, young children reveal some surprisingly advanced moral judgments.

MORAL VERSUS SOCIAL-CONVENTIONAL UNDERSTANDING

Piaget and Kohlberg regarded the young child's moral understanding as superficial and externally motivated. Yet as early as age 3, children have a beginning grasp of justice. Many studies reveal that preschool and young grade school children distinguish *moral rules,* which protect people's rights and welfare, from *social conventions,* arbitrary customs such as dress styles, table manners, and rituals of social interaction (Nucci, 1981; Nucci & Turiel, 1978; Smetana, 1981, 1985). In one study, 2- and 3-year-olds were interviewed about drawings depicting familiar moral and social conventional transgressions. For example, a moral picture showed a child stealing an agemate's apple; a social-conventional picture showed a child eating ice cream with fingers. By 34 months, children viewed moral transgressions as more generalizably wrong (not okay regardless of the setting in which they are committed). And by 42 months, they indicated that moral (but not social-conventional) violations would still be wrong if an adult did not see them and no rules existed to prohibit them (Smetana & Braeges, 1990).

■ *These five school-age children have figured out how to divide up two pizzas fairly among themselves, Already, they have a well-developed sense of distributive justice. (Will Faller)*

How do young children come to make these distinctions? According to Elliott Turiel (1983), not through parental instruction, since adults insist that children conform to social conventions just as often as they press for obedience to moral rules. Instead, children actively make sense of their experiences in both types of situations. They observe that people respond differently to violations of moral rules than breaks with social convention. When a moral offense occurs, children react emotionally, describe their own injury or loss, tell another child to stop, or retaliate. And an adult who intervenes is likely to call attention to the rights and feelings of the victim. In contrast, children often do not respond to violations of social convention. And in these situations, adults tend to demand obedience without explanation, as when they state, "Say the magic word!" or "Don't eat with your fingers" (Smetana, 1989; Turiel, Smetana, & Killen, 1991).

Turiel makes a strong case for early emergence of distinct moral and social-conventional domains of understanding. Yet the very criticism of Kohlberg's theory mentioned earlier—that it overemphasizes individual rights—has also been leveled at the moral–social-conventional distinction (Witherell & Edwards, 1991). Although non-Western children also separate morality from social convention, the dichotomy is often less sharp. For example, 8- to 10-year-old Hindu children agree with their American counterparts that breaking promises, destroying another person's property, and kicking harmless animals are morally wrong. At the same time, they regard food and politeness transgressions, such as eating chicken the day after a father's death or calling parents by their first names, as far more serious than selfish behavior or even family violence (Haidt, Koller, & Diaz, 1993; Shweder, Mahapatra, & Miller, 1990). In India, as in many developing countries, culturally specific practices that strike Western outsiders as arbitrary customs often have profound moral and religious significance.

Clearly, children grapple with the distinction between moral rules and social conventions at a remarkably early age. Yet the boundary drawn between them varies considerably and is a joint product of cognitive development and social experience. We are reminded, once again, that there are both cultural universals and diversity in moral thought.

DISTRIBUTIVE JUSTICE

In everyday life, children frequently experience situations that involve **distributive justice**—beliefs about how to divide up resources fairly. Heated discussions often take place over how much weekly allowance is to be given to siblings of different ages, who has to sit where in the family car on a long trip, and in what way an eight-slice pizza is to be shared by six hungry playmates. William Damon (1977, 1988) has studied changing concepts of distributive justice over early and middle childhood by asking children to resolve dilemmas like the ones just mentioned. His developmental sequence is supported by both cross-sectional and longitudinal evidence (Enright et al., 1984; Enright, Franklin, & Manheim, 1980).

Even 4-year-olds recognize the importance of sharing, but their reasons for doing so often seem contradictory and self-serving. When asked why they gave some of their toys to a playmate, preschoolers typically say something like this: "I shared because if I didn't, she wouldn't play with me" or "I let her have some, but most are for me because I'm older."

Distributive justice
Beliefs about how to divide up resources fairly.

TABLE 12.2

Damon's Sequence of Distributive Justice Reasoning

Basis of Reasoning	Age	Description
Equality	5–6	Fairness involves strictly equal distibution of goods. Special considerations like merit and need are not considered.
Merit	6-7	Fairness is based on deservingness. Children recognize that some people should get more because they have worked harder.
Benevolence	8	Fairness includes special consideration for those who are disadvantaged. More should be given to people in need.

Source: Damon, 1977, 1988.

As children enter middle childhood, they start to express more mature notions of distributive justice (see Table 12.2). At first, their ideas of fairness are based on *equality.* Children in the early school grades are intent on making sure that each person gets the same amount of a treasured resource, such as money, turns in a game, or a delicious treat.[2]

A short time later, children start to view fairness in terms of *merit.* Extra rewards should be given to someone who has worked especially hard or otherwise performed in an exceptional way. Finally, around 8 years, children can reason on the basis of *benevolence.* They recognize that special consideration should be given to those in a condition of disadvantage. Older children say that an extra amount might be given to a child who cannot produce as much or does not get any allowance from his parents. They also adapt their basis of fairness to the situation—for example, relying more on merit when interacting with strangers and more on benevolence when interacting with friends (McGillicuddy-De Lisi, Watkins, & Vinchur, 1994).

According to Damon (1988), parental advice and encouragement support these developing standards of justice, but the give-and-take of peer interaction is especially important. Peer disagreements, along with efforts to resolve them, make children more sensitive to others' perspectives, and this supports their developing ideas of fairness (Kruger, 1993). Advanced distributive justice reasoning, in turn, is associated with more effective social problem solving and a greater willingness to help and share with others (Blotner & Bearison, 1984; McNamee & Peterson, 1986).

Research on children's concepts of distributive justice indicates that they construct complex notions of fairness much earlier than Piaget and Kohlberg believed. In fact, fear of punishment and respect for authority do not even appear as themes in children's distributive justice rationales. Because Damon's dilemmas minimize the relevance of these factors to moral choice, they permit some impressively mature moral reasoning to rise to the surface.

PROSOCIAL REASONING

Return for a moment to Kohlberg's Heinz dilemma, and notice that to help his wife, Heinz has no choice but to break the law and steal. In most everyday situations in which children must decide whether to act prosocially, the cost is not disobeying the law or an authority figure. Instead, it is not satisfying one's own wants or needs. Nancy Eisenberg asked preschoolers through twelfth graders to respond to prosocial dilemmas in which the primary sacrifice in aiding another person is giving up personal desires. Here is a typical one given to younger children:

> One day a girl named Mary was going to a friend's birthday party. On her way she saw a girl who had fallen down and hurt her leg. The girl asked Mary to go to her house and get her parents so the parents could come and take her to the doctor. But if Mary did run and get the child's parents, she would be late for the birthday party and miss the ice cream, cake, and all the games. What should Mary do? Why? (Eisenberg, 1982, p. 231)

[2] Recall from Chapter 6 that in some cultures, equal sharing of goods among children is not common and conservation is greatly delayed (see page 239). It is possible that Damon's sequence of distributive justice reasoning does not represent children's concepts of fairness in all societies.

TABLE 12.3

Eisenberg's Levels of Prosocial Reasoning

Level	Approximate Age	Description
Hedonistic, pragmatic orientation	Preschool, early elementary school	Right behavior satisfies one's own needs. Reasons for helping or not helping refer to gains for the self—for example, "I wouldn't help because I might be hungry."
"Needs of others" orientation	Preschool, elementary school	Concern for the physical, material, and psychological needs of others is expressed in simple terms, without clear evidence of perspective taking or empathic feeling—for example, "He needs it."
Stereotyped, approval-focused orientation	Elementary school and secondary school	Stereotyped images of good and bad persons and concern for approval justify behavior—for example, "He'd like him more if he helped."
Empathic orientation	Later elementary school and secondary school	Reasoning reflects an emphasis on perspective taking and empathic feeling for the other person—for example, "I'd feel bad if I didn't help because he'd be in pain."
Internalized values orientation	Small minority of secondary school students, no elementary school pupils	Justifications for moral choice are based on internalized values, norms, desire to maintain contractual obligations, and belief in the dignity, rights, and equality of all individuals—for example, "I wouldn't feel bad if I didn't help because I'd know that I didn't live up to my values."

Source: Eisenberg, 1982.

Conducting both cross-sectional and longitudinal research, Eisenberg found that responses formed the age-related sequence summarized in Table 12.3 (Eisenberg, Lennon, & Roth, 1983; Eisenberg et al., 1991, 1995; Eisenberg-Berg, 1979).

Notice how Eisenberg's developmental levels resemble Kohlberg's stages. For example, her hedonistic, pragmatic orientation is like Kohlberg's Stage 2, her approval-focused and empathic orientations are like Kohlberg's Stage 3, and her internalized values orientation includes forms of reasoning that seem to match Kohlberg's Stages 4 to 6. But several features of Eisenberg's findings depart from Kohlberg's. Once again, punishment- and authority-oriented reasoning is rare in children's responses. Only occasionally did young children make comments like "If I didn't help, someone would find out and punish me." Also, children's prosocial understanding is clearly advanced when compared to the timing of Kohlberg's stages.

Finally, prosocial dilemmas bring out a form of moral reasoning that Eisenberg calls "empathic." By the late elementary school years, children realize that empathy is an important motivator of prosocial behavior. In one study, 9- and 10-year-olds who easily empathized advanced to higher levels of prosocial understanding during early adolescence (Eisenberg et al., 1987). According to Eisenberg, empathic feelings may encourage more mature prosocial thought and strengthen its realization in everyday behavior. In line with this idea, children and adolescents at higher prosocial levels do tend to respond more altruistically than do agemates who are less advanced (Eisenberg et al., 1991, 1995; Miller et al., 1996). Eisenberg is one researcher who has made a start at putting the cognitive, affective, and behavioral components of morality together.

The research reviewed in the preceding sections reveals that moral understanding in childhood is a rich, diverse phenomenon not completely described by any single theory. Children's responses to a wide range of moral problems, including ones that focus on justice, fair distribution, and prosocial behavior, are needed to comprehensively represent the development of moral thought.

BRIEF REVIEW

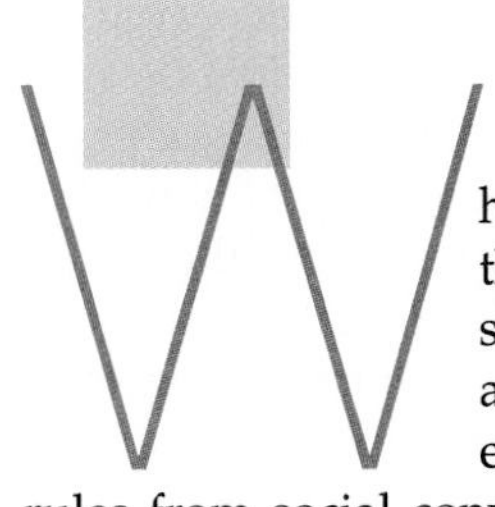

When children are asked to reason about moral problems in which the role of laws and the possibility of punishment are deemphasized, they display moral judgments that are considerably more advanced than predicted by Piaget and Kohlberg. Even preschoolers have a beginning grasp of justice in that they distinguish moral rules from social conventions. During middle childhood, children's notions of how to divide up resources fairly become more differentiated and adapted to the requirements of situations. Prosocial moral dilemmas yield earlier attainment of advanced forms of moral reasoning than Kohlberg's sequence suggests.

Development of Self-Control

The study of moral reasoning tells us what people think they should do and why when faced with a moral problem. But we have already indicated that people's good intentions often fall short. Whether children and adults act in accord with their beliefs depends in part on characteristics we call willpower, firm resolve, or, put more simply, **self-control**. Self-control in the moral domain involves inhibiting an impulse to engage in behavior that violates a moral standard. Sometimes it is called *resistance to temptation.* In the first part of this chapter, we noted that inductive discipline and models who demonstrate as well as verbalize self-controlled behavior foster children's self-control. But these practices become effective only when children develop the ability to resist temptation. When and how does the child's capacity for self-control develop?

BEGINNINGS OF SELF-CONTROL

The beginnings of self-control are supported by cognitive achievements of the second year that we discussed in earlier chapters. To behave in a self-controlled fashion, children must have some ability to think of themselves as separate, autonomous beings who can direct their own actions. And they must also have the representational and memory capacities to internalize a caregiver's directive and apply it to their own behavior (Kopp, 1987).

As these abilities mature, the first glimmerings of self-control appear in the form of **compliance**. Between 12 and 18 months, children start to show clear awareness of caregivers' wishes and expectations and can voluntarily obey simple requests and commands (Kaler & Kopp, 1990; Luria, 1961). And, as every parent knows, they can also decide to do just the opposite! One way toddlers assert their emerging sense of autonomy is by resisting adult directives. But among those who experience warm, sensitive caregiving and reasonable expectations for mature behavior, opposition is far less common than eager, willing compliance, in which the child seems to embrace the parent's agenda (Kochanska, Aksan, & Koenig, 1995). For most toddlers, resistance is gradually transformed into polite refusals and skilled efforts to negotiate compromises with parents over the preschool years (Kuczynski & Kochanska, 1990).

Parents are usually delighted at toddlers' newfound ability to comply, since it indicates that they are ready to learn the rules of social life. Nevertheless, control of the child's actions during the second year depends heavily on prompts from caregivers (Kopp, 1987). According to Vygotsky (1934/1986), children cannot guide their own behavior until they incorporate adult standards into their own speech and use it to instruct the self. Recall from Chapter 6 that this self-directed form of language is called *private speech.* The development of compliance quickly leads to toddlers' first conscience-like verbalizations—for example, correcting the self by saying "no, can't" before touching a light socket, jumping on the sofa, or taking candy from a forbidden dish (Kochanska, 1993).

Researchers typically study self-control by creating situations in the laboratory much like the ones just mentioned. Notice how each calls for **delay of gratification**—waiting for a more appropriate time and place to engage in a tempting act or obtain a desired object. In one study, 18-, 24-, and 30-month-old children were given three delay-of-gratification tasks. In the first, they were asked not to touch an interesting toy telephone that was within arm's reach. In the second, raisins were hidden under cups, and they were instructed to wait until the experimenter said it was all right to pick up a cup and eat a raisin. In the third, they were told not to open a gift until the experimenter had finished her work. As Figure 12.2 shows, on all three problems the ability to delay gratification increased substantially between 18 and 30 months. Furthermore, by 30 months, clear individual differences in the capacity for self-control were present. Consistent with

Self-control
Inhibiting an impulse to engage in behavior that violates a moral standard.

Compliance
Voluntary obedience to requests and commands.

Delay of gratification
Waiting for a more appropriate time and place to engage in a tempting act or obtain a desired object.

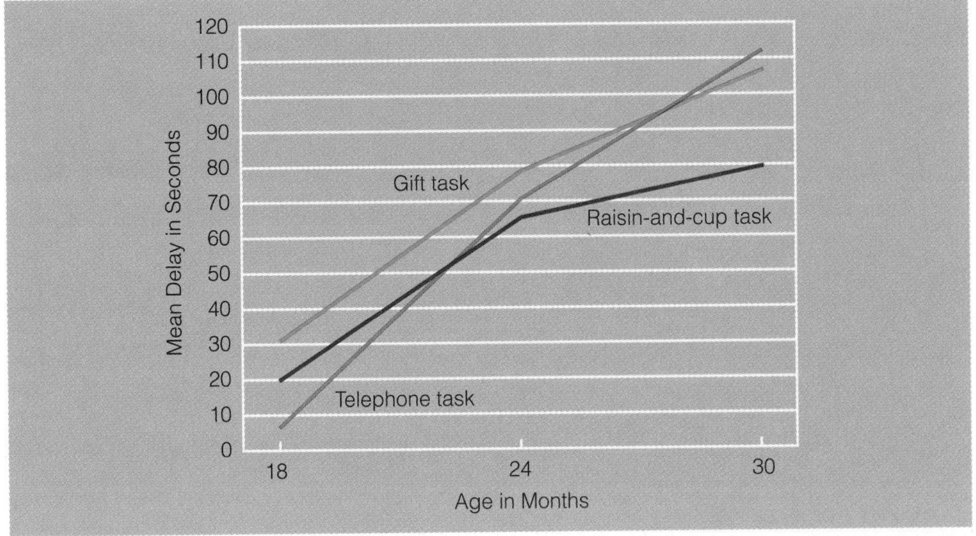

FIGURE 12.2

Age changes in delay of gratification between 18 and 30 months. The capacity for self-control increases dramatically during this period. (Adapted from Vaughn, Kopp, & Krakow, 1984.)

Vygotsky's theory, the single best predictor of them was language development (Vaughn, Kopp, & Krakow, 1984).

Children's ability to engage in socially approved behaviors and to inhibit undesirable behaviors leads caregiver expectations to increase. Heidi Gralinski and Claire Kopp (1993) asked mothers to indicate which things they require or encourage their young children to do and which things they insist they not do between 13 and 30 months of age. As Figure 12.3 reveals, rules expanded from a narrow focus on safety, property, and respect for others to a broader emphasis on the realities of living in a social world. Gradually, mothers placed more emphasis on issues related to family routines, self-care, and independence until, at 30 months, all rules were stressed to the same degree. If you compare these trends with the gains depicted in Figure 12.2, you will see that overall, mothers' expectations dovetail nicely with children's emerging capacity for self-control.

DEVELOPMENT OF SELF-CONTROL IN CHILDHOOD AND ADOLESCENCE

Although the capacity for self-control is in place by the third year, it is not complete. Cognitive development—in particular, improvements in attention and mental representation—permits children to use a variety of effective self-instructional strategies for resisting temptation. As a result, delay of gratification undergoes steady improvement during childhood and adolescence (Mischel & Rodriguez, 1993).

STRATEGIES FOR SELF-CONTROL. Walter Mischel (1974) has studied exactly what children think and say to themselves that promotes gains in resistance to temptation. In several studies, preschoolers were shown two rewards: a highly desirable one that they would have to wait for and a less desirable one that they could have anytime during the waiting period. Informal observations revealed that allocation of attention was especially important in the ability to delay gratification. Rather than focusing on the rewards, the most self-controlled preschoolers used any technique they could think of to divert themselves from the desired objects, including covering their eyes, inventing games with their hands and feet, singing, and even trying to go to sleep!

In everyday situations, preschoolers find it difficult to keep their minds off tempting activities and objects for very long. When their thoughts do turn to an enticing but prohibited goal, the way children mentally represent it has much to do with their success at self-control. Mischel found that teaching children to transform the stimulus in ways that deemphasize its arousing qualities is highly effective in promoting delay of gratification. In one study, some preschoolers were told to think about marshmallows imaginatively as "white and puffy clouds." Others were asked to focus on their realistic, "sweet and chewy properties." Children in the stimulus-transforming, imaginative condition waited much longer before eating the marshmallow reward (Mischel & Baker, 1975).

In the study just described, an experimenter taught young children to use delay-enhancing strategies. How good are they at thinking up these techniques on their own?

The development of self-control is well under way by the time children enter school, where they are frequently required to delay gratification. Waiting to be called on is common event in the lives of these pupils, who have developed strategies for being patient. (D. Wells/ The Image Works)

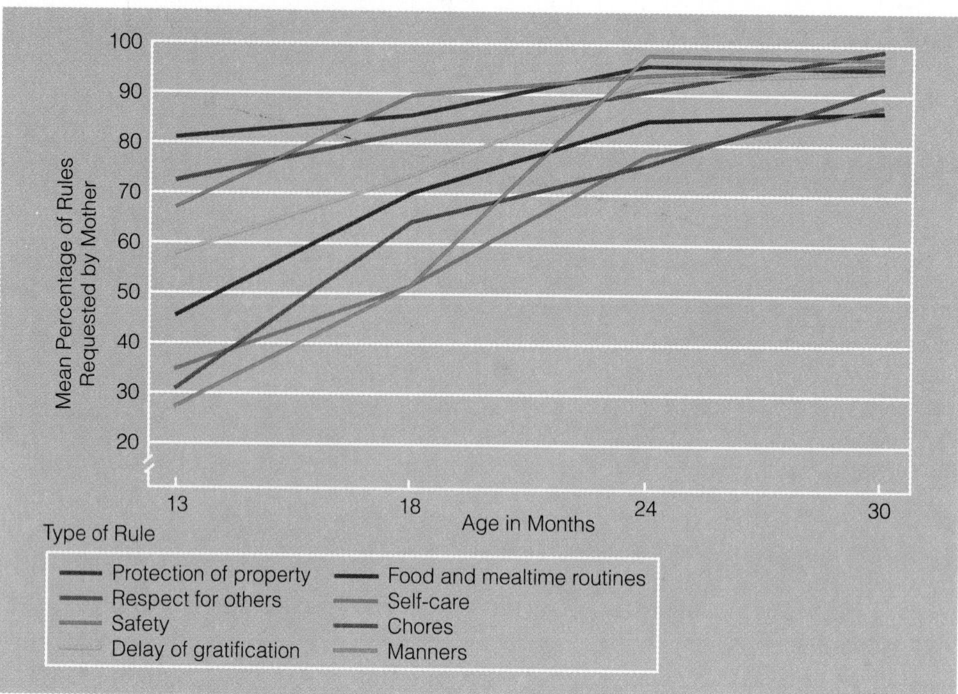

FIGURE 12.3

■ *Percentage of eight types of rules mothers reported asking of their 13- to 30-month-old children. Mothers emphasized safety, property, and respect rules early. As children's capacity for self-control increased, mothers introduced a wider array of rule expectations related to the realities of living in a social world. (From J. H. Gralinski & C. B. Kopp, 1993, "Everyday Rules for Behavior: Mothers' Requests to Young Children,"* Developmental Psychology, *29, p. 579. Copyright © 1993 by the American Psychological Association. Reprinted by permission.)*

Research shows that when an adult refrains from giving preschoolers instructions in how to resist temptation, their ability to wait in delay-of-gratification tasks declines considerably. In contrast, first and second graders do just as well regardless of whether an adult provides them with strategies or not (Toner & Smith, 1977). These findings indicate that not until the early elementary school years are children very good at thinking up their own strategies for resisting temptation. By this time, self-control has been transformed into a flexible capacity for *moral self-regulation*—the ability to monitor one's own conduct, constantly adjusting it as circumstances present opportunities to violate inner standards (Bandura, 1991; Kopp, 1987).

■ KNOWLEDGE OF STRATEGIES. In Chapter 7, we indicated that metacognitive knowledge, or awareness of strategies, plays an important role in the development of self-regulation. When 3- to 11-year-olds were interviewed to find out how much they knew about situational conditions and self-instructions likely to help them do well on a delay-of-gratification task, preschoolers thought of only a few tactics, such as "Close two eyes" and "Talk to the wall." Sometimes they mentioned ineffective techniques, such as looking at the rewards "because it makes me feel good," thereby defeating their own efforts at self-control (Mischel & Mischel, 1983).

Over middle childhood, children suggested an increasingly broad array of successful strategies and explained why they worked by referring to their arousal-reducing properties. But not until the late elementary school years did they mention techniques involving transformations of rewards or their own arousal states. For example, one 11-year-old recommended saying, "The marshmallows are filled with an evil spell." Another said he would tell himself, "I hate marshmallows, I can't stand them. But when the grown-up gets back, I'll tell myself 'I love marshmallows' and eat it" (Mischel & Mischel, 1983, p. 609).

Perhaps awareness of the importance of transforming ideation appears so late in development because it requires the abstract, hypothetical reasoning powers of formal operational thought. But once this advanced metacognitive understanding emerges, it facilitates moral self-regulation. In a study of older children with social adjustment difficulties attending a special summer camp, those who knew that an abstract representation of a reward would help them delay used more effective strategies and were able to wait longer in the presence of tempting objects. Furthermore, their self-regulatory skills generalized to everyday life. Children who performed well in a laboratory delay situation were rated as getting along better with peers throughout the summer (Rodriguez, Mischel, & Shoda, 1989).

INDIVIDUAL DIFFERENCES. Longitudinal research reveals modest stability in children's capacity to manage their behavior in a morally relevant fashion. Mischel and his collaborators found that 4-year-olds able to wait longer in delay-of-gratification tasks were especially adept as adolescents in applying metacognitive and self-regulatory skills to their behavior. Their parents saw them as more verbally fluent and responsive to reason, as better at concentrating and planning ahead, and as coping with stress more maturely. When applying to college, those who had been self-controlled preschoolers scored somewhat higher on the Scholastic Aptitude Test (SAT), although they were no more intelligent than children less able to resist temptation (Mischel, Shoda, & Peake, 1988; Shoda, Mischel, & Peake, 1990).

Researchers believe these enduring individual differences are the combined result of temperamental characteristics and child-rearing practices. Consistent with this idea, impulsive children, who often act without thinking and are hot-tempered when they do not get their way, are more likely to show deficits in moral self-regulation than are their agemates (Kochanska, 1991; Kochanska et al., 1994). Recall that a mismatch between a child's temperamental style and parenting practices can undermine psychological adjustment for many years to come. As we will see in the final section of this chapter, when temperamentally vulnerable children are exposed to highly power-assertive, inconsistent discipline, they display long-term, serious problems in observing standards of conduct. But before we turn to the topic of aggression, you may find it helpful to review the moral changes we have discussed throughout this chapter, which are summarized in the Milestones table on page 490.

The Other Side of Self-Control: Development of Aggression

Beginning in late infancy, all children display aggression from time to time, and as opportunities to interact with siblings and peers increase, aggressive outbursts occur more often. But recall from Chapter 11 that conflicts between young children are far less frequent than friendly, cooperative interaction. An occasional aggressive act is normal and to be expected, and these encounters often become important learning experiences as adults intervene and teach children alternative ways of satisfying desires. Nevertheless, as early as the preschool years, some children show abnormally high rates of aggression. They lash out with verbal insults and physical assaults in situations that appear to involve little or no provocation. Allowed to continue, their belligerent behavior can lead to lasting deficits in moral development and self-control and to an antisocial lifestyle. To understand this process, let's see how aggression develops during childhood and adolescence.

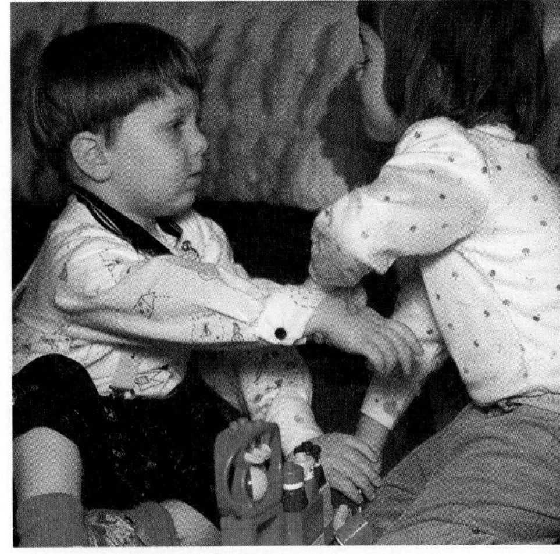

■ *An occasional expression of aggression is normal among young children. These preschoolers display instrumental aggression as they struggle over an attractive toy. Instrumental aggression declines with age as children learn how to compromise and share. (Rita Mannini/Photo Researchers)*

EMERGENCE OF AGGRESSION

During the second half of the first year, infants develop the cognitive capacity to identify sources of anger and frustration and the motor skills to lash out at them (see Chapter 10). As a result, two forms of aggression emerge. The most common is **instrumental aggression**. In this form, children are not deliberately hostile. Instead, they want an object, privilege, or space, and in trying to get it, they push, shout at, or otherwise attack a person who is in the way. The other type, **hostile aggression**, is meant to hurt, as when the child hits, insults, or tattles on a playmate with no other aim in mind than to injure the other person.

Instrumental aggression
Aggression aimed at obtaining an object, privilege, or space with no deliberate intent to harm another person.

Hostile aggression
Aggression intended to harm another person.

Both the form of aggression and the way it is expressed change with age. In a classic study, mothers were asked to keep records of their children's angry outbursts. Physical aggression was gradually replaced by verbal aggression over the preschool years (Goodenough, 1931). Rapid language development contributes to this change, but it is also due to adults' and peers' strong negative reactions to pushing, hitting, and biting (Parke & Slaby, 1983). In another study, aggressive acts of 4- to 7-year-olds were recorded at school. Instrumental aggression declined over this age period, whereas hostile, person-oriented outbursts increased. An interesting finding was that tattling, criticism, and

MILESTONES

Moral Development

Age	Moral Internalization	Moral Construction	Self-Control
1½–2 years	■ Concern with deviations from standards first appears ■ Modeling of a wide variety of prosocial acts begins.		■ Compliance and delay of gratification emerge.
3–6 years	■ Guilt reactions to transgressions first appear. ■ By the end of this period, internalization of many prosocial standards and prohibitions has occurred. 	■ Sensitivity to intentions in making moral judgments is present. ■ Differentiated notions about the legitimacy of authority figures are formed. ■ Distinction between moral rules and social conventions develops. ■ Distributive justice and prosocial moral reasoning are self-serving. ■ At the end of this age period, distributive justice is based on equality.	■ Delay of gratification improves. ■ Adult-provided strategies assist with self-control; children can generate only a few strategies on their own. ■ Self-control is transformed into a flexible capacity for moral self-regulation.
7–11 years	■ Internalization of societal norms continues. 	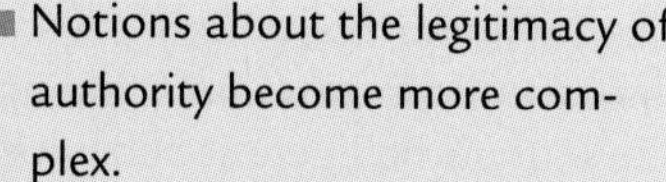 ■ Notions about the legitimacy of authority become more complex. ■ Preconventional responses to Kohlberg's hypothetical moral dilemmas, focusing on rewards, punishment, and the power of authority figures, are common. ■ Distributive justice reasoning includes merit and, eventually, benevolence; basis of fairness is adapted to the situation. ■ Prosocial moral reasoning reflects concern with others' needs and approval.	■ Generation of self-control strategies increases in variety. ■ Awareness of effective self-control strategies and why they work expands.

MILESTONES

Moral Development (continued)

Age	Moral Internalization	Moral Construction	Self-Control
12–adulthood		■ Conventional responses to Kohlberg's hypothetical moral dilemmas, emphasizing human relationships and societal order, increase. ■ Moral thought and action become integrated as individuals move toward Kohlberg's higher stages. ■ Postconventional responses to Kohlberg's hypothetical moral dilemmas, reflecting abstract principles and values, appear among a few highly educated individuals in Western cultures. ■ Prosocial moral reasoning reflects empathic feelings, norms, and abstract values.	■ Moral self-regulation continues to improve

Note: These milestones represent overall age trends. Individual differences exist in the precise age at which each milestone is attained. See Chapter 10, page 396, for additional milestones related to morally relevant emotions of empathy and guilt.

ridicule seldom provoked aggression in 4- and 5-year-olds but often did in 6- and 7-year-olds (Hartup, 1974). Older children seem better able to "read" malicious behavior in others and, as a result, more often respond with a hostile retaliation.

Although children of both sexes show this general pattern of development, on the average boys are more aggressive than girls, a trend that appears in many cultures (Whiting & Edwards, 1988a). In Chapter 13, when we take up sex-related differences in aggression in greater detail, we will see that biological factors—in particular, male sex hormones, or androgens—are influential. At the same time, the development of gender roles is important. As soon as 2-year-olds become dimly aware of gender stereotypes—that males and females are expected to behave differently—aggression drops off in girls but is maintained in boys (Fagot & Leinbach, 1989). Then parents' tendency to discipline boys more harshly magnifies this effect.

From middle childhood on, aggression is a highly stable personality characteristic, especially among boys (Cairns et al., 1989). In a longitudinal investigation that spanned 22 years, very aggressive 8-year-olds became 30-year-olds who were more likely to score high in aggressive inclinations on a personality test, use severe punishment with their children, and be convicted of criminal offenses (see Figure 12.4 on page 492). In this study, the researchers also tracked the aggressive tendencies of participants' family members and found strong continuity across generations. Highly aggressive children were more likely to have parents and grandparents who were antisocial themselves and whose behavior problems were apparent in their own childhoods (Huesmann et al., 1984).

In recent years, researchers have made considerable progress in identifying individual and environmental factors that sustain aggressive behavior. Although some children—especially those who are impulsive and overactive—are clearly at risk for high

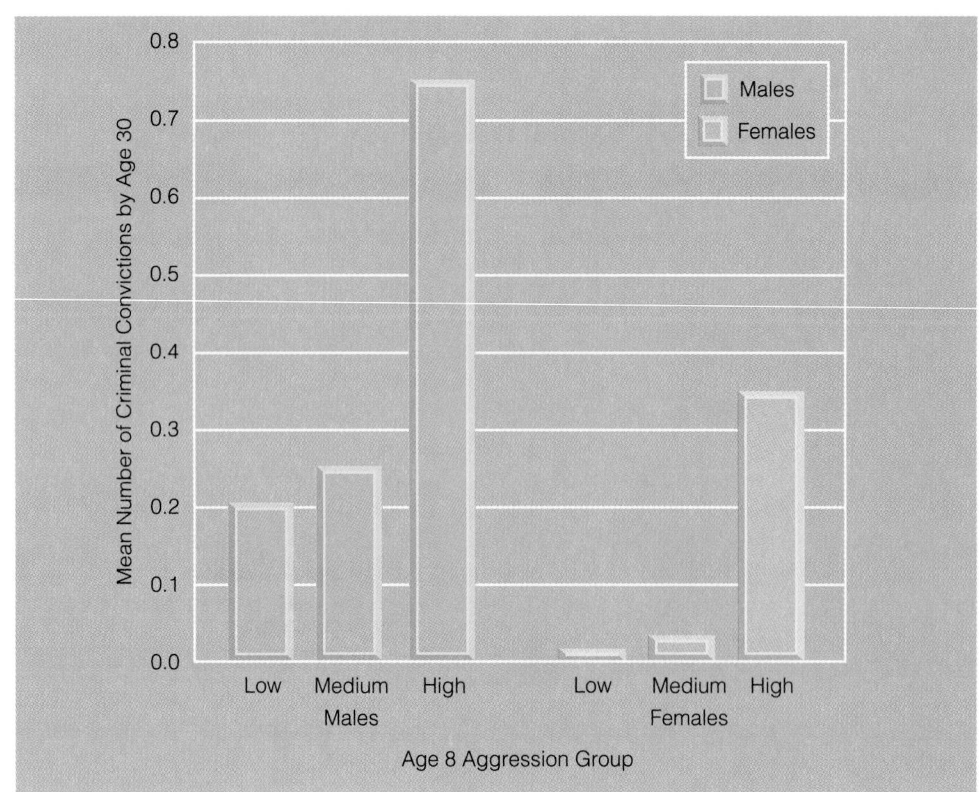

FIGURE 12.4

■ *Relationship of childhood aggression to criminal behavior in adulthood for males and females. (From L. R. Huesmann, L. D. Eron, M. M. Lefkowitz, & L. O. Walder, 1984,* Developmental Psychology, *20, p. 1125. Copyright © 1984 by the American Psychological Association. Reprinted by permission.)*

aggression, whether or not they become so depends on child-rearing conditions. Strife-ridden families, poor parenting practices, aggressive peers, and televised violence are strongly linked to children's antisocial acts. In this chapter, we focus on family and peer influences, reserving the topic of television for Chapter 15. We will also see that community and cultural influences can heighten or reduce children's risk of acquiring a hostile interpersonal style.

THE FAMILY AS TRAINING GROUND FOR AGGRESSIVE BEHAVIOR

The same child-rearing practices that undermine the development of moral internalization and self-control are correlated with aggression. Love withdrawal, power assertion, physical punishment, and inconsistent discipline are linked to antisocial behavior from early childhood through adolescence, in children of both sexes (Parke & Slaby, 1983). Parents who use these tactics fail to teach acceptable alternatives, serve as aggressive models, and frustrate their children's need for nurturance so that they vent their anger on others. These ineffective and destructive techniques are often found together in the same family, compounding their harmful consequences (Olweus, 1980).

Home observations of aggressive children reveal that anger and punitiveness quickly spread from one family member to another, creating a conflict-ridden family atmosphere and an "out-of-control" child. As Figure 12.5 shows, the pattern begins with coercive parental discipline, which is made more likely by stressful life experiences, the parent's own personality, or a temperamentally difficult child. Once the parent threatens, criticizes, and punishes, then the child whines, yells, and refuses until the parent finds the child's behavior to be too much and "gives in." The sequence is likely to be repeated, since at the end of each exchange, both parent and child get relief for stopping the unpleasant behavior of the other. The next time the child misbehaves, the parent is even more coercive and the child more defiant, until one member of the pair "begs off." As these cycles become more frequent, they generate anxiety and irritability among other family members, who soon join in the hostile interactions (Dodge, Pettit, & Bates, 1994; Patterson, Reid, & Dishion, 1992).

Besides fostering aggression in the ways just described, parents can encourage it indirectly, through poor supervision of children's whereabouts. Unfortunately, children from conflict-ridden homes who already display serious antisocial tendencies are most

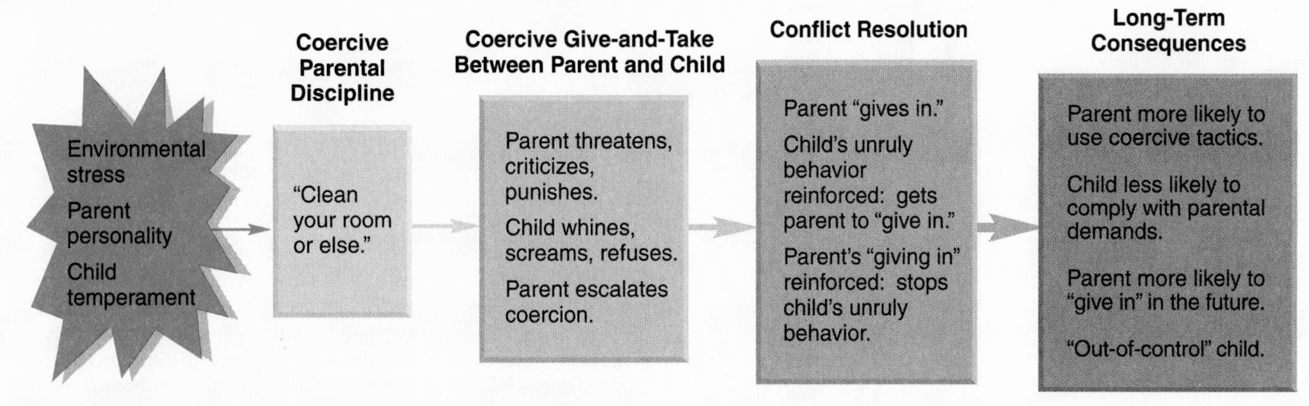

FIGURE 12.5

■ *Coercive interaction pattern that promotes and sustains aggression among family members.*

likely to experience inadequate parental monitoring. As a result, few if any limits are placed on out-of-home activities and peer associations that further their hostile style of responding. Aggressive children typically select antisocial friends like themselves. Talk between them contains frequent coercive statements and attacks, even during videotaping in a laboratory. These friendships provide yet another context in which to practice and strengthen hostile behavior (Dishion, Andrews, & Crosby, 1995; Dishion, Patterson, & Griesler, 1994).

SOCIAL-COGNITIVE DEFICITS AND DISTORTIONS

Children who are products of the family processes just described soon acquire a violent and callous view of the social world. Aggressive children often see hostile intent where it does not exist—in situations where a peer's intentions are unclear, where harm is accidental, and even where a peer is trying to be helpful (Dodge, 1985; Dodge & Somberg, 1987). As a result, they make many unprovoked attacks, which trigger aggressive retaliations. Recall, also, that young people high in antisocial behavior fall behind their agemates in perspective-taking skill, and they are delayed in moral understanding as well (Trevethan & Walker, 1989).

Furthermore, compared to their nonaggressive agemates, aggressive children are convinced that there are more benefits and fewer costs for engaging in hostile acts. They are more likely to think that aggression "works" to produce tangible rewards and reduce teasing, taunting, and other unpleasant behaviors by others (Perry, Perry, & Rasmussen, 1986). And when tempted to aggress, they are more concerned about achieving control, less concerned about a victim's suffering or being disliked by peers, and less likely to evaluate themselves negatively for responding aggressively (Boldizar, Perry, & Perry, 1989). If the sociobiological perspective is correct, however, even these children retain a basic tendency to respond empathically. According to Gibbs (1993), antisocial children may neutralize empathy by using such cognitive-distortion techniques as blaming their victims. Looking back on his burglaries, one delinquent reflected, "If I started feeling bad, I'd say to myself, 'Tough rocks for him. He should have had his house locked better and the alarm on'" (Samenow, 1984, p. 115).

The social-cognitive deficits and distortions just described add further to the long-term maintenance of aggression. In a recent longitudinal study, biased social cognitions were already present in 4-year-olds who had been physically abused. These same children displayed high rates of aggressive behavior after entering kindergarten 6 months later (Dodge, Bates, & Pettit, 1990). As the Social Issues box on page 494 indicates, many aggressive children follow an unfortunate path toward school failure, membership in deviant peer groups, and eventual chronic delinquency and adult criminality.

COMMUNITY AND CULTURAL INFLUENCES

Children's tendency to engage in destructive, injurious behavior increases under certain environmental conditions. When peer group atmospheres are tense and competitive rather than friendly and cooperative, hostility is more likely (DeRosier et al., 1994). These group characteristics are more common in poverty-stricken neighborhoods with a

SOCIAL ISSUES

Juvenile Delinquency

Juvenile delinquents are children and adolescents who engage in illegal acts. Young people under age 21 account for a large proportion of police arrests in the United States—about 30 percent (U.S. Department of Justice, 1995). Yet this official estimate is misleading. It does not tell us how many have committed offenses but have not been caught, how serious their crimes are, and whether many or just a few young people are responsible (Henggeler, 1989).

When adolescents are asked directly, and confidentially, about lawbreaking, almost all admit they are guilty of an offense of one sort or another (Farrington, 1987). But most of the time, they do not commit major crimes. Instead, they engage in petty stealing, disorderly conduct, and acts that are illegal only for minors, such as underage drinking, violating curfews, and running away from home. Both police arrests and self-reports show that delinquency rises over the early teenage years, remains high during middle adolescence, and then declines into young adulthood. What accounts for this trend? As young teenagers spend more time with agemates and less with adults, the desire for peer approval increases. Over time, peers become less influential, moral reasoning matures, and young people enter social contexts (such as marriage, work, and career) that are less conducive to lawbreaking.

For most adolescents, a brush with the law does not forecast long-term antisocial behavior. But teenagers who have many encounters with the police are usually serious offenders. About 12 percent of violent crimes (homicide, rape, robbery, and assault) and 22 percent of property crimes (burglary and theft) are committed by adolescents (U.S. Department of Justice, 1995). A small percentage of young people are responsible, the large majority of whom are boys.

Low verbal intelligence, poor school performance, peer rejection in childhood, and entry into antisocial peer groups are linked to delinquency. How do these factors fit together? One of the most consistent findings about delinquent youths is that their family environments are low in warmth, high in conflict, and characterized by inconsistent discipline. Beginning in early childhood, these forms of child rearing breed antisocial behavior and undermine both cognitive and social competence. Research suggests that the path to chronic delinquency unfolds through the series of steps shown in Figure 12.6.

Treating chronic delinquents requires an approach that recognizes the multiple determinants of delinquency. So far as possible, adolescents are best kept in their own homes and communities to increase the possibility that treatment changes will transfer to their daily environments. Many treatment models exist, including individual therapies and community-based interventions involving halfway houses, day treatment centers, special classrooms, work experience programs, and summer camps. Those that work best are lengthy and intensive and teach cognitive and social skills needed to overcome family, peer, and school difficulties (Guerra, Tolan, & Hammond, 1994).

The hard-core delinquent for whom other efforts have failed may have to be removed from the community and placed in an institution. Overall, the success of institutional programs has not been encouraging. Positive behavior changes typically do not last once young people return to the everyday settings that contributed to their difficulties (Quay, 1987). These disappointing outcomes indicate that the best way to combat antisocial behavior is through prevention, beginning early in life.

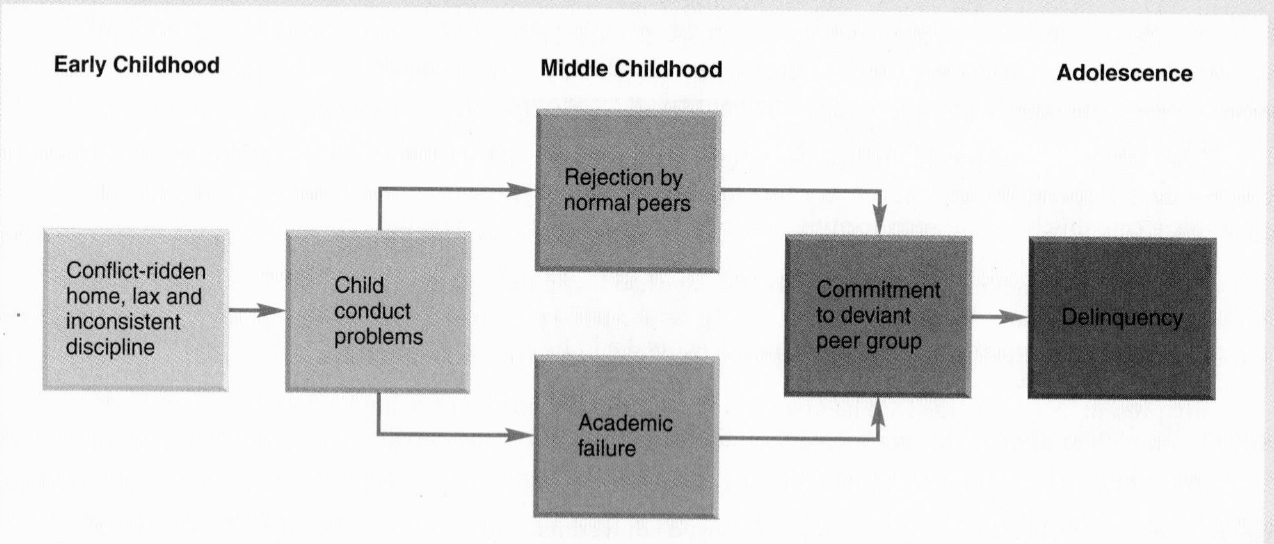

FIGURE 12.6

Developmental path to chronic delinquency. (From G. R. Patterson, B. D. DeBaryshe, & E. Ramsey, 1989, "A Developmental Perspective on Antisocial Behavior," American Psychologist, *44, p. 331. Copyright © 1989 by the* American Psychological Association. *Reprinted by permission.)*

wide range of stressors, including poor-quality schools, limited recreational and employment opportunities, and negative adult role models. In these areas, children and adolescents have easy access to deviant peers and are especially likely to be recruited into antisocial gangs. Among low-income, ethnic minority children, such neighborhoods predict aggression beyond family influences (Kupersmidt et al., 1995). Harsh living conditions are far more prevalent in some societies than others. Recent cross-national comparisons reveal that the United States ranks first in the industrialized world in interpersonal violence and homicides. Glorification of violence in popular culture, ready availability of handguns, and a high poverty rate are believed to be responsible (Hill et al., 1994; Sheley & Wright, 1995).

Ethnic and political prejudices that keep certain groups at the margins of society further magnify the risk of angry, combative responses. In inner-city ghettos and in war-torn areas of the world, large numbers of children live in midst of constant danger, chaos, and deprivation. As the Cultural Influences box on page 496 reveals, these youngsters are at risk for severe emotional stress, deficits in moral reasoning, and behavior problems.

HELPING CHILDREN AND PARENTS CONTROL AGGRESSION

Help for aggressive children must break the cycle of hostilities between family members and promote effective ways of understanding and relating to others. Interventions with preschool and school-age children have been most successful. Once antisocial patterns persist into adolescence, so many factors act to sustain them that treatment is far more difficult (Kazdin, 1995).

COACHING, MODELING, AND REINFORCING ALTERNATIVE BEHAVIORS. Procedures based on social learning theory have been devised to interrupt destructive family interaction. Gerald Patterson (1982) has designed a successful parent training program of this kind. A therapist provides modeling and coaching in child discipline by observing the parent's inept practices, demonstrating alternatives, and insisting that the parent practice them. Parents learn not to give in to an acting-out child and not to escalate forceful attempts to control misbehavior. In addition, they are taught to pair commands with reasons and to replace verbal insults and spankings with more effective strategies, such as time out and withdrawal of privileges. Research reveals that after only a few weeks of such training, antisocial behavior declined and parents began to view their children more positively—gains still evident a year later (Patterson & Fleishman, 1979).

On the child's side, interventions that teach alternative ways of resolving conflict that are incompatible with aggression are helpful. Sessions in which children model and role-play cooperation and sharing and see that these behaviors lead to rewarding social outcomes reduce aggression and increase positive social behavior (Zahavi & Asher, 1978). Once aggressive children begin to change, parents need to be reminded to give them attention and approval for their prosocial acts. The coercive cycles of parents and aggressive children are so pervasive that these children often get punished when they do behave appropriately (Strassberg, 1995).

SOCIAL-COGNITIVE INTERVENTIONS. The social-cognitive deficits of aggressive children prevent them from experiencing empathy to another person's pain and suffering—an important inhibitor of aggressive behavior. Furthermore, since aggressive children have few opportunities to witness family members acting in sensitive, caring ways, they miss early experiences that are vital for promoting empathic responding (see Chapter 10). In such children, empathy may have to be directly taught. In one program, sessions in which children practiced identifying others' feelings and expressing their own reduced hostility among peers and increased cooperation, helping, and generosity (Feshbach & Feshbach, 1982).

Other social-cognitive treatments focus on improving social information processing in antisocial youths. For example, in a program designed to remediate social problem solving deficits, adolescents were taught to attend to relevant, nonhostile social cues; seek additional information before acting; and evaluate potential responses in terms of their effectiveness. The intervention led to increased skill in solving social problems, decreased endorsement of beliefs supporting aggression, and reduced hostile, impulsive behaviors (Guerra & Slaby, 1990).

CULTURAL INFLUENCES

The Impact of Ethnic and Political Violence on Children

On May 27, 1992, Zlata Filipovic, a 10-year-old Bosnian girl, recorded the following reactions to the intensifying Serb attack on the city of Sarajevo in her diary:

> Slaughter! Massacre! Horror! Crime! Blood! Screams! Tears! Despair!
>
> That's what Vaso Miskin Street looks like today. Two shells exploded in the street and one in the market. Mommy was nearby at the time. . . . Daddy and I were beside ourselves because she hadn't come home. I saw some of it on TV but I still can't believe what I actually saw. . . . I've got a lump in my throat and a knot in my tummy. HORRIBLE. They're taking the wounded to the hospital. It's a madhouse. We kept going to the window hoping to see Mommy, but she wasn't back. . . . Daddy and I were tearing our hair out. . . . I looked out the window one more time and . . . I SAW MOMMY RUNNING ACROSS THE BRIDGE. As she came into the house she started shaking and crying. Through her tears she told us how she had seen dismembered bodies. . . . Thank God, Mommy is with us. Thank God. (Filipovic, 1994, p. 55)

Violence stemming from ethnic and political tensions is being felt increasingly around the world. Since World War II, almost all the hundreds of conflicts around the globe have been internal civil wars. Besides being armed encounters, modern wars are usually social upheavals in which well-established ways of life are threatened or destroyed and children are frequent victims (Ressler, 1993).

Children's experiences under conditions of armed conflict are diverse. Some may participate in the fighting, either because they are forced or because they want to please adults. Others are kidnapped, terrorized, or tortured. Those who are bystanders often come under direct fire and may be killed or physically maimed for life. And, as Zlata's diary entry illustrates, many children of war watch in horror as family members, friends, and neighbors flee, are wounded, or die (Ladd & Cairns, 1996).

The initial reactions of most children to these experiences are similar. They include disturbed sleep, difficulty concentrating, decreased interest in pleasurable activities, emotional detachment from parents and friends, repetitive play with traumatic themes, and a heightened state of alertness in response to acute and constant danger.

When war and social crises are temporary, most children are comforted by caregivers' reassuring messages and do not show long-term emotional difficulties. But chronic danger requires children to make substantial adjustments, and their psychological functioning can be seriously impaired. Many children of war lose their sense of safety, acquire a high tolerance for violence, are haunted by terrifying memories, become suspicious of others, and build a pessimistic view of the future (Cairns, 1996).

The extent to which children are negatively affected by war depends on mediating factors. Closeness to wartime events increases the chances of maladjustment. For example, an estimated 50 percent of traumatized 6- to 12-year-old Cambodian war refugees continued to show intense stress reactions when they reached young adulthood (Kinzie et al., 1989). The support and affection of parents is the best safeguard against lasting problems. Unfortunately, many children of war are separated from family members. Sometimes, the child's community can offer protection. For example, Israeli children who lost a parent in battle fared best when they lived in kibbutzim, where many adults knew the child well and felt responsible for his or her welfare (Lifschitz et al., 1977).

When wartime drains families and communities of resources, international organizations need to step in and help children. Until we know how to prevent war, efforts to preserve children's physical and psychological well-being may be the best way to stop transmission of violence to the next generation in many parts of the world (Macksoud, 1994).

■ *This Rwandan refugee child has experienced the trauma of civil war. Here, he watches as his home burns, and he has probably witnessed the wounding and death of family members, friends, and neighbors. If he survives, he is likely to show lasting emotional problems without special support from caring adults. (Michael Simpson/The Picture Cube)*

Training in empathy and social information processing necessarily involves taking the perspectives of others. In Chapter 11, we noted that the antisocial acts of troubled youths could be reduced through coaching and practice in perspective taking. Perhaps this approach is helpful because it promotes empathic responding and accurate interpretation of social cues, which deter aggressive behavior.

■ COMPREHENSIVE APPROACHES. According to some researchers, effective treatment for antisocial children and adolescents needs to be multifaceted, encompassing social understanding, relating to others, and self-control. Although only a few such efforts have been tried, their success supports the power of a comprehensive approach. In one program, called EQUIP, *positive peer culture*—an adult-guided but youth-conducted small-group approach designed to create a climate in which prosocial acts replace antisocial behavior—served as the basis for treatment. It was supplemented with social skills training, anger management training, training to correct cognitive distortions (such as blaming the victim), and moral discussions to promote "catch-up" to age-appropriate moral reasoning (Gibbs, Potter, & Goldstein, 1995). In a recent evaluation, juvenile delinquents who participated in EQUIP displayed improved social skills and conduct during the following year relative to controls receiving no intervention. Also, the more advanced moral reasoning that emerged during group meetings appeared to have a long-term impact on antisocial youths' ability to inhibit lawbreaking behavior (Leeman, Gibbs, & Fuller, 1993).

Yet even multidimensional treatments can fall short if young people remain embedded in hostile home lives, antisocial peer groups, and violent neighborhood settings. Intensive efforts to create nonaggressive environments—at the family, community, and cultural levels—are needed to support the interventions just described and to ensure optimal development of all children. We will return to this theme several times in later chapters.

SUMMARY

MORALITY AS ROOTED IN HUMAN NATURE

- The biological perspective on moral development is represented by a controversial field called **sociobiology**. It assumes that morality is grounded in the genetic heritage of our species, perhaps through prewired emotional reactions. Although human morality cannot be fully explained in this way, the biological perspective reminds us of the adaptive significance of moral behavior.

MORALITY AS THE ADOPTION OF SOCIETAL NORMS

- Psychoanalytic and social learning theories regard moral development as a matter of **internalization**: the adoption of preexisting, ready-made standards of conduct as one's own.
- According to Freud, morality emerges with the resolution of the Oedipus and Electra conflicts during the phallic stage of development. Fear of punishment and loss of parental love lead children to form a **superego** through **identification** with the same-sex parent and to redirect hostile impulses toward the self in the form of guilt.
- Although guilt is an important motivator of moral action, Freud's interpretation of it is no longer widely accepted. In contrast to Freudian predictions, power assertion and love withdrawal do not foster conscience development. Instead, **induction** is far more effective. Recent psychoanalytic ideas place greater emphasis on a positive parent–child relationship and earlier beginnings of morality. However, they retain continuity with Freud's theory in regarding emotion as the basis for moral development.
- Social learning theory views moral behavior as acquired in the same way as other responses: through modeling and reinforcement. Young children readily imitate morally relevant behaviors, including resistance to temptation, if models make their efforts explicit by verbalizing them. Effective models are warm and powerful and practice what they preach. Harsh punishment does not promote moral internalization and socially desirable behavior. Instead, it provides children with aggressive models, leads them to avoid the punishing adult, and can spiral into serious abuse.

MORALITY AS SOCIAL UNDERSTANDING

- In contrast to psychoanalytic and social learning theories, the cognitive-developmental perspective assumes that morality develops through **construction**—actively thinking about right and wrong in situations in which social conflicts arise and deriving new moral understandings.
- Piaget's work was the original inspiration for the cognitive-developmental perspective. He identified two stages of moral understanding: **heteronomous morality**, in which children view moral rules in terms of **realism** and as fixed dictates of authority figures; and **autonomous morality**, in which children use **reciprocity** as a standard of fairness and regard rules as flexible, socially agreed-on principles.

Although Piaget's theory describes the general direction of moral development, it underestimates the moral capacities of young children.

- Piaget's work inspired Kohlberg's expanded theory. Kohlberg presented subjects with **moral dilemmas** that required them to both choose and justify a course of action. As a result, he identified three levels of moral understanding, each of which contains two stages: the **preconventional level**, in which morality is viewed as controlled by rewards, punishments, and the power of authority figures; the **conventional level**, in which conformity to social rules is regarded as necessary to preserve positive human relationships and societal order; and the **postconventional level**, in which individuals define morality in terms of abstract principles and values that apply to all situations and societies. Besides Kohlberg's clinical interview, efficient questionnaire approaches for assessing moral understanding exist. The most recently devised is the **Sociomoral Reflection Measure–Short Form (SRM–SF)**.
- Kohlberg's stages are strongly related to age and form an invariant sequence. However, the influence of situational factors on moral judgment suggests that moral development fits a less tightly organized stage conception than Kohlberg assumed. Piaget's cognitive and Selman's perspective-taking stages are necessary but not sufficient conditions for each advance in moral reasoning. Many experiences contribute to maturity of moral thought, including peer interaction; warm, rational child-rearing practices; and years of schooling.
- Cross-cultural research indicates that a certain level of societal complexity is required for Kohlberg's highest stages. At the same time, his theory does not encompass the full range of moral reasoning in all cultures. Although Kohlberg's theory does not underestimate the moral maturity of females, it emphasizes justice rather than caring as the most central moral ideal. Maturity of moral reasoning is moderately related to a wide variety of moral behaviors.

MORAL REASONING OF YOUNG CHILDREN

- Kohlberg's theory, like Piaget's, underestimates young children's moral understanding. As early as age 3, children have a beginning grasp of justice in that they distinguish moral rules from social conventions. However, this dichotomy is often less pronounced in non-Western cultures. Research on **distributive justice** and prosocial reasoning reveals that when moral dilemmas deemphasize the role of laws and the possibility of punishment, children display some surprisingly sophisticated moral judgments.

DEVELOPMENT OF SELF-CONTROL

- The emergence of **self-control** is supported by self-awareness and representational and memory capacities of the second year. The first glimmerings of self-control appear in the form of **compliance**. Researchers typically study self-control by creating situations in the laboratory that call for **delay of gratification**. The ability to delay increases steadily over the third year. Language development—in particular, use of self-directed speech to guide behavior—is believed to be involved.
- During the preschool years, children profit from adult-provided self-control strategies. Over middle childhood, they produce an increasing variety of strategies themselves and become consciously aware of which ones work well and why. Modest stability in moral self-regulation from childhood to adolescence is believed to be due to the combined influence of temperament and child-rearing practices.

THE OTHER SIDE OF SELF-CONTROL: DEVELOPMENT OF AGGRESSION

- Aggression first appears in late infancy. Over the preschool years, physical forms are replaced by verbal forms, and **instrumental aggression** declines, whereas **hostile aggression** increases. Beginning in middle childhood, aggression is a highly stable characteristic, particularly among boys.
- Although impulsive, overactive children are at risk for high aggression, whether or not they become so depends on child-rearing conditions. Strife-ridden family environments and power-assertive, inconsistent discipline promote self-perpetuating cycles of aggressive behavior. Children who are products of these family processes develop social-cognitive deficits and distortions that add to the long-term maintenance of aggression. Widespread poverty, harsh living conditions, and cultural glorification of violence increase antisocial acts among children and adolescents.
- Among interventions designed to reduce aggression, procedures based on social learning theory that interrupt destructive family processes by training parents in child discipline and teaching children alternative ways of resolving conflict work well in early and middle childhood. Social-cognitive interventions, including empathy, social problem solving, and perspective-taking training, are also beneficial. Comprehensive interventions addressing the multiple factors that sustain antisocial behavior may be the most effective approach to treatment.

IMPORTANT TERMS AND CONCEPTS

sociobiology (p. 462)
internalization (p. 463)
superego (p. 463)
identification (p. 463)
induction (p. 464)
time out (p. 467)
construction (p. 468)
heteronomous morality (p. 470)
realism (p. 470)
autonomous morality (p. 470)
reciprocity (p. 470)
moral dilemma (p. 472)
Sociomoral Reflection Measure–Short Form (SRM–SF) (p. 472)
preconventional level (p. 473)
conventional level (p. 474)
postconventional level (p. 474)
just community (p. 479)
distributive justice (p. 483)
self-control (p. 486)
compliance (p. 486)
delay of gratification (p. 486)
instrumental aggression (p. 489)
hostile aggression (p. 489)

CONNECTIONS for Chapter 12

If you are interested in . . .	turn to . . .	to learn about . . .
Influences on morality	Chapter 10, pp. 394–395	Cognitive and child-rearing influences on empathy
	Chapter 14, pp. 543–546	Styles of child rearing and self-control
	Chapter 15, pp. 594–595	Peer conformity and antisocial behavior in early adolescence
	Chapter 15, pp. 600–603	Television, aggression, and prosocial behavior
	Chapter 15, p. 622	Adolescent employment and work-related values
Modeling and development	Chapter 1, pp. 18–19	Social learning theory
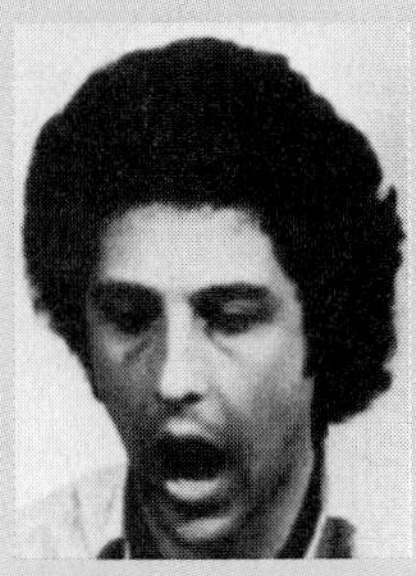	Chapter 4, pp. 139–140	Newborn imitation
	Chapter 6, pp. 215–217, 220–221	Development of imitation during the first 2 years
	Chapter 9, p. 343	Imitation and language development
	Chapter 10, p. 382	Social learning theory, modeling, and emotional development
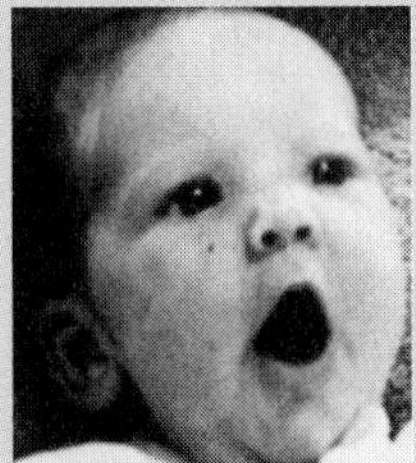	Chapter 13, pp. 515–516	Observational learning, gender stereotyping, gender-role adoption
	Chpater 13, pp. 516–517 Chapter 14, p. 554	Imitation of siblings
	Chapter 15, p. 584	Parental modeling of effective social skills
	Chapter 15, p. 594	Peer modeling
	Chapter 15, pp. 600–603	Television, imitation, and social learning
The concept of construction	Chapter 1, p. 19 Chapter 6, pp. 212–213, 220–221	Piaget's cognitive-developmental theory and construction of knowledge
	Chapter 4, p. 161	Perception as construction
	Chapter 7, pp. 275–277	Constructivist approaches to information processing
	Chapter 10, pp. 413–414	Attachment and construction of internal working models
	Chapter 11, pp. 426–428	Children's theory of mind
	Chapter 11, pp. 428–430, 438–440	Construction of self-concept and identity

13 Development of Sex-Related Differences and Gender Roles

On a typical morning, I observed the following scene during a free-play period at our university laboratory preschool:

Four-year-old Jenny eagerly entered the housekeeping corner and put on a frilly long dress and grown-up-looking high heels. Karen, setting the table nearby, produced whimpering sound effects for the baby doll in the crib. Jenny lifted the doll, sat down in the rocking chair, gently cradled the baby in her arms, and whispered, "You're hungry, aren't you?" A moment later, Jenny announced to Karen, "This baby won't eat. I think she's sick. Ask Rachel if she'll be the nurse." Karen ran off to find Rachel, who was coloring at the art table.

Meanwhile, Nathan called to Tommy, "Wanna play traffic?" Both boys dashed energetically toward the cars and trucks in the block corner. Soon David joined them. "I'll be policeman first!" announced Nathan, who pulled a chair into the center of the block area and climbed on it. "Green light, go!" shouted the young police officer. With this signal, Tommy and David scurried on all fours around the chair, each pushing a large wooden truck. "Red light," exclaimed Nathan, and the trucks screeched to a halt.

"My truck beat yours," announced Tommy to David.

"Only 'cause I need gas," David responded as he pulled off to the side and pretended to fill the tank.

"Let's build a runway for the trucks," suggested Nathan. The three construction engineers began to gather large blocks and boards for the task.

The activity choices and behaviors of these young children reveal that they have already adopted many of the gender-linked standards of their cultural community. Jenny, Karen, and Rachel used dresses, dolls, and household props to act out a stereotypically feminine scene of nurturance. In contrast, Nathan, Tommy, and David's play is active, competitive, and masculine in theme. And already, these preschoolers interact more often with children of their own sex than the other sex.

What causes young children's play and social preferences to become so strongly gender typed, and how do these attitudes and behaviors change with age? Do societal expectations affect the way children think about themselves as masculine and feminine beings, thereby limiting their potential? To what extent do widely held beliefs about the characteristics of males and females reflect reality? Is it true that the average boy is aggressive, competitive, and good at spatial and mathematical skills, whereas the average girl is passive, nurturant, and good at verbal skills? How large are differences between the sexes, and in what ways do biological and environmental factors contribute to them? These are the central questions asked by researchers who study gender typing, and we will answer each of them in this chapter.

Perhaps more than any other area of child development, the study of gender typing has responded to societal change. Largely because of progress in women's rights, over the past 25 years major shifts have occurred in how sex-related differences are regarded. Until the early 1970s, the adoption of gender-typed behavior was viewed as a desirable goal of child rearing and essential for healthy psychological adjustment. Today, many people recognize that some gender-typed characteristics, such as extreme aggressiveness and competitiveness on the part of males and passivity and conformity on the part of females, are serious threats to mental health.

Consistent with this realization, theoretical revision marks the study of gender typing. At one time, psychoanalytic theory offered an influential account of how children acquired "masculine" and "feminine" traits. According to Freud (1925/1961), these attitudes and behaviors were adopted in the same way as other societal standards—through identification with the same-sex parent during the preschool years. Today we know that interactions with other-sex parents, siblings, teachers, and peers, along with examples of gender-appropriate behavior in the surrounding culture, also play powerful roles.

Furthermore, recent research shows that gender typing begins earlier and lasts much longer than Freud believed, continuing into adolescence and even adulthood. Finally, Freud's theory, as well as Erikson's (1950) extension of it, regards gender typing as a natural outcome of biological differences between the sexes. Although debate continues over this assumption, firm commitment to it has not been helpful in the quest to discover how children might be released from gender-based definitions of appropriate behavior. As a result, most researchers have abandoned the psychoanalytic approach in favor of other perspectives.

Social learning theory, with its emphasis on modeling and reinforcement, and cognitive-developmental theory, with its focus on children as active thinkers about their social world, are major current approaches to gender typing. However, neither is sufficient by itself. We will see that a recent information-processing view, *gender schema theory,* combines elements of both theories to explain how children acquire gender-typed knowledge and behavior.

Along with new theories have come new terms. Considerable controversy surrounds the labels *sex* and *gender.* Some researchers use these words interchangeably. Others apply them in a way that makes causal assumptions—*sex* to refer to biologically based differences and *gender* to socially influenced characteristics. Still others object to this convention because our understanding of many differences is still evolving. Also, it perpetuates too strong a dichotomy between nature and nurture (Unger & Crawford, 1993). I use another system that avoids these problems. *Sex related* refers to comparisons between males and females that do not involve any causal inference; we simply say that a difference exists. In contrast, *gender* is used when judgments are being made about either biological or environmental causes (Deaux, 1993).

Throughout this chapter, you will encounter a variety of additional terms. Two of these involve the public face of gender in society. **Gender stereotypes** are widely held beliefs about characteristics deemed appropriate for males and females. **Gender roles** are the reflection of these stereotypes in everyday behavior. **Gender-role identity** is the private face of gender. It refers to perception of the self as relatively masculine or feminine in characteristics, abilities, and behaviors. Finally, **gender typing**, a term already mentioned, is the process of developing gender-linked beliefs, gender roles, and a gender-role identity. As we explore this process, you will see that it is complex and multiply determined. Biological, cognitive, and social factors are involved.

Gender Stereotypes and Gender Roles

Gender stereotypes have appeared in religious, philosophical, and literary works for centuries. For example, in ancient times, Aristotle wrote,

> Woman is more compassionate than man and has a greater propensity to tears. She is, also, more envious, more querulous, more slanderous, and more contentious. Farther still, the female is more dispirited, more despondent, more impudent and more given to falsehood than the male. . . . But the male . . . is more disposed to give assistance in danger, and is more courageous than the female. (Cited in Miles, 1935, p. 700)

Although the past three decades have brought a new level of awareness about the wide range of roles possible for each gender, strong beliefs about differences between males and females remain. In the 1960s, researchers began to ask people what personality characteristics they consider typical of men and women. Widespread agreement emerged in many studies. As Table 13.1 illustrates, **instrumental traits**, reflecting competence, rationality, and assertiveness, were regarded as masculine; **expressive traits**, emphasizing warmth, caring, and sensitivity, were viewed as feminine. Despite intense political activism over gender equality during the 1970s and 1980s, these stereotypes have remained essentially the same (Golombok & Fivush, 1994; Lutz & Ruble, 1995). Furthermore, cross-cultural research on respondents from 30 nations reveals that the

Gender stereotypes
Widely held beliefs about characteristics deemed appropriate for males and females.

Gender roles
The reflection of gender stereotypes in everyday behavior.

Gender-role identity
Perception of the self as relatively masculine or feminine in characteristics, abilities, and behaviors.

Gender typing
The process of developing gender-linked beliefs, gender roles, and a gender-role identity.

Instrumental traits
Masculine-stereotyped personality traits that reflect competence, rationality, and assertiveness.

Expressive traits
Feminine-stereotyped personality traits that reflect warmth, caring, and sensitivity.

TABLE 13.1

Personality Traits Regarded as Stereotypically Masculine and Feminine

Masculine Traits	Feminine Traits
Active	Aware of others' feelings
Acts as a leader	Considerate
Adventurous	Cries easily
Aggressive	Devotes self to others
Ambitious	Emotional
Competitive	Excitable in a major crisis
Doesn't give up easily	Feelings hurt easily
Dominant	Gentle
Feels superior	Home oriented
Holds up well under pressure	Kind
Independent	Likes children
Makes decisions easily	Neat
Not easily influenced	Needs approval
Outspoken	Passive
Rough	Tactful
Self-confident	Understanding of others
Takes a stand	Warm in relations with others

instrumental–expressive dichotomy is a widely held stereotype around the world (Williams & Best, 1990).

Besides personality traits, other gender stereotypes exist. These include physical characteristics (tall, strong, and sturdy for men; soft, dainty, and graceful for women), occupations (truck driver, insurance agent, and chemist for men; elementary school teacher, secretary, and nurse for women), and activities or behaviors (good at fixing things and leader in groups for men; good at child care and decorating the home for women) (Biernat, 1991a; Deaux & Lewis, 1984). The variety of attributes consistently identified as masculine or feminine, their broad acceptance, and their stability over time suggest that gender stereotypes are deeply ingrained patterns of thinking. When do children become aware of them, and what implications do they have for gender-role adoption?

GENDER STEREOTYPING IN EARLY CHILDHOOD

Recall from Chapter 11 that around age 2, children label their own sex and that of other people, using such words as "boy" versus "girl" and "woman" versus "man." As soon as these categories are established, children start to sort out what they mean in terms of activities and behaviors. As a result, a wide variety of gender stereotypes are mastered.

Preschoolers associate many toys, articles of clothing, tools, household items, games, occupations, and even colors (pink and blue) with one sex as opposed to the other (Huston, 1983; Picariello, Greenberg, & Pillemer, 1990). In a study illustrating the range of gender stereotypes acquired at an early age, children as young as 2½ were shown pictures of boys and girls. As each was presented, an adult described it by making a statement about a gender-stereotyped behavior, physical characteristic, activity, or future role—for example, "I can hit you," "I look nice," "I like to play ball," and "When I grow up, I'll be a nurse." Children of both sexes indicated that girls "like to play with dolls," "talk a lot," "never hit," say "I need some help," and later on as grown-ups will "clean the house" and "be a nurse." They also believed that boys "like to help father," say "I can

■ *By age 1½, gender-stereotyped game and toy choices are present, becoming increasingly consistent with age. Already, these 3-year-olds play in highly gender-stereotyped ways. (Left, Erika Stone/Photo Researchers; right, Stephen Marks)*

hit you," and as future adults will "be boss" and "mow the grass" (Kuhn, Nash, & Brucken, 1978).

Even before children can label their own sex and match up statements and objects with male and female figures, they prefer "gender-appropriate" activities. By 1½ years, gender-stereotyped game and toy choices are present (Caldera, Huston, & O'Brien, 1989; Fagot, Leinbach, & Hagan, 1986). Between ages 1 and 3, these preferences become highly consistent for both boys and girls (O'Brien & Huston, 1985).

A striking feature of preschoolers' gender stereotypes is that they operate like blanket rules rather than flexible guidelines. In several studies, researchers labeled a target child as a boy or girl and then provided either gender-typical or gender-atypical information about the target's characteristics. Next, children were asked to rate the target on additional gender-stereotypic attributes. Preschoolers usually relied on only the gender label in making these judgments, ignoring the specific information. For example, when told, "Tommy is a boy. Tommy's best friend is a girl, and Tommy likes to play house," children under age 6 nevertheless said that Tommy would much prefer to play with cars and train engines than sewing machines and dolls (Biernat, 1991a; Martin, 1989).

The rigidity of preschoolers' gender stereotypes helps us understand some commonly observed everyday behaviors. Shown a picture of a Scottish bagpiper wearing a kilt, a 4-year-old is likely to say, "Men don't wear skirts!" At preschool, children can be heard exclaiming that girls don't drive fire engines and can't be police officers and boys don't take care of babies and can't be the teacher. These one-sided judgments are a joint product of gender stereotyping in the environment and young children's cognitive immaturity—in particular, their difficulty integrating conflicting sources of information. Most preschoolers do not yet realize that characteristics *associated* with sex—activities, toys, occupations, hairstyle, and clothing—do not *determine* whether a person is male or female. As we will see later, they have trouble understanding that males and females can be different in terms of their bodies yet similar in many other ways.

GENDER STEREOTYPING IN MIDDLE CHILDHOOD AND ADOLESCENCE

By age 5, gender stereotyping of activities and occupations is well established. During middle childhood and adolescence, knowledge of stereotypes strengthens in the less obvious areas of personality traits and achievement. At the same time, older children begin to realize that gender-stereotypic attributes are associated, not defining, features of gender. As a result, beliefs about the characteristics and capacities of males and females become more flexible.

■ PERSONALITY TRAITS. To assess stereotyping of personality traits, researchers ask children to assign "masculine" adjectives (such as tough, rational, and cruel) and "feminine" adjectives (such as gentle, affectionate, and dependent) to either a male or female stimulus figure. Recall from Chapter 11 that not until middle childhood are children good at sizing up people in terms of psychological dispositions. This same finding carries over to awareness of gender stereotypes.

Research carried out in many countries, including England, Canada, France, Germany, India, Korea, the Netherlands, and the United States, reveals that stereotyping of personality traits increases steadily during the elementary school years, becoming adultlike around age 11 (Beere, 1990; Best et al., 1977). A large Canadian study examined the pattern of children's trait learning and found that the stereotypes acquired first reflected "own-sex favoritism." Kindergartners through second graders had greatest knowledge of trait stereotypes that portrayed their own gender in a positive light. Once trait stereotyping was well under way, elementary school pupils were most familiar with "positive feminine" traits and "negative masculine" traits (Serbin, Powlishta, & Gulko, 1993). In addition to learning specific stereotypes, children seemed to pick up a widely held general impression—that of girls as "sugar and spice and everything nice" and boys as "snakes and snails and puppy dog tails."

■ ACHIEVEMENT AREAS. Shortly after entering elementary school, children figure out which academic subjects and skill areas are "masculine" and which are "feminine." Throughout the school years, they regard reading, art, and music as more for girls and mathematics, athletics, and mechanical skills as more for boys (Eccles, Jacobs, & Harold, 1990; Stein, 1971; Stein & Smithells, 1969). Similar stereotypes can also be found in other cultures. When pupils in Japan, Taiwan, and the United States were asked to name the school subject they liked best, girls were more likely to choose reading and boys mathematics in all three countries. Asked to predict how well they would do in these subjects once they reached high school, boys thought they would do better in mathematics than did girls. In contrast, no sex-related difference in favor of girls emerged in predictions about reading (Lummis & Stevenson, 1990). These findings suggest that by the mid-elementary school years, children have acquired a more general stereotype of achievement as a "masculine" pursuit.

Other subtle forms of achievement stereotyping appear during middle childhood. Recall our discussion of achievement-related attributions in Chapter 11, which indicated that attributing failure to ability as opposed to effort undermines achievement motivation. Elementary school pupils tend to explain the failures of females, particularly in "cross-gender" activities, as due to ability. In contrast, they interpret corresponding male failures more generously, in terms of insufficient effort or learning opportunities (Nemerowicz, 1979).

■ TOWARD GREATER FLEXIBILITY. Clearly, school-age children are knowledgeable about a wide variety of gender stereotypes. At the same time, they develop a more open-minded view of what males and females *can do*.

Look back at how researchers assessed gender stereotyping in the studies described earlier. You will see that almost all used a forced-choice technique in which children had to assign a characteristic to either one gender or the other. In some instances, researchers have also asked whether both genders can display a personality trait or activity—a response that provides a measure of stereotype flexibility. In the Canadian study mentioned earlier, stereotype knowledge and flexibility were assessed, and as Figure 13.1 on page 506 reveals, both increased from kindergarten to sixth grade (Serbin, Powlishta, & Gulko, 1993). Other evidence reveals that school-age children's flexible appreciation that males and females can engage in the same activities and occupations parallels their grasp of social conventions—that many social practices are arbitrary rules arrived at by group consensus, not fixed, immutable laws (Carter & Patterson, 1982).

As gender stereotypes become more flexible and children develop the cognitive capacity to integrate conflicting social cues, they no longer rely on only a gender label to predict what a person will be like. They also consider the individual's unique characteristics. Unlike preschoolers, when school-age children and adolescents are told about a child named Tommy who likes to play house, they notice both his sex and his interest. Realizing that many attributes are shared by boys and girls, older children say that

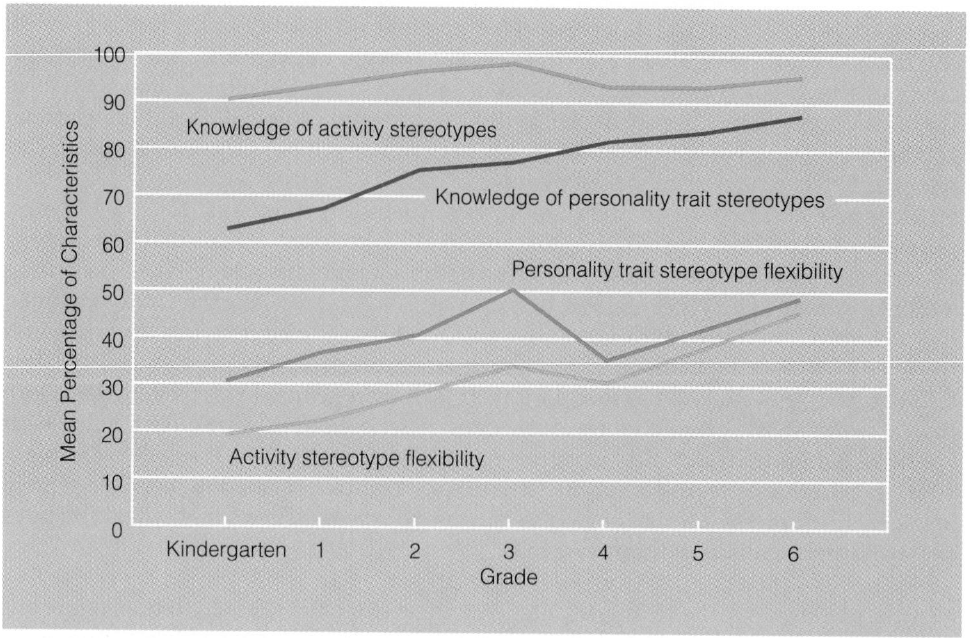

FIGURE 13.1

■ *Changes in knowledge and flexibility of gender stereotypes from kindergarten to sixth grade in a cross-sectional study of over 500 Canadian children. (From L. A. Serbin, K. K. Powlishta, & J. Gulko, 1993, "The Development of Sex Typing in Middle Childhood,"* Monographs of the Society for Research in Child Development, *58 (2, Serial No. 232), p. 35. © The Society for Research in Child Development, Inc. Adapted by permission.)*

Tommy would probably enjoy several other "cross-gender" activities and some gender-typical ones as well (Biernat, 1991a; Martin, 1989).

Nevertheless, acknowledging that boys and girls *can* cross gender lines does not mean that children always *approve* of doing so. In one study, 4- and 8-year-olds and adults were asked how much they would like being friends with an agemate who violated gender-role expectations for behavior (such as a male wearing a dress or a female playing football) and how bad they thought such "transgressions" were. Children and adults were fairly tolerant of "feminine" violations. But most judged "masculine" violations quite harshly—as just as bad as violating a moral rule! Clearly, evaluations of certain "cross-gender" behaviors on the part of males tend to be negative at all ages—a finding that reflects greater social pressure on boys and men to conform to gender roles (Levy, Taylor, & Gelman, 1995).

INDIVIDUAL, SEX-RELATED, AND ETHNIC DIFFERENCES IN GENDER STEREOTYPING

Almost all children acquire extensive knowledge of gender stereotypes by middle childhood. But while they are developing, children differ widely in the makeup of their understanding. Research shows that the various components of gender stereotyping—activities, behaviors, occupations, and personality traits—do not correlate highly (Serbin, Powlishta, & Gulko, 1993). This suggests that gender typing is not unitary. Instead, it is more like "an intricate puzzle that the child pieces together in a rather idiosyncratic way" (Hort, Leinbach, & Fagot, 1991, p. 196). To build a coherent notion of gender, children must assemble many elements, including gender labels, diverse stereotypes, and evaluations of the appropriateness of each. The precise pattern in which they acquire the pieces, the rate at which they do so, and the flexibility of their beliefs vary greatly from child to child (Signorella, 1987).

Group differences in gender stereotyping also exist. The strongest of these is sex-related: boys hold more gender-stereotypic views throughout childhood and adolescence—in studies carried out in the United States and other nations, such as Great Britain and Hungary (Archer, 1992; Levy, Taylor, & Gelman, 1995; Turner, Gervai, & Hinde, 1993). In addition, boys are more likely to devalue the achievements of females and to attribute sex-related differences to physical rather than social causes (Smith & Russell, 1984). However, in a few recent studies, boys and girls did not always differ in these ways (Biernat, 1991b; Serbin, Powlishta, & Gulko, 1993). One heartening possibility is that boys are beginning to view gender roles as encompassing more varied possibilities.

Research including ethnic minorities reveals that black children hold less stereotyped views of females than do white children (Bardwell, Cochran, & Walker, 1986; Kleinke &

Nicholson, 1979). Perhaps this finding is due to aspects of African-American family life. For example, more black than white women with children under 18 are employed (U.S. Bureau of the Census, 1995). This means that African-American children are more likely to have mothers whose lives reflect less traditional gender roles.

Finally, although no social-class differences in gender stereotyping are present in childhood, middle-class individuals tend to hold more flexible gender-stereotyped views than their lower-class counterparts in adolescence and adulthood (Canter & Ageton, 1984; Lackey, 1989; Serbin, Powlishta, & Gulko, 1993). Years of schooling along with a wider array of options in life may contribute to this difference.

GENDER STEREOTYPING AND GENDER-ROLE ADOPTION

Do children's gender-stereotyped patterns of thinking influence gender-role adoption, thereby restricting their experiences and potential? The evidence on this issue is mixed. Gender-typed preferences and behaviors increase sharply over the preschool years—the same period in which children rapidly acquire a wide variety of stereotypes. In addition, boys—the more stereotyped of the two sexes—show greater conformity to their gender role (Bussey & Bandura, 1992; Huston, 1983).

But these parallel patterns of development do not tell us for sure that stereotyping shapes children's behavior. Indeed, research suggests that the relationship is not that clear-cut. Children well versed in gender-related expectations are not always highly gender typed in everyday life (Downs & Langlois, 1988; Serbin, Powlishta, & Gulko, 1993; Weinraub et al., 1984).

Why might this be so? First, some gender-role preferences, such as the desire to play with "gender-appropriate" toys and same-sex playmates, are acquired before children know much about stereotypes. Second, we have already seen that children master the components of gender-stereotyped knowledge in diverse ways, each of which may have different implications for their behavior. Finally, by middle childhood, virtually all children know a great deal about gender stereotypes—knowledge so universal that it cannot predict variation in gender-role adoption.

According to Aletha Huston (1983), gender-typed knowledge and behavior may develop along different lines during the preschool years, perhaps coming together in middle childhood. In support of this idea, stereotype flexibility (rather than knowledge) is a good predictor of gender-role adoption during the school years. Children who believe that many stereotyped expectations are appropriate for both sexes are more likely to cross gender lines in the activities, playmates, and occupational roles they choose for themselves (Serbin, Powlishta, & Gulko, 1993; Signorella, Bigler, & Liben, 1993).

The impact of stereotypes on behavior is likely to become more powerful as children incorporate these ideas into their gender-role identities—self-perceptions about what they can and should do at play, in school, and as future participants in society. But the development of gender-role identity is a topic we treat later in this chapter. For now, let's turn to various influences that promote children's gender-typed beliefs and behavior.

BRIEF REVIEW

During the preschool years, children acquire a wide variety of gender stereotypes about activities, behaviors, and occupations. Stereotypes involving personality traits and achievement areas are added in middle childhood. At the same time, a more flexible view of what males and females can do emerges. Children master the components of gender stereotyping in diverse ways, and the flexibility of their beliefs varies considerably. Group differences in stereotyping also exist. In most studies, boys' judgments are more stereotyped than those of girls, and black children hold less stereotyped views of females than do white children. Social-class differences in stereotyping do not emerge until adolescence. School-age children with a flexible appreciation of gender stereotypes are less gender typed in their preferences and behavior.

Influences on Gender Stereotyping and Gender-Role Adoption

According to social learning theorists, direct teaching is the way gender-stereotyped knowledge and behaviors are transmitted to children. We will see shortly that much research is consistent with this view. Nevertheless, some people argue that biological makeup leads each sex to be uniquely suited to fill particular roles and that most societies do little more than encourage gender differences that are genetically based. Is there evidence to support this idea?

THE CASE FOR BIOLOGY

Although practically no modern theorist would claim that "biology is destiny," serious questions about biological influences on gender typing remain. Two sources of evidence have been used to support the role of biology: (1) cross-cultural similarities in gender stereotypes and gender-role adoption, and (2) the influence of hormones on gender-role behavior. Let's examine each in turn.

Great diversity exists in the extent to which societies promote instrumental traits in males and expressive traits in females. Since this Kenyan boy spends much of his day caring for younger siblings, he often displays help-giving and emotional support. Consequently, he is likely to be less gender stereotyped in personality traits than most boys in other cultures. (Paul Conklin/ Monkmeyer Press)

HOW MUCH CROSS-CULTURAL SIMILARITY EXISTS IN GENDER TYPING? Earlier in this chapter, we noted that the instrumental–expressive dichotomy is reflected in the gender stereotyping of many national groups. Although this finding fits with the idea that social influences simply build on genetic differences between the sexes, we must be cautious in drawing this conclusion.

A close look at cross-cultural findings reveals that most societies promote instrumental traits in males and expressive traits in females, but great diversity exists in the magnitude of this difference (Hendrix & Johnson, 1985; Whiting & Edwards, 1988b). Consider Nyansongo, a small agricultural settlement in Kenya. Nyansongo mothers, who work 4 to 5 hours a day in the gardens, assign the care of young children, the tending of the cooking fire, and the washing of dishes to older siblings. Since children of both sexes perform these duties, girls are relieved of total responsibility for "feminine" tasks and have more time to interact with agemates. Their greater freedom and independence leads them to score higher than girls of other tribal and village cultures in dominance, assertiveness, and playful roughhousing. In contrast, boys' caregiving responsibilities mean that they often display help-giving and emotional support (Whiting & Edwards, 1988a). Among industrialized nations, Sweden is widely recognized as a society in which traditional gender beliefs and behaviors are considerably reduced (see the Cultural Influences box on the following page).

Furthermore, cultural reversals of traditional gender typing exist. Anthropologist Margaret Mead (1935/1963) conducted a classic study of three tribal societies in New Guinea. Among the Arapesh, both men and women were cooperative and nurturant. Among the Mundugamor, both sexes were ruthless and aggressive. And among the Tchambuli, women were dominant and assertive whereas men were passive and dependent.

These examples indicate that experience can have a profound impact on gender typing. Nevertheless, it can still be argued that deviations from traditional gender roles are more the exception than the rule. Biological pressures may still be operating, appearing in behavior as long as cultural pressures against them are not extreme. Because cross-cultural findings are inconclusive, scientists have turned to a more direct test of the importance of biology: research on the impact of sex hormones on gender-role adoption.

SEX HORMONES AND GENDER-ROLE ADOPTION. In Chapters 3 and 5, we discussed how genetic makeup, mediated by hormones, regulates sexual development and body growth in males and females. Sex hormones also affect brain development and neural activity in many animal species, and they do so in humans as well (Hines & Green, 1991). Are hormones, which so pervasively affect body structures, also important in gender-role adoption?

CULTURAL INFLUENCES

Sweden's Commitment to Gender Equality

Of all nations in the world, Sweden is unique in its valuing of gender equality and its social programs that translate this commitment into action. Over a century ago, Sweden's ruling political party adopted equality as a central goal. One social class was not to exploit another, nor one gender another. In the 1960s, Sweden's expanding economy required that women enter the labor force in large numbers. When the question arose as to who would help sustain family life, the Swedish people called on the principle of equality and answered: fathers, just like mothers.

The Swedish "equal-roles family model" maintains that husband and wife should have the same opportunity to pursue a career and be equally responsible for housework and child care. To support this goal, day care centers had to be made available outside the home. Otherwise, a class of less privileged women might be exploited for caregiving and domestic work—an outcome that would contradict the principle of equality. And since full-time employment for both parents often strains a family with young children, Sweden mandated that mothers and fathers with children under age 8 could reduce the length of their working day to 6 hours, with a corresponding reduction in pay but not in benefits (Sandqvist, 1992).

According to several indicators, Sweden's family model is very successful. Maternal employment is extremely high; over 80 percent of mothers with infants and preschoolers work outside the home. Day care centers are numerous, of high quality, and heavily subsidized by the government. And although Swedish fathers do not yet share housework and child care equally with mothers, they are more involved than fathers in North America and other Western European nations. In one international study of 40 countries, Swedish men rated themselves lowest in "masculine" traits. On most, they fell at about the same level as Swedish women, and on some, below them (Hofstede, 1980). These findings provide further evidence that gender roles in Sweden are less differentiated than elsewhere.

Has Sweden's progressive family policy affected the gender beliefs and behaviors of its youths? A study of Swedish and American adolescents found that the "masculine" role was more highly valued than the "feminine" role in both countries. However, this difference was less pronounced in Sweden, where young people regarded each gender as a blend of instrumental and expressive traits. And although Swedish adolescents more often aspired to stereotyped occupations than did their American counterparts, Swedish girls felt considerably better about their gender—a difference that might be due to greater equalization in men's and women's pay scales and a widespread attitude in Sweden that "feminine" work is important to society. Finally, compared to American adolescents, Swedish young people more often viewed gender roles as a matter of learned tasks and domains of expertise rather than inborn personality traits or sets of rights and duties (Intons-Peterson, 1988).

Traditional gender typing is not eradicated in Sweden. But great progress has been made as a result of steadfastly pursuing a program of gender equality for several decades.

Play Styles and Preference for Same-Sex Peers. Experiments with animals reveal that exposure to sex hormones during certain sensitive periods does affect behavior. For example, prenatally administered androgens (male sex hormones) increase active play in both male and female mammals. Androgens also promote male-typical sexual behavior and aggression and suppress maternal caregiving in a wide variety of species (Beatty, 1992).

Eleanor Maccoby (1988, 1990a) argues that at least some of these hormonal effects extend to humans. In the introduction to this chapter, we noted that as early as the preschool years, children seek out playmates of their own sex—a preference observed in a wide variety of cultures and many mammalian species (Beatty, 1992; Whiting & Edwards, 1988a). At age 4, children already spend three times as much time with same-sex than other-sex playmates. By age 6, this ratio has climbed to 11 to 1 (Maccoby & Jacklin, 1987). Throughout the school years, children continue to show a strong preference for same-sex peers, a trend that declines in adolescence when puberty triggers an interest in the other sex (Hayden-Thomson, Rubin, & Hymel, 1987; Serbin, Powlishta, & Gulko, 1993).

Why is sex segregation so widespread and persistent? According to Maccoby, early on, hormones affect play styles, leading to rough, noisy movements among boys and calm, gentle actions among girls. Then, as children begin to interact with peers, they choose partners whose interests and behaviors are compatible with their own. By age 2, girls already appear overwhelmed by boys' rambunctious behavior. When paired with a boy in a laboratory play session, the girl stands idly by while he explores the toys (Jacklin & Maccoby, 1978). Nonhuman primates react similarly. When a male juvenile initiates rough, physical play, male peers join in, whereas females withdraw (Beatty, 1992).

■ *Beginning in the preschool years, children seek out playmates of their own sex. Sex hormones are believed to influence children's play styles, leading to calm, gentle actions in girls and rough, noisy movements in boys. Then preschoolers naturally choose same-sex partners who share their interests and behavior. Social pressures for "gender-appropriate" play and the tendency to evaluate members of one's own sex more positively are also believed to promote gender segregation. (Left, Merritt Vincent/PhotoEdit; right, Michael Newman/PhotoEdit)*

Play-style preferences remain especially powerful in boys' choice of playmates into the elementary school years. When asked whether they would prefer playing with a girl who likes rough, active games or a boy who likes calm, quiet games, preschool and school-age boys choose on the basis of play style rather than gender. Girls' responses are less consistent (Alexander & Hines, 1994). Social pressures for "gender-appropriate" play and cognitive factors—in particular, gender stereotyping and the tendency to evaluate members of one's own sex more positively—are also believed to contribute to gender segregation. But sex hormones are involved—a conclusion that receives further support from studies of exceptional sexual development in humans.

Exceptional Sexual Development. For ethical reasons, we cannot experimentally manipulate hormones in humans to see how they affect behavior. But cases do exist in which hormone levels varied naturally or were modified for medical reasons.

John Money, Anke Ehrhardt, and their collaborators conducted research on children with *congenital adrenal hyperplasia (CAH),* a disorder in which a genetic defect causes the adrenal system to produce unusually high levels of androgens from the prenatal period onward. Although the physical development of boys remains unaffected, CAH girls are usually born with masculinized external genitals. Most undergo surgical correction in infancy or childhood; a few experience it in later life. Continuous drug therapy is used to correct the hormone imbalance (Ehrhardt & Baker, 1974; Money & Ehrhardt, 1972).

Interviewing CAH children and their family members, the researchers found that girls displayed "masculine" gender-role behavior. They liked cars, trucks, and blocks better than dolls; preferred boys as playmates; were uninterested in fantasizing about traditional feminine roles (such as bride and mother); and were less concerned with matters of physical appearance (clothing, jewelry, and hairstyle) than non-CAH girls. Also, both boys and girls with CAH showed higher activity levels, as indicated by greater participation in active sports and outdoor games. Similar outcomes in more recent studies lend additional weight to Money and Ehrhardt's conclusion that prenatal androgen exposure supports "masculine" gender-role behavior (Berenbaum & Snyder, 1995; Hines & Kaufman, 1994).

Critics, however, point out that subtle environmental pressures may have contributed to the findings just described. For example, genital abnormalities, in some cases not corrected until well beyond infancy, may have caused family members to perceive affected girls as boyish and unfeminine and to treat them accordingly (Quadagno, Briscoe, & Quadagno, 1977). And in the course of their medical treatment, girls with CAH were probably told that as adults they might have difficulty conceiving a child. Perhaps they showed little interest in marriage and motherhood because they were unsure of these possibilities in their own lives.

Furthermore, research on individuals reared as members of the other sex because they had ambiguous genitals indicates that in most cases, gender typing is consistent with sex of rearing, regardless of genetic sex (Money, 1985). In instances in which these individuals do decide to switch gender roles, they usually move from "feminine" to "masculine"—to the gender associated with more highly valued characteristics. Consider some striking findings on genetic males born with female-looking genitals because of a prenatal androgen deficiency. In four villages in the Dominican Republic, where this defect is common, all but one of those reared as a girl changed to a masculine gender role in adolescence and young adulthood (Imperato-McGinley et al., 1979). Although the researchers inferred that "androgens make a strong and definite contribution to gender typing" (p. 1236), additional research questions this conclusion. Among the Sambia of Papua New Guinea, sexually ambiguous males reared as females switched gender roles only in response to social pressures—when it became clear that they could not fulfill their cultural destiny of bearing children (Herdt & Davidson, 1988).

Studies of individuals whose mothers took synthetic androgens to prevent miscarriage but whose genitals were unaffected yield mixed results. Some report a rise in "masculine" attributes, including play interests, independence, self-confidence, and aggressive solutions to social problems (Ehrhardt, 1975; Reinisch, 1981). But others show no clear effects (Hines, 1982).

Taken together, research on the impact of sex hormones suggests that they affect some aspects of gender typing. The most uniform findings involve activity level and preference for "gender-appropriate" play and toys (Collaer & Hines, 1995). Since other behavioral outcomes are neither large nor consistent, biological makeup probably plays little role. Finally, it is important to keep in mind that even biological factors can be modified by experience. For example, in animal research, social dominance and environmental stress increase androgen production (Macrides, Bartke, & Dalterio, 1975; Rose, Holaday, & Bernstein, 1976).

THE CASE FOR ENVIRONMENT

A wealth of evidence reveals that environmental factors provide powerful support for gender-role development. As we will see in the following sections, adults view boys and girls differently, and they treat them differently. In addition, children's social contexts—home, school, and community—offer many opportunities to observe people behaving in ways consistent with gender stereotypes. And as soon as children enter the world of the peer group, their agemates encourage conformity to gender roles.

■ **PERCEPTIONS AND EXPECTATIONS OF ADULTS.** When adults are asked to observe neutrally dressed infants who are labeled as either boy or girl, they "see" qualities that fit with the baby's artificially assigned sex. In research of this kind, adults tend to rate infants' physical features and (to a lesser extent) their personality traits in a gender-stereotyped fashion (Stern & Karraker, 1989; Vogel et al., 1991). Among new parents, these gender-biased perceptions seem to be even stronger. In one study, mothers and fathers were interviewed 24 hours after the birth of their first child. Although male and female newborns did not differ in length, weight, or Apgar scores, parents perceived them differently. They rated sons as firmer, larger featured, better coordinated, more alert, stronger, and hardier and daughters as softer, finer featured, more delicate, more awkward, and more inattentive (Rubin, Provenzano, & Luria, 1974).

During childhood and adolescence, parents continue to hold different perceptions and expectations of their sons and daughters. They persist in interpreting children's behavior in stereotyped ways, want their preschoolers to play with "gender-appropriate" toys, and say that boys and girls should be reared differently. For example, when asked about their child-rearing values, parents tend to emphasize achievement, competitiveness, and control of emotion as important for boys. In contrast, they regard warmth, "ladylike" behavior, and close supervision of activities as important for girls. These differences have changed very little over the past several decades (Block, 1983; Brooks-Gunn, 1986; Turner & Gervai, 1995).

■ **TREATMENT BY PARENTS.** Do adults actually treat children in accord with their stereotypical beliefs? A combined analysis of 172 studies reported that on the whole, differences in the way parents socialize boys and girls are not large (Lytton & Romney, 1991). However, this does not mean that parental treatment is unimportant. It simply says that if we sum across age periods and behaviors, we find only a few clear trends.

When the evidence is examined closely, consistent age effects emerge. Younger children receive more direct training in gender roles than do older children—a finding that is not surprising, since gender typing takes place especially rapidly during early childhood (Fagot & Hagan, 1991). And wide variation from study to study suggests that some parents practice differential treatment much more intensely than do others.

Infancy and Early Childhood. In infancy and early childhood, parents encourage a diverse array of "gender-appropriate" play activities and behaviors. As early as the first few months of life—before children can express their own preferences—parents begin to create different environments for boys and girls. Bedrooms are decorated with distinct colors and themes. Guns, cars, tools, and footballs are purchased for boys; dolls, tea sets, jewelry, and jump ropes for girls. A child who makes a special request for a birthday or Christmas present is far more likely to receive it if it is a "gender-consistent" toy (Etaugh & Liss, 1992; Pomerleau et al., 1990; Robinson & Morris, 1986).

Parents also actively reinforce gender-role conformity in young children. For example, they react more positively when a young son as opposed to a daughter plays with cars and trucks, demands attention, runs and climbs, or tries to take toys from others. In contrast, they more often direct play activities, provide help, discuss emotions, and encourage assistance with household tasks when interacting with a daughter (Fagot, 1978; Fagot & Hagan, 1991; Kuebli & Fivush, 1992). Early in development, then, parents provide experiences that encourage assertiveness, exploration, and engagement with the physical world in boys and imitation, dependency, and social orientation in girls.

Middle Childhood. During middle childhood, issues of achievement become more salient to parents as children's skills expand. Observations of mothers and fathers interacting with their school-age children in teaching situations reveal that they demand greater independence from boys than girls. For example, when a child requests help, parents more often ignore or refuse to respond to a son, whereas they offer help right away to a daughter (Rothbart & Rothbart, 1976). And the way parents provide help to each sex differs. They behave in a more mastery-oriented fashion with sons, setting higher standards and pointing out important features of the task. In contrast, they frequently stray from task goals to joke and play with daughters (Block, Block, & Harrington, 1975). Furthermore, during a conversation, parents are likely to interrupt daughters but permit sons to finish their statements, subtly delivering the message that what a boy has to say is more important (Greif, 1979).

Parents also hold gender-differentiated perceptions of and expectations for children's competencies in various school subjects. In longitudinal research on over 2,100 families with school-age children, Jacqueline Eccles, Janet Jacobs, and Rena Harold (1990) found that parents rated daughters as more competent in English than sons; the reverse was true for mathematics and sports. These beliefs were stronger than actual skill differences among the children. In fact, boys and girls in this sample performed equally well in the two academic areas, based on grades and achievement test scores. What else besides overt performance influenced parents' judgments? The researchers discovered that parents' stereotypes about the abilities of males and females played a significant role. The more parents endorsed the idea of gender-specific abilities, the more likely they were to believe that their child was naturally talented in a gender-typical field and would find "other-gender" pursuits to be difficult. These judgments, in turn, influenced children's self-perceptions of ability, the effort they devoted to mastering particular skills, and their later performance (Eccles et al., 1989; Jacobs, 1991). The researchers speculated that this chain of events is likely to affect the occupations that males and females seek out and qualify for. As the Social Issues box on the following page reveals, gender inequality continues to exist in many vocational domains.

Differential treatment by parents extends to the freedom granted children in their everyday lives. During middle childhood, boys are allowed to range farther from home without adult supervision. Assignment of chores reflects this same trend. In many cultures, girls are given tasks, such as food preparation, cleaning, and baby-sitting, that keep them close to home, whereas boys are given responsibilities that take them into the surrounding world, such as yard work and errands (Whiting & Edwards, 1988a). As we noted earlier, when cultural circumstances require children to perform "cross-gender" chores (as is the case in Nyansongo), the range of behaviors practiced expands.

SOCIAL ISSUES

Sex-Related Differences in Vocational Development

Over the past two decades, high school boys' vocational preferences have remained strongly gender stereotyped, whereas girls have expressed increasing interest in occupations traditionally held by men (Sandberg et al., 1991). Nevertheless, women's progress in entering and excelling at male-dominated professions has been slow. As Table 13.2 shows, the percentage of women in engineering, law, medicine, and business executive and managerial positions increased between 1972 and 1994 in the United States. Yet their presence falls far short of men's. Women remain heavily concentrated in the less well paid, traditionally feminine professions of literature, social work, education, and nursing (U.S. Bureau of the Census, 1995). In virtually all fields, their achievements lag behind those of men, who write more books, make more discoveries, hold more positions of leadership, and produce more works of art (Reis, 1991).

As we will see in the final section of this chapter, ability cannot account for these dramatic differences. Instead, gender-stereotyped messages from the social environment play a key role. Although girls' grades are higher than those of boys, they reach adolescence less confident of their abilities and more likely to underestimate their achievement (Bornholt, Goodnow, & Cooney, 1994). During the last two years of high school, the proportion of girls in gifted programs declines (Reis, 1991). When high school students were asked what discouraged them from continuing in gifted programs, parental and peer pressures and attitudes of teachers and counselors ranked high on girls' lists (Read, 1991). Some parents still regard vocational accomplishment as unnecessary for girls and as risking their chances for marriage and motherhood. At times, counselors advise girls not to enroll in advanced math and science courses for similar reasons. And high school teachers tend to view bright male students as more capable than their female counterparts (Blaubergs, 1980; Grau, 1985). Once communicated, these beliefs can be reinforced by peers.

During college, the career aspirations of academically talented females decline further. In one longitudinal study, high school valedictorians were followed over a 10-year period—through college and into the work world. By their sophomore year, young women showed a decline in estimates of their intelligence, whereas young men did not. Women also shifted their expectations toward less demanding careers because of concerns about combining work with motherhood and unresolved questions about their ability. Even though female valedictorians outperformed their male counterparts in college courses, they achieved at lower levels after career entry (Arnold, 1994). Another longitudinal study reported similar outcomes. Educational aspirations of mathematically talented females declined considerably during college, as did the number majoring in the sciences (Benbow & Arjimand, 1990).

These findings reveal a pressing need for programs that sensitize parents, teachers, and school counselors to the special problems girls face in developing and maintaining high career aspirations. Research shows that academically talented girls' aspirations rise in response to career guidance that encourages them to set high goals—ones that match their abilities, interests, and values (Kerr, 1983). Those who continue to achieve have three experiences in common: a college environment that values and supports the accomplishments of women, frequent interaction with faculty and professionals in their chosen fields, and the opportunity to test their abilities in a nurturing environment (Arnold, 1994).

TABLE 13.2

Percentage of Females in Various Professions, 1972, 1983, 1994

Profession	1972	1983	1994
Engineering	0.8	5.8	8.3
Law	3.8	15.8	24.6
Medicine	9.3	15.8	22.3
Business—executive and managerial	17.6	32.4	43.0[a]
Writing, art, entertainment	31.7	42.7	47.8
Social work	55.1	64.3	69.3
Elementary and secondary education	70.0	70.9	74.9
Higher education	28.0	36.3	42.5
Library, museum curatorship	81.6	84.4	81.6
Nursing	92.6	95.8	93.8

Source: U.S. Bureau of the Census, 1995.

[a] This percentage includes executives and managers at all levels. Women make up only 5 to 10 percent of senior management at big firms, although that figure represents a three-fold increase in the past decade.

■ *This Lapp boy of Norway wanders far from home as he tends his family's sled reindeer. The freedom he is granted promotes independence and self-reliance. Because his sisters are given household tasks, they spend much more time under the watchful eye of adults. (Bryan and Cherry Alexander)*

Although these findings might be taken to suggest that girls in Western cultures be granted more freedom and boys assigned more gender-atypical tasks, the consequences of doing so are not so straightforward. For example, when fathers hold stereotypical views and their sons engage in "feminine" housework, boys experience strain in the father–child relationship, feel stressed by their responsibilities, and judge themselves to be less competent (McHale et al., 1990). In contrast, a match between parental values and nontraditional child-rearing practices leads to benefits for children. In one study, 6-year-olds growing up in countercultural families that were committed to gender equality were compared to agemates living in conventional homes or experiencing other countercultural alternatives (for example, communes emphasizing spiritual and pronature values but not gender equality). Children in gender-countercultural homes were less likely to classify objects and occupations in stereotypical ways, and girls more often aspired to nontraditional careers (Weisner & Wilson-Mitchell, 1990).

Mothers versus Fathers. In most aspects of differential treatment of boys and girls, fathers are the ones who discriminate the most. For example, in Chapter 10 we saw that fathers tend to engage in more physically stimulating play with their infant sons than daughters, whereas mothers tend to play in a quieter way with infants of both sexes. In childhood, fathers more than mothers encourage "gender-appropriate" behavior, and they place more pressure to achieve on sons than daughters (Gervai, Turner & Hinde, 1995; Lytton & Romney, 1991).

Parents also seem especially committed to ensuring the gender typing of children of their own sex. While mothers go on shopping trips and bake cookies with their daughters, fathers play catch, help coach the Saturday morning soccer game, and go fishing with their sons. This same-sex-child bias is another aspect of gender-role training that is more pronounced for fathers. When asked whether certain aspects of child rearing are the domain of one parent rather than the other, parents of boys indicated that fathers have a special responsibility to serve as a role model and play companion to their sons (Fagot, 1974).

■ TREATMENT BY TEACHERS. Research shows that in some ways, preschool and elementary school teachers reinforce pupils of both sexes for "feminine" rather than "masculine" behavior. In classrooms, obedience is usually valued and assertiveness is discouraged—by male and female teachers alike (Fagot, 1985a; Oettingen, 1985; Robinson & Canaday, 1978). This "feminine bias" is believed to promote discomfort for boys in school, but it may be equally or even more harmful for girls, who willingly conform with possible long-term negative consequences for their sense of independence and self-esteem.

Teachers also act in ways that maintain and even extend gender roles taught at home. In preschool, they contribute to "gender-appropriate" activity preferences by calling on

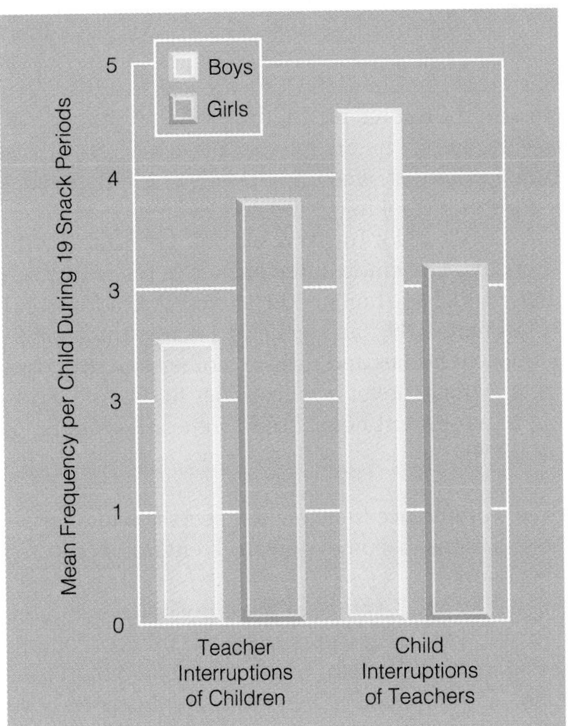

FIGURE 13.2

■ *Interruptions by teachers of children and by children of teachers at snack time in preschool. Children were observed in groups of two boys and two girls at a table with a female teacher. Teachers interrupted girls' conversations more often than boys'. Boys responded in kind; compared to girls, they more often interrupted teachers. (Adapted from Hendrick & Stange, 1991.)*

boys rather than girls to demonstrate how to use a new masculine-stereotyped item (Serbin, Connor, & Iler, 1979). At the same time, they follow parents' lead in interrupting girls more often than boys during conversation, thereby promoting boys' social dominance and girls' passivity. By age 4, children react in kind (see Figure 13.2). Boys interrupt their female teachers more often than girls do (Hendrick & Stange, 1991).

At older ages, teachers react to children's achievement and social behaviors in terms of gender stereotypes. They praise boys for their knowledge, girls for their obedience. And although they discourage aggression and other forms of misbehavior in all children, they do so more frequently and forcefully in boys. Teachers' greater scolding of boys seems to result from an expectation that boys will misbehave more often than girls—a belief based partly on boys' actual behavior and partly on gender stereotypes. When teachers reprimand girls, it is usually for giving a wrong answer (Good & Brophy, 1994).

Just as teachers can promote gender typing, they can do the opposite by modifying the way they communicate with children. For example, when teachers introduce new materials in a non-gender-biased fashion, praise all pupils for independence and persistence, and ignore attention seeking and dependency, children's activity choices and behavior change accordingly (Serbin, Connor, & Citron, 1978; Serbin, Connor, & Iler, 1979). However, girls are more responsive to these interventions than boys are. And most of the time, changes in children's behavior are short lived. As soon as the usual interaction patterns resume in the classroom, children return to their prior ways of responding. Like nontraditional families, schools that are successful in modifying gender typing have clearly articulated philosophies about gender equality that pervade all aspects of classroom life (Berk & Lewis, 1977; Bianchi & Bakeman, 1978).

■ OBSERVATIONAL LEARNING. In addition to direct pressures from adults, numerous gender-typed models are available in children's environments. Although American society has changed to some degree, children come in contact with many real people who conform to traditional gender-role expectations. Reflections of gender in the media are also stereotyped. As we will see in Chapter 15, the way males and females are represented in television programs has changed very little in recent years (Signorielli, 1990). Also, analyses of the content of children's storybooks and textbooks reveal that they continue to portray males and females stereotypically. Boys and men outnumber girls and women as main characters, and males take center stage in most of the exciting and adventurous plot activities. Females, when they do appear as important characters, are often engaged in housekeeping and caring for children. The availability of gender-equitable reading materials for children is increasing, but school texts at the high school level have been especially slow to change (Noddings, 1992).

When children are exposed to nonstereotyped models, they are less traditional in their beliefs and behaviors. As we will see in Chapter 14, children who often see their parents cross traditional gender lines—mothers who are employed or who engage in "masculine" household tasks (repairing appliances, washing the car) and fathers who engage in "feminine" household tasks (ironing, cooking, child care)—are less aware of gender stereotypes (Serbin, Powlishta, & Gulko, 1993; Turner & Gervai, 1995). Girls with career-oriented mothers show special benefits. They more often engage in typically masculine activities (such as physically active play), have higher educational aspirations, and hold nontraditional vocational goals (Hoffman, 1989; Tauber, 1979). Finally, among children of divorced parents, boys in father-absent homes and girls in mother-absent homes are less gender typed, perhaps because they have fewer opportunities to observe traditional gender roles than they would in a two-parent household (Brenes, Eisenberg, & Helmstadter, 1985; Santrock & Warshak, 1979).

■ PEERS. Earlier we noted that children's preference for same-sex peers is widespread. Once formed, sex-segregated peer associations become powerful environments for strengthening traditional beliefs and behaviors.

Observations of preschoolers reveal that by age 3, same-sex peers positively reinforce one another for "gender-appropriate" play by praising, approving, imitating, or joining in the activity of an agemate (Fagot & Patterson, 1969; Langlois & Downs, 1980). In contrast, when preschoolers display "gender-inappropriate" play—for example, when boys play with dolls, or girls with woodworking tools—they are criticized and rebuffed. Peer rejection is greater for boys who frequently engage in "cross-gender" behavior. Their male peers ignore them even when they do enter "masculine" activities (Fagot, 1977).

Boys and girls also develop different styles of social influence in gender-segregated peer groups. To get their way with male peers, boys more often rely on commands, threats, and physical force. In contrast, girls learn to emphasize polite requests and persuasion. These tactics succeed with other girls but not with boys, who start to ignore girls' gentle tactics by school entry (Borja-Alvarez, Zarbatany, & Pepper, 1991; Charlesworth & Dzur, 1987; Leaper, 1991). Consequently, an additional reason that girls may stop interacting with boys is that they do not find it very rewarding to communicate with an unresponsive social partner (Maccoby, 1988, 1990a).

Although children prefer same-sex playmates, mixed-sex interaction does occur, and adults can promote it. When teachers comment approvingly, interaction between boys and girls is sustained on a short-term basis (Serbin, Tonick, & Sternglanz, 1977). Also, changing the design of the preschool classroom by joining gender-typed activity areas (such as blocks and housekeeping) increases mixed-sex play (Kinsman & Berk, 1979). Interaction between boys and girls is encouraged on a long-term basis in classrooms where teaching nonstereotyped values is an important part of the school curriculum (Lockheed, 1986).

Some researchers believe that fostering mixed-sex interaction is a vital means for reducing gender stereotyping and broadening developmental possibilities for both boys and girls (Lloyd & Smith, 1985). However, to be successful, interventions may also need to modify the styles of social influence acquired by children in their same-sex peer relations. Otherwise, boys are likely to dominate and girls to react passively, thereby strengthening traditional gender roles and the stereotypes each sex holds of the other (Lockheed & Harris, 1984).

■ SIBLINGS. Growing up with siblings of the same or other sex also affects gender typing. But compared to peer influences, sibling effects are more complex because their impact depends on birth order and family size (Wagner, Schubert, & Schubert, 1993).

If sibling effects operated just like peer influences, we would expect a family of same-sex siblings to promote traditional gender roles and a family of mixed-sex siblings to do just the opposite. In an observational study of the play behaviors of 4- to 9-year-olds in their homes, the activities of same-sex siblings were highly "gender appropriate." But among mixed-sex siblings, play choices were determined by the sex of the older child. In fact, this effect was so strong that boys with older sisters actually played "house" and "dolls" as much as pairs of sisters did. In contrast, boys with older brothers never engaged in these "feminine" pursuits (Stoneman, Brody, & MacKinnon, 1986).

■ *When siblings are the same sex, they are more likely to be assigned "cross-gender" chores. This father encourages his daughters to help with yard work—a responsibility typically reserved for boys. (MacDonald Photos/Envision)*

But curiously, other research contradicts these findings. For example, when 8- and 9-year-olds were videotaped playing with toys in a laboratory, preference for "other-gender" toys was more common among children whose siblings were all of their own sex (Tauber, 1979). And several studies report that individuals with same-sex siblings are less stereotyped in their interests and personality characteristics than are those from mixed-sex families (Grotevant, 1978; Leventhal, 1970).

How can these conflicting results be explained? Recall from Chapter 10 that an important nonshared family environmental influence on personality development is that siblings often strive to be different from one another. This effect is strongest when children are of the same sex and come from large families. A close look at the research just described reveals that studies reporting a modeling and reinforcement effect (an increase in gender typing among same-sex siblings) were limited to children from small, two-child families. In contrast, those reporting a differentiation effect included children from large families. In homes with many children, a younger child may not emulate an older sibling out of a need to stand out as unique.

In addition, parents may sometimes relax pressures toward gender typing when their children are all of the same sex. Consistent with this idea, mothers are more willing to give their child a gender-atypical toy as a gift if a child has an older, same-sex sibling (Stoneman, Brody, & MacKinnon, 1986). Also, in all-girl and all-boy families, children are more likely to be assigned "cross-gender" chores because no "gender-appropriate" child is available to do the job. Therefore, families in which siblings are all of the same sex may provide some special opportunities to step out of traditional gender roles.

BRIEF REVIEW

Cross-cultural similarities in gender typing are not consistent enough to support a strong role for biology. Prenatally administered androgens promote a variety of "masculine" behaviors in animal species. Studies of children with congenital adrenal hyperplasia (CAH) suggest similar effects in humans for activity level and preference for "masculine" play and toys.

At the same time, powerful environmental influences on gender typing exist. Beginning in infancy, adults view boys and girls differently, and they treat them differently. Parents—especially fathers—actively promote "gender-appropriate" play activities and behavior in young children. During middle childhood, they demand greater independence from boys in achievement situations, hold gender-stereotyped beliefs about children's abilities in school subjects, and grant boys more freedom in their everyday lives. Adoption of traditional gender roles receives further support from teachers, same-sex peers, and models in the surrounding environment. Sibling effects on gender typing are jointly influenced by sex of siblings, birth order, and family size.

Gender-Role Identity

Besides biological and environmental influences, another factor eventually comes to influence gender typing: *gender-role identity,* a person's perception of the self as relatively masculine or feminine in characteristics. By middle childhood, researchers can measure gender-role identity by asking children to rate themselves on personality traits, since at that time, self-concepts begin to emphasize psychological attributes over concrete behaviors (see Chapter 11). Table 13.3 shows some sample items from a gender-role identity questionnaire designed for school-age children, who are asked to evaluate each statement on a four-point scale, from "very true of me" to "not at all true of me" (Boldizar, 1991). Similar methods for assessing gender-role identity are used with adults (Bem, 1974; Spence, Helmreich, & Stapp, 1975).

Individuals differ considerably in the way they respond to these questionnaires. A child or adult with a "masculine" identity scores high on traditionally masculine items (such as ambitious, competitive, and self-sufficient) and low on traditionally feminine ones (such as affectionate, cheerful, and soft-spoken). Someone with a "feminine" identity does just the reverse. Although the majority of individuals view themselves in gender-typed terms, a substantial minority (especially females) have a type of gender-role identity called **androgyny**. They score high on both masculine and feminine personality characteristics (Bem, 1974; Boldizar, 1991).

Research indicates that gender-role identity is a good predictor of psychological adjustment. Masculine and androgynous children and adults have a higher sense of self-esteem, whereas feminine individuals often think poorly of themselves (Alpert-Gillis & Connell, 1989; Boldizar, 1991). In line with their flexible self-definitions, androgynous individuals are more adaptable in behavior—for example, able to show masculine independence or feminine sensitivity, depending on the situation (Taylor & Hall, 1982). And they show greater maturity of moral judgment than individuals with other gender-role orientations (Bem, 1977; Block, 1973).

However, a close look at these findings reveals that the masculine component of androgyny is largely responsible for the superior psychological health of androgynous women over those with traditional identities (Taylor & Hall, 1982; Whitley, 1983). Feminine women seem to have adjustment difficulties because many of their traits are not highly valued by society. Nevertheless, the existence of an androgynous identity demonstrates that masculinity and femininity are not opposites, as many people believe. It is possible for children to acquire a mixture of positive qualities traditionally associated

TABLE 13.3

Sample Items from a Gender-Role Identity Questionnaire for School-Age Children

Personality Trait	Item
Masculine	
Ambitious	I'm willing to work hard to get what I want.
Assertive	It's easy for me to tell people what I think, even when I know they will probably disagree with me.
Competitive	When I play games, I really like to win.
Self-sufficient	I can take care of myself.
Feminine	
Affectionate	When I like someone, I do nice things for them to show them how I feel.
Cheerful	I am a cheerful person.
Soft-spoken	I usually speak softly.
Yielding	When there's a disagreement, I usually give in and let others have their way.

Source: J. P. Boldizar, 1991, "Assessing Sex Typing and Androgyny in Children: The Children's Sex Role Inventory," *Developmental Psychology, 27,* p. 509. Copyright © 1991 by the American Psychological Association. Reprinted by permission.

Androgyny
A type of gender-role identity in which the person scores high on both masculine and feminine personality characteristics.

with each gender—an orientation that may best help them realize their potential. And in a future society in which feminine characteristics are socially rewarded to the same extent as masculine ones, androgyny may very well represent the ideal personality.

EMERGENCE OF GENDER-ROLE IDENTITY

How do children develop gender-role identities that consist of varying mixtures of masculine and feminine characteristics? Both social learning and cognitive-developmental answers exist.

According to social learning theory, *behavior comes before self-perceptions.* Preschoolers first acquire gender-typed responses through modeling and reinforcement. Only later do they organize these behaviors into society's gender-role expectations, which they accept as appropriate for themselves. In contrast, cognitive-developmental theory emphasizes that *self-perceptions come before behavior.* Over the preschool years, children first acquire a cognitive appreciation of the permanence of their sex. They develop **gender constancy**, the understanding that sex remains the same even if clothing, hairstyle, and play activities change. Once formed, children use this idea to guide their actions, and a preference for gender-typed activities appears.

Social learning and cognitive-developmental theories lead to strikingly different predictions about gender-role development. But before we look at what research has to say about the accuracy of each, let's trace the development of gender constancy during the preschool years.

■ DEVELOPMENT OF GENDER CONSTANCY. Lawrence Kohlberg (1966) first proposed that before age 6 or 7, children cannot maintain the constancy of their gender, just as they cannot pass Piagetian conservation problems. Only gradually do they attain this understanding, by moving through three stages of development:

1. **Gender labeling.** During the early preschool years, children can label their own sex and that of others correctly. But when asked such questions as "When you (a girl) grow up, could you ever be a daddy?" or "Could you be a boy if you wanted to?" young children freely answer yes (Slaby & Frey, 1975). In addition, when shown a doll whose hairstyle and clothing are transformed before their eyes, children indicate that the doll's sex is no longer the same (McConaghy, 1979).

2. **Gender stability.** At this stage, children have a partial understanding of the permanence of sex. They grasp its stability over time. But even though they know that male and female babies will eventually become boys and girls and men and women, they continue to insist, as they did at younger ages, that changing hairstyle, clothing, or "gender-appropriate" activities will lead a person to switch sexes as well (Fagot, 1985b; Slaby & Frey, 1975).

3. **Gender consistency.** During the late preschool and early school years, children become certain of the situational consistency of their sex. They know that sex remains constant even if a person decides to dress in "cross-gender" clothes or engage in nontraditional activities (Emmerich, 1981; McConaghy, 1979).

Many studies confirm that gender constancy emerges in the sequence just described. In addition, mastery of gender constancy is associated with attainment of conservation, as Kohlberg assumed (De Lisi & Gallagher, 1991). Yet cognitive immaturity is not the only reason for preschoolers' poor performance on gender constancy tasks. It also results from limited social experience—in particular, lack of opportunity to learn about genital differences between the sexes. In many households in Western cultures, young children do not see members of the other sex naked. Therefore, they distinguish males and females using the only information they do have—the way each gender dresses and behaves. As Figure 13.3 on page 520 shows, children as young as 3 who are aware of genital characteristics usually answer gender-constancy questions correctly (Bem, 1989).

■ HOW WELL DOES GENDER CONSTANCY PREDICT GENDER-ROLE ADOPTION? Is cognitive-developmental theory correct that gender constancy is primarily responsible for children's gender-typed behavior? From findings discussed earlier in this chapter, perhaps you have already concluded that evidence for this assumption is weak. Long before

Gender constancy
The understanding that gender remains the same even if clothing, hairstyle, and play activities change.

Gender labeling
Kohlberg's first stage of gender understanding, in which preschoolers can label the gender of themselves and others correctly.

Gender stability
Kohlberg's second stage of gender understanding, in which preschoolers have a partial understanding of the permanence of gender; they grasp its stability over time.

Gender consistency
Kohlberg's final stage of gender understanding, in which children master gender constancy.

FIGURE 13.3

■ *Percentage of preschoolers with and without genital knowledge who achieved gender constancy in a study of 3- to 5-year-olds. (Adapted from Bem, 1989.)*

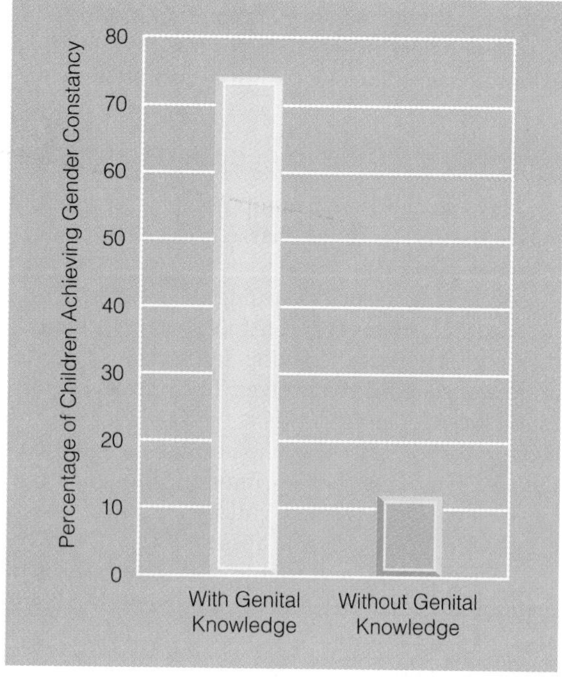

most preschoolers appreciate the permanence of their sex, they show a wide variety of gender-typed responses and are especially attentive to same-sex models (Bussey & Bandura, 1984). "Gender-appropriate" behavior appears so early in the preschool years that modeling and reinforcement must account for its initial appearance. In line with social learning theory, a recent cross-sectional study found that preschoolers first acquired "gender-consistent" play behavior and clear awareness of peer disapproval of "cross-gender" activities. Only later, around age 4, did they apply these social standards to themselves, anticipating feeling good for play with "gender-appropriate" toys and bad for play with "gender-inappropriate" toys. Once these self-evaluative reactions were established, children seemed to use them to guide their own actions. Gender-linked self-evaluations predicted preference for gender-typed play activities (Bussey & Bandura, 1992).

Although gender constancy does not initiate gender-role conformity, the cognitive changes that lead up to it do seem to facilitate gender typing. Preschoolers who reach the stage of gender labeling early show especially rapid development of "gender-appropriate" play preferences and are more knowledgeable about gender stereotypes than are their late-labeling peers (Fagot & Leinbach, 1989; Fagot, Leinbach, & O'Boyle, 1992). Similarly, understanding of gender stability is related to gender stereotyping, preference for same-sex playmates, and choice of "gender-consistent" toys (Martin & Little, 1990). These findings suggest that as soon as children acquire basic gender categories, they use them as the basis for acquiring gender-relevant information and modifying their own behavior.

If a complete understanding of gender constancy is not necessary for gender-role adoption, then just what is its function in development? Considerable debate surrounds this issue. Some researchers believe gender constancy strengthens children's gender typing. According to this view, when a new concept is formed, it should spark increased information seeking and attempts to behave in ways consistent with it (Lutz & Ruble, 1995). Other researchers think gender constancy may free children to experiment with "cross-gender" choices. From this perspective, children who have not attained gender constancy may engage in "gender-appropriate" behavior because they believe that doing so is what makes them a boy or girl. Once gender constancy is achieved, children understand that their sex remains the same regardless of their gender-role preferences. As a result, nontraditional behaviors become less threatening (Bem, 1989; Huston, 1983).

At present, research testing these hypotheses is conflicting. Some studies report that gender constancy leads to a rise in "gender-appropriate" activity choices (Frey & Ruble, 1992; Luecke-Aleksa et al., 1995; Stangor & Ruble, 1989). Others find that it predicts gender-stereotype flexibility (Ullian, 1976; Urberg, 1979). And yet a third set of findings indicates that gender constancy has no impact on preschoolers' already well-developed gender-role preferences (Bussey & Bandura, 1992; Lobel & Menashri, 1993; Martin &

Little, 1990). Whichever position is correct, the impact of gender constancy on gender typing is not great. As we will see in the following section, gender-role adoption is more powerfully affected by children's beliefs about how tight the connection needs to be between their own gender and behavior (Maccoby, 1990b).

GENDER-ROLE IDENTITY DURING MIDDLE CHILDHOOD AND ADOLESCENCE

During middle childhood, boys' and girls' gender-role identities follow different paths of development. Self-ratings on personality traits reveal that from third to sixth grade, boys strengthen their identification with the "masculine" role. In contrast, girls' identification with "feminine" characteristics declines. Although girls' overall orientation still leans toward the feminine side, they are clearly the more androgynous of the sexes (Boldizar, 1991; Serbin, Powlishta, & Gulko, 1993). In early adolescence, the gender-role identities of both sexes become more traditional. Then, by the mid- to late-adolescent years, a move back in the direction of androgyny occurs, a trend that is stronger for girls than boys (Huston & Alvarez, 1990).

Children's activity preferences and behaviors follow a similar pattern. Unlike boys, girls do not increase their preference for gender-typed activities in middle childhood. Instead, they experiment with a wider range of options. Besides cooking, sewing, and baby-sitting, they join organized sports teams, take up science projects, and build forts in the backyard. Then a temporary return to gender-stereotyped interests occurs in early adolescence that eventually declines, especially for girls (Leahy & Eiter, 1980; Stoddart & Turiel, 1985).

These changes are due to a mixture of social and cognitive forces. We have already seen that society attaches greater prestige to "masculine" characteristics. Girls undoubtedly become aware of this as they grow older. As a result, in middle childhood they start to identify with "masculine" traits and are attracted to some typically masculine activities. Messages from adults and agemates are also influential. A girl can act like a "tomboy" with little disapproval from parents and peers, but a boy who behaves like a "sissy" is likely to be ridiculed and rejected.

In early adolescence, puberty magnifies differences in appearance between boys and girls, causing teenagers to spend more time thinking about themselves in gender-linked ways. And when adolescents start to date, they often become more gender typed as a way of increasing their attractiveness to the other sex (Crockett, 1990). Finally, gains in perspective taking lead young teenagers to be very preoccupied with what others think, which adds to gender-role conformity. As young people move toward establishing a mature personal identity, they become less concerned with others' opinions of them and more involved in finding meaningful values to include in their self-definitions (see Chapter 11). As a result, highly stereotypic self-perceptions decline.

During middle childhood, girls feel freer than boys to engage in "cross-gender" activities. These girls participate in a team sport typically reserved for boys and men. (Tony Freeman/PhotoEdit)

■ INDIVIDUAL DIFFERENCES. Although gender-role identity follows the general path of development just described, individual differences exist at all ages, and they are moderately related to gender-role behavior. A more masculine and less feminine identity is associated with a higher sense of overall academic competence as well as better performance on spatial and mathematical tasks (Boldizar, 1991; Newcombe & Dubas, 1992; Signorella & Jamison, 1986). Although girls with feminine orientations are more popular with agemates, masculine-oriented children of both sexes are more assertive and less dependent (Hall & Halberstadt, 1980). At present, androgynous children are not especially advantaged in any of these areas. Instead, a gender-role identity that leans toward the masculine side seems to be the key factor in the majority of positive outcomes for children.

Since these relationships are correlational, we cannot really tell whether masculine and feminine self-perceptions *arise from particular behaviors* (as social learning theory assumes) or *serve as guides for behavior* (as cognitive-developmental theory predicts). According to recent theory and research, the answer is both, as we will see in the following section.

GENDER SCHEMA THEORY

Gender schema theory is an information-processing approach to gender typing that combines social learning and cognitive-developmental features. It also integrates the various elements of the gender-typing process—stereotyping, gender-role identity, and gender-role adoption—into a unified picture of how masculine and feminine orientations emerge and are often strongly maintained (Bem, 1981, 1983; Martin & Halverson, 1981, 1987).

According to gender schema theory, at an early age, children respond to instruction from others, picking up gender-typed preferences and behaviors. At the same time, they start to organize these experiences into gender schemas, or masculine and feminine categories, that they use to interpret their world. As soon as children can label their own sex, they start to select gender schemas that are consistent with it, applying those categories to themselves. As a result, self-perceptions become gender typed and serve as additional gender schemas that children use to process information and guide their own behavior.

Figure 13.4 shows how this network of gender schemas strengthens gender-typed preferences and behaviors. Let's take the example of a child who has been taught that "dolls are for girls" and "trucks are for boys" and who also knows that she is a girl. Our child uses this information to make decisions about how to behave. Because her schemas lead her to conclude that "dolls are for me," when given a doll she approaches it, explores it, and learns more about it. In contrast, on seeing a truck, she uses her gender

■ *Gender schemas can have powerful effects on children's attitudes, behaviors, and learning opportunities. These boys are clearly enjoying playing with this Rubik's Cube. Research shows that when preschoolers like a toy, they tend to assume that children of their own sex will like it more and those of the other sex will like it less. But if an adult were to tell these boys that the cube is a "girl's toy," their desire to play with it would probably diminish. (Alan Carey/The Image Works)*

Gender schema theory
An information-processing approach to gender typing that combines social learning and cognitive-developmental features to explain how environmental pressures and cognitions work together to affect stereotyping, gender-role identity, and gender-role adoption.

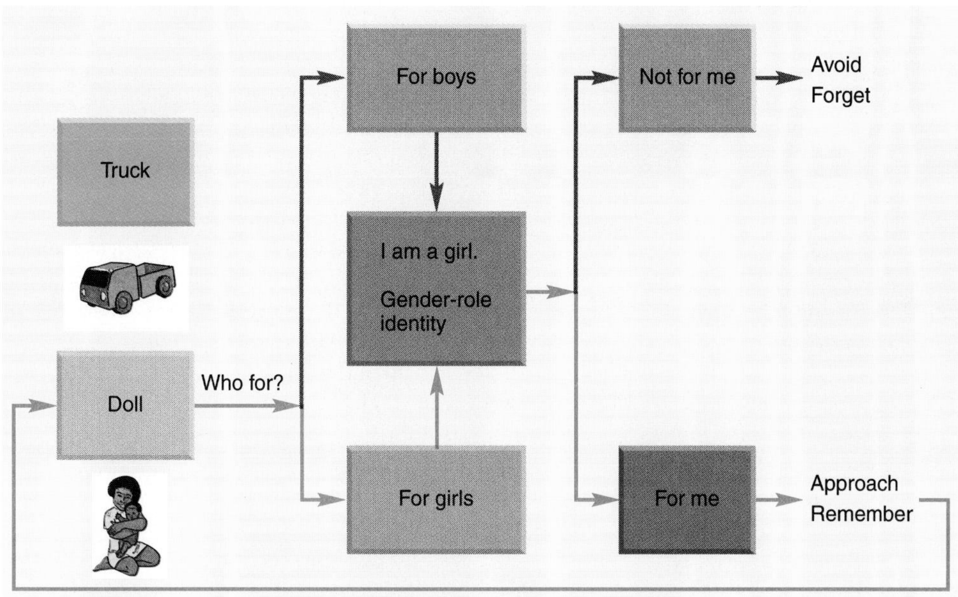

FIGURE 13.4

■ *Impact of gender schemas on gender-typed preferences and behaviors. This girl's network of gender schemas leads her to approach and explore "feminine" toys, such as dolls, and to avoid "masculine" toys, such as trucks. (From C. L. Martin & C. F. Halverson, Jr., 1981, "A Schematic Processing Model of Sex Typing and Stereotyping in Children,"* Child Development, *52, p. 1121. © The Society for Research in Child Development, Inc. Adapted by permission.)*

schemas to conclude that "trucks are not for me" and responds by avoiding the "gender-inappropriate" toy (Martin & Halverson, 1981).

In a series of studies examining this pattern of reasoning, 4- and 5-year-olds were shown unfamiliar, gender-neutral toys varying in attractiveness and asked how much they, other girls, and other boys would like each toy. Children made gender-based predictions. For example, if a girl liked a toy, she assumed that other girls would like it more and boys would like it less, even if it was highly attractive! Next, the researchers showed another group of 4- and 5-year-olds the toys, but this time they labeled some as boys' toys and others as girls' toys and left a third group unlabeled. Once again, children engaged in gender-based reasoning, relying on the label to guide their own liking and their expectations of others. As Figure 13.5 on page 524 shows, highly attractive toys lost their appeal when they were labeled as for the other gender (Martin, Eisenbud, & Rose, 1995).

Gender schema theory explains why gender stereotypes and gender-role preferences are self-perpetuating and how they restrict children's alternatives. The reason is that schema-consistent information is attended to and approached, whereas schema-inconsistent information is ignored, misinterpreted, or actively rejected. Research indicates that when children see others behaving in "gender-inconsistent" ways, they either have difficulty remembering what they have seen or they distort it to make it "gender consistent." For example, when shown a picture of a boy cooking at a stove, many children recall the picture as a girl rather than a boy. And when shown a film that includes a male nurse, they remember him as a doctor (Martin & Halverson, 1983; Signorella & Liben, 1984). The result is that over time, children increase their knowledge of "things for me" that fit with their gender schemas, but they learn much less about "cross-gender" activities and behaviors.

Among children with strong stereotypical beliefs, self-perceptions, and activity preferences, gender-schematic thinking is especially extreme (Carter & Levy, 1991; Levy & Carter, 1989). But gender-schematic thinking could not operate to restrict behavior and learning opportunities if society did not teach children a wide variety of gender-linked associations. Researchers are currently experimenting with ways to reduce children's tendency to view the world in gender-schematic terms. As the From Research to Practice box on page 525 reveals, training in cognitive skills that counteract powerful social messages about gender has produced some impressive results.

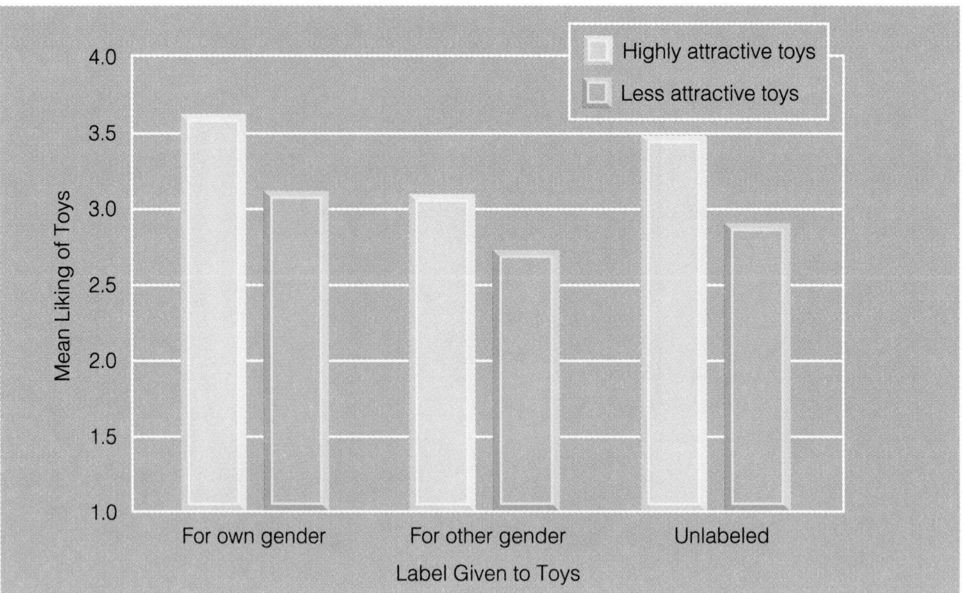

FIGURE 13.5

■ *Four- and 5-year-olds' gender-based reasoning about gender-neutral toys varying in attractiveness. Preschoolers liked toys less when they were labeled for the other gender. Highly attractive toys, especially, lost their appeal in the "other-gender" condition. (From C. L. Martin, L. Eisenbud, & H. Rose, 1995, "Children's Gender-based Reasoning About Toys,"* Child Development, *66, p. 1467. © The Society for Research in Child Development, Inc. Adapted by permission.)*

BRIEF REVIEW

According to social learning theory, behavior precedes self-perceptions in the development of gender-role identity. In contrast, cognitive-developmental theory assumes that self-perceptions emerge first and guide children's behavior. In contrast to cognitive-developmental predictions, gender-typed behavior is present so early in development that gender constancy cannot explain it; modeling and reinforcement must account for its initial appearance. Several cognitive achievements—gender labeling, gender stability, and gender-linked self-evaluations—appear to promote gender-role adoption. However, the importance of gender constancy continues to be debated. During middle childhood, boys strengthen their identification with the "masculine" role, whereas girls become more androgynous. Gender-role identity becomes more traditional in early adolescence, a trend that eventually declines.

Gender schema theory is an information-processing approach to gender typing that combines social learning and cognitive-developmental features. It explains how social pressures and children's cognitions work together to perpetuate gender-linked perceptions and behavior.

To What Extent Do Boys and Girls *Really* Differ in Gender-Stereotyped Attributes?

So far in this chapter, we have examined the relationship of biological, environmental, and cognitive factors to children's gender-typed preferences and behaviors. But we have said little about the extent to which boys and girls actually differ in mental abilities and personality traits on which we might expect them to differ, given the pervasive stereotypes found in our culture. Over the past several decades, there have been thousands of efforts to measure sex-related differences in these characteristics. At the heart of these studies is the age-old nature–nurture debate. Researchers have looked for stable differences between males and females and, from there, have searched for the biological and environmental roots of each variation.

In 1974, Eleanor Maccoby and Carol Jacklin completed a monumental review of sex-related differences. Examining 1,600 studies conducted between 1966 and 1973 and comparing the number that reported differences to the number that did not, they concluded

FROM RESEARCH TO PRACTICE

Reducing Gender Schematic Thinking with Cognitive Interventions

On the first day of school, Mrs. Brown taped blue tags with boys' names and pink tags with girls' names to the corner of each desk in her second-grade classroom. When explaining classroom routines, she told the boys and girls to form separate lines at lunch and recess. During daily lessons, Mrs. Brown made frequent reference to gender. "All the boys should be sitting down!" she exclaimed when the class got too noisy. And as an art activity was about to begin, she directed, "Leanne, please get paper for the girls. Jack, I'd like you to be a good helper for the boys."

In a recent experiment, Rebecca Bigler (1995) had some teachers create "gender classrooms" like Mrs. Brown's by emphasizing gender categories. Other teachers in "control classrooms" were told to refer to children only by their names or treat the class as a unit. After 4 weeks, 6- to 10-year-olds in "gender classrooms" endorsed more gender stereotypes than did controls. They also had a more homogeneous view of each gender group in that they judged all or most members as very similar in personality traits and abilities. Yet as Figure 13.6 shows, the impact of "gender classrooms" was largely limited to one-dimensional thinkers—children who had trouble understanding that a person can belong to more than one social category at once.

According to gender schema theory, environmental influences on gender typing are sustained by cognitive forces. When children who are one-dimensional thinkers encounter an exception to their gender schemas (such as a girl who is good at baseball), they are unlikely to process it, since they cannot separate the activity category "baseball" from the gender category "male." Recall from Chapter 6 that operational thought enables children to classify flexibly by the end of middle childhood (see page 236).

Bigler's findings suggest that it is especially important for teachers to avoid grouping children on the basis of gender during the early years of schooling when classification skills are limited and gender stereotypes are forming. At the same time, training in multiple classification can reduce gender-biased thinking. When 5- to 10-year-olds were taught that ability and interest, not gender, determine whether a person can do a job well, they gained in stereotype flexibility and memory for "gender-inconsistent" information (story characters engaged in "cross-gender" tasks). Interestingly, classification training with gender-neutral stimuli—sorting objects into two categories at once—had the same effect (Bigler & Liben, 1992). Interventions that promote logical reasoning about gender and other aspects of knowledge can help children develop a more gender-equitable view of the world.

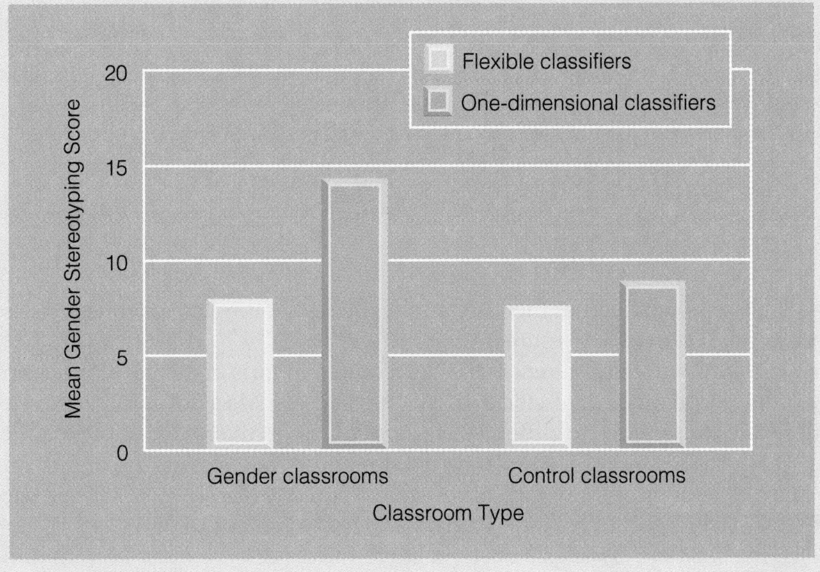

FIGURE 13.6

■ *Children's gender stereotyping in "gender" and "control classrooms." "Gender classrooms" had a powerful impact on 6- to 10-year-olds who were one-dimensional thinkers—unable to see that a person can belong to more than one social category at once. These children endorsed many more stereotypes than did classmates who could classify flexibly. (Adapted from Bigler, 1995.)*

that actual differences were fewer than commonly believed. Convincing evidence, they indicated, could be found in only four areas: verbal abilities (in favor of girls) and spatial abilities, mathematical abilities, and aggression (all in favor of boys).

Maccoby and Jacklin's procedures quickly produced criticisms of their overall findings (Block, 1976). A major shortcoming was that many studies were based on such small and possibly biased samples that some sex-related differences could have gone undetected. Since 1974, many new literature reviews have been conducted. Instead of tabulating the results of individual studies, researchers now reanalyze the data of many investigations together, thereby avoiding the pitfall of giving too much weight to those with small

TABLE 13.4

Sex-Related Differences in Mental Abilities and Personality Traits

Characteristic	Sex-Related Difference
Verbal abilities	Girls show faster early language development and are advantaged in reading and writing achievement throughout the school years.
Spatial abilities	Boys outperform girls in spatial abilities by middle childhood, a difference that persists throughout the life span. However, it is present only on certain types of spatial tasks.
Mathematical abilities	Beginning in adolescence, boys do better than girls on tests of mathematical reasoning. The difference is especially striking among high-achieving pupils. Many more boys perform exceptionally well in math.
School achievement	Girls get better grades than boys in all academic subjects in elementary school, after which the difference declines. In junior high, boys start to show an advantage in mathematics.
Achievement motivation	Sex-related differences in achievement motivation are linked to type of task. Boys perceive themselves as more competent and have higher expectancies of success in "masculine" achievement areas, such as mathematics, sports, and mechanical skills. Girls have higher expectancies and set higher standards for themselves in "feminine" areas, such as English and art.
Emotional sensitivity	Girls are more effective senders and receivers of emotional information. Girls also score higher on self-report measures of empathy, but only between 1 and 2 years are they more empathic in real-life situations.
Fear, timidity, and anxiety	Girls are more fearful and timid than boys, a difference that is present as early as the first year of life. In school, girls are more anxious about failure and try harder to avoid it. In contrast, boys are greater risk takers, a difference reflected in their higher injury rates throughout childhood and adolescence.
Compliance and dependency	Girls are more compliant than boys in response to directives from adults or peers. They also engage in more help seeking from adults and score higher in dependency on personality tests. In contrast, boys are more dominant and assertive.
Activity level	Boys are more active than girls.
Aggression	Boys display more physical and verbal aggression, but the difference is small during childhood. As adolescence approaches, boys continue to rely on overt aggression, whereas girls display more indirect forms of hostility involving social alienation. Adolescent boys are far more likely to become involved in antisocial behavior and violent crime.
Developmental problems	Many types of developmental problems are more common among boys, including speech and language disorders, reading disabilities, and behavior problems such as hyperactivity, hostile acting-out behavior, and emotional and social immaturity. More boys than girls are born with genetic disorders, physical disabilities, and mental retardation.

Sources: Benbow & Stanley, 1980; Crick & Grotpeter, 1995; Eisenberg & Lennon, 1983; Feingold, 1988, 1994; Friedman, 1989; Hall, 1978; Hall & Halberstadt, 1981; Hedges & Nowell, 1995; Hyde, 1984; Hyde & Linn, 1988; Linn & Hyde, 1989; Prior et al., 1993; Reznick et al., 1989; Zahn-Waxler et al., 1992.

samples. This approach has another advantage. Besides telling us whether a sex-related difference exists, it provides an estimate of its size.

Table 13.4 summarizes differences between boys and girls in mental abilities and personality traits, based on current evidence. As you can see, Maccoby and Jacklin's review did underestimate sex-related differences, particularly in the realm of personality. The majority of findings listed in the table are small to moderate in size, making them fairly typical in magnitude for psychological research.[1] Nevertheless, as we will see shortly, a few sex-related differences are large (Eagly, 1995; Hyde & Plant, 1995).

Finally, in considering the size of sex-related differences, we must keep in mind that some have changed over time. For example, during the past several decades, the gender gap has narrowed in all areas of mental ability for which differences have been identified except upper-level mathematics, where boys' advantage has remained constant (Feingold, 1988, 1993; Linn & Hyde, 1989). This trend is a reminder that sex-related differences are not fixed for all time. The general picture of how boys and girls differ may not be the same in a few decades as it is today.

[1] Sex usually accounts for about 5 to 10 percent of individual differences, leaving most to be explained by other factors. This means that on virtually every ability and personality characteristic, the distributions of boys' and girls' scores overlap greatly. Yet even small to moderate differences are meaningful. For example, in instances in which sex is responsible for only 5 percent of individual variation, about 60 percent of one group but only 40 percent of the other group would score above average.

MENTAL ABILITIES

Sex-related differences in mental abilities remain consistent with the findings of Maccoby and Jacklin—favoring girls in verbal skills and boys in spatial and mathematical skills. Many researchers believe heredity is involved in the verbal and spatial disparities, and they have attempted to identify the specific biological processes responsible. But no biological factor operates in an experiential vacuum. For each intellectual ability, we will see that environment plays an important role.

■ VERBAL ABILITIES. Early in development, girls are ahead in language progress. They begin to talk earlier and show faster vocabulary growth during the second year, after which boys catch up (see Chapter 9). Throughout the school years, girls attain higher scores on reading and writing achievement tests and account for a lower percentage of children referred for remedial reading instruction (Halpern, 1992; Mullis et al., 1994). However, girls' advantage on tests of general verbal ability has declined considerably since the 1970s. At present, it is so small that researchers judge it to be negligible (Feingold, 1988; Hyde & Linn, 1988).

Girls' more rapid early language development is difficult to explain in purely environmental terms. The most common biological explanation is their faster rate of physical maturation, believed to promote earlier development of the left cerebral hemisphere, where language functions are housed for most people (see Chapter 5). In animals and humans, the left side of the cortex is slightly larger and more mature in females than males (Diamond et al., 1983).

Although biology may contribute to girls' superior reading performance, experience also seems to be important. Recall that children think of reading as a feminine subject, that parents rate daughters as more competent at it, and that elementary school classrooms are feminine-biased settings in which boys' greater activity level and noncompliance lead them to be targets of teacher disapproval. Consistent with this idea, girls' tendency to learn to read more quickly is reduced in countries where reading and early school learning are regarded as well suited to the masculine gender role (Preston, 1962). Perhaps girls write more fluently than boys because they read books more frequently and generalize what they learn to written expression (Hedges & Nowell, 1995).

■ SPATIAL ABILITIES. Spatial skills involve the ability to mentally manipulate visual information. The male advantage in spatial performance has commanded a great deal of research attention, since it has implications for math and science education and entry into scientific careers.

The study of spatial skills is complicated by the fact that a variety of spatial tasks exist (see Figure 13.7 on page 528). The gender gap is large for *mental rotation tasks,* in which individuals must rotate a three-dimensional figure rapidly and accurately inside their heads. In addition, males do substantially better on *spatial perception tasks,* in which people must determine spatial relationships by considering the orientation of the surrounding environment. Sex-related differences in *spatial visualization tasks,* involving analysis of complex visual forms, are weak or nonexistent (Linn & Petersen, 1985; Voyer, Voyer, & Bryden, 1995). Many strategies can be used to solve these problems. Although males may rely on spatial manipulations, perhaps females come up with other equally effective strategies and, for this reason, do just as well.

Sex-related differences in spatial abilities emerge by middle childhood and persist throughout the life span (Kerns & Berenbaum, 1991). The pattern is consistent enough to suggest a biological explanation. Although many controversial hypotheses have been suggested, recent research has focused on two of them:

1. *The brain lateralization/maturation rate hypothesis.* Earlier we noted that girls' faster rate of physical maturation may lead to earlier specialization of the left hemisphere, which enhances early verbal skills. In contrast, boys' slower maturation rate is believed to promote stronger right-hemispheric specialization during adolescence, a pattern believed to enhance later-emerging spatial abilities (Waber, 1976).

As yet, research testing this theory offers only limited support. Some studies report a slight advantage in spatial skills for late maturing adolescents (Gilger & Ho, 1989; Newcombe & Dubas, 1987). Others, however, find no relationship between maturation rate and mental abilities (Newcombe, Dubas, & Baenninger, 1989). Furthermore, even when

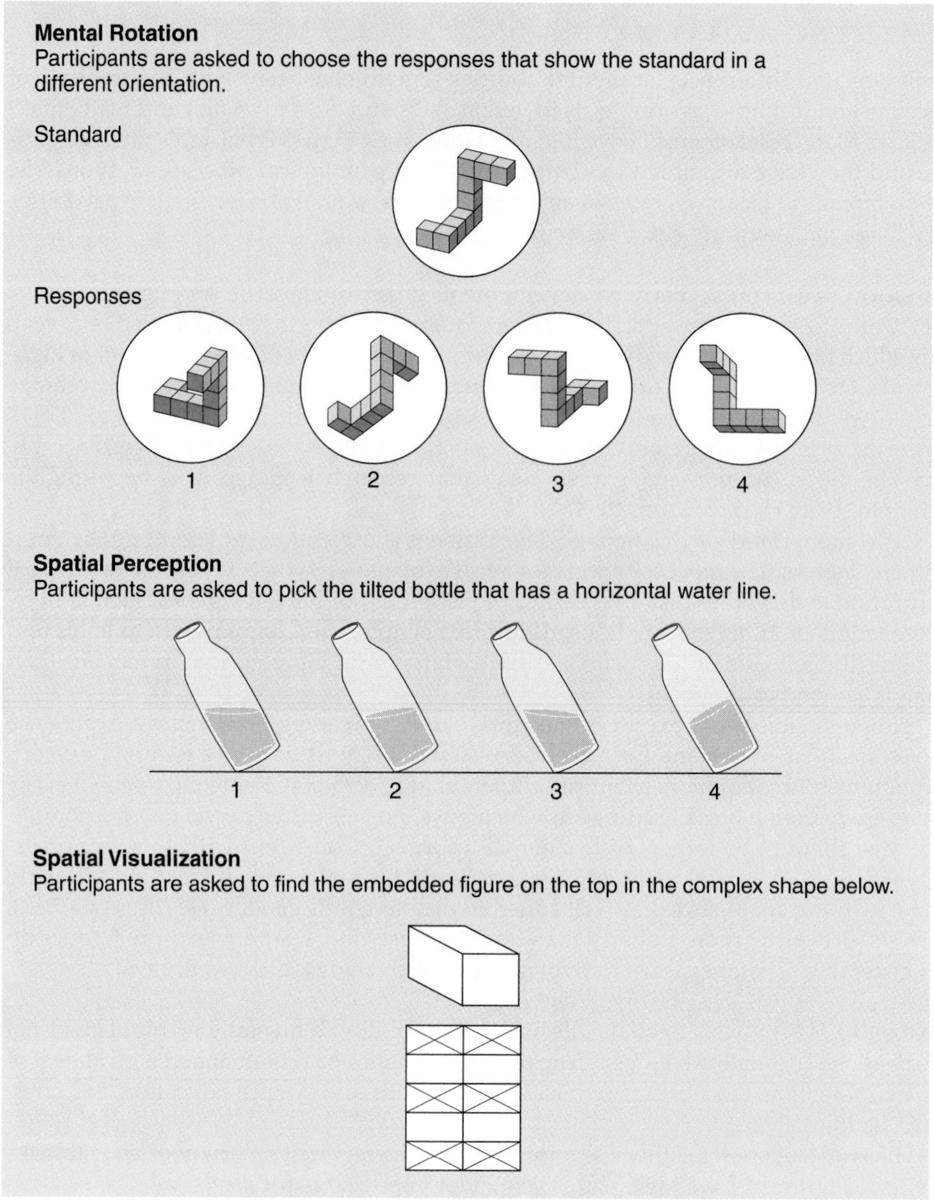

FIGURE 13.7

■ *Types of spatial tasks on which the performance of males and females has been compared. (From M. C. Linn & A. C. Petersen, 1985, "Emergence and Characterization of Sex Differences in Spatial Ability: A Meta-Analysis,"* Child Development, *56, pp. 1482, 1483, 1485. © The Society for Research in Child Development, Inc. Reprinted by permission.)*

late maturers outperform early maturers on spatial tasks, they do not always show greater right-hemispheric specialization (Newcombe & Dubas, 1992).

2. *The prenatal androgen hormone hypothesis.* A second hypothesis is that prenatal exposure to androgen hormones enhances right-hemispheric functioning, thereby accounting for the male advantage in spatial abilities. Consistent with this idea, girls and women whose prenatal androgen levels were abnormally high due to CAH (see page 510) show superior performance on spatial rotation tasks (Collaer & Hines, 1995). Additional evidence indicates that people with severe prenatal deficiencies of either male or female hormones have difficulty with spatial skills (Hier & Crowley, 1982; Netley, 1986).[2]

Studies of hormone variations within normal range are less clear. For example, one investigation reported a link between prenatal androgens and spatial ability at age 4, but only for girls and in the opposite direction expected: The greater the hormone exposure, the lower the spatial score (Finegan, Niccols, & Sitarenios, 1992). These findings suggest that prenatal hormones may affect spatial skills, but they do not operate in a straightforward fashion.

Although less attention has been devoted to the impact of environment, several studies suggest that experience can widen or reduce the gender gap. Boys' early play activities may contribute to their advantage, since children who play with manipulative,

[2] In Chapter 3, we indicated that Turner syndrome girls, who are missing an X chromosome, do poorly on spatial tasks. They are deficient in female sex hormones.

"masculine" toys do better on spatial tasks (Dirks, 1982; Fagot & Littman, 1976). At times, girls' limited exposure to certain scientific principles may prevent them from demonstrating their spatial competencies. In a study in which female college students were taught a relevant physical rule before solving the water-level problem in Figure 13.7, their performance equaled that of males (Liben & Golbeck, 1984). Surprisingly, everyday experience with liquid surfaces, more available to girls and women, seems to work against mastery of this task. Waitresses, housewives, and bartenders do especially poorly. Repeatedly pouring and serving liquids seems to promote an object-relative rather than environment-relative perspective when judging whether a liquid surface is horizontal (Hecht & Proffitt, 1995).

Finally, on spatial rotation tasks for which sex-related differences are largest, females differ only in speed, not accuracy, and training improves their scores substantially (Linn & Petersen, 1985). Perhaps females' greater anxiety about failing in achievement situations contributes to their longer solution time, although less efficient mental strategies are clearly involved (Casey, 1996).

■ *These school-age girls are building models of the Leaning Tower of Pisa and spend much time in their classroom drawing and reading maps. These activities are likely to promote development of spatial abilities during a period in which boys start to outperform girls. (Bob Krist/Leo de Wys Inc.)*

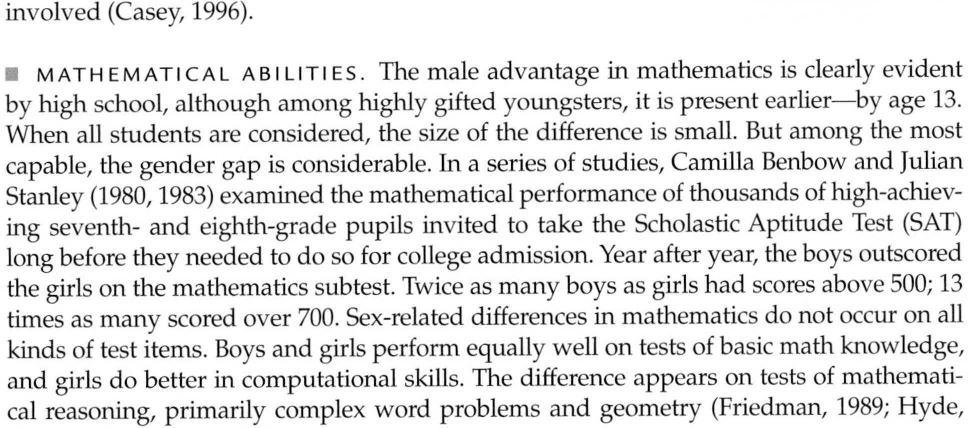

■ MATHEMATICAL ABILITIES. The male advantage in mathematics is clearly evident by high school, although among highly gifted youngsters, it is present earlier—by age 13. When all students are considered, the size of the difference is small. But among the most capable, the gender gap is considerable. In a series of studies, Camilla Benbow and Julian Stanley (1980, 1983) examined the mathematical performance of thousands of high-achieving seventh- and eighth-grade pupils invited to take the Scholastic Aptitude Test (SAT) long before they needed to do so for college admission. Year after year, the boys outscored the girls on the mathematics subtest. Twice as many boys as girls had scores above 500; 13 times as many scored over 700. Sex-related differences in mathematics do not occur on all kinds of test items. Boys and girls perform equally well on tests of basic math knowledge, and girls do better in computational skills. The difference appears on tests of mathematical reasoning, primarily complex word problems and geometry (Friedman, 1989; Hyde, Fenema, & Lamon, 1990).

Some researchers believe the gender gap in mathematics, particularly at the high end of the distribution, is biologically based (Benbow, 1988). One common assumption is that sex-related differences in mathematics are due to differences in spatial skills and that the same biological factors underlie performance in both areas. In support of this view, EEGs taken while junior high school pupils work on spatial tasks suggest that mathematically talented boys have a unique capacity to inhibit regions of the left cortical hemisphere and allow the right hemisphere to take over (Benbow & Lubinski, 1993). Furthermore, adolescent girls and college women who do well on mental rotation tasks tend to score high on the mathematics subtest of the SAT. When individual differences in mental rotation ability are controlled, sex-related differences in SAT math scores are largely eliminated (Casey et al., 1995). In sum, use of efficient, visually based reasoning skills seems to be partly responsible for the greater ease with which males can solve complex mathematical problems (Casey, 1996).

But spatial abilities, as we have seen, are affected by both genetic and environmental factors. Similarly, a variety of social pressures contribute to girls' underrepresentation among the mathematically talented. The mathematics gender gap is related to pupil attitudes and self-esteem. Earlier in this chapter, we noted that long before sex-related differences in math achievement are present, children view math as a masculine subject and parents believe boys are better at it. Furthermore, girls' tendency to attribute their academic failures to low ability (rather than insufficient effort) reduces their self-confidence and promotes high anxiety in achievement situations (see Chapter 11). Girls display this learned-helpless style particularly strongly in mathematics. Over time, girls start to regard math as less useful for their future lives and are more likely than boys to stop taking math courses when they are not mandatory. The end result of this chain of events is that girls are less likely to acquire abstract mathematical concepts and reasoning skills (Linn & Hyde, 1989; Marsh, 1989).

PERSONALITY TRAITS

Sex-related differences in personality are in line with gender stereotypes. Traits most often studied include emotional sensitivity, compliance and dependency, and aggression.

■ EMOTIONAL SENSITIVITY. Females are more emotionally sensitive than males, a difference that appears quite early. Beginning in the preschool years, girls perform slightly better than boys when asked to make judgments of others' emotional states using nonverbal cues (Hall, 1978). Except for anger, girls also express feelings more freely and intensely, using language and facial and body gestures (Hall & Halberstadt, 1981; Saarni, 1993).

It would be reasonable to expect these differences to extend to empathic responding, but so far the evidence is mixed. On self-report measures of empathy, girls and women consistently score higher than boys and men. But when observed for behavioral signs that they are empathizing with the distress of a nearby person, 1- to 2-year-old girls display greater concern than do boys, but preschool- through adolescent-age youngsters show no difference (Eisenberg & Lennon, 1983; Zahn-Waxler et al., 1992; Zahn-Waxler, Robinson, & Emde, 1992).

■ *Girls' greater emotional sensitivity is probably environmentally determined, since boys are just as caring and affectionate in certain situations—for example, when interacting with a cherished pet. (Larry Lawfer/The Picture Cube)*

As with other attributes, both biological and environmental explanations for sex-related differences in emotional sensitivity exist. One possibility is that females are genetically prewired to be more emotionally sensitive as a way of ensuring that they will be well prepared for the caregiving role. Yet research suggests that girls are not naturally more nurturant. Before age 5, boys and girls spend equal amounts of time talking to and playing with a baby in either laboratory or natural environments (Berman, 1986; Fogel et al., 1987). In middle childhood, boys' willingness to relate to infants declines, but they continue to respond with just as much care and affection to pets and elderly relatives (Melson & Fogel, 1988). Furthermore, sex-related differences in emotional sensitivity are not present in adulthood when parents interact with their own babies. In Chapter 10, we saw that fathers are very affectionate with their infants and are just as competent caregivers as mothers. And in Chapter 4, we noted that men and women react similarly to the sound of a crying baby.

Cultural expectations that girls be warm and expressive and boys be distant and controlled seem largely responsible for the gender gap in emotional sensitivity. In infancy, mothers respond more often to a baby girl's happiness and distress than to a boy's (Malatesta et al., 1986; Malatesta & Haviland, 1982). And during childhood, parents place much greater pressure on girls to be kind, considerate, and compassionate (Zahn-Waxler, Cole, & Barrett, 1991). In addition, when talking about past experiences with their preschool children, both mothers and fathers use a greater number and variety of emotion words and are more willing to discuss sadness with their daughters than sons (Fivush, 1991; Kuebli & Fivush, 1992). Taken together, these findings suggest that girls are given far more encouragement to express and reflect on feelings than are boys.

■ COMPLIANCE AND DEPENDENCY. Beginning in the preschool years, girls are more compliant than boys, both to adult and peer demands. Girls also seek help and information from adults more often and score higher in dependency on personality tests (Feingold, 1994; Jacklin & Maccoby, 1978). There is widespread agreement that these patterns of behavior are learned, and they have much to do with activity environments in which boys and girls spend their time.

From an early age, girls are encouraged to participate in adult-structured activities at home and in preschool and, consequently, spend more time near adults. In contrast, boys are attracted to activities in which adults are minimally involved or entirely absent (Powlishta, Serbin, & Moller, 1993). As a result, boys and girls engage in very different social behaviors. Compliance and bids for help and attention appear more often in adult-structured contexts, whereas assertiveness, leadership, and creative use of materials occur more often in unstructured pursuits (Carpenter, 1983).

Ideally, boys and girls should experience a balanced array of activities to develop both the capacity to lead and assert as well as comply with others' directives. In one study, the assertive and compliant tendencies of preschoolers of both sexes were easily modified by assigning them to classroom activities that differed in degree of adult structure (Carpenter, Huston, & Holt, 1986).

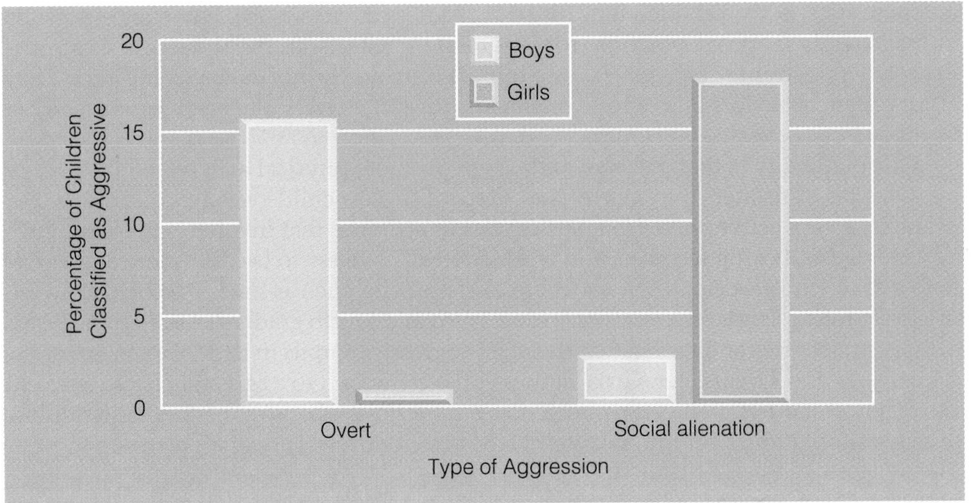

FIGURE 13.8

■ *Percentage of boys and girls who often used overt aggression or aggression directed at social alienation in a study of third through sixth graders. Boys expressed their antagonism directly, through physical and verbal attacks. In contrast, girls used indirect forms of aggression aimed at social alienation. When both types of aggression are considered, girls are just as aggressive as boys. This study also found that like antisocial boys, girls who often try to harm others by damaging peer relationships are at risk for serious adjustment difficulties (see Chapter 12). They report high levels of loneliness, depression, and isolation and are disliked by their peers. (Adapted from Crick & Grotpeter, 1995.)*

■ AGGRESSION. Aggression has attracted more research attention than any other sex-related difference. In Chapter 12, we noted that boys are more aggressive than girls in many cultures. The findings are consistent in study after study: Beginning in the preschool years, boys engage in more physical and verbal aggression, and by adolescence, boys are ten times more likely to be involved in antisocial behavior and violent crime (U.S. Department of Justice, 1995).

Nevertheless, the gender gap in aggression is small in childhood (Hyde, 1984). Also, it tends to appear in particular situations. Physically aggressive acts are especially frequent in boys' interactions with other boys; they occur less often in mixed-sex interaction and hardly at all in girls' play with other girls, which typically stresses cooperation and agreement (Brody & Hall, 1993). And boys are far more likely than girls to retaliate with aggression when they are physically attacked (Darvill & Cheyne, 1981).

As adolescence approaches, boys continue to rely on direct confrontation when provoked by peers. In contrast, girls start to display indirect forms of hostility. In one longitudinal study extending from fourth grade through junior high, children were asked at yearly intervals to describe two recent conflicts with agemates, one same-sex and one other-sex. By seventh grade, the percentage of girls reporting same-sex disputes involving social alienation—malicious gossip, rumor spreading, and exclusion—rose dramatically. Boys never mentioned such conflicts! Unlike direct attacks, these hidden cruelties make it difficult for victims to identify the perpetrator and retaliate. Consequently, they permit girls to behave aggressively while avoiding open conflict, which violates the "feminine" gender role (Cairns et al., 1989).

As Figure 13.8 shows, the percentage of girls who often use these subtle forms of aggression is just as great as the percentage of boys who frequently engage in direct attacks (Crick & Grotpeter, 1995). Since most research focuses on physical and verbal assaults, it underestimates girls' aggressiveness.

Biological Influences. Because males' greater overt aggression is present early in life, generalizes across cultures, and is found in many animal species, almost all researchers agree that biology must be involved. Earlier we mentioned that androgen hormones are related to aggression in animals; they are also believed to play a role in humans. But think back for a moment to our discussion of children with CAH. Although they were exposed to abnormally high levels of androgens during the prenatal period, they were not more aggressive (although they did show higher activity levels). This suggests that in humans, only a predisposition for aggression results from androgen exposure. Researchers currently believe that the impact of male sex hormones is indirect. They affect certain behaviors that, when combined with situational influences, lead to a higher likelihood of aggressive outcomes.

One possibility is that prenatal androgens promote physical activity, which may or may not be translated into aggression, depending on child-rearing conditions. For example, a very active child who participates in activities that involve aggression, such as water fights, boxing matches, and tackle football, is likely to become more aggressive than a child who participates in nonaggressive pursuits, such as track, baseball, or swimming. One study lends support to this idea. Third and fourth graders indicated their own activity preferences and nominated the most aggressive pupils in their class in fall of the school year and 1 year later. Girls showed little attraction to aggressive activities, and their choices did not predict later behavior. But for boys who were neither high nor low in aggression at the beginning of the study, activity preferences had a strong impact. Those who liked activities involving aggressive acts were viewed by peers as much higher in aggression the following year (Bullock & Merrill, 1980).

Another hypothesis is that prenatal hormones influence brain functioning in ways that affect children's emotional reactions. According to this view, hormone levels might induce more frequent displays of excitement, anger, or anxiety, which have an increased likelihood of resulting in aggression in the presence of certain environmental conditions. Indeed, there is evidence that early hormone levels (measured at birth from umbilical cord blood samples) predict excited emotional states for boys during the first 2 years of life, although no relationships exist for girls (Marcus et al., 1985).

Besides the prenatal period, adolescence is a second phase in which hormonal changes have implications for aggressive behavior. Adolescent boys who are high in androgens report more sadness and anxiety, and they also display more aggressive traits, such as hostile reactions to threatening acts from peers, low tolerance for frustration, and rebellious and delinquent behavior (Nottelmann et al., 1987; Olweus, 1980; Susman et al., 1987). In one study, higher estrogens and androgens were linked to more frequent expressions of anger by adolescent girls in a laboratory discussion session with their parents (Inoff-Germain et al., 1988).

Although much more research is needed, the evidence we have so far suggests that there are multiple pathways between hormones and aggression, that each involves a complex series of steps, and that each may vary with the sex and age of the child. It is also clear that whether hormonally induced responses, such as activity level or emotional state, are channeled into aggressive acts depends on environmental conditions.

Environmental Influences. In Chapter 12, we showed how strife-ridden families and coercive child-rearing practices promote aggressive behavior. For several reasons, boys are more likely to be affected by these interaction patterns than girls. Parents more often use physical punishment with boys, which encourages them to adopt the same tactics in their own relationships. In contrast, inductive discipline, which promotes self-control and empathy, is used more often with girls (Block, 1978). In addition, parents are less likely to interpret fighting as aggressive when it occurs among boys. The stereotype reflected in the familiar saying "Boys will be boys" may lead many adults to overlook male hostility unless it is extreme. This sets up conditions in which it is encouraged, or at least tolerated (Condry & Ross, 1985). In view of these findings, it is not surprising that school-age boys expect less parental disapproval and report feeling less guilty for aggressive acts than do girls (Perry, Perry, & Weiss, 1989).

Furthermore, arguing between husband and wife, although stimulating aggression among all family members, seems to have a greater effect on boys. In a study in which 2-year-olds overheard angry verbal exchanges between adults while playing with a familiar peer in a laboratory, girls tended to show fearful, withdrawing reactions, such as freezing in place and covering or hiding their faces. In contrast, boys engaged in more aggression, lashing out at their playmates (Cummings, Iannotti, & Zahn-Waxler, 1985). During the school years, boys report feeling more hostile than do girls after observing angry exchanges between adults (Hennessy, Rabideau, & Cicchetti, 1994).

Putting together all the evidence, we can see that boys have a higher likelihood of becoming embroiled in circumstances that serve as training ground for aggressive and antisocial behavior. Biological predispositions and encouragement from the social environment, acting in complex combination, are responsible.

BRIEF REVIEW

Boys and girls differ in a variety of mental abilities and personality traits. Girls show more rapid early language development and higher reading achievement and are more emotionally sensitive, compliant, and dependent. Boys are advantaged in certain spatial and mathematical skills and are more physically and verbally aggressive. Although biological factors are involved in some characteristics, both boys and girls can acquire all of them, and families, schools, and peers affect the size of each difference. Finally, in view of the many ways in which it is possible for human beings to vary, our overall conclusion must be that males and females are more alike in developmental potential than they are different from each other.

Developing Non-Gender-Stereotyped Children

The Milestones table on page 534 provides an overview of changes in gender typing considered in this chapter. We have seen that children's developmental possibilities can be seriously limited by persistent gender stereotypes in their culture. Although many researchers and laypeople recognize the importance of rearing children who feel free to express their human qualities without fear of violating gender-role expectations, no easy recipe exists for accomplishing this difficult task. It needs to be tackled on many fronts—in the home, at school, and in the wider society.

Throughout our discussion, we have mentioned ways in which gender stereotyping and gender-role adoption can be reduced. But even children who are fortunate enough to grow up in homes and schools that minimize stereotyping will eventually encounter it in the media and in what men and women typically do in the surrounding community. Until societal values change, children need early experiences that repeatedly counteract their readiness to absorb our culture's extensive network of gender-linked associations.

Sandra Bem (1983, 1984) suggests that parents and teachers make a special effort to delay young children's learning of gender-stereotyped messages, since they readily assume that cultural practices determine a person's sex. Adults can begin by eliminating traditional gender roles from their own behavior and from the alternatives they provide for children. For example, mothers and fathers can take turns making dinner, bathing children, and driving the family car, and they can provide sons and daughters with both trucks and dolls and pink and blue clothing. Teachers can make sure that all children spend some time each day in adult-structured and unstructured activities. Also, efforts can be made to shield children from media presentations that indicate males and females differ in what they can do.

Once children notice the wide array of gender stereotypes in their society, parents and teachers can point out exceptions. For example, they can arrange for children to see men and women pursuing nontraditional careers. And they can reason with children, explaining that interests and skills, not sex, should determine a person's occupation. Furthermore, older children can be told about the historical roots and current consequences of gender equalities in our society—why, for example, there has never been a female president, why few fathers stay home with their children, and why stereotyped views of men and women are hard to change. As these efforts help children build concepts of themselves and their social world that are not limited by a masculine–feminine dichotomy, they contribute to the transformation of societal values. And they bring us closer to a time when people will be released from the constraints of traditional gender roles.

MILESTONES

Gender Typing

Age	Gender Stereotyping and Gender-Role Adoption	Gender-Role Identity	Sex-Related Differences in Mental Abilities and Personality Traits
1½–5 years	■ "Gender-appropriate" play preferences emerge and increase. ■ Gender stereotyping of activities, occupations, and behaviors develops. ■ Preference for same-sex peers emerges and increases.	■ Gender constancy develops in a three-stage sequence: gender labeling, gender stability, and gender consistency. ■ By the end of this period, gender-linked self-evaluations develop. 	■ Girls show more rapid language development during the second year, after which boys catch up. ■ Girls' greater emotional sensitivity emerges and persists into adulthood. ■ Girls' greater compliance and dependency is evident. ■ Boys' greater verbal and physical aggression emerges and persists into adulthood.
6–11 years	■ Knowledge of gender stereotypes expands, especially in the areas of personality traits and achievement. ■ Gender stereotyping becomes more flexible. ■ Girls experiment with "cross-gender" activities; boys' preference for "masculine" pursuits increases.	■ "Masculine" gender-role identity strengthens among boys; girls' gender-role identity becomes more androgynous. 	■ Girls are ahead in reading achievement throughout the school years. ■ Boys' advantage in spatial abilities emerges and persists throughout the life span. ■ Boys' greater verbal and physical aggression is sustained; by the end of this age period, girls show a rise in aggressive acts involving social alienation (gossip, rumor spreading, and exclusion).
12–20 years	■ Gender-role conformity increases in early adolescence and then gradually declines, especially for girls. ■ Preference for same-sex peers becomes less pronounced after puberty.	■ Gender-role identities of both sexes become more traditional in early adolescence, a trend that gradually declines, especially for girls. 	■ Boys' advantage in mathematical reasoning emerges. ■ Boys' greater overt aggression translates into much higher involvement in antisocial behavior and violent crime, a trend accounted for by a small number of adolescents.

Note: These milestones represent overall age trends. Individual differences exist in the precise age at which each milestone is attained and in the extent of gender typing.

SUMMARY

GENDER STEREOTYPES AND GENDER ROLES

- Despite progress in women's rights, over the past several decades gender stereotypes have remained essentially the same. **Instrumental traits** continue to be regarded as masculine, **expressive traits** as feminine—a dichotomy that is widely held around the world. Stereotyping of physical characteristics, occupations, and activities is also common.
- Children begin to acquire **gender stereotypes** and **gender roles** early in the preschool years. By middle childhood, they are aware of many stereotypes, including activities, occupations, personality traits, and achievement areas. Preschoolers' understanding of gender stereotypes is rigid and inflexible. Over the elementary school years, children develop a more open-minded view of what males and females can do, although they often do not approve of males who violate gender-role expectations.
- Individual and group differences in children's gender-stereotyped knowledge and flexibility exist. Children acquire the components of gender stereotyping in different patterns and to different degrees. Boys hold more stereotyped views than girls, white children more than black children. Although social-class differences do not exist in childhood, middle-class adolescents hold more flexible views than do their lower-class counterparts.
- Awareness of gender stereotypes is only weakly related to gender-role adoption. Stereotype flexibility, however, is a moderately good predictor of children's willingness to cross gender lines during the school years.

INFLUENCES ON GENDER STEREOTYPING AND GENDER-ROLE ADOPTION

- Cross-cultural similarities in gender stereotypes and gender-role adoption have been used to support the role of biology in **gender typing**. However, great diversity exists in the extent to which cultures endorse the instrumental–expressive dichotomy, and cases of traditional gender-role reversal exist.
- Prenatal androgen levels may underlie sex-related differences in play styles, which contribute to children's preference for same-sex playmates. Research on children with congenital adrenal hyperplasia (CAH) supports this conclusion. However, other "masculine" gender-role preferences of CAH children may be due to environmental pressures. In instances in which children are reared as members of the other sex because of ambiguous genitals, gender typing is usually consistent with sex of rearing, regardless of genetic sex.
- Beginning in infancy, parents hold gender-stereotyped perceptions and expectations of boys and girls and create different environments for them. By the preschool years, parents reinforce their children for many "gender-appropriate" play activities and behaviors. During middle childhood, they demand greater independence from boys in achievement situations, hold gender-stereotyped beliefs about children's abilities in various school subjects, and allow boys more freedom to explore. Fathers differentiate between boys and girls more than mothers do. Also, each parent takes special responsibility for the gender typing of the same-sex child.
- Teachers also encourage gender-typical behaviors and activities, and children have many opportunities to observe traditional gender roles in the surrounding environment. When interacting with children of their own sex, boys and girls receive further reinforcement for "gender-appropriate" play and develop different styles of social influence. The impact of siblings on gender typing varies with birth order and family size. In small, two-child families, younger children tend to imitate the gender-role behavior of their older sibling. In large families, same-sex siblings often strive to be different from one another. As a result, they are likely to be less stereotyped in their interests and personality characteristics.

GENDER-ROLE IDENTITY

- Researchers measure **gender-role identity** by asking children and adults to rate themselves on "masculine" and "feminine" personality traits. Although most people have traditional identities, some are **androgynous**, scoring high on both masculine and feminine characteristics. At present, the masculine component of androgyny is largely responsible for its association with superior psychological adjustment.
- According to social learning theory, preschoolers first acquire gender-typed responses through modeling and reinforcement and only later organize them into cognitions about themselves. Cognitive-developmental theory suggests that **gender constancy** must be achieved before children can develop gender-typed behavior.
- Children master gender constancy by moving through three stages: **gender labeling**, **gender stability**, and **gender consistency**. Understanding of gender constancy is associated with attainment of conservation and opportunities to learn about genital differences between the sexes. In contrast to cognitive-developmental predictions, "gender-appropriate" behavior is acquired long before gender constancy. However, other cognitive attainments—gender labeling, gender stability, and gender-linked self-evaluations—strengthen preschoolers' gender-role adoption.
- During middle childhood, boys strengthen their identification with the "masculine" role, whereas girls become more androgynous. In early adolescence, the gender-role identities of both sexes become more traditional, a trend that gradually becomes less pronounced.
- **Gender schema theory** is an information-processing approach to gender typing that combines social learning and cognitive-developmental features. As children learn gender-typed preferences and behaviors, they form masculine and feminine categories, or gender schemas, that they apply to themselves and use to interpret their world. Schema-consistent information is attended to and approached, whereas schema-inconsistent information is ignored, misinterpreted, or actively rejected. As a result, children learn much more about "gender-appropriate" than "gender-inappropriate" activities and behaviors.

TO WHAT EXTENT DO BOYS AND GIRLS *REALLY* DIFFER IN GENDER-STEREOTYPED ATTRIBUTES?

- Girls are advanced in early language development, score better in reading and writing achievement, and are more emotionally sensitive, compliant, and dependent. Boys do better at certain spatial and mathematical skills and are more physically and verbally aggressive.
- Biological factors are believed to underlie sex-related differences in language development and spatial abilities, but the precise processes involved have not yet been identified. Adult encouragement and learning opportunities contribute importantly to differences in reading and spatial and mathematical skills. Girls' greater emotional sensitivity, compliance, and dependency are largely due to gender-stereotyped expectations and child-rearing practices.
- Prenatal and pubertal hormones appear to contribute to greater physical and verbal aggression in males. However, hormones seem to exert their effects indirectly, by influencing activity level or emotional reactions that increase the likelihood of aggressive behavior under certain conditions. Parents are more likely to use physical punishment with boys and to overlook their aggressive acts. In addition, boys react with greater hostility to strife-ridden family atmospheres than do girls.

DEVELOPING NON-GENDER-STEREOTYPED CHILDREN

- Parents and teachers can counteract young children's readiness to absorb gender-linked associations by delaying access to gender stereotypes. Once children notice gender stereotypes, adults can point out exceptions and discuss the arbitrariness of many gender inequalities in society.

IMPORTANT TERMS AND CONCEPTS

gender stereotypes (p. 502)
gender roles (p. 502)
gender-role identity (p. 502)
gender typing (p. 502)
instrumental traits (p. 502)
expressive traits (p. 502)
androgyny (p. 518)
gender constancy (p. 519)
gender labeling (p. 519)
gender stability (p. 519)
gender consistency (p. 519)
gender schema theory (p. 522)

for Chapter 13

If you are interested in . . .	turn to . . .	to learn about . . .
Sex-related differences in development	Chapter 3, p. 78	Developmental problems
	Chapter 5, p. 172	Motor skills
	Chapter 5, pp. 191–192	Adolescent eating disorders
	Chapter 9, p. 356	Early language development
	Chapter 11, p. 436	Learned helplessness and achievement motivation
	Chapter 11, pp. 452–453	Intimacy of friendship
	Chapter 12, pp. 480–481	Moral reasoning
	Chapter 14, p. 561	Adjustment to divorce and remarriage
	Chapter 14, p. 566	Maternal employment and development
Stereotyping	Chapter 5, pp. 187–188	Homosexuality and social acceptance
	Chapter 5, p. 204	Obesity and social acceptance
	Chapter 11, p. 443	Identity development among ethnic minority adolescents
	Chapter 11, p. 449	Children's understanding of ethnicity and social class
	Chapter 15, pp. 587–588	Physical attractiveness and social acceptance
	Chapter 15, pp. 601–602	Television and ethnic and gender stereotypes
	Chapter 15, p. 616	Teachers' reactions to children's ethnic and social class backgrounds
Biological influences on sexual differentiation and behavior	Chapter 3, p. 73	X and Y chromosomes and sex determination
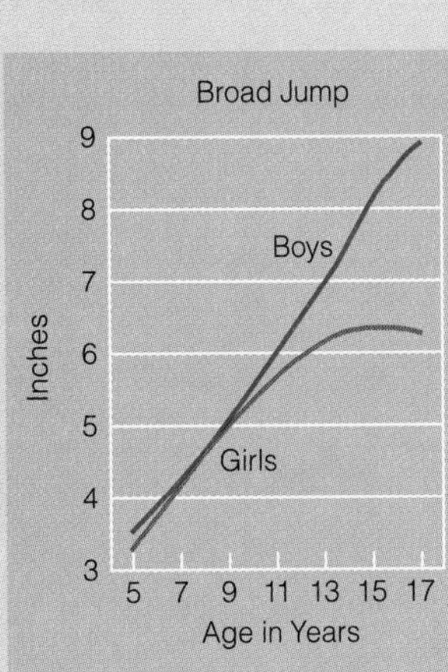	Chapter 3, pp. 80–81	Abnormalities of the sex chromosomes
	Chapter 3, p. 90	Sexual differentation during the prenatal period
	Chapter 5, p. 177	Hormonal influences on sexual maturation at puberty
	Chapter 5, pp. 187–188	Heredity and homosexuality

14 The Family

Take a moment to think back to your own childhood, and jot down a brief description of the first ten memories that come to mind. When I ask my students to do this, about half the events they mention involve their families. This emphasis is not surprising, since the family is the child's first and longest-lasting context for development. Recall from Chapter 5 that compared to other species, human children develop slowly, requiring years of support and instruction before they are ready to be independent. Our gradual journey to maturity has left an imprint on human social organization everywhere: Families are pervasive, and parents are universally important in the lives of children.

Of course, other social settings also mold children's development, but in power and breadth of influence, none equals the family. In previous chapters, we saw that the family introduces children to the physical world through the opportunities it offers for play and exploration of objects. It also creates bonds between people that are unique. The attachments children form with parents and siblings usually last a lifetime, and they serve as models for relationships in the wider world of neighborhood and school. Within the family, children also experience their first social conflicts. Discipline by parents and arguments with siblings provide children with important lessons in compliance and cooperation and opportunities to learn how to influence the behavior of others. Finally, the family is children's first context for learning the language, cognitive skills, and social and moral values of their culture.

We begin our discussion of the family by examining the reasons that this social unit came into being and has survived for thousands of years. Then we describe the current view of the family as a *social system* with many interacting influences on the child. Next, we take a close look at the family as the core socializing agency of society. We consider parents' child-rearing styles, the many factors that shape them, and their consequences for children's development.

In the second half of this chapter, we take up the significance of recent changes in family life that have led to a diversity of family lifestyles. And families of all walks of life are affected by high rates of divorce and remarriage, the dramatic increase in maternal employment, and the need for high-quality day care. Finally, the modern family is especially vulnerable to a breakdown in protective, emotionally supportive parent–child relationships. We conclude by considering the origins and consequences of child maltreatment.

Evolutionary Origins

The human family in its most common form—a lifelong commitment between a man and woman who feed, shelter, and nurture their children until they reach maturity—arose tens of thousands of years ago among our hunting and gathering ancestors. Apes and monkeys also live in social groups, but only rarely do they organize themselves into familylike units. In the few species that do, males and females mate for life, an arrangement that often leads to greater involvement of the male in infant caregiving (Smuts & Gubernick, 1992). But most of the time, nonhuman primate babies cling to and are nursed by their mothers until they can move about independently. After that time, they travel with the larger group for protection but, unlike human children, must forage to feed themselves (Lancaster & Whitten, 1980).

Anthropologists believe that bipedalism—the ability to walk upright on two legs—was an important evolutionary step that led to the human family unit. Once arms were

■ *A lifelong commitment between a man and woman who care for their young until they reach maturity arose tens of thousands of years ago among our hunting-and-gathering ancestors because it enhanced survival. This modern hunting-and-gathering mother of Central Africa cracks recently gathered nuts with her children while the father hunts for game. (I. DeVore/Anthro-Photo)*

freed to carry things, our ancestors found it easier to cooperate and share, especially in providing for the young. Men usually traveled in search of game; women gathered fruit and vegetables that served as a temporary food supply when hunting was unsuccessful. The human family pattern in which a man and woman assumed special responsibility for their own children emerged because it enhanced survival. It ensured a relatively even balance of male hunters and female gatherers within a social group, thereby creating the greatest possible protection against starvation during times when game was scarce (Lancaster & Whitten, 1980). Furthermore, the economic and social obligations of parents to each other and to their children were so important to the survival of early humans that they could not be entrusted to rational thinking alone. The capacity for strong emotional bonds evolved to ensure long-term commitment among family members (Mitchell & Shively, 1984).

Ninety-nine percent of the history of our species was spent in the hunting and gathering stage. Although this form of society no longer characterizes most contemporary cultures, it has left a lasting imprint on modern family life (Lancaster & Whitten, 1980). Indeed, hunters and gatherers who live today as they did in prehistoric times vary in many of the same ways that families in industrialized nations do: in their rate of divorce, in the extent to which men and women share work roles, in fathers' involvement in child rearing, and in their kindness toward children (Hewlett, 1992a).

Functions of the Family

The family unit of our evolutionary ancestors did not just promote the survival of its own members. It also performed vital services for the society. Each of the following functions must be carried out for a society to survive:

1. *Reproduction.* Replacements for dying members must be provided.
2. *Economic services.* Goods and services must be produced and distributed.
3. *Social order.* Procedures must exist for reducing conflict and maintaining orderly conduct.
4. *Socialization.* The young must be trained by mature members to become competent, participating members of society.
5. *Emotional support.* Procedures must exist for binding individuals together, dealing with emotional crises, and fostering a sense of commitment and purpose in each person.

In the early history of our species, families probably served all or most of these functions. But as societies became more complex, the demands placed on the family became too much for it to sustain alone. Consequently, other institutions developed to assist with certain functions, and families became linked to larger social structures. For example, political and legal institutions assumed responsibility for ensuring societal order, and schools built on the family's socialization function. Religious institutions supplemented both child-rearing and emotional support functions by offering family members educational services and a set of common beliefs that enhanced their sense of purpose and shared goals (Parke & Kellam, 1994).

Finally, although some family members still carry out economic tasks together (as in family-run farms and businesses), this function has largely been taken over by institutions that make up the world of work. The modern family consumes far more goods and services than it produces. Consequently, whereas children used to be important contributors to the family's economic well-being, today they are economic liabilities. A conservative estimate of the cost of rearing an American child born in the mid-1990s from birth through 4 years of college is $225,000[1]—one factor that has contributed to the declining birth rate in modern industrialized nations.

Although some functions have been taken over by or are shared with other institutions, three important ones—reproduction, socialization, and emotional support—remain primarily the province of the family. These functions are especially concerned with children, since they include giving birth to, rearing, and nurturing the young. Researchers interested in finding out how modern families fulfill these functions take a **social systems perspective**, viewing the family as a complex set of interacting relationships influenced by the larger social context.

The Family as a Social System

The social systems perspective on family functioning grew out of researchers' efforts to describe and explain the complex patterns of interaction that take place among family members. As we review its features, you will see that it has much in common with Bronfenbrenner's ecological systems theory, discussed in Chapter 1.

When child development specialists first began to study the family in the middle part of this century, they investigated in a very limited way. Most research focused on the mother–child relationship and emphasized one-way effects of maternal treatment on children's behavior. Today, family systems theorists recognize that children are not mechanically shaped by the inputs of others. You already know from earlier chapters that *bidirectional influences* exist in which the behaviors of each family member affect those of others. The very term *family system* implies that the responses of all family members are interrelated (Kantor & Lehr, 1975; Minuchin, 1988). These system influences operate both directly and indirectly.

DIRECT AND INDIRECT INFLUENCES

Recently I witnessed the following two episodes as I passed through the checkout counter at the supermarket:

> Little Danny stood next to tempting rows of candy as his mother lifted groceries from the cart onto the counter. "Pleeeease, can I have it, Mom?" begged Danny, holding up a large package of bubble gum. "Do you have a dollar? Just one?"
>
> "No, not today," his mother answered softly. "Remember, we picked out your special cereal. That's what I need the dollar for." Danny's mother handed him the cereal while gently taking the bubble gum from his hand and returning it to the shelf. "Here, let's pay the man," she said, as she lifted Danny into the empty grocery cart where he could see the checkout counter.

[1] This figure is based on a 1988 estimate, corrected for later inflation (Glick, 1990; U.S. Department of Labor, 1996). It includes basic expenses related to food, housing, clothing, medical care, and education.

Social systems perspective
A view of the family as a complex set of interacting relationships influenced by the larger social context.

Three-year-old Meg sat in the cart while her mother transferred groceries to the counter. Meg turned around, grabbed a bunch of bananas, and started to pull them apart.

"Stop it, Meg!" shouted her mom, who snatched the bananas from Meg's hand. Meg reached for a chocolate bar from a nearby shelf while her mother wrote the check. "Meg, how many times have I told you, DON'T TOUCH!" Loosening the candy from Meg's tight little grip, Meg's mother slapped her hand. Meg's face turned red with anger as she began to wail. "Keep this up, and you'll get it when we get home," threatened Meg's mom as they left the store.

These observations fit with a wealth of research on the family system. Many studies show that when parents (like Danny's mom) are firm but patient, children tend to comply with their requests. And when children cooperate, their parents are likely to be warm and gentle in the future. In contrast, parents (like Meg's mom) who discipline with harshness and impatience have children who refuse and rebel. And because children's misbehavior is stressful for parents, they may increase their use of punishment, leading to more unruliness by the child. In these examples, the behavior of one family member helps sustain a form of interaction in another that either promotes or undermines children's well-being.

According to the social systems perspective, ties to the community are essential for families to function at their best. These adults and children participate in a city project in which they improve a neighborhood park. As they do so, they enrich their community's resources and form networks of social support that they can turn to in times of stress. (Bob Daemmrich/Stock Boston)

The impact of family relationships on child development becomes even more complicated when we consider that interaction between any two members is affected by others present in the setting. Recall from Chapter 1 that Bronfenbrenner called these indirect influences the effect of *third parties.* Researchers have become intensely interested in how a range of relationships—mother with father, parent with sibling, grandparent with parent—modifies the child's direct experiences in the family.

Third parties can serve as effective supports for children's development, or they can undermine children's well-being. For example, when parents are warm and considerate toward each other, mothers and fathers praise and stimulate their children more and nag and scold them less. In contrast, when a marriage is tense and hostile, parents are likely to criticize and punish (Cox et al., 1989; Howes & Markman, 1989; Simons et al., 1992). Disputes between parents over child-rearing issues seem to be particularly harmful. They are linked to a rise in child behavior problems over and above the increase associated with non-child-related marital difficulties (Jouriles et al., 1991).

Yet even when children's adjustment is strained by arguments between their parents, other family members may help restore effective interaction. Grandparents are a case in point. They can promote children's development in many ways—both directly, by responding warmly to the child, and indirectly, by providing parents with child-rearing advice, models of child-rearing skill, and even financial assistance (Cherlin & Furstenberg, 1986). Of course, like any indirect influence, grandparents' involvement can sometimes be negative. Later in this chapter, we will see that when quarrelsome relations exist between grandparents and a divorced custodial parent, children may suffer.

To make matters even more complicated, the social systems perspective views the interplay of forces within the family as constantly adapting to changes in its members. Individuals continue to develop throughout the life span. As a result, interaction is not static, but shifts across time. For example, as children acquire new skills, parents adjust the way they treat their more competent youngsters. Then changes in child rearing pave the way for new achievements and further modifications in family relationships. In fact, no other social unit is required to adjust to such vast changes in its members as is the family.

THE FAMILY SYSTEM IN CONTEXT

The social systems perspective, as we noted earlier, views the family as affected by larger social contexts. Connections to the community—in terms of *formal organizations,* such as school, workplace, day care center, and church or synagogue, as well as *informal social networks* of relatives, friends, and neighbors—influence parent–child relationships. For example, child adjustment problems, particularly those that are related to parental conflict, are more common in urban than rural settings. Although population density and poverty contribute to this finding, fragmented communication networks are also responsible. Psychological disturbance is highest in inner-city areas in which families move often, parks and playgrounds are in disarray, community centers providing leisure-time activities do not exist, and visits among neighbors are rare. In contrast, when family ties to the community are strong—as indicated by regular church attendance and frequent contact with friends and relatives—family stress and child adjustment problems are reduced (Garbarino & Kostelny, 1993).

Why do ties to the community reduce family stress and enhance child development? There are several reasons. First, social support offers interpersonal acceptance. A neighbor or relative who listens and tries to relieve a parent's concern enhances self-esteem. The parent, in turn, is likely to behave more sensitively toward her children. In one study of families experiencing economic strain, social networks affected parenting indirectly by reducing mothers' feelings of depression (Simons et al., 1993). Second, social networks often provide access to valuable information and services. A friend who suggests where a job or housing might be found or who looks after children while the parent attends to other pressing needs helps make the multiple roles of spouse, provider, and caregiver easier to fulfill. Third, links to the community can offer child-rearing controls and role models. Friends and relatives may encourage and demonstrate effective ways of interacting with children and discourage ineffective practices (Cochran, 1993). Finally, as children participate in their parents' social networks, other adults can influence children directly through warmth, stimulation, and exposure to a wider array of competent models.

No single researcher could possibly study all aspects of family functioning included in the social systems perspective at once. However, as we address each piece of the family puzzle in the course of this chapter, we will continually see examples of the many interlocking parts that combine to influence children's development.

BRIEF REVIEW

The human family originated with our hunting and gathering ancestors, for whom it was uniquely suited to promote survival. Important functions of the modern family include reproduction, socialization, and emotional support. According to the social systems perspective, the family consists of a complex network of bidirectional relationships that continually readjust as family members change over time. The quality of these relationships, and therefore children's development, depends in part on links established with formal and informal social supports in the surrounding community.

Socialization Within the Family

Among functions of the family, socialization has been of greatest interest to child development researchers. In previous chapters, we discussed many ways in which parents can foster children's competence—by being sensitive to infants' behaviors and needs; by serving as warm models and reinforcers of mature behavior; by using reasoning, explanation, and inductive discipline to promote morality and self-control; and by attributing children's failures to lack of effort rather than low ability, thereby encouraging a mastery-oriented approach to challenging tasks.

Socialization begins in earnest during the second year, once children are first able to comply with parental directives (see Chapter 12). Effective caregivers pace their demands so they fit with children's capacities. For example, they do not impose a range of "don'ts" on infants. Instead, they put away breakable objects, place barriers across steep staircases, and physically remove babies when they behave in ways that endanger themselves or disturb others. As socialization pressures increase in early childhood, parents vary greatly in how they go about the task. Let's combine the various elements of good child rearing we have already considered into an overall view of effective parenting.

STYLES OF CHILD REARING

In a series of landmark studies, Diana Baumrind gathered information on child-rearing practices by observing parents' interaction with their preschool children at home

TABLE 14.1

A Two-Dimensional Classification of Parenting Styles

	RESPONSIVE	UNRESPONSIVE
DEMANDING	Authoritative parent	Authoritarian parent
UNDEMANDING	Permissive parent	Uninvolved parent

Source: Adapted from E. E. Maccoby & J. A. Martin, 1983, "Socialization in the Context of the Family: Parent–Child Interaction," in E. M. Hetherington (Ed.), *Handbook of Child Psychology: Vol. 4. Socialization, Personality, and Social Development* (4th ed., pp. 1–101). New York: Wiley. Copyright © 1983 by John Wiley & Sons. Reprinted by permission.

and in the laboratory. Two broad dimensions of parenting emerged from the observations. The first is *demandingness.* Some parents establish high standards for their children and insist that their youngsters meet those standards. Other parents demand very little and rarely try to influence their child's behavior. The second dimension is *responsiveness.* Some parents are accepting of and responsive to their children. They frequently engage in open discussions and verbal give-and-take. Others are rejecting and unresponsive.

As Table 14.1 shows, the various combinations of demandingness and responsiveness yield four styles of parenting. Baumrind's research focused on three of them: authoritative, authoritarian, and permissive. The fourth type, the uninvolved style, has been studied by other researchers.

AUTHORITATIVE CHILD REARING. In Baumrind's early research, preschoolers were separated into adjustment categories by psychologists who observed them over several months at nursery school. One group, the "mature" preschoolers, differed sharply from the others in that their parents used a set of child-rearing techniques Baumrind called the **authoritative style**. Authoritative parents make reasonable demands for maturity, and they enforce them by setting limits and insisting on obedience. At the same time, they express warmth and affection, listen patiently to their child's point of view, and encourage participation in family decision making. In sum, authoritative child rearing is a rational, democratic approach that recognizes and respects the rights of both parents and children.

Baumrind's (1967) findings revealed that children of authoritative parents were developing especially well. Ratings by psychologists indicated that they were lively and happy in mood, self-confident in their mastery of new tasks, and self-controlled in their ability to resist engaging in disruptive acts. These children also displayed less traditional gender-role behavior. Boys scored particularly high in friendliness and cooperativeness and girls in independence and desire to master new tasks (Baumrind & Black, 1967). Recent evidence confirms a positive association between authoritative parenting and emotional and social skills during the preschool years (Denham, Renwick, & Holt, 1991).

Researchers who have examined the correlates of authoritative parenting at older ages also report that it is linked to many aspects of competence. These include high self-esteem, social and moral maturity, involvement in school learning, academic achievement in high school, and educational attainment (Block, 1971; Kurdek & Fine, 1994; Lamborn et al., 1991; Luster & McAdoo, 1996; Steinberg et al., 1992, 1994).

AUTHORITARIAN CHILD REARING. Parents who use an **authoritarian style** are also demanding, but they place such a high value on conformity that they are unresponsive—even outright rejecting—when children are unwilling to obey. "Do it because I say so!" is the attitude of these parents. As a result, they engage in very little give-and-take with children, who are expected to accept an adult's word for what is right in an unquestioning manner. If the child does not, authoritarian parents resort to force and punishment. The authoritarian style is clearly biased in favor of parents' needs; children's self-expression and independence are suppressed.

Baumrind (1967, 1971) found that preschoolers with authoritarian parents were anxious, withdrawn, and unhappy. When interacting with peers, they tended to react with hostility when frustrated. Boys, especially, were high in anger and defiance. Girls were dependent and lacking in exploration, and they retreated from challenging tasks.

Authoritative style
A parenting style that is demanding and responsive. A rational, democratic approach in which both parents' and children's rights are respected.

Authoritarian style
A parenting style that is demanding but low in responsiveness to children's rights and needs. Conformity and obedience are valued over open communication.

In adolescence, young people with authoritarian parents continue to be less well adjusted than those exposed to an authoritative style (Steinberg et al., 1994). Nevertheless, teenagers used to authoritarian child rearing do better in school and are less likely to engage in antisocial acts than those with undemanding parents—that is, who use either of the two styles we are about to discuss (Baumrind, 1991; Kurdek & Fine, 1994; Lamborn et al., 1991).

■ PERMISSIVE CHILD REARING. The **permissive style** of child rearing is nurturant and accepting, but it avoids making demands or imposing controls of any kind. Permisive parents allow children to make many of their own decisions at an age when they are not yet capable of doing so. They can eat meals and go to bed when they feel like it and watch as much television as they want. They do not have to learn good manners or do any household chores. And they are permitted to interrupt and annoy others without any parental restraint. Although some permissive parents truly believe this approach to child rearing is best, many others lack confidence in their ability to influence their child's behavior and are disorganized and ineffective in running their households.

Baumrind (1967) found that children of permissive parents were very immature. They had difficulty controlling their impulses and were disobedient and rebellious when asked to do something that conflicted with their momentary desires. They were also overly demanding and dependent on adults, and they showed less persistence on tasks at preschool than children of parents who exerted more control. The link between permissive parenting and dependent, nonachieving behavior was especially strong for boys (Baumrind, 1971).

In adolescence, parental indulgence continues to be related to poor self-control. Permissively reared teenagers are less involved in school learning and use drugs more frequently than do teenagers whose parents communicate clear standards for behavior (Baumrind, 1991; Kurdek & Fine, 1994; Lamborn et al., 1991).

■ UNINVOLVED CHILD REARING. Undemanding parenting combined with indifferent or rejecting behavior constitutes the **uninvolved style**. Uninvolved parents show little commitment to caregiving beyond the minimum effort required to feed and clothe their child. Often these parents are so overwhelmed by the many pressures and stresses in their lives that they have little time and energy to spare for children. As a result, they cope with the demands of parenting by doing what they can to avoid inconvenience. They may respond to the child's demands for easily accessible objects, but any efforts that involve long-term goals, such as establishing and enforcing rules about homework and acceptable social behavior, are weak and fleeting (Maccoby & Martin, 1983).

At its extreme, uninvolved parenting is a form of child maltreatment called *neglect*. Especially when it begins early, it disrupts virtually all aspects of development. Emotionally detached, depressed mothers who show little interest in their babies have children who soon show deficits in many domains, including attachment, cognition, and emotional and social skills (See Chapter 10, page 385). Even when parental disengagement is less pronounced, the development of children is impaired. In one longitudinal study, preschoolers whose mothers were uninvolved as opposed to responsive during the first few years were noncompliant and demanding. Asked to wait while the mother filled out a questionnaire, these children tugged and pulled at her clothing, grabbed her pencil, and sometimes kicked and hit (Martin, 1981).

Uninvolved parenting also works poorly at older ages. Research in Finland and the United States shows that parents who rarely have conversations with their adolescents, take little interest in their life at school, and are seldom aware of their whereabouts have youngsters who are low in tolerance for frustration and emotional control, do poorly in school, lack long-term goals, and are prone to engage in delinquent acts (Baumrind, 1991; Kurdek & Fine, 1994; Lamborn et al., 1991; Pulkkinen, 1982).

WHAT MAKES THE AUTHORITATIVE STYLE SO EFFECTIVE?

Table 14.2 on page 546 summarizes outcomes associated with each of the child-rearing styles we have just considered. The authoritative style predicts child competence

Permissive style
A parenting style that is responsive but undemanding. An overly tolerant approach to child rearing.

Uninvolved style
A parenting style that is both undemanding and unresponsive. Reflects minimal commitment to child rearing.

so consistently that Baumrind believes it causes superior development. But like other correlational findings, this relationship is open to different interpretations (Lewis, 1981). Perhaps parents of mature children use demanding tactics because their youngsters have cooperative, obedient dispositions, not because firm control is an essential ingredient of effective parenting. Yet Baumrind (1983) points out that children often resisted adult directives in authoritative homes, but parents handled this patiently and rationally. They neither gave in to children's unreasonable demands nor responded harshly and arbitrarily. Baumrind emphasizes that not just firm control, but *rational and reasonable* use of firm control, facilitates development.

Nevertheless, children's characteristics contribute to the ease with which parents can apply the authoritative style. Recall from Chapter 10 that temperamentally difficult children are more likely to receive coercive discipline. And when children resist, some parents respond inconsistently, at first by being punitive and later by giving in, thereby reinforcing the child's unruly behavior. Children of parents who go back and forth between authoritarian and uninvolved styles are especially aggressive and irresponsible and do very poorly in school (see Chapter 12). Over time, the relationship between parenting and children's characteristics becomes increasingly bidirectional. An impulsive, noncompliant child makes it very hard for parents to be firm, rational, and consistent, but child-rearing practices can strengthen or reduce difficult behavior (Stice & Barrera, 1995).

Why does an authoritative style support children's competence and help bring the recalcitrant behavior of poorly socialized children under control? There are several reasons. First, control that appears fair and reasonable to the child, not arbitrary, is far more likely to be complied with and internalized. Second, nurturant parents who are secure in the standards they hold for their children provide models of caring concern as well as confident, assertive behavior. They are also more effective reinforcing agents, praising children for striving to meet their expectations and making good use of disapproval, which works best when applied by an adult who has been warm and caring. Finally, authoritative parents make demands that fit with children's ability to take responsibility for their own behavior. As a result, these parents let children know that they are competent individuals who can do things successfully for themselves, and high self-esteem and mature, independent behavior are fostered (Kuczynski et al., 1987).

TABLE 14.2

Relationship of Child-Rearing Styles to Child Outcomes

Child-Rearing Style	Outcomes
Authoritative	■ In childhood, lively and happy mood; high self-esteem and self-control; less traditional gender-role behavior
	■ In adolescence, high self-esteem, social and moral maturity, academic achievement, and educational attainment
Authoritarian	■ In childhood, anxious, withdrawn, and unhappy mood; hostile when frustrated
	■ In adolescence, less well adjusted than agemates exposed to the authoritative style, but better school performance than agemates exposed to permissive or uninvolved styles
Permissive	■ In childhood, impulsive, disobedient, and rebellious; demanding and dependent on adults; poor persistence at tasks
	■ In adolescence, poor self-control and school performance; more frequent drug use than agemates exposed to authoritative or authoritarian styles
Uninvolved	■ In childhood, deficits in attachment, cognition, play, and emotional and social skills; aggressive, acting out behavior
	■ In adolescence, poor self-control and school performance; frequent drug use

ADAPTING CHILD REARING TO CHILDREN'S DEVELOPMENT

Since authoritative parents continually adapt to children's growing competence, their practices change with age. In the following sections, we will see that a gradual lessening of direct control supports development, as long as it is built on continuing parental warmth and involvement in child rearing.

■ PARENTING IN MIDDLE CHILDHOOD: COREGULATION. During middle childhood, the amount of time children spend with parents declines dramatically. In a study in which parents kept diaries of family activities, they reported spending less than half as much time in caregiving, teaching, reading, and playing with 5- to 12-year-olds as they did with preschoolers (Hill & Stafford, 1980). The school-age child's growing independence means that parents must deal with new issues—for example, how to promote responsible behavior and constructive use of leisure time, whether children's friends are good influences, and how to deal with problems at school (Maccoby, 1984a).

Although parents face a new set of concerns, child rearing becomes easier for those who established an authoritative style during the early years (Maccoby, 1984b). Reasoning works more effectively with school-age children because of their greater capacity for logical thinking. Of course, older children sometimes use their cognitive skills to bargain and negotiate—behaviors that can try parents' patience. But parents can appeal to their child's better developed sense of self-esteem, humor, and morality to resolve these difficulties. Perhaps because parents and children have, over time, learned how to resolve conflicts, coercive discipline declines over middle childhood (Maccoby, 1984a).

As children demonstrate that they can take on new responsibilities, parents gradually shift control to the child. This does not mean that they let go entirely. Instead, effective parents of school-age children engage in **coregulation**, a transitional form of supervision in which they exercise general oversight while permitting children to be in charge of moment-by-moment decision making. Coregulation supports and protects school-age children, who are not yet ready for total independence. At the same time, it prepares them for adolescence, when they will make many important decisions themselves.

Coregulation grows out of a cooperative relation between parent and child—one based on mutual respect. Here is a summary of its critical ingredients:

> The parental tasks . . . are threefold. First, [parents] must monitor, guide, and support their children at a distance—that is, when their children are out of their presence; second, they must effectively use the times when direct contact does occur; and third, they must strengthen in their children the abilities that will allow them to monitor their own behavior, to adopt acceptable standards of [good] conduct, to avoid undue risks, and to know when they need parental support and guidance. Children must be willing to inform parents of their whereabouts, activities, and problems so that parents can mediate and guide when necessary. (Maccoby, 1984a, pp. 191–192)

Although school-age children often press for greater independence, they know how much they need their parents' continuing support. In one study, fourth graders described parents as the most influential people in their lives. They often turned to mothers and fathers for affection, advice, enhancement of self-worth, and assistance with everyday problems (Furman & Buhrmester, 1992).

■ PARENTING IN ADOLESCENCE: FOSTERING AUTONOMY. During adolescence, young people in complex societies deal with the need to choose from many options by seeking **autonomy**—establishing themselves as separate, self-governing individuals. Autonomy extends beyond school-age children's capacity to regulate their own behavior in the absence of parental monitoring. It has a vital *emotional component*—relying more on oneself and less on parents for support and guidance. And it also has an important *behavioral component*—making decisions independently by carefully weighing one's own judgment and the suggestions of others to arrive at a well-reasoned course of action (Hill & Holmbeck, 1986; Steinberg & Silverberg, 1986). If you look carefully at the concept of autonomy, you will see that it is closely related to the quest for identity. Research

Coregulation
A transitional form of supervision in which parents exercise general oversight while permitting children to be in charge of moment-by-moment decision making.

Autonomy
A sense of oneself as a separate, self-governing individual. An important developmental task of adolescence that is closely related to the quest for identity.

■ *Adolescent autonomy is effectively achieved in the context of warm parenting. This mother supports her daughter's desire to try new experiences, relaxing control in accord with the adolescent's readiness to take on new responsibilities without threatening the parent–child bond. (Kopstein/Monkmeyer Press)*

suggests that adolescents who successfully establish personally meaningful values and life goals are autonomous. They have given up childish dependence on parents for a more mature, responsible relationship (Frank, Pirsch, & Wright, 1990).

Autonomy receives support from a variety of changes within the adolescent. In Chapter 5, we saw that puberty triggers psychological distancing from parents. In addition, as young people look more mature, they are granted more independence and responsibility. Cognitive development also paves the way toward autonomy. Abstract thinking permits teenagers to solve problems in more mature ways and to foresee the consequences of their actions more clearly. How can parents foster this readiness for autonomy? Controversy surrounds this question.

Take a moment to think back to Erikson's psychosocial theory, discussed in Chapter 1. Like identity, autonomy is a concern that returns at various points during the life cycle. Recall that it is a central task of toddlerhood, and it resurfaces at adolescence, when social expectations demand a new level of self-reliance. Research reveals that autonomy can be arrived at in different ways. When young people feel autonomous yet characterize their relationship with parents as unsupportive, they appear better adjusted than teenagers in conflict-ridden families who do not feel autonomous. This suggests that adolescents in troubled homes benefit when they can separate themselves emotionally from stressful parent–child interaction (Fuhrman & Holmbeck, 1995; Sessa & Steinberg, 1991). But overall, autonomy achieved in the context of warm, supportive parent–child ties is most adaptive. It predicts high self-reliance, work orientation, academic competence, and gains in self-esteem during the adolescent years (Allen et al., 1994; Lamborn & Steinberg, 1993).

These findings suggest that the task for parents and teenagers is not one of just separating. Instead, parents need to gradually relax control in accord with the adolescent's readiness for more freedom without threatening the parent–child bond. An authoritative style begun in childhood encourages this process. Authoritative parents meet the challenges of adolescence by establishing guidelines that are flexible, open to discussion, and implemented in an atmosphere of concern and fairness. It is not hard for them to explain the basis of their decisions, solicit and consider carefully the adolescent's input, and gradually modify their rules as the young person moves closer to adulthood (Steinberg, 1990, 1996). If you return to Chapter 11, you will see that this very blend of connection and independence promotes identity development as well.

SOCIAL-CLASS AND ETHNIC VARIATIONS IN CHILD REARING

Research examining parenting in over 180 societies reveals that a style that is responsive but moderately demanding is the most common pattern around the world. Many cultures seem to have discovered for themselves the link between authoritative parenting and healthy psychological development (Rohner & Rohner, 1981). Nevertheless, in the United States and other Western nations, consistent differences in child rearing exist that are linked to social class and ethnicity.

■ SOCIAL CLASS. When asked about qualities they would like to encourage in their children, parents who work in skilled and semiskilled manual occupations (for example, machinists, truck drivers, and custodians) tend to place a high value on external characteristics, such as obedience, neatness, and cleanliness. In contrast, parents in white-collar and professional occupations tend to emphasize inner psychological traits, such as curiosity, happiness, and self-control. These differences in values are reflected in parenting behaviors. Middle-income parents talk to and stimulate their babies more and grant them greater freedom to explore. When their children are older, they use more warmth, explanations, verbal praise, and inductive discipline. In contrast, low-income parents are more likely to be restrictive. Because they think that infants can easily be spoiled, they often limit the amount of rocking and cuddling they do (Luster, Rhoades, & Haas, 1989). Later on, harsh commands, such as "You do that because I told you to," as well as criticism and physical punishment occur more often in low-income households (Dodge, Pettit, & Bates, 1994).

Social-class differences in child rearing can be understood in terms of different life conditions in low-income and middle-income families. Low-income parents often feel a sense of powerlessness and lack of influence in relationships beyond the home. For example, at work they must obey the rules of others in positions of power and authority. When they get home, their parent–child interaction seems to duplicate these experiences, only with them in the authority roles. In contrast, middle-class parents have a greater sense of control over their own lives. At work, they are used to making independent decisions and convincing others of their point of view. At home, they teach these skills to their children (Greenberger, O'Neil, & Nagel, 1994). The values and behaviors required for success in the world of work are believed to affect parents' ideas about traits important to train in their children, who are expected to enter similar work roles in the future (Kohn, 1979).

■ *Homelessness in the United States has risen over the past two decades. Families like this one travel from place to place in search of employment and a safe and secure place to live. At night, they sleep in the family car. Because of constant stresses and few social supports, homeless children are usually behind in development, have frequent health problems, and show poor psychological adjustment. (Rick Browne/Stock Boston)*

Education also contributes to social-class differences in child rearing. Middle-class parents' interest in verbal stimulation and in fostering the development of children's inner characteristics is supported by years of schooling, during which they observed models of adult–child verbal instruction, acquired advanced verbal skills, and learned to think about abstract, subjective ideas. In research carried out in Mexico, where female school enrollment has recently increased, the more years of education a mother had, the more she stimulated her young child through face-to-face conversation (Richman, Miller, & LeVine, 1992; Uribe, LeVine, & LeVine, 1994).

Furthermore, middle-class parents' greater economic security frees them from the burden of having to worry about making ends meet on a daily basis. As a result, they can devote more energy and attention to their own inner characteristics and those of their children. And they can also provide many more experiences—from toys to special outings to after-school lessons—that encourage these characteristics.

■ POVERTY. When families become so low income that they slip into poverty, then effective parenting and children's development are seriously threatened. Shirley Brice Heath (1990), an anthropologist who has spent many years studying children and families of poverty, describes the case of Zinnia Mae, who grew up in Trackton, a close-knit black community located in a small southeastern American city. As unemployment struck Trackton in the 1980s and citizens moved away, 16-year-old Zinnia Mae caught a ride to Atlanta. Two years later, Heath visited her there. By then, Zinnia Mae was the mother of three children—a 16-month-old daughter named Donna and 2-month-old twin boys. She had moved into a high-rise public housing project, one of eight concrete buildings surrounding a dirt plot scattered with broken swings, seesaws, and benches.

Each of Zinnia Mae's days was much the same. She watched TV and talked with her girlfriends on the phone. The children had only one set meal (breakfast) and otherwise ate whenever they were hungry or bored. Their play space was limited to the living-room sofa and a mattress on the floor. Toys consisted of scraps of a blanket, spoons and food cartons, a small rubber ball, a few plastic cars, and a roller skate abandoned in the building. Zinnia Mae's most frequent words were "I'm so tired." She worried about how

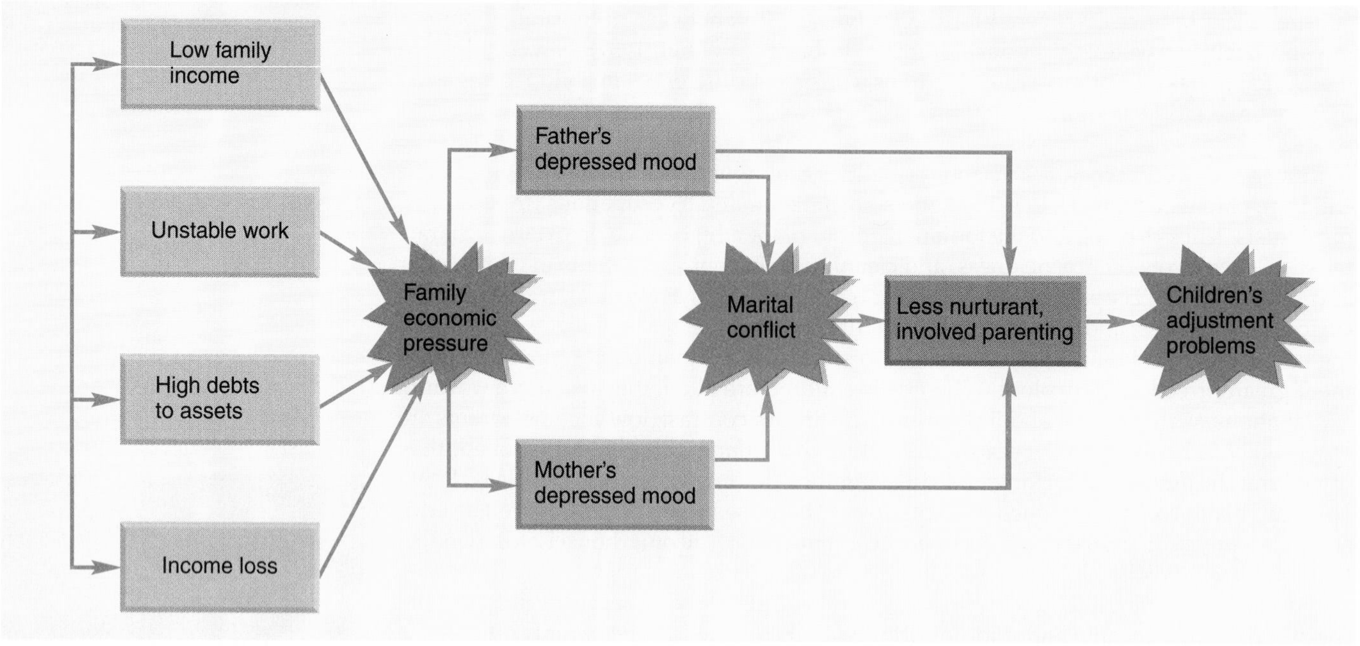

FIGURE 14.1

Pathway from family economic pressure to children's adjustment. When stresses pile up, parents become demoralized. Their depressed mood prompts a rise in marital conflict and a decline in nurturant, involved parenting. Disrupted parenting, in turn, leads to children's adjustment problems. (Adapted from R. D. Conger, K. J. Conger, G. H. Elder, Jr., F. O. Lorenz, R. L. Simons, & L. B. Whitbeck, 1992, "A Family Process Model of Economic Hardship and Adjustment of Early Adolescent Boys," Child Development, 63, p. 528. © The Society for Research in Child Development, Inc. Reprinted by permission.)

to get papers to the welfare office and where to find a baby-sitter so she could go to the laundry or grocery.

At Heath's request, Zinnia Mae agreed to tape record her interactions with her children over a 2-year period. In 500 hours of tape (other than simple directions or questions about what the children were doing), Zinnia Mae started a conversation with Donna and the boys only 18 times. Cut off from community ties and preoccupied with day-to-day survival, Zinnia Mae found it difficult to join in activities with her children. As a result, Donna and her brothers experienced a barren, understimulating home life—one very different from the family and community in which Zinnia Mae herself had grown up.

The constant stresses that accompany poverty gradually weaken the family system. Poor families experience many daily hassles—bills to pay, the car breaking down, loss of welfare and unemployment payments, something stolen from the house, to name just a few. When daily crises arise, parents become depressed, irritable, and distracted, marital conflict rises, parenting becomes less nurturant and involved, and children's development suffers. This sequence of events, summarized in Figure 14.1, has been confirmed in research on adolescents, some of whose parents experienced job instability and declining income (Conger et al., 1992, 1993, 1994). Negative outcomes for children are especially severe in single-parent families, in families living in poor housing located in dangerous neighborhoods, and in homeless families. These circumstances make everyday existence more difficult while reducing social supports that assist parents in coping with economic hardship (Duncan, Brooks-Gunn, & Klebanov, 1994; McLoyd et al., 1994).

ETHNICITY. Ethnic groups often have distinct child-rearing beliefs and practices. Some involve variations in demandingness that appear to be adaptive when viewed in light of cultural values and the context in which parent and child live.

For example, compared to Caucasian-Americans, Chinese adults describe their own parenting techniques and those they experienced as children as more demanding (Berndt et al., 1993). As Figure 14.2 shows, this greater emphasis on control continues to characterize Chinese parents who have immigrated to the United States. It seems to reflect deeply engrained Confucian values stressing strict discipline and respect for elders that have survived rapid social change and migration to a new country (Chao, 1994; Lin & Fu, 1990).

In Hispanic and Asian Pacific Island families, firm insistence on respect for parental authority, particularly that of the father, is paired with unusually high maternal warmth. This combination is believed to promote compliance and deep family commitment in children—strong feelings of loyalty and identification with parents and close relatives (Fracasso & Busch-Rossnagel, 1992; Harrison et al., 1994).

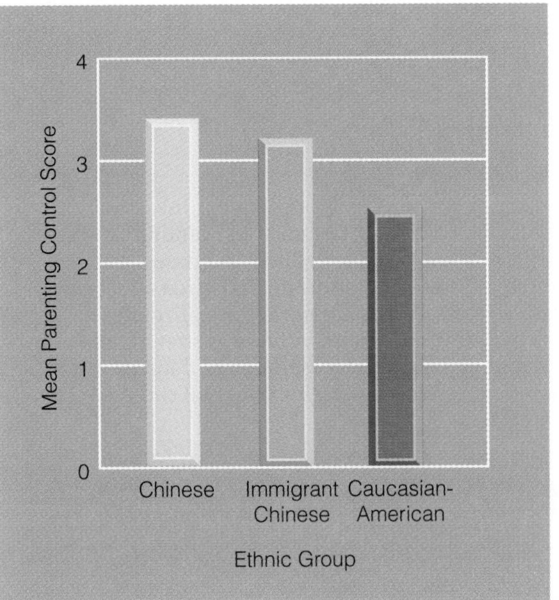

FIGURE 14.2

■ *Self-reported emphasis on control by Chinese, immigrant Chinese, and Caucasian-American parents. In this study, mothers and fathers who were living in Taiwan, who had immigrated from Taiwan to the United States, and who were Caucasian-American citizens were asked to rate their parenting styles. Both groups of Chinese parents emphasized control to a greater extent than did Caucasian-American parents. (Adapted from Lin & Fu, 1990.)*

Although wide variation among African-American families exists, research suggests that black mothers tend to rely on an adult-centered approach in which they expect immediate obedience from children. This trend is stronger for mothers who are younger, less educated, less involved in organized religion, and rearing their children alone (Kelley, Power, & Wimbush, 1992). Strict demands for compliance, however, make sense under certain conditions. When parents have few social supports and live in dangerous neighborhoods, forceful discipline may be necessary to protect children from becoming victims of crime or involved in antisocial activities (Ogbu, 1985).

The family structure and child-rearing customs of certain ethnic minorities buffer the stress and disorganization that result from living in poverty. A case in point is the African-American family, which has managed to survive generations of extreme economic deprivation and racism. A far greater percentage of American black than white children live in poverty, and a greater percentage also experience the strain of parental divorce, widowhood, and out-of-wedlock teenage pregnancy (Children's Defense Fund, 1996). As the Cultural Influences box on the following page indicates, the African cultural tradition of **extended-family households**, in which one or more adult relatives live with the parent-child **nuclear family unit**, is a vital feature of African-American family life that has enabled its members to survive and, in some instances, overcome highly adverse social conditions. Active and involved extended families also characterize other ethnic minorities, such as Asian-American, Native American, and Hispanic groups (Harrison et al., 1994). These families illustrate the remarkable ability of the family unit to use its cultural traditions to support its members under conditions of high life stress.

BRIEF REVIEW

Child-rearing practices can be organized along two dimensions: demandingness and responsiveness. When combined, these characteristics yield four parenting styles: authoritative, authoritarian, permissive, and uninvolved. The authoritative style is linked to many aspects of competence; children experiencing uninvolved child rearing fare least well. Because authoritative parents make reasonable demands and are highly responsive to children's needs, they adapt to children's changing capacities. During middle childhood, effective parents engage in coregulation, a transitional form of supervision in which they exercise general oversight while granting children more decision-making power. In adolescence, warm, supportive parenting in which control is gradually relaxed in accord with adolescents' readiness for greater freedom fosters mature autonomy and positive adjustment.

Extended-family household
A household in which parent and child live with one or more adult relatives.

Nuclear family unit
The part of the family that consists of parents and their children.

CULTURAL INFLUENCES

The African-American Extended Family

The African-American extended family can be traced to the African heritage of most black Americans. In many African societies, newly married couples do not start their own households. Instead, they marry into a large extended family that assists its members with all aspects of daily life. This tradition of a broad network of kinship ties traveled to the United States during the period of slavery. Since then, it has served as a protective shield against the destructive impact of poverty and racial prejudice on African-American family life (McLoyd, 1990). Today, more black than white adults have relatives other than their own children living in the same household. African-American parents also see more kin during the week and perceive them as more important figures in their lives, respecting the advice of relatives and caring deeply about what they think is important (Wilson, 1986).

By providing emotional support and sharing income and essential resources, the African-American extended family helps reduce the stress of poverty and single parenthood. In addition, extended-family members often help with the rearing of children (Pearson et al., 1990). The presence of grandmothers in the households of many African-American teenagers and their infants protects babies from the negative influence of an overwhelmed and inexperienced mother. In one study, black grandmothers displayed more sensitive interaction with the babies of their teenage daughters than did the teenage mothers themselves. The grandmothers also provided basic information about infant development to these young mothers (Stevens, 1984). Furthermore, black adolescent mothers living in extended families are more likely to complete high school and get a job and less likely to be on welfare than mothers living on their own—factors that return to benefit children's well-being (Furstenberg & Crawford, 1978).

For single mothers who were very young at the time of their child's birth, extended family living continues to be associated with more positive adult–child interaction during the preschool years. Otherwise, establishing an independent household with the help of nearby relatives is related to improved child rearing. Perhaps this arrangement permits the more mature mother who has developed effective parenting skills to implement them (Chase-Lansdale, Brooks-Gunn, & Zamsky, 1994). In families with adolescents, kinship support increases the likelihood of authoritative parenting, which, in turn, is related to self-reliance, emotional well-being, and reduced delinquency (Taylor & Roberts, 1995).

Finally, the African-American extended family plays an important role in transmitting black cultural values to children. Compared to African-American nuclear families, extended-family arrangements place more emphasis on cooperation and moral and religious values (Tolson & Wilson, 1990). Older black adults, such as grandparents and great grandparents, are also more likely to possess a strong ethnic identity and to regard educating children about their African heritage as an important part of socialization (Thornton & Taylor, 1988). These influences strengthen family bonds, protect children's development, and increase the chances that the extended-family lifestyle will carry over to the next generation.

■ *Strong bonds with extended-family members have helped to protect the development of many African-American children growing up under conditions of poverty and single parenthood. (Karen Kasmauski/Woodfin Camp & Associates)*

The authoritative style is the most common pattern of child rearing around the world. Nevertheless, consistent social-class differences exist: Low-income parents tend to be more coercive, whereas middle-income parents use more warmth, explanations, and inductive discipline. The constant stresses that accompany poverty undermine effective parenting and children's development. Ethnic variations in child rearing can be understood in terms of cultural values and the context in which families live.

Family Lifestyles and Transitions

Families in industrialized nations have become more pluralistic than ever before—a trend that has been particularly marked in the United States. Today, there are fewer births per family unit, more adults who want to adopt, and more lesbian and gay parents who are open about their sexual orientation. In addition, rapid transitions in family life over the past several decades—a dramatic rise in marital breakup, single-parent households, remarried parents, and employed mothers—have reshaped the family system.

In the following sections, we discuss these changes in the family, emphasizing how each affects family relationships and, ultimately, children's development. In reading about some of these shifts in family life, you may wonder, as many people do, whether the institution of the family is in a state of crisis. Anxiety over family disintegration is not new to our times. Family transitions have always existed; they are simply more numerous and visible today than in the past. Yet rapid social change has intensified pressures on the family. Throughout our discussion, we will see examples of the need for social policies that strengthen kin and community supports, which have sustained the family for centuries.

FROM LARGE TO SMALL FAMILIES

In the mid-1950s, the peak of the post-World War II baby boom, the average number of children in an American family was 3.8. After that time, the birth rate dropped steadily, until it reached 1.8 children per family in the early 1970s, where it remains today (U.S. Bureau of the Census, 1995). Compared to several decades ago, there are many more one- and two-child families, as well as more couples opting to have no children. Experts project that the birth rate will decrease further by the early part of the twenty-first century.

Family size has declined for several reasons. Improved contraception along with legalized abortion make the current period one of greater choice with respect to having children. Also, many more women are experiencing the economic and personal rewards of a career. A family size of one or two children is certainly more compatible with a woman's decision to divide her energies between work and family. Furthermore, more couples are delaying the birth of their first child until they are well established professionally and secure economically (see Chapter 3). Adults who postpone parenthood are likely to have fewer children. Finally, marital instability is another reason contemporary families are smaller. More couples today get divorced before their childbearing plans are complete.

■ **FAMILY SIZE AND PARENT–CHILD INTERACTION.** Overall, a smaller family size has positive effects on parent–child interaction. Parents who have fewer children are more patient and use less punishment. They also have more time to devote to each child's activities, schoolwork, and other special needs. Furthermore, in smaller families, siblings are more likely to be widely spaced (born more than 2 years apart), which adds to the attention and resources parents can invest in each child. Together, these findings may account for the fact that children who grow up in smaller families have somewhat higher intelligence test scores, do better in school, and attain higher levels of education (Blake, 1989; Grant, 1994).

Children's problem behavior also varies with family size. Parents of one or two children sometimes pressure their youngsters too much. As a result, anxiety is more common in small families. In contrast, coercive discipline and reduced supervision probably contribute to higher rates of antisocial behavior and delinquency in families with many children (Wagner, Schubert, & Schubert, 1985).

However, these findings require an important qualification. Large families are usually less well off economically than smaller ones are. Factors associated with low income—crowded housing, poor nutrition, and parental stress—may be responsible for the negative relationship between family size and children's well-being. Indeed, evidence supports this idea. In a study of black South African families experiencing economic hardship, parents who were able to provide greater residential stability and less crowded living quarters had children who were developing more favorably—physically, cognitively, emotionally, and socially (Goduka, Poole, & Aotaki-Phenice, 1992). Furthermore, when children grow up in large, well-to-do families, the unfavorable outcomes typically associated with large family size are reduced (but not eliminated) (Powell & Steelman, 1993).

■ GROWING UP WITH SIBLINGS. Despite a smaller family size than in generations past, 80 percent of American children grow up with at least one sibling. Siblings exert important influences on development, both directly, through relationships with each other, and indirectly, through the effects an additional child has on the behavior of parents. In previous chapters, we examined some consequences of having brothers and sisters, including effects on intelligence, language development, personality, self and social understanding, and gender typing. Now let's look more closely at the quality of the sibling relationship itself.

Emergence of Sibling Relationships. When adults think of sibling ties, images of rivalry often come to mind—brothers and sisters competing for a fair share of parental attention and material resources. The common assumption that jealousy is a key element in sibling interaction originated with psychoanalytic theory, which stressed that each child desires to monopolize the parents' love. Today we know that conflict is only one feature of a rich emotional relationship that starts to build between siblings after a baby's birth.

Longitudinal research on the early development of sibling ties shows that a drop in maternal involvement with the older preschool child occurs after the birth of a baby. As a result, jealousy is often an element in the firstborn's feelings toward the new arrival. Many young children respond by becoming demanding and clingy for a time and engaging in instances of deliberate naughtiness. But positive expressions of affection and concern for the infant also occur. By the end of the baby's first year, siblings have become salient social partners. Preschoolers comfort, share toys with, imitate, and express friendliness toward the infant in addition to anger and ambivalence. During the second year, the younger sibling often imitates the firstborn child. Already, older children have become influential agents of socialization for their brothers and sisters (Dunn & Kendrick, 1982).

Because of their frequency and emotional intensity, sibling interactions become unique contexts in which social competence expands. Between their second and fourth birthdays, younger siblings take a more active role in play. As a result, sibling conversations increase, and their content differs from parent–child interaction. Mothers' statements typically emphasize caregiving and control—for example, providing comforting words, acknowledging children's hurts and fears, and referring to feelings as a way of stopping inappropriate behavior. In contrast, siblings talk more about emotions in playful or humorous ways and call attention to their own wants and needs when conflicts arise (Brown & Dunn, 1992). At least when they are close in age, siblings relate to each other on a more equal footing, much like peers. As a result, the skills acquired during sibling interaction probably contribute to perspective taking, moral maturity, and competence in relating to other children outside the home. In support of this idea positive sibling ties consistently predict favorable adjustment, even among hostile children at risk for social difficulties (Dunn et al., 1994; Stormshak et al., 1996)

Wide individual differences in the quality of sibling relationships appear in the first few weeks after the second child's birth that remain modestly stable from early into middle childhood (Dunn, 1989, 1992). In Chapter 10, we noted that children's temperament affects how positive or conflict-ridden sibling interaction will be. Sibling relationships are also influenced by parental behavior. In one study, mothers who were more positive and playful with a new baby sparked feelings of rivalry in the older child, who acted less friendly toward the infant. In contrast, when mothers were tired and depressed after a second birth, a warm and caring sibling relationship often emerged that seemed to compensate for the mother's withdrawal (Dunn & Kendrick, 1982). Other research reveals that secure infant–mother attachment and warm parenting toward both children predict positive sibling interaction. Cold, intrusive child rearing is associated with sibling antagonism (Stocker & McHale, 1992; Volling & Belsky, 1992). Once established, this match between parent–child and sibling relationships is self-sustaining. Warm parenting fosters considerate sibling interaction, which prompts positive parental behavior in the future. When parents are hostile and coercive, aggression is promoted among all family members (see Chapter 12).

Sibling Relationships in Middle Childhood and Adolescence. During middle childhood, sibling conflict tends to increase. As children participate in a wider range of activities, parents often compare siblings' traits, abilities, and accomplishments. When these evaluations are communicated to children, they heighten sibling rivalry. The child who gets less parental attention, more disapproval, and fewer material resources is likely to express resentment toward a sibling granted more favorable treatment (Brody, Stoneman, & McCoy, 1994; Boer, Goedhart, & Treffers, 1992). In several studies, researchers observed mothers and fathers interacting with their school-age children and then watched the siblings play together. Unequal treatment by both mothers and fathers predicted sibling conflict, but the effect was stronger for fathers. Perhaps because fathers spend less time with children, their favoritism may be more noticeable, thereby triggering greater anger during sibling interactions (Brody, Stoneman, & McCoy, 1992; Brody et al., 1992).

■ *Although sibling rivalry tends to increase in middle childhood, siblings also provide one another with emotional support and help with difficult tasks. (Erika Stone)*

Although conflict rises during the school years, siblings continue to rely on each other for companionship, emotional support, and assistance with everyday tasks. Because of the uniqueness of the sibling relationship, older siblings provide a more effective scaffold for children's learning than do older familiar peers. When researchers had either a sibling or a good friend of the sibling teach a younger child how to build a windmill out of small, interlocking pieces, siblings provided more explanations and encouragement and gave the child more control over the task than did older peers. In part, this occurred because younger children observed, imitated, consulted, asked for explanations, and exerted pressure for task control to a greater extent with siblings. As a result, children taught by siblings performed considerably better on the task (Azmitia & Hesser, 1993).

Like parent–child relationships, sibling interactions adapt to development at adolescence. As younger children mature and become more self-sufficient, they are no longer willing to accept as much direction from their brothers and sisters. Consequently, older siblings' influence declines during the teenage years. Does this mean that quarreling between siblings increases at this time? Usually not. Sibling interaction becomes less intense during adolescence, in both positive and negative feelings. As teenagers become more involved in friendships and romantic partnerships, they invest less time and energy in sibling relationships. Also, adolescents may not want to depend as much on siblings, who are part of the family from which they are trying to establish autonomy (Furman & Buhrmester, 1992; Stocker & Dunn, 1994).

Despite a drop in companionship, attachment between siblings, like closeness to parents, remains strong for most young people. One large survey of high school students found that 77 percent regarded siblings as major influences in their lives (Blyth, Hill, & Thiel, 1982). The quality of sibling interaction at adolescence continues to be affected by other relationships, both within and outside the family. Teenagers whose parents are warm and supportive have more positive sibling ties (Brody et al., 1992). And for children who have difficulty making friends at school, a gratifying sibling relationship can provide compensating emotional supports (East & Rook, 1992).

ONE-CHILD FAMILIES

Without a chance to experience the closeness and conflicts of sibling relationships, are children born into one-child families disadvantaged in development? Many people think so. Parents of only children often report that relatives and friends pressure them to have a second, believing that an only child is destined to be spoiled, self-centered, and selfish. This stereotype has been strengthened by the child-rearing advice of experts, which can be traced as far back as 1907, when G. Stanley Hall remarked, "Being an only child is a disease in itself" (Fenton, 1928, p. 547).

Research indicates that sibling relationships bring many benefits, but they are not essential for healthy development. Only children are as socially competent as

TABLE 14.3

Advantages and Disadvantages of a One-Child Family

Advantages		Disadvantages	
Mentioned By Parents	**Mentioned By Children**	**Mentioned By Parents**	**Mentioned By Children**
Having time to pursue one's own interests and career	Avoiding sibling rivalry	Walking a "tightrope" between healthy attention and overindulgence	Not getting to experience the closeness of a sibling relationship
Less financial pressure	Having more privacy	Having only one chance to "make good" as a parent	Feeling too much pressure from parents to succeed
Not having to worry about "playing favorites" among children	Enjoying greater affluence	Being left childless in case of the child's death	Having no one to help care for parents when they get old
	Having a closer parent–child relationship		

Source: Hawke & Knox, 1978.

other children, and they are advantaged in self-esteem and achievement motivation. Consequently, they do better in school and attain higher levels of education (Falbo, 1992). One reason for these trends may be that only children have somewhat closer relationships with their parents, who exert more pressure for mastery and accomplishment. As long as these demands are not unreasonable, they seem to have positive effects on development (Falbo & Polit, 1986).

Are these findings restricted to Western industrialized countries, where family size is a matter of individual choice? The People's Republic of China has a rigid family policy in which urban couples are given strong economic incentives to have no more than one child. Limited to a single offspring, are Chinese parents rearing a new generation of children with indulgence, making Hall's pronouncement a reality? Refer to the Cultural Influences box on the following page, and you will see that Chinese only children differ very little from their Western counterparts.

Nevertheless, the one-child family has both pros and cons, as does every family lifestyle. In a survey in which only children and their parents were asked what they liked and disliked about living in a single-child family, each mentioned a set of advantages and disadvantages, which are summarized in Table 14.3. The list is useful for Western parents to consider when deciding how many children would best fit their own personal and family life plans.

ADOPTIVE FAMILIES

Today, infertile couples as well as older, single individuals who want a family are turning to adoption in increasing numbers. At the same time, the availability of healthy babies has declined, since fewer young, unwed mothers give up their infants than did in the past (see Chapter 5). Consequently, more people are adopting from foreign countries that have an abundance of unwanted babies. Also, adoption agencies often try to get people to consider older children or children with physical and psychological problems who are badly in need of permanent homes. Over half of prospective parents modify their adoption goals and take one of these youngsters (Schaffer & Kral, 1988).

Although adoptive families are highly diverse, they face common challenges. Waiting many years for parenthood and having no control over when they will get a child leads some people to question their entitlement to be parents, including their right to use firm discipline. And different heredity means that adoptive parents and children are less alike in intelligence and personality than are biological relatives—resemblances that contribute to family harmony. Partly for these reasons, adopted youngsters have more emotional and learning difficulties than do their nonadopted agemates in childhood and adolescence (Verhulst, Althaus, & Versluis-Den Bieman, 1990; Verhulst & Versluis-Den Bieman, 1995).

Yet when we consider that many adopted children had poor prenatal care and stressful early lives, they fare surprisingly well. In a Swedish longitudinal study, researchers followed over 600 babies who were candidates for adoption into adolescence and young adulthood. Some were adopted shortly after birth, some were reared by their biological

CULTURAL INFLUENCES

Only Children in the People's Republic of China

The People's Republic of China has 21 percent of the world's population but only 7 percent of its fertile land. In the late 1970s, the Central Committee of the Communist Party concluded that quality of life for China's citizens would not improve without drastic efforts to control its swelling population. In 1979, it implemented a one-child family policy by encouraging young people to marry late, offering public education about birth control, and providing economic incentives—health care funds, a monetary bonus at the child's birth, and a monthly subsidy until age 14 for only children. As a result, a profound generational change occurred. Although the majority of adults of childbearing age had siblings, most of their children did not. By 1985, 80 to 90 percent of babies born in urban areas and 50 to 60 percent born in rural regions were only children (Tseng et al., 1988).

Critics of the policy complained that it might ruin the character of the Chinese people. In a culture where the most valued qualities in children are good behavior and the ability to get along well with others, media reports predicted that parents and grandparents would engage in pampering and spoiling, causing children to behave like "little emperors" (Falbo, 1992). Researchers soon began to investigate the development of China's new generation of children.

Toni Falbo and Dudly Poston (1993) have conducted the most comprehensive study of the characteristics of Chinese only and non-only children to date. They selected a representative sample of 4,000 third and sixth graders, 1,000 from each of four provinces, each geographically distinct and containing a highly diverse population. The older pupils had been born before implementation of the one-child family policy, the younger pupils afterward. All took verbal and mathematical achievement tests. Parent, teacher, peer, and self-ratings on a variety of attributes provided a measure of personality, which was specially designed to tap the "little emperor" syndrome—whether children were selfish, dependent, uncooperative, and disrespectful of their elders. Finally, children's height and weight were measured to see if the new policy was associated with improved physical development.

Much like findings in Western nations, Chinese only children were advanced in academic achievement. In three of the four provinces, they outscored non-only children in verbal skills. Although differences were less clear in math, only children never scored lower than first and last borns, and they usually did better than at least one of these groups. Only children had few distinguishing personality characteristics. And in two of the provinces, they were physically larger than their classmates. The economic benefits parents received from limiting family size may have resulted in better nutrition and health for children.

Other investigators have focused on fear, anxiety, and depression, based on the assumption that in families where parents want more children, only children might suffer emotionally. Yet only children actually report less distress than do children with siblings (Yang et al., 1995). Why is this so? Perhaps government condemnation promotes tension and unhappiness in families with more than one child. Informal observations suggest that this attitude has spread to children's peer relations. When a dispute arises, only children can sometimes be heard commenting to playmates with siblings: "You shouldn't have been born!" "Your parents should have only one child!"

In sum, Chinese only children seem to be developing as well or better than their counterparts with siblings. Why are so many Chinese adults convinced that only children are "little emperors?" When rapid social change takes place, people used to different conditions may regard the new lifestyle as a threat to the social order. In the case of the one-child family policy, they may incorrectly assume that lack of siblings is the cause of children's difficulties, failing to consider that the large number of only children in China today guarantees that they will dominate *both* success and failure groups.

This mural reminds citizens that limiting family size is a basic national policy in the People's Republic of China. In urban areas, the majority of couples have no more than one child. (Owen Franken/Stock Boston)

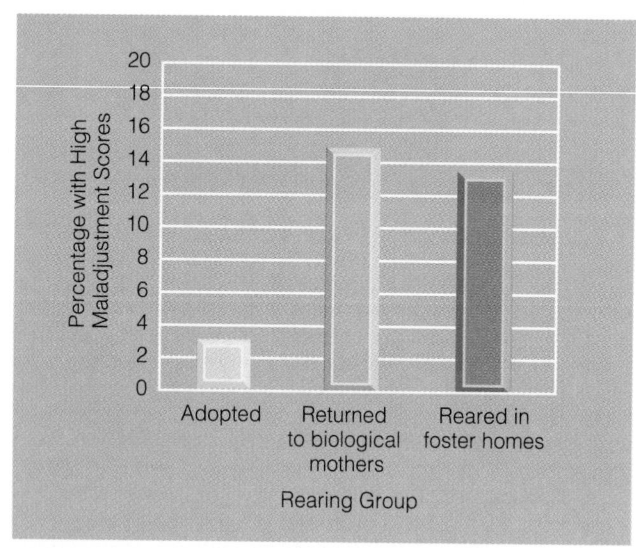

FIGURE 14.3

■ *Percentage of 15-year-olds with high maladjustment scores who were adopted, placed in foster homes, or returned to their biological mothers shortly after birth in a Swedish longitudinal study. All adolescents had been candidates for adoption when they were born. Compared to the other two groups, adopted young people were rated by teachers as having far fewer problems, including anxiety, withdrawal, aggression, inability to concentrate, peer difficulties, and poor school motivation. (Adapted from Bohman & Sigvardsson, 1990.)*

mothers who changed their minds about giving them up, and some were reared in foster homes. As Figure 14.3 shows, adoptees developed much more favorably than children returned to their birth mothers or reared in foster families (Bohman & Sigvardsson, 1990). Furthermore, when children with special needs are adopted at older ages, they usually benefit. From 70 to 80 percent of their parents report high satisfaction with the adoptive experience—a rate that equals that of families adopting healthy infants (Rosenthal, 1992).

By adolescence, adoptees' lives are often complicated by unresolved curiosity about their roots. Some have difficulty accepting the possibility that they may never know their birth parents. Others worry about what they would do if their birth parents suddenly appeared. Nevertheless, the decision to search out birth parents is usually postponed until young adulthood, when marriage and childbirth may trigger it (Schaffer & Kral, 1988). Despite concerns about their origins, most adoptees appear optimistic and well adjusted as adults. By that time, the higher rate of problem behavior evident in childhood disappears. Furthermore, young people who were transracially or transculturally adopted typically develop identities that are healthy blends of their birth and rearing backgrounds (Simon, Altstein, & Melli, 1994).

Clearly, adoption is a satisfying family alternative for most parents and children who experience it. The outcomes are good because of careful pairing of children with parents and guidance provided adoptive families by well-trained social service professionals.

■ *Homosexual parents are as committed to and effective at child rearing as heterosexual parents. Their children are well adjusted, and the large majority develop a heterosexual orientation. (Mark Richards/PhotoEdit)*

GAY AND LESBIAN FAMILIES

Several million American gay men and lesbians are parents, most through previous heterosexual marriages, a few through adoption or reproductive technologies (Hare, 1994). In the past, laws assuming that homosexuals could not be adequate parents led those who divorced a heterosexual partner to lose custody of their children. Today, several states hold that sexual orientation is irrelevant to custody, but in others, fierce prejudice against homosexual parents still prevails.

Families headed by a homosexual parent or a gay or lesbian couple are very similar to those of heterosexuals. Gay and lesbian parents are as committed to and effective at the parental role, and sometimes more so. Indeed, some research indicates that gay fathers are more consistent in setting limits and more responsive to their children's needs than are heterosexual fathers, perhaps because gay men's less traditional gender-role identity fosters involvement with children (Bigner & Jacobsen, 1989a, 1989b). Children of gay and lesbian parents are as well adjusted as other children, and the large majority are heterosexual (Bailey et al., 1995; Flaks et al., 1995; Golombok & Tasker, 1996).

When extended family members have difficulty accepting them, homosexual mothers and fathers often build "families of choice" through friends who assume functions traditionally expected of relatives. But most of the time, parents of gays and lesbians cannot endure a permanent rift. With the passage of time, interactions of homosexual parents with their families of origin become more positive and serve as effective supports in the rearing of children (Hare, 1994; Lewin, 1993).

Partners of homosexual parents usually take on some caregiving responsibilities and are attached to the children. But their involvement varies with the way children were brought into the relationship. When children were adopted or conceived through reproductive technologies, partners tend to be more involved than when children resulted from a previous heterosexual relationship (Hare & Richards, 1993). In a few instances, homosexual partners become joint legal parents of children, an arrangement that enhances family stability (Green & Bozett, 1991).

Overall, children of homosexuals can be distinguished from other children only by issues related to living in a nonsupportive society. The greatest concern of gay and lesbian parents is that their children will be stigmatized by their parents' sexual orientation (Hare, 1994; Lewin, 1993).

DIVORCE

Parental separation and divorce are extremely common in the lives of American children. Between 1960 and 1980, the divorce rate in the United States tripled and then stabilized. Currently, it is the highest in the world (see Figure 14.4). Over 1 million American children experience the separation and divorce of their parents each year. At any given time, about one-fourth of the child population lives in single-parent households. Although the large majority (85 percent) reside with their mothers, the number in father-headed households has increased over the past decade, from 9 to 15 percent (Meyer & Garasky, 1993).

Children spend an average of 5 years in a single-parent home, or almost a third of their total childhood. For many, divorce eventually leads to new family relationships. Two-thirds to three-fourths of divorced parents marry a second time. Half of these children eventually experience a third major change in their family lives—the end of their parents' second marriage (Hetherington & Jodl, 1994).

These figures reveal that divorce is not a single event in the lives of parents and children. Instead, it is a transition that leads to a variety of new living arrangements, accompanied by changes in housing, income, and family roles and responsibilities (Hetherington, 1995). Although marital breakup is quite stressful for children, great variation exists in how children respond. Among the factors that make a difference are the custodial parent's psychological well-being, the child's characteristics, and social supports within the family and surrounding community. Our knowledge has been enriched by several longitudinal studies that have tracked children over many years as well as many short-term investigations. As we look at the impact of divorce, you may find it helpful to refer to the summary in Table 14.4.

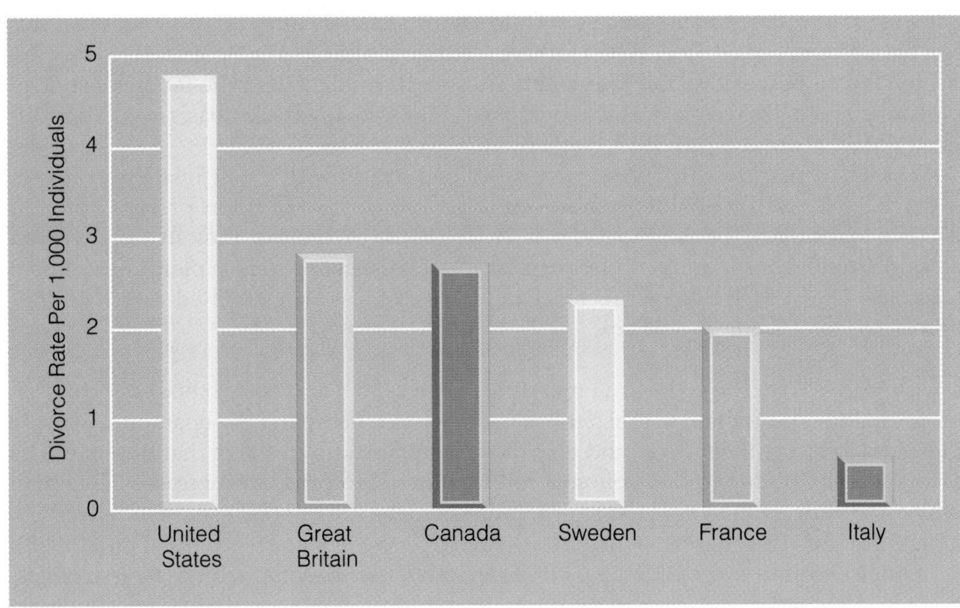

FIGURE 14.4

Divorce rate in six industrialized nations. The divorce rate in the United States is the highest in the world. (Adapted from McKenry & Price, 1995.)

TABLE 14.4

Factors Related to Children's Adjustment to Divorce

Factor	Description
Custodial parents' psychological health	A mature, well-adjusted parent is better able to handle stress, shield the child from conflict, and engage in authoritative parenting.
Child characteristics	
Age	Preschool and early elementary school children often blame themselves and show intense separation anxiety. Older children may also react strongly by engaging in disruptive, antisocial acts. However, some display unusually mature, responsible behavior.
Temperament	Children with difficult temperaments are less able to withstand stress and show longer-lasting difficulties.
Sex	Boys in mother-custody homes experience more severe and longer-lasting problems than do girls.
Social supports	The ability of divorced parents to set aside their hostilities, contact with the noncustodial parent, and positive relationships with extended family members, teachers, and friends lead to improved outcomes for children.

■ IMMEDIATE CONSEQUENCES. The period surrounding divorce is often accompanied by a rise in family conflict as parents try to settle disputes over finances, personal belongings, and child custody. Once one parent moves out, additional events threaten the parent–child relationship. Mother-headed households typically experience a sharp drop in income. Many divorced women lack the education and experience needed for well-paid jobs. Furthermore, half of those supposed to receive child support from the absent father get less than the full amount or none at all (Children's Defense Fund, 1996). Divorced mothers often have to move to new housing for economic reasons, reducing supportive ties to neighbors and friends. When those who were homemakers must find immediate employment, young children are likely to experience inadequate child care while the mother is away and a distracted, unavailable parent while she is at home (Emery & Forehand, 1994; Nelson, 1993).

These life circumstances often lead to a highly disorganized family situation called "minimal parenting." Predictable events and routines—scheduled mealtimes and bedtimes, household chores, and joint parent–child activities—usually disintegrate. As children react with distress and anger to their less secure home lives, discipline may become harsh and inconsistent as mothers try to recapture control of their upset youngsters. Fathers usually spend more time with children immediately after divorce, but often this contact decreases over time. When fathers see their children only occasionally, they are inclined to be permissive and indulgent. This often conflicts with the mother's style of parenting and makes her task of managing the child on a day-to-day basis even more difficult (Furstenberg & Nord, 1985; Hetherington, Cox, & Cox, 1982).

The child-rearing difficulties just described are probably not just the result of divorce, since conflict-ridden parent–child relationships are often present before a divorce takes place (Shaw, Emery, & Tuer, 1993). Nevertheless, they usually worsen around the time of separation. Not surprisingly, children experience painful emotional reactions. The intensity of their feelings and the way these are expressed vary with children's age, temperament, and sex.

Children's Age. The cognitive immaturity of preschool and early school-age children makes it difficult for them to grasp the reasons behind their parents' separation. Because they tend to blame themselves and take the marital breakup as a sign that they could be abandoned by both parents, younger children are often profoundly upset. They may whine and cling, displaying intense separation anxiety. Preschoolers are especially likely to fantasize that their parents will get back together (Wallerstein, Corbin, & Lewis, 1988).

Older children are better able to understand the reasons behind their parents' divorce. They recognize that strong differences of opinion, incompatible personalities, and lack of caring for one another are responsible (Mazur, 1993). The ability to accurately assign blame may reduce some of the pain children feel. Still, many school-age and adolescent youngsters react strongly to the end of their parents' marriage. Particularly when family conflict is high, they are likely to display adjustment difficulties (Borrine et al., 1991; Forehand et al., 1991). Undesirable peer activities that provide an escape from unpleasant home lives, such as running away, truancy, early sexual activity, and delinquent behavior, are common (Doherty & Needle, 1991; Tasker & Richards, 1994).

However, not all older children react this way. For some—especially the oldest child in the family—divorce can trigger more mature behavior. They may willingly take on extra burdens, such as household tasks, care and protection of younger siblings, and emotional support of a depressed, anxious mother. But if these demands are too great, older children may eventually become resentful and withdraw from the family into some of the more destructive behavior patterns just described (Hetherington, 1995; Wallerstein & Kelly, 1980).

Children's Temperament and Sex. In earlier chapters, we noted that temperament can either reduce or increase children's risk for maladjustment. When temperamentally difficult children are exposed to stressful life events and inadequate parenting, their problems are likely to be compounded. In contrast, easy children are less often targets of parental impatience and anger and are also better able to cope with adversity when it hits.

These findings help us understand sex-related differences in children's response to divorce. Girls sometimes show internalizing reactions, such as crying, self-criticism, and withdrawal. More often, they display some demanding, attention-getting behavior. But in mother-custody families, boys experience more serious adjustment difficulties. Recall from Chapter 13 that boys are more active, assertive, and noncompliant than girls to begin with. These behaviors escalate when boys encounter parental conflict and inconsistent discipline (Hetherington, Cox, & Cox, 1982). Longitudinal research in Great Britain and the United States reveals that many sons of divorcing couples were impulsive and undercontrolled long before the marital breakup—behaviors that may have contributed to as well as been caused by their parents' marital problems. As a result, these boys entered the period of family turmoil surrounding divorce with a reduced capacity to cope with family stress (Cherlin et al., 1991; Elliott & Richards, 1991; Hetherington, 1991).

Perhaps because their behavior is so unruly, boys of divorcing parents receive less emotional support and are viewed more negatively by mothers, teachers, and peers. Furthermore, the coercive cycles of interaction that boys often establish with their divorced mothers soon spread to sibling relations. In mother–custody families with sons, quarreling, teasing, hitting, and other negative behaviors toward siblings increase (Baldwin & Skinner, 1989; MacKinnon, 1989). These outcomes compound boys' difficulties. Children of both sexes show declines in achievement during the aftermath of divorce, but school problems are greater for boys (Guidubaldi & Cleminshaw, 1985).

■ LONG-TERM CONSEQUENCES. The majority of children show improved adjustment by 2 years after divorce. Yet a few show persisting emotional distress and declines in school achievement that contribute to serious adjustment difficulties into young adulthood (Chase-Lansdale, Cherlin, & Kiernan, 1995).

Because they are more often exposed to ineffective child rearing, boys and children with difficult temperaments are especially likely to experience lasting behavior problems (Hetherington & Clingempeel, 1992). Among girls, the most consistent long-term consequences have to do with heterosexual behavior—a rise in sexual activity at adolescence, a higher rate of out-of-wedlock births, short-lived sexual relationships in early adulthood, and lack of self-confidence in associations with men (Cherlin, Kiernan, & Chase-Lansdale, 1995; Wallerstein & Corbin, 1989).

The overriding factor in positive adjustment following divorce is effective parenting—in particular, how well the custodial parent handles stress, shields the child from family conflict, and engages in authoritative parenting (Buchanan, Maccoby, & Dornbusch, 1991). Contact with noncustodial fathers is also important. For girls, a good father–child relationship appears to contribute to healthy heterosexual development. For boys, it seems to play a crucial role in overall psychological well-being. In fact, several

■ *Contact with noncustodial fathers is important in children's adjustment to divorce. This divorced father and his daughter enjoy an especially warm relationship during visitation periods—a circumstance that will contribute to her long-term psychological well-being. (David Young-Wolf/PhotoEdit)*

studies reveal that outcomes for sons are better when the father is the custodial parent (Camara & Resnick, 1988; Santrock & Warshak, 1986). Fathers are more likely than mothers to praise a boy's good behavior and less likely to ignore his disruptiveness (Hetherington, Cox, & Cox, 1982). The father's image of greater power and authority may also help him obtain more compliance from a son. Furthermore, boys whose fathers maintain frequent contact have more opportunities to identify with and adopt their father's self-controlled behavior.

Although divorce is painful for children, those who remain in a stressed, intact family are more poorly adjusted than those who have weathered the stormy transition to a single-parent family and are living in low-conflict households (Block, Block, & Gjerde, 1988; Hetherington, Cox, & Cox, 1982). Children whose divorcing parents put aside their disagreements and support each other in their parenting roles have the best chance of growing up competent, stable, and happy. When parental cooperation is not possible, caring extended family members, positive sibling relationships, and warm friendships can reduce the likelihood that divorce will result in long-term disruption (Hetherington, 1995; Jenkins & Smith, 1990).

Schools can also make a difference. Cognitive and social outcomes are improved if preschool and school-age children attend classrooms in which teachers provide consistent structure and create a democratic atmosphere in which warmth is combined with reasonable demands for mature behavior (Hetherington, Cox, & Cox, 1982; Peres & Pasternack, 1991). Note that these are the very ingredients of good parenting associated with favorable adjustment in intact families. Children of divorce clearly benefit from a nurturant, predictable school environment when these experiences are not available at home.

■ DIVORCE MEDIATION, JOINT CUSTODY, AND CHILD SUPPORT. Awareness that divorce is highly stressful for parents and children has led to community-based services aimed at helping them through this difficult time. Parents Without Partners is a national organization with a membership of 180,000. It provides publications, telephone referrals, and programs through local chapters designed to relieve the problems of single parents. Support groups for children are also available, often sponsored by churches, synagogues, schools, and mental health agencies, in which fears and concerns are shared and coping skills are taught. Evaluations of the effectiveness of these programs suggest that they can reduce stress and promote improved communication among family members (Emery, 1988).

Divorce mediation
A series of meetings between divorcing adults and a trained professional, who tries to help them settle disputes. Aimed at avoiding legal battles that intensify family conflict.

Another recently developed intervention is **divorce mediation**. It consists of a series of meetings between divorcing adults and a trained professional, who tries to help them settle disputes, such as property division and child custody. Its purpose is to avoid legal battles that intensify family conflict. In some states, divorce mediation is voluntary. In others, it must be attempted before a case is heard by a judge. Research reveals that it increases out-of-court settlements, compliance with agreements, and feelings of well-being among divorcing parents. Because it reduces family hostilities, divorce mediation probably benefits children, although little research has addressed this issue directly (Emery & Wyer, 1987; Emery, Mathews, & Kitzmann, 1994).

A relatively new child custody option tries to keep both parents involved with children. In **joint custody**, the court grants the mother and father equal say in important decisions about the child's upbringing. Yet many experts have raised questions about the practice. Joint custody results in a variety of living arrangements. In most instances, children reside with one parent and see the other on a fixed schedule, much like the typical sole custody situation. But in other cases, parents share physical custody, and children must move between homes and sometimes school and peers as well. These transitions introduce a new kind of instability that may be especially hard on some children (Johnston, Kline, & Tschann, 1989). The success of joint custody requires a cooperative relationship between divorcing parents. If they continue to quarrel, it prolongs children's exposure to a hostile family atmosphere (Furstenberg & Cherlin, 1991). See the Social Issues box on page 565 for an additional legal practice that poses similar risks to children's well-being.

Finally, many single-parent families depend on child support from the absent parent to relieve financial strain. In response to a recent federal law, all states have established procedures for withholding wages from parents who fail to make these court-ordered payments. Although child support is usually not enough to lift a single-parent family out of poverty, it can ease its burdens substantially. An added benefit is that children are more likely to maintain contact with a noncustodial father if he pays child support (Stephen, Freedman, & Hess, 1993).

BLENDED FAMILIES

Life in a single-parent home is often a temporary condition. Many parents remarry within a few years. Others *cohabit*, or share an intimate sexual relationship and a residence with a partner outside of marriage. Some cohabiting couples eventually marry and some do not. In either case, parent, stepparent, and children form a new family structure called the **blended**, or **reconstituted, family** (Bumpass, Raley, & Sweet, 1995).

For some children, this expanded family network is a positive turn of events that brings with it greater adult attention. But for most, it presents difficult adjustments. Stepparents often use different child-rearing practices than the child is used to, and having to switch to new rules and expectations can be stressful. In addition, children often regard steprelatives as "intruders" into the family (Hetherington & Jodl, 1994). Indeed, their arrival does change interaction with the natural parent. But how well children adapt is, once again, related to the overall quality of family functioning. This varies depending on which parent forms a new relationship and the age and sex of the child. As we will see, older children and girls seem to have the hardest time (see Table 14.5).

■ MOTHER/STEPFATHER FAMILIES. The most frequent form of blended family is a mother/stepfather arrangement, since mothers generally retain custody of the child. Under these conditions, boys usually adjust well. They welcome a stepfather who is warm and involved, who refrains from exerting his authority too quickly, and who offers relief from the coercive cycles of interaction that tend to build with their divorced mothers. Mothers' friction with sons also declines for other reasons—greater economic security, another adult to share child care and household tasks, and an end to loneliness. One study found that less than 2 years after remarriage, boys living in mother/stepfather households were doing almost as well as those in nondivorced families (Hetherington, Cox, & Cox, 1985). In contrast, girls adapt less favorably when custodial mothers find new partners. Stepfathers disrupt the close ties many girls established with their mothers in a single-parent family, and girls often react to the new arrangement with sulky, resistant behavior (Hetherington, 1993; Vuchinich et al., 1991).

Note, however, that age affects these findings. Early adolescents of both sexes find it harder to adjust to blended families (Bray & Berger, 1993; Hetherington, 1993). Young teenagers are in the midst of dealing with their own budding sexuality and establishing autonomy. The presence of a stepparent may make these tasks more difficult. Further-

Joint custody
A child custody arrangement following divorce in which the court grants both parents equal say in important decisions about the child's upbringing.

Blended, or reconstituted, family
A family structure resulting from cohabitation or remarriage that includes parent, child, and steprelatives.

TABLE 14.5

Factors Related to Children's Adjustment to Blended Families

Factor	Description
Form of blended family	Children living in father/stepmother families display more adjustment difficulties than those in mother/stepfather families, perhaps because father-custody children start out with more problems.
Child characteristics	
Age	Early adolescents find it harder to adjust, perhaps because the presence of a stepparent makes it more difficult for them to deal with sexuality and autonomy. Also, compared to children, they are more aware of the impact of remarriage on their own lives.
Sex	Girls display more severe reactions than do boys because of interruptions in close bonds with custodial parents and greater conflict with stepmothers.
Repeated marital transitions	The more marital transitions, the greater the risk of severe and long-lasting adjustment problems.
Social supports	(See Table 14.4.)

more, because adolescents are more aware of the impact of remarriage on their own lives, they may challenge some aspects of it that children simply accept, creating more relationship issues with their steprelatives.

About one-third of adolescent boys and one-fourth of adolescent girls disengage from their stepfamilies, spending little time at home. Instead, they may turn to a friend's family as a "surrogate," extracurricular activities, a job, or peers. When disengagement leads to positive relationships with adults and constructive pursuits, teenagers fare quite well. When it results in involvement with antisocial peers and little adult supervision, it is linked to serious difficulties—poor achievement, school dropout, sexual activity, substance abuse, and delinquency (Hetherington & Jodl, 1994).

■ FATHER/STEPMOTHER FAMILIES. Although only a few studies have focused on father/stepmother families, research consistently reveals more confusion for children under these conditions. In the case of noncustodial fathers, remarriage often leads to reduced contact. They tend to withdraw from their "previous" families, more so if they have daughters rather than sons. When fathers have custody, children typically react negatively to remarriage. One reason is that children living with fathers often start out with more problems. Perhaps the biological mother could no longer handle the unruly child (usually a boy), so the father and his new wife are faced with a youngster who has serious behavior problems. In other instances, the father is granted custody because of a very close relationship with the child, and his remarriage disrupts this bond (Brand, Clingempeel, & Bowen-Woodward, 1988).

Girls, especially, have a hard time getting along with their stepmothers (Hobart & Brown, 1988). Sometimes (as just mentioned) this occurs because the girl's relationship with her father is threatened by the remarriage. In addition, girls often become entangled in loyalty conflicts between their two mother figures. Noncustodial mothers (unlike fathers) are likely to maintain regular contact with children, but frequent visits by mothers are associated with less favorable stepmother–stepdaughter relations. The longer girls live in father/stepmother households, the more positive their interaction with stepmothers becomes. With time and patience they do adjust, and eventually girls benefit from the support of a second mother figure (Brand, Clingempeel, & Bowen-Woodward, 1988).

■ SUPPORT FOR BLENDED FAMILIES. In blended families as in divorce, there are multiple pathways leading to diverse outcomes. Family life education and therapy can help parents and children adapt to the complexities of their new circumstances. Effective approaches encourage stepparents to move into their new roles gradually rather than abruptly. Only when a warm bond has formed between stepparents and stepchildren is

SOCIAL ISSUES ➤ POINT OF VIEW

Should Grandparents Be Awarded Visitation Rights After Parental Divorce?

Before the 1970s, grandparents did not have the right to petition the courts for visitation privileges with their grandchildren after parental separation and divorce. Legally mandated visitation was reserved for parents, who regulated grandparents' access to children. Although grandparent visitation cases occasionally reached the courts, judges were wary about granting these requests. They recognized that intense conflict between parents and grandparents lay behind most petitions and that it was not in the best interests of children to embroil them in intergenerational disputes (Derdeyn, 1985).

In recent years, a rising population of older Americans has led to a broadening of grandparents' rights. Interest groups representing senior citizens have convinced state legislators to support the grandparent–grandchild relationship during an era in which a high rate of marital breakup has threatened extended family ties. Today, all 50 states permit grandparents to seek legal visitation judgments (Bostock, 1994). The new policy is also motivated by a well-intentioned desire on the part of lawmakers to foster children's access to social supports within the family and widespread belief in the specialness of the grandparent–grandchild relationship. As we saw earlier in this chapter, grandparents can promote children's development in many ways—both directly, through their relationship with the child, and indirectly, by providing parents with child-rearing advice, models of child-rearing skill, and financial assistance.

Nevertheless, serious questions have been raised about legalizing children's ties to their grandparents. The most significant factor in how children's development is affected by interaction with grandparents is the quality of the grandparents' relationship with the children's parents. If it is positive, children are likely to benefit. But courtroom battles that turn parents and grandparents into adversaries may close the door to gains that would otherwise result from frequent grandparent–grandchild contact (Thompson et al., 1989). As one therapist observed, in families where parents are divorcing, the behavior of grandparents varies greatly, from constructive help to entanglement in parental battles and efforts to undermine the child's relationship with one and sometimes both parents (Derdeyn, 1985).

In sum, research suggests that the courts should exercise considerable restraint in awarding grandparent visitation rights in divorce cases. Yet statutes providing for grandparent visitation are expanding to include a broader range of circumstances, largely as a result of senior citizen pressure. More laws take the position that grandparents have rights of access to their grandchildren simply as a result of their status as grandparents. As evidence for this trend, in half the states, it is now possible for grandparents to petition for visitation with a child in an intact home (Bostock, 1994).

YOUR POINT OF VIEW . . .

- Visitation rights permit grandparents to seek court orders that limit parents' freedom to control some aspects of family life. How can this shift in power alter family relationships?
- In what ways should grandparent visitation statutes be limited so they protect the best interests of children? Should grandparents' previous and current relationships with family members be considered? How about the reason grandparents filed the petition?

more active parenting possible. In addition, couples often need help in forming a "parenting coalition"—cooperation and consistency in child rearing. By limiting loyalty conflicts, this allows children to benefit from stepparent relationships and increased diversity in their lives (Visher, 1994).

REPEATED MARITAL TRANSITIONS. Unfortunately, many children do not have a chance to settle into a happy blended family, since the divorce rate for second marriages is higher than for first marriages. In a study of fourth-grade boys, the more marital transitions children experienced, the more severe and prolonged their adjustment difficulties (see Figure 14.5 on page 566). Furthermore, parents with poor child-rearing skills and antisocial tendencies (as indicated by arrest records, drug use, and personality tests) were particularly likely to undergo several divorces and remarriages. In the process, they exposed their children to recurring episodes of high family conflict and inconsistent parenting (Capaldi & Patterson, 1991). When marital transitions pile up, they become part of a cluster of negative life events that severely disrupt children's development.

MATERNAL EMPLOYMENT

For many years, divorce has been associated with a high rate of maternal employment, due to financial strains experienced by mothers responsible for maintaining their own families. But over the last several decades, women of all sectors of the population—not just those who are single and poor—have gone to work in increasing numbers.

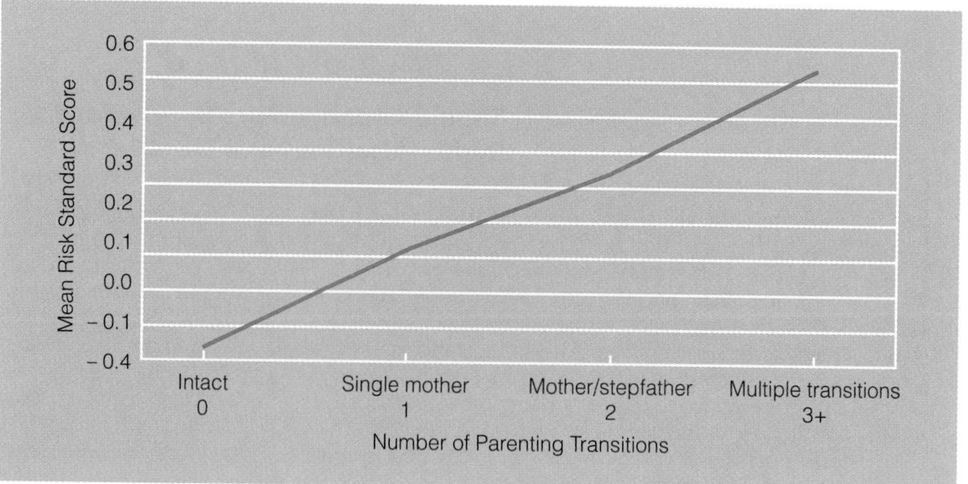

FIGURE 14.5

■ *Boys' risk for poor adjustment by number of parenting transitions. Risk was determined by averaging seven adjustment measures: antisocial behavior, drug use, deviant peer associations, peer rejection, poor academic skills, low self-esteem, and depression. The greater the number of transitions, the higher the risk score. (Adapted from Capaldi & Patterson, 1991.)*

Today, single and married mothers are in the labor market in nearly equal proportions. For children of any age, over 60 percent of their mothers are employed (U.S. Bureau of the Census, 1995).

In Chapter 10, we discussed the impact of maternal employment on infant–mother attachment and concluded that for babies, the consequences depend on the quality of day care and the continuing parent–child relationship. This same conclusion applies to development during later years. In addition, many studies agree that a host of factors—the mother's work satisfaction, the support she receives from her husband, the child's sex, and the social class of the family—have a bearing on whether children show benefits or problems from growing up in an employed-mother family.

■ *As long as this employed mother enjoys her job, remains committed to parenting, and finds satisfactory child care arrangements, her children are likely to develop high self-esteem, positive family and peer relations, and flexible beliefs about gender. And more daily hours spent to doing homework under parental guidance may be an important reason that children of employed mothers get better grades in school. (Michael Newman/PhotoEdit)*

■ MATERNAL EMPLOYMENT AND CHILD DEVELOPMENT. As long as mothers want to work, like their jobs, and have found satisfactory child care arrangements, employment is associated with greater life satisfaction for both low-income and middle-income mothers (Beyer, 1995; Goldberg & Easterbrooks, 1988). Children of mothers who enjoy working and remain committed to parenting show especially positive adjustment—a higher sense of self-esteem, more positive family and peer relations, less gender-stereotyped beliefs, and better grades in school (Hoffman, 1989; Williams & Radin, 1993).

These benefits undoubtedly result from parenting practices. Employed mothers who value their parenting role are more likely to use authoritative child rearing (Greenberger & Goldberg, 1989). Also, children in dual-earner households devote more daily hours to doing homework under parental guidance. And contrary to popular belief, maternal employment does not reduce the total amount of time school-age children and adolescents spend with their mothers, and it results in more time with their fathers (Richards & Duckett, 1994).

A modest increase in fathers' involvement in child care and household duties accompanies maternal employment, and it seems to facilitate a variety of aspects of development (Zaslow, Rabinovich, & Suwalsky, 1991). In a longitudinal study of maternal employment, fathers' early involvement in child care was positively related to intelligence, academic achievement, and mature social behavior for both sons and daughters (Gottfried, 1991). Furthermore, fathers' participation is one of the routes through which children of employed mothers acquire gender-stereotype flexibility (Williams, Radin, & Allegro, 1992).

But there are some qualifiers to these encouraging findings. First, outcomes associated with maternal employment are more positive for daughters than sons. Girls, especially, profit from the image of female competence. Daughters of employed mothers have higher educational aspirations and, in college, are more likely to choose nontraditional careers, such as law, medicine, and physics. In contrast, boys in low-income homes are sometimes adversely affected. They tend to admire their fathers less and interact more negatively with them. These outcomes are probably due to a lingering belief in lower-class homes that when a mother works, the father has failed in his provider role (Hoffman, 1989).

Beyond these sex-related and social-class differences, several other factors make a difference in how children adjust to maternal employment. Women continue to hold less prestigious jobs than men, and they earn less than men in comparable occupations. Because these factors affect income and morale, they are likely to influence how mothers feel and behave with children at the end of the working day. Furthermore, when employment places heavy demands on the mother's schedule, children are at risk for ineffective parenting. Working very long hours and spending little time with school-age children are associated with less favorable outcomes, both cognitively and socially (Moorehouse, 1991). In contrast, part-time employment seems to have benefits for children of all ages, probably because it permits mothers to meet the needs of youngsters with a wide range of characteristics (Alvarez, 1985; Williams & Radin, 1993).

■ SUPPORT FOR EMPLOYED MOTHERS AND FATHERS. The research we have reviewed indicates that as long as mothers have the necessary supports to engage in effective parenting, maternal employment offers children many advantages. In dual-earner families, the husband's willingness to share responsibilities is crucial. Although men assist to a greater extent than they did in the past, women still shoulder most household and child care tasks. If the father helps very little or not at all, the mother carries a double load, at home and at work, leading to fatigue, distress, and reduced time and energy for children.

Besides fathers, work settings, communities, and government policies can help employed mothers in their child-rearing roles. Part-time employment and liberal paid maternity and paternity leaves (including time off when children are ill) would help many women juggle the demands of work and child rearing. Although these workplace supports are widely available in Western Europe and Canada, at present only unpaid employment leave is mandated by U.S. federal law (see Chapter 1, page 36). Finally, high-quality day care is vital for parents' peace of mind and children's healthy development, as we will see in the following section.

DAY CARE

Even more than infants and toddlers, preschoolers spend considerable time away from their parents in day care settings. Figure 14.6 on page 550 shows the varied ways in which American 3- and 4-year-olds are cared for while their parents are at work. About 35 percent spend most of these hours in either their own home or another home, cared for by a relative or nonrelative. The largest proportion—43 percent—attend day care centers. Out-of-home care is especially common during the preschool years because organized child care facilities generally specialize in preschoolers; fewer accommodate infants or provide before- and after-school care for 5- to 13-year-olds. Figure 14.6 also reflects the tremendous shortage of affordable day care in the United States. Twenty-two percent of employed mothers of 3- and 4-year-olds get by without any day care arrangements, a figure that rises to 34 percent and 51 percent for infants and school-age children, respectively (Lombardi, 1993; Willer et al., 1991).

■ DAY CARE AND CHILD DEVELOPMENT. Recall from Chapter 8 that high-quality early intervention can enhance the development of economically disadvantaged children. However, as we noted in Chapter 1, much day care in the United States is not of this high quality. Preschoolers exposed to poor-quality day care, regardless of whether they come from middle- or low-income homes, score lower on measures of cognitive and social skills (Howes, 1988b, 1990; Vandell & Powers, 1983). In contrast, good day care can reduce the negative impact of an underprivileged home life, and it sustains the benefits of growing up in an advantaged family (Phillips et al., 1994).

What are the ingredients of high-quality day care for young children? Several large-scale studies of center- and home-based care reveal that the following factors are especially important: group size (number of children in a single space), caregiver–child ratio, caregiver stability (low turnover), caregivers' educational preparation, and caregivers' personal commitment to learning about and taking care of children. When these characteristics are favorable, adults are more attentive, verbally stimulating, and sensitive to children's needs, and children perform especially well on measures of intelligence, language, and social development (Galinsky et al., 1994; Helburn, 1995; Howes, Phillips, &

FIGURE 14.6

■ *Who's minding America's preschoolers? The chart refers to settings in which 3- and 4-year-olds spend most time while their parents are at work. The "other" category consists mostly of children cared for by their mothers during working hours. Over one-fourth of 3- and 4-year-olds experience more than one type of child care, a fact not reflected in the chart. (Adapted from B. Willer, S. L. Hofferth, E. E. Kisker, P. Divine-Hawkins, E. Farquhar, & F. B. Glantz, 1991, "The Demand and Supply of Child Care in 1990: Joint Findings from the National Child Care Survey 1990 and A Profile of Child Care Settings." Washington, DC: National Association for the Education of Young Children. Reprinted by permission.)*

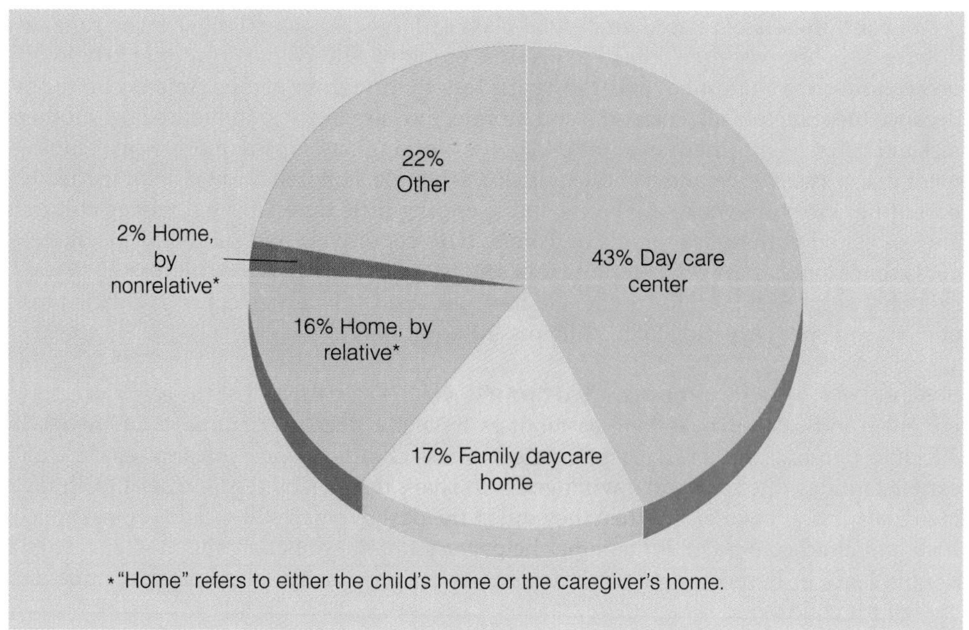

Whitebook, 1992). Other research shows that spacious, well-equipped environments and a rich variety of activities that meet the needs and interests of preschool children also contribute to positive outcomes (Howes, 1988b; Scarr et al., 1993).

Table 14.6 summarizes characteristics of high-quality day care for preschoolers, based on current findings. (Return to Chapter 10, page 417, to review signs of high-quality day care for infants and toddlers.). When these ingredients are absent, children's well-being is compromised. Furthermore, research indicates that parents who place their children in low-quality day care tend to lead stressful lives and use inappropriate child-rearing techniques—factors that, when combined, pose an especially serious risk to children's development (Howes, 1990).

■ DAY CARE POLICIES IN THE UNITED STATES AND OTHER WESTERN NATIONS. As we noted in Chapter 1, the overall state of American day care is alarmingly inadequate. Many caregivers have little or no specialized education for teaching young children, and in some states, 1 adult is permitted to supervise as many as 12 to 15 preschoolers. From 75 to 90 percent of day care homes are unlicensed and therefore not monitored for quality. Caregivers' salaries typically fall below the poverty line, with few if any fringe benefits. As a result, over 40 percent leave their jobs annually (Willer et al., 1991; Zigler & Gilman, 1993). Tax relief to help American parents pay for day care has increased in recent years, but many have difficulty affording it. At current rates, day care fees consume more than 25 percent of the annual earnings of a minimum-wage worker with one young child (Maynard & McGinnis, 1993). Although publicly funded centers for low-income families exist, they fall far short of the need. In some places, waiting lists have swelled into the thousands (Children's Defense Fund, 1996).

In Western Europe, government-supported day care for all 1½- to 3-year-olds up to the age of school entry is widely available. The need for places for infants and toddlers is not as great as in the United States because of generous parental leave policies following the birth of a child. Caregivers are usually paid on the same scale as elementary school teachers, and they receive health insurance and other benefits just like any other citizen. Standards for group size, caregiver–child ratios, and caregiver educational preparation are rigorously set and enforced. Center-based care is the most common form in Western Europe, but many governments also support day care homes by paying caregivers directly, providing training for them, and inspecting for health and safety. Since programs are heavily subsidized, parents pay only a small income-related fee, usually less than 10 percent of the average woman's wages (Kamerman, 1993; Scarr et al., 1993).

Day care is a legal right and nearly as accessible as public schooling in Western European countries. It is one element in a wide array of policies designed to attract mothers back to the labor force after the child's first year while fostering children's development.

TABLE 14.6

Signs of High-Quality Day Care for Preschool Children

Program Characteristic	Signs of Quality
Physical setting	Indoor environment is clean, in good repair, and well-ventilated. Classroom space is divided into richly equipped activity areas, including make-believe play, blocks, science, math, games and puzzles, books, art, and music. Fenced outdoor play space is equipped with swings, climbing equipment, tricycles, and sandbox.
Group size	In preschools and day care centers, group size is no greater than 18 to 20 children with 2 teachers.
Caregiver–child ratio	In day care centers, teacher is responsible for no more than 8 to 10 children. In family day care homes, caregiver is responsible for no more than 6 children.
Daily activities	Most of the time, children work individually or in small groups. Children select many of their own activities and learn through experiences relevant to their own lives. Caregivers facilitate children's involvement, accept individual differences, and adjust expectations to children's developing capacities.
Teacher qualifications	Caregivers have college-level specialized preparation in early childhood development, early childhood education, or a related field.
Relationships with parents	Parents are encouraged to observe and participate. Caregivers talk frequently with parents about children's behavior and development.
Licensing and accreditation	Program is licensed by the state. If a preschool or day care center, accreditation by the National Academy of Early Childhood Programs is evidence of an especially high-quality program. If a day care home, accreditation by the National Association for Family Day Care is evidence of high-quality experiences for children.

Source: National Association for the Education of Young Children, 1991.

Because the United States does not yet have a national day care policy, it lags far behind other industrialized nations in supply, quality, and affordability of day care.

SELF-CARE

Care for school-age children while their parents work also has important implications for development. In recent years, much public concern has been voiced about the estimated 2.4 million 5- to 13-year-olds in the United States who regularly look after themselves during after-school hours (Cain & Hofferth, 1989). Although many return home to an empty house, others "hang out" with peers in the neighborhood or in nearby shopping malls during late afternoons and evenings.

Research on these **self-care children** reveals inconsistent findings. Some studies report that they suffer from low self-esteem, fearfulness, and poor academic achievement, whereas others show no such effects (Padilla & Landreth, 1989). Why these contradictions? The way self-care children spend their time seems to be the crucial factor. Children who have a history of authoritative child rearing, are monitored from a distance by telephone calls, and have regular after-school chores appear responsible and well adjusted. In contrast, those left to their own devices are more likely to bend to peer pressures and engage in antisocial behavior (Steinberg, 1986). Children from single-parent, poverty-stricken homes who look after themselves are at special risk for antisocial involvement. Nevertheless, self-care for these children is no worse than returning home to an overwhelmed, psychologically unavailable mother who offers her child little emotional support (Vandell & Ramanan, 1991).

Parents need to consider children's maturity carefully before deciding on self-care. Before age 8 or 9, children should not be left unsupervised because most are not yet competent to deal with emergencies (Galambos & Maggs, 1991). Unfortunately, when children express discomfort with self-care or are not mature enough to handle it, many

Self-care children
Children who look after themselves during after-school hours.

employed parents have no alternative. After-school programs for 6- to 13-year-olds are rare in American communities. Enrolling children in poor-quality after-school care can undermine their academic and social competence (Vandell & Corasaniti, 1988). In contrast, when after-school programs support academic learning and offer enrichment activities (scouting, music lessons, and organized sports) unavailable to many low-income children, they show improved school performance, peer relations, and psychological adjustment (Posner & Vandell, 1994).

BRIEF REVIEW

Rapid changes in family life have taken place in Western industrialized nations. The recent trend toward a smaller family size is associated with more favorable child development. Nevertheless, most children continue to grow up with at least one brother or sister. Although unequal treatment by parents promotes sibling rivalry, sibling relationships serve as important sources of companionship, emotional support, and assistance and contribute to social competence. Only children are as well adjusted as children with siblings, and they are advantaged in academic achievement and educational attainment. Compared to nonadopted agemates, adopted children have more emotional and learning difficulties in childhood, but this difference disappears by adulthood. Children of lesbian and gay parents develop as favorably as other children, and the majority are heterosexual.

Large numbers of American children experience the divorce of their parents. Although many adjust well by 2 years after the divorce, boys and temperamentally difficult children are likely to display lasting problems. Effective parenting is the most important factor in helping children adapt to life in a single-parent family. When parents cohabit or remarry, daughters, early adolescents, and children living in father/stepmother families display more adjustment difficulties.

Maternal employment is related to high self-esteem, mature social behavior, reduced gender stereotyping, and better grades in school. However, outcomes vary with children's sex and social class, the demands of the mother's job, and the father's participation in child rearing. High-quality day care fosters cognitive, language, and social development. Unfortunately, much day care in the United States is substandard and poses serious risks to children's development.

Vulnerable Families: Child Maltreatment

Families, as we indicated in the first part of this chapter, contribute to the maintenance of society by serving as contexts in which children are loved, protected, and encouraged to develop into competent, caring adults. Throughout our discussion of family transitions, we encountered examples of the many factors, both within and outside the family, that contribute to parents' capacity to be warm, consistent, and appropriately demanding. As we turn now to the topic of child maltreatment, we will see that when these vital supports for effective child rearing break down, children as well as their parents can suffer terribly.

INCIDENCE AND DEFINITIONS

Child maltreatment is as old as the history of humankind, but only recently has there been widespread acceptance that the problem exists, research aimed at understanding it, and programs directed at helping maltreated children and their families. Perhaps this increase in public and professional concern is due to the fact that child maltreatment is especially common in large industrialized nations (Gelles & Cornell, 1983). It occurs so often in the United States that a recent government committee called it a "national emergency." A total of 2.9 million cases were reported to juvenile authorities in 1993, an increase of 132 percent over the previous decade (Children's Defense Fund, 1996). The true figure is surely much higher, since most cases, including ones in which children suffer serious physical injury, go unreported.

Child maltreatment takes the following forms:

1. *Physical abuse*—assaults on children that produce pain, cuts, welts, bruises, burns, broken bones, and other injuries
2. *Sexual abuse*—sexual comments, fondling, intercourse, and other forms of exploitation
3. *Physical neglect*—living conditions in which children do not receive enough food, clothing, medical attention, or supervision
4. *Emotional neglect*—failure of caregivers to meet children's needs for affection and emotional support
5. *Psychological abuse*—actions that seriously damage children's emotional, social, or cognitive functioning

Although all experts recognize that these five types exist, they do not agree on the range of adult behaviors and how frequent and intense they must be to be called maltreatment. Consensus on a definition is important, since if we cannot define abuse and neglect, we are hampered in studying their origins and impact on children and designing effective interventions. The greatest problems arise in the case of subtle, ambiguous behaviors. For example, some experts regard psychological abuse, in which children are ridiculed, humiliated, rejected, scapegoated, or terrorized by an adult, as the most frequent and destructive form, since it accompanies most other types (Grusec & Walters, 1991). Yet definitions of psychological abuse are especially complex and serious in their consequences for children and families. If they are too narrow and include only the most severe instances of mental cruelty, they allow many harmful actions toward children to continue unchecked and untreated. If they are too lenient, they can result in arbitrary, disruptive legal intrusions into family life (Barnett, Manly, & Cicchetti, 1993).

ORIGINS OF CHILD MALTREATMENT

When child maltreatment first became a topic of research in the early 1960s, it was viewed as rooted in adult psychological disturbance. The first studies indicated that adults who abused or neglected their children usually had a history of maltreatment in their own childhoods, unrealistic expectations that children would satisfy their own unmet emotional needs, and poor control of aggressive impulses (Kempe et al., 1962; Spinetta & Rigler, 1972). (See the Social Issues box on page 573 for a discussion of child sexual abuse, which was not recognized as a serious social problem until the 1970s.)

It soon became clear that although child maltreatment was more common among disturbed parents, a single "abusive personality type" did not exist. Sometimes, even "normal" parents harmed their children! Also, parents who were abused as children did not always repeat the cycle with their own youngsters (Kaufman & Zigler, 1989; Simons et al., 1991).

For help in understanding child maltreatment, researchers turned to the social systems perspective on family functioning. They discovered that child abuse and neglect are affected by many interacting variables—at the family, community, and cultural levels. Table 14.7 summarizes factors associated with child maltreatment. The more that are present, the greater the risk that abuse or neglect will occur. Let's examine each set of influences in turn.

THE FAMILY. Within the family, certain children—those whose characteristics make them more of a challenge to rear—have an increased likelihood of becoming targets of abuse. These include premature or very sick babies and children who are temperamentally difficult, inattentive or overactive, or who have other developmental problems. But whether such children are actually maltreated depends on characteristics of parents (Belsky, 1993). In one study, temperamentally difficult children had mothers who believed they could do little to control their child's behavior. Instead, they attributed the

TABLE 14.7

Factors Related to Child Maltreatment

Factor	Description
Parent characteristics	Psychological disturbance; substance abuse; history of abuse as a child; belief in harsh, physical discipline; desire to satisfy unmet emotional needs through the child; unreasonable expectations for child behavior; young age (most under 30); low educational level
Child characteristics	Premature or very sick baby; difficult temperament; inattentiveness and overactivity; and other developmental problems
Family characteristics	Low income; poverty; homelessness; marital instability; social isolation; physical abuse of mother by husband or boyfriend; frequent moves; large, closely spaced families; overcrowded living conditions; disorganized household; lack of steady employment; other signs of high life stress
Community	Characterized by social isolation; few parks, day care centers, preschool programs, recreation centers, and churches to serve as family supports
Culture	Approval of physical force and violence as ways to solve problems

Source: Belsky, 1993; Simons et al., 1991.

child's unruliness to a stubborn or bad disposition, an interpretation that led them to move quickly toward physical force when the child misbehaved (Bugental, Blue, & Cruzcosa, 1989).

Once child abuse gets started, it quickly becomes part of a self-sustaining family pattern. The small irritations to which abusive parents react—a fussy baby, a preschooler who knocks over a glass of milk, or a child who will not mind immediately—soon become bigger ones. Then the harshness of parental behavior increases. By the preschool years, abusive and neglectful parents seldom interact with their children. When they do, they rarely express pleasure and affection; the communication is almost always negative (Trickett et al., 1991).

Most parents, however, have enough self-control not to respond to their children's misbehavior with abuse, and not all children with developmental problems are mistreated. Other factors must combine with these conditions to prompt an extreme parental response. Research reveals that unmanageable parental stress is strongly associated with all forms of maltreatment. Low income, unemployment, marital conflict, overcrowded living conditions, frequent moves, and extreme household disorganization are common in abusive homes. These conditions increase the chances that parents will be so overwhelmed that they cannot meet basic child-rearing responsibilities or will vent their frustrations by lashing out at their children (Pianta, Egeland, & Erickson, 1989).

■ THE COMMUNITY. The majority of abusive parents are isolated from both formal and informal social supports in their communities. There are at least two causes of this social isolation. First, because of their own life histories, many of these parents have learned to mistrust and avoid others. They do not have the skills necessary for establishing and maintaining positive relationships with friends and relatives (Polansky et al., 1985). Second, abusive parents are more likely to live in poverty stricken neighborhoods with high resident mobility that provide few links between family and community, such as parks, day care centers, preschool programs, recreation centers, and churches (Coulton et al., 1995; Garbarino & Kostelny, 1993). For these reasons, they lack "lifelines" to others and have no one to turn to for help during particularly stressful times.

■ THE LARGER CULTURE. One final set of factors—cultural values, laws, and customs—profoundly affects the chances that child maltreatment will occur when parents feel overburdened. Societies that view force and violence as appropriate ways to solve problems set the stage for child abuse. These conditions exist in the United States. Although all 50 states have laws designed to protect children from maltreatment, strong support still exists for the use of physical force in parent–child relations. For example, during the past quarter century, the U.S. Supreme Court has twice upheld the right of

SOCIAL ISSUES

Child Sexual Abuse

Until recently, child sexual abuse was viewed as a rare occurrence. When children came forward with it, adults often thought that the children had fantasized the experience, and their claims were not taken seriously. In the 1970s, efforts by professionals along with widespread media attention caused child sexual abuse to be recognized as a serious national problem. Over 200,000 cases are reported each year.

CHARACTERISTICS OF ABUSERS AND VICTIMS. Sexual abuse is committed against children of both sexes, but more often against girls than boys. Its incidence is highest in middle childhood, but it also occurs at younger and older ages. Few children experience only a single episode. For some, the abuse begins early in life and continues for many years (Burkhardt & Rotatori, 1995). Generally, the abuser is male—a parent or someone whom the parent knows well. Often it is a father, stepfather, or live-in boyfriend; somewhat less often, an uncle or older brother. In a few instances, mothers are the offenders, more often with sons than daughters. If a nonrelative is responsible, it is usually someone the child has come to know and trust (Alter-Reid et al., 1986).

In the overwhelming majority of cases, the abuse is serious. Children are subjected to intercourse, oral-genital contact, fondling, and forced stimulation of the adult. Abusers make the child comply in a variety of distasteful ways, including deception, bribery, verbal intimidation, and physical force (Gomez-Schwartz, Horowitz, & Cardarelli, 1990).

You may be wondering how any adult—especially, a parent or close relative—could possibly violate a child sexually. Many offenders deny their own responsibility. They blame the abuse on the willing participation of a seductive youngster. Yet children are not capable of making a deliberate, informed decision to enter into a sexual relationship! Even at older ages, they are not free to say yes or no. Instead, abusers tend to have characteristics that predispose them toward sexual exploitation. They have great difficulty controlling their impulses, may suffer from psychological disorders, and are often addicted to alcohol and drugs. Furthermore, they tend to pick out victims who are unlikely to defend themselves—children who are physically weak, emotionally deprived, and socially isolated (Faller, 1990).

Reported cases of child sexual abuse are strongly linked to poverty, marital instability, and resulting weakening of family ties. Children who live in homes where there is a history of constantly changing characters—repeated marriages, separations, and new partners—are especially vulnerable. But community surveys reveal that middle-class children in relatively stable homes are also victims. Economically advantaged families are simply more likely to escape detection. Intense pressure toward secrecy and feelings of confusion and guilt prevent most children from seeking help (Gomez-Schwartz, Horowitz, & Cardarelli, 1990).

CONSEQUENCES FOR CHILDREN. The adjustment problems of child sexual abuse victims are often severe. Depression, low self-esteem, mistrust of adults, feelings of anger and hostility, and difficulties in getting along with peers are common. Younger children often react with sleep difficulties, loss of appetite, and generalized fearfulness. Adolescents sometimes run away or show suicidal reactions, substance abuse, and delinquency (Kendall-Tackett, Williams, & Finkelhor, 1993).

Sexually abused children frequently display sexual knowledge and behavior beyond that which is appropriate for their age. They have learned from their abusers that sexual overtures are acceptable ways to get attention and rewards. As they move toward young adulthood, they tend to be promiscuous and to enter into unhealthy relationships. Females are likely to choose husbands who abuse both them and their children (Faller, 1990). As mothers, they often show poor parenting skills, abusing and neglecting their own children (Pianta, Egeland, & Erickson, 1989). In this way, the harmful impact of sexual abuse is transmitted to the next generation.

PREVENTION AND TREATMENT. Treating victims of child sexual abuse is difficult. Once the abuse is revealed, the reactions of family members—anxiety about harm to the child, anger toward the abuser, and sometimes hostility toward the victim for telling—can increase children's distress. Since sexual abuse typically appears in the midst of other serious family problems, long-term therapy with both children and parents is usually necessary (Doyle, 1994; Gomez-Schwartz, Horowitz, & Cardarelli, 1990).

The best way to reduce the suffering of child sexual abuse victims is to prevent it from continuing. Children's testimony, as we noted in Chapter 7, is currently being taken more seriously by the courts. In schools, sex education programs can help children recognize inappropriate sexual advances and encourage them to report these actions. Finally, educating teachers, caregivers, and other adults who work with children about the signs and symptoms of sexual abuse can help ensure that victimized children are identified early and receive the help they need.

So there really was a monster in her bedroom.

For many kids, there's a real reason to be afraid of the dark.

Last year in Indiana, there were 6,912 substantiated cases of sexual abuse. The trauma can be devastating for the child and for the family. So listen closely to the children around you.

If you hear something you don't want to believe, perhaps you should. For helpful information on child abuse prevention, contact the LaPorte County Child Abuse Prevention Council, 7451 Johnson Road, Michigan City, IN 46360. (219) 874-0007

LaPorte County Child Abuse Prevention Council

As this poster points out, child sexual abuse, until recently regarded as a product of children's vivid imaginations, is a devastating reality. Victims are in urgent need of protection and treatment. (La Porte County Child Abuse Protection Council)

school officials to use corporal punishment to discipline children. Crime rates have risen in American cities, and television sets beam graphic displays of violence into family living rooms. In view of the widespread acceptance of violent behavior in American culture, it is not surprising that over 90 percent of American parents report using slaps and spankings to discipline their children (Staub, 1996). In countries where physical punishment is not accepted, such as China, Japan, Luxembourg, and Sweden, child abuse is rare (Zigler & Hall, 1989).

CONSEQUENCES OF CHILD MALTREATMENT

The family circumstances of maltreated children impair the development of emotional self-regulation, self-concept, and social skills. Over time, these youngsters show serious learning and adjustment problems, including difficulties with peers, academic failure, severe depression, substance abuse, and delinquency (Hotaling et al., 1988; Simons, Conger, & Whitbeck, 1988).

What explains these damaging consequences? Think back to our discussion of the effects of hostile cycles of parent–child interaction in Chapter 12. These are especially severe for abused children. Indeed, a family characteristic strongly associated with child abuse is domestic violence, in which mothers are repeatedly brutalized (physically and psychologically) by their partners (McCloskey, Figueredo, & Koss, 1995). Clearly, the home lives of abused children overflow with opportunities to learn to use aggression as a way of solving problems. The low warmth and control to which neglected children are exposed also promote aggressive, acting-out behavior (Miller et al., 1993).

Furthermore, demeaning parental messages, in which children are ridiculed, humiliated, rejected, or terrorized, result in low self-esteem, high anxiety, self-blame, and efforts to escape from extreme psychological pain—at times severe enough to lead to suicide attempts in adolescence (Briere, 1992; Sternberg et al., 1993). At school, maltreated children are serious discipline problems. Their noncompliance, poor motivation, and cognitive immaturity interfere with academic achievement—an outcome that further undermines their chances for life success (Eckenrode, Laird, & Doris, 1993).

PREVENTING CHILD MALTREATMENT

Since child maltreatment is embedded within families, communities, and society as a whole, efforts to prevent it must be directed at each of these levels. Many approaches have been suggested. These include interventions that teach high-risk parents effective child-rearing and disciplinary strategies, high school child development courses that include direct experience with children, and broad social programs that have as their goal full employment and better economic conditions for low-income families.

We have already seen that providing social supports to families is very effective in easing parental stress. It is not surprising that this approach sharply reduces child maltreatment. Research indicates that an affectionate, trusting relationship with another person is the most important factor in preventing mothers with childhood histories of abuse from repeating the cycle with their own youngsters (Caliso & Milner, 1992; Egeland, Jacobvitz, & Sroufe, 1988). Parents Anonymous, a national organization that has as its main goal helping child-abusing parents learn constructive parenting practices, does so largely through providing social supports to families. Each of its local chapters offers self-help group meetings, daily telephone calls, and regular home visits to relieve social isolation and teach child-rearing skills.

Crisis intervention services also exist in many communities. Nurseries offer temporary child care when parents feel they are about to lose control, and telephone hot lines provide immediate help to parents under stress and refer them to appropriate community agencies when long-term assistance is warranted.

Other preventive approaches include announcements in newspapers and magazines and on television and radio that are designed to educate people about child maltreatment and tell them where to seek help. Besides these efforts, changes in the overall attitudes and practices of American culture are needed. Many experts believe that child maltreatment cannot be eliminated

Public service announcements help prevent child abuse by educating people about the problem and informing them of where to seek help. This poster reminds adults that degrading remarks can hit as hard as a fist. (Courtesy San Francisco Child Abuse Council)

as long as violence is widespread and corporal punishment continues to be regarded as an acceptable child-rearing alternative (Gil, 1987; Zigler & Hall, 1989).

Although more cases reach the courts than in decades past, child maltreatment remains a crime that is difficult to prove. Most of the time, the only witnesses are the child victims themselves or other loyal family members. Even in court cases in which the evidence is strong, judges hesitate to impose the ultimate safeguard against further harm: permanent removal of the child from the family.

There are several reasons for this reluctant attitude. First, in American society, government intervention into family life is viewed as a last resort, to be used only when there is near certainty that a child will be denied basic care and protection. Second, despite destructive family relationships, maltreated children and their parents are usually attached to one another. Most of the time, neither desires separation. Finally, the American legal system tends to regard children as parental property rather than as human beings in their own right, and this has also stood in the way of court-ordered protection (Hart & Brassard, 1987).

Even with intensive treatment, some adults persist in their abusive acts. An estimated 1,500 American children (half of them under 1 year of age) die from maltreatment each year (Children's Defense Fund, 1996). In cases where parents are unlikely to change their behavior, taking the drastic step of separating parent from child and legally terminating parental rights is the only reasonable course of action.

Child maltreatment is a distressing and horrifying topic. When we consider how often it occurs in the United States, a society that claims to place a high value on the dignity and worth of the individual, it is even more appalling. Yet there is reason to be optimistic. Great strides have been made in understanding and preventing child maltreatment over the last several decades.

SUMMARY

EVOLUTIONARY ORIGINS

- The human family can be traced to our hunting-and-gathering origins. When bipedalism evolved and arms were freed to carry things, our ancestors found it easier to cooperate and share, especially in providing food for the young. A single male became committed to a female and their joint offspring, a relationship that enhanced survival.

FUNCTIONS OF THE FAMILY

- Besides promoting the survival of its own members, the family performs essential functions for society. In complex societies, these are largely restricted to reproduction, socialization, and emotional support.

THE FAMILY AS A SOCIAL SYSTEM

- Modern researchers view the family from a **social systems perspective**—as a complex set of interacting relationships affected by the larger social context. Bidirectional influences exist in which the behaviors of each family member affect those of others. Connections to the community—through formal organizations and informal social networks—promote effective family interaction and enhance children's development.

SOCIALIZATION WITHIN THE FAMILY

- Two broad dimensions, demandingness and responsiveness, describe individual differences in the way parents go about the task of socialization. When combined, they yield four styles of parenting. The **authoritative style**, which is both demanding and responsive, promotes cognitive, emotional, and social competence from early childhood into adolescence. The **authoritarian style**, which is high in demandingness but low in responsiveness, is associated with anxious, withdrawn, dependent child behavior. The **permissive style** is responsive but undemanding; children who experience it typically show poor self-control and achievement. Finally, the **uninvolved style** is low in both demandingness and responsiveness. It disrupts virtually all aspects of development.
- As children get older, a gradual lessening of control supports development, as long as parental warmth and involvement in child rearing are maintained. In middle childhood, effective parents engage in **coregulation**, exerting general oversight while permitting children to be in charge of moment-by-moment decision making. During adolescence, mature **autonomy** is fostered by parenting that grants young people independence in accord with their readiness for it while maintaining close family ties.
- The authoritative style is the most common form of child rearing in many cultures around the world. Nevertheless, in many societies, differences in child rearing are linked to social class and ethnicity. Effective parenting, along with children's development, is seriously undermined by the stress and disorganization of living in poverty. **Extended family households**, in which one or more adult relatives live with the parent–child **nuclear family unit**, are common among ethnic minorities and protect children's development under conditions of high life stress.

FAMILY LIFESTYLES AND TRANSITIONS

- Over the past several decades, family lifestyles have become more diverse, and rapid transitions in family life have taken place in industrialized nations. The trend toward smaller families has positive consequences for parent–child interaction and children's development. Nevertheless, most children still grow up with at least one sibling. Because of their emotional intensity and frequency of interaction, sibling relationships promote many aspects of social competence. Unequal parental treatment increases sibling rivalry. During adolescence, sibling relationships become less intense, but attachment to siblings remains strong for most young people.
- Contrary to popular belief, sibling relationships are not essential for normal development. Only children are as well adjusted as children with siblings, and they are advantaged in school achievement and educational attainment.
- Infertile couples and older, single individuals often turn to adoption as a way of starting a family. Although adopted children have more emotional and learning difficulties than do their nonadopted agemates, by adulthood this difference disappears. Most parents who adopt children with physical or psychological problems report high satisfaction with the adoptive experience. Young people who were transracially or transculturally adopted typically develop healthy identities that combine their birth and rearing backgrounds.
- Gay and lesbian parents are as committed to and effective at child rearing as heterosexuals, and sometimes more so. Their children are well adjusted and largely heterosexual.
- Divorce is extremely common in the lives of American children. Although painful emotional reactions usually accompany the period surrounding divorce, children with difficult temperaments and boys in mother-custody homes react more strongly and are more likely to show lasting adjustment problems. The most consistent long-term effects for girls involve heterosexual behavior in adolescence and young adulthood. The overriding factor in positive adjustment following divorce is good parenting. Contact with the noncustodial parent is also important. Because **divorce mediation** helps parents resolve their disputes, it can reduce children's exposure to conflict. **Joint custody** is a controversial practice that requires a cooperative relationship between divorcing parents to be successful.
- When divorced parents enter new relationships through cohabitation or remarriage, children must adapt to a **blended**, or **reconstituted, family**. How well children do depends on which parent remarries and on the age and sex of the child. Girls, older children, and children in father/stepmother families display the greatest problems. Because repeated marital transitions expose children to recurring episodes of family conflict and inconsistent parenting, they severely disrupt development.
- As long as mothers enjoy their work and remain committed to parenting, maternal employment is associated with favorable consequences for children, including a higher sense of self-esteem, more positive family and peer relations, and less gender-stereotyped beliefs. However, outcomes are more positive for daughters than sons, and boys in low-income homes sometimes show adverse effects. The father's willingness to share responsibilities and workplace supports, such as part-time employment and generous parental leave, help mothers juggle the multiple demands of work and child rearing.
- American children experience a diverse array of day care arrangements while their parents are at work. Center-based care is the most common form during the preschool years. Research indicates that when group size is small, caregiver–child ratios are generous, caregiver turnover is low, and caregivers are well educated, they communicate in more stimulating and responsive ways. As a result, many aspects of development are fostered. The United States lags far behind other Western nations in supply, quality, and affordability of day care services.
- During middle childhood, millions of children look after themselves during after-school hours. When **self-care children** have a history of authoritative child rearing and are monitored from a distance, they fare well. In contrast, children left to their own devices are at risk for antisocial behavior. High-quality day care for school-age children is not widely available in the United States.

VULNERABLE FAMILIES: CHILD MALTREATMENT

- Child maltreatment is related to factors within the family, community, and larger culture. Child and parent characteristics often feed on one another to produce abusive behavior. Unmanageable parental stress and social isolation greatly increase the chances that abuse and neglect will occur. When a society approves of force and violence as appropriate means for solving problems, child abuse is promoted.

IMPORTANT TERMS AND CONCEPTS

social systems perspective (p. 541)
authoritative style (p. 544)
authoritarian style (p. 544)
permissive style (p. 545)
uninvolved style (p. 545)
coregulation (p. 547)
autonomy (p. 547)
extended-family household (p. 551)
nuclear family unit (p. 551)
divorce mediation (p. 562)
joint custody (p. 563)
blended, or reconstituted, family (p. 563)
self-care children (p. 569)

for Chapter 14

If you are interested in . . .	turn to . . .	to learn about . . .
Social support and development	Chapter 1, p. 25	Ecological systems theory and the importance of social support for development
	Chapter 3, p. 106	Social support in natural, or prepared, childbirth
	Chapter 5, pp. 181–182	Social support and adolescent reactions to pubertal changes
	Chapter 8, pp. 329–330	Social support for parents in early intervention programs
	Chapter 10, p. 413	Social support for parents and security of attachment
	Chapter 11, pp. 450–451, 453	Children's friendships as sources of social support
	Chapter 15, pp. 611–614	Peer social support and adjustment to school transitions
Cultural variations in child rearing	Chapter 1, p. 28	Adult encouragement of infant sharing among the !Kung
	Chapter 4, p. 128	Cultural variations in infant sleeping arrangements
	Chapter 4, pp. 144–145	Maternal stimulation of African and West Indian babies' motor development
	Chapter 8, p. 322	Transracial adoption: When black children grow up in white homes
	Chapter 10, p. 401	Asian and Caucasian mothers' styles of interacting with their infants
	Chapter 10, p. 409	Cultural variations in patterns of attachment
	Chapter 15, p. 586	Cultural variations in parental encouragement of children's play
	Chapter 15, p. 621	Japanese and Taiwanese parents' encouragement of achievement
Siblings and development	Chapter 8, p. 327	Family size, birth order, and intelligence
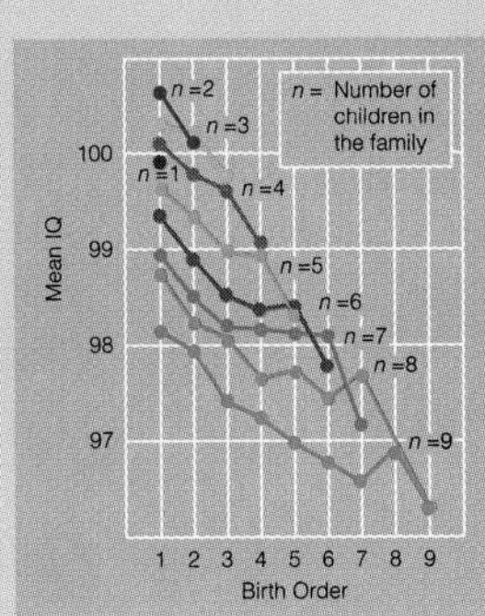	Chapter 10, p. 402	Temperament and sibling relationships
	Chapter 13, pp. 516–517	Sibling influences on gender-role adoption

15 Peers, Media, and Schooling

Four 6-year-old pupils are gathered around one of the computers in their first-grade classroom, using LOGO, a flexible computer language in which numerical instructions yield geometric shapes, to draw a snowman on the screen. As John assumes control of the keyboard, the children consider how large to make the snowman's hat. Their conversation is richly woven with ideas and joint efforts at problem solving:

Kevin: Small.
John: Two. [referring to units specifying size in LOGO]
Andrew: Shh, listen to what Cathie says. What number?
Cathie: I don't know. John, I think you should decide. It's your hat.
Kevin: Should take four.
Cathie: I think that would be too big, wouldn't it?
Kevin: You've never took four before.
Andrew: Do three . . . It'll be too big.
John: I say two.
Cathie: If you say two, put in two, John. Put in two. [John draws the square.] That's fine, isn't it?

[Now the children decide on a length for the brim.]

Andrew: Two . . . One . . .
John: Try one.
Kevin: And then do another one?
Cathie: Well, it's got to go to the corner, and one past . . .
John: Right, two. . . . Will I go forward?
John: I say two.
Cathie: If you say two, put in two, John. Put in two. [John draws the square.] That's fine, isn't it? (Hughes & Macleod, 1986, pp. 197–198)

In creating the snowman, these young children cooperate to reach a common goal, generate alternative strategies for solution, extend their knowledge of mathematical estimation, and begin to master a technology that plays a central role in the economic and leisure life of their society. Their cognitive and social competencies illustrate the importance of three contexts for development. Beginning at an early age, socialization in the family is supplemented by experiences in the wider world of peers, media, and school.

In all human societies, children spend many hours in one another's company. In no culture are they reared entirely by adults. In Chapter 11, we saw how one special type of peer relationship, friendship, contributes uniquely to development. In this chapter, we take a broader look at how peer sociability changes with age, the many factors that support it, and its profound significance for psychological adjustment. Next we turn to television and computers, reviewing what is known about the effects of these captivating electronic devices on children's cognitive and social skills. Finally, our discussion addresses the school, an institution established to assist the family in transmitting culturally valued knowledge to the next generation. We consider how class and school size, educational philosophy, teacher–pupil interaction, and the ability mix of pupils affect educational experiences in classrooms. We conclude with an evaluation of the success of American schools in equipping young people to keep pace with their counterparts in other industrialized nations and preparing them for productive work lives.

The Importance of Peer Relations

Are peer relations crucial for development, and how do they add to children's experiences with caring adults? To find out for sure, we would need to study a group of children reared only by parents, comparing their competencies to children growing up under typical conditions. These circumstances rarely occur naturally and are unethical to arrange experimentally among humans. But scientists who have conducted such studies with nonhuman primates report that although peer bonds are usually not as intense as attachments to parents, their impact on social competence is considerable. For example, maternally reared rhesus monkeys with no peer contact display immature play, excessive aggression and fearfulness, and less cooperation at maturity (Harlow, 1969).

Parent and peer associations seem to complement one another. The parent–child bond emphasizes caregiving and affection, providing children with the security they need to enter the world of peers. Peer interaction, in turn, consists mainly of play and socializing, permitting children to expand social skills first acquired within the family (Hartup & Moore, 1990). Peer relations are also flexible enough so that they can fill in, at least to some extent, for the early parent–child bond. In a special type of investigation called **peer-only rearing**, researchers reared rhesus monkey infants in groups without adults. When given a choice between their preferred peer (the one they most often sought closeness to during rearing), a familiar peer, and an unfamiliar peer, peer-only reared monkeys spent most time near the preferred peer. In addition, the preferred peer served as a source of security, reducing distress more effectively than did other agemates (Higley et al., 1992).

Nevertheless, peer-only reared monkeys do not develop as well as their counterparts with typical parental and peer upbringing. In the study just described, they spent much of their time either clinging to or hovering near their preferred agemate in novel environments, constantly seeking reassurance. Perhaps for this reason, peer-only reared monkeys display some behavior problems as they get older, including increased dominant and submissive (as opposed to friendly) interaction with unfamiliar agemates, reduced exploration, and deficient sexual behavior (Goy & Goldfoot, 1974). Nevertheless, within their familiar peer group, peer-only reared monkeys do develop socially competent behavior, and they are far better off than monkeys reared in isolation (Suomi & Harlow, 1978).

Do these findings generalize to human children? A unique parallel to peer-only rearing research suggests that in large measure, they do. In the 1940s, Anna Freud and Sophie Dann (1951) studied six young German-Jewish orphans whose parents had been murdered in the Nazi gas chambers shortly after the children's birth. The children remained together in a concentration camp for several years, without close ties to adults. When World War II ended, they were brought to England and cared for in a country house until they could adjust to their new surroundings. Observations revealed that they were passionately attached to other members of their group, becoming upset when separated, even for brief moments. They were also intensely prosocial, freely sharing, comforting, and offering assistance to one another. At the same time, they showed many anxious symptoms, including intense thumb sucking, restlessness, immature play, and periods of aggression toward as well as complete dependency on their caregivers. As they built trusting relationships with adults, the children's play, language, and exploration developed rapidly. In sum, peers serve as vital sources of security in threatening situations and contribute to many aspects of development. But they do so more effectively when they are preceded by a warm, supportive relationship with a caregiver.

Before we turn to the development of peer sociability, a word of caution is in order. Strictly speaking, the term *peer* means equal in rank or standing. Consistent with this definition, investigators have focused on children close in age, largely because observing is easiest in age-graded settings, such as day care centers, schools, and summer camps. Yet in the neighborhood, where children's activities are harder to track, more than half their contacts are with children who differ in age by at least a year (Ellis, Rogoff, & Cromer, 1981). And in cultures where children are not segregated by age for schooling and recreation, cross-age interaction is even more common (Weisner & Gallimore, 1977; Whiting & Edwards, 1988a). We will consider what is known about mixed-age peer interaction as

Peer-only rearing
A type of study in which nonhuman primates are reared together from birth without adults.

our discussion proceeds. But the heavy research emphasis on agemates limits what we currently know about the diversity of children's peer experiences.

Development of Peer Sociability

Peer sociability begins early in cultures where children have regular contact with one another during the first year of life. Observations of infant playmates reveal that signs of peer interaction are already present. Gradually, these evolve into the more complex, better coordinated social exchanges of the childhood and adolescent years. The development of peer sociability is supported by and contributes to important cognitive, language, and emotional milestones that we discussed in previous chapters.

INFANT AND TODDLER BEGINNINGS

When pairs of infants are brought together in a laboratory, looking accompanied by touching is present at 3 to 4 months, peer-directed smiles and babbles by 6 months. These isolated social acts increase until by the second half of the first year, an occasional reciprocal exchange occurs in which babies smile, laugh, gesture, or otherwise imitate each other's behavior (Vandell & Mueller, 1995; Vandell, Wilson, & Buchanan, 1980).

Between 1 and 2 years, isolated acts decline, and coordinated interaction occurs more often. Older toddlers also combine several behaviors, such as looking, vocalizing, gesturing, and smiling, into a single social act (Bronson, 1981). By age 2, when both the mother and a peer are present, attempts to engage the peer in play occur more often than initiations to the mother (Eckerman, Whatley, & Kutz, 1975).

Nevertheless, we must be careful not to exaggerate infants' and toddlers' social capacities. Even in laboratory playrooms where these young playmates have little else to capture their attention, peer social contacts do not occur often, and sustained interaction is rare. Furthermore, the rise in reciprocal exchanges over the second year consists largely of imitations of the other child's actions, such as jumping, chasing, or banging a toy. Not until age 2 to 2½ do children frequently use words to affect a peer's behavior, as when they say "Let's play chase," or engage in complementary roles, such as feeding a doll that another child is holding (Eckerman, Davis, & Didow, 1989; Howes & Matheson, 1992).

But peer sociability is present in the first 2 years, and research suggests that it is fostered by the early infant–caregiver relationship. From interacting with sensitive, responsive adults, babies learn how to send and interpret emotional signals in their first peer associations (Vandell & Mueller, 1995). Consistent with this idea, infants with a warm parental relationship engage in more extended peer exchanges (Vandell & Wilson, 1987). These children, in turn, display more socially competent behavior during the preschool years (Howes, 1988a; Howes & Matheson, 1992).

THE PRESCHOOL YEARS

Between ages 2 and 5, the amount and quality of peer interaction changes greatly. In the early part of this century, Mildred Parten (1932) observed young children in nursery school and noticed a dramatic rise with age in joint, interactive play. She concluded that social development proceeds in a three-step sequence. It begins with **nonsocial activity**—unoccupied, onlooker behavior and solitary play. Then it shifts to a form of limited social participation called **parallel play**, in which a child plays near other children with similar materials but does not try to influence their behavior. At the highest level are two forms of true social interaction. The first is **associative play**, in which children engage in separate activities, but they interact by exchanging toys and commenting on one another's behavior. The second is **cooperative play**—a more advanced type of interaction in which children orient toward a common goal, such as acting out a make-believe theme or working on the same product, for example, a sand castle or painting.

Recent longitudinal research indicates that these play forms emerge in the order suggested by Parten, but they do not form a developmental sequence in which later-appearing ones replace earlier ones (Howes & Matheson, 1992). Instead, all types coexist during

Nonsocial activity
Unoccupied, onlooker behavior and solitary play.

Parallel play
A form of limited social participation in which the child plays near other children with similar materials but does not interact with them.

Associative play
A form of true social participation in which children engage in separate activities, but they interact by exchanging toys and commenting on one another's behavior.

Cooperative play
A form of true social participation in which children's actions are directed toward a common goal.

■ *These children are engaged in parallel play. Although they sit side by side and use similar materials, they do not try to influence one another's behavior. Parallel play remains frequent and stable over the preschool years. Working puzzles or engaging in other similar activities encourages it. (George Doodwin/ Monkmeyer Press)*

the preschool years (see Table 15.1). Furthermore, although nonsocial activity declines with age, it is still the most frequent form of behavior among 3- to 4-year-olds. Even among kindergartners it continues to take up as much as a third of children's free play time. Also, solitary and parallel play remain fairly stable from 3 to 6 years, and together, these categories account for as much of the young child's play as highly social, cooperative interaction. Social development during the preschool years is not just a matter of eliminating nonsocial and partially social activity from the child's behavior.

We now understand that it is the *type,* rather than the amount, of solitary and parallel play that changes during early childhood. In studies of preschoolers' play in Taiwan and the United States, researchers rated the cognitive maturity of nonsocial, parallel, and cooperative play by applying the categories shown in Table 15.2. Within each of Parten's play types, older children displayed more cognitively mature behavior than did younger children (Pan, 1994; Rubin, Watson, & Jambor, 1978).

These findings are helpful in responding to the concerns of some parents, who wonder if a young child who spends much time playing alone is developing normally. Only *certain kinds* of nonsocial activity—aimless wandering, hovering near peers, and functional play involving immature, repetitive motor action—are cause for concern during the preschool years (Coplan et al., 1994). Most nonsocial play of preschoolers is not of this kind. Instead, it is positive and constructive, and teachers and caregivers encourage it when they set out art materials, puzzles, and building toys during free play. Children who spend much time in these activities are not maladjusted. Instead, they are bright children who, when they do play with peers, show socially skilled behavior (Rubin, 1982).

In Chapter 6, we noted that *sociodramatic play* (or make-believe with peers) becomes especially common during the preschool years. This advanced form of cooperative play requires sophisticated cognitive, emotional, and social skills, and it also enhances them. In joint make-believe, preschoolers act out and respond to one another's pretend feelings. Their play is rich in references to emotional states. Young children also explore and gain control of fear-arousing experiences when they play doctor or dentist or pretend to search for monsters in a magical forest. As a result, they are better able to understand the feelings of others and regulate their own. Finally, to collectively create and manage complex plots, preschoolers must resolve their disputes through negotiation and compromise—experiences that contribute greatly to their ability to get along with others (Howes, 1992; Singer & Singer, 1990).

MIDDLE CHILDHOOD AND ADOLESCENCE

When formal schooling begins, children are exposed to agemates who differ in many ways, including achievement, ethnicity, religion, interests, and personality. Contact with a wider variety of peers probably contributes to elementary school children's increasing

TABLE 15.1

Changes in Parten's Social Play Types from Preschool to Kindergarten

Play Type	Preschool 3–4 Years	Kindergarten 5–6 Years
Nonsocial activity	41%	34%
Unoccupied, onlooker behavior	(19)	(14)
Solitary play	(22)	(20)
Parallel play	22	23
Cooperative play	37	43

Sources: Preschool percentages are averages of those reported by Barnes (1971); Rubin, Maioni, & Hornung (1976); Rubin, Watson, & Jambor (1978); and Smith (1978). Kindergarten figures are averages of those reported by Barnes (1971) and Rubin, Watson, & Jambor (1978).

awareness that others have viewpoints different from their own (see Chapter 11). Peer communication, in turn, profits from improved perspective taking. Children of this age are better at accurately interpreting others' emotions and intentions and taking them into account in peer dialogues. In addition, their ability to understand the complementary roles of several players permits the transition to rule-oriented games in middle childhood (refer again to Table 15.2).

School-age children apply their greater awareness of prosocial norms to peer interaction. Recall from Chapter 12 that sharing, helping, and other prosocial acts increase in middle childhood. In addition, younger and older children differ in the way they go about helping agemates. Kindergartners move right in and give assistance, regardless of whether it is desired or not. In contrast, school-age children offer to help and wait for a peer to accept it before behaving prosocially. During adolescence, agemates work on tasks more cooperatively—staying on task, exchanging ideas freely, asking for opinions, and acknowledging one another's contributions (Hartup, 1983). In line with children's greater sensitivity to prosocial expectations, the overall incidence of aggression drops off in middle childhood, although (as we indicated in Chapter 13) its form makes a difference. Verbal insults among boys and social ostracism among girls continue into adolescence, whereas physical attacks decline.

■ *Rough-and-tumble play can be distinguished from aggression by its good-natured quality. In our evolutionary past, it may have been important for the development of fighting skills. (Nancy Sheehan/The Picture Cube)*

As children enter middle childhood, another form of peer interaction becomes increasingly common. Watch children at play in a public park or schoolyard, and you will see that they sometimes wrestle, roll, hit, and run after one another while smiling and laughing. This friendly chasing and play-fighting is called **rough-and-tumble play**. Research indicates that it is a good-natured, sociable activity that is quite distinct from aggressive fighting. Children in many cultures engage in it with peers whom they like especially well, and they continue interacting after a rough-and-tumble episode rather than separating, as they do at the end of an aggressive encounter. Sometimes parents and teachers mistake rough-and-tumble for real fighting and try to intervene. In these instances, children often respond, "It's all right, we're only playing." School-age youngsters are quite good at telling the difference between playful wrestling and a true aggressive attack (Costabile et al., 1991; Smith & Hunter, 1992).

Rough-and-tumble occurs more often among boys. When girls display it, they usually run and chase, whereas boys wrestle and hit. The similarity of these behaviors to the play of young mammals of many species suggests that this form of interaction has some adaptive value. In our evolutionary past, it may have been important for the development of dominance and fighting skills. Consistent with this idea, by age 11 children choose rough-and-tumble partners who are not only likable but similar in strength to themselves (Humphreys & Smith, 1987). And adolescent boys who often play-fight are rated as "tougher" by their classmates (Pellegrini, 1995).

Over middle childhood, children interact increasingly often with peers until, by midadolescence, more time is spent with them than with any other social partners (Csikszentmihalyi & Larson, 1984). Common interests, novel play activities, and opportunities to interact on an equal footing make peer interaction especially gratifying. As adolescence draws to a close, most young people emerge from their peer experiences proficient in many complex social behaviors.

Rough-and-tumble play
A form of peer interaction involving friendly chasing and play-fighting that, in our evolutionary past, may have been important for the development of fighting skill.

TABLE 15.2

Developmental Sequences of Cognitive Play Categories

Play Type	Ages at Which Especially Common	Definition	Examples
Functional play	1–2 years	Simple, repetitive motor movements with or without objects	Running around a room, rolling a car back and forth, kneading clay with no intent to make something
Constructive play	3–6 years	Creating or constructing something	Making a house out of toy blocks, drawing a picture, putting together a puzzle
Make-believe play	3–7 years	Acting out everyday and imaginary roles	Playing house, school, or police officer; acting out fairy-tales or television characters.
Games with rules	6–11 years	Understanding and following rules in play activities	Playing board games, cards, hopscotch, baseball.

Source: Rubin, Fein, & Vandenberg, 1983.

Influences on Peer Sociability

What can adults do to promote peer sociability? In the following sections, we will see that parental encouragement affects child–child interaction. So do situational factors that adults can influence, such as play materials and age mix of children. And cultural values make a difference as well.

PARENTAL ENCOURAGEMENT

During the preschool years, children are limited in their ability to find playmates on their own. They depend on parents to help them establish rewarding peer associations. Parents influence children's peer relations in many ways. One is through the neighborhood they choose to live in. Neighborhoods differ in the extent to which they permit easy contact among children. When children live some distance from one another and cannot gather on their own, parents must act as social planners and "booking agents," scheduling play activities at home, taking children to community settings such as the library or pool, and enrolling them in preschool and other organized activities that offer contact with peers (Parke et al., 1994). Parents who frequently arrange informal peer play activities tend to have preschoolers with larger peer networks and who display more prosocial behavior with agemates. In providing opportunities for peer play, parents show children how to initiate their own peer contacts and encourage them to be good "hosts" who are concerned about their playmates' needs (Ladd & Hart, 1992).

Parents also influence their children's social relations by offering advice and guidance about how to interact with playmates (Russell & Finnie, 1990). Furthermore, in earlier chapters, we discussed many examples of how parents' own social behavior provides preschoolers with models of how to act toward others. Child-rearing styles are strongly associated with the quality of children's peer interactions. In one study, mothers who often used unclear commands and negatives ("Don't" or "No, you can't") and who rarely made polite suggestions ("Please . . ." or "Why don't you . . .") in toddlerhood had 5-year-olds who were aggressive and unsuccessful in influencing agemates (Kochanska, 1992).

PLAY MATERIALS

Quantity of play materials has a major impact on young children's peer interaction. Fights and quarrels increase when preschoolers are confined to a relatively small space and there are not enough toys to go around (Smith & Connolly, 1980).

Peer interaction also varies with the toys available. Art, construction materials, blocks, and puzzles tend to be associated with solitary and parallel play, open-ended and relatively unstructured objects with cooperative play (Farver, Kim, & Lee, 1995). Type of open-ended materials also makes a difference. Preschoolers use realistic toys (trucks, dolls, and tea sets) to act out everyday roles, such as mother, doctor, and baby. In contrast, nonspecific materials (pipe cleaners, cardboard cylinders, and paper bags) encourage fantastic role play, such as pirate and creature from outer space. Fantastic roles, in turn, prompt more complex social interaction, especially planning statements, as in "I'll be the pirate and you be the prisoner" or "Watch out! Now I'm going to jump ship!" Since fantastic make-believe does not follow familiar everyday scripts, children devote more time to planning each episode and explaining to peer companions what they are doing (McLoyd, Warren, & Thomas, 1984).

AGE MIX OF CHILDREN

The theories of Piaget and Vygotsky, which we discussed in Chapter 6, suggest different benefits from interacting with same-age as opposed to different-age peers. Piaget (1932/1965) emphasized experiences with children equal in status who challenge one another's viewpoints, thereby fostering cognitive, social, and moral development. In contrast, Vygotsky (1930–1935/1978) believed that children profit from interacting with older, more capable peers, who encourage more advanced skills in their younger counterparts.

Beginning in infancy, experience with older children seems to foster peer interaction. Babies with older siblings are more socially responsive to same-age playmates, both positively and negatively. They more often laugh and imitate as well as hit, push, and grab than do infants without brothers and sisters (Vandell & Mueller, 1995). And 12-month-olds who are around older children at least once a week are more likely to make social contact with a peer (Vandell, 1996). As skills in relating to agemates improve, they return to enhance other relationships. Preschoolers whose interactions with a best friend are especially cooperative develop more positive relationships with younger siblings (Kramer & Gottman, 1992).

Children interact differently with same-age and different-age youngsters. In several studies, preschool and early elementary school children played or worked on problem-solving tasks. Mixed-age conditions led to a greater quantity and complexity of interaction by younger children, along with special accommodations by older children, who reduced their rate of communication and assumed more responsibility for the task (Brody, Graziano, & Musser, 1983; Howes & Farver, 1987). Nevertheless, the oldest children in mixed-age settings prefer same-age companions, perhaps because they have more compatible play interests and experience more cooperative interaction. Younger children's interaction with same-age partners is also more intense and harmonious, but they often turn to older peers because of their superior knowledge and exciting play ideas.

■ *These children of Kenya, East Africa, learn to play a game with the guidance of a more mature peer. Mixed-age interaction supports the development of new competencies in younger children and prosocial behavior in their older companions. (Owen Franken/Stock Boston)*

By middle childhood, children are consciously aware of the unique functions of older, younger, and same-age peers. They say they prefer to form friendships with agemates; to seek help, comfort, and instruction from older children; and to give help and sympathy to younger ones (French, 1984). Children clearly profit from both same-age and mixed-age relationships. From interacting with coequals, they learn to cooperate and resolve conflicts, and they develop important moral notions of justice and reciprocity (see Chapters 11 and 12). In addition, younger children acquire new competencies from their older companions, and when more mature children teach their less mature counterparts, they practice nurturance, guidance, and other prosocial behaviors.

CULTURAL VALUES

Culture shapes environments in which children's interaction and play activities take place. In collectivist societies that stress group harmony, peer sociability takes different forms than in individualistic cultures like the United States. For example, children in India generally play in large groups that require high levels of cooperation. Much of their behavior during make-believe and early games is imitative, occurs in unison, and involves close physical contact. In a game called Atiya Piatiya, children sit in a circle, join hands, and swing while they recite a jingle. In Bhatto Bhatto, they act out a script about a trip to the market that involves touching each other's elbows and hands as they pretend to cut and share a tasty vegetable (Roopnarine et al., 1994). Similarly, Marquesan preschoolers of Polynesia gather in groups of as many as ten children. Familiar, highly scripted activities reduce opportunities for disagreement. Older, dominant children help keep younger children oriented toward group goals through persuasion and, sometimes, shaming when they drift off into self-centered play (Martini, 1994).

Cultural beliefs about the importance of play also affect the quantity and quality of peer associations. Caregivers who view play as mere entertainment are less likely to provide props and encourage pretend than those who value its cognitive and educational benefits (Farver & Wimbarti, 1995a, 1995b). Korean-American parents, who emphasize task persistence as the means to academic success, have preschoolers who spend less time at joint make-believe and more time unoccupied and in parallel play than do their Caucasian-American counterparts. A cultural deemphasis on individuality and self-expression may also contribute to Korean-American children's reduced involvement in social pretending (Farver, Kim, & Lee, 1995).

During adolescence, peer contact rises in all cultures, but it is particularly high in industrialized nations, where young people spend most of each weekday with agemates in school. Teenagers also spend much out-of-class time together, especially in the United States. American teenagers average 18 nonschool hours per week with peers, compared to 12 hours for Japanese and 9 hours for Taiwanese adolescents (Fuligni & Stevenson, 1995). Higher rates of maternal employment and less demanding academic standards in the United States probably account for this difference.

BRIEF REVIEW

Experiments with rhesus monkeys reveal that peer interaction is a vital source of social competence. Peer sociability begins in infancy as isolated smiles, gestures, and babbles evolve into coordinated interaction. During the preschool years, cooperative play increases, but solitary and parallel play are also common. Within each of these play types, children's activities become more cognitively complex. During middle childhood and adolescence, gains in communication skills and greater awareness of social norms contribute to advances in peer interaction. In our evolutionary past, rough-and-tumble play may have been important for the development of dominance and fighting skill.

Parents influence young children's peer relations by arranging peer play activities and teaching and modeling effective social skills. Richly equipped play environments, nonspecific toys, and same-age peers promote highly positive, cooperative child–child interaction. Mixed-age contact permits older children to practice prosocial skills and younger children to learn from more mature partners. Cultural values influence the quantity and quality of peer associations.

Peer Acceptance

As we all know from our own childhoods, some children are more desirable peer companions than others. The term peer acceptance refers to likability—the extent to which a child is viewed by agemates as a worthy social partner. Researchers usually assess it with self-report measures called **sociometric techniques**. For example, children may be asked to nominate several peers in their class whom they especially like or dislike, to indicate for all possible pairs of classmates which one they prefer to play with, or to rate each peer on a scale from "like very much" to "like very little." Children as young as age 4 can answer these questions reliably (Hymel, 1983).

Sociometric techniques yield four different categories of social acceptance: **popular children**, who get many positive votes; **rejected children**, who are actively disliked; **controversial children**, who get a large number of positive and negative votes; and **neglected children**, who are seldom chosen, either positively or negatively. About two-thirds of pupils in a typical elementary school classroom fit one of these categories. The remaining one-third are *average* in peer acceptance; they do not receive extreme scores (Coie, Dodge, & Coppotelli, 1982).

Peer acceptance is a powerful predictor of current as well as later psychological adjustment. Rejected children, especially, are unhappy, alienated, poorly achieving children with a low sense of self-esteem. Both teachers and parents view them as having a wide range of emotional and social problems. Peer rejection during middle childhood is also strongly associated with poor school performance, absenteeism, dropping out, antisocial behavior, and delinquency in adolescence and criminality in young adulthood (DeRosier, Kupersmidt, & Patterson, 1994; Ollendick et al., 1992; Parker & Asher, 1987). In contrast, research on the outcomes of neglected peer status suggests that it carries much less risk of long-term psychological difficulties. And at present, we have little evidence on how controversial children, who are both liked and disliked, fare in the long run.

Although poor peer acceptance predicts a wide variety of later life problems and certainly may contribute to them, keep in mind that the evidence just described is correlational. Therefore, peer relations may not be a major causal factor. Instead, they may be linked to psychological adjustment through other prior influences, such as children's personality characteristics, parenting practices, or some combination of the two. Indeed, warm support, explanations, and well-coordinated communication tend to characterize the child rearing of popular children; high life stress, power-assertive discipline, and dialogue with frequent interruptions and talkovers characterize the home lives of rejected children (Black & Logan, 1995; Dekovic & Janssens, 1992; Putallaz & Heflin, 1990). At the same time, we will see that popular and rejected youngsters' styles of interaction prompt very different reactions from agemates, which probably compound the impact of family influences. In the following sections, we consider factors in the peer situation that increase the chances that a child will fall into one rather than another peer acceptance category.

ORIGINS OF ACCEPTANCE IN THE PEER SITUATION

What leads one child to be liked, a second to be disliked, and a third to evoke neither positive nor negative reactions from peers? To explore this question, researchers have correlated many child characteristics with sociometric scores. They have also conducted short-term longitudinal research to isolate the behavioral causes of different types of peer acceptance. But before we turn to these findings, let's look at the significance of an important nonbehavioral attribute for children's popularity: their physical appearance.

■ PHYSICAL APPEARANCE. In Chapter 5, we indicated that physical attractiveness has an important bearing on peer acceptance. Recall that children and adolescents who deviate from society's standards of physical beauty as a result of obesity or pubertal timing are less well accepted by peers.

Although the strong preference in our culture for a lithesome female body and a muscular male physique is probably learned (see Chapter 5), partiality for certain facial features emerges so early that it may be built in. Three- to 6-month-old infants look longer at faces judged attractive as opposed to unattractive by adults, regardless of the age, race, and sex of the model (Langlois et al., 1991). By 12 months, they vary their

Sociometric techniques
Self-report measures that ask peers to evaluate one another's likability.

Popular children
Children who get many positive votes on sociometric measures of peer acceptance.

Rejected children
Children who are actively disliked and get many negative votes on sociometric measures of peer acceptance.

Controversial children
Children who get a large number of positive and negative votes on sociometric measures of peer acceptance.

Neglected children
Children who are seldom chosen, either positively or negatively, on sociometric measures of peer acceptance.

behavior in response to attractiveness, showing more positive affect and involved play and less withdrawal toward an attractive as opposed to unattractive unfamiliar adult (Langlois, Roggman, & Rieser-Danner, 1990).

During early and middle childhood, children have different expectations of attractive and unattractive agemates. When asked to guess the characteristics of unfamiliar peers from their photographs, they attribute friendliness, smartness, and niceness to those who are good-looking and aggressiveness and other negative behaviors to those who are unattractive (Adams & Crane, 1980; Langlois & Stephan, 1977). Attractiveness is also associated with popularity and behavior ratings among children who know each other well, although these relationships are stronger for girls than boys (Langlois & Styczynski, 1979).

Parents show this "beauty is best" bias as well (Adams, 1978; Ritts, Patterson, & Tubbs, 1992). In one study, African-American, Caucasian-American, and Mexican-American mothers of attractive newborns expressed more affection toward their babies, whereas those of less attractive newborns displayed more routine caregiving and attention to other people. Mothers also regarded unattractive infants as interfering more in parents' lives (Langlois et al., 1995).

Do children derive their opinions about attractive and unattractive agemates from the way they actually behave or from stereotypes held by adults? To investigate this question, Judith Langlois and Chris Downs (1979) assigned 3- to 5-year-olds to the following same-age, same-sex pairs: two attractive children, two unattractive children, and one attractive and one unattractive child. Then they observed each pair in a laboratory play session. By age 5, unattractive children more often aggressed against their partners than attractive children did. These findings indicate that unattractive children actually display some of the negative behaviors peers attribute to them. However, since differences did not appear until the end of the preschool years, it is possible that unattractive children responded as they did because of others' prior reactions to their physical appearance.

In sum, beginning early in life, a preference for attractive over unattractive children translates into differential adult and peer treatment. Then children may respond in kind to the way they are treated, thereby sustaining the prejudices of their social world.

■ SOCIAL BEHAVIOR. Already we have suggested that social behavior plays a powerful role in peer acceptance. A wealth of research indicates that popular, rejected, controversial, and neglected children interact with agemates in distinct ways.

Popularity is consistently associated with social competence. Well-liked children are effective social problem solvers and communicate with peers in sensitive, friendly, and cooperative ways (Newcomb, Bukowski, & Pattee, 1993). When they do not understand another child's reaction, they are likely to ask for an explanation. If they disagree with a play partner in a game, they go beyond voicing their displeasure; they suggest what the other child could do instead. When they want to enter an ongoing play group, they adapt their behavior to the flow of peer activity (Gottman, Gonso, & Rasmussen, 1975; Ladd & Price, 1987).

Rejected children, in contrast, display a wide range of negative social behaviors. But not all of these disliked children look the same. At least two subtypes exist. **Rejected-aggressive children**, the largest subgroup, show severe conduct problems—high rates of conflict, hostility, and hyperactive, inattentive, and impulsive behavior. They are also deficient in several social-cognitive skills that we discussed in Chapter 11. For example, they are more likely than other children to be poor perspective takers, to misinterpret the innocent behaviors of others as hostile, and to blame others for their social difficulties (Crick & Ladd, 1993; Dekovic & Gerris, 1994). In contrast, **rejected-withdrawn children**, a smaller subgroup, are passive and socially awkward. These children, especially, feel lonely, hold negative expectations for how peers will treat them, and are very concerned about being scorned and attacked (Bierman, Smoot, & Aumiller, 1993; Rabiner, Keane, & MacKinnon-Lewis, 1993; Stewart & Rubin, 1995). Because of their inept, submissive style of interaction, rejected-withdrawn children are at risk for abuse at the hands of bullies (see the From Research to Practice box on the following page).

Consistent with the mixed peer opinion they engender, controversial children display a blend of positive and negative social behaviors. Like rejected-aggressive children, they are hostile and disruptive, but they also engage in positive, prosocial acts. Even though they are disliked by some peers, controversial children have some qualities

Rejected-aggressive children
A subgroup of rejected children who engage in high rates of conflict, hostility, and hyperactive, inattentive, and impulsive behavior.

Rejected-withdrawn children
A subgroup of rejected children who are passive and socially awkward.

FROM RESEARCH TO PRACTICE

Bullies and Their Victims

Follow the activities of aggressive children over a school day, and you will see that they reserve their hostilities for a small number of peers who consistently serve in the role of victims. What is it about these children that invites and sustains attacks against them? Answers to this question are important, since efforts to reduce victimized children's chances of being targeted for abuse would help to control peer aggression.

In one of the most comprehensive studies of the aggressor–victim relationship, Dan Olweus (1978, 1984) asked Swedish teachers to nominate adolescent male bullies, their "whipping boys," and well-adjusted classmates. Then judgments of each group's characteristics were obtained from teachers, mothers, peers, and the boys themselves. Compared to bullies and well-adjusted adolescents, whipping boys were chronically anxious (at home and at school), low in self-esteem, ostracized by peers, physically weak, and afraid to defend themselves.

These findings suggest that victimized children might be attacked more than others because they are perceived as weak and likely to provide their aggressors with rewarding consequences. Indeed, frequently victimized children often reinforce their attackers by giving in to their demands, crying, assuming defensive postures, and failing to fight back. They also have histories of resistant attachment and maternal overprotectiveness that may contribute to their radiation of anxious vulnerability (Olweus, 1993; Troy & Sroufe, 1987).

By elementary school, 10 to 20 percent of children are harassed by aggressive agemates, and peers view these targets differently. They expect victims to give up desirable objects, show signs of distress, and fail to retaliate far more often than nonvictims. In addition, children feel less discomfort at the prospect of causing pain and suffering to victims than nonvictims. These reactions are especially strong for boys and aggressive children (Perry, Williard, & Perry, 1990). In sum, peers are convinced they will succeed at attacking a victimized child and minimize the possibility of harmful consequences.

Aggression and victimization are not polar opposites. Some of the most extreme victims are also very aggressive, picking fights and getting others into trouble (Boulton & Smith, 1994; Olweus, 1978). Perhaps these children foolishly provoke stronger agemates, who then prevail over them. Although both aggressive and victimized children are rejected by peers, these highly aggressive–highly abused youngsters are the most despised, placing them at severe risk for maladjustment.

Interventions that change victimized children's negative opinions of themselves and that teach them to respond in nonreinforcing ways to their attackers (for example, with assertiveness and humor to teasing) are vital. Nevertheless, the findings just described should not be taken to imply that victimized children are to blame for their abuse. Instead, the responsibility lies with bullies who brutally taunt and assault and adults who supervise children's interactions. Inviting students to participate in developing a school code of conduct against bullying, enlisting parents' assistance in changing behavior, and moving aggressive children to another class or school in extreme cases can reduce bully–victim problems (Olweus, 1994).

that protect them from social exclusion. As a result, they appear to be relatively happy and comfortable with their peer relationships (Newcomb, Bukowski, & Pattee, 1993; Parkhurst & Asher, 1992).

Finally, perhaps the most surprising finding on peer acceptance is that neglected children, once thought to be in need of treatment, are usually well adjusted. Although they engage in low rates of interaction and are considered shy by their classmates, they are not less socially skilled than average children. They do not report feeling especially lonely or unhappy about their social life, and when they want to, they can break away from their usual pattern of playing by themselves (Crick & Ladd, 1993; Wentzel & Asher, 1995). Neglected children's status probably reflects their lack of visibility to agemates. They remind us that there are other paths to emotional well-being besides the outgoing, gregarious personality style so highly valued in our culture.

HELPING REJECTED CHILDREN

A variety of interventions aimed at improving the peer relations and psychological adjustment of rejected children have been developed. Most are based on social learning theory and involve coaching, modeling, and reinforcement of positive social skills, such as how to begin interacting with a peer, cooperate in play, and respond to another child with friendly emotion and approval. Several of these programs have produced gains in social competence and peer acceptance that were still present from several weeks to a year later (Bierman, 1986; Lochman et al., 1993; Mize & Ladd, 1990).

Some researchers believe that these interventions might be even more effective when combined with other treatments. Often rejected children are poor students, and their low academic self-esteem magnifies their negative reactions to teachers and classmates.

Intensive academic tutoring improves their school achievement and social acceptance (Coie & Krehbiel, 1984). In addition, techniques designed to reduce rejected-aggressive children's antisocial behavior are helpful. In one study, including verbal prohibitions against antisocial acts and negative consequences for engaging in them in a social-skills coaching program led to better social acceptance than a program that focused only on teaching positive social behaviors (Bierman, Miller, & Stabb, 1987).

Social-cognitive interventions, such as training in perspective taking and social problem solving, have also produced favorable outcomes. Furthermore, increasing rejected children's expectations for social success is often necessary. Many conclude, after repeated rebuffs from peers, that no matter how hard they try, they will never be liked. Rejected children seem to make better use of the social skills they do have when they believe peers will accept them (Rabiner & Coie, 1989).

Finally, we have seen that the problems rejected children experience may originate, at least in part, within the family. Therefore, interventions that focus on the individual child may not be sufficient. If the quality of parent–child interaction is not changed, rejected children may soon return to their old behavior patterns. The most successful approach to treatment may involve replacing coercive cycles with effective parenting techniques (see Chapter 12) in addition to promoting improved peer relations.

BRIEF REVIEW

Peer acceptance is a powerful predictor of long-term psychological adjustment. Rejected children, especially, display serious academic and behavior problems. Physical attractiveness is related to likability. Differential treatment of physically attractive and unattractive children may affect the way they behave, thereby sustaining peer opinion. Children's social behavior is a major determinant of peer acceptance. Popular children interact in a cooperative, friendly fashion; rejected children behave antisocially and ineptly; and controversial children display a mixture of positive and negative social behaviors. Although neglected children engage in low rates of peer interaction, they are usually socially competent and well adjusted. Interventions that train social skills, provide academic tutoring, reduce antisocial behavior, and change social cognitions lead to improved social acceptance of rejected children.

Peer Groups

If you watch children in the schoolyard or neighborhood, you will see that groups of three to a dozen often gather. The organization of these collectives changes greatly with age. By the end of middle childhood, children display a strong desire for group belongingness. Together, they generate unique values and standards for behavior. They also create a social structure of leaders and followers that ensures group goals will be met. When these characteristics are present, a **peer group** is formed (Hartup, 1983).

In Chapter 11, we saw how friendships in middle childhood and adolescence contribute to the development of trust and sensitivity. Children's experiences in peer groups also provide a unique context for social learning—one in which children practice cooperation, leadership, and followership and develop a sense of loyalty to collective goals. Through these experiences, children experiment with and learn about the functioning of social organizations.

PEER GROUP FORMATION

A classic study by Muzafer Sherif and his colleagues (1961), called the Robbers Cave experiment, illustrates how peer groups form and their functions in children's lives. Fifth-grade boys were brought to a summer campground called Robbers Cave, divided

Peer group
Peers who form a social unit by generating unique values and standards of behavior and a social structure of leaders and followers.

■ *Peer groups first form in middle childhood. These boys have probably established a social structure of leaders and followers as they gather often for joint activities, such as bike riding and basketball. Their body language suggests that they feel a strong sense of group belonging. (R. Sidney/The Image Works)*

into two clusters of 11 members each, and removed to separate campsites. Although friendships quickly developed, a strong group structure did not emerge until the camp staff arranged activities that required cooperation. Backpacking trips and opportunities to improve swimming and athletic areas led the campers to create a division of labor. Soon several boys with superior skills took on greater status—one for his cooking, another for his athletic ability, and a third for his entertaining personality. Over time, a clear ranking of leaders and followers emerged.

As the group structure took shape, the boys at each campsite developed distinct notions of appropriate behavior and ways of doing things. For example, one group generated a "norm of toughness." They engaged in rowdiness and swearing, suppressed any signs of pain when injured, and refused treatment for cuts and scratches. In contrast, a "norm of good behavior" arose in the other group. These boys were considerate and used clean language. At each campsite, group members coined nicknames for one another and used special language styles. Eventually the groups took names for themselves: the Rattlers and the Eagles. The boys in each displayed a strong group identity.

The next phase of Sherif's study showed that a group's norms and social structures develop further, based on its relationship with "outsiders." The camp counselors arranged for a tournament of competitive games. Sparked by intergroup rivalry, new leaders and normative behaviors appeared. Among the Rattlers, a large bully emerged as a hero, who led the group in insulting and retaliating against the outgroup, with each successful attack intensifying group solidarity. Over time, the Rattlers and Eagles stereotyped each other as nasty and sneaky, reactions that further magnified the social distance between the groups.

In the final phase of the study, the camp staff tried to create friendly interaction between the groups. Joint recreational activities, however, were disasters, providing opportunities for each group to continue berating the other. But once the counselors planned events with superordinate goals, intergroup hostility began to subside. In one instance, the water supply "broke down," and in another, a truck preparing to get food for the hungry campers "stalled." As a result, all campers joined forces to solve common problems, negative stereotyping declined, and new friendships emerged that cut across group lines.

The Robbers Cave experiment reveals that peer groups form when individuals perceive that others share similar goals. Norms and social structures emerge and change in the service of common motivations. Although racial and ethnic differences often promote prejudice and stereotyping, Sherif's study shows that competition for highly desired resources is enough to evoke deep-seated hostilities. Superordinate goals can reduce intergroup hatred and promote positive attitudes and relationships. Now let's take a closer look at two features that are essential for peer group cohesion: norms and social structures.

■ *These teenage girls have a unique dress code, probably speak to each other in distinct ways, and engage in behaviors that separate them from other cliques and the adult world. Cliques serve as the main context for peer interaction during adolescence, permitting young people to acquire new social skills and experiment with values and roles in the absence of adult monitoring. (David Young-Wolff/ PhotoEdit)*

GROUP NORMS

Group norms are evident by the end of elementary school and strengthen during the teenage years, when peer groups become more tightly knit and exclusive. Adolescent peer groups are organized around **cliques**, small groups of about five to seven members who are good friends and, therefore, usually alike in age, ethnicity, and social class (see Chapter 11). In early adolescence, cliques are limited to same-sex members, but by the midadolescent years, mixed-sex groups become common. The cliques within a typical high school can be identified by their interests and social status, as the well-known "popular" and "unpopular" groups in virtually every school reveal (Cairns et al., 1995; Gillmore et al., 1996). Once formed, cliques develop dress codes, ways of speaking, and behaviors that separate them from one another and from the adult world.

Sometimes adolescents form a larger, more loosely organized group called a **crowd**. Unlike the more intimate clique, membership in a crowd is based on reputation and stereotype. Whereas the clique serves as the main context for direct interaction, the crowd grants the adolescent an identity within the larger social structure of the school. In a typical high school, for example, the "jocks" are very involved in athletics; the "brains" worry about their grades; and the "workers" have part-time jobs and lots of spending money. The "druggies" use drugs on more than a one-time basis, while the "greasers" wear dark jackets, cross the street to smoke cigarettes, and feel alienated from most aspects of school life (Brown, 1990; Urberg et al., 1995).

What influences the assortment of teenagers into cliques and crowds with particular normative characteristics? Research reveals that family influences are important. In a study of 8,000 ninth to twelfth graders, adolescents who described their parents as authoritative (warm and demanding) were members of "brain," "jock," and "popular" groups that accepted both the adult and peer reward systems of the school. In contrast, boys whose parents were permissive (warm but undemanding) valued interpersonal relationships and aligned themselves with the "fun culture," or "partyer" crowd. And teenagers who viewed their parents as uninvolved (low in warmth and demandingness) more often affiliated with "partyer" and "druggie" crowds, suggesting lack of identification with adult reward systems (Durbin et al., 1993).

These findings indicate that many peer group norms are extensions of ones acquired at home. But once adolescents join a clique or crowd, it can modify their beliefs and behaviors. For example, when adolescents associate with peers who have authoritative parents, their friends' competence "rubs off" on them. Authoritative parenting within

Clique
A small group of about five to seven members who are good friends.

Crowd
A large, loosely organized group consisting of several cliques with similar normative characteristics.

the peer network is associated with better academic performance and lower levels of delinquency and substance abuse, beyond the impact of authoritativeness in the teenager's own home (Fletcher et al., 1995). However, the positive impact of having academically and socially skilled peers is greatest for teenagers whose own parents are authoritative. And the negative impact of having antisocial, drug-using friends is strongest for teenagers whose parents use less effective child-rearing styles (Mounts & Steinberg, 1995). In sum, family experiences affect the extent to which adolescents become like their peers over time.

In early adolescence, as interest in dating increases, boys' and girls' cliques come together. The merger takes place slowly. At junior high school dances and parties, clusters of boys and girls can be seen standing on opposite sides of the room, watching but seldom interacting. As mixed-sex cliques form and "hang out" together, they provide a supportive context for boys and girls to get to know each other, offering models for how to interact with the opposite sex and opportunities to do so without having to be intimate. Gradually, the larger group divides into couples, several of whom spend time together, going to parties and movies. By late adolescence, boys and girls feel comfortable enough about approaching each other directly that the mixed-sex clique is no longer needed and disappears (Padgham & Blyth, 1990).

Just as cliques gradually decline in importance, so do crowds. As adolescents formulate their own personal values and goals, they no longer feel a strong need to wear a "badge" that broadcasts, through dress, language, and preferred activities, who they are. Nevertheless, both cliques and crowds serve vital functions during the teenage years. The clique provides a context for acquiring new social skills and for experimenting with values and roles in the absence of adult monitoring. The crowd offers adolescents the security of a temporary identity as they separate from the family and begin to construct a coherent sense of self (Brown, 1990).

GROUP SOCIAL STRUCTURES

In all groups, members differ in power or status, an arrangement that fosters division of responsibilities and smooth, cooperative interaction. Group norms and social structures are related. Leaders are generally the major norm setters, and the ideas of high-status peers are usually sufficient to alter the group's opinion (Adler & Adler, 1995). How do leaders and followers emerge in children's groups?

Ethological research reveals that group social structures are sometimes based on toughness or assertiveness. A **dominance hierarchy** is a stable ordering of individuals that predicts who will win when conflict arises between group members. Observations of arguments, threats, and physical attacks between children reveal a consistent lineup of winners and losers as early as the preschool years. This hierarchy becomes increasingly stable during middle childhood and adolescence, especially among boys (Pettit et al., 1990; Savin-Williams, 1979).

Like dominance relations among animals, those among human children serve the adaptive function of limiting aggression among group members. Once a dominance hierarchy is clearly established, hostility is rare. When it occurs, it is very restrained, often taking the form of playful verbal insults that can be accepted cheerfully by the target (Fine, 1980). This gradual replacement of friendly insults for more direct hostility may help children and adolescents learn how to control their aggressive impulses.

Think back to the Robbers Cave study, and you will see that group structures are not always a matter of the largest and strongest children rising to the top. When group goals involve the conquest of "outsiders," a structure based on dominance is likely to emerge, as it did when the Rattlers and Eagles played competitive games. At other times, quite different personal qualities become relevant. In a study of fourth- to sixth-grade Girl Scout troups, girls who emerged as informal leaders had traits reflecting an effective managerial style. They were friendly, thoughtful, organized, and quick to suggest new ideas. Often they were popular and physically attractive as well (Edwards, 1994). Many group structures also depend on talents that support important normative activities, such as knowing what to do on a camp-out or being a skilled athlete or debater (Savin-Williams, 1980). Since peer groups vary widely in their normative concerns, social power accrues to different young people in different situations.

Dominance hierarchy
A stable ordering of group members that predicts who will win under conditions of conflict.

Peer Relations and Socialization

We have seen that peer interaction contributes to a wide variety of skills that help children and adolescents adapt successfully to their social worlds. Just how do peers socialize one another? As we will see in the following sections, they use some of the same techniques that parents do: reinforcement, modeling, and direct pressures to conform to certain expectations.

PEER REINFORCEMENT AND MODELING

Children's responses to one another serve as reinforcers, modifying the extent to which they display certain behaviors. Turn back to Chapter 13, page 516, to review how peers reinforce gender-role behavior. Peer reinforcement begins early and increases with age. Children often use it for positive ends. Those who engage in attentive, approving, and affectionate social acts are likely to receive similar behaviors in return (Leiter, 1977).

However, children are just as receptive to peer reinforcement for antisocial responses as they are for prosocial behavior. In the From Research to Practice box on page 589, we showed that the hostile acts of bullies are repeatedly reinforced by the passivity of their victims. Children who retaliate and succeed at getting an aggressor to retreat punish that child's actions. At the same time, their own behavior is rewarded. A striking finding of observational research on preschoolers is a steady increase in aggressive behavior on the part of initially nonaggressive children who counterattack in the face of peer hostility (Patterson, Littman, & Bricker, 1967). Peer feedback is an important means through which children's aggression is enhanced as well as controlled, and even mild-mannered children can learn to behave aggressively from being targets of hostile attacks.

Besides dispensing reinforcers, peers provide one another with models of a broad array of social behaviors. Peer imitation is common throughout the preschool years, but by middle childhood it declines (Grusec & Abramovitch, 1982). Recall from Chapter 12 that once children internalize the rules of social life, they no longer need to rely so heavily on observations of others for information about how to behave.

The powerful effects of peer reinforcement and modeling have led researchers to experiment with peers as agents of behavior change. Socially competent children can be trained to encourage improved social skills in less competent peers, and both show gains in social maturity (Strain, 1977). Peers can also tutor less knowledgeable children at school, teaching, modeling and reinforcing academic skills. Carefully planned peer tutoring programs in which tutors are trained and supervised by adult teachers promote self-esteem and learning in both tutors and tutees. Peer tutoring is especially effective with low-income ethnic minority pupils who are achieving poorly in school (Bargh & Schul, 1980; Strickland & Ascher, 1992).

PEER CONFORMITY

Conformity to peer pressure is greater during adolescence than in childhood or young adulthood—a finding that is not surprising when we consider how much time teenagers spend together. But contrary to popular belief, adolescence is not a period in which young people blindly do what their peers ask. Peer conformity is a complex process that varies with the adolescent's age and need for social approval and with the situation.

In one study of nearly 400 junior and senior high students, adolescents reported that they felt greatest pressure to conform to the most obvious behaviors of their peers: dressing and grooming like everyone else and participating in social activities, such as dating and going to parties (see Figure 15.1). Peer pressure to engage in proadult behavior, such as getting good grades and cooperating with parents, was also strong. Although pressure toward misconduct rose in early adolescence, compared to other areas it was low. Many teenagers said that their friends actively discouraged antisocial acts. These findings

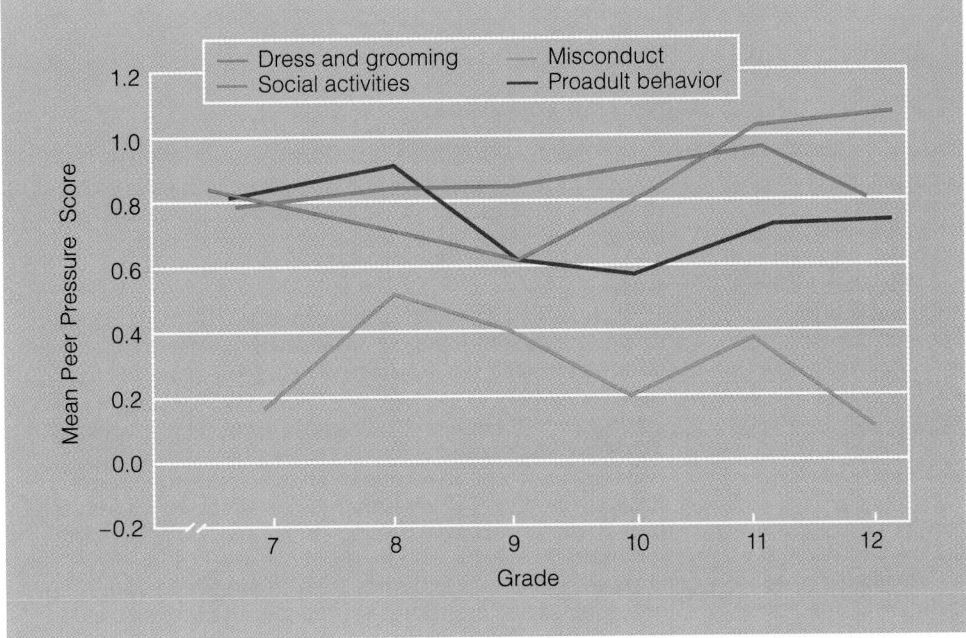

FIGURE 15.1

■ *Grade changes in perceived peer pressure in four areas of behavior in a cross-sectional study of junior and senior high school students. Overall, teenagers felt greatest pressure to conform to dress and grooming styles and social activities. Pressure to engage in proadult behavior was also strong. Although peer pressure toward misconduct peaked in early adolescence, it was relatively low. (From B. B. Brown, M. J. Lohr, & E. L. McClenahan, 1986, "Early Adolescents' Perceptions of Peer Pressure,"* Journal of Early Adolescence, *6, p. 147. Reprinted by permission.)*

show that peer and parental pressures often act in concert, toward desirable ends! Finally, peer pressures were only modestly related to teenagers' values and behaviors. Clearly, these young people did not always follow the dictates of peers (Brown, Lohr, & McClenahan, 1986).

Perhaps because of greater concern with what their friends think of them, early adolescents are more likely than younger or older individuals to give in to peer pressure (Brown, Clasen, & Eicher, 1986). Yet when parents and peers disagree, even young teenagers do not consistently rebel against their families. Instead, parents and peers differ in their spheres of greatest influence. Parents have more impact on teenagers' basic life values and educational plans (Sebald, 1986). Peers are more influential in short-term, day-to-day matters, such as type of dress, taste in music, and choice of friends.

Adolescents' personal characteristics also made a difference. Young people who feel competent and worthwhile are less likely to fall in line behind peers who engage in early sex, delinquency, and frequent drug use (see the Social Issues box on page 596). Research on poverty-stricken Brazilian street youths illustrates how family connectedness encourages this sense of well-being. As Figure 15.2 on page 597 shows, 9- to 18-year-olds who worked at street jobs and returned to their families at night or on weekends reported more social supports and fewer problem behaviors than did homeless youths with fragmented family ties. Asked to describe a typical day for a working and a homeless youth, teenage informants gave these accounts:

> [Working street youth]: If he's in school, he goes to school and when classes end, he buys peanuts and asks his mother to roast them. Then, he goes to the soccer field or plays cards until 5:30, when he goes out to sell [the peanuts] and gets home at 4:00 A.M.
>
> [Homeless street youth]: When we go to sleep it's about 5 in the morning; we wake up around 2 or 3 in the afternoon. You wake up, get up, wash your face, if you have money you have breakfast, go out to steal, then you start to sell the stuff and the money all goes on drugs, because on the street it's all drugs! . . . Then, you get high, you're all set, then you come down and sleep. (Campos et al., 1994, pp. 321–322)

Family support seemed to serve as an antidote to unfavorable peer pressures on the street, with profound consequences for development.

Before we turn to the impact of media on children, you may find it helpful to examine the Milestones table on page 598, which summarizes the development of peer relations.

SOCIAL ISSUES

Adolescent Substance Use and Abuse

In the United States, teenage alcohol and drug use is pervasive—higher than in any other industrialized nation (Newcomb & Bentler, 1989). By age 14, 56 percent of young people have already tried cigarette smoking, 81 percent drinking, and 39 percent at least one illegal drug (usually marijuana). By the end of high school, 15 percent are regular cigarette users, 32 percent have engaged in heavy drinking at least once, and over 43 percent have experimented with illegal drugs. Of these, about a third have tried at least one highly addictive and toxic substance, such as amphetamines, cocaine, phencyclidine (PCP), or heroin (U.S. Department of Health and Human Services, 1994).

Surprisingly, these high figures represent a decline in adolescent alcohol and drug use during the past decade, a period in which the media gave greater attention to the hazards of these substances (see Figure 15.3). Why do so many young people subject themselves to the health risks associated with alcohol and drugs? Part of the reason is cultural. Modern adolescents live in a drug-dependent society. They see adults using caffeine to wake up in the morning, cigarettes to cope with daily hassles, a drink to calm down in the evening, and additional remedies to relieve stress and physical illness.

For most young people, drug use simply reflects their intense curiosity about "adultlike" behaviors. One longitudinal study revealed that the majority of teenagers dabbled in alcohol as well as tobacco and marijuana. These *experimenters* were not headed for a life of decadence and addiction, as many adults believe. Instead, they were psychologically healthy, sociable, inquisitive adolescents who were actually better adjusted throughout their childhoods than *abstainers*—teenagers who never used drugs at all (Shedler & Block, 1990). In a society in which substance use is commonplace, it appears that some involvement with drugs is normal and to be expected.

Yet adolescent drug experimentation should not be taken lightly. Because most drugs impair perception and thought processes, a single heavy dose can lead to permanent injury or death. And a worrisome minority of teenagers move from substance use to abuse —taking drugs regularly, requiring increasing amounts to achieve the same effect, and finding themselves unable to stop (Kandel & Yamaguchi, 1993). Four percent of high school seniors are daily drinkers, and almost as many indicate that they took an illegal drug on a daily basis over the past month (U.S. Department of Health and Human Services, 1994).

In contrast to experimenters, drug abusers are seriously troubled young people who are inclined to express their unhappiness through antisocial acts. Additional longitudinal evidence shows that their impulsive, disruptive style is often evident in early childhood and seems to be perpetuated by a variety of other interrelated factors, including low-income backgrounds, family mental health problems, parental drug use, lack of parental involvement and support, and poor school performance. By early adolescence, peer encouragement—friends who use drugs, urge the young person to do so, and provide access to illegal substances—is a strong predictor of substance abuse, probably because at-risk teenagers seek out deviant agemates. Once an adolescent associates with drug-using peers, his or her own substance use approaches their level (Chassin et al., 1996; Dobkin et al., 1995; Stice & Barrera, 1995).

School-based programs that promote effective parenting (including monitoring of teenagers' activities) and that teach adolescents skills for resisting peer pressure reduce drug experimentation to some degree (Steinberg, Fletcher, & Darling, 1994). But some drug taking seems to be inevitable. Therefore, interventions that prevent adolescents from endangering themselves and others when they do experiment are essential. Many communities offer weekend on-call transportation services that any young person can contact for a safe ride home, with no questions asked. Providing appealing substitute activities, such as drug-free video arcades, dances, and sports activities, is also helpful. And educating teenagers about the dangers of drugs and alcohol is vital, since an increase in perceived risk closely paralleled the gradual decline in substance use in recent years (O'Malley, Johnston, & Bachman, 1995).

Drug abuse, as we have seen, occurs for quite different reasons than does occasional use. Therefore, different strategies are needed to deal with it. Hospitalization is often a necessary and even lifesaving first step. Once the young person is weaned from the drug, therapy to treat impulsiveness, antisocial behavior, and family problems and academic and vocational training to improve life success and satisfaction are generally needed. Not much is known about the best way to treat adolescent drug abuse. Even the most comprehensive programs have relapse rates that are alarmingly high—from 35 to 70 percent (Newcomb & Bentler, 1989).

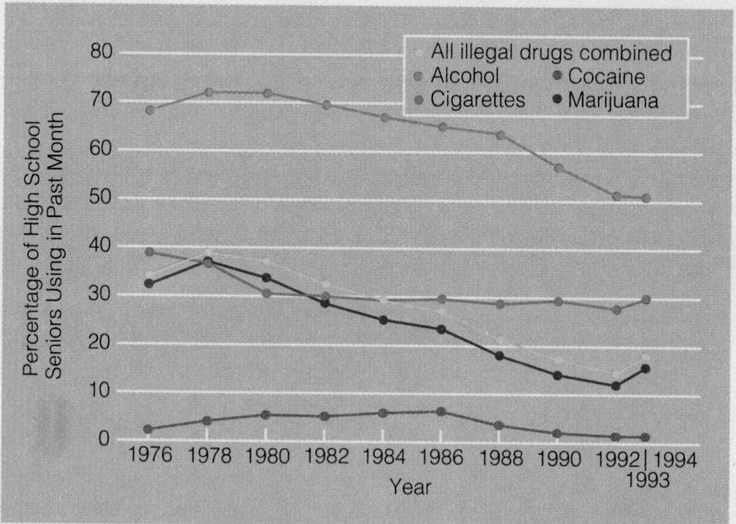

FIGURE 15.3

■ *Percentages of high school seniors reporting use of alcohol, cigarettes, and illegal drugs in the past month, 1976–1993. Substance use continues to be widespread among adolescents, although overall it has declined during the past decade. However, the sharp increase from 1992 to 1993—largely accounted for by marijuana and cigarette smoking—has sounded a note of alarm. (From U.S. Department of Health and Human Services, 1994.)*

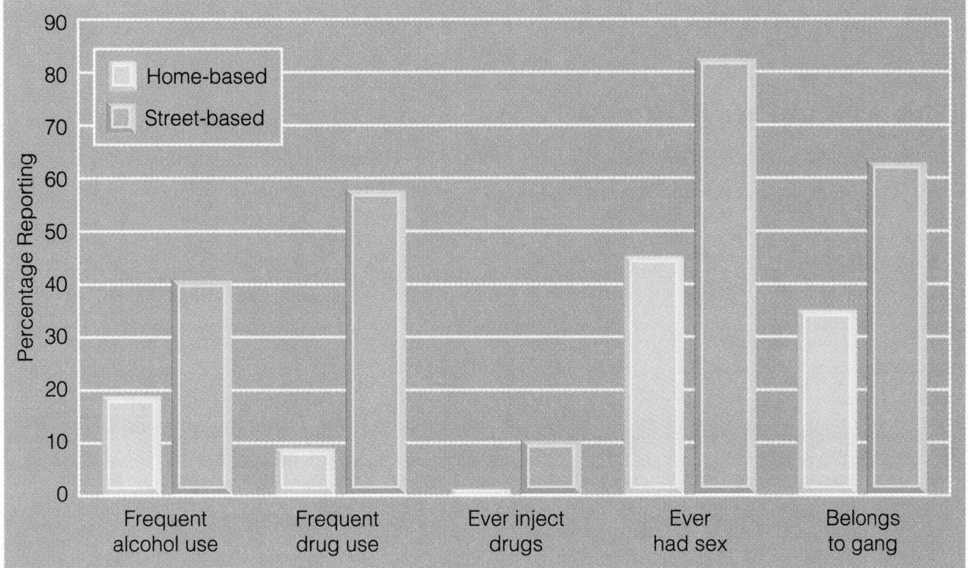

FIGURE 15.2

■ *Problem behaviors of Brazilian street youths who either worked at street jobs and returned to their families (home-based) or lived on the streets and had fragmented family ties (street-based). The greater social support available to home-based youths appeared to promote resistance to peer pressures, reducing problem behaviors. (Adapted from Campos et al., 1994.)*

BRIEF REVIEW

By the end of middle childhood, peer groups form, through which children and adolescents learn about the functioning of social organizations. Group norms foster a sense of belongingness. Group social structures lead to a division of responsibility and offer practice in leader and follower roles. Adolescent peer groups are organized around cliques, small groups of good friends, and crowds, large, loosely organized groups based on reputation and stereotype. The clique provides a setting in which adolescents learn social skills and try out new values and roles. The crowd offers a temporary identity as teenagers work on constructing their own. When group goals emphasize competitiveness, dominance often determines leader–follower roles. Otherwise, group structures depend on managerial skills and talents that support important normative activities.

Children socialize one another through reinforcement, modeling, and direct pressures to conform to peer expectations. The powerful effects of peer reinforcement and modeling have inspired social skills and tutoring programs in which peers serve as agents of behavior change. Conformity to peer pressure rises in adolescence, but teenagers do not mindlessly "follow the crowd." Peers have a more powerful impact on everyday matters of dress and social behavior, parents on basic life values and educational plans.

Television

Exposure to television is almost universal in the United States and other Western industrialized nations. Ninety-eight percent of American homes have at least one television set, over 50 percent have two or more, and a TV set is switched on in a typical household for an average of nearly 8 hours per day (Comstock, 1993). Although the popularity of television is widespread, there is good reason to be concerned about its effects on children and youths. In an unusual investigation, residents of a small Canadian town were studied just before TV reception became available in their community and then 2 years later. School-age children showed a decline in reading ability and creative thinking, a rise in gender-stereotyped beliefs, and an increase in verbal and physical aggression during play. In addition, a sharp drop in adolescents' community participation followed the arrival of television (Williams, 1986).

Worrisome findings like these have been reported in hundreds of studies over the past four decades. But they are not an inherent part of the medium itself. Instead, they

MILESTONES

Development of Peer Relations

Age	Peer Sociability	Peer Groups	Peer Socialization
Birth–2 years	■ Isolated social acts increase over the first year and are gradually replaced by coordinated interaction.		■ At the end of this period, peer reinforcement and modeling are evident.
2½–6 years	■ At the beginning of this period, children use words to affect a peer's behavior. ■ Parallel play appears, remains stable from 3 to 6 years, and becomes more cognitively mature. ■ Cooperative play increases—especially sociodramatic play. ■ Rough-and-tumble play emerges.	■ Dominance hierarchies emerge.	■ Peer modeling and reinforcement increase.
7–11 years	■ Peer communication skills improve, including interpreting and responding to the emotions and intentions of others. ■ Ability to understand the complementary roles of several players improves, permitting the transition to rule-oriented games. ■ Peer interaction becomes more prosocial, and aggression (in the form of physical attacks) declines. ■ Rough-and-tumble play becomes more common.	■ Peer groups with distinct norms and social structures emerge. ■ Dominance hierarchies become more stable.	■ As children internalize social rules, peer modeling declines.
12–20 years	■ Peer interaction becomes more cooperative. ■ More time is spent with peers than any other partners.	■ Peer groups become more tightly knit and exclusive, organized around cliques. ■ Large, loosely organized crowds form, based on reputation and stereotype.	■ Conformity to peer pressure increases and gradually declines.

Note: These milestones represent overall age trends. Individual differences exist in the precise age at which each milestone is attained.

result from the way it is used in our society. As our discussion proceeds, we will see that television has as much potential for good as for ill. If the content of TV programming were improved and adults capitalized on it to enhance children's interest in their everyday worlds, television could be a powerful, cost-effective means of strengthening cognitive, emotional, and social development.

HOW MUCH TELEVISION DO CHILDREN VIEW?

The amount of time children in the United States devote to television is extraordinary. Regular viewing typically begins between 2 and 3 years of age at about 1½ hours a day, a figure that rises to 4 hours by age 12 and then declines slightly during adolescence. The average American school-age child watches 28 hours per week (Comstock, 1993). When we consider how much time the set is on during school holidays and summer vacations, children spend more time watching television than they do in any other waking activity, including going to school and interacting with family members or peers.

Children differ in their attraction to television. Boys watch slightly more TV than do girls (Huston et al., 1990). And children with lower IQs, who come from low-income families, and who are members of poverty-stricken ethnic minorities tend to watch the most (Huston, Watkins, & Kunkel, 1989). Excessive TV viewing is also associated with adjustment problems, such as family and peer difficulties (Liebert, 1986).

DEVELOPMENT OF TELEVISION LITERACY

When watching TV programs, children are confronted with a rapid stream of people, objects, places, words, and sounds. Television, or film, has its own specialized code of conveying information. Researchers liken the task of cracking this code to that of learning to read, calling it **television literacy**. Although the symbolic learning required to understand television is not as great as that demanded by reading, it is still considerable.

Television literacy has two parts. The first involves understanding the form of the message. Children must master the meaning of a variety of visual and auditory effects, such as camera zooms, panoramic views, fade-outs, split screens, instant replays, and sound effects. Second, they must process the content of the message, constructing an accurate story line by integrating scenes, character behavior, and dialogue. These two parts are really interdependent, since television form provides essential cues to a program's content (Fitch, Huston, & Wright, 1993).

During early and middle childhood, children are captivated by TV's salient perceptual features. When a program contains quickly paced character movement, special effects, loud music, nonhuman speech, or children's voices, they become highly attentive. At other times, they look away, play with toys, or talk to others in the same room (Rice, Huston, & Wright, 1982). While involved in other activities, preschoolers follow the TV soundtrack. They turn back to the set when they hear cartoon characters and puppets speaking and certain words, such as "Big Bird" and "cookie," that signal the content is likely to be interesting and meaningful to them (Alwitt et al., 1980).

Clearly, young children are selective and strategic processors of televised information, but how much do they really understand? Not a great deal. Before age 8, children have difficulty integrating separate scenes into a continuous story line. As a result, they often do not relate a TV character's behavior to prior intentions and later consequences (Collins et al., 1978). Other TV forms are confusing as well, such as fades, which signal the passage of time, and instant replays, which preschoolers take as repeated events (Anderson & Smith, 1984; Rice, Huston, & Wright, 1986).

Furthermore, young children find it hard to judge the reality of TV material. At ages 2 and 3, they do not discriminate televised images from real objects; they say a bowl of popcorn on television would spill if the TV were turned upside down (Flavell et al., 1990). By age 4, they have mastered this distinction, and they judge TV reality according to whether the images resemble people and objects in the everyday world. Consequently, they consider human actors "real" and cartoon characters "unreal." Around age 5, children start to make finer distinctions about television reality. They say that news and documentaries depict real events and that fictional programs are "just for TV." But not until age 7 do they fully grasp the unreality of TV fiction—that characters do not retain their roles in real life and that their behavior is scripted and rehearsed (Wright et al., 1994).

Television literacy
The task of learning television's specialized symbolic code of conveying information.

■ *Although television has the potential to support development, too often it teaches that aggression is an acceptable way to solve problems. Viewing violent TV is consistently linked to antisocial behavior in children and adolescents. (Mary Kate Denny/PhotoEdit)*

Cognitive development and experience in watching TV lead to gains in television literacy. Understanding of cinematic forms and memory for information important to plot comprehension increase sharply from middle childhood to adolescence. In addition, older children can draw inferences about televised material. For example, fifth to eighth graders recognize that a character who at first seems like a "good guy" but who unexpectedly behaves callously and aggressively is really a double-dealing "bad guy" in the end. In contrast, younger children find it difficult to reconcile their initially positive expectations with the character's eventual bad behavior. Consequently, they evaluate the character and his actions much more favorably (Collins, 1983).

In sum, preschool and early school-age children assimilate televised information piecemeal, have an incomplete understanding of its reality, and are unable to critically evaluate it. These factors increase the chances that they will imitate and believe what they see on the screen. Let's take a close look at the impact of TV on children's social learning.

TELEVISION AND SOCIAL LEARNING

Since the 1950s, researchers and public citizens have been concerned about the attitudes and behaviors that television cultivates in child and adolescent viewers. Most studies have focused on the implications of TV violence for the development of antisocial conduct. Still others have addressed the power of TV to teach undesirable gender and ethnic stereotypes. In addition, a growing body of evidence illustrates TV's as yet untapped potential to contribute to children's cognitive and social competence.

■ AGGRESSION. The National Television Violence Study, a recent large-scale survey of the amount, nature, and context of TV violence in the United States, concluded that violence pervades American TV (see Figure 15.4). Fifty-seven percent of programs between 6 A.M. and 11 P.M. contain violent scenes, often in the form of repeated aggressive acts against a victim that go unpunished. In fact, most violent portrayals do not show victims experiencing any serious physical harm, and few condemn violence or depict alternative ways of solving problems. To the contrary, over one-third of violent TV scenes are embedded in humor, a figure that rises to two-thirds for children's shows. Violent content is 9 percent above average in children's programming, and cartoons are the most violent TV fare of all (Mediascope, 1996).

Reviewers of thousands of studies have concluded that television violence provides children with "an extensive how-to course in aggression" (Comstock & Paik, 1994; Hearold, 1986; Huston et al., 1992; Slaby et al., 1995, p. 163). The case is strengthened by the fact that research using a wide variety of research designs, methods, and participants has yielded similar findings. In addition, the relationship of TV violence to mean-spiritedness and hostile behavior remains the same after many factors that might otherwise account for this association are controlled, such as IQ, social class, school achievement, and child-rearing practices (Donnerstein, Slaby, & Eron, 1994).

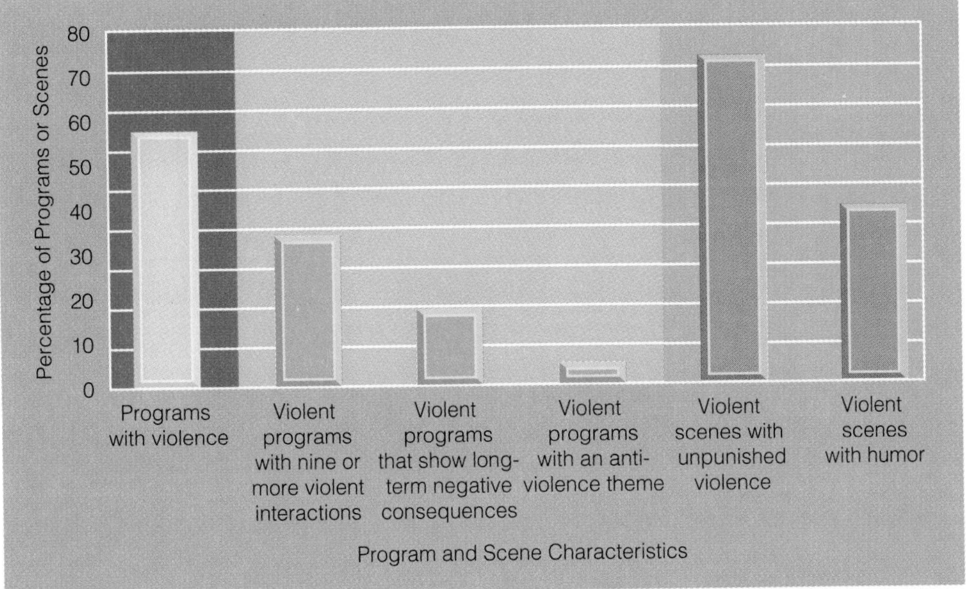

FIGURE 15.4

■ *Violent characteristics of American television programming, derived from a large, representative sample of over 3,000 programs broadcast between 6 A.M. and 11 P.M. Violence occurs in the majority of programs. It often consists of repeated aggressive acts that go unpunished and that are embedded in humor. Only rarely do programs show long-term negative consequences of violence or present it in the context of an antiviolence theme. (Adapted from Mediascope, 1996.)*

Violent programming not only creates short-term difficulties in family and peer relations, but has long-term effects as well. Longitudinal research reveals that highly aggressive children have a greater appetite for violent TV. As they watch more, they become increasingly likely to resort to hostile ways of solving problems, a spiraling pattern of learning that contributes to serious antisocial acts by adolescence and young adulthood (Slaby et al., 1995). In the most extensive longitudinal study conducted to date, boys who watched many violent programs at age 8 were more likely to be rated by peers as highly aggressive at age 19 and to have committed serious criminal acts by age 30 (see Figure 15.5 on page 602) (Huesmann, 1986; Lefkowitz et al., 1972).

Television violence also "hardens" children to aggression, making them more willing to tolerate it in others. In a well-known study, fifth graders watched either an aggressive detective show or a nonaggressive baseball game. Then each participant was left "in charge" of two younger children (who were supposedly playing in a nearby room and could be watched on a video monitor) and told to notify the experimenter if anything went wrong. A prepared film showed the younger children becoming increasingly hostile toward each other and destructive of property. Participants who had seen the aggressive film took much longer to seek help, and many tolerated all but the most violent acts among their charges (Drabman & Thomas, 1976).

Furthermore, compared to light viewers, heavy viewers of violent TV believe that there is much more violence and danger in society, an effect that is especially strong for children who perceive televised aggression as realistic and relevant to their own lives (Donnerstein, Slaby, & Eron, 1994; Gerbner et al., 1979). These findings indicate that violent television modifies children's attitudes toward social reality so they increasingly match what they see on TV. Children begin to think of the world as a mean and scary place where aggressive acts are a widespread and acceptable means for solving problems.

■ ETHNIC AND GENDER STEREOTYPES. Television conveys stereotypes that are common in American society. African-Americans and other ethnic minorities are underrepresented on TV. When they appear, they are often segregated in situation comedies or depicted negatively, as villains or victims of violence (Graves, 1993; Huston et al., 1992). Similarly, men greatly outnumber women in prime-time dramatic and children's programs and are usually the main characters. Women are often cast in "feminine" roles, such as wife, mother, nurse, teacher, or secretary, and as victims (Signorielli, 1990, 1993). Even formal features of TV sometimes reflect gender stereotypes. For example, TV toy commercials aimed at boys have more scene shifts, rapid cuts, blaring music, and sound effects, conveying a masculine image of "fast, sharp, and loud." Those aimed at girls emphasize camera fades and background music, conveying a "feminine" image of "gradual, soft, and fuzzy." By first grade, children can tell from these features whether an ad is meant for boys or girls (Huston et al., 1984).

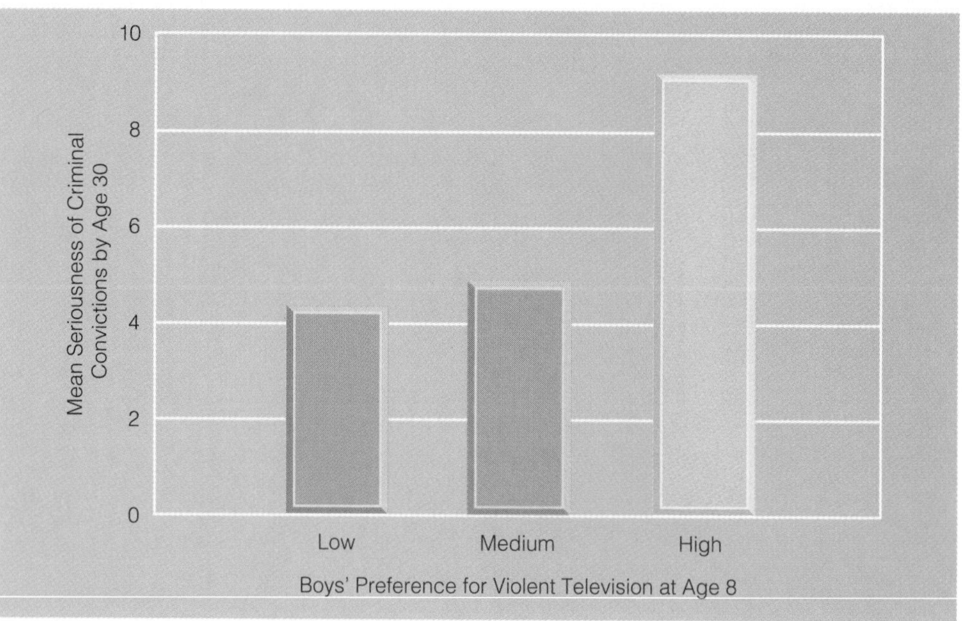

FIGURE 15.5

■ *Relationship between boys' violent television viewing at age 8 and seriousness of criminal convictions by age 30. Boys who watched many violent programs were more likely to have committed serious criminal acts in adolescence and early adulthood.(From L. R. Huesmann, 1986, "Psychological Processes Promoting the Relation Between Exposure to Media Violence and Aggressive Behavior by the Viewer,"* Journal of Social Issues, *42, p. 129. Reprinted by permission.)*

Are children's attitudes toward other people affected by TV's stereotyped portrayals? Much like the association between televised violence and aggressive behavior, a bidirectional relationship between TV viewing and gender stereotyping may exist. Adolescents who hold strong gender-stereotyped beliefs are especially attracted to TV programs with stereotyped characters (Friedrich-Cofer et al., 1978). At the same time, television viewing is linked to gains in children's endorsement of many gender stereotypes (Signiorelli, 1993). The little evidence that exists on TV's impact on ethnic stereotyping is mixed. In one study, exposure to African-Americans on prime-time TV evoked more negative attitudes in black children—a finding that might be explained by the way African-Americans were depicted (Dorr, Graves, & Phelps, 1980). However, positive portrayals of African-Americans and other ethnic minorities in cartoons and children's programs lead to more favorable views and greater willingness to form ethnically diverse friendships (Graves, 1993).

■ CONSUMERISM. Television commercials directed at children "work" by increasing product sales. Although children can distinguish a TV program from a commercial as early as 3 years of age, below age 8 they seldom grasp the selling purpose of the ad. They think commercials are well-intentioned efforts by film makers to be helpful to viewers (Levin, Petros, & Petrella, 1982). Around age 8 or 9, most children understand that commercials are meant to persuade, and by age 11, they realize that advertisers will resort to clever techniques to sell their products. As a result, children become increasingly skeptical of the truthfulness of commercial messages (Ward, Wackman, & Wartella, 1977).

Nevertheless, even older children and adolescents find many commercials alluring. In a study of 8- to 14-year-old boys, celebrity endorsement of a racing toy made the product more attractive, and live racetrack images led to exaggerated estimates of the toy's positive features (Ross et al., 1984). Sugary foods make up about 80 percent of advertising aimed at children. When parents give in to children's demands, young TV viewers come to prefer these snacks and are convinced by TV messages that they are healthy (Gorn & Goldberg, 1982). The ease with which television advertising can manipulate children's beliefs and preferences has raised questions about whether child-directed commercials, especially those aimed at young children, constitute fair and ethical practice by the broadcasting industry (Huston, Watkins, & Kunkel, 1989).

■ PROSOCIAL BEHAVIOR. Many TV programs include acts of cooperating, helping, and comforting. A large-scale review of research on prosocial television leaves little doubt that it can increase children's prosocial behavior (Hearold, 1986). But the evidence also highlights some important qualifications to TV's prosocial impact. Almost all the findings are short term and limited to situations quite similar to those shown on TV (Liebert & Sprafkin, 1988). In addition, television programs often mix prosocial and antisocial intentions and behavior. Recall that young children have difficulty integrating these elements.

As a result, they usually attend to the characters' aggressions and miss the prosocial message, and their antisocial behavior rises accordingly. Prosocial TV has positive effects only when it is free of violent content (Liss, Reinhardt, & Fredriksen, 1983).

Finally, parents who use authoritative child rearing rather than commands and physical force have children who watch more prosocial programs (Abelman, 1985). Consequently, children from families that already promote social and moral maturity probably benefit most from prosocial television.

TELEVISION, ACADEMIC LEARNING, AND IMAGINATION

Since the early days of television, educators have been interested in its potential for strengthening school performance, especially among low-income children who enter kindergarten behind their middle-class peers. "Sesame Street," the most popular educational program for young children, was created for public television with this goal in mind. Its founders believed that by using fast-paced action, lively sound effects, and humorous characters to stress letter and number recognition, counting, vocabulary, and basic concepts, they could enhance children's academic development (Liebert & Sprafkin, 1988).

Research shows that "Sesame Street" works well as an academic tutor. During the program's first year, researchers evaluated its effectiveness on a diverse sample of 950 preschoolers. As Figure 15.6 shows, the more children watched, the more they gained on tests designed to measure the program's learning goals (Ball & Bogatz, 1970). A second study revealed that when regular viewers from urban low-income families entered first grade, teachers rated them as better prepared for school than their light-viewing counterparts (Bogatz & Ball, 1972). Recent findings are consistent with these early evaluations. For example, "Sesame Street" viewing is positively related to vocabulary development among preschoolers varying widely in social class (Rice et al., 1990).

In other respects, however, the rapid-paced format of "Sesame Street" and other children's programs has been criticized. It has not earned high marks in the area of imagination and creativity. Longitudinal research reveals that more TV viewing at ages 3 and 4 is associated with less elaborate make-believe play in older preschoolers and lower creativity scores in elementary school children (Singer & Singer, 1981, 1983). In experiments designed to see which kinds of TV programs promote imaginative play, gains occurred only for slow-paced, nonviolent material with a clear story line, not for rapid-paced, disconnected bits of information (Huston-Stein et al., 1981; Tower et al., 1979).

Some experts argue that because television presents such complete data to the senses, in heavy doses it encourages reduced mental effort and shallow information processing. Too much television also takes up time children would otherwise spend in activities that

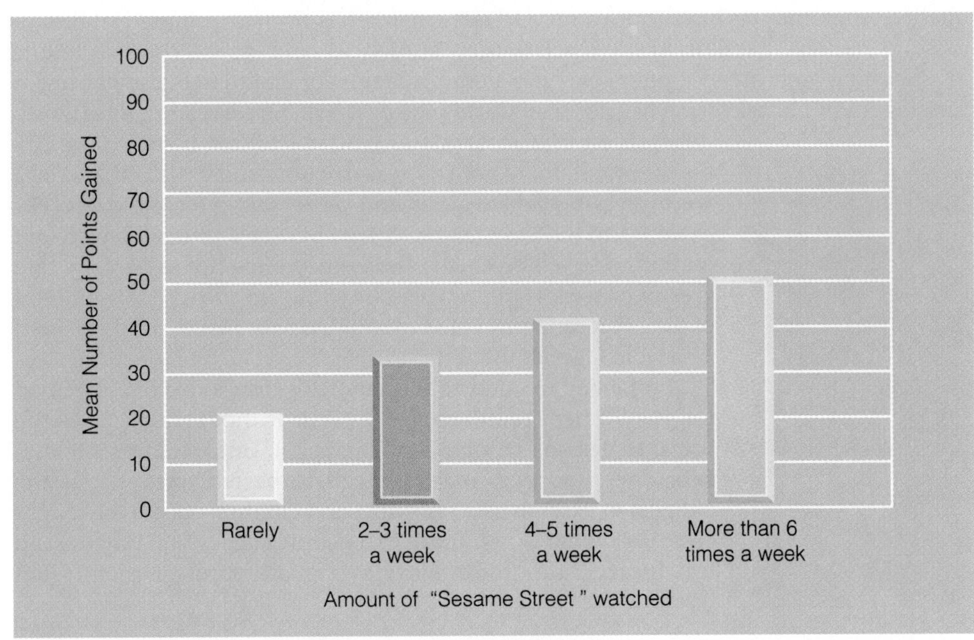

FIGURE 15.6

■ *Relationship between amount of "Sesame Street" viewing and preschoolers' gains on tests of basic academic knowledge. The more children watched, the more points they gained. (From Ball & Bogatz, 1970.)*

TABLE 15.3

Parental Strategies for Regulating Children's TV Viewing

Strategy	Description
Limit TV viewing.	Avoid using TV as a baby-sitter. Provide clear rules that limit what children can watch—for example, an hour a day and only certain programs—and stick to the rules.
Refrain from using TV as a reinforcer.	Do not use television to reward or punish children, a practice that increases its attractiveness.
Encourage child-appropriate viewing.	Encourage children to watch programs that are child-appropriate, informative, and prosocial.
Explain televised information to children.	As much as possible, watch with children, helping them understand what they see. When adults express disapproval of on-screen behavior, raise questions about the realism of televised information, and encourage children to discuss it, they teach children to evaluate TV content rather than accept it uncritically.
Link televised content to everyday learning.	Build on TV programs in constructive ways, encouraging children to move away from the set into active engagement with their surroundings. For example, a program on animals might spark a trip to the zoo, a visit to the library for books about animals, or new ways of observing and caring for the family pet.
Model good viewing practices.	Avoid excess television viewing, especially violent programs, yourself. Parental viewing patterns influence children's viewing patterns.
Use authoritative child rearing.	Respond to children with warmth and reasonable demands for mature behavior. Children who experience these practices prefer programs with prosocial content and are less attracted to violent TV.

Source: Slaby et al., 1995.

require sustained concentration and active thinking, such as reading, playing, and interacting with adults and peers (Singer & Singer, 1990). However, television can support cognitive development as long as children's viewing is not excessive and programs are specially designed to take into account their developmental needs.

IMPROVING CHILDREN'S TELEVISION

Improving children's television is an especially challenging task. Over time, high-quality programming has dropped off and advertising has risen as commercial broadcasting stations have tried to reach larger audiences and boost profits. Public broadcasting and cable TV offer some excellent programs for children. But government funding for public television has declined during the past two decades, and cable (which depends on user fees) is less available to low-income families. Furthermore, there are fewer restrictions today than there once were on program content and advertising for children. For example, in the past, characters in children's programs were not permitted to sell products. Today they often do—a strategy that greatly increases children's desire to buy. In addition, the amount of time that can be devoted to commercials during child-oriented TV is no longer limited.

Professional organizations and citizens groups have pressed for government regulation of TV, but without success (see the Social Issues box on the following page). Until children's television does improve, parents need to be educated about the dangers of excessive TV viewing, and children need to be taught critical viewing skills. Table 15.3 lists strategies that parents can use to regulate children's viewing and protect them from harmful TV.

■ *In this home, the television is turned off, and an older child engages in an art activity while her younger sister looks on and learns from her. Using television to promote children's prosocial behavior and active engagement with the surrounding world is a great challenge for parents in the United States, given the antisocial content of many programs. (Dusty Willison/International Stock)*

SOCIAL ISSUES ➤ POINT OF VIEW

Should the Federal Government Regulate Television to Protect Children's Development?

The average American child finishing elementary school has seen more than 100,000 violent acts on television, a figure that climbs to over 200,000 by the end of the teenage years (Gerbner & Signorielli, 1990). TV violence on normal commercial television has remained relatively constant over the past two decades. But recent changes in the media world have increased children's exposure. Over 60 percent of American families are cable subscribers, and nearly half own VCRs—rates that are rapidly increasing. Children with cable or VCR access can see films with far more graphic violence and sexual content than are shown on commercial TV (Huston et al., 1992). Although the greatest concern is with violence, we have seen that TV messages fostering ethnic and gender stereotyping and uncritical consumerism are also damaging to children.

Many organizations concerned with the well-being of children and families have recommended government regulation of TV. But the First Amendment right to free speech has made the federal government reluctant to place limits on television content. Consequently, professionals and committed legislators have sought ways to counteract the harmful impact of television that are consistent with the First Amendment—for example, requiring a minimum amount of educational programming for children and insisting on antiviolence public service announcements.

Broadcasters, whose profits are at risk, are against any government restrictions. Whereas other industries must face the scrutiny of the media, the television industry has been able to control the way TV violence research is presented. To protect itself, it has perpetuated a variety of myths—that violent programming is simply a reflection of society, a response to popular demand, or a problem of parental irresponsibility. Consequently, the gap between research and public understanding has been far greater for television than for other public health threats, such as cigarette smoking and drunk driving (Donnerstein, Slaby, & Eron, 1994).

Instead of regulatory control, a voluntary film rating system is in place, based on the familiar movie codes G, PG, PG-13, R, X, and now NC-17 (no children under 17). Although ratings are important, the current system is largely based on offensiveness rather than harmfulness. As a result, some very violent films, such as graphic horror movies, receive PG ratings, despite studies indicating that their content can be very disturbing to young viewers (Wilson, Linz, & Randall, 1990). In addition, the context of violent acts—their realism, intensity, motivation, and consequences—is not considered in the ratings. To be useful to parents, ratings must provide far more information on the kind and scope of violence presented. And parents need to know that although ratings may reduce the appropriateness of programs in their eyes, they make shows more appealing to some children (Mediascope, 1996).

Parents face an awesome task in monitoring and controlling children's TV viewing, given the extent of harmful messages on the screen. The television industry needs to take a more responsible attitude toward limiting such content. Public education about the impact of television on children's development is vital, since consumer pressure is a powerful instrument of change. Government regulation consistent with the First Amendment combined with public insistence that broadcasters generate their own remedies would transform TV into part of the solution to violence and other social ills in the United States.

YOUR POINT OF VIEW . . .

- Contact the National Foundation to Improve Television, a nonprofit organization, at 60 State Street, Boston, MA 02109, telephone (617) 523-6353, to find out about its initiatives to reduce the impact of television violence on children. Are its recommendations consistent with the First Amendment? Why or why not?
- Telephone the Harvard Community Health Organization at (617) 859-5030 and order its Violence Prevention Kit, at a cost of $10. What strategies does this community use to help protect children from TV and other sources of violence?

Computers

Today, computers are a familiar fixture in the everyday lives of children and adolescents, offering a wide range of entertainment and learning tools. By 1994, over 98 percent of American public schools had integrated computers into their instructional programs. And as computer technology became increasingly affordable, the number of American homes with at least one computer increased 36-fold between 1981 and 1993, from 750,000 to 27 million (U.S. Bureau of the Census, 1995).

Children and adolescents are fascinated by computers. They generally prefer them to television, perhaps because computers combine the visual and auditory liveliness of TV with an active role for the user. As one child commented, "It's fun because you get to control it. TV controls itself" (Greenfield, 1984, p. 128). What is the impact of this interactive medium on the human mind and the world we live in? Many researchers believe that one way to answer this question is to study how computers affect children—their impact on cognitive development, academic achievement, everyday activities, and social behavior.

ADVANTAGES OF COMPUTERS

Most research on computers and child development has been carried out in classrooms, where computer use can be easily observed. The findings reveal that computers can have rich educational and social benefits. Children as young as 3 years of age like computer activities and can type in simple commands on a standard keyboard. Yet they do not find the computer so captivating that it diverts them from other worthwhile play activities (Campbell & Schwartz, 1986). Furthermore, preschool and elementary school pupils prefer to use computers socially. Small groups often gather around the machine. Children take turns and help one another figure out next steps, as illustrated in the vignette at the beginning of this chapter. Children are far more likely to collaborate when working with the computer than with paper and pencil (Clements, Nastasi, & Swaminathan, 1993). The common belief that computers channel children into solitary pursuits is unfounded.

What do children learn from computers? This depends on what they do with them. Three major uses of computers in classrooms are computer-assisted instruction, word processing, and programming.

■ COMPUTER-ASSISTED INSTRUCTION. In **computer-assisted instruction (CAI)**, children acquire new knowledge and practice academic skills with the help of learning software. The unique features of many CAI programs make them effective and absorbing ways to learn. For example, pupils can begin at points that match their current level of mastery, and programs are often written to intervene when children's responses indicate that special help is needed. Also, multiple communication modes of text, graphics, animation, voice, and music enhance children's attention and interest. Most CAI programs provide drill and practice on basic academic skills. A few emphasize rote memorization less and discovery learning, reasoning, and problem solving more. For example, in one, children operate a lemonade stand and learn about economic principles of cost, profit, supply, and demand in a familiar context.

Reviews of hundreds of studies reveal that as long as children use them regularly over a period of several months, drill-and-practice programs are successful in improving reading and mathematics skills during the early elementary school years (Clements & Nastasi, 1992; Fletcher-Flinn & Gravatt, 1995; Lepper & Gurtner, 1989). The individualization and repetition offered by drill-and-practice software is especially beneficial for pupils with learning difficulties (Niemiec & Walberg, 1987). However, these applications tap only a small part of the computer's instructional potential and children's cognitive capacities. When drill-and-practice activities are overemphasized, they can subtract from children's opportunities to learn through active, meaningful experimentation (Clements, Nastasi, & Swaminathan, 1993).

■ WORD PROCESSING. Children can use word processing programs as soon as they begin to read and write. When the computer becomes part of the language arts curriculum, it permits children to write freely and try out letters and words without having to struggle with handwriting at the same time. In addition, children can plan and revise the text's meaning and style as well as check their spelling. As a result, they worry less about making mistakes, and their written products tend to be longer and of higher quality (Clements, 1995).

In the early stages of learning to write, word processing is especially effective in encouraging better written prose, but it is not as helpful with the mechanics of writing. For example, first graders learn to spell more accurately when they write by hand than when they type (Cunningham & Stanovich, 1990). This suggests that word processing should not replace the traditional mode of writing instruction. Instead, it is best used to build on and enhance it.

■ PROGRAMMING. Programming offers children the highest degree of control over the computer, since they must tell it what to do. Specially designed computer languages,

Computer-assisted instruction (CAI)
Use of computers to transmit new knowledge and practice academic skills.

■ *Computers provide learning environments that are cognitively stimulating and socially interactive. Special steps are needed to ensure that girls and minority pupils have equal access to them. When classrooms emphasize cooperative learning and software is designed with the interests of girls in mind, they become enthusiastic users. (Stephen Marks)*

such as LOGO, are available to introduce children to programming skills. Research shows that computer programming leads to improvements in concept formation, problem solving, and creativity (Clements, 1995; Clements & Nastasi, 1992). Also, since children must detect errors in their programs to get them to work, programming helps them reflect on their own thought processes, leading to gains in metacognitive knowledge and self-regulation (Clements, 1990; Miller & Emihovich, 1986). Finally, children who know how to program are more aware of the uses of computers and how they function (Pea & Kurland, 1984). As a result, they are better prepared to participate in a society in which computers are becoming increasingly important in everyday life.

In the studies just mentioned, teachers were always available to encourage and support children's efforts. They questioned, prompted, and modeled, providing a vital scaffold for mastery of programming skills. Furthermore, in open-ended programming contexts like LOGO, children are especially likely to formulate and solve problems collaboratively, persist in the face of challenge, appear self-motivated rather than externally motivated, and display positive attitudes toward learning (Nastasi & Clements, 1992, 1994). Consistent with Vygotsky's theory, social interaction surrounding challenging computer programming tasks fosters an internal reward system for mastery and a wide variety of higher cognitive processes.

As Figure 15.7 on page 608 indicates, drill and practice on basic skills accounts for slightly more than half of elementary school pupils' classroom computer use. In junior high and high school, computers more often serve as a tool for accomplishing complex academic tasks, such as writing, analyzing data, and solving problems, and for computer literate—in word processing, programming, keyboarding, and data base and spreadsheet programs (Becker, 1991). Yet the research we have reviewed confirms that with the right kind of software and adult assistance, elementary school pupils can use the computer in remarkably sophisticated ways. In the process, they reap intellectual and social benefits.

■ COMMUNICATIONS TECHNOLOGY. New communications technology is available through electronic mail (e-mail) and other computer-based services. A recent survey revealed that 16 percent of teachers make use of the internet in classroom instruction (National Education Association, 1995). As a result, children and adolescents can interact with other students around the world, and collaborative relationships can be built among schools and community institutions. As yet, little research on the impact of communications technology on children's development exists. But one study highlights the power of electronic conversations to enhance understanding of other cultures. Groups of six to nine classrooms from different regions of the United States and foreign countries, formed "learning circles." Pupils in each class planned a project and consulted with the other classes and teachers in their circle over the Internet to complete it. In return for this help, each class assisted their learning circle partners with their projects.

Informal examination of children's e-mail messages revealed a broadening of horizons about other people and places. For example, a time zone difference led pupils in

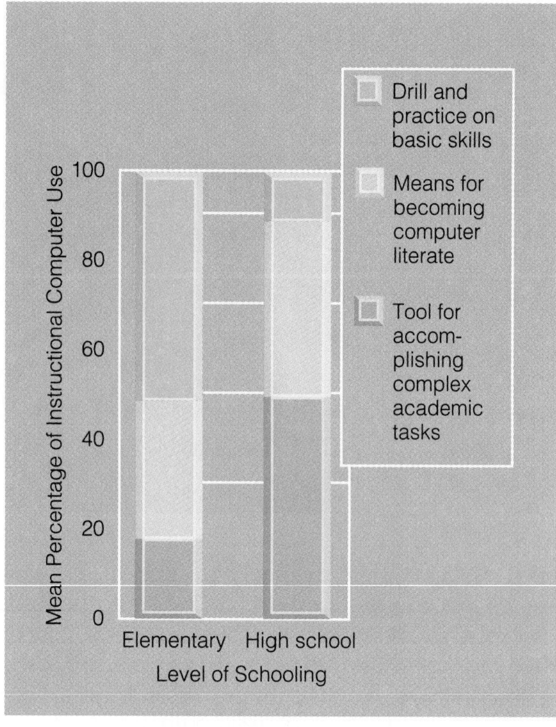

FIGURE 15.7

■ *Classroom instructional use of computers by level of schooling, based on a survey of computer coordinatrs in a nationally represented sample of American schools. In elementary school, computers are most often used for drill and practice on basic skills. In high school, they largely serve as a tool for accomplishing complex academic tasks and for becoming computer literate–in word processing, programing, keyboarding, and data base spreadsheet programs. (Adapted from Becker, 1991.)*

Kansas to receive a message from Japan written on a day that had not yet arrived. Children in an Australian school described Christmas celebrations in the middle of their summer season. Pupils in Persian Gulf nations wrote candidly about their fears as one circle discussed the problems of world peace and security. And a project on the whaling industry became more complex when children who depend on whales as their primary source of food contributed to it (Reis, 1992).

CONCERNS ABOUT COMPUTERS

Although computers provide children with many learning advantages, they raise serious concerns as well. Computers appear most often in the homes and schools of economically well-off pupils (Rocheleau, 1995). Furthermore, high-IQ pupils are attracted to problem-solving software and dislike the frequent feedback of drill-and-practice programs. In contrast, lower-IQ pupils like computer activities with lively animation and graphics and are uncomfortable with the lack of structure in problem-solving software (although with adult and peer support, they benefit from it) (Clements, Nastasi, & Swaminathan, 1993). As a result, some experts believe that computers are widening the difference in intellectual skills between lower- and middle-income children.

Furthermore, by the end of middle childhood, boys spend more time with computers than do girls. Parents of sons are more likely than parents of daughters to install a computer in the home. Even when girls have ready access to computers, much software is unappealing to them because it emphasizes themes of war, violence, and male-dominated sports. Girls' reduced involvement with computers may contribute to sex-related differences in math achievement and interest in scientific careers that emerge by adolescence (see Chapter 13). Yet girls' tendency to retreat from computers can be overcome, since the gender gap is declining (Rocheleau, 1995). When teachers present computers in the context of cooperative rather than competitive learning and software is designed with the interests of girls in mind, they become enthusiastic users (Hawkins & Sheingold, 1986).

Finally, video games account for most out-of-school, recreational use of computers by children and adolescents, especially boys. Many parents are seriously concerned about the allure of these fast-paced electronic amusements. They fear that their youngsters will become overly involved as well as more aggressive because of the games' highly violent content. The limited evidence available indicates that videogame use is related to aggressive behavior, although a causal link has not yet been established (Fling et al., 1992; Schutte et al., 1988).

BRIEF REVIEW

American children spend more time watching TV than they do in any other waking activity. Before age 8, children have difficulty processing televised information accurately. Heavy TV viewing promotes aggressive behavior, indifference to real-life violence, and a fearful view of the world; ethnic and gender stereotypes; and a naive belief in the truthfulness of advertising. Although the right kind of televised content can encourage prosocial behavior, academic skills, and imaginative thinking, the positive potential of the TV medium remains largely untapped.

Computers have become increasingly common in the lives of children. At school, children often collaborate on computer activities. Computer-assisted instruction, word processing, programming, and electronic communications each offer unique educational benefits. Nevertheless, the advantages of computers are more accessible to children who are economically well off, high in IQ, and male.

Schooling

Unlike the informal world of peer relations, the school is a formal institution designed to transmit knowledge and skills children need to become productive members of society. Children spend many hours in school—6 hours a day, 5 days a week, 36 weeks of the year—totaling, altogether, about 15,000 hours by high school graduation. In earlier chapters, we noted that schools are vital forces in children's development, affecting their modes of remembering, reasoning, problem solving, and social and moral understanding. How do schools exert such a powerful impact? Research looking at schools as complex social systems—their class and student body size, educational philosophies, teacher–pupil interaction patterns, and the larger cultural context in which they are embedded—provides important insights into this question.

CLASS AND STUDENT BODY SIZE

The physical plants of all schools are similar: Each has classrooms, hallways, a playground, and a lunchroom. But they are also different. Schools vary widely in the number of pupils they accommodate in each class and the school as a whole—factors that profoundly affect life at school.

Is there an optimal class size that fosters effective pupil learning? Reviews of research indicate that as classes drop below 15 or 20 pupils, academic achievement improves. Above this threshold, however, class size has little impact on children's performance (Cooper, 1989; Glass et al., 1982). A recent experiment confirmed this conclusion. Kindergartners in 76 elementary schools were randomly assigned to three class types: small (15 to 20 pupils), regular (22 to 25 pupils), and regular plus aide (22 to 25 pupils with the assistance of a full-time teacher's aide), arrangements that continued into third grade. Small-class pupils scored higher in reading and math achievement during each year, an effect that was particularly strong for minority pupils. The presence of a teacher's aide in regular-size classes had no consistent effect. Finally, even after all pupils returned to regular-size classes in fourth and fifth grade, children who had experienced the small classes remained ahead in achievement (Achilles et al., 1993; Finn & Achilles, 1990).

Why is small class size beneficial? Teachers of fewer children spend less time disciplining and more time granting pupils individual attention, and pupils' relationships are more positive and cooperative. Also, when class size is small, both teachers and pupils are more satisfied with their school experiences. The learning advantages of small classes are greatest in the early years of schooling, when children require more adult assistance (Blatchford & Mortimore, 1994).

By the time students reach secondary school, they no longer spend most of their time in a single, self-contained classroom. Instead, they move from one class to another and have access to many activities outside regular academic instruction. As a result, the relevant physical context becomes the school as a whole. One feature of the general school environment that is consistently related to adolescents' behavior is student body size. A greater percentage of students in small than large high schools are actively involved in the extracurricular life of their schools. Schools of 500 to 700 students or less promote personalized conditions because there are fewer people to ensure that clubs, sports events, and social activities will function. As a result, young people enter a greater number and variety of activities and hold more positions of responsibility and leadership. In contrast, plenty of students are available to fill activity slots in large schools, so only a small elite can be genuinely active (Barker & Gump, 1964; Lindsay, 1984).

In view of these findings, it is not surprising that adolescents in small schools report a greater sense of personal responsibility, competence, and challenge from their extracurricular experiences. This is true even for "marginal" students—those with low IQs, academic difficulties, and poverty-stricken backgrounds—who otherwise display little commitment to school life (Willems, 1967). A special advantage of small schools is that potential dropouts are far more likely to join in activities, gain recognition for their abilities, and remain until graduation. Small schools are not associated with gains in achievement, but the experiences they offer are equally important. Longitudinal research reveals that the sense of social obligation engendered in small high schools carries over to community participation in adult life (Berk, 1992b).

EDUCATIONAL PHILOSOPHIES

Each teacher brings to the classroom an educational philosophy that plays a major role in children's learning experiences. Two philosophical approaches have been studied extensively: traditional and open classrooms. They differ in what children are taught, the way they are believed to learn, the extent to which decision making rests with teacher or child, and how academic progress is evaluated.

TRADITIONAL VERSUS OPEN CLASSROOMS.

In a **traditional classroom**, children are relatively passive in the learning process. The teacher is the sole authority for knowledge, rules, and decision making and does most of the talking. Pupils spend most of their time at their desks—listening, responding when called on, and completing teacher-assigned tasks. Their progress is evaluated by how well they keep pace with a common set of expectations for everyone in their grade.

In an **open classroom**, children are viewed as active agents in their own development. The teacher assumes a flexible authority role, sharing decision making with pupils, who learn at their own pace. Children are evaluated by considering their progress in relation to their own prior development. How well they compare to same-age pupils is less important. A glance inside the door of an open classroom reveals richly equipped learning centers, small groups of pupils working on tasks they choose themselves, and a teacher who moves from one area to another, guiding and supporting in response to children's individual needs (Minuchin & Shapiro, 1983).

During the past few decades, the pendulum in American education has swung back and forth between these two approaches. In the 1960s and early 1970s, open education gained in popularity, inspired by Piaget's view of children as active, motivated learners. Then, as high school students' scores on the Scholastic Aptitude Test (SAT) declined over the 1970s, a "back to basics" movement arose. As a result, classrooms returned to traditional, teacher-directed instruction, a style still prevalent today.

The combined results of many studies reveal that children in traditional classrooms have a slight edge in terms of academic achievement. But open settings are associated with other benefits. Open-classroom pupils are more independent, and they value and respect individual differences in their classmates more. Pupils in open environments also like school better than those in traditional classrooms, and their attitudes toward school become increasingly positive as they spend more time there (Walberg, 1986). In contrast, the high teacher structure and lack of pupil autonomy in traditional classrooms seem to contribute to a general decline in motivation throughout the school years (Eccles et al., 1993b; Skinner & Belmont, 1993).

Whole-class, teacher-directed instruction in academic skills, previously not encountered until first grade or later, has become increasingly common in American preschools and kindergartens. When training in basic skills is emphasized at such an early age, it is

Traditional classroom
A classroom based on the educational philosophy that children are passive learners who acquire information presented by teachers. Pupils are evaluated on the basis of how well they keep up with a uniform set of standards for everyone in their grade.

Open classroom
A classroom based on the educational philosophy that children are active agents in their own development and learn at different rates. Teachers share decision making with pupils. Pupils are evaluated in relation to their own prior development.

especially detrimental to intrinsic motivation and other aspects of emotional well-being. A recent study revealed that compared to children in teacher-directed classrooms, 3- to 6-year-olds in child-centered classrooms perceived their abilities to be higher, had higher expectations for task success, more often preferred challenging problems, and were less likely to seek adult approval or worry about school. These findings held for both low-income and middle-income children (Stipek et al., 1995).

■ NEW PHILOSOPHICAL DIRECTIONS. Although much research has focused on the traditional–open dichotomy, it actually oversimplifies the real world of classroom differences. The philosophies of some teachers fall somewhere in between. These teachers want to foster high achievement as well as independence, positive social relationships, and excitement about learning. Turn back to Chapter 6, page 252, to reread the description of the Kamehameha Elementary Education Project (KEEP), an approach based on Vygotsky's sociocultural theory that represents this intermediate point of view. KEEP has been highly successful in fostering both achievement and enthusiasm for learning among ethnic minority pupils. Recall from Chapter 6 that sociocultural theory has inspired other educational innovations, including reciprocal teaching and cooperative learning (see pages 250–253). These methods emphasize the importance of rich, socially communicative environments and collaboration on challenging, meaningful activities for children to learn at their best.

Yet another influential philosophy combines Vygotsky's theory with other major perspectives to reshape the classroom into a small society of learners—a system created from within by teachers and children and sustained from without by the larger social context. See the Cultural Influences box on page 612 for the remarkable story of a small Italian city that restructured its schools to support early childhood development. The Reggio Emilia approach is inspiring educators in many nations to rethink educational practices for young children.

SCHOOL TRANSITIONS

Besides size and educational philosophy, an additional structural feature of schooling has important implications for pupils' academic performance and adjustment: the timing of transitions from one school level to the next. Many American 5- and 6-year-olds are already accustomed to school-like settings, since they have attended preschool and day care centers. Still, entering kindergarten is a major milestone. Parents take pride in their children's readiness for greater independence and responsibility. At the same time, they worry about how well prepared their youngsters are for a more earnest approach to learning. Children, in turn, must accommodate to new physical settings, adult authorities, daily schedules, peer companions, and academic challenges.

■ EARLY ADJUSTMENT TO SCHOOL. In a study of factors that predict effective transition to kindergarten, Gary Ladd and Joseph Price (1987) gathered observational and interview data on children at the end of preschool and during their kindergarten year. Both child and setting characteristics ensuring supportive ties to peers were major contributors to favorable school adjustment. Children who engaged in cooperative play and friendly interaction with agemates in preschool seemed to transfer these skills to kindergarten. They were better liked by peers and rated by teachers as more involved in classroom life. The presence of preschool friends in kindergarten also enhanced adaptation. Perhaps familiar agemates served as a secure base from which to develop new ties, enhancing children's peer acceptance and feelings of comfort in the classroom. Finally, children who retained more out-of-school peer relationships viewed school more favorably after kindergarten entry. The continuity of these nonschool ties may have provided children with a greater sense of stability in their otherwise changing social environments.

In a second investigation, additional factors having to do with peer relationships emerged as contributors to school adjustment. Pupils with more preschool experience scored higher on school readiness tests, were rated by teachers as better prepared for school, and showed increasingly positive school attitudes over the kindergarten year. In addition, the extent to which children made new friends at school and kept them predicted gains in achievement. As children formed new bases of social support in kindergarten, they seemed to integrate themselves into the environment in ways that fostered academic competence (Ladd, 1990).

CULTURAL INFLUENCES

The Reggio Emilia Approach to Early Childhood Education

In Reggio Emilia, a small town in north-central Italy, an extraordinary city-run early childhood program has captured the attention of educators worldwide. Capitalizing on the enthusiasm and commitment of parents who began to build their own preschool using materials left over from the rubble of World War II, founder Loris Malaguzzi (1993) devised a city-funded educational system that, today, includes 22 preschools for 3- to 6-year-olds and 13 centers for infants and toddlers. Among important influences on the Reggio Emilia program are Piaget's cognitive-developmental theory, Vygotsky's sociocultural theory, Gardner's theory of multiple intelligences, and Bronfenbrenner's ecological systems theory.

Reggio Emilia education views the child as a complex, capable being who learns from exploring the physical world and, especially, from interacting with others (Gandini, 1993). The approach is based on strong community ties; parents, teachers, administrative staff, and government officials join forces to support the efforts of the school. Parents meet with teachers and other staff members for program planning, and they volunteer in classrooms. Teachers routinely collaborate with other teachers and with specially trained educational advisers called *pedagogistas* in devising new ways to assist children's learning.

Pairs of teachers stay with the same class of children for 3 years, and each classroom is arranged to promote small-group interaction. Together, these features grant children extended opportunities to develop meaningful relationships with adults and peers. Because teachers get to know children especially well, they teach more effectively.

The *atelierista,* a full-time specialist and artist, is responsible for implementing a central component of the Reggio Emilia curriculum. In a special room, or set of rooms, called the *atelier,* the atelierista supports teachers and children as they work with a wide variety of artistic media—drawings, paintings, photographs, clay, audio- or videotapes, music, and transcriptions of conversations. Children are encouraged to represent everything they think about, including such challenging concepts as shadows, feelings, growth, time, and motion. The atelierista stores the products to document children's activities and progress. Then children, parents, and teachers can return to reflect on and reconsider them. As one atelierista explained, "First, [the atelier] provides a place for children to become masters of . . . all the symbolic languages. Second, it helps teachers understand how children invent . . . [many] paths to communication . . . ." (Vecchi, 1993).

An additional feature of Reggio Emilia education is an emphasis on long-term, multifaceted projects that offer a broad, integrative framework for exploration and social interaction. Parents, teachers, pedagogistas, and atelieristas meet to select project themes, which must (1) allow for both individual and collective contributions, (2) provide general goals, within which children decide on subgoals, (3) promote lively dialogue, and (4) permit many modes of representation. For example, in an 8-week project based on the theme of long-jumping, children engaged in many interconnected learning experiences. These included designing and building a long-jump track; planning, advertising, and holding an Olympic sports event; experimenting with the relation between running speed and jumping distance; and communicating their knowledge through diverse symbol systems (Forman, 1993).

Children's enthusiasm and involvement and the complexity and originality of their products attest to the success of Reggio Emilia schools. Besides drawing on well-researched theories, the approach explicitly recognizes that supportive relationships with members of the educational system and community must be present for teachers to create ideal conditions for children's learning.

These findings suggest a variety of ways to prepare preschoolers for the challenges of kindergarten—both before and during the transitional period. These include encouraging positive social skills during the early years, arranging for children to attend preschool, and helping them establish and maintain peer ties both in and out of school. In planning the composition of kindergarten classrooms, educators might also consider grouping children to maximize contact with friends. As we will see shortly, rewarding peer associations continue to be important in successful adaptation to school change at later ages.

■ SCHOOL TRANSITIONS IN ADOLESCENCE. A second important period of school transition occurs during adolescence, when students typically move from an intimate, self-contained elementary school classroom to a much larger, impersonal secondary school. There they must shift from one class to the next throughout the day and become accustomed to a student body size three to four times larger than that of their previous school. During adolescence, school transitions can drastically alter academic and social experiences in ways that have long-term consequences for development.

Research reveals that with each school change—from elementary to middle or junior high and then to high school—adolescents' course grades decline. The drop is partly due to tighter academic standards. At the same time, the transition to secondary school often brings with it less personal attention, more whole-class instruction, and less chance to

Moving from a small, self-contained elementary school classroom to a large, impersonal secondary school is stressful for adolescents. School grades, extracurricular participation, and self-esteem decline, especially for girls. (M. Antman/The Image Works)

participate in classroom decision making. In view of these changes, it is not surprising that students report that their junior high teachers care less about them, are less friendly, and grade less fairly than did their elementary school teachers (Eccles et al., 1993b). Focusing on math classes, one group of researchers found that students moving from an elementary school classroom high in support to a junior high classroom low in support showed a sharp decline in their liking for the subject. When the direction of change was reversed—from classrooms low in support to ones high in support—attitudes toward the subject improved (Midgley, Feldlaufer, & Eccles, 1989).

Inevitably, the transition to secondary school requires students to readjust their feelings of self-confidence and self-worth as academic expectations are revised and they enter a more complex social world. In a comprehensive study, Roberta Simmons and Dale Blyth (1987) discovered that the timing of school transition is important, especially for girls. The researchers followed over 300 adolescents living in a large midwestern city from sixth to tenth grade. Some were enrolled in school districts with a 6–3–3 grade organization (a K–6 elementary school, a 3-year junior high, and a 3-year high school). These students made two school changes during adolescence, one to junior high and one to high school. A comparison group attended schools with an 8–4 organization. They made only one school transition, from a K–8 elementary school to high school.

For the sample as a whole, grade point averages dropped and feelings of anonymity increased after each transition. Participation in extracurricular activities declined more in the 6–3–3 than in the 8–4 arrangement, although the drop was greater for girls. Sex-related differences in self-esteem were even more striking. As Figure 15.8 on page 614 shows, boys' self-esteem increased steadily, except in 6–3–3 schools, where it leveled off after entry into high school. Girls in the 6–3–3 arrangement fared especially poorly. Their self-esteem declined with each school change. In contrast, their 8–4 counterparts gained in feelings of self-worth throughout the secondary school years.

These findings show that any school transition is likely to temporarily depress adolescents' psychological well-being, but the earlier it occurs, the more dramatic and long lasting its impact. Girls in 6–3–3 schools fared poorest, the researchers argued, because movement to junior high tended to occur at the same time as other life changes—namely, the onset of puberty and dating. Adolescents who have to cope with added life transitions, such as family disruption, a decline in parental work status, or a shift in residence around the time they change schools, are at greatest risk for academic and emotional difficulties (Flanagan & Eccles, 1993).

Poorly achieving and poverty-stricken young people show an especially sharp drop in school performance after the transition to junior high school. They are likely to turn to peers, whose values they describe as becoming increasingly antisocial, for the support they lack in other spheres of school life (Seidman et al., 1994). For some, school transition initiates a downward spiral in academic performance and school involvement that eventually leads to failure and dropping out (Simmons, Black, & Zhou, 1991).

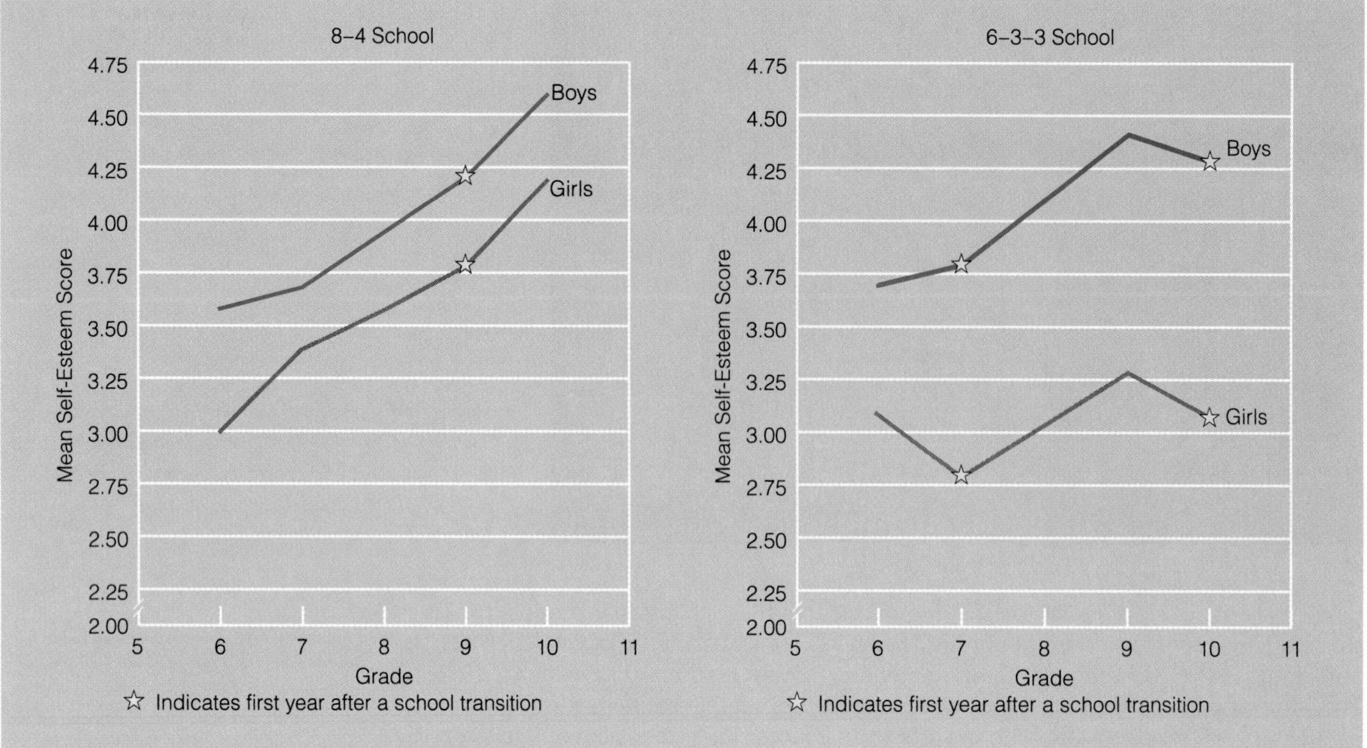

FIGURE 15.8

■ *Self-esteem from sixth to tenth grade by school type for boys and girls. In this longitudinal study of over 300 adolescents, self-esteem increased steadily for both sexes in the 8–4 school arrangement. Girls in 6–3–3 schools fared especially poorly. Their self-esteem dropped sharply after each school change. (Adapted from Simmons & Blyth, 1987.)*

■ HELPING ADOLESCENTS ADJUST TO SCHOOL TRANSITIONS. As with the preschool to kindergarten transition, there are ways to ease the strain of moving from elementary to secondary school. Since most students do better in an 8–4 school arrangement, school districts thinking about reorganization should seriously consider this plan.[1] When this is not possible, smaller social units can be formed within large schools to relieve students' feelings of anonymity. Some schools use a "team" or "house" approach that reduces the size of the young person's reference group, permitting closer relations with teachers and peers and greater extracurricular involvement (Berk, 1992; Eccles et al., 1993a).

Other less extensive changes in the school environment are also helpful. During the first year after a school transition, homerooms can be provided in which teachers offer academic and personal counseling and work closely with parents to promote favorable school adjustment. Students can also be assigned to classes with several familiar peers or a constant group of new peers—arrangements that promote emotional security and social support. In one study, high school freshmen experiencing these interventions showed considerably better academic performance and psychological adjustment at the end of the school year than did controls. These benefits were long lasting. A follow-up after 4 years revealed that only half as many students in the intervention group had dropped out of school (Felner & Adan, 1988).

TEACHER–PUPIL INTERACTION

The classroom is a complex social system in which a myriad of interactions take place each day. Teachers play a central role in this highly social environment, engaging in as many as 1,000 exchanges with pupils from the time the bell rings in the morning until dismissal in the afternoon (Jackson, 1968). A vast amount of research exists on teacher–pupil interaction, the majority of which focuses on its significance for academic achievement.

[1] Recall from Chapter 5 (page 184) that girls who reach puberty early fare better in K–6 schools where they are relieved of pressures from older adolescents to become involved in dating, sexual activity, and drug experimentation before they are ready. Although the 8–4 arrangement is best for the majority of adolescents, early maturing girls require extra support under these conditions.

■ *The quality of teachers' instructional messages affects pupils' involvement in academic lessons. Emphasizing higher-level thinking—analyzing, synthesizing, and applying ideas and concepts—promotes participation and learning. (Stephen Marks)*

■ CLASSROOM MANAGEMENT AND QUALITY OF INSTRUCTION. Class time devoted to academic instruction and pupil involvement in academic work is consistently related to achievement test scores (Brophy & Good, 1986). But for pupils to learn effectively in an environment as crowded and distracting as the classroom, teachers must arrange conditions that make work possible. Teachers' classroom management skills are strongly related to academic achievement (Good & Brophy, 1994). Effective classroom managers arrange conditions in which activities flow easily from one to the next and few discipline problems arise. As a result, pupils spend more time learning, which is reflected in their performance.

Besides management skills, the quality of teachers' instructional messages affects children's task involvement and learning. A disappointing finding is that American elementary school teachers emphasize rote, repetitive drill more than higher-level thinking, such as analyzing, synthesizing, and applying ideas and concepts (Dossey et al., 1988). But individual differences do exist, and both simple and complex instruction occurs in all classrooms to some degree. Observing fifth-grade teachers, Susan Stodolsky (1988) found that instructional style varied according to the subject matter being taught. Lower-level cognitive activity was especially common during math, in the form of memorization of number facts and computational routines. In contrast, teachers emphasized both low- and high-level cognitive processes in social studies. Within each subject, pupils were far more attentive when given complex tasks than basic memory exercises. And overall, their involvement was greater in social studies than in math. This suggests that introducing more complex activities (as long as they fit with pupils' current abilities) is likely to increase both children's engagement in academic lessons and their achievement.

So far, we have considered one-way effects of teachers on pupils. But as you already know, social interaction is bidirectional; each participant influences the behavior of the other. Teachers do not interact in the same way with all children. Some get more attention, praise, and criticism than others. Teachers' reactions to pupils depend on the extent to which children's behavior matches the academic and conduct expectations of the school. Well-behaved, high-achieving pupils experience positive interactions with their teachers. They are frequently called on to share ideas, and they receive more praise. In contrast, teachers especially dislike children who combine low achievement with active, disruptive behavior. These unruly pupils are often criticized and are rarely asked to contribute to class discussion. When they seek special help or permission, their requests are usually denied (Good & Brophy, 1994).

■ TEACHER EXPECTATIONS FOR CHILDREN'S PERFORMANCE. Unfortunately, once teachers' attitudes toward pupils are established, they are in danger of becoming more extreme than is warranted by children's behavior. If teachers rigidly treat pupils in ways that match their impressions, they may engage in discriminatory practices that have long-term consequences for children's motivation and achievement. A special concern is that an educational **self-fulfilling prophecy**[2] can be set in motion. In other words, pupils may adopt teachers' positive or negative views and start to live up to them.

In the 1960s, Robert Rosenthal and Lenore Jacobson (1968) conducted a famous experiment in which they tested this hypothesis. First, pupils in an elementary school took an IQ test, and teachers were falsely informed that test results could identify children expected to "bloom," or show an intellectual growth spurt, during the following months. Each teacher was provided with a list of "bloomers" in her class (children randomly chosen by the researchers). Then the IQ test was given again at the end of the school year. Results indicated that first and second graders for whom teachers expected gains actually showed them. But no self-fulfilling prophecy effects appeared among third through sixth graders.

Rosenthal and Jacobson's study was soon criticized on methodological grounds, and many other investigations failed to confirm its findings. Later, it became clear that teachers, especially those who are self-confident and experienced, will reject experimenter-provided expectancies if they do not match their firsthand observations (Carter et al., 1987). Research that has done most to advance our understanding of self-fulfilling prophecies focuses on teachers' naturally formed expectancies, their impact on teacher–pupil interaction, and their consequences for children's learning. Findings reveal that although teachers interact differently with high and low achievers, in most cases their behavior is a reality-based response to pupils' learning needs and does not cause children to do better or worse in school. But sometimes teachers do harbor unfair judgments of children. Unfortunately, they are usually biased in a negative direction, resulting in more unfavorable classroom experiences and achievement than would otherwise occur (Brophy, 1983).

Self-fulfilling prophecies interact in complex ways with teacher and pupil characteristics. When teachers emphasize competition and frequently make public comparisons among pupils, children are very aware of teacher opinion, increasing the likelihood that it will affect their performance (Weinstein et al., 1987). Furthermore, teachers who regard low-achieving pupils as limited by ability rather than effort or learning opportunities are likely to provide them with little encouragement for mastering challenging tasks. And when teachers have a strong fear of losing control of their class, they are especially likely to initiate negative self-fulfilling prophecies. They do so by avoiding public communication with disruptive, low-achieving pupils and giving them feedback that is abrupt, inconsistent, and not based on the quality of their work (Cooper, 1979). Withdrawn children may also be prime candidates for biased teacher expectancies. Since they rarely approach teachers, they provide little information about what they are like as learners. This makes it easier for teachers who hold inappropriate expectancies to sustain them (Jones & Gerig, 1994).

■ TEACHERS' REACTIONS TO CHILDREN'S ETHNIC AND SOCIAL-CLASS BACKGROUNDS. Teachers sometimes respond in stereotyped ways to low-income and ethnic minority pupils, making them especially susceptible to negative self-fulfilling prophecies. In Chapter 11, we noted that African-American and Mexican-American children often receive less favorable feedback from teachers than do white children, a circumstance that undermines their achievement motivation. One study found that as early as the preschool years, teachers provided less verbal stimulation in classes of low-income than middle-income children (Quay & Jarrett, 1986).

Recall from Chapter 8 that ethnic minority children often have unique language customs, knowledge, and skills that differ sharply from those valued at school. Teachers who are unaware of this fact may interpret the minority pupil's behavior as uncooperative when it is not. For this reason, it is vital that teachers understand the values and practices that culturally different children bring to the classroom. Then they can adjust learning experiences to take account of the child's background, and negative self-fulfilling prophecies with serious consequences for the school performance of minority children can be avoided.

Educational self-fulfilling prophecy
The idea that pupils may adopt teachers' positive or negative attitudes toward them and start to live up to these views.

[2] Most research on self-fulfilling prophecies focuses on the teacher–pupil relationship, but the effect can occur in other social contexts, such as parent–child and peer interaction. Try to think of other findings we have discussed in this and earlier chapters that can be viewed as self-fulfilling prophecies.

ABILITY GROUPING

In many schools, pupils are ability grouped, or tracked, into classes in which children of similar achievement levels are taught together. The practice is designed to ease teachers' task of having to meet a wide range of academic needs in the same learning environment. Yet teachers' treatment of different ability groups may be an especially powerful source of self-fulfilling prophecies. In low-ability groups, pupils experience more drill on basic facts and skills, less discussion, a slower learning pace, and less time on academic work. Gradually, children in low groups show a drop in self-esteem, are viewed by themselves and others as "not smart," and limit their friendship choices to children within their own group. For these reasons, ability grouping can widen the gap between high and low achievers (Dornbusch, Glasgow, & Lin, 1996; Gamoran et al., 1995). At least into the early years of secondary school, mixed-ability classes are desirable. Research suggests that they do not stifle the more able students, and they have intellectual and social benefits for poorly performing youngsters (Oakes, Gamoran, & Page, 1992).

By the time adolescents enter high school, some tracking is unavoidable because certain aspects of instruction must dovetail with the young person's future educational and career plans. In the United States, high school students are counseled into a college preparatory, vocational, or general education sequence. Unfortunately, educational inequalities of earlier years tend to be perpetuated. Low-income minority students are assigned in large numbers to noncollege tracks. One study found that a good student from an economically disadvantaged family had only half as much chance of ending up in an academically oriented program as a student of equal ability from a middle-class background (Vanfossen, Jones, & Spade, 1987).

High school students are separated into academic and vocational tracks in virtually all industrialized nations. But the American system differs from those of Western Europe, China, and Japan in important respects. In those countries, students take a national examination to determine their placement in high school. The outcome usually fixes future possibilities for the young person. In the United States, educational decisions are more fluid. Students who are not assigned to a college preparatory track or who do poorly in high school can still get a college education. But by the adolescent years, social-class differences in quality of education and academic achievement have already sorted American students more drastically than is the case in other countries. In the end, many young people do not benefit from this more open system. Compared to other developed nations, the United States has a higher percentage of high school dropouts and adolescents with very limited academic skills (Hamilton, 1990; McAdams, 1993).

TEACHING PUPILS WITH SPECIAL NEEDS

So far, we have seen that effective teachers flexibly adjust their teaching strategies to accommodate pupils with a wide range of abilities and characteristics. These adjustments, however, are especially challenging when children have learning difficulties. Over the past two decades, extra steps have been taken to create appropriate learning environments for these pupils. The Individuals with Disabilities Education Act (Public Law 101-475), first passed in 1975 and revised in 1990, mandates that schools place children who require special supports for learning in the "least restrictive" environments that meet their educational needs. The goal of the law is to better prepare pupils for participation in society by providing educational experiences as similar as possible to those of the majority.

According to PL 101-475, school districts must offer an array of options for special needs children. Among these are separate schools, self-contained classrooms in regular school buildings, and integration into classes serving pupils without disabilities. The term **mainstreaming** refers to this last alternative. PL 101-475 recognizes that regular classroom placement is not appropriate for all children and does not require it. But since passage of the law, a rapid increase in mainstreaming has occurred. Some mainstreamed pupils are mildly mentally retarded—children whose IQs fall between 55 and 70 and who also show problems in adaptive behavior (Grossman, 1983). But most are pupils with **learning disabilities**—those with a specific learning disorder (for example, in reading, writing, or math computation) that results in poor school achievement. Learning-disabled pupils are average or above-average in IQ, and their problems cannot be

Mainstreaming
The integration of pupils with learning difficulties into regular classrooms for all or part of the school day.

Learning disabilities
Specific learning disorders (for, example, in reading, writing, or math computation) that result in poor school achievement, despite an average or above-average IQ.

traced to any obvious physical or emotional difficulty or to environmental disadvantage. Instead, faulty brain functioning is believed to underlie their difficulties (Hammill, 1990). Some of the disorders run in families, suggesting that they are at least partly genetic (Pennington & Smith, 1988). In most instances, the cause is unknown.

Does mainstreaming accomplish its dual goal of providing more appropriate academic experiences and integrated participation in classroom life? At present, research findings are not positive on either of these points. Achievement differences between mainstreamed pupils and those taught in self-contained classrooms are not great (MacMillan, Keogh, & Jones, 1986). Furthermore, mainstreamed children are often rejected by peers. Those who are mentally retarded are overwhelmed by the social skills of their classmates; they cannot interact quickly or adeptly in a conversation or game. And the processing deficits of some children with learning disabilities also lead to problems in social awareness and responsiveness (Rourke, 1988). As a result, these children report considerable dissatisfaction with their peer experiences and intense feelings of loneliness (Taylor, Asher, & Williams, 1987).

Does this mean that mainstreaming is not a good way to serve children with special learning needs? This extreme conclusion is not warranted. Many regular classroom teachers do not have the training or the time to give these pupils all the help they need. Often these children do best when they receive instruction in a resource room for part of the day and in the regular classroom for the remainder. In the resource room, a special education teacher works with pupils individually and in small groups. Then, depending on their abilities, children are mainstreamed for different subjects and amounts of time. This flexible approach makes it more likely that the unique academic needs of each child will be served (Keogh, 1988; Lerner, 1989).

Once children enter the regular classroom, teachers must make a special effort to promote peer acceptance. When instruction is carefully individualized and teachers minimize comparisons with higher-achieving classmates, mainstreamed pupils show gains in self-esteem and achievement (Madden & Slavin, 1983). Also, cooperative learning experiences in which a mainstreamed child and several classmates work together on the same task have been found to promote friendly interaction and improved social acceptance (Scruggs & Mastropieri, 1994). Finally, teachers can prepare children for the arrival of a special-needs pupil. Under these conditions, mainstreaming may lead to gains in emotional sensitivity, perspective taking, and prosocial behavior among classmates that break down social barriers and promote early integration of individuals with disabilities into the mainstream of American life.

BRIEF REVIEW

Schools are powerful forces in children's development. In class sizes below 15 or 20 pupils, academic achievement is higher. A student body size of 500 to 700 students or less promotes adolescents' extracurricular participation. Pupils in traditional classrooms are slightly advantaged in achievement; those in open classrooms are more independent, tolerant of individual differences, and excited about learning. New philosophical directions based on Vygotsky's sociocultural theory are inspiring methods that stress social communication and collaboration as vital for learning. School transitions create new adjustment problems. Supportive ties to peers ease entry into kindergarten. The earlier school transition takes place in adolescence, the more likely it is to depress psychological well-being, especially among girls.

Teachers who are effective classroom managers and who provide cognitively stimulating activities enhance children's involvement and academic performance. Educational self-fulfilling prophecies are likely to occur when teachers emphasize competition and comparisons among pupils, have difficulty controlling the class, and engage in ability grouping. Disruptive, low-achieving pupils, withdrawn children, and low-income ethnic minority pupils are especially susceptible. To be effective, mainstreaming must be carefully tailored to meet the academic and social needs of children with learning difficulties.

How Well Educated Are American Young People?

Our discussion of schooling has focused largely on what teachers can do in classrooms to support the education of children and adolescents. Yet many factors, both within and outside schools, affect children's learning. Societal values, school resources, quality of teaching, and parental encouragement all play important roles. Nowhere are these multiple influences more apparent than when schooling is examined in cross-cultural perspective.

CROSS-NATIONAL RESEARCH ON ACADEMIC ACHIEVEMENT

American students fare unevenly when their achievement is compared to students in other industrialized nations. In international studies of mathematics and science achievement, young people from Hong Kong, Japan, Korea, and Taiwan have consistently been among the top performers, whereas Americans have scored no better than at the mean (Husén, 1967; International Education Association, 1988; Lapointe, Askew, & Mead, 1992: Lapointe, Mead, & Askew, 1992; McKnight et al., 1987). In the most recent assessments, American 9- and 13-year-olds fell slightly below the international average in mathematics and science. Although the scores of many nations were tightly bunched,[3] the performance of the United States was mediocre. In other subjects, the United States compares more favorably. For example, in reading, American 9-year-olds and 13-year-olds were among the highest scoring, with only minimal differences existing between top-performing countries (National Center for Education Statistics, 1994).

In an effort to identify factors that support high achievement, researchers have looked closely at Asian nations. In a series of large-scale studies, Harold Stevenson, Shin-Ying Lee, and James Stigler examined the achievement of elementary school children in Japan, Taiwan, and the United States. In one investigation, nearly 1,500 first and fifth graders were selected to represent children in three metropolitan areas: Sendai (Japan), Taipei (Taiwan), and Minneapolis. Math and reading achievement were measured with tests based on content common to all three locations. In addition, the researchers observed in classrooms and interviewed the children as well as their parents and teachers. Findings revealed that Asian children were far ahead of their American counterparts in math achievement at the beginning of elementary school, a difference that became stronger with increasing grade level. Less extreme gaps occurred in reading, in which Taiwanese children scored highest, Japanese children lowest, and American children in between (Stevenson, 1992; Stevenson & Lee, 1990).

Pupils in the investigation just described were tested in 1980. Over the following decade, the researchers returned to the three sites to look for possible changes in students' performance. In 1984 and 1990, first graders were restudied when they reached fifth and eleventh grade, respectively. To supplement this longitudinal sample, in 1990, several thousand fifth and eleventh graders were given achievement tests in each city. As Figure 15.9(a) on page 620 shows, from 1980 to 1990, Japanese and Taiwanese fifth graders remained ahead of Americans in math achievement, and the gap between Taiwanese and American pupils widened. Furthermore, American pupils fell behind both groups of Asian pupils in reading achievement, while Japanese pupils took the lead (see Figure 15.9b). Finally, longitudinal trends in Figure 15.9(c) reveal that the math achievement of

[3] Often the news media report international comparisons in achievement in terms of the highest- to lowest-ranked nations. Ranks are not a trustworthy way to compare countries, since small differences in score often translate into large differences in ranks. Also, when the math performance of college-bound high school seniors is considered, the United States falls among the lowest-scoring nations. But once again, we must interpret this finding cautiously, since the percentage of high school seniors taking math classes varies enormously among countries. For example, only a small, highly select group of students is still enrolled in top-scoring Hong Kong and Japan (Bracey, 1996).

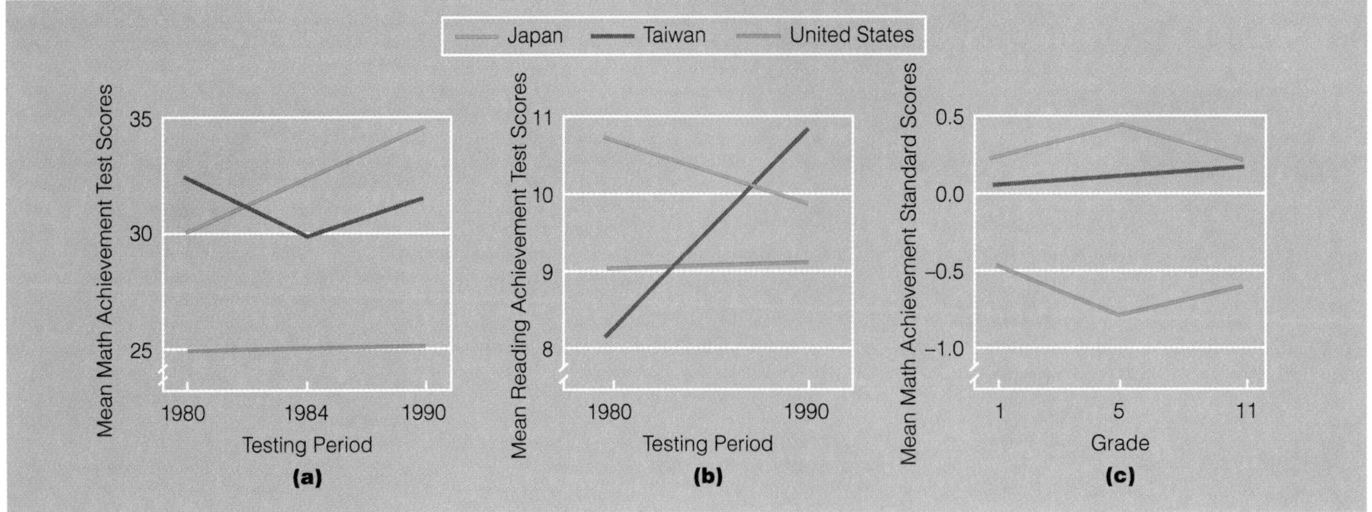

FIGURE 15.9

■ *Math and reading achievement at three testing periods in Japan, Taiwan, and the United States. (a) From 1980 to 1990, Japanese fifth graders maintained their lead over American fifth graders in math achievement, and the gap between Taiwanese and American children increased. (b) American fifth graders fell behind both Asian groups in reading achievement. Japanese fifth graders, who scored lowest in 1980, did best in 1990. (c) A longitudinal follow-up of first graders when they reached fifth and eleventh grades revealed that the math achievement of American students did not improve. (From H. W. Stevenson, C. Chen, & S-Y. Lee, 1993, "Mathematics Achievement of Chinese, Japanese, and American Children: Ten Years Later,"* Science, *259, p. 54. Copyright © 1993 by the AAAS. Reprinted by permission.)*

American students did not improve as they moved from first to eleventh grade (Stevenson, Chen, & Lee, 1993).

Why do American students fall behind their Asian counterparts in academic accomplishments? A common assumption is that Asian pupils are high achievers because they are "smarter," but this is not true. They do not do better on intelligence tests than their American agemates (Stevenson et al., 1985). Instead, as the Cultural Influences box on the following page explains, a wide variety of social forces combine to foster a stronger commitment to learning in many Asian families and schools.

By the turn of the twenty-first century, many more jobs in the United States will demand high levels of literacy and technical knowledge. School reforms are currently underway, aimed at helping young people master the language, math, and science skills necessary to meet work force needs. Perhaps as a result of these efforts, the achievement of American elementary and secondary school students has improved over the past decade in math and science, in reading and writing less so (Mullis et al., 1994). Effective educational change, however, must take into account the life background and future goals of students. Simply toughening academic standards is likely to further discourage many low-income, poorly achieving young people, who can only fall farther behind under these conditions (Parrish, 1991). As we will see next, besides strengthening academic instruction, special efforts are needed in the area of vocational education to help noncollege-bound youths prepare for productive work roles.

■ *Japanese children achieve considerably better than their American counterparts for a variety of reasons. A longer school day permits frequent alternation of academic instruction with pleasurable activity. This approach probably makes learning easier and more enjoyable. (Eiji Miyazawa/Black Star Publishing Company)*

CULTURAL INFLUENCES

Education in Japan, Taiwan, and the United States

Why do Asian children perform so well academically? Research examining societal, school, and family conditions in Japan, Taiwan, and the United States provides some answers.

CULTURAL VALUING OF ACADEMIC ACHIEVEMENT. In Japan and Taiwan, natural resources are limited. Progress in science and technology is essential for economic well-being. Since a well-educated work force is necessary to meet this goal, children's mastery of academic skills is vital. In the United States, attitudes toward academic achievement are far less unified. Many Americans believe it is more important to encourage children to feel good about themselves and to explore various areas of knowledge than to perform well in school.

EMPHASIS ON EFFORT. Japanese and Taiwanese parents and teachers believe that all children have the potential to master challenging academic tasks if they work hard enough. In contrast, many more of their American counterparts regard native ability as the key to academic success (Stevenson, 1992). These differences in attitude may contribute to the fact that American parents are less inclined to encourage activities at home that might enhance school performance. Japanese and Taiwanese children spend more free time studying, reading, and playing academic-related games than do children in the United States (Stevenson & Lee, 1990). In high school, Asian students continue to devote more time to academic pursuits, whereas American students spend more time working and socializing—factors related to both cross-cultural and individual differences in achievement (Fuligni & Stevenson, 1995).

INVOLVEMENT OF PARENTS IN EDUCATION. Asian parents devote many hours to helping their children with homework. American parents spend very little and, at least while their children are in elementary school, do not regard homework as especially important. Overall, American parents are far more satisfied with the quality of their children's education, hold lower standards for their children's academic performance, and are less concerned about how well their youngsters are doing in school (Stevenson, Chen, & Lee, 1993; Stevenson & Lee, 1990).

HIGH-QUALITY EDUCATION FOR ALL. Unlike American teachers, Japanese and Taiwanese teachers do not make early educational decisions on the basis of achievement. There are no separate ability groups or tracks in elementary school. Instead, all pupils receive the same nationally mandated high-quality instruction. In the United States, wide variation in quality of schooling exists. Low-income, ethnic minority children have a much higher likelihood of attending under-equipped schools offering poor-quality instruction than do their middle-income counterparts.

COHERENT LESSONS THAT ACTIVELY INVOLVE CHILDREN IN LEARNING. Academic lessons in Japanese and Taiwanese classrooms are particularly well organized and presented in ways that capture children's attention and actively involve them. Japanese and Taiwanese teachers assume the role of knowledge guide rather than dispenser of information. Each daily lesson begins with an engaging practical problem and, like a good story, has an introduction, conclusion, and consistent theme. Discussion is frequent as Asian teachers stimulate children to explain and evaluate their solutions. Compared to American classrooms, topics in mathematics are treated in greater depth, and there is less repetition of material taught the previous year (Stevenson & Lee, 1990).

MORE TIME DEVOTED TO INSTRUCTION. In Japan and Taiwan, the school year is over 50 days longer than in the United States, and much more time is devoted to academic pursuits, especially mathematics. Furthermore, time is used more effectively in Asian classrooms. In one comparison of elementary school academic lessons, the teacher was the leader of the child's activity 90 percent of the time in Taiwan, 74 percent in Japan, but only 46 percent in the United States. Most often, American children worked on their own at their desks, which often resulted in loss of focus on the purpose of the activity. In contrast, Japanese and Taiwanese teachers alternated between short seatwork periods and group discussion of problems, thereby embedding independent work into the larger lesson and keeping children involved. Furthermore, Asian schools are not regimented places, as many Americans believe. An 8-hour school day and effective use of class time permits extra recesses and a longer lunch period, with plenty of time for play, social interaction, field trips, and extracurricular activities (Stevenson, 1992, 1994).

COMMUNICATION BETWEEN TEACHERS AND PARENTS. Japanese and Taiwanese teachers get to know their pupils especially well. They teach the same children for 2 or 3 years and make visits to the home once or twice a year. Continuous communication between teachers and parents takes place with the aid of small notebooks that children carry back and forth every day and in which messages about assignments, academic performance, and behavior are written. No such formalized system of frequent teacher–parent communication exists in the United States (Stevenson & Lee, 1990).

Do Japanese and Taiwanese young people pay a price for the pressure placed on them to succeed? By high school, academic work often displaces other experiences, since Asian adolescents must pass a highly competitive entrance exam to be admitted to college. Yet in Chapter 11, we noted that the highest performing Asian students are very well adjusted. Although the educational system of one society cannot simply be transplanted to cure the ills of another, awareness of the ingredients of Asian success has prompted Americans to rethink current educational practices.

MAKING THE TRANSITION FROM SCHOOL TO WORK

Approximately 25 percent of American adolescents graduate from high school without plans to go to college. Although they have a much better chance of finding employment than those who drop out, non-college-bound youths have fewer work opportunities than they did several decades ago. More than one-fourth of high school graduates younger than age 20 who do not continue their education are unemployed (U.S. Bureau of the Census, 1995). When they do find work, most are limited to low-paid, unskilled jobs. In addition, they have few alternatives to turn to for vocational counseling and job placement as they make the transition from school to work (Bailey, 1993).

American employers prefer to hire young adults, regarding the recent high school graduate as insufficiently prepared for a demanding, skilled occupation. Indeed, there is some truth to this conclusion. During high school, almost half of American adolescents are employed—a greater percentage than in any other developed country. But most of these are middle-class students in pursuit of spending money rather than vocational training. Low-income teenagers who need to contribute to family income find it harder to get jobs (Children's Defense Fund, 1996).

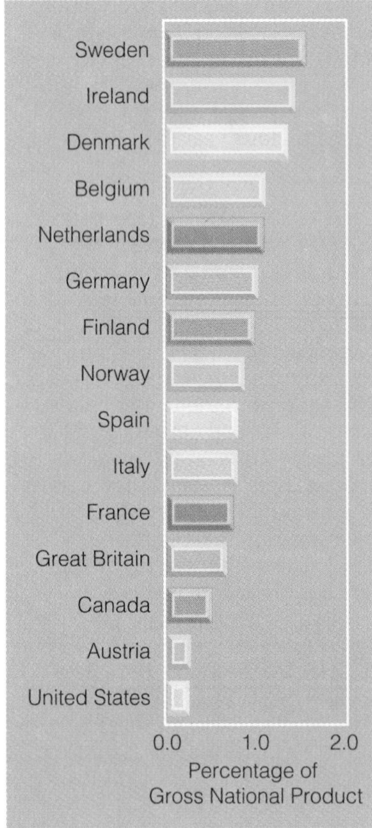

FIGURE 15.10

■ *Percentage of gross national product devoted to vocational training in Western Europe, Canada, and the United States. The United States invests far less in vocational training for its non-college-bound young people than do many other countries. (Clark, 1992.)*

Furthermore, the jobs adolescents hold are limited to low-level repetitive tasks that provide little contact with adult supervisors and do not prepare them for well-paid careers. A heavy commitment to such jobs is actually harmful. High school students who work more than 15 hours a week have poorer school attendance, lower grades, and less time for extracurricular activities. They also report more drug and alcohol use and feel more distant from their parents. And perhaps because of the menial nature of their jobs, employed teenagers tend to become cynical about work life. Many admit to having stolen from their employers (Greenberger & Steinberg, 1986; Steinberg & Dornbusch, 1991).

When work experiences are specially designed to meet educational and vocational goals, outcomes are very different. Work–study programs are related to positive school and work attitudes, improved achievement, and lower dropout rates among teenagers whose low-income backgrounds and weak academic skills make them especially vulnerable to unemployment (Owens, 1982; Steinberg, 1984). Yet high-quality vocational preparation for American adolescents who do not go to college is scarce. Unlike Western European nations, the United States has no widespread training system to prepare its youths for business and industrial occupations or manual trades. The federal government does support some job-training programs, but most are too short to make a difference in the lives of poorly skilled adolescents, who need intensive training and academic remediation before they are ready to enter the job market. And at present, these programs serve only a small minority of young people who need assistance (Children's Defense Fund, 1996). As Figure 15.10 shows, the United States invests far less in vocational training than do many other countries.

Inspired by successful programs in western Europe, youth apprenticeship strategies that coordinate on-the-job training with classroom instruction are being considered as an important dimension of educational reform in the United States. Bringing together the worlds of schooling and work offers many benefits. These include helping non-college-bound adolescents establish productive lives right after graduation; motivating at-risk youths, who learn more effectively when basic skills are linked to everyday experiences; and contributing to the nation's economic growth (Bailey, 1993; Hamilton, 1993).

Nevertheless, implementing an apprenticeship system poses major challenges. Among these are overcoming the reluctance of employers to assume part of the responsibility for youth vocational training; creating institutional structures that ensure cooperation between schools and businesses; and finding ways to prevent underprivileged youths from being concentrated in the lowest-skilled apprenticeship placements, a circumstance that would perpetuate current social inequalities (Bailey, 1993; Hamilton, 1993). Pilot apprenticeship projects are being tried, in an effort to surmount these difficulties and break down the dichotomy that exists between learning and working in the United States. Young people well prepared for an economically and personally satisfying vocation are much more likely to become productive citizens, devoted family members, and contented adults. The support of schools, communities, and society as a whole can contribute greatly to a positive outcome.

SUMMARY

THE IMPORTANCE OF PEER RELATIONS

- Research with nonhuman primates suggests that parent and peer relations complement one another. The parent–child bond provides children with the security to enter the world of peers. Peer interaction, in turn, permits children to expand the social skills they have begun to acquire within the family. Studies of **peer-only rearing** reveal that peer relations can, to some extent, fill in for the early parent–child bond. However, peer-only reared monkeys do not develop as well as their counterparts with typical parental and peer upbringing.

DEVELOPMENT OF PEER SOCIABILITY

- Peer sociability begins in infancy with isolated social acts that are gradually replaced by coordinated exchanges in the second year of life. During the preschool years, interactive play with peers increases. According to Parten, **nonsocial activity** shifts to **parallel play** and then to **associative** and **cooperative play**. However, research indicates that these play forms do not form a developmental sequence in which later-appearing ones replace earlier ones. Instead, all coexist among preschoolers. Sociodramatic play becomes especially common and enhances cognitive, emotional, and social skills.
- During middle childhood, peer interaction is more sensitively tuned to others' perspectives and increasingly governed by prosocial norms. In addition, **rough-and-tumble play** becomes more common. In our evolutionary past, this friendly chasing and play-fighting may have been important for the development of fighting skill. In adolescence, peers show greater skill at working on tasks cooperatively.

INFLUENCES ON PEER SOCIABILITY

- Parents influence young children's peer relations by creating opportunities for agemates to get together, offering advice and guidance about how to interact with playmates, and modeling effective social skills.
- Situational factors affect peer sociability. When toys and space are in short supply, negative interactions increase. Cooperative play occurs more often when preschoolers play with open-ended, relatively unstructured materials. Mixed-age interaction provides older children with practice in prosocial behavior and younger children with opportunities to learn from their older companions. Same-age peers engage in more intense and harmonious exchanges.
- In collectivist cultures, large-group imitative play involving acting out of highly scripted activities is common. When caregivers value the cognitive and educational benefits of make-believe and stress individuality and self-expression, social pretending occurs more often.

PEER ACCEPTANCE

- **Sociometric techniques** are used to distinguish four types of peer acceptance: **popular children**, who are liked by many agemates; **rejected children**, who are actively disliked; **controversial children**, who are both liked and disliked; and **neglected children**, who are seldom chosen, either positively or negatively. Rejected children often experience lasting adjustment difficulties.
- Physical attractiveness is related to peer acceptance. Attractive and unattractive children may respond in kind to the way they are treated, sustaining peer opinion.
- The most powerful predictor of peer acceptance is social behavior. Popular children communicate with agemates in sensitive, friendly, and cooperative ways. At least two subtypes of peer rejection exist. **Rejected-aggressive** children are hostile, hyperactive, inattentive, and impulsive, whereas **rejected-withdrawn** children are passive and socially awkward. Controversial children display a blend of positive and negative social behaviors. Although neglected children often choose to play by themselves, they are socially competent and well adjusted.
- Interventions that improve the peer acceptance of rejected children include coaching in social skills, academic remediation, and social-cognitive interventions that enhance perspective taking and expectancies for social success.

PEER GROUPS

- By the end of middle childhood, **peer groups** with unique norms and social structures of leaders and followers emerge. In adolescence, tightly organized peer groups called **cliques** become common. Sometimes several cliques form a larger, more loosely organized group called a **crowd** that grants the adolescent an identity within the larger social structure of the school. Teenagers' choice of a peer group results from a blend of family and peer influences.
- Group social structures sometimes consist of **dominance hierarchies**, which serve the adaptive function of limiting aggression among group members. In many instances, leadership is not based on dominance, but rather on managerial skills and talents that support important normative activities of the group.

PEER RELATIONS AND SOCIALIZATION

- Peers serve as socialization agents through reinforcement, modeling, and direct pressures to conform to social behaviors. Peer conformity is strongest during early adolescence. However, peers seldom demand total conformity, and most peer pressures do not conflict with important adult values.

TELEVISION

- Children spend more time watching TV than in any other waking activity. Heavy viewers tend to have lower IQs, come from low-income families, and have adjustment problems. Cognitive development and experience in watching TV gradually lead to gains in **television literacy** during middle childhood and adolescence.
- Televised violence promotes short- and long-term increases in aggressive behavior, tolerance of aggression in others, and a hostile and dangerous view of the world. TV also conveys stereotypes that affect children's beliefs about ethnicity and gender. Children are easily manipulated by TV commercials. Not until age 8 or 9 do they understand the selling purpose of the ads.

- Television can foster prosocial behavior as long as it is free of violent content. Appropriately designed programs also have the potential for promoting academic learning and imagination.

COMPUTERS

- Computers can have rich cognitive and social benefits. In classrooms, pupils often use computers collaboratively. During the early elementary school years, **computer-assisted instruction (CAI)** leads to gains in academic achievement, and word processing results in longer, higher-quality written prose. Experience with computer programming promotes a wide variety of higher cognitive processes. Computer-based communications technology can broaden children's understanding of other people and places. Nevertheless, computers may be widening gaps in intellectual skills between low-income and middle-income children and boys and girls.

SCHOOLING

- Schools powerfully influence many aspects of development. As class size drops below 15 or 20 pupils, academic achievement improves. In small high schools, adolescents are more actively involved in extracurricular activities and develop a sense of social obligation that carries over to community participation in adult life.
- Teachers' educational philosophies play a major role in children's learning experiences. Pupils in **traditional classrooms** are advantaged in academic achievement. Those in **open classrooms** tend to be independent learners who respect individual differences and have more positive attitudes toward school. New philosophical approaches based on Vygotsky's sociocultural theory emphasize the importance of rich, socially communicative environments and collaboration on challenging, meaningful activities.
- Supportive ties to peers are related to favorable adjustment to kindergarten. School transitions in adolescence can also be stressful. With each school change, course grades decline and feelings of anonymity increase. Girls experience more adjustment difficulties after the elementary to junior high transition, since other life changes (puberty and the beginning of dating) tend to occur at the same time.
- Patterns of teacher–pupil interaction affect children's academic progress. Teachers who are effective classroom managers have pupils who achieve especially well. Instruction that encourages higher-level thinking promotes pupil interest and involvement in classroom activities. **Educational self-fulfilling prophecies** are most likely to occur when teachers emphasize competition and public evaluation, view poorly achieving pupils as limited by ability rather than effort, and fear losing control of the class. Low-income and ethnic minority children and pupils in low ability groups are especially vulnerable to negative self-fulfilling prophecies.
- Teachers face special challenges in meeting the needs of children with learning difficulties. Pupils with mild mental retardation and **learning disabilities** are often integrated into regular classrooms for all or part of the school day. The success of **mainstreaming** depends on carefully tailoring instruction to meet pupils' learning needs and promoting peer acceptance.

HOW WELL EDUCATED ARE AMERICAN YOUNG PEOPLE?

- In cross-national comparisons of academic achievement, students in Asian nations are consistently among the top performers in mathematics and science, whereas Americans score no better than average. A strong cultural commitment to learning is responsible for the academic success of Japanese and Taiwanese pupils.
- Besides strengthening academic standards, the United States needs to help its non-college-bound high school graduates make an effective transition from school to work. Unlike Western European young people, American adolescents have no widespread vocational training system to assist them in preparing for challenging, well-paid careers in business, industry, and manual trades.

IMPORTANT TERMS AND CONCEPTS

peer-only rearing (p. 580)
nonsocial activity (p. 581)
parallel play (p. 581)
associative play (p. 581)
cooperative play (p. 581)
rough-and-tumble play (p. 583)
sociometric techniques (p. 587)
popular children (p. 587)
rejected children (p. 587)
controversial children (p. 587)
neglected children (p. 587)
rejected-aggressive children (p. 588)
rejected-withdrawn children (p. 588)
peer group (p. 590)
clique (p. 592)
crowd (p. 592)
dominance hierarchy (p. 593)
television literacy (p. 599)
computer-assisted instruction (CAI) (p. 606)
traditional classroom (p. 610)
open classroom (p. 610)
educational self-fulfilling prophecy (p. 616)
mainstreaming (p. 617)
learning disabilities (p. 617)

CONNECTIONS for Chapter 15

If you are interested in . . .	turn to . . .	to learn about . . .
Peer interaction	Chapter 6, pp. 247–248	Peer interaction and cognitive development
	Chapter 11, pp. 449–453	Friendship in childhood and adolescence
	Chapter 11, pp. 453–457	Social problem solving
	Chapter 12, pp. 477–478	Peer interaction and moral reasoning
	Chapter 13, p. 516	Peer interaction and gender-role adoption
	Chapter 14, pp. 567–568	High-quality day care and social skills
Peer acceptance	Chapter 5, pp. 183–184	Early versus late pubertal maturation and peer acceptance
	Chapter 5, p. 204	Peer rejection of obese children
	Chapter 7, p. 270	Peer rejection of children with attention-deficit hyperactivity disorder
	Chapter 12, p. 494	Peer rejection of aggressive children
	Chapter 13, p. 516	Peer rejection of children who engage in "gender-inappropriate" behavior
Educational philosophies	Chapter 5, pp. 189, 190	Sex education
	Chapter 6, p. 246	Piaget's cognitive-developmental theory and education
	Chapter 6, pp. 250–253	Vygotsky's sociocultural theory and education
	Chapter 7, p. 288	Whole language versus basic skills approaches to teaching reading
	Chapter 8, pp. 328–331	Approaches to early intervention
	Chapter 9, pp. 375–376	Bilingual education in the United States
	Chapter 12, p. 479	Teaching moral values in the public schools

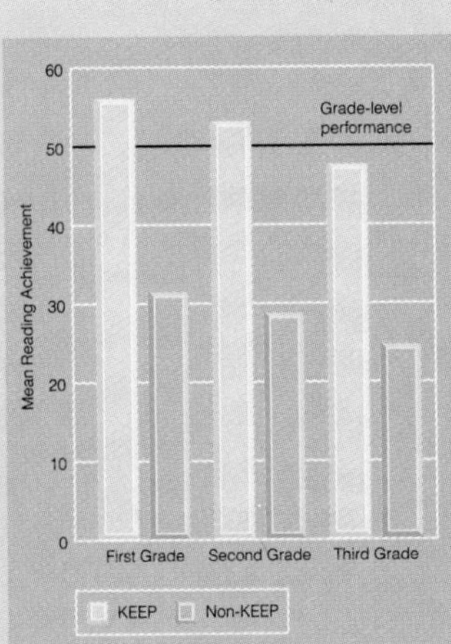

Glossary

A

AB search error The error made by 8- to 12-month-olds after an object is moved from hiding place A to hiding place B. Infants in Piaget's Substage 4 search for it only in the first hiding place (A).

Accommodation That part of adaptation in which old schemes are adjusted and new ones created to produce a better fit with the environment. Distinguished from *assimilation.*

Achievement motivation The tendency to persist at challenging tasks.

Adaptation In Piaget's theory, the process of building schemes through direct interaction with the environment. Made of two complementary activities: *assimilation* and *accommodation.*

Affordances The action possibilities a situation offers an organism with certain motor capabilities. Discovery of affordances is believed to guide perceptual development.

Age of viability The age at which the fetus can first survive if born early. Occurs sometime between 22 and 26 weeks.

Allele Each of two forms or more of a gene located at the same place on the autosomes.

Amnion The inner membrane that forms a protective covering around the prenatal organism and encloses it in amniotic fluid, which helps keep temperature constant and provides a cushion against jolts caused by the mother's movement.

Androgens Hormones produced chiefly by the testes, and in smaller quantities by the adrenal glands, that influence the pubertal growth spurt, the appearance of body hair, and male sex characteristics.

Androgyny A type of gender-role identity in which the person scores high on both masculine and feminine personality characteristics.

Animistic thinking The belief that inanimate objects have lifelike qualities, such as thoughts, wishes, feelings, and intentions. A characteristic of Piaget's preoperational stage.

Anorexia nervosa An eating disorder in which individuals (usually females) starve themselves because of a compulsive fear of getting fat.

Apgar Scale A rating used to assess the newborn baby's physical condition immediately after birth.

Applied behavior analysis A set of practical procedures that combines reinforcement, modeling, and the manipulation of situational cues to change behavior.

Assimilation That part of adaptation in which the external world is interpreted in terms of current schemes. Distinguished from *accommodation.*

Associative play A form of true social participation in which children engage in separate activities, but they interact by exchanging toys and commenting on one another's behavior. Distinguished from *nonsocial activity, parallel play,* and *cooperative play.*

Attachment The strong affectional tie that humans feel toward special people in their lives.

Attachment Q-set An efficient method for assessing the quality of the attachment bond in which a parent or an expert informant sorts a set of 90 descriptors of attachment-related behaviors on the basis of how descriptive they are of the child. The resulting profile indicates the degree to which the child displays secure-base behavior.

Attention-deficit hyperactivity disorder A childhood disorder involving inattention, impulsivity, and excessive motor activity. Often leads to academic failure and social problems.

Attribution retraining An approach to intervention in which attributions of learned helpless children are modified through feedback that encourages them to believe in themselves and persist in the face of task difficulty.

Attributions Common, everyday explanations for the causes of behavior.

Authoritarian style A parenting style that is demanding but low in responsiveness to children's rights and needs. Conformity and obedience are valued over open communication. Distinguished from *authoritative, permissive,* and *uninvolved styles.*

Authoritative style A parenting style that is demanding and responsive. A rational, democratic approach in which both parents' and children's rights are respected. Distinguished from *authoritarian* and *permissive parents.*

Autobiographical memory Long-lasting memory for one-time events that are particularly meaningful in terms of the life story each of us creates about ourselves.

Autonomous morality Piaget's second stage of moral development, in which children view rules as flexible, socially agreed-on principles that can be revised to suit the will of the majority.

Autonomy A sense of oneself as a separate, self-governing individual. An important developmental task of adolescence that is closely related to the quest for identity.

Autosomes The 22 matching chromosome pairs in each human cell.

Autostimulation theory The theory that REM sleep provides stimulation necessary for central nervous system development in young infants.

Avoidant attachment The quality of insecure attachment characterizing infants who are usually not distressed by parental separation and who avoid the parent when she returns. Distinguished from *secure, resistant,* and *disorganized/disoriented attachment.*

B

Babbling Repetition of consonant–vowel combinations in long strings, beginning around 6 months of age.

Basic emotions Emotions that can be directly inferred from facial expressions, such as happiness, interest, surprise, fear, anger, sadness, and disgust.

Basic-skills approach An approach to beginning reading instruction that emphasizes training in phonics—the basic rules for translating written symbols into sounds—and simplified reading materials. Distinguished from *whole-language approach.*

Behavioral genetics A field of study devoted to uncovering the hereditary and environmental origins of individual differences in human traits and abilities.

Behaviorism An approach that views directly observable events—stimuli and responses—as the appropriate focus of study and the development of behavior as taking place through classical and operant conditioning.

Belief-desire theory of mind The theory of mind that emerges around age 3 to 4 in which both beliefs and desires determine behavior and that closely resembles the everyday psychology of adults.

Biased sampling Failure to select participants who are representative of the population of interest in a study.

Binocular depth cues Depth cues that rely on each eye receiving a slightly different view of the visual field; the brain blends the two images, creating three-dimensionality.

Blended, or reconstituted, family A family structure resulting from cohabitation or remarriage that includes parent, child, and steprelatives.

Body Image Conception of and attitude toward one's physical appearance.

Brain plasticity The ability of other parts of the brain to take over functions of damaged regions.

Breech position A position of the baby in the uterus that would cause the buttocks or feet to be delivered first.

Broca's area A language structure located in the frontal lobe of the cerebral cortex that controls language production.

Bulimia An eating disorder in which individuals (mainly females) go on eating binges followed by deliberate vomiting, other purging techniques such as heavy doses of laxatives, and strict dieting.

C

Canalization The tendency of heredity to restrict the development of some characteristics to just one or a few outcomes.

Cardinality A principle specifying that the last number in a counting sequence indicates the quantity of items in the set.

Carrier A heterozygous individual who can pass a harmful gene to his or her offspring.

Catch-up growth Physical growth that returns to its genetically determined path after being delayed by environmental factors.

Categorical self Early classification of the self according to salient ways in which people differ, such as age, sex, and physical characteristics.

Categorical speech perception The tendency to perceive a range of sounds that belong to the same phonemic class as identical.

Centration The tendency to focus on one aspect of a situation to the neglect of other important features. A characteristic of Piaget's preoperational stage.

Cephalocaudal trend An organized pattern of physical growth and motor control that proceeds from head to tail.

Cerebellum A brain structure that aids in balance and control of body movements.

Cerebral cortex The largest structure of the human brain that accounts for the highly developed intelligence of the human species.

Child development A field of study devoted to understanding all aspects of human growth from conception through adolescence.

Child social indicators Periodic measures of children's health, living conditions, achievement, and psychological well-being that lend insight into their overall status in a community, state, or nation.

Chorion The outer membrane that forms a protective covering around the prenatal organism. It sends out tiny fingerlike villi, from which the placenta begins to emerge.

Chromosomes Rodlike structures in the cell nucleus that store and transmit genetic information.

Chronosystem In ecological systems theory, temporal changes in children's environments, which produce new conditions that affect development. These changes can be imposed externally or arise from within the organism, since children select, modify, and create many of their own settings and experiences.

Circular reaction In Piaget's theory, a means of building schemes in which infants try to repeat a chance event caused by their own motor activity.

Classical conditioning A form of learning that involves associating a neutral stimulus with a stimulus that leads to a reflexive response.

Clinical interview A method in which the researcher uses flexible, open-ended questions to probe for the participant's point of view.

Clinical method A method in which the researcher attempts to understand the unique individual child by combining interview data, observations, test scores, and sometimes psychophysiological assessments.

Clique A small group of about five to seven members who are good friends.

Codominance A pattern of inheritance in which both alleles, in a heterozygous combination, are expressed.

Cognitive maps Mental representations of large-scale environments.

Cognitive-developmental theory An approach introduced by Piaget that views the child as actively building mental structures and cognitive development as taking place in stages.

Cohort effects The effects of cultural-historical change on the accuracy of findings: Children born in one period of time are influenced by particular cultural and historical conditions.

Compliance Voluntary obedience to requests and commands.

Componential analysis A research procedure aimed at clarifying the cognitive processes responsible for intelligence test scores by correlating them with laboratory measures designed to assess the speed and effectiveness of information processing.

Comprehension In language development, the words and word combinations that children understand. Distinguished from *production.*

Comprehension monitoring Sensitivity to how well one understands a spoken or written message.

Computer-assisted instruction (CAI) Use of computers to transmit new knowledge and practice academic skills.

Concordance rate The percentage of instances in which both members of a twin pair show a trait when it is present in one twin.

Concrete operational stage Piaget's third stage, during which thought is logical, flexible, and organized in its application to concrete information. However, the capacity for abstract thinking is not yet present. Spans the years from 7 to 11.

Conditioned response (CR) In classical conditioning, an originally reflexive response that is produced by a conditioned stimulus (CS).

Conditioned stimulus (CS) In classical conditioning, a neutral stimulus that through pairing with an unconditioned stimulus (UCS) leads to a new response (CR).

Confluence model A view that regards mental development as a function of family size, birth order, and spacing—factors that affect the quality of the environment each child experiences within the family.

Conservation The understanding that certain physical characteristics of objects remain the same, even when their outward appearance changes.

Construction The process of moral development in which children actively attend to and interrelate multiple aspects of situations in which social conflicts arise and derive new moral understandings.

Constructivist approach An approach to cognitive development in which children discover virtually all knowledge about the world through their own activity. Consistent with Piaget's cognitive-developmental theory. Distinguished from *nativist approach.*

Continuous development A view that regards development as a cumulative process of adding on more of the same types of skills that were there to begin with. Distinguished from *discontinuous development.*

Contrast sensitivity A general principle accounting for early pattern preferences, which states that if babies can detect a difference in contrast between two patterns, they will prefer the one with more contrast.

Control deficiency The inability to execute a mental strategy effectively. Distinguished from *production* and *utilization deficiencies.*

Control processes, or mental strategies Procedures that operate on and transform information, increasing the efficiency of thinking and the chances that information will be retained.

Controversial children Children who get a large number of positive and negative votes on sociometric measures of peer acceptance. Distinguished from *popular, neglected,* and *rejected children.*

Conventional level Kohlberg's second level of moral development, in which moral understanding is based on conforming to social rules to ensure positive human relationships and societal order.

Convergent thinking The generation of a single correct answer to a problem. Type of cognition emphasized on intelligence tests. Distinguished from *divergent thinking.*

Cooing Pleasant vowel-like noises made by infants beginning around 2 months of age.

Cooperative learning A learning environment structured into groups of peers who work together toward a common goal. Distinguished from *nonsocial activity, parallel play,* and *associative play.*

Cooperative play A form of true social participation in which children's actions are directed toward a common goal. Distinguished from *nonsocial activity, parallel play,* and *associative play.*

Coregulation A transitional form of supervision in which parents exercise general oversight while permitting children to be in charge of moment-by-moment decision making.

Corpus callosum The large bundle of fibers that connects the two hemispheres of the brain.

Correlation coefficient A number, ranging from +1.00 to –1.00, that describes the strength and direction of the relationship between two variables. The size of the number shows the strength of the relationship. The sign of the number (+ or –) refers to the direction of the relationship.

Correlational design A research design in which the investigator gathers information without altering participants' experiences and examines relationships between variables. Does not permit inferences about cause and effect.

Creativity The ability to produce work that is original (that others have not thought of before) and that is appropriate (sensible or useful in some way).

Cross-sectional design A research design in which groups of participants of different ages are studied at the same point in time. Distinguished from *longitudinal design.*

Crossing over Exchange of genes between chromosomes next to each other during meiosis.

Crowd A large, loosely organized group consisting of several cliques with similar normative characteristics.

Crystallized intelligence In Cattell's theory, a form of intelligence that depends on culturally loaded, fact-oriented information. Distinguished from *fluid intelligence.*

Cumulative deficit hypothesis A view that attributes the age-related decline in IQ among poverty-stricken ethnic minority children to the compounding effects of underprivileged rearing conditions.

D

Debriefing Providing a full account and justification of research activities to participants in a study in which deception was used.

Deferred imitation The ability to remember and copy the behavior of models who are not immediately present.

Delay of Gratification Waiting for a more appropriate time and place to engage in a tempting act or obtain a desired object.

Deoxyribonucleic acid (DNA) Long, double-stranded molecules that make up chromosomes.

Dependent variable The variable the researcher expects to be influenced by the independent variable in an experiment.

Deprivation dwarfism A growth disorder observed between 2 and 15 years of age. Characterized by substantially below average stature, weight that is usually appropriate for height, immature skeletal age, and decreased GH secretion. Caused by emotional deprivation.

Developmental psychology A branch of psychology devoted to understanding all changes that human beings experience throughout the life span.

Differentiation theory The view that perceptual development involves the detection of increasingly fine-grained, invariant features in the environment.

Difficult child A child whose temperament is such that he or she is irregular in daily routines, is slow to accept new experiences, and tends to react negatively and intensely. Distinguished from *easy child* and *slow-to-warm-up child.*

Discontinuous development A view in which new and different ways of interpreting and responding to the world emerge at particular time periods. Assumes that development takes place in stages. Distinguished from *continuous development.*

Discrepancy theory A theory of emotional development in which a child's reaction to a novel stimulus is determined by the degree of similarity between the stimulus and a scheme of a familiar object, to which the stimulus is compared.

Dishabituation Increase in responsiveness after stimulation changes.

Disorganized/disoriented attachment The quality of insecure attachment characterizing infants who respond in a confused, contradictory fashion when reunited with the parent. Distinguished from *secure, avoidant,* and *resistant attachment.*

Distance curve A growth curve that plots the average height and weight of a sample of children at each age. Shows typical yearly progress toward mature body size.

Distributive justice Beliefs about how to divide up resources fairly.

Divergent thinking The generation of multiple and unusual possibilities when faced with a task or problem. Associated with creativity. Distinguished from *convergent thinking.*

Divorce mediation A series of meetings between divorcing adults and a trained professional, who tries to help them settle disputes. Aimed at avoiding legal battles that intensify family conflict.

Dizygotic twins. See *fraternal twins.*

Domain-general changes Similar transformations across all types of knowledge, resulting in the perfection of general reasoning abilities. Distinguished from *domain-specific changes.*

Domain-specific changes Distinct transformations within each type of knowledge, resulting in the perfection of separate, specialized abilities. Distinguished from *domain-general changes.*

Dominance hierarchy A stable ordering of group members that predicts who will win under conditions of conflict.

Dominant cerebral hemisphere The hemisphere of the brain responsible for skilled motor action. The left hemisphere is dominant in right-handed individuals. In left-handed individuals, the right hemisphere may be dominant, or motor and language skills may be shared between the hemispheres.

Dominant–recessive inheritance A pattern of inheritance in which, under heterozygous conditions, the influence of only one allele is apparent.

Drive reduction model of attachment A behaviorist view that regards the mother's satisfaction of the baby's hunger (primary drive) as the basis for the infant's preference for her (secondary drive).

Dynamic assessment An innovative approach to testing consistent with Vygotsky's concept of the zone of proximal development. Using a pretest–intervene–retest procedure, introduces purposeful teaching into the testing situation to find out what the child can attain with social support.

Dynamic systems theory A theory that views new motor skills as reorganizations of previously mastered skills that lead to more effective ways of exploring and controlling the environment. Motor development is jointly influenced by central nervous system maturation, movement possibilities of the body, environmental supports for the skill, and the task the child has in mind.

E

Easy child A child whose temperament is such that he or she quickly establishes regular routines in infancy, is generally cheerful, and adapts easily to new experiences. Distinguished from *difficult child* and *slow-to-warm-up child.*

Ecological systems theory Bronfenbrenner's approach, which views the child as developing within a complex system of relationships affected by multiple levels of the environment, from immediate settings of family and school to broad cultural values and programs.

Educational self-fulfilling prophecy The idea that pupils may adopt teachers' positive or negative attitudes toward them and start to live up to these views.

Ego In Freud's theory, the rational part of personality that reconciles the demands of the id, the external world, and the conscience.

Elaboration The memory strategy of creating a relation between two or more items that are not members of the same category.

Embryo The prenatal organism from 2 to 8 weeks after conception, during which time the foundations of all body structures and internal organs are laid down.

Emotional display rules Rules that specify when, where, and how it is culturally appropriate to express emotions.

Emotional self-regulation Strategies for adjusting our emotional state to a comfortable level of intensity so we can remain productively engaged in our surroundings.

Empathy The ability to understand the feelings of others and respond with complementary emotions.

Epiphyses Growth centers in the bones where new cartilage cells are produced and gradually harden.

Episodic memory Memory for personally experienced events.

Equilibration In Piaget's theory, back-and-forth movement between cognitive equilibrium and disequilibrium throughout development, which leads to more effective schemes. Describes how assimilation and accommodation work together to produce cognitive change.

Estrogens Hormones produced chiefly by the ovaries that cause the breasts, uterus, and vagina to mature and the body to take on feminine proportions during puberty.

Ethnography A method in which the researcher attempts to understand the unique values and social processes of a culture or a distinct social group by living with its members and taking field notes for an extended period of time.

Ethological theory of attachment A theory formulated by Bowlby, which views the infant's emotional tie to the familiar caregiver as an evolved response that promotes survival.

Ethology An approach concerned with the adaptive, or survival, value of behavior and its evolutionary history.

Event sampling An observational procedure in which the researcher records all instances of a particular behavior during a specified time period.

Exosystem In ecological systems theory, settings that do not contain children but that affect their experiences in immediate settings. Examples are parents' workplace and health and welfare services in the community.

Expansions Adult responses that elaborate on a child's utterance, increasing its complexity.

Experimental design A research design in which the investigator randomly assigns participants to treatment conditions. Permits inferences about cause and effect.

Expressive style A style of early language learning in which toddlers use language mainly to talk about the feelings and needs of themselves and other people. Distinguished from *referential style.*

Expressive traits Feminine-stereotyped personality traits that reflect warmth, caring, and sensitivity.

Extended family household A household in which parent and child live with one or more adult relatives.

Extinction In classical conditioning, decline of the conditioned response (CR), as a result of presenting the conditioned stimulus (CS) enough times without the unconditioned response (UCS).

F

Factor analysis A complicated statistical procedure that combines scores from many separate test items into a few factors, which substitute for the separate scores. Used to identify mental abilities that contribute to performance on intelligence tests.

Fast mapping Connecting a new word with an underlying concept after only a brief encounter.

Fetal alcohol effects (FAE) The condition of children who display some but not all of the detects of fetal alcohol syndrome. Usually their mothers drank alcohol in smaller quantities during pregnancy.

Fetal alcohol syndrome (FAS) A set of defects that results when women consume large amounts of alcohol during most or all of pregnancy. Includes mental retardation, slow physical growth, and facial abnormalities.

Fetus The prenatal organism from the beginning of the third month to the end of pregnancy, during which time completion of body structures and dramatic growth in size takes place.

Field experiment A research design in which participants are randomly assigned to treatment conditions in natural settings.

Fluid intelligence In Cattell's theory, a form of intelligence that requires very little specific knowledge but involves the ability to see complex relationships and solve problems. Distinguished from *crystallized intelligence.*

Fontanels Six soft spots that separate the bones of the skull at birth.

Formal operational egocentrism A form of egocentrism present during the formal operational stage involving an inability to distinguish the abstract perspectives of self and other.

Formal operational stage Piaget's final stage, in which adolescents develop the capacity for abstract, scientific thinking. Begins around age 11.

Fraternal, or dizygotic, twins Twins resulting from the release and fertilization of two ova. They are genetically no more alike than ordinary siblings. Distinguished from *identical,* or *monozygotic, twins.*

Functionalist approach A theoretical perspective that regards emotions as central, adaptive forces in all aspects of human activity.

Fuzzy-trace theory A theory that posits two encoding systems, one that automatically reconstructs information into a fuzzy version called a *gist,* especially useful for reasoning, and a second that retains a verbatim version adapted for answering questions about specifics.

G

Gametes Human sperm and ova, which contain half as many chromosomes as a regular body cell.

Gender consistency Kohlberg's final stage of gender understanding, in which children master gender constancy.

Gender constancy The understanding that gender remains the same even if clothing, hairstyle, and play activities change.

Gender labeling Kohlberg's first stage of gender understanding, in which preschoolers can label the gender of themselves and others correctly.

Gender roles The reflection of gender stereotypes in everyday behavior.

Gender schema theory An information-processing approach to gender typing that combines social learning and cognitive-developmental features to explain how environmental pressures and cognitions work together to affect stereotyping, gender-role identity, and gender-role adoption.

Gender stability Kohlberg's second stage of gender understanding, in which preschoolers have a partial understanding of the permanence of gender; they grasp its stability over time.

Gender stereotypes Widely held beliefs about characteristics deemed appropriate for males and females.

Gender typing The process of developing gender-linked beliefs, gender roles, and a gender-role identity.

Gender-role identity Perception of the self as relatively masculine or feminine in characteristics, abilities, and behaviors.

Gene A segment of a DNA molecule that contains instructions for production of various proteins that contribute to growth and functioning of the body.

General factor, or "g" In Spearman's theory of intelligence, a common factor representing abstract reasoning power that underlies a wide variety of test items.

General growth curve Curve that represents overall changes in body size—rapid growth during infancy, slower gains in early and middle childhood, and rapid growth once more during adolescence.

Generalized other A blend of what we imagine important people in our lives think of us; determines the content of self-concept.

Genetic counseling Counseling that helps couples assess the likelihood of giving birth to a baby with a hereditary disorder.

Genetic imprinting A pattern of inheritance in which alleles are imprinted, or chemically marked, in such a way that one pair member is activated, regardless of its makeup.

Genetic–environmental correlation The idea that heredity influences the environments to which individuals are exposed.

Genotype The genetic makeup of the individual.

Gist A fuzzy representation of information that preserves essential content without details, is less likely to be forgotten than a verbatim representation, and requires less mental effort to use.

Glial cells Cells serving the function of myelinization.

Goodness-of-fit model Thomas and Chess's model, which states that an effective match, or "good fit," between child-rearing practices and a child's temperament leads to favorable development and psychological adjustment. When a "poor fit" exists, the outcome is distorted development and maladjustment.

Grammar The component of language concerned with syntax, the rules by which words are arranged into sentences, and morphology, the use of grammatical markers that indicate number, tense, case, person, gender, and other meanings.

Grammatical morphemes Small markers that change the meaning of sentences, as in "John*'s* dog" and "he *is* eating."

Growth hormone (GH) A pituitary hormone that affects the development of all body tissues, except the central nervous system and the genitals.

H

Habituation A gradual reduction in the strength of a response as the result of repetitive stimulation.

Heritability estimate A statistic that measures the extent to which individual differences in complex traits, such as intelligence and personality, are due to genetic factors.

Heteronomous morality Piaget's first stage of moral development, in which children view rules as having a permanent existence, as unchangeable, and as requiring strict obedience.

Heterozygous Having two different alleles at the same place on a pair of chromosomes. Distinguished from *homozygous.*

Hierarchical classification The organization of objects into classes and subclasses on the basis of similarities and differences between the groups.

Home Observation for Measurement of the Environment (HOME) A checklist for gathering information about the quality of children's home lives through observation and parental interviews. Infancy, preschool, and middle childhood versions exist.

Homozygous Having two identical alleles at the same place on a pair of chromosomes. Distinguished from *heterozygous.*

Horizontal décalage Development within a Piagetian stage. Gradual mastery of logical concepts during the concrete operational stage is an example.

Hostile aggression Aggression intended to harm another person.

Human development An interdisciplinary field of study devoted to understanding all changes that human beings experience throughout the life span.

Hypothalamus A structure located at the base of the brain that initiates and regulates pituitary secretions.

Hypothesis A prediction about behavior drawn from a theory.

Hypothetico-deductive reasoning A formal operational problem-solving strategy in which adolescents begin with a general theory of all possible factors that could affect an outcome in a problem and deduce specific hypotheses, which they test in an orderly fashion.

I

Id In Freud's theory, the part of personality that is the source of basic biological needs and desires.

Identical, or monozygotic, twins Twins that result when a zygote, during the early stages of cell duplication, divides in two. They have the same genetic makeup.

Identification In Freud's theory, the process leading to formation of the superego in which children take the same-sex parent's characteristics into their personality.

Identity A well-organized conception of the self made up of values, beliefs, and goals to which the individual is solidly committed.

Identity achievement The identity status of individuals who have explored and committed themselves to self-chosen values and goals. Distinguished from *moratorium, identity foreclosure,* and *identity diffusion.*

Identity diffusion The identity status of individuals who do not have firm commitments to values and goals and are not actively trying to reach them.

Identity foreclosure The identity status of individuals who have accepted ready-made values and goals that authority figures have chosen for them. Distinguished from *identity achievement, moratorium,* and *identity foreclosure.*

Illocutionary intent What a speaker means to say, regardless of whether the form of the utterance is perfectly consistent with it.

Imaginary audience Adolescents' belief that they are the focus of everyone else's attention and concern.

Imitation Learning by copying the behavior of another person. Also called *modeling* or *observational learning.*

Independent variable The variable manipulated by the researcher in an experiment by randomly assigning participants to treatment conditions.

Induction A type of discipline in which the effects of the child's misbehavior on others are communicated to the child.

Infant mortality The number of deaths in the first year of life per 1,000 live births.

Infantile amnesia The inability of older children and adults to remember experiences that happened before age 3.

Information processing An approach that views the human mind as a symbol-manipulating system through which information flows and that regards cognitive development as a continuous process.

Informed consent The right of research participants, including children, to have explained to them all aspects of a study that may affect their willingness to participate in language they can understand.

Inhibited child A child who withdraws and displays negative emotion to novel stimuli. Distinguished from *uninhibited child.*

Instrumental aggression Aggression aimed at obtaining an object, privilege, or space with no deliberate intent to harm another person. Distinguished from *hostile aggression.*

Instrumental traits Masculine-stereotyped personality traits that reflect competence, rationality, and assertiveness.

Intelligence quotient (IQ) A score that permits an individual's performance on an intelligence test to be compared to the typical performance of same-age individuals.

Intentional, or goal-directed, behavior A sequence of actions in which schemes are deliberately combined to solve a problem.

Interactional synchrony A sensitively tuned "emotional dance," in which the caregiver responds to infant signals in a well-timed, appropriate fashion and both partners match emotional states, especially the positive ones.

Intermodal perception Perception that combines information from more than one sensory system.

Internal working model A set of expectations derived from early caregiving experiences concerning the availability of attachment figures, their likelihood of providing support during times of stress, and the self's interaction with those figures that affect all future close relationships.

Internalization The process of moral development in which children adopt preexisting, ready-made standards for right action as their own.

Intersubjectivity A process whereby two participants who begin a task with different understandings arrive at a shared understanding.

Invariant features Features that remain stable in a constantly changing perceptual world.

Investment theory of creativity Sternberg and Lubart's theory, in which investment in novel projects depends on the availability of diverse intellectual, personality, motivational, and environmental resources, each of which must be present at some minimum level.

Invisible displacement task A type of object-hiding task in which the object is moved from one place to another while out of sight.

J

Joint custody A child custody arrangement following divorce in which the court grants both parents equal say in important decisions about the child's upbringing.

Just community Kohlberg's approach to moral education, in which a small society of teachers and students practice a democratic way of life.

K

Kaufman Assessment Battery for Children (K-ABC) An individually administered intelligence test that measures two broad types of processing skills: simultaneous and sequential processing. The one of the few tests to be grounded in an explicit cognitive theory.

Kinetic depth cues Depth cues created by movements of the body or of objects in the environment.

Kinship studies Studies comparing the characteristics of family members to determine the importance of heredity in complex human characteristics.

Kwashiorkor A disease usually appearing between 1 and 3 years of age that is caused by a diet low in protein. Symptoms include an enlarged belly, swollen feet, hair loss, skin rash, and irritable, listless behavior.

L

Laboratory experiment An experiment conducted in the laboratory, which permits the maximum possible control over treatment conditions.

Language acquisition device (LAD) In Chomsky's theory, a biologically based, innate system for picking up language that permits children, as soon as they have acquired sufficient vocabulary, to combine words into grammatically consistent utterances and to understand the meaning of sentences they hear.

Language-making capacity (LMC) According to Slobin's theory, a built-in set of cognitive procedures for analyzing language that supports the discovery of grammatical regularities.

Lanugo A white, downy hair that covers the entire body of the fetus, helping the vernix stick to the skin.

Lateralization Specialization of functions of the two hemispheres of the cortex.

Learned helplessness Attributions that credit success to luck and failure to low ability. Leads to low expectancies of success and anxious loss of control in the face of challenging tasks. Distinguished from *mastery-oriented attributions.*

Learning disabilities Specific learning disorders (for, example, in reading, writing, or math computation) that result in poor school achievement, despite an average or above-average IQ.

Level I–Level II theory Jensen's controversial theory, which states that ethnic and social-class differences in IQ are due to genetic differences in higher-order, abstract forms of intelligence (Level II) rather than basic memory skills (Level I).

Levels-of-processing model A model of mental functioning in which retention of information depends on the depth to which it is analyzed. Attentional resources determine processing capacity.

Lexical contrast theory A theory that attributes semantic development to two principles: conventionality, children's natural desire to acquire the words and word meanings of their language community; and contrast, children's discovery of meanings by contrasting new words with ones currently in their vocabulary.

Long-term memory In Atkinson and Shiffrin's store model, the part of the mental system that contains our permanent knowledge base.

Longitudinal design A research design in which one group of participants is studied repeatedly at different ages. Distinguished from *cross-sectional design.*

Longitudinal-sequential design A research design with both longitudinal and cross-sectional components in which groups of participants born in different years are followed over time.

M

Macrosystem In ecological systems theory, the values, laws, and customs of a culture that influence experiences and interactions at lower levels of the environment.

Mainstreaming The integration of pupils with learning difficulties into regular classrooms for all or part of the school day.

Make-believe play A type of play in which children pretend, acting out everyday and imaginary activities.

Marasmus A disease usually appearing in the first year of life that is caused by a diet low in all essential nutrients. Leads to a wasted condition of the body.

Mastery-oriented attributions Attributions that credit success to high ability and failure to insufficient effort. Leads to high self-esteem and a willingness to approach challenging tasks. Distinguished from *learned helplessness.*

Matching A procedure for assigning participants with similar characteristics in equal numbers to treatment conditions in an experiment. Ensures that groups will be equivalent on factors likely to distort the results.

Maturation A genetically determined, naturally unfolding course of growth.

Mechanistic theories Theories that regard the child as a passive reactor to environmental inputs. Distinguished from *organismic theory.*

Meiosis The process of cell division through which gametes are formed and in which the number of chromosomes in each cell is halved.

Menarche First menstruation.

Mental representation An internal image of an absent object or a past event.

Mental space, or M-space In Case's neo-Piagetian theory

of cognitive development, a construct similar to working memory. It expands with brain maturation, exercise of strategies, and formation of central conceptual structures, which permit the child to move up to a new Piagetian stage.

Mesosystem In ecological systems theory, connections among children's immediate settings.

Metacognition Awareness and understanding of various aspects of thought.

Metalinguistic awareness The ability to think about language as a system.

Microgenetic design A research design in which change is tracked from the time it begins until it stabilizes, as participants master an everyday or novel task.

Microsystem In ecological systems theory, the activities and interaction patterns in the child's immediate surroundings.

Mitosis The process of cell duplication, in which each new cell receives an exact copy of the original chromosomes.

Modifier genes Genes that modify the effect of another gene on a characteristic by either enhancing or diluting its effects.

Modular view of the mind A domain-specific, nativist view that regards the mind as a collection of separate modules—genetically prewired, independent, special purpose systems, each of which is equipped with structures for making sense of a certain type of information.

Monozygotic twins See *identical twins.*

Moral dilemma A conflict situation presented to research participants, who are asked to decide both what the main actor should do and why. Used to assess the development of moral reasoning.

Moratorium The identity status of individuals who are exploring alternatives in an effort to find values and goals to guide their life. Distinguished from *identity achievement, identity diffusion,* and *identity foreclosure.*

Motherese, or child-directed speech The form of language adopted by adults when speaking to infants and toddlers that is made up of short sentences with high-pitched, exaggerated intonation, clear pronunciation, and distinct pauses between speech segments.

Mutation A sudden but permanent change in a segment of DNA.

Myelinization A process in which neural fibers are coated with an insulating fatty sheath (called myelin) that improves the efficiency of message transfer.

N

Nativist approach An approach to cognitive development in which children are born with substantial innate knowledge, which guides their interpretations of reality and gets cognitive development off to a speedy, efficient start. Consistent with a modular view of the mind. *Distinguished from constructivist approach.*

Natural experiment A research design in which the investigator studies already existing treatments in natural settings by carefully selecting groups of participants with similar characteristics.

Natural, or prepared, childbirth An approach designed to reduce pain and medical intervention and to make childbirth a rewarding experience for parents.

Naturalistic observation A method in which the researcher goes into the natural environment to observe the behavior of interest. Distinguished from *structured observation.*

Nature-nurture controversy Disagreement among theorists about whether genetic or environmental factors are the most important determinants of development and behavior.

Neglected children Children who are seldom chosen, either positively or negatively, on sociometric measures of peer acceptance. Distinguished from *popular, rejected,* and *controversial children.*

Neonatal Behavioral Assessment Scale (NBAS) A test developed to assess the behavioral status of the infant during the newborn period.

Neurons Nerve cells that store and transmit information in the brain.

Niche-picking A type of genetic-environmental correlation in which individuals actively choose environments that complement their heredity.

Noble savage Rousseau's view of the child as naturally endowed with an innate plan for orderly, healthy growth.

Non-rapid-eye-movement (NREM) sleep A "regular" sleep state in which the body is quiet and heart rate, breathing, and brain wave activity are slow and regular. Distinguished from *rapid-eye-movement (REM) sleep.*

Nonorganic failure to thrive A growth disorder usually present by 18 months of age that is caused by lack of affection and stimulation.

Nonshared environmental influences Environmental influences that make children living in the same family different from one another. Distinguished from *shared environmental influences.*

Nonsocial activity Unoccupied, onlooker behavior and solitary play. Distinguished from *parallel, associative,* and *cooperative play.*

Normative approach An approach in which age-related averages are computed to represent the typical child's development.

Nuclear family unit The part of the family that consists of parents and their children.

O

Obesity A greater than 20 percent increase over average body weight, based on the child's age, sex, and physical build.

Object permanence The understanding that objects continue to exist when they are out of sight.

Observer bias The tendency of observers who are aware of the purposes of a study to see and record what is expected rather than participants' actual behaviors.

Observer influence The tendency of participants to react to the presence of an observer and behave in unnatural ways.

Open classroom A classroom based on the educational philosophy that children are active agents in their own development and learn at different rates. Teachers share decision making with pupils. Pupils are evaluated in relation to their own prior development. Distinguished from *traditional classroom.*

Operant conditioning A form of learning in which a spontaneous behavior is followed by a stimulus that changes the probability that the behavior will occur again.

Operant conditioning model of attachment A behaviorist view that regards the mother's contingent reinforcement of the baby's social behavior as the basis for the infant's preference for her.

Operations In Piaget's theory, mental representations of actions that obey logical rules.

Ordinality A principle specifying order (more-than and less-than) relationships among quantities.

Organismic theories Theories that assume the existence of psychological structures inside the child that underlie and control development. Distinguished from *mechanistic theories.*

Organization In Piaget's theory, the internal rearrangement and linking together of schemes so that they form a strongly interconnected cognitive system. In information processing, the memory strategy of grouping information into meaningful chunks.

Overextension An early vocabulary error in which a word is applied too broadly, to a wider collection of objects and events than is appropriate. Distinguished from *underextension.*

Overregularization Application of regular grammatical rules to words that are exceptions. For example, saying "mouses" instead of "mice."

P

Parallel play A form of limited social participation in which the child plays near other children with similar materials but does not interact with them. Distinguished from *nonsocial activity, associative play,* and *cooperative play.*

Peer group Peers who form a social unit by generating unique values and standards of behavior and a social structure of leaders and followers.

Peer-only rearing A type of study in which nonhuman primates are reared together from birth without adults.

Perception-bound Being easily distracted by the concrete, perceptual appearance of objects. A characteristic of Piaget's preoperational stage.

Permissive style A parenting style that is responsive but undemanding. An overly tolerant approach to child rearing. Distinguished from *authoritative, authoritarian,* and *uninvolved styles.*

Person perception The way individuals size up people with whom they are familiar in everyday life.

Personal fable Adolescents' belief that they are special and unique. Leads them to conclude that others cannot possibly understand their thoughts and feelings. May promote a sense of invulnerability to danger.

Perspective taking The capacity to imagine what other people may be thinking and feeling.

Phenotype The individual's physical and behavioral characteristics, which are determined by both genetic and environmental factors.

Phoneme The smallest speech unit that can be distinguished perceptually.

Phonological store A special part of working memory that permits us to retain speech-based information. Supports early vocabulary development.

Phonology The component of language concerned with understanding and producing speech sounds.

Physical causality The causal action one object exerts on another through contact.

Pictorial depth cues Depth cues artists use to make a painting look three-dimensional, such as receding lines, texture changes, and overlapping objects.

Pincer grasp The well-coordinated grasp emerging at the end of the first year, involving thumb and forefinger opposition.

Pituitary gland A gland located near the base of the brain that releases hormones affecting physical growth.

Placenta The organ that separates the mother's bloodstream from the embryo or fetal bloodstream but permits exchange of nutrients and waste products.

Planning Thinking out a sequence of acts ahead of time and allocating attention accordingly to reach a goal.

Pleiotropism The influence of a single gene on more than one characteristic.

Polygenic inheritance A pattern of inheritance involving many genes that applies to characteristics that vary continuously among people.

Popular children Children who get many positive votes on sociometric measures of peer acceptance. Distinguished from *rejected, controversial,* and *neglected children.*

Postconventional level Kohlberg's highest level of moral development, in which individuals define morality in terms of abstract principles and values that apply to all situations and societies.

Practical intelligence Abilities apparent in the real world, not in testing situations, that involve "knowing how" rather than "knowing that."

Practice effects Changes in participants' natural responses as a result of repeated testing.

Pragmatics The component of language concerned with how to engage in effective and appropriate communication with others.

Preconventional level Kohlberg's first level of moral development, in which moral understanding is based on rewards, punishment, and the power of authority figures.

Preformationism Medieval view of the child as a miniature adult.

Prenatal diagnostic methods Methods that permit detection of developmental problems before birth.

Preoperational egocentrism A form of egocentrism present during the preoperational stage involving the inability to distinguish the symbolic viewpoints of others from one's own.

Preoperational stage Piaget's second stage, in which rapid development of representation takes place. However, thought is not yet logical. Spans the years from 2 to 7.

Prereaching The poorly coordinated, primitive reaching movements of newborn babies.

Preterm Infants born several weeks or more before their due date.

Primary mental abilities In Thurstone's theory of intelligence, seven distinct mental abilities identified through factor analysis (verbal meaning, perceptual speed, reasoning, number, rote memory, word fluency, and spatial visualization).

Primary sexual characteristics Physical features that involve the reproductive organs (ovaries, uterus, and vagina in females; penis, scrotum, and testes in males).

Principle of mutual exclusivity The assumption by children in the early stages of vocabulary growth that words mark entirely separate (nonoverlapping) categories.

Private speech Self-directed speech that children use to plan and guide their own behavior.

Production In language development, the words and word combinations that children use. Distinguished from *comprehension.*

Production deficiency The failure to use a mental strategy in situations where it could be helpful. Distinguished from *control* and *utilization deficiencies.*

Programmed cell death Death of many neurons during the peak period of development in any brain area to make room for growth of neural fibers that form synaptic connections.

Project Head Start A federal program that provides low-income children with a year or two of preschool education before school entry and that encourages parent involvement in children's development.

Propositional thought A type of formal operational reasoning in which adolescents evaluate the logic of verbal statements without making reference to real-world circumstances.

Prosocial, or altruistic, behavior Actions that benefit another person without any expected reward for the self.

Protection from harm The right of research participants to be protected from physical or psychological harm.

Protodeclarative A preverbal gesture through which infants make an assertion about an object by touching it, holding it up, or pointing to it.

Protoimperative A preverbal gesture in which infants point, reach, and make sounds to get another person to do something.

Proximodistal trend An organized pattern of physical growth and motor control that proceeds from the center of the body outward.

Psychoanalytic perspective An approach to personality development introduced by Sigmund Freud that assumes children move through a series of stages in which they confront conflicts between biological drives and social expectations. The way these conflicts are resolved determines psychological adjustment.

Psychometric approach An approach to cognitive development that focuses on the construction of tests to assess mental abilities.

Psychophysiological methods Methods that measure the relation between physiological processes and behavior. Among the most common are measures of autonomic nervous system activity (such as heart rate and respiration) and measures of brain functioning (such as the electroencephalogram [EEG], event-related potentials [ERPs], and functional magnetic resonance imaging [fMRI]).

Psychosexual theory Freud's theory, which emphasizes that how parents manage children's sexual and aggressive drives during the first few years is crucial for healthy personality development.

Psychosocial theory Erikson's theory, which emphasizes that the demands of society at each Freudian stage not only promote the development of a unique personality, but also ensure that individuals acquire attitudes and skills that help them become active, contributing members of their society.

Puberty Biological changes during adolescence that lead to an adult-sized body and sexual maturity.

Public policy Laws and government programs designed to improve current conditions.

Punishment In operant conditioning, removing a desirable stimulus or presenting an unpleasant one to decrease the occurrence of a response.

Random assignment An evenhanded procedure for assigning participants to treatment groups, such as drawing numbers out of a hat or flipping a coin. Increases the chances that participants' characteristics will be equally distributed across treatment conditions in an experiment.

Range of reaction Each person's unique, genetically determined response to a range of environmental conditions.

Rapid-eye-movement (REM) sleep An "irregular" sleep state in which brain wave activity is similar to that of the waking state; eyes dart beneath the lids; heart rate, blood pressure, and breathing are uneven; and slight body movements occur. Distinguished from *rapid-eye-movement (REM) sleep.*

Realism A view of rules as external features of reality rather than cooperative principles. Characterizes Piaget's heteronomous stage.

Recall A type of memory that involves remembering a stimulus that is not present. Distinguished from *recognition.*

Recasts Adult responses that restructure a child's incorrect speech into appropriate form.

Reciprocal teaching A method of teaching based on Vygotsky's theory in which a teacher and two to four pupils form a collaborative learning group. Dialogues occur that create a zone of proximal development in which reading comprehension improves.

Reciprocity A standard of fairness in which individuals express the same concern for the welfare of others as they do for themselves.

Recognition A type memory that involves noticing whether a stimulus is identical or similar to one previously experienced. Distinguished from *recall.*

Reconstruction A memory process in which complex, meaningful material is reinterpreted in terms of existing knowledge.

Recursive thought The self-embedded form of perspective taking that involves thinking about what another person is thinking.

Referential communication skills The ability to produce clear verbal messages and to recognize when the meaning of others' messages is unclear.

Referential style A style of early language learning in which toddlers use language mainly to label objects. Distinguished from *expressive style.*

Reflex An inborn, automatic response to a particular form of stimulation.

Rehearsal The memory strategy of repeating information.

Reinforcer In operant conditioning, a stimulus that increases the occurrence of a response.

Rejected children Children who are actively disliked and get many negative votes on sociometric measures of peer acceptance. Distinguished from *popular, controversial,* and *neglected children.*

Rejected-aggressive children A subgroup of rejected children who engage in high rates of conflict, hostility, and hyperactive, inattentive, and impulsive behavior. Distinguished from *rejected-withdrawn children.*

Rejected-withdrawn children A subgroup of rejected children who are passive and socially awkward. Distinguished from *rejected-aggressive children.*

Reliability The consistency, or repeatability, of measures of behavior.

Resistant attachment The quality of insecure attachment characterizing infants who remain close to the parent before departure and display angry, resistive behavior when she returns. Distinguished from *secure, avoidant,* and *disorganized/disoriented attachment.*

Reticular formation A brain structure that maintains alertness and consciousness.

Reversibility The ability to mentally go through a series of steps and then return to the starting point. In Piaget's theory, part of every logical operation.

Rh factor A protein that, when present in the fetus's blood but not in the mother's, can cause the mother to build up antibodies. If these return the fetus's system, they destroy red blood cells, reducing the oxygen supply to organs and tissues.

Risks-versus-benefits ratio A comparison of the costs of a research study to participants in terms of inconvenience and possible psychological or physical injury against its value for advancing knowledge and improving conditions of life. Used in assessing the ethics of research.

Rough-and-tumble play A form of peer interaction involving friendly chasing and play-fighting that, in our evolutionary past, may have been important for the development of fighting skill.

S

Scaffolding A changing quality of support over a teaching session in which adults adjust the assistance they provide to fit the child's current level of performance. Direct instruction is offered when a task is new; less help is provided as competence increases.

Scheme In Piaget's theory, a specific structure, or organized way of making sense of experience, that changes with age.

Scripts General representations of what occurs and when it occurs in a particular situation. A basic means through which children (and adults) organize and interpret everyday experiences.

Secondary sexual characteristics Features visible on the outside of the body that serve as signs of sexual maturity but do not involve the reproductive organs (for example, breast development in females, appearance of underarm and pubic hair in both sexes).

Secular trends in physical growth Changes in body size and rate of growth from one generation to the next.

Secure attachment The quality of attachment characterizing infants who are distressed by parental separation and easily comforted by the parent when she returns. Distinguished from *resistant, avoidant,* and *disorganized/disoriented attachment.*

Secure base The use of the familiar caregiver as a base from which the infant confidently explores the environment and to which the infant returns for emotional support.

Selective attrition Selective loss of participants during an investigation, resulting in a biased sample.

Self-care children Children who look after themselves during after-school hours.

Self-concept The sum total of attributes, abilities, attitudes, and values that an individual believes defines who he or she is.

Self-conscious emotions Emotions that involve injury to or enhancement of the sense of self. Examples are shame, embarrassment, guilt, envy, and pride.

Self-control Inhibiting an impulse to engage in behavior that violates a moral standard.

Self-esteem An aspect of self-concept that involves judgments about one's own worth and the feelings associated with those judgments.

Self-recognition Perception of the self as a separate being, distinct from people and objects in the surrounding world.

Self-regulation The process of continuously monitoring progress toward a goal, checking outcomes, and redirecting unsuccessful efforts.

Semantic bootstrapping Relying on the semantic properties of words to figure out basic grammatical regularities.

Semantic memory The vast, intricately organized knowledge system in long-term memory.

Semantics The component of language concerned with understanding the meaning of words and word combinations.

Sensitive period A time span that is optimal for certain capacities to emerge and in which the individual is especially responsive to environmental influences.

Sensorimotor egocentrism A form of egocentrism present in infancy that involves a merging of the self with the surrounding world, an absence of the understanding that the self is an object in a world of objects.

Sensorimotor stage Piaget's first stage, during which infants "think" with their eyes, ears, hands, and other sensorimotor equipment. Spans the first 2 years of life.

Sensory register In Atkinson and Shiffrin's store model, the first part of the mental system through which information flows, where sights and sounds are represented directly but held only briefly.

Separation anxiety An infant's distressed reaction to the departure of the familiar caregiver.

Serial position effect In memory tasks involving lists of items, the tendency to remember ones at the beginning and end better than those in the middle.

Seriation The ability to arrange items along a quantitative dimension, such as length or weight.

Sex chromosomes The twenty-third pair of chromosomes, which determines the sex of the child. In females, called XX; in males, called XY.

Shading A conversational strategy in which a change of topic is initiated gradually by modifying the focus of discussion.

Shape constancy Perception of an object's shape as the same, despite changes in the shape of its retinal image.

Shared environmental influences Environmental influences that pervade the general atmosphere of the home and affect all children living in it to the same extent.

Short-term memory In Atkinson and Shiffrin's store model, the central processing unit of the mental system, where information is consciously operated on using control processes, or mental strategies.

Size constancy Perception of an object's size as the same, despite changes in the size of its retinal image.

Skeletal age An estimate of physical maturity based on development of the bones of the body.

Skill theory Fischer's theory, in which each Piagetian stage is viewed as an extended period of skill learning in which the child acquires new competencies on specific tasks, integrates them with others, and gradually transforms them into more general, higher-order skills. As a result, the child moves up to a new Piagetian stage.

Slow-to-warm-up child A child whose temperament is such that he or she is inactive, shows mild, low-key reactions to environmental stimuli, is negative in mood, and adjusts slowly to new experiences. Distinguished from *easy child* and *difficult child.*

Small for date Infants whose birth weight is below normal when length of pregnancy is taken into account. May be full term or *preterm.*

Social cognition Thinking about the self, other people, and social relationships.

Social comparisons Judgments of abilities, behavior, appearance, and other characteristics in relation to those of others.

Social learning theory An approach that emphasizes the role of modeling, or observational learning, in the development of behavior.

Social policy Any planned set of actions directed at solving a social problem or attaining a social goal.

Social problem solving Resolving social conflicts in ways that are both acceptable to others and beneficial to the self.

Social referencing Relying on another person's emotional reaction to appraise an uncertain situation.

Social smile The smile evoked by the stimulus of the human face. First appears between 6 and 10 weeks.

Social systems perspective A view of the family as a complex set of interacting relationships influenced by the larger social context.

Sociobiology A field that assumes many complex social behaviors, including morally relevant prosocial acts, are rooted in our genetic heritage and have evolved because of their survival value.

Sociocultural theory Vygotsky's sociocultural theory, in which children acquire the ways of thinking and behaving that make up a community's culture through cooperative dialogues with more knowledgeable members of that society.

Sociodramatic play The make-believe play with others that is underway by age 2½.

Sociometric techniques Self-report measures that ask peers to evaluate one another's likability.

Sociomoral Reflection Measure–Short Form (SRM-SF) A questionnaire for assessing moral understanding in which individuals rate the importance of moral values addressed by brief questions and explain their ratings. Does not require research participants to read and think about lengthy moral dilemmas.

Specific factor, or "s" In Spearman's theory of intelligence, a mental ability factor that is unique to a particular task.

Specimen record An observational procedure in which the researcher records a description of the participant's entire stream of behavior for a specified time period.

Speech registers Language adaptations to social expectations.

Spermarche First ejaculation of seminal fluid.

Stage A qualitative change in thinking, feeling, and behaving that characterizes a particular time period of development.

Stanford-Binet Intelligence Scale An individually administered intelligence test that is the modern descendent of Alfred Binet's first successful test for children. Measures general intelligence and four factors: verbal reasoning, quantitative reasoning, abstract/visual (spatial) reasoning, and short-term memory.

States of arousal Different degrees of sleep and wakefulness.

States rather than transformations The tendency to treat the initial and final states in a problem as completely unrelated. A characteristic of Piaget's preoperational stage.

Store model Atkinson and Shiffrin's model of mental functioning, which views information as being held in three parts of the system for processing: the sensory register, short-term memory, and long-term memory.

Strange Situation A procedure involving short separations from and reunions with the parent that assesses the quality of the attachment bond.

Stranger anxiety The infant's expression of fear in response to unfamiliar adults. Appears in many babies after 7 months of age.

Strategy-choice model Siegler's model, which shows how strategies change over time as children master a diverse array of tasks. From multiple strategies available, children choose adaptively, striking a balance between accuracy and speed until answers are strongly associated problems and can be retrieved automatically.

Structure-of-intellect model Guilford's 180-factor model of intelligence, which classifies each intellectual task according to three dimensions: content, mental operation, and product.

Structured interview A method in which the researcher asks each participant the same questions in the same way.

Structured observation A method in which the researcher sets up a situation that evokes the behavior of interest and observes it in a laboratory. Distinguished from *naturalistic observation.*

Sudden infant death syndrome (SIDS) Death of a seemingly healthy baby, who stops breathing during the night, without apparent cause.

Superego In Freud's theory, the part of the personality that is the seat of conscience and is often in conflict with the id's desires.

Synapses The gap between neurons, across which chemical messages are sent.

Synaptic pruning Loss of connective fibers by seldom-stimulated neurons, thereby returning them to an uncommitted state so they can support the development of future skills.

Syntactic bootstrapping Observing how words are used syntactically, in the structure of sentences, to deduce their meanings.

T

Tabula rasa Locke's view of the child as a blank slate whose character is shaped by experience.

Telegraphic speech Children's two-word utterances that, like a telegram, leave out smaller and less important words.

Television literacy The task of learning television's specialized symbolic code of conveying information.

Temperament Stable individual differences in quality and intensity of emotional reaction.

Teratogen Any environmental agent that causes damage during the prenatal period.

Theory An orderly, integrated set of statements that describes, explains, and predicts behavior.

Theory of mind A coherent understanding of people as mental beings that children revise as they encounter and make sense of new evidence. Includes children's knowledge of mental activity and their appreciation that people can have different perceptions, thoughts, and feelings about the same event.

Theory of multiple intelligences Gardner's theory, which identifies seven independent intelligences on the basis of distinct sets of processing operations applied in culturally meaningful activities (linguistic, logico-mathematical, musical, spatial, bodily-kinesthetic, interpersonal, intrapersonal).

Three-stratum theory of intelligence Carroll's theory, which represents the structure of intelligence as a pyramid, with "g" at the top; eight broad, biologically based abilities at the second stratum; and narrower manifestations of these abilities at the lowest stratum that result from experience with particular tasks. The most comprehensive classification of mental abilities to be confirmed by factor analytic research.

Thyroxine A hormone released by the thyroid gland that is necessary for central nervous system development and body growth.

Time out A form of mild punishment in which children are removed from the immediate setting until they are ready to act appropriately.

Time sampling An observational procedure in which the researcher records whether or not certain behaviors occur during a sample of short time intervals.

Traditional classroom A classroom based on the educational philosophy that children are passive learners who acquire information presented by teachers. Pupils are evaluated on the basis of how well they keep up with a uniform set of standards for everyone in their grade. Distinguished from *open classroom.*

Transductive reasoning Reasoning from one particular event to another particular event, instead of from general to particular or particular to general. A characteristic of Piaget's preoperational stage.

Transitive inference The ability to seriate—or arrange items along a quantitative dimension—mentally.

Triarchic theory of intelligence Sternberg's theory, which states that information processing skills, prior experience with tasks, and contextual (or cultural) factors interact to determine intelligent behavior.

Turnabout A conversational strategy in which the speaker not only comments on what has just been said but also adds a request to get the partner to respond again.

Ulnar grasp The clumsy grasp of the young infant, in which the fingers close against the palm.

Umbilical cord The long cord connecting the prenatal organism to the placenta that delivers nutrients and removes waste products.

Unconditioned response (UCR) In classical conditioning, a reflexive response that is produced by an unconditioned stimulus (UCS).

Unconditioned stimulus (UCS) In classical conditioning, a stimulus that leads to a reflexive response.

Underextension An early vocabulary error in which a word is applied too narrowly, to a smaller number of objects or events than is appropriate.

Uninhibited child A child who approaches and displays positive emotion to novel stimuli.

Uninvolved style A parenting style that is both undemanding and unresponsive. Reflects minimal commitment to child rearing. Distinguished from *authoritative, authoritarian,* and *permissive styles.*

Utilization deficiency The failure to benefit from using a mental strategy. Distinguished from *control* and *production deficiencies.*

V

Validity The extent to which measures in a research study accurately reflect what the investigator intended to measure.

Velocity curve A growth curve that plots the average amount of growth at each yearly interval for a sample of children. Clarifies the timing of growth spurts.

Vernix A white, cheeselike substance covering the fetus and preventing the skin from chapping due to constant exposure to the amniotic fluid.

Visual acuity Fineness of visual discrimination.

Visual cliff An apparatus used to study depth perception in infants. Consists of a glass-covered table and a central platform, from which babies are encouraged to crawl. Patterns placed beneath the glass create the appearance of a shallow and deep side.

W

Washout effect The loss of IQ and achievement gains resulting from early intervention within a few years after the program ends.

Wechsler Intelligence Scale for Children–III (WISC-III) An individually administered intelligence test that includes a measure of both general intelligence and a variety of verbal and performance scores.

Wernicke's area A language structure located in the temporal lobe of the cortex that is responsible for interpreting language.

Whole-language approach An approach to beginning reading instruction that parallels children's natural language learning and keeps reading materials whole and meaningful. Distinguished from *basic-skills approach.*

Working memory In the levels of processing model, the conscious pool of attentional resources from which our information-processing activities draw.

X

X-Linked Inheritance A pattern of inheritance in which a recessive gene is carried on the X chromosome. Males are more likely to be affected.

Z

Zone of proximal development In Vygotsky's theory, a range of tasks that the child cannot yet handle alone but can do with the help of more skilled partners.

Zygote The union of sperm and ovum at conception.

References

A

Aaron, R., & Powell, G. (1982). Feedback practices as a function of teacher and pupil race during reading groups instruction. *Journal of Negro Education, 51,* 50–59.

Abbott, S. (1992). Holding on and pushing away: Comparative perspectives on an eastern Kentucky child-rearing practice. *Ethos, 20,* 33–65.

Abbotts, B., & Osborn, L. M. (1993). Immunization status and reasons for immunization delay among children using public health immunization clinics. *American Journal of Diseases of Children, 147,* 965–968.

Abelman, R. (1985). Styles of parental disciplinary practices as a mediator of children's learning from prosocial television portrayals. *Child Study Journal, 15,* 131–145.

Abramovitch, R., Freedman, J. L., Henry, K., & Van Brunschot, M. (1995). Children's capacity to agree to psychological research: Knowledge of risks and benefits and voluntariness. *Ethics & Behavior, 5,* 25–48.

Abramovitch, R., Freedman, J. L., Thoden, K., & Nikolich, C. (1991). Children's capacity to consent to participation in psychological research: Some empirical findings. *Child Development, 62,* 1100–1109.

Abravanel, E., & Sigafoos, A. D. (1984). Exploring the presence of imitation during early infancy. *Child Development, 55,* 381–392.

Achenbach, T. M., & Howell, C. (1993). Are American children's problems getting worse? A 13-year comparison. *Journal of the American Academy of Child and Adolescent Psychiatry, 32,* 1145–1154.

Achenbach, T. M., Phares, V., Howell, C. T., Rauh, V. A., & Nurcombe, B. (1990). Seven-year outcome of the Vermont intervention program for low-birth-weight infants. *Child Development, 61,* 1672–1681.

Achenbach, T. M., & Weisz, J. R. (1975). A longitudinal study of developmental synchrony between conceptual identity, seriation, and transitivity of color, number, and length. *Child Development, 46,* 840–848.

Achilles, C. M., Nye, B. A., Zaharias, J. B., & Fulton, B. D. (1993). *The Lasting Benefits Study (LBS) in grades 4 and 5 (1990–1991): A legacy from Tennessee's four-year (K–3) class size study (1985–1989), Project STAR.* Paper presented at the North Carolina Association for Research in Education, Greensboro, NC.

Ackerman, B. P. (1978). Children's understanding of speech acts in unconventional frames. *Child Development, 49,* 311–318.

Ackerman, B. P. (1993). Children's understanding of the speaker's meaning in referential communication. *Journal of Experimental Child Psychology, 55,* 56–86.

Ackerman, S. H., Keller, S. E., Schleifer, S. J., Shindledecker, R. D., Camerino, M., Hofer, M. A., Weiner, H., & Stein, M. (1988). Premature maternal separation and lymphocyte function. *Brain and Behavior Immunology, 2,* 161–165.

Ackil, J. K., & Zaragoza, M. S. (1995). Developmental differences in eyewitness suggestibility and memory for source. *Journal of Experimental Child Psychology, 60,* 57–83.

Acredolo, L. P., & Goodwyn, S. W. (1990). Sign language in babies: The significance of symbolic gesturing for understanding language development. In R. Vasta (Ed.), *Annals of child development* (Vol. 7, pp. 1–42). Greenwich, CT: JAI Press.

Adams, G. R. (1978). Racial membership and physical attractiveness effects on preschool teachers' expectations. *Child Study Journal, 8,* 29–41.

Adams, G. R., & Crane, P. (1980). An assessment of parents' and teachers' expectations of preschool children's social preference for attractive or unattractive children and adults. *Child Development, 51,* 224–231.

Adams, R. J. (1987). An evaluation of color preference in early infancy. *Infant Behavior and Development, 10,* 143–150.

Adler, P. A., & Adler, P. (1995). Dynamics of inclusion and exclusion in preadolescent cliques. *Social Psychology Quarterly, 58,* 145–162.

Adolph, K. E., Eppler, M. A., & Gibson, E. J. (1993). Crawling versus walking infants' perception of affordances for locomotion over sloping surfaces. *Child Development, 64,* 1158–1174.

Ahlsten, G., Cnattingius, S., & Lindmark, G. (1993). Cessation of smoking during pregnancy improves fetal growth and reduces infant morbidity in the neonatal period: A population-based prospective study. *Acta Paediatrica, 82,* 177–181.

Ainsworth, M. D. S., Blehar, M., Waters, E., & Wall, S. (1978). *Patterns of attachment.* Hillsdale, NJ: Erlbaum.

Alan Guttmacher Institute. (1994). *Sex and America's teenagers.* New York: Author.

Albers, L. L., & Katz, V. L. (1991). Birth setting for low-risk pregnancies. *Journal of Nurse-Midwifery, 36,* 215–220.

Albert, R. S. (1994). The achievement of eminence: A longitudinal study of exceptionally gifted boys and their families. In R. F. Subotnik & K. D. Arnold (Eds.), *Beyond Terman: Contemporary studies of giftedness and talent* (pp. 282–315). Norwood, NJ: Ablex.

Ales, K. L., Druzin, M. L., & Santini, D. L. (1990). Impact of advanced maternal age on the outcome of pregnancy. *Surgery, Gynecology & Obstetrics, 171,* 209–216.

Alessandri, S. M., Sullivan, M. W., & Lewis, M. (1990). Violation of expectancy and frustration in early infancy. *Developmental Psychology, 26,* 738–744.

Alexander, G. M., & Hines, M. (1994). Gender labels and play styles: Their relative contribution to children's selection of playmates. *Child Development, 65,* 869–879.

Allen, J. P., Hauser, S. T., Bell, K. L., & O'Connor, T. G. (1994). Longitudinal assessment of autonomy and relatedness in adolescent–family interactions as predictors of adolescent ego development and self-esteem. *Child Development, 65,* 179–194.

Allen, L. F., Palomares, R. S., DeForest, P., Sprinkle, B., & Reynolds, C. R. (1991). The effects of intrauterine cocaine exposure: Transient or teratogenic? *Archives of Clinical Neuropsychology, 6,* 133–146.

Alpert-Gillis, L. J., & Connell, J. P. (1989). Gender and sex-role influences on children's self-esteem. *Journal of Personality, 57,* 97–114.

Alsaker, F. D. (1995). Timing of puberty and reactions to pubertal changes. In M. Rutter (Ed.), *Psychosocial disturbances in young people* (pp. 37–82). New York: Cambridge University Press.

Alter-Reid, K., Gibbs, M. S., Lachenmeyer, J. R., Sigal, J., & Massoth, N. A. (1986). Sexual abuse of children: A review of empirical findings. *Clinical Psychology Review, 6,* 249–266.

Altshuler, J. L., & Ruble, D. N. (1989). Developmental changes in children's awareness of strategies for coping with uncontrollable stress. *Child Development, 60,* 1337–1349.

Alvarez, W. F. (1985). The meaning of maternal employment for mothers and their perceptions of their three-year-old children. *Child Development, 56,* 350–360.

Alwitt, L. F., Anderson, D. R., Lorch, E. P., & Levin, S. R. (1980). Preschool children's visual attention to attributes of television. *Human Communication Research, 7,* 52–67.

Amabile, T. M. (1982). Children's artistic creativity: Detrimental effects of competition in a field setting. *Personality and Social Psychology Bulletin, 8,* 573–578.

Amabile, T. M. (1983). *The social psychology of creativity.* New York: Springer-Verlag.

Ambuel, B. (1995). Adolescents, unintended pregnancy, and abortion: The struggle for a compassionate social policy. *Current Directions in Psychological Science, 4,* 1–5.

American Psychiatric Association (1994). *Diagnostic and statistical manual of mental disorders* (4th ed.). Washington, DC: Author.

American Psychological Association. (1992). Ethical principles of psychologists and code of conduct. *American Psychologist, 44,* 1597–1611.

Ames, C. (1990, April). *Achievement goals and classroom structure: Developing a learning orientation.* Paper presented at the meeting of the American Educational Research Association, Boston.

Amiel-Tison, C. (1985). Pediatric contribution to the present knowledge on the neurobehavioral status of infants at birth. In J. Mehler & R. Fox (Eds.), *Neonate cognition: Beyond the blooming buzzing confusion* (pp. 365–380). Hillsdale, NJ: Erlbaum.

Anand, K. (1990). The biology of pain perception in newborn infants. In D. Tyler & E. Krane (Eds.), *Advances in pain research therapy* (pp. 113–155). New York: Raven Press.

Anderson, D. R., & Smith, R. (1984). Young children's TV viewing: The problem of cognitive continuity. In F. J. Morrison, C. Lord, & D. P. Keating (Eds.), *Applied developmental psychology* (Vol. 1, pp. 115–163). Orlando, FL: Academic Press.

Anderson, E. S. (1984). The acquisition of sociolinguistic knowledge: Some evidence from children's verbal role play. *Western Journal of Speech Communication, 48,* 125–144.

Anderson, G. C. (1991). Current knowledge about skin-to-skin (kangaroo) care for preterm infants. *Journal of Perinatology, 11,* 216–226.

Andersson, B-E. (1989). Effects of public day care—A longitudinal study. *Child Development, 60,* 857–866.

Andersson, B-E. (1992). Effects of day-care on cognitive and socioemotional competence of thirteen-year-old Swedish schoolchildren. *Child Development, 63,* 20–36.

Andrews, S. R., Blumenthal, J. B., Johnson, D. L., Kahn, A. J., Ferguson, C. J., Lasater, T. M., Malone, P. E., & Wallace, D. B. (1982). The skills of mothering: A study of parent–child development centers. *Monographs of the Society for Research in Child Development, 47*(6, Serial No. 198).

Anglin, J. M. (1993). Vocabulary development: A morphological analysis. *Monographs of the Society for Research in Child Development, 58*(10, Serial No. 238).

Antell, S. E., & Keating, D. P. (1983). Perception of numerical invariance in neonates. *Child Development, 54,* 695–701.

Antonarakis, S. E. (1992). The meiotic stage of nondisjunction in trisomy 21: Determination by using DNA polymorphisms. *American Journal of Human Genetics, 50,* 544–550.

Apgar, V. (1953). A proposal for a new method of evaluation in the newborn infant. *Current Research in Anesthesia and Analgesia, 32,* 260–267.

Arbuthnot, J., Sparling, Y., Faust, D., & Kee, W. (1983). Logical and moral development in preadolescent children. *Psychological Reports, 52,* 209–210.

Archer, J. (1992). Childhood gender roles: Social content and organization. In H. McGurk (Ed.), *Childhood social development* (pp. 31–62). Hillsdale, NJ: Erlbaum.

Archer, S. L. (1982). The lower age boundaries of identity development. *Child Development, 53,* 1551–1556.

Archer, S. L. (1989a). Gender differences in identity development: Issues of process, domain, and timing. *Journal of Adolescence, 2,* 117–138.

Archer, S. L. (1989b). The status of identity: Reflections on the need for intervention. *Journal of Adolescence, 12,* 345–359.

Archer, S. L., & Waterman, A. S. (1990). Varieties of identity diffusions and foreclosures: An exploration of subcategories of the identity statuses. *Journal of Adolescent Research, 5,* 96–111.

Arcus, D., & Kagan, J. (1995). Temperament and craniofacial variation in the first two years. *Child Development, 66,* 1529–1540.

Ariès, P. (1962). *Centuries of childhood.* New York: Random House.

Arnold, K. D. (1994). The Illinois Valedictorian Project: Early adult careers of academically talented male and female high school students. In R. F. Subotnik & K. D. Arnold (Eds.), *Beyond Terman: Contemporary longitudinal studies of giftedness and talent* (pp. 24–51) Norwood NJ: Ablex.

Aronfreed, J. (1968). *Conduct and conscience.* New York: Academic Press.

Arsenio, W. F., & Kramer, R. (1992). Victimizers and their victims: Children's conceptions of the mixed emotional consequences of moral transgressions. *Child Development, 63,* 915–927.

Arterberry, M. E., Craton, L. G., & Yonas, A. (1993). Infants' sensitivity to motion-carried information for depth and object properties. In C. E. Granrud (Ed.), *Visual perception and cognition in infancy* (pp. 215–234). Hillsdale, NJ: Erlbaum.

Arterberry, M. E., Yonas, A., & Bensen, A. S. (1989). Self-produced locomotion and the development of responsiveness to linear perspective and texture gradients. *Developmental Psychology, 25,* 976–982.

Artman, L., & Cahan, S. (1993). Schooling and the development of transitive inference. *Developmental Psychology, 29,* 753–759.

Asendorpf, J. B., Warkentin, V., & Baudonniere, P. (1996). Self-awareness and other-awareness II: Mirror self-recognition, social contingency awareness, and synchronic imitation. *Developmental Psychology, 32,* 313–321.

Ashmead, D. H., Davis, D. L., Whalen, T., & Odom, R. D. (1991). Sound localization and sensitivity to interaural time differences in human infants. *Child Development, 62,* 1211–1226.

Ashmead, D. H., McCarty, M. E., Lucas, L. S., & Belvedere, M. C. (1993). Visual guidance in infants' reaching toward suddenly displaced targets. *Child Development, 64,* 1111–1127.

Ashmead, D. H., & Perlmutter, M. (1980). Infant memory in everyday life. In M. Perlmutter (Ed.), *New directions for child development* (Vol. 10, pp. 1–16). San Francisco: Jossey-Bass.

Aslin, R. N. (1987). Visual and auditory development in infancy. In J. D. Osofsky (Ed.), *Handbook of infant development* (2nd ed., pp. 5–97). New York: Wiley.

Aslin, R. N. (1993). Perception of visual direction in human infants. In C. E. Granrud (Ed.), *Visual perception and cognition in infancy* (pp. 91–119). Hillsdale, NJ: Erlbaum.

Astington, J. W. (1991). Intention in the child's theory of mind. In C. Moore & D. Frye (Eds.), *Children's theories of mind* (pp. 157–172). Hillsdale, NJ: Erlbaum.

Astington, J. W. (1995). Commentary: Talking it over with my brain. In J. H. Flavell, F. L. Green, & E. R. Flavell, Young children's knowledge about thinking. *Monographs of the Society for Research in Child Development, 60* (1, Serial No. 243).

Astington, J. W., & Gopnik, A. (1991). Theoretical explanations of children's understanding of the mind. *British Journal of Developmental Psychology, 9,* 7–31.

Astley, S. J., Clarren, S. K., Little, R. E., Sampson, P. D., & Daling, J. R. (1992). Analysis of facial shape in children gestationally exposed to marijuana, alcohol, and/or cocaine. *Pediatrics, 89,* 67–77.

Atkinson-King, K. (1973). Children's acquisition of phonological stress contrasts. *UCLA Working Papers in Phonetics,* 25.

Atkinson, R. C., & Shiffrin, R. M. (1968). Human memory: A proposed system and its control processes. In K. W. Spence & J. T. Spence (Eds.), *Advances in the psychology of learning and motivation* (Vol. 2, pp. 90–195). New York: Academic Press.

Au, T. K., Dapretto, M., & Song, Y-K. (1994). Input vs. constraints: Early word acquisition in Korean and English. *Journal of Memory and Language, 33,* 567–582.

Au, T. K., Sidle, A. L., & Rollins, K. B. (1993). Developing an intuitive understanding of conservation and contamination: Invisible particles as a plausible mechanism. *Developmental Psychology, 29,* 286–299.

August, D., & Garcia, E. E. (1988). *Language minority education in the United States.* Springfield, IL: Charles C Thomas.

Avis, J., & Harris, P. (1991). Belief–desire reasoning among Baka children: Evidence for a universal conception of mind. *Child Development, 62,* 460–467.

Azmitia, M. (1988). Peer interaction and problem solving: When are two heads better than one? *Child Development, 59,* 87–96.

Azmitia, M., & Hesser, J. (1993). Why siblings are important agents of cognitive development: A comparison of siblings and peers. *Child Development, 64,* 430–444.

Azmitia, M., & Montgomery, R. (1993). Friendship, transactive dialogues, and the development of scientific reasoning. *Social Development, 2,* 202–2211

B

Baddeley, A. D. (1992). Working memory. *Science, 255,* 556–559.

Baddeley, A. D. (1994). The magic number seven: Still magic after all these years? *Psychological Review, 101,* 353–356.

Baer, J. (1991). *Creativity and divergent thinking: A task-specific approach.* Hillsdale, NJ: Erlbaum.

Bahrick, L. E. (1983). Infants' perception of substance and temporal synchrony in multimodal events. *Infant Behavior and Development, 6,* 429–451.

Bahrick, L. E. (1988). Intermodal learning in infancy: Learning on the basis of two kinds of invariant relations in audible and visible events. *Child Development, 59,* 197–209.

Bahrick, L. E. (1992). Infants' perceptual differentiation of amodal and modality-specific audio-visual relations. *Journal of Experimental Child Psychology, 53,* 180–199.

Bai, D. L., & Bertenthal, B. I. (1992). Locomotor status and the development of spatial search skills. *Child Development, 63,* 215–226.

Bailey, J. M., Bobrow, D., Wolfe, M., & Mikach, S. (1995). Sexual orientation of adult sons of gay fathers. *Developmental Psychology, 31,* 124–129.

Bailey, J. M., & Pillard, R. C. (1991). A genetic study of male sexual orientation. *Archives of General Psychiatry, 43,* 808–812.

Bailey, J. M., Pillard, R. C., Neale, M. C., & Agyei, Y. (1993). Heritable factors influence sexual orientation in women. *Archives of General Psychiatry, 50,* 217–223.

Bailey, R. C. (1990). Growth of African pygmies in early childhood. *New England Journal of Medicine, 323,* 1146.

Bailey, T. (1993). Can youth apprenticeship thrive in the United States? *Educational Researcher, 22*(3), 4–10.

Baillargeon, R. (1987). Object permanence in 3.5- and 4.5-month-old infants. *Developmental Psychology, 23,* 655–664.

Baillargeon, R. (1993). The object concept revisited: New directions in the investigation of infants' physical knowledge. In C. E. Granrud (Ed.), *Carnegie–Mellon Symposia on Cognition* (Vol. 23, pp. 265–315). Hillsdale, NJ: Erlbaum.

Baillargeon, R. (1994a). How do infants learn about the physical world? *Current Directions in Psychological Science, 3,* 133–140.

Baillargeon, R. (1994b). Physical reasoning in infancy. In M. S. Gazzaniga (Ed.), *The cognitive neurosciences* (pp. 181–204). Cambridge, MA: MIT Press.

Baillargeon, R. (1995). A model of physical reasoning in infancy. In C. K. Rovee-Collier & L. P. Lipsitt (Eds.), *Advances in infancy research* (Vol. 9, pp. 305–371). Norwood, NJ: Ablex.

Baillargeon, R., & DeVos, J. (1991). Object permanence in young infants: Further evidence. *Child Development, 62,* 1227–1246.

Baillargeon, R., Graber, M., DeVos, J., & Black, J. (1990). Why do young infants fail to search for hidden objects? *Cognition, 36,* 255–284.

Baillargeon, R., Needham, A., & DeVos, J. (1992). The development of young infants' intuitions about support. *Early Development and Parenting, 1,* 68–78.

Baird, P., & Sadovnick, A. D. (1987). Life expectancy in Down syndrome. *Journal of Pediatrics, 110,* 849–854.

Bakeman, R., Adamson, L. B., Konner, M., & Barr, R. G. (1990). !Kung infancy: The social context of object exploration. *Child Development, 61,* 794–809.

Baker, C. (1993). *Foundations of bilingual education and bilingualism.* Clevedon, England: Multilingual Matters.

Baker-Ward, L., Gordon, B. N., Ornstein, P. A., Larus, D. M., & Clubb, P. A. (1993). Young children's long-term retention of a pediatric examination. *Child Development, 64,* 1519–1533.

Baker-Ward, L., Ornstein, P. A., & Holden, D. J. (1984). The expression of memorization in early childhood. *Journal of Experimental Child Psychology, 37,* 555–575.

Baldwin, D. V., & Skinner, M. L. (1989). Structural model for antisocial behavior: Generalization to single-mother families. *Developmental Psychology, 25,* 45–50.

Baldwin, J. M. (1895). *Mental development in the child and the race: Methods and processes.* New York: Macmillan.

Baldwin, J. M. (1897). *Social and ethnic interpretations in mental development: A study in social psychology.* New York: Macmillan.

Ball, S., & Bogatz, G. A. (1970). *The first year of "Sesame Street": An evaluation.* Princeton, NJ: Educational Testing Service.

Ballard, B. D., Gipson, M. T., Guttenberg, W., & Ramsey, K. (1980). Palatability of food as a factor influencing obese and normal-weight children's eating habits. *Behavior Research and Therapy, 18,* 598–600.

Band, E. B., & Weisz, J. R. (1988). How to feel better when it feels bad: Children's perspectives on coping with everyday stress. *Developmental Psychology, 24,* 247–253.

Bandura, A. (1967). Behavioral psychotherapy. *Scientific American, 216,* 78–86.

Bandura, A. (1977). *Social learning theory.* Englewood Cliffs, NJ: Prentice-Hall.

Bandura, A. (1986). *Social foundations of thought and action: A social cognitive theory.* Englewood Cliffs, NJ: Prentice-Hall.

Bandura, A. (1989). Social cognitive theory. In R. Vasta (Ed.), *Annals of child development* (Vol. 6, pp. 1–60). Greenwich, CT: JAI Press.

Bandura, A. (1991). Social cognitive theory of moral thought and action. In W. M. Kurtines & J. L. Gewirtz (Eds.), *Handbook of moral behavior and development* (Vol. 1, pp. 45–103). Hillsdale, NJ: Erlbaum.

Bandura, A. (1992). Perceived self-efficacy in cognitive development and functioning. *Educational Psychologist, 28,* 117–148.

Banis, H. T., Varni, J. W., Wallander, J. L., Korsch, B. M., Jay, S. M., Adler, R., Garcia-Temple, E., & Negrete, V. (1988). Psychological and social adjustment of obese children and their families. *Child: Care, Health, and Development, 14,* 157–173.

Banks, M. S. (1980). The development of visual accommodation during early infancy. *Child Development, 51,* 646–666.

Banks, M. S., & Bennett, P. J. (1988). Optical and photoreceptor immaturities limit the spatial and chromatic vision of human neonates. *Journal of the Optical Society of America, 5,* 2059–2079.

Banks, M. S., & Ginsburg, A. P. (1985). Early visual preferences: A review and new theoretical treatment. In H. W. Reese (Ed.), *Advances in child development and behavior* (Vol. 19, pp. 207–246). New York: Academic Press.

Banks, M. S., & Salapatek, P. (1981). Infant pattern vision: A new approach based on the contrast sensitivity function. *Journal of Experimental Child Psychology, 31,* 1–45.

Banks, M. S., & Salapatek, P. (1983). Infant visual perception. In M. M. Haith & J. J. Campos (Eds.), *Handbook of child psychology: Vol. 2. Infancy and developmental psychobiology* (4th ed., pp. 436–571). New York: Wiley.

Banks, M. S., & Shannon, E. (1993). Spatial and chromatic visual efficiency in human neonates. In C. Granrud (Ed.), *Visual perception and cognition in infancy* (pp. 1–46). Hillsdale, NJ: Erlbaum.

Bard, K. A. (1992). Intentional behavior and intentional communication in young free-ranging orangutans. *Child Development, 63,* 1186–1197.

Bardwell, J. R., Cochran, S. W., & Walker, S. (1986). Relationship of parental education, race, and gender to sex role stereotyping in five-year-old kindergartners. *Sex Roles, 15,* 275–281.

Barenboim, C. (1977). Developmental changes in the interpersonal cognitive system from middle childhood to adolescence. *Child Development, 48,* 1467–1474.

Barenboim, C. (1981). The development of person perception in childhood and adolescence: From behavioral comparisons to psychological constructs to psychological comparisons. *Child Development, 52,* 129–144.

Bargh, J. A., & Schul, Y. (1980). On the cognitive benefits of peer teaching. *Journal of Educational Psychology, 72,* 593–604.

Barker, D. J. P., Gluckman, P. D., Godfrey, K. M., Harding, J. E., Owens, J. A., & Robinson, J. S. (1993). Fetal nutrition and cardiovascular disease in adult life. *Lancet, 341,* 938–941.

Barker, R. G., & Gump, P. V. (1964). *Big school, small school: High school size and student behavior.* Stanford, CA: Stanford University Press.

Barkley, R. A. (1990). *Attention deficit hyperactivity disorder: A handbook for diagnosis and treatment.* New York: Guilford.

Barkley, R. A. (1994). Impaired delayed responding: A unified theory of attention-deficit hyperactivity disorder. In R. A. Barkley (Ed.), *Disruptive behavior disorders in childhood* (pp. 11–57). New York: Plenum.

Barkley, R. A., DuPaul, G. J., & Costello, A. J. (1993). Stimulant medications. In J. Werry & M. Aman (Eds.), *Handbook of pediatric psychopharmacology* (pp. 205–237). New York: Plenum.

Barnes, K. E. (1971). Preschool play norms: A replication. *Developmental Psychology, 5,* 99–103.

Barnes-Josiah, D., & Augustin, A. (1995). Secular trend in the age at menarche in Haiti. *American Journal of Human Biology, 7,* 357–362.

Barnett, D., Manly, J., & Cicchetti, D. (1993). Defining child maltreatment: The interface between policy and research. In D. Cicchetti & S. Toth (Eds.), *Child abuse, child development, and social policy* (pp. 7–73). Norwood, NJ: Ablex.

Barnett, W. S. (1993). Benefit-cost analysis of preschool education: Findings from a 25-year follow-up. *American Journal of Orthopsychiatry, 63,* 500–508.

Barnett, W. S. (1993). New wine in old bottles: Increasing the coherence of early childhood care and educational policy. *Early Childhood Research Quarterly, 8,* 519–558.

Baron-Cohen, S. (1991). Do people with autism understand what causes emotion? *Child Development, 62,* 385–395.

Barr, H. M., Streissguth, A. P., Darby, B. L., & Sampson, P. D. (1990). Prenatal exposure to alcohol, caffeine, tobacco, and aspirin: Effects on fine and gross motor performance in 4-year-old children. *Developmental Psychology, 26,* 339–348.

Barr, R. G., Konner, M., Bakeman, R., & Adamson, L. (1991). Crying in !Kung San infants: A test of the cultural specificity hypothesis. *Developmental Medicine and Child Neurology, 33,* 601–610.

Barrera, M. E., & Maurer, D. (1981a). Discrimination of strangers by the three-month-old. *Child Development, 52,* 559–563.

Barrera, M. E., & Maurer, D. (1981b). Recognition of mother's photographed face by the three-month-old infant. *Child Development, 52,* 714–716.

Barrett, K. C., & Campos, J. J. (1987). Perspectives on emotional development II: A functionalist approach to emotions. In J. D. Osofsky (Ed.), *Handbook of infant development* (2nd ed., pp. 555–578). New York: Wiley.

Barron, F. (1988). Putting creativity to work. In R. J. Sternberg (Ed.), *The nature of creativity: Contemporary psychological perspectives* (pp. 76–98). New York: Cambridge University Press.

Bartlett, F. C. (1932). *Remembering.* Cambridge: Cambridge University Press.

Barton, M. E., & Tomasello, M. (1991). Joint attention and conversation in mother-infant–sibling triads. *Child Development, 62,* 517–529.

Basinger, K. S., Gibbs, J. C., & Fuller, D. (1995). Context and the measurement of moral judgment. *International Journal of Behavioral Development, 18,* 537–556.

Bastian, H. (1993). Personal beliefs and alternative childbirth choices: A survey of 552 women who planned to give birth at home. *Birth, 20,* 186–192.

Bates, E. (1979). *The emergence of symbols: Cognition and communication in infancy.* New York: Academic Press.

Bates, E. (1995). *Modularity, domain specificity, and the development of language.* Unpublished manuscript, University of California, San Diego.

Bates, E., Bretherton, I., & Snyder, L. (1988). *From first words to grammar.* New York: Cambridge University Press.

Bates, E., & MacWhinney, B. (1987). Competition, variation, and language learning. In B. MacWhinney (Ed.), *Mechanisms of language acquisition* (pp. 157–193). Hillsdale, NJ: Erlbaum.

Bates, E., Marchman, V., Thal, D., Fenson, L. Dale, P., Reznick, J. S., Reilly, J., & Hartung, J. (1994). Developmental and stylistic variation in the composition of early vocabulary. *Journal of Child Language, 21,* 85–123.

Bauer, P. J. (1996). What do infants recall of their lives? Memory for specific events by one- to two-year-olds. *American Psychologist, 51,* 29–41.

Bauer, P. J., & Dow, G. A. A. (1994). Episodic memory in 16- and 20-month-old children: Specifics are generalized, but not forgotten. *Developmental Psychology, 30,* 403–417.

Bauer, P. J., & Mandler, J. M. (1989a). Taxonomies and triads: Conceptual organization in one- to two-year-olds. *Cognitive Psychology, 21,* 156–184.

Bauer, P. J., & Mandler, J. M. (1989b). One thing follows another: Effects of temporal structure on 1- to 2-year-olds' recall of events. *Developmental Psychology, 25,* 197–206.

Bauer, P. J., & Mandler, J. M. (1992). Putting the horse before the cart: The use of temporal order in recall of events by one-year-old children. *Developmental Psychology, 28,* 441–452.

Baumeister, R. F. (1990). Identity crisis. In R. M. Lerner, A. C. Petersen, & J. Brooks-Gunn (Eds.), *The encyclopedia of adolescence* (Vol. 1, pp. 518–521). New York: Garland.

Baumrind, D. (1967). Child care practices anteceding three patterns of preschool behavior. *Genetic Psychology Monographs, 75,* 43–88.

Baumrind, D. (1971). Current patterns of parental authority. *Developmental Psychology Monograph, 4* (1, Pt. 2).

Baumrind, D. (1983). Rejoinder to Lewis's reinterpretation of parental firm control effects: Are authoritative families really harmonious? *Psychological Bulletin, 94,* 132–142.

Baumrind, D. (1991). The influence of parenting style on adolescent competence and substance use. *Journal of Early Adolescence, 11,* 56–95.

Baumrind, D. (1995). Commentary on sexual orientation: Research and social policy implications. *Developmental Psychology, 31,* 130–136.

Baumrind, D., & Black, A. E. (1967). Socialization practices associated with dimensions of competence in preschool boys and girls. *Child Development, 38,* 291–327.

Bayley, N. (1969). *Bayley Scales of Infant Development.* New York: The Psychological Corporation.

Beal, C. R. (1990). The development of text evaluation and revision skills. *Child Development, 61,* 247–258.

Beatty, W. W. (1992). Gonadal hormones and sex differences in nonresproductive behaviors. In A. A. Gerall, H. Moltz, & I. L. Ward (Eds.), *Handbook of behavioral neurobiology: Vol. 11. Sexual differentiation* (pp. 85–128). New York: Plenum.

Beauchamp, G. K., Cowart, B. J., Mennella, J. A., & Marsh, R. R. (1994). Infant salt taste: Developmental, methodological, and contextual factors. *Developmental Psychobiology, 27,* 353–365.

Beck, M. (1994, January 17). How far should we push Mother Nature? *Newsweek,* pp. 54–57.

Becker, H. J. (1991). How computers are used in United States schools: Basic data from the 1989 I.E.A. Computers in Education Survey. *Journal of Educational Computing Research, 7,* 407–420.

Becker, J. (1989). Preschoolers' use of number words to denote one-to-one correspondence. *Child Development, 60,* 1147–1157.

Becker, J. (1990). Processes in the acquisition of pragmatic competence. In G. Conti-Ramsden & C. Snow (Eds.), *Children's language* (Vol. 7, pp. 7–24). Hillsdale, NJ: Erlbaum.

Becker, J. (1993). Young children's numerical use of number words: Counting in many-to-one situations. *Developmental Psychology, 29,* 458–465.

Beere, C. A. (1990). *Gender roles: A handbook of tests and measures.* New York: Greenwood Press.

Begley, S. (1995, October 9). Promises, promises. *Newsweek,* pp. 60–62.

Behrend, D. A. (1988). Overextensions in early language comprehension: Evidence from a signal detection approach. *Journal of Child Language, 15,* 63–75.

Behrend, D. A., Rosengren, K. S., & Perlmutter, M. (1992). The relation between private speech and parental interactive style. In R. M. Diaz & L. E. Berk (Eds.), *Private speech: From social interaction to self-regulation* (pp. 85–100). Hillsdale, NJ: Erlbaum.

Behrman, R. E., & Vaughan, V. C. (1987). *Nelson textbook of pediatrics* (13th ed.). Philadelphia: Saunders.

Beilin, H. (1978). Inducing conservation through training. In G. Steiner (Ed.), *Psychology of the twentieth century* (Vol. 7, pp. 260–289). Munich: Kindler.

Beilin, H. (1992). Piaget's enduring contribution to developmental psychology. *Developmental Psychology, 28,* 191–204.

Belkin, L. (1992, July 28). Childless couples hang on to last hope, despite law. *The New York Times,* pp. B1–B2.

Bell, A., Weinberg, M., & Hammersmith, S. (1981). *Sexual Preference: Its development in men and women.* Bloomington: Indiana University Press.

Bell, M. A., & Fox, N. A. (1992). The relations between frontal brain electrical activity and cognitive development during infancy. *Child Development, 63,* 1142–1163.

Bell, S. M., & Ainsworth, M. D. S. (1972). Infant crying and maternal responsiveness. *Child Development, 43,* 1171–1190.

Bell-Dolan, D. J., Foster, S. L., & Sikora, D. M. (1989). Effects of sociometric testing on children's behavior and loneliness in school. *Developmental Psychology, 25,* 306–311.

Bellinger, D., Leviton, A., Waternaux, C., Needleman, H., & Rabinowitz, M. (1987). Longitudinal analysis of prenatal and postnatal lead exposure and early cognitive development. *New England Journal of Medicine, 316,* 1037–1043.

Bellinger, D., Sloman, J., Leviton, A., Rabinowitz, M., Needleman, H. L., & Waternaux, C. (1991). Low level lead exposure and children's cognitive function in the preschool years. *Pediatrics, 87,* 219–227.

Belmont, L., & Marolla, F. A. (1973). Birth order, family size, and intelligence. *Science, 182,* 1096–1101.

Belsky, J. (1993). Etiology of child maltreatment: A developmental ecological analysis. *Psychological Bulletin, 114,* 413–434.

Belsky, J., & Braungart, J. M. (1991). Are insecure-avoidant infants with extensive day-care experience less stressed by and more independent in the Strange Situation? *Child Development, 62,* 567–571.

Belsky, J., Fish, M., & Isabella, R. A. (1991). Continuity and discontinuity in infant negative and positive emotionality: Family antecedents and attachment consequences. *Developmental Psychology, 27,* 421–431.

Belsky, J., Rovine, M., & Taylor, D. G. (1984). The Pennsylvania infant and family development project, III. The origins of individual differences in infant–mother attachment: Maternal and infant contributions. *Child Development, 55,* 718–728.

Bem, S. L. (1974). The measurement of psychological androgyny. *Journal of Consulting and Clinical Psychology, 42,* 155–162.

Bem, S. L. (1977). On the utility of alternative procedures for assessing psychological androgyny. *Journal of Consulting and Clinical Psychology, 45,* 196–205.

Bem, S. L. (1981). Gender schema theory: A cognitive account of sex typing. *Psychological Review, 88,* 354–364.

Bem, S. L. (1983). Gender schema theory and its implications for child development: Raising gender aschematic children in a gender-schematic society. *Signs: Journal of Women in Culture and Society, 8,* 598–616.

Bem, S. L. (1984). Androgyny and gender schema theory: A conceptual and empirical integration. In R. A. Dienstbier & T. B. Sonderegger (Eds.), *Nebraska Symposium on Motivation* (Vol. 34, pp. 179–226). Lincoln: University of Nebraska Press.

Bem, S. L. (1989). Genital knowledge and gender constancy in preschool children. *Child Development, 60,* 649–662.

Benacerraf, B. R., Green, M. F., Saltzman, D. H., Barss, V. A., Penso, C. A., Nadel, A. S., Heffner, L. J., Stryker, J. M., Sandstrom, M. M., & Frigoletto, F. D., Jr. (1988). Early amniocentesis for prenatal cytogenetic evaluation. *Radiology, 169,* 709–710.

Benbow, C. P. (1986). Physiological correlates of extreme intellectual precocity. *Neuropsychologia, 24,* 719–725.

Benbow, C. P. (1988). Sex differences in mathematical reasoning ability in intellectually talented preadolescents: Their nature, effects, and possible causes. *Behavioral and Brain Science, 11,* 169–232.

Benbow, C. P., & Arjimand, O. (1990). Predictors of high academic achievement in mathematics and science by mathematically talented students: A longitudinal study. *Journal of Educational Psychology, 82,* 430–441.

Benbow, C. P., & Lubinski, D. (1993). Psychological profiles of the mathematically talented: Some sex differences and evidence supporting their biological basis. In G. R. Bock & K. Ackrill (Eds.), *The origins and development of high ability* (Ciba Foundation Symposium 178, pp. 44–59).

Benbow, C. P., & Stanley, J. C. (1980). Sex differences in mathematical ability: Fact or artifact? *Science, 210,* 1262–1264.

Benbow, C. P., & Stanley, J. C. (1983). Sex differences in mathematical reasoning: More facts. *Science, 222,* 1029–1031.

Bench, R. J., Collyer, Y., Mentz, L., & Wilson, I. (1976). Studies in infant behavioural audiometry: I. Neonates. *Audiology, 15,* 85–105.

Bendersky, M., & Lewis, M. (1994). Environmental risk, biological risk, and developmental outcome. *Developmental Psychology, 30,* 484–494.

Benedict, R. (1934a). Anthropology and the abnormal. *Journal of Genetic Psychology, 10,* 59–82.

Benedict, R. (1934b). *Patterns of culture.* Boston: Houghton Mifflin.

Benoit, D., & Parker, K. C. H. (1994). Stability and transmission of attachment across three generations. *Child Development, 65,* 1444–1456.

Benson, J. B., & Haith, M. M. (1995). Future-oriented processes: A foundation for planning behavior in infants and toddlers. *Infancia y Aprendizaje, 57,* 127–140.

Berenbaum, S. A., & Snyder, E. (1995). Early hormonal influences on childhood sex-typed activity and playmate preferences: Implications for the development of sexual orientation. *Developmental Psychology, 31,* 31–42.

Berg, W. K., & Berg, K. M. (1987). Psychophysiological development in infancy: State, startle, and attention. In J. Osofsky (Ed.), *Handbook of infant development* (2nd ed., pp. 238–317). New York: Wiley.

Berk, L. E. (1985). Relationship of caregiver education to child-oriented attitudes, job satisfaction, and behaviors toward children. *Child Care Quarterly, 14,* 103–129.

Berk, L. E. (1992a). Children's private speech: An overview of theory and the status of research. In R. M. Diaz & L. E. Berk (Eds.), *Private speech: From social interaction to self-regulation* (pp. 17–53). Hillsdale, NJ: Erlbaum.

Berk, L. E. (1992b). The extracurriculum. In P. W. Jackson (Ed.), *Handbook of research on curriculum* (pp. 1002–1043). New York: Macmillan.

Berk, L. E. (1994a, November). Vygotsky's theory: The importance of make-believe play. *Young Children, 50,* 30–39.

Berk, L. E. (1994b, November). Why children talk to themselves. *Scientific American, 271*(5), 78–83.

Berk, L. E., & Landau, S. (1993). Private speech of learning disabled and normally achieving children in classroom academic and laboratory contexts. *Child Development, 64,* 556–571.

Berk, L. E., & Lewis, N. G. (1977). Sex role and social behavior in four school environments. *Elementary School Journal, 77,* 205–217.

Berk, L. E., & Spuhl, S. T. (1995). Maternal interaction, private speech, and task performance in preschool children. *Early Childhood Research Quarterly, 10,* 145–169.

Berk, L. E., & Winsler, A. (1995). *Scaffolding children's learning: Vygotsky and early childhood education.* Washington, DC: National Association for the Education of Young Children.

Berkey, C. S., Wang, X., Dockery, D. W., & Ferris, B. G., Jr. (1994). Adolescent height growth of U.S. children. *Annals of Human Biology, 21,* 435–442.

Berko, J. (1958). The child's learning of English morphology. *Word, 14,* 150–177.

Berko Gleason, J. (1993). Language development: An overview and a preview. In J. Berko Gleason (Ed.), *The development of language* (3rd ed., pp. 1–37). New York: Macmillan.

Berkowitz, M. W., & Gibbs, J. C. (1983). Measuring the developmental features of moral discussion. *Merrill-Palmer Quarterly, 29,* 399–410.

Berman, P. (1980). Are women more responsive than men to the young? A review of developmental and situational variables. *Psychological Bulletin, 88,* 668–695.

Berman, P. W. (1986). Young children's responses to babies: Do they foreshadow differences between maternal and paternal styles? In A. Fogel & G. F. Melson (Eds.), *Origins of nurturance* (pp. 25–51). Hillsdale, NJ: Erlbaum.

Bermejo, V. (1996). Cardinality development and counting. *Developmental Psychology, 32,* 263–268.

Berndt, T. J. (1988). The nature and significance of children's friendships. In R. Vasta (Ed.), *Annals of child development* (Vol. 5, pp. 155–186). Greenwich, CT: JAI Press.

Berndt, T. J., Cheung, P. C., Lau, S., Hau, K-T., & Lew, W. J. F. (1993). Perceptions of parenting in mainland China, Taiwan, and Hong Kong: Sex differences and societal differences. *Developmental Psychology, 29,* 156–164.

Berndt, T. J., & Hoyle, S. G. (1985). Stability and change in childhood and adolescent friendships. *Developmental Psychology, 21,* 1007–1015.

Berndt, T. J., & Keefe, K. (1995). Friends' influence on adolescents' adjustment to school. *Child Development, 66,* 1312–1329.

Berndt, T. J., & Perry, T. B. (1990). Distinctive features and effects of early adolescent friendships. In R. Montemayor, G. R. Adams, & T. P. Gullotta (Eds.), *From childhood to adolescence: A transitional period?* (pp. 269–287). Newbury Park, CA: Sage.

Berney, B. (1993). Round and round it goes: The epidemiology of childhood lead poisoning, 1950–1990. *Milbank Quarterly, 71,* 3–39.

Bernier, J. C., & Siegel, D. H. (1994). Attention-deficit hyperactivity disorder: A family ecological systems perspective. *Families in Society, 75,* 142–150.

Berrueta-Clement, J. R., Schweinhart, L. J., Barnett, W. S., Epstein, A. S., & Weikart, D. P. (1984). Changed lives: The effects of the Perry Preschool Program on youths through age 19. *Monographs of the High/Scope Research Foundation, 8.*

Bertenthal, B. I. (1993). Infants' perception of biomechanical motions: Instrinsic image and knowledge-based constraints. In C. Granrud (Ed.), *Visual perception and cognition in infancy* (pp. 175–214). Hillsdale, NJ: Erlbaum.

Bertenthal, B. I., & Campos, J. J. (1987). New directions in the study of early experience. *Child Development, 58,* 560–567.

Bertenthal, B. I., Campos, J. J., & Barrett, K. (1984). Self-produced locomotion: An organizer of emotional, cognitive, and social development in infancy. In R. Emde & R. Harmon (Eds.), *Continuities and discontinuities in development* (pp. 174–210). New York: Plenum.

Bertenthal, B. I., Campos, J. J., & Haith, M. M. (1980). Development of visual organization: The perception of subjective contours. *Child Development, 51,* 1077–1080.

Bertenthal, B. I., Proffitt, D. R., Kramer, S. J., & Spetner, N. B. (1987). Infants' encoding of kinetic displays varying in relative coherence. *Developmental Psychology, 23,* 171–178.

Bertenthal, B. I., Proffitt, D. R., Spetner, N. B., & Thomas, M. A. (1985). The development of infant sensitivity to biomechanical motions. *Child Development, 56,* 531–543.

Best, D. L. (1993). Inducing children to generate mnemonic organizational strategies: An examination of long-term retention and materials. *Developmental Psychology, 29,* 324–336.

Best, D. L., & Ornstein, P. A. (1986). Children's generation and communication of mnemonic organizational strategies. *Developmental Psychology, 22,* 845–853.

Best, D. L., Williams, J. E., Cloud, J. M., Davis, S. W., Robertson, L. S., Edwards, J. R., Giles, H., & Fowles, J. (1977). Development of sex-trait stereotypes among young children in the United States, England, and Ireland. *Child Development, 48,* 1375–1384.

Betz, C. (1994, March). Beyond time-out: Tips from a teacher. *Young Children, 49*(3), 10–14.

Beunen, G. P., Malina, R. M., Van't Hof, M. A., Simons, J., Ostyn, M., Renson, R., & Van Gerven, D. (1988). *Adolescent growth and motor performance.* Champaign, IL: Human Kinetics.

Beyer, S. (1995). Maternal employment and children's academic achievement: Parenting styles as mediating variable. *Developmental Review, 15,* 212–253.

Beyth-Marom, R., Austin, L., Fischhoff, B., Palmgren, C., & Jacobs-Quadrel, M. (1993). Perceived consequences of risky behaviors: Adults and adolescents. *Developmental Psychology, 29,* 549–563.

Bhatt, R. S., Rovee-Collier, C. K. & Weiner, S. (1994). Developmental changes in the interface between perception and memory retrieval. *Developmental Psychology, 30,* 151–162.

Bialystok, E. (1986). Factors in the growth of linguistic awareness. *Child Development, 57,* 498–510.

Bianchi, B. D., & Bakeman, R. (1978). Sex-typed affiliation preferences observed in preschoolers: Traditional and open school differences. *Child Development, 49,* 910–912.

Bickerton, D. (1981). *Roots of language.* Ann Arbor, MI: Karoma.

Bickerton, D. (1990). *Language & species.* Chicago: University of Chicago Press.

Bierman, K. L. (1986). Process of change during social skills training with preadolescents and its relation to treatment outcome. *Child Development, 57,* 230–240.

Bierman, K. L., Miller, C. L., & Stabb, S. D. (1987). Improving the social behavior and peer acceptance of rejected boys: Effects of social skill training with instructions and prohibitions. *Journal of Consulting and Clinical Psychology, 55,* 194–200.

Bierman, K. L., Smoot, D. L., & Aumiller, K. (1993). Characteristics of aggressive-rejected, aggressive (nonrejected), and rejected (nonaggressive) boys. *Child Development, 64,* 139–151.

Biernat, M. (1991a). A multi-component, developmental analysis of sex-typing. *Sex Roles, 24,* 567–586.

Biernat, M. (1991b). Gender stereotypes and the relationship between masculinity and femininity: A developmental analysis. *Journal of Personality and Social Psychology, 61,* 351–365.

Bigelow, B. J. (1977). Children's friendship expectations: A cognitive-developmental study. *Child Development, 48,* 246–253.

Bigelow, B. J., & LaGaipa, J. J. (1975). Children's written descriptions of friendship: A multidimensional analysis. *Developmental Psychology, 11,* 857–858.

Bigler, R. S. (1995). The role of classification skill in moderating environmental influences on children's gender stereotyping: A study of the functional use of gender in the classroom. *Child Development, 66,* 1072–1087.

Bigler, R. S., & Liben, L. S. (1992). Cognitive mechanisms in children's gender stereotyping: Theoretical and educational implications of a cognitive-based intervention. *Child Development, 63,* 1351–1363.

Bigler, R. S., & Liben, L. S. (1993). A cognitive-developmental approach to racial stereotyping and reconstructive memory in Euro-American children. *Child Development, 64,* 1507–1518.

Bigner, J. J., & Jacobsen, R. B. (1989a). Parenting behaviors of homosexual and heterosexual fathers. *Journal of Homosexuality, 18,* 173–186.

Bigner, J. J., & Jacobsen, R. B. (1989b). The value of children to gay and straight fathers. *Journal of Homosexuality, 18,* 163–172.

Bijeljac-Babic, R., Bertoncini, J., & Mehler, J. (1993). How do 4-day-old infants categorize multisyllable utterances? *Developmental Psychology, 29,* 711–721.

Birch, E. E. (1993). Stereopsis in infants and its developmental relation to visual acuity. In K. Simons (Ed.), *Early visual development: Normal and abnormal* (pp. 224–236). New York: Oxford University Press.

Birch, L. L., & Fisher, J. A. (1995). Appetite and eating behavior in children. *Pediatric Clinics of North America, 42,* 931–953.

Birch, L. L., Zimmerman, S., & Hind, H. (1980). The influence of social-affective context on preschool children's food preferences. *Child Development, 51,* 856–861.

Birenbaum-Carmeli, D. (1995). Maternal smoking during pregnancy: Social, medical, and legal perspectives on the conception of a human being. *Health Care for Women International, 16,* 57–73.

Birnholz, J. C., & Benacerraf, B. R. (1983). The development of human fetal hearing. *Science, 222,* 516–518.

Bischof-Köhler, D. (1991). The development of empathy in infants. In M. E. Lamb & H. Keller (Eds.), *Infant development: Perspectives from German-speaking countries* (pp. 1–33). Hillsdale, NJ: Erlbaum.

Bischofshausen, S. (1985). Developmental differences in schema dependency for temporally ordered story events. *Journal of Psycholinguistic Research, 14,* 543–556.

Bishop, S. M., & Ingersoll, G. M. (1989). Effects of marital conflict and family structure on the self-concepts of pre- and early adolescents. *Journal of Youth and Adolescence, 18,* 25–38.

Bivens, J. A., & Berk, L. E. (1990). A longitudinal study of the development of elementary school children's private speech. *Merrill-Palmer Quarterly, 36,* 443–463.

Bjorklund, D. F. (1995). *Children's thinking: Developmental function and individual differences* (2nd ed.). Pacific Grove, CA: Brooks/Cole.

Bjorklund, D. F., & Coyle, T. R. (1995). Utilization deficiencies in the development of memory strategies. In F. E. Weinert & W. Schneider (Eds.), *Research on memory development: State of the art and future directions* (pp. xxx–xxx). Hillsdale, NJ: Erlbaum.

Bjorklund, D. F., & Harnishfeger, K. K. (1987). Developmental differences in the mental effort requirements for the use of an organizational strategy in free recall. *Journal of Experimental Child Psychology, 44,* 109–125.

Bjorklund, D. F., & Jacobs, J. W. (1985). Associative and categorical processes in children's memory: The role of automaticity in the development of organization in free recall. *Journal of Experimental Child Psychology, 39,* 599–617.

Bjorklund, D. F., & Muir, J. E. (1988). Children's development of free recall: Remembering on their own. In R. Vasta (Ed.), *Annals of child development* (Vol. 5, pp. 79–123). Greenwich, CT: JAI Press.

Bjorklund, D. F., Schneider, W., Cassel, W. S., & Ashley, E. (1994). Training and extension of a memory strategy: Evidence for utilization deficiencies in high- and low-IQ children. *Child Development, 65,* 951–965.

Black, B., & Logan, A. (1995). Links between communication patterns in mother–child, father–child, and child–peer interactions and children's social status. *Child Development, 66,* 255–271.

Blake, I. K. (1994). Language development and socialization in young African-American children. In P. M. Greenfield & R. R. Cocking (Eds.), *Cross-cultural roots of minority child development* (pp. 167–195). Hillsdale, NJ: Erlbaum.

Blake, J. (1989). *Family size and achievement.* Berkeley: University of California Press.

Blake, J., & Boysson-Bardies, B. de (1992). Patterns in babbling: A cross-linguistic study. *Journal of Child Language, 19,* 51–74.

Blanchard, M., & Main, M. (1979). Avoidance of the attachment figure and social-emotional adjustment in day-care infants. *Developmental Psychology, 15,* 445–446.

Blanchard, R., Zucker, K. J., Bradley, S. J., & Hume, C. S. (1995). Birth order and sibling sex ratio in homosexual male adolescents and probably prehomosexual feminine boys. *Developmental Psychology, 31,* 22–30.

Blanck, G. (1990). Vygotsky: The man and his cause. In L. C. Moll (Ed.), *Vygotsky and education* (pp. 31–58). New York: Cambridge University Press.

Blasi, A. (1990). Kohlberg's theory and moral motivation. In D. Schrader (Ed.), *New directions for child development* (No. 47, pp. 51–57). San Francisco: Jossey-Bass.

Blass, E. M., & Ciaramitaro, V. (1994). A new look at some old mechanisms in human newborns: Taste and tactile determinants of state, affect, and action. *Monographs of the Society for Research in Child Development, 59*(1, Serial No. 239).

Blass, E. M., Ganchrow, J. R., & Steiner, J. E. (1984). Classical conditioning in newborn humans 2–48 hours of age. *Infant Behavior and Development, 7,* 223–235.

Blatchford, P., & Mortimore, P. (1994). The issue of class size for young children in schools: What can we learn from research? *Oxford Review of Education, 20,* 411–428.

Blatt, M., & Kohlberg, L. (1975). The effects of classroom moral discussion upon children's level of moral judgment. *Journal of Moral Education, 4,* 129–161.

Blaubergs, M. S. (1980, March). Sex-role stereotyping and gifted girls' experience and education. *Roeper Review, 2*(3), 13–15.

Blewitt, P. (1994). Understanding categorical hierarchies: The earliest levels of skill. *Child Development, 65,* 1279–1298.

Block, G., & Abrams, B. (1993). Vitamin and mineral status of women of childbearing potential. *Annals of the New York Academy of Sciences, 678,* 255–265.

Block, J. (1971). *Lives through time.* Berkeley, CA: Bancroft Books.

Block, J. H. (1973). Conceptions of sex role: Some cross-cultural and longitudinal perspectives. *American Psychologist, 28,* 512–526.

Block, J. H. (1976). Issues, problems, and pitfalls in assessing sex differences: A critical review of "The Psychology of Sex Differences." *Merrill-Palmer Quarterly, 22,* 283–308.

Block, J. H. (1978). Another look at sex differentiation in the socialization behaviors of mothers and fathers. In J. Sherman & F. L. Denmark (Eds.), *Psychology of women: Future directions for research* (pp. 29–87). New York: Psychological Dimensions.

Block, J. H. (1983). Differential premises arising from differential socialization of the sexes: Some conjectures. *Child Development, 54,* 1335–1354.

Block, J., Block, J. H., & Gjerde, P. F. (1988). Parental functioning and home environment in families of divorce: Prospective and concurrent analyses. Journal of the American Academy of Child and Adolescent Psychiatry, 27, 207–213.

Block, J. H., Block, J., & Harrington, D. (1975). *Sex role typing and instrumental behavior: A developmental study.* Paper presented at the annual meeting of the Society for Research in Child Development, Denver.

Block, J., & Robins, R. W. (1994). A longitudinal study of consistency and change in self-esteem from early adolescence to early adulthood. *Child Development, 64,* 909–923.

Bloom, B. S. (Ed.). (1985). *Developing talent in young people.* New York: Ballantine.

Bloom, L. (1970). *Language development: Form and function in emerging grammars.* Cambridge, MA: MIT Press.

Bloom, L. (1990). Developments in expression: Affect and speech. In N. Stein & T. Trabasso (Eds.), *Psychological and biological approaches to emotion* (pp. 215–245). Hillsdale, NJ: Erlbaum.

Bloom, L., Lahey, M., Liften, K., & Fiess, K. (1980). Complex sentences: Acquisition of syntactic connections and the semantic relations they encode. *Journal of Child Language, 7,* 235–256.

Blotner, R., & Bearison, D. J. (1984). Developmental consistencies in socio-moral knowledge: Justice reasoning and altruistic behavior. *Merrill-Palmer Quarterly, 30,* 349–367.

Blumstein, S. E. (1995). *The neurobiology of language.* San Diego: Academic Press.

Blyth, D. A., Hill, J., & Thiel, K. (1982). Early adolescents' significant others: Grade and gender differences in perceived relationships with familial and nonfamilial adults and young people. *Journal of Youth and Adolescence, 11,* 425–450.

Blyth, D. A., Simmons, R. G., & Zakin, D. F. (1985). Satisfaction with body image for early adolescent females: The impact of pubertal timing within different school environments. *Journal of Youth and Adolescence, 14,* 207–225.

Bodrova, E. & Leong, D. J. (1996). *Tools of the mind: The Vygotskian approach to early childhood education.* Englewood Cliffs, NJ: Merrill.

Boer, F., Goedhart, A. W., & Treffers, P. D. A. (1992). Siblings and their parents. In F. Boer & J. Dunn (Eds.), *Children's sibling relationships* (pp. 41–54). Hillsdale, NJ: Erlbaum.

Bogatz, G. A., & Ball, S. (1972). *The second year of "Sesame Street": A continuing evaluation.* Princeton, NJ: Educational Testing Service.

Bohannon, J. N., III. (1993). Theoretical approaches to language acquisition. In J. Berko Gleason (Ed.), *The development of language* (3rd ed., pp. 239–297). New York: Macmillan.

Bohannon, J. N., III, & Stanowicz, L. (1988). The issue of negative evidence: Adult responses to children's language errors. *Developmental Psychology, 24,* 684–689.

Bohannon, J. N., III, & Symons, V. (1988, April). *Conversational conditions of children's imitation.* Paper presented at the biennial Conference on Human Development, Charleston, SC.

Bohman, M., & Sigvardsson, S. (1990). Outcome in adoption: Lessons from longitudinal studies. D. M. Bordzkinsky & M. D. Schechter (Eds.), *The psychology of adoption* (pp. 93–106). New York: Oxford University Press.

Boismier, J. D. (1977). Visual stimulation and wake–sleep behavior in human neonates. *Developmental Psychobiology, 10,* 219–227.

Boldizar, J. P. (1991). Assessing sex typing and androgyny in children: The children's sex role inventory. *Developmental Psychology, 27,* 505–515.

Boldizar, J. P., Perry, D. G., & Perry, L. C. (1989). Outcome values and aggression. *Child Development, 60,* 571–579.

Bonvillian, J., Nelson, K. E., & Charrow, V. (1976). Language and language-related skills in deaf and hearing children. *Sign Language Studies, 12,* 211–250.

Booth, C. L., Rose-Krasnor, L., & Rubin, K. H. (1991). Relating preschoolers' social competence and their mothers' parenting behaviors to early attachment security and high-risk status. *Journal of Social and Personal Relationships, 8,* 363–382.

Borja-Alvarez, T., Zarbatany, L., & Pepper, S. (1991). Contributions of male and female guests and hosts to peer group entry. *Child Development, 62,* 1079–1090.

Borke, H. (1975). Piaget's mountains revisited: Changes in the egocentric landscape. *Developmental Psychology, 11,* 240–243.

Borkowski, J. G., Carr, M., Rellinger, E., & Pressley, M. (1990). Self-regulated cognition: Interdependence of metacognition, attributions, and self-esteem. In B. Jones & L. Idol (Eds.), *Dimensions of thinking and cognitive instruction* (pp. 53–92). Hillsdale, NJ: Erlbaum.

Bornholt, L. J., Goodnow, J. J., & Cooney, G. H. (1994). Influences of gender stereotypes on adolescents' perceptions of their own achievement. *American Educational Research Journal, 31,* 675–692.

Bornstein, M. H. (1989). Sensitive periods in development: Structural characteristics and causal interpretations. *Psychological Bulletin, 105,* 179–197.

Bornstein, M. H. (1992). Perception across the life span. In M. H. Bornstein & M. E. Lamb (Eds.), *Developmental psychology: An advanced textbook* (pp. 155–209). Hillsdale, NJ: Erlbaum.

Bornstein, M. H., Kessen, W., & Weiskopf, S. (1976). The categories of hue in infancy. *Science, 191,* 201–202.

Bornstein, M. H., & Lamb, M. E. (1992). *Development in infancy: An introduction* (3rd ed.). New York: McGraw-Hill.

Bornstein, M. H., Tal, J., Rahn, C., Galperín, C. Z., Pêcheux, M., Lamour, M., Toda, S., Azuma, H., Ogino, M., & Tamis-LeMonda, C. S. (1992a). Functional analysis of the contents of maternal speech to infants of 5 and 13 months in four cultures: Argentina, France, Japan, and the United States. *Developmental Psychology, 28,* 593–603.

Bornstein, M. H., Vibbert, M., Tal, J., & O'Donnell, K. (1992b). Toddler language and play in the second year: Stability, covariation, and influences of parenting. *First Language, 12,* 323–338.

Borrine, M. L., Handal, P. J., Brown, N. Y., & Searight, H. R. (1991). Family conflict and adolescent adjustment in intact, divorced, and blended families. *Journal of Consulting and Clinical Psychology, 59,* 753–755.

Borstelmann, L. J. (1983). Children before psychology: Ideas about children from antiquity to the late 1800s. In W. Kessen (Ed.), *Handbook of child psychology: Vol. 1. History, theory, and methods* (4th ed., pp. 1–40). New York: Wiley.

Bostock, C. (1994). Does the expansion of grandparent visitation rights promote the best interests of the child?: A survey of grandparent visitation laws in fifty states. *Columbia Journal of Law and Social Problems, 27,* 319–373.

Bouchard, C. (1994). *The genetics of obesity.* Boca Raton, FL: CRC Press.

Bouchard, T. J., Jr., Lykken, D. T., McGue, M., Segal, N. L., & Tellegen, A. (1990). Sources of human psychological differences: The Minnesota Study of Twins Reared Apart. *Science, 250,* 223–228.

Bouchard, T. J., Jr., & McGue, M. (1981). Familial studies of intelligence: A review. *Science, 212,* 1055–1058.

Bouchard, T. J., Jr., & Segal, N. L. (1985). Environment and IQ. In B. B. Wolman (Ed.), *Handbook of intelligence* (pp. 391–464). New York: Wiley.

Boukydis, C. F. Z. (1985). Perception of infant crying as an interpersonal event. In B. M. Lester & C. F. Z. Boukydis (Eds.), *Infant crying* (pp. 187–215). New York: Plenum.

Boukydis, C. F. Z., & Burgess, R. L. (1982). Adult physiological response to infant cries: Effects of temperament of infant, parental status and gender. *Child Development, 53,* 1291–1298.

Boulton, M. J., & Smith, P. K. (1994). Bully/victim problems in middle-school children: Stability, self-perceived competence, peer perceptions and peer acceptance. *British Journal of Developmental Psychology, 12,* 315–329.

Bower, C., & Stanley, F. J. (1992). Periconceptional vitamin supplementation and neural tube defects: Evidence from a case-control study in Western Australia and a review of recent publications. *Journal of Epidemiological and Community Health, 46,* 157–162.

Bowerman, M. (1973). *Early syntactic development: A cross-linguistic study with special reference to Finnish.* Cambridge: Cambridge University Press.

Bowerman, M. (1989). Learning a semantic system: What role do cognitive predispositions play? In M. Rice & R. Schiefelbusch (Eds.), *The teachability of language* (pp. 133–170). Baltimore: Paul H. Brookes.

Bowlby, J. (1969). *Attachment and loss: Vol. 1. Attachment.* New York: Basic Books.

Bowlby, J. (1980). *Attachment and loss: Vol. 3. Loss.* New York: Basic Books.

Boyer, K., & Diamond, A. (1992). Development of memory for temporal order in infants and young children. In A. Diamond (Ed.), *Development and neural bases of higher cognitive function* (pp. 267–317). New York: New York Academy of Sciences.

Boyes, M. C., & Allen, S. G. (1993). Styles of parent–child interaction and moral reasoning in adolescence. *Merrill-Palmer Quarterly, 39,* 551–570.

Boyes, M. C., & Chandler, M. (1992). Cognitive development, epistemic doubt, and identity formation in adolescence. *Journal of Youth and Adolescence, 21,* 277–304.

Boysson-Bardies, B. de, & Vihman, M. M. (1991). Adaptation to language: Evidence from babbling and first words in four languages. *Language, 67,* 297–319.

Brabeck, M. (1983). Moral judgment: Theory and research on differences between males and females. *Developmental Review, 3,* 274–291.

Bracey, G. W. (1996). International comparisons and the condition of American education. *Educational Researcher, 25*(1), 5–11.

Brackbill, Y., McManus, K., & Woodward, L. (1985). *Medication in maternity: Infant exposure and maternal information.* Ann Arbor: University of Michigan Press.

Brackbill, Y., & Nichols, P. L. (1982). A test of the confluence model of intellectual development. *Developmental Psychology, 18,* 192–198.

Braddick, O. (1993). Orientation and motion-selective mechanisms in infants. In K. Simons (Ed.), *Early visual development: Normal and abnormal* (pp. 163–177). New York: Oxford University Press.

Bradley, R. H., & Caldwell, B. M. (1976). The relation of infants' home environments to mental test performance at fifty-four months: A follow-up study. *Child Development, 47,* 1172–1174.

Bradley, R. H., & Caldwell, B. M. (1979). Home Observation for Measurement of the Environment: A revision of the preschool scale. *American Journal of Mental Deficiency, 84,* 235–244.

Bradley, R. H., & Caldwell, B. M. (1981). The HOME Inventory: A validation of the preschool scale for black children. *Child Development, 52,* 708–710.

Bradley, R. H., & Caldwell, B. M. (1982). The consistency of the home environment and its relation to child development. *International Journal of Behavioral Development, 5,* 445–465.

Bradley, R. H., Caldwell, B. M., & Rock, S. L. (1988). Home environment and school performance: A ten-year follow-up and examination of three models of environmental action. *Child Development, 59,* 852–867.

Bradley, R. H., Caldwell, B. M., Rock, S. L., Hamrick, H. M., & Harris, P. (1988). Home Observation for Measurement of the Environment: Development of a home inventory for use with families having children 6 to 10 years old. *Contemporary Educational Psychology, 13,* 58–71.

Bradley, R. H., Caldwell, B. M., Rock, S. L., Ramey, C. T., Barnard, K. E., Gray, C., Hammond, M. A., Mitchell, S., Gottfried, A., Siegel, L., & Johnson, D. L. (1989). Home environment and cognitive development in the first 3 years of life: A collaborative study involving six sites and three ethnic groups in North America. *Developmental Psychology, 25,* 217–235.

Bradley, R. H., Whiteside, L., Mundfrom, D. J., Casey, P. H., Kelleher, K. J., & Pope, S. K. (1994). Contribution of early intervention and early caregiving experiences to resilience in low-birthweight, premature children living in poverty. *Journal of Clinical Child Psychology, 23,* 425–434.

Braine, L. G., Schauble, L., Kugelmass, S., & Winter, A. (1993). Representation of depth by children: Spatial strategies and lateral biases. *Developmental Psychology, 29,* 466–479.

Braine, M. D. S. (1976). Children's first word combinations. *Monographs of the Society for Research in Child Development, 41*(1, Serial No. 164).

Braine, M. D. S. (1992). What sort of innate structure is needed to "bootstrap" into syntax? *Cognition, 45,* 77–100.

Brainerd, C. J. (1978). *Piaget's theory of intelligence.* Englewood Cliffs, NJ: Prentice-Hall.

Brainerd, C. J., & Gordon, L. L. (1994). Development of verbatim and gist memory for numbers. *Developmental Psychology, 30,* 163–177.

Brainerd, C. J., & Reyna, V. F. (1990). Gist is the grist: Fuzzy-trace theory and the new intuitionism. *Developmental Review, 10,* 3–47.

Brainerd, C. J., & Reyna, V. F. (1993). Memory independence and memory interference in cognitive development. *Psychological Review, 100,* 42–67.

Brainerd, C. J., & Reyna, V. F. (1995). Learning rate, learning opportunities, and the development of forgetting. *Developmental Psychology, 31,* 251–262.

Brand, E., Clingempeel, W. E., & Bowen-Woodward, K. (1988). Family relationships and children's psychological adjustment in stepmother and stepfather families: Findings and conclusions from the Philadelphia Stepfamily Research Project. In E. M. Hetherington & J. D. Arasteh (Eds.), *Impact of divorce, single parenting, and stepparenting on children* (pp. 299–324). Hillsdale, NJ: Erlbaum.

Brandt, L. P. A., & Nielsen, C. V. (1992). Job stress and adverse outcome of pregnancy: A causal link or recall bias? *American Journal of Epidemiology, 135,* 302–311.

Bransford, J. D., Stein, B. S., Shelton, T. S., & Owings, R. A. (1981). Cognition and adaptation: The importance of learning to learn. In J. Harvey (Ed.), *Cognition, social behavior, and the environment* (pp. 93–110). Hillsdale, NJ: Erlbaum.

Braungart, J. M., Fulker, D. W., & Plomin, R. (1992). Genetic mediation of the home environment during infancy: A sibling adoption study of the HOME. *Developmental Psychology, 28,* 1048–1055.

Braungart, J. M., Plomin, R., DeFries, J. C., & Fulker, D. W. (1992). Genetic influence on tester-rated infant temperament as assessed by Bayley's Infant Behavior Record: Nonadoptive and adoptive siblings and twins. *Developmental Psychology, 28,* 40–47.

Braverman, P. K., & Strasburger, V. C. (1993). Adolescent sexual activity. *Clinical Pediatrics, 32,* 658–668.

Braverman, P. K., & Strasburger, V. C. (1994). Sexually transmitted diseases. *Clinical Pediatrics, 33,* 26–37.

Bray, J. H., & Berger, S. H. (1993). Developmental issues in Stepfamilies Research Project: Family relationships and parent–child interactions. *Journal of Family Psychology, 7,* 7–17.

Brazelton, T. B. (1984). *Neonatal Behavioral Assessment Scale.* Philadelphia: Lippincott.

Brazelton, T. B., Koslowski, B., & Tronick, E. Z. (1976). Neonatal behavior among urban Zambians and Americans. *Journal of the American Academy of Child Psychiatry, 15,* 97–107.

Brazelton, T. B., Nugent, J. K., & Lester, B. M. (1987). Neonatal Behavioral Assessment Scale. In J. D. Osofsky (Ed.), *Handbook of infant development* (2nd ed., pp. 780–817). New York: Wiley.

Bread for the World Institute. (1994). *Hunger 1994.* Silver Spring, MD: Author.

Brenes, M. E., Eisenberg, N., & Helmstadter, G. C. (1985). Sex role development of preschoolers from two-parent and one-parent families. *Merrill-Palmer Quarterly, 31,* 33–46.

Brennan, W. M., Ames, E. W., & Moore, R. W. (1966). Age differences in infants' attention to patterns of different complexities. *Science, 151,* 354–356.

Brenner, D., & Hinsdale, G. (1978). Body build stereotypes and self-identification in three age groups of females. *Adolescence, 13,* 551–562.

Bretherton, I. (1992). The origins of attachment theory: John Bowlby and Mary Ainsworth. *Developmental Psychology, 28,* 759–775.

Bretherton, I., Fritz, J., Zahn-Waxler, C., & Ridgeway, D. (1986). Learning to talk about emotions: A functionalist perspective. *Child Development, 57,* 529–548.

Briere, J. N. (1992). *Child abuse trauma.* Newbury Park, CA: Sage.

Broberg, A., Lamb, M. E., & Hwang, P. (1990). Inhibition: Its stability and correlates in 16- to 40-month-old children. *Child Development, 61,* 1153–1163.

Brody, G. H., Graziano, W. G., & Musser, L. M. (1983). Familiarity and children's behavior in same-age and mixed-age peer groups. *Developmental Psychology, 19,* 568–576.

Brody, G. H., Stoneman, Z., & McCoy, J. K. (1992). Associations of maternal and paternal direct and differential behavior with sibling relationships: Contemporaneous and longitudinal analyses. *Child Development, 63,* 82–92.

Brody, G. H., Stoneman, Z., & McCoy, J. K. (1994). Forecasting sibling relationships in early adolescence from child temperaments and family processes in middle childhood. *Child Development, 65,* 771–784.

Brody, G. H., Stoneman, Z., McCoy, J. K., &Forehand, R. (1992). Contemporaneous and longitudinal associations of sibling conflict with family relationship assessments and family discussions about sibling problems. *Child Development, 63,* 391–400.

Brody, L. R., & Hall, J. A. (1993). Gender and emotion. In M. Lewis & J. M. Haviland (Eds.), *Handbook of emotions* (pp. 447–460). New York: Guilford.

Brody, N. (1987). Jensen, Gottfredson, and the black–white difference in intelligence test scores. *Behavioral and Brain Sciences, 10,* 507–508.

Brody, N. (1992). *Intelligence* (2nd ed.). San Diego: Academic Press.

Brody, N. (1994). Psychometric theories of intelligence. In R. J. Sternberg (Ed.), *Encyclopedia of human intelligence* (pp. 868–875). New York: Macmillan.

Broman, S. H. (1983). Obstetric medications. In C. C. Brown (Ed.), *Childhood learning disabilities and prenatal risk* (pp. 56–64). New York: Johnson & Johnson.

Bronfenbrenner, U. (1979). *The ecology of human development: Experiments by nature and design.* Cambridge, MA: Harvard University Press.

Bronfenbrenner, U. (1989). Ecological systems theory. In R. Vasta (Ed.), *Annals of child development* (Vol. 6, pp. 187–251). Greenwich, CT: JAI Press.

Bronfenbrenner, U. (1993). The ecology of cognitive development: Research models and fugitive findings. In. R. H. Wozniak & K. W. Fischer (Eds.), *Development in context* (pp. 3–44). Hillsdale, NJ: Erlbaum.

Bronfenbrenner, U. (1995). The bioecological model from a life course perspective: Reflections of a participant observer. In P. Moen, G. H. Elder, Jr., & K. Lüscher (Eds.), *Examining lives in context* (pp. 599–618). Washington, DC: American Psychological Association.

Bronfenbrenner, U., & Ceci, S. J. (1994). Nature–nurture reconceptualized in developmental perspective: A bioecological model. *Psychological Review, 101,* 568–586.

Bronfenbrenner, U., & Crouter, A. C. (1983). The evolution of environmental models in developmental research. In W. Kessen (Ed.), *Handbook of child psychology: Vol. 1. History, theory and methods* (pp. 357–476). New York: Wiley.

Bronfenbrenner, U., & Neville, P. R. (1995). America's children and families: An international perspective. In S. L. Kagan & B. Weissbourd (Eds.), *Putting families first* (pp. 3–27). San Francisco: Jossey-Bass.

Bronson, G. W. (1991). Infant differences in rate of visual encoding. *Child Development, 62,* 44–54.

Bronson, W. C. (1981). *Toddlers' behaviors with agemates: Issues of interaction, cognition,* and affect. Norwood, NJ: Ablex.

Brooks, J., & Lewis, M. (1976). Infants' responses to strangers: Midget, adult, and child. *Child Development, 47,* 323–332.

Brooks-Gunn, J. (1986). The relationship of maternal beliefs about sex typing to maternal and young children's behavior. *Sex Roles, 14,* 21–35.

Brooks-Gunn, J. (1988a). Antecedents and consequences of variations in girls' maturational timing. *Journal of Adolescent Health Care, 9,* 365–373.

Brooks-Gunn, J. (1988b). The impact of puberty and sexual activity upon the health and education of adolescent girls and boys. *Peabody Journal of Education, 64,* 88–113.

Brooks-Gunn, J., McCarton, C. M., Casey, P. H., McCormick, M. C., Bauer, C. R., Bernbaum, J. C., Tyson, J., Swanson, M., Bennett, F. C., Scott, D. T., Tonascia, J., & Meinert, C. L. (1994). Early intervention in low-birth-weight premature infants. *Journal of the American Medical Association, 272,* 1257–1262.

Brooks-Gunn, J., & Reiter, E. O. (1990). The role of pubertal processes in the early adolescent transition. In S. Feldman & G. Elliott (Eds.), *At the threshold: The developing adolescent* (pp. 16–53). Cambridge, MA: Harvard University Press.

Brooks-Gunn, J., & Ruble, D. N. (1980). Menarche: The interaction of physiology, cultural, and social factors. In A. J. Dan, E. A. Graham, & C. P. Beecher (Eds.), *The menstrual cycle: A synthesis of interdisciplinary research* (pp. 141–159). New York: Springer-Verlag.

Brooks-Gunn, J., & Ruble, D. N. (1983). The experience of menarche from a developmental perspective. In J. Brooks-Gunn & A. C. Peterson (Eds.), *Girls at puberty* (pp. 155–177). New York: Plenum.

Brooks-Gunn, J., & Warren, M. P. (1989). Biological and social contributions to negative affect in young adolescent girls. *Child Development, 60,* 40–55.

Brooks-Gunn, J., Warren, M. P., Samelson, M., & Fox, R. (1986). Physical similarity of and disclosure of menarcheal status to friends: Effects of grade and pubertal status. *Journal of Early Adolescence, 6,* 3–14.

Brophy, J. E. (1983). Research on the self-fulfilling prophecy and teacher expectations. *Journal of Educational Psychology, 75,* 631–661.

Brophy, J. E., & Good, T. L. (1986). Teacher behavior and student achievement. In M. C. Wittrock (Ed.), *Handbook of research on teaching* (3rd ed., pp. 328–375). New York: Macmillan.

Brown, A. L., & Campione, J. C. (1972). Recognition memory for perceptually similar pictures in preschool children. *Journal of Experimental Psychology, 95,* 55–62.

Brown, A. L., & Ferrara, R. A. (1985). Diagnosing zones of proximal development. In J. Wertsch (Ed.), *Culture, communication, and cognition* (pp. 273–305). New York: Cambridge University Press.

Brown, A. L., Bransford, J. D., Ferrara, R. A., & Campione, J. C. (1983). Learning, remembering and understanding. In J. H. Flavell & E. M. Markman (Eds.), *Handbook of child psychology: Vol. 3. Cognitive development* (4th ed., pp. 77–166). New York: Wiley.

Brown, A. L., Smiley, S. S., Day, J. D., Townsend, M., & Lawton, S. Q. C. (1977). Intrusion of a thematic idea in children's recall of prose. *Child Development, 48,* 1454–1466.

Brown, A. L., Smiley, S. S., & Lawton, S. Q. C. (1978). The effects of experience on the selection of suitable retrieval cues for studying texts. *Child Development, 49,* 829–835.

Brown, A. M. (1990). Development of visual sensitivity to light and color vision in human infants: A critical review. *Vision Research, 30,* 1159–1188.

Brown, B. (1990). Peer groups. In S. Feldman & G. Elliott (Eds.), *At the threshold: The developing adolescent* (pp. 171–196). Cambridge, MA: Cambridge University Press.

Brown, B. B., Clasen, D., & Eicher, S. (1986). Perceptions of peer pressure, peer conformity dispositions, and self-reported behavior among adolescents. *Developmental Psychology, 22,* 521–530.

Brown, B. B., Lohr, M. J., & McClenahan, E. L. (1986). Early adolescents' perceptions of peer pressure. *Journal of Early Adolescence, 6,* 139–154.

Brown, J. R., & Dunn, J. (1992). Talk with your mother or your sibling? Developmental changes in early family conversations about feelings. *Child Development, 63,* 336–349.

Brown, R. (1973). *A first language: The early stages.* Cambridge, MA: Harvard University Press.

Brown, R., & Hanlon, C. (1970). Derivational complexity and order of acquisition in child speech. In J. R. Hayes (Ed.), *Cognition and the development of language* (pp. 11–53). New York: Wiley.

Brownell, C. A., & Carriger, M. S. (1990). Changes in cooperation and self-other differentiation during the second year. *Child Development, 61,* 1164–1174.

Bruck, M., Ceci, S. J., Francouer, E., & Renick, A. (1995). Anatomically detailed dolls do not facilitate preschoolers' reports of a pediatric examination involving genital touching. *Journal of Experimental Psychology: Applied, 1,* 95–109.

Bruner, J. S. (1983). *Child's talk: Learning to use language.* Oxford: Oxford University Press.

Buchanan, C. M., Eccles, J. S., & Becker, J. B. (1992). Are adolescents the victims of raging hormones? Evidence for activational effects of hormones on moods and behavior at adolescence. *Psychological Bulletin, 111,* 62–107.

Buchanan, C. M., Maccoby, E. E., & Dornbusch, S. M. (1991). Caught between parents: Adolescents' experience in divorced homes. *Child Development, 62,* 1008–1029.

Buck, G. M., Cookfair, D. L., Michalek, A. M., Nasca, P. C., Standfast, S. J., Sever, L. E., & Kramer, A. A. (1989). Intrauterine growth retardation and risk of sudden infant death syndrome (SIDS). *American Journal of Epidemiology, 129,* 874–884.

Bugental, D. B., Blue, J., Cortez, V., Fleck, K., & Rodriquez, A. (1992). Influences of a witnessed affect of information processing in children. *Child Development, 63,* 774–786.

Bugental, D. B., Blue, J., & Cruzcosa, M. (1989). Perceived control over caregiving outcomes: Implications for child abuse. Developmental Psychology, 25, 532–539.

Buhrmester, D., & Furman, W. (1987). The development of companionship and intimacy. *Child Development, 58,* 1101–1115.

Buhrmester, D., & Furman, W. (1990). Perceptions of sibling relationships during middle childhood and adolescence. *Child Development, 61,* 1387–1398.

Bullock, D., & Merrill, L. (1980). The impact of personal preference on consistency through time: The case of childhood aggression. *Child Development, 51,* 808–814.

Bullock, M., & Lutkenhaus, P. (1990). Who am I? The development of self-understanding in toddlers. *Merrill-Palmer Quarterly, 36,* 217–238.

Bumpass, L. L., Raley, R. K., & Sweet, J. A. (1995). The changing character of stepfamilies: Implications of cohabitation and nonmarital childbearing. *Demography, 32,* 425–436.

Burhans, K. K., & Dweck, C. S. (1995). Helplessness in early childhood: The role of contingent worth. *Child Development, 66,* 1719–1738.

Burkett, G., Yasin, S. Y., Palow, D., LaVoie, L., & Martinez, M. (1994). Patterns of cocaine binging: Effect on pregnancy. *American Journal of Obstetrics and Gynecology, 171,* 372–379.

Burkhardt, S. A., & Rotatori, A. F. (1995). *Treatment and prevention of childhood sexual abuse.* Washington, DC: Taylor & Francis.

Burns, S. M., & Brainerd, C. J. (1979). Effects of constructive and dramatic play on perspective taking in very young children. *Developmental Psychology, 15,* 512–521.

Burton, B. K. (1992). Limb anomalies associated with chorionic villus sampling. *Obstetrics and Gynecology, 79* (Pt. 1), 726–730.

Bushnell, E. W. (1985). The decline of visually guided reaching during infancy. *Infant Behavior and Development, 8,* 139–155.

Bushnell, E. W., & Boudreau, J. P. (1993). Motor development and the mind: The potential role of motor abilities as a determinant of aspects of perceptual development. *Child Development, 64,* 1005–1021.

Buss, A. H., & Plomin, R. (1984). *Temperament: Early developing personality traits.* Hillsdale, NJ: Erlbaum.

Bussey, K. (1992). Lying and truthfulness: Children's definitions, standards, and evaluative reactions. *Child Development, 63,* 129–137.

Bussey, K., & Bandura, A. (1984). Influence of gender constancy and social power on sex-linked modeling. *Journal of Personality and Social Psychology, 47,* 1292–1302.

Bussey, K., & Bandura, A. (1992). Self-regulatory mechanisms governing gender development. *Child Development, 63,* 1236–1250.

Butler, G. E., McKie, M., & Ratcliffe, S. G. (1990). The cyclical nature of prepubertal growth. *Annals of Human Biology, 17,* 177–198.

Butler, R., & Ruzany, N. (1993). Age and socialization effects on the development of social comparison motives and normative ability assessment in kibbutz and urban children. *Child Development, 64,* 532–543.

Bybee, J., & Slobin, D. (1982). Rules and schemes in the development and use of the English past tense. *Language, 58,* 265–289.

Byrd, D. M., & Gholson, B. (1985). Reading, memory, and metacognition. *Journal of Educational Psychology, 77,* 428–436.

Byrne, D. F. (1973). The development of role taking in adolescence. Dissertation *Abstracts International, 34,* 56478. (University Microfilms No. 74–11, 314).

C

Cadoff, J. (1995, March). Can we prevent SIDS? *Parents, 70*(3), 30–31, 35.

Cain, K. M., & Dweck, C. S. (1995). The relation between motivational patterns and achievement cognitions through the elementary school years. *Merrill-Palmer Quarterly, 41,* 25–52.

Cain, V. S., & Hofferth, S. L. (1989). Parental choice of self-care for school-age children. *Journal of Marriage and the Family, 51,* 65–77.

Caine, N. (1986). Behavior during puberty and adolescence. In G. Mitchell & J. Erwin (Eds.), *Comparative primate biology: Vol. 2A. Behavior, conservation, and ecology* (pp. 327–361). New York: Alan R. Liss.

Cairns, E. (1996). *Children and political violence.* Cambridge: Blackwell.

Cairns, R. B. (1983). The emergence of developmental psychology. In W. Kessen (Ed.), *Handbook of child psychology: Vol. 1. History, theory, and methods* (4th ed., pp. 41–102). New York: Wiley.

Cairns, R. B. (1992). The making of a developmental science: The contributions and intellectual heritage of James Mark Baldwin. *Developmental Psychology, 28,* 17–24.

Cairns, R. B., Cairns, B. D., Neckerman, H. J., Ferguson, L. L., & Gariépy, J-L. (1989). Growth and aggression: 1. Childhood to early adolescence. *Developmental Psychology, 25,* 320–330.

Cairns, R. B., Leung, M. C., Buchanan, L., & Cairns, B. D. (1995). Friendships and social networks in childhood and adolescence: Fluidity, reliability, and interrelations. *Child Development, 66,* 1330–1345.

Caldas, S. J. (1993). Current theoretical perspectives on adolescent pregnancy and childbearing in the United States. *Journal of Adolescent Research, 8,* 4–20.

Caldera, Y. M., Huston, A. C., & O'Brien, M. (1989). Social interactions and play patterns of parents and toddlers with feminine, masculine, and neutral toys. *Child Development, 60,* 70–76.

Caldwell, B. M., & Bradley, R. H. (1994). Environmental issues in developmental follow-up research. In S. L. Friedman & H. C. Haywood (Eds.), *Developmental follow-up* (pp. 235–256). San Diego: Academic Press.

Caliso, J., & Milner, J. (1992). Childhood history of abuse and child abuse screening. *Child Abuse and Neglect, 16,* 647–659.

Camara, K. A., & Resnick, G. (1988). Interparental conflict and cooperation: Factors moderating children's post-divorce adjustment. In E. M. Hetherington & J. D. Arasteh (Ed.), *Impact of divorce, single parenting, and step-parenting on children* (pp. 169–195). Hillsdale, NJ: Erlbaum.

Camarata, S., & Leonard, L. B. (1986). Young children pronounce object words more accurately than action words. *Journal of Child Language, 13,* 51–65.

Campbell, F. A., & Ramey, C. T. (1991). The Carolina Abecedarian Project. In M. Burchinal (Chair), *Early experience and children's competencies: New findings from four longitudinal studies.* Symposium presented at the biennial meeting of the Society for Research in Child Development, Seattle, WA.

Campbell, F. A., & Ramey, C. T. (1994). Effects of early intervention on intellectual and academic achievement: A follow-up study of children from low-income families. *Child Development, 65,* 684–698.

Campbell, P. F., & Schwartz, S. S. (1986). Microcomputers in the preschool: Children, parents, and teachers. In P. Campbell & G. Fein (Eds.), *Young children and microcomputers* (pp. 45–60). Englewood Cliffs, NJ: Prentice-Hall.

Campbell, R., & Sais, E. (1995). Accelerated metalinguistic (phonological) awareness in bilingual children. *British Journal of Developmental Psychology, 13,* 61–68.

Campbell, S. B., Cohn, J. F., & Meyers, T. (1995). Depression in first-time mothers: Mother–infant interaction and depression chronicity. *Developmental Psychology, 31,* 349–357.

Campos, J. J., & Bertenthal, B. I. (1989). Locomotion and psychological development. In F. Morrison, K. Lord, & D. Keating (Eds.), *Applied developmental psychology* (Vol. 3, pp. 229–258). New York: Academic Press.

Campos, J. J., Caplovitz, K. B., Lamb, M. E., Goldsmith, H. H., Stenberg, C. (1983). Socioemotional development. In M. M. Haith & J. J. Campos (Eds.), *Handbook of child psychology: Vol. 3. Infancy and developmental psychobiology* (pp. 783–915). New York: Wiley.

Campos, J. J., Kermoian, R., & Zumbahlen, M. R. (1992). Socioemotional transformation in the family system following infant crawling onset. In N. Eisenberg & R. A. Fabes (Eds.), *New directions for child development* (No. 55, pp. 25–40). San Francisco: Jossey-Bass.

Campos, R., Raffaelli, M., Ude, W., Greco, M., Ruff, A., Rolf, J., Antunes, C. M., Halsey, N., Greco, D., & Street Youth Study Group. (1994). Social networks and daily activities of street youth in Belo Horitzonte, Brazil. *Child Development, 65,* 319–330.

Campos, R. G. (1989). Soothing pain-elicited distress in infants with swaddling and pacifiers. *Child Development, 60,* 781–792.

Camras, L. A., Oster, H., Campos, J. J., Miyake, K., & Bradshaw, D. (1992). Japanese and American infants' responses to arm restraint. *Developmental Psychology, 28,* 578–583.

Camras, L. A., & Sachs, V. B. (1991). Social referencing and caretaker expressive behavior in a day care setting. *Infant Behavior and Development, 14,* 27–36.

Canfield, R. L., & Haith, M. M. (1991). Young infants' visual expectations for symmetric and asymmetric stimulus sequences. *Developmental Psychology, 27,* 198–208.

Canick, J. A., & Saller, D. N., Jr. (1993). Maternal serum screening for aneuploidy and open fetal defects. *Obstetrics and Gynecology Clinics of North America, 20,* 443–454.

Canter, R. J., & Ageton, S. S. (1984). The epidemiology of adolescent sex-role attitudes. *Sex Roles, 11,* 657–676.

Capaldi, D. M., & Patterson, G. R. (1991). Relation of parental transitions to boys' adjustment problems: I. A linear hypothesis. II. Mothers at risk for transitions and unskilled parenting. *Developmental Psychology, 27,* 489–504.

Capelli, C. A., Nakagawa, N., & Madden, C. M. (1990). How children understand sarcasm: The role of context and intonation. *Child Development, 61,* 1824–1841.

Caplan, M., Vespo, J., Pedersen, J., & Hay, D. F. (1991). Conflict and its resolution in small groups of one- and two-year-olds. *Child Development, 62,* 1513–1524.

Cardon, L. R., Fulker, D. W., DeFries, J. C., & Plomin, R. (1992). Continuity and change in general cognitive ability from 1 to 7 years of age. *Developmental Psychology, 28,* 64–73.

Carey, S. (1978). The child as word learner. In M. Halle, G. Miller, & J. Bresnan (Eds.), *Linguistic theory and psychological reality* (pp. 264–293). Cambridge, MA: MIT Press.

Carey, S., & Spelke, E. (1994). Domain-specific knowledge and conceptual change. In L. A. Hirschfeld & S. A. Gelman (Eds.), *Mapping the mind* (pp. 169–200). New York: Cambridge University Press.

Carlson, V., Cicchietti, D., Barnett, D., & Braunwald, K. (1989). Disorganized/disoriented attachment relationship in maltreated infants. *Child Development, 25,* 525–531.

Caron, A. J., Caron, R. F., & MacLean, D. J. (1988). Infant discrimination of naturalistic emotional expressions: The role of face and voice. *Child Development, 59,* 603–616.

Carpenter, C. J. (1983). Activity structure and play: Implications for socialization. In M. Liss (Ed.), *Social and cognitive skills: Sex roles and children's play* (pp. 117–145). New York: Academic Press.

Carpenter, C. J., Huston, A. C., & Holt, W. (1986). Modification of preschool sex-typed behaviors by participation in adult-structured activities. *Sex Roles, 14,* 603–615.

Carr, M., Borkowski, J. G., & Maxwell, S. E. (1991). Motivational components of underachievement. *Developmental Psychology, 27,* 108–118.

Carr, S., Dabbs, J., & Carr, T. (1975). Mother–infant attachment: The importance of the mother's visual field. *Child Development, 46,* 331–338.

Carr, M., & Schneider, W. (1991). Long-term maintenance of organizational strategies in kindergarten children. *Contemporary Educational Psychology, 16,* 61–75.

Carraher, T., Schliemann, A. D., & Carraher, D. W. (1988). Mathematical concepts in everyday life. In G. B. Saxe & M. Gearhart (Eds.), *New directions for child development* (Vol. 41, pp. 71–87). San Francisco: Jossey-Bass.

Carroll, J. B. (1993). *Human cognitive abilities: A survey of factor-analytic studies.* New York: Cambridge University Press.

Carruth, B. R., Goldberg, D. L., & Skinner, J. D. (1991). Do parents and peers mediate the influence of television advertising on food-related purchases? *Journal of Adolescent Research, 6,* 253–271.

Carter, D. B., & Levy, G. D. (1991). Gender schemas and the salience of gender: Individual differences in nonreversal discrimination learning. *Sex Roles, 25,* 555–567.

Carter, D. B., & Patterson, C. J. (1982). Sex roles as social conventions: The development of children's conceptions of sex-role stereotypes. *Developmental Psychology, 18,* 812–824.

Carter, K., Sabers, D., Cushing, K., Pinnegar, S., & Berliner, D. C. (1987). Processing and using information about students: A study of expert, novice, and postulant teachers. *Teaching & Teacher Education, 3,* 147–157.

Casaer, P. (1993). Old and new facts about perinatal brain development. *Journal of Child Psychology and Psychiatry, 34,* 101–109.

Case, R. (1977). Responsiveness to conservation training as a function of induced subjective uncertainty, M-space, and cognitive style. *Canadian Journal of Behavioral Sciences, 9,* 12–25.

Case, R. (1978). Intellectual development from birth to adulthood: A neo-Piagetian approach. In R. S. Siegler (Ed.), *Children's thinking: What develops?* (pp. 37–71). Hillsdale, NJ: Erlbaum.

Case, R. (1985). *Intellectual development: A systematic reinterpretation.* New York: Academic Press.

Case, R. (1992a). *The mind's staircase.* Hillsdale, NJ: Erlbaum.

Case, R. (1992b). The role of the frontal lobes in the regulation of cognitive development. *Brain and Cognition, 20,* 51–73.

Case, R., & Griffin, S. (1990). Child cognitive development: The role of central conceptual structures in the development of scientific and social thought. In C. A. Hauert (Ed.), *Developmental psychology: Cognitive, perceptuo-motor and neuropsychological perspectives* (pp. 193–230). Amsterdam: North Holland.

Case, R., Griffin, S., McKeough, A., & Okamoto, Y. (1992). Parallels in the development of children's social, numerical, and spatial thought. In R. Case (Ed.), *The mind's staircase* (pp. 269–284). Hillsdale, NJ: Erlbaum.

Casey, M. B. (1996). Understanding individual differences in spatial ability within females: A nature/nurture interactions framework. *Developmental Review, 16.*

Casey, M. B., Nuttall, R., Pezaris, E., & Benbow, C. P. (1995). The influence of spatial ability on gender differences in mathematics college entrance test scores across diverse samples. *Developmental Psychology, 31,* 697–705.

Casey, M. B., Tivnan, T., Riley, E., & Spenciner, L. (1991). Differentiating preschoolers' sequential planning ability from their general intelligence: A study of organization, systematic responding, and efficiency in young children. *Journal of Applied Developmental Psychology, 12,* 19–32.

Caspi, A., & Silva, P. A. (1995). Temperamental qualities at age three predict personality traits in young adulthood: Longitudinal evidence from a birth cohort. *Child Development, 66,* 486–498.

Caspi, A., Elder, G. H., Jr., & Bem, D. J. (1987). Moving against the world: Life-course patterns of explosive children. *Developmental Psychology, 23,* 308–313.

Caspi, A., Elder, G. H., Jr., & Bem, D. J. (1988). Moving away from the world: Life-course patterns of shy children. *Developmental Psychology, 24,* 824–831.

Caspi, A., Lynam, D., Moffitt, T. E., & Silva, P. A. (1993). Unraveling girls' delinquency: Biological, dispositional, and contextual contributions to adolescent misbehavior. *Developmental Psychology, 29,* 19–30.

Cassidy, J., & Berlin, L. J. (1994). The insecure/ambivalent pattern of attachment: Theory and research. *Child Development, 65,* 971–991.

Cassidy, J., Parke, R. D., Butkovsky, L., & Braungart, J. M. (1992). Family–peer connections: The roles of emotional expressiveness within the family and children's understanding of emotions. *Child Development, 63,* 603–618.

Cassidy, S. B. (1995). Uniparental disomy and genomic imprinting as causes of human genetic disease. *Environmental and Molecular Mutagenesis, 25,* 13–20.

Catherwood, D., Crassini, B., & Freiberg, K. (1989). Infant response to stimuli of similar hue and dissimilar shape: Tracing the origins of the categorization of objects by hue. *Child Development, 60,* 752–762.

Cattell, J. M. (1890). Mental tests and measurements. *Mind, 15,* 373–381.

Cattell, R. B. (1971). *Abilities: Their structure, growth and action.* Boston: Houghton Mifflin.

Cattell, R. B. (1987). *Intelligence: Its structure, growth and action.* Amsterdam: North-Holland.

Cauce, A. M. (1987). School and peer competence in early adolescence: A test of domain-specific self-perceived competence. *Developmental Psychology, 23,* 287–291.

Caudill, W. (1973). Psychiatry and anthropology: The individual and his nexus. In L. Nader & T. W. Maretzki (Eds.), *Cultural illness and health: Essays in human adaptation* (Anthropological Studies 9, pp. 67–77). Washington, DC: American Anthropological Association.

Cazden, C. (1984). *Effective instructional practices in bilingual education.* Washington, DC: National Institute of Education.

Ceci, S. J. (1990). *On intelligence . . . More or less.* Englewood Cliffs, NJ: Prentice-Hall.

Ceci, S. J. (1991). How much does schooling influence general intelligence and its cognitive components? A reassessment of the evidence. *Developmental Psychology, 27,* 703–722.

Ceci, S. J., & Bruck, M. (1993). Suggestibility of the child witness: A historical review and synthesis. *Psychological Bulletin, 113,* 403–439.

Ceci, S. J., & Bruck, M. (1995). *Jeopardy in the courtroom: A scientific analysis of children's testimony.* Washington, DC: American Psychological Association.

Ceci, S. J., Leichtman, M. D., & Bruck, M. (1994). The suggestibility of children's eyewitness reports: Methodological issues. In F. Weinert & W. Schneider (Eds.), *Memory development: State of the art and future directions* (pp. 323–347). Hillsdale, NJ: Erlbaum.

Ceci, S. J., & Liker, J. (1986). Academic and nonacademic intelligence: An experimental separation. In R. J. Sternberg & R. K. Wagner (Eds.), *Practical intelligence: Nature and origins of competence in the everyday world* (pp. 119–142). New York: Cambridge University Press.

Ceci, S. J., & Roazzi, A. (1994). The effects of context on cognition: Postcards from Brazil. In R. J. Sternberg (Ed.), *Mind in context* (pp. 74–101). New York: Cambridge University Press.

Cernoch, J. M., & Porter, R. H. (1985). Recognition of maternal axillary odors by infants. *Child Development, 56,* 1593–1598.

Chadwick, E. G., & Yogev, R. (1995). Pediatric AIDS. In G. E. Gaull (Ed.), *Pediatric Clinics of North America* (Vol. 42, No. 4, pp. 969–992). Philadelphia: Saunders.

Chalmers, J. B., & Townsend, M. A. R. (1990). The effects of training in social perspective taking on socially maladjusted girls. *Child Development, 61,* 178–190.

Chamberlain, M. C., Nichols, S. L., & Chase, C. H. (1991). Pediatric AIDS: Comparative cranial MRI and CT scans. *Pediatric Neurology, 7,* 357–362.

Chanarin, I. (1994). Adverse effects of increased dietary folate: Relation to measures to reduce the incidence of neural tube defects. *Clinical and Investigative Medicine, 17,* 244–252.

Chandler, M. J. (1973). Egocentrism and antisocial behavior: The assessment and training of social perspective-taking skills. *Developmental Psychology, 9,* 326–332.

Chandler, M. J. (1988). Doubt and developing theories of mind. In J. W. Astington, P. L. Harris, & D. R. Olson (Eds.), *Developing theories of mind* (pp. 387–413). New York: Cambridge University Press.

Chandra, R. K. (1991). Interactions between early nutrition and the immune system. In *Ciba Foundation Symposium* (No. 156, pp. 77–92). Chichester, England: Wiley.

Chaney, C. (1992). Language development, metalinguistic skills, and print awareness in 3-year-old children. *Applied Psycholinguistics, 13,* 485–514.

Chang, H. (1992). *Adolescent life and ethos: An ethnography of a U.S. high school.* Washington, DC: Falmer.

Chao, R. K. (1994). Beyond parental control and authoritarian parenting style: Understanding Chinese parenting through the cultural notion of training. *Child Development, 65,* 1111–1119.

Chapman, K. L., Leonard, L. B., & Mervis, C. B. (1986). The effect of feedback on young children's inappropriate word usage. *Journal of Child Language, 13,* 101–117.

Chapman, M., & Lindenberger, U. (1988). Functions, operations, and décalage in the development of transitivity. *Developmental Psychology, 24,* 542–551.

Chapman, M., & Skinner, E. A. (1989). Children's agency beliefs, cognitive performance, and conceptions of effort and ability: Individual and developmental differences. *Child Development, 60,* 1229–1238.

Chapman, M., Zahn-Waxler, C., Iannotti, R., & Cooperman, G. (1987). Empathy and responsibility in the motivation of children's helping. *Developmental Psychology, 23,* 140–145.

Charlesworth, W. R., & Dzur, C. (1987). Gender comparisons of preschoolers' behavior and resource utilization in group problem-solving. *Child Development, 58,* 191–200.

Charo, R. A. (1994). USA: New York surrogacy law. *Lancet, 440,* 361.

Chase, C., Teele, D. W., Klein, J. O., & Rosner, B. A. (1995). Behavioral sequelae of otitis media for infants at one year of age and their mothers. In D. J., Lim, C. D. Bluestone, J. O. Klein, J. D. Nelson, & P. L. Ogra (Eds.), *Recent advances in otitis media.* Ontario, Canada: Decker.

Chase-Lansdale, P. L., & Brooks-Gunn, J. (Eds.). (1994). *Escape from poverty: What makes a difference for children?* New York: Cambridge University Press.

Chase-Lansdale, P. L., Brooks-Gunn, J., & Zamsky, E. S. (1994). Young African-American multigenerational families in poverty: Quality of mothering and grandmothering. *Child Development, 65,* 373–393.

Chase-Lansdale, P. L., Cherlin, A. J., & Kiernin, K. E. (1995). The long-term effects of parental divorce on the mental health of young children. *Child Development, 66,* 1614–1634.

Chassin, L., Curran, P. J., Hussong, A. M., & Colder, C. R. (1996). The relation of parent alcoholism to adolescent substance use: A longitudinal follow-up study. *Journal of Abnormal Psychology, 105,* 70–80.

Chatkupt, S., Mintz, M., Epstein, L. G., Bhansali, D., & Koenigsberger, M. R. (1989). Neuroimaging studies in children with human immunodeficiency virus type 1 infection. *Annals of Neurology, 26,* 453.

Chen, X., Rubin, K. H., & Li, Z. (1995). Social functioning and adjustment in Chinese children: A longitudinal study. *Developmental Psychology, 31,* 531–539.

Cherlin, A. J., & Furstenberg, F. F., Jr. (1986). *The new American grandparent.* New York: Basic Books.

Cherlin, A. J., Furstenberg, F. F., Jr., Chase-Lansdale, P. L., Kiernan, K. E., Robins, P. K., Morrison, D. R., & Teitler, J. O. (1991). Longitudinal studies of effects of divorce on children in Great Britain and the United States. *Science, 252,* 1386–1389.

Cherlin, A. J., Kiernan, K. E., & Chase-Lansdale, P. L. (1995). Parental divorce in childhood and demographic outcomes in young adulthood. *Demography, 32,* 299–318.

Cherny, S. S. (1994). Home environmental influences on general cognitive ability. In J. C. DeFries, R. Plomin, & D. W. Fulker (Eds.), *Nature and nurture during middle childhood* (pp. 262–280). Cambridge, MA: Blackwell.

Chess, S., & Thomas, A. (1984). *Origins and evolution of behavior disorders.* New York: Brunner/Mazel.

Chi, M. T. H. (1978). Knowledge structures and memory development. In R. S. Siegler (Ed.), *Children's thinking: What develops?* (pp. 73–96). Hillsdale, NJ: Erlbaum.

Chi, M. T. H., & Ceci, S. J. (1987). Content knowledge: Its role, representation, and restructuring in memory development. In H. W. Reese (Ed.), *Advances in child development and behavior* (Vol. 20, pp. 91–142). Orlando, FL: Academic Press.

Children's Defense Fund. (1990, April). Improving the health of Medicaid-eligible children. *CDF Reports, 11*(8), 1–2.

Children's Defense Fund. (1992). *The state of America's children yearbook, 1992.* Washington, DC: Author.

Children's Defense Fund. (1996). *The state of America's children yearbook, 1996.* Washington, DC: Author.

Childs, C. P., & Greenfield, P. M. (1982). Informal modes of learning and teaching: The case of Zinacanteco weaving. In N. Warren (Ed.), *Advances in cross-cultural psychology* (Vol. 2, pp. 269–316). London: Academic Press.

Chisholm, J. S. (1989). Biology, culture, and the development of temperament: A Navajo example. In J. K. Nugent, B. M. Lester, & T. B. Brazelton (Eds.), *Biology, culture, and development* (Vol. 1, pp. 341–364). Norwood, NJ: Ablex.

Chiu, L-H. (1992-1993). Self-esteem in American and Chinese (Taiwanese) children. *Current Psychology: Research and Reviews, 11,* 309–313.

Choi, S. (1991). Early acquisition of epistemic meaning in Korean: A study of sentence-ending suffixes in the spontaneous speech of three children. *First Language, 11,* 93–120.

Chomsky, N. (1957). *Syntactic structures.* The Hague: Mouton.

Chomsky, N. (1959). Review of B. F. Skinner's *Verbal Behavior. Language, 35,* 26–129.

Chomsky, N. (1976). *Reflections on language.* London: Temple Smith.

Chomsky, N. (1981). *Lectures on government and binding.* Dordrecht, Holland: Foris.

Chomsky, N. (1988). *Language and problems of knowledge.* Cambridge, MA: MIT Press.

Christie, D. J., & Schumacher, G. M. (1975). Developmental trends in the abstraction and recall of relevant versus irrelevant thematic information from connected verbal materials. *Child Development, 46,* 598–602.

Cicchetti, D., & Aber, J. L. (1986). Early precursors of later depression: An organizational perspective. In L. P. Lipsitt & C. Rovee-Collier (Eds.), *Advances in infancy research* (Vol. 4, pp. 87–137). Norwood, NJ: Ablex.

Cicchetti, D., & Garmezy, N. (1993). Prospects and promises in the study of resilience. *Development and Psychopathology, 5,* 497–502.

Clancy, P. (1985). Acquisition of Japanese. In D. I. Slobin (Ed.), *The crosslinguistic study of language acquisition: Vol. 1. The data* (pp. 323–524). Hillsdale, NJ: Erlbaum.

Clancy, P. (1989). Form and function in the acquisition of Korean wh- questions. *Journal of Child Language, 16,* 323–347.

Clark, C. S. (1992, October 23). Youth apprenticeships. *CQ Researcher,* pp. 907–923.

Clark, E. V. (1973). Nonlinguistic strategies and the acquisition of word meanings. *Cognition, 2,* 161–182.

Clark, E. V. (1983). Meanings and concepts. In P. H. Mussen (Ed.), *Handbook of child psychology: Vol. 3. Cognitive development* (pp. 787–840). New York: Wiley.

Clark, E. V. (1990). On the pragmatics of contrast. *Journal of Child Language, 17,* 417–431.

Clark, E. V. (1993). *The lexicon in acquisition.* Cambridge: Cambridge University Press.

Clark, E. V. (1995). The lexicon and syntax. In J. L. Miller & P. D. Eimas (Eds.), *Speech, language, and communication* (pp. 303–337). San Diego: Academic Press.

Clark, M. L. (1991). Social identity, peer relations, and academic competence of African-American adolescents. *Education and Urban Society, 24,* 41–52.

Clarke-Stewart, K. A. (1978). Recasting the Lone Stranger. In J. Glick & K. A. Clarke-Stewart (Eds.), *The development of social understanding* (pp. 109–176). New York: Gardner Press.

Clarke-Stewart, K. A. (1989). Infant day care: Maligned or malignant? *American Psychologist, 44,* 266–273.

Claude, D., & Firestone, P. (1995). The development of ADHD boys: A 12-year follow-up. *Canadian Journal of Behavioural Science, 27,* 226–249.

Clausen, J. A. (1975). The social meaning of differential physical and sexual maturation. In S. E. Dragastin & G. H. Elder (Eds.), *Adolescence in the life cycle: Psychological change and the social context* (pp. 25–47). New York: Halsted.

Clements, D. H. (1990). Metacomponential development in a Logo programming environment. *Journal of Educational Psychology, 82,* 141–149.

Clements, D. H. (1995). Teaching creativity with computers. *Educational Psychology Review, 7,* 141–161.

Clements, D. H., & Nastasi, B. K. (1992). Computers and early childhood education. In M. Gettinger, S. N. Elliott, & T. R. Kratochwill (Eds.), *Advances in school psychology: Preschool and early childhood treatment directions* (pp. 187–246). Hillsdale, NJ: Erlbaum.

Clements, D. H., Nastasi, B. K., & Swaminathan, S. (1993, January). Young children and computers: Crossroads and directions from research. *Young Children, 48*(2), 56–64.

Clifford, M. M. (1988). Failure tolerance and academic risk taking in ten- to twelve-year-old students. *British Journal of Educational Psychology, 58,* 15–27.

Clifton, R. K., Rochat, P., Robin, D. J., & Berthier, N. E. (1994). Multimodal perception in the control of infant reaching. *Journal of Experimental Psychology: Human perception and Performance, 20,* 876–886.

Clifton, R. K., Perris, E., & Bullinger, A. (1991). Infants' perception of auditory space. *Developmental Psychology, 27,* 161–171.

Clopton, N. A., & Sorell, G. T. (1993). Gender differences in moral reasoning: Stable or situational? *Psychology of Women Quarterly, 17,* 85–101.

Coakley, J. (1990). *Sport and society: Issues and controversies* (4th ed.). St. Louis: Mosby.

Cochran, M. (1993). Personal networks in the ecology of human development. In M. Cochran, M. Larner, D. Riley, L. Gunnarsson, & C. R. Henderson, Jr. (Eds.), *Extending families: The social networks of parents and their children* (pp. 1–33). New York: Cambridge University Press.

Coe, C. L., Lubach, G. R., Schneider, M. L., Dierschke, D. J., & Ershler, W. B. (1992). Early rearing conditions alter immune responses in the developing infant primate. *Pediatrics, 90,* 505–509.

Cohen, F. L. (1984). *Clinical genetics in nursing practice.* Philadelphia: Lippincott.

Cohen, F. L. (1993a). Epidemiology of HIV infection and AIDS in children. In F. L. Cohen & J. D. Durham (Eds.), *Women, children, and HIV/AIDS* (pp. 137–155). New York: Springer.

Cohen, F. L. (1993b). HIV infection and AIDS: An overview. In F. L. Cohen & J. D. Durham (Eds.), *Women, children, and HIV/AIDS* (pp. 3–30). New York: Springer.

Cohen, S., & Williamson, G. M. (1991). Stress and infectious disease in humans. *Psychological Bulletin, 109,* 5–24.

Cohn, D. A., Cowan, P. A., Cowan, C. P., & Pearson, J. (1992). Mothers' and fathers' working models of childhood attachment relationships, parenting styles, and child behavior. *Development and Psychopathology, 4,* 417–432.

Coie, J. D., & Krehbiel, G. (1984). Effects of academic tutoring on the social status of low-achieving, socially rejected children. *Child Development, 55,* 1465–1478.

Coie, J. D., Dodge, K. A., & Coppotelli, H. (1982). Dimensions and types of social status: A cross-age perspective. *Developmental Psychology, 18,* 557–570.

Colby, A., & Kohlberg, L. (1987). *The measurement of moral judgment: Theoretical foundations and research validation* (Vol. 1). Cambridge: Cambridge University Press.

Colby, A., Kohlberg, L., Gibbs, J.C., & Lieberman, M. (1983). A longitudinal study of moral judgment. *Monographs of the Society for Research in Child Development, 48* (1–2, Serial No. 200).

Cole, D. A. (1991). Change in self-perceived competence as a function of peer and teacher evaluation. *Developmental Psychology, 27,* 682–688.

Cole, M. (1990). Cognitive development and formal schooling: The evidence from cross-cultural research. In L. C. Moll (Ed.), *Vygotsky and education* (pp. 89–110). New York: Cambridge University Press.

Coles, C. D., Platzman, K. A., Smith, I., James, M. E., & Falek, A. (1992). Effects of cocaine and alcohol use in pregnancy on neonatal growth and neurobehavioral status. *Neurotoxicology and Teratology, 14,* 23–33.

Collaer, M. L., & Hines, M. (1995). Human behavioral sex differences: A role for gonadal hormones during early development? *Psychological Bulletin, 118,* 55–107.

Collard, R. (1971). Exploratory and play behaviors of infants reared in an institution and in lower and middle class homes. *Child Development, 42,* 1003–1015.

Collins, J. A. (1994). Reproductive technology—the price of progress. *New England Journal of Medicine, 331,* 270–271.

Collins, R. (1993, January). Head Start: Steps toward a two-generation program strategy. *Young Children, 48*(2), 25–33.

Collins, W. A. (1983). Children's processing of television content: Implications for prevention of negative effects. *Prevention in Human Services, 2,* 53–66.

Collins, W. A., Wellman, H., Keniston, A. H., & Westby, S. D. (1978). Age-related aspects of comprehension and inference from a televised dramatic narrative. *Child Development, 49,* 389–399.

Colombo, J. (1993). *Infant cognition: Predicting later intellectual functioning.* Newbury Park, CA: Sage.

Colombo, J. (1995). On the neural mechanisms underlying developmental and individual differences in visual fixation in infancy. *Developmental Review, 15,* 97–135.

Comstock, G. A. (1993). The medium and society: The role of television in American life. In G. L. Berry & J. K. Asamen (Eds.), *Children and television* (pp. 117–131). Newbury Park, CA: Sage.

Comstock, G. A., & Paik, H. (1994). The effects of television violence on antisocial behavior: A meta-analysis. *Communication Research, 21,* 269–277.

Condry, J. C., & Ross, D. F. (1985). Sex and aggression: The influence of gender label on the perception of aggression in children. *Child Development, 56,* 225–233.

Conger, R. D., Conger, K. J., Elder, G. H., Jr., Lorenz, F. O., Simons, R. L., & Whitbeck, L. B. (1992). A family process model of economic hardship and adjustment of early adolescent boys. *Child Development, 63,* 527–541.

Conger, R. D., Conger, K. J., Elder, G. H., Jr., Lorenz, F. O., Simons, R. L., & Whitbeck, L. B. (1993). Family economic stress and adjustment of early adolescent girls. *Developmental Psychology, 29,* 206–219.

Conger, R. D., Ge, X., Elder, G. H., Jr., Lorenz, F. O., & Simons, R. L. (1994). Economic stress, coercive family process, and developmental problems of adolescents. *Child Development, 65,* 541–561.

Conger, R.D., Patterson, G. R., & Ge, X. (1995). It takes two to replicate: A mediational model for the impact of parents' stress on adolescent adjustment. *Child Development, 66,* 80–97.

Connolly, J. A., & Doyle. A. B. (1984). Relations of social fantasy play to social competence in preschoolers. *Developmental Psychology, 20,* 797–806.

Connolly, J. A., Doyle, A. B., & Reznick, E. (1988). Social pretend play and social interaction in preschoolers. *Journal of Applied Developmental Psychology, 9,* 301–313.

Connor, E. M., Sperling, R. S., Gelber, R., Kiselev, P., Scott, G., & Sullivan, M. J. (1995). Reduction of maternal–infant transmission of human immunodeficiency virus 1 with zidovudine treatment. *Obstetrical and Gynecological Survey, 50,* 253–255.

Conoley, J. C. (1990). Review of the K-ABC: Reflecting the unobservable. *Journal of Psychoeducational Assessment, 8,* 369–375.

Constanzo, P. R., & Woody, E. Z. (1979). Externality as a function of obesity in children: Pervasive style or eating-specific attribute? *Journal of Personality and Social Psychology, 37,* 2286–2296.

Cooke, R. A. (1982). The ethics and regulation of research involving children. In B. B. Wolman (Ed.), *Handbook of developmental psychology* (pp. 149–172). Englewood Cliffs, NJ: Prentice-Hall.

Cooley, C. H. (1902). Human nature and the social order. New York: Scribner.

Coon, H., Fulker, D. W., DeFries, J. C., & Plomin, R. (1990). Home environment and cognitive ability of 7-year-old children in the Colorado Adoption Project: Genetic and environmental etiologies. *Developmental Psychology, 26,* 459–468.

Cooper, H. M. (1979). Pygmalion grows up: A model for teacher expectation communication and performance. *Review of Educational Research, 49,* 389–410.

Cooper, H. M. (1989). Does reducing student-to-instructor ratios affect achievement? *Educational Psychologist, 24,* 79–98.

Cooper, R. P., & Aslin, R. N. (1990). Preference for infant-directed speech in the first month after birth. *Child Development, 61,* 1584–1595.

Cooper, R. P., & Aslin, R. N. (1994). Developmental differences in infant attention to the spectral properties of infant-directed speech. *Child Development, 65,* 1663–1677.

Coplan, R. J., Rubin, K. H., Fox, N. A., Calkins, S. D., & Stewart, S. L. (1994). Being alone, playing alone, and acting alone: Distinguishing among reticence and passive and active solitude in young children. *Child Development, 65,* 129–137.

Copper, R. L., Goldenberg, R. L., Creasy, R. K., DuBard, M. B., Davis, R. O., Entman, S. S., Iams, J. D., & Cliver, S. P. (1993). A multicenter study of preterm birth weight and gestational age-specific neonatal mortality. *American Journal of Obstetrics and Gynecology, 168,* 78–84.

Corah, N. L., Anthony, E. J., Painter, P., Stern, J. A., & Thurston, D. L. (1965). Effects of perinatal anoxia after seven years. *Psychological Monographs, 79* (3, No. 596).

Coren, S., & Halpern, D. F. (1991). Left-handedness: A marker for decreased survival fitness. *Psychological Bulletin, 109,* 90–106.

Cornell, E. H., & Bergstrom, L. I. (1983). Serial-position effects in infants' recognition memory. *Memory and Cognition, 11,* 494–499.

Cornell, E. H., & Gottfried, A. W. (1976). Intervention with premature human infants. *Child Development, 47,* 32–39.

Corrigan, R. (1987). A developmental sequence of actor-object pretend play in young children. *Merrill-Palmer Quarterly, 33,* 87–106.

Corwin, M. J., Lester, B. M., Sepkoski, C., Peucker, M., Kayne, H., & Golub, H. L. (1995). Newborn acoustic cry characteristics of infants subsequently dying of sudden infant death syndrome. *Pediatrics, 96,* 73–77.

Costabile, A., Smith, P. K., Matheson, L., Aston, J., Hunter, T., & Boulton, M. (1991). Cross-national comparison of how children distinguish serious and playful fighting. *Developmental Psychology, 27,* 881–887.

Cotton, P. (1990). Sudden infant death syndrome: Another hypothesis offered but doubts remain. *Journal of the American Medical Association, 263,* 2865, 2869.

Cotton, P. (1994). Smoking cigarettes may do developing fetus more harm than ingesting cocaine, some experts say. *Journal of the American Medical Association, 271,* 576–577.

Coulton, C. J., Korbin, J. E., Su, M., & Chow, J. (1995). Community level factors and child maltreatment rates. *Child Development, 66,* 1262–1276.

Courage, M. L., & Adams, R. J. (1990). Visual acuity assessment from birth to three years using the acuity card procedures: Cross-sectional and longitudinal samples. *Optometry and Vision Science, 67,* 713–718.

Cox, D. R., Green, E. D., Lander, E. S., Cohen, D., & Myers, R. M. (1994). Assessing mapping progress in the Human Genone Project. *Science, 265,* 2031.

Cox, M. J., Owen, M. T., Henderson, V. K., & Lewis, J. M. (1989). Marriage, adult adjustment, and early parenting. *Child Development, 60,* 1015–1024.

Cox, M. J., Owen, M. T., Henderson, V. K., & Margand, N. A. (1992). Prediction of infant–father and infant–mother attachment. *Developmental Psychology, 28,* 474–483.

Craik, F. I. M., & Lockhart, R. S. (1972). Levels of processing: A framework for memory research. *Journal of Verbal Learning and Verbal Behavior, 11,* 671–684.

Craik, F. I. M., & Tulving, E. (1975). Depth of processing and the retention of words in episodic memory. *Journal of Experimental Psychology: General, 104,* 268–294.

Crain-Thoreson, C., & Dale, P. S. (1992). Do early talkers become early readers? Linguistic precocity, preschool language, and emergent literacy. *Developmental Psychology, 28,* 421–429.

Cratty, B. J. (1986). *Perceptual and motor development in infants and children* (3rd ed.). Englewood Cliffs, NJ: Prentice-Hall.

Creatsas, G. K., Vekemans, M., Horejsi, J., Uzel, R., Lauritzen, C., & Osler, M. (1995). Adolescent sexuality in Europe a multicentric study. *Adolescent and Pediatric Gynecology, 8,* 59–63.

Crick, N. R., & Dodge, K. A. (1994). A review and reformulation of social information-processing mechanisms in children's social adjustment. *Psychological Bulletin, 115,* 74–101.

Crick, N. R., & Grotpeter, J. K. (1995). Relational aggression, gender, and social-psychological adjustment. *Child Development, 66,* 710–722.

Crick, N. R., & Ladd, G. W. (1993). Children's perceptions of their peer experiences: Attributions, loneliness, social anxiety, and social avoidance. *Developmental Psychology, 29,* 244–254.

Crockett, L. J. (1990). Sex role and sex-typing in adolescence. In R. M. Lerner, A. C. Petersen, & J. Brooks-Gunn (Eds.), *The encyclopedia of adolescence* (Vol. 2, pp. 1007–1017). New York: Garland.

Crook, C. K., & Lipsitt, L. P. (1976). Neonatal nutritive sucking: Effects of taste stimulation upon sucking rhythm and heart rate. *Child Development, 47,* 518–522.

Crowe, H. P., & Zeskind, P. S. (1992). Psychophysiological and perceptual responses to infant cries varying in pitch: Comparison of adults with low and high scores on the child abuse potential inventory. *Child Abuse & Neglect, 16,* 19–29.

Crystal, D. S., Chen, C., Fuligni, A. J., Stevenson, H. W., Hsu, C-C., Ko, H-J., Kitamura, S., & Kimura, S. (1994). Psychological maladjustment and academic achievement: A cross-cultural study of Japanese, Chinese, and American high school students. *Child Development, 65,* 738–753.

Csikzentmihalyi, M. (1988). Motivation and creativity: Toward a synthesis of structural and energistic approaches to cognition. *New Ideas in Psychology, 6,* 159–176.

Csikszentmihalyi, M., & Larson, R. (1984). *Being adolescent: Conflict and growth in the teenage years.* New York: Basic Books.

Cummings, E. M., & Cicchetti, D. (1990). Towards a transactional model of relations between attachment and depression. In M. Greenberg, D. Cicchetti, & E. M. Cummings (Eds.), *Attachment in the preschool years: Theory, research, and intervention* (pp. 339–372). Chicago: University of Chicago Press.

Cummings, E. M., & Davies, P. T. (1994). Maternal depression and child development. *Journal of Child Psychology and Psychiatry, 35,* 73–112.

Cummings, E. M., Iannotti, R. J., & Zahn-Waxler, C. (1985). Influence of conflict between adults on the emotions and aggression of young children. *Developmental Psychology, 21,* 495–507.

Cummings, E. M., & Zahn-Waxler, C. (1992). Emotions and the socialization of aggression: Adults' angry behavior and children's arousal and aggression. In A. Fraczek & H. Zumkley (Eds.), *Socialization and aggression* (pp. 61–84). New York: Springer-Verlag.

Cunningham, A. E., & Stanovich, K. E. (1990). Early spelling acquisition: Writing beats the computer. *Journal of Educational Psychology, 82,* 159–162.

Curtiss, S. (1977). *Genie: A psycholinguisitc study of a modern-day "wild child."* New York: Academic Press.

Curtiss, S. (1989). The independence and task-specificity of language. In M. H. Bornstein & J. S. Bruner (Eds.), *Interaction in human development* (pp. 105–137). Hillsdale, NJ: Erlbaum.

Czeizel, A. E., & Dudas, I. (1992). Prevention of the first occurrence of neural tube defects by periconceptional vitamin supplementation. *New England Journal of Medicine, 327,* 1832–1835.

D

Dahl, R. E., Scher, M. S., Williamson, D. E., Robles, N., & Day, N. (1995). A longitudinal study of prenatal marijuana use. Effects on sleep and arousal at age 3 years. *Archives of Pediatric and Adolescent Medicine, 149,* 145–150.

Damon, W. (1977). *The social world of the child.* San Francisco: Jossey-Bass.

Damon, W. (1988). *The moral child.* New York: Free Press.

Damon, W. (1995). *Greater expectations: Overcoming the culture of indulgence in America's homes and schools.* New York: Free Press.

Damon, W., & Hart, D. (1988). *Self-understanding in childhood and adolescence.* New York: Cambridge University Press.

Danforth, J. S., Barkley, R. A., & Stokes, T. F. (1990). Observations of parent–child interactions with hyperactive children: Research and clinical applications. *Clinical Psychology Review, 11,* 703–727.

Daniels, K., & Taylor, K. (1993). Secrecy and openness in donor insemination. *Politics and Life Sciences, 12,* 155–170.

Dannemiller, J. L. (1989). A test of color constancy in 9- and 20-week-old human infants following simulated illuminant changes. *Developmental Psychology, 25,* 171–184.

Dannemiller, J. L., & Stephens, B. R. (1988). A critical test of infant pattern preference models. *Child Development, 59,* 210–216.

Danziger, S., & Danziger, S. (1993). Child poverty and public policy: Toward a comprehensive antipoverty agenda. *Daedelus, 122,* 57–84.

Darvill, D., & Cheyne, J. A. (1981, March). *Sequential analysis of responses to aggression: Age and sex effects.* Paper presented at the biennial meeting of the Society for Research in Child Development, Boston.

Darwin, C. (1877). Biographical sketch of an infant. *Mind, 2,* 285–294.

Darwin, C. (1936). *On the origin of species by means of natural selection.* New York: Modern Library. (Original work published 1859)

Das Eiden, R., Teti, D. M., & Corns, D. M. (1995). Maternal working models of attachment, marital adjustment, and the parent–child relationship. *Child Development, 66,* 1504–1518.

Das Gupta, P., & Bryant, P. E. (1989). Young children's causal inferences. *Child Development, 60,* 1138–1146.

Davidson, P., & Youniss, J. (1991). Which comes first, morality or identity? In W. M. Kurtines & J. L. Gewirtz (Eds.), *Handbook of moral behavior and development* (Vol. 1, pp. 105–121). Hillsdale, NJ: Erlbaum.

Davidson, R. J. (1994). Asymmetric brain function, affective style, and psychopathology: The role of early experience and plasticity. *Development and Psychopathology, 6,* 741–758.

Davidson, R. J., & Fox, N. A. (1989). Frontal brain asymmetry predicts infants' response to maternal separation. *Journal of Abnormal Psychology, 98,* 127–131.

Day, S. (1993, May). Why genes have a gender. *New Scientist, 138*(1874), 34–38.

De Lisi, R., & Gallagher, A. M. (1991). Understanding gender stability and constancy in Argentinean children. *Merrill-Palmer Quarterly, 37,* 483–502.

de Villiers, J. G., & de Villiers, P. A. (1973). A cross-sectional study of the acquisition of grammatical morphemes in child speech. *Journal of Psycholinguistic Research, 2,* 267–278.

de Villiers, P. A., & de Villiers, J. G. (1992). Language development. In M. H. Bornstein & M. E. Lamb (Eds.), *Developmental psychology: An advanced textbook* (3rd ed., pp. 337–418). Hillsdale, NJ: Erlbaum.

Deary, I. J. (1995). Auditory inspection time and intelligence: What is the direction of causation? *Developmental Psychology, 31,* 237–250.

Deater-Deckard, K., Scarr, S., McCartney, K., & Eisenberg, M. (1994). Paternal separation anxiety: Relationships with parenting stress, child-rearing attitudes, and maternal anxieties. *Psychological Science, 5,* 341–346.

Deaux, K. (1993). Commentary: Sorry, wrong number—A reply to Gentile's call. *Psychological Science, 4,* 125–126.

Deaux, K., & Lewis, L. L. (1984). Structure of gender stereotypes: Interrelationships among components and gender label. *Journal of Personality and Social Psychology, 46,* 991–1004.

DeCasper, A. J., & Spence, M. J. (1986). Prenatal maternal speech influences newborns' perception of speech sounds. *Infant Behavior and Development, 9,* 133–150.

DeGroot, A. D. (1951). War and the intelligence of youth. *Journal of Abnormal and Social Psychology, 46,* 596–597.

Dekovic, M., & Gerris, J. R. M. (1994). Developmental analysis of social cognitive and behavioral differences between popular and rejected children. *Journal of Applied Developmental Psychology, 15,* 367–386.

Dekovic, M., & Janssens, J. M. A. M. (1992). Parents' child-rearing style and child's sociometric status. *Developmental Psychology, 28,* 925–932.

Delecki, J. (1985). Principles of growth and development. In P. M. Hill (Ed.), *Human growth and development throughout life* (pp. 33–48). New York: Wiley.

Delgado-Gaitan, C. (1992). School matters in the Mexican-American home: Socializing children to education. *American Educational Research Journal, 29,* 495–515.

Delgado-Gaitan, C. (1994). Socializing young children in Mexican-American families: An intergenerational perspective. In P. M. Greenfield & R. R. Cocking (Eds.), *Cross-cultural roots of minority child development* (pp. 55–86). Hillsdale, NJ: Erlbaum.

DeLoache, J. S. (1987). Rapid change in symbolic functioning of very young children. *Science, 238,* 1556–1557.

DeLoache, J. S. (1991). Symbolic functioning in very young children: Understanding of pictures and models. *Child Development, 62,* 736–752.

DeLoache, J. S., & Todd, C. M. (1988). Young children's use of spatial categorization as a mnemonic strategy. *Journal of Experimental Child Psychology, 46,* 1–20.

DeLoache, J. S., Kolstad, V., & Anderson, K. N. (1991). Physical similarity and young children's understanding of scale models. *Child Development, 62,* 111–126.

DeMarie-Dreblow, D. (1991). Relation between knowledge and memory: A reminder that correlation does not imply causality. *Child Development, 62,* 484–498.

DeMarie-Dreblow, D., & Miller, P. H. (1988). The development of children's strategies for selective attention: Evidence for a transitional period. *Child Development, 59,* 1504–1513.

Denham, S. A., Renwick, S. M., & Holt, R. W. (1991). Working and playing together: Prediction of preschool social-emotional competence from mother-child interaction. *Child Development, 62,* 242–249.

Denham, S. A., Zoller, D., & Couchoud, E. (1994). Socialization of preschoolers' emotion understanding. *Developmental Psychology, 30,* 928–936.

Dennis, W. (1960). Causes of retardation among institutionalized children: Iran. *Journal of Genetic Psychology, 96,* 47–59.

Dennis, W. (1973). *Children of the Creche.* New York: Appleton-Century-Crofts.

Dennis, W., & Najarian, P. (1957). Infant development under environmental handicap. *Psychological Monographs, 71,* 1–13.

Derdeyn, A. P. (1985). Grandparent visitation rights: Rendering family dissension more pronounced? *American Journal of Orthopsychiatry, 55,* 277–287.

DeRosier, M. E., Cillessen, A. H. N., Coie, J. D., & Dodge, K. A. (1994). Group social context and children's aggressive behavior. *Child Development, 65,* 1068–1079.

DeRosier, M. E., Kupersmidt, J. B., & Patterson, C. J. (1994). Children's academic and behavioral adjustment as a function of the chronicity and proximity of peer rejection. *Child Development, 65,* 1799–1813.

Deutsch, W., & Pechmann, T. (1982). Social interaction and the development of definite descriptions. *Cognition, 11,* 159–184.

Devlin, B., Fienberg, S. E., Resnick, D. P., & Roeder, K. (1995). Galton redux: Intelligence, race and society: A review of "The Bell Curve: Intelligence and Class Structure in American Life." *American Statistician, 90,* 1483–1488.

deVries, M. W. (1984). Temperament and infant mortality among the Masai of East Africa. *American Journal of Psychiatry, 141,* 1189–1194.

Dewsbury, D. A. (1992). Comparative psychology and ethology: A reassessment. *American Psychologist, 47,* 208–215.

Diamond, A. (1991). Neuropsychological insights into the meaning of object concept development. In S. Carey & R. Gelman (Eds.), *The epigenesis of mind: Essays on biology and knowledge* (pp. 67–110). Hillsdale, NJ: Erlbaum.

Diamond, A. Cruttenden, L, & Neiderman, D. (1994). AB with multiple wells: 1. Why are multiple wells sometimes easier than two wells? 2. Memory or memory + inhibition. *Developmental Psychology, 30,* 192–205.

Diamond, A., Hurwitz, W., Lee, E. Y., Bockes, T., Grover, W., & Minarcik, C. (1996). Cognitive deficits on frontal cortex tasks in children with early treated PKU: Results of two years of longitudinal study. *Journal of Neuroscience, 15.*

Diamond, M., Johnson, R., Young, D., & Singh, S. (1983). Age-related morphologic differences in the rat cerebral cortex and hippocampus: Male–female; right–left. *Experimental Neurology, 81,* 1–13.

Dias, M. G., & Harris, P. L. (1990). The influence of imagination on reasoning by young children. *British Journal of Developmental Psychology, 8,* 305–318.

Diaz, R. M., & Berk, L. E. (1995). A Vygotskian critique of self-instructional training. *Development and Psychopathology, 7,* 369–392.

Dick-Read, G. (1959). *Childbirth without fear.* New York: Harper & Brothers.

Dickinson, D. K. (1984). First impressions: Children's knowledge of words gained from a single exposure. *Applied Psycholinguistics, 5,* 359–373.

Diekstra, R. F. W., Kienhorst, C. W. M., & de Wilde, E. J. (1995). Suicide and suicidal behaviour among adolescents. In M. Rutter & D. J. Smith (Eds.), *Psychosocial disorders in young people* (pp. 686–761). Chicester, England: Wiley.

Diener, M. L., Goldstein, L. H., & Mangelsdorf, S. C. (1995). The role of prenatal expectations in parents' reports of infant temperament. *Merrill-Palmer Quarterly, 41,* 172–190.

Dietz, W. H., Jr., Bandini, L. G., & Gortmaker, S. (1990). Epidemiologic and metabolic risk factors for childhood obesity. *Klinische Pädiatrie, 202,* 69–72.

DiLalla, L. F., Kagan, J., & Reznick, J. S. (1994). Genetic etiology of behavioral inhibition among 2-year-old children. *Infant Behavior and Development, 17,* 405–412.

Dirks, J. (1982). The effect of a commercial game on children's Block Design scores on the WISC-R test. *Intelligence, 6,* 109–123.

Dishion, T. J., Andrews, D. W., & Crosby, L. (1995). Antisocial boys and their friends in early adolescence: Relationship characteristics, quality, and interactional processes. *Child Development, 66,* 139–151.

Dishion, T. J., Patterson, G. R., & Griesler, P. C. (1994). Peer adaptations in the development of antisocial behavior: A confluence model. In L. R. Huesmann (Ed.), *Current perspectives on aggressive behavior* (pp. 61–95). New York: Plenum.

Dittrichova, J., Brichacek, V., Paul, K., & Tautermannova, M. (1982). The structure of infant behavior: An analysis of sleep and waking in the first months of life. In W. W. Hartup (Ed.), *Review of child development research* (Vol. 6, pp. 73–100). Chicago: University of Chicago Press.

Dixon, R. A., & Lerner, R. M. (1992). A history of systems in developmental psychology. In M. H. Bornstein & M. E. Lamb (Eds.), *Developmental psychology: An advanced textbook* (3rd ed., pp. 3–58). Hillsdale, NJ: Erlbaum.

Dlugosz, L., & Bracken, M. B. (1992). Reproductive effects of caffeine: A review and theoretical analysis. *Epidemiological Review, 14,* 83–100.

Doberczak, T., Kandall, S. R., & Friedmann, P. (1993). Relationships between maternal methadone dosage, maternal-neonatal methadone levels, and neonatal withdrawal. *Obstetrics & Gynecology, 81,* 936–939.

Dobkin, P. L., Tremblay, R. E., Másse, L. C., & Vitaro, F. (1995). Individual and peer characteristics in predicting boys' early onset of substance abuse: A seven-year longitudinal study. *Child Development, 66,* 1198–1214.

Dodd, B. J. (1972). Effects of social and vocal stimulation on infant babbling. *Developmental Psychology, 7,* 80–83.

Dodge, K. A. (1985). A social information processing model of social competence in children. In M. Perlmutter (Ed.), *Minnesota Symposia on Child Psychology* (Vol. 18, pp. 77–125). Hillsdale, NJ: Erlbaum.

Dodge, K. A., Bates, J. E., & Pettit, G. S. (1990). Mechanisms in the cycle of violence. *Science, 250,* 1678–1683.

Dodge, K. A., Pettit, G. S., & Bates, J. E. (1994). Socialization mediators of the relation between socioeconomnic status and child conduct problems. *Child Development, 65,* 649–665.

Dodge, K. A., Pettit, G. S., McClaskey, C. L., & Brown, M. M. (1986). Social competence in children. *Monographs of the Society for Research in Child Development, 51*(2, Serial No. 213).

Dodge, K. A., & Price, J. M. (1994). On the relation between social information processing and socially competent behavior in early school-aged children. *Child Development, 65,* 1385–1397.

Dodge, K. A., & Somberg, D. R. (1987). Hostile attributional biases among aggressive boys are exacerbated under conditions of threats to the self. *Child Development, 58,* 213–224.

Dodwell, P. C., Humphrey, G. K., & Muir, D. W. (1987). Shape and pattern perception. In P. Salapatek & L. Cohen (Eds.), *Handbook of infant perception* (Vol. 2, pp. 1–77). Orlando, FL: Academic Press.

Doherty, W. J., & Needle, R. H. (1991). Psychological adjustment and substance use among adolescents before and after a parental divorce. *Child Development, 62,* 328–337.

Dolgin, K. G., & Behrend, D. A. (1984). Children's knowledge about animates and inanimates. *Child Development, 55,* 1646–1650.

Dollaghan, C. (1985). Child meets word: "Fast mapping" in preschool children. *Journal of Speech and Hearing Research, 28,* 449–454.

Donnerstein, E., Slaby, R. G., & Eron, L. D. (1994). The mass media and youth aggression. In L. D. Eron, J. H. Gentry, & P. Schlegel (Eds.), *Reason to hope: A psychosocial perspective on violence and youth* (pp. 219–250). Washington, DC: American Psychological Association.

Dornbusch, S. M., Glasgow, K. L., & Lin, I-C. (1996). The social structure of schooling. *Annual Review of Psychology, 47,* 401–429.

Dorr, A., Graves, S. B., & Phelps, E. (1980). Television literacy for young children. *Journal of Communication, 30*(3), 71–83.

Dorris, M. (1989). *The broken cord.* New York: Harper & Row.

Dossey, J. A., Mullis, I. V. S., Lindquist, M. M., & Chambers, D. L. (1988). *The Mathematics Report Card: Are we measuring up?* Princeton, NJ: Educational Testing Service.

Douglas, V. I. (1983). Attentional and cognitive problems. In M. Rutter (Ed.), *Developmental neuropsychiatry* (pp. 280–329). New York: Guilford.

Downey, G., & Walker, E. (1989). Social cognition and adjustment in children at risk for psychopathology. *Developmental Psychology, 25,* 835–845.

Downs, A. C., & Fuller, M. J. (1991). Recollections of spermarche: An exploratory investigation. *Current Psychology: Research and Reviews, 10,* 93–102.

Downs, A. C., & Langlois, J. H. (1988). Sex typing: Construct and measurement issues. *Sex Roles, 18,* 87–100.

Doyle, C. (1994). *Child sexual abuse.* London: Chapman & Hall.

Drabman, R. S., Cordua, G. D., Hammer, D., Jarvie, G. J., & Horton, W. (1979). Developmental trends in eating rates of normal and overweight preschool children. *Child Development, 50,* 211–216.

Drabman, R. S., & Thomas, M. H. (1976). Does watching violence on television cause apathy? *Pediatrics, 57,* 329–331.

Draper, P., & Cashdan, E. (1988). Technological change and child behavior among the !Kung. *Ethnology, 27,* 339–365.

Droege, K. L., & Stipek, D. J. (1993). Children's use of dispositions to predict classmates' behavior. *Developmental Psychology, 29,* 646–654.

Drotar, D. (1992). Personality development, problem solving, and behavior problems among preschool children with early histories of nonorganic failure-to-thrive: A controlled study. *Developmental and Behavioral Pediatrics, 13,* 266–273.

Drotar, D., Eckerle, D., Satola, J., Pallotta, J., & Wyatt, B. (1990). Maternal interactional behavior with nonorganic failure-to-thrive infants: A case comparison study. *Child Abuse and Neglect, 14,* 41–51.

Drotar, D., & Sturm, L. (1988). Prediction of intellectual development in young children with early histories of nonorganic failure-to-thrive. *Journal of Pediatric Psychology, 13,* 281–296.

Dubas, J. S., & Petersen, A. C. (1993). Female pubertal development. In M. Sugar (Ed.), *Female adolescent development* (2nd ed., pp. 3–26). New York: Brunner/Mazel.

DuBois, D. L., & Hirsch, B. J. (1990). School and neighborhood friendship patterns of black and whites in early adolescence. *Child Development, 61,* 524–536.

Dubow, E. F., & Luster, T. (1990). Adjustment of children born to teenage mothers: The contribution of risk and protective factors. *Journal of Marriage and the Family, 52,* 393–404.

Dubow, E. F., & Tisak, J. (1989). The relation between stressful life events and adjustment in elementary school children: The role of social support and social problem-solving skills. *Child Development, 60,* 1412–1423.

Dubow, E. F., Tisak, J., Causey, D., Hryshko, A., & Reid, G. (1991). A two-year longitudinal study of stressful life events, social support, and social problem-solving skills: Contributions to children's behavioral and academic adjustment. *Child Development, 62,* 583–599.

Duncan, G. J., Brooks-Gunn, J., & Klebanov, P. K. (1994). Economic deprivation and early childhood development. *Child Development, 65,* 296–318.

Dunham, P. J., & Dunham, F. (1992). Lexical development during middle infancy: A mutually driven infant–caregiver process. *Developmental Psychology, 28,* 414–420.

Dunham, P. J., Dunham, F., & Curwin, A. (1993). Joint-attentional states and lexical acquisition at 18 months. *Developmental Psychology, 29,* 827–831.

Dunn, J. (1989). Siblings and the development of social understanding in early childhood. In P. G. Zukow (Ed.), *Sibling interaction across cultures* (pp. 106–116). New York: Springer-Verlag.

Dunn, J. (1992). Sisters and brothers: Current issues in developmental research. In F. Boer & J. Dunn (Eds.), *Children's sibling relationships* (pp. 1–17). Hillsdale, NJ: Erlbaum.

Dunn, J. (1994). Temperament, siblings, and the development of relationships. In W. B. Carey & S. C. McDevitt (Eds.), *Prevention and early intervention* (pp. 50–58). New York: Brunner/Mazel.

Dunn, J., Brown, J. R., & Maguire, M. (1995). The development of children's moral sensibility: Individual differences and emotion understanding. *Developmental Psychology, 31,* 649–659.

Dunn, J., Brown, J., Slomkowski, C. T., & Youngblade, L. (1991). Young children's understanding of other people's feelings and beliefs: Individual differences and their antecedents. *Child Development, 62,* 1352–1366.

Dunn, J., & Kendrick, C. (1982). *Siblings: Love, envy and understanding.* Cambridge, MA: Harvard University Press.

Dunn, J., & Plomin, R. (1990). *Separate lives: Why siblings are so different.* New York: Basic Books.

Dunn, J., Slomkowski, C., & Beardsall, L. (1994). Sibling relationships from the preschool period through middle childhood and early adolescence. *Developmental Psychology, 30,* 315–324.

Dunn, J., Slomkowski, C., Beardsall, L., & Rende, R. (1994). Adjustment in middle childhood and early adolescence: Links with earlier and contemporary sibling relationships. *Journal of Child Psychology and Psychiatry, 35,* 491–504.

Dunn, J. T. (1993). Iodine supplementation and the prevention of cretinism. *Annals of the New York Academy of Sciences, 678,* 158–168.

Dunst, C. J., & Linderfelt, B. (1985). Maternal ratings of temperament and operant learning in two- to three-month-old infants. *Child Development, 56,* 555–563.

Durbin, D. L., Darling, N., Steinberg, L., & Brown, B. B. (1993). Parenting style and peer group membership among European-American adolescents. *Journal of Research on Adolescence, 3,* 87–100.

Dweck, C. S. (1991). Self-theories and goals: Their role in motivation, personality and development. In R. Dienstbier (Ed.), *Nebraska Symposia on Motivation* (Vol. 36, pp. 199–235). Lincoln: University of Nebraska Press.

Dweck, C. S., & Leggett, E. L. (1988). A social-cognitive approach to motivation and personality. *Psychological Review, 95,* 256–273.

Dye-White, E. (1986). Environmental hazards in the work setting: Their effect on women of child-bearing age. *American Association of Occupational Health and Nursing Journal, 34,* 76–78.

E

Eagly, A. H. (1995). The science and politics of comparing women and men. *American Psychologist, 50,* 145–158.

East, P. L., & Rook, K. S. (1992). Compensatory patterns of support among children's peer relationships: A test using school friends, nonschool friends, and siblings. *Developmental Psychology, 28,* 168–172.

Ebeling, K. S., & Gelman, S. A. (1994). Children's use of context in interpreting "big" and "little." *Child Development, 65,* 1178–1192.

Eberhart-Phillips, J. E., Frederick, P. D., & Baron, R. C. (1993). Measles in pregnancy: A descriptive study of 58 cases. *Obstetrics and Gynecology, 82,* 797–801.

Eccles, J. S., & Harold, R. D. (1991). Gender differences in sport involvement: Applying the Eccles' expectancy-value model. *Journal of Applied Sport Psychology, 3,* 7–35.

Eccles, J. S., Jacobs, J. E., & Harold, R. D. (1990). Gender-role stereotypes, expectancy effects, and parents' role in the socialization of gender differences in self-perceptions and skill acquisition. *Journal of Social Issues, 46,* 183–201.

Eccles, J. S., Midgley, C. Wigfield, A., Buchanan, C. M., Reuman, D., Flanagan, C., & Mac Iver, D. (1993a). Development during adolescence: The impact of stage–environment fit on young adolescents' experiences in schools and in families. *American Psychologist, 48,* 90–101.

Eccles, J. S., Wigfield, A., Flanagan, C., Miller, C., Reuman, D., & Yee, D. (1989). Self-concepts, domain values, and self-esteem: Relations and changes at early adolescence. *Journal of Personality and Social Psychology, 57,* 283–310.

Eccles, J. S., Wigfield, A., Midgley, C., Reuman, D., Mac Iver, D., & Feldlaufer, H. (1993b). Negative effects of traditional middle schools on students' motivation. *Elementary School Journal, 93,* 553–574.

Eckenrode, J., Laird, M., & Doris, J. (1993). School performance and disciplinary problems among abused and neglected children. *Developmental Psychology, 29,* 53–62.

Eckerman, C. O., Davis, C. C., & Didow, S. M. (1989). Toddlers' emerging ways of achieving social coordination with a peer. *Child Development, 60,* 440–453.

Eckerman, C. O., Whatley, J. L., & Kutz, S. L. (1975). Growth of social play with peers during the second year of life. *Developmental Psychology, 11,* 42–49.

Eder, R. A. (1989). The emergent personologist: The structure and content of 3 1/2-, 5 1/2-, and 7 1/2-year-olds' concepts of themselves and other persons. *Child Development, 60,* 1218–1228.

Eder, R. A. (1990). Uncovering young children's psychological selves: Individual and developmental differences. *Child Development, 61,* 849–863.

Edwards, C. A. (1994). Leadership in groups of school-age girls. *Developmental Psychology, 30,* 920–927.

Edwards, C. P. (1978). Social experiences and moral judgment in Kenyan young adults. *Journal of Genetic Psychology, 133,* 19–30.

Edwards, C. P. (1981). The comparative study of the development of moral judgment and reasoning. In R. L. Munroe, R. Munroe, & B. B. Whiting (Eds.), *Handbook of cross-cultural human development* (pp. 501–528). New York: Garland.

Edwards, J. N. (1991). New conceptions: Biosocial innovations and the family. *Journal of Marriage and the Family, 53,* 349–360.

Egeland, B., & Hiester, M. (1995). The long-term consequences of infant day-care and mother–infant attachment. *Child Development, 66,* 474–485.

Egeland, B., Jacobvitz, D., & Sroufe, L. A. (1988). Breaking the cycle of abuse. *Child Development, 59,* 1080–1088.

Ehrhardt, A. A. (1975). Prenatal hormone exposure and psychosexual differentiation. In E. J. Sachar (Ed.), *Topics in psychoendocrinology* (pp. 67–82). New York: Grune & Stratton.

Ehrhardt, A. A., & Baker, S. W. (1974). Fetal androgens, human central nervous system differentiation, and behavior sex differences. In R. C. Friedman, R. M. Richart, & R. L. VandeWiele (Eds.), *Sex differences in behavior* (pp. 33–51). New York: Wiley.

Eilers, R. E., & Oller, D. K. (1994). Infant vocalizations and the early diagnosis of severe hearing impairment. *Journal of Pediatrics, 124,* 199–203.

Eisenberg, N. (1982). The development of reasoning regarding prosocial behavior. In N. Eisenberg (Ed.), *The development of prosocial behavior* (pp. 219–249). New York: Academic Press.

Eisenberg, N., Carlo, G., Murphy, B., & Van Court, P. (1995). Prosocial development in late adolescence: A longitudinal study. *Child Development, 66,* 1179–1197.

Eisenberg, N., & Fabes, R. A. (1995). The relation of young children's vicarious emotional responding to social competence, regulation, and emotionality. *Cognition and Emotion, 9,* 203–228.

Eisenberg, N., Fabes, R. A., Carolo, G., Speer, A. L., Switzer, G., Karbon, M., & Troyer, D. (1993). The relations of empathy-related emotions and maternal practices to children's comforting behavior. *Journal of Experimental Child Psychology, 55,* 131–150.

Eisenberg, N., Fabes, R. A., Murphy, B., Maszk, P., Smith, M., & Karbon, M. (1995). The role of emotionality and regulation in children's social functioning: A longitudinal study. *Child Development, 66,* 1360–1384.

Eisenberg, N., Fabes, R. A., Nyman, M., Bernzweig, J., & Pinuelas, A. (1994). The relations of emotionality and regulation to children's anger-related reactions. *Child Development, 65,* 109–128.

Eisenberg, N., & Lennon, R. (1983). Sex differences in empathy and related capacities. *Psychological Bulletin, 94,* 100–131.

Eisenberg, N., Lennon, R., & Roth, K. (1983). Prosocial development: A longitudinal study. *Developmental Psychology, 19,* 846–855.

Eisenberg, N., & Miller, P. A. (1987). The relation of empathy to prosocial and related behaviors. *Psychological Bulletin, 101,* 91–119.

Eisenberg, N., Miller, P. A., Shell, R., McNalley, & Shea, C. (1991). Prosocial development in adolescence: A longitudinal study. *Developmental Psychology, 27,* 849–857.

Eisenberg, N., Shell, R., Pasternack, J., Lennon, R., Beller, R., & Mathy, R. M. (1987). Prosocial development in middle childhood: A longitudinal study. *Developmental Psychology, 23,* 712–718.

Eisenberg-Berg, N. (1979). Development of children's prosocial moral judgment. *Developmental Psychology, 15,* 128–137.

Ekman, P., & Friesen, W. (1972). Constants across culture in the face of emotion. *Journal of Personality and Social Psychology, 17,* 124–129.

Elardo, R., Bradley, R. H., & Caldwell, B. M. (1975). The relation of infants' home environments to mental test performance from six to thirty-six months: A longitudinal analysis. *Child Development, 46,* 71–76.

Elardo, R., Bradley, R. H., & Caldwell, B. M. (1977). A longitudinal study of the relation of infants' home environments to language development at age 3. *Child Development, 48,* 595–603.

Elder, G. H., Jr. (1974). *Children of the Great Depression.* Chicago: University of Chicago Press.

Elder, G. H., Jr., & Caspi, A. (1988). Human development and social change: An emerging perspective on the life course. In N. Bolger, A. Caspi, G. Downey, & M. Moorehouse (Eds.), *Persons in context: Developmental processes* (pp. 77–113). Cambridge: Cambridge University Press.

Elder, G. H., Jr., Caspi, A., & Van Nguyen, T. (1986). Resourceful and vulnerable children: Family influences in hard times. In R. K. Silbereisen, K. Eysferth, & G. Rodinger (Eds.), *Development as action in context: Problem behavior and normal youth development* (pp. 167–186). New York: Springer-Verlag.

Elder, G. H., Jr., & Clipp, E. (1988). Wartime losses and social bonding: Influences across 40 years in men's lives. *Psychiatry, 51,* 177–198.

Elder, G. H., Jr., & Hareven, T. K. (1993). Rising above life's disadvantage: From the Great Depression to war. In G. H. Elder, Jr., J. Modell, & R. D. Parke (Eds.),

Children in time and place (pp. 47–72). Cambridge, England: Cambridge University Press.

Elder, G. H., Jr., Liker, J. K., & Cross, C. E. (1984). Parent–child behavior in the Great Depression: Life course and intergenerational influences. In P. B. Baltes & O. G. Brim (Eds.), *Life-span development and behavior* (Vol. 6, pp. 109–158). New York: Academic Press.

Elder, G. H., Jr., Van Nguyen, T., & Caspi, A. (1985). Linking family hardship to children's lives. *Child Development, 56,* 361–375.

Elias, M. J., Gara, M., Ubriaco, M., Rothman, P. A., Clabby, J. F., & Schuyler, T. (1986). Impact of preventive social problem solving intervention on children's coping with middle-school stressors. *American Journal of Community Psychology, 14,* 259–276.

Elicker, J., Englund, M., & Sroufe, L. A. (1992). Predicting peer competence and peer relationships in childhood from early parent–child relationships. In R. D. Parke & G. W. Ladd (Eds.), *Family–peer relationships: Modes of linkage* (pp. 77–106). Hillsdale, NJ: Erlbaum.

Elkind, D., & Bowen, R. (1979). Imaginary audience behavior in children and adolescence. *Developmental Psychology, 15,* 33–44.

Elliott, B. J., & Richards, M. P. M. (1991). Children and divorce: Educational performance and behaviour before and after parental separation. *International Journal of Law and the Family, 5,* 258–276.

Elliott, E. S., & Dweck, C. S. (1988). Goals: An approach to motivation and achievement. *Journal of Personality and Social Psychology, 54,* 5–12.

Ellis, S., Rogoff, B., & Cromer, C. (1981). Age segregation in children's social interactions. *Developmental Psychology, 17,* 399–407.

Ellsworth, C. P., Muir, D. W., & Hains, S. M. J. (1993). Social competence and person-object differentiation: An analysis of the still-face effect. *Developmental Psychology, 29,* 63–73.

Elsen, H. (1994). Phonological constraints and overextensions. *First Language, 14,* 305–315.

Emde, R. N. (1992). Individual meaning and increasing complexity: Contributions of Sigmund Freud and René Spitz to developmental psychology. *Developmental Psychology, 28,* 347–359.

Emde, R. N., Bioringen, Z., Clyman, R. B., & Oppenheim, D. (1991). The moral self of infancy: Affective core and procedural knowledge. *Developmental Review, 11,* 251–270.

Emde, R. N., & Buchsbaum, H. K. (1990). "Didn't you hear my mommy?" Autonomy with connectedness in moral self-emergence. In D. Cicchetti & M. Beeghly (Eds.), *Development of the self through transition* (pp. 35–60). Chicago: University of Chicago Press.

Emde, R. N., Plomin, R., Robinson, J., Corley, R., DeFries, J., Fulker, D. W., Reznick, J. S., Campos, J., Kagan, J., & Zahn-Waxler, C. (1992). Temperament, emotion, and cognition at fourteen months: The MacArthur Longitudinal Twin Study. *Child Development, 63,* 1437–1455.

Emery, R. E. (1988). *Marriage, divorce, and children's adjustment.* Newbury Park, CA: Sage.

Emery, R. E., & Forehand, R. (1994). Parental divorce and children's well-being: A focus on resilience. In R. J. Haggerty, L. R. Sherrod, N. Garmezy, & M. Rutter (Eds.), *Stress, risk, and resilience in children and adolescents* (pp. 64–99). New York: Cambridge University Press.

Emery, R. E., Mathews, S. G., & Kitzmann, K. M. (1994). Child custody mediation and litigation: Parents' satisfaction and functioning a year after settlement. *Journal of Consulting and Clinical Psychology, 62,* 124–129.

Emery, R. E., & Wyer, M. M. (1987). Divorce mediation. *American Psychologist, 42,* 472–480.

Emmerich, W. (1981). Non-monotonic developmental trends in social cognition: The case of gender constancy. In S. Strauss (Ed.), *U-shaped behavioral growth* (pp. 249–269). New York: Academic Press.

Emory, E. K., & Toomey, K. A. (1988). Environmental stimulation and human fetal responsibility in late pregnancy. In W. P. Smotherman & S. R. Robinson (Eds.), *Behavior of the fetus* (pp. 141–161). Caldwell, NJ: Telford.

Engliert, C. S., & Palincsar, A. S. (1991). Reconsidering instructional research in literacy from a sociocultural perspective. *Learning Disabilities Research and Practice, 6,* 225–229.

Enright, R. D., Bjerstedt, A., Enright, W. F., Levy, W. M., Jr., Lapsley, D. K., Buss, R. R., Harwell, M., & Zindler, M. (1984). Distributive justice development: Cross-cultural, contextual, and longitudinal evaluations. *Child Development, 55,* 1737–1751.

Enright, R. D., Franklin, C. C., & Manheim, L. A. (1980). Children's distributive justice reasoning: A standardized and objective scale. *Developmental Psychology, 16,* 193–202.

Enright, R. D., Lapsley, D. K., & Shukla, D. (1979). Adolescent egocentrism in early and late adolescence. *Adolescence, 14,* 687–695.

Enright, R. D., & Sutterfield, S. J. (1980). An ecological validation of social cognitive development. *Child Development, 51,* 156–161.

Epstein, C. J. (Ed.). (1993). *The phenotypic mapping of Down syndrome and other aneuploid conditions.* New York: Wiley-Liss.

Epstein, H. T. (1980). EEG developmental stages. *Developmental Psychobiology, 13,* 629–631.

Epstein, L. H., McCurley, J., Wing, R. R., & Valoski, A. (1990). Five-year follow-up of family-based treatments for childhood obesity. *Journal of Consulting and Clinical Psychology, 58,* 661–664.

Epstein, L. H., Wing, R. R., Koeske, R., & Valoski, A. (1987). Long-term effects of family-based treatment of childhood obesity. *Journal of Consulting and Clinical Psychology, 55,* 91–95.

Erdley, C. A., & Dweck, C. S. (1993). Children's implicit personality theories as predictors of their social judgments. *Child Development, 64,* 863–878.

Erikson, E. H. (1950). *Childhood and society.* New York: Norton.

Erikson, E. H. (1968). *Identity, youth, and crisis.* New York: Norton.

Ervin-Tripp, S. (1991). Play in language development. In B. Scales, M. Almy, A. Nicolopoulou, & S. Ervin-Tripp (Eds.), *Play and the social context of development in early care and education* (pp. 84–97). New York: Teachers College Press.

Eskenazi, B. (1993). Caffeine during pregnancy: Grounds for concern? *Journal of the American Medical Association, 270,* 2973–2974.

Espenschade, A., & Eckert, H. (1974). Motor development. In W. R. Warren & E. R. Buskirk (Eds.), *Science and medicine of exercise and sport* (pp. 329–330). New York: Harper & Row.

Etaugh, C., & Liss, M. B. (1992). Home, school, and playroom: Training grounds for adult gender roles. *Sex Roles, 26,* 129–147.

Etzel, B., & Gewirtz, J. (1967). Experimental modification of caretaker-maintained high rate operant crying in a 6- and a 20-week-old infant (Infans tyrannotearus): Extinction of crying with reinforcement of eye contact and smiling. *Journal of Experimental Child Psychology, 5,* 303–317.

Eveleth, P. B., & Tanner, J. M. (1990). *Worldwide variation in human growth* (2nd ed.). Cambridge: Cambridge University Press.

F

Fabes, R. A., Eisenberg, N., & Eisenbud, L. (1993). Behavioral and physiological correlates of children's reactions to others in distress. *Developmental Psychology, 29,* 655–663.

Fabes, R. A., Eisenberg, N., Karbon, M., Troyer, D., & Switzer, G. (1994). The relations of children's emotion regulation to their vicarious emotional responses and comforting behaviors. *Child Development, 27,* 858–866.

Fabes, R. A., Eisenberg, N., Nyman, M., & Michealieu, Q. (1991). Young children's appraisals of others' spontaneous emotional reactions. *Developmental Psychology, 27,* 858–866.

Fabricius, W. V., & Wellman, H. M. (1993). Two roads diverged: Young children's ability to judge distance. *Child Development, 64,* 399–414.

Facchinetti, F., Battaglia, C., Benatti, R., Borella, P., & Genazzani, A. R. (1992).

Oral magnesium supplementation improves fetal circulation. *Magnesium Research, 3,* 179–181.

Fackelmann, K. A. (1992, November 28). Finding Marfan syndrome in the womb. *Science News, 142*(22), 382.

Fagan, J. F., III. (1973). Infant's delayed recognition memory and forgetting. *Journal of Experimental Child Psychology, 16,* 424–450.

Fagan, J. F., III, & Detterman, D. K. (1992). The Fagan Test of Infant Intelligence: A technical summary. *Journal of Applied Developmental Psychology, 13,* 173–193.

Fagan, J. F., III, & Singer, L. T. (1979). The role of simple feature differences in infants' recognition of faces. *Infant Behavior and Development, 2,* 39–45.

Fagan, J. F., III, & Singer, L. T. (1983). Infant recognition memory as a measure of intelligence. In L. P. Lipsitt (Ed.), *Advances in infancy research* (Vol. 2, pp. 31–78). Norwood, NJ: Ablex.

Fagen, J. W., & Rovee-Collier, C. K. (1983). Memory retrieval: A time-locked process in infancy. *Science, 222,* 1349–1351.

Fagot, B. I. (1974). Sex differences in toddlers' behavior and parental reaction. *Developmental Psychology, 10,* 554–558.

Fagot, B. I. (1977). Consequences of moderate cross-gender behavior in preschool children. *Child Development, 48,* 902–907.

Fagot, B. I. (1978). The influence of sex of child on parental reactions to toddler children. *Child Development, 49,* 459–465.

Fagot, B. I. (1985a). Beyond the reinforcement principle: Another step toward understanding sex role development. *Developmental Psychology, 21,* 1097–1104.

Fagot, B. I. (1985b). Changes in thinking about early sex role development. *Developmental Review, 5,* 83–98.

Fagot, B. I., & Hagan, R. I. (1991). Observations of parent reactions to sex-stereotyped behaviors: Age and sex effects. *Child Development, 62,* 617–628.

Fagot, B. I., & Kavanaugh, K. (1990). The prediction of antisocial behavior from avoidant attachment classifications. *Child Development, 61,* 864–873.

Fagot, B. I., & Leinbach, M. D. (1989). The young child's gender schema: Environmental input, internal organization. *Child Development, 60,* 663–672.

Fagot, B. I., Leinbach, M. D., & Hagan, R. I. (1986). Gender labeling and the adoption of sex-typed behaviors. *Developmental Psychology, 22,* 440–443.

Fagot, B. I., Leinbach, M. D., & O'Boyle, C. (1992). Gender labeling, gender stereotyping, and parenting behaviors. *Developmental Psychology, 28,* 225–230.

Fagot, B. I., & Littman, I. (1976). Relation of pre-school sex-typing to intellectual performance in elementary school. *Psychological Reports, 39,* 699–704.

Fagot, B. I., & Patterson, G. R. (1969). An in vivo analysis of reinforcing contingencies for sex-role behaviors in the preschool child. *Developmental Psychology, 1,* 563–568.

Fahrmeier, E. D. (1978). The development of concrete operations among the Hausa. *Journal of Cross-Cultural Psychology, 9,* 23–44.

Fairburn, C. G., & Beglin, S. J. (1990). Studies of the epidemiology of bulimia nervosa. *American Journal of Psychiatry, 147,* 401–408.

Falbo, T. (1992). Social norms and the one-child family: Clinical and policy implications. In F. Boer & J. Dunn (Eds.), *Children's sibling relationships* (pp. 71–82). Hillsdale, NJ: Erlbaum.

Falbo, T., & Polit, D. (1986). A quantitative review of the only-child literature: Research evidence and theory development. *Psychological Bulletin, 100,* 176–189.

Falbo, T., & Poston, D. L., Jr. (1993). The academic, personality, and physical outcomes of only children in China. *Child Development, 64,* 18–35.

Faller, K. C. (1990). *Understanding child sexual maltreatment.* Newbury Park, CA: Sage.

Fantz, R. L. (1961). The origin of form perception. *Scientific American, 204,* 66–72.

Faraone, S. V., Biederman, J., Chen, W. J., Milberger, S., Warburton, R., & Tsuang, M. T. (1995). Genetic heterogeneity in attention-deficit hyperactivity disorder (ADHD): Gender, psychiatric comorbidity, and maternal ADHD. *Journal of Abnormal Psychology, 104,* 334–345.

Farrar, M. J. (1990). Discourse and the acquisition of grammatical morphemes. *Journal of Child Language, 17,* 607–624.

Farrar, M. J., & Goodman, G. S. (1992). Developmental changes in event memory. *Child Development, 63,* 173–187.

Farrington, D. P. (1987). Epidemiology. In H. C. Quay (Ed.), *Handbook of juvenile delinquency* (pp. 33–61). New York: Wiley.

Farver, J. M. (1993). Cultural differences in scaffolding pretend play: A comparison of American and Mexican mother–child and sibling–child pairs. In K. MacDonald (Ed.), *Parent–child play* (pp. 349–366). Albany, NY: SUNY Press.

Farver, J. M., & Branstetter, W. H. (1994). Preschoolers' prosocial responses to their peers' distress. *Developmental Psychology, 30,* 334–341.

Farver, J. M., Kim, Y. K., & Lee, Y. (1995). Cultural differences in Korean- and Anglo-American preschoolers' social interaction and play behaviors. *Child Development, 66,* 1088–1099.

Farver, J. M., & Wimbarti, S. (1995a). Indonesian toddlers' social play with their mothers and older siblings. *Child Development, 66,* 1493–1503.

Farver, J. M., & Wimbarti, S. (1995b). Paternal participation in toddlers' pretend play. *Social Development, 4,* 19–31.

Feagans, L. V., Kipp. E., & Blood, I. (1994). The effects of otitis media on the attention skills of day-care-attending toddlers. *Developmental Psychology, 30,* 701–708.

Feagans, L. V., & Proctor, A. (1994). The effects of mild illness in infancy on later development: The sample case of the effects of otitis media (middle ear effusion). In C. B. Fisher & R. M. Lerner (Eds.), *Applied developmental psychology* (pp. 139–173). New York: McGraw-Hill.

Feagans, L. V., Sanyal, M., Henderson, F., Collier, A., & Appelbaum, M. I. (1987). The relationship of middle ear disease in early childhood to later narrative and attention skills. *Journal of Pediatric Psychology, 12,* 581–594.

Featherman, D. (1980). Schooling and occupational careers: Constancy and change in worldly success. In O. Brim, Jr., & J. Kagan (Eds.), *Constancy and change in human development* (pp. 675–738). Cambridge, MA: Harvard University Press.

Fein, G. G., Gariboldi, A., & Boni, R. (1993). The adjustment of infants and toddlers to group care: The first six months. *Early Childhood Research Quarterly, 8,* 1–14.

Feingold, A. (1988). Cognitive gender differences are disappearing. *American Psychologist, 43,* 95–103.

Feingold, A. (1993). Cognitive gender differences: A developmental perspective. *Sex Roles, 29,* 91–112.

Feingold, A. (1994). Gender differences in personality: A meta-analysis. *Psychological Bulletin, 116,* 429–456.

Feinman, S. (1982). Social referencing in infancy. *Merrill-Palmer Quarterly, 28,* 445–470.

Feis, C. L., & Simons, C. (1985). Training preschool children in interpersonal cognitive problem-solving skills: A replication. *Prevention in Human Services, 3,* 59–70.

Feldhusen, J. F. (1986). A conception of giftedness. In R. J. Sternberg & J. E. Davidson (Eds.), *Conceptions of giftedness* (pp. 112–127). New York: Cambridge University Press.

Feldman, D. H., & Goldsmith, L. T. (1991). *Nature's gambit.* New York: Teachers College Press.

Felner, R. D., & Adan, A. M. (1988). The School Transitional Environment Project: An ecological intervention and evaluation. In R. H. Price, E. L. Cowan, R. P. Lorion, & J. Ramos-McKay (Eds.), *14 ounces of prevention: A casebook for practitioners* (pp. 111–122). Washington, DC: American Psychological Association.

Fenson, L., Dale, P. S., Reznick, J. S., Bates, E., Thal, D. J., & Pethick, S. J. (1994). Variability in early communicative development. *Monographs of the Society for Research in Child Development, 59*(5, Serial No. 242).

Fenton, N. (1928). The only child. *Journal of Genetic Psychology, 35,* 546–556.

Ferguson, L. R. (1978). The competence and freedom of children to make choices regarding participation in research: A statement. *Journal of Social Issues, 34,* 114–121.

Fergusson, D. M., Horwood, L. J., & Shannon, F. T. (1987). Breastfeeding and subsequent social adjustment in six- to eight-year-old children. *Journal of Child Psychology and Psychiatry, 28,* 378–386.

Fernald, A. (1993). Approval and disapproval: Infant responsiveness to vocal affect in familiar and unfamiliar languages. *Child Development, 64,* 637–656.

Fernald, A., & Morikawa, H. (1993). Common themes and cultural variations in Japanese and American mothers' speech to infants. *Child Development, 64,* 637–656.

Fernald, A., Taeschner, T., Dunn, J., Papousek, M., Boysson-Bardies, B., & Fukui, I. (1989). A cross-language study of prosodic modifications in mothers' and fathers' speech to preverbal infants. *Journal of Child Language, 16,* 477–502.

Feshbach, N. D., & Feshbach, S. (1982). Empathy training and the regulation of aggression: Potentialities and limitation. *Academic Psychology Bulletin, 4,* 399–413.

Feuerstein, R. (1979). *Dynamic assessment of retarded performers: The learning potential assessment device: Theory, instruments, and techniques.* Baltimore: University Park Press.

Feuerstein, R. (1980). *Instrumental enrichment.* Baltimore: University Park Press.

Field, T. M., (1994). The effects of mother's physical and emotional unavailability on emotion regulation. In N. A. Fox (Ed.), The development of emotion regulation: Biological and behavioral considerations. *Monographs of the Society for Research in Child Development, 59*(2–3, Serial No. 240).

Field, T. M., Fox, N. A., Pickens, J., & Nawrocki, T. (1995). Relative right frontal EEG activation in 3- to 6-month-old infants of "depressed" mothers. *Developmental Psychology, 31,* 358–363.

Field, T. M., Schanberg, S. M., Scafidi, F., Bauer, C. R., Vega-Lahr, N., Garcia, R., Nystrom, J., & Kuhn, C. M. (1986). Effects of tactile/kinesthetic stimulation on preterm neonates. *Pediatrics, 77,* 654–658.

Field, T. M., Woodson, R., Greenberg, R., & Cohen, D. (1982). Discrimination and imitation of facial expressions by neonates. *Science, 218,* 179–181.

Fiese, B. (1990). Playful relationships: A contextual analysis of mother–toddler interaction and symbolic play. *Child Development, 61,* 1648–1656.

Filipovic, Z. (1994). *Zlata's diary: A child's life in Sarajevo.* New York: Penguin.

Fine, B. A. (1990). *Strategies in genetic counseling: Reproductive genetics and new technologies.* White Plains, NY: March of Dimes Birth Defects Foundation.

Fine, G. A. (1980). The natural history of preadolescent male friendship groups. In H. C. Foot, A. J. Chapman, & J. R. Smith (Eds.), *Friendship and social relations in children* (pp. 293–320). Chichester, England: Wiley.

Finegan, J. K., Niccols, G. A., & Sitarenios, G. (1992). Relations between prenatal testosterone levels and cognitive abilities at 4 years. *Developmental Psychology, 28,* 1075–1089.

Finn, J. D., & Achilles, C. M. (1990). Answers and questions about class size: A statewide experiment. *American Educational Research Journal, 27,* 557–577.

Fischer, K. W., & Bidell, T. (1991). Constraining nativist inferences about cognitive capacities. In S. Carey & R. Gelman Eds.), *The epigenesis of mind: Essays on biology and cognition* (pp. 199–235). Hillsdale, NJ: Erlbaum.

Fischer, K. W., & Farrar, M. J. (1987). Generalizations about generalizations: How a theory of skill development explains both generality and specificity. *International Journal of Psychology, 22,* 643–677.

Fischer, K. W., & Pipp, S. L. (1984). Processes of cognitive development: Optimal level and skill acquisition. In R. J. Sternberg (Ed.), *Mechanisms of cognitive development* (pp. 45–80). New York: Freeman.

Fischer, K. W., & Rose, S. P. (1994). Dynamic development of coordination of components in brain and behavior: A framework for theory. In G. Dawson & K. W. Fischer (Eds.), *Human behavior and the developing brain* (pp. 3–66). New York: Guilford.

Fischer, K. W., & Rose, S. P. (1995, Fall). Concurrent cycles in the dynamic development of brain and behavior. *SRCD Newsletter,* pp. 3–4, 15–16.

Fischman, M. G., Moore, J. B., & Steele, K. H. (1992). Children's one-hand catching as a function of age, gender, and ball location. *Research Quarterly for Exercise and Sport, 63,* 349–355.

Fisher, C. B., & Rosendahl, S. (1990). Psychological risks and remedies of research participation. In C. B. Fisher & W. W. Tryon (Eds.), *Ethics in applied developmental psychology* (pp. 43–59). Norwood, NJ: Ablex.

Fisher, J. A., & Birch, L. L. (1995). 3–5 year-old children's fat preferences and fat consumption are related to parental adiposity. *Journal of the American Dietetic Association, 95,* 759–764.

Fishler, K., & Koch, R. (1991). Mental development in Down syndrome mosaicism. *American Journal on Mental Retardation, 96,* 345–351.

Fitch, M., Huston, A. C., & Wright, J. C. (1993). From television forms to genre schemata: Children's perceptions of television reality. In G. L. Berry & J. K. Asamen (Eds.), *Children and television* (pp. 38–52). Newbury Park, CA: Sage.

Fitzgerald, J. (1987). Research on revision in writing. *Review of Educational Research, 57,* 481–506.

Fivush, R. (1984). Learning about school: The development of kindergartners' school scripts. *Child Development, 55,* 1697–1709.

Fivush, R. (1991). Gender and emotion in mother-child conversations about the past. *Journal of Narrative and Life History, 1,* 325–341.

Fivush, R. (1993). Developmental perspectives on autobiographical recall. In G. S. Goodman & B. L. Bottoms (Eds.), *Child victims, child witnesses: Understanding and improving testimony* (pp. 1–24). New York: Guilford.

Fivush, R. (1995). Language, narrative, and autobiography. *Consciousness and Cognition, 4,* 100–103.

Fivush, R., & Hamond, N. R. (1989). Time and again: Effects of repetition and retention interval on two year olds' event recall. *Journal of Experimental Child Psychology, 47,* 259–273.

Fivush, R., Haden, C., & Adam, S. (1995). Structure and coherence of preschoolers' personal narratives over time: Implications for childhood amnesia. *Journal of Experimental Child Psychology, 60,* 32–56.

Fivush, R., Kuebli, J., & Clubb, P. A. (1992). The structure of events and event representations: A developmental analysis. *Child Development, 63,* 188–201.

Fivush, R., & Reese, E. (1992). The social construction of autobiographical memory. In M. A. Conway, D. C. Rubin, H. Spinnler, & W. A. Wagenaar (Eds.), *Theoretical perspectives on autobiographical memory* (pp. 115–132). Ultrecht, Netherlands: Kluwer.

Flake, A. W., & Harrison, M. R. (1995). Fetal surgery. *Annual Review of Medicine, 46,* 67–78.

Flaks, D. K., Ficher, I., Masterpasqua, F., & Joseph, G. (1995). Lesbians choosing motherhood: A comparative study of lesbian and heterosexual parents and their children. *Developmental Psychology, 31,* 105–114.

Flanagan, C. A., & Eccles, J. S. (1993). Changes in parents' work status and adolescents' adjustment at school. *Child Development, 64,* 246–257.

Flavell, J. H. (1963). *The developmental psychology of Jean Piaget.* New York: Van Nostrand.

Flavell, J. H. (1985). *Cognitive development* (2nd ed.). Englewood Cliffs, NJ: Prentice-Hall.

Flavell, J. H. (1992). Cognitive development: Past, present, and future. *Developmental Psychology, 28,* 998–1005.

Flavell, J. H. (1993). The development of children's understanding of false belief and the appearance–reality distinction. *International Journal of Psychology, 28,* 595–604.

Flavell, J. H., Botkin, P. T., Fry, C. L., Jr., Wright, J. W., & Jarvis, P. E. (1968). *The development of role-taking and communication skills in children.* New York: Wiley.

Flavell, J. H., Flavell, E. R., Green, F. L., & Korfmacher, J. E. (1990). Do young children think of television images as pictures or real objects? *Journal of Broadcasting and Electronic Media, 34,* 399–419.

Flavell, J. H., Green, F. L., & Flavell, E. R. (1987). Development of knowledge about the appearance–reality distinction. *Monographs of the Society for Research in Child Development, 51*(1, Serial No. 212).

Flavell, J. H., Green, F. L., & Flavell, E. R. (1989). Young children's ability to differentiate appearance–reality and level 2 perspectives in the tactile modality. *Child Development, 60,* 201–213.

Flavell, J. H., Green, F. L., & Flavell, E. R. (1993). Children's understanding of the stream of consciousness. *Child Development, 64,* 387–398.

Flavell, J. H., Green, F. L., & Flavell, E. R. (1995). Young children's knowledge about thinking. *Monographs of the Society for Research in Child Development, 60*(1, Serial No. 243).

Fletcher, A. C., Darling, N. E., Steinberg, L., & Dornbusch, S. M. (1995). The company they keep: Relation of adolescents' adjustment and behavior to their friends' perceptions of authoritative parenting in the social network. *Developmental Psychology, 31,* 300–310.

Fletcher-Flinn, C. M., & Gravatt, B. (1995). The efficacy of computer-assisted instruction (CAI): A meta-analysis. *Journal of Educational Computing Research, 12,* 219–242.

Fling, S., Smith, L., Rodriguez, T., Thornton, D., Atkins, E., & Nixon, K. (1992). Videogames, aggression, and self-esteem: A survey. *Social Behavior and Personality, 20,* 39–46.

Fodor, J. A. (1983). *The modularity of mind.* Cambridge, MA: MIT Press.

Fogel, A., Melson, G. F., Toda, S., & Mistry, T. (1987). Young children's responses to unfamiliar infants. *International Journal of Behavioral Development, 10,* 1071–1077.

Fogel, A., Toda, S., & Kawai, M. (1988). Mother–infant face-to-face interaction in Japan and the United States: A laboratory comparison using 3-month-old infants. *Developmental Psychology, 24,* 398–406.

Fonagy, P., Steele, H., & Steele, M. (1991). Maternal representations of attachment during pregnancy predict the organization of infant–mother attachment at one year of age. *Child Development, 62,* 891–905.

Food Research and Action Center. (1991). *Community Childhood Hunger Identification Project.* Washington, DC: Author.

Ford, C., & Beach, F. (1951). *Patterns of sexual behavior.* New York: Harper & Row.

Forehand, R., Wierson, M., Thomas, A. M., Fauber, R., Armistead, L., Kempton, T., & Long, N. (1991). A short-term longitudinal examination of young adolescent functioning following divorce: The role of family factors. *Journal of Abnormal Child Psychology, 19,* 97–111.

Forman, E. A., & McPhail, J. (1993). Vygotskian perspective on children's collaborative problem-solving activities. In E. A. Forman, N. Minick, & C. A. Stone (Eds.), *Contexts for learning* (pp. 323–347). New York: Cambridge University Press.

Forman, G. (1993). Multiple symbolization in the long jump project. In C. Edwards, L. Gandini, & G. Forman (Eds.), *The hundred languages of children: The Reggio Emilia approach to early childhood education* (pp. 171–188). Norwood, NJ: Ablex.

Forrest, J. D., & Singh, S. (1990). The sexual and reproductive behavior of American women, 1982–1988. *Family Planning Perspectives, 22,* 206–214.

Fortier, I., Marcoux, S., & Beaulac-Baillargeon, L. (1993). Relation of caffeine intake during pregnancy to intrauterine growth retardation and preterm birth. *American Journal of Epidemiology, 137,* 931–940.

Fortier, I., Marcoux, S., & Brisson, J. (1994). Passive smoking during pregnancy and the risk of delivering a small-for-gestational-age infant. *American Journal of Epidemiology, 139,* 294–301.

Fox, C. H. (1994). Cocaine use in pregnancy. *Journal of the American Board of Family Practice, 7,* 225–228.

Fox, N. A. (1991). If it's not left, it's right: Electroencephalograph asymmetry and the development of emotion. *American Psychologist, 46,* 863–872.

Fox, N. A., Bell, M. A., & Jones, N. A. (1992). Individual differences in response to stress and cerebral asymmetry. *Developmental Neuropsychology, 8,* 161–184.

Fox, N. A., Calkins, S. D., & Bell, M. A. (1994). Neural plasticity and development in the first two years of life: Evidence from cognitive and socioemotional domains of research. *Development and Psychopathology, 6,* 677–696.

Fox, N. A., & Davidson, R. J. (1986). Taste-elicited changes in facial signs of emotion and the asymmetry of brain electrical activity in newborn infants. *Neuropsychologia, 24,* 417–422.

Fox, N. A., & Field, T. M. (1989). Individual differences in young children's adjustment to preschool. *Journal of Applied Developmental Psychology, 10,* 527–540.

Fox, N. A., & Fitzgerald, H. E. (1990). Autonomic function in infancy. *Merrill-Palmer Quarterly, 36,* 27–51.

Fox, N. A., Kimmerly, N. L., & Schafer, W. D. (1991). Attachment to mother/attachment to father: A meta-analysis. *Child Development, 62,* 210–225.

Fracasso, M. P., & Busch-Rossnagel, N. A. (1992). Parents and children of Hispanic origin. In M. E. Procidano & C. B. Fisher (Eds.), *Contemporary families: A handbook for school professionals* (pp. 93–98). New York: Teachers College Press.

Francis, P. L., & McCroy, G. (1983). *Bimodal recognition of human stimulus configurations.* Paper presented at the biennial meeting of the Society for Research in Child Development, Detroit.

Frank, S. J., Pirsch, L. A., & Wright, V. C. (1990). Late adolescents' perceptions of their relationships with their parents: Relationships among deidealization, autonomy, relatedness, and insecurity and implications for adolescent adjustment and ego identity status. *Journal of Youth and Adolescence, 19,* 571–588.

Frankel, K. A., & Bates, J. E. (1990). Mother–toddler problem solving: Antecedents in attachment, home behavior, and temperament. *Child Development, 61,* 810–819.

Frazier, M. M. (1994). Issues, problems and programs in nurturing the disadvantaged and culturally different talented. In K. A. Heller, F. J., Jonks, & H. A. Passow (Eds.), *International handbook of research and development of giftedness and talent* (pp. 685–692). Oxford: Pergamon Press.

Frederiksen, J. R., & Warren, B. M. (1987). A cognitive framework for developing expertise in reading. In R. Glaser (Ed.), *Advances in instructional psychology* (Vol. 3, pp. 1–39). Hillsdale, NJ: Erlbaum.

Freedman, D. G., & Freedman, N. (1969). Behavioral differences between Chinese-American and European-American newborns. *Nature, 224,* 1227.

Freeman, D. (1983). *Margaret Mead and Samoa: The making and unmaking of an anthropological myth.* Cambridge, MA: Harvard University Press.

French, D. C. (1984). Children's knowledge of the social functions of younger, older, and same-age peers. *Child Development, 55,* 1429–1433.

Freud, A., & Dann, S. (1951). An experiment in group upbringing. *Psychoanalytic Study of the Child, 6,* 127–168.

Freud, S. (1961). Some psychological consequences of the anatomical distinction between the sexes. In J. Strachey (Ed.), *Standard edition of the complete psychological works of Sigmund Freud* (Vol. 19, pp. 248–258). London: Hogarth Press. (Original work published 1925)

Freud, S. (1973). *An outline of psychoanalysis.* London: Hogarth. (Original work published 1938)

Freud, S. (1974). *The ego and the id.* London: Hogarth. (Original work published 1923)

Frey, K. S., & Ruble, D. N. (1992). Gender constancy and the "cost" of sex-typed behavior: A test of the conflict hypothesis. *Developmental Psychology, 28,* 714–721.

Fried, P. A. (1993). Prenatal exposure to tobacco and marijuana: Effects during pregnancy, infancy, and early childhood. *Clinical Obstetrics and Gynecology, 36,* 319–337.

Fried, P. A., & Makin, J. E. (1987). Neonatal behavioral correlates of prenatal exposure to marijuana, cigarettes, and alcohol in a low risk population. *Neurobehavioral Toxicology and Teratology, 9,* 1–7.

Fried, P. A., & Watkinson, B. (1990). 36- and 48-month neurobehavioral follow-up of children prenatally exposed to marijuana, cigarettes, and alcohol. *Journal of Developmental and Behavioral Pediatrics, 11,* 49–58.

Friedman, J. A., & Weinberger, H. L. (1990). Six children with lead poisoning. *American Journal of Diseases of Children, 144,* 1039–1044.

Friedman, L. (1989). Mathematics and the gender gap: A meta-analysis of recent studies on sex differences in mathematical tasks. *Review of Educational Research, 59,* 185–214.

Friedman, M., & Weiss, E. (1993, December). America's vaccine crisis. *Parents,* pp. 39–43.

Friedman, S. L., Scholnick, E. K., & Cocking, R. R. (1987). Reflections on reflections: What planning is and how it develops. In S. L. Friedman, E. K. Scholnick, & R. R. Cocking (Eds.), *Blueprints for thinking: The role of planning in cognitive development* (pp. 515–534). New York: Cambridge University Press.

Friedrich-Cofer, L. K., Tucker, C. J., Norris-Baker, C., Farnsworth, J. B., Fisher, D. P., Hannington, C. M., & Hoxie, K. (1978). *Perceptions by adolescents of television heroines.* Paper presented at the annual meeting of the Southwestern Psychological Association, New Orleans.

Friel-Patti, S., & Finitzo-Hieber, T. (1990). Language learning in a prospective study of otitis media with effusion in the first two years of life. *Journal of Speech and Hearing Research, 33,* 188–194.

Friend, M., & Davis, T. L. (1993). Appearance–reality distinction: Children's understanding of the physical and affective domains. *Developmental Psychology, 29,* 907–914.

Frodi, A. (1985). When empathy fails: Aversive infant crying and child abuse. In B. M. Lester & C. F. Z. Boukydis (Eds.), *Infant crying: Theoretical and research perspectives* (pp. 263–277). New York: Plenum.

Froggatt, P., Beckwith, J. B., Schwartz, P. J., Valdes-Dapena, M., & Southall, D. P. (1988). Cardiac and respiratory mechanisms that might be responsible for sudden infant death syndrome. *Annals of the New York Academy of Sciences, 533,* 421–426.

Froom, J., & Culpepper, L. (1991). Otitis media in day-care children: A report from the International Primary Care Network. *Journal of Family Practice, 32,* 289–294.

Fuchs, I., Eisenberg, N., Hertz-Lazarowitz, R., & Sharabany, R. (1986). Kibbutz, Israeli city, and American children's moral reasoning about prosocial moral conflicts. *Merrill-Palmer Quarterly, 32,* 37–50.

Fuhrman, T., & Holmbeck, G. N. (1995). A contextual-moderator analysis of emotional autonomy and adjustment in adolescence. *Child Development, 66,* 793–811.

Fujinaga, T., Kasuga, T., Uchida, N., & Saiga, H. (1990). Long-term follow-up study of children developmentally retarded by early environmental deprivation. *Genetic, Social and General Psychology Monographs, 116,* 37–104.

Fuligni, A. J., & Stevenson, H. W. (1995). Time use and mathematics achievement among American, Chinese, and Japanese high school students. *Child Development, 66,* 830–842.

Furman, W., & Buhrmester, D. (1992). Age and sex differences in perceptions of networks of personal relationships. *Child Development, 63,* 103–115.

Furstenberg, F. F., Jr., & Cherlin, A. J. (1991). *Divided families.* Cambridge, MA: Harvard University Press.

Furstenberg, F. F., Jr., & Crawford, D. B. (1978). Family support: Helping teenagers to cope. *Family Planning Perspectives, 10,* 322–333.

Furstenberg, F. F., Jr., & Nord, C. W. (1985). Parenting apart: Patterns of childrearing after marital disruption. *Journal of Marriage and the Family, 47,* 893–904.

Furstenberg, F. F., Jr., Brooks-Gunn, J., & Chase-Landsdale, L. (1989). Teenaged pregnancy and childbearing. *American Psychologist, 44,* 313–320.

Furstenberg, F. F., Jr., Brooks-Gunn, J., & Morgan, S. P. (1987). *Adolescent mothers and their children in later life.* Cambridge: Cambridge University Press.

Furstenberg, F. F., Jr., Levine, J. A., & Brooks-Gunn, J. (1990). The children of teenage mothers: Patterns of early childbearing in two generations. *Family Planning Perspectives, 22,* 54–61.

Fuson, K. C. (1988). *Children's counting and concepts of number.* New York: Springer-Verlag.

Fuson, K. C. (1990). Issues in place-value and multidigit addition and subtraction learning and teaching. *Journal of Research in Mathematics Education, 21,* 273–280.

Fuson, K. C. (1992). Research on learning and teaching addition and subtraction of whole numbers. In G. Leinhardt, R. T. Putnam, & R. A. Hattrup (Eds.), *The analysis of arithmetic for mathematics teaching* (pp. 53–187). Hillsdale, NJ: Erlbaum.

Fuson, K. C., & Kwon, Y. (1992). Korean children's understanding of multidigit addition and subtraction. *Child Development, 63,* 491–506.

G

Gaddis, A., & Brooks-Gunn, J. (1985). The male experience of pubertal change. *Journal of Youth and Adolescence, 14,* 61–69.

Gaensbauer, T. J. (1980). Anaclitic depression in a three-and-one-half month-old child. *American Journal of Psychiatry, 137,* 841–842.

Gagan, R. J. (1984). The families of children who fail to thrive: Preliminary investigations of parental deprivation among organic and non-organic cases. *Child Abuse and Neglect, 8,* 93–103.

Galambos, N. L., & Maggs, J. L. (1991). Children in self-care: Figures, facts, and fiction. In J. V. Lerner & N. L. Galambos (Eds.), *Employed mothers and their children* (pp. 131–157). New York: Garland.

Galin, D., Johnstone, J., Nakell, L., & Herron, J. (1979). Development of the capacity for tactile information transfer between hemispheres in normal children. *Science, 204,* 1330–1332.

Galinsky, E., Howes, C., Kontos, S., & Shinn, M. (1994). *The study of children in family child care and relative care: Highlights of findings.* New York: Families and Work Institute.

Galler, J. R., Ramsey, C. F., Morley, D. S., Archer, E., & Salt, P. (1990). The long-term effects of early kwashiorkor compared with marasmus. IV. Performance on the National High School Entrance Examination. *Pediatric Research, 28,* 235–239.

Galler, J. R., Ramsey, F., & Solimano, G. (1985a). A follow-up study of the effects of early malnutrition on subsequent development: I. Physical growth and sexual maturation during adolescence. *Pediatric Research, 19,* 518–523.

Galler, J. R., Ramsey, F., & Solimano, G. (1985b). A follow-up study of the effects of early malnutrition on subsequent development: II. Fine motor skills in adolescence. *Pediatric Research, 19,* 524–527.

Galler, J. R., Ramsey, F., Solimano, G., Kucharski, L. T., & Harrison, R. (1984). The influence of early malnutrition on subsequent behavioral development: IV. Soft neurological signs. *Pediatric Research, 18,* 826–832.

Gallimore, R., & Tharp, R. G. (1990). Teaching mind in society: Teaching, schooling, and literate discourse. In L. C. Moll (Ed.), *Vygotsky and education* (pp. 175–205). New York: Cambridge University Press.

Gallistel, C. R., & Gelman, R. (1992). Preverbal and verbal counting and computation. *Cognition, 44,* 43–74.

Galotti, K. M., Kozberg, S. F., & Farmer, M. C. (1991). Gender and developmental differences in adolescents' conceptions of moral reasoning. *Journal of Youth and Adolescence, 20,* 13–30.

Galton, F. (1883). *Inquiries into human faculty and its development.* London: Macmillan.

Gamoran, A., Nystrand, M., Berends, M., & LePore, P. C. (1995). An organizational analysis of the effect of ability grouping. *American Educational Research Journal, 32,* 687–715.

Gandini, L. (1993). Fundamentals of the Reggio Emilia approach to early childhood education. *Young Children, 49*(1), 4–8.

Gandour, M. J. (1989). Activity level as a dimension of temperament in toddlers: Its relevance for the organismic specificity hypothesis. *Child Development, 60,* 1092–1098.

Gannon, S., & Korn, S. J. (1983). Temperament, cultural variation, and behavior disorder in preschool children. *Child Psychiatry and Human Development, 13,* 203–212.

Garbarino, J., & Kostelny, K. (1992). Child maltreatment as a community problem. *Child Abuse and Neglect, 16,* 455–464.

Garbarino, J., & Kostelny, K. (1993). Neighborhood and community influences on parenting. In T. Luster & L. Okagaki (1993). *Parenting: An ecological perspective* (pp. 203–226). Hillsdale, NJ: Erlbaum.

Gardner, H. (1980). *Artful scribbles: The significance of children's drawings.* New York: Basic Books.

Gardner, H. (1983). *Frames of mind.* New York: Basic Books.

Gardner, H. (1993). *Multiple intelligences: The theory in practice.* New York: Basic Books.

Gardner, M. J., Snee, M. P., Hall, A. J., Powell, C. A., Downes, S., & Terrell, J. D. (1990). Leukemia cases linked to fathers' radiation dose. *Nature, 343,* 423–429.

Gardner, R. A., &, Gardner, B. T. (1969). Teaching sign language to a chimpanzee. *Science, 165,* 664–672.

Garland, A. F., & Zigler, E. (1993). Adolescent suicide prevention: Current research and social policy implications. *American Psychologist, 48,* 169–182.

Garmezy, N. (1991). Resilience and vulnerability to adverse developmental outcomes associated with poverty. *American Behavioral Scientist, 34,* 416–430.

Garmezy, N. (1993). Children in poverty: Resilience despite risk. *Psychiatry,* 56, 127–136.

Garmon, L. C., Basinger, K. S., Gregg, V. R., & Gibbs, J. C. (1995, April.) *Gender differences in stage and expression of moral judgment.* Paper presented at the biennial meeting of the Society for Research in Child Development, Indianapolis.

Garmon, L. C., Basinger, K. S., Gregg, V. R., & Gibbs, J. C. (1996). Gender differences in stage and expression of moral judgment. *Merrill-Palmer Quarterly, 42,* 418–437.

Garner, D. M. (1993). Pathogenesis of anorexia nervosa. *Lancet, 341,* 1631–1635.

Garner, P. W., Jones, D. C., & Miner, J. L. (1994). Social competence among low-income preschoolers: Emotion socialization practices and social cognitive correlates. *Child Development, 65,* 622–637.

Garvey, C. (1974). Requests and responses in children's speech. *Journal of Child Language, 2,* 41–60.

Garvey, C. (1990). *Play.* Cambridge, MA: Harvard University Press.

Garwood, S. G., Phillips, D., Hartman, A., & Zigler, E. F. (1989). As the pendulum swings: Federal agency programs for children. *American Psychologist, 44,* 434–440.

Gaskins, S. (1994). Symbolic play in a Mayan village. *Merrill-Palmer Quarterly, 40,* 344–359.

Gathercole, S. E., Willis, C. S., Emslie, H., & Baddeley, A. D. (1992). Phonological memory and vocabulary development during the early school years: A longitudinal study. *Developmental Psychology, 28,* 887–898.

Gathercole, V. C. (1987). The contrastive hypothesis for the acquisition of word meaning: A reconsideration of the theory. *Journal of Child Language, 14,* 493–531.

Gauvain, M., & Rogoff, B. (1989a). Collaborative problem solving and children's planning skills. *Developmental Psychology, 25,* 139–151.

Gauvain, M., & Rogoff, B. (1989b). Ways of speaking about space: The development of children's skill in communicating spatial knowledge. *Cognitive Development, 4,* 295–307.

Geary, D. C. (1994). *Children's mathematical development.* Washington, DC: American Psychological Association.

Geary, D. C. (1995). Reflections of evolution and culture in children's cognition. *American Psychologist, 50,* 24–37.

Geary, D. C., Bow-Thomas, C. C., Fan, L., & Siegler, R. S. (1993). Even before formal instruction, Chinese children outperform American children in mental addition. *Cognitive Development, 8,* 517–529.

Geary, D. C., & Burlingham-Dubree, M. (1989). External validation of the strategy choice model for addition. *Journal of Experimental Child Psychology, 47,* 175–192.

Gekoski, M. J., Rovee-Collier, C. K., & Carulli-Rabinowitz, V. (1983). A longitudinal analysis of inhibition of infant distress: The origins of social expectations? *Infant Behavior and Development, 6,* 339–351.

Gellatly, A. R. H. (1987). Acquisition of a concept of logical necessity. *Human Development, 30,* 32–47.

Gelles, R. J., & Cornell, C. P. (1983). International perspectives on child abuse. *Child Abuse & Neglect, 7,* 375–386.

Gelman, R. (1972). Logical capacity of very young children: Number invariance rules. *Child Development, 43,* 75–90.

Gelman, R. (1990). First principles organize attention to and learning about relevant data: Number and animate–inanimate distinction as examples. *Cognitive Science, 14,* 79–106.

Gelman, R., & Shatz, M. (1978). Appropriate speech adjustments: The operation of conversational constraints on talk to two-year-olds. In M. Lewis & L. A. Rosenblum (Eds.), *Interaction, conversation, and the development of language* (pp. 27–61). New York: Wiley.

Gentner, D., & Rattermann, M. J. (1991). Language and the career of similarity. In S. A. Gelman & J. P. Byrnes (Eds.), *Perspectives on language and thought: Interrelations in development* (pp. 225–277). Cambridge: Cambridge University Press.

George, C., Kaplan, N., & Main, M. (1985). *The Adult Attachment Interview.* Unpublished manuscript, University of California at Berkeley.

Gerbner, G., Gross, L., Signorielli, N., Morgan, M., & Jackson-Beeck, M. (1979). The demonstration of power: Violence Profile No. 10. *Journal of Communication, 29*(3), 177–195.

Gerbner, G., & Signorielli, N. (1990). *Violence profile, 1967 through 1988–1989. Enduring patterns.* Unpublished manuscript, Annenberg School of Communication, University of Pennsylvania, Philadelphia.

Gershman, E. S., & Hayes, D. S. (1983). Differential stability of reciprocal friendships and unilateral relationships among preschool children. *Merrill-Palmer Quarterly, 29,* 169–177.

Gershon, E. S., Targum, S. D., Kessler, L. R., Mazure, C. M., & Bunney, W. E., Jr. (1977). Genetics studies and biologic strategies in affective disorders. *Progress in Medical Genetics, 2,* 103–164.

Gervai, J., Turner, P. J., & Hinde, R. A. (1995). Gender-related behaviour, attitudes, and personality in parents of young children in England and Hungary. *International Journal of Behavioral Development, 18,* 105–126.

Gesell, A. (1933). Maturation and patterning of behavior. In C. Murchison (Ed.), *A handbook of child psychology.* Worcester, MA: Clark University Press.

Gesell, A., & Ilg, F. L. (1949). The child from five to ten. In A. Gesell & F. Ilg (Eds.), *Child development* (pp. 394–454). New York: Harper & Row.

Gettinger, M., Doll, B., & Salmon, D. (1994). Effects of social problem solving, goal setting, and parent training on children's peer relations. *Journal of Applied Developmental Psychology, 15,* 141–163.

Getzels, J., & Csikszentmihalyi, M. (1976). *The creative vision: A longitudinal study of problem-finding in art.* New York: Wiley.

Gewirtz, J. (1969). Mechanisms of social learning: Some roles of stimulation and behavior in early human development. In D. A. Goslin (Eds.), *Handbook of socialization theory and research* (pp. 57–212). Skokie, IL: Rand McNally.

Gewirtz, J. L., & Boyd, E. F. (1977a). Does maternal responding imply reduced infant crying? A critique of the 1972 Bell and Ainsworth report. *Child Development, 48,* 1200–1207.

Gewirtz, J. L., & Boyd, E. F. (1977b). In reply to the rejoinder to our critique of the 1972 Bell and Ainsworth report. *Child Development, 48,* 1217–1218.

Ghiglieri, M. P. (1988). *East of the mountains of the moon: Chimpanzee society in the African rain forest.* New York: Free Press.

Gibbs, J. C. (1991). Toward an integration of Kohlberg's and Hoffman's theories of morality. In W. M. Kurtines & J. L. Gewirtz (Eds.), *Handbook of moral behavior and development* (Vol. 1, pp. 183–222). Hillsdale, NJ: Erlbaum.

Gibbs, J. C. (1993). Moral-cognitive interventions. In A. P. Goldstein & C. R. Huff (Eds.), *The gang intervention handbook* (pp. 159–185). Champaign, IL: Research Press.

Gibbs, J. C. (1994). The cognitive developmental perspective. In W. M. Kurtines & J. L. Gewirtz (Eds.), *Moral development: An introduction* (pp. 27–48). Boston: Allyn and Bacon.

Gibbs, J. C. (1995). The cognitive developmental perspective. In W. M. Kurtines & J. L. Gewirtz (Eds.), *Moral development: An introduction* (pp. 27–48). Boston: Allyn and Bacon.

Gibbs, J. C., Basinger, K. S., & Fuller, D. (1992). *Moral maturity: Measuring the development of sociomoral reflection.* Hillsdale, NJ: Erlbaum.

Gibbs, J. C., Clark, P. M., Joseph, J. A., Green, J. L., Goodrick, T. S., & Makowski, D. G. (1986). Relations between moral judgment, moral courage, and field independence. *Child Development, 57,* 185–193.

Gibbs, J. C., Potter, G. B., & Goldstein, A. P. (1995). *The EQUIP program: Teaching youth to think and act responsibly through a peer-helping approach.* Champaign, IL: Research Press.

Gibbs, J. C., & Schnell, S. V. (1985). Moral development "versus" socialization. *American Psychologist, 40,* 1071–1080.

Gibson, D., & Harris, A. (1988). Aggregated early intervention effects for Down's syndrome persons: Patterning and longevity of benefits. *Journal of Mental Deficiency Research, 32,* 1–7.

Gibson, E. J. (1970). The development of perception as an adaptive process. *American Scientist, 58,* 98–107.

Gibson, E. J. (1988). Exploratory behavior in the development of perceiving, acting, and the acquiring of knowledge. *Annual Review of Psychology, 39,* 1–41.

Gibson, E. J., & Walk, R. D. (1960). The "visual cliff." *Scientific American, 202,* 64–71.

Gibson, J. J. (1979). *The ecological approach to visual perception.* Boston: Houghton Mifflin.

Gil, D. G. (1987). Maltreatment as a function of the structure of social systems. In M. R. Brassard, R. Germain, & S. N. Hart (Eds.), *Psychological maltreatment of children and youth* (pp. 159–170). New York: Pergamon Press.

Gilfillan, M. C., Curtis, L., Liston, W. A., Pullen, I., Whyte, D. A., & Brock, D. J. H. (1992). Prenatal screening for cystic fibrosis. *Lancet, 340,* 214–216.

Gilger, J. W., & Ho, H-Z. (1989). Gender differences in adult spatial information processing: Their relationship to pubertal timing, adolescent activities, and sex-typing of personality. *Cognitive Development, 4,* 197–214.

Gilligan, C. F. (1982). *In a different voice.* Cambridge, MA: Harvard University Press.

Gillmore, M. R., Hawkins, J. D., Day, L. E., & Catalano, R. F. (1996). Friendship and deviance: New evidence on an old controversy. *Journal of Early Adolescence,* 16.

Ginsburg, H. P., & Opper, S. (1988). *Piaget's theory of intellectual development* (3rd ed.). Englewood Cliffs, NJ: Prentice-Hall.

Glass, G. V., Cahen, L. S., Smith, M. L., & Filby, N. N. (1982). *School class size.* Beverly Hills, CA: Sage.

Gleitman, L. R. (1990). The structural sources of verb meanings. *Language Acquisition, 1,* 3–55.

Glick, J. (1975). Cognitive development in cross-cultural perspective. In F. Horowitz (Ed.), *Review of child development research* (Vol. 4, pp. 595–654). Chicago: University of Chicago Press.

Glick, P. C. (1990). American families: As they are and were. Sociology and Social Research, 74, 139–145.

Glover, J. A. (1977). Risky shift and creativity. *Social Behavior and Personality, 5,* 317–320.

Gnepp, J. (1983). Children's social sensitivity: Inferring emotions from conflicting cues. *Developmental Psychology, 19,* 805–814.

Goduka, I. N., Poole, D. A., & Aotaki-Phenice, L. (1992). A comparative study of black South African children from three different contexts. *Child Development, 63,* 509–525.

Goelman, H. (1986). The language environments of family day care. In S. Kilmer (Ed.), *Advances in early education and day care* (Vol. 4, pp. 153–179). Greenwich, CT: JAI Press.

Goffin, S. G. (1988, March). Putting our advocacy efforts into a new context. *Young Children, 43*(3), 52–56.

Goldberg, W. A., & Easterbrooks, M. A. (1988). Maternal employment when children are toddlers and kindergartners. In A. E. Gottfried & A. W. Gottfried (Eds.), *Maternal employment and children's development: Longitudinal research.* New York: Plenum.

Goldfield, B. A. (1987). The contributions of child and caregiver to referential and expressive language. *Applied Psycholinguistics, 8,* 267–280.

Goldin-Meadow, S., & Morford, M. (1985). Gesture in early language: Studies of deaf and hearing children. *Merrill-Palmer Quarterly, 31,* 145–176.

Goldin-Meadow, S., & Mylander, C. (1983). Gestural communication in deaf children: Noneffect of parental input on language development. *Science, 221,* 372–374.

Goldsmith, D. F., & Rogoff, B. (1995). Sensitivity and teaching by dysphoric and nondysphoric women in structured versus unstructured situations. *Developmental Psychology, 31,* 388–394.

Goldsmith, H. H. (1987). Roundtable: What is temperament? Four approaches. *Child Development, 58,* 505–529.

Goleman, D. (1980, February). 1,528 little geniuses and how they grew. *Psychology Today, 13*(9), 28–53.

Golinkoff, R. M. (1983). The preverbal negotiation of failed messages: Insights into the transition period. In R. M. Golinkoff (Ed.), *The transition of prelinguistic to linguistic communication* (pp. 57–78). Hillsdale, NJ: Erlbaum.

Golinkoff, R. M., Hirsh-Pasek, K., Bailey, L. M., & Wenger, N. R. (1992). Young children and adults use lexical principles to learn new nouns. *Developmental Psychology, 28,* 99–108.

Golombok, S., & Fivush, R. (1994). *Gender development.* New York: Cambridge University Press.

Golomb, C., & Galasso, L. (1995). Make believe and reality: Explorations of the imaginary realm. *Developmental Psychology, 31,* 800–810.

Golombok, S., Cook, R., Bish, A., & Murray, C. (1995). Families created by the new reproductive technologies: Quality of parenting and social and emotional development of the children. *Child Development, 66,* 285–298.

Golombok, S., & Tasker, F. L. (1996). Do parents influence the sexual orientation of their children? Findings from a longitudinal study of lesbian families. *Developmental Psychology, 32,* 3–11.

Gomez-Schwartz, B., Horowitz, J. M., & Cardarelli, A. P. (1990). *Child sexual abuse: Initial effects.* Newbury Park, CA: Sage.

Göncü, A. (1993). Development of intersubjectivity in the dyadic play of preschoolers. *Early Childhood Research Quarterly, 8,* 99–116.

Good, T. L., & Brophy, J. E. (1994). *Looking in classrooms* (6th ed.). New York: HarperCollins.

Goodall, J. (1990). *Through a window: My thirty years with the chimpanzees of Gombe.* Boston: Houghton Mifflin.

Goodenough, F. L. (1931). *Anger in young children.* Minneapolis: University of Minnesota Press.

Goodman, G. S., Hirschman, J. E., Hepps, D., & Rudy, L. (1991). Children's memory for stressful events. *Merrill-Palmer Quarterly, 37,* 109–158.

Goodman, G. S., & Tobey, A. E. (1994). Memory development within the context of child sexual abuse investigations. In C. B. Fisher & R. M. Lerner (Eds.), *Applied developmental psychology* (pp. 46–75). New York: McGraw-Hill.

Goodman, K. S. (1986). *What's whole in whole language?* Portsmouth, NH: Heinemann.

Goodman, S. H., Brogan, D., Lynch, M. E., & Fielding, B. (1993). Social and emotional competence in children of depressed mothers. *Child Development, 64,* 516–531.

Goodman, S. H., Gravitt, G. W., Jr., & Kaslow, N. J. (1995). Social problem solving: A moderator of the relation between negative life stress and depression symptoms in children. *Journal of Abnormal Child Psychology, 23,* 473–485.

Goossens, F. A., & van IJzendoorn, M. H. (1990). Quality of infants' attachments to professional caregivers: Relation to infant–parent attachment and day-care characteristics. *Child Development, 61,* 832–837.

Gopnik, A., & Choi, S. (1990). Do linguistic differences lead to cognitive differences? A cross-linguistic study of semantic and cognitive development. *First Language, 11,* 199–215.

Gopnik, A., & Choi, S. (1995). Names, relational words, and cognitive development in English and Korean speakers: Nouns are not always learned before verbs. In A. Gopnik & S. Choi (Eds.), *Beyond names for things: Children's acquisition of verbs* (pp. 63–80). Hillsdale, NJ: Erlbaum.

Gopnik, A., & Meltzoff, A. N. (1986). Relations between semantic and cognitive development in the one-word stage: The specificity hypothesis. *Child Development, 57,* 1040–1053.

Gopnik, A., & Meltzoff, A. N. (1987a). The development of categorization in the second year and its relation to other cognitive and linguistic developments. *Child Development, 58,* 1523–1531.

Gopnik, A., & Meltzoff, A. N. (1987b). Language and thought in the young child: Early semantic developments and their relationships to object permanence, means–ends understanding, and categorization. In K. Nelson & A. Van Kleeck (Eds.), *Children's language* (Vol. 6, pp. 191–212). Hillsdale, NJ: Erlbaum.

Gopnik, A., & Meltzoff, A. N. (1992). Categorization and naming: Basic-level sorting in eighteen-month-olds and its relation to language. *Child Development, 63,* 1091–1103.

Gopnik, A., & Wellman, H. M. (1994). The theory theory. In L. A. Hirschfeld & S. A. Gelman (Eds.), *Mapping the mind* (pp. 257–293). New York: Cambridge University Press.

Gordon, P., & Chafetz, J. (1990). Verb-based versus class-based accounts of actionality effects in children's comprehension of passives. *Cognition, 36,* 227–254.

Gorman, J., Leifer, M., & Grossman, G. (1993). Nonorganic failure to thrive: Maternal history and current maternal functioning. *Journal of Clinical Child Psychology, 22,* 327–336.

Gorn, G. J., & Goldberg, M. E. (1982). Behavioral evidence of the effects of televised food messages on children. *Journal of Consumer Research, 9,* 200–205.

Gortmaker, S. L., Dietz, W. H., & Cheung, L. W. Y. (1990). Inactivity, diet, and the fattening of America. *Journal of the American Dietetic Association, 90,* 1247–1252.

Gortmaker, S. L., Must, A., Perrin, J. M., Sobol, A. M., & Dietz, W. H., Jr. (1993). Social and economic consequences of overweight in adolescence and young adulthood. *New England Journal of Medicine, 329,* 1008–1012.

Goswami, V., & Bryant, P. (1990). *Phonological skills and learning to read.* Hillsdale, NJ: Erlbaum.

Gottesman, I. I. (1963). Genetic aspects of intelligent behavior. In N. R. Ellis (Ed.), *Handbook of mental deficiency* (pp. 253–296). New York: McGraw-Hill.

Gottesman, I. I., Carey, G., & Hanson, D. R. (1983). Pearls and perils in epigenetic psychopathology. In S. B. Guze, E. J. Earls, & J. E. Barrett (Eds.), *Childhood psychopathology and development* (pp. 287–300). New York: Raven Press.

Gottfried, A. E. (1991). Maternal employment in the family setting: Developmental and environmental issues. In J. V. Lerner & N. L. Galambos (Eds.), *Employed mothers and their children* (pp. 63–84). New York: Garland.

Gottfried, A. E., Gottfried, A. W., & Bathurst, K. (1988). Maternal employment, family environment, and children's development: Infancy through the school years. In A. E. Gottfried & A. W. Gottfried (Eds.), *Maternal employment and children's development: Longitudinal research* (pp. 11–58). New York: Plenum.

Gottlieb, G. (1991). Experiential canalization of behavioral development: Theory. *Developmental Psychology, 27,* 4–13.

Gottman, J. M., Gonso, J., & Rasmussen, B. (1975). Social interaction, social competence, and friendship in children. *Child Development, 46,* 709–718.

Goy, R. W., & Goldfoot, D. A. (1974). Experiential and hormonal factors influencing development of sexual behavior in the male rhesus monkey. In R. O. Schmitt & F. G. Worden (Eds.), *The neurosciences* (pp. 571–581). Cambridge, MA: MIT Press.

Graber, J. A., Brooks-Gunn, J., Paikoff, R. L. & Warren, M. P. (1994). Prediction of eating problems: An 8-year study of adolescent girls. *Developmental Psychology, 30,* 823–834.

Graham, F. K., Ernhart, C. B., Thurston, D. L., & Craft, M. (1962). Development three years after perinatal anoxia and other potentially damaging newborn experiences. *Psychological Monographs, 76*(3, No. 522).

Graham, P. (1979). Epidemiological studies. In H. C. Quay & J. S. Werry (Eds.), *Psychopathological disorders of childhood* (pp. 185–246). New York: Wiley.

Graham, S., Doubleday, C., & Guarino, P. A. (1984). The development of relations between perceived controllability and the emotions of pity, anger, and guilt. *Child Development, 55,* 561–565.

Gralinski, J. H., & Kopp, C. B. (1993). Everyday rules for behavior: Mothers' requests to young children. *Developmental Psychology, 29,* 573–584.

Grant, J. P. (1994). *The state of the world's children 1994.* New York: Oxford University Press for UNICEF.

Grant, J. P. (1995). *The state of the world's children 1995.* New York: Oxford University Press for UNICEF.

Grantham-McGregor, S., Powell, C., Walker, S., Chang, S., & Fletcher, P. (1994). The long-term follow-up of severely malnourished children who participated in an intervention program. *Child Development, 65,* 428–439.

Grattan, M. P., De Vos, E., Levy, J., & McClintock, M. K. (1992). Asymmetric action in the human newborn: Sex differences in patterns of organization. *Child Development, 63,* 273–289.

Grau, P. N. (1985). Counseling the gifted girl. *Gifted Child Today, 38,* 8–11.

Gravel, J. S., & Wallace, I. F. (1992). Listening and language at 4 years of age: Effects of early otitis media. *Journal of Speech and Hearing Research, 35,* 588–595.

Graves, S. B. (1993). Television, the portrayal of African Americans, and the development of children's attitudes. In G. L. Berry & J. K. Asamen (Eds.), *Children and television* (pp. 179–190). Newbury Park, CA: Sage.

Gray, C. E. (1966). A measurement of creativity in Western civilization. *American Anthropologist, 68,* 1384–1417.

Green, G. D., & Bozett, F. W. (1991). Lesbian mothers and gay fathers. In J. C. Gonsiorek & J. D. Weinrich (Eds.), *Homosexuality* (pp. 197–214). Newbury Park, CA: Sage.

Green, J. A., Jones, L. E., & Gustafson, G. E. (1987). Perception of cries by parents and nonparents: Relation to cry acoustics. *Developmental Psychology, 23,* 370–382.

Green, R. (1987). *The "sissy boy" syndrome and the development of homosexuality.* New Haven, CT: Yale University Press.

Greenberger, E., & Goldberg, W. A. (1989). Work, parenting, and the socialization of children. *Developmental Psychology, 25,* 22–35.

Greenberger, E., O'Neil, R., & Nagel, S. K. (1994). Linking workplace and homeplace: Relations between the nature of adults' work and their parenting behaviors. *Developmental Psychology, 30,* 990–1002.

Greenberger, E., & Steinberg, L. (1986). *When teenagers work.* New York: Basic Books.

Greenbowe, T., Herron, J. D., Lucas, C., Nurrenbern, S., Staver, J. R., & Ward, C. R. (1981). Teaching preadolescents to act as scientists: Replication and extension of an earlier study. *Journal of Educational Psychology, 73,* 705–711.

Greenfield, P. (1992, June). *Notes and references for developmental psychology.* Conference on Making Basic Texts in Psychology More Culture-Inclusive and Culture-Sensitive, Western Washington University, Bellingham, WA.

Greenfield, P. M. (1994). Independence and interdependence as developmental scripts: Implications for theory, research, and practice. In P. M. Greenfield & R. R. Cocking (Eds.), *Cross-cultural roots of minority child development* (pp. 1–37). Hillsdale, NJ: Erlbaum.

Greenfield, P. M. (1984). *Mind and media: The effects of television, video games, and computers.* Cambridge, MA: Harvard University Press.

Greeno, J. G. (1989). A perspective on thinking. *American Psychologist, 44,* 134–141.

Greenough, W. T., & Black, J. E. (1992). Induction of brain structure by experience: Substrates for cognitive development. In M. R. Gunnar & C. A. Nelson (Eds.), *Minnesota Symposia on Child Psychology* (pp. 155–200). Hillsdale, NJ: Erlbaum.

Greenough, W. T., Black, J. E., & Wallace, C. S. (1987). Experience and brain development. *Child Development, 58,* 539–559.

Greenough, W. T., Wallace, C. S., Alcantara, A. A., Anderson, B. J., Hawrylak, N., Sirevaag, A. M., Weiler, I. J., & Withers, G. S. (1993). Development of the brain: Experience affects the structure of neurons, glia, and blood vessels. In N. J. Anastasiow & S. Harel (Eds.), *At-risk infants: Interventions, families, and research* (pp. 173–185). Baltimore: Paul H. Brookes.

Greif, E. B. (1979). *Sex differences in parent–child conversations: Who interrupts who?* Paper presented at the annual meeting of the Society for Research in Child Development, Boston.

Gregg, V., Gibbs, J. C., & Fuller, D. (1994). Patterns of developmental delay in moral judgment by male and female delinquents. *Merrill-Palmer Quarterly, 40,* 538–553.

Gribble, P. A., Cowen, E. L., Wyman, P. A., Work, W. C., Wannon, M., & Raoof, A. (1993). Parent and child views of parent–child relationship qualities and resilient outcomes among urban children. *Journal of Child Psychology and Psychiatry, 34,* 507–519.

Grisso, T. (1992). Minors' assent to behavioral research without parental consent. In B. Stanley & J. E. Sieber (Eds.), *Social research on children and adolescents: Ethical issues* (pp. 109–139). Newbury Park, CA: Sage.

Grodzinsky, G. M., & Diamond, R. (1992). Frontal lobe functioning in boys with attention-deficit hyperactivity disorder. *Developmental Neuropsychology, 8,* 427–445.

Grolnick, W. S., & Slowiaczek, M. L. (1994). Parents' involvement in children's schooling: A multidimensional conceptualization and motivational model. *Child Development, 65,* 237–252.

Grossman, H. J. (Ed.). (1983). *Classification in mental retardation.* Washington, DC: American Association on Mental Deficiency.

Grossmann, K., Grossmann, K. E., Spangler, G., Suess, G., & Unzner, L. (1985). Maternal sensitivity and newborns' orientation responses as related to quality of attachment in Northern Germany. In I. Bretherton & E. Waters (Eds.), Growing points of attachment theory and research. *Monographs of the Society for Research in Child Development, 50*(1–2, Serial No. 209).

Grotevant, H. D. (1978). Sibling constellations and sex-typing of interests in adolescence. *Child Development, 49,* 540–542.

Grotevant, H. D., & Cooper, C. R. (1981). *Assessing adolescent identity in the areas of occupation, religion, politics, friendships, dating, and sex roles: Manual for administration and coding of the interview.* Austin: University of Texas Press.

Grotevant, H. D., & Cooper, C. R. (1988). The role of family experience in career exploration during adolescence. In P. Baltes, D. Featherman, & R. Lerner (Eds.), *Life-span development and behavior* (Vol. 8, pp. 231–258). Hillsdale, NJ: Erlbaum.

Grusec, J. E. (1988). *Social development: History, theory, and research.* New York: Springer-Verlag.

Grusec, J. E. (1992). Social learning theory and developmental psychology: The legacies of Robert Sears and Albert Bandura. *Developmental Psychology, 28,* 776–786.

Grusec, J. E., & Abramovitch, R. (1982). Imitation of peers and adults in a natural setting: A functional analysis. *Child Development, 53,* 636–642.

Grusec, J. E., Kuczynski, L., Rushton, J., & Simutis, Z. (1979). Learning resistance to temptation through observation. *Developmental Psychology, 15,* 233–240.

Grusec, J. E., & Walters, G. C. (1991). Psychological abuse and childrearing belief systems. In R. H. Starr, Jr., & D. A. Wolfe (Eds.), *The effects of child abuse and neglect* (pp. 186–202). New York: Guilford.

Guerra, N. G., & Slaby, R. G. (1990). Cognitive mediators of aggression in adolescent offenders: 2. Intervention. *Developmental Psychology, 26,* 269–277.

Guerra, N. G., Tolan, P. H., & Hammond, W. R. (1994). Prevention and treatment of adolescent violence. In L. D. Eron, J. H. Gentry, & P. Schlegel (Eds.), *Reason to hope: A psychosocial perspective on violence and youth* (pp. 383–403). Washington, DC: American Psychological Association.

Guidubaldi, J., & Cleminshaw, H. K. (1985). Divorce, family health and child adjustment. *Family Relations, 34,* 35–41.

Guilford, J. P. (1967). *The nature of human intelligence.* New York: McGraw-Hill.

Guilford, J. P. (1985). The structure-of-intellect model. In B. B. Wolman (Ed.), *Handbook of intelligence* (pp. 225–266). New York: Wiley.

Guilford, J. P. (1988). Some changes in the structure-of-intellect model. *Educational and Psychological Measurement, 48,* 1–4.

Gunnar, M. R., & Nelson, C. A. (1994). Event-related potentials in year-old infants: Relations with emotionality and cortisol. *Child Development, 65,* 80–94.

Gurucharri, C., & Selman, F. L. (1982). The development of interpersonal understanding during childhood, preadolescence, and adolescence: A longitudinal follow-up study. *Child Development, 53,* 924–927.

Gustafson, G. E., Green, J. A., & Cleland, J. W. (1994). Robustness of individual identity in the cries of human infants. *Developmental Psychobiology, 27,* 1–9.

Gustafson, G. E., & Harris, K. L. (1990). Women's responses to young infants' cries. *Developmental Psychology, 26,* 144–152.

Guyer, B., Strolino, D. M., Ventura, S. J., & Singh, G. K. (1995). Annual summary of vital statistics - 1995. *Pediatrics, 96,* 1029–1039.

H

Haan, N., Aerts, E., & Cooper, B. (1985). *On moral grounds: The search for practical morality.* New York: New York University Press.

Haas, J. E., Taylor, J. A., Bergman, A. B., Vanbelle, G., Felgenhauer, J. L., Siebert, J. R., & Benjamin, D. R. (1993). Relationship between epidemiologic risk factors and clinicopathologic findings in the sudden infant death syndrome. *Pediatrics, 91,* 106–112.

Hack, M. B., Taylor, H. G., Klein, N., Eiben, R., Schatschneider, C., & Mercuri-Minich, N. (1994). School-age outcomes in children with birth weights under 750 g. *New England Journal of Medicine, 331,* 753–759.

Hadjistavropoulos, H. D., Craig, K. D., Grunau, R. V. E., & Johnston, C. C. (1994). Judging pain in newborns: Facial and cry determinants. *Journal of Pediatric Psychology, 19,* 485–491.

Hadwin, J., & Perner, J. (1991). Pleased and surprised: Children's cognitive theory of emotion. *British Journal of Developmental Psychology, 9,* 215–234.

Haglund, B., Cnattingius, S., & Otterbladolausson, P. (1995). Sudden infant death syndrome in Sweden, 1983–1990: Season at death, age at death, and maternal smoking. *American Journal of Epidemiology, 142,* 619–624.

Hahn, W. K. (1987). Cerebral lateralization of function: From infancy through childhood. *Psychological Bulletin, 101,* 376–392.

Haidt, J., Koller, S. H., & Diaz, M. G. (1993). Affect, culture, and morality, or is it wrong to eat your dog? *Journal of Personality and Social Psychology, 65,* 613–628.

Haier, R. J., Nuechterlein, K. H., Hazlett, E., Wu, J. C., Paek, J., Browning, H. L., & Buchsbaum, M. S. (1988). Cortical glucose metabolic rate correlates of abstract reasoning and attention studied with positron emission tomography. *Intelligence, 12,* 199–217.

Haier, R. J., Siegel, B., Tang, C., Abel, L., & Buchsbaum, M. S. (1992). Intelligence and changes in regional cerebral glucose metabolic rate following learning. *Intelligence, 16,* 415–426.

Haight, W. L., & Miller, P. J. (1993). *Pretending at home: Early development in a sociocultural context.* Albany, NY: SUNY Press.

Hainline, L. (1993). Conjugate eye movements of infants. In K. Simons (Ed.), *Early visual development: Normal and abnormal* (pp. 47–55). New York: Oxford University Press.

Haith, M. M., Wentworth, N., & Canfield, R. L. (1993). The formation of expectations in early infancy. In C. Rovee-Collier & L. P. Lipsitt (Eds.), *Advances in infancy research* (Vol. 8, pp. 251–297). Norwood, NJ: Ablex.

Hakuta, K. (1986). *Mirror of language.* New York: Basic Books.

Hakuta, K., Ferdman, B. M., & Diaz, R. M. (1987). Bilingualism and cognitive development: Three perspectives. In S. Rosenberg (Ed.), *Advances in applied psycholinguistics: Vol. 2. Reading, writing, and language learning* (pp. 284–319). New York: Cambridge University Press.

Hakuta, K., & Garcia, E. E. (1989). Bilingualism and education. *American Psychologist, 44,* 374–379.

Hale, S., Fry, A. F., & Jessie, K. A. (1993). Effects of practice on speed of information processing in children and adults: Age sensitivity and age invariance. *Developmental Psychology, 29,* 880–892.

Halford, G. S. (1993). *Children's understanding: The development of mental models.* Hillsdale, NJ: Erlbaum.

Hall, D. G. (1996). Preschoolers' default assumptions about word meaning: Proper names designate unique individuals. *Developmental Psychology, 32,* 177–186.

Hall, G. S. (1904). *Adolescence* (Vols. 1–2). New York: Appleton-Century-Crofts.

Hall, J. A. (1978). Gender effects in decoding nonverbal cues. *Psychological Bulletin, 85,* 845–857.

Hall, J. A., & Halberstadt, A. G. (1980). Masculinity and femininity in children: Development of the Children's Attributes Questionnaire. *Developmental Psychology, 16,* 270–280.

Hall, J. A., & Halberstadt, A. G. (1981). Sex roles and nonverbal communication skills. *Sex Roles, 7,* 273–287.

Hall, W. S. (1989). Reading comprehension. *American Psychologist, 44,* 157–161.

Halliday, J. L., Watson, L. F., Lumley, J., Danks, D. M., & Sheffield, L. S. (1995). New estimates of Down syndrome risks at chorionic villus sampling, amniocentesis, and live birth in women of advanced maternal age from a uniquely defined population. *Prenatal Diagnosis, 15,* 455–465.

Halmi, K. A. (1987). Anorexia nervosa and bulimia. In V. B. Van Hasselt & M. Hersen (Eds.), *Handbook of adolescent psychology* (pp. 265–287). New York: Pergamon Press.

Halpern, D. F. (1992). *Sex differences in cognitive abilities* (2nd ed.). Hillsdale, NJ: Erlbaum.

Halverson, H. M. (1931). An experimental study of prehension in infants by means of systematic cinema records. *Genetic Psychology Monographs, 10,* 107–286.

Hamelin, K., & Ramachandran, C. (1993, June). Kangaroo care. *Canadian Nurse, 89*(6), 15–17.

Hamer, D. H., Hu, S., Magnuson, V. L., Hu, N., & Pattatucci, A. M. L. (1993). A linkage between DNA markers on the X chromosome and male sexual orientation. *Science, 261,* 321–327.

Hamilton, S. F. (1990). *Apprenticeship for adulthood: Preparing youth for the future.* New York: Free Press.

Hamilton, S. F. (1993). Prospects for an American-style youth apprenticeship system. Educational Researcher, 22(3), 11–16.

Hammersley, M. (1992). *What's wrong with ethnography?* New York: Routledge.

Hammill, D. D. (1990). On defining learning disabilities: An emerging consensus. *Journal of Learning Disabilities, 23,* 74–84.

Handler, A. S., Mason, E. D., Rosenberg, D. L., & Davis, F. G. (1994). The relationship between exposure during pregnancy to cigarette smoking and cocaine use and placenta previa. *American Journal of Obstetrics and Gynecology, 170,* 884–889.

Hanigan, W. C., Morgan, A. M., Stahlberg, L. K., & Hiller, J. L. (1990). Tentorial hemorrhage associated with vacuum extraction. *Pediatrics, 85,* 534–539.

Hanna, E., & Meltzoff, A. N. (1993). Peer imitation by toddlers in laboratory, home, and day-care contexts: Implications for social learning and memory. *Developmental Psychology, 29,* 701–710.

Hare, J. (1994). Concerns and issues faced by families headed by a lesbian couple. *Families in Society, 43,* 27–35.

Hare, J., & Richards, L. (1993). Children raised by lesbian couples: Does context of birth affect father and partner involvement? *Family Relations, 42,* 249–255.

Harlow, H. F. (1969). Age-mate or peer affectional system. In D. S. Lehrman, R. A. Hinde, & E. Shaw (Eds.), *Advances in the study of behavior* (Vol. 2, pp. 333–383). New York: Academic Press.

Harlow, H. F., & Zimmerman, R. (1959). Affectional responses in the infant monkey. *Science, 130,* 421–432.

Härnqvist, K. (1968). Changes in intelligence from 13 to 18. *Scandinavian Journal of Psychology, 9,* 50–82.

Harris, R. T. (1991, March–April). Anorexia nervosa and bulimia nervosa in female adolescents. *Nutrition Today, 26*(2), 30–34.

Harris, S., Mussen, P. H., & Rutherford, E. (1976). Some cognitive, behavioral, and personality correlates of maturity of moral judgment. *Journal of Genetic Psychology, 128,* 123–135.

Harrison, A. O., Wilson, M. N., Pine, C. J., Chan, S. Q., & Buriel, R. (1994). Family ecologies of ethnic minority children. In G. Handel & G. G. Whitchurch (Eds.), *The psychosocial interior of the family* (pp. 187–210). New York: Aldine De Gruyter.

Hart, B. (1991). Input frequency and children's first words. *First Language, 11,* 289–300.

Hart, B., & Risley, T. R. (1995). *Meaningful differences in the everyday experience of young American children.* Baltimore: Paul H. Brookes.

Hart, S. N., & Brassard, M. R. (1987). A major threat to children's mental health. *American Psychologist, 42,* 87–92.

Harter, S. (1982). The perceived competence scale for children. *Child Development, 53,* 87–97.

Harter, S. (1983). Developmental perspectives on the self-system. In E. M. Hetherington (Ed.), *Handbook of child psychology: Vol. 4. Socialization, personality, and social development* (4th ed., pp. 275–385). New York: Wiley.

Harter, S. (1986). Processes underlying the construction, maintenance, and enhancement of self-concept in children. In S. Suhls & A. Greenwald (Eds.), *Psychological perspectives of the self* (Vol. 3, pp. 136–182). Hillsdale, NJ: Erlbaum.

Harter, S. (1990). Issues in the assessment of the self-concept of children and adolescents. In A. LaGreca (Ed.), *Through the eyes of a child* (pp. 292–325). Boston: Allyn and Bacon.

Harter, S., & Buddin, B. J. (1987). Children's understanding of the simultaneity of two emotions: A five-stage developmental acquisition sequence. *Developmental Psychology, 23,* 388–399.

Harter, S., Wright, K., & Bresnick, S. (1987, April). *A developmental sequence of the emergence of self affects: The understanding of pride and shame.* Paper presented at the biennial meeting of the Society for Research in Child Development, Baltimore.

Hartup, W. W. (1974). Aggression in childhood: Developmental perspectives. *American Psychologist, 29,* 336–341.

Hartup, W. W. (1983). Peer relations. In E. M. Hetherington (Ed.), *Handbook of child psychology: Vol. 4. Socialization, personality, and social development* (4th ed., pp. 103–196). New York: Wiley.

Hartup, W. W. (1996). The company they keep: Friendships and their developmental significance. *Child Development, 67,* 1–13.

Hartup, W. W., French, D. C., Laursen, B., Johnston, M. K., & Ogawa, J. R. (1993). Conflict and friendship relations in middle childhood: Behavior in a closed-field situation. *Child Development, 64,* 445–454.

Hartup, W. W., & Moore, S. G. (1990). Early peer relations: Developmental significance and prognostic implications. *Early Childhood Research Quarterly, 5,* 1–17.

Hashimoto, K., Noguchi, M., & Nakatsuji, N. (1992). Mouse offspring derived from fetal ovaries or reaggregates which were cultured and transplanted into adult females. *Development: Growth & Differentiation, 34,* 233–238.

Hauth, J. C., Goldenberg, R. L., Parker, C. R., Cutter, G. R., & Cliver, S. P. (1995). Low-dose aspirin—lack of association with an increase in abruptio placentae or perinatal mortality. *Obstetrics and Gynecology, 85,* 1055–1058.

Hawke, S., & Knox, D. (1978). The one-child family: A new life-style. *The Family Coordinator, 27,* 215–219.

Hawkins, J. N. (1994). Issues of motivation in Asian education. In H. F. O'Neil, Jr., & M. Drillings (Eds.), *Motivation: Theory and research* (pp. 101–115). Hillsdale, NJ: Erlbaum.

Hawkins, J. N., & Sheingold, K. (1986). The beginnings of a story: Computers and the organization of learning in classrooms. In J. A. Culbertson & L. L. Cunningham

(Eds.), *Microcomputers and education* (85th yearbook of the National Society for the Study of Education, pp. 40–58). Chicago: University of Chicago Press.

Hay, D. F. (1984). Social conflict in early childhood. In G. Whitehurst (Ed.), *Annals of child development* (Vol. 1, pp. 1–44). Greenwich, CT: JAI Press.

Hay, D. F., Caplan, M., Castle, J., & Stimson, C. A. (1991). Does sharing become increasingly "rational" in the second year of life? *Developmental Psychology, 27,* 987–993.

Hayden-Thomson, L., Rubin, K. H., & Hymel, S. (1987). Sex preferences in sociometric choices. *Developmental Psychology, 23,* 558–562.

Hayes, C. D. (1982). *Making policies for children: A study of the federal process.* Washington, DC: National Academy Press.

Hayes, C. D. (Ed.). (1987). *Risking the future: Adolescent sexuality, pregnancy, and childbearing* (Vol. 1). Washington, DC: National Academy Press.

Hayes, C. D., Palmer, J., & Zaslow, M. (1990). *Who cares for America's children? Child care policy for the 1990s.* Washington, DC: National Academy Press.

Hayes, R. M. (1989). Homeless children. In F. J. Macchiarola & A. Gartner (Eds.), Caring for America's children. *Proceedings of the Academy of Political Science, 37*(32), 58–69.

Hayne, H., & Rovee-Collier, C. K. (1995). The organization of reactivated memory in infancy. *Child Development, 66,* 893–906.

Hayne, H., Rovee-Collier, C. K., & Perris, E. E. (1987). Categorization and memory retrieval by three-month-olds. *Child Development, 58,* 750–767.

Haynes, S. N. (1991). Clinical applications of psychophysiological assessment: An introduction and overview. *Psychological Assessment, 3,* 307–308.

Hayslip, B., Jr. (1994). Stability of intelligence. In R. J. Sternberg (Ed.), *Encyclopedia of human intelligence* (Vol. 2, pp. 1019–1026). New York: Macmillan.

Hearold, S. (1986). A synthesis of 1,043 effects of television on social behavior. In G. Comstock (Ed.), *Public communications and behavior* (Vol. 1, pp. 65–133). New York: Academic Press.

Heath, S. B. (1982). Questioning at home and at school: A comparative study. In G. Spindler (Ed.), *Doing the ethnography of schooling: Educational anthropology in action* (pp. 102–127). New York: Holt.

Heath, S. B. (1989). Oral and literate traditions among black Americans living in poverty. *American Psychologist, 44,* 367–373.

Heath, S. B. (1990). The children of Trackton's children: Spoken and written language and social change. In J. Stigler, G. Herdt, & R. A. Shweder (Eds.), *Cultural psychology: Essays on comparative human development* (pp. 496–519). New York: Cambridge University Press.

Hebb, D. O. (1949). *The organization of behavior.* New York: Wiley.

Hecht, H., & Proffitt, D. R. (1995). The price of expertise: Effects of experience on the water-level task. *Psychological Science, 6,* 90–95.

Hedges, L. V., & Nowell, A. (1995). Sex differences in mental test scores: Variability and numbers of high-scoring individuals. *Science, 269,* 41–45.

Heinl, T. (1983). *The baby massage book.* London: Coventure.

Heinonen, O. P., Slone, D., & Shapiro, S. (1977). *Birth defects and drugs in pregnancy.* Littleton, MA: PSG Publishing.

Helburn, S. W. (Ed.). (1995). *Cost, quality and child outcomes in child care centers.* Denver: University of Colorado.

Held, R. (1993). What can rates of development tell us about underlying mechanisms? In C. E. Granrud (Ed.), *Visual perception and cognition in infancy* (pp. 75–89). Hillsdale, NJ: Erlbaum.

Hendrick, J., & Stange, T. (1991). Do actions speak louder than words? An effect of the functional use of language on dominant sex role behavior in boys and girls. *Early Childhood Research Quarterly, 6,* 565–576.

Hendrix, L., & Johnson, G. D. (1985). Instrumental and expressive socialization: A false dichotomy. *Sex Roles, 13,* 581–595.

Henggeler, S. W. (1989). *Delinquency in adolescence.* Newbury Park, CA: Sage.

Hennessy, K. D., Rabideau, G. J., & Cicchetti, D. (1994). Responses of physically abused and nonabused children to different forms of interadult anger. *Child Development, 65,* 815–828.

Henry, B., Moffitt, T. E., Caspi, A., Langley, J., & Silva, P. A. (1994). On the "remembrance of things past": A longitudinal evaluation of the retrospective method. *Psychological Assessment, 6,* 92–101.

Herdt, G. H., & Davidson, J. (1988). The Sambia "Turnim-Man": Sociocultural and clinical aspects of gender formation in male pseudohermaphrodites with 5-alpha-reductase deficiency in Papua, New Guinea. *Archives of Sexual Behavior, 17,* 33–56.

Hernandez, D. J. (1994, Spring). Children's changing access to resources: A historical perspective. *Social Policy Report of the Society for Research in Child Development, 8*(1).

Herrnstein, R. J., & Murray, C. (1994). *The bell curve: Intelligence and class structure in American life.* New York: Free Press.

Hershberger, S. L., & D'Augelli, A. R. (1995). The impact of victimization on the mental health and suicidality of lesbian, gay, and bisexual youths. *Developmental Psychology, 31,* 65–74.

Hetherington, E. M. (1991). The role of individual differences and family relationships in children's coping with divorce and remarriage. In P. A. Cowan & M. Hetherington (Eds.), *Family transitions* (pp. 165–194). Hillsdale, NJ: Erlbaum.

Hetherington, E. M. (1993). An overview of the Virginia Longitudinal Study of Divorce and Remarriage: A focus on early adolescence. *Journal of Family Psychology, 7,* 39–56.

Hetherington, E. M., & Clingempeel, W. G. (1992). Coping with marital transitions: A family systems perspective. *Monographs of the Society for Research in Child Development, 57*(2–3, Serial No. 227).

Hetherington, E. M., Cox, M. J., & Cox, R. (1982). Effects of divorce on parents and children. In M. E. Lamb (Ed.), *Nontraditional families: Parenting and child development* (pp. 233–288). Hillsdale, NJ: Erlbaum.

Hetherington, E. M., Cox, M. J., & Cox, R. (1985). Long-term effects of divorce and remarriage on the adjustment of children. *Journal of the American Academy of Child and Adolescent Psychiatry, 24,* 518–530.

Hetherington, E. M., & Jodl, K. M. (1994). Stepfamilies as settings for child development. In A. Booth & J. Dunn (Eds.), *Stepfamilies: Who benefits? Who does not?* (pp. 55–79). Hillsdale, NJ: Erlbaum.

Hetherington, P. (1995, March). *The changing American family and the well-being of children.* Master lecture presented at the biennial meeting of the Society for Research in Child Development, Indianapolis.

Hetherington, S. E. (1990). A controlled study of the effect of prepared childbirth classes on obstetric outcomes. *Birth, 17,* 86–90.

Hewlett, B. S. (Ed.). (1992a). *Father–child relations.* New York: Aldine De Gruyter.

Hewlett, B. S. (1992b). Husband–wife reciprocity and the father–infant relationship among Aka pygmies. In B. S. Hewlett (Ed.), *Father–child relations: Cultural and biosocial contexts* (pp. 153–176). New York: Aldine De Gruyter.

Heyman, G. D., & Dweck, C. S. (1992). Achievement goals and intrinsic motivation: Their relation and their role in adaptive motivation. *Motivation and Emotion, 16,* 231–247.

Heyman, G. D., Dweck, C. S., & Cain, K. M. (1992). Young children's vulnerability to self-blame and helplessness: Relationship to beliefs about goodness. *Child Development, 63,* 401–415.

Heyns, B. (1978). *Summer learning and the effects of schooling.* San Diego: Academic Press.

Hickey, T. L., & Peduzzi, J. D. (1987). Structure and development of the visual system. In P. Salapatek & L. Cohen (Eds.), *Handbook of infant perception: Vol. 1. From sensation to perception* (pp. 1–42). New York: Academic Press.

Hier, D. B., & Crowley, W. F. (1982). Spatial ability in androgen-deficient men. *New England Journal of Medicine, 302,* 1202–1205.

Higgins, A. (1991). The just community approach to moral education: Evolution of the idea and recent findings. In W. M. Kurtines & J. L. Gewirtz (Eds.), *Handbook of moral behavior and development* (Vol. 3, pp. 111–141). Hillsdale, NJ: Erlbaum.

Higgins, A. (1995). Educating for justice and community: Lawrence Kohlberg's vision of moral education. In W. M. Kurtines & J. L. Gewirtz (Eds.), *Moral development: An introduction* (pp. 49–81). Boston: Allyn and Bacon.

Higley, J. D., Hopkins, W. D., Thompson, W. W., Byrne, E. A., Hirsch, R. M., & Suomi, S. J. (1992). Peers as primary attachment sources in yearling rhesus monkeys (*Macaca mulatta*). *Developmental Psychology, 28,* 1163–1171.

Hill, C. R., & Stafford, F. P. (1980). Parental care of children: Time diary estimate of quantity, predictability, and variety. Journal of Human Resources, 15, 219–239.

Hill, H. M., Soriano, F. I., Chen, S. A., & LaFromboise, T. D. (1994). Sociocultural factors in the etiology and prevention of violence among ethnic minority youth. In L. D. Eron, J. H. Gentry, & P. Schlegel (Eds.), *Reason to hope* (pp. 59–97). Washington, DC: American Psychological Association.

Hill, J., & Holmbeck, G. N. (1986). Attachment and autonomy during adolescence. In G. Whitehurst (Ed.), *Annals of child development* (Vol. 3, pp. 145–189). Greenwich, CT: JAI Press.

Hill, P. M., & Humphrey, P. (1982). *Human growth and development throughout life: A nursing perspective.* New York: Delmar.

Hillier, L., Hewitt, K. L., & Morrongiello, B. A. (1992). Infants' perception of illusions in sound localization: Reaching to sounds in the dark. *Journal of Experimental Child Psychology, 53,* 159–179.

Hinde, R. A. (1989). Ethological and relationships approaches. In R. Vasta (Ed.), *Annals of child development* (Vol. 6, pp. 251–285). Greenwich, CT: JAI Press.

Hinde, R. A., Stevenson-Hinde, J., & Tamplin, A. (1985). Characteristics of 3- to 4-year-olds assessed at home and their interactions in preschool. *Developmental Psychology, 21,* 130–140.

Hines, M. (1982). Prenatal gonadal hormones and sex differences in human behavior. *Psychological Bulletin, 92,* 56–80.

Hines, M., & Green, R. (1991). Human hormonal and neural correlates of sex-typed behaviors. *Review of Psychiatry, 10,* 536–555.

Hines, M., & Kaufman, F. R. (1994). Androgen and the development of human sex-typical behavior: Rough-and-tumble play and sex of preferred playmates in children with congenital adrenal hyperplasia (CAH). *Child Development, 65,* 1042–1053.

Hirschi, T., & Hindelang, M. J. (1977). Intelligence and delinquency: A revisionist view. *American Sociological Review, 42,* 571–587.

Hirsh-Pasek, K., Kemler Nelson, D. G., Jusczyk, P. W., Cassidy, K. W., Druss, B., & Kennedy, L. (1987). Clauses are perceptual units for young infants. *Cognition, 26,* 269–286.

Hiscock, M., & Kinsbourne, M. (1987). Specialization of the cerebral hemispheres: Implications for learning. *Journal of Learning Disabilities, 20,* 130–143.

Hobart, C., & Brown, D. (1988). Effects of prior marriage children on adjustment in remarriages: A Canadian study. *Journal of Comparative Family Studies, 19,* 381–396.

Hodges, J., & Tizard, B. (1989). Social and family relationships of ex-institutional adolescents. *Journal of Child Psychology and Psychiatry, 30,* 77–97.

Hodges, R. M., & French, L. A. (1988). The effect of class and collection labels on cardinality, class-inclusion, and number conservation tasks. *Child Development, 59,* 1387–1396.

Hofferth, S. L. (1995). Who enrolls in Head Start? A demographic analysis of Head Start–eligible children. *Early Childhood Research Quarterly, 9,* 243–268.

Hoffman, L. W. (1989). Effects of maternal employment in the two-parent family. *American Psychologist, 44,* 283–292.

Hoffman, L. W. (1991). The influence of the family environment on personality: Accounting for sibling differences. *Psychological Bulletin, 110,* 187–203.

Hoffman, L. W. (1994). Commentary on Plomin, R. (1994). A proof and a disproof questioned. *Social Development, 3,* 60–63.

Hoffman, M. L. (1980). Moral development in adolescence. In J. Adelson (Ed.), *Handbook of adolescent psychology* (pp. 295–343). New York: Wiley.

Hoffman, M. L. (1981). Is altruism part of human nature? *Journal of Personality and Social Psychology, 40,* 121–137.

Hoffman, M. L. (1983). Affective and cognitive processes in moral internalization. In E. T. Higgins, D. N. Ruble, & W. W. Hartup (Eds.), *Social cognition and social development: A sociocultural perspective* (pp. 236–274). Cambridge: Cambridge University Press.

Hoffman, M. L. (1984). Interaction of affect and cognition in empathy. In C. E. Izard, J. Kagan, & R. B. Zajonc (Eds.), *Emotions, cognition, and behavior* (pp. 103–131). Cambridge: Cambridge University Press.

Hoffman, M. L. (1988). Moral development. In M. H. Bornstein & M. E. Lamb (Eds.), *Developmental psychology: An advanced textbook* (2nd ed., pp. 497–548). Hillsdale, NJ: Erlbaum.

Hoffman, M. L. (1991). Empathy, cognition, and social action. In W. M. Kurtines & J. L. Gewirtz (Eds.), *Handbook of moral behavior and development* (Vol. 1, pp. 275–303). Hillsdale, NJ: Erlbaum.

Hoffner, C., & Badzinski, D. M. (1989). Children's integration of facial and situational cues to emotion. *Child Development, 60,* 411–422.

Hofstede, G. (1980). *Culture's consequences: International differences in work-related values.* London: Sage.

Hofsten, C. von. (1984). Developmental changes in the organization of prereaching movements. *Developmental Psychology, 20,* 378–388.

Hofsten, C. von. (1989). Motor development as the development of systems: Comments on the special section. *Developmental Psychology, 25,* 950–953.

Hofsten, C. von, & Spelke, E. S. (1985). Object perception and object-directed reaching in infancy. *Journal of Experimental Psychology: General, 114,* 198–212.

Holcomb, T. F. (1990). Fourth graders' attitudes toward AIDS issues: A concern for the elementary school counselor. *Elementary School Guidance & Counseling, 25,* 83–90.

Holden, G. W. (1983). Avoiding conflict: Mothers as tacticians in the supermarket. *Child Development, 54,* 233–240.

Holden, G. W., & West, M. J. (1989). Proximate regulation by mothers: A demonstration of how differing styles affect young children's behavior. *Child Development, 60,* 64–69.

Holmbeck, G. N., & Hill, J. P. (1991). Conflictive engagement, positive affect, and menarche in families with seventh-grade girls. *Child Development, 62,* 1030–1048.

Holmbeck, G. N., Waters, K. A., & Brookman, R. R. (1990). Psychosocial correlates of sexually transmitted diseases and sexual activity in black adolescent females. *Journal of Adolescent Research, 5,* 431–448.

Holmes, L. B. (1993). Report on the National Institute of Child Health and Human Development workshop on chorionic villus sampling and limb and other defects. *Teratology, 48,* 7–13.

Holzman, C., & Paneth, N. (1994). Maternal cocaine use during pregnancy and perinatal outcomes. *Epidemiologic Reviews, 16,* 315–334.

Honzik, M. P., Macfarlane, J. W., & Allen, L. (1948). The stability of mental test performance between two and eighteen years. *Journal of Experimental Education, 17,* 309–329.

Hook, E. B. (1982). Epidemiology of Down syndrome. In S. M. Pueschel & J. E. Rynders (Eds.), *Down syndrome: Advances in biomedicine and the behavioral sciences* (pp. 21–43). Cambridge, MA: Ware Press.

Hook, E. B. (1988). Evaluation and projection of rates of chromosome abnormalities in chorionic villus studies (c.v.s.). *American Journal of Human Genetics Supplement, 43,* A108.

Hopkins, B., & Westra, T. (1988). Maternal handling and motor development: An intracultural study. *Genetic, Social and General Psychology Monographs, 14,* 377–420.

Hopkins-Tanne, J. (1994). U.S. campaign for women to take folic acid to prevent birth defects. *British Medical Journal, 308,* 223.

Horgan, D. (1978). The development of the full passive. *Journal of Child Language, 5,* 65–80.

Horn, J. M. (1983). The Texas Adoption Project: Adopted children and their intellectual resemblance to biological and adoptive parents. *Child Development, 54,* 268–275.

Horner, T. M. (1980). Two methods of studying stranger reactivity in infants: A review. *Journal of Child Psychology and Psychiatry, 21,* 203–219.

Horowitz, F. D. (1987). *Exploring developmental theories: Toward a structural/behavioral model of development.* Hillsdale, NJ: Erlbaum.

Horowitz, F. D. (1992). John B. Watson's legacy: Learning and environment. *Developmental Psychology, 28,* 360–367.

Hort, B. E., Leinbach, M. D., & Fagot, B. I. (1991). Is there coherence among the cognitive components of gender acquisition? *Sex Roles, 24,* 195–207.

Horton, R. (1995, July 13). Is homosexuality inherited? *New York Review of Books,* pp. 36–41.

Hotaling, G. T., Finkelhor, D., Kirkpatrick, J. T., & Strauss, M. A. (Eds.). (1988). *Family abuse and its consequences: New directions in research.* Newbury Park, CA: Sage.

Howe, M. L., & Courage, M. L. (1993). On resolving the enigma of infantile amnesia. *Psychological Bulletin, 113,* 305–326.

Howe, M. L., Courage, M. L., & Bryant-Brown, L. (1995). Reinstating preschoolers' memories. *Developmental Psychology, 29,* 854–869.

Howes, C. (1988a). Peer interaction of young children. *Monographs of the Society for Research in Child Development, 53*(1, Serial No. 217).

Howes, C. (1988b). Relations between early child care and schooling. *Developmental Psychology, 24,* 53–57.

Howes, C. (1990). Can the age of entry into child care and the quality of child care predict adjustment in kindergarten? *Developmental Psychology, 26,* 292–303.

Howes, C. (1992). *The collaborative construction of pretend.* Albany, NY: SUNY Press.

Howes, C., & Farver, J. (1987). Social pretend play in 2-year-olds: Effects of age of partner. *Early Childhood Research Quarterly, 2,* 305–314.

Howes, C., & Matheson, C. C. (1992). Sequences in the development of competent play with peers: Social and social pretend play. *Developmental Psychology, 28,* 961–974.

Howes, C., Phillips, D. A., & Whitebook, M. (1992). Thresholds of quality: Implications for the social development of children in center-based child care. Child Development, 63, 449–460.

Howes, C., Rodning, C., Galluzzo, D. C., & Myers, L. (1988). Attachment and child care: Relationships with mother and caregiver. *Early Childhood Research Quarterly, 3,* 403–416.

Howes, P., & Markman, H. J. (1989). Marital quality and child functioning: A longitudinal investigation. *Child Development, 60,* 1044–1051.

Hubel, D. H., & Wiesel, T. N. (1970). The period of susceptibility to the physiological effects of unilateral eye closure in kittens. *Journal of Physiology, 206,* 419–436.

Hudson, J. A., & Fivush, R. (1991). As time goes by: Sixth graders remember a kindergarten experience. *Applied Cognitive Psychology, 5,* 347–360.

Hudson, J. A., Fivush, R., & Kuebli, J. (1992). Scripts and episodes: The development of event memory. *Applied Cognitive Psychology, 6,* 483–505.

Hudson, J. A., & Nelson, K. (1983). Effects of script structure on children's story recall. *Developmental Psychology, 19,* 625–635.

Hudson, J. A., Shapiro, L. R., & Sosa, B. B. (1995). Planning in the real world: Preschool children's scripts and plans for familiar events. *Child Development, 66,* 984–998.

Hudspeth, W. J., & Pribram, K . H. (1992). Psychophysiological indices of cerebral maturation. *International Journal of Psychophysiology, 12,* 19–29.

Huesmann, L. R. (1986). Psychological processes promoting the relation between exposure to media violence and aggressive behavior by the viewer. *Journal of Social Issues, 42,* 125–139.

Huesmann, L. R., Eron, L. D., Lefkowitz, M. M., & Walder, L. O. (1984). Stability of aggression over time and generations. *Developmental Psychology, 20,* 1120–1134.

Hughes, M., & Macleod, H. (1986). Part II: Using LOGO with very young children. In R. Lawler, B. D. Boulay, M. Hughes, & H. Macleod (Eds.), *Cognition and computers: Studies in learning* (pp. 179–219). Chichester, England: Ellis Horwood.

Hughes, W. (1975). *Skin color identification and preference among children in Sweden and America: A comparative analysis.* Uppsala, Sweden: University of Uppsala, Department of Educational Research, School of Education.

Humphrey, T. (1978). Function of the nervous system during prenatal life. In U. Stave (Ed.), *Perinatal physiology* (pp. 651–683). New York: Plenum.

Humphreys, A. P., & Smith, P. K. (1987). Rough and tumble, friendship, and dominance in schoolchildren: Evidence for continuity and change with age. *Child Development, 58,* 201–212.

Humphreys, L. G. (1989). Intelligence: Three kinds of instability and their consequences for policy. In R. L. Linn (Ed.), *Intelligence* (pp. 193–216). Urbana: University of Illinois Press.

Hunt, J. McV. (1961). *Intelligence and experience.* New York: Ronald Press.

Hunt, J. McV., Mohandessi, K., Ghodessi, M., & Akeyama, M. (1976). The psychological development of orphanage-reared infants: Interventions with outcomes (Tehran). *Genetic Psychology Monographs, 94,* 177–226.

Hunter, J. E., & Hunter, R. F. (1984). Validity and utility of alternative predictors of job performance. *Psychological Bulletin, 96,* 72–98.

Huntington, L., Hans, S. L., & Zeskind, P. S. (1990). The relations among cry characteristics, demographic variables, and developmental test scores in infants prenatally exposed to methadone. *Infant Behavior and Development, 13,* 533–538.

Hura, S. L., & Echols, C. H. (1996). The role of stress and articulatory difficulty in children's early productions. *Developmental Psychology, 32,* 165–176.

Husén, T. (1967). *International study of achievement in mathematics: A comparison of twelve countries.* New York: Wiley.

Huston, A. C. (1983). Sex-typing. In E. M. Hetherington (Ed.), *Handbook of child psychology: Vol. 4. Socialization, personality, and social development* (4th ed., pp. 387–467). New York: Wiley.

Huston, A. C. (Ed.). (1991). *Children in poverty: Child development and public policy.* Cambridge, England: Cambridge University Press.

Huston, A. C. (1994, Summer). Children in poverty: Designing research to affect policy. *Social Policy Report of the Society for Research in Child Development, 8*(2).

Huston, A. C., & Alvarez, M. M. (1990). The socialization context of gender role development in early adolescence. In R. Montemayor, G. R. Adams, & T. P. Gullotta (Eds.), *From childhood to adolescence: A transitional period?* (pp. 156–179). Newbury Park, CA: Sage.

Huston, A. C., Donnerstein, E., Fairchild, H., Feshbach, N. D., Katz, P. A., Murray, J. P., Rubinstein, E. A., Wilcox, B. L., & Zuckerman, D. (1992). *Big world, small screen: The role of television in American society.* Lincoln: University of Nebraska Press.

Huston, A. C., Greer, D., Wright, J. C., Welch, R., & Ross, R. (1984). Children's comprehension of televised formal features with masculine and feminine connotations. *Developmental Psychology, 20,* 707–716.

Huston, A. C., Watkins, B. A., & Kunkel, D. (1989). Public policy and children's television. *American Psychologist, 44,* 424–433.

Huston, A. C., Wright, J. C., Rice, M. L., Kerkman, D., & St. Peters, M. (1990). Development of television viewing patterns in early childhood: A longitudinal investigation. *Developmental Psychology, 26,* 409–420.

Huston-Stein, A. C., Fox, S., Greer, D., Watkins, B. A., & Whitaker, J. (1981). The effects of TV action and violence on children's social behavior. *Journal of Genetic Psychology, 138,* 183–191.

Huttenlocher, J., Haight, W., Bryk, A., Seltzer, M., & Lyons, T. (1991). Early vocabulary growth: Relation to language input and gender. *Developmental Psychology, 27,* 236–248.

Huttenlocher, P. R. (1994). Synaptogenesis in human cerebral cortex. In G. Dawson & K. W. Fischer (Eds.), *Human behavior and the developing brain* (pp. 137–152). New York: Guilford.

Hyde, J. S. (1984). How large are gender differences in aggression? A developmental meta-analysis. *Developmental Psychology, 20,* 722–736.

Hyde, J. S., Fenema, E., & Lamon, S. J. (1990). Gender differences in mathematics performance: A meta-analysis. *Psychological Bulletin, 107,* 139–155.

Hyde, J. S., & Linn, M. C. (1988). Gender differences in verbal ability: A meta-analysis. *Psychological Bulletin, 104,* 53–69.

Hyde, J. S., & Plant, E. A. (1995). Magnitude of psychological gender differences: Another side to the story. *American Psychologist, 50,* 159–161.

Hymel, S. (1983). Preschool children's peer relations: Issues in sociometric assessment. *Merrill-Palmer Quarterly, 19,* 237–260.

Hynd, G. W., Horn, K. L., Voeller, K. K., & Marshall, R. M. (1991). Neurobiological basis of attention-deficit hyperactivity disorder (ADHD). *School Psychology Review, 20,* 174–186.

I

Imperato-McGinley, J., Peterson, R. E., Gautier, T., & Sturla, E. (1979). Steroid 5 alpha-reductase deficiency in man: An inherited form of male pseudohermaphroditism. *Science, 186,* 1213–1243.

Infante-Rivard, C., Fernández, A., Gauthier, R., & Rivard, G. E. (1993). Fetal loss associated with caffeine intake before and during pregnancy. *Journal of the American Medical Association, 270,* 2940–2943.

Ingram, D. (1986). Phonological development: Production. In P. Fletcher & M. Garman (Eds.), *Language acquisition* (2nd ed., pp. 223–239). Cambridge: Cambridge University Press.

Inhelder, B., & Piaget, J. (1958). *The growth of logical thinking from childhood to adolescence: An essay on the construction of formal operational structures.* New York: Basic Books. (Original work published 1955)

Inoff-Germain, G., Arnold, G. S., Nottelman, E. D., Susman, E. J., Cutler, G. B., Jr., & Crousos, G. P. (1988). Relations between hormone levels and observational measures of aggressive behavior of young adolescents in family interactions. *Developmental Psychology, 24,* 129–139.

International Education Association. (1988). *Science achievement in seventeen countries: A preliminary report.* Oxford: Pergamon Press.

Intons-Peterson, M. J. (1988). *Gender concepts of Swedish and American youth.* Hillsdale, NJ: Erlbaum.

Irgens, L. M., Markestad, T. Baste, V., Schreuder, P., Skjaerven, R., & Oyen, N. (1995). Sleeping position and sudden infant death syndrome in Norway 1967–1991. *Archives of Disease in Childhood, 72,* 478–482.

Irvine, J. J. (1986). Teacher–student interactions: Effects of student race, sex, and grade level. *Journal of Educational Psychology, 78,* 14–21.

Isabella, R. A. (1993). Origins of attachment: Maternal interactive behavior across the first year. *Child Development, 64,* 605–621.

Isabella, R. A., & Belsky, J. (1991). Interactional synchrony and the origins of infant–mother attachment: A replication study. *Child Development, 62,* 373–384.

Izard, C. E. (1979). *The maximally discriminative facial movement scoring system.* Unpublished manuscript, University of Delaware.

Izard, C. E. (1991). *The psychology of emotions.* New York: Plenum.

Izard, C. E., Fantauzzo, C. A., Castle, J. M., Haynes, O. M., Rayias, M. F., & Putnam, P. H. (1995). The ontogeny and significance of infants' facial expressions in the first 9 months of life. *Developmental Psychology, 31,* 997–1013.

Izard, C. E., Hembree, E. A., & Huebner, R. R. (1987). Infants' emotion expressions to acute pain. *Developmental Psychology, 23,* 105–113.

Izard, C. E., & Malatesta, C. Z. (1987). Perspectives on emotional development I: Differential emotions theory of early emotional development. In J. D. Osofsky (Ed.), *Handbook of infant development* (2nd ed., pp. 494–554). New York: Wiley.

Izard, C. E., Porges, S. W., Simons, R. F., Haynes, O. M., Hyde, C., Parisi, M., & Cohen, B. (1991). Infant cardiac activity: Developmental changes and relations with attachment. *Developmental Psychology, 27,* 432–439.

J

Jacklin, C. N., & Maccoby, E. E. (1978). Social behavior at thirty-three months in same-sex and mixed-sex dyads. *Child Development, 49,* 557–569.

Jackson, P. W. (1968). *Life in classrooms.* New York: Holt, Rinehart & Winston.

Jacobs, J. E. (1991). Influence of gender stereotypes on parent and child mathematics attitudes. *Journal of Educational Psychology, 83,* 518–527.

Jacobson, S. W., Fein, G. G., Jacobson, J. L., Schwartz, P. M., & Dowler, J. (1985). The effect of intrauterine PCB exposure on visual recognition memory. *Child Development, 56,* 853–860.

Jacobson, J. L., Jacobson, S. W., Fein, G., Schwartz, P. M., & Dowler, J. (1984). Prenatal exposure to an environmental toxin: A test of the multiple effects model. *Developmental Psychology, 20,* 523–532.

Jacobson, J. L., Jacobson, S. W., & Humphrey, H. E. B. (1990). Effects of in utero exposure to polychlorinated biphenyls on cognitive functioning in young children. *Journal of Pediatrics, 116,* 38–45.

Jacobson, J. L., Jacobson, S. W., Padgett, R. J., Brumitt, G. A., & Billings, R. L. (1992). Effects of prenatal PCB exposure on cognitive processing efficiency and sustained attention. *Developmental Psychology, 28,* 297–306.

Jacobson, S. W., Jacobson, J. L., Sokol, R. J., Martier, S. S., & Ager, J. W. (1993). Prenatal alcohol exposure and infant information processing ability. *Child Development, 64,* 1706–1721.

Jadack, R. A., Hyde, J. S., Moore, C. F., & Keller, M. L. (1995). Moral reasoning about sexually transmitted diseases. *Child Development, 66,* 167–177.

James, W. (1963). *Psychology.* New York: Fawcett. (Original work published 1890)

Jameson, S. (1993). Zinc status in pregnancy: The effect of zinc therapy on perinatal mortality, prematurity, and placental ablation. *Annals of the New York Academy of Sciences, 678,* 178–192.

Jamin, J. R. (1994). Language and socialization of the child in African families living in France. In P. M. Greenfield & R. R. Cocking (Eds.), *Cross-cultural roots of minority child development* (pp. 147–166). Hillsdale, NJ: Erlbaum.

Jarrold, C., Carruthers, P., Smith, P. K., & Boucher, J. (1994). Pretend play: Is it metarepresentational? *Mind & Language, 9,* 445–468.

Jaskiewicz, J. A., & McAnarney, E. R. (1994). Pregnancy during adolescence. *Pediatrics in Review, 15,* 32–38.

Jencks, C. (1972). *Inequality: A reassessment of the effect of family and schooling in America.* New York: Basic Books.

Jenkins, J. M., & Astington, J. W. (1996). Cognitive factors and family structure associated with theory of mind development in young children. *Developmental Psychology, 32,* 70–78.

Jenkins, J. M., & Smith, M. A. (1990). Factors protecting children living in disharmonious homes. *Journal of the American Academy of Child and Adolescent Psychiatry, 29,* 60–69.

Jensen, A. R. (1969). How much can we boost IQ and scholastic achievement? *Harvard Educational Review, 39,* 1–123.

Jensen, A. R. (1973). *Educability and group differences.* New York: Harper & Row.

Jensen, A. R. (1974). Cumulative deficit: A testable hypothesis. *Developmental Psychology, 10,* 996–1019.

Jensen, A. R. (1980). *Bias in mental testing.* New York: Free Press.

Jensen, A. R. (1985). The nature of the black-white difference on various psychometric tests: Spearman's hypothesis. *Behavioral and Brain Sciences, 8,* 193–219.

Jensen, A. R. (1988). Speed of information processing and population differences. In

S. H. Irvine & J. W. Berry (Eds.), *Human abilities in cultural context* (pp. 105–145). New York: Cambridge University Press.

Jensen, A. R., & Figueroa, R. A. (1975). Forward and backward digit-span interaction with race and IQ: Predictions from Jensen's theory. *Journal of Educational Psychology, 67,* 882–893.

Jensen, A. R., & Reynolds, C. R. (1982). Race, social class and ability patterns on the WISC-R. *Personality and Individual Differences, 3,* 423–438.

Jensen, A. R., & Whang, P. A. (1994). Speed of accessing arithmetic facts in long-term memory: A comparison of Chinese-American and Anglo-American children. *Contemporary Educational Psychology, 19,* 1–12.

Johanson, R. B., Rice, C., Coyle, M., Arthur, J., Anyanwu, L., Ibrahim, J., Warwick, A., Redman, C. W. E., & O'Brien, P. M. S. (1993). A randomised prospective study comparing the new vacuum extractor policy with forceps delivery. *British Journal of Obstetrics and Gynaecology, 100,* 524–530.

Johnson, J. E., & Hooper, F. E. (1982). Piagetian structuralism and learning: Two decades of educational application. *Contemporary Educational Psychology, 7,* 217–237.

Johnson, J. S., & Newport, E. L. (1989). Critical period effects in second language learning: The influence of maturational state on the acquisition of English as a second language. *Cognitive Psychology, 21,* 60–99.

Johnson, S. L., & Birch, L. L. (1994). Parents' and children's adiposity and eating style. *Pediatrics, 94,* 653–661.

Johnson, S. P., & Aslin, R. N. (1995). Perception of object unity in 2-month-old infants. *Developmental Psychology, 31,* 739–745.

Johnston, J. R., & Slobin, D. I. (1979). The development of locative expressions in English, Italian, Serbo-Croatian, and Turkish. *Journal of Child Language, 16,* 531–547.

Johnston, J. R., Kline, M., & Tschann, J. M. (1989). Ongoing postdivorce conflict: Effects on children of joint custody and frequent access. *American Journal of Orthopsychiatry, 59,* 576–592.

Jones, C. P., & Adamson, L. B. (1987). Language use in mother–child–sibling interactions. *Child Development, 58,* 356–366.

Jones, E. F., Forrest, J. D., Goldman, N., Henshaw, S. K., Lincoln, R. Rosoff, J. I., Westoff, C. F., & Wulf, D. (1988). Teenage pregnancy in developed countries: Determinants and policy implications. *Family Planning Perspectives, 17,* 53–63.

Jones, G. P., & Dembo, M. H. (1989). Age and sex role differences in intimate friendships during childhood and adolescence. *Merrill-Palmer Quarterly, 35,* 445–462.

Jones, M. C. (1965). Psychological correlates of somatic development. *Child Development, 36,* 899–911.

Jones, M. C., & Bayley, N. (1950). Physical maturing among boys as related to behavior. *Journal of Educational Psychology, 41,* 129–148.

Jones, M. C., & Mussen, P. H. (1958). Self-conceptions, motivations, and interpersonal attitudes of early- and late-maturing girls. *Child Development, 29,* 491–501.

Jones, M. G., & Gerig, T. M. (1994). Silent sixth-grade students: Characteristics, achievement, and teacher expectations. *Elementary School Journal, 95,* 169–182.

Jones, S. S., & Raag, T. (1989). Smile production in older infants: The importance of a social recipient for the facial signal. *Child Development, 60,* 811–818.

Jordan, B. (1993). *Birth in four cultures.* Prospect Heights, IL: Waveland.

Jorgensen, M., & Keiding, N. (1991). Estimation of spermarche from longitudinal spermaturia data. *Biometrics, 47,* 177–193.

Josselson, R. (1994). The theory of identity development and the question of intervention. In S. L. Archer (Ed.), *Interventions for adolescent identity development* (pp. 12–25). Thousand Oaks, CA: Sage.

Jouriles, E. N., Murphy, C. M., Farris, A. M., Smith, D. A., Richters, J. E., & Waters, E. (1991). Marital adjustment, parental disagreements about child rearing, and behavior problems in boys: Increasing the specificity of the marital assessment. *Child Development, 62,* 1424–1433.

Jusczyk, P. W. (1995). Language acquisition: Speech sounds and phonological development. In J. L. Miller & P. D. Eimas (Eds.), *Handbook of perception and cognition: Vol. 11. Speech, language, and communication* (pp. 263–301). Orlando, FL: Academic Press.

Jusczyk, P. W., & Aslin, R. N. (1995). Infants' detection of the sound patterns of words in fluent speech. *Cognitive Psychology, 29,* 1–23.

Jusczyk, P. W., Charles-Luce, J., & Luce, P. A. (1994). Infants' sensitivity to high frequency vs. low-frequency phonetic sequences in the native language. *Journal of Memory and Language, 33,* 630–645.

Jusczyk, P. W., Cutler, A., & Redanz, N. (1993). Preference for the predominant stress patterns of English words. *Child Development, 64,* 675–687.

Jusczyk, P. W., & Krumhansl, C. (1993). Pitch and rhythmic patterns affecting infants' sensitivity to musical phrase structure. *Journal of Experimental Psychology: Human Perception and Performance, 19,* 1–14.

K

Kagan, J. (1987). Introduction. In J. Kagan & S. Lamb (Eds.), *The emergence of morality in young children* (pp. ix–xx). Chicago: University of Chicago Press.

Kagan, J. (1989). *Unstable ideas: Temperament, cognition, and self.* Cambridge, MA: Cambridge University Press.

Kagan, J. (1992). Behavior, biology, and the meanings of temperamental constructs. *Pediatrics, 90,* 510–513.

Kagan, J., Arcus, D., Snidman, N., Feng, W. Y., Hendler, J., & Greene, S. (1994). Reactivity in infants: A cross-national comparison. *Developmental Psychology, 30,* 342–345.

Kagan, J., Kearsley, R. B., & Zelazo, P. R. (1978). *Infancy: Its place in human development.* Cambridge, MA: Harvard University Press.

Kagan, J., Klein, R. E., Finley, G. E., Rogoff, B., & Nolan, E. (1979). A cross-cultural study of cognitive development. *Monographs of the Society for Research in Child Development, 44*(5, Serial No. 180).

Kagan, J., & Snidman, N. (1991). Temperamental factors in human development. *American Psychologist, 46,* 856–862.

Kahn, P. H., Jr. (1992). Children's obligatory and discretionary moral judgments. *Child Development, 63,* 416–430.

Kail, R. (1988). Developmental functions for speeds of cognitive processes. *Journal of Experimental Child Psychology, 45,* 339–364.

Kail, R. (1991). Processing time declines exponentially during childhood and adolescence. *Developmental Psychology, 27,* 259–266.

Kail, R. (1993). The role of a global mechanism in developmental change in speed of processing. In M. L. Howe & R. Pasnak (Eds.), *Emerging themes in cognitive development: Vol. 1. Foundations.* New York: Springer-Verlag.

Kail, R., & Park, Y. (1992). Global developmental change in processing time. *Merrill-Palmer Quarterly, 38,* 525–541.

Kail, R., & Park, Y. (1994). Processing time, articulation time, and memory span. *Journal of Experimental Child Psychology, 57,* 281–291.

Kail, R., & Salthouse, T. A. (1994). Processing speed as a mental capacity. *Acta Psychologica, 86,* 199–225.

Kaitz, M., Meirov, H., Landman, I., & Eidelman, A. I. (1993a). Infant recognition by tactile cues. *Infant Behavior and Development, 16,* 333–341.

Kaitz, M., Meschulach-Sarfaty, O., Auerbach, J., & Eidelman, A. (1988). A reexamination of newborns' ability to imitate facial expressions. *Developmental Psychology, 24,* 3–7.

Kaitz, M., Shiri, S., Danziger, S., Hershko, Z., & Eidelman, A. I. (1993b). Fathers can also recognize their newborns by touch. *Infant Behavior and Development, 17,* 205–207.

Kaler, S. R., & Kopp, C. B. (1990). Compliance and comprehension in very young toddlers. *Child Development, 61,* 1997–2003.

Kamerman, S. B. (1993). International perspectives on child care policies and programs. *Pediatrics, 91,* 248–252.

Kandel, D. B. (1978). Homophily, selection, and socialization in adolescent friendships. *American Journal of Sociology, 84,* 427–436.

Kandall, S. R., Gaines, J., Habel, L., Davidson, G., & Jessop, D. (1993). Relationship of maternal substance abuse to subsequent sudden infant death syndrome in offspring. *Journal of Pediatrics, 123,* 120–126.

Kandel, D. B., Raveis, V. H., & Davies, M. (1991). Suicidal ideation in adolescence: Depression, substance use, and other risk factors. *Journal of Youth and Adolescence, 20,* 289–309.

Kandel, D. B., & Yamaguchi, K. (1993). From beer to crack: Developmental patterns of drug involvement. *American Journal of Public Health, 83,* 851–855.

Kanner, A. D., Feldman, S. S., Weinberger, D. A., & Ford, M. E. (1987). Uplifts, hassles, and adaptational outcomes in early adolescents. *Journal of Early Adolescence, 7,* 371–394.

Kantor, D., & Lehr, W. (1975). *Inside the family.* San Francisco: Jossey-Bass.

Kaplan, R. M. (1985). The controversy related to the use of psychological tests. In B. B. Wolman (Ed.), *Handbook of intelligence* (pp. 465–504). New York: Wiley.

Karadsheh, R. (1991, March). *This room is a junkyard! Children's comprehension of metaphorical language.* Paper presented at the biennial meeting of the Society for Research in Child Development, Seattle, WA.

Karmiloff-Smith, A. (1992). *Beyond modularity: A developmental perspective on cognitive science.* Cambridge, MA: MIT Press.

Kassebaum, N. L. (1994). Head Start: Only the best for America's children. *American Psychologist, 49,* 123–126.

Katchadourian, H. (1977). *The biology of adolescence.* San Francisco: Freeman.

Katchadourian, H. (1990). Sexuality. In S. S. Feldman & G. R. Elliott (Eds.), *At the threshold: The developing adolescent* (pp. 330–351). Cambridge, MA: Harvard University Press.

Kaufman, A. S., Kamphaus, R. W., & Kaufman, N. L. (1985). New directions in intelligence testing: The Kaufman Assessment Battery for Children (K-ABC). In B. B. Wolman (Ed.), *Handbook of intelligence* (pp. 663–698). New York: Wiley.

Kaufman, A. S., & Kaufman, N. L. (1983). *Kaufman Assessment Battery for Children: Administration and scoring manual.* Circle Pines, MN: American Guidance Service.

Kaufman, J., & Zigler, E. F. (1989). The intergenerational transmission of child abuse. In D. Cicchetti & V. Carlson (Eds.), *Child maltreatment: Theory and research on the causes and consequences of child abuse and neglect* (pp. 129–150). Cambridge, MA: Cambridge University Press.

Kavanaugh, R. D., & Harris, P. L. (1994). Imagining the outcome of pretend transformations: Assessing the competence of normal children and children with autism. *Developmental Psychology, 30,* 847–854.

Kawasaki, C., Nugent, J. K., Miyashita, H., Miyahara, H., & Brazelton, T. B. (1994). The cultural organization of infants' sleep. *Children's Environments, 11,* 135–141.

Kaye, K., Elkind, L., Goldberg, D., & Tytun, A. (1989). Birth outcomes for infants of drug abusing mothers. *New York State Journal of Medicine, 89,* 256–261.

Kaye, K., & Marcus, J. (1981). Infant imitation: The sensory-motor agenda. *Developmental Psychology, 17,* 258–265.

Kazdin, A. (1995). *Conduct disorders in childhood and adolescence* (2nd ed.). Thousand Oaks, CA: Sage.

Kearins, J. M. (1981). Visual spatial memory in Australian aboriginal children of desert regions. *Cognitive Psychology, 13,* 434–460.

Keating, D. (1979). Adolescent thinking. In J. Adelson (Ed.), *Handbook of adolescent psychology* (pp. 211–246). New York: Wiley.

Keating, D., & Clark, L. V. (1980). Development of physical and social reasoning in adolescence. *Developmental Psychology, 16,* 23–30.

Keen, C. L., & Zidenberg-Cherr, S. (1994). Should vitamin–mineral supplements be recommended for all women with childbearing potential? *American Journal of Clinical Nutrition, 59,* 532S–539S.

Keeney, T. J., Canizzo, S. R., & Flavell, J. H. (1967). Spontaneous and induced verbal rehearsal in a recall task. *Child Development, 38,* 953–966.

Keil, F. C. (1986). Conceptual domains and the acquisition of metaphor. *Cognitive Development, 1,* 72–96.

Keil, F. C. (1989). *Concepts, kinds, and cognitive development.* Cambridge, MA: MIT Press.

Keller, A., Ford, L. H., & Meacham, J. A. (1978). Dimensions of self-concept in preschool children. *Developmental Psychology, 14,* 483–489.

Keller, M., & Wood, P. (1989). Development of friendship reasoning: A study of interindividual differences and intraindividual change. *Developmental Psychology, 25,* 820–826.

Kelley, M. L., Power, T. G., & Wimbush, D. D. (1992). Determinants of disciplinary practices in low-income black mothers. *Child Development, 63,* 573–582.

Kellman, P. J. (1993). Kinematic foundations of infant visual perception. In C. E. Granrud (Ed.), *Visual perception and cognition in infancy* (pp. 121–173). Hillsdale, NJ: Erlbaum.

Kemp, J. S., & Thach, B. T. (1993). A sleep position-dependent mechanism for infant death on sheepskins. *American Journal of Diseases of Children, 147,* 642–646.

Kempe, C. H., Silverman, B. F., Steele, P. W., Droegemueller, P. W., & Silver, H. K. (1962). The battered-child syndrome. *Journal of the American Medical Association, 181,* 17–24.

Kendall-Tackett, K. A., Williams, L. M., & Finkelhor, D. (1993). Impact of sexual abuse on children: A review and synthesis of recent empirical studies. *Psychological Bulletin, 113,* 164–180.

Kendler, K. S., & Robinette, C. D. (1983). Schizophrenia in the National Academy of Science—National Research Council twin registry: A 16-year update. *American Journal of Psychiatry, 140,* 1551–1563.

Kennell, J., Klaus, M., McGrath, S., Robertson, S., & Hinkley, C. (1991). Continuous emotional support during labor in a U.S. hospital. *Journal of the American Medical Association, 265,* 2197–2201.

Keogh, B. K. (1988). Improving services for problem learners. *Journal of Learning Disabilities, 21,* 6–11.

Kerkman, D. D., & Siegler, R. S. (1993). Individual differences and adaptive flexibility in lower-income children's strategy choices. *Learning and Individual Differences, 5,* 113–136.

Kermoian, R., & Campos, J. J. (1988). Locomotor experience: A facilitator of spatial cognitive development. *Child Development, 59,* 908–917.

Kerns, K. A., & Berenbaum, S. A. (1991). Sex differences in spatial ability in children. *Behavior Genetics, 21,* 383–396.

Kerr, B. A. (1983). Raising the career aspirations of gifted girls. *Vocational Guidance Quarterly, 32,* 37–43.

Kerr, M., Lambert, W. W., Stattin, H., & Klackenberg-Larsson, I. (1994). Stability of inhibition in a Swedish longitudinal sample. *Child Development, 65,* 138–146.

Kessen, W. (1967). Sucking and looking: Two organized congenital patterns of behavior in the human newborn. In H. W. Stevenson, E. H. Hess, & H. L. Rheingold (Eds.), *Early behavior: Comparative and developmental approaches* (pp. 147–179). New York: Wiley.

Ketterlinus, R. D., Henderson, S. H., & Lamb, M. E. (1990). Maternal age, sociodemographics, prenatal health and behavior: Influences on neonatal risk status. *Journal of Adolescent Health Care, 11,* 423–431.

Kim, K., & Spelke, E. S., (1992). Infants' sensitivity to effects of gravity on visible object motion. *Journal of Experimental Psychology: Human Perception and Performance, 18,* 385–393.

Kinsman, C. A., & Berk, L. E. (1979). Joining the block and housekeeping areas: Changes in play and social behavior. *Young Children, 35*(1), 66–75.

Kinzie, J. D., Sack, W., Angell, R., Clarke, G., & Ben, R. (1989). A three-year follow-up of Cambodian young people traumatized as children. *Journal of the American Academy of Child and Adolescent Psychiatry, 28,* 501–504.

Kirby, D. (1992). School-based programs to reduce sexual risk-taking. *Journal of School Health, 62,* 280–287.

Kirby, D., Short, L., Collins, J., Rugg, D., Kolbe, L., Howard, M., Miller, B., Sonenstein, F., & Zabin, L. S. (1994). School-based programs to reduce sexual behaviors: A review of effectiveness. *Public Health Reports, 109*(3), 339–360.

Kisker, E. E. (1985). Teenagers talk about sex, pregnancy, and contraception. *Family Planning Perspectives, 17,* 83–90.

Kitchener, K. S., Lynch, C. L., Fischer, K. W., & Wood, P. K. (1993). Developmental range of reflective judgment: The effect of contexual support and practice on developmental stage. *Developmental Psychology, 29,* 893–906.

Klahr, D. (1992). Information-processing approaches to cognitive development. In M. H. Bornstein & M. E. Lamb (Eds.), *Developmental psychology: An advanced textbook* (3rd ed., pp. 273–335). Hillsdale, NJ: Erlbaum.

Kleinke, C. L., & Nicholson, T. A. (1979). Black and white children's awareness of de facto race and sex differences. *Developmental Psychology, 15,* 84–86.

Klimes-Dougan, B., & Kistner, J. (1990). Physically abused preschoolers' responses to peers' distress. *Developmental Psychology, 26,* 599–602.

Klineberg, O. (1963). Negro–white differences in intelligence test performance: A new look at an old problem. *American Psychologist, 18,* 198–203.

Klonoffcohen, H. S., Edelstein, S. L., Lefkowitz, E. S., Srinivasan, I. P., Kaegi, D., Chang, J. C., & Wiley, K. J. (1995). The effect of passive smoking and tobacco exposure through breast milk on sudden infant death syndrome. *Journal of the American Medical Association, 273,* 795–798.

Knittle, J. L., & Hirsch, J. (1968). Effect of early nutrition on the development of rat epididymal fat pads: Cellularity and metabolism. *Journal of Clinical Investigation, 47,* 2091–2098.

Knobloch, H., & Pasamanick, B. (Eds.). (1974). *Gesell and Amatruda's Developmental Diagnosis.* Hagerstown, MD: Harper & Row.

Kochanska, G. (1991). Socialization and temperament in the development of guilt and conscience. *Child Development, 62,* 1379–1392.

Kochanska, G. (1992). Children's interpersonal influence with mothers and peers. *Developmental Psychology, 28,* 491–499.

Kochanska, G. (1993). Toward a synthesis of parental socialization and child temperament in early development of conscience. *Child Development, 64,* 325–347.

Kochanska, G. (1995). Children's temperament, mothers' discipline, and security of attachment: Multiple pathways to emerging internalization. *Child Development, 66,* 597–615.

Kochanska, G., & Aksan, N. (1995). Mother–child mutually positive affect, the quality of child compliance to requests and prohibitions, and maternal control as correlates of early internalization. *Child Development, 66,* 597–615.

Kochanska, G., Aksan, N., & Koenig, A. L. (1995). A longitudinal study of the roots of preschoolers' conscience: Committed compliance and emerging internalization. *Child Development, 66,* 1752–1769.

Kochanska, G., Casey, R. J., & Fukumoto, A. (1995). Toddlers' sensitivity to standard violations. *Child Development, 66,* 643–656.

Kochanska, G., DeVet, K., Goldman, M., Murray, K., & Putnam, S. P. (1994). Maternal reports of conscience development and temperament in young children. *Child Development, 65,* 852–868.

Kochanska, G., Kuczynski, L., & Radke-Yarrow, M. (1989). Correspondence between mothers' self-reported and observed child-rearing practices. *Child Development, 60,* 56–63.

Kochanska, G., & Radke-Yarrow, M. (1992). Inhibition in toddlerhood and the dynamics of the child's interaction with an unfamiliar peer at age five. *Child Development, 63,* 325–335.

Kohlberg, L. (1969). Stage and sequence: The cognitive-developmental approach to socialization. In D. A. Goslin (Ed.), *Handbook of socialization theory and research* (pp. 347–480). Chicago: Rand McNally.

Kohlberg, L. (1984). *Essays on moral development. Vol. 2: The psychology of moral development.* San Francisco: Harper & Row.

Kohlberg, L., Levine, C., & Hewer, A. (1983). *Moral stages: A current formulation and a response to critics.* Basel: Karger.

Kohn, M. L. (1979). The effects of social class on parental values and practices. In D. Reiss & H. A. Hoffman (Eds.), *The American family: Dying or developing?* (pp. 45–68). New York: Plenum.

Kojima, H. (1986). Childrearing concepts as a belief-value system of the society and the individual. In H. Stevenson, H. Azuma, & K. Hakuta (Eds.), *Child development and education in Japan* (pp. 39–54). New York: Freeman.

Kohlberg, L. (1966). A cognitive-developmental analysis of children's sex-role concepts and attitudes. In E. E. Maccoby (Ed.), *The development of sex differences* (pp. 82–173). Stanford, CA: Stanford University Press.

Kohlberg, L. (1976). Moral stages and moralization: The cognitive-developmental approach. In T. Lickona (Ed.), *Moral development and behavior: Theory, research, and social issues* (pp. 31–53). New York: Holt.

Kolberg, R. (1993). Human embryo cloning reported. *Science, 262,* 652–653.

Kopp, C. B. (1987). The growth of self-regulation: Caregivers and children. In N. Eisenberg (Ed.), *Contemporary topics in developmental psychology* (pp. 34–55). New York: Wiley.

Kopp, C., & Kaler, S. R. (1989). Risk in infancy. *American Psychologist, 44,* 224–230.

Kotovsky, L., & Baillargeon, R. (1995). *Should a stationary object be displaced when hit by a moving object? Reasoning about collision events in 2.5-month-old infants.* Unpublished manuscript, University of Illinois at Urbana–Champaign.

Kozol, J. (1991). *Savage inequalities.* New York: Crown.

Kozulin, A. (1990). *Vygotsky's psychology: A biography of ideas.* Cambridge, MA: Harvard University Press.

Kramer, L., & Gottman, J. M. (1992). Becoming a sibling: "With a little help from my friends." *Developmental Psychology, 28,* 685–699.

Kranzler, J. H., & Jensen, A. R. (1989). Inspection time and intelligence: A meta-analysis. *Intelligence, 13,* 329–347.

Krebs, D., & Gillmore, J. (1982). The relationship among the first stages of cognitive development, role-taking abilities, and moral development. *Child Development, 53,* 877–886.

Kreipe, R. E., Churchill, B. H., & Strauss, J. (1989). Long-term outcome of adolescents with anorexia nervosa. *American Journal of Diseases of Children, 143,* 1322–1327.

Kreitler, S., & Kreitler, H. (1987). Conceptions and processes of planning: The development of perspective. In S. L. Friedman, E. K. Scholnick, & R. R. Cocking (Eds.), *Blueprints for thinking: The role of planning in cognitive development* (pp. 205–272). Cambridge: Cambridge University Press.

Kreutzer, M. A., Leonard, C., & Flavell, J. H. (1975). An interview study of children's knowledge about memory. *Monographs of the Society for Research in Child Development, 40*(1, Serial No. 159).

Krevans, J., & Gibbs, J. C. (in press). Parents' use of inductive discipline: Relations to children's empathy and prosocial behavior. *Child Development.*

Kristjansson, B., & Fried, P. A. (1989). Maternal smoking during pregnancy affects children's vigilance performance. *Drug and Alcohol Dependency, 24,* 11–19.

Kroger, J. (1995). The differentiation of "firm" and "developmental" foreclosure identity statuses: A longitudinal study. *Journal of Adolescent Research, 10,* 317–337.

Kruger, A. C. (1993). Peer collaboration: Conflict, cooperation, or both? *Social Development, 2,* 165–182.

Krumhansl, C. L., & Jusczyk, P. W. (1990). Infants' perception of phrase structure in music. *Psychological Science, 1,* 70–73.

Ku, L. C., Sonenstein, F. L., & Pleck, J. H. (1993). Factors influencing first intercourse for teenage men. *Public Health Reports, 108,* 680–694.

Kuczaj, S. A., II. (1986). Thoughts on the intentional basis of early object word extension: Evidence from comprehension and production. In S. A. Kuczaj, II, & M. D. Barrett (Eds.), *The development of word meaning* (pp. 99–120). New York: Springer-Verlag.

Kuczynski, L. (1984). Socialization goals and mother–child interaction: Strategies for long-term and short-term compliance. *Developmental Psychology, 20,* 1061–1073.

Kuczynski, L., & Kochanska, G. (1990). Development of children's noncompliance strategies from toddlerhood to age 5. *Developmental Psychology, 26,* 398–408.

Kuczynski, L., & Kochanska, G. (1995). Function and content of maternal demands: Developmental significance of early demands for competent action. *Child Development, 66,* 616–628.

Kuczynski, L., Kochanska, G., Radke-Yarrow, M., & Girnius-Brown, O. (1987). A developmental interpretation of young children's noncompliance. *Developmental Psychology, 23,* 799–806.

Kuebli, J., & Fivush, R. (1992). Gender differences in parent-child conversations about past emotions. *Sex Roles, 27,* 683–698.

Kuhl, P. K., Williams, K. A., Lacerda, F., Stevens, K. N., & Lindblom, B. (1992). Linguistic experience alters phonetic perception in infants by 6 months of age. *Science, 255,* 606–608.

Kuhn, D. (1989). Children and adults as intuitive scientists. *Psychological Review, 96,* 674–689.

Kuhn, D. (1992). Cognitive development. In M. H. Bornstein & M. E. Lamb (Eds.), *Developmental psychology: An advanced textbook* (3rd ed., pp. 211–272). Hillsdale, NJ: Erlbaum.

Kuhn, D. (1993). Connecting scientific and informal reasoning. *Merrill-Palmer Quarterly, 39,* 74–103.

Kuhn, D. (1995). Microgenetic study of change: What has it told us? *Psychological Science, 6,* 133–139.

Kuhn, D., Amsel, E., & O'Loughlin, M. (1988). *The development of scientific thinking* skills. Orlando, FL: Academic Press.

Kuhn, D., Garcia-Mila, M., Zohar, A., & Andersen, C. (1995). Strategies of knowledge acquisition. *Monographs of the Society for Research in Child Development, 60*(245, Serial No. 4).

Kuhn, D., Ho, V., & Adams, C. (1979). Formal reasoning among pre- and late adolescents. *Child Development, 50,* 1128–1135.

Kuhn, D., Nash, S. C., & Brucken, L. (1978). Sex role concepts of two- and three-year-olds. *Child Development, 49,* 445–451.

Kunzinger, E. L., III. (1985). A short-term longitudinal study of memorial development during early grade school. *Developmental Psychology, 21,* 642–646.

Kupersmidt, J. B., DeRosier, M. E., & Patterson, C. P. (1995). Similarity as the basis for children's friendships: The roles of sociometric status, aggressive and withdrawn behavior, academic achievement, and demographic characteristics. *Journal of Social & Personal Relationships, 12,* 439–452.

Kupersmidt, J. B., Griesler, P. C., De Rosier, M. E., Patterson, C. J., & Davis, P. W. (1995). Childhood aggression and peer relations in the context of family and neighborhood factors. *Child Development, 66,* 360–375.

Kurdek, L. A. (1980). Developmental relations among children's perspective-taking, moral judgment, and parent-rated behavior. *Merrill-Palmer Quarterly, 26,* 103–121.

Kurdek, L. A. (1978). Relationship between cognitive perspective-taking and teachers' ratings of children's classroom behavior in grades one through four. *Journal of Genetic Psychology, 132,* 21–27.

Kurdek, L. A., & Fine, M. A. (1994). Family acceptance and family control as predictors of adjustment in young adolescents: Linear, curvilinear, or interactive effects? *Child Development, 65,* 1137–1146.

Kurth, A. (1993). Reproductive issues, pregnancy, and childbearing in HIV-infected women. In F. L. Cohen & J. D. Durham (Eds.), *Women, children, and HIV/AIDS* (pp. 137–155). New York: Springer.

L

LaBarre, W. (1954). *The human animal.* Chicago: University of Chicago Press.

Lackey, P. N. (1989). Adults' attitudes about assignments of household chores to male and female children. *Sex Roles, 20,* 271–281.

Ladd, G. W. (1990). Having friends, keeping friends, making friends, and being liked by peers in the classroom: Predictors of children's early school adjustment? *Child Development, 61,* 1081–1100.

Ladd, G. W., & Cairns, E. (1996). Children: Ethnic and political violence. *Child Development, 67,* 14–18.

Ladd, G. W., & Hart, C. H. (1992). Creating informal play opportunities: Are parents' and preschoolers' initiations related to children's competence with peers? *Developmental Psychology, 28,* 1179–1187.

Ladd, G. W., & Price, J. M. (1987). Predicting children's social and school adjustment following the transition from preschool to kindergarten. *Child Development, 58,* 1168–1189.

Lagercrantz, H., & Slotkin, T. A. (1986). The "stress" of being born. *Scientific American, 254,* 100–107.

Lamaze, F. (1958). *Painless childbirth.* London: Burke.

Lamb, M. E. (1976). Interaction between eight-month-old children and their fathers and mothers. In M. E. Lamb (Ed.), *The role of the father in child development* (pp. 307–327). New York: Wiley.

Lamb, M. E. (1987). *The father's role: Cross-cultural perspectives.* Hillsdale, NJ: Erlbaum.

Lamb, M. E., & Oppenheim, D. (1989). Fatherhood and father–child relationships: Five years of research. In S. H. Cath, A. Gurwitt, & L. Gunsberg (Eds.), *Fathers and their families* (pp. 11–26). Hillsdale, NJ: Erlbaum.

Lamb, M. E., Sternberg, K. J., & Prodromidis, M. (1992). Nonmaternal care and the security of infant–mother attachment: A reanalysis of the data. *Infant Behavior and Development, 15,* 71–83.

Lamb, M. E., Thompson, R. A., Gardner, W., Charnov, E. L., & Connell, J. P. (1985). *Infant–mother attachment: The origins and developmental significance of individual differences in Strange Situation behavior.* Hillsdale, NJ: Erlbaum.

Lamborn, S. D., & Steinberg, L. (1993). Emotional autonomy redux: Revisiting Ryan and Lynch. *Child Development, 64,* 483–499.

Lamborn, S. D., Mounts, N. S., Steinberg, L., & Dornbusch, S. M. (1991). Patterns of competence and adjustment among adolescents from authoritative, authoritarian, indulgent, and neglectful families. *Child Development, 62,* 1049–1065.

Lampl, M. (1993). Evidence of altatory growth in infancy. *American Journal of Human Biology, 5,* 641–652.

Lampl, M., Veldhuis, J. D., & Johnson, M. L. (1992). Saltation and stasis: A model of human growth. *Science, 258,* 801–803.

Lancaster, J. B., & Whitten, P. (1980). Family matters. *The Sciences, 20,* 10–15.

Landau, R. (1982). Infant crying and fussing. *Journal of Cross-Cultural Psychology, 13,* 427–443.

Landau, S., Lorch, E. P., & Milich, R. (1992). Visual attention to and comprehension of television in attention-deficit hyperactivity disordered and normal boys. *Child Development, 63,* 928–937.

Landau, S., Pryor, J. B., & Haefli, K. (1995). Pediatric HIV: School-based sequelae and curricular interventions for infection prevention and social acceptance. *School Psychology Review, 24,* 213–229.

Landesman, S., & Ramey, C. (1989). Developmental psychology and mental retardation: Integrating scientific principles with treatment practices. *American Psychologist, 44,* 409–415.

Lane, D. M., & Pearson, D. A. (1982). The development of selective attention. *Merrill-Palmer Quarterly, 28,* 317–337.

Lange, G., & Pierce, S. H. (1992). Memory-strategy learning and maintenance in preschool children. *Developmental Psychology, 28,* 453–462.

Langlois, J. H., & Downs, A. C. (1979). Peer relations as a function of physical attractiveness: The eye of the beholder or behavioral reality? *Child Development, 50,* 409–418.

Langlois, J. H., & Downs, A. C. (1980). Mothers, fathers, and peers as socialization agents of sex-typed play behaviors in young children. *Child Development, 51,* 1237–1247.

Langlois, J. H., Ritter, J. M., Casey, R. J., & Sawin, D. B. (1995). Infant attractiveness predicts maternal behaviors and attitudes. *Developmental Psychology, 31,* 464–472.

Langlois, J. H., Ritter, J. M., Roggman, L. A., & Vaughn, L. S. (1991). Facial diversity and infant preferences for attractive faces. *Developmental Psychology, 27,* 79–84.

Langlois, J. H., Roggman, L. A., & Rieser-Danner, L. A. (1990). Infants' differential social responses to attractive and unattractive faces. *Developmental Psychology, 26,* 153–159.

Langlois, J. H., & Stephan, C. (1977). The effects of physical attractiveness and ethnicity on children's behavioral attributions and peer preferences. *Child Development, 48,* 1694–1698.

Langlois, J. H., & Stephan, C. W. (1981). Beauty and the beast: The role of physical attractiveness in peer relationships and social behavior. In S. S. Brehm, S. M. Kassin, & S. X. Gibbons (Eds.), *Developmental social psychology: Theory and research* (pp. 152–168). New York: Oxford University Press.

Langlois, J. H., & Styczynski, L. E. (1979). The effects of physical attractiveness on the behavioral attributions and peer preferences of acquainted children. *International Journal of Behavioral Development, 2,* 325–342.

Lapointe, A. E., Askew, J. M., & Mead, N. A. (1992). *Learning mathematics.* Princeton, NJ: Educational Testing Service.

Lapointe, A. E., Mead, N. A., & Askew, J. M. (1992). *Learning science.* Princeton, NJ: Educational Testing Service.

Lapsley, D. K. (1990). Egocentrism theory and the "new look" at the imaginary audience and personal fable in adolescence. In R. M. Lerner, A. C. Petersen, & J. Brooks-Gunn (Eds.), *The encyclopedia of adolescence* (pp. 281–286). New York: Garland.

Lapsley, D. K., Jackson, S., Rice, K., & Shadid, G. (1988). Self-monitoring and the "new look" at the imaginary audience and personal fable: An ego-developmental analysis. *Journal of Adolescent Research, 3,* 17–31.

Lapsley, D. K., Milstead, M., Quintana, S., Flannery, D., & Buss, R. (1986). Adolescent egocentrism and formal operations: Tests of a theoretical assumption. *Developmental Psychology, 22,* 800–807.

Lapsley, D. K., Rice, K. G., & FitzGerald, D. P. (1990). Adolescent attachment, identity, and adjustment to college: Implications for the continuity of adaptation hypothesis. *Journal of Counseling and Development, 68,* 561–565.

Larson, R., & Ham, M. (1993). Stress and "storm and stress" in early adolescence: The relationship of negative events with dysphoric affect. *Developmental Psychology, 29,* 130–140.

Larson, R., & Lampman-Petraitis, C. (1989). Daily emotional states as reported by children and adolescents. *Child Development, 60,* 1250–1260.

Laudenslager, M. L., & Reite, M. R. (1984). Loss and separations: Immunological consequences and health implications. In P. Shaver (Ed.), *Review of personality and social psychology* (Vol. 5, pp. 285–311). Beverly Hills, CA: Sage.

Laupa, M. (1991). Children's reasoning about three authority attributes: Adult status, knowledge, and social position. *Developmental Psychology, 27,* 321–329.

Laupa, M. (1995). "Who's in charge?" Preschool children's concepts of authority. *Early Childhood Research Quarterly, 9,* 1–7.

Laupa, M., & Turiel, E. (1993). Children's concepts of authority and social contexts. *Journal of Educational Psychology, 85,* 191–197.

Lazar, I., & Darlington, R. (1982). Lasting effects of early education: A report from the Consortium for Longitudinal Studies. *Monographs of the Society for Research in Child Development, 47*(2–3, Serial No. 195).

Leahy, R. L., & Eiter, M. (1980). Moral judgment and the development of real and ideal androgynous self-image during adolescence and young adulthood. *Developmental Psychology, 16,* 362–370.

Leaper, C. (1991). Influence and involvement in children's discourse. *Child Development, 62,* 797–811.

Lee, C. L., & Bates, J. E. (1985). Mother–child interaction at age two years and perceived difficult temperament. *Child Development, 56,* 1314–1325.

Lee, S. H., Ewert, D. P., Frederick, P. D., & Mascola, L. (1992). Resurgence of congenital rubella syndrome in the 1990s. *Journal of the American Medical Association, 267,* 2616–2620.

Lee, V. E., Brooks-Gunn, J., & Schnur, E. (1988). Does Head Start work? A 1-year follow-up comparison of disadvantaged children attending Head Start, no preschool, and other preschool programs. *Developmental Psychology, 24,* 210–222.

Lee, V. E., Brooks-Gunn, J., Schnur, E., & Liaw, F. (1990). Are Head Start effects sustained? A longitudinal follow-up comparison of disadvantaged children attending Head Start, no preschool, and other preschool programs. *Child Development, 61,* 495–507.

Leekam, S. (1993). Children's understanding of mind. In M. Bennett (Ed.), *The development of social cognition* (pp. 26–61). New York: Guilford.

Leeman, L. W., Gibbs, J. C., & Fuller, D. (1993). Evaluation of a multi-component group treatment program for juvenile delinquents. *Aggressive Behavior, 19,* 281–292.

Lefkowitz, M. M., Eron, L. D., Walder, L. O., & Huesmann, L. R. (1972). Television violence and child aggression: A follow-up study. In G. A. Comstock & E. A. Rubinstein (Eds.), *Television and social behavior* (Vol. 3, pp. 35–135). Washington, DC: U.S. Government Printing Office.

Lehman, D. R., & Nisbett, R. E. (1990). A longitudinal study of the effects of undergraduate training on reasoning. *Developmental Psychology, 26,* 952–960.

Lehnert, K. L., Overholser, J. C., & Spirito, A. (1994). Internalized and externalized anger in adolescent suicide attempters. *Journal of Adolescent Research, 9,* 105–119.

Leichtman, M. D., & Ceci, S. J. (1995). The effect of stereotypes and suggestions on preschoolers' reports. *Developmental Psychology, 31,* 568–578.

Leiter, M. P. (1977). A study of reciprocity in preschool play groups. *Child Development, 48,* 1288–1295.

LeMare, L. J., & Rubin, K. H. (1987). Perspective taking and peer interaction: Structural and developmental analyses. *Child Development, 58,* 306–315.

Lemire, R. J., Loeser, J. D., Leech, R. W., & Alvord, E. C. (1975). *Normal and abnormal development of the human nervous system.* New York: Harper & Row.

Lempert, H. (1989). Animacy constraints on preschoolers' acquisition of syntax. *Child Development, 60,* 237–245.

Lenneberg, E. H. (1967). *Biological foundations of language.* New York: Wiley.

Leonard, M. F., Rhymes, J. P., & Solnit, A. J. (1986). Failure to thrive in infants: A family problem. *American Journal of Diseases of Children, 111,* 600–612.

Lepper, M. R., & Gurtner, J. (1989). Children and computers: Approaching the twenty-first century. American Psychologist, 44, 170–178.

Lerner, J. W. (1989). Educational interventions in learning disabilities. *Journal of the American Academy of Child and Adolescent Psychiatry, 28,* 326–331.

Lerner, R. M., & Brackney, B. (1978). The importance of inner and outer body parts attitudes in the self-concept of late adolescents. *Sex Roles, 4,* 225–238.

Lerner, R. M., & Schroeder, C. (1971). Physique identification, preference, and aversion in kindergarten children. *Developmental Psychology, 5,* 538.

Leslie, A. M. (1987). Pretense and representation: The origins of "theory of mind." *Psychological Review, 94,* 412–426.

Leslie, A. M. (1988). Some implications of pretense for mechanisms underlying the child's theory of mind. In J. W. Astington, P. L. Harris, & D. R. Olson (Eds.), *Developing theories of mind* (pp. 19–46). New York: Cambridge University Press.

Lester, B. M. (1985). Introduction: There's more to crying than meets the ear. In B. M. Lester & C. F. Z. Boukydis (Eds.), *Infant crying* (pp. 1–27). New York: Plenum.

Lester, B. M. (1987). Developmental outcome prediction from acoustic cry analysis in term and preterm infants. *Pediatrics, 80,* 529–534.

Lester, B. M., & Dreher, M. (1989). Effects of marijuana use during pregnancy on newborn cry. *Child Development, 60,* 765–771.

Lester, B. M., Kotelchuck, M., Spelke, E., Sellers, M. J., & Klein, R. E. (1974). Separation protest in Guatemalan infants: Cross-cultural and cognitive findings. *Developmental Psychology, 10,* 79–85.

LeVay, S. (1993). *The sexual brain.* Cambridge, MA: MIT Press.

Leventhal, G. S. (1970). Influence of brothers and sisters on sex role behavior. *Journal of Personality and Social Psychology, 16,* 452–465.

Levin, S. R., Petros, T. V., & Petrella, F. W. (1982). Preschoolers' awareness of television advertising. *Child Development, 53,* 933–937.

Levine, L. E. (1983). Mine: Self-definition in 2-year-old boys. *Developmental Psychology, 19,* 544–549.

Levine, L. J. (1995). Young children's understanding of the causes of anger and sadness. *Child Development, 66,* 697–709.

LeVine, R. A., Dixon, S., LeVine, S., Richman, A., Leiderman, P. H., Keefer, C. H., & Brazelton, T. B. (1994). *Child care and culture: Lessons from Africa.* New York: Cambridge University Press.

Levitt, A. G., & Utmann, J. G. A. (1992). From babbling towards the sound systems of English and French: A longitudinal two-case study. *Journal of Child Language, 19,* 19–49.

Levitt, A. G., & Wang, Q. (1991). Evidence for language-specific rhythmic influences in the reduplicative babbling of French- and English-learning infants. *Language and Speech, 34,* 235–249.

Levy, G. D., & Carter, D. B. (1989). Gender schema, gender constancy, and gender-role knowledge: The roles of cognitive factors in preschoolers' gender-role stereotype attributions. *Developmental Psychology, 25,* 444–449.

Levy, G. D., Taylor, M. G., & Gelman, S. A. (1995). Traditional and evaluative aspects of flexibility in gender roles, social conventions, moral rules, and physical laws. *Child Development, 66,* 515–531.

Levy-Shiff, R., & Israelashvili, R. (1988). Antecedents of fathering: Some further exploration. *Developmental Psychology, 24,* 434–440.

Lewin, E. (1993). *Lesbian mothers.* Ithaca, NY: Cornell University Press.

Lewis, C. C. (1981). The effects of parental firm control: A reinterpretation of findings. *Psychological Bulletin, 90,* 547–563.

Lewis, M. (1991). Ways of knowing: Objective self-awareness or consciousness. *Developmental Review, 11,* 231–243.

Lewis, M. (1992a). *Shame: The exposed self.* New York: Free Press.

Lewis, M. (1992b). The self in self-conscious emotions (commentary on self-evaluation in young children). *Monographs of the Society for Research in Child Development, 57*(1, Serial No. 226).

Lewis, M., & Brooks, J. (1978). Self-knowledge and emotional development. In M. Lewis & L. A. Rosenblum (Ed.), *The development of affect* (pp. 205–226). New York: Plenum.

Lewis, M., & Brooks-Gunn, J. (1979). *Social cognition and the acquisition of self.* New York: Plenum.

Lewis, M., Alessandri, S. M., & Sullivan, M. W. (1992). Differences in shame and pride as a function of children's gender and task difficulty. *Child Development, 63,* 630–638.

Lewis, M., Ramsay, D. S., & Kawakami, K. (1993). Differences between Japanese infants and Caucasian American infants in behavioral and cortisol response to inoculation. *Child Development, 64,* 1722–1731.

Lewis, M., Sullivan, M. W., & Ramsay, D. S. (1992). Individual differences in anger and sad expressions during extinction: Antecedents and consequences. *Infant Behavior and Development, 15,* 443–452.

Lewis, M., Sullivan, M. W., Stanger, C., & Weiss, M. (1989). Self development and self-conscious emotions. *Child Development, 60,* 146–156.

Lewis, M., Sullivan, M. W., & Vasen, A. (1987). Making faces: Age and emotion differences in the posing of emotional expressions. *Developmental Psychology, 23,* 690–697.

Lewontin, R. C. (1976). Race and intelligence. In N. J. Block & G. Dworkin (Eds.), *The IQ controversy* (pp. 78–92). New York: Pantheon Books.

Li, C. Q., Windsor, R. A., & Perkins, L. (1993). The impact on infant birth weight and gestational age of cotinine-validated smoking reduction during pregnancy. *Journal of the American Medical Association, 269,* 1519–1524.

Liaw, F., & Brooks-Gunn, J. (1993). Patterns of low-birth-weight children's cognitive development. *Developmental Psychology, 29,* 1024–1035.

Liben, L. S., & Downs, R. M. (1986). *Children's production and comprehension of maps: Increasing graphic literacy.* Washington, DC: National Institute of Education.

Liben, L. S., & Golbeck, S. L. (1984). Performance on Piagetian horizontality and verticality tasks: Sex-related differences in knowledge of relevant physical phenomena. *Developmental Psychology, 20,* 595–606.

Lickona, T. (1976). Research on Piaget's theory of moral development. In T. Lickona (Ed.), *Moral development and behavior* (pp. 219–240). New York: Holt, Rinehart & Winston.

Lickona, T. (1991). *Educating for character.* New York: Bantam.

Lidz, C. S. (1991). *Practitioner's guide to dynamic assessment.* New York: Guilford.

Liebert, R. M. (1986). Effects of television on children and adolescents. *Developmental and Behavioral Pediatrics, 7,* 43–48.

Liebert, R. M., & Sprafkin, J. (1988). *The early window: Effects of television on children and youth* (3rd ed.). New York: Pergamon Press.

Lifschitz, M., Berman, D., Galili, A., & Gilad, D. (1977). Bereaved children: The effects of mother's perception and social system organization on their short-range adjustment. *Journal of Child Psychiatry, 16,* 272–284.

Light, P., & Perrett-Clermont, A. (1989). Social context effects in learning and testing. In A. R. H. Gellatly, D. Rogers, & J. Sloboda (Eds.), *Cognition and social worlds* (pp. 99–112). Oxford: Clarendon Press.

Lillard, A. S. (1993). Pretend play skills and the child's theory of mind. *Child Development, 64,* 348–371.

Limber, S. P., & Flekkøy, M. G. (1995). The U.N Convention on the Rights of the Child: Its relevance for social scientists. Social Policy Report of the Society for Research in *Child Development, 9*(2).

Lin, C. C., & Fu, V. R. (1990). A comparison of child-rearing practices among Chinese, immigrant Chinese, and Caucasian-American parents. *Child Development, 61,* 429–433.

Lindell, S. G. (1988). Education for childbirth: A time for change. *Journal of Obstetrics, Gynecology, and Neonatal Nursing, 17,* 108–112.

Lindsay, P. (1984). High school size, participation in activities, and young adult social participation: Some enduring effects of schooling. *Educational Evaluation and Policy Analysis, 6,* 73–83.

Linn, M. C., & Hyde, J. S. (1989). Gender, mathematics, and science. *Educational Researcher, 18,* 17–27.

Linn, M. C., & Petersen, A. C. (1985). Emergence and characterization of sex differences in spatial ability: A meta-analysis. *Child Development, 56,* 1479–1498.

Linn, S., Lieberman, E., Schoenbaum, S. C., Monson, R. R., Stubblefield, P. G., & Ryan, K. J. (1988). Adverse outcomes of pregnancy in women exposed to diethylstilbestrol in utero. *Journal of Reproductive Medicine, 33,* 3–7.

Lipsitt, L. P. (1990). Learning and memory in infants. *Merrill-Palmer Quarterly, 36,* 53–66.

Lipsitt, L. P., & Werner, J. S. (1981). The infancy of human learning processes. In E. S. Gollin (Ed.), *Developmental plasticity* (pp. 101–133). New York: Academic Press.

Liss, M. B., Reinhardt, L. C., & Fredriksen, S. (1983). TV heroes: The impact of rhetoric and deeds. *Journal of Applied Developmental Psychology, 4,* 175–187.

Litowitz, B. (1977). Learning to make definitions. *Journal of Child Language, 8,* 165–175.

Little, J. & Thompson, B. (1988). Descriptive epidemiology. In I. MacGillivray, D. M. Campbell, & B. Thompson (Eds.), *Twinning and twins* (pp. 37–66). New York: Wiley.

Livesley, W. J., & Bromley, D. B. (1973). *Person perception in childhood and adolescence.* New York: Wiley.

Livson, N., & Peskin, H. (1980). Perspectives on adolescence from longitudinal research. In J. Adelson (Ed.), *Handbook of adolescent psychology* (pp. 47–98). New York: Wiley.

Lloyd, B., & Smith, C. (1985). The social representation of gender and young children's play. *British Journal of Developmental Psychology, 3,* 65–73.

Lloyd, P., Boada, H., & Forns, H. (1992). New directions in referential communication research. *British Journal of Developmental Psychology, 10,* 385–403.

Lobel, T. E., & Menashri, J. (1993). Relations of conceptions of gender-role transgressions and gender constancy to gender-typed toy preferences. *Developmental Psychology, 29,* 150–155.

Lochman, J. E., Coie, J. D., Underwood, M. K., & Terry, R. (1993). Effectiveness of a social relations intervention program for aggressive and nonaggressive, rejected children. *Journal of Consulting and Clinical Psychology, 61,* 1053–1058.

Locke, J. (1892). Some thoughts concerning education. In R. H. Quick (Ed.), *Locke on education* (pp. 1–236). Cambridge: Cambridge University Press. (Original work published 1690)

Locke, J. L. (1989). Babbling and early speech: Continuity and individual differences. *First Language, 9,* 191–206.

Lockheed, M. E. (1986). Reshaping the social order: The case of gender segregation. *Sex Roles, 14,* 617–628.

Lockheed, M. E., & Harris, A. M. (1984). Cross-sex collaborative learning in elementary classrooms. *American Educational Research Journal, 21,* 275–294.

Lockman, J. J. (1990). Perceptual motor coordination in infancy. In C-A. Hauert (Ed.), *Developmental psychology: Cognitive, perceptuomotor, and neuropsychological perspectives* (pp. 85–111). New York: Plenum Press.

Loehlin, J. C. (1992). *Genes and environment in personality development.* Newbury Park, CA: Sage.

Loehlin, J. C., Horn, J. M., & Willerman, L. (1989). Modeling IQ change: Evidence from the Texas Adoption Project. *Child Development, 60,* 993–1004.

Loehlin, J. C., Willerman, L., & Horn, J. M. (1988). Human behavior genetics. *Annual Review of Psychology, 38,* 101–133.

Lombardi, J. (1993). Looking at the child care landscape. *Pediatrics, 91,* 179–188.

Lord, S. E., Eccles, J. S., & McCarthy, K. A. (1994). Surviving the junior high transition: Family processes and self-perceptions as protective and risk factors. *Journal of Early Adolescence, 14,* 162–199.

Lorenz, K. Z. (1943). Die angeborenen Formen möglicher Erfahrung. *Zeitschrift für Tierpsychologie, 5,* 235–409.

Lorenz, K. Z. (1952). *King Solomon's ring.* New York: Crowell.

Losey, K. M. (1995). Mexican-American students and classroom interaction: An overview and critique. *Review of Educational Research, 65,* 283–318.

Loveland, K. A. (1987). Behavior of young children with Down syndrome before the mirror: Exploration. *Child Development, 58,* 768–778.

Lozoff, B. (1989). Nutrition and behavior. *American Psychologist, 44,* 231–236.

Lozoff, B., Wolf, A., Latz, S., & Paludetto, R. (1995, March). *Cosleeping in Japan, Italy, and the U.S.: Autonomy versus interpersonal relatedness.* Paper presented at the biennial meeting of the Society for Research in Child Development, Indianapolis.

Lubart, T. I. (1994). Creativity. In R. J. Sternberg (Ed.), *Thinking and problem solving* (pp. 289–332). San Diego: Academic Press.

Lubart, T. I., & Sternberg, R. J. (1995). An investment approach to creativity: Theory and data. In S. M. Smith, T. B. Ward, & R. A. Finke (Eds.), *The creative cognition approach* (pp. 271–302). Cambridge, MA: MIT Press.

Lucariello, J., & Nelson, K. (1985). Slot-filler categories as memory organizers for young children. *Developmental Psychology, 21,* 272–282.

Ludemann, P. M. (1991). Generalized discrimination of positive facial expressions by seven- and ten-month-old infants. *Child Development, 62,* 55–67.

Luecke-Aleksa, D., Anderson, D. R., Collins, P. A., & Schmitt, K. L. (1995). Gender constancy and television viewing. *Developmental Psychology, 31,* 773–780.

Lummis, M., & Stevenson, H. W. (1990). Gender differences in beliefs about achievement: A cross-cultural study. *Developmental Psychology, 26,* 254–263.

Luria, A. R. (1961). *The role of speech in the regulation of normal and abnormal behavior.* New York: Pergamon Press.

Luria, A. R. (1966). *The human brain and psychological processes.* New York: Harper & Row.

Luster, T., & Dubow, E. (1992). Home environment and maternal intelligence as predictors of verbal intelligence: A comparison of preschool and school-age children. *Merrill-Palmer Quarterly, 38,* 151–175.

Luster, T., & McAdoo, H. (1996). Family and child influences on educational attainment: A secondary analysis of the High/Scope Perry Preschool data. *Developmental Psychology, 32,* 26–39.

Luster, T., Rhoades, K., & Haas, B. (1989). The relation between parental values and parenting behavior. Journal of Marriage and the Family, 51, 139–147.

Luthar, S. S., & Zigler, E. (1991). Vulnerability and competence: A review of research on resilience in childhood. *American Journal of Orthopsychiatry, 6,* 6–22.

Lutz, S. E., & Ruble, D. N. (1995). Children and gender prejudice: Context, motivation, and the development of gender conception. In R. Vasta (Ed.), *Annals of child development* (Vol. 10, pp. 131–166). London: Jessica Kingsley.

Lyon, T. D., & Flavell, J. H. (1994). Young children's understanding of "remember" and "forget." *Child Development, 65,* 1357–1371.

Lyons-Ruth, K., Connell, D. B., Grunebaum, H. U., & Botein, S. (1990). Infants at social risk: Maternal depression and family support services as mediators of infant development and security of attachment. *Child Development, 61,* 85–98.

Lysynchuk, L. M., Pressley, M., & Vye, N. J. (1990). Reciprocal teaching improves standardized reading-comprehension performance in poor comprehenders. *Elementary School Journal, 90,* 469–484.

Lytton, H., & Romney, D. M. (1991). Parents' sex-related differential socialization of boys and girls: A meta-analysis. *Psychological Bulletin, 109,* 267–296.

M

Maccoby, E. E. (1984a). Middle childhood in the context of the family. In W. A. Collins (Ed.), *Development during middle childhood* (pp. 184–239). Washington, DC: National Academy Press.

Maccoby, E. E. (1984b). Socialization and developmental change. *Child Development, 55,* 317–328.

Maccoby, E. E. (1988). Gender as a social category. *Developmental Psychology, 24,* 755–765.

Maccoby, E. E. (1990a). Gender and relationships. *American Psychologist, 45,* 513–520.

Maccoby, E. E. (1990b). The role of gender identity and gender constancy in sex-differentiated development. In D. Schrader (Ed.), *New directions for child development* (No. 47, pp. 5–20). San Francisco: Jossey-Bass.

Maccoby, E. E., & Jacklin, C. N. (1974). *The psychology of sex differences.* Stanford, CA: Stanford University Press.

Maccoby, E. E., & Jacklin, C. N. (1987). Gender segregation in childhood. In E. H. Reese (Ed.), *Advances in child development and behavior* (Vol. 20, pp. 239–287). New York: Academic Press.

Maccoby, E. E., & Martin, J. A. (1983). Socialization in the context of the family. In E. M. Hetherington (Ed.), *Handbook of Child Psychology: Vol. 4. Socialization, personality, and social development* (pp. 1–101). New York: Wiley.

Macfarlane, J. (1971). From infancy to adulthood. In M. C. Jones, N. Bayley, J. W. Macfarlane, & M. P. Honzik (Eds.), *The course of human development* (pp. 406–410). Waltham, MA: Xerox College Publishing.

MacKinnon, C. E. (1989). An observational investigation of sibling interactions in married and divorced families. *Developmental Psychology, 25,* 36–44.

Macksoud, M. (1994, March–April). Children in war. *World Health, 47*(2), 36–44.

MacMillan, D. L., Keogh, B. K., & Jones, R. L. (1986). Special educational research on mildly handicapped learners. In M. C. Wittrock (Ed.), *Handbook of research on teaching* (3rd ed., pp. 686–724). New York: Macmillan.

Macrides, R., Bartke, A., & Dalterio, S. (1975). Strange females increase plasma testosterone levels in male mice. *Science, 189,* 1104–1105.

MacTurk, R., Vietze, P., McCarthy, M., McQuiston, S., & Yarrow, L. (1985). The organization of exploratory behavior in Down syndrome and nondelayed infants. *Child Development, 56,* 573–581.

Madden, N., & Slavin, R. (1983). Mainstreaming students with mild handicaps: Academic and social outcomes.

Review of Educational Research, 53, 519–569.

Magai, C., & McFadden, S. H. (1995). *The role of emotions in social and personality development: History, theory, and research.* New York: Plenum.

Main, M., & Cassidy, J. (1988). Categories of response to reunion with the parent at age 6: Predictable from infant attachment classifications and stable over a 1-month period. *Developmental Psychology, 24,* 415–426.

Main, M., & Goldwyn, R. (1994). *Interview-based adult attachment classifications: Related to infant–mother and infant–father attachment.* Unpublished manuscript, University of California, Berkeley.

Main, M., & Solomon, J. (1990). Procedures for identifying infants as disorganized/disoriented during the Ainsworth Strange Situation. In M. Greenberg, D. Cicchetti, & M. Cummings (Eds.), *Attachment in the preschool years: Theory, research, and intervention* (pp. 121–160). Chicago: University of Chicago Press.

Makin, J. W., Fried, P. A., & Watkinson, B. (1991). A comparison of active and passive smoking during pregnancy: Long-term effects. *Neurotoxicology and Teratology, 13,* 5–12.

Makin, J. W., & Porter, R. H. (1989). Attractiveness of lactating females' breast odors to neonates. *Child Development, 60,* 803–810.

Malaguzzi, L. (1993). History, ideas, and basic philosophy. In C. Edwards, L. Gandini, & G. Forman (Eds.), *The hundred languages of children: The Reggio Emilia approach to early childhood education* (pp. 41–89). Norwood, NJ: Ablex.

Malatesta, C. Z., & Haviland, J. M. (1982). Learning display rules: The socialization of emotion expression in infancy. *Child Development, 53,* 991–1003.

Malatesta, C. Z., Grigoryev, P., Lamb, C., Albin, M., & Culver, C. (1986). Emotion socialization and expressive development in preterm and full-term infants. *Child Development, 57,* 316–330.

Malatesta-Magai, C. Z., Izard, C. E., & Camras, L. A. (1991). Conceptualizing early infant affect: Emotions as fact, fiction or artifact? In K. Strongman (Ed.), *International review of studies on emotion* (pp. 1–36). New York: Wiley.

Malina, R. M. (1975). *Growth and development: The first twenty years in man.* Minneapolis: Burgess Publishing.

Malina, R. M. (1990). Physical growth and performance during the transition years (9–16). In R. Montemayor, G. R. Adams, & T. P. Gullotta (Eds.), *From childhood to adolescence: A transitional period?* (pp. 41–62). Newbury Park, CA: Sage.

Malina, R. M., & Bouchard, C. (1991). *Growth, maturation, and physical activity.* Champaign, IL: Human Kinetics.

Malloy, M. H., & Hoffman, H. J. (1995). Prematurity, sudden infant death syndrome, and age of death. *Pediatrics, 96,* 464–471.

Malloy, M. H., Kao, T., & Lee, Y. J. (1992). Analyzing the effect of prenatal care on pregnancy outcome: A conditional approach. *American Journal of Public Health, 82,* 448–453.

Maloney, M., & Kranz, R. (1991). *Straight talk about eating disorders.* New York: Facts on File.

Mandler, J. M. (1984). *Stories, scripts, and scenes: Aspects of schema theory.* Hillsdale, NJ: Erlbaum.

Mandler, J. M. (1992a). The foundations of conceptual thought in infancy. *Cognitive Development, 7,* 273–285.

Mandler, J. M. (1992b). How to build a baby: II. Conceptual primitives. *Psychological Review, 99,* 587–604.

Mandler, J. M., Bauer, P. J., & McDonough, L. (1991). Separating the sheep from the goats: Differentiating global categories. *Cognitive Psychology, 23,* 263–298.

Mandler, J. M., & McDonough, L. (1993). Concept formation in infancy. *Cognitive Development, 8,* 291–318.

Mandler, J. M., & Robinson, C. A. (1978). Developmental changes in picture recognition. *Journal of Experimental Child Psychology, 26,* 122–136.

Mangelsdorf, S. C., Gunnar, M., Kestenbaum, R., Lang, S., & Andreas, D. (1990). Infant proneness-to-distress temperament, maternal personality, and mother–infant attachment: Associations and goodness of fit. *Child Development, 61,* 830–831.

Mant, C. M., & Perner, J. (1988). The child's understanding of commitment. *Developmental Psychology, 24,* 343–351.

Maqsud, M. (1977). The influence of social heterogeneity and sentimental credibility on moral judgments of Nigerian Muslim adolescents. *Journal of Cross-Cultural Psychology, 8,* 113–122.

Maratsos, M. P. (1983). Some current issues in the study of the acquisition of grammar. In P. H. Mussen (Ed.), *Handbook of child psychology* (Vol. 3, pp. 707–786). New York: Wiley.

Maratsos, M. P. (1989). Innateness and plasticity in language acquisition. In M. L. Rice & R. L. Schiefelbusch (Eds.), *The teachability of language* (pp. 105–125). Baltimore: Paul H. Brookes.

Maratsos, M. P., & Chalkley, M. A. (1980). The internal language of children's syntax: The ontogenesis and representation of syntactic categories. In K. Nelson (Ed.), *Children's language* (Vol. 2, pp. 127–214). New York: Gardner Press.

Marcella, S., & McDonald, B. (1990). The infant walker: An unappreciated household hazard. *Connecticut Medicine, 54,* 127–129.

Marcia, J. E. (1980). Identity in adolescence. In J. Adelson (Ed.), *Handbook of adolescent psychology* (pp. 159–187). New York: Wiley.

Marcia, J. E. (1988). Identity and intervention. *Journal of Adolescence, 12,* 401–410.

Marcia, J. E., Waterman, A. S., Matteson, D. R., Archer, S. L., & Orlofsky, J. L. (1993). *Ego identity: A handbook for psychosocial research.* New York: Springer-Verlag.

Marcus, G. F. (1995). Children's overregularization of English plurals: A quantitative analysis. *Journal of Child Language, 22,* 447–459.

Marcus, G. F. (1993). Negative evidence in language acquisition. *Cognition, 46,* 53–85.

Marcus, G. F., Pinker, S., Ullman, M., Hollander, M., Rosen, T. J., & Xu, F. (1992). Overregularization in language acquisition. *Monographs of the Society for Research in Child Development, 57*(4, Serial No. 228).

Marcus, J., Maccoby, E. E., Jacklin, C. N., & Doering, C. H. (1985). Individual differences in mood in early childhood: Their relation to gender and neonatal sex steroids. *Developmental Psychobiology, 18,* 327–340.

Marini, Z., & Case, R. (1989). Parallels in the development of preschoolers' knowledge about their physical and social worlds. *Merrill-Palmer Quarterly, 35,* 63–87.

Marini, Z., & Case, R. (1994). The development of abstract reasoning about the physical and social world. *Child Development, 65,* 147–159.

Markman, E. M. (1989). *Categorization and naming in children.* Cambridge, MA: MIT Press.

Markman, E. M. (1992). Constraints on word learning: Speculations about their nature, origins, and domain specificity. In M. R. Gunnar & M. P. Maratsos (Eds.), *Minnesota Symposia on Child Psychology* (Vol. 25, pp. 59–101). Hillsdale, NJ: Erlbaum.

Markovits, H., & Vachon, R. (1989). Reasoning with contrary-to-fact propositions. *Journal of Experimental Child Psychology, 47,* 398–412.

Markovits, H., & Vachon, R. (1990). Conditional reasoning, representation, and level of abstraction. *Developmental Psychology, 26,* 942–951.

Markstrom-Adams, C., & Adams, G. R. (1995). Gender, ethnic group, and grade differences in psychosocial functioning during middle adolescence? *Journal of Youth and Adolescence, 24,* 397–417.

Markus, H. R., & Kitayama, S. (1991). Culture and the self: Implications for cognition, emotion, and motivation. *Psychological Review, 98,* 224–253.

Marsh, D. T., Serafica, F. C., & Barenboim, C. (1981). Interrelationships among perspective taking, interpersonal problem solving, and interpersonal functioning. *Journal of Genetic Psychology, 138,* 37–48.

Marsh, H. W. (1989). Sex differences in the development of verbal and mathematics constructs: The High School and Beyond study. *American Educational Research Journal, 26,* 191–225.

Marsh, H. W. (1990). The structure of academic self-concept: The Marsh/Shavelson model. *Journal of Educational Psychology, 82,* 623–636.

Marsh, H. W., Barnes, J., Cairns, L., & Tidman, M. (1984). Self-description questionnaire: Age and sex effects in the structure and level of self-concept for preadolescent children. *Journal of Educational Psychology, 76,* 940–956.

Marsh, H. W., Craven, R. G., & Debus, R. (1991). Self-concepts of young children 5 to 8 years of age: Measurement and multidimensional structure. *Journal of Educational Psychology, 83,* 377–392.

Marsh, H. W., & Gouvernet, P. J. (1989). Multidimensional self-concepts and perceptions of control: Construct validation of responses by children. *Journal of Educational Psychology, 81,* 57–69.

Marsh, H. W., Smith, I. D., & Barnes, J. (1985). Multidimensional self-concepts: Relations with sex and academic achievement. *Journal of Educational Psychology, 77,* 581–596.

Marshall, E. (1995). Gene therapy's growing pains. *Science, 269,* 1050–1052.

Martin, C. L. (1989). Children's use of gender-related information in making social judgments. *Developmental Psychology, 25,* 80–88.

Martin, C. L., Eisenbud, L., & Rose, H. (1995). Children's gender-based reasoning about toys. *Child Development, 66,* 1453–1471.

Martin, C. L., & Halverson, C. F., Jr. (1981). A schematic processing model of sex typing and stereotyping in children. *Child Development, 52,* 1119–1134.

Martin, C. L., & Halverson, C. F., Jr. (1983). The effects of sex-typing schemas on young children's memory. *Child Development, 54,* 563–574.

Martin, C. L., & Halverson, C. F., Jr. (1987). The role of cognition in sex role acquisition. In D. B. Carter (Ed.), *Current conceptions of sex roles and sex typing: Theory and research* (pp. 123–137). New York: Praeger.

Martin, C. L., & Little, J. K. (1990). The relation of gender understanding to children's sex-typed preferences and gender stereotypes. *Child Development, 61,* 1427–1439.

Martin, G. B., & Clark, R. D., III. (1982). Distress crying in neonates: Species and peer specificity. *Developmental Psychology, 18,* 3–9.

Martin, J. A. (1981). A longitudinal study of the consequences of early mother-infant interaction: A microanalytic approach. *Monographs of the Society for Research in Child Development, 46* (3, Serial No. 190).

Martin, J. B. (1987). Molecular genetics: Applications to the clinical neurosciences. *Science, 298,* 765–772.

Martin, R. M. (1975). Effects of familiar and complex stimuli on infant attention. *Developmental Psychology, 11,* 178–185.

Martin, R. P., Olejnik, S., & Gaddis, L. (1994). Is temperament an important contributor to schooling outcomes in elementary school? Modeling effects of temperament and scholastic ability on academic achievement. In W. B. Carey & S. C. McDevitt (Eds.), *Prevention and early intervention* (pp. 59–68). New York: Brunner/Mazel.

Martin, S. L., Ramey, C. T., & Ramey, S. (1990). The prevention of a randomized trial of educational day care. *American Journal of Public Health, 80,* 844–847.

Martini, M. (1994). Peer interactions in Polynesia: A view from the Marquesas. In J. L. Roopnarine, J. E. Johnson, & F. H. Hooper (Eds.), *Children's play in diverse cultures* (pp. 73–103). Albany, NY: SUNY Press.

Marzolf, D. P., & DeLoache, J. S. (1994). Transfer in young children's understanding of spatial representations. *Child Development, 65,* 1–15.

Masataka, N. (1992). Motherese in a signed language. *Infant Behavior and Development, 15,* 453–460.

Mason, M. G., & Gibbs, J. C. (1993a). Role-taking opportunities and the transition to advanced moral judgment. *Moral Education Forum, 18,* 1–12.

Mason, M. G., & Gibbs, J. C. (1993b). Social perspective taking and moral judgment among college students. *Journal of Adolescent Research, 8,* 109–123.

Massey, C. M., & Gelman, R. (1988). Preschoolers' ability to decide whether a photographed unfamiliar object can move itself. *Developmental Psychology, 24,* 307–317.

Masur, E. F. (1995). Infants' early verbal imitation and their later lexical development. *Merrill-Palmer Quarterly, 41,* 286–306.

Masur, E. F., McIntyre, C. W., & Flavell, J. H. (1973). Developmental changes in apportionment of study time among items in a multi-trial free recall task. *Journal of Experimental Child Psychology, 15,* 237–246.

Matas, L., Arend, R., & Sroufe, L. A. (1978). Continuity of adaptation in the second year: The relationship between quality of attachment and later competence. *Child Development, 49,* 547–556.

Matheny, A. P., Jr. (1989). Temperament and cognition: Relations between temperament and mental test scores. In G. A. Kohnstamm, J. E. Bates, & M. K. Rothbart (Eds.), *Temperament in childhood* (pp. 263–282). New York: Wiley.

Matias, R., & Cohn, J. F. (1993). Are MAX-specified infant facial expressions during face-to-face interaction consistent with differential emotions theory? *Developmental Psychology, 29,* 524–531.

Matsumoto, D. (1990). Cultural similarities and differences in display rules. *Motivation and Emotion, 14,* 195–214.

Mattson, S. N., Jernigan, T. L., & Riley, E. P. (1994). MRI and prenatal alcohol exposure: Images provide insight into FAS. *Alcohol Health & Research World, 18,* 49–52.

Matute-Bianchi, M. E. (1986). Ethnic identities and patterns of school success and failure among Mexican-descent and Japanese-American students in a California high school: An ethnographic analysis. *American Journal of Education, 95,* 233–255.

Mayers, M. M., Davenny, K., Schoenbaum, E. E., Feingold, A. R., Selwyn, P. A., Robertson, V., Ou, C. Y., Rogers, M. F., & Naccarato, M. (1991). A prospective study of infants of human immunodeficiency virus seropositive and seronegative women with a history of intravenous drug use or of intravenous drug-using sex partners, in the Bronx, New York City. *Pediatrics, 88,* 1248–1256.

Mayes, L. C., & Zigler, E. (1992). An observational study of the affective concomitants of mastery in infants. *Journal of Child Psychology and Psychiatry, 33,* 659–667.

Maynard, R., & McGinnis, E. (1993). Policies to meet the need for high quality child care. In A. Booth (Ed.), *Child care for the '90s* (pp. 189–208). Hillsdale, NJ: Erlbaum.

Mazur, E. (1993). Developmental differences in children's understanding of marriage, divorce, and remarriage. *Journal of Applied Developmental Psychology, 14,* 191–212.

Mazzocco, M. M. M., Nord, A. M., van Doorninck, W., Green, C. L., Kovar, C. G., & Pennington, B. F. (1994). Cognitive development among children with early-treated phenylketonuria. *Developmental Neuropsychology, 10,* 133–151.

McAdams, R. P. (1993). *Lessons from abroad: How other countries educate their children.* Lancaster, PA: Technomic.

McAnarney, E. R., Kreipe, R. E., Orr, D. P., & Comerci, G. D. (1992). *Textbook of adolescent development.* Philadelphia: Saunders.

McCabe, A. E., & Peterson, C. (1988). A comparison of adults' versus children's spontaneous use of *because* and *so. Journal of Genetic Psychology, 149,* 257–268.

McCabe, A. E., & Siegel, L. S. (1987). The stability of training effects in young children's class inclusion reasoning. *Merrill-Palmer Quarterly, 33,* 187–194.

McCall, R. B. (1977). Childhood IQs as predictors of adult educational and occupational status. *Science, 197,* 482–483.

McCall, R. B. (1993). Developmental functions for general mental performance. In D. K. Detterman (Ed.), *Current topics in human intelligence* (Vol. 3, pp. 3–29). Norwood, NJ: Ablex.

McCall, R. B., Appelbaum, M. I., & Hogarty, P. S. (1973). Developmental changes in mental performance. *Monographs of the Society for Research in Child Development, 38*(3, Serial No. 150).

McCall, R. B., & Carriger, M. S. (1993). A meta-analysis of infant habituation and recognition memory performance as predictors of later IQ. *Child Development, 64,* 57–79.

McCall, R. B., Kennedy, C. B., & Appelbaum, M. I. (1977). Magnitude of discrepancy and the distribution of attention in infants. *Child Development, 48,* 772–785.

McCartney, K. (1984). The effect of quality of day care environment upon children's language development. *Developmental Psychology, 20,* 244–260.

McCloskey, L. A., Figueredo, A. J., & Koss, M. P. (1995). The effects of systemic family violence on children's mental health. *Child Development, 66,* 1239–1261.

McConaghy, M. J. (1979). Gender permanence and the genital basis of gender: Stages in the development of constancy of gender identity. *Child Development, 50,* 1223–1226.

McConaghy, N., & Silove, D. (1992). Do sex-linked behaviors in children influence relationships with their parents? *Archives of Sexual Behavior, 21,* 469–479.

McCormick, C. M., & Maurer, D. M. (1988). Unimanual hand preferences in 6-month-olds: Consistency and relation to familial-handedness. *Infant Behavior and Development, 11,* 21–29.

McCormick, M. C., Gortmaker, S. L., & Sobol, A. M. (1990). Very low birth weight children: Behavior problems and school difficulty in a national sample. *Journal of Pediatrics, 117,* 687–693.

McCune, L. (1993). The development of play as the development of consciousness. In M. H. Bornstein & A. O'Reilly (Eds.), *New directions for child development* (No. 59, pp. 67–79). San Francisco: Jossey-Bass.

McCune, L. (1995). A normative study of representational play at the transition to language. *Developmental Psychology, 31,* 198–206.

McGee, L. M., & Richgels, D. J. (1996). *Literacy's beginnings: Supporting young readers and writers.* Boston: Allyn and Bacon.

McGhee, P. E. (1979). *Humor: Its origin and development.* San Francisco: Freeman.

McGhee-Bidlack, B. (1991). The development of noun definitions: A metalinguistic analysis. *Journal of Child Language, 18,* 417–434.

McGillicuddy-De Lisi, A. V., Watkins, C., & Vinchur, A. J. (1994). The effect of relationship on children's distributive justice reasoning. *Child Development, 65,* 1694–1700.

McGilly, K., & Siegler, R. S. (1990). The influence of encoding and strategic knowledge on children's choices among serial recall strategies. *Developmental Psychology, 26,* 931–941.

McGinty, M. J., & Zafran, E. I. (1988). *Surrogacy: Constitutional and legal issues.* Cleveland: Ohio Academy of Trial Lawyers.

McGraw, K. O., Durm, M. W., & Durnam, M. R. (1989). The relative salience of sex, race, age, and glasses in children's social perception. *Journal of Genetic Psychology, 150,* 251–267.

McGroarty, M. (1992, March). The societal context of bilingual education. *Educational Researcher, 21*(2), 7–9.

McGue, M., Bouchard, T. J., Jr., Iacono, W. G., & Lykken, D. T. (1993). Behavioral genetics of cognitive ability: A life-span perspective. In R. Plomin & G. E. McClearn (Eds.), *Nature, nurture, and psychology* (pp. 59–76). Washington, DC: American Psychological Association.

McGuinness, D., & Pribram, K. H. (1980). The neuropsychology of attention: Emotional and motivational controls. In M. C. Wittcock (Ed.), *The brain and psychology* (pp. 95–139). New York: Academic Press.

McGuire, K. D., & Weisz, J. R. (1982). Social cognition and behavior correlates of preadolescent chumship. *Child Development, 53,* 1483–1484.

McHale, S. M., Bartko, W. T., Crouter, A. C., & Perry-Jenkins, M. (1990). Children's housework and psychosocial functioning: The mediating effects of parents' sex-role behaviors and attitudes. *Child Development, 61,* 68–81.

McKenna, J., Mosko, S., Richard, C., Drummond, S., Hunt, L., Cetel, M. B., & Arpaia, J. (1994). Experimental studies of infant–parent co-sleeping: Mutual physiological and behavioral influences and their relevance to SIDS (sudden infant death syndrome). *Early Human Development, 38,* 187–201.

McKenna, M. C., Stratton, B. D., Grindler, M. C., & Jenkins, S. J. (1995). Differential effects of whole language and traditional instruction on reading attitudes. *Journal of Reading Behavior, 27,* 19–43.

McKenry, P. C., & Price, S. J. (1995). Divorce: A comparative perspective. In B. B. Ingoldsby & S. Smith (Eds.), *Families in multicultural perspective* (pp. 187–212). New York: Guilford.

McKey, R. H., Condelli, L., Ganson, H., Barrett, B. J., McConkey, C., & Plantz, M. C. (1985). *The impact of Head Start on children, families, and communities.* Washington, DC: U.S. Government Printing Office.

McKnight, C. C., Crosswhite, F. J., Dossey, J. A., Kifer, E., Swafford, J. O., Travers, K. J., & Cooney, T. J. (1987). *The underachieving curriculum: Assessing U.S. school mathematics from an international perspective.* Champaign, IL: Stipes.

McKusick, V. A. (1995). *Mendelian inheritance in man: Catalogs of autosomal dominant, autosomal recessive, and X-linked phenotypes* (10th ed.). Baltimore: Johns Hopkins University Press.

McLean, D. F., Timajchy, K. H., Wingo, P. A., & Floyd, R. L. (1993). Psychosocial measurement: Implications of the study of preterm delivery in black women. *American Journal of Preventive Medicine, 9,* 39–81.

McLoyd, V. C. (1990). The impact of economic hardship on black families and children: Psychological distress, parenting, and socioemotional development. *Child Development, 61,* 311–346.

McLoyd, V. C., Jayaratne, T. E., Ceballo, R., & Borquez, J. (1994). Unemployment and work interruption among African American single mothers: Effects on parenting and adolescent socioemotional functioning. *Child Development, 65,* 562–589.

McLoyd, V. C., Warren, D., & Thomas, E. A. C. (1984). Anticipatory and fantastic role enactment in preschool triads. *Developmental Psychology, 20,* 807–814.

McManus, I. C., Sik, G., Cole, D. R., Mellon, A. F., Wong, J., & Kloss, J. (1988). The development of handedness in children. *British Journal of Developmental Psychology, 6,* 257–273.

McMichael , A. J., Baghurst, P. A., & Wigg, N. R. (1988). Port Pirie Cohort Study: Environmental exposure to lead and children's abilities at the age of four years. *New England Journal of Medicine, 319,* 468–475.

McNamee, S., & Peterson, J. (1986). Young children's distributive justice reasoning, behavior, and role taking: Their consistency and relationship. *Journal of Genetic Psychology, 146,* 399–404.

MCR Vitamin Study Research Group. (1991). Prevention of neural tube defects: Results of the Medical Research Council Vitamin Study. *Lancet, 338,* 131–137.

Mead, G. H. (1934). *Mind, self, and society.* Chicago: University of Chicago Press.

Mead, M. (1928). *Coming of age in Samoa.* Ann Arbor, MI: Morrow.

Mead, M. (1963). *Sex and temperament in three primitive societies.* New York: Morrow. (Original work published 1935)

Mead, M., & Newton, N. (1967). Cultural patterning of perinatal behavior. In S. Richardson & A. Guttmacher (Eds.), *Childbearing: Its social and psychological aspects* (pp. 142–244). Baltimore: Williams & Wilkins.

Mebert, C. J. (1991). Dimensions of subjectivity in parents' ratings of infant temperament. *Child Development, 62,* 352–361.

Mediascope, Inc. (1996). *National Television Violence Study: Executive summary 1994–1995.* Studio City, CA: Author.

Mehler, J., Jusczyk, P. W., Lambertz, G., Halsted, N., Bertoncini, J., & Amiel-Tison, C. (1988). A precursor of language acquisition in young infants. *Cognition, 29,* 143–178.

Meilman, P. W. (1979). Cross-sectional age changes in ego identity status during adolescence. *Developmental Psychology, 15,* 230–231.

Melnikow, J., & Alemagno, S. (1993). Adequacy of prenatal care among inner-city women. *Journal of Family Practice, 37,* 575–582.

Melson, G. F., & Fogel, A. (1988, January). Learning to care. *Psychology Today, 22*(1), 39–45.

Meltzoff, A. N. (1988). Infant imitation after a 1-week delay: Long-term memory for novel acts and multiple stimuli. *Developmental Psychology, 24,* 470–476.

Meltzoff, A. N. (1990). Towards a developmental cognitive science. *Annals of the New York Academy of Sciences,* 608, 1–37.

Meltzoff, A. N. (1994). What infant memory tells us about infantile amnesia: Long-term recall and deferred imitation. *Journal of Experimental Child Psychology, 59,* 497–515.

Meltzoff, A. N. (1995). Understanding the intentions of others: Re-enactment of intended acts by 18-month-old children. *Developmental Psychology, 31,* 838–850.

Meltzoff, A. N., & Borton, R. W. (1979). Intermodal matching by human neonates. *Nature, 282,* 403–404.

Meltzoff, A. N., & Kuhl, P. K. (1994). Faces and speech: Intermodal processing of biologically relevant signals in infants and adults. In D. J. Lewkowicz & R. Lickliter (Eds.), *The development of intersensory perception: Comparative perspectives* (pp. 335–369). Hillsdale, NJ: Erlbaum.

Meltzoff, A. N., & Moore, M. K. (1977). Imitation of facial and manual gestures by human neonates. *Science, 198,* 75–78.

Meltzoff, A. N., & Moore, M. K. (1992). Early imitation within a functional framework: The importance of person, identity, movement, and development. *Infant Behavior and Development, 15,* 479–505.

Meltzoff, A. N., & Moore, M. K. (1994). Imitation, memory, and the representation of persons. *Infant Behavior and Development, 17,* 83–99.

Meltzoff, A., & Gopnik, A. (1993). The role of imitation in understanding persons and developing a theory of mind. In S. Baron-Cohen & H. Tager-Flusberg (Eds.), *Understanding other minds* (pp. 335–366). Oxford: Oxford University Press.

Menn, L., & Stoel-Gammon, C. (1993). Phonological development: Learning sounds and sound patterns. In J. Berko Gleason (Ed.), *The development of language* (pp. 65–113). New York: Macmillan.

Mennella, J. A., & Beauchamp, G. K. (1991). Maternal diet alters the sensory qualities of human milk and the nursling's behavior. *Pediatrics, 88,* 737–744.

Menyuk, P. (1977). *Language and maturation.* Cambridge, MA: MIT Press.

Menyuk, P. (1986). Predicting speech and language problems with persistent otitis media. In J. F. Kavanaugh (Ed.), *Otitis media and child development* (pp. 83–96). Parkton, MD: York Press.

Menyuk, P., Liebergott, J. W., & Schultz, M. C. (1995). *Early language development in full-term and premature infants.* Hillsdale, NJ: Erlbaum.

Meredith, N. V. (1978). *Human body growth in the first ten years of life.* Columbia, SC: State Printing.

Mervis, C. B. (1987). Child-basic object categories and early lexical development. In U. Neisser (Ed.), *Concepts and conceptual development: Ecological and intellectual factors in categorization* (pp. 201–233). Cambridge: Cambridge University Press.

Mervis, C. B., Golinkoff, R. M., & Bertrand, J. (1994). Two-year-olds readily learn multiple labels for the same basic-level category. *Child Development, 65,* 1163–1177.

Meyer, D. R., & Garasky, S. (1993). Custodial fathers: Myths, realities, and child support policy. *Journal of Marriage and the Family, 55,* 73–79.

Meyer-Bahlburg, H. F. L., Ehrhardt, A. A., Rosen, L. R., Gruen, R. S., Veridiano, N. P., Vann, F. H., & Neuwalder, H. F. (1995). Prenatal estrogens and the development of homosexual orientation. *Developmental Psychology, 31,* 12–21.

Michael, R. T., Gagnon, J. H., Laumann, E. O., & Kolata, G. (1994). *Sex in America.* Boston: Little, Brown.

Michel, C. (1989). Radiation embryology. *Experientia, 45,* 69–77.

Michelena, M. I. de, Burstein, E., Lama, J. R., & Vásquez, J. C. (1993). Paternal age as a risk factor for Down syndrome. *American Journal of Medical Genetics, 45,* 679–682.

Micheli, R. (1985, June). Water babies. *Parents, 60*(6), 8–13.

Midgley, C., Feldlaufer, H., & Eccles, J. S. (1989). Student/teacher relations and attitudes toward mathematics before and after the transition to junior high school. *Child Development, 60,* 981–992.

Miles, C. (1935). Sex in social psychology. In C. Murchison (Ed.), *Handbook of social psychology* (pp. 699–704). Worcester, MA: Clark University Press.

Milgram, N. A., & Palti, G. (1993). Psychosocial characteristics of resilient children. *Journal of Research in Personality, 27,* 207–221.

Milich, R., & Lorch, E. P. (1994). Television viewing methodology to understand cognitive processing of ADHD children. In K. Gadow & I. Bialer (Eds.), *Advances in clinical child psychology* (Vol. 16, pp. 177–202). New York: Plenum.

Miller, G. E., & Emihovich, C. (1986). The effects of mediated programming instruction on preschool children's self-monitoring. *Journal of Educational Computing Research, 2,* 283–297.

Miller, J. G. (1994). Cultural diversity in the morality of caring: Individually oriented versus duty-based interpersonal moral codes. *Cross-cultural Research: The Journal of Comparative Social Science, 28,* 3–39.

Miller, J. M., Boudreaux, M. C., & Regan, F. A. (1995). A case-control study of cocaine use in pregnancy. *American Journal of Obstetrics and Gynecology, 172,* 180–185.

Miller, K. F., & Baillargeon, R. (1990). Length and distance: Do preschoolers think that occlusion brings things together? *Developmental Psychology, 26,* 103–114.

Miller, L. T., & Vernon, P. A. (1992). The general factor in short-term memory, intelligence, and reaction time. *Intelligence, 16,* 5–29.

Miller, N. B., Cowan, P. A., Cowan, C. P., Hetherington, E. M., & Clingempeel, W. G. (1993). Externalizing in preschoolers and early adolescents: A cross-study replication of a family model. *Developmental Psychology, 29,* 3–16.

Miller, P., & Sperry, L. L. (1987). The socialization of anger and aggression. *Merrill-Palmer Quarterly, 33,* 1–31.

Miller, P. A., Eisenberg, N., Fabes, R. A., & Shell, R. (1996). Relations of moral reasoning and vicarious emotion to young children's prosocial behavior toward peers and adults. *Developmental Psychology, 32,* 210–219.

Miller, P. H. (1993). *Theories of developmental psychology* (3rd ed.). New York: Freeman.

Miller, P. H., & Bigi, L. (1979). The development of children's understanding of attention. *Merrill-Palmer Quarterly, 25,* 235–250.

Miller, P. H., Haynes, V. F., DeMarie-Dreblow, D., & Woody-Ramsey, J. (1986). Children's strategies for gathering information in three tasks. *Child Development, 57,* 1429–1439.

Miller, P. H., Kessel, F. S., & Flavell, J. H. (1970). Thinking about people thinking about people thinking about . . . : A study of social cognitive development. *Child Development, 41,* 613–623.

Miller, P. H., & Seier, W. L. (1994). Strategy utilization deficiencies in children: When, where, and why. In H. W. Reese (Ed.), *Advances in child development and behavior* (Vol. 25, pp. 107–156). New York: Academic Press.

Miller, P. H., Seier, W. L., Probert, J. S., & Aloise, P. A. (1991). Age differences in the capacity demands of a strategy among spontaneously strategic children. *Journal of Experimental Child Psychology, 52,* 149–165.

Miller, P. H., Woody-Ramsey, J., & Aloise, P. A. (1991). The role of strategy effortfulness in strategy effectiveness. *Developmental Psychology, 27,* 738–745.

Miller, P. H., & Zalenski, R. (1982). Preschoolers' knowledge about attention. *Developmental Psychology, 18,* 871–875.

Miller, S. A. (1997). *Developmental research methods* (2nd ed.). Englewood Cliffs, NJ: Prentice-Hall.

Miller, S. A., & Davis, T. L. (1992). Beliefs about children: A comparative study of mothers, teachers, peers, and self. *Child Development, 63,* 1251–1265.

Miller-Jones, D. (1989). Culture and testing. *American Psychologist, 44,* 360–366.

Mills, D. L., Coffey-Corina, S. A., & Neville, H. J. (1993). Language acquisition and cerebral specialization in 20-month-old infants. *Journal of Cognitive Neuroscience, 5,* 317–334.

Mills, D. L., Coffey-Corina, S. A., & Neville, H. J. (1994). Variability in cerebral organization during primary language acquisition. In G. Dawson & K. W. Fischer (Eds.), *Human behavior and the developing brain* (pp. 427–455). New York: Guilford.

Mills, R., & Grusec, J. E. (1989). Cognitive, affective, and behavioral consequences of praising altruism. *Merrill-Palmer Quarterly, 35,* 299–326.

Minuchin, P. P. (1988). Relationships within the family: A systems perspective on development. In R. A. Hinde & J. Stevenson-Hinde (Eds.), *Relationships within families: Mutual influences* (pp. 7–26). New York: Oxford University Press.

Minuchin, P. P., & Shapiro, E. K. (1983). The school as a context for social development. In E. M. Hetherington (Ed.), *Handbook of child psychology: Vol. 4. Socialization, personality, and social development* (4th ed., pp. 197–274). New York: Wiley.

Mischel, H. N., & Liebert, R. M. (1966). Effects of discrepancies between observed and imposed reward criteria on their acquisition and transmission. *Journal of Personality and Social Psychology, 3,* 45–53.

Mischel, H. N., & Mischel, W. (1983). The development of children's knowledge of self-control strategies. *Child Development, 54,* 603–619.

Mischel, W. (1974). Processes in delay of gratification. In L. Berkowitz (Ed.), *Advances in experimental social psychology* (Vol. 7, pp. 249–292). New York: Academic Press.

Mischel, W., & Baker, N. (1975). Cognitive appraisals and transformations in delay behavior. *Journal of Personality and Social Psychology, 31,* 254–261.

Mischel, W., & Rodriguez, M. L. (1993). Psychological distance in self-imposed delay of gratification. In R. R. Cocking & K. A. Renninger (Eds.), *The development and meaning of psychological distance* (pp. 109–122). Hillsdale, NJ: Erlbaum.

Mischel, W., Shoda, Y., & Peake, P. K. (1988). The nature of adolescent competencies predicted by preschool delay of gratification. *Journal of Personality and Social Psychology, 54,* 687–696.

Mitchell, G., & Shively, C. (1984). Natural and experimental studies of nonhuman primate and other animal families. In R. D. Parke (Ed.), *Review of child development research* (Vol. 7, pp. 20–41). Chicago: University of Chicago Press.

Miyake, K., Chen, S., & Campos, J. J. (1985). Infant temperament, mother's mode of interaction, and attachment in Japan: An interim report. In I. Bretherton & E. Waters (Eds.), Growing points of attachment theory and research. *Monographs of the Society for Research in Child Development, 50*(1–2, Serial No. 209).

Mize, J., & Ladd, G. W. (1988). Predicting preschoolers' peer behavior and status from their interpersonal strategies: A comparison of verbal and enactive responses to hypothetical social dilemmas. *Developmental Psychology, 24,* 782–788.

Mize, J., & Ladd, G. W. (1990). A cognitive-social learning approach to social skill training with low-status preschool children. *Developmental Psychology, 26,* 388–397.

Moely, B. E. (1977). Organizational factors in the development of memory. In R. V. Kail & J. W. Hagen (Eds.), *Perspectives on the development of memory and cognition* (pp. 203–236). Hillsdale, NJ: Erlbaum.

Moerk, E. L. (1992). *A first language taught and learned.* Baltimore: Paul H. Brookes.

Moll, I. (1994). Reclaiming the natural line in Vygotsky's theory of cognitive development. *Human Development, 37,* 333–342.

Moll, L. C., & Whitmore, K. (1993). Vygotsky in classroom practice: Moving from individual transmission to social transaction. In E. A. Forman, N. Minick, & C. A. Stone (Eds.), *Contexts for learning* (pp. 19–42). New York: Oxford University Press.

Money, J. (1985). Pediatric sexology and hermaphroditism. *Journal of Sex and Marital Therapy, 11,* 139–156.

Money, J. (1993). Specific neurocognitional impairments associated with Turner (45,X) and Klinefelter (47,XXY) syndromes: A review. *Social Biology, 40,* 147–151.

Money, J., & Ehrhardt, A. A. (1972). *Man and woman, boy and girl.* Baltimore: Johns Hopkins University Press.

Monroe, S., Goldman, P., & Smith, V. E. (1988). *Brothers: Black and poor—A true story of courage and survival.* New York: Morrow.

Montemayor, R., & Eisen, M. (1977). The development of self-conceptions from childhood to adolescence. *Developmental Psychology, 13,* 314–319.

Moon, S. M., & Feldhusen, J. F. (1994). The Program for Academic and Creative Enrichment (PACE): A follow-up study ten years later. In R. F. Subotnik & K. D. Arnold (Eds.), *Beyond Terman: Contemporary longitudinal studies of giftedness and talent* (pp. 375–400). Norwood, NJ: Ablex.

Moore, E. G. J. (1986). Family socialization and the IQ test performance of traditionally and transracially adopted black children. *Developmental Psychology, 22,* 317–326.

Moore, K. L., & Persaud, T. V. N. (1993). *Before we are born* (4th ed.). Philadelphia: Saunders.

Moore, M. T. (1985). The relationship between the originality of essays and variables in the problem-discovery process: A study of creative and noncreative middle school students. *Research in the Teaching of English, 19,* 84–95.

Moorehouse, M. J. (1991). Linking maternal employment patterns to mother–child activities and children's school competence. *Developmental Psychology, 27,* 295–303.

Moran, G. F., & Vinovskis, M. A. (1986). The great care of godly parents: Early childhood in Puritan New England. In A. B. Smuts & J. W. Hagen (Eds.), History and research in child development. *Monographs of the Society for Research in Child Development, 50*(4–5, Serial No. 211), pp. 24–37.

Morelli, G., Rogoff, B., Oppenheim, D., & Goldsmith, D. (1992). Cultural variation in infants' sleeping arrangements: Questions of independence. *Developmental Psychology, 28,* 604–613.

Morgan, J. L., Bonama, K. M., & Travis, L. L. (1995). Negative evidence on negative evidence. *Developmental Psychology, 31,* 180–197.

Morgan, J. L., & Saffran, J. R. (1995). Emerging integration of sequential and suprasegmental information in preverbal speech segmentation. *Child Development, 66,* 911–936.

Morgane, P. J., Austin-LaFrance, R., Bronzino, J., Tonkiss, J., Diaz-Cintra, S., Cintra, L., Kemper, T., & Galler, J. R. (1993). Prenatal malnutrition and development of the brain. *Neuroscience and Biobehavioral Reviews, 17,* 91–128.

Moroney, J. T., & Allen, M. H. (1994). Cocaine and alcohol use in pregnancy. In O. Devinsky, F. Feldmann, & B. Hainline (Eds.), *Neurological complications of pregnancy* (pp. 231–242). New York: Raven Press.

Morrison, F. J., Smith, L., & Dow-Ehrensberger, M. (1995). Education and cognitive development: A natural experiment. *Developmental Psychology, 31,* 789–799.

Morrongiello, B. A. (1986). Infants' perception of multiple-group auditory patterns. *Infant Behavior and Development, 9,* 307–319.

Morton, J., & Johnson, M. H. (1991). CONSPEC and CONLERN: A two-process theory of infant face recognition. *Psychological Review, 98,* 164–181.

Moshman, D., & Franks, B. A. (1986). Development of the concept of inferential validity. *Child Development, 57,* 153–165.

Moss, M., Colombo, J., Mitchell, D. W., & Horowitz, F. D. (1988). Neonatal behavioral organization and visual processing at three months. *Child Development, 59,* 1211–1220.

Mott, F. L., & Marsiglio, W. (1985). Early childbearing and completion of high school. *Family Planning Perspectives, 17,* 234–237.

Mounts, N. S., & Steinberg, L. (1995). An ecological analysis of peer influence on adolescent grade point average and drug use. *Developmental Psychology, 31,* 915–922.

Muecke, L., Simons-Morton, B., Huang, I. W., & Parcel, G. (1992). Is childhood obesity associated with high-fat foods and low physical activity? *Journal of School Health, 62,* 19–23.

Mullen, M. K. (1994). Earliest recollections of childhood: A demographic analysis. *Cognition, 52,* 55–79.

Mullis, I. V. S., Dossey, J. A., Campbell, J. R., Gentile, C. A., O'Sullivan, C., & Latham, A. S. (1994). *NAEP 1992 trends in academic progress.* Washington, DC: U.S. Government Printing Office.

Munro, G., & Adams, G. R. (1977). Ego identity formation in college students and working youth. *Developmental Psychology, 13,* 523–524.

Murett-Wagstaff, S., & Moore, S. G. (1989). The Hmong in America: Infant behavior and rearing practices. In J. K. Nugent, B. M. Lester, & T. B. Brazelton (Eds.), *Biology, culture, and development* (Vol. 1, pp. 319–339). Norwood, NJ: Ablex.

Murray, A. D. (1985). Aversiveness is in the mind of the beholder. In B. M. Lester & C. F. Z. Boukydis (Eds.), *Infant crying* (pp. 217–239). New York: Plenum.

Murray, A. D., Johnson, J., & Peters, J. (1990). Fine-tuning of utterance length to preverbal infants: Effects on later language development. *Journal of Child Language, 17,* 511–525.

Murry, V. M. (1992). Incidence of first pregnancy among black adolescent females over three decades. *Youth & Society, 23,* 478–506.

Mussen, P., & Eisenberg-Berg, N. (1977). *Roots of caring, sharing, and helping.* San Francisco: Freeman.

N

Nachtigall, R. D. (1993). Secrecy: An unresolved issue in the practice of donor insemination. *American Journal of Obstetrics and Gynecology, 168,* 1846–1851.

Naigles, L. G., & Gelman, S. A. (1995). Overextensions in comprehension and production revisited: Preferential-looking in a study of dog, cat, and cow. *Journal of Child Language, 22,* 19–46.

Naigles, L. R., & Hoff-Ginsberg, E. (1995). Input to verb learning: Evidence for the plausibility of syntactic bootstrapping. *Developmental Psychology, 31,* 827–837.

Nánez, J., Sr. (1987). Perception of impending collision in 3- to 6-week-old infants. *Infant Behavior and Development, 11,* 447–463.

Nánez, J., Sr., & Yonas, A. (1994). Effects of luminance and texture motion on infant defensive reactions to optical collision. *Infant Behavior and Development, 17,* 165–174.

Narvaez, D., & Rest, J. (1995). The four components of acting morally. In W. M. Kurtines & J. L. Gewirtz (Eds.), *Moral development: An introduction* (pp. 385–400). Boston: Allyn and Bacon.

Nastasi, B. K., & Clements, D. H. (1992). Social-cognitive behaviors and higher-order thinking in educational computer environments. *Learning and Instruction, 2,* 215–238.

Nastasi, B. K., & Clements, D. H. (1994). Effectance motivation, perceived scholastic competence, and higher-order thinking in two cooperative computer environments. *Journal of Educational Computing Research, 10,* 249-275.

Nastasi, B. K., Clements, D. H., & Battista, M. T. (1990). Social-cognitive interactions, motivation, and cognitive growth in Logo programming and CAI problem-solving environments. *Journal of Educational Psychology, 82,* 1–9.

National Association for the Education of Young Children. (1991). *Accreditation criteria and procedures of the National Academy of Early Childhood Programs* (rev. ed.). Washington, DC: Author.

National Center for Education Statistics. (1994). *The condition of education 1994.* Washington, DC: U.S. Government Printing Office.

National Center for Health Statistics. (1995). *Advance report of final natality statistics* (Vol. 44). Washington, DC: U.S. Government Printing Office.

National Commission for the Protection of Human Subjects. (1977). *Report and recommendations: Research involving children.* Washington, DC: U.S. Government Printing Office.

National Education Association. (1995). *Education technology survey.* Washington, DC: Author.

Needham, A., & Baillargeon, R. (1995). *Reasoning about support in 3-month-old infants.* Unpublished manuscript, University of Illinois at Urbana–Champaign.

Needleman, H. L., Schell, A., Bellinger, D., Leviton, A., & Allred, E. N. (1990). The long-term effects of exposure to low doses of lead in childhood. *New England Journal of Medicine, 322,* 83–88.

Neier, A. (1994, February 14). Watching rights (the use of official languages). *Nation,* p. 187.

Neisser, U. (1967). *Cognitive psychology.* Englewood Cliffs, NJ: Prentice-Hall.

Neisser, U., Boodoo, G., Bouchard, T. J., Jr., Boykin, A. W., Brody, N., Ceci, S. J., Halpern, D. F., Loehlin, J. C., Perloff, R., Sternberg, R. J., & Urbina, S. (1996). Intelligence: Knowns and unknowns. *American Psychologist, 51,* 77–101.

Nelson, C. A. (1993). Neural correlates of recognition memory in the first postnatal year of life. In G. Dawson & K. Fischer (Eds.), *Human behavior and the developing brain* (pp. 269–313). New York: Guilford.

Nelson, C. A. (1995). The ontogeny of human memory: A cognitive neuroscience perspective. *Developmental Psychology, 31,* 723–738.

Nelson, G. (1993). Risk, resistance, and self-esteem: A longitudinal study of elementary school-aged children from mother-custody and two-parent families. *Journal of Divorce and Remarriage, 19,* 99–119.

Nelson, K. (1973). Structure and strategy in learning to talk. *Monographs of the Society for Research in Child Development, 38*(1–2, Serial No. 149).

Nelson, K. (1976). Some attributes of adjectives used by young children. *Cognition, 4,* 13–30.

Nelson, K. (1981). Individual differences in language development: Implications for development and language. *Developmental Psychology, 17,* 170–187.

Nelson, K. (1993). The psychological and social origins of autobiographical memory. *Psychological Science, 1,* 1–8.

Nelson, K., & Gruendel, J. (1981). Generalized event representations: Basic building blocks of cognitive development. In M. Lamb & A. Brown (Eds.), *Advances in developmental psychology* (Vol. 1, pp. 131–158). Hillsdale, NJ: Erlbaum.

Nelson, K., & Gruendel, J. (1986). Children's scripts. In K. Nelson (Ed.), *Event knowledge: Structure and function in development* (pp. 21–46). Hillsdale, NJ: Erlbaum.

Nelson, K. E. (1989). Strategies for first language teaching. In M. L. Rice & R. L. Schiefelbusch (Eds.), *The teachability of language* (pp. 263–310). Baltimore: Paul H. Brookes.

Nelson, K. E., & Kosslyn, S. M. (1976). Recognition of previously labeled or unlabeled pictures by 5-year-olds and adults. *Journal of Experimental Child Psychology, 21,* 40–45.

Nelson-Le Gall, S. A. (1985). Motive-outcome matching and outcome foreseeability: Effects on attribution of intentionality and moral judgments. *Developmental Psychology, 21,* 332–337.

Nemerowicz, G. M. (1979). *Children's perceptions of gender and work roles.* New York: Praeger.

Netley, C. T. (1986). Summary overview of behavioural development in individuals with neonatally identified X and Y aneuploidy. *Birth Defects, 22,* 293–306.

Neville, H. J. (1991). Neurobiology of cognitive and language processing: Effects on early experience. In K. R. Gibson, & A. C. Petersen (Eds.), *Brain maturation and cognitive development: Comparative and cross-cultural perspectives* (pp. 355–380). New York: Aldine De Gruyter.

Neville, H. J., Coffey, S. A., Holcomb, P. J., & Tallal, P. (1993). The neurobiology of sensory and language processing in language-impaired children. *Journal of Cognitive Neuroscience, 5,* 235–253.

Newcomb, A. F., & Bagwell, C. (1995). Children's friendship relations: A meta-analytic review. *Psychological Bulletin, 117,* 306–347.

Newcomb, A. F., Bukowski, W. M., & Pattee, L. (1993). Children's peer relations: A meta-analytic review of popular, rejected, neglected, controversial, and average sociometric status. *Psychological Bulletin, 113,* 99–128.

Newcomb, M. D., & Bentler, P. M. (1989). Substance use and abuse among children and teenagers. *American Psychologist, 44,* 242–248.

Newcombe, N. (1982). Development of spatial cognition and cognitive development. In R. Cohen (Ed.), *Children's conceptions of spatial relationships* (pp. 65–81). San Francisco: Jossey-Bass.

Newcombe, N., & Dubas, J. S. (1987). Individual differences in cognitive ability: Are they related to timing of puberty? In R. M. Lerner & T. T. Foch (Eds.), *Biological–psychosocial interactions in early adolescence: A life-span perspective* (pp. 249–302). Hillsdale, NJ: Erlbaum.

Newcombe, N., & Dubas, J. S. (1992). A longitudinal study of predictors of spatial ability in adolescent females. *Child Development, 63,* 37–46.

Newcombe, N., Dubas, J. S., & Baenninger, M. A. (1989). Associations of timing of puberty, spatial ability, and lateralization in adult women. *Child Development, 60,* 246–254.

Newcombe, N., & Fox, N. A. (1994). Infantile amnesia: Through a glass darkly. *Child Development, 65,* 31–40.

Newcombe, N., & Huttenlocher, J. (1992). Children's early ability to solve perspective-taking problems. *Developmental Psychology, 28,* 635–643.

Newman, L. S. (1990). Intentional and unintentional memory in young children: Remembering vs. playing. *Journal of Experimental Child Psychology, 50,* 243–258.

Newnham, J. P., Evans, S. F., Michael, C. A., Stanley, F. J., & Landau, L. I. (1993). Effects of frequent ultrasound during pregnancy: A randomized controlled trial. *Lancet, 342,* 887–890.

Newport, E. L. (1991). Contrasting conceptions of the critical period for language. In S. Carey & R. Gelman (Eds.), *The epigenesis of mind: Essays on biology and cognition* (pp. 111–130). Hillsdale, NJ: Erlbaum.

Newson, J., & Newson, E. (1975). Intersubjectivity and the transmission of culture: On the social origins of symbolic functioning. *Bulletin of the British Psychological Society, 28,* 437–446.

Nicholls, A. L., & Kennedy, J. M. (1992). Drawing development: From similarity of features to direction. *Child Development, 63,* 227–241.

Nicholls, J. G. (1978). The development of concepts of effort and ability, perception of academic attainment, and the understanding that difficult tasks require more ability. *Child Development, 49,* 800–814.

Nichols, M. R. (1993). Paternal perspectives of the childbirth experience. *Maternal–Child Nursing Journal, 21,* 99–108.

Nichols, R. C. (1978). Heredity and environment: Major findings from twin studies of ability, personality, and interests. *Home, 29,* 158–173.

Nicolopoulou, A. (1993). Play, cognitive development, and the social world: Piaget, Vygotsky, and beyond. *Human Development, 36,* 1–23.

Nidorf, J. F. (1985). Mental health and refugee youths: A model for diagnostic training. In T. C. Owen (Ed.), *Southeast Asian mental health: Treatment, prevention, services, training, and research* (pp. 391–427). Washington, DC: National Institute of Mental Health.

Niemiec, R., & Walberg, H. J. (1987). Comparative effects of computer-assisted instruction: A synthesis of reviews. *Journal of Educational Computing Research, 3,* 19–37.

Nilsson, L., & Hamberger, L. (1990). *A child is born.* New York: Delacorte.

Noddings, N. (1992). Gender and the curriculum. In P. W. Jackson (Ed.), *Handbook of research on curriculum* (pp. 659–684). New York: Macmillan.

Norbeck, J. S., & Tilden, V. P. (1983). Life stress, social support, and emotional disequilibrium in complications of pregnancy: A prospective, multivariate study. *Journal of Health and Social Behavior, 24,* 30–46.

Nottelmann, E. D. (1987). Competence and self-esteem during transition from childhood to adolescence. *Developmental Psychology, 23,* 441–450.

Nottlemann, E. D., Inoff-Germain, G., Susman, E. J., & Chrousos, G. P. (1990). Hormones and behavior at puberty. In J. Bancroft & J. M. Reinisch (Eds.), *Adolescence and puberty* (pp. 88–123). New York: Oxford University Press.

Nottelmann, E. D., & Jensen, P. S. (1995). Comorbidity of disorders in children and adolescents. In T. H. Ollendick & R. J. Prinz (Eds.), *Advances in clinical child psychology* (pp. 109–155). New York: Plenum.

Nottelmann, E. D., Susman, E. J., Blue, J. H., Inoff-Germain, G., Dorn, L. D., Loriaux, D. L., Cutler, G. B., Jr., & Chrousos, G. P. (1987). Gonadal and adrenal hormone correlates of adjustment in early adolescence. In R. M. Lerner & T. T. Foch (Eds.), *Biological-psychosocial interactions in early adolescence: A life-span perspective* (pp. 303–323). Hillsdale, NJ: Erlbaum.

Nowakowski, R. S. (1987). Basic concepts of CNS development. *Child Development, 58,* 568–595.

Nucci, L. (1981). Conceptions of personal issues: A domain distinct from moral or societal concepts. *Child Development, 52,* 114–121.

Nucci, L., & Turiel, E. (1978). Social interactions and the development of social concepts in preschool children. *Child Development, 49,* 400–407.

Nuckolls, K. B., Cassel, J., & Kaplan, B. H. (1972). Psychosocial assets, life crisis, and the prognosis of pregnancy. *American Journal of Epidemiology, 95,* 431–441.

Nunnally, J. C. (1982). The study of human change: Measurement, research strategies, and methods of analysis. In B. B. Wolman (Ed.), *Handbook of developmental psychology* (pp. 133–148). Englewood Cliffs, NJ: Prentice-Hall.

O

O'Brien, M., & Huston, A. C. (1985). Development of sex-typed play behavior in toddlers. *Developmental Psychology, 21,* 866–871.

O'Connor, B. B. (1993). The home birth movement in the United States. *Journal of Medicine and Philosophy, 18,* 147–174.

O'Connor, B. P. (1995). Identity development and perceived parental behavior as sources of adolescent egocentrism. *Journal of Youth and Adolescence, 24,* 205–227.

O'Keefe, B. J., & Benoit, P. J. (1982). Children's arguments. In J. R. Cox & C. A. Willard (Eds.), *Advances in argumentation theory and research* (pp. 154–183). Carbondale: Southern Illinois University Press.

O'Mahoney, J. F. (1989). Development of thinking about things and people: Social and nonsocial cognition during adolescence. *Journal of Genetic Psychology, 150,* 217–224.

O'Malley, P. M., Johnston, L. D., & Bachman, J. G. (1995). Adolescent substance use: Epidemiology and implications for public policy. *Pediatric Clinics of North America, 42*(2), 241–260.

O'Neill, D. K., Astington, J. W., & Flavell, J. H. (1992). Young children's understanding of the role that sensory experiences play in knowledge acquisition. *Child Development, 63,* 474–490.

O'Reilly, A. W. (1995). Using representations: Comprehension and production of actions with imagined objects. *Child Development, 66,* 999–1010.

O'Reilly, A. W., & Bornstein, M. H. (1993). Caregiver–child interaction in play. In M. H. Bornstein & A. W. O'Reilly (Eds.), *New directions for child development* (No. 59, pp. 55–66). San Francisco: Jossey-Bass.

Oakes, J., Gamoran, A., & Page, R. N. (1992). Curriculum differentiation: Opportunities, outcomes, and meanings. In P. W. Jackson (Ed.), *Handbook of research on curriculum* (pp. 570–608). New York: Macmillan.

Oakes, L. M. (1994). Development of infants' use of continuity cues in their perception of causality. *Developmental Psychology, 30,* 869–879.

Oakes, L. M., & Cohen, L. B. (1995). Infant causal perception. In C. K. Rovee-Collier & L. P. Lipsitt (Eds.), *Advances in infancy research* (Vol. 9, pp. 1–54). Norwood, NJ: Ablex.

Oakes, L. M., Madole, K. L., & Cohen, L. B. (1991). Infants' object examining: Habituation and categorization. *Cognitive Development, 6,* 377–392.

Oakland, T., & Parmelee, R. (1985). Mental measurement of minority-group children. In B. B. Wolman (Ed.), *Handbook of intelligence* (pp. 699–736). New York: Wiley.

Oates, R. K. (1984). Similarities and differences between nonorganic failure to thrive and deprivation dwarfism. *Child Abuse and Neglect, 8,* 438–445.

Oates, R. K., Peacock, A., & Forrest, D. (1985). Long-term effects of nonorganic failure to thrive. *Pediatrics, 75,* 36–40.

Oberg, C. N. (1988, Spring). Children and the uninsured. *Social Policy Report* (Society for Research in Child Development), 3(No. 1).

Ochs, E. (1988). *Culture and language development: Language acquisition and language socialization in a Samoan village.* Cambridge: Cambridge University Press.

Ochse, R. (1990). *Before the gates of excellence: The determinants of creative genius.* New York: Cambridge University Press.

Oettingen, G. (1985). The influence of kindergarten teachers on sex differences in behavior. *International Journal of Behavioral Development, 8,* 3–13.

Offer, D. (1988). *The teenage world: Adolescents' self-image in ten countries.* New York: Plenum.

Ogbu, J. U. (1985). A cultural ecology of competence among inner-city blacks. In M. B. Spencer, G. K. Brookins, & W. R. Allen (Eds.), *Beginnings: The social and affective development of black children* (pp. 45–66). Hillsdale, NJ: Erlbaum.

Ogbu, J. U. (1988). Black education: A cultural-ecological perspective. In H. P. McAdoo (Ed.), *Black families* (pp. 169–186). Beverly Hills, CA: Sage.

Ogbu, J. U. (1994). From cultural differences to differences in cultural frame of reference. In P. M. Greenfield & R. Cocking (Eds.), *Cross-cultural roots of minority child development* (pp. 365–391). Hillsdale, NJ: Erlbaum.

Okagaki, L., & Sternberg, R. J. (1993). Parental beliefs and children's school performance. *Child Development, 64,* 36–56.

Ollendick, T. H., Weist, M. D., Borden, M. C., & Greene, R. W. (1992). Sociometric status and academic, behavioral, and psychological adjustment: A five-year longitudinal study. *Journal of Consulting and Clinical Psychology, 60,* 80–87.

Oller, D. K., & Eilers, R. E. (1988). The role of audition in infant babbling. *Child Development, 59,* 441–449.

Olweus, D. (1978). *Aggression in the schools: Bullies and whipping boys.* Washington, DC: Hemisphere.

Olweus, D. (1980). Familial and temperamental determinants of aggressive behavior in adolescent boys: A causal analysis. *Developmental Psychology, 16,* 644–666.

Olweus, D. (1984). Aggressors and their victims: Bullying at school. In N. Frude & H. Gault (Eds.), *Disruptive behaviors in schools* (pp. 57–76). New York: Wiley.

Olweus, D. (1993). *Bullying at school.* Oxford: Blackwell.

Olweus, D. (1994). Bullying at school: Basic facts and effects of a school based intervention program. *Journal of Child Psychology and Psychiatry, 35,* 1171–1190.

Omer, H., & Everly, G. S. (1988). Psychological factors in preterm labor: Critical review and theoretical synthesis. *American Journal of Psychiatry, 145,* 1507–1513.

Ornstein, P. A. (1995, August 22). Personal communication.

Ornstein, P. A., Naus, M. J., & Liberty, C. (1975). Rehearsal and organizational processes in children's memory. *Child Development, 46,* 818–830.

Ornstein, P. A., Shapiro, L. R., Clubb, P. A., & Follmer, A. (1996). The influence of prior knowledge on children's memory for salient medical experiences. In N. Stein, P. A. Ornstein, C. J. Brainerd, & B. Tversky (Eds.), *Memory for everyday and emotional events.* Hillsdale, NJ: Erlbaum.

Osherson, D. N., & Markman, E. M. (1975). Language and the ability to evaluate contradictions and tautologies. *Cognition, 2,* 213–226.

Oster, H., Hegley, D., & Nagel, L. (1992). Adult judgments and fine grained analysis of infant facial expressions: Testing the validity of a priori coding formulas. *Developmental Psychology, 28,* 1115–1131.

Ottenberg, S. (1994). Initiations. In P. K. Bock (Ed.), *Handbook of psychological anthropology* (pp. 351–377). Westport, CT: Greenwood Press.

Owen, M. T., & Cox, M. J. (1988). Maternal employment and the transition to parenthood. In A. E. Gottfried & A. W. Gottfried (Eds.), *Maternal employment and children's development: Longitudinal research* (pp. 85–119). New York: Plenum.

Owen, M. T., Easterbrooks, M. A., Chase-Lansdale, L., & Goldberg, W. A. (1984). The relation between maternal employment status and the stability of attachments to mother and father. *Child Development, 55,* 1894–1901.

Owens, R. (1996). *Language development: An introduction* (4th ed.). New York: Merrill.

Owens, T. (1982). Experience-based career education: Summary and implications of research and evaluation findings. *Child and Youth Services Journal, 4,* 77–91.

P

Padgham, J. J., & Blyth, D. A. (1990). Dating during adolescence. In R. M. Lerner, A. C. Peterson, & J. Brooks-Gunn (Eds.), *The encyclopedia of adolescence* (Vol. 1, pp. 196–198). New York: Garland.

Padilla, M. L., & Landreth, G. L. (1989). Latchkey children: A review of the literature. *Child Welfare, 68,* 445–454.

Page, D. C., Mosher, R., Simpson, E. M., Fisher, E. M. C., Mardon, G., Pollack, J., McGillivray, B., de la Chapelle, A., & Brown, L. G. (1987). The sex-determining region of the human Y chromosome encodes a finger protein. *Cell, 51,* 1091–1104.

Paget, K. F., & Kritt, D. (1986). The development of the conceptual organization of self. *Journal of Genetic Psychology, 146,* 333–341.

Paikoff, R. L., & Brooks-Gunn, J. (1991). Do parent–child relationships change during puberty? *Psychological Bulletin, 110,* 47–66.

Palincsar, A. S. (1992, April). *Beyond reciprocal teaching: A retrospective and prospective view.* Raymond B. Cattell Early Career Award Address at the annual meeting of the American Educational Research Association, San Francisco.

Palincsar, A. S., & Brown, A. L. (1984). Reciprocal teaching of comprehension-fostering and comprehension-monitoring activities. *Cognition and Instruction, 1,* 117–175.

Palincsar, A. S., Brown, A. L., & Campione, J. C. (1993). First-grade dialogues for knowledge-acquisition and use. In E. A. Forman, N. Minick, & C. A. Stone (Eds.), *Contexts for learning* (pp. 43–57). New York: Oxford University Press.

Palincsar, A. S., & Klenk, L. (1992). Fostering literacy learning in supportive contexts. *Journal of Learning Disabilities, 25,* 211–225.

Pan, H. W. (1994). Children's play in Taiwan. In J. L. Roopnarine, J. E. Johnson, & F. H. Hooper (Eds.), *Children's play in diverse cultures* (pp. 31–50). Albany, NY: SUNY Press.

Papini, D. R. (1994). Family interventions. In S. L. Archer (Ed.), *Interventions for adolescent identity development* (pp. 47–61). Thousand Oaks, CA: Sage.

Parikh, B. (1980). Development of moral judgment and its relation to family environmental factors in Indian and American families. *Child Development, 51,* 1030–1039.

Paris, S. G., Lawton, T. A., Turner, J. C., & Roth, J. L. (1991). A developmental perspective on standardized achievement testing. *Educational Researcher, 20*(5), 12–20.

Parke, R. D. (1977). Punishment in children: Effects, side effects, and alternative strategies. In H. L. Hom, Jr., & A. Robinson (Eds.), *Psychological processes in early education* (pp. 71–97). New York: Academic Press.

Parke, R. D., Burks, V. M., Carson, J. L., Neville, B., & Boyum, L. A. (1994). Family–peer relationships: A tripartite model. In R. D. Parke & S. G. Kellam (Eds.), *Exploring family relationships with other social contexts* (pp. 115–145). Hillsdale, NJ: Erlbaum.

Parke, R. D., & Kellam, S. G. (Eds.) (1994). *Exploring family relationships with other social contexts.* Hillsdale, NJ: Erlbaum.

Parke, R. D., & Slaby, R. G. (1983). The development of aggression. In E. M. Hetherington (Ed.), *Handbook of child psychology: Vol. 4. Socialization, personality, and social development* (4th ed., pp. 547–641). New York: Wiley.

Parke, R. D., & Tinsley, B. R. (1981). The father's role in infancy: Determinants of involvement in caregiving and play. In

M. E. Lamb (Ed.), *The role of the father in child development* (pp. 429–458). New York: Wiley.

Parke, R. D., & Walters, R. H. (1967). Some factors determining the efficacy of punishment for inducing response inhibition. *Monographs of the Society for Research in Child Development, 32*(1, Serial No. 109).

Parker, J. G., & Asher, S. R. (1987). Peer relations and later personal adjustment: Are low-accepted children at risk? *Psychological Bulletin, 102,* 357–389.

Parker, J. G., & Asher, S. R. (1993). Friendship and friendship quality in middle childhood: Links with peer group acceptance and feelings of loneliness and social dissatisfaction. *Developmental Psychology, 29,* 611–621.

Parkhurst, J. T., & Asher, S. R. (1992). Peer rejection in middle school: Subgroup differences in behavior, loneliness, and interpersonal concerns. *Developmental Psychology, 28,* 231–241.

Parrish, L. H. (1991). Community resources and dropout prevention. In L. L. West (Ed.), *Effective strategies for dropout prevention of at-risk youth* (pp. 217–232). Gaithersburg, MD: Aspen.

Parsons, J. E., Adler, T. F., & Kaczala, C. M. (1982). Socialization of achievement attitudes and beliefs: Parental influences. *Child Development, 53,* 310–321.

Parten, M. (1932). Social participation among preschool children. *Journal of Abnormal and Social Psychology, 27,* 243–269.

Pascual-Leone, J. (1970). A mathematical model for the transition rule in Piaget's developmental stages. *Acta Psychologia, 32,* 301–345.

Pascual-Leone, J. (1987). Organismic processes for neo-Piagetian theories: A dialectical causal account of cognitive development. *International Journal of Psychology, 22,* 531–570.

Passman, R. H. (1987). Attachments to inanimate objects: Are children who have security blankets insecure? *Journal of Consulting and Clinical Psychology, 55,* 825–830.

Patterson, C. J. (1995). Sexual orientation and human development: An overview. *Developmental Psychology, 31,* 3–11.

Patterson, G. R. (1982). *Coercive family processes.* Eugene, OR: Castilia Press.

Patterson, G. R., & Fleishman, M. J. (1979). Maintenance of treatment effects: Some considerations concerning family systems and follow-up data. *Behavior Therapy, 10,* 168–185.

Patterson, G. R., DeBaryshe, B. D., & Ramsey, E. (1989). A developmental perspective on antisocial behavior. *American Psychologist, 44,* 329–335.

Patterson, G. R., Littman, R. A., & Bricker, W. (1967). Assertive behavior in children: A step toward a theory of aggression. *Monographs of the Society for Research in Child Development, 35*(5, Serial No. 113).

Patterson, G. R., Reid, J. B., & Dishion, T. J. (1992). *Antisocial boys.* Eugene, OR: Castalia.

Patteson, D. M., & Barnard, K. E. (1990). Parenting of low birth weight infants: A review of issues and interventions. *Infant Mental Health Journal, 11,* 37–56.

Pea, R. D., & Kurland, D. M. (1984). On the cognitive effects of learning computer programming. *New Ideas in Psychology, 2,* 137–168.

Pearson, D. A., & Lane, D. M. (1990). Visual attention movements: A developmental study. *Child Development, 61,* 1779–1795.

Pearson, J. L., Hunter, A. G., Ensminger, M. E., & Kellam, S. G. (1990). Black grandmothers in multigenerational households: Diversity in family structure and parenting involvement in the Woodlawn community. *Child Development, 61,* 434–442.

Peckham, C. S., & Logan, S. (1993). Screening for toxoplasmosis during pregnancy. *Archives of Disease in Childhood, 68,* 3–5.

Pederson, D. R., & Moran, G. (1995). A categorical description of infant–mother relationships in the home and its relation to Q-sort measures of infant–mother interaction. In E. Waters, B. E. Vaughn, G. Posada, & K. Kondo-Ikemura (Eds.), Caregiving, cultural, and cognitive perspectives on secure-base behavior and working models: New growing points of attachment theory and research. *Monographs of the Society for Research in Child Development, 60*(2–3, Serial No. 244).

Peevers, B. H., & Secord, P. F. (1973). Developmental changes in attribution of descriptive concepts to persons. *Journal of Personality and Social Psychology, 27,* 120–128.

Pellegrini, A. D. (1995). A longitudinal study of boys' rough-and-tumble play and dominance during early adolescence. *Journal of Applied Developmental Psychology, 16,* 77–93.

Penner, S. G. (1987). Parental responses to grammatical and ungrammatical utterances. *Child Development, 58,* 376–384.

Pennington, B. F., Bender, B., Puck, M., Salbenblatt, J., & Robinson, A. (1982). Learning disabilities in children with sex chromosome anomalies. *Child Development, 53,* 1182–1192.

Pennington, B. F., & Smith, S. D. (1988). Genetic influences on learning disabilities: An update. *Journal of Consulting and Clinical Psychology, 56,* 817–823.

Pepler, D. J., & Ross, H. S. (1981). The effects of play on convergent and divergent problem solving. *Child Development, 52,* 1202–1210.

Perelle, I. B., & Ehrman, L. (1994). An international study of human handedness: The data. *Behavior Genetics, 24,* 217–227.

Peres, Y., & Pasternack, R. (1991). To what extent can the school reduce the gaps between children raised by divorced and intact families? *Journal of Divorce and Remarriage, 15,* 143–158.

Perfetti, C. A. (1988). Verbal efficiency in reading ability. In M. Daneman, G. E. MacKinnon, & T. G. Waller (Eds.), *Reading research: Advances in theory and practice* (Vol. 6, pp. 109–143). San Diego: Academic Press.

Perleth, C., & Heller, K. A. (1994). The Munich Longitudinal Study of Giftedness. In R. F. Subotnik & K. D. Arnold (Eds.), *Beyond Terman: Contemporary studies of giftedness and talent* (pp. 77–114). Norwood, NJ: Ablex.

Perlmutter, M. (1984). Continuities and discontinuities in early human memory: Paradigms, processes, and performances. In R. V. Kail, Jr., & N. R. Spear (Eds.), *Comparative perspectives on the development of memory* (pp. 253–287). Hillsdale, NJ: Erlbaum.

Perner, J. (1988). Higher-order beliefs and intentions in children's understanding of social interaction. In J. W. Astington, P. L. Harris, & D. R. Olson (Eds.), *Developing theories of mind* (pp. 271–294). New York: Cambridge University Press.

Perner, J. (1991). *Understanding the representational mind.* Cambridge, MA: MIT Press.

Perry, D. G., Perry, L. C., & Rasmussen, P. (1986). Cognitive social learning mediators of aggression. *Child Development, 57,* 700–711.

Perry, D. G., Perry, L. C., & Weiss, R. J. (1989). Sex differences in the consequences that children anticipate for aggression. *Developmental Psychology, 25,* 171–184.

Perry, D. G., Williard, J. C., & Perry, L. C. (1990). Peers' perceptions of the consequences that victimized children provide aggressors. *Child Development, 61,* 1310–1325.

Peshkin, A. (1978). *Growing up American: Schooling and the survival of the community.* Chicago: University of Chicago Press.

Peterson, C. C., Peterson, J. L., & Seeto, D. (1983). Developmental changes in ideas about lying. *Child Development, 54,* 1529–1535.

Peterson, L. (1982). An alternative perspective to norm-based explanations of modeling and children's generosity: A reply to Lipscomb, Larrieu, McAllister, and Bregman. *Merrill-Palmer Quarterly, 28,* 283–290.

Pettit, G. S., Bakshi, A., Dodge, K. A., & Coie, J. D. (1990). The emergence of social dominance in young boys' play groups: Developmental differences and behavioral correlates. *Developmental Psychology, 26,* 1017–1025.

Pettito, L. A., & Marentette, P. F. (1991). Babbling in the manual mode: Evidence for the ontogeny of language. *Science, 251,* 1493–1496.

Phelps, K. E., & Woolley, J. D. (1994). The form and function of young children's magical beliefs. *Developmental Psychology, 30,* 385–394.

Phillips, D. A. (1987). Socialization of perceived academic competence among highly competent children. *Child Development, 58,* 1308–1320.

Phillips, D. A., Howes, C., & Whitebook, M. (1992). The social policy context of child care: Effects on quality. *American Journal of Community Psychology, 20,* 25–51.

Phillips, D. A., Voran, M., Kisker, E., Howes, C., & Whitebook, M. (1994). Child care for children in poverty: Opportunity or inequity? *Child Development, 65,* 472–492.

Phillips, D. A., & Zimmerman, M. (1990). The developmental course of perceived competence and incompetence among competent children. In R. Sternberg & J. Kolligian (Eds.), *Competence considered* (pp. 41–66). New Haven: Yale University Press.

Phillips, K., & Fulker, D. W. (1989). Quantitative genetic analysis of longitudinal trends in adoption designs with application to IQ in the Colorado Adoption Project. *Behavior Genetics, 19,* 621–658.

Phillips, O. P., & Elias, S. (1993). Prenatal genetic counseling issues in women of advanced reproductive age. *Journal of Women's Health, 2,* 1–5.

Phinney, J. S. (1989). Stages of ethnic identity development in minority group adolescents. *Journal of Early Adolescence, 9,* 34–49.

Phinney, J., & Alipuria, L. (1990). Ethnic identity in college students from four ethnic groups. *Journal of Adolescence, 13,* 171–183.

Piaget, J. (1926). *The language and thought of the child.* New York: Harcourt, Brace & World. (Original work published 1923)

Piaget, J. (1928). *Judgment and reasoning in the child.* New York: Harcourt, Brace & World. (Original work published 1926)

Piaget, J. (1929). *The child's conception of physical causality.* New York: Harcourt, Brace & World. (Original work published 1926)

Piaget, J. (1930). *The child's conception the world.* New York: Harcourt, Brace & World. (Original work published 1926)

Piaget, J. (1950). *The psychology of intelligence.* New York: International Universities Press.

Piaget, J. (1951). *Play, dreams, and imitation in childhood.* New York: Norton. (Original work published 1945)

Piaget, J. (1952a). Jean Piaget (autobiographical sketch). In E. G. Boring, H. S. Langfeld, H. Werner, & R. M. Yerkes (Eds.), *A history of psychology in autobiography* (pp. 237–256). Worcester, MA: Clark University Press.

Piaget, J. (1952b). *The origins of intelligence in children.* New York: International Universities Press. (Original work published 1936)

Piaget, J. (1954). *The construction of reality in the child.* New York: Free Press.

Piaget, J. (1965). *The moral judgment of the child.* New York: Free Press. (Original work published 1932)

Piaget, J. (1967). *Six psychological studies.* New York: Vintage.

Piaget, J. (1971). *Biology and knowledge.* Chicago: University of Chicago Press.

Piaget, J. (1985). *The equilibration of cognitive structures: The central problem of intellectual development.* Chicago: University of Chicago Press.

Piaget, J., & Inhelder, B. (1956). *The child's conception of space.* London: Routledge & Kegan Paul. (Original work published 1948)

Piaget, J., & Inhelder, B. (1969). *The psychology of the child.* London: Routledge & Kegan Paul. (Original work published 1967)

Piaget, J., Inhelder, B., & Szeminska, A. (1960). *The child's conception of geometry.* New York: Basic Books. (Original work published 1948)

Pianta, R. C., Egeland, B., & Erickson, M. F. (1989). The antecedents of maltreatment: Results of the Mother-Child Interaction Research Project. In D. Cicchetti & V. Carlson (Eds.), *Child maltreatment* (pp. 203–253). New York: Cambridge University Press.

Pianta, R. C., Sroufe, L. A., & Egeland, B. (1989). Continuity and discontinuity in maternal sensitivity at 6, 24, and 42 months in a high-risk sample. *Child Development, 60,* 481–487.

Piatt, B. (1993). *Only English? Law and language policy in the United States.* Albuquerque: University of New Mexico Press.

Picariello, M. L., Greenberg, D. N., & Pillemer, D. B. (1990). Children's sex-related stereotyping of colors. *Child Development, 61,* 1453–1460.

Pick, A. D., & Frankel, G. W. (1974). A developmental study of strategies of visual selectivity. *Child Development, 45,* 1162–1165.

Pick, H. L., Jr. (1989). Motor development: The control of action. *Developmental Psychology, 25,* 867–870.

Pickens, J., & Field, T. M. (1993). Facial expressivity in infants of depressed mothers. *Developmental Psychology, 25,* 867–870.

Pickens, J., Field, T., Nawrocki, T., Martinez, A., Soutullo, D., & Gonzalez, J. (1994). Full-term and preterm infants' perception of face–voice synchrony. *Infant Behavior and Development, 17,* 447–455.

Pike, K. M., & Rodin, J. (1991). Mothers, daughters, and disordered eating. *Journal of Abnormal Psychology, 100,* 198–204.

Pillemer, D. B., & White, S. H. (1989). Childhood events recalled by children and adults. In H. W. Reese (Ed.), *Advances in child development and behavior* (Vol. 21, pp. 297–340). New York: Academic Press.

Pillow, B. H. (1988a). The development of children's beliefs about the mental world. *Merrill-Palmer Quarterly, 34,* 1–32.

Pillow, B. H. (1988b). Early understanding of perception as a source of knowledge. *Journal of Experimental Child Psychology, 47,* 116–129.

Pillow, B. H. (1991). Understanding of biased social cognition. *Developmental Psychology, 27,* 539–551.

Pine, J. M. (1995). Variation in vocabulary development as a function of birth order. *Child Development, 66,* 272–281.

Pinker, S. (1981). On the acquisition of grammatical morphemes. *Journal of Child Language, 8,* 477–484.

Pinker, S. (1984). *Language learnability and language development.* Cambridge, MA: Harvard University Press.

Pinker, S. (1994). *The language instinct: How the mind creates language.* New York: William Morrow.

Pinker, S., Lebeaux, D. S., & Frost, L. A. (1987). Productivity and constraints in the acquisition of the passive. *Cognition, 26,* 195–267.

Pinto, J., & Davis, P. V. (1991, April). *The categorical perception of human gait in 3- and 5-month-old infants.* Paper presented at the biennial meeting of the Society for Research in Child Development, Seattle, WA.

Pipes, P. L. (1989). *Nutrition in infancy and childhood* (4th ed.). St. Louis: Mosby.

Pipp, S., & Haith, M. M. (1984). Infant visual responses to pattern: Which metric predicts best? *Journal of Experimental Child Psychology, 38,* 373–379.

Pipp, S., Easterbrooks, M. A., & Brown, S. R. (1993). Attachment status and complexity of infants' self- and other-knowledge when tested with mother and father. *Social Development, 2,* 1–14.

Pipp, S., Easterbrooks, M. A., & Harmon, R. J. (1992). The relation between attachment and knowledge of self and mother in one- to three-year-old children. *Child Development, 63,* 738–750.

Plomin, R. (1990). *Nature and nurture: An introduction to behavior genetics.* Pacific Grove, CA: Brooks/Cole.

Plomin, R. (1994a). The Emanuel Miller Memorial Lecture 1993: Genetic research and identification of environmental influences. *Journal of Child Psychology and Psychiatry, 35,* 817–834.

Plomin, R. (1994b). Genetics and children's experiences in the family. *Journal of Child Psychology and Psychiatry, 36,* 33–68.

Plomin, R. (1994c). *Genetics and experience: The interplay between nature and nurture.* Thousand Oaks, CA: Sage.

Plomin, R. (1994d). Nature, nurture, and social development. *Social Development, 3,* 37–53.

Plomin, R., & DeFries, J. C. (1983). The Colorado Adoption Project. *Child Development, 54,* 276–289.

Plomin, R., Chipuer, H. M., & Loehlin, J. C. (1990). Behavior genetics and personality. In L. A. Pervin (Ed.), *Handbook of personality theory and research* (pp. 225–243). New York: Guilford.

Plomin, R., Owen, J. J., & McGuffin, P. (1994). The genetic basis of complex human behaviors. *Science, 264,* 1733–1739.

Plomin, R., Reiss, D., Hetherington, E. M., & Howe, G. W. (1994). Nature and nurture: Genetic contributions to measures of the family environment. *Developmental Psychology, 30,* 32–43.

Plumert, J. M. (1994). Flexibility in children's use of spatial and categorical organizational strategies in recall. *Developmental Psychology, 30,* 738–747.

Plumert, J. M., Pick, H. L., Jr., Marks, R. A., Kintsch, A. S., & Wegesin, D. (1994). Locating objects and communicating about locations: Organizational differences in children's searching and direction-giving. *Developmental Psychology, 30,* 443–453.

Plunkett, K. (1993). Lexical segmentation and vocabulary growth in early language acquisition. *Journal of Child Language, 20,* 43–60.

Podrouzek, W., & Furrow, D. (1988). Preschoolers' use of eye contact while speaking: The influence of sex, age, and conversational partner. *Journal of Psycholinguistic Research, 17,* 89–93.

Poets, C. F., Schlaud, M., Keemann, W. J., Rudolph, A., Diekmann, U., & Sens, B. (1995). Sudden infant death and maternal cigarette smoking—results from the Lower Saxony Perinatal Working Group. *European Journal of Pediatrics, 154,* 326–329.

Polansky, N. A., Gaudin, J. M., Ammons, P. W., & Davis, K. B. (1985). The psychological ecology of the neglectful mother. *Child Abuse & Neglect, 9,* 265–275.

Polit, D. F., Quint, J. C., & Riccio, J. A. (1988). *The challenge of service teenage mothers: Lessons from Project Redirection.* New York: Manpower Demonstration Research Corporation.

Polka, L., & Werker, J. F. (1994). Developmental changes in perception of non-native vowel contrasts. *Journal of Experimental Psychology: Human Perception and Performance, 20,* 421–435.

Pollitt, E., Gorman, K. S., Engle, P. L., Martorell, R., & Rivera, J. (1993). Early supplementary feeding and cognition. *Monographs of the Society for Research in Child Development, 58*(7, Serial No. 235).

Pollock, L. (1987). *A lasting relationship: Parents and children over three centuries.* Hanover, NH: University Press of New England.

Pomerleau, A., Bolduc, D., Malcuit, G., & Cossette, L. (1990). Pink or blue: Environmental gender stereotypes in the first two years of life. *Sex Roles, 22,* 359–367.

Porges, S. W. (1991). Autonomic regulation and attention. In B. A. Campbell, H. Hayne, & R. Richardson (Eds.), *Attention and information processing in infants and adults* (pp. 201–223). Hillsdale, NJ: Erlbaum.

Porges, S. W., Doussard-Roosevelt, J. A., & Maiti, A. K. (1994). Vagal tone and the physiological regulation of emotion. In N. A. Fox (Ed.), The development of emotion regulation: Biological and behavioral considerations. *Monographs of the Society for Research in Child Development, 59*(2–3, Serial No. 240).

Porter, R. H., Makin, J. W., Davis, L. B., & Christensen, K. M. (1992). An assessment of the salient olfactory environment of formula-fed infants. *Physiology & Behavior, 50,* 907–911.

Posada, G., Gao, Y., Wu, F., Posada, R., Tascon, M., Schöelmerich, A., Sagi, A., Kondo-Ikemura, K., Haaland, W., & Synnevaag, B. (1995). The secure-base phenomenon across cultures: Children's behavior, mothers' preferences, and experts' concepts. In E. Waters, B. E. Vaughn, G. Posada, & K. Kondo-Ikemura (Eds.), Caregiving, cultural, and cognitive perspectives on secure-base behavior and working models: New growing points of attachment theory and research. *Monographs of the Society for Research in Child Development, 60*(2–3, Serial No. 244).

Posner, J. K., & Vandell, D. L. (1994). Low-income children's after-school care: Are there beneficial effects of after-school programs? *Child Development, 64,* 440–456.

Post, G. B., & Kemper, H. C. G. (1993). Nutrient intake and biological maturation during adolescence: The Amsterdam growth and health longitudinal study. *European Journal of Clinical Nutrition, 47,* 400–408.

Poulin-Dubois, D., Serbin, L. A., Kenyon, B., & Derbyshire, A. (1994). Infants' intermodal knowledge about gender. *Developmental Psychology, 30,* 436–442.

Powell, B., & Steelman, L. C. (1993). The educational benefits of being spaced out: Sibship density and educational progress. *American Sociological Review, 58,* 367–381.

Power, F. C., Higgins, A., & Kohlberg, L. (1989). *Lawrence Kohlberg's approach to moral education.* New York: Columbia University Press.

Powers, S. I., Hauser, S. T., & Kilner, L. A. (1989). Adolescent mental health. *American Psychologist, 44,* 200–208.

Powlishta, K. K., Serbin, L. A., Doyle, A., & White, D. R. (1994). Gender, ethnic, and body type biases: The generality of prejudice in childhood. Developmental *Psychology, 30,* 526–536.

Powlishta, K. K., Serbin, L. A., & Moller, L. C. (1993). The stability of individual differences in gender typing: Implications for understanding gender segregation. *Sex Roles, 29,* 723–737.

Pratt, M. W., Green, D., & MacVicar, J. (1992). The mathematical parent: Parental scaffolding, parenting style, and learning outcomes in long-division mathematics homework. *Journal of Applied Developmental Psychology, 24,* 832–839.

Prechtl, H. F. R. (1958). Problems of behavioral studies in the newborn infant. In D. S. Lehrmann, R. A. Hinde, & E. Shaw (Eds.), *Advances in the study of behavior* (Vol. 1, pp. 75–98). New York: Academic Press.

Prechtl, H. F. R., & Beintema, D. (1965). *The neurological examination of the full-term newborn infant.* London: William Heinemann Medical Books.

Preisser, D. A., Hodson, B. W., & Paden, E. P. (1988). Developmental phonology: 18–29 months. *Journal of Speech and Hearing Disorders, 53,* 125–130.

Premack, A. J. (1976). *Why chimps can read.* New York: Harper & Row.

Pressley, M. (1982). Elaboration and memory development. *Child Development, 53,* 296–309.

Pressley, M. (1992). How not to study strategy discovery. *American Psychologist, 47,* 1240–1241.

Pressley, M. (1994). State-of-the-science primary-grades reading instruction or whole language? *Educational Psychologist, 29,* 211–215.

Pressley, M. (1995a). *Advanced educational psychology for educators, researchers, and policymakers.* New York: HarperCollins.

Pressley, M. (1995b). More about the development of self-regulation: Complex, long-term, and thoroughly social. *Educational Psychologist, 30,* 207–212.

Pressley, M., Cariglia-Bull, T., Deane, S., & Schneider, W. (1987). Short-term memory, verbal competence, and age as predictors of imagery instructional effectiveness. *Journal of Experimental Child Psychology, 43,* 194–211.

Pressley, M., & El-Dinary, P. B. (Eds.). (1993). Strategies instruction [Special issue]. *Elementary School Journal, 94*(2).

Preston, R. C. (1962). Reading achievement of German and American children. *School and Society, 90,* 350–354.

Previc, F. H. (1991). A general theory concerning the prenatal origins of cerebral lateralization. *Psychological Review, 98,* 299–334.

Preyer, W. (1888). *The mind of the child* (2 vols.). New York: Appleton. (Original work published 1882)

Prior, M., Smart, D., Sanson, A., & Oberklaid, F. (1993). Sex differences in psychological adjustment from infancy to 8 years. *Journal of the American Academy of Child and Adolescent Psychiatry, 32,* 291–304.

Proffitt, D. R., & Bertenthal, B. I. (1990). Converging operations revisited: Assessing what infants perceive using discrimination measures. *Perception & Psychophysics, 47,* 1–11.

Proos, L. A. (1993). Anthropometry in adolescence—secular trends, adoption, ethnic and environmental differences. *Hormone Research, 39,* 18–24.

Provisional Committee on Pediatric AIDS, American Academy of Pediatrics. (1995). Perinatal human immunodeficiency virus testing. *Pediatrics, 95,* 303–307.

Pryor, J. B., & Reeder, G. D. (1993). Collective and individual representations of HIV/AIDS stigma. In J. B. Pryor & G. D. Reeder (Eds.), *The social psychology of HIV infection* (pp. 263–286). Hillsdale, NJ: Erlbaum.

The Psychological Corporation. (1993). *Assessment focus.* San Antonio, TX: Author.

Pulkkinen, L. (1982). Self-control and continuity from childhood to late adolescence. In P. B. Baltes & O. G. Brim, Jr. (Eds.), *Life-span development and behavior* (Vol. 4, pp. 63–105). New York: Academic Press.

Putallaz, M., & Heflin, A. H. (1990). Parent–child interaction. In S. R. Asher & J. D. Coie (Eds.), *Peer rejection in childhood* (pp. 189–216). Cambridge: Cambridge University Press.

Q

Qazi, Q. H., Sheikh, T. M., Fikrig, S., & Menikoff, H. (1988). Lack of evidence for craniofacial dysmorphism in perinatal human immunodeficiency virus infection. *Journal of Pediatrics, 112,* 7–11.

Quadagno, D. M., Briscoe, R., & Quadagno, J. S. (1977). Effect of perinatal gonadal hormones on selected nonsexual behavior patterns: A critical assessment of the nonhuman and human literature. *Psychological Bulletin, 84,* 62–80.

Quadrel, M. J., Fischhoff, B., & Davis, W. (1993). Adolescent (in)vulnerability. *American Psychologist, 48,* 102–116.

Quay, H. C. (1987). Institutional treatment. In H. C. Quay (Ed.), *Handbook of juvenile delinquency* (pp. 244–265). New York: Wiley.

Quay, L. C., & Jarrett, O. S. (1986). Teachers' interactions with middle- and lower-SES preschool boys and girls. *Journal of Educational Psychology, 78,* 495–498.

Quintero, R. A., Puder, K. S., & Cotton, D. B. (1993). Embryoscopy and fetoscopy. *Obstetrics and Gynecology Clinics of North America, 20,* 563–581.

R

Rabiner, D. L., & Coie, J. (1989). Effect of expectancy inductions on rejected children's acceptance by unfamiliar peers. *Developmental Psychology, 25,* 450–457.

Rabiner, D. L., Keane, S. P., & MacKinnon-Lewis, C. (1993). Children's beliefs about familiar and unfamiliar peers in relation to their sociometric status. *Developmental Psychology, 29,* 236–243.

Radke-Yarrow, M., & Zahn-Waxler, C. (1984). Roots, motives and patterns in children's prosocial behavior. In J. Reykowski, J. Karylowski, D. Bar-Tel, & E. Staub (Eds.), *The development and maintenance of prosocial behaviors: International perspectives on positive mortality* (pp. 81–99). New York: Plenum.

Radziszewska, B., & Rogoff, B. (1988). Influence of adult and peer collaboration on the development of children's planning skills. *Developmental Psychology, 24,* 840–848.

Räihä, N. C. R., & Axelsson, I. E. (1995). Protein nutrition during infancy. *Pediatric Clinics of North America, 42,* 745–763.

Ramey, C. T., & Campbell, F. A. (1984). Preventive education for high-risk children: Cognitive consequences of the Carolina Abecedarian Project. *American Journal of Mental Deficiency, 88,* 515–523.

Ramey, C. T., & Ramey, S. L. (1990). Intensive educational intervention for children of poverty. *Intelligence, 14,* 1–9.

Ramphal, C. (1962). *A study of three current problems in education.* Unpublished doctoral dissertation, University of Natal, India.

Ramsay, D. S. (1985). Fluctuations in unimanual hand preference in infants following the onset of duplicated babbling. *Developmental Psychology, 21,* 318–324.

Ramsay, D. S., & McCune, L. (1984). *Fluctuations in bimanual handedness in the second year of life.* Unpublished manuscript, Rutgers University.

Ramsay, M., Gisel, E. G., & Boutry, M. (1993). Non-organic failure to thrive: Growth failure secondary to feeling-skills disorder. *Developmental Medicine and Child Neurology, 35,* 285–297.

Ramsey, P. G. (1991). Young children's awareness and understanding of social class differences. *Journal of Genetic Psychology, 152,* 71–82.

Ramsey, P. G. (1995, September). Growing up with the contradictions of race and class. *Young Children, 50*(6), 18–22.

Rand, Y., & Kaniel, S. (1987). Group administration of the LPAD. In C. S. Lidz (Ed.), *Dynamic assessment: An interactional approach to evaluating learning potential* (pp. 196–214). New York: Guilford.

Rapport, M. D., & Kelly, K. L. (1993). Psychostimulant effects on learning and cognitive function in children with attention deficit hyperactivity disorder: Findings and implications. In J. L. Matson (Ed.), *Hyperactivity in children: A handbook* (pp. 97–136). Boston: Allyn and Bacon.

Rast, M., & Meltzoff, A. N. (1995). Memory and representation in young children with Down syndrome: Exploring deferred imitation and object permanence. *Development and Psychopathology, 7,* 393–407.

Ratcliffe, S. G., Pan, H., & McKie, M. (1992). Growth during puberty in the XYY boy. *Annals of Human Biology, 19,* 579–587.

Ratner, N. B. (1993). Atypical language development. In J. Berko Gleason (Ed.), *The development of language* (pp. 325–368). New York: Macmillan.

Ratner, N., & Bruner, J. S. (1978). Social exchange and the acquisition of language. *Journal of Child Language, 5,* 391–402.

Rayner, K., & Pollatsek, A. (1989). *The psychology of reading.* Englewood Cliffs, NJ: Prentice-Hall.

Read, C. R. (1991). Achievement and career choices: Comparisons of males and females. *Roeper Review, 13,* 188–193.

Rees, M. (1993). Menarche when and why? *Lancet, 342,* 1375–1376.

Reese, H. W. (1977). Imagery and associative memory. In R. V. Kail & J. W. Hagen (Eds.), *Perspectives on the development of memory and cognition* (pp. 113–116). Hillsdale, NJ: Erlbaum.

Reich, P. A. (1986). *Language development.* Englewood Cliffs, NJ: Prentice-Hall.

Reinisch, J. M. (1981). Prenatal exposure to synthetic progestins increases potential for aggression in humans. *Science, 211,* 1171–1173.

Reis, M. (1992). Making connections from urban schools. *Education and Urban Society, 24,* 477–488.

Reis, S. M. (1991). The need for clarification in research designed to examine gender differences in achievement and accomplishment. *Roeper Review, 13,* 193–198.

Reiser, J., Yonas, A., & Wikner, K. (1976). Radial localization of odors by human neonates. *Child Development, 47,* 856–859.

Reisman, J. E. (1987). Touch, motion, and proprioception. In P. Salapatek & L. Cohen (Eds.), *Handbook of infant perception: Vol. 1. From sensation to perception* (pp. 265–303). Orlando, FL: Academic Press.

Renzulli, J. (1986). The three-ring conception of giftedness: A developmental model for creative productivity. In R. Sternberg & J. Davidson (Eds.), *Conceptions of giftedness* (pp. 51–92). New York: Cambridge University Press.

Repke, J. T. (1992). Drug supplementation in pregnancy. *Current Opinion in Obstetrics and Gynecology, 4,* 802–806.

Resnick, L. B. (1989). Developing mathematical knowledge. *American Psychologist, 44,* 162–169.

Ressler, E. M. (1993). *Children in war.* New York: UNICEF.

Rest, J. R. (1979). *Development in judging moral issues.* Minneapolis: University of Minnesota Press.

Rest, J. R. (1983). Morality. In J. H. Flavell & E. M. Markman (Ed.), *Handbook of child psychology: Vol. 3. Cognitive development* (4th ed., pp. 556–629). New York: Wiley.

Rest, J. R. (1986). *Moral development: Advances in research and theory.* New York: Praeger.

Rest, J. R., & Narvaez, D. (1991). The college experience and moral development. In W. M. Kurtines & J. L. Gewirtz (Eds.), *Handbook of moral behavior and development* (Vol. 2, pp. 229–245). Hillsdale, NJ: Erlbaum.

Revelle, G. L., Karabenick, J. D., & Wellman, H. M. (1981). *Comprehension monitoring in preschool children.* Paper presented at the biennial meeting of the Society for Research in Child Development, Boston.

Reyna, V. F., & Brainerd, C. J. (1992). A fuzzy-trace theory of reasoning and remembering: Paradoxes, patterns, and parallelism. In A. Healy, S. Kosslyn, & R. Shiffrin (Eds.), *From learning processes to cognitive processes* (Vol. 2, pp. 235–259). Hillsdale, NJ: Erlbaum.

Reyna, V. F., & Kiernan, B. (1994). Development of gist versus verbatim memory in sentence recognition: Effects of lexical familiarity, semantic content, encoding instructions, and retention interval. *Developmental Psychology, 30,* 178–191.

Reznick, J. S., Gibbons, J. L., Johnson, M. O., & McDonough, P. M. (1989). Behavioral inhibition in a normative sample. In J. S. Reznick (Ed.), *Perspectives on behavioral inhibition* (pp. 25–49). Chicago: University of Chicago Press.

Reznick, J. S., & Goldfield, B. A. (1992). Rapid change in lexical development in comprehension and production. *Developmental Psychology, 28,* 406–413.

Rheingold, H., Gewirtz, J., & Ross, H. (1959). Social conditioning of vocalizations in the infant. *Journal of Comparative and Physiological Psychology, 52,* 68–72.

Ricard, M., & Kamberk-Kilicci, M. (1995). Children's empathic responses to emotional complexity. *International Journal of Behavioral Development, 18,* 211–225.

Ricciardelli, L. A. (1992). Bilingualism and cognitive development: Relation to threshold theory. *Journal of Psycholinguistic Research, 21,* 301–316.

Riccio, C. A., Hynd, G. W., Cohen, M. J., & Gonzalez, J. J. (1993). Neurological basis of attention deficit hyperactivity disorder. *Exceptional Children, 60,* 118–124.

Ricciuti, H. N. (1993). Nutrition and mental development. *Current Directions in Psychological Science, 2,* 43–46.

Ricco, R. B. (1989). Operational thought and the acquisition of taxonomic relations involving figurative dissimilarity. *Developmental Psychology, 25,* 996–1003.

Rice, M. L., Huston, A. C., & Wright, J. C. (1982). The forms of television: Effects on children's attention, comprehension, and social behavior. In D. Pearl, L. Bouthilet, & J. Lazar (Eds.), *Television and behavior: Ten years of scientific progress and implications for the eighties* (Vol. 2, pp. 24–38). Washington, DC: U.S. Government Printing Office.

Rice, M. L., Huston, A. C., & Wright, J. C. (1986). Replays as repetitions: Young children's interpretation of television forms. *Journal of Applied Developmental Psychology, 7,* 61–76.

Rice, M. L., Huston, A. C., Truglio, R., & Wright, J. (1990). Words from "Sesame Street": Learning vocabulary while viewing. *Developmental Psychology, 26,* 421–428.

Rice, M. L., & Woodsmall, L. (1988). Lessons from television: Children's word learning when viewing. *Child Development, 59,* 420–429.

Richards, D. D., & Siegler, R. S. (1986). Children's understandings of the attributes of life. *Journal of Experimental Child Psychology, 42,* 1–22.

Richards, M. H., & Duckett, E. (1994). The relationship of maternal employment to early adolescent daily experience with and without parents. *Child Development, 65,* 225–236.

Richardson, S. A., Koller, H., & Katz, M. (1986). Factors leading to differences in the school performance of boys and girls. *Developmental and Behavioral Pediatrics, 7,* 49–55.

Richman, A. L., Miller, P. M., & LeVine, R. A. (1992). Cultural and educational variations in maternal responsiveness. *Developmental Psychology, 28,* 614–621.

Ridley, C. A., & Vaughn, R. (1982). Interpersonal problem solving: An intervention program for preschool children. *Journal of Applied Developmental Psychology, 3,* 177–190.

Riese, M. L. (1987). Temperament stability between the neonatal period and 24 months. *Developmental Psychology, 23,* 216–222.

Ritts, V., Patterson, M. L., & Tubbs, M. E. (1992). Expectations, impressions, and judgments of physically attractive students: A review. *Review of Educational Research, 62,* 413–426.

Robbins, L. C. (1963). The accuracy of parental recall of aspects of child development and of child rearing practices. *Journal of Abnormal and Social Psychology, 66,* 261–270.

Robert, M. (1989). Reduction of demand characteristics in the measurement of certainty during modeled conservation. *Journal of Experimental Child Psychology, 47,* 451–466.

Roberton, M. A. (1984). Changing motor patterns during childhood. In J. R. Thomas (Ed.), *Motor development during childhood and adolescence* (pp. 48–90). Minneapolis: Burgess Publishing.

Roberts, J. E., Burchinal, M. R., & Campbell, F. (1994). Otitis media in early childhood and patterns of intellectual development and later academic performance. *Journal of Pediatric Psychology, 19,* 347–367.

Roberts, R. J., Jr., & Aman, C. J. (1993). Developmental differences in giving directions: Spatial frames of reference and mental rotation. *Child Development, 64,* 1258–1270.

Robinson, B. E., & Canaday, H. (1978). Sex-role behaviors and personality traits of male day care teachers. *Sex Roles, 4,* 853–865.

Robinson, C. C., & Morris, J. T. (1986). The gender-stereotyped nature of Christmas toys received by 36-, 48-, and 60-month-old children: A comparison between non-requested vs. requested toys. *Sex Roles, 15,* 21–32.

Robinson, E. J., & Mitchell, P. (1994). Young children's false-belief reasoning: Interpretation of messages is not easier than the classic task. *Developmental Psychology, 30,* 67–72.

Robinson, J. L., Kagan, J., Reznick, J. S., & Corley, R. (1992). The heritability of inhibited and uninhibited behavior: A twin study. *Developmental Psychology, 28,* 1030–1037.

Rochat, P. (1992). Self-sitting and reaching in 5- to 8-month-old infants: The impact of posture and its development on early eye–hand coordination. *Journal of Motor Behavior, 24,* 210–220.

Rochat, P., & Goubet, N. (1995). Development of sitting and reaching in 5- to 6-month-old infants. *Infant Behavior and Development, 18,* 53–68.

Roche, A. F. (1979). Secular trends in stature, weight, and maturation. In A. F. Roche (Ed.), Secular trends in human growth, maturation, and development. *Monographs of the Society for Research in Child Development, 44*(3–4, Serial No. 179).

Roche, A. F. (1981). The adipocyte-number hypothesis. *Child Development, 52,* 31–43.

Rocheleau, B. (1995). Computer use by school-age children: Trends, patterns, and predictors. *Journal of Educational Computing Research, 12,* 1–17.

Rodriguez, M. L., Mischel, W., & Shoda, Y. (1989). Cognitive and personality variables in the delay of gratification of older children at risk. *Journal of Personality and Social Psychology, 57,* 358–367.

Roe, K. V., Roe, A., Drivas, A., & Bronstein, R. (1990). A curvilinear relationship between maternal vocal stimulation and three-month-olds' cognitive processing: A cross-cultural phenomenon. *Infant Mental Health Journal, 11,* 175–189.

Roffwarg, H. P., Muzio, J. N., & Dement, W. C. (1966). Ontogenetic development of the human sleep-dream cycle. *Science, 152,* 604–619.

Roggman, L. A., Langlois, J. H., Hubbs-Tait, L., & Rieser-Danner, L. A. (1994). Infant day-care, attachment, and the "file drawer problem." *Child Development, 65,* 1429–1443.

Rogoff, B. (1990). Apprenticeship in thinking. New York: Oxford University Press.

Rogoff, B., & Chavajay, P. (1995). What's become of research on the cultural basis of cognitive development? *American Psychologist, 50,* 859–877.

Rogoff, B., & Mistry, J. (1985). Memory development in cultural context. In M. Pressley & C. Brainerd (Eds.), *Cognitive learning and memory in children* (pp. 117–142). New York: Springer-Verlag.

Rogoff, B., Mistry, J., Göncü, A., & Mosier, C. (1993). Guided participation in cultural activity by toddlers and caregivers. *Monographs of the Society for Research in Child Development, 58*(8, Serial No. 236).

Rogoff, B., & Waddell, K. J. (1982). Memory for information organized in a scene by children from two cultures. *Child Development, 53,* 1224–1228.

Rohner, R. P., & Rohner, E. C. (1981). Parental acceptance-rejection and parental control: Cross-cultural codes. *Ethnology, 20,* 245–260.

Roland, A. (1988). *In search of self in India and Japan: Toward a cross-cultural psychology.* Princeton, NJ: Princeton University Press.

Roopnarine, J. L., Hossain, Z., Gill, P., & Brophy, H. (1994). Play in the East Indian context. In J. L. Roopnarine, J. E. Johnson, & F. H. Hooper (Eds.), *Children's play in diverse cultures* (pp. 9–30). Albany, NY: SUNY Press.

Roopnarine, J. L., Talukder, E., Jain, D., Joshi, P., & Srivastave, P. (1990). Characteristics of holding, patterns of play, and social behaviors between parents and infants in New Delhi, India. *Developmental Psychology, 26,* 667–673.

Roper Starch Worldwide. (1994). *A national survey of 252 males and 251 females.* New York: Author.

Rosa, R. W. (1993). Retinoid embryopathy in humans. In G. Koren (Ed.), *Retinoids in clinical practice* (pp. 77–109). New York: Marcel Dekker.

Rose, R. J. (1995). Genes and human behavior. *Annual Review of Psychology, 46,* 625–654.

Rose, R. M., Holaday, J. W., & Bernstein, I. S. (1976). Plasma testosterone, dominance rank and aggressive behavior in male rhesus monkeys. *Nature, 231,* 366–368.

Rose, S. A. (1988). Shape recognition in infancy: Visual integration of sequential information. *Child Development, 59,* 1161–1176.

Rose, S. A., & Feldman, J. F. (1995). Prediction of IQ and specific cognitive abilities at 11 years from infancy measures. *Developmental Psychology, 31,* 685–696.

Rosen, A. B., & Rozin, P. (1993). Now you see it, now you don't: The preschool child's conception of invisible particles in the context of dissolving. *Developmental Psychology, 29,* 300–311.

Rosen, K. S., & Rothbaum, F. (1993). Quality of parental caregiving and security of attachment. *Developmental Psychology, 29,* 358–367.

Rosen, W. D., Adamson, L. B., & Bakeman, R. (1992). An experimental investigation of infant social referencing: Mothers' messages and gender differences. *Developmental Psychology, 28,* 1172–1178.

Rosenberg, M. (1979). *Conceiving the self.* New York: Basic Books.

Rosengren, K. S., & Hickling, A. K. (1994). Seeing is believing: Children's explanations of commonplace, magical, and extraordinary transformations. *Child Development, 65,* 1605–1626.

Rosenstein, D., & Oster, H. (1988). Differential facial responses to four basic tastes in newborns. *Child Development, 59,* 1555–1568.

Rosenthal, D. A. (1987). Ethnic identity development in adolescents. In J. S. Phinney & M. J. Rotheram (Eds.), *Children's ethnic socialization* (pp. 156–179). Newbury Park, CA: Sage.

Rosenthal, J. A. (1992). *Special-needs adoption: A study of intact families.* New York: Praeger.

Rosenthal, R., & Jacobson, L. (1968). *Pygmalion in the classroom: Teacher expectation and pupils' intellectual development.* New York: Holt, Rinehart & Winston.

Ross, G. S. (1980). Categorization in 1- to 2-year-olds. *Developmental Psychology, 16,* 391–396.

Ross, H. S., & Goldman, B. D. (1977). Infants' sociability toward strangers. *Child Development, 48,* 638–642.

Ross, R. P., Campbell, T., Huston-Stein, A., & Wright, J. C. (1984). Nutritional misinformation of children: A developmental and experimental analysis of the effects of televised food commercials. *Journal of Applied Developmental Psychology, 1,* 329–347.

Rotenberg, K. J., Simourd, L., & Moore, D. (1989). Children's use of a verbal–nonverbal consistency principle to infer truth and lying. *Child Development, 60,* 309–322.

Rothbart, M. K. (1981). Measurement of temperament in infancy. *Child Development, 52,* 569–578.

Rothbart, M. K., & Rothbart, M. (1976). Birth-order, sex of child and maternal help giving. *Sex Roles, 2,* 39–46.

Rothbaum, F., Rosen, K. S., Pott, M., & Beatty, M. (1995). Early parent–child relationships and later problem behavior: A longitudinal study. *Merrill-Palmer Quarterly, 41,* 133–151.

Rotheram-Borus, M. J. (1993). Biculturalism among adolescents. In M. Bernal & G. Knight (Eds.), *Ethnic identity* (pp. 81–102). Albany, NY: SUNY Press.

Rothman, K. J., Moore, L.L., Singer, M.R., Nguyen, U.S., Manneno, S. & Milunsky, A. (1995). Teratogenicity of high vitamin A intake. *New England Journal of Medicine, 333,* 1369-1373.

Rourke, B. P. (1988). Socioemotional disturbances of learning disabled children. *Journal of Consulting and Clinical Psychology, 56,* 801–810.

Rousseau, J. J. (1955). *Emile.* New York: Dutton. (Original work published 1762)

Rovee-Collier, C. K. (1987). Learning and memory. In J. D. Osofsky (Ed.), *Handbook of infant development* (2nd ed., pp. 98–148). New York: Wiley.

Rovee-Collier, C. K., & Hayne, H. (1987). Reactivation of infant memory: Implications for cognitive development. In H. W. Reese (Ed.), *Advances in child development and behavior* (Vol. 20, pp. 185–238). New York: Academic Press.

Rovee-Collier, C. K., & Shyi, G. (1992). A functional and cognitive analysis of infant long-term retention. In C. J. Brainerd, M. L. Howe, & V. Reyna (Eds.), *Development of long-term retention* (pp. 3–55). New York: Springer-Verlag.

Royce, J. M., Darlington, R. B., & Murray, H. W. (1983). Pooled analyses: Findings across studies. In Consortium for Longitudinal Studies (Ed.), *As the twig is bent: Lasting effects of preschool programs* (pp. 411–459). Hillsdale, NJ: Erlbaum.

Rozin, P. (1990). Development in the food domain. *Developmental Psychology, 26,* 555–562.

Rubin, J. Z., Provenzano, F. J., & Luria, Z. (1974). The eye of the beholder: Parents' views on sex of newborns. *American Journal of Orthopsychiatry, 44,* 512–519.

Rubin, K. H. (1982). Nonsocial play in preschoolers: Necessarily evil? *Child Development, 53,* 651–657.

Rubin, K. H., Fein, G. G., & Vandenberg, B. (1983). Play. In E. M. Hetherington (Ed.), *Handbook of child psychology: Vol. 4. Socialization, personality, and social development* (4th ed., pp. 693–744). New York: Wiley.

Rubin, K. H., & Krasnor, L. R. (1985). Social-cognitive and social behavioral perspectives on problem solving. In M. Perlmutter (Ed.), *Minnesota Symposia on Child Psychology* (Vol. 18, pp. 1–68). Hillsdale, NJ: Erlbaum.

Rubin, K. H., Maioni, T. L., & Hornung, M. (1976). Free play behaviors in middle- and lower-class preschoolers: Parten and Piaget revisited. *Child Development, 47,* 414–419.

Rubin, K. H., Watson, K. S., & Jambor, T. W. (1978). Free-play behaviors in preschool and kindergarten children. *Child Development, 49,* 534–536.

Ruble, D. N., Boggiano, A. K., Feldman, N. S., & Loebl, J. H. (1980). Developmental analysis of the role of social comparison in self-evaluation. *Developmental Psychology, 16,* 105–115.

Ruff, H. A., & Lawson, K. R. (1990). Development of sustained, focused attention in young children during free play. *Developmental Psychology, 26,* 85–93.

Ruff, H. A., Lawson, K. R., Parrinello, R., & Weissberg, R. (1990). Long-term stability of individual differences in sustained attention in the early years. *Child Development, 61,* 60–75.

Ruff, H. A., Saltarelli, L. M., Capozzoli, M., & Dubiner, K. (1992). The differentiation of activity in infants' exploration of objects. *Developmental Psychology, 28,* 851–861.

Ruffman, T., Perner, J., Olson, D. R., & Doherty, M. (1993). Reflecting on scientific thinking: Children's understanding of the hypothesis–evidence relation. *Child Development, 64,* 1617–1636.

Ruiz, R. (1988). Bilingualism and bilingual education in the United States. In C. B. Paulston (Ed.), *International handbook of bilingualism and bilingual education* (pp. 539–560). New York: Greenwood Press.

Rumbaugh, D. M. (1977). *Language learning by a chimpanzee: The Lana project.* New York: Academic Press.

Runco, M. A. (1987). The generality of gifted performance in gifted and nongifted children. *Gifted Child Quarterly, 31,* 121–125.

Runco, M. A. (1992a). Children's divergent thinking and creative ideation. *Developmental Review, 12,* 233–264.

Runco, M. A. (1992b). The evaluative, valuative, and divergent thinking of children. *Journal of Creative Behavior, 25,* 311–319.

Runco, M. A. (1993). Divergent thinking, creativity, and giftedness. *Gifted Child Quarterly, 37,* 16–22.

Runco, M. A., & Okuda, S. M. (1988). Problem, discovery, divergent thinking, and the creative process. *Journal of Youth and Adolescence, 17,* 211–220.

Russell, A., & Finnie, V. (1990). Preschool children's social status and maternal instructions to assist group entry. *Developmental Psychology, 26,* 603–611.

Russell, J. A. (1990). The preschooler's understanding of the causes and consequences of emotion. *Child Development, 61,* 1872–1881.

Rutter, M. (1985). Resilience in the face of adversity: Protective factors and resistance to psychiatric disorder. *British Journal of Psychiatry, 147,* 598–611.

Rutter, M. (1987). Psychosocial resilience and protective mechanisms. *American Journal of Orthopsychiatry, 57,* 316–331.

Ryan, K. J. (1989). Ethical issues in reproductive endocrinology and infertility. *American Journal of Obstetrics and Gynecology, 160,* 1415–1417.

Ryynänen, M., Kirkinen, P., Mannermaa, A, & Saarikoski, S. (1995). Carrier diagnosis of the fragile X syndrome—a challenge in antenatal clinics. *American Journal of Obstetrics and Gynecology, 172,* 1236–1239.

S

Saarni, C. (1989). Children's understanding of strategic control of emotional expression in social transactions. In C. Saarni & P. L. Harris (Eds.), *Children's understanding of emotion* (pp. 181–208). New York: Cambridge University Press.

Saarni. C. (1993). Socialization of emotion. In M. Lewis & J. M. Haviland (Eds.), *Handbook of emotions* (pp. 435–446). New York: Guilford.

Sadler, T. W. (1995). *Langman's medical embryology (7th ed.).* Baltimore: Williams & Wilkins.

Salapatek, P. (1975). Pattern perception in early infancy. In L. B. Cohen & P. Salapatek (Eds.), *Infant perception: From sensation to cognition* (pp. 133–248). New York: Academic Press.

Salapatek, P., & Cohen, L. (Eds.). (1987). *Handbook of infant perception: Vol 2. From perception to cognition.* Orlando, FL: Academic Press.

Samenow, S. E. (1984). *Inside the criminal mind.* New York: Random House.

Sameroff, A. J., Seifer, R., Baldwin, A., & Baldwin, C. (1993). Stability of intelligence from preschool to adolescence: The influence of social and family risk factors. *Child Development, 64,* 80–97.

Sampson, R. J., & Laub, J. H. (1993). *Crime in the making: Pathways and turning points through life.* Cambridge, MA: Harvard University Press.

Samson, L. F. (1988). Perinatal viral infections and neonates. *Journal of Perinatal Neonatal Nursing, 1,* 56–65.

Samuels, S. J. (1985). Toward a theory of automatic information processing in reading: Updated. In H. Singer & R. B. Ruddell (Eds.), *Theoretical models and processes of reading* (3rd ed., pp. 719–721). Newark, DE: International Reading Association.

Sandberg, D. E., Ehrhardt, A. A., Ince, S. E., & Meyer-Bahlberg, H. F. L. (1991). Gender differences in children's and adolescent's career aspirations. *Journal of Adolescent Research, 6,* 371–386.

Sandqvist, K. (1992). Sweden's sex-role scheme and commitment to gender equality. In S. Lewis, D. N. Izraeli, & H. Hottsmans (Eds.), *Dual-earner families: International perspectives.* London: Sage.

Sanson, A. V., Smart, D. F., Prior, M., Oberklaid, F., & Pedlow, R. (1994). The structure of temperament from age 3 to 7 years: Age, sex, and sociodemographic influences. *Merrill-Palmer Quarterly, 40,* 233–252.

Santrock, J. W., & Warshak, R. A. (1979). Father custody and social development in boys and girls. *Journal of Social Issues, 35,* 112–125.

Santrock, J. W., & Warshak, R. A. (1986). Development of father custody relationships and legal/clinical considerations in father-custody families. In M. E. Lamb (Ed.), *The father's role: Applied perspectives* (pp. 135–166). New York: Wiley.

Sarason, I. G. (1980). *Test anxiety: Theory, research, and applications.* Hillsdale, NJ: Erlbaum.

Saudino, K., & Eaton, W. O. (1991). Infant temperament and genetics: An objective twin study. *Child Development, 62,* 1167–1174.

Savage-Rumbaugh, E. S., Murphy, J., Sevcik, R. A., Brakke, K. E., Williams, S. L., & Rumbaugh, D. M. (1993). Language comprehension in ape and child. *Monographs of the Society for Research in Child Development, 58*(3–4, Serial No. 233).

Savage-Rumbaugh, E. S., Sevcik, R. A., Brakke, K. E., Rumbaugh, D. M., & Greenfield, P. (1990). Symbols: Their communicative use, comprehension, and combination by bonobos (*Pan paniscus*). In C. Rovee-Collier & L. P. Lipsitt (Eds.), *Advances in infancy research* (Vol. 6, pp. 221–271). Norwood, NJ: Ablex.

Savin-Williams, R. C. (1979). Dominance hierarchies in groups of early adolescents. *Child Development, 50,* 923–935.

Savin-Williams, R. C. (1980). Dominance hierarchies in groups of middle to late adolescent males. *Journal of Youth and Adolescence, 9,* 75–85.

Savin-Williams, R. C. (1990). *Gay and lesbian youth: Expresssions of identity.* New York: Hemisphere.

Savin-Williams, R. C., & Berndt, T. J. (1990). Friendship and peer relations. In S. S. Feldman & G. R. Elliott (Eds.), *At the threshold: The developing adolescent* (pp. 277–307). Cambridge, MA: Harvard University Press.

Saxe, G. B. (1985). Effects of schooling on arithmetical understandings: Studies with Oksapmin children in Papua, New Guinea. *Journal of Educational Psychology, 77,* 503–513.

Saxe, G. B. (1988, August–September). Candy selling and math learning. *Educational Researcher, 17*(6), 14–21.

Saywitz, K. J. (1987). Children's testimony: Age-related patterns of memory errors. In S. J. Ceci, M. P. Toglia, & D. F. Ross (Eds.), *Children's eyewitness memory* (pp. 36–52). New York: Springer-Verlag.

Saywitz, K. J., & Nathanson, R. (1993). Children's testimony and their perceptions of stress in and out of the courtroom. *Child Abuse & Neglect, 17,* 613–622.

Scarr, S. (1985). Constructing psychology: Making facts and fables for our times. *American Psychologist, 40,* 499–512.

Scarr, S., & McCartney, K. (1983). How people make their own environments: A theory of genotype environment effects. *Child Development, 54,* 424–435.

Scarr, S., & Weinberg, R. A. (1976). IQ test performance of black children adopted by white families. *American Psychologist, 31,* 726–739.

Scarr, S., & Weinberg, R. A. (1978). The influence of "family background" on intellectual attainment. *American Sociological Review, 43,* 674–692.

Scarr, S., & Weinberg, R. A. (1983). The Minnesota Adoption Studies: Genetic differences and malleability. *Child Development, 54,* 260–267.

Scarr, S., Phillips, D. A., & McCartney, K. (1990). Facts, fantasies, and the future of child care in America. *Psychological Science, 1,* 26–35.

Scarr, S., Phillips, D., McCartney, K., & Abbott-Shim, M. (1993). Quality of child care as an aspect of family and child care policy in the United States. *Pediatrics, 91,* 182–188.

Schachter, F. F., & Stone, R. K. (1985). Difficult sibling, easy sibling: Temperament and the within-family environment. *Child Development, 56,* 1335–1344.

Schaefer, M., Hatcher, R. P., & Bargelow, P. D. (1980). Prematurity and infant stimulation. *Child Psychiatry and Human Development, 10,* 199–212.

Schaffer, H. R. (1979). Acquiring the concept of the dialogue. In M. H. Bornstein & W. Kessen (Eds.), *Psychological development from infancy: Image to intention* (pp. 279–305). Hillsdale, NJ: Erlbaum.

Schaffer, H. R., & Emerson, P. E. (1964). The development of social attachments in infancy. *Monographs of the Society for Research in Child Development, 29*(3, Serial No. 94).

Schaffer, J., & Kral, R. (1988). Adoptive families. In C. S. Chilman, E. W. Nunnally, & F. M. Cox (Eds.), *Variant family forms* (pp. 165–184). Newbury Park, CA: Sage.

Schaie, K. W., & Hertzog, C. (1982). Longitudinal methods. In B. B. Wolman

(Ed.), *Handbook of developmental psychology* (pp. 91–115). Englewood Cliffs, NJ: Prentice-Hall.

Schaivi, R. C., Theilgaard, A., Owen, D., & White, D. (1984). Sex chromosome anomalies, hormones, and aggressivity. *Archives of General Psychiatry, 41,* 93–99.

Schanberg, S., & Field, T. M. (1987). Sensory deprivation stress and supplemental stimulation in the rat pup and preterm human neonate. *Child Development, 58,* 1431–1447.

Schauble, L. (1996). The development of scientific reasoning in knowledge-rich contexts. *Developmental Psychology, 32,* 102–119.

Schieffelin, B. B., & Ochs, E. (1987). *Language socialization across cultures.* New York: Cambridge University Press.

Schifter, T., Hoffman, J. M., Hatten, H. P., & Hanson, M. W. (1994). Neuroimaging in infantile autism. *Journal of Child Neurology, 9,* 155–161.

Schlegel, A., & Barry, H., III. (1991). *Adolescence: An anthropological inquiry.* New York: Free Press.

Schneider, W., & Bjorklund, D. F. (1992). Expertise, aptitude, and strategic remembering. *Child Development, 63,* 461–473.

Schneider, W., & Pressley, M. (1989). *Memory development between 2 and 20.* New York: Springer-Verlag.

Schnur, E., Brooks-Gunn, J., & Shipman, V. C. (1992). Who attends programs serving poor children? The case of Head Start attendees and nonattendees. *Journal of Applied Developmental Psychology, 13,* 405–421.

Scholl, T. O., Heidiger, M. L., & Belsky, D. H. (1996). Prenatal care and maternal health during adolescent pregnancy: A review and meta-analysis. *Journal of Adolescent Health, 15,* 444–456.

Scholnick, E. K. (1995, Fall). Knowing and constructing plans. *SRCD Newsletter,* pp. 1–2, 17.

Schonfeld, D. J., Johnson, S. R., Perrin, E. C., O'Hare, L. L. & Cicchetti, D. V. (1993). Understanding of acquired immunodeficiency syndrome by elementary school children—A developmental survey. *Pediatrics, 92,* 389–395.

Schramm, W., Barnes, D., & Bakewell, J. (1987). Neonatal mortality in Missouri home births. *American Journal of Public Health, 77,* 930–935.

Schultz, R. T., Cho, N. K., Staib, L. H., & Kier, L. E. (1994). Brain morphology in normal and dyslexic children: The influence of sex and age. *Annals of Neurology, 35,* 732–742.

Schunk, D. H. (1983). Ability versus effort attributional feedback: Differential effects on self-efficacy and achievement. *Journal of Educational Psychology, 75,* 848–856.

Schunk, D. H., & Zimmerman, B. J. (Eds.). (1994). *Self-regulation of learning and performance.* Englewood Cliffs, NJ: Erlbaum.

Schutte, N. S., Malouff, J. M., Post-Gorden, J. C., & Rodasta, A. L. (1988). Effects of playing videogames on children's aggressive and other behaviors. *Journal of Applied Social Psychology, 18,* 454–460.

Schwanenflugel, P. J., Fabricius, W. V., & Alexander, J. (1994). Developing theories of mind: Understanding concepts and relations between mental activities. *Child Development, 65,* 1546–1563.

Scribner, S. (1986). Thinking in action: Some characteristics of practical thought. In R. J. Sternberg & R. K. Wagner (Eds.), *Practical intelligence: Nature and origins of competence in the everyday world* (pp. 13–30). New York: Cambridge University Press.

Scruggs, T. E., & Mastropieri, M. A. (1994). Successful mainstreaming in elementary science classes: A qualitative study of three reputational cases. *American Educational Research Journal, 31,* 785–811.

Sears, R. R., Maccoby, E. E., & Levin, H. (1957). *Patterns of child rearing.* New York: Harper & Row.

Seay, B., Alexander, B. K., & Harlow, H. F. (1964). Maternal behavior of socially deprived rhesus monkeys. *Journal of Abnormal and Social Psychology, 69,* 345–354.

Sebald, H. (1986). Adolescents' shifting orientation toward parents and peers: A curvilinear trend over recent decades. *Journal of Marriage and the Family, 48,* 5–13.

Segal, L. B., Oster, H., Cohen, M., Caspi, B., Myers, M., & Brown, D. (1995). Smiling and fussing in seven-month-old preterm and full-term black infants in the still-face situation. *Child Development, 66,* 1829–1843.

Seidman, E., Allen, L., Aber, J. L., Mitchell, C., & Feinman, J. (1994). The impact of school transitions in early adolescence on the self-system and perceived social context of poor urban youth. *Child Development, 65,* 507–522.

Seifer, R., Sameroff, A. J., Barrett, L. C., & Krafchuk, E. (1994). Infant temperament measured by multiple observations and mother report. *Child Development, 65,* 1478–1490.

Seifer, R., & Schiller, M. (1995). The role of parenting sensitivity, infant temperament, and dyadic interaction in attachment theory and assessment. In E. Waters, B. E. Vaughn, G. Posada, & K. Kondo-Ikemura (Eds.), Caregiving, cultural, and cognitive perspectives on secure-base behavior and working models: New growing points of attachment theory and research. *Monographs of the Society for Research in Child Development, 60*(2–3, Serial No. 244).

Seifer, R., Schiller, M., Sameroff, A. J., Resnick, S., & Riordan, K. (1996). Attachment, maternal sensitivity, and infant temperament during the first year of life. *Developmental Psychology, 32,* 12–25.

Seitz, V., & Apfel, N. H. (1993). Adolescent mothers and repeated childbearing: Effects of a school-based intervention program. *American Journal of Orthopsychiatry, 63,* 572–581.

Seitz, V., & Apfel, N. H. (1994). Effects of a school for pregnant students on the incidence of low-birthweight deliveries. *Child Development, 65,* 666–676.

Seitz, V., Apfel, N. H., & Rosenbaum, L. K. (1991). Effects of an intervention program for pregnant adolescents: Educational outcomes at two years postpartum. *American Journal of Community Psychology, 6,* 911–930.

Seligman, M. E. P. (1975). *Helplessness: On depression, development, and death.* San Francisco: Freeman.

Seligmann, J. (1991, December 9). Condoms in the classroom. *Newsweek,* p. 61.

Seligmann, J. (1994, May 4). The pressure to lose. *Newsweek,* pp. 60–61.

Selman, R. L. (1976). Social-cognitive understanding: A guide to educational and clinical practice. In T. Lickona (Ed.), *Moral development and behavior: Theory, research, and social issues* (pp. 299–316). New York: Holt, Rinehart & Winston.

Selman, R. L. (1980). *The growth of interpersonal understanding.* New York: Academic Press.

Selman, R. L. (1981). The child as a friendship philosopher. In S. R. Asher & J. M. Gottman (Eds.), *The development of friendships* (pp. 242–272). New York: Cambridge University Press.

Selman, R. L., & Byrne, D. F. (1974). A structural-developmental analysis of levels of role taking in middle childhood. *Child Development, 45,* 803–806.

Seltzer, V., & Benjamin, F. (1990). Breastfeeding and the potential for human immunodeficiency virus transmission. *Obstetrics and Gynecology, 75,* 713–715.

Serbin, L. A., Connor, J. M., & Citron, C. C. (1978). Environmental control of independent and dependent behaviors in preschool girls and boys: A model for early independence training. *Sex Roles, 4,* 867–875.

Serbin, L. A., Connor, J. M., & Iler, I. (1979). Sex-stereotyped and nonstereotyped introductions of new toys in the preschool classroom: An observational study of teacher behavior and its effects. *Psychology of Women Quarterly, 4,* 261–265.

Serbin, L. A., Powlishta, K. K., & Gulko, J. (1993). The development of sex typing in middle childhood. *Monographs of the Society for Research in Child Development, 58*(2, Serial No. 232).

Serbin, L. A., Tonick, I. J., & Sternglanz, S. H. (1977). Shaping cooperative cross-sex play. *Child Development, 48,* 924–929.

Service, R. F. (1994). Genome mapping: Closing in on human and mouse maps. *Science, 264,* 1404.

Sessa, F. M., & Steinberg, L. (1991). Family structure and the development of autonomy during adolescence. *Journal of Early Adolescence, 11,* 38–55.

Sever, J. L. (1983). Maternal infections. In C. C. Brown (Ed.), *Childhood learning disabilities and prenatal risk* (pp. 31–38). New York: Johnson & Johnson.

Shachar, H., & Sharan, S. (1994). Talking, relating, and achieving: Effects of cooperative learning and whole-class instruction. *Cognition and Instruction, 12,* 313–353.

Shaffer, D., Garland, A., Gould, M., Fisher, P., & Trautman, P. (1988). Preventing teenage suicide: A critical review. *Journal of the American Academy of Child and Adolescent Psychiatry, 27,* 675–687.

Shagle, S. C., & Barber, B. K. (1993). Effects of family, marital, and parent–child conflict on adolescent self-derogation and suicidal ideation. *Journal of Marriage and the Family, 55,* 964–974.

Shahar, S. (1990). *Childhood in the Middle Ages.* London: Routledge & Kegan Paul.

Shainess, N. (1961). A re-evaluation of some aspects of femininity through a study of menstruation: A preliminary report. *Comparative Psychiatry, 2,* 20–26.

Shalala, D. E. (1993). Giving pediatric immunizations the priority they deserve. *Journal of the American Medical Association, 269,* 1844–1845.

Shaw, D. S., Emery, R. E., & Tuer, M. D. (1993). Parental functioning and children's adjustment in families of divorce: A prospective study. *Journal of Abnormal Child Psychology, 21,* 119–134.

Shaw, G. M., Schaffer, D., Velie, E. M., Morland, K., & Harris, J. A. (1995). Periconceptional vitamin use, dietary folate, and the occurrence of neural tube defects. *Epidemiology, 6,* 219–226.

Shedler, J., & Block, J. (1990). Adolescent drug use and psychological health: A longitudinal inquiry. *American Psychologist, 45,* 612–630.

Sheingold, K. (1973). Developmental differences in intake and storage of visual information. *Journal of Experimental Child Psychology, 16,* 1–11.

Sheley, J. F., & Wright, J. D. (1995). *In the line of fire.* New York: Aldine De Gruyter.

Shelov, S. P. (1993). *Caring for your baby and young child: Birth to age 5.* New York: Bantam.

Sherif, M., Harvey, O. J., White, B. J., Hood, W. R., & Sherif, C. W. (1961). *The Robbers Cave experiment: Intergroup conflict and cooperation.* Norman: University of Oklahoma Press.

Sherman, M., & Key, C. B. (1932). The intelligence of isolated mountain children. *Child Development, 3,* 279–290.

Shettles, L. B., & Rorvik, D. M. (1984). *How to choose the sex of your baby.* New York: Doubleday.

Shields, P. J., & Rovee-Collier, C. K. (1992). Long-term memory for context-specific category information at six months. *Child Development, 63,* 245–259.

Shiffrin, R. M., & Atkinson, R. C. (1969). Storage and retrieval processes in long-term memory. *Psychological Review, 76,* 179–193.

Shiller, V., Izard, C. E., & Hembree, E. A. (1986). Patterns of emotion expression during separation in the Strange Situation. *Developmental Psychology, 22,* 378–382.

Shinn, M. W. (1900). *The biography of a baby.* Boston: Houghton Mifflin.

Shipman, G. (1971). The psychodynamics of sex education. In R. Muuss (Ed.), *Adolescent behavior and society* (pp. 326–339). New York: Random House.

Shoda, Y., Mischel, W., & Peake, P. K. (1990). Predicting adolescent cognitive and self-regulatory competencies from preschool delay of gratification: Identifying diagnostic conditions. *Developmental Psychology, 26,* 978–986.

Shonkoff, J. P. (1995, September). Child care for low-income families. *Young Children, 50*(6), 63–65.

Shulman, S., Elicker, J., & Sroufe, A. (1994). Stages of friendship growth in preadolescence as related to attachment history. *Journal of Social and Personal Relationships, 11,* 341–361.

Shultz, T. R. (1980). Development of the concept of intention. In W. A. Collins (Ed.), *Minnesota Symposia on Child Psychology* (Vol. 13, pp. 131–164). Hillsdale, NJ: Erlbaum.

Shurtleff, D. B., & Lemire, R. J. (1995). Epidemiology, etiologic factors, and prenatal diagnosis of open spinal dysraphism. *Neurosurgery Clinics of North America, 6,* 183–193.

Shweder, R. A., Mahapatra, M., & Miller, J. G. (1990). Culture and moral development. In J. Stigler, R. A. Shweder, & G. Herdt (Eds.), *Cultural psychology: Essays on comparative human development* (pp. 130–204). New York: Cambridge University Press.

Siebert, J. M., Garcia, A., Kaplan, M., & Septimus, A. (1989). Three model pediatric AIDS programs: Meeting the needs of children, families, and communities. In J. M. Siebert & R. A. Olson (Eds.), *Children, adolescents, and AIDS* (pp. 25–60). Lincoln: University of Nebraska Press.

Siegel, A. W. (1981). The externalization of cognitive maps by children and adults: In search of ways to ask better questions. In L. S. Liben, A. H. Patterson, & N. Newcombe (Eds.), *Spatial representation and behavior across the life span* (pp. 167–194). New York: Academic Press.

Siegler, R. S. (1983). Information processing approaches to development. In W. Kessen (Ed.), *Handbook of child psychology: Vol. 1. History, theory, and methods* (pp. 129–212). New York: Wiley.

Siegler, R. S. (1986). Unities in strategy choices across domains. In M. Perlmutter (Ed.), *Minnesota Symposia on Child Psychology* (Vol. 19, pp. 1–48). Hillsdale, NJ: Erlbaum.

Siegler, R. S. (1989). How domain-general and domain-specific knowledge interact to product strategy choices. *Merrill-Palmer Quarterly, 35,* 1–26.

Siegler, R. S. (1991). *Children's thinking* (2nd ed.). Englewood Cliffs, NJ: Prentice-Hall.

Siegler, R. S. (1992). The other Alfred Binet. *Developmental Psychology, 28,* 179–190.

Siegler, R. S., & Crowley, K. (1991). The microgenetic method: A direct means for studying cognitive development. *American Psychologist, 46,* 606–620.

Siegler, R. S., & Crowley, K. (1992). Microgenetic methods revisited. *American Psychologist, 47,* 1241–1243.

Siegler, R. S., & Jenkins, E. (1989). *How children discover new strategies.* Hillsdale, NJ: Erlbaum.

Siegler, R. S., & Munakata, Y. (1993, Winter). Beyond the immaculate transition: Advances in the understanding of change. *Newsletter of the Society for Research in Child Development.*

Siegler, R. S., & Richards, D. D. (1980). *College students' prototypes of children's intelligence.* Paper presented at the annual meeting of the American Psychological Association, New York.

Siegler, R. S., & Richards, D. D. (1982). The development of intelligence. In R. J. Sternberg (Ed.), *Handbook of human intelligence* (pp. 897–971). Cambridge: Cambridge University Press.

Siegler, R. S., & Robinson, M. (1982). The development of numerical understandings. In H. W. Reese & L. P. Lipsitt (Eds.), *Advances in child development and behavior* (Vol. 16, pp. 241–312). New York: Academic Press.

Siegler, R. S., & Shrager, J. (1984). Strategy choices in addition and subtraction: How do children know what to do? In C. Sophian (Ed.), *Origins of cognitive skills* (pp. 229–294). Hillsdale, NJ: Erlbaum.

Sigelman, C. Maddock, A., Epstein, J., & Carpenter, W. (1993). Age differences in understandings of disease causality: AIDS, colds, and cancer. *Child Development, 64,* 272–284.

Sigman, M. (1995). Nutrition and child development: More food for thought. *Current Directions in Psychological Science, 4,* 52–55.

Sigman, M., & Kasari, C. (1995). Joint attention across contexts in normal and autistic children. In C. Moore & P. J. Dunham (Eds.), *Joint attention: Its origins and role in development* (pp. 189–203). Hillsdale, NJ: Erlbaum.

Signorella, M. L. (1987). Gender schemata: Individual differences and context effects. In L. S. Liben & M. L. Signorella (Eds.), *Children's gender schemata* (pp. 23–37). San Francisco: Jossey-Bass.

Signorella, M. L., Bigler, R. S., & Liben, L. S. (1993). Developmental differences in children's gender schemata about others: A meta-analytic review. *Developmental Review, 13,* 147–183.

Signorella, M. L., & Jamison, W. (1986). Masculinity, femininity, androgyny, and cognitive performance: A meta-analysis. *Psychological Bulletin, 100,* 207–228.

Signorella, M. L., & Liben, L. S. (1984). Recall and reconstruction of gender-related pictures: Effects of attitude, task difficulty, and age. *Child Development, 55,* 393–405.

Signorielli, N. (1990). Children, television, and gender roles. *Journal of Adolescent Health Care, 11,* 50–58.

Signorielli, N. (1993). Television, the portrayal of women, and children's attitudes. In G. L. Berry & J. K. Asamen (Eds.), *Children and television: Images in a changing sociocultural world* (pp. 229–242). Newbury Park, CA: Sage.

Simmons, R. G., & Blyth, D. A. (1987). Moving into adolescence. New York: Aldine De Gruyter.

Simmons, R. G., Black, A., & Zhou, Y. (1991). African-American versus white children and the transition to junior high school. *American Journal of Education, 99,* 481–520.

Simon, R., Altstein, H., & Melli, M. S. (1994). *The case for transracial adoption.* Washington, DC: American University Press.

Simons, R. L., Conger, R. D., & Whitbeck, L. B. (1988). A multistage social learning model of the influences of family and peers upon adolescent substance use. *Journal of Drug Issues, 18,* 293–316.

Simons, R. L., Lorenz, R. O., Conger, R. D., & Wu, C-I. (1992). Support from spouse as a mediator and moderator of the disruptive influence of economic strain on parenting. *Child Development, 63,* 1282–1301.

Simons, R. L., Lorenz, F. O., Wu, C-I., & Conger, R. D. (1993). Social network and marital support as mediators and moderators of the impact of stress and depression on parental behavior. *Developmental Psychology, 29,* 368–381.

Simons, R. L., Whitbeck, L. B., Conger, R. D., & Chyi-In, W. (1991). Intergenerational transmission of harsh parenting. *Developmental Psychology, 27,* 159–171.

Simonton, D. K. (1988). *Scientific genius: A psychology of science.* New York: Cambridge University Press.

Simpson, S. A., & Harding, A. E. (1993). Predictive testing for Huntington's disease after the gene. *Journal of Medical Genetics, 30,* 1036–1038.

Singer, D. G., & Singer, J. L. (1990). *The house of make-believe.* Cambridge, MA: Harvard University Press.

Singer, J. L., & Singer, D. G. (1981). *Television, imagination, and aggression: A study of preschoolers.* Hillsdale, NJ: Erlbaum.

Singer, J. L., & Singer, D. G. (1983). Psychologists look at television. *American Psychologist, 38,* 826–834.

Singer, N. G., & Sattler, J. M. (1994). Stanford-Binet Intelligence Scale, Fourth Edition. In R. J. Sternberg (Ed.), *Encyclopedia of human intelligence* (Vol. 2, pp. 1033–1038). New York: Macmillan.

Sitskoorn, M. M., & Smitsman, A. W. (1995). Infants' perception of dynamic relations between objects: Passing through or support? *Developmental Psychology, 31,* 437–447.

Sivard, R. L. (1993). World military and social expenditures (15th ed.). Leesburg, VA: WMSE Publications.

Skinner, B. F. (1957). *Verbal behavior.* New York: Appleton-Century-Crofts.

Skinner, E. A., & Belmont, M. J. (1993). Motivation in the classroom: Reciprocal effects of teacher behavior and student engagement across the school year. *Journal of Educational Psychology, 85,* 571–581.

Skodak, M., & Skeels, H. M. (1949). A follow-up study of one hundred adopted children. *Journal of Genetic Psychology, 75,* 85–125.

Skouteris, H., McKenzie, B. E., & Day, R. H. (1992). Integration of sequential information for shape perception by infants: A developmental study. *Child development, 63,* 1164–1176.

Slaby, R. G., & Frey, K. S. (1975). Development of gender constancy and selective attention to same-sex models. *Child Development, 46,* 849–856.

Slaby, R. G., Roedell, W. C., Arezzo, D., & Hendrix, K. (1995). *Early violence prevention.* Washington, DC: National Association for the Education of Young Children.

Slade, A. (1987). A longitudinal study of maternal involvement and symbolic play during the toddler period. *Child Development, 58,* 367–375.

Slater, A. M., Mattock, A., & Brown, E. (1990). Size constancy at birth: Newborn infants' responses to retinal and real size. *Journal of Experimental Child Psychology, 49,* 314–322.

Slater, A. M., & Morison, V. (1985). Shape constancy and slant perception at birth. *Perception, 14,* 337–344.

Slobin, D. I. (1982). Universal and particular in the acquisition of language. In L. R. Gleitman & H. E. Wanner (Eds.), *Language acquisition: The state of the art* (pp. 128–170). Cambridge: Cambridge University Press.

Slobin, D. I. (1985). Crosslinguistic evidence for the language-making capacity. In D. I. Slobin (Ed.), *The crosslinguistic study of language acquisition: Vol. 2. Theoretical issues* (pp. 1157–1256). Hillsdale, NJ: Erlbaum.

Smetana, J. G. (1981). Preschool children's conceptions of moral and social rules. *Child Development, 52,* 1333–1336.

Smetana, J. G. (1985). Preschool children's conceptions of transgressions: Effects of varying moral and conventional domain-related attributes. *Developmental Psychology, 21,* 18–29.

Smetana, J. G. (1989). Toddlers' social interactions in the context of moral and conventional transgressions in the home. *Developmental Psychology, 25,* 499–508.

Smetana, J. G., & Braeges, J. L. (1990). The development of toddlers' moral and conventional judgments. *Merrill-Palmer Quarterly, 36,* 329–346.

Smiley, P. A., & Dweck, C. S. (1994). Individual differences in achievement goals among young children. *Child Development, 65,* 1723–1743.

Smith, C. L., & Tager-Flusberg, H. (1982). Metalinguistic awareness and language development. *Journal of Experimental Child Psychology, 34,* 449–468.

Smith, H. (1992). The detrimental health effects of ionizing radiation. *Nuclear Medicine Communications, 13,* 4–10.

Smith, J., & Prior, M. (1995). Temperament and stress resilience in school-age children: A within-families study. *Journal of the American Academy of Child and Adolescent Psychiatry, 34,* 168–179.

Smith, J., & Russell, G. (1984). Why do males and females differ? Children's beliefs about sex differences. *Sex Roles, 11,* 1111–1119.

Smith, L. D. (1992). On prediction and control: B. F. Skinner and the technological ideal of science. *American Psychologist, 47,* 216–223.

Smith, M. C. (1978). Cognizing the behavior stream: The recognition of intentional action. *Child Development, 49,* 736–743.

Smith, P. K., & Connolly, K. J. (1980). *The ecology of preschool behaviour.* Cambridge: Cambridge University Press.

Smith, P. K., & Hunter, T. (1992). Children's perceptions of playfighting, playchasing and real fighting: A cross-national study. *Social Development, 1,* 211–229.

Smith, S. (Ed.). (1995). Two-generation programs for families in poverty: A new intervention strategy. *Advances in applied developmental psychology* (Vol. 9). Norwood, NJ: Ablex.

Smolucha, F. (1992). Social origins of private speech in pretend play. In R. M. Diaz & L. E. Berk (Eds.), *Private speech: From social interaction to self-regulation* (pp. 123–141). Hillsdale, NJ: Erlbaum.

Smuts, B. B., & Gubernick, D. J. (1992). Male–infant relationships in nonhuman primates: Paternal investment or mating effort? In B. S. Hewlett (Ed.), *Father–child relations: Cultural and biosocial contexts* (pp. 1–30). New York: Aldine De Gruyter.

Smyth, R. (1995). Conceptual perspective-taking and children's interpretation of pronouns in reported speech. *Journal of Child Language, 22,* 171–187.

Snarey, J. R. (1995). In a communitarian voice: The sociological expansion of Kohlbergian theory, research, and practice. In W. M. Kurtines & J. L. Gewirtz (Eds.), *Moral development: An introduction* (pp. 109–134). Boston: Allyn and Bacon.

Snarey, J. R., Reimer, J., & Kohlberg, L. (1985). The development of social-moral reasoning among kibbutz adolescents: A longitudinal cross-cultural study. *Developmental Psychology, 20,* 3–17.

Snidman, N., Kagan, J., Riordan, L., & Shannon, D. C. (1995). Cardiac function and behavioral reactivity. *Psychophysiology, 32,* 199–207.

Sobesky, W. E. (1983). The effects of situational factors on moral judgments. *Child Development, 54,* 575–584.

Society for Research in Child Development. (1993). Ethical standards for research with children. In *Directory of Members* (pp. 337–339). Ann Arbor, MI: Author.

Sockett, H. (1992). The moral aspects of the curriculum. In P. W. Jackson (Ed.), *Handbook of research on curriculum* (pp. 543–569). New York: Macmillan.

Sodian, B., Taylor, C., Harris, P. L., & Perner, J. (1991). Early deception and the child's theory of mind: False trails and genuine markers. *Child Development, 62,* 468–483.

Sodian, B., & Wimmer, H. (1987). Children's understanding of inference as a source of knowledge. *Child Development, 58,* 424–433.

Soken, H. H., & Pick, A. D. (1992). Intermodal perception of happy and angry expressive behaviors by seven-month-old infants. *Child Development, 63,* 787–795.

Sommer, K., Whitman, T. L., Borkowski, J. G., Schellenbach, C., Maxwell, S., & Keogh, D. (1993). Cognitive readiness and adolescent parenting. *Developmental Psychology, 29,* 389–398.

Sommerville, J. (1982). *The rise and fall of childhood.* Beverly Hills, CA: Sage.

Sonenstein, F. L., Pleck, J. H., & Ku, L. C. (1991). Levels of sexual activity among adolescent males in the United States. *Family Planning Perspectives, 23,* 162–167.

Sonnenschein, S. (1986a). Development of referential communication: Deciding that a message is uninformative. *Developmental Psychology, 22,* 164–168.

Sonnenschein, S. (1986b). Development of referential communication skills: How familiarity with a listener affects a speaker's production of redundant messages. *Developmental Psychology, 22,* 549–552.

Sonnenschein, S. (1988). The development of referential communication: Speaking to different listeners. *Child Development, 59,* 694–702.

Sontag, C. W., Baker, C. T., & Nelson, V. L. (1958). Mental growth and personality development: A longitudinal study. *Monographs of the Society for Research in Child Development,* 23(2, Serial No. 68).

Sophian, C. (1988). Early developments in children's understanding of number: Inferences about numerosity and one-to-one correspondence. *Child Development, 59,* 1397–1414.

Sophian, C. (1995). Representation and reasoning in early numerical development: Counting, conservation, and comparisons between sets. *Child Development, 66,* 559–577.

Sorce, J., Emde, R., Campos, J., & Klinnert, M. (1985). Maternal emotional signaling: Its effect on the visual cliff behavior of 1-year-olds. *Developmental Psychology, 21,* 195–200.

Sosa, R., Kennell, J., Klaus, M., Robertson, S., & Urrutia, J. (1980). The effect of a supportive companion on perinatal problems, length of labor, and mother–infant interaction. *New England Journal of Medicine, 303,* 597–600.

Sostek, A. M., Smith, Y. F., Katz, K. S., & Grant, E. G. (1987). Developmental outcome of preterm infants with intraventricular hemorrhage at one and two years of age. *Child Development, 58,* 779–786.

Southern, W. T., Jones, E. D., & Stanley, J. C. (1994). Acceleration and enrichment: The context and development of program options. In K. A. Heller, F. J., Jonks, & H. A. Passow (Eds.), *International handbook of research and development of giftedness and talent* (pp. 387–409). Oxford: Pergamon Press.

Spätling, L., & Spätling, G. (1988). Magnesium supplementation in pregnancy: A double-blind study. *British Journal of Obstetrics and Gynecology, 95,* 120–125.

Spearman, C. (1927). *The abilities of man: Their nature and measurement.* New York: Macmillan.

Speer, J. R., & Flavell, J. H. (1979). Young children's knowledge of the relative difficulty of recognition and recall memory tasks. *Developmental Psychology, 15,* 214–217.

Speicher, B. (1994). Family patterns of moral judgment during adolescence and early adulthood. *Developmental Psychology, 30,* 624–632.

Spelke, E. S. (1987). The development of intermodal perception. In P. Salapatek & L. Cohen (Eds.), *Handbook of infant perception: Vol. 2. From perception to cognition* (pp. 233–273). Orlando, FL: Academic Press.

Spelke, E. S. (1990). Principles of object perception. *Cognitive Science, 14,* 29–56.

Spelke, E. S. (1994). Initial knowledge: Six suggestions. *Cognition, 50,* 431–445.

Spelke, E. S., Breinlinger, K., Jacobson, K., & Phillips, A. (1993). Gestalt relations and object perception: A developmental study. *Perception, 22,* 1483–1501.

Spelke, E. S., Breinlinger, K., Macomber, J., & Jacobson, K. (1992). Origins of knowledge. *Psychological Review, 99,* 605–632.

Spelke, E. S., Hofsten, C. von, & Kestenbaum, R. (1989). Object perception in infancy: Interaction of spatial and kinetic information for object boundaries. *Developmental Psychology, 25,* 185–196.

Spellacy, W. N., Miller, S. J., & Winegar, A. (1986). Pregnancy after 40 years of age. *Obstetrics and Gynecology, 68,* 452–454.

Spence, J. T., Helmreich, R., & Stapp, J. (1975). Ratings of self and peers on sex role attributes and their relation to self-esteem and conceptions of masculinity and femininity. *Journal of Personality and Social Psychology, 32,* 29–39.

Spence, M. J., & DeCasper, A. J. (1987). Prenatal experience with low-frequency maternal voice sounds influences neonatal perception of maternal voice samples. *Infant Behavior and Development, 10,* 133–142.

Spencer, C., Blades, M., & Morsley, K. (1989). *The child in the physical environment.* Chichester, England: Wiley.

Spencer, M. B., & Dornbusch, S. M. (1990). Challenges in studying minority youth. In S. S. Feldman & G. R. Elliott (Eds.), *At the threshold: The developing adolescent* (pp. 123–146). Cambridge, MA: Harvard University Press.

Spinetta, J., & Rigler, D. (1972). The child-abusing parent: A psychological review. *Psychological Bulletin, 77,* 296–304.

Spitz, R. A. (1946). Anaclitic depression. *Psychoanalytic Study of the Child, 2,* 313–342.

Spivack, G., & Shure, M. B. (1974). *Social adjustment of young children: A cognitive approach to solving real-life problems.* San Francisco: Jossey-Bass.

Spivack, G., & Shure, M. B. (1985). ICPS and beyond: Centripetal and centrifugal forces. *American Journal of Community Psychology, 13,* 226–243.

Spock, B., & Rothenberg, M. B. (1992). *Dr. Spock's baby and child care.* New York: Pocket Books.

Sroufe, L. A. (1979). The ontogenesis of emotion. In J. D. Osofsky (Ed.), *Handbook of infant development* (pp. 462–516). New York: Wiley.

Sroufe, L. A. (1985). Attachment classification from the perspective of infant–caregiver relationships and infant temperament. *Child Development, 56,* 1–14.

Sroufe, L. A. (1988). A developmental perspective on day care. *Early Childhood Research Quarterly, 3,* 293–292.

Sroufe, L. A., & Waters, E. (1976). The ontogenesis of smiling and laughter: A perspective on the organization of development in infancy. *Psychological Review, 83,* 173–189.

Sroufe, L. A., & Wunsch, J. P. (1972). The development of laughter in the first year of life. *Child Development, 43,* 1324–1344.

Sroufe, L. A., Egeland, B., & Kreutzer, T. (1990). The fate of early experience following developmental change: Longitudinal approaches to individual adaptation. *Child Development, 61,* 1363–1373.

St James-Roberts, I. (1989). Persistent crying in infancy. *Journal of Child Psychology and Psychiatry, 30,* 189–195.

St James-Roberts, I., & Halil, T. (1991). Infant crying patterns in the first year: Normal community and clinical findings. *Journal of Child Psychology and Psychiatry, 32,* 951–968.

St. Peters, M., Fitch, M., Huston, A. C., Wright, J. C., & Eakins, D. J. (1991). Television and families: What do young children watch with their parents? *Child Development, 62,* 1409–1423.

Stack, D. M., & Muir, D. W. (1992). Adult tactile stimulation during face-to-face interactions modulates five-month-olds' affect and attention. *Child Development, 63,* 1509–1525.

Stahl, S. A. (1992). Saying the "p" word: Nine guidelines for effective phonics instruction. *The Reading Teacher, 45,* 618–625.

Stahl, S. A., McKenna, M. C., & Pagnucco, J. R. (1994). The effects of whole-language instruction: An update and reappraisal. *Educational Psychologist, 29,* 175–185.

Stangor, C., & Ruble, D. N. (1989). Differential influences of gender schemata and gender constancy on children's information processing and behavior. *Social Cognition, 7,* 353–372.

Stankov, L., Horn, J. L., Roy, T. (1980). On the relationship between Gf/Gc theory and Jensen's Level I/Level II theory. *Journal of Educational Psychology, 72,* 796–809.

Stark, L. J., Allen, K. D., Hurst, M., Nash, D. A., Rigney, B., & Stokes, T. F. (1989). Distraction: Its utilization and efficacy with children undergoing dental treatment. *Journal of Applied Behavior Analysis, 22,* 297–307.

Starkey, P., Spelke, E. S., & Gelman, R. (1983). Detection of intermodal numerical correspondences by human infants. *Science, 10,* 179–181.

Stattin, H., & Magnusson, D. (1990). *Pubertal maturation in female development.* Hillsdale, NJ: Erlbaum.

Staub, E. (1996). Cultural-societal roots of violence. *American Psychologist, 51,* 117–132.

Stechler, G., & Halton, A. (1982). Prenatal influences on human development. In B. B. Wolman (Ed.), *Handbook of developmental psychology* (pp. 175–189). Englewood Cliffs, NJ: Prentice-Hall.

Stein, A. H. (1971). The effects of sex-role standards for achievement and sex-role preference on three determinants of achievement motivation. *Developmental Psychology, 4,* 219–231.

Stein, A. H., & Smithells, J. (1969). Age and sex differences in children's sex-role standards about achievement. *Developmental Psychology, 1,* 252–259.

Stein, B. E., & Meredith, M. A. (1993). *The merging of the senses.* Cambridge, MA: MIT Press.

Stein, Z., Susser, M., Saenger, G., & Marolla, F. (1975). *Famine and human development: The Dutch hunger winter of 1944–1945.* New York: Oxford University Press.

Steinberg, L. D. (1984). The varieties and effects of work during adolescence. In M. Lamb, A. Brown, & B. Rogoff (Eds.), *Advances in developmental psychology* (Vol. 3, pp. 1–37). Hillsdale, NJ: Erlbaum.

Steinberg, L. D. (1986). Latchkey children and susceptibility to peer pressure: An ecological analysis. *Developmental Psychology, 22,* 433–439.

Steinberg, L. D. (1987). The impact of puberty on family relations: Effects of pubertal status and pubertal timing. *Developmental Psychology, 23,* 451–460.

Steinberg, L. D. (1990). Interdependence in the family: Autonomy, conflict, and harmony in the parent–adolescent relationship. In S. S. Feldman & G. R. Elliott (Eds.), *At the threshold: The developing adolescent* (pp. 255–276). Cambridge, MA: Harvard University Press.

Steinberg, L. D. (1996). Adolescence (4th ed.). New York: McGraw-Hill.

Steinberg, L. D., & Dornbusch, S. M. (1991). Negative correlates of part-time employment during adolescence: Replication and elaboration. *Developmental Psychology, 27,* 304–313.

Steinberg, L. D., Fletcher, A., & Darling, N. (1994). Parental monitoring and peer influences on adolescent substance use. *Pediatrics, 93,* 1060–1064.

Steinberg, L. D., Lamborn, S. D., Darling, N., Mounts, N. S., & Dornbusch, S. M. (1994). Over-time changes in adjustment and competence among adolescents from authoritative, authoritarian, indulgent, and neglectful families. *Child Development, 65,* 754–770.

Steinberg, L. D., Lamborn, S. D., Dornbusch, S. M., & Darling, N. (1992). Impact of parenting practices on adolescent achievement: Authoritative parenting, school involvement, and encouragement to succeed. *Child Development, 63,* 1266–1281.

Steinberg, L. D., & Silverberg, S. (1986). The vicissitudes of autonomy in early adolescence. *Child Development, 57,* 841–851.

Steiner, J. E. (1979). Human facial expression in response to taste and smell stimulation. In H. W. Reese & L. P. Lipsitt (Eds.), *Advances in child development and behavior* (Vol. 13, pp. 257–295). New York: Academic Press.

Steiner, M. (1990). Postpartum psychiatric disorders. *Canadian Journal of Psychiatry, 35,* 89–95.

Steinhausen, H. C., Willms, J., & Spohr, H-L. (1993). Long-term psychopathological and cognitive outcome of children with fetal alcohol syndrome. *Journal of the American Academy of Child and Adolescent Psychiatry, 32,* 990–994.

Stenberg, C., & Campos, J. (1990). The development of anger expressions in infancy. In N. Stein, B. Leventhal, & T. Trabasso (Eds.), *Psychological and biological approaches to emotion* (pp. 247–282). Hillsdale, NJ: Erlbaum.

Stenberg, C., Campos, J., & Emde, R. (1983). The facial expression of anger in seven-month-old infants. *Child Development, 54,* 178–184.

Stephen, E. H., Freedman, V. A., & Hess, J. (1993). Near and far: Contact of children with their non-residential fathers. *Journal of Divorce & Remarriage, 20,* 171–191.

Stern, D. N. (1985). *The interpersonal world of the infant: A view from psychoanalysis and developmental psychology.* New York: Basic Books.

Stern, M., & Karraker, K. H. (1989). Sex stereotyping of infants: A review of gender labeling studies. *Sex Roles, 20,* 501–522.

Sternberg, K. J., Lamb, M. E., Greenbaum, C., Cicchetti, D., Dawud, S., Cortes, R. M., Krispin, O., & Lorey, F. (1993). Effects of domestic violence on children's behavior problems and depression. *Developmental Psychology, 29,* 44–52.

Sternberg, R. J. (1977). *Intelligence, information processing, and analogical reasoning.* Hillsdale, NJ: Erlbaum.

Sternberg, R. J. (1982, April). Who's intelligent? *Psychology Today, 16*(4), 30–39.

Sternberg, R. J. (1984). Evaluation of the Kaufman Assessment Battery for Children from an information processing perspective. *Journal of Special Education, 18,* 269–279.

Sternberg, R. J. (1985). *Beyond IQ: A triarchic theory of human intelligence.* New York: Cambridge University Press.

Sternberg, R. J. (1986). A triarchic theory of intellectual giftedness. In R. Sternberg & J. Davidson (Eds.), *Conceptions of giftedness* (pp. 223–243). New York: Cambridge University Press.

Sternberg, R. J. (1988). A triarchic view of intelligence in cross-cultural perspective. In S. H. Irvine & J. W. Berry (Eds.), *Human abilities in cultural context* (pp. 60–85). New York: Cambridge University Press.

Sternberg, R. J. (1989). Intelligence, wisdom, and creativity: Their natures and interrelationships. In R. L. Linn (Ed.), *Intelligence: Measurement, theory, and public* policy (pp. 119–146). Urbana: University of Illinois Press.

Sternberg, R. J., & Detterman, D. K. (1986). *What is intelligence?* Norwood, NJ: Ablex.

Sternberg, R. J., & Grigorenko, E. L. (1993). Thinking styles and the gifted. *Roeper Review, 16,* 122–130.

Sternberg, R. J., & Lubart, T. I. (1991a). An investment theory of creativity and its development. *Human Development, 34,* 1–31.

Sternberg, R. J., & Lubart, T. I. (1991b). Creating creative minds. *Phi Delta Kappan, 72*(8), 608–614.

Sternberg, R. J., & Lubart, T. I. (1995). *Defying the crowd.* New York: Basic Books.

Sternberg, R. J., Wagner, R. K., Williams, W. M., & Horvath, J. A. (1995). Testing common sense. *American Psychologist, 50,* 912–927.

Stetsenko, A., Little, T. D., Oettingen, G., & Baltes, P. B. (1995). Agency, control, and means–ends beliefs about school performance in Moscow children: How similar are they to beliefs of Western children? *Developmental Psychology, 31,* 285–299.

Stevens, J. H. (1984). Black grandmothers' and black adolescent mothers' knowledge about parenting. *Developmental Psychology, 20,* 1017–1025.

Stevenson, H. W. (1992, December). Learning from Asian schools. *Scientific American, 267*(6), 32–38.

Stevenson, H. W. (1994). Extracurricular programs in East Asian schools. *Teachers College Record, 95,* 389–407.

Stevenson, H. W., Chen, C., & Lee, S-Y. (1993). Mathematics achievement of Chinese, Japanese, and American children: Ten years later. *Science, 259,* 53–58.

Stevenson, H. W., & Lee, S-Y. (1990). Contexts of achievement: A study of American, Chinese, and Japanese children. *Monographs of the Society for Research in Child Development, 55*(1–2, Serial No. 221).

Stevenson, H. W., Stigler, J. W., Lee, S., Lucker, G. W., Litamura, S., & Hsu, C. (1985). Cognitive performance and academic achievement of Japanese, Chinese, and American children. *Child Development, 56,* 718–734.

Stevenson, R., & Pollitt, C. (1987). The acquisition of temporal terms. *Journal of Child Language, 14,* 533–545.

Stewart, D. A. (1982). *Children with sex chromosome aneuploidy: Follow-up studies.* New York: Alan R. Liss.

Stewart, S. L., & Rubin, K. H. (1995). The social problem-solving skills of anxious-withdrawn children. *Development and Psychopathology, 7,* 323–336.

Stice, E., & Barrera, M., Jr. (1995). A longitudinal examination of the reciprocal relations between perceived parenting and adolescents' substance use and externalizing behaviors. *Developmental Psychology, 31,* 322–334.

Stillman, R. J. (1982). In utero exposure to diethylstilbestrol: Adverse effects on the reproductive tract and reproductive performance in male and female offspring. *American Journal of Obstetrics and Gynecology, 142,* 905–921.

Stipek, D. J. (1981). Children's perceptions of their own and their classmates' ability. *Journal of Educational Psychology, 73,* 404–410.

Stipek, D. J., & MacIver, D. (1989). Developmental change in children's assessment of intellectual competence. *Child Development, 60,* 531–538.

Stipek, D. J., Feiler, R., Daniels, D., & Milburn, S. (1995). Effects of different instructional approaches on young children's achievement and motivation. *Child Development, 66,* 209–223.

Stipek, D. J., Gralinski, J. H., & Kopp, C. B. (1990). Self-concept development in the toddler years. *Developmental Psychology, 26,* 972–977.

Stipek, D. J., Recchia, S., & McClintic, S. (1992). Self-evaluation in young children. *Monographs of the Society for Research in Child Development, 57* (1, Serial No. 226).

Stoch, M. B., Smythe, P. M., Moodie, A. D., & Bradshaw, D. (1982). Psychosocial outcome and CT findings after growth undernourishment during infancy: A 20-year developmental study. *Developmental Medicine and Child Neurology, 24,* 419–436.

Stocker, C. M., & Dunn, J. (1994). Sibling relationships in childhood and adolescence. In J. C. DeFries, R. Plomin, & D. W. Fulker (Eds.), *Nature and nurture in middle childhood* (pp. 214–232). Cambridge, MA: Blackwell.

Stocker, C. M., & McHale, S. M. (1992). The nature and family correlates of preadolescents' perceptions of their sibling relationships. *Journal of Social and Personal Relationships, 9,* 179–195.

Stockman, I. J., & Vaughn-Cooke, F. (1992). Lexical elaboration in children's locative action expressions. *Child Development, 63,* 1104–1125.

Stoddart, T., & Turiel, E. (1985). Children's concepts of cross-gender activities. *Child Development, 56,* 1241–1252.

Stodolsky, S. S. (1974). How children find something to do in preschools. *Genetic Psychology Monographs, 90,* 245–303.

Stodolsky, S. S. (1988). *The subject matters.* Chicago: University of Chicago Press.

Stoel-Gammon, C., & Otomo, K. (1986). Babbling development of hearing-impaired and normally hearing subjects. *Journal of Speech and Hearing Disorders, 51,* 33–41.

Stone, L. (1977). *The family, sex, and marriage in England, 1500–1800.* New York: Harper & Row.

Stoneman, Z., Brody, G. H., & MacKinnon, C. E. (1986). Same-sex and cross-sex siblings: Activity choices, roles, behavior, and gender stereotypes. *Sex Roles, 15,* 495–511.

Stormshak, E. A., Bellanti, C. J., Bierman, K. L., & Conduct Problems Prevention Research Group. (1996). The quality of sibling relationships and the development of social competence and behavioral control in aggressive children. *Developmental Psychology, 32,* 79–89.

Story, M., French, S. A., Resnick, M. D., & Blum, R. W. (1995). Ethnic/racial and socioeconomic differences in dieting behaviors and body image perceptions in adolescents. *International Journal of Eating Disorders, 18,* 173–179.

Strain, P. S. (1977). An experimental analysis of peer social initiation on the behavior of withdrawn preschool children: Some training and generalization effects. *Journal of Abnormal Child Psychology, 5,* 445–455.

Strasburger, V. C. (1989). Adolescent sexuality and the media. *Adolescent Gynecology, 36,* 747–773.

Strassberg, Z. (1995). Social information processing in compliance situations by mothers of behavior-problem boys. *Child Development, 66,* 376–389.

Strassberg, Z., Dodge, K., Pettit, G. S., & Bates, J. E. (1994). Spanking in the home and children's subsequent aggression toward kindergarten peers. *Development and Psychopathology, 6,* 445–461.

Strauss, M. S., & Curtis, L. E. (1984). Development of numerical concepts in infancy. In C. Sophian (Ed.), *Origins of cognitive skills: The Eighteenth Annual Carnegie Symposium on Cognition* (pp. 131–155). Hillsdale, NJ: Erlbaum.

Streissguth, A. P., Barr, H. M., Sampson, P. D., & Bookstein, F. L. (1994). Prenatal alcohol and offspring development: The first fourteen years. *Drug & Alcohol Dependence, 36,* 89–99.

Streissguth, A. P., Barr, H. M., Sampson, P. D., Darby, B. L., & Martin, D. C. (1989). IQ at age 4 in relation to maternal alcohol use and smoking during pregnancy. *Developmental Psychology, 25,* 3–11.

Streissguth, A. P., Treder, R., Barr, H. M., Shepard, T., Bleyer, W. A., Sampson, P. D., & Martin, D. (1987). Aspirin and acetaminophen use by pregnant women and subsequent child IQ and attention decrements. *Teratology, 35,* 211–219.

Streitmatter, J. (1993). Gender differences in identity development: An examination of longitudinal data. *Adolescence, 28,* 55–66.

Strickland, D. S., & Ascher, C. (1992). Low-income African-American children and public schooling. In P. W. Jackson (Ed.), *Handbook of research on curriculum* (pp. 609–625). New York: Macmillan.

Strober, M., McCracken, J., & Hanna, G. (1990). Affective disorders. In R. M. Lerner, A. C. Petersen, & J. Brooks-Gunn (Eds.), *The encyclopedia of adolescence* (Vol. 1, pp. 18–25). New York: Garland.

Strutt, G. F., Anderson, D. R., & Well, A. D. (1975). A developmental study of the effects of irrelevant information on speeded classification. *Journal of Experimental Child Psychology, 20,* 127–135.

Stunkard, A. J., & Sørenson, T. I. A. (1993). Obesity and socioeconomic status—a complex relation. *New England Journal of Medicine, 329,* 1036–1037.

Stunkard, A. J., Sørenson, T. I. A., Hanis, C., Teasdale, T. W., Chakraborty, R., Schull, W. J., & Schulsinger, F. (1986). An adoption study of human obesity. *New England Journal of Medicine, 314,* 193–198.

Subbotsky, E. V. (1994). Early rationality and magical thinking in preschoolers: Space and time. *British Journal of Developmental Psychology, 12,* 97–108.

Suess, G. J., Grossmann, K. E., & Sroufe, L. A. (1992). Effects of infant attachment to mother and father on quality of adaptation in preschool: From dyadic to individual organisation of self. *International Journal of Behavioral Development, 15,* 43–65.

Sullivan, H. S. (1953). *The interpersonal theory of psychiatry.* New York: Norton.

Sullivan, L. W. (1987). The risks of the sickle-cell trait: Caution and common sense. *New England Journal of Medicine, 317,* 830–831.

Sullivan, M. L. (1993). Culture and class as determinants of out-of-wedlock childbearing and poverty during late adolescence. *Journal of Research on Adolescence, 3,* 295–316.

Sullivan, S. A., & Birch, L. L. (1990). Pass the sugar, pass the salt: Experience dictates preference. *Developmental Psychology, 26,* 546–551.

Sullivan, S. A., & Birch, L. L. (1994). Infant dietary experience and acceptance of solid foods. *Pediatrics, 93,* 271–277.

Suomi, S. J., & Harlow, H. F. (1978). Early experience and social development in rhesus monkeys. In M. E. Lamb (Ed.) *Social and personality development* (pp. 252–271). New York: Holt, Rinehart & Winston.

Super, C. M. (1981). Behavioral development in infancy. In R. H. Monroe, R. L. Monroe, & B. B. Whiting (Eds.), *Handbook of cross-cultural human development* (pp. 181–270). New York: Garland.

Super, C. M., & Harkness, S. (1982). The infant's niche in rural Kenya and metropolitan America. In L. L. Adler (Ed.), *Cross-cultural research at issue* (pp. 247–255). New York: Academic Press.

Susman, E. J., Inoff-Germain, G., Nottelmann, E. D., Loriaux, D. L., Cutler, G. B., Jr., & Chrousos, G. P. (1987). Hormones, emotional dispositions, and aggressive attributes in young adolescents. *Child Development, 58,* 1114–1134.

Swanson, H. L. (1990). Influence of metacognitive knowledge and aptitude on problem solving. *Journal of Educational Psychology, 82,* 306–314.

Swanson, H. S. W. (1993). Donor anonymity in artificial insemination: Is it still necessary? *Columbia Journal of Law and Social Problems, 27,* 151–190.

Szepkouski, G. M., Gauvain, M., & Carberry, M. (1994). The development of planning skills in children with and without mental retardation. *Journal of Applied Developmental Psychology, 15,* 187–206.

T

Tager-Flusberg, H. (1993). Putting words together: Morphology and syntax in the preschool years. In J. Berko Gleason (Ed.), *The development of language* (pp. 151–193). New York: Macmillan.

Tager-Flusberg, H., & Sullivan, K. (1994). Predicting and explaining behavior: A comparison of autistic, mentally retarded and normal children. *Journal of Child Psychology and Psychiatry, 35,* 1059–1075.

Taitz, L. S. (1983). *The obese child.* Boston: Blackwell.

Takahashi, K. (1990). Are the key assumptions of the "Strange Situation" procedure universal? A view from Japanese research. *Human Development, 33,* 23–30.

Takanishi, R., DeLeon, P., & Pallak, M. S. (1983). Psychology and public policy affecting children, youth, and families. *American Psychologist, 38,* 67–69.

Tamis-LeMonda, C. S., & Bornstein, M. H. (1989). Habituation and maternal encouragement of attention in infancy as predictors of toddler language, play and representational competence. *Child Development, 60,* 738–751.

Tamis-LeMonda, C. S., & Bornstein, M. H. (1994). Specificity in mother–toddler language–play relations across the second year. *Developmental Psychology, 30,* 283–292.

Tanner, J. M. (1990). *Foetus into man* (2nd ed.). Cambridge, MA: Harvard University Press.

Tanner, J. M., & Inhelder, B. (Eds.). (1956). *Discussions on child development* (Vol. 1). London: Tavistock.

Tanner, J. M., & Whitehouse, R. H. (1975). Revised standards for triceps and subscapular skinfolds in British children. *Archives of Disease in Childhood, 50,* 142–145.

Tanner, J. M., Whitehouse, R. H., Cameron, N., Marshall, W. A., Healey, M. J. R., & Goldstein, H. (1983). *Assessment of skeletal maturity and prediction of adult height* (TW2 Method), (2nd. ed.). London: Academic Press.

Tasker, F. L., & Richards, M. P. M. (1994). Adolescents' attitudes toward marriage and marital prospects after parental divorce: A review. *Journal of Adolescent Research, 9,* 340–362.

Tauber, M. A. (1979). Parental socialization techniques and sex differences in children's play. *Child Development, 50,* 225–234.

Taylor, A. R., Asher, S. R., & Williams, G. A. (1987). The social adaptation of mainstreamed mildly retarded children. *Child Development, 58,* 1321–1334.

Taylor, B. J. (1991). A review of epidemiological studies of sudden infant death syndrome in southern New Zealand. *Journal of Paediatric Child Health, 27,* 344–348.

Taylor, J. A., & Sanderson, M. (1995). A reexamination of the risk factors for the sudden infant death syndrome. *Journal of Pediatrics, 126,* 887–891.

Taylor, M., Cartwright, B. S., & Bowden, T. (1991). Perspective taking and theory of mind: Do children predict interpretive diversity as a function of differences in observers' knowledge? *Child Development, 62,* 1334–1351.

Taylor, M., Esbensen, B. M., & Bennett, R. T. (1994). Children's understanding of knowledge acquisition: The tendency for children to report that they have always known what they have just learned. *Child Development, 65,* 1581–1604.

Taylor, M. C., & Hall, J. A. (1982). Psychological androgyny: Theories, methods, and conclusions. *Psychological Bulletin, 92,* 347–366.

Taylor, R. D., & Roberts, D. (1995). Kinship support and maternal and adolescent well-being in economically disadvantaged African-American families. *Child Development, 66,* 1585–1597.

Teberg, A. J., Walther, F. J., & Pena, I. C. (1988). Mortality, morbidity, and outcome of the small-for-gestational-age infant. *Seminar in Perinatology, 12,* 84–94.

Tedder, J. L. (1991). Using the Brazelton Neonatal Assessment Scale to facilitate the parent-infant relationship in a primary care setting. *Nurse Practitioner, 16,* 27–36.

Teele, D. W., Klein, J. O., Chase, C., Menyuk, P., Rosner, B. A., & the Greater Boston Otitis Media Study Group. (1990). Otitis media in infancy and intellectual ability, school achievement, speech, and language at age 7 years. *Journal of Infectious Diseases, 162,* 685–694.

Temple, C. M., & Carney, R. A. (1995). Patterns of spatial functioning in Turner's syndrome. *Cortex, 31,* 109–118.

Tennes, K., Emde, R., Kisley, A., & Metcalf, D. (1972). The stimulus barrier in early infancy: An exploration of some formulations of John Benjamin. In R. Holt and E. Peterfreund (Eds.), *Psychoanalysis and contemporary science* (Vol. 1, pp. 206–234). New York: Macmillan.

Terman, L., & Oden, M. H. (1959). *Genetic studies of genius: Vol. 4. The gifted group at midlife.* Stanford, CA: Stanford University Press.

Terrace, H. S., Petitto, L. A., Sanders, R. J., & Bever, T. G. (1980). On the grammatical capacity of apes. In K. E. Nelson (Ed.), *Children's language* (Vol. 2, pp. 371–495). New York: Cambridge University Press.

Tessler, M. (1991). *Making memories together: The influence of mother–child joint encoding on the development of autobiographical memory style.* Unpublished doctoral dissertation, City University of New York Graduate Center.

Teti, D. M., Gelfand, D. M., Messinger, D. S., & Isabella, R. (1995). Maternal depression and the quality of early attachment: An examination of infants, preschoolers, and their mothers. *Developmental Psychology, 31,* 364–376.

Thakwray, D. E., Smith, M. C., Bodfish, J. W., & Meyers, A. W. (1993). A comparison of behavioral and cognitive-behavioral interventions for bulimia nervosa. *Journal of Consulting and Clinical Psychology, 61,* 639–645.

Thapar, A., Gottesman, I. I., Owen, M. J., O'Donovan, M. C., & McGuffin, P. (1994). The genetics of mental retardation. *British Journal of Psychiatry, 164,* 747–758.

Tharp, R. G. (1989). Psychocultural variables and constants: Effects on teaching and learning in schools. *American Psychologist, 44,* 349–359.

Tharp, R. G. (1994). Intergroup differences among Native Americans in socialization and child cognition: An ethnogenetic analysis. In P. M. Greenfield & R. Cocking (Eds.), *Cross-cultural roots of minority child development* (pp. 87–105). Hillsdale, NJ: Erlbaum.

Tharp, R. G., & Gallimore, R. (1988). *Rousing minds to life: Teaching, learning, and schooling in social context.* New York: Cambridge University Press.

Thatcher, R. W. (1991). Maturation of human frontal lobes: Physiological evidence for staging. *Developmental Neuropsychology, 7,* 397–419.

Thatcher, R. W. (1994). Cyclic cortical reorganization: Origins of human cognitive development. G. Dawson & K. W. Fischer (Eds.), *Human behavior and the developing brain* (pp. 232–266). New York: Guilford.

Thelen, E. (1983). Learning to walk is still an "old" problem: A reply to Zelazo. *Journal of Motor Behavior, 15,* 139–161.

Thelen, E. (1989). The (re)discovery of motor development: Learning new things from an old field. *Developmental Psychology, 25,* 946–949.

Thelen, E. (1992). Development as a dynamic system. *Current Directions in Psychological Science, 1,* 189–193.

Thelen, E. (1994). Three-month-old infants can learn task-specific patterns of interlimb coordination. *Psychological Science, 5,* 280–285.

Thelen, E. (1995). Motor development: A new synthesis. *American Psychologist, 50,* 79–95.

Thelen, E., & Adolph, K. E. (1992). Arnold Gesell: The paradox of nature and nurture. *Developmental Psychology, 28,* 368–380.

Thelen, E., Corbetta, D., Kamm, K., Spencer, J. P., Schneider, K., & Zernicke, R. F. (1993). The transition to reaching: Mapping intention and intrinsic dynamics. *Child Development, 64,* 1058–1098.

Thelen E., Fisher, D. M., & Ridley-Johnson, R. (1984). The relationship between physical growth and a newborn reflex. *Infant Behavior and Development, 7,* 479–493.

Theorell, K., Prechtl, H. F. R., & Vos, J. (1974). A polygraphic study of normal and abnormal newborn infants. *Neuropaediatrie, 5,* 279–317.

Thoman, E. B., & Ingersoll, E. W. (1993). Learning in premature infants. *Developmental Psychology, 29,* 692–700.

Thoman, E. B., & Whitney, M. P. (1990). Behavioral states in infants: Individual differences and individual analyses. In J. Colombo & J. Fagen (Eds.), *Individual differences in infancy* (pp. 113–135). Hillsdale, NJ: Erlbaum.

Thomas, A., & Chess, S. (1977). *Temperament and development.* New York: Brunner/Mazel.

Thomas, A., Chess, S., & Birch, H. G. (1968). *Temperament and behavior disorders in children.* New York: New York University Press.

Thomas, A., Chess, S., & Birch, H. G. (1970, August). The origins of personality. *Scientific American, 223*(2), 102–109.

Thomas, N. G., & Berk, L. E. (1981). Effects of school environments on the development of young children's creativity. *Child Development, 52,* 1152–1162.

Thomas, R. M. (1992). *Comparing theories of child development* (3rd ed.). Belmont, CA: Wadsworth.

Thompson, J. G., & Myers, N. A. (1985). Inferences and recall at ages four and seven. *Child Development, 56,* 1134–1144.

Thompson, L. A., Detterman, D. K., & Plomin, R. (1991). Associations between cognitive abilities and scholastic achievement: Genetic overlap but environmental differences. *Psychological Science, 2,* 158–165.

Thompson, R. A. (1990a). On emotion and self-regulation. In R. A. Thompson (Ed.), *Nebraska Symposium on Motivation* (Vol. 36, pp. 383–483). Lincoln: University of Nebraska Press.

Thompson, R. A. (1990b). Vulnerability in research: A developmental perspective on research risk. *Child Development, 61,* 1–16.

Thompson, R. A. (1992). Developmental changes in research risk and benefit: A changing calculus of concerns. In B. Stanley & J. E. Sieber (Eds.), *Social research on children and adolescents: Ethical issues* (pp. 31–64). Newbury Park, CA: Sage.

Thompson, R. A. (1994). Emotion regulation: A theme in search of definition. In N. A. Fox (Ed.), The development of emotion regulation: Biological and behavioral considerations. *Monographs of the Society for Research in Child Development, 59*(2–3, Serial No. 240).

Thompson, R. A., Lamb, M., & Estes, D. (1982). Stability of infant–mother attachment and its relationship to changing life circumstances in an unselected middle-class sample. *Child Development, 53,* 144–148.

Thompson, R. A., & Limber, S. (1991). "Social anxiety" in infancy: Stranger wariness and separation distress. In H. Leitenberg (Ed.), *Handbook of social and evaluation anxiety* (pp. 85–137). New York: Plenum.

Thompson, R. A., Tinsley, B. R., Scalora, M. J., & Parke, R. D. (1989). Grandparents' visitation rights: Legalizing the ties that bind. *American Psychologist, 44,* 1217–1222.

Thorndike, R. L., Hagen, E. P., & Sattler, J. M. (1986). *The Stanford-Binet Intelligence Scale: Fourth edition. Guide for administering and scoring.* Chicago: Riverside Publishing.

Thornton, M., & Taylor, R. (1988). Black American perceptions of black Africans. *Ethnic and Racial Studies, 11,* 139–150.

Thurstone, L. L. (1938). *Primary mental abilities.* Chicago: University of Chicago Press.

Tietjen, A., & Walker, L. (1985). Moral reasoning and leadership among men in a Papua, New Guinea village. *Developmental Psychology, 21,* 982–992.

Tizard, B., & Hodges, J. (1978). The effect of early institutional rearing on the development of eight-year-old children. *Journal of Child Psychology and Psychiatry, 19,* 99–118.

Tizard, B., & Rees, J. (1975). The effect of early institutional rearing on the behaviour problems and affectional relationships of four-year-old children. *Journal of Child Psychology and Psychiatry, 16,* 61–73.

Tolarova, M. (1986). Cleft lip and palate and isolated cleft palate in Czechoslovakia. *Advances in Bioscience, 61,* 251–268.

Tolson, T. F. J., & Wilson, M. N. (1990). The impact of two- and three-generational black family structure on perceived family climate. *Child Development, 61,* 416–428.

Tomasello, M. (1995). Language is not an instinct. *Cognitive Development, 10,* 131–156.

Tomasello, M., & Akhtar, N. (1995). Two-year-olds use pragmatic cues to differentiate reference to objects and actions. *Cognitive Development, 10,* 201–224.

Tomasello, M., & Barton, M. (1994). Learning words in nonostensive contexts. *Developmental Psychology, 30,* 639–650.

Tomasello, M., Mannle, S., & Kruger, A. C. (1986). Linguistic environment of 1- to 2-year-old twins. *Developmental Psychology, 22,* 169–176.

Toner, I. J., & Smith, R. A. (1977). Age and overt verbalization in delay maintenance behavior in children. *Journal of Experimental Child Psychology, 24,* 123–128.

Torrance, E. P. (1980). *The Torrance Tests of Creative Thinking.* New York: Scholastic Testing Service.

Torrance, E. P. (1988). The nature of creativity as manifest in its testing. In R. J. Sternberg (Ed.), *The nature of creativity: Contemporary psychological perspectives* (pp. 43–75). New York: Cambridge University Press.

Touris, M., Kromelow, S., & Harding, C. (1995). Mother–firstborn attachment and the birth of a sibling. *American Journal of Orthopsychiatry, 65,* 293–297.

Touwen, B. C. L. (1978). Variability and stereotype in normal and deviant development. In J. Apley (Ed.), *Care of the handicapped child* (pp. 99–110). Philadelphia: Lippincott.

Touwen, B. C. L. (1984). Primitive reflexes—conceptual or semantic problem? In H. F. R. Prechtl (Ed.), *Continuity of neural functions from prenatal to postnatal life* (Clinics in Developmental Medicine, No. 94, pp. 115–125). Philadelphia: Lippincott.

Tower, R. B., Singer, D. G., Singer, J. L., & Biggs, A. (1979). Differential effects of television programming on preschoolers' cognition, imagination, and social play. *American Journal of Orthopsychiatry, 49,* 265–281.

Trause, M. A. (1977). Stranger responses: Effects of familiarity, stranger's approach, and sex of infant. *Child Development, 48,* 1657–1661.

Trevethan, S. D., & Walker, L. J. (1989). Hypothetical versus real-life moral reasoning among psychopathic and delinquent youth. *Development and Psychopathology, 1,* 91–103.

Triandis, H. C. (1989). The self and social behavior in differing cultural contexts. *Psychological Review, 96,* 506–520.

Trickett, P. K., Aber, J. L., Carlson, V., & Cicchetti, D. (1991). Relationship of socioeconomic status to the etiology and developmental sequelae of physical child abuse. *Developmental Psychology, 27,* 148–158.

Trinkoff, A., & Parks, P. L. (1993). Prevention strategies for infant walker-related injuries. *Public Health Reports, 108,* 784–788.

Trivers, R. L. (1971). The evolution of reciprocal altruism. *Quarterly Review of Biology, 46,* 35–57.

Tronick, E. Z. (1989). Emotions and emotional communication in infants. *American Psychologist, 44,* 115–123.

Tronick, E. Z., & Cohn, J. F. (1989). Infant–mother face-to-face interaction: Age and gender differences in coordination and the occurrence of miscoordination. *Child Development, 60,* 85–92.

Tronick, E. Z., Thomas, R. B., & Daltabuit, M. (1994). The Quechua manta pouch: A caretaking practice for buffering the Peruvian infant against the multiple stressors of high altitude. *Child Development, 65,* 1005–1013.

Troy, M., & Sroufe, L. A. (1987). Victimization among preschoolers: Role of attachment relationship history. *Journal of the American Academy of Child and Adolescent Psychiatry, 26,* 166–172.

Tseng, W., Kuotai, T., Hsu, J., Jinghua, C., Lian, Y., & Kameoka, V. (1988). Family planning and child mental health in China: The Nanjing Survey. *American Journal of Psychiatry, 145,* 1396–1403.

Tudge, J. R. H. (1992). Processes and consequences of peer collaboration: A Vygotskian analysis. *Child Development, 63,* 1364–1379.

Tudge, J. R. H., & Winterhoff, P. A. (1993). Vygotsky, Piaget, and Bandura: Perspectives on the relations between the social world and cognitive development. *Human Development, 36,* 61–81.

Tulving, E. (1972). Episodic and semantic memory. In E. Tulving & W. Donaldson (Eds.), *Organization of memory* (pp. 382–403). New York: Academic Press.

Tulviste, P. (1991). *Cultural-historical development of verbal thinking: A psychological study.* Commack, NY: Nova Science Publishers.

Tunmer, W. E., & Nesdale, A. R. (1982). The effects of digraphs and pseudo-words on phonemic segmentation in young children. *Journal of Applied Psycholinguistics, 3,* 299–311.

Turiel, E. (1983). *The development of social knowledge: Morality and convention.* New York: Cambridge University Press.

Turiel, E., Smetana, J. G., & Killen, M. (1991). Social contexts in social cognitive development. In W. M. Kurtines & J. L. Gewirtz (Eds.), *Handbook of moral behavior and development* (Vol. 2, pp. 307–332). Hillsdale, NJ: Erlbaum.

Turk, J. (1995). Fragile X syndrome. *Archives of Diseases of Children, 72,* 3–5.

Turkheimer, E., & Gottesman, I. I. (1991). Individual differences and the canalization of human behavior. *Developmental Psychology, 27,* 18–22.

Turner, P. J., & Gervai, J. (1995). A multidimensional study of gender typing in preschool children and their parents: Personality, attitudes, preferences, behavior, and cultural differences. *Developmental Psychology, 31,* 759–772.

Turner, P. J., Gervai, J. & Hinde, R. A. (1993). Gender typing in young children: Preferences, behaviour and cultural differences. *British Journal of Developmental Psychology, 11,* 323–342.

Tyc, V. L., Fairclough, D., Fletcher, B., & Leigh, L. (1995). Children's distress during magnetic resonance imaging procedures. *Children's Health Care, 24,* 5–19.

Tzuriel, D. (1989). Inferential thinking modifiability in young socially disadvantaged and advantaged children. *International Journal of Dynamic Assessment and Instruction, 1,* 65–80.

U

U.S. Bureau of the Census (1995). *Statistical abstract of the United States* (115th ed.). Washington, DC: U.S. Government Printing Office.

U.S. Centers for Disease Control. (1992). *HIV/AIDS surveillance.* Washington, DC: U.S. Government Printing Office.

U.S. Centers for Disease Control. (1994). *HIV/AIDS surveillance.* Washington, DC: U.S. Government Printing Office.

U.S. Centers for Disease Control. (1995). *HIV/AIDS surveillance.* Washington, DC: U.S. Government Printing Office.

U.S. Conference of Mayors. (1994). *Status report on hunger and homelessness in America's cities: 1994.* Washington, DC: U.S. Government Printing Office.

U.S. Department of Health and Human Services. (1995a). *Advance data from vital and health statistics of the National Center for Health Statistics.* Washington, DC: U.S. Government Printing Office.

U.S. Department of Health and Human Services. (1995b). *Vital statistics of the United States, 1992.* Washington, DC: U.S. Government Printing Office.

U.S. Department of Health and Human Services, National Institute on Drug Abuse. (1994). *National survey results on drug use from Monitoring the Future study: Vol. 1. Secondary school students.* Washington, DC: U.S. Government Printing Office.

U.S. Department of Justice. (1995). *Crime in the United States.* Washington, DC: U.S. Government Printing Office.

U.S. Department of Labor, Bureau of Labor Statistics (1996, February). *Consumer Price Index. Monthly Labor Review, 119*(2).

U.S. Office of Management and Budget. (1995). *Budget of the United States government.* Washington, DC: U.S. Government Printing Office.

Udry, J. R. (1990). Hormonal and social determinants of adolescent sexual initiation. In J. Bancroft & J. M. Reinisch (Eds.), *Adolescence and puberty* (pp. 70–87). New York: Oxford University Press.

Ullian, D. Z. (1976). The development of conceptions of masculinity and femininity. In B. Lloyd & J. Archer (Eds.), *Exploring sex differences* (pp. 25–47). London: Academic Press.

Underwood, M. K., Coie, J. D., & Herbsman, C. R. (1992). Display rules for anger and aggression in school-age children. *Child Development, 63,* 366–380.

Unger, R. K., & Crawford, M. (1993). Sex and gender—The troubled relationship between terms and concepts. *Psychological Science, 4,* 122–124.

Unger, R., Kreeger, L., & Christoffel, K. K. (1990). Childhood obesity: Medical and familial correlates and age of onset. *Clinical Pediatrics, 29,* 368–372.

United Nations. (1991). *World population trends and policies: 1991 monitoring report.* New York: Author.

Urberg, K. A. (1979, March). *The development of androgynous sex-role concepts in young children.* Paper presented at the biennial meeting of the Society for Research in Child Development, San Francisco.

Urberg, K. A., Degirmencioglue, S. M., Tolson, J. M., & Halliday-Scher, K. (1995). The structure of adolescent peer networks. *Developmental Psychology, 31,* 540–547.

Uribe, F. M. T., LeVine, R. A., & LeVine, S. E. (1994). Maternal behavior in a Mexican community: The changing environments of children. In P. M. Greenfield & R. R. Cocking (Eds.), *Cross-cultural roots of minority child development* (pp. 41–54). Hillsdale, NJ: Erlbaum.

Uttal, D. H., & Wellman, H. M. (1989). Young children's representation of spatial information acquired from maps. *Developmental Psychology, 25,* 128–138.

Užgiris, I. C., & Hunt, J. McV. (1975). *Assessment in infancy: Ordinal scales of psychological development.* Urbana: University of Illinois Press.

V

Vaidyanathan, R. (1988). Development of forms and functions of interrogatives in children: A language study of Tamil. *Journal of Child Language, 15,* 533–549.

Valian, V. V . (1986). Syntactic categories in the speech of young children. *Developmental Psychology, 22,* 562–579.

Valian, V. V. (1993). *Parental replies: Linguistic status and didactic role.* Cambridge, MA: MIT Press.

Valian, V. (1996). *Parental replies: Linguistic status and didactic role.* Cambridge, MA: MIT Press.

van Dam, M., & van IJzendoorn, M. H. (1988). Measuring attachment security: Concurrent and predictive validity on the parental attachment Q-set. *Journal of Genetic Psychology, 149,* 447–457.

van den Boom, D. C. (1995). Do first-year intervention effects endure? Follow-up during toddlerhood of a sample of Dutch irritable infants. *Child Development, 66,* 1798–1816.

van den Boom, D. C., & Hoeksma, J. B. (1994). The effect of infant irritability on mother–infant interaction: A growth-curve analysis. *Developmental Psychology, 30,* 581–590.

Van de Perre, P., Simonson, A., Hitimana, D., Davis, F., Msellati, P., Mukamabano, J., Van Goethem, C., Karita, E., & Lepage, P. (1993). Infective and anti-infective properties of breastmilk from HIV-1-infected women. *Lancet, 341,* 914–918.

van der Veer, R., & Valsiner, J. (1991). *Understanding Vygotsky: A quest for synthesis.* London: Routledge.

Van Dyke, D. C., Lang, D. J., Heide, F., van Duyne, S., & Soucek, M. J. (Eds.). (1990). *Clinical perspectives in the management of Down syndrome.* New York: Springer-Verlag.

van IJzendoorn, M. H. (1995a). Adult attachment representations, parental responsiveness, and infant attachment: A meta-analysis on the predictive validity of the Adult Attachment Interview. *Psychological Bulletin, 117,* 387–403.

van IJzendoorn, M. H. (1995b). Of the way we are: On temperament, attachment, and the transmission gap: A rejoinder to Fox (1995). *Psychological Bulletin, 117,* 411–415.

van IJzendoorn, M. H., & Bakermans-Kranenburg, M. J. (1996). Adult Attachment Interview classifications in mothers, fathers, adolescents, and clinical groups: A meta-analytic search for normative data. *Journal of Consulting and Clinical Psychology, 64.*

van IJzendoorn, M. H., & Kroonenberg, P. M. (1988). Cross-cultural patterns of attachment: A meta-analysis of the Strange Situation. *Child Development, 59,* 147–156.

van IJzendoorn, M. H., Goldberg, S., Kroonenberg, P. M., & Frenkel, O. J. (1992). The relative effects of maternal and child problems on the quality of attachment: A meta-analysis of attachment in clinical samples. *Child Development, 63,* 840–858.

van IJzendoorn, M. H., Kranenburg, M. J., Zwart-Woudstra, A., van Busschbach, A. M., & Lambermon, M. W. E. (1991). Parental attachment and children's socio-emotional development: Some findings on the validity of the adult attachment interview in The Netherlands. *International Journal of Behavioral Development, 14,* 375–394.

Vandell, D. L. (1996). *Social behavior and interaction in 6- to 12-month-olds.* Unpublished manuscript, University of Texas at Dallas.

Vandell, D. L., & Corasaniti, M. A. (1988). The relation between third-graders' after school care and social, academic, and emotional functioning. *Child Development, 59,* 868–875.

Vandell, D. L., & Hembree, S. E. (1994). Peer social status and friendship: Independent contributors to children's social and academic adjustment. *Merrill-Palmer Quarterly, 40,* 461–477.

Vandell, D. L., & Mueller, E. C. (1995). Peer play and friendships during the first two years. In H. C. Foot, A. J. Chapman, & J. R. Smith (Eds.), *Friendship and social relations in children* (pp. 181–208). New Brunswick, NJ: Transaction.

Vandell, D. L., & Powers, C. (1983). Day care quality and children's free play activities. *American Journal of Orthopsychiatry, 53,* 293–300.

Vandell, D. L., & Ramanan, J. (1991). Children of the National Longitudinal Survey of Youth: Choices in after-school care and child development. *Developmental Psychology, 27,* 637–643.

Vandell, D. L., & Wilson, K. S. (1987). Infants' interactions with mother, sibling, and peer: Contrasts and relations between interaction systems. Child Development, 58, 176–186.

Vandell, D. L., Wilson, K. S., & Buchanan, N. R. (1980). Peer interaction in the first year of life: An examination of its structure, content, and sensitivity to toys. *Child Development, 51,* 481–488.

Vanfossen, B., Jones, J., & Spade, J. (1987). Curriculum tracking and status maintenance. *Sociology of Education, 60,* 104–122.

Vasudev, J., & Hummel, R. C. (1987). Moral stage sequence and principled reasoning in an Indian sample. *Human Development, 30,* 105–118.

Vaughn, B. E., Bradley, C. F., Joffe, L. S., Seifer, R., & Barglow, P. (1987). Maternal characteristics measured prenatally are predictive of ratings of temperamental "difficulty" on the Carey Infant Temperament Questionnaire. *Developmental Psychology, 23,* 152–161.

Vaughn, B. E., Kopp, C. B., & Krakow, J. B. (1984). The emergence and consolidation of self-control from eighteen to thirty months of age: Normative trends and individual differences. *Child Development, 55,* 990–1004.

Vaughn, B. E., Stevenson-Hinde, J., Waters, E., Kotsaftis, A., Lefever, G. B., Shouldice, A., Trudel, M., & Belsky, J. (1992). Attachment security and temperament in infancy and early childhood: Some conceptual clarifications. *Developmental Psychology, 28,* 463–473.

Vaughn, B. E., & Waters, E. (1990). Attachment behavior at home and in the lab: Q-sort observations and Strange Situation classifications of one-year-olds. *Child Development, 61,* 1965–1973.

Vecchi, V. (1993). The role of the atelierista. In C. Edwards, L. Gandini, & G. Forman (Eds.), *The hundred languages of children: The Reggio Emilia approach to early childhood education* (pp. 119–127). Norwood, NJ: Ablex.

Ventura, S. J. (1989). Trends and variations in first births to older women in the United States, 1970–86. *Vital and Health Statistics* (Series 21). Hyattsville, MD: U.S. Department of Health and Human Services.

Verhulst, F. C., Althaus, M., & Versluis-Den Bieman, H. J. M. (1990). Problem behavior in international adoptees: I. An epidemiological study. *Journal of the American Academy of Child and Adolescent Psychiatry, 29,* 94–103.

Verhulst, F. C., & Versluis-den Bieman, H. J. M. (1995). Developmental course of problem behaviors in adolescent adoptees. *Journal of the American Academy of Child and Adolescent Psychiatry,* 34, 151–159.

Vernon, P. A. (1981). Level I and Level II: A review. *Educational Psychologist, 16,* 45–64.

Vernon, P. A. (1987). Level I and Level II revisited. In S. Modgil & C. Modgil (Eds.), *Arthur Jensen: Consensus and controversy* (pp. 17–24). New York: Falmer Press.

Vernon, P. A. (1993). Intelligence and neural efficiency. In D. K. Detterman (Ed.), *Current topics in human intelligence* (Vol. 3, pp. 171–187). Norwood, NJ: Ablex.

Vernon, P. A., & Mori, M. (1992). Intelligence, reaction times, and peripheral nerve conduction velocity. *Intelligence, 8,* 273–288.

Vihman, M. M. (1993). Phonological development. In J. E. Bernthal & N. Bankson (Eds.), *Articulation disorders* (pp. 63–146). Englewood Cliffs, NJ: Prentice-Hall.

Vihman, M. M., Kay, E., Boysson-Bardies, B. de, Durand, C., & Sundberg, U. (1994). External sources of individual differences? A cross-linguistic analysis of the phonetics of mothers' speech to 1-year-old children. *Developmental Psychology, 30,* 651–662.

Visher, J. S. (1994). Stepfamilies: A work in progress. *American Journal of Family Therapy, 22,* 337–344.

Vitaro, F., & Pelletier, D. (1991). Assessment of children's social problem-solving skills in hypothetical and actual conflict situations. *Journal of Abnormal Child Psychology, 19,* 505–518.

Vogel, D. A., Lake, M. A., Evans, S., & Karraker, H. (1991). Children's and adults' sex-stereotyped perceptions of infants. *Sex Roles, 24,* 605–616.

Vohr, B. R., & Garcia-Coll, C. T. (1988). Follow-up studies of high-risk low-birth-weight infants: Changing trends. In H. E. Fitzgerald, B. M. Lester, & M. W. Yogman (Eds.), *Theory and research in behavioral pediatrics* (pp. 1–65). New York: Plenum.

Volling, B. L., & Belsky, J. (1992). Contribution of mother–child and father–child relationships to the quality of sibling interaction: A longitudinal study. *Child Development, 63,* 1209–1222.

Vorhees, C. V. (1986). Principles of behavioral teratology. In E. P. Riley & C. V. Vorhees (Eds.), *Handbook of behavioral teratology* (pp. 23–48). New York: Plenum.

Vorhees, C. V., & Mollnow, E. (1987). Behavioral teratogenesis: Long-term influences on behavior from early exposure to environmental agents. In J. D. Osofsky (Ed.), *Handbook of infant development* (2nd ed., pp. 913–971). New York: Wiley.

Voydanoff, P., & Donnelly, B. W. (1990). *Adolescent sexuality and pregnancy.* Newbury Park, CA: Sage.

Voyer, D., Voyer, S., & Bryden, M. P. (1995). Magnitude of sex differences in spatial abilities: A meta-analysis and consideration of critical variables. *Psychological Bulletin, 117,* 250–270.

Vuchinich, S., Hetherington, E. M., Vuchinich, R. A., & Clingempeel, W. G. (1991). Parent-child interaction and gender differences in early adolescents' adaptation to stepfamilies. Developmental Psychology, 27, 618–626.

Vurpillot, E. (1968). The development of scanning strategies and their relation to visual differentiation. *Journal of Experimental Child Psychology, 6,* 632–650.

Vygotsky, L. S. (1978). *Mind in society: The development of higher mental processes.* Cambridge, MA: Harvard University Press. (Original works published 1930, 1933, and 1935)

Vygotsky, L. S. (1986). *Thought and language* (A. Kozulin, Trans.). Cambridge, MA: MIT Press. (Original work published 1934)

W

Waber, D. P. (1976). Sex differences in cognition: A function of maturation rate? *Science, 192,* 572–574.

Wachs, T. D. (1975). Relation of infants' performance on Piaget scales between twelve and twenty-four months and their Stanford-Binet performance at thirty-one months. *Child Development, 46,* 929–935.

Wachs, T. D. (1994). Commentary on Plomin, R. (1994). Genetics, nurture and social development: An alternative viewpoint. *Social Development, 3,* 66–70.

Wachs, T. D., Signman, M. Bishry, Z., Moussa, W., Neumann, C., Buibo, N., & McDonald, M. A. (1992). Caregiver–child interaction patterns in two cultures in relation to nutritional intake. *International Journal of Behavioral Development, 15,* 1–8.

Waddington, C. H. (1957). *The strategy of the genes.* London: Allen and Unwin.

Wagner, B. M., & Phillips, D. A. (1992). Beyond beliefs: Parent and child behaviors and children's perceived academic competence. *Child Development, 63,* 1380–1391.

Wagner, M. E., Schubert, H. J. P., & Schubert, D. S. P. (1985). Family size effects: A review. *Journal of Genetic Psychology, 146,* 65–78.

Wagner, M. E., Schubert, H. J. P., & Schubert, D. S. P. (1993). Sex-of-sibling effects: Part 1. Gender role, intelligence, achievement, and creativity. In Hayne W. Reese (Ed.), *Advances in child development and behavior* (Vol. 24, pp. 181–214). San Diego: Academic Press.

Wagner, R. K., & Sternberg, R. J. (1990). Street smarts. In K. E. Clark & M. B. Clark (Eds.), *Measures of leadership* (pp. 493–504). West Orange, NJ: Leadership Library of America.

Walberg, H. J. (1986). Synthesis of research on teaching. In M. C. Wittrock (Ed.), *Handbook of research on teaching* (3rd ed., pp. 214–229). New York: Macmillan.

Walden, T. A., & Ogan, T. A. (1988). The development of social referencing. *Child Development, 59,* 1230–1240.

Waldman, I. D., Weinberg, R. A., & Scarr, S. (1994). Racial-group differences in IQ in the Minnesota Transracial Adoption Study: A reply to Levin and Lynn. *Intelligence, 19,* 29–44.

Walk, R. D., & Gibson, E. J. (1961). A comparative and analytic study of visual depth perception. *Psychological Monographs, 75*(15, Serial No. 519).

Walker, D., Greenwood, C., Hart, B., & Carta, J. (1994). Prediction of school outcomes based on early language production and socioeconomic factors. *Child Development, 65,* 606–621.

Walker, L. J. (1980). Cognitive and perspective-taking prerequisites for moral development. *Child Development, 51,* 131–139.

Walker, L. J. (1988). The development of moral reasoning. In R. Vasta (Ed.), *Annals of child development* (Vol. 5, pp. 33–78). Greenwich, CT: JAI Press.

Walker, L. J. (1989). A longitudinal study of moral reasoning. *Child Development, 60,* 157–166.

Walker, L. J. (1995). Sexism in Kohlberg's moral psychology? In W. M. Kurtines & J. L. Gewirtz (Eds.), *Moral development: An introduction* (pp. 83–107). Boston: Allyn and Bacon.

Walker, L. J., & Richards, B. S. (1979). Stimulating transitions in moral reasoning as a function of stage of cognitive development. *Developmental Psychology, 15,* 95–103.

Walker, L. J., & Taylor, J. H. (1991a). Family interactions and the development of moral reasoning. *Child Development, 62,* 264–283.

Walker, L. J., & Taylor, J. H. (1991b). Stage transitions in moral reasoning: A longitudinal study of developmental processes. *Developmental Psychology, 27,* 330–337.

Walker-Andrews, A. S. (1986). Intermodal perception of expressive behaviors: Relation of eye and voice? *Developmental Psychology, 22,* 373–377.

Walker-Andrews, A. S., & Grolnick, W. (1983). Discrimination of vocal expressions by young infants. *Infant Behavior and Development, 6,* 491–498.

Waller, M. B. (1993, January). Helping crack-affected children succeed. *Educational Leadership, 50*(4), 57–60.

Wallerstein, J. S., & Corbin, S. B. (1989). Daughters of divorce: Report from a ten-year follow-up. *American Journal of Orthopsychiatry, 59,* 593–604.

Wallerstein, J. S., Corbin, S. B., & Lewis, J. M. (1988). Children of divorce: A ten-year study. In E. M. Hetherington & J. Arasteh (Eds.), *Impact of divorce, single parenting, and stepparenting on children* (pp. 198–214). Hillsdale, NJ: Erlbaum.

Wallerstein, J. S., & Kelly, J. B. (1980). *Surviving the break-up: How children and parents cope with divorce.* New York: Basic Books.

Walsh, M. E., & Bibace, R. (1991). Children's conceptions of AIDS: A developmental analysis. *Journal of Pediatric Psychology, 16,* 273–285.

Walters, R. H., & Andres, D. (1967). *Punishment procedures and self-control.* Paper presented at the annual meeting of the American Psychological Association, Washington, D.C.

Walton, G. E., & Bower, T. G. R. (1993). Amodal representations of speech in infants. *Infant Behavior and Development, 16,* 233–243.

Wanska, S. K., & Bedrosian, J. L. (1985). Conversational structure and topic performance in mother–child interaction. *Journal of Speech and Hearing Research, 28,* 579–584.

Warburton, D. (1989). The effect of maternal age on the frequency of trisomy: Change in meiosis or in utero selection? In T. J. Hassold & C. J. Epstein (Eds.), *Molecular and cytogenetic studies of nondisjunction* (pp. 165–181). New York: Alan R. Liss.

Ward, S., Wackman, D., & Wartella, E. (1977). *How children learn to buy: The development of consumer information-processing skills.* Beverly Hills, CA: Sage.

Wark, G. R., & Krebs, D. L. (1996). Gender and dilemma differences in real-life moral judgment. *Developmental Psychology, 32,* 220–230.

Warren, A. R., & Tate, C. S. (1992). Egocentrism in children's telephone conversations. In R. M. Diaz & L. E. Berk (Eds.), *Private speech: From social interaction to self-regulation* (pp. 245–264). Hillsdale, NJ: Erlbaum.

Wartner, U. G., Grossmann, K., Fremmer-Bombik, E., & Suess, G. (1994).

Attachment patterns at age six in south Germany: Predictability from infancy and implications for preschool behavior. *Child Development, 65,* 1014–1027.

Wasserman, G., Graziano, J. H., Factor-Litvac, P., Popovac, D., Morina, N. & Musabegovic, A. (1992). Independent effects of lead exposure and iron deficiency anemia on developmental outcome at age 2 years. *Journal of Pediatrics, 121,* 695–703.

Waterman, A. S. (1985). Identity in context of adolescent psychology. In A. S. Waterman (Ed.), *New Directions for Child Development* (No. 30, pp. 5–24). San Francisco: Jossey-Bass.

Waterman, A. S. (1989). Curricula interventions for identity change: Substantive and ethical considerations. *Journal of Adolescence, 12,* 389–400.

Waters, E., Vaughn, B. E., Posada, G., & Kondo-Ikemura K. (Eds.). (1995). Caregiving, cultural, and cognitive perspectives on secure-base behavior and working models: New growing points of attachment theory and research. *Monographs of the Society for Research in Child Development, 60*(2–3, Serial No. 244).

Watson, D. J. (1989). Defining and describing whole language. *Elementary School Journal, 90,* 129–141.

Watson, J. B., & Raynor, R. (1920). Conditioned emotional reactions. *Journal of Experimental Psychology, 3,* 1–14.

Waxman, S. R., & Hatch, T. (1992). Beyond the basics: Preschool children label objects flexibly at multiple hierarchical levels. *Journal of Child Language, 19,* 153–166.

Waxman, S. R., & Senghas, A. (1992). Relations among word meanings in early lexical development. *Developmental Psychology, 28,* 862–873.

Weber-Fox, C. M., & Neville, H. J. (1992). Maturational constraints on cerebral specialization for language processing: ERP and behavioral evidence in bilingual speakers. *Society for Neuroscience Abstracts, 18.*

Wechsler, D. (1989). *Manual for the Wechsler Preschool and Primary Scale of Intelligence–Revised.* New York: The Psychological Corporation.

Wechsler, D. (1991). *Manual for the Wechsler Intelligence Test for Children–III.* New York: The Psychological Corporation.

Wegman, M. E. (1994). Annual summary of vital statistics—1993. *Pediatrics, 95,* 792–803.

Wehren, A., De Lisi, R., & Arnold, M. (1981). The development of noun definition. *Journal of Child Language, 8,* 165–175.

Weideger, P. (1976). *Menstruation and menopause.* New York: Knopf.

Weinberg, M. K., & Tronick, E. Z. (1994). Beyond the face: An empirical study of infant affective configurations of facial, vocal, gestural, and regulatory behaviors. *Child Development, 65,* 1503–1515.

Weinberg, R. A., Scarr, S., & Waldman, I. D. (1992). The Minnesota Transracial Adoption Study: A follow-up of IQ test performance at adolescence. *Intelligence, 16,* 117–135.

Weinraub, M., Clemens, L. P., Sockloff, A., Ethridge, T., Gracely, E., & Myers, B. (1984). The development of sex role stereotypes in the third year: Relationships to gender labeling, gender identity, sex-typed toy preference, and family characteristics. *Child Development, 55,* 1493–1503.

Weinstein, R. S., Marshall, H. H., Sharp, L., & Botkin, M. (1987). Pygmalion and the student: Age and classroom differences in children's awareness of teacher expectations. Child Development, 58, 1079–1093.

Weisberg, R. W. (1993). *Creativity: Beyond the myth of genius.* New York: Freeman.

Weisner, T. S., & Gallimore, R. (1977). My brother's keeper: Child and sibling caretaking. *Current Anthropology, 18,* 169–190.

Weisner, T. S., & Wilson-Mitchell, J. E. (1990). Nonconventional family life-styles and sex typing in six-year-olds. *Child Development, 61,* 1915–1933.

Weiss, B., Dodge, K. A., Bates, J. E., & Pettit, G. S. (1992). Some consequences of early harsh discipline: Child aggression and a maladaptive social information processing style. *Child Development, 63,* 1321–1335.

Weisz, J. R., Chaiyasit, W., Weiss, B., Eastman, K. L., & Jackson, E. W. (1995). A multimethod study of problem behavior among Thai and American children in school: Teacher reports versus direct observations. *Child Development, 66,* 402–415.

Wellman, H. M. (1977). Preschoolers' understanding of memory relevant variables. *Child Development, 48,* 13–21.

Wellman, H. M. (1985). The child's theory of mind: The development of conceptions of cognition. In S. R. Yussen (Ed.), *The growth of reflection in children* (pp. 169–206). Orlando, FL: Academic Press.

Wellman, H. M. (1990). *The child's theory of mind.* Cambridge, MA: MIT Press.

Wellman, H. M., & Banerjee, M. (1991). Mind and emotion: Children's understanding of the emotional consequences of beliefs and desires. *British Journal of Developmental Psychology, 9,* 191–214.

Wellman, H. M., & Bartsch, K. (1988). Young children's reasoning about beliefs. *Cognition, 30,* 239–277.

Wellman, H. M., & Gelman, S. A. (1992). Cognitive development: Foundational theories of core domains. *Annual Review of Psychology, 43,* 337–375.

Wellman, H. M., & Hickling, A. K. (1994). The mind's "I": Children's conception of the mind as an active agent. *Child Development, 65,* 1564–1580.

Wellman, H. M., Somerville, S. C., & Haake, R. J. (1979). Development of search procedures in real-life spatial environments. *Developmental Psychology, 15,* 530–542.

Wellman, H. M., & Woolley, J. (1990). From simple desires to ordinary beliefs: The early development of everyday psychology. *Cognition, 35,* 245–275.

Welsh, M. C., Pennington, B. F., Ozonoff, S., Rouse, B., & McCabe, E. R. B. (1990). Neuropsychology of early-treated phenylketonuria: Specific executive function deficits. *Child Development, 61,* 1697–1713.

Wentzel, K. R., & Asher, S. R. (1995). The academic lives of neglected, rejected, popular, and controversial children. *Child Development, 66,* 754–763.

Werker, J. F., & Pegg, J. E. (1992). Infant speech perception and phonological acquisition. In C. A. Ferguson, L. Menn, & C. Stoel-Gammon (Eds.), *Phonological development: Models, research, implications* (pp. 285–311). Timonium, MD: York Press.

Werner, E. E. (1989). Children of the Garden Island. *Scientific American, 260*(4), 106–111.

Werner, E. E. (1993). Risk, resilience, and recovery: Perspectives from the Kauai Longitudinal Study. *Development and Psychopathology, 5,* 503–515.

Werner, E. E., & Smith, R. S. (1982). Vulnerable but invincible. New York: McGraw-Hill.

Werner, E. E., & Smith, R. S. (1992). *Overcoming the odds: High risk children from birth to adulthood.* Ithaca, NY: Cornell University Press.

Wertsch, J. V., & Tulviste, P. (1992). L. S. Vygotsky and contemporary developmental psychology. *Developmental Psychology, 28,* 548–557.

Whalen, C. K., & Henker, B. (1991). Therapies for hyperactive children: Comparisons, combinations, and compromises. *Journal of Consulting and Clinical Psychology, 59,* 126–137.

Whalen, C. K., Henker, B., Burgess, S., & O'Neil, R. (1995). Young people talk about AIDS: "When you get sick, you stay sick." *Journal of Clinical Child Psychology, 24,* 338–345.

Wheeler, M. D. (1991). Physical changes of puberty. *Endocrinology and Metabolism Clinics of North America, 20,* 1–14.

White, B. (1990). *The first three years of life.* New York: Prentice-Hall.

White, B., & Held, R. (1966). Plasticity of sensorimotor development in the human infant. In J. F. Rosenblith & W. Allinsmith (Eds.), *The causes of behavior* (pp. 60–70). Boston: Allyn and Bacon.

White, K. R., Taylor, M. J., & Moss, V. D. (1992). Does research support claims about the benefits of involving parents in early intervention programs? *Review of Educational Research, 62,* 91–125.

White, R. W. (1959). Motivation reconsidered: The concept of competence. *Psychological Review, 66,* 297–333.

White, S. H. (1976). The active organism in theoretical behaviorism. *Human Development, 19,* 99–107.

White, S. H. (1992). G. Stanley Hall: From philosophy to developmental psychology. *Developmental Psychology, 28,* 25–34.

Whitebook, M., Howes, C., & Phillips, D. (1990). *Who cares? Child care teachers and the quality of care in America.* Oakland, CA: Child Care Employee Project.

Whitehurst, G. J., Arnold, D. S., Epstein, J. N., Angell, A. L., Smith, M., & Fischel, J. E. (1994). A picture book reading intervention in day care and home for children from low-income families. *Developmental Psychology, 30,* 679–689.

Whitehurst, G. J., Fischel, J. E., Caulfield, M. B., DeBaryshe, B. D., & Valdez-Menchaca, M. C. (1989). Assessment and treatment of early expressive language delay. In P. R. Zelazo & R. Barr (Eds.), *Challenges to developmental paradigms: Implications for assessment and treatment* (pp. 113–135). Hillsdale, NJ: Erlbaum.

Whitehurst, G. J., & Vasta, R. (1975). Is language acquired through imitation? *Journal of Psycholinguistic Research, 4,* 37–59.

Whiting, B., & Edwards, C. P. (1988a). *Children of different worlds.* Cambridge, MA: Harvard University Press.

Whiting, B., & Edwards, C. P. (1988b). A cross-cultural analysis of sex differences in the behavior of children aged 3 through 11. In G. Handel (Ed.), *Childhood socialization* (pp. 281–297). New York: Aldine De Gruyter.

Whiting, J. W. M., Burbank, V. K., & Ratner, M. S. (1986). The duration of maidenhood across cultures. In J. B. Lancaster & B. Hamburg (Eds.), *School-age pregnancy and parenthood: Biosocial dimensions* (pp. 273–302). New York: Aldine De Gruyter.

Whitley, B. E. (1983). Sex role orientation and self-esteem: A critical meta-analytic review. *Journal of Personality and Social Psychology, 44,* 765–778.

Whitney, M. P., & Thoman, E. B. (1993). Early sleep patterns of premature infants are differentially related to later developmental disabilities. *Journal of Developmental and Behavioral Pediatrics, 14,* 71–80.

Whitney, M. P., & Thoman, E. B. (1994). Sleep in premature and full-term infants from 24-hour home recordings. *Infant Behavior and Development, 17,* 223–234.

Wigfield, R. E., Fleming, P. J., Berry, P. J., Rudd, P. T., & Golding, J. (1992). Can the fall in Avon's sudden infant death rate be explained by changes in sleeping position? *British Medical Journal, 304,* 282–283.

Wilcox, A. J., & Skjoerven, R. (1992). Birth weight and perinatal mortality: The effect of gestational age. *American Journal of Public Health, 83,* 378–382.

Wilcox, A. J., Weinberg, C. R., & Baird, D. D. (1995). Timing of sexual intercourse in relation to ovulation: Effects on the probability of conception, survival of the pregnancy, and sex of the baby. *New England Journal of Medicine, 333,* 1517–1519.

Wille, D. E. (1991). Relation of preterm birth with quality of infant–mother attachment at one year. *Infant Behavior and Development, 14,* 227–240.

Willems, E. P. (1967). Sense of obligation to high school activities as related to school size and marginality of student. *Child Development, 38,* 1247–1260.

Willer, B., Hofferth, S. L., Kisker, E. E., Divine-Hawkins, P., Farquhar, E., & Glantz, F. B. (1991). *The demand and supply of child care in 1990: Joint findings from the National Child Care Survey 1990 and A Profile of Child Care Settings.* Washington, DC: National Association for the Education of Young Children.

Willerman, L. (1979). Effects of families on intellectual development. *American Psychologist, 34,* 923–929.

Williams, C. S., Buss, K. A., & Eskenazi, B. (1992). Infant resuscitation is associated with an increased risk of left-handedness. *American Journal of Epidemiology, 136,* 277–286.

Williams, E., & Radin, N. (1993). Paternal involvement, maternal employment, and adolescents' academic achievement: An 11-year follow-up. *American Journal of Orthopsychiatry, 63,* 306–312.

Williams, E., Radin, N., & Allegro, T. (1992). Sex-role attitudes of adolescents reared primarily by their fathers: An 11-year follow-up. *Merrill-Palmer Quarterly, 38,* 457–476.

Williams, J. E., & Best, D. L. (1990). *Measuring sex stereotypes: A multination study.* Newbury Park, CA: Sage.

Williams, T. M. (1986). *The impact of television: A natural experiment in three communities.* Orlando, FL: Academic Press.

Willinger, M. (1995). Sleep position and sudden infant death syndrome. *Journal of the American Medical Association, 273,* 818–819.

Wilson, B. J., Linz, D., & Randall, B. (1990). Applying social science research to film ratings: A shift from offensiveness to harmful effects. *Journal of Broadcasting and Electronic Media, 34,* 443–468.

Wilson, E. O. (1975). *Sociobiology: The new synthesis.* Cambridge, MA: Harvard University Press.

Wilson, M. N. (1986). The black extended family: An analytical consideration. *Developmental Psychology, 22,* 246–258.

Wilson, R. S. (1983). The Louisville Twin Study: Developmental synchronies in behavior. *Child Development, 54,* 298–316.

Wilson, W. J. (1987). *The truly disadvantaged: The inner city, the underclass, and public policy.* Chicago: University of Chicago Press.

Wimmer, H., & Hartl, M. (1991). Against the Cartesian view on mind: Young children's difficulty with own false beliefs. *British Journal of Developmental Psychology, 9,* 125–138.

Windle, M. A. (1994). A study of friendship characteristics and problem behaviors among middle adolescents. *Child Development, 65,* 1764–1777.

Winer, G., Craig, R. K., & Weinbaum, E. (1992). Adults' failure on misleading weight-conservation tests: A developmental analysis. *Developmental Psychology, 28,* 109–120.

Winick, M., & Noble, A. (1966). Cellular response in rats during malnutrition at various ages. *Journal of Nutrition, 89,* 300–306.

Winn, S., Roker, D., & Coleman, J. (1995). Knowledge about puberty and sexual development in 11–16 year-olds: Implications for health and sex education in schools. *Educational Studies, 21,* 187–201.

Winner, E. (1986, August). Where pelicans kiss seals. *Psychology Today, 20*(8), 25–35.

Winner, E. (1988). *The point of words: Children's understanding of metaphor and irony.* Cambridge, MA: Harvard University Press.

Winthrop, R. H. (1991). *Dictionary of concepts in cultural anthropology.* New York: Greenwood Press.

Wintre, M. G., & Vallance, D. D. (1994). A developmental sequence in the comprehension of emotions: Intensity, multiple emotions, and valence. *Developmental Psychology, 30,* 509–514.

Witelson, S. F., & Kigar, D. L. (1988). Anatomical development of the corpus callosum in humans: A review with reference to sex and cognition. In D. L. Molfese & S. J. Segalowitz (Eds.), *Brain lateralization in children* (pp. 35–57). New York: Guilford.

Witherell, C. S., & Edwards, C. P. (1991). Moral versus social-conventional reasoning: A narrative and culture critique. *Journal of Moral Education, 20,* 293–304.

Wolf, A. W., Jimenez, E., & Lozoff, B. (1994). No evidence of developmental ill effects of low-level lead exposure in a developing country. *Developmental and Behavioral Pediatrics, 15,* 224–231.

Wolf, A., & Lozoff, B. (1989). Object attachment, thumbsucking, and the passage to sleep. *Journal of the American Academy of Child and Adolescent Psychiatry, 28,* 287–292.

Wolff, P. H. (1966). The causes, controls and organization of behavior in the neonate. *Psychological Issues, 5*(1, Serial No. 17).

Wolfner, G. Faust, D., & Dawes, R. (1993). The use of anatomical dolls in sexual abuse evaluations: The state of the science. *Applied and Preventive Psychology, 2,* 1–11.

Wong-Fillmore, L., Ammon, P., McLaughlin, B., & Ammon, M. S. (1985). *Learning English through bilingual instruction.* Rosslyn, VA: National Clearinghouse for Bilingual Education.

Wood, D. J. (1989). Social interaction as tutoring. In M. H. Bornstein & J. S. Bruner (Eds.), *Interaction in human development.* Hillsdale, NJ: Erlbaum.

Woody-Ramsey, J., & Miller, P. H. (1988). The facilitation of selective attention in preschoolers. *Child Development, 59,* 1497–1503.

Woolley, J. D., & Wellman, H. M. (1990). Young children's understanding of realities, nonrealities, and appearances. *Child Development, 61,* 946–961.

Woolley, J. D., & Wellman, H. M. (1992). Children's conception of dreams. *Cognitive Development, 7,* 365–380.

Wright, J. C., Huston, A. C., Reitz, A. L., & Piemyat, S. (1994). Young children's perceptions of television reality: Determinants and developmental differences. *Developmental Psychology, 30,* 229–239.

Wright, J. W. (Ed.). (1995). *The universal almanac 1995.* Kansas City: Andrews and McMeel.

Wyman, P. A., Cowen, E. L., Work, W. C., Raoof, A., Gribble, P. A., Parker, G. R., & Wannon, M. (1992). Interviews with children who experienced major life stress: Family and child attributes that predict resilient outcomes. *Journal of the American Academy of Child and Adolescent Psychiatry, 31,* 904–910.

Y

Yang, B., Ollendick, T. H., Dong, Q., Xia, Y., & Lin, L. (1995). Only children and children with siblings in the People's Republic of China: Levels of fear, anxiety, and depression. *Child Development, 66,* 1301–1311.

Yarrow, M. R., Campbell, J. D., & Burton, R. V. (1970). Recollections of childhood: A study of the retrospective method. *Monographs of the Society for Research in Child Development, 35*(5, Serial No. 138).

Yarrow, M. R., Scott, P. M., & Waxler, C. Z. (1973). Learning concern for others. *Developmental Psychology, 8,* 240–260.

Yazigi, R. A., Odem, R. R., & Polakoski, K. L. (1991). Demonstration of specific binding of cocaine to human spermatozoa. *Journal of the American Medical Association, 266,* 1956–1959.

Yeates, K. O., MacPhee, D., Campbell, F. A., & Ramey, C. T. (1983). Maternal IQ and home environment as determinants of early childhood intellectual competence: A developmental analysis. *Developmental Psychology, 19,* 731–739.

Yeates, K. O., Schultz, L. H., & Selman, R. L. (1991). The development of interpersonal negotiation strategies in thought and action: A social-cognitive link to behavioral adjustment and social status. *Merrill-Palmer Quarterly, 37,* 369–405.

Yogman, M. W. (1981). Development of the father–infant relationship. In H. Fitzgerald, B. Lester, & M. W. Yogman (Eds.), *Theory and research in behavioral pediatrics* (Vol. 1, pp. 221–279). New York: Plenum.

Yonas, A., Granrud, E. C., Arterberry, M. E., & Hanson, B. L. (1986). Infants' distance perception from linear perspective and texture gradients. *Infant Behavior and Development, 9,* 247–256.

Yonas, A., & Hartman, B. (1993). Perceiving the affordance of contact in four- and five-month-old infants. *Child Development, 64,* 298–308.

Youngblade, L. M., & Dunn, J. (1995). Individual differences in young children's pretend play with mother and sibling: Links to relationships and understanding of other people's feelings and beliefs. *Child Development, 66,* 1472–1492.

Younger, B. A. (1985). The segregation of items into categories by ten-month-old infants. *Child Development, 56,* 1574–1583.

Younger, B. A. (1993). Understanding category members as "the same sort of thing": Explicit categorization in ten-month infants. *Child Development, 64,* 309–320.

Youniss, J. (1980). *Parents and peers in social development: A Piagetian-Sullivan perspective.* Chicago: University of Chicago Press.

Youniss, J., & Smollar, J. (1986). *Adolescent relations with mothers, fathers, and friends.* Chicago: University of Chicago Press.

Yuill, N. (1993). Understanding of personality and dispositions. In M. Bennett (Ed.), *The development of social cognition* (pp. 87–110). New York: Guilford.

Yuill, N., & Perner, J. (1988). Intentionality and knowledge in children's judgments of actor's responsibility and recipient's emotional reaction. *Developmental Psychology, 24,* 358–365.

Z

Zabin, L. S., & Hayward, S. C. (1993). *Adolescent sexual behavior and childbearing.* Newbury Park, CA: Sage.

Zahavi, S., & Asher, S. R. (1978). The effect of verbal instructions on preschool children's aggressive behavior. *Journal of School Psychology, 16,* 146–153.

Zahn-Waxler, C., Cole, P. M., & Barrett, K. C. (1991). Guilt and empathy: Sex differences and implications for the development of depression. In J. Garber & K. A. Dodge (Eds.), *The development of emotion regulation and dysregulation* (pp. 243–272). Cambridge: Cambridge University Press.

Zahn-Waxler, C., Cole, P. M., Welsh, J. D., & Fox, N. A. (1995). Psychophysiological correlates of empathy and prosocial behaviors in preschool children with behavior problems. *Development and Psychopathology, 7,* 27–48.

Zahn-Waxler, C., Iannotti, R. J., Cummings, E. M., & Denham, S. (1990). Antecedents of problem behaviors in children of depressed mothers. *Development and Psychopathology, 2,* 271–291.

Zahn-Waxler, C., Kochanska, G., Krupnick, J., & McKnew, D. (1990). Patterns of guilt in children of depressed and well mothers. *Developmental Psychology, 26,* 51–59.

Zahn-Waxler, C., & Radke-Yarrow, M. (1990). The origins of empathic concern. *Motivation and Emotion, 14,* 107–130.

Zahn-Waxler, C., Radke-Yarrow, M., & King, R. M. (1979). Childrearing and children's prosocial initiations toward victims of distress. *Child Development, 50,* 319–330.

Zahn-Waxler, C., Radke-Yarrow, M., Wagner, E., & Chapman, M. (1992). Development of concern for others. *Developmental Psychology, 28,* 126–136.

Zahn-Waxler, C., & Robinson, J. (1995). Empathy and guilt: Early origins of feelings of responsibility. In J. P. Tangney & K. W. Fischer (Eds.), *Self-conscious emotions* (pp. 143–173). New York: Guilford.

Zahn-Waxler, C., Robinson, J. L., & Emde, R. N. (1992). The development of empathy in twins. *Developmental Psychology, 28,* 1038–1047.

Zajonc, R. B. (1976). Family configuration and intelligence. *Science, 192,* 227–236.

Zajonc, R. B., & Markus, G. B. (1975). Birth order and intellectual development. *Psychological Review, 82,* 74–88.

Zajonc, R. B., Markus, H., & Markus, G. B. (1979). The birth order puzzle. *Journal of Personality and Social Psychology, 37,* 1325–1341.

Zametkin, A. J. (1995). Attention-deficit disorder: Born to be hyperactive? *Journal of the American Medical Association, 273,* 1871–1874.

Zaslow, M. J., Rabinovich, B. A., & Suwalsky, J. T. (1991). From maternal employment to child outcomes: Preexisting group differences and moderating variables. In J. V. Lerner & N. L. Galambos (Eds.), *Employed mothers and their children* (pp. 237–282). New York: Garland.

Zelazo, N. A., Zelazo, P. R., Cohen, K. M., & Zelazo, P. D. (1993). Specificity of practice effects on elementary neuromotor patterns. *Developmental Psychology, 29,* 686–691.

Zelazo, P. R. (1983). The development of walking: New findings on old assumptions. *Journal of Motor Behavior, 2,* 99–137.

Zelazo, P. R., Zelazo, N. A., & Kolb, S. (1972). "Walking" in the newborn. *Science, 176,* 314–315.

Zeskind, P. S., & Ramey, C. T. (1978). Fetal malnutrition: An experimental study of its consequences on infant development in two caregiving environments. *Child Development, 49,* 1155–1162.

Zeskind, P. S., & Ramey, C. T. (1981). Preventing intellectual and interactional sequelae of fetal malnutrition: A longitudinal, transactional, and synergistic approach to development. *Child Development, 52,* 213–218.

Zhang, J., Cai, W., & Lee, D. J. (1992). Occupational hazards and pregnancy outcomes. *American Journal of Industrial Medicine, 21,* 397–408.

Zigler, E. F., Abelson, W. D., & Seitz, V. (1973). Motivational factors in the performance of economically disadvantaged children on the Peabody Picture Vocabulary Test. *Child Development, 44,* 294–303.

Zigler, E. F., & Finn-Stevenson, M. (1992). Applied developmental psychology. In M. H. Bornstein & M. E. Lamb (Eds.), *Developmental psychology: An advanced textbook* (3rd ed., pp. 677–729). Hillsdale, NJ: Erlbaum.

Zigler, E. F., & Gilman, E. (1993). Day care in America: What is needed? *Pediatrics, 91,* 175–178.

Zigler, E. F., & Hall, N. W. (1989). Physical child abuse in America: Past, present, and future. In D. Cicchetti & V. Carlson (Eds.), *Child maltreatment* (pp. 203–253). New York: Cambridge University Press.

Zigler, E. F., & Seitz, V. (1982). Social policy and intelligence. In R. J. Sternberg (Ed.), *Handbook of human intelligence* (pp. 586–641). Cambridge: Cambridge University Press.

Zigler, E., & Styfco, S. J. (1993). Using research and theory to justify and inform Head Start expansion. *Social Policy Report, 7*(2), 1–20.

Zigler, E. F., & Styfco, S. J. (1994). Head Start: Criticisms in a constructive context. *American Psychologist, 49,* 127–132.

Zigler, E. F., & Styfco, S. J. (1995). Is the Perry Preschool better than Head Start? Yes and no. *Early Childhood Research Quarterly, 9,* 269–287.

Zimmerman, B. J. (1990). Self-regulation learning and academic achievement: An overview. *Educational Psychologist, 25,* 3–18.

Zimmerman, M. A., & Arunkumar, R. (1994). Resiliency research: Implications for schools and policy. *Social Policy Report of the Society for Research in Child Development, 8*(4).

Name Index

C

I

J

K

L

M

S

T

U

V

W

Y

Z

Subject Index

A

B

C

D

E

F

G

N

S

T